The Playbill® Broadway Yearbook

Sixth Annual Edition
2009–2010

Robert Viagas
Editor

Amy Asch
Assistant Editor

Kesler Thibert
Art Director

Aubrey Reuben   Brian Mapp   Joe Marzullo
Photographers

David Gewirtzman
Production Coordinator

Samantha Souza
Photo Coordinator

The Playbill Broadway Yearbook: Sixth Annual Edition, June 1, 2009–May 31, 2010
Robert Viagas, Editor

©2010 Playbill® Incorporated
All rights reserved.

No part of this publication may be reproduced or transmitted in any form or by any means, electronic or mechanical, including photocopy, recording or any information storage or retrieval system now known or to be invented, without permission in writing from the publishers, except by a reviewer who wishes to quote brief passages in connection with a review written for inclusion in a magazine, newspaper or broadcast.

All PLAYBILL® covers in this book are from the magazine's archives.

ISBN 978-1-4234-9277-1
ISSN 1932-1945

Published by PLAYBILL® BOOKS
525 Seventh Avenue, Suite 1801
New York, NY 10018
Email: yearbook@playbill.com
Internet: www.playbill.com

Published in 2010 by Applause Theatre & Cinema Books
An Imprint of Hal Leonard Corporation
7777 West Bluemound Road
Milwaukee, WI 53213

Trade Book Division Editorial Offices
19 West 21st Street, New York, NY 10010

www.applausepub.com

Preface to the Sixth Edition

Assembling each year's *Playbill Broadway Yearbook* is a little like building a battleship out of toothpicks. But what makes the effort worthwhile, even a joy and an adventure, is the *Alice in Wonderland*-like journey through the backstages of Broadway taken by myself and the *Yearbook* staff.

You've let us know that you like seeing all the PLAYBILL covers and surveying production photos from all the shows—the short runs as well as the blockbusters.

But we also know that the Scrapbook pages have become the heart and soul of the *Yearbook*, with their blog-like accounts of life on the other side of the stage doors.

This year we continued our quest to locate Correspondents who are not the usual suspects:

• Tessa Netting, one of the young ballerinas in *Billy Elliot*, who supplied us with hilarious photos of life in the dressing rooms at the Imperial.
• Even after her show *Looped* closed, star Valerie Harper (encouraged by *Yearbook* alumnus Michael Mulheren) created a mini memoir of what it was like to embody Tallulah Bankhead on stage each night.
• Zachary James, who plays the funereal butler Lurch in *The Addams Family*, showed his sprightly side with a panel of photos of him and his young friend Adam Riegler ("Pugsley") making faces—in and out of character—for the camera.
• Young Chris Chalk, who plays Denzel Washington's son in *Fences*, tells about all the things he learned watching Washington and co-star Viola Davis deal with the script, the director, the audience and even with rabid fans at the stage door.
• January LaVoy, the Correspondent from *Enron*, also delivered her Scrapbook after the show had closed, and there is a wistfulness about this groundbreaking show that closed too soon that many stage performers will share.
• The indefatigable Kris Koop Ouellette, who was out of her show *Phantom of the Opera* for several months with an illness, stayed in contact with the cast and, upon her return, delivered a Scrapbook full of wonderful backstage stories in her patented breathless style—and with a fresh batch of exclusive backstage photos including a rare pic of the Phantom unmasked. She is the only Correspondent who has written for all six editions so far.
• Erin Mackey offers glimpses of what it was like to work with timeless talents like Barbara Cook, Vanessa Williams and Stephen Sondheim on *Sondheim on Sondheim*.
• Tony nominee Christiane Noll offers photos and memories—including the cast's weekly Saturday Night Surprise dress-up parties—from the labor of love that was *Ragtime*.

THE 2009-2010 YEARBOOK COMMITTEE
Top (Standing L-R): Brian Mapp, David Gewirtzman, Samantha Souza
Seated: Robert Viagas
Bottom (L): Amy Asch (R): Joe Marzullo
Not pictured: Kesler Thibert

• One of the last Scrapbooks to arrive was Sean Patrick Doyle's from *La Cage aux Folles*, but it turned out to be well worth the wait. One of the "notorious and dangerous" Cagelles, he supplied his show's chapter with priceless backstage photos and what may be the single best quote in the book. In answering the question "Who Wore the Least?" he replied that the Cagelles' costumes are so sheer, "You can see our SOULS in some of those outfits."

These are just a few samples. The sixth edition of *The Playbill Broadway Yearbook* glitters with dozens more, reflecting our best participation yet from the good folks who create that Broadway magic every night. My personal delight at collaborating with talented people also extends to the great folks in the offices of PLAYBILL who conjure up a new *Yearbook* each fall:

David Gewirtzman, who tracks all the hundreds of actors' comings and goings from and to dozens of shows. Let me draw your attention to the elegant and witty "Alumni" and "Transfer Students" logos he designs for each show, among his many jobs on the *Yearbook*.

Amy Asch, a proofreader of superhuman ability, who can discern a "Michele" from a "Michelle" at 40 paces.

Brian Mapp, our group photographer who got more Broadway people to smile than almost any show out there.

Graphic designer Kesler Thibert's back cover "puzzle" is just a small part of his artistry throughout the book. Samantha Souza tirelessly sets up photo shoots and tracks down all those names for the stage crew and faculty pictures.

Finally, we extend a special welcome to celebrity lensman Joe Marzullo, who succeeded veteran Aubrey Reuben at midseason as photographer of opening nights and special events. As I write this we've already begun work on the seventh edition of the *Yearbook*. See you in 2011!

Robert Viagas
June 2010

Special Thanks

Special thanks to Amy Asch, David Gewirtzman, Samantha Souza, Brian Mapp, Joe Marzullo, Kesler Thibert, Aubrey Reuben, Pam Karr, Greg Kalafatas, Martha Graebner, Maria Somma, Matt Blank, Andrew Gans, Kenneth Jones, Ernio Hernandez, Adam Hetrick, Bobby Maguire, Brynn Cox, Tripp Phillips, Catherine Ryan, Ben Viagas and Jean Kroeper Murphy whose help made this year's edition possible.

We also thank the Sixth Edition *Yearbook* Correspondents who shared their stories with such wit and insight: Donna Marie Asbury, Lisa Banes, William Joseph Barnes, Derrick Baskin, Catherine Blades, Corbin Bleu, Patrick Boll, Catherine Brunell, Sharna Burgess, Lisa Buxbaum, Blanca Camacho, Chris Chalk, Jill Cordle, Riley Costello, Adam Dannheisser, Diane DiVita, Sean Patrick Doyle, Ryan Duncan, John Treacy Egan, Russell Fischer, Arthur Gaffin, Maija Garcia, David Alan Grier, Jean Michelle Grier, Valerie Harper, Hunter Ryan Herdlicka, Jon Michael Hill, Lisa Ho, Marin Ireland, Zachary James, Luka Kain, Jay Klaitz, January LaVoy, Beth Leavel, Ray Lee, Frank Lombardi, Alyse Alan Louis, Erin Mackey, Jeffrey Kuhn, David McDonald, Marti McIntosh, Bryce McDonald, Kimber Monroe, Tessa Netting, Christiane Noll, Kris Koop Ouellette (for the sixth time), Justin Peck, Daniel Quadrino, Vanessa Ray, Rondi Reed, Tory Ross (for the third time), Laurissa Romain, Christina Sajous, Steve Schepis, Timothy R. Semon, Kelly Sheehan, J. Robert Spencer, Shanna Spinello, Chelsea Morgan Stock, Rebecca & Damon Sugden, Janet Takami, Jason Viarengo (for the third time), John Wernke and Robin Windsor.

And we thank the folks on each show who shared their photographs and other artwork that lent extra sparkle to the Scrapbook pages: Catherine Brunell, Samanthe Burrow, Gary Cooper, Jennifer Evans, Steve Fenn, Zachary James, January LaVoy, John Mara, Marti McIntosh, Robert Petkoff, James Romick, Tory Ross, Janet Takami, Tomas Vrzala, Peter James Zielinski, Alissa Zulvergold.

Also the Broadway press agents who helped set up interviews and photo sessions and helped track down the names of all the people in the crew photos: especially Chris Boneau, Adrian Bryan-Brown, Michael Hartman, Richard Kornberg, Jeffrey Richards, Marc Thibodeau, Philip Rinaldi, Sam Rudy, Tony Origlio, Rick Miramontez and their respective staffs.

Plus Joan Marcus, Paul Kolnik, Carol Rosegg, Anita Shevett, Steve Shevett and all the fine professional photographers whose work appears on these pages.

And, most of all, thanks to the great show people of Broadway who got into the spirit of the *Yearbook* and took time out of their busy days to pose for our cameras. There's no people like them.

Yearbook User's Manual

Which Shows Are Included? *The Playbill Broadway Yearbook 2009-2010* covers the Broadway season, that ran, as per tradition, from June 1, 2009 to May 31, 2010. Each of the seventy-one shows that played at a Broadway theatre under a Broadway contract during that time are highlighted in this edition. That includes new shows that opened during that time, like *American Idiot*; shows from last season that ran into this season, like *Billy Elliot*; older shows from seasons past that closed during this season, like *Avenue Q*; and older shows from seasons past that ran throughout this season and continue into the future (and into the next *Yearbook*), like *The Phantom of the Opera*.

How Is It Decided Which Credits Page Will Be Featured? Each show's credits page (which PLAYBILL calls a "billboard page") changes over the year as cast members come and go. We use the opening-night billboard page for most new shows. For most shows that carry over from the previous season, we use the billboard page from the first week in October. Occasionally, sometimes at the request of the producer, we use a billboard page from another part of the season, especially when a major new star joins the cast.

What Are "Alumni" and "Transfer Students"? Over the course of a season some actors leave a production; others take their places. To follow our *Yearbook* concept, the ones who left a show before the date of the billboard page are listed as "Alumni"; the ones who joined the cast are called "Transfer Students." If you see a photo appearing in both "Alumni" and "Transfer Students" sections, it's not a mistake; it just means that they went in and out of the show during the season and were not present on the billboard date.

What Is a "Correspondent" and How Is One Chosen? We ask each show to appoint a Correspondent to record anecdotes of backstage life at his or her production. Sometimes the show's press agent picks the Correspondent; sometimes the company manager, the stage manager or the producer does the choosing. Each show gets to decide for itself. A few shows decline to provide a Correspondent, fail to respond to our request, or miss the deadline. Correspondents bring a richness of experience to the job and help tell the story of backstage life on Broadway from many different points of view.

Who Gets Their Pictures in the Yearbook? Everyone who works on Broadway can get a picture in the *Yearbook*. That includes actors, producers, writers, designers, assistants, stagehands, ushers, box office personnel, stage doormen and anyone else employed at a Broadway show or a support organization. PLAYBILL maintains a database of headshots of all Broadway actors and most creators. We send our staff photographers to all opening nights and all major Broadway-related events. We also offer to schedule in-theatre photo shoots at every production. No one is required to appear in the *Yearbook*, but all are invited. A few shows declined to host a photo shoot this year or were unable to provide material by our deadline. We hope that those still running will join us in 2011.

TABLE OF CONTENTS

Preface iii
Special Thanks iv
Season Timeline vi
Head of the Class ix

THE SHOWS:

Accent on Youth 374
The Addams Family 1
After Miss Julie 11
All About Me 16
American Idiot 21
August: Osage County 28
Avenue Q 32
A Behanding in Spokane 37
Billy Elliot, The Musical 41
Blithe Spirit 374
Brighton Beach Memoirs 51
Burn the Floor 54
Bye Bye Birdie 60
Chicago 69
Collected Stories 76
Come Fly Away 79
Enron 85
Everyday Rapture 91
Exit the King 374
Fela! 97
Fences 104
Finian's Rainbow 109
God of Carnage 117
Guys and Dolls 121
Hair 127
Hamlet 135
In the Heights 140
In the Next Room 148
Irena's Vow 374
Irving Berlin's White Christmas 152
Jersey Boys 158
Joe Turner's Come and Gone 374
La Cage aux Folles 164
Lend Me a Tenor 171
The Lion King 176
The Little Mermaid 184
A Little Night Music 191

Looped 198
Mamma Mia! 202
Mary Poppins 211
Mary Stuart 374
Memphis 219
Million Dollar Quartet 227
The Miracle Worker 232
Next Fall 236
Next to Normal 240
9 to 5: The Musical 245
The Norman Conquests 252
Oleanna 256
The Phantom of the Opera 261
The Philanthropist 374
Present Laughter 270
Promises, Promises 276
Race 282
Ragtime 286
reasons to be pretty 374
Red 294
Rock of Ages 298
The Royal Family 305
Shrek The Musical 310
Sondheim on Sondheim 318
South Pacific 324
A Steady Rain 332
Superior Donuts 335
The 39 Steps 340
Time Stands Still 345
A View from the Bridge 349
Waiting for Godot 374
West Side Story 354
White Christmas (see Irving Berlin's
   White Christmas)
Wicked 362
Wishful Drinking 371
Short Runs 374

SPECIAL EVENTS AND AWARDS 375
FACULTY 394
IN MEMORIAM 422
INDEX 423

Timeline 2009-2010

Opening Nights, News Headlines and Other Significant Milestones of the Season

June 7, 2009 The 63rd annual Tony Awards are given at Radio City Music Hall. *Billy Elliot, The Musical* is named Best Musical, *God of Carnage* is named Best Play, and Best Revival awards go to *Hair* and *The Norman Conquests*. Host Neil Patrick Harris helps deliver the highest-rated Tony Awards broadcast in three years.

June 14, 2009 With the closing of *Joe Turner's Come and Gone*, the Belasco Theatre is taken off the market for a planned year-long multi-million-dollar renovation by The Shubert Organization.

June 18, 2009 The Tony Awards announce retirement of the Best Special Theatrical Event award, which had been given sporadically since 2001.

July 14, 2009 The Tony Awards announce that most journalists, including First Night critics, will be removed from the list of voters, supposedly to reduce "conflicts of interest." Several journalists protest that they are the only ones without a conflict of interest, but henceforth only industry professionals will be allowed to vote on the annual awards. Eight months later the Tonys will restore the vote to members of the New York Drama Critics Circle only.

July 27, 2009 John Cudia becomes the twelfth actor to play the title role of *The Phantom of the Opera* on Broadway, succeeding Howard McGillin, who holds the worldwide record of 2,544 performances in the role.

August 2, 2009 Broadway gets its first production of the new season, *Burn the Floor*, Jason Gilkison's dance revue that has been refining itself in various forms on international tours for the past decade. This production features the team of Maksim Chmerkovskiy and Karina Smirnoff of the hit TV show "Dancing with the Stars."

August 5, 2009 Garth Drabinsky and Myron Gottlieb, co-founders of Broadway producing company Livent Inc. that produced 1990s hits such as *Ragtime* and *Show Boat* are sentenced to prison terms of seven and six years respectively for accounting fraud in connection with the failed company.

August 7, 2009 Broadway producer Rocco Landesman is confirmed as chairman of the National Endowment for the Arts, leaving his post as president of the theatre-owning company Jujamcyn. Among his many achievements in a long career: head producer of *The Producers* and pitcher for that show's championship softball team in the Broadway Show League.

August 7, 2009 The Tony-winning revival of *Hair*, which seemed like such a financial long shot in January that extra producers were brought aboard to share the cost, announces that it has recouped its entire $5.76 million investment in a little over four months of performances, one of the quickest paybacks for a musical in modern Broadway history.

August 20, 2009 Two songs that had been performed in Spanish in the revival of *West Side Story* revert to English. They are "A Boy Like That" ("Un Hombre Asi") and "I Feel Pretty" ("Me Siento Hermosa") whose Stephen Sondheim lyrics had been rendered in Spanish for this production by Lin-Manuel Miranda. Director/librettist Arthur Laurents issued a statement explaining, "From the outset, the Spanish in *West Side Story* was an experiment. It's been an ongoing process of finding what worked and what didn't, and it still continues." The Spanish sung by the Sharks street gang in "Tonight" ("Quintet") was kept.

(L-R): *Bye Bye Birdie* lyricist Lee Adams, leading lady Gina Gershon, director/choreographer Robert Longbottom, composer Charles Strouse and leading man John Stamos at the ribbon cutting ceremony in the front entrance of the rebuilt Henry Miller's Theatre on July 28, 2009.

September 9, 2009 Jordan Roth, the 33-year-old scion of the producing Roth family, is named president of Jujamcyn Theaters, the third-largest theatre owner on Broadway. Roth joined Jujamcyn in 2005 as resident producer and became vice president in 2006. He succeeds Rocco Landesman, who was named chairman of the National Endowment for the Arts in August.

September 9, 2009 First season debut of the hit TV series "Glee," about life among high school theatre and music students. The series stars Lea Michele (*Spring Awakening*) and Matthew Morrison (*Light in the Piazza*), and will go on to feature many Broadway stars as guests.

September 13, 2009 In a dramatic reversal, producers of the Tony-winning Broadway musical *Avenue Q* take to the stage of the Golden Theatre on what was to have been the show's closing night to announced that it would take the unusual step of moving Off-Broadway, and will reopen at New World Stages October 9. *Avenue Q* racked up 2,534 Broadway performances.

September 17, 2009 *Phantom of the Opera*, already the longest-running show in Broadway history, notches its 9,000th performance.

Week ending September 20, 2009 Keith Huff's two-hander drama, *A Steady Rain*, sets a record for highest one-week gross for any non-musical production ever on Broadway: $1.17 million, beating the $1.06 million record set by Billy Crystal's *700 Sundays* in 2005.

September 22, 2009 The original cast recording of the Tony Award-winning musical *Jersey Boys* is certified platinum by the Recording Industry Association of America, meaning it has sold more than one million copies in the U.S.

September 23, 2009 Hugh Jackman and Daniel Craig are in the headlines when they stop a preview performance of *A Steady Rain* to scold an audience member whose phone rang repeatedly. Jackman tried addressing the person in character to turn off the phone. When it rang again a few minutes later, Craig broke character to say, "We can wait, just get the phone."

September 29, 2009 Jackman and Craig reach the opening night of *A Steady Rain*, playing a pair of Chicago cops whose willingness to blink at corruption leads to disaster.

October 1, 2009 Michael McKean stars as a Vietnam draft evader who finally finds something worth fighting for in *Superior Donuts*, the latest drama from Tracy Letts, the Pulitzer- and Tony-winning author of 2007's *August: Osage County*.

October 4, 2009 *Star Wars* co-star Carrie Fisher shares the warts-and-all story of her train-wreck life as the child of Hollywood royalty Debbie Reynolds and Eddie Fisher in a one-woman show titled *Wishful Drinking*.

October 6, 2009 Jude Law stars as Shakespeare's melancholy Dane in a revival of *Hamlet* memorable for its "To be or not to be" soliloquy delivered in a snowfall. The 400-year-old play goes on to sell out and ends its limited run in the black. It's the 66th Broadway production of the classic on record since 1761.

October 8, 2009 Rosemary Harris, Jan Maxwell, John Glover and Ana Gasteyer star in Manhattan Theatre Club's revival of Edna Ferber and George S. Kaufman's 1927 comedy classic, *The Royal Family*, about a family of over-the-top Broadway actors.

October 11, 2009 *Oleanna*, David Mamet's drama about a female college student who accuses her professor of sexual harassment, gets a short-lived Broadway revival, starring Bill

Timeline 2009-2010

Pullman and Julia Stiles. It's the second opening in four days for director Doug Hughes, who also staged *The Royal Family*.

October 15, 2009 Rebuilt from (below) the ground up, the 1918 vintage Henry Miller's Theatre reopens with Roundabout Theatre Company's production of *Bye Bye Birdie*. Gina Gershon, John Stamos, Bill Irwin and Nolan Gerard Funk star in the first Broadway revival of the 1960 musical about a rock singer whose manager plans one last publicity stunt before he's drafted into the army.

October 19, 2009 The new musical *Memphis* tells the story of an early 1950s white deejay (Chad Kimball) who tries to bring black rock 'n' roll to a wider audience in the title city. Along the way he falls in love with a black singer (Montego Glover). The show has music by rocker David Bryan, a book by Joe DiPietro and lyrics by both.

October 22, 2009 Sienna Miller, Jonny Lee Miller and Marin Ireland star in *After Miss Julie*, Patrick Marber's new take on August Strindberg's 1888 play about sex and class, with the story relocated to 1945 England.

October 25, 2009 Opening night for a revival of *Brighton Beach Memoirs*, which is planned to run in alternating repertory with another Neil Simon play, *Broadway Bound*. The two plays share a setting and many characters. Producer Emanuel Azenberg envisioned the twin productions as a "victory lap" for the 82-year-old Simon, but audiences don't respond as expected. The production closes abruptly on its first weekend, and the second production is scratched.

October 29, 2009 The first Broadway revival in half a century for *Finian's Rainbow*, the show tune-packed 1947 musical about an Irishman and his daughter who come to America on a magical quest. The Burton Lane/Fred Saidy/E.Y. Harburg show stars Jim Norton, Kate Baldwin, Cheyenne Jackson, Christopher Fitzgerald, Chuck Cooper and Terri White.

November 5, 2009 *The Lion King* gives its 5,000th Broadway performance.

November 2009 Comedian Dame Edna Everage and singer Michael Feinstein pretend to battle over use of the title *All About Me* for their forthcoming Broadway shows. After a flurry of press releases they "agree" to merge their shows as a single odd-couple production, scheduled for spring.

November 15, 2009 Transfer of a hit Kennedy Center revival of *Ragtime*, the Lynn Ahrens/Stephen Flaherty musical based on E.L. Doctorow's novel about blacks, whites and other immigrants colliding in 1906 New York. The production stars Christiane Noll, Robert Petkoff and Quentin Earl Darrington.

November 19, 2009 Laura Benanti and Michael Cerveris are featured in Sarah Ruhl's

(Left): Who is that dirty hippie in the patched jeans performing March 27, 2010, with the cast of *Hair* at the Inner Circle Gala? It is (right) billionaire New York Mayor Michael Bloomberg (with Diana DeGarmo).

drama *In the Next Room, or the vibrator play*, about a 19th century doctor whose experiments with the latest electrical invention—the vibrator—revolutionize his practice and transform his marriage in an unexpected way.

November 22, 2009 *Irving Berlin's White Christmas* gets its second annual holiday production. This year's leads are Melissa Errico, Tony Yazbeck, Mara Davi and James Clow.

November 23, 2009 *Fela!*, a biographical musical celebration of Nigerian musical pioneer and political activist Fela Anikulapo Kuti, transfers from an acclaimed run Off-Broadway. Sahr Ngaujah alternates in the leading role with Kevin Mambo. Also featured: Tony winner Lillias White and Saycon Sengbloh.

November 30, 2009 Long-running musical *Wicked* becomes the first Broadway show in history to gross more than $2 million in a single week. Increased ticket prices, continued popularity and a holiday weekend all contribute to the milestone.

December 6, 2009 Playwright David Mamet confronts the issue of racial prejudice in America with his new drama, *Race*, about a law firm with one white partner and one black partner who take the case of a white man charged with a sex crime against a black woman. James Spader, David Alan Grier, Kerry Washington and Richard Thomas comprise the cast, directed by the author.

December 7-8, 2009 At the 21st annual Gypsy of the Year competition, Hugh Jackman and Daniel Craig smash all fundraising records, collecting $1,549,953 in six weeks of curtain appeals at their hit Broadway drama *A Steady Rain*.

December 10, 2009 The Broadway League releases its latest audience survey which yields several interesting statistics. Nearly 40 percent of tickets in 2008-09 were bought over the Internet; nearly a quarter of the audience consisted of international visitors; average household income of theatregoers was $195,700; the average age of theatergoers rose slightly to 42.2 years.

December 13, 2009 Film actress Catherine Zeta-Jones makes her Broadway debut as Desiree Armfeldt in a revival of the Stephen Sondheim/Hugh Wheeler musical *A Little Night Music* that co-stars Broadway icon Angela Lansbury as her disapproving mother.

December 17, 2009 The Broadway League and the Service Employees International Union Local 32BJ—which includes porters, cleaners and bathroom attendants at more than two dozen Broadway theatres—reach a tentative three-year contract agreement, raising pay and increasing producer-paid coverage of family health benefits.

December 25, 2009 Official release date for the film version of the Tony-winning musical *Nine*, directed by Rob Marshall and starring Daniel Day-Lewis, Penélope Cruz, Judi Dench, Nicole Kidman, Marion Cotillard and Sophia Loren.

December 31, 2009 In the midst of a vicious recession, Broadway manages to close the books on its first-ever calendar year to gross more than $1 billion. The feat came in a year when attendance actually declined from 12.32 million to 11.95 million, and when playing weeks (the number of shows multiplied by the number of weeks they played) declined from 1,653 to 1,440. Higher prices and more people buying prime seats to big musicals accounted for the increase at the box office.

Early January 2010 For the first time in decades, a show-related album tops the Billboard chart. British singer Susan Boyle's rendition of "I Dreamed a Dream" from *Les Misérables* wowed the U.K. TV amateur show "Britain's Got Talent" in April 2009. The resulting CD, also titled "I Dreamed a Dream," opened at No. 1 on the Billboard album chart, and stayed there for five weeks, selling more than 3 million copies.

January 10, 2010 The comedy caper *The 39 Steps* closes after 771 performances, but not before announcing that it will follow in the footsteps of *Avenue Q* and reopen Off-Broadway—

Timeline 2009-2010

joining the puppet musical at the New World Stages complex.

January 21, 2010 Victor Garber eases into the dressing gown of aging matinee idol Garry Essendine in Roundabout Theatre Company's revival of Noël Coward's *Present Laughter*. Harriet Harris plays his tart-tongued secretary and Brooks Ashmanskas leaps across the stage as mad young playwright Roland Maule.

January 24, 2010 Liev Schreiber and Scarlett Johansson star in Gregory Mosher's revival of Arthur Miller's *A View From the Bridge*, about a Brooklyn longshoreman who loves his teen-aged niece a little bit too much.

January 25, 2010 Corbin Bleu becomes the first actor from the popular Disney *High School Musical* franchise to make a Broadway debut. He steps into the leading role of Usnavi in the long-running musical *In the Heights*.

January 28, 2010 Laura Linney, Alicia Silverstone, Brian d'Arcy James and Eric Bogosian star in *Time Stands Still*, the first new Broadway drama of the 2010's. Donald Margulies' drama presents two American journalists trying to sort out their lives after they are forced to return home from covering the Iraq War.

January 31, 2010 The cast album of the 2009 *West Side Story* revival (with its Spanish lyrics) wins the Grammy Award for Best Musical Show Album. A highlight of the 52nd Annual Grammy broadcast on CBS-TV is a performance by the rock group Green Day, joined by the cast of their upcoming Broadway musical *American Idiot*.

February 2, 2010 The film adaptation of the Broadway musical *Nine* is nominated for four Oscars including Best Supporting Actress (Penélope Cruz) and Best Original Song, for Maury Yeston's "Take It All," which was added to the film score. It wins none of the awards.

February 2, 2010 Evaluating the first year of the pedestrian plaza in Times Square that closed Broadway to traffic between 42nd and 47th Streets, Mayor Michael Bloomberg says that traffic congestion has not necessarily improved, as was hoped, but pedestrian injuries in the area have decreased. The mall stays.

March 3, 2010 Oscar nominee Abigail Breslin and Tony nominee Alison Pill play Helen Keller and teacher Annie Sullivan in a revival of William Gibson's *The Miracle Worker*, directed by Kate Whoriskey.

March 4, 2010 Christopher Walken returns to Broadway after ten years, playing a man searching for his lost hand in the world premiere of Martin McDonagh's gruesome comedy, *A Behanding in Spokane*, alongside Zoe Kazan, Anthony Mackie and Sam Rockwell.

March 11, 2010 A gay couple is split over a question of religion in Geoffrey Nauffts' drama *Next Fall*, which transfers from Off-Broadway's Naked Angels company. Patrick Breen and Patrick Heusinger play the couple, with Sheryl Kaller directing.

March 14, 2010 Valerie Harper channels eccentric film icon Tallulah Bankhead in Matthew Lombardo's play *Looped*, recreating a studio ses-

Composer Stephen Sondheim (center, flanked by, L-R, longtime collaborators James Lapine and John Weidman) becomes emotional at the announcement that Broadway's Henry Miller's Theatre will be renamed for him as an 80th birthday present. See March 22, 2010.

sion at which Bankhead tried to re-record (or "loop") a line of dialogue for one of her last films.

March 18, 2010 Australian drag comedienne Dame Edna joins forces with cabaret singer Michael Feinstein for *All About Me*, an odd-couple semi-vaudeville/semi-musical about their lives and careers, with a script by Feinstein, Barry Humphries and Christopher Durang, and staging by Casey Nicholaw.

March 22, 2010 Roundabout Theatre Com-pany announces Henry Miller's Theatre will be renamed the Stephen Sondheim Theatre. The announcement comes from his longtime writing partners James Lapine and John Weidman at a gala performance marking the composer's 80th birthday.

March 25, 2010 Director/choreographer Twyla Tharp, who had a hit with *Movin' Out*, an all-dancing musical based on the Billy Joel songbook, gives a similar treatment to the Frank Sinatra songbook in *Come Fly Away*, about four lovelorn couples. The corps features John Selya, Keith Roberts, Karine Plantadit and Holley Farmer.

April 1, 2010 Alfred Molina and Eddie Redmayne star in the U.S. debut of *Red*, John Logan's hit London drama about abstract impressionist painter Mark Rothko.

April 4, 2010 Stanley Tucci directs a revival of *Lend Me a Tenor*, Ken Ludwig's farce about the backstage chaos that erupts at an Ohio opera house when the star tenor fails to show up for an all-important benefit gala. Among the cast: Anthony LaPaglia, Tony Shalhoub, Jan Maxwell, Mary Catherine Garrison and Jennifer Laura Thompson.

April 8, 2010 Nathan Lane and Bebe Neuwirth co-star as Gomez and Morticia Addams in the musical *The Addams Family*, based on the cheerfully macabre drawings of Charles Addams, and the 1960s TV series they inspired. Andrew Lippa wrote the music and lyrics, with book by Marshall Brickman and Rick Elice. Directed by Jerry Zaks, the cast also features Carolee Carmello, Kevin Chamberlin, Jackie Hoffman and Terrence Mann.

April 11, 2010 The musical *Million Dollar Quartet* recreates a legendary 1956 recording session at which a young Elvis Presley jammed with future stars Johnny Cash, Carl Perkins and Jerry Lee Lewis. Directed by Eric Schaeffer, the production moves to Broadway from a sold-out Chicago run.

April 12, 2010 The musical *Next to Normal* wins the Pulitzer Prize for Drama.

April 18, 2010 Transfer of Menier Chocolate Factory's London revival of the Jerry Herman and Harvey Fierstein's musical *La Cage aux Folles* starring Douglas Hodge and Kelsey Grammer.

April 20, 2010 Songs from the rock group Green Day tell the story of *American Idiot*, a new rock musical using songs from the album of the same name, along with "21st Century Breakdown." John Gallagher Jr. and Rebecca Naomi Jones are among those featured in the cast.

April 22, 2010 Celebrating the 80th birthday of composer/lyricist Stephen Sondheim, Roundabout Theatre Company hosts *Sondheim on Sondheim*, a revue in which Sondheim discusses his work (on film) while the songs are performed by a cast that includes Barbara Cook, Vanessa Williams, Norm Lewis, Euan Morton, Leslie Kritzer and Tom Wopat.

April 25, 2010 Kristin Chenoweth, Sean Hayes, Brooks Ashmanskas and Katie Finneran are featured in a revival of the Burt Bacharach-Hal David-Neil Simon musical *Promises, Promises*, based on the Oscar-winning film, *The Apartment*.

April 26, 2010 Denzel Washington and Viola Davis star in Kenny Leon's revival of August Wilson's Pulitzer-winning drama *Fences*, about a former Negro League baseball player who struggles now as a garbage man.

April 27, 2010 Norbert Leo Butz stars in the Broadway transfer of Lucy Prebble's hit London drama *Enron*, about the real-life collapse of the American energy company of the same name.

April 28, 2010 Linda Lavin and Sarah Paulson play two female writers with help and challenge each other in the Broadway debut of Donald Margulies' *Collected Stories*, originally produced by Manhattan Theatre Club Off-Broadway. It's Margulies' second Broadway opening in three months.

May 1, 2010 Faisal Shahzad, a naturalized U.S. citizen from Pakistan, fails in an attempt to explode a terrorist car bomb in Times Square. The S.U.V. containing fireworks, gasoline and propane tanks was parked on West 45th Street next to the building that houses the Minskoff Theatre. A street vendor alerted police to the smoking vehicle, prompting a shutdown and partial evacuation of a section of the Broadway theatre district. The bomb fizzles and Shahzad is arrested and tried for the crime.

May 24, 2010 The Broadway League announces that Broadway shows earned a landmark $1.02 billion in 2009-2010.

June 13, 2010 The 64th Annual Tony Awards are broadcast live from Radio City Music Hall.

—*Robert Viagas*

Head of the Class
Trends, Extraordinary Achievements and Peculiar Coincidences of the Season

Most Tony Awards to a Play: *Red* (6).
Most Tony Awards to a Musical: *Memphis* (4).
Shortest Run: *Brighton Beach Memoirs* (9 performances).
An Acting Challenge: Everywhere you looked, performers were playing...performers. Douglas Hodge won a Tony playing a cabaret singer in *La Cage aux Folles*. Valerie Harper played Tallulah Bankhead in *Looped*. Catherine Zeta-Jones played a touring actress in *A Little Night Music*. Savannah Wise played Evelyn Nesbit in *Ragtime*. Carrie Fisher played herself in *Wishful Drinking*. *Memphis* presented a fictional singer, played by Montego Glover, while a quartet of actors played the *Million Dollar Quartet* of Elvis Presley, Jerry Lee Lewis, Carl Perkins and Johnny Cash. Victor Garber played a character Noël Coward based on himself in *Present Laughter*. *The Royal Family* topped them all by portraying an entire acting clan.
The Color of the Season: Red. David Mamet's *Race* turned on a red dress. The title character of *Fela!* was accused of being a "Red." Dame Edna and just about every other leading lady sported a bright red dress. And, of course, the most lauded new drama of the season was titled *Red* and each night left the stage drenched in crimson paint.
Awards They Should Give: #1 Best New Showtune: Our nominees: "Memphis Lives in Me" from *Memphis*. "God" from *Sondheim on Sondheim*. "The Moon and Me" from *The Addams Family*.
Stars Come Out: Kristin Chenoweth, Barbara Cook, Daniel Craig, Viola Davis, Dame Edna Everage, Michael Feinstein, Gina Gershon, Kelsey Grammer, Valerie Harper, Rosemary Harris, Sean Hayes, Hugh Jackman, Scarlett Johansson, Nathan Lane, Angela Lansbury, Lucy Liu, Bebe Neuwirth, John Stamos, Christopher Walken, Denzel Washington, Vanessa Williams, Catherine Zeta-Jones, et al.
New Musicals with Original Scores: Only two: *The Addams Family* and *Memphis*.
New PLAYS with Original Scores: Several, including *The Royal Family* with incidental music by Maury Yeston, *Fences* with incidental music by Branford Marsalis, and *Enron*, with songs by Lucy Prebble and Adam Cork.
Awards They Should Give: #2 Best Special Effects: Our nominees: Uncle Fester flies to the moon in *The Addams Family*. Filmed images of Stephen Sondheim at home flash on ever-rearranging screen blocks in *Sondheim on Sondheim*. The massive tentacles of a giant squid reach out and embrace Terrence Mann in *The Addams Family*. Og the Leprechaun makes apples, books and other objects appear and disappear in *Finian's Rainbow*. What look like a thousand video screens spangling the three-story set comment on the action in *American Idiot*. A racist senator is transformed from a white man to a black man before the audience's eyes in *Finian's Rainbow*. Extraordinary Girl flies in *American Idiot*.
La Cage or Addams Family? Grown child

Broadway's Longest Runs
By number of performances. Asterisk (*) indicates show still running as of May 31, 2010. Totals are for original runs except where otherwise noted.

* *The Phantom of the Opera* 9299
Cats 7485
Les Misérables 6680
A Chorus Line 6137
Oh! Calcutta! (Revival) 5959
* *Chicago* (Revival) 5616
Beauty and the Beast 5461
* *The Lion King* 5248
Rent 5123
Miss Saigon 4097
* *Mamma Mia!* 3586
42nd Street 3486
Grease 3388
Fiddler on the Roof 3242
Life With Father 3224
Tobacco Road 3182
Hello, Dolly! 2844
* *Wicked* 2734
My Fair Lady 2717
Hairspray 2642

wants oddball family to welcome painfully straitlaced future in-laws for what turns out to be a hilariously uncomfortable get-acquainted dinner party. Conservative would-be father-in-law is outraged by what he sees, but repressed future mother-in-law lets down her hair and everything works out okay.
Shows That Brought the Band Onstage: *All About Me, Come Fly Away, Chicago, Fela!, Memphis, Ragtime*.
Strangest New Trend: Sippy cups for adults at theatre bars.
Awards They Should Give: #3 Best New Rendition of an Old Song in a Revival or Jukebox Musical: Our nominees: The title song of *American Idiot*. "How Are Things in Glocca Morra?" in *Finian's Rainbow*. "A Fact Can Be a Beautiful Thing" in *Promises, Promises*. "Liaisons" in *A Little Night Music*.
Tribute Shows That End With Big Picture of the Subject Hanging Over the Stage: *Million Dollar Quartet, Come Fly Away, Sondheim on Sondheim*.
Oddest Program Note: "Eddie Fisher: Thanks for bringing your drug dealer to my opening in Berkeley. His notes were inspirational."
Coups de Theatre: Jude Law declaims Shakespeare's "To be or not to be" speech in a snowstorm in *Hamlet*. Christopher Walken narrates, in his often-imitated style, how he lost his hand to a pack of "hillbillies" in *A Behanding in Spokane*. In the same show, the scene in which the revolting contents of Walken's mysterious suitcase are revealed. Katie Finneran steals the show by showing off her "owl" jacket in a single scene in *Promises, Promises*. Hugh Jackman, as a corrupt Chicago cop, gradually realizes he is no longer in the driver's seat and is going to lose his career, his family and his freedom in *A Steady Rain*. Viola Davis erupts when Denzel Washington brings home his love child for her to raise in *Fences*. For those who were able to see it in the in-the-round arrangement of the Circle in the Square Theatre, the look on Abigail Breslin's face at the family water pump in *The Miracle Worker* when she, as blind-and-deaf Helen Keller, finally awakens to the connection between water and the sign for water. Kelsey Grammer and Douglas Hodge share a sweet kiss at the curtain of *La Cage aux Folles*. Levi Kreis kicks away his piano stool and really gets down to business playing Jerry Lee Lewis in *Million Dollar Quartet*.

Angela Lansbury brings a lifetime of experience to her rendition of "Liaisons" in *A Little Night Music*. Chuck Cooper heads a quartet singing and dancing a song about mankind's favorite pastime in "The Begat" from *Finian's Rainbow*. Sienna Miller provocatively displays her legs to Jonny Lee Miller as her father's chauffeur in *After Miss Julie*. Chad Kimball explains why nothing can seduce him into leaving his hometown in "Memphis Lives in Me" from *Memphis*. Norbert Leo Butz conveys the dizzying hubris of seemingly endless success in *Enron*. In the same play, actors in dinosaur masks begin feasting on the doomed company's ever-mounting debts. Alfred Molina and Eddie Redmayne athletically prep and prime a huge new crimson canvas in *Red*. Kevin Chamberlin levitates off the ground and flirts with the moon in *The Addams Family*. Patrick Breen finds himself suddenly alone with his male lover's macho father in *Next Fall*.

Laura Linney and Brian d'Arcy James at the bittersweet moment when they realize they can't stay together any longer in *Time Stands Still*. Karine Plantadit gets thrown around like a rag doll in *Come Fly Away*. Anthony LaPaglia teaches Justin Bartha to sing like a virtuoso in *Lend Me a Tenor*. In the same show, LaPaglia and Jan Maxwell have a savagely comic lovers' quarrel. Christina Sajous takes flight in *American Idiot*. The residents of Sweet Apple, Ohio, make their entrance in color-coded sherbet-hued costumes in *Bye Bye Birdie*. Dame Edna plays it more or less straight for a moment, giving a searing rendition of "The Ladies Who Lunch" in *All About Me*. In David Mamet's clipped, muscular monologue from *Race*, David Alan Grier lays out why blacks hate whites. Michael Cerveris first demonstrates his wondrous new device in *In the Next Room*. And, in the same play, the final moments in which he finally opens up emotionally to his wife, played by Laura Benanti, in their frozen garden. Stephen Sondheim, on video in *Sondheim on Sondheim*, recounting how his mother told him that her greatest regret in life was giving birth to him.

Autographs

The Addams Family

First Preview: March 8, 2010. Opened: April 8, 2010.
Still running as of May 31, 2010.

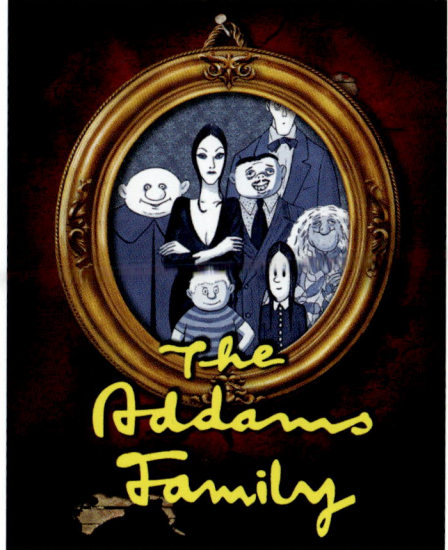

CAST

THE ADDAMS FAMILY

Gomez Addams	NATHAN LANE
Morticia Addams	BEBE NEUWIRTH
Uncle Fester	KEVIN CHAMBERLIN
Grandma	JACKIE HOFFMAN
Wednesday Addams	KRYSTA RODRIGUEZ
Pugsley Addams	ADAM RIEGLER
Lurch	ZACHARY JAMES

THE BEINEKE FAMILY

Mal Beineke	TERRENCE MANN
Alice Beineke	CAROLEE CARMELLO
Lucas Beineke	WESLEY TAYLOR

THE ADDAMS ANCESTORS

ERICK BUCKLEY, RACHEL DE BENEDET,
MATTHEW GUMLEY, FRED INKLEY,
MORGAN JAMES, CLARK JOHNSEN,
BARRETT MARTIN, JESSICA LEA PATTY,
LIZ RAMOS, CHARLIE SUTTON,
ALÉNA WATTERS

All puppetry is performed by members of
the *Addams Family* Company.

STANDBY

Standby for Gomez Addams and Mal Beineke:
MERWIN FOARD

Continued on next page

LUNT-FONTANNE THEATRE

UNDER THE DIRECTION OF
JAMES M. NEDERLANDER AND JAMES L. NEDERLANDER

Stuart Oken   Roy Furman   Michael Leavitt   Five Cent Productions
Stephen Schuler   Decca Theatricals   Scott M. Delman   Stuart Ditsky   Terry Allen Kramer   Stephanie P. McClelland
James L. Nederlander   Eva Price   Jam Theatricals/Mary Lu Roffe   Pittsburgh CLO/Gutterman-Swinsky
Vivek Tiwary/Gary Kaplan   The Weinstein Company/Clarence, LLC   Adam Zotovich/Tribe Theatricals

by Special Arrangement with
Elephant Eye Theatrical
present

Nathan Lane   Bebe Neuwirth

in

The Addams Family
A NEW MUSICAL

Book by
Marshall Brickman & Rick Elice

Music and Lyrics by
Andrew Lippa

Based on Characters Created by
Charles Addams

Starring
**Terrence Mann   Carolee Carmello
Kevin Chamberlin**

With
**Jackie Hoffman   Zachary James   Adam Riegler
Wesley Taylor** and **Krysta Rodriguez**

Merwin Foard   Jim Borstelmann   Erick Buckley   Colin Cunliffe   Rachel de Benedet
Valerie Fagan   Matthew Gumley   Fred Inkley   Morgan James   Clark Johnsen   Barrett Martin
Jessica Lea Patty   Liz Ramos   Samantha Sturm   Charlie Sutton   Aléna Watters

Lighting Design by	Sound Design by	Puppetry by
Natasha Katz	**Acme Sound Partners**	**Basil Twist**

Hair Design by	Make-up Design by	Special Effects by
Tom Watson	**Angelina Avallone**	**Gregory Meeh**

Orchestrations	Music Director	Dance Arrangements	Vocal Arrangements & Incidental Music
Larry Hochman	**Mary-Mitchell Campbell**	**August Eriksmoen**	**Andrew Lippa**

Casting	Press Representative	Marketing	Music Coordinator
Telsey + Company	**The Publicity Office**	**Type A Marketing**	**Michael Keller**

Production Supervisor	Production Management	General Management
Beverley Randolph	**Aurora Productions**	**101 Productions, Ltd.**

Creative Consultant
Jerry Zaks

Choreography by
Sergio Trujillo

Directed and Designed by
Phelim McDermott & Julian Crouch

4/8/10

(L-R): Adam Riegler, Jackie Hoffman, Bebe Neuwirth, Nathan Lane, Kevin Chamberlin, Krysta Rodriguez and Zachary James

Photo by Joan Marcus

The Addams Family

MUSICAL NUMBERS

ACT ONE

Overture	Orchestra
"When You're an Addams"	The Addams Family, Ancestors
"Pulled"	Wednesday, Pugsley
"Where Did We Go Wrong"	Morticia, Gomez
"One Normal Night"	Company
"Morticia"	Gomez, Male Ancestors
"What If"	Pugsley
"Full Disclosure"	Company
"Waiting"	Alice
"Full Disclosure – Part 2"	Company

ACT TWO

Entr'acte	Orchestra
"Just Around the Corner"	Morticia, Ancestors
"The Moon and Me"	Uncle Fester, Female Ancestors
"Happy/Sad"	Gomez
"Crazier Than You"	Wednesday, Lucas
"Let's Not Talk About Anything Else But Love"	Mal, Gomez, Uncle Fester, Grandma
"In the Arms"	Mal, Alice
"Live Before We Die"	Gomez, Morticia
"Tango de Amor"	Morticia, Gomez, Company
"Move Toward the Darkness"	Company

(L-R): Bebe Neuwirth and Carolee Carmello
Photo by Joan Marcus

Cast Continued

UNDERSTUDIES

For Gomez Addams: JIM BORSTELMANN
For Morticia Addams: RACHEL DE BENEDET, JESSICA LEA PATTY
For Uncle Fester: JIM BORSTELMANN, ERICK BUCKLEY
For Wednesday Addams: MORGAN JAMES, JESSICA LEA PATTY
For Pugsley Addams: MATTHEW GUMLEY
For Grandma: VALERIE FAGAN
For Lurch: FRED INKLEY, BARRETT MARTIN
For Mal Beineke: FRED INKLEY
For Alice Beineke: VALERIE FAGAN, MORGAN JAMES
For Lucas Beineke: COLIN CUNLIFFE, CLARK JOHNSEN

SWINGS

JIM BORSTELMANN, COLIN CUNLIFFE, VALERIE FAGAN, SAMANTHA STURM

Dance Captain: LIZ RAMOS
Puppet Performance Captain: COLIN CUNLIFFE
Assistant Dance Captain: COLIN CUNLIFFE

ORCHESTRA

Conductor: MARY-MITCHELL CAMPBELL
Associate Conductor: CHRIS FENWICK
Concertmaster: VICTORIA PATERSON
Violin: SEAN CARNEY
Viola: HIROKO TAGUCHI
Cello: ALLISON SEIDNER
Lead Trumpet: TONY KADLECK
Trumpet: BUD BURRIDGE
Trombones/Tuba: RANDY ANDOS
Reed 1: ERICA VON KLEIST
Reed 2: CHARLES PILLOW
Reed 3: MARK THRASHER
French Horn: ZOHAR SCHONDORF
Drums: DAMIEN BASSMAN
Bass: DAVE KUHN
Keyboard 1: CHRIS FENWICK
Keyboard 2: WILL VAN DYKE
Guitars: JIM HERSHMAN
Percussion: BILLY MILLER

Music Coordinator: MICHAEL KELLER
Music Copying:
KAYE-HOUSTON MUSIC/
ANNE KAYE & DOUG HOUSTON

The Addams Family

THE MAN BEHIND THE FAMILY

The musical *The Addams Family* is inspired by the creations of the legendary American cartoonist Charles Addams, who lived from 1912 until 1988. In 1933, when he was just 21, his work was published in *The New Yorker*, and over the course of nearly six decades, he became one of the magazine's most cherished contributors.

Bizarre, macabre and weird are all words that have been used to describe Charles Addams' cartoons. Yet adjectives such as charming, enchanting and tender can just as accurately be employed to depict the same body of work, as well as the man himself. His unique style and wonderfully crafted cartoons enabled his work to transcend such dichotomies for his millions of fans worldwide.

Charles Addams is most widely known for his characters that came to be called The Addams Family, a group that evolved into multiple television shows, motion pictures and now this Broadway musical. Gomez, Morticia, Uncle Fester, Wednesday, Pugsley,

"Are you unhappy, darling?" "Oh yes, yes! Completely."

Grandma and Lurch existed in various forms and aspects of Addams' cartoons dating back to the 1930's but were not actually named by him until the early 1960's, when the television series was created. Surprisingly, The Addams Family characters appear in only a small number of the artist's several thousand works. The majority of his cartoons are occupied by hundreds of other characters, but there is little doubt that those that come to life on this stage are his most beloved creations.

Over 15 books of his drawings have been published around the world, including the new collection, *The Addams Family: An Evilution*, the first complete history of The Addams Family, including more than 200 cartoons, many never previously published. The collection also includes Addams' own incisive character descriptions (originally penned for the benefit of the television show producers) that remind us where these oddly lovable characters came from and, in doing so, offer a lasting tribute to one of America's greatest humorists.

To learn more about Charles Addams, his life and his legacy, please visit our gallery in the second floor lounge.

All artwork © Charles Addams with permission of the Tee and Charles Addams Foundation

The Addams Family

Nathan Lane
Gomez Addams

Bebe Neuwirth
Morticia Addams

Terrence Mann
Mal Beineke

Carolee Carmello
Alice Beineke

Kevin Chamberlin
Uncle Fester

Jackie Hoffman
Grandma

Zachary James
Lurch

Adam Riegler
Pugsley Addams

Wesley Taylor
Lucas Beineke

Krysta Rodriguez
Wednesday Addams

Merwin Foard
Standby Gomez Addams, Standby Mal Beineke

Jim Borstelmann
Swing

Erick Buckley
Ancestor

Colin Cunliffe
Swing, Puppet Performance Captain, Assistant Dance Captain

Rachel De Benedet
Ancestor

Valerie Fagan
Swing

Matthew Gumley
Ancestor

Fred Inkley
Ancestor

Morgan James
Ancestor

Clark Johnsen
Ancestor

Barrett Martin
Ancestor

Jessica Lea Patty
Ancestor

Liz Ramos
Ancestor, Dance Captain

Samantha Sturm
Swing

Charlie Sutton
Ancestor

Aléna Watters
Ancestor

Marshall Brickman
Book

Rick Elice
Book

Andrew Lippa
Music and Lyrics

Phelim McDermott
Director/Designer

Julian Crouch
Director/Designer

Jerry Zaks
Creative Consultant

Sergio Trujillo
Choreographer

Tom Clark, Mark Menard and Nevin Steinberg, Acme Sound Partners
Sound Designer

The Addams Family

 Natasha Katz *Lighting Designer*
 Basil Twist *Puppetry*
 Tom Watson *Hair and Wig Designer*
 Angelina Avallone *Make-up Designer*
 Gregory Meeh *Special Effects Designer*
 Mary-Mitchell Campbell *Music Director*
 Larry Hochman *Orchestrations*

 Bernard Telsey, Telsey + Company *Casting*
 Michael Keller *Music Coordinator*
 Beverley Randolph *Production Supervisor*
 Heidi Miami Marshall *Associate Director*
 Dontee Kiehn *Associate Choreographer*
 Wendy Orshan, 101 Productions, Ltd. *General Manager*
 Stuart Oken *Producer*

 Roy Furman *Producer*
 Michael Leavitt *Producer*
 Terry Allen Kramer *Producer*
 Stephanie P. McClelland/ Green Curtain Productions *Producer*
 James L. Nederlander *Producer*
 Arny Granat, Jam Theatricals *Producer*
 Steve Traxler, Jam Theatricals *Producer*

 Van Kaplan, Executive Producer, Pittsburgh CLO *Producer*
 Jay and Cindy Gutterman *Producer*
 Morton Swinsky *Producer*
 Bob Weinstein, The Weinstein Company *Producer*
 Harvey Weinstein, The Weinstein Company *Producer*
 Adam Zotovich *Producer*

 Carl Moellenberg, Tribe Theatricals *Producer*
 Wendy Federman, Tribe Theatricals *Producer*
 Jamie deRoy, Tribe Theatricals *Producer*
 Larry Hirschhorn, Tribe Theatricals *Producer*

BOX OFFICE STAFF (L-R): Joe Olcese, Tom Waxman, Gregg Collichio

The Playbill Broadway Yearbook 2009-2010

The Addams Family

HAIR DEPARTMENT
(L-R): Whitney Adkins Mvondo, Barry Ernst (Hair and Make-Up Supervisor), Suzanne Storey

STAGE DOOR STAFF
(L-R): Bob Garner, John Sheppard

SANDBAR CONCESSIONS STAFF
(L-R): Ray West, Miles Seligman, Paul Ruggiero (Concessions Manager), Mike Anthony

CREW
(L-R): Paul Wimmer (Production Carpenter), David Gotwald (Production Sound), Jeremy Wahlers (Asst. Electrician), Holli Shevett (Deck Sound), Bryan Davis (Fly Automation), Mike Hyman (Head Electrician), Steve Long (Asst. Electrician), David Brickman (Spot Op), Scott Silvian (Asst. Sound), Brendan Lynch (Spot Op), Danny Viscardo (Props)

CHILDREN'S GUARDIAN
Katy Lathan (Children's Guardian) with actors Adam Riegler (left) and Matthew Gumley (right)

MERCHANDISE STAFF / ENCORE MERCHANDISING
(L-R): Elie Berkowitz, Christine Penski, Kathleen Mueller, Brooke Forman, Matt Rodriguez

ASSOCIATE DIRECTOR
Steve Bebout

STAGE MANAGEMENT
(L-R): Zac Chandler (Asst. Stage Manager), Allison A. Lee (Asst. Stage Manager), Beverley Randolph (Production Supervisor), Scott Taylor Rollison (Stage Manager)

The Addams Family

FRONT OF HOUSE STAFF
Front Row (L-R): Madeline Flores, Mildred Villano, Jessica Gonzalez (Chief Usher), Stephanie Martinez, Tracey Malinowski (House Manager)

Middle Row (L-R): Sharon Grant, Rosalind Joyce, Maritza Perez, Melissa Ocasio, Jason Fonseca (Porter), Carmella Cambio, Kathleen Ryan, Paul Perez, Angalic Cortes, Joey Cintron, Lauren Banyai

Back Row (L-R): Greg MacDonald, Hector Aguilar, Georgie Colon, Sheron James-Richardson, Philip Zhang, David Ocasio, Barry Jenkins (Head Porter), Roberto Calderon

ORCHESTRA
Front Row (L-R): Erica Von Kleist, Jim Hershman, Victoria Paterson, Hiroko Taguchi, Mary-Mitchell Campbell (Music Director/Conductor)

Middle Row (L-R): Chris Fenwick (Associate Conductor), Charles Pillow, Allison Seidner, Sean Carney, Damien Bassman

Back Row (L-R): Will Van Dyke, Mark Thrasher, Craig Johnson, Bud Burridge, Randy Andos, Billy Miller, Dave Kuhn

WARDROBE DEPARTMENT
Front Row (L-R): Alicia Aballi, Andrea Gonzalez (Asst. Wardrobe Supervisor), Jennifer Barnes, Ceili Clemens, Maria Goya

Middle Row (L-R): Mark Jones, Ronald Tagert, Linda Lee (Wardrobe Supervisor), Paula Davis

Back Row (L-R): Adele Miskie, John Webber, Ken Brown

STAFF FOR THE ADDAMS FAMILY

GENERAL MANAGEMENT
101 PRODUCTIONS, LTD.
Wendy Orshan   Jeffrey M. Wilson
David Auster
Elie Landau

COMPANY MANAGER
Sean Free

PRODUCTION MANAGEMENT
AURORA PRODUCTIONS
Gene O'Donovan, Ben Heller,
Rachel Sherbill, Jarid Sumner, Melissa Mazdra,
Amanda Raymond, Graham Forden,
Liza Luxenberg, Janelle Coats

GENERAL PRESS REPRESENTATIVE
THE PUBLICITY OFFICE
Marc Thibodeau
Jeremy Shaffer   Michael S. Borowski
Matthew Fasano

The Playbill Broadway Yearbook 2009-2010

The Addams Family

CASTING
TELSEY + COMPANY
Bernie Telsey CSA, Will Cantler CSA, David Vaccari CSA,
Bethany Knox CSA, Craig Burns CSA,
Tiffany Little Canfield CSA, Rachel Hoffman CSA,
Carrie Rosson CSA, Justin Huff CSA, Bess Fifer CSA,
Patrick Goodwin CSA, Abbie Brady-Dalton

PRODUCTION SUPERVISOR .....**Beverley Randolph**
Stage Manager ....Scott Taylor Rollison
Assistant Stage Manager ....Allison A. Lee
Associate Company Manager ....Chris D'Angelo
Associate Directors ....Heidi Miami Marshall,
Steve Bebout
Drama League Directing Fellow ....David F. Chapman
Associate Choreographer ....Dontee Kiehn
Associate Scenic Designer ....Frank McCullough
Associate Costume Designers ....MaryAnn D. Smith,
David Kaley
Associate Lighting Designer ....Yael Lubetzky
Automated Lighting Programmer ....Aland Henderson
Associate Sound Designer ....Jason Crystal
Associate Special Effects Designer ....Jeremy Chernick
Associate Puppetry Designer ....Ceili Clemens
Assistant Scenic Designers ....Lauren Alvarez,
Jeffrey Hinchee, Christine Peters,
Rob Thirtle
Assistant Costume Designer ....Sarah Laux
Assistant Lighting Designer ....Joel Shier
Assistant Make-up Designer ....Jorge Vargas
Costume Assistant ....Jennifer A. Jacob
Assistant in Puppetry ....Meredith Miller
Production Carpenter ....Paul T. Wimmer
Assistant Carpenter/Automation ....Bill Partello
Flyman ....Bryan S. Davis
Production Electrician ....J. Michael Pitzer
Head Electrician ....Mike Hyman
Assistant Electrician ....Jeremy Wahlers
Lead Follow Spot ....Stephen R. Long
Production Props ....Denise J. Grillo
Assistant Props ....Kevin Crawford
Production Sound ....David Gotwald
Assistant Sound ....Scott Silvian
Advance Sound ....Darin Stillman
Wardrobe Supervisor ....Linda Lee
Assistant Wardrobe Supervisor ....Andrea Gonzalez
Mr. Lane's Dresser ....Ken Brown
Ms. Neuwirth's Dresser ....Paula Davis
Dressers ....Jennifer Barnes, Ceili Clemens,
Del Miskie, Ronald Tagert,
John Webber
Hair & Make-up Supervisor ....Barry Ernst
Hair Dressers ....Suzanne Storey,
Whitney Adkins Mvondo
Music Coordinator ....Michael Keller
Music Preparation ....Kaye-Houston Music, Inc./
Anne Kaye, Doug Houston
Music Preparation Assistants ....Russell Driscoll,
Ernst Ebell, III,
Arthur Koening, Barry Lille
Electronic Music Programmer ....James Abbott
Additional Orchestrations ....August Eriksmoen,
Danny Troob
Additional Drum & Percussion
Arrangements ....Damien Bassman
Music Interns ....Ben Krauss, Tim Rosser

Children's Guardian ....Katy Lathan
Stage Management
Production Assistants ....Zac Chandler,
CJ LaRoche, Jenn McNeil,
Alison Roberts, Deanna Weiner
Company Management
Assistants ....Johnny Milani, Kathleen Mueller
Lighting Design Production Assistant ....Alec Thorne
Sound Design Production Assistant ....Jessica Bauer
Assistant to Mr. Oken ....Missy Greenberg
Assistant to Mr. Furman ....Eileen Williams
Assistant to Mr. Leavitt ....Erlinda Vo
Assistant to Mr. Lippa ....Will Van Dyke
Assistant to Mr. Lane ....Andrea Wolfson
Legal Counsel ....Levine, Plotkin & Menin LLP/
Loren Plotkin, Esq., Susan Mindell,
Conrad Rippy, Cris Criswell
Accountant ....Rosenberg, Neuwirth,
& Kuchner, CPAs/
Christopher Cacace
Comptroller ....Jana Jevnikar
Advertising ....Serino Coyne/
Sandy Block, Angelo Desimini,
Matt Upshaw
Marketing ....Type A Marketing/
Anne Rippey, Nick Pramik
Interactive Marketing ....Situation Interactive/
Damian Bazadona, John Lanasa,
Jeremy Kraus, Jenn Elston
Educational Program ....Camp Broadway
101 Productions, Ltd. Staff ....Ingrid Kloss,
Meredith Morgan, Michael Rudd,
Mary Six Rupert, Christine Stump
Children's Tutoring ....On Location Education/
Alan Simon, Muriel Kester
Banking ....City National Bank/Anne McSweeney
Insurance ....DeWitt Stern, Inc./Peter Shoemaker
Physical Therapy ....PhysioArts/Jennifer R. Green
Orthopedist ....David S. Weiss, MD
Immigration ....Traffic Control Group, Inc./David King
Merchandising ....Encore Merchandising, Inc./
Joey Boyles, Chris Paseka,
Maryana Geller
Production Photographer ....Joan Marcus
Payroll Services ....Castellana Services, Inc.
Music Intern ....Adam Wiggins

www.theaddamsfamilymusical.com

CREDITS
Scenery by Hudson Scenic Studios, Inc., Showman Fabricators, Chicago Scenic Studios, Inc. Automated scenery by Hudson Scenic Studios. Lighting equipment and special lighting effects from PRG Lighting. Sound equipment from Masque Sound. Costumes executed by Eric Winterling, Carelli Costumes, Jennifer Love. Costume painting by Jeffrey Fender. Props by the Paragon Innovation Group, Jerard Studios, Craig Grigg, Daedalus Design & Production, Zoe Morsette, ICBA, Inc. Men's shirts by Cego Custom Shirt. Millinery by Hugh Hanson for Carelli Costumes and Arnold S. Levine, Inc. Custom footwear by LaDuca Productions, Ltd.; Pluma Handmade Dance Footwear; Worldtone Dance; and Sam Vasili Custom Shoes. "Fester" custom work by Izquierdo Studio. "Grandma's" shawl by Vanessa Theriault. Additional men's tailoring by Paul Chang, Chicago. Special effects by Jauchem & Meeh,

Inc. Flying by Foy Aerographic® Services. Make-up provided by M•A•C. Mr. Mann's wardrobe provided by Brooks Brothers. Cell phones courtesy of Nokia. Emergen-C super energy booster provided by Alacer Corp. Onstage merchandising by George Fenmore.

"Addams Family Theme" by Vic Mizzy, published by Unison Music Company (ASCAP). Administered by Next Decade Entertainment, Inc. All rights reserved, used by permission.

THE ADDAMS FAMILY rehearsed at
New 42nd Street Rehearsal Studios.

PUPPETRY BUILT BY
TANDEM OTTER PRODUCTIONS
Barbara Busackino, Project Manager
Ceili Clemens, Build Manager
BUILDERS: TV Alexander, Liz Cherry, Duncan Gillis, Kristin Gdula, Michael Kerns, Matthew Leabo, Vito Leanza, Nara Lesser, Laura Manns, Eric Novak, Adam Pagdon, Travis Pickett, Jon Mark Ponder, Jessica Scott, Ted Southern, Nikki Taylor
BUILD INTERNS: Rebecca Aldridge, Katherine Allen, Baxley Andresen, Lydia Andrien, Rachel Borg, Ariel Brickman, Reva Castillenti, Camille Chan, Katie Clarkson, Bevan Dunbar, Morgan Filteau, Ben Finer, Lynnette Franklin, Lauren Gouse, Peter Howard, Nina Kelsch, Trey Kirchoff, Lindsay Limauro, Elizabeth Liu, Jonothan Lyons, Hannah Mossop, Tiffany J. Plante, Adena Rice, Emily Rosen, Jessica Silas, Samantha Simoes, Millie Taylor, Cherise R. Ward, Bethany Willet

Souvenir merchandise by
Encore Merchandising, Inc.

Original cast album coming soon from
Decca Records.

Chairman ....James M. Nederlander
President ....James L. Nederlander

Executive Vice President
Nick Scandalios

Vice President
Corporate Development
Charlene S. Nederlander

Senior Vice President
Labor Relations
Herschel Waxman

Vice President
Jim Boese

Chief Financial Officer
Freida Sawyer Belviso

STAFF FOR THE LUNT-FONTANNE
House Manager ....Tracey Malinowski
Treasurer ....Joe Olcese
Assistant Treasurer ....Gregg Collichio
House Carpenter ....Terry Taylor
House Electrician ....Dennis Boyle
House Propertyman ....Andrew Bentz
House Flyman ....Matt Walters
House Engineers ....Robert MacMahon,
Joseph Riccio III

The Addams Family
SCRAPBOOK

1. Bebe Neuwirth at the premiere party.
2. Carolee Carmello takes her bow on opening night.
3. Adam Riegler and Yearbook correspondent Zachary James mug for the camera backstage.
4. Creative consultant Jerry Zaks.
5. Cast members Krysta Rodriguez and Wesley Taylor at the opening night after-party at the Marriott Marquis Hotel.

Correspondent: Zachary James, "Lurch"

Opening Night Gifts: Flashlight, plaster hand, Charles Addams cartoons.

Most Exciting Celebrity Visitor: John Astin, TV's Gomez Addams.

Who Got the Gypsy Robe: Jim Borstelmann.

Actor Who Performed the Most Roles in This Show: Liz Ramos—Ancestor, Bird, Star, Monster under the bed, Tassle.

Who Has Done the Most Shows in Their Career: Nathan Lane, 18.

Favorite Moment During Each Performance: Carolee Carmello singing "Waiting."

Favorite In-Theatre Gathering Place: The Water Cooler Club, The Baja Dune, Grandma's Attic, Upper Lobby for Dance Clean-Up, Snack time in the Hair Room.

Favorite Off-Site Hangout: Bond 45

Favorite Snack Food: Chocolate covered potato chips from Speach Family Candy.

Mascot: Cubby Bernstein.

Favorite Therapy: Physical Therapy with Jen.

Most Memorable Ad-Lib: Tie among "I gotta package from Spain" and "I hear that Tiger Woods is hot to trot" and "I'm gonna go up to my room and get me some Dick…Clark."

Record Number of Cell Phone Rings, Cell Phone Photos, Tweeting or Texting Incidents During a Performance: Who can count?

Web Buzz on This Show: We have a lot of webs in our show. They weren't included in the out-of-town tryout but add a nice touch to our Broadway set on the staircases and chandelier.

Memorable Press Encounter: Michael Riedel.

Memorable Stage Door Fan Encounters: Wesley being told he had an ugly headshot. Countless people saying they can't wait to replace us when they graduate and/or move to NYC. "I'm Russell from Facebook."

Latest Audience Arrival: A tour group bus got stuck in the Lincoln tunnel and arrived around 8:30.

Who Wore the Heaviest/Hottest Costume: Kevin Chamberlin as Uncle Fester.

Who Wore the Least: Adam Riegler as Pugsley.

The Playbill Broadway Yearbook 2009-2010

The Addams Family
SCRAPBOOK

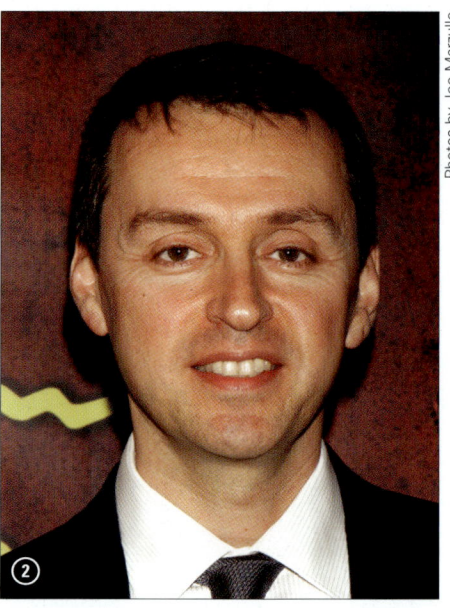

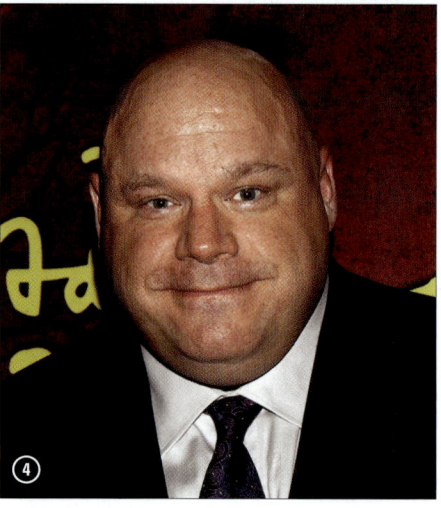

2009-2010 AWARDS

DRAMA DESK AWARD
Outstanding Set Design
(Phelim McDermott, Julian Crouch
and Basil Twist)

OUTER CRITICS CIRCLE AWARD
Outstanding Set Design—Play or Musical
(Phelim McDermott & Julian Crouch)

1. (Front L-R): Nathan Lane and Bebe Neuwirth with cast members on stage during opening night curtain calls.
2. Songwriter Andrew Lippa.
3. Charlotte d'Amboise, cast member Terrence Mann, and their daughters Josephine and Shelby attending the opening night after-party.
4. Cast member Kevin Chamberlin.

Fastest Costume Change: Wednesday from Yellow Dress to Black Dress in our out-of-town tryout.
The ladies from Ghosts to puppeteers to bathing beauties.
Busiest Day at the Box Office: The day after we opened.
Catchphrases Only the Company Would Recognize: "Showtime, Terry's here!"
Which Orchestra Member Played the Most Instruments: Damien Bassman and his array of percussion instruments
Which Orchestra Member Played the Most Consecutive Performances Without A Sub: Damien Bassman, Will Van Dyke, Allison Seidner.
Best In-House Parody Lyrics: "When you're an Addams, you blame it on the bossa nova." "Move toward the exit."
Memorable Directorial Notes: "We need to give the puppets a break."
"Don't EVER do that again!"
Company In-Jokes: Tombstones Comedy Club.
Company Legend: Bebe Neuwirth.
Understudy Anecdote: The foiled Times Square Car Bomb trapped Zach James on the subway for an hour and a half until after "places." Fred Inkley was dressed and ready to go on as Lurch when Zach burst in the stage door to find they had been holding the curtain due to the bomb scare. The show went on as normal. Just a half hour later than usual.

Nicknames: Moishe, Bebela, Gummels, Uncle Nathan, Couch, Gower.
Sweethearts Within the Company: Cousin It and Tassle.
Embarrassing Moment: When the blackout curtain came down on Wesley (Lucas) during "Crazier Than You" and he had to dive under it to finish the song. When the house didn't fall down and we had to walk around it.
Ghostly Encounter Backstage: The Oriental Theatre in Chicago. Google "Iroquois Theatre Fire" for more info!
Superstitions That Turned Out To Be True: Bad dress rehearsal, great opening.
Coolest Thing About Being in This Show: Playing iconic and beloved characters.
Fan Club Info: We have a fan club?!

After Miss Julie

First Preview: September 18, 2009. Opened: October 22, 2009.
Closed December 6, 2009 after 40 Previews and 53 Performances.

CAST
(in order of appearance)
Christine .... MARIN IRELAND
John .... JONNY LEE MILLER
Miss Julie .... SIENNA MILLER

PLACE
The kitchen of a large country estate outside London.

TIME
July 26, 1945. Night and the morning after. The British Labour Party won their famous "landslide" election victory on this night. The triumph of the Labour Party over Winston Churchill's Conservative Party swept a new government into power with the promise of radical change and reform.

UNDERSTUDIES
For John:
RYAN McCARTHY
For Miss Julie/Christine:
LISA VELTEN SMITH

Additional voices by PAUL O'BRIEN, SANDRA SHIPLEY, DANIEL STEWART

Production Stage Manager:
JAMES FITZSIMMONS
Stage Manager:
BRYCE McDONALD

AMERICAN AIRLINES THEATRE
ROUNDABOUT THEATRE COMPANY
Todd Haimes, Artistic Director
Harold Wolpert, Managing Director
Julia C. Levy, Executive Director

In association with Sonia Friedman Productions and Ostar Productions

Present

Sienna Miller   Jonny Lee Miller
Marin Ireland

in

A version of Strindberg's Miss Julie
By
Patrick Marber

| Set Design | Costume Design | Lighting Design | Original Music and Sound Design |
| Allen Moyer | Michael Krass | Mark McCullough | David Van Tieghem |

| Wig Design | Dialect Coach | Fight Director | Production Stage Manager |
| Paul Huntley | Deborah Hecht | Thomas Schall | James FitzSimmons |

| Casting | Production Management | General Manager | Press Representative |
| Jim Carnahan, C.S.A. | Aurora Productions | Rebecca Habel | Boneau/Bryan-Brown |

| Director of Marketing & Sales Promotion | Founding Director | Associate Artistic Director |
| David B. Steffen | Gene Feist | Scott Ellis |

Directed by
Mark Brokaw

World Stage Premiere presented at the Donmar Warehouse, London, on November 20th 2003
Support for new plays generously provided by The Andrew W. Mellon Foundation and The Harold and Mimi Steinberg Charitable Trust.
Roundabout Theatre Company is a member of the League of Resident Theatres.
www.roundabouttheatre.org

(L-R): Jonny Lee Miller and Sienna Miller.

After Miss Julie

Sienna Miller
Miss Julie

Jonny Lee Miller
John

Marin Ireland
Christine

Ryan McCarthy
u/s John

Jonny Lee Miller and Marin Ireland.
Photo by Joan Marcus

Lisa Velten Smith
u/s Christine, Miss Julie

August Strindberg
Author of Miss Julie

Patrick Marber
Playwright

Mark Brokaw
Director

Allen Moyer
Set Design

Paul Huntley
Hair and Wig Design

Sonia Friedman Productions

Bill Haber, Ostar Productions

Jim Carnahan
Casting

Gene Feist
Founding Director, Roundabout Theatre Company

Todd Haimes
Artistic Director, Roundabout Theatre Company

ROUNDABOUT THEATRE COMPANY STAFF
ARTISTIC DIRECTOR .... **TODD HAIMES**
MANAGING DIRECTOR .... **HAROLD WOLPERT**
EXECUTIVE DIRECTOR .... **JULIA C. LEVY**
ASSOCIATE ARTISTIC DIRECTOR .. **SCOTT ELLIS**

ARTISTIC STAFF
DIRECTOR OF ARTISTIC DEVELOPMENT/
  DIRECTOR OF CASTING .... Jim Carnahan
Artistic Consultant .... Robyn Goodman
Resident Director .... Doug Hughes
Associate Artists ..... Scott Elliott, Bill Irwin, Joe Mantello,
              Mark Brokaw, Kathleen Marshall
Literary Manager .... Jill Rafson
Casting Director .... Carrie Gardner
Casting Associate .... Kate Boka
Casting Associate .... Stephen Kopel
Artistic Assistant .... Amy Ashton
Literary Associate .... Josh Fiedler
The Blanche and Irving Laurie Foundation
  Theatre Visions Fund Commissions .... Julia Cho,
              Stephen Karam, Lewis Black,
              Nathan Louis Jackson
Educational Foundation of
  America Commissions .... Bekah Brunstetter,
              Lydia Diamond, Diana Fithian,
              Julie Marie Myatt

New York State Council
  on the Arts Commission .... Nathan Louis Jackson
Roundabout Commissions .... Steven Levenson,
              Robert Lopez & Kristen Anderson-Lopez
Artistic Intern .... Benjamin Izzo
Casting Interns .... Kyle Bosley, Jillian Cimini,
              Erin Drake, Andrew Femenella,
              Lauren Lewis, Quinn Meyers
Script Readers .... Jay Cohen, Hillary Dixler,
              Nicholas Stimler

EDUCATION STAFF
EDUCATION DIRECTOR .... Greg McCaslin
Education Program Manager .... Jennifer DiBella
Education Associate
  for Theatre-Based Programs .... Jay Gerlach
Education Coordinator .... Aliza Greenberg
Education Dramaturg .... Ted Sod
Teaching Artists .... Cynthia Babak,
              Victor Barbella, LaTonya Borsay,
              Mark Bruckner, Joe Clancy, Vanessa Davis,
              Joe Doran, Elizabeth Dunn-Ruiz,
              Janet Edwards, Kevin Free, Tony Freeman,
              Sheri Graubert, Matthew A.J. Gregory,
              Melissa Gregus, Adam Gwon, Devin Haqq,
              Carrie Heitman, Karla Hendrick, Jim Jack,
              Jason Jacobs, Lisa Renee Jordan,
              Jamie Kalama, Alvin Keith, Tami Mansfield,
              Erin McCready, Deidre O'Connor,
              Andrew Ondrejcak, Maya Parra, Laura Poe,
              Jennifer Rathbone, Leah Reddy,
              Amanda Rehbein, Bernita Robinson,
              Christopher Rummel, Cassy Rush,
              Nick Simone, Heidi Stallings, Daniel Sullivan,
              Carl Tallent, Vickie Tanner, Jolie Tong,
              Cristina Vaccaro, Jennifer Varbalow,
              Leese Walker, Eric Wallach, Christina Watanabe,
              Gail Winar, Conwell Worthington, III
Teaching Artist Apprentices .... Carrie Ellman-Larsen,
              Deanna Frieman, Meghan O'Neill
Education Interns .... Nicole Bournas-Ney,
              Mandy Menaker

ADMINISTRATIVE STAFF
GENERAL MANAGER .... Sydney Beers
Associate Managing Director .... Greg Backstrom
General Manager,
  American Airlines Theatre .... Rebecca Habel
General Manager, Steinberg Center .... Rachel E. Ayers
Human Resources Manager .... Stephen Deutsch
Operations Manager .... Valerie D. Simmons
Associate General Manager .... Maggie Cantrick
Office Manager .... Scott Kelly
Management Associate .... Jill K. Boyd

After Miss Julie

Archivist	Tiffany Nixon
Receptionists	Dee Beider, Raquel Castillo, Elisa Papa, Allison Patrick, Monica Sidorchuk
Messenger	Darnell Franklin
Management Interns	Samara Harand, Jennifer Levine

FINANCE STAFF

DIRECTOR OF FINANCE	Susan Neiman
Assistant Controller	John LaBarbera
Accounts Payable Administrator	Frank Surdi
Financial Associate	Yonit Kafka
Business Office Assistant	Joshua Cohen
Business Interns	Davin DeSantis, Stephanie Jaccarino, Laura Marshall

DEVELOPMENT STAFF

Director, Institutional Giving	Julie K. D'Andrea
Director, Special Events	Steve Schaeffer
Director, Major Gifts	Joy Pak
Director, Patron Programs	Amber Jo Manuel
Manager, Donor Information Systems	Lise Speidel
Manager, Patron Programs	Tyler Ennis
Manager, Telefundraising	Gavin Brown
Manager, Corporate Relations	Roxana Petzold
Associate Manager, Patron Programs	Marisa Perry
Special Events Associate	Ashley Firestone
Patron Services Associate	David Pittman
Institutional Giving Associate	Nick Nolte
Development Assistants	Ryan Hallett, Nick Luckenbaugh
Assistant to the Executive Director	Jason Butler
Major Gifts Intern	Kayla Carpenter
Special Events Intern	Amy Rosenfeld

INFORMATION TECHNOLOGY STAFF

IT DIRECTOR	Antonio Palumbo
IT Associate	Dylan Norden
IT Associate	Jim Roma
DIRECTOR DATABASE OPERATIONS	Wendy Hutton
Database Administrator/Programmer	Revanth Anne

MARKETING STAFF

DIRECTOR OF MARKETING AND SALES PROMOTION	David B. Steffen
Associate Director of Marketing	Tom O'Connor
Marketing/Publications Manager	Margaret Casagrande
Assistant Director of Marketing	Stefanie Schussel
Marketing Manager	Shannon Marcotte
Website Consultant	Keith Powell Beyland
Director of Telesales Special Promotions	Marco Frezza
Telesales Manager	Anthony Merced
Telesales Office Coordinator	Patrick Pastor
Marketing Interns	H.L. Ray, Sean Burpee

TICKET SERVICES STAFF

Director of Sales Operations	Charlie Garbowski, Jr.
Ticket Services Manager	Ellen Holt
Subscription Manager	Ethan Ubell
Box Office Managers	Edward P. Osborne, Jaime Perlman, Krystin MacRitchie, Nicole Nicholson
Group Sales Manager	Jeff Monteith
Assistant Box Office Managers	Robert Morgan, Andrew Clements, Scott Falkowski, Catherine Fitzpatrick
Assistant Ticket Services Managers	Robert Kane, Bill Klemm, Lindsay Ericson
Customer Services Coordinator	Thomas Walsh
Ticket Services	Solangel Bido, Arianna Boykins, Lauren Cartelli, Joseph Clark, Barbara Dente, Nisha Dhruna, Adam Elsberry, James Graham, Kara Harrington, Tova Heller, Nicki Ishmael, Kate Longosky, Michelle Maccarone, Elisa Mala, Mead Margulies, Chuck Migliaccio, Carlos Morris, Kayrose Pagan, Thomas Protulipac, Jessica Pruett-Barnett, Kaia Rafoss, Josh Rozett, Ben Schneider, Kenneth Senn, Heather Siebert, Nalane Singh, Lillian Soto, Ron Tobia, Jacklyn Verbitski, Hannah Weitzman
Intern	Melissa Cohen

SERVICES

Counsel	Paul, Weiss, Rifkind, Wharton and Garrison LLP, Charles H. Googe Jr., Carol M. Kaplan
Counsel	Rosenberg & Estis
Counsel	Andrew Lance, Gibson, Dunn, & Crutcher, LLP
Counsel	Harry H. Weintraub, Glick and Weintraub, P.C.
Counsel	Stroock & Stroock & Lavan LLP
Counsel	Daniel S. Dokos, Weil, Gotschal & Manges LLP
Immigration Counsel	Mark D. Koestler and Theodore Ruthizer
Government Relations	Law Offices of Claudia Wagner LLC
House Physicians	Dr. Theodore Tyberg, Dr. Lawrence Katz
House Dentist	Neil Kanner, D.M.D.
Insurance	DeWitt Stern Group, Inc.
Accountant	Lutz & Carr CPAs, LLP
Advertising	Spotco/ Drew Hodges, Jim Edwards, Tom Greenwald, Kyle Hall, Cory Spinney
Interactive Marketing	Situation Interactive/ Damian Bazadona, John Lanasa, Ryan Klink, Kristen Butler
Events Photography	Anita and Steve Shevett
Production Photographer	Joan Marcus
Theatre Displays	King Displays, Wayne Sapper
Lobby Refreshments	Sweet Concessions
Merchandising	Spotco Merch/ James Decker

MANAGING DIRECTOR EMERITUS ....Ellen Richard

Roundabout Theatre Company
231 West 39th Street, New York, NY 10018
(212) 719-9393.

GENERAL PRESS REPRESENTATIVES
BONEAU/BRYAN-BROWN
Adrian Bryan-Brown
Matt Polk   Jessica Johnson   Amy Kass
Emily Meagher

STAFF FOR AFTER MISS JULIE

Company Manager	Carly DiFulvio
Production Stage Manager	James FitzSimmons
Stage Manager	Bryce McDonald
Production Management by	Aurora Productions/ Gene O'Donovan, W. Benjamin Heller II, Rachel Sherbill, Jarid Sumner, Steve Rosenberg, Melissa Mazdra, Amy Merlino Coey, Amanda Raymond, Graham Forden, Liza Luxenberg
Etiquette/Movement Consultant	Frank Ventura
Assistant Director	Alec Strum
Associate Scenic Designer	Warren Karp
Associate Costume Designer	Tracy Christensen
Associate Lighting Designer	Driscoll Otto
Associate Sound Designer	Jill BC DuBoff
Assistant Sound Designer	Sam Doerr
Make-Up Design by	Angelina Avallone
Production Properties	Peter Sarafin
Production Carpenter	Glenn Merwede
Production Electrician	Barb Bartel
Running Properties	Robert W. Dowling II
Sound Operator	Dann Wojnar
Music Search Supervisor	Hank Aberle
Wardrobe Supervisor	Susan J. Fallon
Hair and Wig Supervisor	Manuela LaPorte
Dresser	Kat Martin
Wardrobe Dayworker	Lauren Galitelli
Assistant Make-Up Artist	Jorge Vargas
Production Assistant	Katherine Wallace
SDC Observer	Alexis Jacknow
IA Apprentice	Sarah K. Conyers
Scenery Constructed by	Great Lakes Scenic Studios
Costumes Constructed by	Eric Winterling, Scafati, Helen Uffner, Vintage Clothing
Select Costume Pieces by	Virginia Johnson
Lighting Equipment Provided by	PRG Lighting, a division of Production Resource Group LLC
Sound Equipment Provided by	Sound Associates
Prop Furniture	Tom Carroll Scenery
Special Effects	Craig Grigg and Subrosa Machine
Cast Iron Range	Yorkshire Ranges
UK Prop Shopper	Tracey Clarke
Special Thanks to	Marie-Claire Martineau and Teruyo Takagi

M•A•C
Official Makeup of Roundabout Theatre Company

AMERICAN AIRLINES THEATRE STAFF

Company Manager	Carly DiFulvio
House Carpenter	Glenn Merwede
House Electrician	Brian Maiuri
House Properties	Robert W. Dowling II
House Sound	Dann Wojnar
IA Apprentice	Sarah K. Conyers
Wardrobe Supervisor	Susan J. Fallon
Box Office Manager	Ted Osborne
Assistant Box Office Manager	Robert Morgan
House Manager	Steve Ryan
Associate House Manager	Zipporah Aguasvivas
Head Usher	Jacklyn Rivera
House Staff	Ilia Diaz, Anne Ezell, Adam Wier, Rebecca Knell, James Watanachaiyot, Ernesto Sanchez, Celia Perez, Kareem McRae, Crystal Suarez, Fatimah Robinson, Paul Krasner
Security	Julious Russell
Additional Security provided by	Gotham Security
Maintenance	Jerry Hobbs, Daniel Pellew, Willie Philips, Magali Western
Lobby Refreshments	Sweet Concessions

After Miss Julie

MANAGEMENT
(L-R): Carly DiFulvio, Rebecca Habel, James FitzSimmons, Kate Wallace, Bryce McDonald

BOX OFFICE
(L-R): Ted Osborne, Solangel Bido, Mead Margulies

CREW
Front Row (L-R): Kat Martin, Dann Wojnar, Sarah K. Conyers, Susan Fallon

Back Row (L-R): Jay Penfield, Barb Bartel, Glenn Merwede, Robert Dowling

After Miss Julie
Scrapbook

Correspondent: Marin Ireland, "Christine"
Opening Night Gifts: Straight razors from Jonny.
Most Exciting Celebrity Visitor: Twiggy. She loved the show!
Special Backstage Ritual: Sienna and Jonny doing a "boogie" offstage.
Favorite Moment During Each Performance (On Stage or Off): Company cuddle at five minutes.
Favorite In-Theatre Gathering Place: Traproom for Sunday brunch! Or stage right wings, for some reason.
Favorite Off-Site Hangout: Joe Allen's.
Favorite Snack Food: Coconut water.
Mascot: Porgy
Favorite Therapy: Grether's pastilles.
Fastest Costume Change: Sienna, from uptown Julie to morning-after Julie in about 30 seconds.
Who Wore the Heaviest/Hottest Costume: Jonny's wool suits.
Catchphrase Only the Company Would Recognize: "What's the stench??"
Memorable Directorial Note: Something about a "boner"...Freudian slip!
Nickname: "Teeny" (Julie's nickname for Christine.)
Coolest Thing About Being in This Show: We're all Millers! My mother's maiden name is Miller, so that makes three of us!

1. Yearbook correspondent Marin Ireland with co-star Jonny Lee Miller on opening night.
2. Sienna Miller at the American Airlines Theatre for the premiere.
3. The marquee of the American Airlines Theatre during the show's run.
4. Understudies Lisa Velten Smith and Ryan McCarthy.
5. Ireland, Miller and Miller take a curtain call on opening night.
6. Director Mark Brokaw (L) and playwright Patrick Marber.

Photos by Aubrey Reuben

The Playbill Broadway Yearbook 2009-2010

All About Me

First Preview: February 22, 2010. Opened: March 18, 2010.
Closed April 4, 2010 after 27 Previews and 20 Performances.

HENRY MILLER'S THEATRE

Jeffrey Richards Jerry Frankel Eagle Productions LLC
Jamie deRoy/Remmel T. Dickinson Richard Winkler/Dan Frishwasser Mallory Factor
Cheryl Lachowicz Chris Yegen Judith Resnick Jon Bierman
Christopher Hart Productions CTM Media Group Stewart F. Lane/Bonnie Comley
Michael Filerman Barry & Carole Kaye/Irv Welzer Terry Allen Kramer Terrie J. Lootens
Stein & Gunderson Productions WenSheJack Productions Mickey Conlon

present

Dame Edna

in

ALL ABOUT ME

A Showbiz Entertainment

Written by
Christopher Durang and Barry Humphries

Conceived by
**Barry Humphries,
with Lizzie Spender and Terrence Flannery**

With
Gregory Butler   Jodi Capeless   Jon-Paul Mateo

| Scenic & Costume Design | Lighting Design | Sound Design |
| Anna Louizos | Howell Binkley | Peter Fitzgerald |

| Dame Edna's Gowns | Video Design | Production Stage Manager |
| Stephen Adnitt | Chris Cronin | James W. Gibbs |

| Orchestrations | Additional Arrangements | Music Coordinator | Casting |
| John Oddo | Glen Kelly | Michael Keller | Telsey + Co |

| Technical Supervision | General Press Representative | General Management | Associate Producers |
| Hudson Theatrical Associates/ Neil Mazzella | Jeffrey Richards Associates Irene Gandy/Alana Karpoff | Stuart Thompson Productions | Jeremy Scott Blaustein Rae Rothfield |

Music Supervisor
Rob Bowman

Directed by
Casey Nicholaw

3/18/10

CAST
(in order of appearance)

DAME EDNA

Stage Manager	JODI CAPELESS
Bruno	GREGORY BUTLER
Benito	JON-PAUL MATEO
Stage Manager	FRANCESCA RUSSELL

Barry Humphries is appearing with the permission of Actors' Equity Association.

UNDERSTUDY

For Bruno/Benito/Stage Manager, Dance Captain:
PATRICK WETZEL

(L-R): Gregory Butler, Dame Edna and Jon-Paul Mateo

Continued on next page

All About Me

First Preview: February 22, 2010. Opened: March 18, 2010.
Closed April 4, 2010 after 27 Previews and 20 Performances.

CAST
(in order of appearance)

MICHAEL FEINSTEIN

Stage Manager	JODI CAPELESS
Bruno	GREGORY BUTLER
Benito	JON-PAUL MATEO
Stage Manager	FRANCESCA RUSSELL

UNDERSTUDY
For Bruno/Benito/Stage Manager, Dance Captain:
PATRICK WETZEL

HENRY MILLER'S THEATRE

Jeffrey Richards Jerry Frankel Eagle Productions LLC
Jamie deRoy/Remmel T. Dickinson Richard Winkler/Dan Frishwasser Mallory Factor
Cheryl Lachowicz Chris Yegen Judith Resnick Jon Bierman
Christopher Hart Productions CTM Media Group Stewart F. Lane/Bonnie Comley
Michael Filerman Barry & Carole Kaye/Irv Welzer Terry Allen Kramer Terrie J. Lootens
Stein & Gunderson Productions WenSheJack Productions Mickey Conlon

present

Michael Feinstein

in

ALL ABOUT ME

A Showbiz Entertainment

Written by
Christopher Durang and Michael Feinstein

Conceived by
**Michael Feinstein,
with Lizzie Spender and Terrence Flannery**

With
Gregory Butler   Jodi Capeless   Jon-Paul Mateo

Scenic & Costume Design	Lighting Design	Sound Design
Anna Louizos	Howell Binkley	Peter Fitzgerald

Video Design	Production Stage Manager
Chris Cronin	James W. Gibbs

Orchestrations	Additional Arrangements	Music Coordinator	Casting
John Oddo	Glen Kelly	Michael Keller	Telsey + Co

Technical Supervision	General Press Representative	General Management	Associate Producers
Hudson Theatrical Associates/ Neil Mazzella	Jeffrey Richards Associates Irene Gandy/Alana Karpoff	Stuart Thompson Productions	Jeremy Scott Blaustein Rae Rothfield

Music Supervisor
Rob Bowman

Directed by
Casey Nicholaw

3/18/10

Michael Feinstein

Photo by Joan Marcus

Continued on next page

All About Me

ORIGINAL SONGS

"Make That Piano Sing"	Music by Matthew Sklar, lyrics by Chad Beguelin
"Niceness"	Music by Nick Rowley, lyrics by Barry Humphries
"We Get Along Amazingly Well"	Music by Michael Feinstein, lyrics by Glen Kelly and Barry Humphries
"I'm Forcing Myself"	Music by Wayne Barker, lyrics by Barry Humphries
"The Dingo Ate My Baby"	Music by Michael Feinstein, lyrics by Barry Humphries
"The Koala Song"	Music and lyrics by Michael Feinstein
"Medley Song"	Music and lyrics by Michael Feinstein
"All About Me"	Music by Matthew Sklar, lyrics by Chad Beguelin
"The Gladdy Song"	Music by Michael Feinstein, lyrics by Barry Humphries and Michael Feinstein

ORCHESTRA

Conductor: ROB BOWMAN
Music Coordinator: MICHAEL KELLER
Reeds: DAVID MANN, AARON HEICK, MARK VINCI, RON JANNELLI
Trumpets: CRAIG JOHNSON, BRIAN PARESCHI, KENNY RAMPTON
Trombones: JOHN FEDCHOCK, BIRCH JOHNSON
Piano: ROB BOWMAN
Bass: DAVID FINCK
Drums: ALBIE BERK
Music Copying: KAYE-HOUSTON MUSIC/ ANNE KAYE AND DOUG HOUSTON

Dame Edna

Michael Feinstein

Gregory Butler
Bruno

Jodi Capeless
Stage Manager

Jon-Paul Mateo
Benito

Patrick Wetzel
u/s Stage Manager/ Bruno/Benito

Christopher Durang
Author

Barry Humphries
Author, Co-Conceiver

Casey Nicholaw
Director/ Choreographer

Anna Louizos
Scenic and Costume Design

Howell Binkley
Lighting Design

Chris Cronin
Video Design

Michael Keller
Music Coordinator

Bernard Telsey, Telsey + Company
Casting

Neil A. Mazzella/ Hudson Theatrical Associates
Technical Supervision

Stuart Thompson Productions
General Management

Jeffrey Richards
Producer

Jerry Frankel
Producer

Jamie deRoy
Producer

Stewart F. Lane and Bonnie Comley
Producers

All About Me

Remmel T. Dickinson
Producer

Mallory Factor
Producer

Michael Filerman
Producer

Irving Welzer
Producer

Terry Allen Kramer
Producer

Wendy Federman
Producer

Jeremy Scott Blaustein
Associate Producer

CREW
(L-R): Dorion Fuchs, Jordan Gable, Paul Ashton, Cleon D. Byerly, Jake Hall, Josh Weitzman, Ed Chapman, James Gibbs, Steve Beers, Markus Fokken, Kimberly Baird, Judy Badame, Francesca Russell

---

STAFF FOR *ALL ABOUT ME*

GENERAL MANAGEMENT
STUART THOMPSON PRODUCTIONS
Stuart Thompson James Triner David Turner

COMPANY MANAGER
Cassidy J. Briggs

GENERAL PRESS REPRESENTATIVE
JEFFREY RICHARDS ASSOCIATES
Irene Gandy
Alana Karpoff Elon Rutberg Diana Rissetto

CASTING
TELSEY + COMPANY, C.S.A.
Bernie Telsey CSA, Will Cantler CSA, David Vaccari CSA, Bethany Knox CSA, Craig Burns CSA, Tiffany Little Canfield CSA, Rachel Hoffman CSA, Carrie Rosson CSA, Justin Huff CSA, Bess Fifer CSA, Patrick Goodwin CSA, Abbie Brady-Dalton

PRODUCTION MANAGEMENT
HUDSON THEATRICAL ASSOCIATES
Neil Mazzella Sam Ellis Irene Wang

PRODUCTION STAGE MANAGER JAMES W. GIBBS

The Playbill Broadway Yearbook 2009-2010

All About Me

Stage Manager	Francesca Russell
Assistant Director	Matt Williams
Associate Scenic Designer	Mike Carnahan
Assistant Scenic Designer	Hilary Noxon
Associate Lighting Designer	Ryan O'Gara
Associate Costume Designer	Heather Dunbar
Assistant Costume Designer	Aimee M. Dombo
Assistant Sound Designer	Domonic Sack
Props	Kathy Fabian/Propstar
Propstar Associates	Tim Ferro, Carrie Mossman
Propstar Assistants	Jessica Provencale, Edward Morris
Production Assistants	Brian Bogin, Quinn M. Corbin
Moving Light Programmer	Chris Herman
Animator	Matt Anderson
Automation	Paul Ashton
Flyman	Jordan Gable
Followspot Operators	Dorion Fuchs, Jocelyn Smith
Sound Operator	Ed Chapman
Deck Sound	Aaron Straus
Assistant Sound	Jake Hall
Wardrobe Supervisor	Kimberly Baird
Dressers	Judy Badame, Cleon Byerly
Hair Supervisor	Markus Fokken
Orchestrators	Bill Elliot, Dick Lieb, Jonathan Tunick, Doug Walter, William Waranoff
Special Media and Creative Content	Andy Drachenberg
Assistant to Barry Humphries & Lizzie Spender	Nicola Pedlingham
Assistant to Michael Feinstein	Andy Brattain
General Management Assistants	Megan Curren, Brittany Levasseur
General Management Interns	Andrew Lowy, Erin Byrne
Assistants to Jeffrey Richards	Michael Crea, Will Trice
Advertising	Serino Coyne, Inc./ Greg Corradetti, Tom Callahan, Robert Jones, Danielle Boyle
Interactive Marketing	Damian Bazadona, John Lanasa, Miriam Naggar, Victoria Gettler
Banking	City National/Michele Gibbons
Accountants	Fried & Kowgios CPA's LLP/ Robert Fried, CPA
Controller	Galbraith & Co/ Sarah Galbraith, Tabitha Falcone
Legal Counsel	Lazarus & Harris LLP./ Scott R. Lazarus, Esq., Robert C. Harris, Esq.
Insurance	DeWitt Stern Group
Payroll	Castellana Services Inc.
Transportation	IBA Limousines
Dame Edna Honorary Understudy	Scott Mason
Company Mascots	Skye, Franco, Phoenix, Alexander & Smokey, Mecca

CREDITS

Scenery and automation constructed by Hudson Scenic Studio. Lighting equipment from PRG Lighting. Sound and video by Sound Associates. Pianos by Steinway & Sons and The Piano Exchange. Upholstery by Mimi New York and Sarah Bird. Flame treatment by Turning Star Inc. Hosiery and undergarments by Bra*Tenders. Flowers by George Vallo/Porta Fiori Flowers. Theatre display by King Display. Sickness relief by Emergen-C.

"Strike Up the Band" by George Gershwin and Ira Gershwin. Published by W B Music Corp. All rights reserved. Used by permission. "The Lady Is a Tramp" by Richard Rodgers and Lorenz Hart. Published by Chappel & Co., All rights reserved. Used by permission. Used by special arrangement with The Rodgers and Hammerstein Organization and the Family Trust u/w of Richard Rodgers, www.rnh.com. All rights reserved. "My Romance" music by Richard Rodgers, lyrics by Lorenz Hart. Used by special arrangement with The Rodgers and Hammerstein Organization and the Family Trust u/w of Richard Rodgers. All rights reserved. "As Long As She Needs Me" by Lionel Bart. Published by Hollis Music. All rights reserved. Used by permission. "You Make Me Feel So Young" by Mack Gordon and Josef Myrow. Published by WB Music Corp. All rights reserved. Used by permission. *Oklahoma!* medley includes songs from Rodgers and Hammerstein's *Oklahoma!* Music by Richard Rodgers, lyrics by Oscar Hammerstein II. Used by special arrangement with The Rodgers and Hammerstein Organization and the Family Trust u/w of Richard Rodgers. All rights reserved. "Single Ladies (Put a Ring on It)" by Thaddis Harrell, Christopher Stewart, Beyonce Knowles, Terius Nash. Published by 2082 Music Publishing, B Day Publishing, EMI April Music Inc., Sony ATV Harmony, Suga Wuga Music Inc., WB Music Corp., Songs of Peer, Ltd. and March Ninth Music Publishing. All rights reserved. Used by permission. "But the World Goes Round" by John Kander and Fred Ebb. Published by EMI Unart Catalog Inc. All rights reserved. Used by permission. "Great Balls of Fire" by Otis Blackwell and Jack Hammer. Published by Unichappell Music Inc., Mijac Music, Chappell & Co., Inc. and Mystical Light Music. All rights reserved. Used by permission. "What Did I Have That I Don't Have" by Burton Lane and Alan Jay Lerner. Published by Chappell & Co., Inc. All rights reserved. Used by permission. "What Kind of Fool Am I" by Leslie Bricusse and Anthony Newley. Published by Ludlow Music. All rights reserved. Used by permission. "Ladies Who Lunch" by Stephen Sondheim. Published by The Herald Square Music Co. All rights reserved. Used by permission. Overture includes selections from *Sweet Charity, A Chorus Line, Funny Girl, The Phantom of the Opera, Sunday in the Park With George, Send in the Clowns, Rent, Sweeney Todd: The Demon Barber of Fleet Street, Cabaret, West Side Story, Gypsy* and *Chicago*. "New York, New York" composed by John Kander, with lyrics by Fred Ebb. "And All That Jazz" music by John Kander. Lyrics by Fred Ebb ©1973 (Renewed), Unichappell Music Inc. (BMI) and Kander & Ebb, Inc. All rights administered by Unichappell Music Inc. All rights reserved. Used by permission. "Sunday in the Park With George," "Send in the Clowns" and "The Ballad of Sweeney Todd" music and lyrics by Stephen Sondheim ©1975, 1979, 1984 Rilting Music, Inc. (ASCAP). All rights administered by WB Music Corp. All rights reserved. Used by permission. Overture from *Cats*: Copyright ©1991 by the Really Useful Group LTD. This selection is used by special arrangement with Williamson Music, on behalf of Faber Music Limited, www.williamsonmusic.com. All rights reserved. Medley includes selections from "We Could Make Such Beautiful Music Together" music composed by Katzman and lyrics by Robert Sour. "Tea for Two" music by Vincent Youmans and lyrics by Irving Caesar. ©1924 (Renewed), Irving Caesar Music Corp. (ASCAP) and WB Music Corp. All rights administered by WB Music Corp. All rights reserved. Used by permission. "Friendship" by Cole Porter, ©1934 (Renewed), Chappell & Co., Inc. (ASCAP). All rights reserved. Used by permission. "How About You?" by Burton Lane, lyrics by Ralph Freed. "I Loves You Porgy" music by George Gershwin and lyrics by DuBose Heyward and Ira Gershwin. ©1935 (Renewed), George Gershwin Music (ASCAP), Dubose and Dorothy Heyward Memorial Fund Pub. (ASCAP) and Ira Gershwin Music (ASCAP). All rights administered by WB Music Corp. All rights reserved. Used by permission. "Side by Side" lyrics by Gus Kahn and music by Harry M. Woods. "Wind Beneath My Wings" written by Larry Henley and Jeff Silbar. "I'll Be There" by Berry Gordy. "Thank You For Being a Friend" by Andrew Gold. "You Go To My Head" by J. Fred Coots with lyrics by Haven Gillespie. "I Get a Kick Out of You" Cole Porter, ©1934 (Renewed), WB Music Corp. (ASCAP). All rights reserved. Used by permission. "Rehab" by Amy Winehouse. "One More for the Road" by Harold Arlen and Johnny Mercer. "YMCA" by Henri Belolo, Jacques Morali and Victor Willis. "A You're Adorable" music by Sid Lippman and lyrics by Buddy Kaye and Fred Wise. "See Me Feel Me" by Pete Townshend. "Touch Me in the Morning" by Ronald Miller and Michael Masser. "Old Folks at Home" by Stephen Foster. "Up a Lazy River" by Hoagy Carmichael and Sidney Arodin. "Old Man River" by Jerome Kern and Oscar Hammerstein II. "A Couple of Swells" music and lyrics by Irving Berlin. This selection is used by special arrangement with The Rodgers and Hammerstein Organization, the Family Trust u/w of Richard Rodgers and the Estate of Irving Berlin. All rights reserved. "My Funny Valentine" music by Richard Rodgers, lyrics by Lorenz Hart. This selection is used by special arrangement with The Rodgers and Hammerstein Organization, the Family Trust u/w of Richard Rodgers and the Estate of Irving Berlin. All rights reserved.

Makeup provided by M•A•C.

Rehearsed at the New 42nd Street Studios.

SPECIAL THANKS
Hilton Times Square, Andrew Ross, WMD & NP (AUS)

www.AllAboutMeBroadway.com
www.BroadwaysBestShows.com

HENRY MILLER'S THEATRE
SYDNEY BEERS   GREG BACKSTROM
General Manager   Associate Managing Director
VALERIE SIMMONS
Operations Manager

STAFF FOR THE HENRY MILLER'S THEATRE

House Manager	Johannah-Joy G. Magyawe
Treasurer	Jaime Perlman
House Carpenter	Steve Beers
House Electrician	Josh Weitzman
House Properties	Andrew Forste
Engineer	Deosarran
Assistant House Manager	Bobby Wolf
Assistant Treasurers	Andrew Clements, Carlos Morris, Ronnie Tobias
Security	Gotham Security
Maintenance	C+W Cleaning Services Inc.
Lobby Refreshments by	Sweet Concessions

American Idiot

First Preview: March 24, 2010. Opened: April 20, 2010.
Still running as of May 31, 2010.

CAST
(in order of appearance)

Johnny	JOHN GALLAGHER JR.
Will	MICHAEL ESPER
Tunny	STARK SANDS
Heather	MARY FABER
Whatsername	REBECCA NAOMI JONES
St. Jimmy	TONY VINCENT
The Extraordinary Girl	CHRISTINA SAJOUS
Ensemble	DECLAN BENNETT, ANDREW CALL, GERARD CANONICO, MIGUEL CERVANTES, JOSHUA HENRY, BRIAN CHARLES JOHNSON, LESLIE McDONEL, CHASE PEACOCK, THEO STOCKMAN, BEN THOMPSON, ALYSHA UMPHRESS, LIBBY WINTERS

Standby for Johnny, Will, Tunny: VAN HUGHES

UNDERSTUDIES

For Johnny: CHASE PEACOCK
For Will: DECLAN BENNETT
For Tunny: BEN THOMPSON
For Heather: LESLIE McDONEL, LIBBY WINTERS
For Whatsername: LESLIE McDONEL, CHRISTINA SAJOUS
For St. Jimmy: ANDREW CALL, JOSHUA KOBAK
For The Extraordinary Girl: ASPEN VINCENT, LIBBY WINTERS

Continued on next page

ST. JAMES THEATRE
A JUJAMCYN THEATRE

JORDAN ROTH
President

PAUL LIBIN
Producing Director

JACK VIERTEL
Creative Director

Tom Hulce & Ira Pittelman
Ruth and Stephen Hendel   Vivek J. Tiwary and Gary Kaplan   Aged In Wood and Burnt Umber
Scott M. Delman   Latitude Link   HOP Theatricals and Jeffrey Finn   Larry Welk
Bensinger Filerman and Moellenberg Taylor   Allan S. Gordon and Élan V. McAllister
Berkeley Repertory Theatre

In Association with
Awaken Entertainment   John Pinckard and John Domo

Present

american IDIOT

Music by
Green Day

Lyrics by
Billie Joe Armstrong

Book by
Billie Joe Armstrong and **Michael Mayer**

John Gallagher Jr.
Stark Sands   Michael Esper
Rebecca Naomi Jones   Christina Sajous   Mary Faber
and
Tony Vincent

with

Declan Bennett   Andrew Call   Gerard Canonico   Miguel Cervantes   Joshua Henry   Van Hughes
Brian Charles Johnson   Joshua Kobak   Lorin Latarro   Omar Lopez-Cepero   Leslie McDonel
Chase Peacock   Theo Stockman   Ben Thompson   Alysha Umphress   Aspen Vincent   Libby Winters

Scenic Design	Costume Design	Lighting Design	Sound Design	Video/Projection Design
Christine Jones	Andrea Lauer	Kevin Adams	Brian Ronan	Darrel Maloney

Casting	Production Stage Manager	Technical Supervisor	Music Coordinator
Jim Carnahan, C.S.A. Carrie Gardner, C.S.A.	James Harker	Hudson Theatrical Associates	Michael Keller

General Management	Press Representative	Marketing
Abbie M. Strassler	The Hartman Group	Type A Marketing

Music Director	Associate Choreographer	Associate Director
Carmel Dean	Lorin Latarro	Johanna McKeon

Associate Producers
SenovvA   Tix Productions   Tracy Straus and Barney Straus   Lorenzo Thione and Jay Kuo
Pat Magnarella   Christopher Maring

Musical Supervision, Arrangements, and Orchestrations
Tom Kitt

Choreographer
Steven Hoggett

Director
Michael Mayer

World Premiere produced by Berkeley Repertory Theatre, September 2009
Tony Taccone, Artistic Director   Susan Medak, Managing Director

4/20/10

(L-R): Michael Esper, Stark Sands and John Gallagher Jr.

Photo by Paul Kolnik

American Idiot

SONG LIST

1. "American Idiot" ....Company
2. "Jesus of Suburbia"
   a. "Jesus of Suburbia" ....John Gallagher Jr. and Michael Esper
   b. "City of the Damned" ....Stark Sands, John Gallagher Jr., Michael Esper and Company
   c. "I Don't Care" ....John Gallagher Jr., Michael Esper, Stark Sands and Company
   d. "Dearly Beloved" ....Mary Faber and Men
   e. "Tales of Another Broken Home" ....John Gallagher Jr., Michael Esper, Stark Sands, Mary Faber and Company
3. "Holiday" ....John Gallagher Jr., Stark Sands, Theo Stockman and Company
4. "Boulevard of Broken Dreams" ....John Gallagher Jr., Rebecca Naomi Jones, Stark Sands and Men
5. "Favorite Son" ....Joshua Henry and Women
6. "Are We the Waiting" ....Stark Sands, Joshua Henry and Company
7. "St. Jimmy" ....John Gallagher Jr., Tony Vincent and Company
8. "Give Me Novacaine" ....Michael Esper, Stark Sands and Company
9. "Last of the American Girls"/"She's a Rebel" ....John Gallagher Jr., Rebecca Naomi Jones, Michael Esper, Chase Peacock, Tony Vincent and Company
10. "Last Night on Earth" ....Tony Vincent, Rebecca Naomi Jones, Mary Faber and Company
11. "Too Much Too Soon" ....Theo Stockman, Alysha Umphress, Michael Esper and Mary Faber
12. "Before the Lobotomy" ....Stark Sands, Chase Peacock, Joshua Henry and Ben Thompson
13. "Extraordinary Girl" ....Christina Sajous, Stark Sands and Company
14. "Before the Lobotomy" (reprise) ....Stark Sands, Chase Peacock, Joshua Henry, Ben Thompson and Company
15. "When It's Time" ....John Gallagher Jr.
16. "Know Your Enemy" ....Tony Vincent, Michael Esper, John Gallagher Jr. and Company
17. "21 Guns" ....Rebecca Naomi Jones, Christina Sajous, Mary Faber, Stark Sands, John Gallagher Jr., Michael Esper and Company
18. "Letterbomb" ....Rebecca Naomi Jones and Women
19. "Wake Me Up When September Ends" ....John Gallagher Jr., Michael Esper, Stark Sands and Company
20. "Homecoming"
    a. "The Death of St. Jimmy" ....Tony Vincent and John Gallagher Jr.
    b. "East 12th Street" ....John Gallagher Jr., Gerard Canonico, Theo Stockman and Company
    c. "Nobody Likes You" † ....Michael Esper and Company
    d. "Rock and Roll Girlfriend" * ......Miguel Cervantes, Mary Faber, Michael Esper and Company
    e. "We're Coming Home Again" .....John Gallagher Jr., Stark Sands, Michael Esper and Company
21. "Whatsername" ....John Gallagher Jr. and Company

† Lyrics by Mike Dirnt
* Lyrics by Tré Cool

Cast Continued

SWINGS
JOSHUA KOBAK, LORIN LATARRO, OMAR LOPEZ-CEPERO, ASPEN VINCENT

BAND
Conductor/Keyboard/Accordion: CARMEL DEAN
Drums/Percussion: TREY FILES
Guitar 1: MICHAEL AARONS
Guitar 2: ALEC BERLIN
Bass: DAN GRENNES
Violin: CENOVIA CUMMINS
Viola: ALISSA SMITH
Cello: AMY RALSKE
Associate Conductor: JARED STEIN
Music Coordinator: MICHAEL KELLER
Keyboard Programmer: RANDY COHEN

TIME: The Recent Past
PLACE: Jingletown, USA

Developed by Berkeley Repertory Theatre, November-December 2008, and New York Stage and Film and the Powerhouse Theater at Vassar, July 2009.

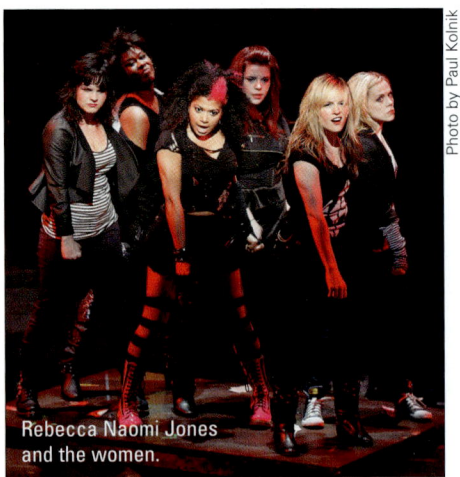
Rebecca Naomi Jones and the women.
Photo by Paul Kolnik

John Gallagher Jr.
Johnny

Tony Vincent
St. Jimmy

Stark Sands
Tunny

Michael Esper
Will

Rebecca Naomi Jones
Whatsername

Christina Sajous
The Extraordinary Girl

Mary Faber
Heather

American Idiot

Declan Bennett
Ensemble

Andrew Call
Ensemble

Gerard Canonico
Ensemble

Miguel Cervantes
Ensemble

Joshua Henry
Ensemble

Van Hughes
Standby for Johnny, Will, Tunny

Brian Charles Johnson
Ensemble

Joshua Kobak
Swing

Omar Lopez-Cepero
Swing

Leslie McDonel
Ensemble

Chase Peacock
Ensemble

Theo Stockman
Ensemble

Ben Thompson
Ensemble

Alysha Umphress
Ensemble

Aspen Vincent
Swing

Libby Winters
Ensemble

Carmel Dean
Music Director

Mike Dirnt, Billie Joe Armstrong, Tré Cool/Green Day
Music (Green Day); Book & Lyrics (Billie Joe Armstrong)

Michael Mayer
Director, Book

Steven Hoggett
Choreographer

Tom Kitt
Music Supervisor/ Arrangements/ Orchestrations

Christine Jones
Scenic Design

Andrea Lauer
Costume Design

Kevin Adams
Lighting Design

Brian Ronan
Sound Design

Jim Carnahan
Casting

Lorin Latarro
Associate Choreographer

Liz Caplan Vocal Studios, LLC
Production Vocal Supervisor

Neil A. Mazzella, Hudson Theatrical Associates
Technical Supervisor

Michael Keller
Music Coordinator

Tom Hulce
Producer

Ira Pittelman
Producer

Ruth Hendel
Producer

Robyn Goodman, Aged in Wood
Producer

American Idiot

Walt Grossman,
Aged in Wood
Producer

Judi Krupp,
Burnt Umber
Producer

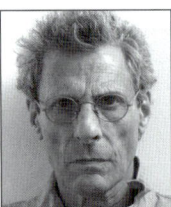
Bill Gerber,
Burnt Umber
Producer

Ralph Bryan,
Latitude Link
Producer

2009-2010 AWARDS

DRAMA DESK AWARD
Outstanding Director of a Musical
(Michael Mayer)

OUTER CRITICS CIRCLE AWARD
Outstanding Lighting Design (Play or Musical)
(Kevin Adams)

ACTORS' EQUITY EXTRAORDINARY EXCELLENCE
IN DIVERSITY ON BROADWAY AWARD

Larry Kaye,
HOP Theatricals
Producer

Jeffrey Finn
Producer

Chris Bensinger
Producer

Michael Filerman
Producer

Carl Moellenberg
Producer

Allan S. Gordon
Producer

Élan V. McAllister
Producer

Tony Taccone,
Artistic Director,
Berkeley Repertory
Theatre
Producer

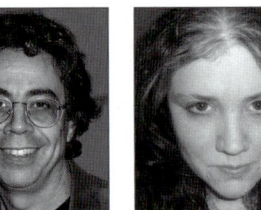
Jennifer Maloney,
Awaken
Entertainment
Producer

Sean Wing
Ensemble

(L-R): Stark Sands, John Gallagher Jr., Michael Esper and the ensemble

Photo by Paul Kolnik

American Idiot

Tony Vincent as St. Jimmy
Photo by Paul Kolnik

STAFF FOR *AMERICAN IDIOT*

GENERAL MANAGER
Abbie M. Strassler

COMPANY MANAGER
Kimberly Helms

GENERAL PRESS REPRESENTATIVE
THE HARTMAN GROUP
Michael Hartman
Leslie Baden   Alyssa Hart

MARKETING
TYPE A MARKETING
Anne Rippey   Nick Pramik   Janette Rouch

TECHNICAL SUPERVISION
HUDSON THEATRICAL ASSOCIATES
Neil A. Mazzella   Sam Ellis

PRODUCTION VOCAL SUPERVISOR
Liz Caplan Vocal Studios, LLC

Production Stage Manager	James Harker
Stage Manager	Freda Farrell
Assistant Stage Manager	Bethany Russell
Assistant Company Manager	Rachel Scheer
Dance Captain	Lorin Latarro
Assistant Dance Captain	Ben Thompson
Assistant Director	Austin Regan
Associate Set Designer	Edward Coco
Assistant Set Designer	Damon Pelletier
Associate Costume Designer	Chloe Chapin
Assistant Costume Designer	Janice Lopez
Associate Lighting Designer	Aaron Sporer
Assistant Lighting Designer	Benjamin Travis
Assistant to the Lighting Designer	Barbara Samuels
Associate Sound Designer	Ashley Hanson
Associate Video/Projection Designer	Dan Scully
Assistant Editor	Nico Sarudiansky
Moving Light Programmer	Victor Seastone
Video and Projection Programmer	Jeff Cady/SenovvA
Video and Projection Assistant	Alex Marshall/SenovvA
Production Carpenter	Donald J. Oberpriller
Flyman	Dave Brown
Flying Automation/Deck Carpenter	Mark Diaz
Production Electrician	Greg Husinko
Head Electrician	Eric Abbott
Followspots	Sue Pelkofer, Tom Maloney, Bob Miller
Production Sound Operator	David Dignazio
Assistant Sound	Cody Spencer
Deck Sound	Joe Lenihan
Production Video/Deck Audio	Greg Peeler
Production Property Supervisor	Joseph P. Harris Jr.
Head Properties	Eric Castaldo
Wardrobe Supervisor	Angela Simpson
Assistant Wardrobe Supervisor	Jaki Harris
Dressers	Meredith Benson, Ryan Oslak, Danny Paul, Julienne Schubert-Blechman, Jack Scott, Yleana Nuñez
Hair Designer	Brandon Dailey
Wig Designer	Leah Loukas
Makeup Designer	Amy Jean Wright
Hair Supervisor	Kevin Maybee
Craft Artisan	Jennilee Houghton
Costume Interns	Amy Sutton, Matt Allemon, Mikaela Holmes
Costume Shoppers	Paloma Young, Kara Harmon
Assistant Synthesizer Programmer	Bryan Cook
Music Preparation	Colleen Darnall
Management Associate	Scott Armstrong
Assistant to Mr. Hulce	Christopher Maring
Assistant to Mr. Pittelman	Dorothy Evins
Stage Management Interns	Clinton Harwood, Katie Klehr White
Production Office Interns	Jamie Caplan, Amanda Gagnon
Casting Associate	Jillian Cimini
Advertising	Serino Coyne, Inc./Tom Callahan, Scott Johnson, Kristina Curatolo
Interactive Marketing	Situation Interactive/Damian Bazadona, Christopher Powers, John Lanasa, Eric Bornemann, Jessica Dacchille
Press Associates	Michelle Bergmann, Nicole Capatasto, Tom D'Ambrosio, Juliana Hannett, Bethany Larsen, Matt Ross, Frances White, Wayne Wolfe
Banking	JP Morgan Chase
Payroll	Castellana Services, Inc./Lance Castellana
Accountant	Fried & Kowgios Partners CPA's LLP/Robert Fried CPA
Comptroller	Galbraith & Co., Inc/Sarah Galbraith
Insurance	Tanenbaum Harber of Florida/Carol Bressi-Cilona
Legal Counsel	Lazarus & Harris, LLP/Scott R. Lazarus, Esq., Robert C. Harris, Esq.
Physical Therapy	Performing Arts Physical Therapy/Sean Gallagher
Massage Therapist	Russ Beasley
Group Sales	Telecharge Group Sales
Merchandising	Bravado
Media Licensing	Eric Kulberg
Production Photography	Doug Hamilton
Opening Night Coordination	Suzanne Tobak
Travel Agency	Tzell Travel/The "A" Team, Road Rebel

Flying by Foy

CREDITS AND ACKNOWLEDGEMENTS

Scenery and automation by Hudson Scenic Studio, Inc. Lighting equipment from Hudson Sound and Light LLC. Sound equipment from Masque Sound. Video technology and production by SenovvA, Inc. TV/displays provided by Sony Electronics, Inc. Media server technology by Green Hippotizers. Specialty props provided by The Spoon Group. Prosthetics constructed by Denscape Designs. Denim courtesy of Levis. Additional costumes by Donna Langman Costumes, John Kristiansen New York Inc., Saint Laurie Merchant Tailors NYC, World Tone Shoes. Hair products provided by Bumble and Bumble, LLC, and Pravana. Makeup provided by M•A•C. Custom in-ear monitors provided by Ultimate Ears. Keyboards by Yamaha. Guitar strings provided by Ernie Ball. Guitars provided by Gibson and Epiphone Guitar Company. Cymbals by Agop Cymbals. Drumsticks by Pro-Mark Sticks. Opening audio sequence by Ira Pittelman and Wayne Hyde.

Rehearsed at the New 42nd Street Studios

SPECIAL THANKS

Adrienne Armstrong, Chris Bilheimer, Chris Dugan, Lorrin Golembieski, Doug Goodman, Brian Bumbery, Tom Pearl and the staff of Berkeley Rep. Theatre, Carole Pittelman, Bill Schneider, Maggie Whitaker, Wayne Hyde, Bryan Smith, Derek Brooks, Andrew Hans Buscher and Jordan Roth.

www.AmericanIdiotOnBroadway.com

JUJAMCYN THEATERS

JORDAN ROTH
President

PAUL LIBIN	**JACK VIERTEL**
Producing Director	Creative Director
DANIEL ADAMIAN	**JENNIFER HERSHEY**
General Manager	Director of Operations
MEREDITH VILLATORE	**JERRY ZAKS**
Chief Financial Officer	Resident Director

STAFF FOR THE ST. JAMES THEATRE

Manager	Daniel Adamian
Associate Manager	Jeff Hubbard
Treasurer	Vincent Sclafani
Carpenter	Timothy McDonough Jr.
Propertyman	Timothy McDonough
Electrician	Albert Sayers
Engineer	Anthony Pastore

American Idiot
SCRAPBOOK

(L-R): Mary Faber, "Yearbook" correspondent Christina Sajous, Michael Esper, John Gallagher Jr., Stark Sands, Rebecca Naomi Jones, Tony Vincent and Cast on stage during the opening night curtain call.

Correspondent: Christina Sajous, "The Extraordinary Girl"

Memorable Letter, Fax or Note: Whoopi Goldberg attended our opening, and then the following day she sent the cast/crew two boxes of Ruby et Violette cookies with a note that said, "You blew me away! Whoopi!" We still have her note posted in the "St. Timmy" tech room/office till this day. I personally received fan mail from someone who saw and connected deeply with our show. In return, I sent him an *American Idiot* Playbill autographed by the cast.

Opening Night Gifts: Opening night felt like Christmas!!! We received tons of gifts. To name a few: the producers gave each of us mp3 players with a cast photo attached to decorate the outside. So cool! We received posters from our assistant designer Chloe, and another one from an artist named Louisa Bertman who drew the entire cast and creative team. The drawings really do capture a striking resemblance. Billie Joe and Adrienne Armstrong surprised us with real silver dogtags that read, "Rage and Love." Our vocal coach Liz Caplan, who says clear vodkas are better for the voice, gave us little bottles of Grey Goose and Grether's Pastilles. Lastly, Stark Sands presented everyone with a green toy soldier, each one missing a leg. Hilarious!!!!!!

Most Exciting Celebrity Visitors: We've had many other celebrities attend the show: Donald Trump, Serena Williams, Robin Wright, Helen Hunt, Liza Minnelli, Clive Davis, Michelle Pfeiffer, David Schwimmer, Steven Spielberg, Courtney Love, Mark Sanchez, Joel Grey, and his daughter Jennifer Grey, Mandy Patinkin, William Finn, Jesse Tyler Ferguson, Michael Greif, and the cast of "Glee." This is to name the few that we either met backstage or heard were in the audience. I wouldn't be surprised if many others attended, but remained anonymous.

Who Got the Gypsy Robe: The Gypsy Robe was scheduled to be presented to Lorin Latarro, the associate choreographer, swing and past Gypsy Robe winner. However, she opted to pass the title along to Andrew Call (who was second to having the most Broadway credits). So classy of her! Andrew wore that robe proudly as he ran around in a circle three times, while each of us touched it.

Who Has Done the Most Shows in Their Career: Lorin Latarro has performed in thirteen Broadway shows! Wow!

Special Backstage Rituals: Before the curtain rises for each show, the cast huddle together in a circle, put our hands in the middle and shout, "One, two, three It's fuck time!" We have been carrying that tradition since our run in Berkeley. Another habit: A number of people get together at five minutes to "places" and do military-style push-ups. Also, the girls who perform in "Favorite Son" tap each other on the butts before we enter from upstage center.

Favorite Moments During Each Performance: We all look forward to "It's fuck time" and "American Idiot," because it prepares us for the most emotional, physically demanding, high octane, outrageous, badassssss, punk performance of our lives.

Favorite In-Theatre Gathering Place: The St. James theatre does not have a greenroom, so Tim McDonough's tech office has become our primary gathering place. We renamed the office "St. Timmy." There is always a TV on the sports channel, and snacks available on the counter, which is conveniently amazing since this cast loves to eat!

Favorite Off-Site Hangouts: We often visit Angus McIndoe's which is right next door, Smith's on Eighth Avenue, Emmett's Bar and Restaurant on Eighth Avenue, and The Standard Beer Garden in the Meat Packing District, to name a few.

Favorite Snack Food: In St. Timmy's room

Green Day's Billie Joe Armstrong, Tré Cool and Mike Dirnt take a bow on the St. James stage at the premiere.

American Idiot
SCRAPBOOK

1. (L-R): Cast members Libby Winters, Christina Sajous, Rebecca Naomi Jones, Mary Faber, and Alysha Umphress at the Roseland cast party.
2. The marquee of the St. James Theatre.
3. (L-R): Choreographer Steven Hoggett and director Michael Mayer on opening night.

there is always an assortment of bagels, muffins, cookies, Girl Scout cookies, cake, cupcakes, brownies, Twizzlers, jelly beans, mixed nuts, pretzels, cheese, slices of deli meat, and an occasional banana, apples and grapes. Also, we tend to snack on Läkerol Pastilles like they're candy.

Mascot: The show doesn't have a mascot, but our Broadway League Softball team does. Cast member and captain of our team, Miguel Cervantes has a dog named Tabasco who attends every game we play in Central Park. So far, we are undefeated, so I guess Tabasco is good luck.

Favorite Therapy: The choreography in this show is highly physical and athletic, so we visit the physical therapist Sean P. Gallagher, and our in-house massage god Russ Beasley. The massage appointments for Russ are always booked the moment the list hits the callboard. Whiplash!!! Also, we depend on the therapy of Throat-Coat tea, Grether's Pastilles, Läkerols,

steamers, Entertainers Secret, and honey sticks.

Parody Lyric: The song "Extraordinary Girl" has been renamed "Extraordinary Risk." Also, Brian Charles Johnson, Chase Peacock, and Johnny Gallagher Jr. collaborated on a rap song called "San Francisco Nights Are Cold," dedicated to our cast and the experience we had during the Berkeley run in California.

Web Buzz: I'm not on Twitter, but I know some of my castmates are, and every day there is a response to our show that has been documented by fans. Also, there is an "*American Idiot* on Broadway" fan page on Facebook with more than 25,000 friends as of the end of May 2010.

Memorable Press Encounters: In California we did a punk photo shoot in front of a 7-Eleven parking lot where we had the freedom to dance, chug beers, smoke cigarettes, munch on beef jerky, sing loudly and play guitar.

Memorable Stage Door Fan Encounters: It has only been about nine weeks since previews and already I have seen a handful of the same faces in the audience. We literally have fans that devote their time to our show at least once a week. Seriously!!!! To name a few: Lauren (her hair is lavender), Hollis (she has a bob haircut with pink streaks. She comes at least once a week and sometimes she will commit to a matinee and evening show all in one day), Jillian (she is always a lucky winner of the lottery tickets for our show), Catrina (not only does she support our show, but she attends our softball games every Thursday) and, lastly, Justin Nelson (he travels from Utah. He literally saw the show 10 times in Berkeley, and 3 times in NYC).

Catchphrases Only the Company Would Recognize: "Fierce!" "Sensible." "Is it?" "That's what SHE said." "That's what HE said." "In the Burnt Park!" "It's fuck time!" "What though…?" "Daaaaaaaaamn!" "In the fire, oooooh!" "Eeeeyah!"

Memorable Directorial Note: Nothing specific comes to mind, but we love when Michael Mayer expresses his dislikes by using words like, "hideous!" "ewwww!" "heinous!" and "bad!", which he delivers in the most loving and entertaining way. We love it!!

Nicknames: They call me "X" or "X-Tina." Gerard Canonico is "G-Rard." Ben Thompson is "Bentensity." Rebecca Naomi Jones is "Reblacka" or "Little Girl Legs." Theo Stockman is "Theocracy." Joshua Henry is "Chocothunder." Brian Charles Johnson is "Babyface." Libby Winters is "Lilly." Leslie McDonel is "Sissy." Andrew Call is "Relentless." Miguel Cervantes is "Miguelito." Carmel Dean is "Carmie" or "Aussie." Chase Peacock is "Peacock." Tony Vincent is "TV." Mary Faber is "Fabes." Declan Bennett is "Is It." Jared Stein is "Vegan." Van Hughes is "Vanny." Alysha Umphress is "Black Girl" or "Pusssssssy." Stark Sands is "Starky" or "Murderball." Michael Esper is "Mikey" or "Esper." Johnny Gallagher Jr. is "JGJ" or "Gallagher." Aspen Vincent is "Tiny" or "Aspeena." Omar Lopez-Cepero is "Ohms." Joshua Kobak is "Kobak." Lorin Latarro is "Latarro." And Sean Wing is "Wing."

Sweethearts Within the Company: Michael Esper and Libby Winters just became exclusive. Woo hoo! Prior to casting: Van Hughes and Leslie McDonel (exclusive), Tony and Aspen Vincent (married), Jared Stein and Kimberly Helms (exclusive).

Embarrassing Moment: It's embarrassing any time we slip on the garbage on stage.

Coolest Things About Being in This Show: *American Idiot* has changed the demographic of audience members who attend theatre. Instead of the parents dragging the children to shows, it is the children dragging their parents. We literally built this show from the ground up, and it's amazing to see how much it has grown into this amazing beast. Lastly, we are not only fans of Green Day, but we have become their family. It's a relationship that the cast and I will cherish forever.

August: Osage County

First Preview: October 30, 2007. Opened: December 4, 2007.
Closed June 28, 2009 after 18 Previews and 648 Performances.

 **THE MUSIC BOX**
239 W. 45th Street
A Shubert Organization Theatre
Philip J. Smith, *Chairman*   Robert E. Wankel, *President*

Jeffrey Richards   Jean Doumanian   Steve Traxler   Jerry Frankel
Ostar Productions   Jennifer Manocherian   The Weinstein Company
Debra Black/Daryl Roth   Ronald & Marc Frankel/Barbara Freitag
Rick Steiner/Staton Bell Group

PRESENT

Phylicia Rashad

in

AUGUST: OSAGE COUNTY

BY

Tracy Letts

with

Elizabeth Ashley   Anne Berkowitz   Guy Boyd   John Cullum
Kimberly Guerrero   Brian Kerwin   Mariann Mayberry   Michael Milligan
Amy Morton   Sally Murphy   Troy West   Frank Wood

SCENIC DESIGN	COSTUME DESIGN	LIGHTING DESIGN	SOUND DESIGN
Todd Rosenthal	**Ana Kuzmanic**	**Ann G. Wrightson**	**Richard Woodbury**

ORIGINAL MUSIC	DRAMATURG	ORIGINAL CASTING
David Singer	**Edward Sobel**	**Erica Daniels**

CASTING	FIGHT CHOREOGRAPHER	DIALECT COACH
Stuart Howard, Amy Schecter & Paul Hardt	**Chuck Coyl**	**Cecilie O'Reilly**

PRODUCTION STAGE MANAGER/PRODUCTION SUPERVISOR	TECHNICAL SUPERVISOR
Jane Grey	**Theatersmith, Inc./Smitty**

PRESS REPRESENTATIVE	GENERAL MANAGEMENT
Jeffrey Richards Associates	**Richards/Climan, Inc.**

DIRECTED BY

Anna D. Shapiro

"August: Osage County" was commissioned by Steppenwolf Theatre Company, and the World Premiere was presented at Steppenwolf Theatre Company, Chicago, IL. Martha Lavey, Artistic Director and David Hawkanson, Executive Director
The Producers wish to express their appreciation to the Theatre Development Fund for its support of this production.

6/28/09

CAST

Beverly Weston	JOHN CULLUM
Violet Weston	PHYLICIA RASHAD
Barbara Fordham	AMY MORTON
Bill Fordham	FRANK WOOD
Jean Fordham	ANNE BERKOWITZ
Ivy Weston	SALLY MURPHY
Karen Weston	MARIANN MAYBERRY
Mattie Fae Aiken	ELIZABETH ASHLEY
Charlie Aiken	GUY BOYD
Little Charles	MICHAEL MILLIGAN
Johnna Monevata	KIMBERLY GUERRERO
Steve Heidebrecht	BRIAN KERWIN
Sheriff Deon Gilbeau	TROY WEST

SETTING

A large country home outside Pawhuska, Oklahoma, 60 miles northwest of Tulsa, Oklahoma.

UNDERSTUDIES/STANDBYS

For Bill, Steve, Charles, Beverly, Sheriff Deon Gilbeau: FRANK DEAL
For Violet, Mattie Fae: SUSANNE MARLEY
For Charles, Beverly: STEPHEN PAYNE
For Barbara, Karen, Ivy: DEE PELLETIER
For Little Charles, Bill, Steve, Sheriff Deon Gilbeau: AARON SEROTSKY
For Johnna, Ivy, Karen: KRISTINA VALADA-VIARS
For Jean: EMILY WALTON

(L-R): Phylicia Rashad and Amy Morton

Photo by Robert J. Saferstein

August: Osage County

Phylicia Rashad
Violet Weston

Elizabeth Ashley
Mattie Fae Aiken

Anne Berkowitz
Jean Fordham

Guy Boyd
Charlie

John Cullum
Beverly Weston

Kimberly Guerrero
Johnna Monevata

Brian Kerwin
Steve Heidebrecht

Mariann Mayberry
Karen Weston

Michael Milligan
Little Charles

Amy Morton
Barbara Fordham

Sally Murphy
Ivy Weston

Troy West
Sheriff Deon Gilbeau

Frank Wood
Bill Fordham

Frank Deal
u/s Charles, Steve, Bill, Beverly, Sheriff Deon Gilbeau

Susanne Marley
u/s Violet, Mattie Fae

Stephen Payne
u/s Charles, Beverly

Dee Pelletier
u/s Barbara, Karen, Ivy

Aaron Serotsky
u/s Bill, Steve, Little Charles, Sheriff

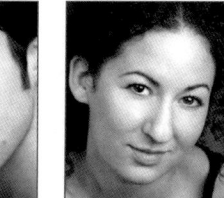
Kristina Valada-Viars
u/s Johnna, Ivy, Karen

Emily Walton
u/s Jean

Tracy Letts
Playwright

Anna D. Shapiro
Director

Todd Rosenthal
Set Design

Ana Kuzmanic
Costume Design

Ann G. Wrightson
Lighting Design

Richard Woodbury
Sound Design

David Singer
Original Music

Chuck Coyl
Fight Choreographer

Christopher C. Smith, Smitty/ Theatersmith, Inc.
Technical Supervisor

David R. Richards and Tamar Haimes, Richards/Climan, Inc.
General Manager

Jeffrey Richards
Producer

Jean Doumanian
Producer

Steve Traxler
Producer

Jerry Frankel
Producer

August: Osage County

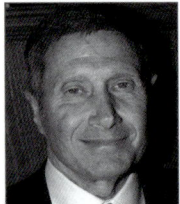

Bill Haber,
Ostar Productions
Producer

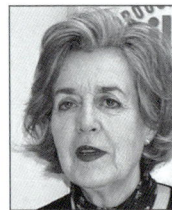

Jennifer
Manocherian
Producer

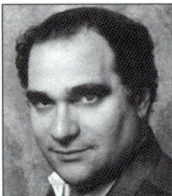

Bob Weinstein,
The Weinstein
Company
Producer

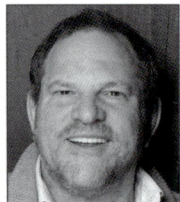

Harvey Weinstein,
The Weinstein
Company
Producer

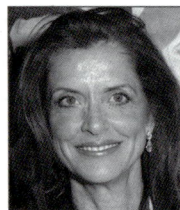

Debra Black
Producer

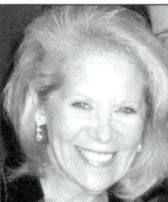

Daryl Roth
Producer

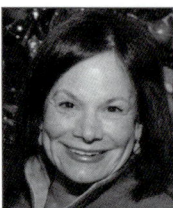

Barbara Freitag
Producer

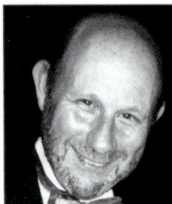

Rick Steiner
Producer

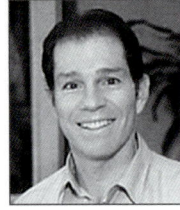

Dan Staton,
Staton Bell Group
Producer

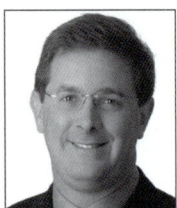

Marc Bell,
Staton Bell Group
Producer

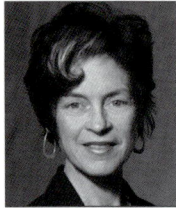

Martha Lavey
*Artistic Director,
Steppenwolf Theatre
Company*

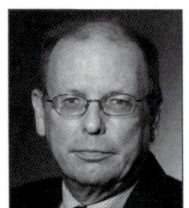

David Hawkanson
*Executive Director,
Steppenwolf Theatre
Company*

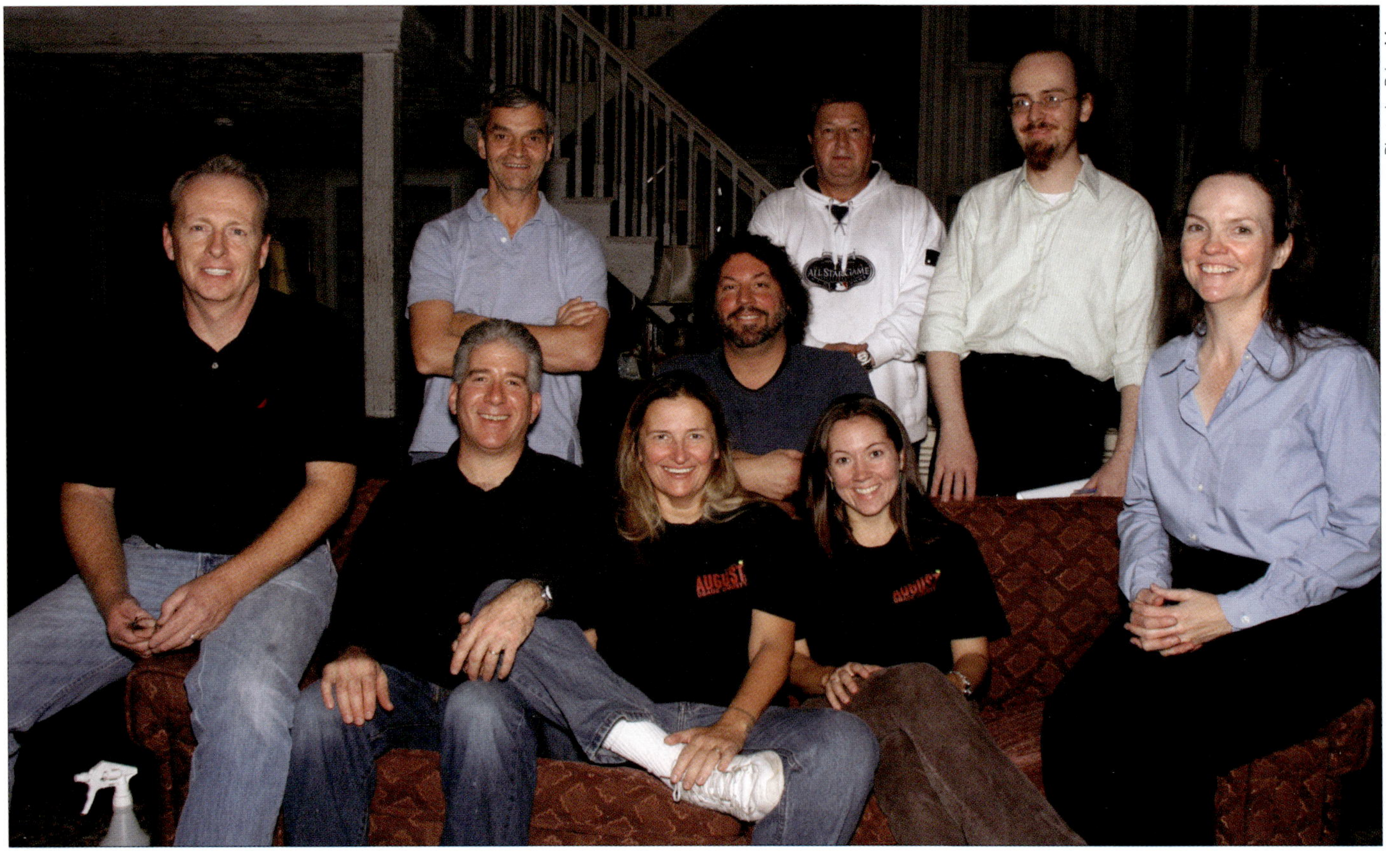

Photo by Brian Mapp

CREW
Front Row (L-R): Bill Rowland, Neil Rosenberg, Jane Grey, Cambra Overend, Valerie Spradling

Back Row (L-R): Kim Garnett, Rob Bevenger, Dennis Maher, Liam O'Brien

August: Osage County

FRONT OF HOUSE STAFF
Front Row (L-R): Kenneth Kelly, Lottie Dennis, Jenna Scanlon

Middle Row (L-R): Joseph Amato, Jonathan Shulman, Joseph Lopez, Steven Staszewski, Dennis Scanlon

Back Row (L-R): Nicholas Stavola, Christopher Caron, Michael Composto

STAFF FOR *AUGUST: OSAGE COUNTY*

GENERAL MANAGEMENT
RICHARDS/CLIMAN, INC.
David R. Richards   Tamar Haimes

GENERAL PRESS REPRESENTATIVE
JEFFREY RICHARDS ASSOCIATES/IRENE GANDY
Alana Karpoff   Elon Rutberg
Shane Marshall Brown   Diana Rissetto

ASSISTANT PRODUCER
Patrick Daly

COMPANY MANAGER
MARY MILLER

PRODUCTION STAGE MANAGER/ PRODUCTION SUPERVISOR	Jane Grey
Stage Manager	Cambra Overend
TECHNICAL SUPERVISOR	Christopher C. Smith
Assistant Director	Henry Wishcamper
Assistant Set Designers	Kevin Depinet, Matthew D. Jordan, Martin Andrew Orlowicz, Stephen T. Sorenson
Assistant Costume Designer	Amelia Dombrowski
Assistant Lighting Designer(s)	Kathleen Dobbins/ Carl Faber, Kristina Kloss
Assistant Sound Designer	Joanna Lynne Staub
Assistant to Mr. Traxler	Brandi Preston
General Management Associate	Jeromy Smith
General Management Assistant	Cesar Hawas
Production Assistant	Catherine Mancuso
Associate to Jeffrey Richards	Jeremy Scott Blaustein
Assistant to Jeffrey Richards	Christopher Taggart
Production Carpenter	Don Oberpriller
Production Electrician	Neil McShane
Production Props	Neil Rosenberg
Production Sound	Valerie Spradling
House Carpenter	Dennis Maher
House Electrician	William Rowland
House Props	Kim Garnett
Wardrobe Supervisor	Leah Redmond
Dresser	Kim Prentice
Dialect Coach	Cecilie O'Reilly
Advertising	SpotCo./ Drew Hodges, Jim Edwards Stephen Sosnowski, Tim Falotico
Website Design/ Internet Marketing	Situation Marketing/ Damian Bazadona, John Lanasa, Steve Tate
Marketing Consultant	Ken Davenport
Banking	JP Morgan Chase Bank/ Richard Callian, Margaret Wong
Accountants	FK Partners/ Robert Fried, Elliott Aronstam
Legal Counsel	Lazarus & Harris, LLP/ Scott R. Lazarus, Esq., Robert C. Harris, Esq., Diane Viale
Insurance	DeWitt Stern Group, Inc./Joe Bower
Payroll	CSI/Lance Castellana
Group Sales	Broadway Inbound, Inc.
Merchandising	Desiree
Production Photographers	Joan Marcus, Robert J. Saferstein
Physical Therapy	Performing Arts Physical Therapy
Consulting Orthopedist	Dr. Phillip Bauman
Company Mascots	Joker, Lottie, Mr. Moon, Skye and Buster, Mecca, Che

CREDITS
Scenery constructed by Hudson Scenic Studios. Lighting equipment by PRG Lighting. Sound equipment by Sound Associates. Additional props by The Spoon Group. Hair by Kat Venture and Wyatt of Blondies NYC. Ms. Parsons' and Ms. Ashley's dresses by Timberlake Studios. Major League Baseball® footage used with permission of Major League Baseball Properties, Inc. "Little Charles" music and lyrics by David Singer. "Sanford and Son Theme" words and music by Quincy Jones. Copyright ©1972 Hee Bee Dooinit Music (ASCAP). Worldwide rights for Hee Bee Dooinit Music administered by Cherry Lane Music Publishing Company, Inc. (ASCAP). "Lay Down Sally" (Eric Patrick Clapton, Marcy Levy and George E. Terry) ©(Renewed), Throat Music Ltd. (PRS) and Eric Patrick Clapton (PRS). All rights on behalf of Throat Music Ltd. and Eric Patrick Clapton administered by Warner-Tamerlane Publishing Corp. All rights on behalf of Throat Music Ltd. administered by WB Music Corp. All rights reserved. Used by permission. Permissions cleared by B/Z Rights & Permission, Inc.

SPECIAL THANKS
Roundabout Theatre Company, Richard Thomas, Linda Emond, Cathy Taylor, Jay Geneske, Russell Poole, Michael Brosilow and Kimberly Tompkins, Ricola, Emergen-C.

STEPPENWOLF THEATRE COMPANY
Founders: Terry Kinney, Jeff Perry and Gary Sinise
Ensemble Members: Joan Allen, Kevin Anderson, Alana Arenas, Randall Arney, Kate Arrington, Ian Barford, Robert Breuler, Gary Cole, Kathryn Erbe, K. Todd Freeman, Frank Galati, Francis Guinan, Moira Harris, Jon Hill, Tim Hopper, Tom Irwin, Ora Jones, Tina Landau, Martha Lavey, Tracy Letts, John Mahoney, John Malkovich, Mariann Mayberry, James Vincent Meredith, Laurie Metcalf, Amy Morton, Sally Murphy, Austin Pendleton, Yasen Peyankov, Martha Plimpton, Rondi Reed, Molly Regan, Anna D. Shapiro, Eric Simonson, Lois Smith, Rick Snyder, Jim True-Frost, Alan Wilder

THE SHUBERT ORGANIZATION, INC.
Board of Directors

Philip J. Smith Chairman	**Robert E. Wankel** President
Wyche Fowler, Jr.	**John W. Kluge**
Lee J. Seidler	**Michael I. Sovern**

Stuart Subotnick

Elliot Greene Chief Financial Officer	**David Andrews** Senior Vice President – Shubert Ticketing
Juan Calvo Vice President and Controller	**John Darby** Vice President – Facilities
Peter Entin Vice President – Theatre Operations	**Charles Flateman** Vice President – Marketing
Anthony LaMattina Vice President – Audit & Production Finance	**Brian Mahoney** Vice President – Ticket Sales

D.S. Moynihan
Vice President – Creative Projects

House Manager .... Jonathan Shulman

Avenue Q

First Preview: July 10, 2003. Opened: July 31, 2003.
Closed September 13, 2009 after 22 Previews and 2534 Performances. (Transferred to an Off-Broadway run.)

GOLDEN THEATRE
A Shubert Organization Theatre
Philip J. Smith, *Chairman* Robert E. Wankel, *President*

Kevin McCollum Robyn Goodman Jeffrey Seller
Vineyard Theatre and The New Group
present

Avenue Q The Musical

Music and Lyrics by
Robert Lopez and Jeff Marx

Book by
Jeff Whitty

Based on an Original Concept by
Robert Lopez and Jeff Marx

with

Christian Anderson, Jennifer Barnhart, Ann Harada, Nicholas Kohn,
Anika Larsen, Robert McClure, Danielle K. Thomas

Puppets Conceived and Designed by
Rick Lyon

Set Design	Costume Design	Lighting Design	Sound Design
Anna Louizos	Mirena Rada	Howell Binkley	Acme Sound Partners

Animation Design	Music Director and Incidental Music	Music Coordinator
Robert Lopez	Gary Adler	Michael Keller

General Manager	Technical Supervisor	Production Stage Manager
John Corker	Brian Lynch	Christine M. Daly

Press Representative	Marketing	Casting	Associate Producers
Sam Rudy Media Relations	Scott A. Moore	Cindy Tolan	Sonny Everett Walter Grossman Mort Swinsky

Music Supervision, Arrangements and Orchestrations by
Stephen Oremus

Choreographer
Ken Roberson

Directed by
Jason Moore

Avenue Q was supported by a residency and public staged reading at the 2002 O'Neill Music Theatre Conference of the Eugene O'Neill Theater Center, Waterford, CT

www.avenueq.com

9/13/09

CAST
(in order of appearance)

Princeton, Rod .... ROBERT McCLURE
Brian .... NICHOLAS KOHN
Kate Monster, Lucy & others ..... ANIKA LARSEN
Nicky, Trekkie Monster, Bear
  & others .... CHRISTIAN ANDERSON
Christmas Eve .... ANN HARADA
Gary Coleman .... DANIELLE K. THOMAS
Mrs. T., Bear & others ... JENNIFER BARNHART
Ensemble ...MINGLIE CHEN, SETH RETTBERG

Place: an outer borough of New York City
Time: the present

UNDERSTUDIES

For Princeton, Rod; Brian;
Nicky, Trekkie Monster, Bear & others:
SETH RETTBERG, MATT SCHREIBER
For Kate Monster, Lucy & others:
JENNIFER BARNHART, MINGLIE CHEN,
SHARON WHEATLEY
For Mrs. T., Bear & others:
MINGLIE CHEN, JASMIN WALKER,
SHARON WHEATLEY
For Christmas Eve:
MINGLIE CHEN
For Gary Coleman:
JASMIN WALKER

Continued on next page

The final Broadway cast

Photo by Carol Rosegg

Avenue Q

Cast Continued

SWINGS
MATT SCHREIBER,
JASMIN WALKER, SHARON WHEATLEY

DANCE CAPTAIN
SETH RETTBERG

BAND
Keyboard/Conductor:
GARY ADLER
Keyboard/Associate Conductor:
MARK HARTMAN
Reeds:
PATIENCE HIGGINS
Drums:
MICHAEL CROITER
Bass:
MARYANN McSWEENEY
Guitars:
BRIAN KOONIN

PUPPET COACH
MATT SCHREIBER

(L-R): Jennifer Barnhart, Lucy the Slut, Trekkie Monster and Christian Anderson
Photo by Carol Rosegg

Christian Anderson
Nicky, Trekkie Monster, Bear & others

Jennifer Barnhart
Mrs. T., Bear & others

Ann Harada
Christmas Eve

Nicholas Kohn
Brian

Anika Larsen
Kate Monster, Lucy & others

Robert McClure
Princeton, Rod

Danielle K. Thomas
Gary Coleman

Minglie Chen
Ensemble

Seth Rettberg
Ensemble; Dance Captain

Matt Schreiber
u/s Nicky, Trekkie Monster, Bear & others

Jasmin Walker
Swing

Sharon Wheatley
Swing

Jeff Marx and Robert Lopez
Music and Lyrics, Original Concept, Animation Design

Jeff Whitty
Book

Jason Moore
Director

Ken Roberson
Choreographer

Stephen Oremus
Music Supervision/ Arrangements/ Orchestrations

Rick Lyon
Puppet Design

Anna Louizos
Set Designer

Avenue Q

Mirena Rada
Costume Design

Howell Binkley
Lighting Designer

Tom Clark, Mark Menard and Nevin Steinberg, Acme Sound Partners
Sound Designer

Gary Adler
Music Director/ Conductor/ Incidental Music

Michael Keller
Music Coordinator

Brian Lynch/ Theatretech, Inc.
Technical Supervisor

John Corker
General Manager

Kevin McCollum
Producer

Robyn Goodman
Producer

Jeffrey Seller
Producer

Douglas Aibel, Artistic Director, Vineyard Theatre
Producer

Scott Elliott, Founding Artistic Director, The New Group
Producer

Sonny Everett
Associate Producer

Mort Swinsky
Associate Producer

Carey Anderson
Kate Monster, Lucy & others

Carmen Ruby Floyd
Swing

Carla Renata
Gary Coleman

Jonathan Root
Ensemble

Ann Sanders
Christmas Eve

Benjamin Schrader
Ensemble

Rashidra Scott
Gary Coleman

Howie Michael Smith
Princeton, Rod

CLOSING NIGHT SURPRISE
(L-R): Producer Kevin McCollum, co-songwriter Robert Lopez, director Jason Moore, librettist Jeff Whitty and co-songwriter Jeff Marx on the stage of the Golden Theatre after the final Broadway performance, having just made the surprise announcement that *Avenue Q* would be moving Off-Broadway, opening at New World Stages on October 9, 2009.

Avenue Q

ELECTRICS AND SOUND
Front Row (L-R): Jennifer Lerner, Gretchen Metzloff, Sylvia Yoshioka, Elspeth Appleby

Back Row (L-R): Craig Caccamise, A.J. Giegerich, Joe Pfifferling

FRONT OF HOUSE STAFF
Front Row: Helen Bentley

Second Row (L-R): Patricia Byrne, Nilsa Nairn, Chip Jorgensen, Carolyne "Mrs. Jones" Jones-Barnes

Third Row (L-R): Veronica Morrissey, Shelia Miller, Mae Smith, Cookie Harlin, Felicia Masias, Scott Key, Peter Cooke

Back Row: Yuri Fernandez

MANAGEMENT
(L-R): Beverly Jenkins, Matt Schreiber, Nick Lugo, Christine Daly

CARPENTRY AND PROPS
Seated (L-R): Elise Viola, Jane Pien, Stephen McDonald

Standing (L-R): Tom Anderson, Justin Garvey

CREW
Front Row (L-R): Beverly Jenkins, Jennifer Lerner, Sylvia Yoshioka

Middle Row (L-R): Stephen McDonald, Gretchen Metzloff, Christine Daly, A.J. Giegerich, Elspeth Appleby, Kathy Guida, Jill Heller, Tom Anderson

Back Row (L-R): Nick Lugo, Matt Schreiber, Jane Pien, Charles Zarobinski, Craig Caccamise, Justin Garvey, Elise Viola, Joe Pfifferling

Avenue Q

WARDROBE
(L-R): Jill Heller and Kathy Guida

Staff For *AVENUE Q*

GENERAL MANAGER
John Corker

GENERAL PRESS REPRESENTATIVE
Sam Rudy Media Relations
Sam Rudy — Dale R. Heller

DIRECTOR OF MARKETING
Scott Moore

CASTING
Cindy Tolan
Adam Caldwell, Casting Associate

COMPANY MANAGEMENT
Andrew Jones — Nick Lugo

PRODUCTION
STAGE MANAGER .... **Christine M. Daly**
Technical Supervision .... Brian Lynch/Theatretech, Inc.
Stage Manager .... James Darrah
Assistant Stage Manager .... Matt Schreiber
Resident Director .... Evan Ensign
Assistant Director .... Jen Bender
Associate Conductor .... Mark Hartman
Dance Captain .... Seth Rettberg
Puppet Coach .... Matt Schreiber
Production Assistant .... Alexis Prussack
Assistant to Mr. Corker .... Kim Vasquez
Management Assistant .... Michael Bolgar
Management Intern .... Jessica Fried
Associate Set Designer .... Todd Potter
Assistant Costume Designer .... Elizabeth Bourgeois
Associate Lighting Designer/
 Programmer .... Timothy F. Rogers
Assistant Lighting Designers .... Douglas Cox, Ryan O'Gara
Production Carpenter .... Justin Garvey
House Carpenter .... Charles Zarobinski
Flyman .... Tom Anderson
Production Electrician .... Craig Caccamise
House Electrician .... Sylvia Yoshioka
Head Electrician .... Jennifer Lerner
Video Programmer .... Paul Vershbow
Sound Board Operator .... Elspeth Appleby
Follow Spot Operators ..... Joe Pfifferling, A.J. Giegerich
Deck Electrician .... Gretchen Metzloff
Production Properties Master .... Ron Groomes
House Properties .... Stephen McDonald
Wardrobe Supervisor .... Kathy Guida
Dresser .... Jill Heller
Puppet Wrangler .... Jane Pien
Puppet Builders .... The Lyon Puppets
  Rick Lyon, Andrea Detwiler
  Vanessa Gifford, Deborah Glassberg
  Michelle Hickey, Michael Latini
  Adam Pagdon, Laura Parè
  David Regan, Sara Schmidt Boldon
  James Vogel, James W. Wojtal, Jr.
  Entirely Different Design
  Tim Hawkins, Susan Pitocchi
Music Copying .... Emily Grishman/Alex Lacamoire
Keyboard Programmer .... Mark Hartman
Synthesizer Program Consultant .... Andrew Barrett
Costume Draper .... Karl Ruckdeschel
Assistants to Set Designer .... Heather Dunbar, Donyale Werle
Puppet Wig Consultant .... Carla Muniz
Makeup Consultant .... Danielle Arminio
Sound and Video Design Effects .... Brett Jarvis
Animation/Video Production .... Sound Associates, Inc.
Advertising .... Spotco
  Drew Hodges, Jim Edwards
  Peter Duffy, Y Darius Suyama
Web Design .... Situation Marketing
  Damian Bazadona
Concessions .... Creative Goods, Inc.
  Pete Milano
Legal Counsel .... Levine, Plotkin, Menin LLP
  Loren Plotkin, Susan Mindell
Accounting .... FK Partners
  Robert Fried
Bookkeeper .... Joseph S. Kubala
Insurance .... D.R. Reiff & Associates
  Sonny Everett, Dennis Reiff
Banking .... JP Morgan Chase
Payroll .... CSI Payroll Services, Inc
  Lance Castellana
Production Photographers .... Nicholas Reuchel
  Carol Rosegg
Theatre Displays .... King Displays Inc.

The Producing Office
Kevin McCollum — Jeffrey Seller
John Corker — Debra Nir
Caitlyn Thomson

Aged In Wood
Robyn Goodman — Stephen Kocis
Josh Fiedler — Jessica White

Vineyard Theatre
Douglas Aibel, Artistic Director
Jennifer Garvey-Blackwell, Executive Director
Sarah Stern, Associate Artistic Director
Reed Ridgley, General Manager

The New Group
Artistic Director: Scott Elliott
Executive Director: Geoffrey Rich
Assoc. Artistic Director: Ian Morgan
Assoc. Executive Director: Amanda Brandes

Credits
Puppets built by The Lyon Puppets. Scenery by Centerline Studios Inc. 59th Street Bridge Photograph from *Panoramic New York* used with special permission by Richard Berenholtz. Stage portals by Atlas Scenic Studios. Lighting equipment by Fourth Phase. Sound equipment by ProMix Inc. Chain motors provided by Hudson Scenic. Christmas Eve wedding dress electrified by International Robotics/Mannetron. Ricola natural herb cough drops courtesy of Ricola USA, Inc. Props built by Prism Productions Services, Inc., Tom Carroll Scenery and Ken Larson. Animation operating system provided by ScharffWeissberg.

Avenue Q has not been authorized or approved in any manner by The Jim Henson Company or Sesame Workshop, which have no responsibility for its content.

Quote from "Something's Coming" (Bernstein/Sondheim) by permission of Leonard Bernstein Music Publishing Company LLC. (ASCAP).

Special Thanks
Amanda Green, Amy Kohn, Arthur Novell, Bobbi Brown Cosmetics, BMI Lehman Engel Musical Theatre Workshop, Brett Jarvis, Brian Yorkey, Chelsea Studios, Cheryl Henson, Craig Shemin, Doug Aibel, Ed Christie, Jana Zielonka, Jane Henson, Jean Banks, Jennifer Silver, Esq., Jodi Peikoff, Esq., John Buzzetti, Julia Sullivan, Kai Production Strategies, Kristen Anderson, Lara McLean, Manhattan Theatre Club, Maury Yeston, Nicole Rivera, Paulette Haupt, Peter Franklin, Pro-Mark Drumsticks and Mallets, Scott Elliott, Seth Goldstein, Splashlight Studios, Steven Greenberg, Teresa Focarile, The York Theatre, Lee Johnson.

Any donations received during this performance will be given to Broadway Cares/Equity Fights AIDS.

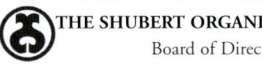

THE SHUBERT ORGANIZATION, INC.
Board of Directors

Gerald Schoenfeld — **Philip J. Smith**
Chairman — President

Wyche Fowler, Jr. — **John W. Kluge**

Lee J. Seidler — **Michael I. Sovern**

Stuart Subotnick

Robert E. Wankel
Executive Vice President

Peter Entin — **Elliot Greene**
Vice President – — Vice President –
Theatre Operations — Finance

David Andrews — **John Darby**
Vice President – — Vice President –
Shubert Ticketing Services — Facilities

D.S. Moynihan
Vice President - Creative Projects

A Behanding in Spokane

First Preview: February 15, 2010. Opened: March 4, 2010.
Still running as of May 31, 2010.

CAST
(in order of appearance)

Carmichael	CHRISTOPHER WALKEN
Mervyn	SAM ROCKWELL
Marilyn	ZOE KAZAN
Toby	ANTHONY MACKIE
Stage Manager	LISA BUXBAUM

UNDERSTUDIES
For Carmichael:
GLENN FLESHLER
For Mervyn:
DASHIELL EAVES
For Marilyn:
MEREDITH FORLENZA
For Toby:
TORY KITTLES

GERALD SCHOENFELD THEATRE
236 West 45th Street
A Shubert Organization Theatre
Philip J. Smith, *Chairman*   **Robert E. Wankel**, *President*

ROBERT FOX   CAROLE SHORENSTEIN HAYS
DEBRA BLACK   STEPHANIE P. McCLELLAND   OSTAR
ROGER BERLIND   SCOTT RUDIN   SHUBERT ORGANIZATION

IN ASSOCIATION WITH
ROBERT G. BARTNER   LORRAINE KIRKE   JAMIE deROY/RACHEL NEUBURGER

PRESENT

**CHRISTOPHER WALKEN
SAM ROCKWELL
ANTHONY MACKIE
ZOE KAZAN**

IN

A BEHANDING IN SPOKANE

BY

MARTIN McDONAGH

SCENIC AND COSTUME DESIGN
SCOTT PASK

LIGHTING DESIGN
BRIAN MacDEVITT

ORIGINAL MUSIC & SOUND DESIGN
DAVID VAN TIEGHEM

CASTING	PRESS REPRESENTATIVE	ADVERTISING
JIM CARNAHAN, C.S.A.	BONEAU/BRYAN-BROWN	SPOTCO

TECHNICAL SUPERVISOR	GENERAL MANAGEMENT	PRODUCTION STAGE MANAGER	ASSOCIATE PRODUCERS
THEATERSMITH, INC.	NINA LANNAN ASSOCIATES MAGGIE BROHN	FRANK LOMBARDI	ERICH JUNGWIRTH RICHARD JORDAN

DIRECTED BY
JOHN CROWLEY

A BEHANDING IN SPOKANE IS PRESENTED IN ASSOCIATION WITH ATLANTIC THEATER COMPANY.

3/4/10

(L-R): Christopher Walken, Anthony Mackie and Zoe Kazan

Photo by Joan Marcus

A Behanding in Spokane

Christopher Walken
Carmichael

Sam Rockwell
Mervyn

Anthony Mackie
Toby

Zoe Kazan
Marilyn

Dashiell Eaves
Understudy

Glenn Fleshler
Understudy

Meredith Forlenza
Understudy

Tory Kittles
Understudy

Martin McDonagh
Playwright

John Crowley
Director

Scott Pask
Scenic and Costume Design

Brian MacDevitt
Lighting Design

Jim Carnahan
Casting

Chris Smith/Theatersmith, Inc.
Production Management

Nina Lannan Associates
General Management

Robert Fox
Producer

Carole Shorenstein Hays
Producer

Debra Black
Producer

Stephanie P. McClelland
Producer

Roger Berlind
Producer

Scott Rudin
Producer

Philip J. Smith, Chairman, The Shubert Organization
Producer

Robert E. Wankel, President, The Shubert Organization
Producer

Jamie deRoy
Producer

Neil Pepe
Artistic Director, Atlantic Theater Company

CREW
Front Row (L-R): Timmy McWilliams, Beverly Edwards, Tim Eaker, Lisa Buxbaum

Middle Row (L-R): Frank Lombardi, Heidi Brown, Neil Rosenberg

Back Row (L-R): John Kilgore, Steve Dow, Leslie Ann Kilian, Geoffrey Polischuk, Mike Ward, Kathleen Gallagher, Rachel Garrett

A Behanding in Spokane

FRONT OF HOUSE STAFF

STAFF FOR *A BEHANDING IN SPOKANE*

COMPANY MANAGER
Beverly Edwards
Associate Company Manager .... Steve Dow

GENERAL PRESS REPRESENTATIVE
BONEAU/BRYAN-BROWN
Chris Boneau   Susanne Tighe
Christine Olver

CASTING
JIM CARNAHAN CASTING
Jim Carnahan CSA, Kate Boka, Carrie Gardner CSA,
Stephen Kopel, Jillian Cimini

PRODUCTION
STAGE MANAGER .... **Frank Lombardi**
Stage Manager .... Lisa Buxbaum
Assistant Director .... JV Mercanti
Production Assistant .... Timothy Eaker
Associate Scenic Designer .... Antje Ellerman
Assistant Scenic Designer .... Lauren Alvarez
Assistant to Scott Pask .... Warren Stiles
Associate Costume Designer .... Valerie Ramshur
Associate Lighting Designer .... Jennifer Schriever
Associate Sound Designer .... David Sanderson
Automated Lighting Programmer ...... Timothy F. Rogers

Make-up Design .... Angelina Avallone
Prosthetic Effects Design ...... Prosthetic Renaissance, Inc.
Mike Marino

House Carpenter .... Timmy McWilliams
Production Electrician .... Michael Ward
House Electrician .... Leslie Ann Kilian
Production Properties .... Kathy Fabian/Propstar
Head Properties .... Neil Rosenberg
House Properties .... Heidi Brown
Production Sound .... Brien Brannigan

Wardrobe Supervisor .... Kathleen Gallagher
Dressers .... Rachel Garrett, Geoffrey Polischuk
Propstar Assistants .... Tim Ferro, Carrie Mossman
Prosthetic Renaissance Assistants .... Hayes Vilandry,
Chris Kelly
Specialty Prop Artisan .... Craig Grigg
Advertising .... SPOTCO
Drew Hodges, Jim Edwards,
Tom Greenwald, Jim Aquino, Stacey Maya
Website Design/Online Marketing Strategy ...... SPOTCO
Sara Fitzpatrick, Matt Wilstein,
Marc Mettler, Christina Sees
Comptroller .... Kenny Noth/Galbraith & Company
Accountants .... Robert Fried CPA,
Fried & Kowgios CPAS LLP
General Management Associates .... David Roth,
Danielle Saks
General Management Interns .... Austin Nathaniel,
Jason Vanderwoude
Production Photographer .... Joan Marcus
Insurance .... AON/Albert G. Ruben Company Inc.
Claudia Kauffman
Banking .... City National Bank, Michele Gibbons
Payroll .... Castellana Services, Inc.
Travel Agent .... Tzell Travel/The "A" Team, Andi Henig
Legal Counsel .... Davis Wright Tremaine LLP
M. Graham Coleman, Robert J. Driscoll
Immigration
Counsel .... Kramer Levin Naftalis & Frankel LLP
Mark D. Koestler, Esq.
Guitarist .... Brien Brannigan
Associate to Mr. Fox .... Sarah Richardson
Transportation .... IBA Limousine, Danny Ibanez

www.BehandinginSpokane.com

CREDITS
Scenery constructed by Showmotion Inc. Costumes by Jennifer Love Costumes, Hochi Asiatico, Jenai Chin, Manhattan Wardrobe Supplies. Lighting equipment by PRG Lighting. Sound equipment supplied by Masque Sound. Prosthetics sculpted by Prosthetic Renaissance, SPS Effects, Laura Gravenstine, Kathleen McDermott. Flame treatment by Turning Star, Inc. Rehearsed at Hilton Theatre Rehearsal Studios.

THE SHUBERT ORGANIZATION, INC.
Board of Directors

Philip J. Smith   **Robert E. Wankel**
Chairman   President

Wyche Fowler, Jr.   **John W. Kluge**

Lee J. Seidler   **Michael I. Sovern**

Stuart Subotnick

Elliot Greene   **David Andrews**
Chief Financial   Senior Vice President –
Officer   Shubert Ticketing

Juan Calvo   **John Darby**
Vice President   Vice President –
and Controller   Facilities

Peter Entin   **Charles Flateman**
Vice President –   Vice President –
Theatre Operations   Marketing

Anthony LaMattina   **Brian Mahoney**
Vice President –   Vice President –
Audit & Production Finance   Ticket Sales

D.S. Moynihan
Vice President – Creative Projects

Theatre Manager .... David M. Conte

A Behanding in Spokane
SCRAPBOOK

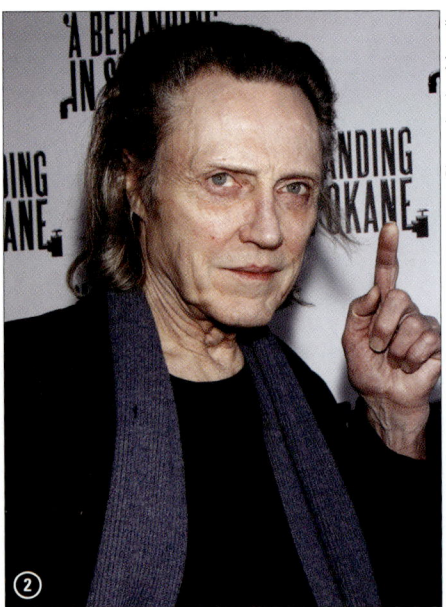

Photos by Joe Marzullo

Correspondents: Frank Lombardi and Lisa Buxbaum, Stage Managers
Most Exciting Celebrity Visitors: Robert De Niro, Dustin Hoffman, David Bowie, Sting, and the Grand Chief of the Cree Nation.
Who Has Done the Most Shows in Their Career: Christopher Walken.
Special Backstage Rituals: Sam Rockwell shadow boxing before each entrance.
Favorite Moment During Each Performance (On Stage or Off): The audience reaction to the suitcase opening and the hands coming out.
Favorite In-Theatre Gathering Place: Basement for our Sunday brunches.
Favorite Off-Site Hangout: Glass House Tavern.
Favorite Snack Foods: Toasted peanut butter & jelly sandwiches; pretzels.
Mascot: Joshua, our propman's son.
Favorite Therapies: Ice packs and tea & organic honey.
Memorable Ad-Libs: Chris Walken aiming his gun at a patron taking a photo. Neil Rosenberg, our propman, coming onstage to re-light the candle that accidentally went out.
Memorable Press Encounter: The unveiling of Christopher Walken's caricature at Sardi's.
Memorable Stage Door Fan Encounter: Radioman
Fastest Costume Change: Anthony Mackie on opening night when his car was 30 minutes late to half-hour call due to an accident.
Who Wore the Least: Zoe Kazan, especially when she was drenched with the water Chris poured on her.
Catchphrases Only the Company Would Recognize: "Don't forget to set your 'cocks' forward tonight."
Company In-Joke: "Why don't you go shtand over there."
Company Legend: Christopher Walken.
Nicknames: "Sammy Waffles" / "Peaches."
Embarrassing Moment: The phone cord not being attached to the wall.
Coolest Thing About Being in This Show: Being able to use "motherfucker" freely.

1. Zoe Kazan on opening night.
2. Christopher Walken at Bar Americain for the cast party.
3. (L-R): Anthony Mackie, Zoe Kazan, Sam Rockwell and Christopher Walken meet the press at Sardi's.
4. Director John Crowley at the premiere.
5. Author Martin McDonagh at Bar Americain.

Billy Elliot

First Preview: October 1, 2008. Opened: November 13, 2008.
Still running as of May 31, 2010.

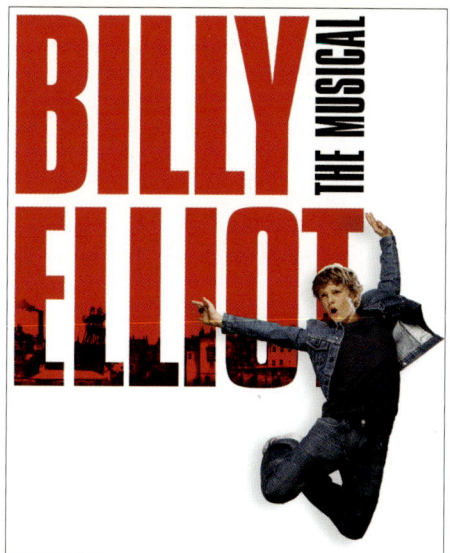

CAST

Billy	DAVID ALVAREZ, TOMMY BATCHELOR, TRENT KOWALIK, KIRIL KULISH
Mrs. Wilkinson	HAYDN GWYNNE
Dad	GREGORY JBARA
Grandma	CAROLE SHELLEY
Tony	WILL CHASE
George	JOEL HATCH
Michael	TREVOR BRAUN, KEEAN JOHNSON
Debbie	MARIA CONNELLY
Small Boy	MITCHELL MICHALISZYN, MATTHEW MINDLER
Big Davey	DANIEL ORESKES
Lesley	DONNA LYNNE CHAMPLIN
Scab/Posh Dad	RICK HILSABECK
Mum	LEAH HOCKING
Mr. Braithwaite	THOMMIE RETTER
Tracey Atkinson	RUBY RAKOS
Older Billy/Scottish Dancer	STEPHEN HANNA
Mr. Wilkinson	KEVIN BERNARD
Pit Supervisor	JEFF KREADY
Clipboard Woman	LIZ PEARCE
"Expressing Yourself" Dancers	KEVIN BERNARD, DONNA LYNNE CHAMPLIN, DAVID HIBBARD, JEFF KREADY, DAVID LARSEN, DARRELL GRAND MOULTRIE, ROBBIE ROBY, MATT TRENT

Continued on next page

IMPERIAL THEATRE
249 West 45th Street
A Shubert Organization Theatre
Philip J. Smith, *Chairman*   Robert E. Wankel, *President*

UNIVERSAL PICTURES STAGE PRODUCTIONS   WORKING TITLE FILMS   OLD VIC PRODUCTIONS
in association with WEINSTEIN LIVE ENTERTAINMENT present

BILLY ELLIOT THE MUSICAL
Based on the Universal Pictures/Studio Canal Film

HAYDN GWYNNE   GREGORY JBARA
CAROLE SHELLEY   WILL CHASE

And Introducing
DAVID ALVAREZ   TOMMY BATCHELOR   TRENT KOWALIK   KIRIL KULISH

With
TREVOR BRAUN • MARIA CONNELLY • STEPHEN HANNA • JOEL HATCH • LEAH HOCKING • KEEAN JOHNSON • THOMMIE RETTER
KEVIN BERNARD • DONNA LYNNE CHAMPLIN • SAMANTHA CZULADA • KYLE DesCHAMPS • EBONI EDWARDS • DAVID EGGERS
BRIANNA FRAGOMENI • GREG GRAHAM • ERIC GUNHUS • IZZY HANSON-JOHNSTON • DAVID HIBBARD • RICK HILSABECK • AARON KABURICK
CARA KJELLMAN • KARA KLEIN • DAVID KOCH • JEFF KREADY • DAVID LARSEN • MERLE LOUISE • MARINA MICALIZZI • MITCHELL MICHALISZYN
MATTHEW MINDLER • DARRELL GRAND MOULTRIE • TESSA NETTING • MADDY NOVAK • KARA OATES • DANIEL ORESKES • LIZ PEARCE
RUBY RAKOS • RACHEL RESHEFF • ROBBIE ROBY • HOLLY TAYLOR • MATT TRENT • NATALIE WISDOM • DANIKA YAROSH

Press Representative THE HARTMAN GROUP   *General Management* NINA LANNAN ASSOCIATES/DEVIN KEUDELL   *Advertising* SPOTCO

Production Stage Manager BONNIE L. BECKER   *Music Contractor* MICHAEL KELLER   *Production Supervisors* ARTHUR SICCARDI   PATRICK SULLIVAN

Adult Casting Director TARA RUBIN CASTING   *Children's Casting Director* NORA BRENNAN   *Resident Director* BT McNICHOLL

Associate Set Designer PAUL ATKINSON   *Associate Costume Designer* CLAIRE MURPHY   *Associate Lighting Designer (Programmer)* VIC SMERDON   *Associate Sound Designer* JOHN OWENS

Associate Choreographer KATHRYN DUNN   *Assistant Choreographer* NIKKI BELSHER   *Hair, Wig and Make-Up Designer* CAMPBELL YOUNG

Musical Supervision and Orchestrations by MARTIN KOCH   *Music Director* DAVID CHASE

Costume Design by NICKY GILLIBRAND   *Lighting Design by* RICK FISHER   *Sound Design by* PAUL ARDITTI

Executive Producers DAVID FURNISH   ANGELA MORRISON

Produced by
TIM BEVAN   ERIC FELLNER   JON FINN   SALLY GREENE

Associate Director JULIAN WEBBER

Set Design by IAN MacNEIL

Choreography by PETER DARLING

Directed by STEPHEN DALDRY

Book and Lyrics by LEE HALL

Music by ELTON JOHN

PROUDLY SPONSORED BY FIDELITY INVESTMENTS

10/1/09

The Miners Association

Photo by David Scheinmann

The Playbill Broadway Yearbook 2009-2010

Billy Elliot

MUSICAL NUMBERS

ACT 1
"The Stars Look Down" (The Eve of the Miners' Strike 1984) ....Full Company
"Shine" ....Mrs. Wilkinson, Ballet Girls, Billy
"We'd Go Dancing" ....Grandma, Men's Ensemble
"Solidarity" ....Full Company
"Expressing Yourself" ....Billy, Michael, Ensemble
"Dear Billy" (Mum's Letter) ....Billy, Mrs. Wilkinson, Mum
"Born to Boogie" ....Billy, Mrs. Wilkinson, Mr. Braithwaite
"Angry Dance" ....Billy, Men's Ensemble

ACT 2
Six Months Later

"Merry Christmas, Maggie Thatcher" ....Full Company
"Deep Into the Ground" ....Dad, Full Company
"He Could Go and He Could Shine" ....Dad, Tony, Ensemble
"Electricity" ....Billy
"Once We Were Kings" ....Full Company
"Dear Billy" (Billy's Reply) ....Billy, Mum
"Company Celebration" ....Full Company

David Alvarez with Police Shields
Photo by David Scheinmann

ORCHESTRA
Conductor:
DAVID CHASE
Associate Conductor:
SHAWN GOUGH
Assistant Conductor:
HOWARD JOINES
Reeds:
EDDIE SALKIN, RICK HECKMAN, MIKE MIGLIORE, JAY BRANDFORD
Trumpets:
JAMES DELA GARZA, JOHN DENT, ALEX HOLTON
Trombones:
DICK CLARK, JACK SCHATZ
French Horns:
ROGER WENDT, EVA CONTI
Keyboards:
JOSEPH JOUBERT, SHAWN GOUGH
Guitar:
JJ McGEEHAN
Bass:
RANDY LANDAU
Drums:
GARY SELIGSON
Percussion:
HOWARD JOINES
Music Coordinator:
MICHAEL KELLER

In addition to playing trumpets, French horns and trombones, the brass section of the *Billy Elliot* Orchestra is also playing cornets, flugel horns, tenor horns and euphoniums. These unique brass instruments are the same instruments played in the Easington Colliery Band, which was founded in 1913. Brass players with band experience were encouraged by management to come from the west of Durham to work in the Colliery and play in the band, which continues to perform to this day.

Cast Continued

ENSEMBLE
KEVIN BERNARD,
DONNA LYNNE CHAMPLIN, ERIC GUNHUS,
STEPHEN HANNA, DAVID HIBBARD,
RICK HILSABECK, LEAH HOCKING,
AARON KABURICK, JEFF KREADY,
DAVID LARSEN, MERLE LOUISE,
DARRELL GRAND MOULTRIE,
DANIEL ORESKES, LIZ PEARCE,
THOMMIE RETTER, MATT TRENT

BALLET GIRLS
EBONI EDWARDS,
IZZY HANSON-JOHNSTON,
MARINA MICALIZZI, TESSA NETTING,
KARA OATES, MADDY NOVAK,
RUBY RAKOS, RACHEL RESHEFF,
HOLLY TAYLOR, DANIKA YAROSH

SWINGS
SAMANTHA CZULADA, KYLE DesCHAMPS,
DAVID EGGERS, BRIANNA FRAGOMENI,
GREG GRAHAM, CARA KJELLMAN,
KARA KLEIN, DAVID KOCH,
NATALIE WISDOM

UNDERSTUDIES
For Mrs. Wilkinson:
LEAH HOCKING, LIZ PEARCE
For Dad:
RICK HILSABECK, DANIEL ORESKES
For Grandma:
MERLE LOUISE
For Tony:
JEFF KREADY, DAVID LARSEN
For George:
ERIC GUNHUS, DAVID HIBBARD
For Debbie:
IZZY HANSON-JOHNSTON
For Mum:
DONNA LYNNE CHAMPLIN, LIZ PEARCE
For Mr. Braithwaite:
GREG GRAHAM, ERIC GUNHUS,
DAVID HIBBARD
For Older Billy/Scottish Dancer:
KYLE DesCHAMPS, MATT TRENT

DANCE CAPTAINS
GREG GRAHAM, CARA KJELLMAN

Haydn Gwynne is appearing with the permission of Actors' Equity Association pursuant to an exchange program between American Equity and UK Equity.

Billy Elliot

 Haydn Gwynne *Mrs. Wilkinson*
 Gregory Jbara *Dad*
 Carole Shelley *Grandma*
 Will Chase *Tony*
 David Alvarez *Billy*
 Tommy Batchelor *Billy*
 Trent Kowalik *Billy*

 Kiril Kulish *Billy*
 Trevor Braun *Michael*
 Maria Connelly *Debbie*
 Stephen Hanna *Older Billy; Scottish Dancer*
 Joel Hatch *George*
 Leah Hocking *Mum*
 Keean Johnson *Michael*

 Thommie Retter *Mr. Braithwaite*
 Kevin Bernard *Mr. Wilkinson; Ensemble*
 Donna Lynne Champlin *Lesley*
 Samantha Czulada *Swing*
 Kyle DesChamps *Swing*
 Eboni Edwards *Ballet Girl*
 David Eggers *Swing*

 Brianna Fragomeni *Swing*
 Greg Graham *Swing/Dance Captain*
 Eric Gunhus *Ensemble*
 Izzy Hanson-Johnston *Ballet Girl*
 David Hibbard *Ensemble*
 Rick Hilsabeck *Posh Dad/Scab; Ensemble*
 Aaron Kaburick *Ensemble*

 Cara Kjellman *Swing/Dance Captain*
 Kara Klein *Swing*
 David Koch *Swing*
 Jeff Kready *Pit Supervisor; Ensemble*
 David Larsen *Ensemble*
 Merle Louise *Ensemble*
 Marina Micalizzi *Ballet Girl*

Billy Elliot

Mitchell Michaliszyn
Small Boy

Matthew Mindler
Small Boy

Darrell Grand Moultrie
Ensemble

Tessa Netting
Ballet Girl

Maddy Novak
Ballet Girl

Kara Oates
Ballet Girl

Daniel Oreskes
Big Davey; Ensemble

Liz Pearce
Clipboard Woman; Ensemble

Ruby Rakos
Ballet Girl

Rachel Resheff
Ballet Girl

Robbie Roby
Ensemble

Holly Taylor
Ballet Girl

Matt Trent
Ensemble

Natalie Wisdom
Swing

Danika Yarosh
Ballet Girl

Elton John
Music

Lee Hall
Book & Lyrics

Stephen Daldry
Director

Peter Darling
Choreographer

Ian MacNeil
Set Design

Nicky Gillibrand
Costume Design

Rick Fisher
Lighting Design

Paul Arditti
Sound Design

Martin Koch
Musical Supervision & Orchestrations

David Chase
Music Director

Michael Keller
Music Coordinator

Tara Rubin Casting
Casting

BT McNicholl
Resident Director

Nina Lannan Associates
General Management

Arthur Siccardi Theatrical Services, Inc.
Production Supervisor

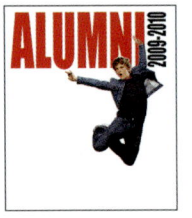

Juliette Allen Angelo
Ballet Girl

David Bologna
Michael

Grady McLeod Bowman
"Expressing Yourself" Dancer, Ensemble

Heather Ann Burns
Ballet Girl

Billy Elliot

 Cynthia Darlow *Ensemble*

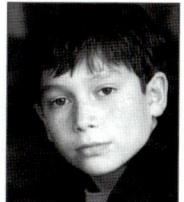 Frank Dolce *Michael*

 Santino Fontana *Tony*

 Meg Guzulescu *Ballet Girl*

 Joshua Horner *"Expressing Yourself" Dancer, Ensemble, Swing*

 Donnie Kehr *Scab/Posh Dad, Ensemble*

 Stephanie Kurtzuba *Lesley, "Expressing Yourself" Dancer, Ensemble*

 Caroline London *Ballet Girl*

 Kerry O'Malley *Mum, Ensemble*

 Jayne Paterson *Clipboard Woman, Ensemble*

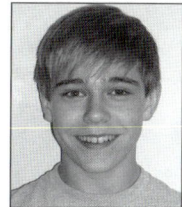 Tanner Pflueger *Billy*

 Corrieanne Stein *Ballet Girl*

 Jamie Torcellini *"Expressing Yourself" Dancer, Ensemble*

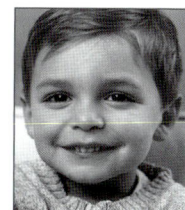 Luke Trevisan *Small Boy*

 Grant Turner *"Expressing Yourself" Dancer, Ensemble*

 Casey Whyland *Tracey Atkinson, Ballet Girl*

 Erin Whyland *Debbie*

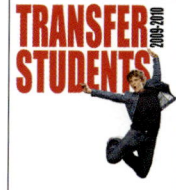

 Grady McLeod Bowman *"Expressing Yourself" Dancer, Ensemble*

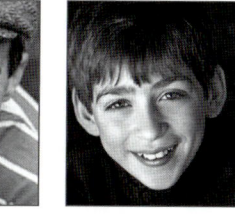 Brad Bradley *"Expressing Yourself" Dancer, Ensemble*

Jacob Clemente *Billy, Tall Boy/Posh Boy*

 Michael Dameski *Billy*

 Ava DeMary *Ballet Girl*

 C.K. Edwards *"Expressing Yourself" Dancer, Ensemble*

 Tim Federle *Dance Captain, Swing*

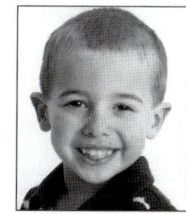 Seth Fromowitz *Small Boy*

 Chelsea Galembo *Swing*

 Meg Guzulescu *Ballet Girl*

 Kate Hennig *Mrs. Wilkinson*

 Kylend Hetherington *Tall Boy/Posh Boy*

 Georgi James *Ballet Girl*

 Donnie Kehr *Scab/Posh Dad, Ensemble*

 Alex Ko *Billy*

 Stephanie Kurtzuba *Lesley, Mum, "Expressing Yourself" Dancer, Ensemble*

 Liam Redhead *Billy*

Billy Elliot

Jake Evan Schwencke
Michael

Matthew Serafini
Swing

Easton Smith
Older Billy/ Scottish Dancer, Ensemble

Amber Stone
Lesley, "Expressing Yourself" Dancer, Ensemble

Dayton Tavares
Billy

Heather Tepe
Swing

Luke Trevisan
Small Boy

Grant Turner
"Expressing Yourself" Dancer, Ensemble

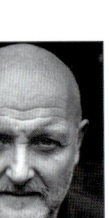
Philip Whitchurch
Dad

BOX OFFICE
(L-R): John Zameryka, Kiki Lenoue

STAGE MANAGERS
(L-R): MK Flynt, Scott Rowen, Bonnie Becker, Charlie Underhill

CREW
Front Row (L-R): Nanette Golia, Diego Irazarry, Jackie Pietro, Tim Miller, Stephanie Vetter, Susan Corrado, Margo Lawless, Terri Purcell, Duduzile Mitall, Marcia McIntosh

Back Row (L-R): Mel McClintock, Danny Terrell, Brian Hutchinson, Pete Donovan, Michael Taylor, Joel Deruyter, Mike Wojchik, John Cooper, Ben Horrigan, David Bornstein, Reg Vessey, Justin Sanok, Wally Bullard, Jay Gill, Paul Ludick, Leah Redmond, Michael Berglund

ORCHESTRA
Front Row (L-R): John Dent, Howard Joines, James Delagarza, Dick Clark, Randy Landau

Back Row (L-R): J.J. McGeehan, Joseph Joubert, Alex Holton, David Chase, Jack Schatz, Roger Wendt, Eva Conti

Billy Elliot

FRONT OF HOUSE STAFF
Front Row (L-R): Chris Caoili, Fran Barberetti, Delores Danska, Joe Pullara

Second Row (L-R): Georgina Vellacorta, Fhara Lynch

Third Row (L-R): Gerry Belitsis, Martin Werner, Lois Fernandez, Crystal Walker

Back Row: Dennis Norwood

STAFF FOR BILLY ELLIOT THE MUSICAL

GENERAL MANAGEMENT
NINA LANNAN ASSOCIATES
Devin Keudell

COMPANY MANAGER
Gregg Arst
Associate Company Manager .... Carol M. Oune
Assistant Company Manager .... Ashley Berman

GENERAL PRESS REPRESENTATIVE
THE HARTMAN GROUP
Michael Hartman
Juliana Hannett   Frances Connelly

CHILDREN'S CASTING
NORA BRENNAN

ADULT CASTING
TARA RUBIN CASTING
Tara Rubin CSA, Eric Woodall CSA, Dale Brown,
Merri Sugarman CSA, Laura Schutzel CSA,
Paige Blansfield, Kaitlin Shaw

Production Stage Manager .... Bonnie L. Becker
Stage Manager .... Charles Underhill
Assistant Stage Managers .... Scott Rowen, Mary Kathryn Flynt

Supervising Dialect Coach (UK) .... William Conacher
Resident Dialect Coach .... Ben Furey

Dance Captains .... Greg Graham, Cara Kjellman
Acro Captain .... Kyle DesChamps
Choreographic Supervision .... Ellen Kane
Staging and Dance Assistant .... Lee Proud

Associate Set Designer .... Paul Atkinson
Assistant Set Designer .... Jaimie Todd
Associate Costume Designer (UK) .... Claire Murphy
Associate Costume Designer (US) .... Brian Russman
Assistant Costume Designer (US) .... Rebecca Lustig
Assistant to Ms. Gillibrand .... Rachel Attridge
Associate Lighting Designer (UK) .... Vic Smerdon
Associate Lighting Designer (US) .... Daniel Walker
Assistant Lighting Designer (US) .... Kristina Kloss
Associate Sound Designer (UK) .... John Owens
Associate Sound Designer (US) .... Tony Smolenski IV
Moving Light Programmer (US) .... David Arch
Costume Shopper (UK) .... Bryony Fayers
Props Shoppers (UK) .... Kathy Anders, Lisa Buckley

Fight Director .... David S. Leong

Production Carpenter .... Gerard Griffin
Production Flyman .... Brian Hutchinson
Production Automation Carpenter ...... Charles Heulitt III
Production Electrician .... Jimmy Maloney, Jr.
Head Electrician .... Kevin Barry
Assistant Electrician .... Brad Robertson
Production Props Supervisor .... Joseph Harris, Jr.
Head Propmaster .... David Bornstein
Assistant Propmaster .... Reg Vessey
Production Sound .... Bob Biasetti
Special Effects Consultant .... Greg Meeh

Wardrobe Supervisor .... Terri Purcell
Associate Wardrobe Supervisor .... Nanette Golia
Dressers .... Michael Berglund, Kenneth Brown, Charles Catanese, Lyssa Everett, Margiann Flanagan, Jay Gill, Joby Horrigan, Margo Lawless, Paul Ludick, Melanie McClintock, Jeannie Naughton, Duduzile Ndlovu-Mitall, Lisa Preston, Jessica Scoblick, Pat Sullivan
Hair & Makeup Supervisor .... Susan Corrado
Assistant Hair Supervisor .... Monica Costea
Hair Dresser .... Cory McCutcheon
Head Children's Guardian .... Robert Wilson
Assistant Head Guardian .... Amanda Grundy
Guardians .... Elizabeth Daniels, John V. Fahey, John Funk, Andy Gale, Annie Grappone
Production Assistants .... Emily Andres, Andrew Gottlieb, Alison M. Roberts

Rehearsal Pianists .... Joseph Joubert, Aron Accurso
Music Copying/Library Services (US) ..... Emily Grishman Music Preparation
Children's Tutoring .... On Location Education/ Alan Simon, Jodi Green
Tutors .... Jennifer Cutler, Irene Karasik, Alla Markova, Alana Serignese, Rachel Truman
Box Office Staff .... Bill Carrick, Paul Blaber, Carlin Blum, Greer Bond, Bryan Cobb, Brian Goode, John Zameryka
Ballet Instructors .... Finis Jhung, Francois Perron
Acrobatic Instructor .... Hector Salazar
Physical Therapy .... PhysioArts/Jenni Green
Company Physical Therapists .... Sarah Bingham, Ryanne Glasper, Suzanne Lynch
Orthopedic Consultant .... Dr. Phillip Bauman
Pediatric/ENT Consultant .... Dr. Barry Kohn
Health & Safety Consultants .... Eric D. Wallace, Greg Petruska

Advertising .... SPOTCO/ Drew Hodges, Jim Edwards, Tom Greenwald, Jim Aquino, Stacey Maya
Marketing .... Allied Live/ Laura Matalon, Tanya Grubich, Meghan Zaneski, Sara Rosenzweig
International Marketing Consultants .... AKA/ Adam Kenwright, Liz Furze, Richard Howle, Adam Jay
Interactive Marketing Agency .... Situation Interactive/ Damian Bazadona, Jenn Elston
Production Videographer .... Suspension Productions/ Joe Locarro
Production Photographers .... David Scheinmann, Carol Rosegg
Accountant .... FK Partners/Robert Fried
Comptroller .... Sarah Galbraith and Co./ Sarah Galbraith
Immigration .... Kramer Levin Naftalis & Frankel LLP/ Mark D. Koestler, Esq., Allison Gray, Esq.
Legal Counsel .... Loeb & Loeb/ Seth Gelblum

The Playbill Broadway Yearbook 2009-2010   47

Billy Elliot

	Franklin, Weinrib, Rudell & Vassallo, PC/ Elliot H. Brown
General Management Associates	Steve Dow, Libby Fox, David Roth
General Management Interns	Danielle Saks, Ryan Conway
Production Supervisor Intern	Lenora Hartley
Lighting Intern	Trent Suidgeest
Sound Intern	Rachel O'Connor
Press Associates	Leslie Baden, Tom D'Ambrosio, Matt Ross, Matt Shea, Wayne Wolfe
Children's Casting Assistant	Jamie Tuss
Payroll Services	Castellana Services, Inc.
Travel Agent	Tzell Travel/ The "A" Team, Andi Henig
Housing	Premier Relocation Solutions/ Christine Sodikoff
Banking	Bank of America/Glen Rylko
Insurance	AON/ Albert G. Ruben Insurance Services, Inc./ Susan M. Weiss
Structural Engineering Consultant	McLaren Engineering Group/ Bill Gorlin
Demolition Services	JRM Construction Management, LLC/ Philip R. Arnold, Jr.
Theatre Displays	BAM Signs
Merchandising	Encore Merchandising/ Joey Boyles, Chris Paseka, Maryanna Geller, Jessie Bello, Claire Newhouse
Opening Night Coordination	The Lawrence Company Events, Inc./ Michael Lawrence
Directing Interns	Emilia Horn, Kate Roosa, Samantha Williams

FOR UNIVERSAL PICTURES STAGE PRODUCTIONS

President and COO, Universal Studios	Ron Meyer
Chairman	Marc Shmuger
Co-Chairman	David Linde
President of Production	Donna Langley
Co-President of Production and EVP	Jimmy Horowitz
President of Marketing and Distribution	Adam Fogelson
President of Marketing	Eddie Egan
SVP, Production Finance	Arturo Barquet
Legal Affairs	Keith Blau

FOR WORKING TITLE FILMS

Head of Marketing	David Livingstone
Marketing Executive	Susan Butterly
Vice President, Legal and Business Affairs	Gráinne McKenna
President of Production (U.S.)	Liza Chasin
Head of Film	Debra Hayward
Head of Development	Natascha Wharton
Head of Production	Michelle Wright
Head of Legal and Business Affairs	Sheeraz Shah
Finance Director	Tim Easthill
Assistant to Eric Fellner	Cara Shine
Assistant to Tim Bevan	Chloe Dorigan
Assistant to Angela Morrison	Tash Amis
Associate Producer	Marieke Spencer
Head of Finance, *Billy Elliot*	Shefali Ghosh
Assistant to Jon Finn	Katie Goodson-Thomas

FOR OLD VIC PRODUCTIONS

Chief Executive	Sally Greene
Executive Producer	Joseph Smith
Finance Director	Vanessa Harrison
Administrator	Becky Barber
Assistant to Sally Greene	Emily Blacksell
Administrative Assistant	Sophie Netchaef
Legal Representative	David Friedlander

CREDITS

Scenery constructed and automation equipment provided by Hudson Scenic Studios, Inc. Back wall by Souvenir Scenic Studios, Ltd. Miners' banner by Alaister Brotchie. Flying by Foy. Lighting equipment from PRG Lighting. Sound equipment by Masque Sound. Puppets designed and contracted by the Wright Stuff Theatre of Puppets. Costumes constructed by Mark Costello, London; Tricorne NYC; Jennifer Love Costumes; Baracath Customwear; Douglas Earl Costumes; David Quinn. Custom knitwear by Maria Ficalora and Karen Eifert. Custom footwear by T.O. Dey and Capezio. Millinery and costume crafts by Rodney Gordon, Inc. Undergarments provided by Bra*Tenders. "Express" dress puppet frames and Maggie Thatcher tank by Sophie Jones. Dancing dresses by Phil Reynolds Costumes, London. Ballet Girls clothing by Airy Fairy Costuming. Fabric painting and costume distressing by Nicola Killeen Textiles and Jeff Fender. Wigs made by Campbell Young Associates. Incidental and small props by the Spoon Group. Soft goods props by Mariah Hale. Musical instruments provided by Manny's Music, Pearl Drums, Mesa Boogie Guitar Amplifiers, Eden Electronics and Ernie Ball. Natural herb cough drops supplied by Ricola USA, Inc. Rehearsed at New 42nd Street Studios. Rehearsal scenery and props by the Technical Office Pty, Australia, and Adelaide Festival Centre Trust Workshops.

Billy Elliot on Broadway originally rehearsed at the Little Shubert Theatre, NYC; Ripley-Grier Studios, NYC; 3 Mills Studio, London.

Make-up Provided by
MAKE UP FOR EVER

To learn more about the production, please visit
www.BillyElliotBroadway.com

To become the next Billy Elliot, please visit
www.BeBilly.com

SPECIAL THANKS

The producers wish to thank the following partners for their generous support: HOTEL MELA, FIDELITY, CAPEZIO, STEPS ON BROADWAY.

Special thanks to Cass Jones (technical director Aus.); Stephen Rebbeck (technical director UK); Dennis Crowley; Maggie Brohn; Mark Vogeley, Michael Stewart and staff of the Little Shubert Theatre; Stanislav Iavorski and the staff of Ripley-Grier Studios; Steve Roath and the staff of Chelsea Studios; Chuck Vassallo and the staff of the Professional Performing Arts School, New York City; American Ballet Theatre; Youth America Grand Prix (YAGP); Ann Willis Ratray (Acting Consultant); Joan Lader; Ray Hesselink; Tim Federle; Callie Carter; Sara Brians; Stacy Caddell; Fred Lassen; Dorothy Medico and Dorothy's School of Dance – Long Island; Laurie Rae Waugh of Acocella Group; Lisa Schuller of Halstead Property, LLC; Marie-Claire Martineau of Maison International; the "Victoria Posse": Jackie Morgan, John Caswell, Tiffany Horton, Donald Ross, Peter Waterman, Gemma Thomas, Sarah Askew, Marian Lynch, Sian Farley; Treagus Stoneman Associates, Ltd.; Louise Withers and Associates; David Blandon; Diane Dawson; Donna Distefano Jewelry. With thanks to the National Coal Mining Museum for England, Wakefield, W. Yorkshire.

Working Title Films would like to thank Ron Meyer, Marc Shmuger, David Linde, Jimmy Horowitz, Donna Langley, Rick Finkelstein, Arturo Barquet, Allison Ganz, Stephanie Sperber, Stephanie Testa and Jonathan Treisman at Universal Pictures; Peter Bennett-Jones and Greg Brenman at Tiger Aspect Pictures; David Thompson at the BBC and Tessa Ross; Luke Lloyd Davies; Janine Shalom; all at Working Title Films for their continuing help and support; and especially to all the people who worked on the film *Billy Elliot*.

Old Vic Productions would like to thank Eric Fellner, Tim Bevan, Elton John, David Furnish, Lee Hall, Stephen Daldry, Peter Darling, Angela Morrison, Jon Finn and all at Working Title Films, Arthur Cohen, David Friedlander, Robert Reed, Marieke Spencer, Jimmy Horowitz, John Barlow, Adam Kenwright, Janine Shalom, and most of all, to David, Kiril and Trent.

Elton John would like to thank Lee Hall, Stephen Daldry, David Furnish, Matt Still, Eric Fellner, Tim Bevan, Jon Finn, Sally Greene, Angela Morrison, Frank Presland, Keith Bradley, Clive Banks, Todd Interland, Davey Johnstone, Bob Birch, Guy Babylon, John Mahon, Nigel Olsen. And a special thanks to Liam, James and George for bringing Billy to life on stage.

 **THE SHUBERT ORGANIZATION, INC.**
Board of Directors

Philip J. Smith Chairman	**Robert E. Wankel** President
Wyche Fowler, Jr.	**John W. Kluge**
Lee J. Seidler	**Michael I. Sovern**

Stuart Subotnick

Elliot Greene Chief Financial Officer	**David Andrews** Senior Vice President – Shubert Ticketing
Juan Calvo Vice President and Controller	**John Darby** Vice President – Facilities
Peter Entin Vice President – Theatre Operations	**Charles Flateman** Vice President – Marketing
Anthony LaMattina Vice President – Audit & Production Finance	**Brian Mahoney** Vice President – Ticket Sales

D.S. Moynihan
Vice President – Creative Projects

House Manager	Joseph Pullara

Billy Elliot
SCRAPBOOK

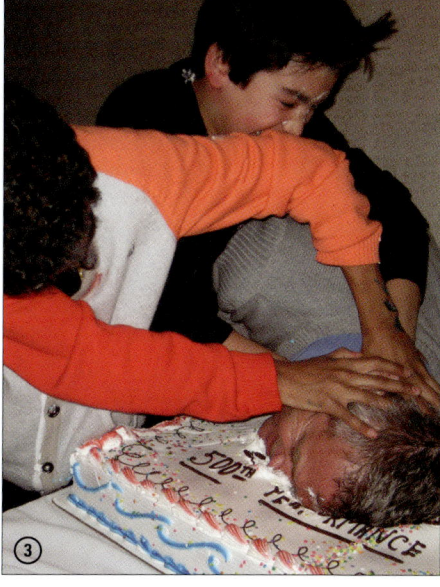

Correspondent: Tessa Netting, "Susan Parks" ("the spastic starfish ballet girl")
Tony Awards: Ten, baby! And who could forget "the Billy speech" by our three originals, Trent Kowalik, David Alvarez and Kiril Kulish: "I'd like to thank my dad, my mom, and my three sisters...." Ask any cast member to quote it. Hilarious.
One-Year Anniversary: Lots of cake, party hats, pictures, games of tag, and champagne (shirley temples for the kids of course) at the back of house in the Imperial Theatre.
500th Performance Party: At the Glass House Tavern, Stephen Daldry lovingly smashed Liam Redhead and Alex Ko's faces into our huge cake...but we all still ate it!
Most Exciting Celebrity Visitors: For the ballet girls: Ashley Argota or Corbin Bleu (he's right next door at *In the Heights*!). For the adults: Kate Winslet. For ME, Thommie Retter, and Seth Fromowitz: Mark Sanchez, quarterback for the New York Jets. I was in heaven.
"Easter Bonnet" Sketch (2009): (Headed by David Koch and Liz Pearce) The 105-year-old original *Ziegfeld Follies* girl, Doris Eaton Travis, taught the ballet girls "Ballin' the Jack" after a mock "ballet girl audition."
"Broadway on Broadway": Haydn Gwynne, Thommie Retter, Tommy Batchelor, and the ballet girls performed "Shine" with Cara Kjellman, Liz Pearce, and Kerry O'Malley singing back-up!
"Gypsy of the Year": (Headed by Aaron Kaburick and Donna Lynne Champlin) We sang a parody to the song "Goodnight and Thank You" from *Evita*, poking fun at the number of injuries and replacements we have had in our large cast, as well as honoring all of our doctors and physical therapists!
Macy's Thanksgiving Day Parade: Kate Hennig, Thommie Retter, Trent Kowalik, and the ballet girls performed "Shine" in the freezing cold, VERY early in the morning! But it was totally worth it...AND we got a special caroling surprise from the cast of *Hair*!
"Carols for a Cure" Carol: "Incredible Phat (the Coldest Night of the Year)."
Holidays: For every holiday, our backstage area is decorated tremendously by our swings, including the incredible artwork of guardian John Funk. Christmas: Secret Santa. Valentine's Day: Secret Admirer with a reveal party. Halloween: All of the kids dress up and go 'trick-or-treating' to all of the dressing rooms around the theatre, ending in the HORRIFYING Haunted House of the Men's Ensemble dressing room with terrifying screams, magical illusions, scary surprises...and Aaron Kaburick wearing a dress!
Special Backstage Rituals: Before every show I have a long, detailed handshake with whoever is playing Michael (either Jake Schwencke or Trevor Braun, it varies)...I must say it attracts quite a crowd and with Philip Whitchurch being a fan favorite.
Also, before "Shine" all of the ballet girls have many different 'bird chants' that they do with each other.
Favorite In-Theatre Gathering Places: Jamming to Lady Gaga in the Boys' Dressing Room (Tra Ga's forever); playing pranks in the Men's quick change area near wardrobe; doing homework on the stairwell or in the bathroom; chilling outside the stage door on 46th Street where we play pranks on passersby with fake rats and money glued to the sidewalk!!
Favorite Off-Site Hangouts: The park on 43rd Street; Dave & Busters (me and Mikey Dameski are the champions...Dayton Tavares and Liam Redhead would disagree); paintball trips, Junior's, movie trips (Harry Potter movie premiere...dressed up of course), hanging out at cast members' apartments.
Favorite Snack Foods: The famous brownies of Izzy Hanson-Johnston's mom, Dirt and Sand for the ballet girls (made by me), Oreos, anything chocolate, Pinkberry (Jay) and Red

1. Tommy Batchelor and the ballet girls performing "Shine" at "Broadway on Broadway."
2. Yearbook Correspondent Tessa Netting and Trent Kowalik react calmly and maturely to Kowalik's Tony Award for Best Actor.
3. At the 500th performance party, director Stephen Daldry gets his face mashed into the cake.
4. Members of the show's Broadway League softball team, The Wankers, in Central Park.

Photos courtesy Tessa Netting

The Playbill Broadway Yearbook 2009-2010   49

Billy Elliot
SCRAPBOOK

1. The swings of *Billy Elliot*.
2. (L-R): Ruby Rakos and Rachel Resheff in the ballet girl dressing room (someone was talking too loudly...).
3. Izzy Hanson-Johnston backstage in sound.

Mango (that sadly closed) and...Bagel Saturday is now EVERY SATURDAY! YES!
Mascot: In the words of Margo Lawless, "NEWS CHICKENNNN!!"
Teams: Softball: The Wankers. Bowling: The Strikers.
Favorite Therapy: PHYSIO ARTS! They fix us.
Special Items: Jeff Kready's comb, Marina Micalizzi's guava lotion, Bri Fragomeni's silly bandz, Eric Gunhus's coal, Mitchell Michaliszyn's 'Bunny', Seth Fromowitz's candy cigarettes, Grady Bowman's wig, Santino Fontana's long pauses (that's not an item but oh well).
Memorable Moments: Kyle DesChamps' movie 'The Legend of Black Dung'; 'Luxury' performed by Maria Connelly, Bri Fragomeni, and Samantha Czulada; Donnie Kehr playing "Pinball Wizard" on his accordion during the Super Bowl; Kiril Kulish attempting to rap; Erin Whyland and Juliette Angelo playing 'America's Next Top Model' with dresser Jeannie Naughton; Danika Yarosh's 'handcuff dance'; Grant Turner and Aaron Kaburick leading ballet girl warm-up with a combination to "Lady Marmalade"; Easton Smith carrying cast members up the stairs; watching Liz Pearce act in Luke Trevisan's 'movie'; playing intense games of 'Bippity Bippity Bop' and 'Zip Zap Zop' with Natalie Wisdom; constantly beating Trent Kowalik and David Alvarez at video games; me and Tommy Batchelor slicking our hair back with butter; Will Chase's face he makes at the cast during his 'Broadway Cares' collection speech.
Memorable Quotes: "One dark, stormy night...three men sat in a cave...one said, JACK, tell us a story! And this is the story he told..." —Ballet girl dresser Marcia
"ACTIVATE." —Kyle DesChamps
"I am going to assign you clubs...Scores, Lace, Private Eyes...GO!" —Georgi James
"You piss yourself." —Kara Oates
"In my mom's car..." —Rachel Resheff
"FREE THE CHICKEN! (From the Chicken Napper) —Ballet Girls
Memorable Stage Door Fan Encounter: Once a fan approached me and Trent Kowalik and asked where Billy Elliot was (because he thought Billy was real).
Catchphrases Only the Company Would Recognize: "What's the party?"
"It's Saturday night on BroadWAY!"
"Have a good Express" (made famous by Trevor Braun).
Tom's "Pum pum pum pum pum pum" song; "Sulphur"; "Ghost in the graveyard"; "Nivia".
In-Jokes: I would like to say to all of the ballet girls so this is in writing: I AM NOT A MAN!
Best In-House Parody Lyrics: For one performance Tommy Batchelor was Billy and during "Electricity" he started singing his own lyrics by mistake! Instead of "It's like that there's a music, playing in your ear..." he sang "It's like that there's a car, about to run you over...."
Tales From the Put-In: As recounted by Jake Schwencke: "During a put-in, I did not have shorts underneath my pants as I have during the show to get the tutu on. So stupidly, during the scene, I pulled my pants down..."
Also, after Dad discovers Billy (the scene after "Solidarity"), when Dad exits there is usually a stair placed underneath the truck upstage since there is such a huge drop. During one put-in the stair was forgotten...and Greg Jbara totally wiped out! Onstage we heard a huge CRASH and were wondering WHAT just happened?
Nicknames: These are the nicknames that I share with current/past cast members: D-Man (David Bologna), Pie Eater (Casey Whyland), Midget Fawn (Keean Johnson), Mad Dog (David Alvarez), Frankie Hooks (Frank Dolce), Gradar (Grady Bowman), Ronald (Jacob Clemente), Gorgeous (Kylend Hetherington), Chris Kanye (C.K. Edwards), Kokopuff (Alex Ko), and Carlos (Jake Schwencke).
Embarrassing Moments: I'm pretty sure almost every cast member has fallen at some point during the "Finale"...I know I have, about a MILLION times.
Ghostly Encounters Backstage: In the ballet girl dressing room we have a ghost named Fred. We leave him candy during the holidays.
Superstitions That Turned Out To Be True: Squeezing the Chicken with Carole Shelley and the ballet girls. We've squeezed it every day, every show, since the first preview and the one day we didn't squeeze it the show stopped five times!
Coolest Thing About Being in This Show: Our cast is so close, like one, big family. We go through a LOT of people coming and going and it's sad to say goodbye, but then you get to meet even more wonderful people. I love them all so much.

Brighton Beach Memoirs (The Neil Simon Plays)

First Preview: October 2, 2009. Opened: October 25, 2009.
Closed November 1, 2009 after 25 Previews and 9 Performances.

CAST
(in order of speaking)

Young Eugene Morris Jerome	NOAH ROBBINS
Blanche Morton	JESSICA HECHT
Kate Jerome	LAURIE METCALF
Laurie Morton	GRACIE BEA LAWRENCE
Nora Morton	ALEXANDRA SOCHA
Stanley Jerome	SANTINO FONTANA
Jack Jerome	DENNIS BOUTSIKARIS

SYNOPSIS OF SCENES
Act I
Brighton Beach, Brooklyn, New York
September, late 1930s, 6:30pm

Act II
Friday, a week later
About 6:45pm

UNDERSTUDIES
For Jack Jerome:
ADAM GRUPPER
For Stanley Jerome:
JÜRGEN HOOPER
For Blanche:
FINNERTY STEEVES
For Young Eugene Jerome:
COBY GETZUG
For Nora and Laurie:
BRIDGET MEGAN CLARK

NEDERLANDER THEATRE
UNDER THE DIRECTION OF
JAMES M. NEDERLANDER AND JAMES L. NEDERLANDER

Ira Pittelman Max Cooper Jeffrey A. Sine Scott Delman Ruth Hendel
Roy Furman Ben Sprecher/Wendy Federman Scott Landis
and Emanuel Azenberg
present

THE NEIL SIMON PLAYS

Laurie Metcalf
Dennis Boutsikaris Santino Fontana Jessica Hecht
Josh Grisetti Gracie Bea Lawrence Allan Miller Noah Robbins Alexandra Socha

Scenic Design	Costume Design	Lighting Design
John Lee Beatty	Jane Greenwood	Brian MacDevitt

Sound Design	Hair & Wig Design	Technical Supervision
Fitz Patton & Josh Schmidt	Tom Watson	Hudson Theatrical Associates

Casting	Press Representative	Associate Producer
Jay Binder / Jack Bowdan	Boneau / Bryan-Brown	Sheila Steinberg

General Manager	Production Supervisor
John E. Gendron	Barclay Stiff

Directed by
David Cromer

The producers wish to express their appreciation to the Theatre Development Fund for its support of this production.

(Clockwise, from Top Left): Santino Fontana, Laurie Metcalf, Dennis Boutsikaris, Jessica Hecht, Alexandra Socha, Gracie Bea Lawrence and Noah Robbins.

Brighton Beach Memoirs (The Neil Simon Plays)

 Laurie Metcalf
Kate Jerome

 Dennis Boutsikaris
Jack Jerome

 Santino Fontana
Stanley Jerome

 Jessica Hecht
Blanche Morton-Gross

 Josh Grisetti
Adult Eugene Morris Jerome in *Broadway Bound*

 Gracie Bea Lawrence
Laurie Morton

 Allan Miller
Ben Epstein in *Broadway Bound*

 Noah Robbins
Young Eugene Morris Jerome

 Alexandra Socha
Nora Morton

 Ari Brand
u/s Adult Eugene Morris Jerome

 Bridget Megan Clark
u/s Laurie Morton, Nora Morton

 Coby Getzug
u/s Young Eugene Morris Jerome

 Adam Grupper
u/s Jack Jerome

 Jürgen Hooper
u/s Stanley Jerome

 Herbert Rubens
u/s Ben Epstein

 Finnerty Steeves
u/s Blanche Morton

 Neil Simon
Playwright

 David Cromer
Director

 John Lee Beatty
Scenic Design

 Jane Greenwood
Costume Design

 Brian MacDevitt
Lighting

 Josh Schmidt
Co-Sound Design

 Tom Watson
Hair and Wig Design

 Stephen Gabis
Dialect Coach

 Jay Binder
Casting

 Jack Bowdan
Casting

 Neil A. Mazzella/Hudson Theatrical Associates
Technical Supervision

 Emanuel Azenberg
Producer

 Ira Pittelman
Producer

 Max Cooper
Producer

 Ruth Hendel
Producer

 Roy Furman
Producer

 Ben Sprecher
Producer

 Wendy Federman
Producer

 Scott Landis
Producer

Brighton Beach Memoirs (The Neil Simon Plays)

CREW
Front Row (L-R): Christopher Pantuso, Katie Beatty

Back Row (L-R): Jill Heller, Rodd Sovar, Gayle Palmieri, Kathryn Guida, James vanBergen

MANAGERS
(L-R): Kelly Beaulieu (Production Assistant), Michael Padden (Assistant Director), Brandon Kahn (Stage Manager), Chelsea Salyer (Assistant Company Manager), Barclay Stiff (Production Supervisor), John E. Gendron (General Manager)

Photos by Barclay Stiff

Editor's Note: *The Neil Simon Plays* were announced as revivals of two Neil Simon plays, *Brighton Beach Memoirs* and *Broadway Bound*, which share a setting and many characters. They were to have been presented in repertory with largely the same cast. However, after the quick closing of *Brighton Beach Memoirs*, *Broadway Bound* was cancelled.

2009-2010 AWARD

DRAMA DESK AWARD
Outstanding Featured Actor in a Play
(Santino Fontana)

GENERAL MANAGEMENT
JOHN E. GENDRON

GENERAL PRESS REPRESENTATIVE
BONEAU/BRYAN-BROWN
Chris Boneau   Jim Byk   Kelly Guiod

CASTING
JAY BINDER CASTING
Jay Binder CSA
Jack Bowdan CSA, Mark Brandon, Sara Schatz CSA, Nikole Vallins
Assistants: Karen Young, Patrick Bell

Production Supervisor	Barclay Stiff
Stage Manager	Brandon Kahn
Assistant Company Manager	Chelsea Salyer
Assistant Director	Michael Padden
Assistant Scenic Designer	Kacie Hultgren
Associate Costume Designer	Jennifer Moeller
Associate Lighting Designer	Peter Hoerburger
Lighting Programmer	Marc Polimeni
Associate Sound Designer	David Stollings
Assistant Sound Designer	David Koch
Production Carpenter	Joe Ferreri Sr.
Production Electrician	Richard Beck
Advance Electrician	James Maloney
Production Sound Engineer	James vanBergen
Production Properties Supervisor	George Wagner
Properties Supervisor	Christopher Pantuso
Wardrobe Supervisor	Kathryn Guida
Dressers	Jill Heller, Gayle Palmieri, Rodd Sovar
Hair Supervisor	Katie Beatty
Child Wrangler	Jessica Azenberg
Production Assistant	Kelly Beaulieu
Management Assistant	Errolyn Rosa
Assistants to Mr. MacDevitt	Josh Starr, Laura Schock
Accountant	Fried & Kowgios CPAs LLP/ Robert Fried
Comptroller	Elliott Aronstam
Advertising	Serino Coyne Inc./ Angelo Desimini, Tom Callahan, Cara Christman, Matt Upshaw
Interactive Marketing	Situation Interactive/ Damian Bazadona, John Lanasa, Chris Powers, Eric Bornemann
Legal Counsel	Levine Plotkin & Menin, LLP/ Loren Plotkin, Susan Mindell, Cris Criswell
Merchandising	Max Merchandising
Banking	JP Morgan Chase
Insurance	DeWitt Stern Group/Peter Shoemaker
Payroll Service	Castellana Services Inc.
Tutoring	On Location Education
Opening Night Coordination	The Lawrence Company/ Joanna Cepler
Voice/Speech Consultant	Stephen Gabis

CREDITS

Scenery by Hudson Scenic Studio, Inc. Lighting equipment by Hudson Sound and Light LLC. Sound equipment by Sound Associates, Inc. Costumes constructed by Eric Winterling, Inc.

SPECIAL THANKS

Nancy Rabatin from The City Quilter. Coffee makers generously provided by Keurig. Breads generously provided by Eli's Bread. Moda Fabrics. And thanks to Austin Pendleton.

NEDERLANDER

Chairman	James M. Nederlander
President	James L. Nederlander

Executive Vice President
Nick Scandalios

Vice President	Senior Vice President
Corporate Development	Labor Relations
Charlene S. Nederlander	**Herschel Waxman**

Vice President	Chief Financial Officer
Jim Boese	**Freida Sawyer Belviso**

STAFF FOR THE NEDERLANDER THEATRE

House Manager	Louise Angelino
Treasurer	Gary Kenny
Assistant Treasurer	Keshave Sattaur
House Carpenter	Joseph Ferreri Sr.
Flyman	Joseph Ferreri Jr.
House Electrician	Richard Beck
House Properties	William Wright

Burn the Floor

First Preview: July 25, 2009. Opened: August 2, 2009.
Closed January 10, 2010 after 8 Previews and 185 Performances.

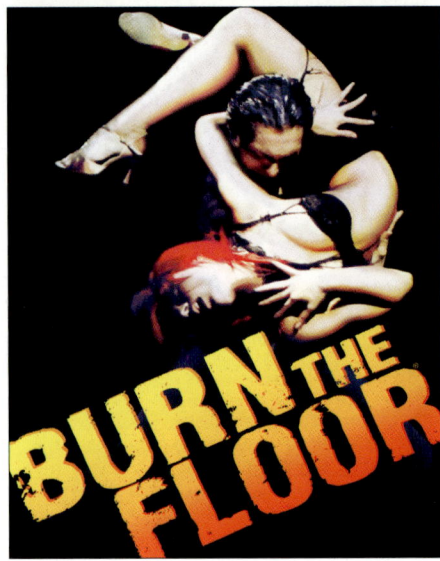

DANCE NUMBERS
ACT I
Inspirations

Ballroom Beat	Cha Cha
Let's Face the Music and Dance	Viennese Waltz
History Repeating	Viennese Waltz, Foxtrot, Swing, Lindy, Jive, Samba, Rumba, Cha Cha, Samba
Magalena	Samba
Slip into Something More Comfortable	Rumba
Weather Storm/The Ballroom Boys	Rumba
Fishies	Jive, Cha Cha
Nights in White Satin	Viennese Waltz
Pastorale	Waltz

Things That Swing

Sway	Cha Cha, Swing
It Don't Mean a Thing (If It Ain't Got That Swing)	Quickstep
I Just Want to Make Love to You	Swing
The Dirty Boogie	Jive, Lindy, Swing
I'm a Ding Dong Daddy	Quickstep, Lindy, Jive, Swing

ACT II
The Latin Quarter

Cariño	Cha Cha
Si tu Supieras	Rumba
Sing Sing Sing (with a Swing)	Salsa, Samba
Tanguera	Tango
Matador	Paso Doble
España Cañí	Paso Doble

Continued on next page

LONGACRE THEATRE
220 West 48th Street
A Shubert Organization Theatre
Philip J. Smith, *Chairman*   Robert E. Wankel, *President*

HARLEY MEDCALF   JOE WATSON
RICHARD LEVI   RICHARD FRANKEL   TOM VIERTEL   STEVEN BARUCH   MARC ROUTH
RAISE THE ROOF ONE
and
TOPPALL/STEVENS/MILLS   BENIGNO/KLEIN   CALDWELL/ALLEN
CARRPAILET/DANZANSKY   BUD MARTIN   THE PRODUCTION STUDIO   SCHAFFERT/SCHNUCK
and
CARRIE ANN INABA

by special arrangement with
DANCE PARTNER INC.
present

BURN THE FLOOR

with
SHARNA BURGESS   HENRY BYALIKOV   KEVIN CLIFTON   SASHA FARBER   JEREMY GARNER
GORDANA GRANDOSEK   PATRICK HELM   SARAH HIVES   MELANIE HOOPER   PETA MURGATROYD
GISELLE PEACOCK   NURIA SANTALUCIA   SARAH SORIANO   DAMON SUGDEN   REBECCA SUGDEN
TRENT WHIDDON   DAMIAN WHITEWOOD   ROBIN WINDSOR
and
RICKY ROJAS and REBECCA TAPIA
special guest stars
KARINA SMIRNOFF and MAKSIM CHMERKOVSKIY

SCENIC DESIGN	LIGHTING DESIGN	COSTUME DESIGN	SOUND DESIGN
RAY KLAUSEN	RICK BELZER	JANET HINE*	PETER J. FITZGERALD

*based on the original design by John Van Gastel

PRODUCTION MANAGEMENT	PRODUCTION STAGE MANAGER
PETER FULBRIGHT	BRUCE BOLTON
MUSIC CONSULTANT	MUSIC COORDINATOR
CHARLIE HULL	JOHN MILLER
GENERAL MANAGER	PRESS REPRESENTATIVE
FRANKEL GREEN THEATRICAL MANAGEMENT	BONEAU/BRYAN-BROWN
JOE WATSON	

ASSOCIATE PRODUCERS
DAN FRISHWASSER   PETA ROBY   NIC NOTLEY   BRAD BAUNER
CREATIVE CONSULTANT
RAJ KAPOOR
DIRECTED AND CHOREOGRAPHED BY
JASON GILKISON

8/2/09

(L-R): Sharna Burgess and Patrick Helm
Photo by Kevin Berne

Burn the Floor

(L-R): Peta Murgatroyd and Damian Whitewood

Photo by Joan Marcus

Dance Numbers Continued

Contemporary

Burn for You . . . . .Rumba
Club le Narcisse . . . . .Cha Cha
After All . . . . .Waltz, Tango, Paso Doble, Rumba
Proud Mary . . . . .Jive
Turn the Beat Around . . . . .Cha Cha

Conductor & Percussion: HENRY SORIANO
Music Coordinator: JOHN MILLER
Percussion: ROGER SQUITERO
Saxophone: DAVID MANN
Violin/Guitar: EARL MANEEIN

Karina Smirnoff
Dancer

Maksim Chmerkovskiy
Dancer

Sharna Burgess
Dancer

Henry Byalikov
Dancer

Kevin Clifton
Dancer

Sasha Farber
Dancer

Jeremy Garner
Dancer

Gordana Grandosek
Dancer

Patrick Helm
Dancer

Sarah Hives
Dancer

Melanie Hooper
Dancer

Peta Murgatroyd
Dancer

Giselle Peacock
Dancer

Nuria Santalucia
Dancer

Sarah Soriano
Dancer

Damon Sugden
Dancer

Rebecca Sugden
Dancer

Trent Whiddon
Dancer

Damian Whitewood
Dancer

Robin Windsor
Dancer

Ricky Rojas
Vocalist

Burn the Floor

 Rebecca Tapia — *Vocalist*
 Jason Gilkison — *Director/Choreographer*
 Ray Klausen — *Scenic Designer*
 Richard Frankel, Frankel Green Theatrical Management — *General Manager*
 Laura Green, Frankel Green Theatrical Management — *General Manager*
 John Miller — *Music Coordinator*
 Carrie Ann Inaba — *Producer*

 Thomas Viertel, The Frankel/Viertel/Baruch/Routh Group — *Producer*
 Steven Baruch, The Frankel/Viertel/Baruch/Routh Group — *Producer*
 Marc Routh, The Frankel/Viertel/Baruch/Routh Group — *Producer*
 Jean Doumanian, Raise The Roof One — *Producer*
 Harriet Newman Leve, Raise The Roof One — *Producer*
 Jennifer Manocherian, Raise The Roof One — *Producer*
 Lauren Stevens, Toppall/Stevens/Mills — *Producer*

 Allan S. Gordon, The Production Studio — *Producer*
 Élan V. McAllister, The Production Studio — *Producer*
 Greg Schaffert, Schaffert/Schnuck — *Producer*
 Terry Schnuck, Schaffert/Schnuck — *Producer*

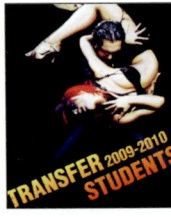
 MiG Ayesa — *Vocalist*
 Irina Boubnovskaia — *Dancer*
 Artem Chigvintsev — *Dancer*
 Anya Garnis — *Dancer*
 Karen Hauer — *Dancer*
 Kym Johnson — *Dancer*

 Pasha Kovalev — *Dancer*
 Mary Murphy — *Dancer*
 Mirko Sciolan — *Dancer*
 Vaidas Skimelis — *Dancer*
 Emma Slater — *Dancer*
 Katarina Stumpfova — *Dancer*
 Gary Wright — *Dancer*

Burn the Floor

WARDROBE DEPARTMENT

STAGE CREW

USHERS AND FRONT OF HOUSE STAFF

PRESS AND MANAGEMENT
(L-R): Jackie Green (Press Office), Kelly Guiod (Press Office), Liz Halakan (Assistant Company Manager), Adam Miller (Company Manager), Bob Reilly (House Manager)

STAFF FOR DANCE PARTNER, INC.

Founder and Producer	Harley Medcalf
Director and Choreographer	Jason Gilkison
Company Manager	Peta Roby
Executive Producer	Nic Notley
Music Consultant	Charlie Hull
Production Stage Manager	Bruce Bolton
Wardrobe Supervisor	Catherine Mayne
Wardrobe Deputy	Bret Hooper
USA Marketing	Maria Brunner, Insight Management
Company Accountant	Gordon Davis
Assistant Accountant	Rita Yao
Personal Assistant to Mr. Medcalf	Jaccinta Medcalf
Ass't. to Jason Gilkison	Clare Clifton
Accounting Services	East Bay Business Services/Marcia Hyman
Payroll Service	Team Services, Inc.
Immigration	RAZco Visas/Ron Zeelens
Music Clearances	Evan Greenspan, Gillian Jones
Merchandising	Broadway NY Marketing Group/Adam Gordon, David Eck
Insurance	DeWitt Stern Group
Travel	Rod Thomas at Qantas
Freight	Chris Seroukas, Soundmoves
Photography	Lindsay Hebbard, Mark Kitaoka, Tracy Martin, Louise Rojas
Banking	USA: City National Bank/Darlene Huntley; Australia: NAB Private/Daniela Siataga
Costume Makers	Sharon Brown, Marie Dowsett

The Playbill Broadway Yearbook 2009-2010

Burn the Floor

Creative Consultant	Kieron Kulik
Sound Engineer	Derek Wilson
Lighting Programmer	Scott Rogers

STAFF FOR BURN THE FLOOR

GENERAL MANAGEMENT
FRANKEL GREEN THEATRICAL MANAGEMENT
Richard Frankel   Laura Green   Joe Watson
Leslie Ledbetter

COMPANY MANAGER
Sammy Ledbetter

GENERAL PRESS REPRESENTATIVE
BONEAU/BRYAN-BROWN
Chris Boneau   Jackie Green   Kelly Guiod

PRODUCTION MANAGER
TECH PRODUCTION SERVICES, INC.
Peter Fulbright   Mary Duffe
Colleen Houlehen   Kate Baker

Company Management Assistant	Andrew Michaelson
Management Intern	Carrie Brinker
Production Carpenter	Erik Hansen
Production Electrician	Michael W. Brown
Assistant Electrician	Barbara Bartel
Production Sound Engineer	Wallace Flores
Wardrobe Supervisor	Penny Davis
Dressers	Ginny Hounsell, Laura Totero
Assistant to Mr. Baruch	Sonja Soper
Assistant to Mr. Viertel	Tania Senewiratne
Advertising	Serino Coyne, Inc./ Sandy Block, Roger Micone, Miriam Naggar, Ryan Cunningham
Director of Marketing & Promotions	Allied Live, LLC/ Tanya Grubich, Laura Matalon, Whitney Manalio, Elyce Henkin
Online Advertising, Marketing & Design	Art Meets Commerce/ Jim Glaub, Ryan Greer, Laurie Connor, Kevin Keating, Brad Coffman, Mark Seeley
Marketing	Leanne Schanzer Promotions, Inc./ Leanne Schanzer, Justin Schanzer, Kara Laviola, Michell Mazzei
Specialty Press Representatives	Act-e Marketing Solutions/ Carmen Sepulveda, Cova Najera Wei Zhou/Weiber Services, Inc.
Production Photography	Joan Marcus
Theatre Displays	King Displays
Insurance	DeWitt Stern Group, Inc.
Legal Counsel	Patricia Crown, Esq.; Carter Ann McGowan
Banking	JP Morgan Chase Bank
Accounting	Fried & Kowgios Partners, CPAs, LLP
Group Sales	Theatre Direct International 1.800.BROADWAY x2 /212-541-8457 x2

FRANKEL GREEN THEATRICAL MANAGEMENT STAFF

Finance Director	Michael Naumann
Assistant to Mr. Frankel	Heidi Libby
Assistant to Mr. Routh	Katie Adams
Assistant to Ms. Green	Joshua A. Saletnik
Assistant to Joe Watson	Liz Halakan
Assistant Finance Director	Sue Bartelt
Finance Associate	Heather Allen
Information Technology Manager	Roddy Pimentel
Sales and Marketing Director	Ronni Mandell
Director of Business Affairs	**Michael Sinder**
Business Affairs Assistant	Dario Dalla Lasta
Booking	On the Road Booking, LLC/ Simma Levine, President
Office Manager	Emily Wright
Receptionists	Christina Cataldo, Allison Raines
Interns	Tonianne Cincotta, Chelsea Laverack, Nina Lutwick, Alex Parra, Katie Pope, Samantha Schecter, Claudia Stuart

CREDITS AND ACKNOWLEDGEMENTS

Scenery built by Showmotion. Softgoods by Mark Hoffman. Lighting equipment from Hudson Sound and Light, LLC. Sound equipment from Sound Associates. Fiberoptic lighting by TPR Enterprises, Ltd.

WITH LOVE AND THANKS TO
Sir Elton John
Jessica Lingotti, Jason Fripp, Leigh Evans, Jason Seifert, Martine Munro, Peter Simpson, Peter Skillman, Janelle Mason, Glen Caruba, Ben Bruno, Sergio Kolomiers, Giorgio and Louise Rojas, Felix Rappaport, Mike Grose, Sue Maloney, our lifetime friends at Kansai Television, Tama Home, all past members of BURN THE FLOOR who made this journey possible, plus Sabrina, Jaccinta and Maria Medcalf.

Cover Photo by Lindsay Hebberd

MUSIC CREDITS

"**New Beginnings/BTF Guns**" Charlie Hull-Dance Partnership Pty Ltd. "**Ballroom Beat**" Charlie Hull-Dance Partnership Pty Ltd. "**Let's Face the Music and Dance**" words and music by Irving Berlin. "**History Repeating**" written by Alex Gifford; Chrysalis Music. "**Slip Into Something More Comfortable**" written by Mark Blackburn, Frederick Karger, Julius Waters, Robert Wells; Universal Music-Z Tunes LLC on behalf Imagem London Ltd., Barton Music Corp. "**Weather Storm**" written by Craig McKenzie Armstrong, Robert Del Naja, Curtis Harmon, Nellee Hooper, James Lloyd, Grantley Marshall, Cameron J. Murray, Cedric Napoleon, Andrew Lee Vowles; Universal Music-MGB Songs on behalf of G.W. JR Music, Inc./Universal Island Music Ltd. on behalf of Island Music Ltd., EMI Virgin Music, Outer National Publishing o/b/o Pieces of a Dream, Inc. "**The Ballroom Boys**" Charlie Hull-Dance Partnership Pty Ltd. "**Fishies**" written by Felix Riebl, Henry James Angus; The Cat Empire Music, by arrangement with Ocean Park Music Group. "**Nights in White Satin**" written by Hayward; The Richmond Organization. "**Pastorale**" written by Lovland; Universal Music Publishing. "**Sway**" Beltran, Ruiz, Rosas, Girnbel; Peer Music. "**It Don't Mean a Thing (If It Ain't Got That Swing)**" written by Duke Ellington and Irving Mills, used by permission of EMI Mills Music Inc., Sony/ATV Music Publishing LLC as successor in interest to Famous Music. "**I Just Wanna Make Love to You**" written by Willie Dixon; Bug Music Inc. "**The Dirty Boogie**" written by Brian Setzer; Setzersongs. "**I'm a Ding Dong Daddy**" written by Phil Baxter, used by permission EMI Feist Catalogue Inc. "**BTF Entracte**" Charlie Hull-Dance Partnership Pty Ltd. "**Cariño**" written by Mongo Santamaria, Neil Creque, Manny Benito, Cory Rooney, Jennifer Lopez, Jose Sanchez, Frank Rodriguez, Guillermo Edgehill Jr.; Bug Music Inc. on behalf of Mongo Music Ltd. Sony/ATV Songs LLC. "**Si tu Supieras**" written by Kike Santander, Foreign Imported Productions and Publishing Inc. "**Sing Sing Sing (with a Swing)**" Louis Prima, used by permission of EMI Robbins Catalog Inc. "**Bordello**" Charlie Hull-Dance Partnership Pty Ltd. "**Tanguera**" written by Mores-Warner Chappell Music Publishing. "**Fanfare Paso Doble**" Charlie Hull-Dance Partnership Pty Ltd. "**España Cañí**" traditional arr. Charlie Hull, Dance Partnership Pty Ltd. "**Burn for You**" written by John Farnham, Ross Fraser, Phillip Buckle; Universal Music-MGB Songs on behalf of Universal Music Publ. MGB Australia Pty/Universal-Polygram Int. Publ., Inc. on behalf of Offkey Music and T.W.O. Polygram Music Publ. Pty. Ltd. "**Club le Narcisse**" written by M. McLaren, L. Gorman, D. Hakagen/Bourgoin-Sony/ATV Music Publishing LLC, Chrysalis Music Publishing, Chrysalis. "**After All**" written by Tom Snow, Dean Pritchard; used by permission of EMI Intertrax Music Inc. and Snow Music, Karen Schauben Music Administration. "**Proud Mary**" written by John C. Fogerty; courtesy of Jondora Music, used by permission of Concord Music Group. "**Turn the Beat Around**" written by Jackson and Jackson-Warner Chappell Music Inc.

PERCUSSION AND DRUM SETS COURTESY OF PEARL

THE SHUBERT ORGANIZATION, INC.
Board of Directors

Philip J. Smith Chairman	**Robert E. Wankel** President
Wyche Fowler, Jr.	**John W. Kluge**
Lee J. Seidler	**Michael I. Sovern**

Stuart Subotnick

Elliot Greene Chief Financial Officer	**David Andrews** Senior Vice President – Shubert Ticketing
Juan Calvo Vice President and Controller	**John Darby** Vice President – Facilities
Peter Entin Vice President – Theatre Operations	**Charles Flateman** Vice President – Marketing
Anthony LaMattina Vice President – Audit & Production Finance	**Brian Mahoney** Vice President – Ticket Sales

D.S. Moynihan
Vice President – Creative Projects

Burn the Floor
SCRAPBOOK

Correspondents: Dancers Sharna Burgess, Robin Windsor, Rebecca & Damon Sugden.

Opening Night Gifts: By far the most interesting are from our Japanese fans—everything from personalized, bedazzled clothes pegs to questionable designer underwear, but champagne and flowers are always popular.

Most Exciting Celebrity Visitors: Recently on Broadway Jennifer Lopez and Marc Anthony came to the show, said they absolutely loved it and J Lo even enjoyed our version of her song "Cariño." In San Francisco when the incomparable Rita Moreno came backstage after the show she dropped to her knees and told us this show belonged on Broadway (so we took her advice).

In Las Vegas, we were thrilled when Liza Minnelli came backstage and in her excitement hugged every sweaty dancer until she looked like she had just done the show with us. In L.A. Rene Russo came backstage after the show before we had even changed from finale costumes and saw more than she really wanted to.

Who Has Done the Most Shows in Their Career: In the current cast, Damon & Rebecca Sugden have been with the company since 1999. They have done more shows than they would really like to count.

Special Backstage Rituals: There are two essential rituals before every show. At hour call there is a rowdy meeting of the 'hacky sack' committee until half-hour to determine the winner (loser) of the 'fish' and other embarrassing consequences. (We have photos, but I don't think we should share…)

Five minutes before every show we gather on stage behind the curtain to do a BTF version of a Japanese Shinto blessing we call the Chen Chen. We feel it brings our energies together and connects us to deliver a heartfelt and honest show. It sets the mood and resets our minds and bodies.

Favorite Moment During Each Performance: The standing ovation and curtain call as we all stand arm in arm. –Rebecca Sugden

The powerful moment when I place a blindfold on Peta for her complete trust in "Weather storm." –Robin Windsor

I have so many favorite moments from all our amazing and different dancers. I watch Ricky Rojas sing 'Fishies' every night. His character and feel makes me smile. Another special moment is 'Pastorale' performed by the elegant, graceful Damon & Rebecca Sugden. They take me on a journey, pulling at my heartstrings every time I watch from the wings. The love and honesty mesmerizes me and I fight back tears, it's devastatingly beautiful. –Sharna Burgess

Favorite In-Theatre Gathering Place: Behind the curtain at five minutes and in the basement for the hacky circle.

Favorite Off-Site Hangout: The bar at Time Hotel has hosted a few shindigs. Otherwise it varies every week.

Favorite Snack Food: Do coffee or Red Bull count?

Mascot: The fluorescent orange fish formerly

1. (L-R): Producer Carrie Ann Inaba and dancers Maksim Chmerkovsky and Karina Smirnoff at a press preview at the Longacre.
2. Director/choreographer Jason Gilkison (R) at the opening night with Nigel Lythgoe.

known as George now reincarnated as Fred is awarded to the hacky sack player deemed the worst of the night/week/season to be worn around the neck as a tie to a special event or an entire travel day.

Favorite Therapy: Sleep, Massage, Chiro, Ben-Gay, Double Espresso!!!

Most Memorable Ad-Lib: Patrick (my dance partner) had a costume issue, but I didn't know until I was already on stage, partnerless. There were two other couples doing matching partner work choreography…then there was me doing my own thing, embarrassing myself. I nearly killed him for not coming on. –Sharna Burgess
I attempted to dance my part and my partner's when left alone with a chair and a spotlight for what seemed an eternity. –Robin Windsor.

Web Buzz: Feedback on Facebook and Twitter has been awesome.

Memorable Press Encounter: We were shocked at the number of press who attended the preview media call and the sea of flashbulbs at our opening night party. We normally associate that amount of media interest in our established markets in Asia and Australia.

Record Number of Cell Phone Rings, Cell Phone Photos or Texting Incidents During a Performance: On Broadway, the ushers are so well trained and strict with cameras and phones being turned off or taken away. In China at the Great Hall however, there were thousands of cameras, phones and tripods that the poor ushers were beside themselves trying to prevent illegal filming.

Memorable Stage Door Fan Encounters: We are amazed to see a number of dance fans returning to the show four or more times.

Fastest Costume Change: Fastest quick change for all cast at the same time is under 60 seconds. Fastest quick change for just one person is vocalist Rebecca Tapia from 'Proud Mary' to 'Turn the Beat Around' at just over 30 seconds.

Busiest Day at the Box Office: On August 16 we broke the record at the Longacre Theatre for ticket sales.

Who Wore the Heaviest/Hottest Costume: The pure wool British tailored 'tails' really have the boys hot under the collar.

Who Wore the Least: The girls in "Narcisse" wear negligee inspired costumes, which also has the boys pretty hot under the collar.

Catchphrases Only the Company Would Recognize: "Carrrrn" means hurry up and get on stage. "Slab" is a penalty for a number of offences, for which the offender must buy a case of beer. "Botch" is when you mess up in hacky sack. Among many others.

Memorable Directorial Note: "Stop, Stop, Stop, Stop, Stop"

Understudy Anecdote: "Don't get sick"

Nicknames: Bruce "Manbearpig," Catherine "Supercaffs," Henry "Lou Diamond Fillipino" Robin "Bobby," Patrick "Patch," Earl "Girl," Sarah "Sass," Gordana "Goga," Damon & Rebecca "Snuggies."

Sweethearts Within the Company: Three married couples, one engaged couple, other romantically involved couples who have met through the show.

Embarrassing Moments: In the "History" number, I've danced on stage all fierce in my Cyd Charisse-inspired costume, absolutely giving it when suddenly I found myself falling backwards, pulling my partner, Patrick on top of me. As we're on the floor, all I could think was "Why did this have to happen on the night J Lo and Marc Anthony are watching?"… I certainly pick my moments. –Sharna Burgess

Ghostly Encounters Backstage: We once saw a 'pale apparition' backstage, then we realized it was just Kevin.

Coolest Thing About Being in This Show: A lot of the cast members have been touring with the show a long time because we have so much fun together on stage and off. We love our dance form, we are the first ballroom dance show of this kind on Broadway.

Fan Club Info: www.burnthefloor.com Also most of the cast are happy to chat on Facebook and Twitter.

Bye Bye Birdie

First Preview: September 10, 2009. Opened: October 15, 2009.
Closed January 24, 2010 after 40 Previews and 117 Performances.

CAST
(in order of appearance)

Mr. Harry MacAfee	BILL IRWIN
Mrs. MacAfee	DEE HOTY
Randolph MacAfee	JAKE EVAN SCHWENCKE
Kim MacAfee	ALLIE TRIMM
Conrad Birdie	NOLAN GERARD FUNK
Albert Peterson	JOHN STAMOS
Rose Alvarez	GINA GERSHON
The Teenagers	ALLISON STRONG, JULIA KNITEL, EMMA ROWLEY, JESS LePROTTO, DANIEL QUADRINO, PAUL PILCZ, DEANNA CIPOLLA, KEVIN SHOTWELL, RILEY COSTELLO, CATHERINE BLADES, JILLIAN MUELLER
Ursula Merkle	BRYNN WILLIAMS
The Fan Club Girls	ALLISON STRONG, JULIA KNITEL, EMMA ROWLEY, DEANNA CIPOLLA, CATHERINE BLADES, JILLIAN MUELLER
Mrs. Mae Peterson	JAYNE HOUDYSHELL
Hugo Peabody	MATT DOYLE
Reporters/Parents	PAULA LEGGETT CHASE, JOHN TREACY EGAN, COLLEEN FITZPATRICK, TODD GEARHART, PATTY GOBLE, SUZANNE GRODNER, NATALIE HILL, DAVID McDONALD, JC MONTGOMERY, TIMOTHY SHEW
Mayor Garfein	TIMOTHY SHEW
Mrs. Edna Garfein	PATTY GOBLE
Mrs. Merkle	SUZANNE GRODNER

Continued on next page

HENRY MILLER'S THEATRE
ROUNDABOUT THEATRE COMPANY
Todd Haimes, Artistic Director
Harold Wolpert, Managing Director
Julia C. Levy, Executive Director

Present

John Stamos   Gina Gershon
and **Bill Irwin**

in

Book by
Michael Stewart

Music by
Charles Strouse

Lyrics by
Lee Adams

with

Jayne Houdyshell   Dee Hoty

Matt Doyle   Jake Evan Schwencke   Allie Trimm
Catherine Blades   Paula Leggett Chase   Deanna Cipolla   Riley Costello   John Treacy Egan
Colleen Fitzpatrick   Todd Gearhart   Patty Goble   Suzanne Grodner   Robert Hager
Nina Hennessey   Natalie Hill   Julia Knitel   Jess LeProtto   David McDonald   JC Montgomery
Jillian Mueller   Paul Pilcz   Daniel Quadrino   Emma Rowley   Timothy Shew   Kevin Shotwell
Allison Strong   Bethany Ann Tesarck   Jim Walton   Brynn Williams   Branch Woodman

and

Nolan Gerard Funk
as Conrad Birdie

Set Design	Costume Design	Lighting Design	Sound Design	Projection Design
Andrew Jackness	Gregg Barnes	Ken Billington	Acme Sound Partners	Howard Werner

Musical Director	Music Coordinator	Hair & Wig Design	Makeup Designer	Production Stage Manager
David Holcenberg	Howard Joines	David Brian Brown	Angelina Avallone	Peter Hanson

Casting	Associate Director	Technical Supervisor	Executive Producer	Press Representative
Jim Carnahan C.S.A. & Kate Boka	Tom Kosis	Steve Beers	Sydney Beers	Boneau/Bryan-Brown

Director of Marketing & Sales Promotion	Founding Director	Associate Artistic Director
David B. Steffen	Gene Feist	Scott Ellis

Orchestrations by Jonathan Tunick
Music Supervisor/Vocal and Dance Arrangements by David Chase
Directed and Choreographed by **Robert Longbottom**

Bank of America is Proud to Support Roundabout Theatre Company
Lead support provided by Roundabout's Musical Theatre Production Fund partners:
Perry and Marty Granoff, The Kaplen Foundation, Peter and Leni May, John and Gilda McGarry, Tom and Diane Tuft.
Generous support also provided by The Blanche and Irving Laurie Foundation.
Roundabout Theatre Company is a member of the League of Resident Theatres.
www.roundabouttheatre.org

10/15/09

(L-R): John Stamos and Gina Gershon

Photo by Joan Marcus

Bye Bye Birdie

SCENES & MUSICAL NUMBERS

ACT ONE

Overture/Prologue
"We Love You Conrad" .... The Fan Club Girls
Scene 1: **The Office of Almaelou Music Corporation**
"An English Teacher" .... Rose Alvarez
Scene 2: **Sweet Apple, Ohio**
"The Telephone Hour" .... The Teenagers
Scene 3: **Kim MacAfee's Bedroom**
"How Lovely to Be a Woman" .... Kim MacAfee
Scene 4: **The MacAfee Living Room**
Scene 5: **Pennsylvania Railroad Station**
"Put on a Happy Face" .... Albert Peterson and the Fan Club Girls
Scene 6: **On Track 9**
"A Healthy, Normal American Boy" .... Rose Alvarez and Albert Peterson, the Fan Club Girls, the Reporters
Scene 7: **Sweet Apple Railroad Station**
"One Boy" .... Kim MacAfee, Hugo Peabody, Helen, Alice and Rose Alvarez
Scene 8: **Courthouse Steps**
"Honestly Sincere" .... Conrad Birdie
Scene 9: **The MacAfee Kitchen**
"Hymn for a Sunday Evening" .... The MacAfees
Scene 10: **Onstage, Central Movie Theatre**
"One Last Kiss" .... Conrad Birdie, the MacAfees, TV Quartet, Full Company

ACT TWO

Scene 1: **Kim MacAfee's Bedroom**
"What Did I Ever See in Him?" .... Rose Alvarez and Kim MacAfee
Scene 2: **The MacAfee Living Room**
"Kids" .... Mr. MacAfee, Mrs. MacAfee and Randolph MacAfee
"A Lot of Livin' to Do" .... Conrad Birdie, Kim MacAfee and The Teenagers
Scene 3: **In the Streets of Sweet Apple**
Scene 4: **Maude's Roadside Retreat**
"Baby, Talk to Me" .... Albert Peterson, Men's Quartet
Scene 5: **Exterior of Maude's Roadside Retreat**
Scene 6: **The Old School Yard**
"Spanish Rose" .... Rose Alvarez
Scene 7: **Sweet Apple Railroad Station**
"Rosie" .... Albert Peterson and Rose Alvarez
Scene 8: **Finale**
"Bye Bye Birdie" .... Full Company

ORCHESTRA

Conductor: DAVID HOLCENBERG
Associate Conductor: MAT EISENSTEIN
Music Coordinator: HOWARD JOINES
Music Director/Keyboard: DAVID HOLCENBERG
Reeds: LES SCOTT, RALPH OLSEN, THOMAS CHRISTENSEN, MARK THRASHER
Trumpets: DONALD DOWNS, STU SATALOF, BARRY DANIELIAN
Trombone: VINCENT FANUELE
Drums: PAUL PIZZUTI
Bass: RAY KILDAY
Guitar: SCOTT KUNEY
Viola: KENNETH BURWARD-HOY, LIUH-WEN TING
Cello: SARAH SEIVER, MAIRI DORMAN-PHANEUF
Synthesizer Programmer: BRUCE SAMUELS
Music Copying:
EMILY GRISHMAN MUSIC PREPARATION
– KATHARINE EDMONDS/ EMILY GRISHMAN

Cast Continued

Gloria Rasputin .... PAULA LEGGETT CHASE
TV Quartet ..... MATT DOYLE, JESS LePROTTO, DANIEL QUADRINO, KEVIN SHOTWELL
TV Stage Manager .... DAVID McDONALD
Charles Maude .... JIM WALTON
Bar Quartet .... JOHN TREACY EGAN, DAVID McDONALD, JC MONTGOMERY, TIMOTHY SHEW
and
WILL JORDAN as Ed Sullivan

SWINGS

Teen Male Swing: ROBERT HAGER
Adult Female Swing: NINA HENNESSY
Teen Female Swing: BETHANY ANN TESARCK
Adult Male Swing: BRANCH WOODMAN

UNDERSTUDIES

For Albert Peterson: TODD GEARHART
For Rose Alvarez: NATALIE HILL
For Conrad Birdie: ROBERT HAGER
For Mr. Harry MacAfee: JIM WALTON
For Mrs. MacAfee: COLLEEN FITZPATRICK
For Kim MacAfee: CATHERINE BLADES
For Randolph MacAfee: RILEY COSTELLO
For Mrs. Mae Peterson: SUZANNE GRODNER
For Hugo Peabody: DANIEL QUADRINO
For Gloria Rasputin: NINA HENNESSY
For Ursula Merkle: JULIA KNITEL

Dance Captain: JULIA KNITEL

Production Stage Manager: PETER HANSON
Stage Manager: JON KRAUSE

Nolan Gerard Funk and company perform "Honestly Sincere"

Photo by Joan Marcus

Bye Bye Birdie

 John Stamos
Albert Peterson

 Gina Gershon
Rose Alvarez

 Bill Irwin
Mr. Harry MacAfee

 Nolan Gerard Funk
Conrad Birdie

 Jayne Houdyshell
Mrs. Mae Peterson

 Dee Hoty
Mrs. MacAfee

 Matt Doyle
Hugo Peabody, TV Quartet

 Jake Evan Schwencke
Randolph MacAfee

 Allie Trimm
Kim MacAfee

 Catherine Blades
Teenager, Fan Club Girl

 Deanna Cipolla
Teenager, Fan Club Girl

 Paula Leggett Chase
Reporter, Parent, Gloria Rasputin

 Riley Costello
Teenager

 John Treacy Egan
Reporter, Parent, Bar Quartet

 Colleen Fitzpatrick
Reporter, Parent

 Todd Gearhart
Reporter, Parent

 Patty Goble
Reporter, Parent, Mrs. Edna Garfein

 Suzanne Grodner
Reporter, Parent, Mrs. Merkle

 Robert Hager
Teen Male Swing

 Nina Hennessey
Adult Female Swing

 Natalie Hill
Reporter, Parent

 Julia Knitel
Teenager, Fan Club Girl

 Jess LeProtto
Teenager, TV Quartet

 David McDonald
Reporter, Parent, TV Stage Manager, Bar Quartet

 JC Montgomery
Reporter, Parent, Bar Quartet

 Jillian Mueller
Teenager, Fan Club Girl

 Paul Pilcz
Teenager

 Daniel Quadrino
Teenager, TV Quartet

 Emma Rowley
Teenager, Fan Club Girl

 Timothy Shew
Reporter, Parent, Bar Quartet, Mayor Garfein

 Kevin Shotwell
Teenager, TV Quartet

 Allison Strong
Teenager, Fan Club Girl

 Bethany Ann Tesarck
Teen Female Swing

 Jim Walton
Charles Maude

 Brynn Williams
Ursula Merkle

Bye Bye Birdie

Branch Woodman
Adult Male Swing

Michael Stewart
Book

Charles Strouse
Music

Lee Adams
Lyrics

Robert Longbottom
Director, Choreographer

Gregg Barnes
Costume Design

Ken Billington
Lighting Design

Tom Clark, Mark Menard and Nevin Steinberg, Acme Sound Partners
Sound Designer

David Holcenberg
Music Director

Howard Joines
Music Coordinator

Jonathan Tunick
Orchestrations

David Chase
Music Supervisor

David Brian-Brown
Hair & Wigs

Angelina Avallone
Make-up Design

Tom Kosis
Associate Director

Pamela Remler
Associate Choreographer

Jim Carnahan
Casting

Gene Feist
Founding Director, Roundabout Theatre Company

Todd Haimes
Artistic Director, Roundabout Theatre Company

Neil McCaffrey
Randolph MacAfee

BOX OFFICE STAFF
Seated: Carlos Morris

Standing (L-R): Ronnie Tobia, Jaime Perlman

FRONT OF HOUSE STAFF
Front Row (L-R): Kristopher Kaye, Chris Brucato, Caroline Carbo

Middle Row (L-R): Jehan O. Young, Bobby Wolf, Johannah-Joy Magyawe, Sabrina Nan Miller

Back Row (L-R): Candice Schnurr, Christine Schisano, Zoey Martinson, Brittanie Bond, Karen Murray

The Playbill Broadway Yearbook 2009-2010

Bye Bye Birdie

WARDROBE DEPARTMENT
(L-R): Nadine Hettel, Vicki Grecki, Stacey Sarmiento, Mary Ann Oberpriller, Suzanne Lunney-Delahunt, Joe Hickey, Tara Delahunt, Kimberly Mark

CARPENTERS
(L-R): Paul Ashton, Dan Hoffman

PROP DEPARTMENT
Seated (L-R): Andrew Forste, Dan Mendelhoff
Standing (L-R): Ben Barnes, Joe Buck

HAIR DEPARTMENT
(L-R): Jennifer Pendergraft, Vanessa Anderson, Joshua First

STAGE MANAGEMENT
Seated: Peter Hanson
Standing (L-R): Jon Krause, Rachel Bauder

ELECTRICS DEPARTMENT
Seated (L-R): James Patrick Pummill, Robert Hager (Actor), Jocelyn Smith
Standing (L-R): Dorion Fuchs, Paul Coltoff, Peter Guernsey, Josh Weitzman, Aaron Straus

Bye Bye Birdie

ORCHESTRA
Front Row (L-R): Tom Christensen, Ralph Olsen, Paul Pizzuti

Middle Row (L-R): Summer Boggess, Ken Burward-Hoy, Sarah Seiver, Liuh-Wen Ting, Les Scott, Stu Satalof, Vinny Fanuele

Back Row (L-R): Ray Kilday, Mark Thrasher, David Holcenberg, Barry Danielian, Don Downs

ROUNDABOUT THEATRE COMPANY STAFF	
ARTISTIC DIRECTOR	TODD HAIMES
MANAGING DIRECTOR	HAROLD WOLPERT
EXECUTIVE DIRECTOR	JULIA C. LEVY
ASSOCIATE ARTISTIC DIRECTOR	SCOTT ELLIS

ARTISTIC STAFF
DIRECTOR OF ARTISTIC DEVELOPMENT/
  DIRECTOR OF CASTING .... Jim Carnahan
Artistic Consultant .... Robyn Goodman
Resident Director .... Doug Hughes
Associate Artists .... Scott Elliott, Bill Irwin, Joe Mantello, Mark Brokaw, Kathleen Marshall
Literary Manager .... Jill Rafson
Casting Director .... Carrie Gardner
Casting Associate .... Kate Boka
Casting Associate .... Stephen Kopel
Artistic Assistant .... Amy Ashton
Literary Associate .... Josh Fiedler
The Blanche and Irving Laurie Foundation
  Theatre Visions Fund Commissions .... Julia Cho, Stephen Karam, Lewis Black, Nathan Louis Jackson
Educational Foundation of
  America Commissions .... Bekah Brunstetter, Lydia Diamond, Diana Fithian, Julie Marie Myatt
New York State Council
  on the Arts Commission .... Nathan Louis Jackson
Roundabout Commissions .... Steven Levenson, Robert Lopez & Kristen Anderson-Lopez
Artistic Intern .... Benjamin Izzo
Casting Interns .... Kyle Bosley, Jillian Cimini, Erin Drake, Andrew Femenella, Lauren Lewis, Quinn Meyers
Script Readers .... Jay Cohen, Hillary Dixler, Nicholas Stimler

EDUCATION STAFF
EDUCATION DIRECTOR .... Greg McCaslin
Education Program Manager .... Jennifer DiBella
Education Associate
  for Theatre-Based Programs .... Jay Gerlach
Education Coordinator .... Aliza Greenberg
Education Dramaturg .... Ted Sod
Teaching Artists .... Cynthia Babak, Victor Barbella, LaTonya Borsay, Mark Bruckner, Joe Clancy, Vanessa Davis, Joe Doran, Elizabeth Dunn-Ruiz, Janet Edwards, Kevin Free, Tony Freeman, Sheri Graubert, Matthew A.J. Gregory, Melissa Gregus, Adam Gwon, Devin Haqq, Carrie Heitman, Karla Hendrick, Jim Jack, Jason Jacobs, Lisa Renee Jordan, Jamie Kalama, Alvin Keith, Tami Mansfield, Erin McCready, Deidre O'Connor, Andrew Ondrejcak, Maya Parra, Laura Poe, Jennifer Rathbone, Leah Reddy, Amanda Rehbein, Bernita Robinson, Christopher Rummel, Cassy Rush, Nick Simone, Heidi Stallings, Daniel Sullivan, Carl Tallent, Vickie Tanner, Jolie Tong, Cristina Vaccaro, Jennifer Varbalow, Leese Walker, Eric Wallach, Christina Watanabe, Gail Winar, Conwell Worthington, III
Teaching Artist Apprentices .... Carrie Ellman-Larsen, Deanna Frieman, Meghan O'Neill
Education Interns .... Nicole Bournas-Ney, Mandy Menaker

ADMINISTRATIVE STAFF
GENERAL MANAGER .... Sydney Beers
Associate Managing Director .... Greg Backstrom
General Manager,
  American Airlines Theatre .... Rebecca Habel
General Manager, Steinberg Center .... Rachel E. Ayers
Human Resources Manager .... Stephen Deutsch
Operations Manager .... Valerie D. Simmons
Associate General Manager .... Maggie Cantrick
Office Manager .... Scott Kelly
Management Associate .... Jill K. Boyd
Archivist .... Tiffany Nixon
Receptionists .... Dee Beider, Raquel Castillo, Elisa Papa, Allison Patrick, Monica Sidorchuk
Messenger .... Darnell Franklin
Management Interns .... Samara Harand, Jennifer Levine

FINANCE STAFF
DIRECTOR OF FINANCE .... Susan Neiman
Assistant Controller .... John LaBarbera
Accounts Payable Administrator .... Frank Surdi
Financial Associate .... Yonit Kafka
Business Office Assistant .... Joshua Cohen
Business Interns .... Davin DeSantis, Stephanie Jaccarino, Laura Marshall

DEVELOPMENT STAFF
Director, Institutional Giving .... Julie K. D'Andrea
Director, Special Events .... Steve Schaeffer
Director, Major Gifts .... Joy Pak
Director, Patron Programs .... Amber Jo Manuel
Manager, Donor Information Systems .... Lise Speidel
Manager, Patron Programs .... Tyler Ennis
Manager, Telefundraising .... Gavin Brown
Manager, Corporate Relations .... Roxana Petzold
Associate Manager, Patron Programs .... Marisa Perry
Special Events Associate .... Ashley Firestone
Patron Services Associate .... David Pittman
Institutional Giving Associate .... Nick Nolte
Development Assistants .... Ryan Hallett, Nick Luckenbaugh
Assistant to the Executive Director .... Jason Butler
Major Gifts Intern .... Kayla Carpenter
Special Events Intern .... Amy Rosenfield

INFORMATION TECHNOLOGY STAFF
IT DIRECTOR .... Antonio Palumbo

Bye Bye Birdie

IT Associate	Dylan Norden
IT Associate	Jim Roma
DIRECTOR DATABASE OPERATIONS	Wendy Hutton
Database Administrator/Programmer	Revanth Anne

MARKETING STAFF

DIRECTOR OF MARKETING AND SALES PROMOTION	David B. Steffen
Associate Director of Marketing	Tom O'Connor
Marketing/Publications Manager	Margaret Casagrande
Assistant Director of Marketing	Stefanie Schussel
Marketing Manager	Shannon Marcotte
Website Consultant	Keith Powell Beyland
Director of Telesales Special Promotions	Marco Frezza
Telesales Manager	Anthony Merced
Telesales Office Coordinator	Patrick Pastor
Marketing Interns	H.L. Ray, Sean Burpee

TICKET SERVICES STAFF

DIRECTOR OF SALES OPERATIONS	Charlie Garbowski, Jr.
Ticket Services Manager	Ellen Holt
Subscription Manager	Ethan Ubell
Box Office Managers	Edward P. Osborne, Jaime Perlman, Krystin MacRitchie, Nicole Nicholson
Group Sales Manager	Jeff Monteith
Assistant Box Office Managers	Robert Morgan, Andrew Clements, Scott Falkowski, Catherine Fitzpatrick
Assistant Ticket Services Managers	Robert Kane, Bill Klemm, Lindsay Ericson
Customer Services Coordinator	Thomas Walsh
Ticket Services	Solangel Bido, Arianna Boykins, Lauren Cartelli, Joseph Clark, Barbara Dente, Nisha Dhruna, Adam Elsberry, James Graham, Kara Harrington, Tova Heller, Nicki Ishmael, Kate Longosky, Elisa Mala, Mead Margulies, Chuck Migliaccio, Carlos Morris, Kayrose Pagan, Thomas Protulipac, Jessica Pruett-Barnett, Kaia Rafoss, Josh Rozett, Ben Schneider, Kenneth Senn, Heather Siebert, Nalane Singh, Lillian Soto, Ron Tobia, Hannah Weitzman
Intern	Melissa Cohen

SERVICES

Counsel	Paul, Weiss, Rifkind, Wharton and Garrison LLP, Charles H. Googe Jr., Carol M. Kaplan
Counsel	Rosenberg & Estis
Counsel	Andrew Lance, Gibson, Dunn, & Crutcher, LLP
Counsel	Harry H. Weintraub, Glick and Weintraub, P.C.
Counsel	Stroock & Stroock & Lavan LLP
Counsel	Daniel S. Dokos, Weil, Gotshal & Manges LLP
Immigration Counsel	Mark D. Koestler and Theodore Ruthizer
Government Relations	Law Offices of Claudia Wagner LLC
House Physicians	Dr. Theodore Tyberg, Dr. Lawrence Katz
House Dentist	Neil Kanner, D.M.D.
Insurance	DeWitt Stern Group, Inc.
Accountant	Lutz & Carr CPAs, LLP
Advertising	Spotco/Drew Hodges, Jim Edwards, Tom Greenwald, Kyle Hall, Cory Spinney
Interactive Marketing	Situation Interactive/Damian Bazadona, John Lanasa, Ryan Klink, Kristen Butler
Events Photography	Anita and Steve Shevett
Production Photographer	Joan Marcus
Theatre Displays	King Displays, Wayne Sapper
Lobby Refreshments	Sweet Concessions
Merchandising	Spotco Merch/James Decker

MANAGING DIRECTOR EMERITUS ....Ellen Richard

Roundabout Theatre Company
231 West 39th Street, New York, NY 10018
(212) 719-9393.

GENERAL PRESS REPRESENTATIVES
BONEAU/BRYAN-BROWN
Adrian Bryan-Brown
Matt Polk   Jessica Johnson   Amy Kass
Emily Meagher

STAFF FOR BYE BYE BIRDIE

Company Manager	Denise Cooper
Company Manager Assistant	Ellen Campion
Production Stage Manager	Peter Hanson
Stage Manager	Jon Krause
Associate Director	Tom Kosis
Associate Choreographer	Pamela Remler
Assistant Choreographer	Chad Schiro
Dance Captain	Julia Knitel
Associate Set Designer	Melissa Shakun
Assistant Set Designers	Sia Balabanova, Veronica Kimmel, Sean Tribble
Assistant to the Set Designer	David Towlun
Associate Costume Designer	Matthew Pachtman
Costume Assistant	Tescia Seufferlein
Assistant to the Costume Designer	Mitchell Travers
Costume Shoppers	Brenda Abbandandolo, Noah Marin
Costume Interns	Alice Garfield, Kathleen Doyle
Associate Lighting Designer	Paul Toben
Assistant Lighting Designer	Anthony Pearson
Associate Sound Designer	Nick Borisjuk
Production Sound Engineer	Patrick Pummill
Associate Projection Designer	Jason Lindahl
Projection Programmer	Phil Gilbert
Rehearsal Pianist	Mat Eisenstein
Rehearsal Drummer	Paul Pizzuti
Production Carpenter	Dan Hoffman
Automation Carpenter	Paul Ashton
Carpenter	Donald Roberts
Flyman	Steve Jones
Production Electrician	Josh Weitzman
Assistant Production Electrician	John Wooding
Moving Light Programmer	Tim Rogers
Followspot Operators	Paul Coltoff, Dorion Fuchs, Erica Warmbrunn
Deck Electrician	Jocelyn Smith
Deck Sound	Jocelyn Smith, Aaron Straus
House Properties	Andrew Forste
Properties Running Crew	Ben Barnes, Dan Mendelhoff, Nelson Vaughn
Production Properties Coordinator	Kathy Fabian, Propstar Inc.
Associate Production Properties	Tim Ferro, Scott Keclik
Wardrobe Supervisor	Nadine Hettel
Dressers	Tara Delahunt, Joe Godwin, Victoria Grecki, Joe Hickey, Mary Ann Oberpriller, Suzanne Lunney-Delahunt, Kimberly Mark, Stacey Sarmiento
Hair and Wig Supervisor	Vanessa Anderson
Hair Assistant	Jennifer Pendergraft
Children's Tutoring Provided by	On Location Education
Child Wranglers	Lauren J. Benn, Jill Valentine
Company Management Assistant	Dave Solomon
Production Assistants	Rachel Bauder, McKenzie Murphy
Physical Therapy	PhysioArts

CREDITS

Scenery fabrication and automation by Hudson Scenic Studio, Inc. Lighting equipment and projections by PRG Lighting. Audio equipment by PRG Audio. Costumes by Tricorne, Inc.; EuroCo Costumes, Inc.; John David Ridge; Katrina Patterns; Maria Ficalora Knitwear, Ltd.; Marsha Kuligowski; Eleanor Wolfe Marclana. Millinery by Lynne Mackey, Inc.; Tanen Co. Uniform Hats. Custom fabric painting and dyeing by Jeff Fender, Ellen Steingraeber. Custom footwear by J.C. Theatrical, Worldtone Dance, LaDuca Shoes. Special thanks to Bra*Tenders for hosiery and undergarments. Eyewear provided by Dr. Wayne Goldberg. Ms. Houdyshell's coat provided by Ritz Furs. Epiphone Limited Wilshire guitars, Epiphone Blues custom amps and Baldwin piano courtesy of Gibson Guitar. Specialty prop construction by Tom Carroll Scenery; Cigar Box Studios, Inc.; Daedalus Design and Production, Inc.; Aardvark Interiors; Turning Star, Inc.; Costume Armour; Propstar. Effects engineering by Technical Design Services, Inc.; Backyard Visions, Inc. Upholstery by Sarah Bird, Propstar; V. Ramos Upholstery, Inc. Photography by David J. Giesbrecht Photography. Footage clips provided by Getty Images.

SPECIAL THANKS

Carolyn Rossi Copeland (Strouse IP Executive Producer), Mary Kickel (Executive Assistant to Mr. Strouse).

Make-up provided by M•A•C.

HENRY MILLER'S THEATRE STAFF

Operations Manager	Valerie D. Simmons
House Manager	Johannah-Joy G. Magyawe
Box Office Manager	Jaime Perlman
Assistant Box Officer Manager	Andrew Clements
House Carpenter	Steve Beers
House Electrician	Josh Weitzman
House Properties	Andrew Forste
Engineer	Deosarran
Security	Gotham Security
Maintenance	C+W Cleaning Services Inc.
Lobby Refreshments by	Sweet Concessions

Bye Bye Birdie
Scrapbook (Adults)

Adult Correspondent: John Treacy Eagan, "Reporter, Parent, Bar Quartet"

Memorable Opening Night Advice: We were lucky to have songwriters Lee Adams and Charles Strouse with us on opening night. They came around to our dressing rooms and gave everyone a pep talk, a "break a leg" kind of thing.

Opening Night Gifts: John Stamos gave everyone a personalized Flip camera engraved, "Happy opening, love John." It was an amazing gift from a generous guy. All the kids used them to film us and each other. Because we're a "green" theatre, we also got "green" aluminum water bottles printed with the *Bye Bye Birdie* logo.

Most Exciting Celebrity Visitors and What They Did/Said: One night during previews the set broke down and John Stamos decided to fill in with a talkback to the audience. But Don Rickles and Bob Saget were in the audience and memorably heckled him.

Who Got the Gypsy Robe: Ours went to Paula Leggett Chase.

"Gypsy of the Year" Sketch: We did a "Glee"-style version of "Bohemian Rhapsody" with some of the kids and the adults. John helped raise money for "Gypsy of the Year" by auctioning off his glasses and visits backstage.

Actor Who Performed the Most Roles in This Show: Jim Walton seemed to play every civil servant in Sweet Apple, Ohio, including a cop, a bartender, a train conductor and a doctor.

Actor Who Has Done the Most Shows in His/Her Career: Probably Paula, since she got the Gypsy Robe. But Tim Shew and Jim Walton did a bunch of shows, too. We've got a lot of legends in this show.

Special Backstage Ritual: We had a ritual every Saturday at 7:30 PM called the Toilet Paper Runway. We would roll toilet paper down the halls and members of the cast had to come up with a category or buzzword, then people would make costumes suiting that buzzword out of things they found in their dressing rooms: newspapers, trash, whatever was on hand. It was a great thing to look forward to each week. When they announced we were closing the buzzword was "unemployment," and some of the adult women dressed as charwomen. The humor helped take some of the sting out.

Favorite Moment During Each Performance: I love when the guys sing "Talk to Me."

Favorite In-Theatre Gathering Place: The new theatre does have a greenroom with a kitchenette, and we all pile in there when there are birthdays. John Stamos has a very open-door policy in his dressing room and people like to hang out with him.

Favorite Off-Site Hangout: Café Un Deux Trois as a group. The kids tend to go places together.

1. (L-R): Songwriters Lee Adams and Charles Strouse arrive for the premiere.
2. Stars Gina Gershon and John Stamos arrive at the Hard Rock Cafe for the opening night party.
3. Ingenue Allie Trimm on opening night.

Favorite Snack Food: John brings in miniature cannoli.

Favorite Therapy: Jen Green comes from Physio/Arts twice a week. They are amazing!

Record Number of Cell Phone Rings, Cell Phone Photos, Tweeting or Texting Incidents During a Performance: I have not heard one phone go off, maybe because we're underground. Every now and then you see a camera.

Web Buzz: We were encouraged to Tweet so we've had a lot of Tweeting, which has been kind of fun. It's a great way to connect with the audience.

Memorable Press Encounters: Some of the kids from the original 1960 production periodically come back to see the show, and meet their kid counterparts and take pictures with them. One girl became a female bodybuilder.

Memorable Stage Door Fan Encounter: A lovely lady who is a big fan of people who appeared in the revival of *1776* always shows up with cookies. Now I'm on her cookie list.

Fastest Costume Change: Between the New York press conference ("American Boy") and the arrival in Sweet Apple, the entire company goes off and immediately comes back in what we call our cupcake costumes. One family is the blue family, another is the orange family, et cetera. When the idea first came up, we thought they would write some extra music to cover the change but director Robert Longbottom said no, we were going to do it right on the music that was already there. So the dressers stand ready and we pretty much make it each night without a hitch.

Company Legends: The quick change.

Who Wore the Heaviest/Hottest Costume: Bill Irwin when he dresses as George Washington during "The Ed Sullivan Show."

Who Wore the Least: Nolan comes out in nothing but briefs at one point, and Gina has the changing scene where she goes down to her underwear.

Catchphrases Only the Company Would Recognize: "Ka-kak." "Citation!"

Best In-House Parody Lyric: In "An English Teacher": "…Mrs. Albert Peterson/Mrs. Fly Paper Trapper Peterson,/ The English Patient's wife."

Understudy Anecdote: Robbie Hager had to go on for Conrad one night and they had to take him shopping because we didn't have clothes that fit him.

Nickname: "Underfoot": Bethany Tesarck.

Ghostly Encounter Backstage: There's a strange smell sometimes, but I think that's the ghost of the sewer system of Manhattan.

Coolest Things About Being in This Show: It hasn't been on Broadway in 50 years. We really are a company that enjoys each other and we're having such a good time. We have a lot of laughs. It's been a really fun experience.

Other Anecdotes: We had some really great moments in rehearsal. Bobby used the device of having the kids teach the adults the choreography by Paula Leggett Chase. So we all broke into little pods and our own children taught us. It was like a little challenge trying to see who would get it.

On John Stamos' birthday, the fantastic Bill Irwin came in and did a whole little show for him. It was amazing. We all got to see an original show created by Bill Irwin.

Bye Bye Birdie
Scrapbook (Kids)

Teen Correspondents: Riley Costello, Catherine Blades and Daniel Quadrino

Memorable Opening Night Note: Charles Strouse and Lee Adams wrote the company a very sweet note thanking us for our hard work.

Opening Night Gifts: John Stamos gave everyone in the company a customized flip video with a *Bye Bye Birdie* cover.

Most Exciting Celebrity Visitors: We have met probably the entire cast of "Full House"... but the overall most exciting guest who had everyone starstruck was the amazing Kristin Chenoweth.

Special Backstage Ritual: The girls do a very special dance in the vocal booth with Gina during the overture. "CROWN ON...CROWN OFF!"

Favorite In-Theatre Gathering Place: The teen dressing rooms are always a fun place to have a random dance party during a false fire alarm!

Favorite Off-Site Hangouts: Bryant Park, HB burger/chophouse and Yum Yum Bankok!

Favorite Therapies: Throat Coat, Ricola, and lots of physical therapy.

Most Memorable Ad-Lib: In the first scene, Gina always changes the breed of dog, which is supposed to be a cocker spaniel. The most memorable one was, "But he was a three-legged, diabetic DALMATIAN!"

Memorable Press Encounter: The box office opening when every seat in our house for the first preview was $10!

Latest Audience Arrival: We swear that we have seen people walking in during "Honestly Sincere."

Fastest Costume Change: Well, the whole company rides off on the treadmill and has to change their entire costume from a New York news reporter to a Sweet Apple citizen in about 20 seconds.

Catchphrases Only the Company Would Recognize: "WALL-E!!!!" "Skida BO BOO-BOO, JELLY CATS!!!" "Hey! You look like you're going on a cruise!!!" "CiCi."

Embarrassing Moments: During an intense dance move Riley farted and everyone erupted in laughter, including our director.

Coolest Thing About Being in This Show: Being in such a great cast with such amazing people, and a really supportive creative team.

Other Memorable Story: Watching "Glee" with members of the cast!

1. Nolan Gerard Funk outside Henry Miller's Theatre with the cast for a press event at the opening of the box office.

2. Curtain calls on opening night (L-R): Dee Hoty, John Stamos, Gina Gershon, Bill Irwin and Allie Trimm.

3. Cast members dressed to the nines for the cast party after the premiere.

Chicago

First Preview: October 23, 1996. Opened: November 14, 1996.
Still running as of May 31, 2010.

THE CAST
(in order of appearance)

Velma Kelly	DEIDRE GOODWIN
Roxie Hart	ASHLEE SIMPSON-WENTZ
Fred Casely	GREGORY BUTLER
Sergeant Fogarty	ADAM ZOTOVICH
Amos Hart	RAYMOND BOKHOUR
Liz	NICOLE BRIDGEWATER
Annie	SOLANGE SANDY
June	DONNA MARIE ASBURY
Hunyak	NILI BASSMAN
Mona	JILL NICKLAUS
Matron "Mama" Morton	ROZ RYAN
Billy Flynn	BRENT BARRETT
Mary Sunshine	R. LOWE
Go-To-Hell Kitty	MELISSA RAE MAHON
Harry	SHAWN EMAMJOMEH
Doctor	JASON PATRICK SANDS
Aaron	JAMES T. LANE
The Judge	JASON PATRICK SANDS
Bailiff	BRIAN O'BRIEN
Martin Harrison	MICHAEL CUSUMANO
Court Clerk	BRIAN O'BRIEN
The Jury	SHAWN EMAMJOMEH

THE SCENE:
Chicago, Illinois. The late 1920s.

Continued on next page

AMBASSADOR THEATRE
A Shubert Organization Theatre
Philip J. Smith, *Chairman* Robert E. Wankel, *President*

Barry & Fran Weissler
in association with
Kardana/Hart Sharp Entertainment
present

**Ashlee Simpson-Wentz Deidre Goodwin
Brent Barrett
Raymond Bokhour**

in

CHICAGO

Lyrics by **Fred Ebb** Music By **John Kander** Book by **Fred Ebb & Bob Fosse**

Original Production Directed and Choreographed by **Bob Fosse**
Based on the play by Maurine Dallas Watkins

with
Roz Ryan R. Lowe

and

Donna Marie Asbury Nili Bassman Nicole Bridgewater Gregory Butler
Michael Cusumano Shawn Emamjomeh Gabriela Garcia David Kent
James T. Lane J. Loeffelholz Melissa Rae Mahon Sharon Moore
Jill Nicklaus Brian O'Brien Jason Patrick Sands
Solange Sandy Brian Spitulnik Adam Zotovich

Supervising Music Director **Rob Fisher** Music Director **Leslie Stifelman**
Scenic Design **John Lee Beatty** Costume Design **William Ivey Long** Lighting Design **Ken Billington**
Sound Design **Scott Lehrer** Orchestrations **Ralph Burns** Dance Music Arrangements **Peter Howard**
Script Adaptation **David Thompson** Musical Coordinator **Seymour Red Press** Hair Design **David Brian Brown**
Casting **Duncan Stewart** Original Casting **Jay Binder**
Technical Supervisor **Arthur Siccardi** Dance Supervisor **Gary Chryst** Production Stage Manager **David Hyslop**
Associate Producer **Alecia Parker** Presented in association with **Live Nation**
General Manager **B.J. Holt** Press Representative **Jeremy Shaffer / The Publicity Office**

Based on the presentation by City Center's Encores!℠

Choreography by **Ann Reinking**
in the style of Bob Fosse

Directed by **Walter Bobbie**

Cast Recording on RCA Victor

11/30/09

Amra-Faye Wright (center) as Velma Kelly

Photo by Catherine Ashmore

Chicago

MUSICAL NUMBERS

ACT I
"All That Jazz"	Velma and Company
"Funny Honey"	Roxie
"Cell Block Tango"	Velma and the Girls
"When You're Good to Mama"	Matron
"Tap Dance"	Roxie, Amos and Boys
"All I Care About"	Billy and Girls
"A Little Bit of Good"	Mary Sunshine
"We Both Reached for the Gun"	Billy, Roxie, Mary Sunshine and Company
"Roxie"	Roxie and Boys
"I Can't Do It Alone"	Velma
"My Own Best Friend"	Roxie and Velma

ACT II
Entr'acte	The Band
"I Know a Girl"	Velma
"Me and My Baby"	Roxie and Boys
"Mister Cellophane"	Amos
"When Velma Takes the Stand"	Velma and Boys
"Razzle Dazzle"	Billy and Company
"Class"	Velma and Matron
"Nowadays"	Roxie and Velma
"Hot Honey Rag"	Roxie and Velma
Finale	Company

ORCHESTRA
Orchestra Conducted by
LESLIE STIFELMAN
Associate Conductor:
SCOTT CADY
Assistant Conductor:
JOHN JOHNSON
Woodwinds:
SEYMOUR RED PRESS, JACK STUCKEY, RICHARD CENTALONZA
Trumpets:
GLENN DREWES, DARRYL SHAW
Trombones:
DAVE BARGERON, BRUCE BONVISSUTO
Piano:
SCOTT CADY
Piano, Accordion:
JOHN JOHNSON
Banjo:
JAY BERLINER
Bass, Tuba:
RONALD RAFFIO
Violin:
MARSHALL COID
Drums, Percussion:
RONALD ZITO

Cast Continued

UNDERSTUDIES
For Roxie Hart:
MELISSA RAE MAHON, JILL NICKLAUS
For Velma Kelly:
DONNA MARIE ASBURY, NICOLE BRIDGEWATER, SOLANGE SANDY
For Billy Flynn:
JASON PATRICK SANDS, BRIAN O'BRIEN
For Amos Hart:
JAMES T. LANE, ADAM ZOTOVICH
For Matron "Mama" Morton:
DONNA MARIE ASBURY, NICOLE BRIDGEWATER
For Mary Sunshine:
J. LOEFFELHOLZ
For Fred Casely and "Me and My Baby":
DAVID KENT, BRIAN O'BRIEN, BRIAN SPITULNIK

For all other roles:
GABRIELA GARCIA, DAVID KENT, SHARON MOORE, BRIAN SPITULNIK

DANCE CAPTAINS
GREGORY BUTLER, GABRIELA GARCIA

"Tap Dance" specialty performed by
JAMES T. LANE, BRIAN O'BRIEN and JASON PATRICK SANDS.
"Me and My Baby" specialty performed by
MICHAEL CUSUMANO and JAMES T. LANE.
"Nowadays" whistle performed by
JASON PATRICK SANDS.

Original Choreography for "Hot Honey Rag" by
BOB FOSSE

Ashlee Simpson-Wentz as Roxie Hart

Chicago

 Ashlee Simpson-Wentz — *Roxie*
 Deidre Goodwin — *Velma Kelly*
 Brent Barrett — *Billy Flynn*
 Raymond Bokhour — *Amos Hart*
 Roz Ryan — *Matron "Mama" Morton*
 R. Lowe — *Mary Sunshine*
 Donna Marie Asbury — *June*

 Nili Bassman — *Hunyak*
 Nicole Bridgewater — *Liz*
 Gregory Butler — *Fred Casely/Dance Captain*
 Michael Cusumano — *Martin Harrison*
 Shawn Emamjomeh — *Harry/The Jury*
 Gabriela Garcia — *Swing/Dance Captain*
 David Kent — *Swing*

 James T. Lane — *Aaron*
 J. Loeffelholz — *Standby Mary Sunshine*
 Melissa Rae Mahon — *Go-To-Hell Kitty*
 Sharon Moore — *Swing*
 Jill Nicklaus — *Mona*
 Brian O'Brien — *Bailiff/Court Clerk*
 Jason Patrick Sands — *Doctor/The Judge*

 Solange Sandy — *Annie*
 Brian Spitulnik — *Swing*
 Adam Zotovich — *Sergeant Fogarty*
 John Kander & Fred Ebb — *Music; Book/Lyrics*
 Bob Fosse — *Book*
 Walter Bobbie — *Director*

 Ann Reinking — *Choreographer*
 John Lee Beatty — *Set Design*
 William Ivey Long — *Costume Designer*
 Ken Billington — *Lighting Designer*
 Scott Lehrer — *Sound Design*
 Rob Fisher — *Supervising Music Director*
 Seymour Red Press — *Music Coordinator*

Chicago

Duncan Stewart
Casting Director

Arthur Siccardi,
Theatrical Services
Inc.
Technical Supervisor

Barry & Fran Weissler
Producers

Morton Swinsky/
Kardana Productions
Producer

R. Bean
Mary Sunshine

Eddie Bennett
*Bailiff, Court Clerk,
"Tap Dance"
Specialty*

Dylis Croman
Annie

Charlotte d'Amboise
Roxie Hart

Bryn Dowling
Roxie Hart

Jennifer Dunne
Mona

Tom Riis Farrell
Amos Hart

Samantha Harris
Roxie Hart

Tom Hewitt
Billy Flynn

Bonnie Langford
Roxie Hart

Kecia Lewis-Evans
*Matron "Mama"
Morton*

Dan LoBuono
*Bailiff, Court Clerk,
"Tap Dance"
Specialty*

Terra C. MacLeod
Velma Kelly

Bianca Marroquin
Roxie Hart

Pilar Millhollen
Swing

Josh Rhodes
Sergeant Fogarty

Jerry Springer
Billy Flynn

Sofia Vergara
*Matron "Mama"
Morton*

Chandra Wilson
*Matron "Mama"
Morton*

Amra-Faye Wright
Velma Kelly

Eddie Bennett
Swing

Brenda Braxton
Velma Kelly

Dylis Croman
Mona

Tom Riis Farrell
Amos Hart

Ruthie Henshall
Roxie Hart

Tom Hewitt
Billy Flynn

Dan LoBuono
*Aaron, Fred Casely,
"Me and My Baby"
Specialty, "Tap
Dance" Specialty*

Terra C. MacLeod
Velma Kelly

Chicago

Bianca Marroquin
Roxie Hart

Pilar Millhollen
Swing

Greg Reuter
Bailiff, Court Clerk, "Tap Dance" Specialty

Matthew Settle
Billy Flynn

D. Vogel
Mary Sunshine

Terri White
Matron "Mama" Morton

Michelle T. Williams
Roxie Hart

Amra-Faye Wright
Velma Kelly

FRONT OF HOUSE STAFF
Front Row (L-R): Anthony Grandison (Bartender), Dorothea Bentley (Chief Usher), Danielle Banyai (Usher), Elizabeth Ulmer (Bartender)

Second Row (L-R): Manuel Levine (House Manager), Timothy Newsome (Usher), Chris Holmes (Bar Manager)

Third Row (L-R): Carol Bokun (Usher), Julie Pazmino (Usher), Tasha Allen (Usher), Tyrone Hendrix (Ticket Taker), Marilyn Wasbotten (Usher)

Fourth Row (L-R): David Loomis (Merchandise), Nicholas Fusco (Usher), Belen Bekker (Usher), Susan Snow (Usher)

Back Row (L-R): Lane Beauchamp (Merchandise), Dennis Cintron (Usher), Rita Sussman (Infrared Rep.), Bobbi Parker (Usher)

WARDROBE AND HAIR
Front Row (L-R): Kathy Dacey (Dresser), Cleopatra Matheos (Dresser)

Back Row (L-R): Kevin Woodworth (Wardrobe Supervisor), Jenna Brauer (Hair Supervisor), Rick Meadows (Dresser)

Chicago

STAGE MANAGEMENT
(L-R): Terrence J. Witter (Stage Manager), David Hyslop (Production Stage Manager), Mindy Farbrother (Stage Manager)

COMPANY MANAGER
Alexandra Gushin Agosta

STAFF FOR CHICAGO

GENERAL MANAGEMENT
B.J. Holt, General Manager
Nina Skriloff, International Manager

PRESS REPRESENTATIVE
THE PUBLICITY OFFICE
Jeremy Shaffer   Marc Thibodeau   Michael Borowski

Production Stage Manager	David Hyslop
Company Manager	Alexandra Gushin Agosta
Stage Managers	Terrence J. Witter, Mindy Farbrother
Associate General Manager	Hilary Hamilton
General Management Associate	Stephen Spadaro
Assistant Director	Jonathan Bernstein
Associate Lighting Designer	John McKernon
Assistant Choreographer	Debra McWaters
Assistant Set Designers	Eric Renschler, Shelley Barclay
Wardrobe Supervisor	Kevin Woodworth
Hair Supervisor	Jenna Brauer
Costume Assistant	Donald Sanders
Personal Asst to Mr. Billington	Jon Kusner
Assistant to Mr. Lehrer	Thom Mohrman
Production Carpenter	Joseph Mooneyham
Production Electrician	James Fedigan
Head Electrician	Luciana Fusco
Front Lite Operator	Michael Guggino
Production Sound Engineer	John Montgomery
Production Props	Paula Zwicky
Dressers	Jo-Ann Bethell, Kathy Dacey, Paula Davis, Rick Meadows, Eric Concklin
Banking	Chase Manhattan, Stephanie Dalton
Music Prep	Chelsea Music Services, Inc. Donald Oliver & Evan Morris
Payroll	Castellana Services, Inc.
Accountants	Rosenberg, Newirth & Kuchner Mark D'Ambrosi, Marina Flom
Insurance	Industrial Risk Specialists
Counsel	Seth Gelblum/Loeb & Loeb
Art Design	Spot Design
Advertising	SpotCo: Drew Hodges, Jim Edwards, Sara Fitzpatrick, Tom McCann, Josh Fraenkel
Press Assistant	Matthew Fasano
Education	Students Live/Amy Weinstein
Merchandising	Dewynters Advertising Inc.
Displays	King Display

NATIONAL ARTISTS MANAGEMENT CO.

Vice President of Marketing	Todd Stuart
Chief Financial Officer	Bob Williams
Manager of Accounting/Admin.	Marian Albarracin
Assistant to Mrs. Weissler	Brett England
Assistant to Mr. Weissler	Diana Glazer
Director of Marketing	Ken Sperr
Director of Promotions	Daya Wolterstorff
Receptionist	Michelle Coleman

SPECIAL THANKS
Additional legal services provided by Jay Goldberg, Esq. and Michael Berger, Esq. Emer'gen-C is the official health and energy drink mix of *Chicago*. Dry cleaning by Ernest Winzer Cleaners. Hosiery and undergarments provided by Bra*Tenders. Tuxedos by Brioni. Ike Behar tuxedo shirts provided by BBRAXTON Exceptional Grooming for Exceptional Men.

CREDITS
Lighting equipment by PRG Lighting. Scenery built and painted by Hudson Scenic Studios. Specialty Rigging by United Staging & Rigging. Sound equipment by PRG Audio. Shoulder holster courtesy of DeSantis Holster and Leather Goods Co. Period cameras and flash units by George Fenmore, Inc. Colibri lighters used. Bible courtesy of Chiarelli's Religious Goods, Inc. Black pencils by Dixon-Ticonderoga. Gavel courtesy of The Gavel Co. Zippo lighters used. Garcia y Vega cigars used. Hosiery by Donna Karan. Shoes by T.O. Dey. Orthopaedic Consultant, David S. Weiss, M.D.

 THE SHUBERT ORGANIZATION, INC.
Board of Directors

Philip J. Smith Chairman	**Robert E. Wankel** President
Wyche Fowler, Jr.	**John W. Kluge**
Lee J. Seidler	**Michael I. Sovern**

Stuart Subotnick

Elliot Greene Chief Financial Officer	**David Andrews** Senior Vice President – Shubert Ticketing
Juan Calvo Vice President and Controller	**John Darby** Vice President – Facilities
Peter Entin Vice President – Theatre Operations	**Charles Flateman** Vice President – Marketing
Anthony LaMattina Vice President – Audit & Production Finance	**Brian Mahoney** Vice President – Ticket Sales

D.S. Moynihan
Vice President – Creative Projects

House Manager .... Patricia Berry

Chicago
SCRAPBOOK

Correspondent: Donna Marie Asbury, "June"
Memorable Note: Glenn Close sent the girls a lovely note thanking us because we helped her with a surprise for her husband!
Anniversary Parties and Gifts: We love when our producers throw us a party at their house in the summer. It's gorgeous out there. They have a pool and the food is always amazing. Oh and we got a *Chicago* "Snuggie" for Christmas!
Most Exciting Celebrity Visitor: Beyoncé! She said we were all amazing.
"Gypsy of the Year" Sketch: Brian O'Brien wrote it. It was a take off of "A Boy Like That" with our amazing Ryan Lowe singing the "Maria" part in her key!!! *Chicago* won best skit!
Actors Who Perform the Most Roles in This Show: Gabriela Garcia, Sharon Moore, David Kent and Brian Spitulnik. They're our fabulous swings!
Who Has Done the Most Shows in Their Career: Brian O'Brien!
Special Backstage Rituals: We all have our favorite spots to stretch right before the show. Shawn Emamjomeh and I are usually stage left, and Melissa Rae Mahon has her yoga mat on stage right. Also people do the *New York Times* crossword puzzle, and online Scrabble on Facebook!
Favorite Moment During Each Performance: When you hear "a-five, six, seven, eight!"… and Velma coming up from the elevator. Best entrance in musical theatre!
Favorite In-Theatre Gathering Place: The wardrobe room, or on the stairs leading up to our dressing rooms.
Favorite Off-Site Hangout: Natsumi…location, location, location.
Favorite Snack Foods: Well we have a chocolate tin in the wardrobe room, and we love "Bagel Sunday!"
Mascots: We have lots of dogs. Boris, Bianca, Ruby, Berger, Stevie, Ellie, Marcus, Chloe, Emmy and Quinn.
Favorite Therapies: We always have Ricolas, Pain Aid, Advil, ice packs and Emergen-C.
Memorable Ad-Lib: Deidre Goodwin was playing Velma in the scene with Mama Morton leading up to the song "Class." And instead of saying "…and now my shoes!" she said "…and now my idea!" Mama Morton then replied: "Well you shouldn't have left your idea layin' around!"
Record Number of Cell Phone Rings, Cell Phone Photos or Texting Incidents During a Performance: It's not so bad anymore. We do see the occasional light coming from someone's phone while they are texting.
Memorable Press Encounter: We always love being a part of "Broadway On Broadway." The press treats us like rock stars!
Cast Response to Web Buzz on the Show: It's always interesting when they announce who's going to be in our show, and then to read everyone's reaction to it!
Busiest Day at the Box Office: Friday night, or Saturday matinee and evening.

(L-R): Cast members Bonnie Langford, Kecia Lewis-Evans, Raymond Bokhour, director Walter Bobbie, Brent Barrett, lighting designer Ken Billington and Deidre Goodwin toast the cake backstage at The Ambassador Theatre to celebrate the show's thirteenth anniversary.

Fastest Costume Change: That's one of the best things about *Chicago*…no costume changes!
Who Wore the Heaviest/Hottest Costume: Amos Hart!
Who Wore the Least: Have you seen our show? Probably Melissa Rae Mahon who plays "Kitty."
Catchphrases Only the Company Would Recognize: "This is Bullsh*t!" "What the who!"
Sweethearts Within the Company: Leslie Stifelman and Melissa Rae Mahon! They met while doing the show and were married on New Year's Day 2010!
Orchestra Members Who Played the Most Instruments: Seymour Red Press, Richard Centalonza and Jack Stuckey. Our woodwinds section.
Orchestra Member Who Played the Most Consecutive Performances Without a Sub: Our banjo player, Jay Berliner.
Best In-House Parody Lyrics: When we are walking up the stairs after the show, and the band is still playing, we always sing "By Mennen," because it sounds just like the old commercial.
Memorable Directorial Note: "Pass the ball! Don't DROP the ball!"
Company In-Jokes: The ball is across the street at the Eugene O'Neill!
Company Legend: Greg Butler—our amazing Dance Captain and "Fred Casely." We call him "Lord of the Dance." He teaches all of our female stars that come into the show. He is an inspiration. His body isn't bad to look at either!
Tales From the Put-in: When Ashlee Simpson-Wentz joined our show, at her put-in we had her entire family (including Jessica), and her baby Bronx kept making all of these cute baby sounds the whole time! Ashlee just kept on going. We thought if her baby can't distract her, then she was ready for New York audiences.
Understudy Anecdote: Well, for a while when I would go on for Velma, after doing the cartwheel, my right breast would come out of the top of my dress. Needless to say, I tape them in now.
Nicknames: Greg Butler has a few: "G-But," "Captain Butler," "Mary-Kate" and "Becky."
We call Gabriela Garcia either "Gabita" or "Sanchez" (because she's the future wife of Mark Sanchez).
We call our Production Stage Manager David Hyslop "PSM" (pronounced "pizm").
Superstitions That Turned Out To Be True: No real superstitions. Although sometimes it feels like there's a little Gremlin in the theatre!
Coolest Thing About Being in This Show: There is always someone new and interesting in *Chicago*. It's given all of us an opportunity to work with some amazing people.

Collected Stories

First Preview: April 9, 2010. Opened: April 28, 2010.
Still running as of May 31, 2010.

CAST
(in alphabetical order)

Ruth Steiner ....LINDA LAVIN
Lisa Morrison ....SARAH PAULSON

TIME:

Act I
Scene One: September 1990
Scene Two: May 1991
Scene Three: August 1992

Act II
Scene One: December 1994
Scene Two: October 1996
Scene Three: Later that night

PLACE:

The Greenwich Village apartment of Ruth Steiner

Stage Manager ....TIMOTHY R. SEMON

UNDERSTUDIES

For Lisa Morrison: ANNE BOWLES
For Ruth Steiner: KIT FLANAGAN

MANHATTAN THEATRE CLUB
SAMUEL J. FRIEDMAN THEATRE

ARTISTIC DIRECTOR
LYNNE MEADOW

EXECUTIVE PRODUCER
BARRY GROVE

PRESENTS

COLLECTED STORIES

A PLAY

BY
DONALD MARGULIES

WITH
LINDA LAVIN **SARAH PAULSON**

SCENIC DESIGN
SANTO LOQUASTO

COSTUME DESIGN
JANE GREENWOOD

LIGHTING DESIGN
NATASHA KATZ

ORIGINAL MUSIC & SOUND DESIGN
OBADIAH EAVES

WIG DESIGN
PAUL HUNTLEY

CASTING
DAVID CAPARELLIOTIS

PRODUCTION STAGE MANAGER
LAURIE GOLDFEDER

DIRECTED BY
LYNNE MEADOW

GENERAL MANAGER
FLORIE SEERY

ASSOCIATE ARTISTIC DIRECTOR
MANDY GREENFIELD

DIRECTOR OF ARTISTIC DEVELOPMENT
JERRY PATCH

DIRECTOR OF MARKETING
DEBRA WAXMAN-PILLA

PRESS REPRESENTATIVE
BONEAU/BRYAN-BROWN

PRODUCTION MANAGER
KURT GARDNER

DIRECTOR OF CASTING
NANCY PICCIONE

DIRECTOR OF DEVELOPMENT
JILL TURNER LLOYD

MANHATTAN THEATRE CLUB WISHES TO EXPRESS ITS APPRECIATION TO THEATRE DEVELOPMENT FUND FOR ITS SUPPORT OF THIS PRODUCTION.

4/28/10

(L-R): Linda Lavin and Sarah Paulson

Photo by Joan Marcus

Collected Stories

Linda Lavin
Ruth Steiner

Sarah Paulson
Lisa Morrison

Anne Bowles
u/s Lisa Morrison

Kit Flanagan
u/s Ruth Steiner

Donald Margulies
Playwright

Lynne Meadow
*Director/
Artistic Director,
Manhattan Theatre
Club*

Santo Loquasto
Scenic Design

Jane Greenwood
Costume Design

Natasha Katz
Lighting Design

Obadiah Eaves
*Original Music &
Sound Design*

Paul Huntley
Wig Design

Barry Grove
*Executive Producer,
Manhattan Theatre
Club*

BOX OFFICE
(L-R): David Dillon, Jeffrey Davis

FRONT OF HOUSE STAFF
Front Row (L-R): Wendy Wright, Patricia Polhill, Jim Joseph, Richard Ponce

Back Row (L-R): Jackson Ero, Ed Brashear, John Wyffels, Tom Jarus, Dinah Glorioso, Adrian Zambrano

STAGE CREW

Back Row (L-R):
Derek Moreno, Michael Growler (sort of),
Joe Hickey, Lou Shapiro, Jason Dodds,
Chris Wiggins, Laurie Goldfeder,
Timothy Semon

Front Row (L-R):
Tim Walters, Natasha Steinhagen,
Ian Harbor, Seth Shepsle

Collected Stories

MANHATTAN THEATRE CLUB STAFF

Artistic Director	Lynne Meadow
Executive Producer	Barry Grove
General Manager	Florie Seery
Associate Artistic Director	Mandy Greenfield
Director of Artistic Development	Jerry Patch
Artistic Consultant	Daniel Sullivan
Director of Artistic Administration/ Assistant to the Artistic Director	Amy Gilkes Loe
Artistic Associate	Lisa McNulty
Artistic Assistant	Rebecca Kahane
Administrative Assistant	Nicki Hunter
Assistant to the Executive Producer	Emily Hammond
Director of Casting	Nancy Piccione
Casting Associate	Kelly Gillespie
Literary Manager/Sloan Project Manager	Annie MacRae
Play Development Assistant	Alex Barron
Director of Development	Jill Turner Lloyd
Director, Individual Giving	Jeremy Blocker
Director, Institutional Giving	Roger Kingsepp
Director, Special Events	Antonello Di Benedetto
Manager, Individual Giving	Emily Fleisher
Manager, Institutional Giving	Andrea Gorzell
Development Associate/ Individual Giving	Allison Taylor
Development Associate/ Institutional Giving	Laurel Bear
Development Associate/ Special Events	Samantha Mascali
Patrons' Liaison	Chad Jones
Director of Marketing	Debra Waxman-Pilla
Assistant Director of Marketing	Sunil Ayyagari
Marketing Associate	Caitlin Baird
Director of Finance	Jeffrey Bledsoe
Human Resources Manager	Darren Robertson
Finance Associate	Adam Cook
Business Assistant	Andrew Kao
IT Manager	Mendy Sudranski
Receptionist/Studio Coordinator	Thatcher Stevens
Associate General Manager	Lindsey Brooks Sag
Company Manager/ NY City Center	Erin Moeller
General Management Assistant	Gillian Campbell
Director of Subscriber Services	Robert Allenberg
Associate Subscriber Services Manager	Andrew Taylor
Subscriber Services Representatives	Mark Bowers, Rosanna Consalva Sarto, Kevin Sullivan, Amber Wilkerson
Director of Telesales and Telefunding	George Tetlow
Assistant Manager	Terrence Burnett
Telemarketing Staff	Stephen Brown, Kel Haney, Kate Sessions
Director of Education	David Shookhoff
Asst. Director of Education/ Coordinator, Paul A. Kaplan Theatre Management Program	Amy Harris
Education Assistant, TheatreLink Coordinator	Julia Davis
Education Assistant	Kelli Bragdon
MTC Teaching Artists	Stephanie Alston, Carl Capatoro, Chris Ceraso, Charlotte Colavin, Dominic Colon, Allison Daugherty, Gilbert Girion, Andy Goldberg, Elise Hernandez, Jeffrey Joseph, Julie Leedes, Kate Long, Louis D. Moreno, Andres Munar, Melissa Murray, Angela Pietropinto, Alexa Polmer, Alfonso Ramirez, Carmen Rivera, Judy Tate, Candido Tirado, Joe White
Theatre Management Interns	Katie Chambers, Tal Drori, Annah Feinberg, Teresa Fisher, Courtney Hammond, Barbara Harrison, Katie Higham, Robert Intile, Matthew Kagen, Michelle Karst, Alicia Mangelsdorf, Gabe Miner, Alison Novelli, Nicole Tingir, Matthew Troillett
Production Manager	Kurt Gardner
Associate Production Manager	Joshua Helman
Assistant Production Manager	Kelsey Martinez
Properties Supervisor	Scott Laule
Assistant Properties Supervisor	Julia Sandy
Props Carpenter	Peter Grimes
Costume Supervisor	Erin Hennessy Dean

GENERAL PRESS REPRESENTATION
BONEAU/BRYAN-BROWN

Chris Boneau	Aaron Meier
Christine Olver	Emily Meagher

Script Readers......Elizabeth Dudgeon, Aaron Grunfeld, Liz Jones, Portia Krieger, Rachel Slaven, Rebecca Stang

SERVICES

Accountants	ERE, LLP
Advertising	SpotCo/Drew Hodges, Tom Greenwald, Jim Edwards, Beth Watson, Tim Falotico
Web Design	Calico Systems
Legal Counsel	Charles H. Googe, Jr.; Carol M. Kaplan/ Paul, Weiss, Rifkind, Wharton and Garrison LLP
Real Estate Counsel	Marcus Attorneys
Labor Counsel	Harry H. Weintraub/ Glick and Weintraub, P.C.
Immigration Counsel	Theodore Ruthizer/ Kramer, Levin, Naftalis & Frankel, LLP
Sponsorship Consultant	Above the Title Entertainment/ Jed Bernstein
Insurance	Dewitt Stern Group, Inc./ Anthony Pittari
Maintenance	Reliable Cleaning
Production Photographer	Joan Marcus
Event Photography	Bruce Glikas
Cover Art	John Ritter
Cover Design	SpotCo
Theatre Displays	King Displays

PRODUCTION STAFF FOR *COLLECTED STORIES*

Company Manager	Seth Shepsle
Production Stage Manager	Laurie Goldfeder
Stage Manager	Timothy R. Semon
Assistant Director	Hilary Adams
Associate Scenic Designer	Jenny B. Sawyers
Assistant Scenic Designer	Yoki Lai
Associate Costume Designer	Wade Laboissonniere
Associate Lighting Designer	Aaron Spivey
Associate Sound Designer	Brandon Wolcott
Video Designer	Rocco DiSanti
Make-Up Designer	Angelina Avallone
Hair/Make-Up Supervisor	Natasha Steinhagen
Dressers	Derek Moreno, Polly Noble
Light Board Programmer	Mark Davidson

CREDITS

Scenery fabrication by Hudson Scenic Studio. Lighting and projection equipment provided by PRG Lighting. Sound equipment provided by Masque Sound.

For more information visit
www.ManhattanTheatreClub.com

MANHATTAN THEATRE CLUB SAMUEL J. FRIEDMAN THEATRE STAFF

Theatre Manager	Jim Joseph
Assistant House Manager	Richard Ponce
Box Office Treasurer	David Dillon
Assistant Box Office Treasurers	Jeffrey Davis, John Skelly
Head Carpenter	Chris Wiggins
Head Propertyman	Timothy Walters
Sound Engineer	Louis Shapiro
Master Electrician	Jeff Dodson
Wardrobe Supervisor	Michael Growler
Apprentices	Jason Dodds, Ian Harbor
Chief Engineer	Deosarran
Maintenance Engineers	Ricky Deosarran, Maximo Perez
Security	Allied Barton
Lobby Refreshments	Sweet Concessions

SCRAPBOOK

Correspondent: Timothy R. Semon, Stage Manager
Most Exciting Celebrity Visitor: Joan Rivers
Who Has Done the Most Shows in Their Career: Linda Lavin, of course.
Favorite In-Theatre Gathering Place: Linda's dressing room.
Favorite Off-Site Hangout: Glass House Tavern.
Favorite Snack Food: Grapes.
Catchphrase Only the Company Would Recognize: "I WUV YOU."
Sweethearts Within the Company: Laurie & Tim.

Come Fly Away

First Preview: March 1, 2010. Opened: March 25, 2010.
Still running as of May 31, 2010.

CAST
(in order of appearance)

Betsy	LAURA MEAD
Marty	CHARLIE NESHYBA-HODGES
Vico	ALEXANDER BRADY
Sid	JOHN SELYA
Kate	KARINE PLANTADIT
Slim	RIKA OKAMOTO
Hank	KEITH ROBERTS
Chanos	MATTHEW STOCKWELL DIBBLE
Babe	HOLLEY FARMER
Featured Vocalist	HILARY GARDNER

Wednesday Matinee and Saturday Matinee

Betsy	ASHLEY TUTTLE
Marty	JEREMY COX
Vico	ALEXANDER BRADY
Sid	CODY GREEN
Kate	MARIELYS MOLINA
Slim	KRISTINE BENDUL
Hank	JOEL PROUTY
Chanos	RON TODOROWSKI
Babe	LAURIE KANYOK
Featured Vocalist	ROSENA M. HILL

THE ENSEMBLE
TODD BURNSED, CAROLYN DOHERTY, HEATHER HAMILTON, MEREDITH MILES, ERIC MICHAEL OTTO, JUSTIN PECK

Continued on next page

MARQUIS THEATRE
UNDER THE DIRECTION OF JAMES M. NEDERLANDER AND JAMES L. NEDERLANDER

JAMES L. NEDERLANDER NICHOLAS HOWEY W.A.T., LTD.
TERRY ALLEN KRAMER PATRICK CATULLO/JON B. PLATT JERRY FRANKEL RONALD FRANKEL/MARC FRANKEL ROY FURMAN
ALLAN S. GORDON/ELAN McALLISTER JAM THEATRICALS STEWART F. LANE/BONNIE COMLEY MARGO LION/DARYL ROTH
HAL LUFTIG/YASUHIRO KAWANA PITTSBURGH CLO/GSFD SPARK PRODUCTIONS THE WEINSTEIN COMPANY BARRY AND FRAN WEISSLER

Present

Concept and Book by
TWYLA THARP

Vocals by
FRANK SINATRA

COME FLY AWAY
A NEW MUSICAL

BY SPECIAL ARRANGEMENT WITH THE FRANK SINATRA FAMILY AND FRANK SINATRA ENTERPRISES

Starring
MATTHEW STOCKWELL DIBBLE   HOLLEY FARMER   LAURA MEAD   CHARLIE NESHYBA-HODGES
RIKA OKAMOTO   KARINE PLANTADIT   KEITH ROBERTS   JOHN SELYA

With
ALEXANDER BRADY   TODD BURNSED   CAROLYN DOHERTY   HEATHER HAMILTON
MEREDITH MILES   ERIC MICHAEL OTTO   JUSTIN PECK

KRISTINE BENDUL   COLIN BRADBURY   JEREMY COX   AMANDA EDGE   CODY GREEN
LAURIE KANYOK   MARIELYS MOLINA   JOEL PROUTY   RON TODOROWSKI   ASHLEY TUTTLE

and
Featured Vocalists
HILARY GARDNER   ROSENA M. HILL

Scenic Design	Costume Design	Lighting Design	Sound Design
JAMES YOUMANS	KATHERINE ROTH	DONALD HOLDER	PETER McBOYLE

Additional Orchestrations & Arrangements by	Original Music Supervisor	Music Supervisor & Music Coordinator	Conductor/Pianist
DON SEBESKY / DAVE PIERCE	SAM LUTFIYYA	PATRICK VACCARIELLO	RUSS KASSOFF

Casting	Press Representatives	Marketing
STUART HOWARD, AMY SCHECTER, PAUL HARDT	THE HARTMAN GROUP / ELLEN JACOBS ASSOCIATES	SCOTT A. MOORE

Creative Consultant	Production Executive	Resident Director
CHARLES PIGNONE	RANDALL A. BUCK	KIM CRAVEN

Production Stage Manager	Technical Supervisor	General Management
RICK STEIGER	DAVID BENKEN	THE CHARLOTTE WILCOX COMPANY

Conceived, Choreographed and Directed by
TWYLA THARP

World Premiere at Alliance Theatre, Atlanta, GA
Susan V. Booth, Artistic Director   Thomas Pechar, Managing Director

3/25/10

(Front, L-R): John Selya, Holley Farmer, Matthew Stockwell Dibble and Company

Photo by Joan Marcus

Come Fly Away

MUSICAL NUMBERS

ACT I

"Moonlight Becomes You"	Marty and Betsy
"Come Fly With Me"	Company
"I've Got the World on a String"	Company
"Let's Fall in Love"	Marty and Betsy
"I've Got You Under My Skin"	Vico and Company
"Summer Wind"	Hank and Kate
"Fly Me to the Moon"	Hank, Kate and Ensemble Men
"I've Got a Crush On You"	Sid and Babe
"Body and Soul"	Chanos, Sid, Babe and Ensemble
"It's Alright With Me"	Company
"You Make Me Feel So Young"	Marty and Betsy
"September of My Years"	Sid
"Witchcraft"	Sid, Babe and Ensemble Men
"Yes Sir, That's My Baby"	Chanos, Slim and Ensemble
"Learnin' the Blues"	Hank, Kate, Slim and Ensemble Women
"That's Life"	Hank and Kate
"Nice 'n' Easy"	Marty, Betsy, Vico and Ensemble Women
"Makin' Whoopee"	Marty, Betsy, Slim and Ensemble
"Jumpin' at the Woodside"	Company

ACT II

"Saturday Night Is the Loneliest Night"	Company
"I'm Gonna Live 'Til I Die"	Sid, Chanos, Hank, Marty and Company
"Pick Yourself Up"	Marty, Betsy, Chanos and Slim
"Wave"	Chanos and Slim
"Let's Face the Music and Dance"	Hank, Kate and Ensemble
"Teach Me Tonight"	Sid and Babe
"Take Five"	Sid, Babe, Marty, Betsy and Ensemble
"Just Friends"	Hank and Kate
"Lean Baby"	Kate and Ensemble Men
"Makin' Whoopee" (reprise)	Kate, Chanos, Slim, Marty, Betsy and Ensemble
"One for My Baby"	Hank and Kate
"My Funny Valentine"	Marty and Betsy
"Air Mail Special"	Vico and Sid
"My Way"	Company
"New York, New York"	Company

Mr. Sinatra's original arrangements by Nelson Riddle, Don Costa, Gordon Jenkins, Quincy Jones, Johnny Mandel, Neal Hefti, Torrie Zito, Sam Nestico, Emuir Deodato and Ernie Freeman.

Cast Continued

ALTERNATES/SWINGS
KRISTINE BENDUL, COLIN BRADBURY, JEREMY COX, AMANDA EDGE, CODY GREEN, LAURIE KANYOK, MARIELYS MOLINA, JOEL PROUTY, RON TODOROWSKI, ASHLEY TUTTLE

DANCE CAPTAIN
ALEXANDER BRADY

ASSISTANT DANCE CAPTAIN
COLIN BRADBURY

Matthew Stockwell Dibble appears with the permission of Actors' Equity Association.

THE BAND
Conductor/Piano: RUSS KASSOFF
Reed I: JERRY DODGION
Reed II: JIMMY COZIER
Reed III: P.J. PERRY
Reed IV: DAVE NOLAND
Reed V: FRANK BASILE
Trumpet I: DAVE STAHL
Trumpet II: EARL GARDNER
Trumpet III: LARRY MOSES
Trumpet IV: RICHIE VITALE
Trombone I: JOHN MOSCA
Trombone II: MARK MILLER
Trombone III: CLARENCE BANKS
Trombone IV: JEFF NELSON
Bass: JAY ANDERSON
Guitar: JAMES CHIRILLO
Drums: WARREN ODZE
Percussion: HILARY GARDNER, ROSENA M. HILL
Music Coordinator: PATRICK VACCARIELLO

MUSIC COPYING
EMILY GRISHMAN MUSIC PREPARATION – EMILY GRISHMAN/KATHARINE EDMONDS HOLLY CARROLL

Matthew Stockwell Dibble
Chanos

Holley Farmer
Babe

Laura Mead
Betsy

Charlie Neshyba-Hodges
Marty

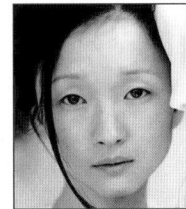
Rika Okamoto
Slim

Karine Plantadit
Kate

Keith Roberts
Hank

Come Fly Away

John Selya
Sid

Hilary Gardner
Featured Vocalist

Rosena M. Hill
Featured Vocalist Alternate

Alexander Brady
Vico, Dance Captain

Todd Burnsed
Ensemble

Carolyn Doherty
Ensemble

Heather Hamilton
Ensemble

Meredith Miles
Ensemble

Eric Michael Otto
Ensemble

Justin Peck
Ensemble

Kristine Bendul
Alternate Slim

Colin Bradbury
Swing, Assistant Dance Captain

Jeremy Cox
Alternate Marty

Amanda Edge
Swing

Cody Green
Alternate Sid

Laurie Kanyok
Alternate Babe

Marielys Molina
Alternate Kate

Joel Prouty
Alternate Hank

Ron Todorowski
Alternate Chanos

Ashley Tuttle
Alternate Betsy

Twyla Tharp
Conception, Direction, Choreography

Frank Sinatra
Vocals

James Youmans
Scenic Design

Donald Holder
Lighting Design

Peter McBoyle
Sound Design

Don Sebesky
Additional Orchestrations and Arrangements

Dave Pierce
Additional Orchestrations and Arrangements

Patrick Vaccariello
Music Supervisor/Music Coordinator

Russ Kassoff
Conductor/Pianist

Randall A. Buck
Production Executive

David Benken
Technical Supervisor

Kim Craven
Resident Director

The Charlotte Wilcox Company
General Manager

James L. Nederlander
Producer

Terry Allen Kramer
Producer

The Playbill Broadway Yearbook 2009-2010

Come Fly Away

 Patrick Catullo, *Producer*
 Jon B. Platt, *Producer*
 Jerry Frankel, *Producer*
 Roy Furman, *Producer*

2009-2010 AWARDS

Drama Desk Award
Outstanding Choreography
(Twyla Tharp)

Fred and Adele Astaire Award
Outstanding Male Dancer
(Charlie Neshyba-Hodges)

 Allan S. Gordon, *Producer*
 Élan V. McAllister, *Producer*
 Arny Granat, Jam Theatricals, *Producer*
 Steve Traxler, Jam Theatricals, *Producer*
 Stewart F. Lane and Bonnie Comley, *Producer*
 Margo Lion, *Producer*

 Daryl Roth, *Producer*
 Hal Luftig, *Producer*
 Yasuhiro Kawana, *Producer*
 Van Kaplan, Pittsburgh CLO, *Producer*
 Jay and Cindy Gutterman, GSFD, *Producer*
 Mort Swinsky, GSFD, *Producer*

 Bob Weinstein, The Weinstein Company, *Producer*
 Harvey Weinstein, The Weinstein Company, *Producer*
 Barry and Fran Weissler, *Producer*
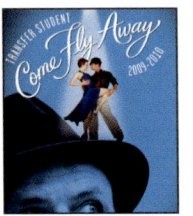 Mark Myars, *Alternate/Swing*

MUSIC CREDITS

Air Mail Special written by Benny Goodman, Jimmy Mundy and Charles Christian. Used by permission of Rytvoc, Inc. (ASCAP), Regent Music Corp. and Ragbag Music Publ. Corp. ©1941. **Body and Soul**, Frank Eyton, John Green, Edward Heyman and Robert B. Sour. Range Road Music Inc. o/b/o itself and Quartet Music, WB Music Corp., and Drurupetal Music. **Come Fly With Me** (Sammy Cahn and Jimmy Van Heusen), ©1958 (renewed), Cahn Music Co. (ASCAP) and Maraville Music Corp. (ASCAP). All rights on behalf of Cahn Music Co. administered by WB Music Corp. **Fly Me to the Moon (In Other Words)** words and music by Bart Howard, TRO ©1954 (renewed), Hampshire House Publishing Corp., New York, NY. International copyright secured. Made in U.S.A. All rights reserved including public performance for profit. **I'm Gonna Live Till I Die** words and music by Al Hoffman, Walter Kent and Manny Kurtz. Copyright ©1950 (renewed) by Al Hoffman Songs, Inc., Barton Music Corp., Walter Kent Music and Mann Curtis Music Company. **I've Got a Crush On You** (George Gershwin and Ira Gershwin), ©1930 (renewed), WB Music Corp. (ASCAP). **I've Got the World on a String** music by Harold Arlen, lyrics by Ted Koehler. Published by S.A. Music (ASCAP). Published and administered in Canada by EMI Mills Music, Inc. (ASCAP). **I've Got You Under My Skin** words and music by Cole Porter, ©1936 by Chappell & Company, Inc. Copyright renewed. Assigned to Robert H. Montgomery, Jr., trustee of the Cole Porter Musical & Literary Property Trusts, Chappell & Co., publisher. International copyright secured. **It's All Right With Me** words and music by Cole Porter, ©1953 by Cole Porter. Copyright renewed. Assigned to Robert H. Montgomery, Jr., trustee of the Cole Porter Musical & Literary Property Trusts, Chappell & Co., publisher. International copyright secured. **Jumpin' at the Woodside** (Count Basie and Jon Hendricks), ©1959 (renewed) WB Music Corp. (ASCAP). **Just Friends** written by John Klenner and Sam M. Lewis. Published and administered by EMI Robbins Catalog Inc. (ASCAP). **Lean**

Come Fly Away

Baby by Roy Alfred and Billy May. Used by permission of Morley Music Co. (ASCAP). **Learnin' the Blues** (Dolores "Vicki" Silvers), Barton Music Corp. **Let's Face the Music and Dance** music and lyrics by Irving Berlin. Used by special arrangement with The Rodgers and Hammerstein Organization on behalf of the Estate of Irving Berlin. **Let's Fall in Love** by Ted Koehler and Harold Arlen ©1933 by Bourne Co. (ASCAP). Copyright renewed. International copyright secured. **Makin' Whoopee** by Walter Donaldson and Gus Kahn. Donaldson Publishing Co., LLC, and Gilbert Keyes Music Company. All rights on behalf of Gilbert Keyes Music Company administered by WB Music Corp. **Moonlight Becomes You** written by Johnny Burke and James Van Heusen, ©1942 Sony/ATV Harmony (ASCAP). **My Funny Valentine** music and lyrics by Richard Rodgers and Lorenz Hart, ©1937 (renewed), Chappell & Co., Inc. (ASCAP) and Williamson Music, Inc. (ASCAP). Used by special arrangement with The Rodgers and Hammerstein Organization on behalf of the Family Trust u/w Richard Rodgers. **My Way** written by Paul Anka, Claude Francois, Jacques Revaux and Gilles Thibault. Chrysalis Standards, Inc. (BMI), Architectural Music Co. (BMI), and Jingoro Co. (BMI). **New York, New York (Theme)** written by John Kander and Fred Ebb. Published and administered EMI Unart Catalog Inc. (BMI). **Nice 'n' Easy** written by Lew Spence, Alan Bergman and Marilyn Bergman. Spirit Two Music, Inc. on behalf of Lew Spence Music and Threesome Music Company (ASCAP). **One for My Baby (And One More for the Road)** by Johnny Mercer and Harold Arlen. Used by permission of Harwin Music Co. (ASCAP). **Pick Yourself Up** (Dorothy Fields and Jerome Kern). Used by permission of Shapiro, Bernstein & Co., Inc. o/b/o Aldi Music. Universal Music Publishing. **Saturday Night Is the Loneliest Night in the Week** (Sammy Cahn and Jule Styne), ©1944 (renewed). Cahn Music Co. (ASCAP) and Producers Music Publ. Co., Inc. (ASCAP). All rights on behalf of Cahn Music Co. administered by WB Music Corp. All rights on behalf of Producers Music Publ. Co., Inc. administered by Chappell & Co., Inc. **The September of My Years** (Sammy Cahn and Jimmy Van Heusen), ©1965 (renewed), Cahn Music Co. (ASCAP) and Van Heusen Music Corp. (ASCAP). All rights on behalf of Cahn Music Co. administered by WB Music Corp. **Summer Wind** (Johnny Mercer, Henry Mayer and Hans Bradtke), ©1965 (renewed), the Johnny Mercer Foundation (ASCAP) and Edition Primus Rolf Budde KG (GEMA). All rights administered by WB Music Corp. **Take Five** written by Paul Desmond, published in the United States by Desmond Music Company. Published in Canada by Derry Music Company. **Teach Me Tonight** (Sammy Cahn and Gene De Paul), ©1954 (renewed), Cahn Music Co. (ASCAP) and The Hub Music Co., Inc. (ASCAP). All rights on behalf of Cahn Music Co. administered by WB Music Corp. **That's Life** (Dean Kay, Kelly L. Gordon), Universal-Polygram Int. Publ., Inc. ©1964, renewed 1992. **Wave** music and lyrics by Antonio Carlos Jobim, published by Corcovado Music Corp. (BMI). **Witchcraft** by Carolyn Leigh and Cy Coleman. Used by permission of Morley Music Co. (ASCAP). **Yes Sir, That's My Baby** by Walter Donaldson and Gus Kahn, ©1925 Donaldson Publishing Co., LLC, and Gilbert Keyes Music Company (ASCAP). All rights on behalf of Gilbert Keyes Music Company administered by WB Music Corp. **You Make Me Feel So Young** (Josef Joe Myrow and Mack Gordon), ©1946 (renewed), WB Music Corp. (ASCAP). All rights reserved. Used by permission.

STAFF FOR *COME FLY AWAY*

GENERAL MANAGEMENT
CHARLOTTE WILCOX COMPANY
Charlotte W. Wilcox
Seth Marquette
Matthew W. Krawiec   Dina S. Friedler
Steve Supeck   Margaret Wilcox

COMPANY MANAGER
Heidi Neven

ASSISTANT COMPANY MANAGER
Michael Bolgar

GENERAL PRESS REPRESENTATIVE
THE HARTMAN GROUP
Michael Hartman
Tom D'Ambrosio   Michelle Bergmann

CASTING
STUART HOWARD ASSOCIATES, LTD.
Stuart Howard   Amy Schecter   Paul Hardt

Production Stage Manager	Rick Steiger
Stage Manager	Lisa Dawn Cave
Assistant Stage Manager	Kevin Bertolacci
Assistant to Mr. Nederlander	Ken Happel
Associate Director, W.A.T. Ltd	Ann Tuomey DePiro
Assistant to Ms. Tharp	Roy Chicas
Associate Set Designer	Jerome Martin
Associate Costume Designer	Amy Clark
Assistants to the Costume Designer	Mike Floyd, Caitlin Hunt
Associate Lighting Designers	Jeanne Koenig, Caroline Chao
Moving Light Programmer	Joseph Allegro
Associate Sound Designer	David Patridge
Assistant Sound Designer	Daniel Fiandaca
Assistant Production Manager	Rose Palombo
Assistant to the Production Manager	Canara Price
Head Carpenter	Jeff Zink
Automation Carpenter	Michael Shepp, Jr.
Production Electrician	James Maloney
Head Electrician	Brad Robertson
Followspot Operator	Justin McClintock
Head Sound	Dillon Cody
Assistant Sound	Daniel Hochstine
Production Props	Jerry L. Marshall
Wardrobe Supervisor	Edmund Harrison
Assistant Wardrobe Supervisor	Jennifer Griggs
Dressers	Tim Greer, Kay Gowenlock, Maggie Horkey, Jeannie Naughton
Stitcher	Sue Hamilton
Production Assistants	Morgan Hartley, Jennifer O'Byrne
Rehearsal Programmer	Joe DeVico
Rehearsal Pianist	Jim Laev
Legal Counsel	Levine, Plotkin & Menin LLP/ Loren Plotkin, Cris Criswell, Susan Mindell, Conrad Rippy
Accountant	Rosenberg, Neuwirth & Kushner, CPA's/ Mark A. D'Ambrosi, Jana Jevnikar
Advertising	SpotCo/Drew Hodges, Jim Edwards, Tom McCann
Website Design	Josh Fraenkel, Tom Greenwald SpotCo/ Sara Fitzpatrick, Matt Wilstein, Mark Mettler
Dance Press Representative Staff	Dulce Shultz
Music Clearance	Jill Meyers Music Consultants
Payroll Services	Castellana Services, Inc.
Production Photographer	Joan Marcus
Banking	City National Bank/Michele Gibbons
Insurance Consultant	Stockbridge Risk Management
Insurance	Reiff & Associates, LLC./ Dennis Reiff, Regina Newsome
Physical Therapy	PhysioArts/Jennifer Green
Massage Therapist	Russell Beasley
Orthopedist	Phillip Bauman, MD
Consulting Physician	Dr. Karen Thorton
Group Sales	Nederlander Group Sales
Merchandise	Creative Goods/ Pete Milano, Mike D'Arcy
Information Management Services	Marion Finkler Taylor
Travel Services	Tzell Travel/Andi Henig
Theatre Displays	King Displays, Inc.

CREDITS

Scenery by Hudson Scenic, I. Weiss NY and Showman Fabrication. Automation by Hudson Scenic. Lighting equipment from Production Resource Group. Sound equipment from Production Resource Group. Costumes by Eric Winterling, Saint Laurie Merchant Tailors NYC. Undergarments by Bra*Tenders. Custom footwear by LaDuca, T.O. Dey, JC Theatrical, Zoraide. Custom headwear by Lynne Mackey Studio, Worth and Worth. Custom jewelry by Abby Kong. Special thanks to Alliance Costume Shop, Mark Happel, John Kristiansen. Music consultation by Frank Sinatra Enterprises. Piano by Steinway & Sons.

To learn more about the production, please visit ComeFlyAway.com

Rehearsed at New 42nd Street Studios

Chairman .... James M. Nederlander
President .... James L. Nederlander

Executive Vice President
Nick Scandalios

Vice President	Senior Vice President
Corporate Development	Labor Relations
Charlene S. Nederlander	**Herschel Waxman**

Vice President	Chief Financial Officer
Jim Boese	**Freida Sawyer Belviso**

STAFF FOR THE MARQUIS THEATRE

Manager	David Calhoun
Associate Manager	Austin Nathaniel
Treasurer	Rick Waxman
Assistant Treasurer	John Rooney
Carpenter	Joseph P. Valentino
Electrician	James Mayo
Property Man	Scott Mecionis

Come Fly Away
SCRAPBOOK

1. (Front L-R): Nancy Sinatra and Twyla Tharp at curtain call on opening night amid a shower of confetti.
2. Keith Roberts and Karine Plantadit arrive at Roseland for the cast party.
3. John Selya and guest at Roseland.
4. (L-R): Cast members Justin Peck ("Yearbook" Correspondent), Eric Michael Otto, Carolyn Doherty, Heather Hamilton, and Meredith Miles on opening night.

Correspondent: Justin Peck, Ensemble
Opening Night Gift: Communal fedora from Twyla.
Most Exciting Celebrity Visitors: Toss up between the Cake Boss with a cake for us and Katie Holmes with Tom and Suri Cruise.
Who Got the Gypsy Robe and What They Put on It: Kristine Bendul. Nothing yet but leaning towards a hood with a fedora attached.
Special Backstage Rituals: Unity Moment. High-tens at stage left. Biscuit and Booby Dance. Second Act PT room re-coup. Darts.
Favorite Moment During Each Performance: Alex's solo castles.
Favorite In-Theatre Gathering Place: PT room (a.k.a. the Spa and Rejuvenation Room).
Favorite Off-Site Hangout: Gordon Biersch @ BuckHead.
Favorite Snack Foods: Beer and tequila.
Mascot: Button, the mutt.
Favorite Therapy: PhysioArts and Mr. Russ.
Memorable Stage Door Fan Encounter: Sequined piano/American flag-vest gentleman from New Orleans who absolutely adored the show.
Latest Audience Arrival: One quarter of the audience missed the show entirely due to the May 1 bomb scare.
Fastest Costume Change: Betsy before "New York, New York."
Who Wore the Heaviest/Hottest Costume: Holley takes it with "The Fifth Grader," her enormous boa that's the weight of a 10-year-old.
Who Wore the Least: Everyone. But, by a small margin, Meredith.
Catchphrases Only the Company Would Recognize: "We'll take it from the button!" "Bird fly by." "Kan kan kan kan k kan-kan kan kan k kan." "It's party time!!!!!!!!!!!!!!" "Scrim out!!"
Best In-House Parody Lyric: "You make me feel so...."
Memorable Directorial Note: "Don't feed the dog."
Company In-Jokes: "Fraulein! Schtick peel, oh, ein schpeck." "Haha, we'll just put some duct tape on it." "Back in the day, you could have biscuit." "I stole some silver." Said in a pirate accent: "Arrr, Morgan!!"
Nicknames: "Johnny Biscuit." "Ginger B." "Mergatroid." "Nancy." "Bangkok Ladyboy."
Sweethearts Within the Company: Alex and Rika.
Embarrassing Moments: John's pants splitting four times on stage.
Superstition That Turned Out To Be True: The show is going AGMA.
Also: In Atlanta, Twyla saved us from hours of schlepping laundry on the bus to the laundromat on our day off by giving us laundry service.
Coolest Things About Being in This Show: We're all together again. Seeing the seniors in the audience re-living the music of their dating days. Being done at 10 PM.

Enron

First Preview: April 8, 2010. Opened: April 27, 2010.
Closed May 9, 2010 after 22 Previews and 16 Performances.

CAST

Jeffrey Skilling	NORBERT LEO BUTZ
Kenneth Lay	GREGORY ITZIN
Claudia Roe	MARIN MAZZIE
Andy Fastow	STEPHEN KUNKEN
Employee/News Reporter/ Analyst	JORDAN BALLARD
Security Guard/Trader	BRANDON J. DIRDEN
Lehman Brother/Trader/Employee/ Board Member	RIGHTOR DOYLE
Lehman Brother/Trader/Arthur Andersen/ Police Officer	ANTHONY HOLDS
Lawyer/Trader	TY JONES
Lawyer/Trader	IAN KAHN
Employee/News Reporter/Hewitt	JANUARY LaVOY
Senator/Trader/Analyst/Judge	TOM NELIS
Daughter	MADISYN SHIPMAN
(Thurs., Fri. & Sun. eve.)	MARY STEWART SULLIVAN
(Mon. & Tues. eve., Sat. mat. & eve., Sun. mat.)	
Trader/Analyst/Court Officer	JEFF SKOWRON
Sheryl Sloman/Congresswoman/ Irene Gant	LUSIA STRUS
Trader/Analyst/Ramsay	NOAH WEISBERG

SETTING
The action takes place in Houston, Texas, between 1992 and the present day.

UNDERSTUDIES/STANDBYS
BEN HARTLEY, ELLYN MARIE MARSH

DANCE CAPTAIN
BEN HARTLEY

BROADHURST THEATRE
235 West 44th Street
A Shubert Organization Theatre
Philip J. Smith, *Chairman*   Robert E. Wankel, *President*

Jeffrey Richards Jerry Frankel Matthew Byam Shaw ACT Productions Neal Street
Beverly Bartner & Norman Tulchin Lee Menzies Bob Boyett Scott M. Delman INFINITY Stages
JK Productions The Araca Group Jamie deRoy Mallory Factor Michael Filerman
Ian Flooks Ronald Frankel James Fuld Jr. Dena Hammerstein Jam Theatricals Rodger H. Hess
Sharon Karmazin Cheryl Lachowicz OSTAR Parnassus Enterprise Jon B. Platt Judith Resnick
Daryl Roth Stein and Gunderson Company Anita Waxman The Weinstein Company
Barry & Carole Kaye Stewart F. Lane & Bonnie Comley Fran & Barry Weissler
and The Shubert Organization

present

the Headlong Theatre
Chichester Festival Theatre and Royal Court Theatre Production

of

by
Lucy Prebble

Starring
Norbert Leo Butz
Gregory Itzin   Marin Mazzie   Stephen Kunken
Jordan Ballard   Brandon J. Dirden   Rightor Doyle   Ben Hartley   Anthony Holds
Ty Jones   Ian Kahn   January LaVoy   Ellyn Marie Marsh   Tom Nelis   Madisyn Shipman
Jeff Skowron   Lusia Strus   Mary Stewart Sullivan   Noah Weisberg

Lighting Design	Composition and Sound Design	Video and Projection Design
Mark Henderson	Adam Cork	Jon Driscoll

Choreography	Casting	Production Stage Manager
Scott Ambler	Telsey + Company	Barclay Stiff

Technical Supervision	Press Representative	Associate Producer	General Management
Hudson Theatrical Associates	Jeffrey Richards Associates Irene Gandy/Alana Karpoff	Jeremy Scott Blaustein	Richards/Climan, Inc.

Set and Costume Design
Anthony Ward

Directed By
Rupert Goold

The Producers wish to express their appreciation to the Theatre Development Fund for its support of this production.

4/27/10

Norbert Leo Butz, as Jeffrey Skilling, floats on what seems like an ever-rising sea of stock prices.

Enron

Norbert Leo Butz
Jeffrey Skilling

Gregory Itzin
Kenneth Lay

Marin Mazzie
Claudia Roe

Stephen Kunken
Andy Fastow

Jordan Ballard
*Employee/
News Reporter/
Analyst*

Brandon J. Dirden
*Security Guard/
Trader*

Rightor Doyle
*Lehman Brother/
Trader/Employee/
Board Member*

Anthony Holds
*Lehman Brother/
Trader/Arthur
Andersen/
Police Officer*

Ty Jones
Lawyer/Trader

Ian Kahn
Lawyer/Trader

January LaVoy
*Employee/
News Reporter/
Hewitt*

Tom Nelis
*Senator/Trader/
Analyst/Judge*

Madisyn Shipman
Daughter

Jeff Skowron
*Trader/Analyst/
Court Officer*

Lusia Strus
*Sheryl Sloman/
Congresswoman/
Irene Grant*

Mary Stewart
Sullivan
Daughter

Noah Weisberg
*Trader/Analyst/
Ramsay*

Ben Hartley
*Assistant
Choreographer/
Dance Captain/
Understudy*

Ellyn Marie Marsh
Understudy

Lucy Prebble
Playwright

Rupert Goold
Director

Anthony Ward
*Set & Costume
Design*

Mark Henderson
Lighting Design

Adam Cork
*Composition and
Sound Design*

Jon Driscoll
*Video & Projection
Design*

Bernard Telsey,
Telsey + Company
Casting

Neil Mazzella,
Hudson Theatrical
Associates
*Technical
Supervision*

Jeffrey Richards
Producer

David R. Richards and Tamar Haimes,
Richards/Climan, Inc.
General Management

Jerry Frankel
Producer

Caro Newling for
Neal Street
Producer

Bob Boyett
Producer

Darren Bagert,
Infinity Stages
Producer

Jamie deRoy
Producer

Enron

Mallory Factor
Producer

Michael Filerman
Producer

James Fuld Jr.
Producer

Arny Granat,
Jam Theatricals
Producer

Steve Traxler,
Jam Theatricals
Producer

Sharon Karmazin
Producer

Jon B. Platt
Producer

Daryl Roth
Producer

Anita Waxman
Producer

Bob Weinstein,
The Weinstein Company
Producer

Harvey Weinstein,
The Weinstein Company
Producer

Stewart F. Lane and Bonnie Comley
Producers

Philip J. Smith,
Chairman,
The Shubert Organization
Producer

Barry and Fran Weissler
Producers

Jeremy Scott Blaustein
Associate Producer

EVENING DOORMAN
Joe Trapasso

BOX OFFICE
(L-R): Clifford Cobb (Head Treasurer), Noreen Morgan (Assistant Treasurer) and Mike Lynch (Assistant Treasurer)

STAGE AND COMPANY MANAGEMENT
(L-R): Barclay Stiff (Production Stage Manager), Mary Miller (Company Manager), Matthew Farrell (Stage Manager)

FRONT OF HOUSE AND USHERS

Enron

STAGE CREW
(L-R): Valerie Spradling, Ron Vitelli, Charles DeVerna, Brian "Boomer" Bullard, Scott Monroe, Brian McGarty

HAIR SUPERVISOR
Erin Lunsford working with cast member Madisyn Shipman

WARDROBE
(L-R): Jeff Johnson, Tree Sarvay, Julian Arango, Vicki Grecki, Rob Bevenger (Wardrobe Supervisor)

Photos by Barclay Stiff

STAFF FOR ENRON

GENERAL MANAGEMENT
RICHARDS/CLIMAN, INC.
David R. Richards   Tamar Haimes

COMPANY MANAGER
MARY MILLER

GENERAL PRESS REPRESENTATIVE
JEFFREY RICHARDS ASSOCIATES
IRENE GANDY/ALANA KARPOFF
Elon Rutberg   Diana Rissetto

CASTING
TELSEY + COMPANY
Bernie Telsey CSA, Will Cantler CSA, David Vaccari CSA, Bethany Knox CSA, Craig Burns CSA, Tiffany Little Canfield CSA, Rachel Hoffman CSA, Carrie Rosson CSA, Justin Huff CSA, Bess Fifer CSA, Patrick Goodwin CSA, Abbie Brady-Dalton

PRODUCTION MANAGEMENT
HUDSON THEATRICAL ASSOCIATES
Neil Mazzella   Irene Wang

PRODUCTION STAGE MANAGER	Barclay Stiff
Stage Manager	Matthew Farrell
Associate Director	Sophie Hunter
Assistant Choreographer	Ben Hartley
Associate Scenic Designer	Christine Peters
Associate Costume Designer	Patrick Bevilacqua
Associate Lighting Designer	Michael Jones
Associate Sound Designer	Chris Cronin
Video Programmer	Chris Herman
Vocal Coach	David Shrubsole
Production Properties Supervisor	Faye Armon
Assistants to Jeffrey Richards	Michael Crea, Will Trice
Associate General Managers	Michael Sag, Jeromy Smith
General Management Assistant	Cesar Hawas
Production Office Intern	Travis Ferguson
Company Management Assistant	Kyle Bonder
General Management Intern	Julianna Slaten
Production Assistant	Kelly Beaulieu
Child Supervisor	Allison Sherry
Production Carpenter	Todd Frank
Production Electrician	Fraser Weir
Production Sound	Valerie Spradling
Production Props	Scott Monroe
House Carpenter	Brian McGarty
House Electrician	Charles DeVerna
House Props	Ronni Vitelli
House Flyman	Brian Bullard
Wardrobe Supervisor	Rob Bevenger
Hair Consultant	Katie Beatty
Makeup Consultant	Ashley Ryan
Dressers	Julian Andres Arango, Victoria Grecki, Jeff Johnson, Tree Sarvay
Prop Shoppers	Kate Costin, Marina Guzman
Costume Shoppers	Michael Graller, Nicole Moody
Advertising	Serino Coyne, Inc./ Greg Corradetti, Tom Callahan, Robert Jones, Danielle Boyle
Interactive Marketing Services	Situation Interactive/ Damian Bazadona, John Lanasa, Miriam Naggar, Victoria Gettler
Creative Director, Broadway's Best Shows	Andy Drachenberg
Banking	City National Bank/Michele Gibbons
Accountants	FK Partners/Robert Fried, CPA
Comptroller	Elliott Aronstam
Legal Counsel	Lazarus & Harris, LLP/ Scott R. Lazarus, Esq., Robert C. Harris, Esq.
Insurance	DeWitt Stern Group, Inc./ Jolyon F. Stern, Joseph Bower
Payroll	CSI/Lance Castellana
Video Clearance	Nan Halperin
Music Clearance	Melody Silverman
Company Mascots	Skye, Franco, Mecca

Rehearsed at the New 42nd Street Studios

CREDITS

Scenery constructed by Hudson Theatrical Associates. Lighting equipment by Hudson Sound & Light LLC. Sound equipment by Sound Associates. Costumes by Jennifer Love Costumes, Vogue 2 Embroidery, Sake Studio Services/Michael Santulli. Video footage supplied by ITN Source and ITN Source/Reuters. Special thanks to Bra*Tenders for hosiery and undergarments.

SPECIAL THANKS

Paul Smithyman, Lincoln Center Theater, Marilyn Armon. Coffee makers and K-cups generously provided by Keurig.

www.EnronBroadway.com
www.BroadwaysBestShows.com

 THE SHUBERT ORGANIZATION, INC.
Board of Directors

Philip J. Smith Chairman	**Robert E. Wankel** President
Wyche Fowler, Jr.	**John W. Kluge**
Lee J. Seidler	**Michael I. Sovern**

Stuart Subotnick

Elliot Greene Chief Financial Officer	**David Andrews** Senior Vice President – Shubert Ticketing
Juan Calvo Vice President and Controller	**John Darby** Vice President – Facilities
Peter Entin Vice President – Theatre Operations	**Charles Flateman** Vice President – Marketing
Anthony LaMattina Vice President – Audit & Production Finance	**Brian Mahoney** Vice President – Ticket Sales

D.S. Moynihan
Vice President – Creative Projects

House Manager .... Hugh Barnett

Enron
Scrapbook

Correspondent: January LaVoy, "Employee"/"News Reporter"/"Hewitt"

Memorable Opening Night Letter: Actually, it was the beautiful closing night letter from our director and playwright in London—a letter in which they chronicled something specific about each member of the company that they cherished and would miss—that was the most memorable to me.

Opening Night Gifts: It was a bit overwhelming, but I will say that someone in the cast (it might have been me and my roommate, Jordan Ballard) got aluminum water bottles for the entire cast with the *Enron* logo and our opening date inscribed on them. Everybody loved it.

Which Actor Performed the Most Roles in This Show: I'm not positive, but I think it was Tony Holds—Employee, Lehman Brother, Arthur Andersen, Raptor, Prison Guard.

Who Has Done the Most Shows in Their Career: Wow. We've got a lot of "actor's actors" in the cast...Greg? Marin? Norbert? Everybody works A LOT.

Special Backstage Rituals: None of our backstage rituals are PG enough to be printed in public.

Favorite Moment During Each Performance (On Stage or Off): The four guys who played our Raptors—Rightor, Noah, Jeff and Tony—had to keep the raptor heads on, even offstage, for much of Act II. There is not much in this world funnier than watching dinosaurs in business suits engaged in casual conversation.

Favorite Theatre Gathering Place: Many of us loved sitting on our fire escapes—which connected many of the dressing rooms—and overlooking 44th Street. It really feels like the center of it all. In fact, the day we moved into the Broadhurst, a bunch of us got together and climbed out our windows onto the fire escapes and screamed and whooped and hollered. (We also had a lot of Broadway debuts in our show.) I think the IATSE guys across the street (at *American Idiot*) thought we'd lost our minds.

Favorite Off-Site Hangouts: If we weren't at Angus, you could find us at Un Deux Trois. (Thanks, Jose!)

Favorite Snack Food: In the four weeks that we rehearsed *Enron* at 42nd Street Studios, we had no less than six birthdays, each with an accompanying cake. We had at least three more in the theatre. I think we all began to feel a sense of entitlement about cake.

Favorite Therapy: We did enjoy our PT. Very physical show.

Most Memorable Ad-Lib: "F@%k Ben Brantley" (which was said onstage, in the clear, at our final performance).

Internet Buzz: Ummm...suffice it to say, it didn't measure up to the size of our...run.

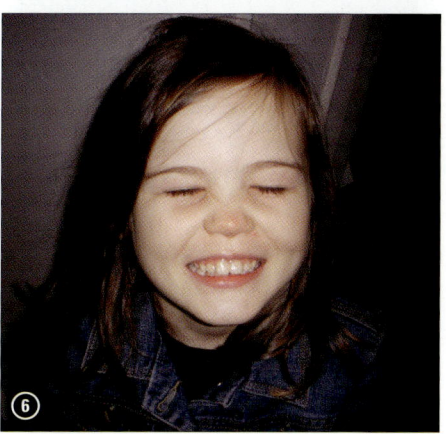

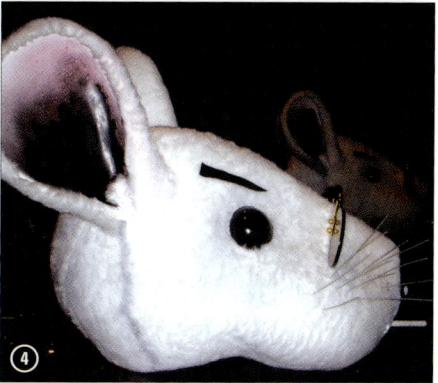

1. A member of the company doing his best to relax in one of the Raptor masks.
2. Looking up from the stage.
3. Greg Itzin and Noah Weisberg backstage.
4. Another of the show's many masks.
5. Noah Weisberg, Ian Kahn and Jeff Skowron.
6. Mary Stewart Sullivan.

Enron
Scrapbook

Record Number of Cell Phone Rings or Texting Incidents During a Performance: I can't say for sure, but I can tell you that the large group of food-poisoned patrons we had at our first preview has to be some sort of record. According to our PA, it was five people in four separate ambulances. Apparently they just kept dropping. We had no idea.

Mascot: Benita.

Fastest Costume Change: Rightor Doyle, from Lehman Brother to Raptor in 10.3 seconds.

Who Wore the Heaviest/Hottest Costume: Once again, I've gotta say the Raptors. (I always feel like I'm talking about a musical group.) Honestly though, it is not an exaggeration to say that some of those guys bled for the show.

Who Wore the Least: Someone (who shall remain nameless) stripped down to nothing at the end of Act I during our final performance. You know who you are.

Catchphrases Only the Company Would Recognize: "Frenryn."
"Popocatepetl copper plated kettle."
"Ameeeeeezing!" (also, "Marin aMeeeezing")
"Where's Ty? Hello...I work here."
"My boy Ben wants books."
"Gold."
"Suck it and see."
"Curtsey and Stretch."
"P. Diddy's Mom."

Memorable Directorial Note: "Be savage."

Company In-Joke: We're going to start a shadow company called *Guys and Dolls*. It will eat our debt.

Understudy Anecdote: I will say that in the sad minutes after we got our closing notice, we were trying to cheer each other up by joking, "Hey—at least they've cancelled the understudy rehearsal on Thursday...right?"

Nicknames: Who needs nicknames with real names like Rightor, Noah, January, Rupert, Ian, Lusia, Barclay...

Superstition That Turned Out To Be True: Never let anyone say that your show is "the most anticipated" anything.

Coolest Things About Being in This Show: Every. Last. Thing.
But if I have to get specific—being handed a light saber and a pair of sunglasses every night for the Texas vs. California number. I think that theatre actors rarely get to feel as badass as we did.

1. (L-R): Steve Kunken, January LaVoy, Rightor Doyle and Ben Hartley.
2. Ty Jones reads an emotional letter from the director and playwright after the closing was announced.
3. "Why"—the *Enron* slogan.
4. The interior of the Broadhurst Theatre.

Photos courtesy January LaVoy

Everyday Rapture

First Preview: April 19, 2010. Opened: April 29, 2010.
Still running as of May 31, 2010.

CAST
(in order of appearance)
SHERIE RENE SCOTT
LINDSAY MENDEZ
BETSY WOLFE
EAMON FOLEY

UNDERSTUDIES
RILEY COSTELLO, NATALIE WEISS

Production Stage Manager:
RICHARD C. RAUSCHER
Stage Manager:
BRYCE McDONALD

MUSICIANS
Conductor/Piano: MARCO PAGUIA
Drums: CLINT DE GANON
Bass: BRIAN HAMM
Guitar: JOHN BENTHAL
Violin/Guitar: JOE BRENT

Synthesizer Programmer: RANDY COHEN
Music Copying: COLLEEN DARNALL

AMERICAN AIRLINES THEATRE

ROUNDABOUT THEATRE COMPANY
Todd Haimes, Artistic Director
Harold Wolpert, Managing Director
Julia C. Levy, Executive Director

Presents

The Second Stage Theatre Production of

Sherie Rene Scott

in

EVERYDAY RAPTURE

by
Dick Scanlan and Sherie Rene Scott

with
Eamon Foley   Lindsay Mendez   Betsy Wolfe

Set Design	Costume Design	Lighting Design	Sound Design	Projection Design
Christine Jones	Tom Broecker	Kevin Adams	Ashley Hanson / Kurt Eric Fischer / Brian Ronan	Darrel Maloney

Orchestrations/Arrangements	Music Supervisor	Musical Director	Music Coordinator
Tom Kitt	Michael Rafter	Marco Paguia	Michael Keller

Production Stage Manager	Production Management	Original Casting
Richard C. Rauscher	Aurora Productions	MelCap Casting

Additional Casting	General Manager	Press Representative
Jim Carnahan, C.S.A.	Rebecca Habel	Boneau/Bryan-Brown

Director of Marketing & Sales Promotion	Founding Director	Associate Artistic Director
David B. Steffen	Gene Feist	Scott Ellis

Choreography by
Michele Lynch

Directed by
Michael Mayer

Roundabout Theatre Company would like to thank Amanda Dubois, Fox Theatricals, Tom Hulce and Ira Pittelman, Sh-K-Boom Records and Thomas Schumacher for their participation in the development of *Everyday Rapture*.

Roundabout Theatre Company is a member of the League of Resident Theatres.
www.roundabouttheatre.org

4/29/09

Sherie Rene Scott and her theatrical trunk.

Photo by Carol Rosegg

Everyday Rapture

   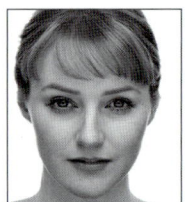   

Sherie Rene Scott | Eamon Foley | Lindsay Mendez | Betsy Wolfe | Riley Costello *Understudy* | Natalie Weiss *Understudy* | Dick Scanlan *Co-Author*

Michael Mayer *Director* | Michele Lynch *Choreographer* | Christine Jones *Set Design* | Kevin Adams *Lighting Design* | Brian Ronan *Sound Design* | Tom Kitt *Orchestrations & Arrangements* | Michael Keller *Music Coordinator*

Jim Carnahan *Additional Casting* | Carole Rothman *Artistic Director, Second Stage Theatre* | Gene Feist *Founding Director, Roundabout Theatre Company* | Todd Haimes *Artistic Director, Roundabout Theatre Company*

BOX OFFICE
Solangel Bido, Robert Morgan, Heather Siebert

WARDROBE
Susan Fallon, Manuela LaPorte, Lauren Gallitelli

92   The Playbill Broadway Yearbook 2009-2010

Everyday Rapture

STAGE AND COMPANY MANAGEMENT

Carly DiFulvio,
Richard C. Rauscher,
McKenzie Murphy,
Bryce McDonald

MUSICIANS

(L-R): Joseph Brent,
John Benthal,
Marco Paguia

CREW

(Standing L-R): Robert Dowling,
Sarah K. Conyers,
Barb Bartel,
Glenn Merwede,
Dann Wojnar,
Jason McKenna,
(Sitting): Jocelyn Smith

Everyday Rapture

USHERS
Rebecca Knell, Kareem McRae, Crystal Suarez

ROUNDABOUT THEATRE COMPANY STAFF
ARTISTIC DIRECTOR .... TODD HAIMES
MANAGING DIRECTOR .... HAROLD WOLPERT
EXECUTIVE DIRECTOR .... JULIA C. LEVY
ASSOCIATE ARTISTIC DIRECTOR ... SCOTT ELLIS

ARTISTIC STAFF
DIRECTOR OF ARTISTIC DEVELOPMENT/
  DIRECTOR OF CASTING .... Jim Carnahan
Artistic Consultant .... Robyn Goodman
Resident Director .... Doug Hughes
Associate Artists ..... Scott Elliott, Bill Irwin, Joe Mantello,
  Mark Brokaw, Kathleen Marshall
Literary Manager .... Jill Rafson
Casting Director .... Carrie Gardner
Casting Associate .... Kate Boka
Casting Associate .... Stephen Kopel
Artistic Assistant .... Amy Ashton
Literary Associate .... Josh Fiedler
The Blanche and Irving Laurie Foundation
  Theatre Visions Fund Commissions .... Julia Cho,
  Stephen Karam, Lewis Black,
  Nathan Louis Jackson
Educational Foundation of
  America Commissions .... Bekah Brunstetter,
  Lydia Diamond, Diana Fithian,
  Julie Marie Myatt
New York State Council
  on the Arts Commission .... Nathan Louis Jackson
Roundabout Commissions .... Steven Levenson,
  Robert Lopez & Kristen Anderson-Lopez
Artistic/Literary Intern .... Liz Malta
Casting Interns .... Kyle Bosley, Jillian Cimini,
  Erin Drake, Andrew Femenella,
  Lauren Lewis, Quinn Meyers
Script Readers .... Jay Cohen, Hillary Dixler,
  Nicholas Stimler

EDUCATION STAFF
EDUCATION DIRECTOR .... Greg McCaslin
Associate Education Director .... Jennifer DiBella
Education Associate
  for Theatre-Based Programs .... Jay Gerlach
Education Program Associate .... Aliza Greenberg
Education Dramaturg .... Ted Sod
Teaching Artists .... Cynthia Babak, Victor Barbella,
Grace Bell, LaTonya Borsay,
Mark Bruckner, Joe Clancy, Vanessa Davis,
Joe Doran, Elizabeth Dunn-Ruiz,
Carrie Ellman-Larsen, Kevin Free,
Tony Freeman, Deanna Frieman,
Natalie Gold, Sheri Graubert,
Matthew A.J. Gregory, Melissa Gregus,
Adam Gwon, Devin Haqq,
Carrie Heitman, Karla Hendrick,
Jim Jack, Jason Jacobs, Lisa Renee Jordan,
Jamie Kalama, Alvin Keith,
Tami Mansfield, Erin McCready, Kyle McGinley,
Andrew Ondrejcak, Meghan O'Neill,
Laura Poe, Nicole Press, Jennifer Rathbone,
Leah Reddy, Amanda Rehbein,
Bernita Robinson, Christopher Rummel,
Cassy Rush, Nick Simone, Heidi Stallings,
Daniel Sullivan, Carl Tallent, Vickie Tanner,
Jolie Tong, Cristina Vaccaro, Jennifer Varbalow,
Leese Walker, Eric Wallach, Michael Warner,
Christina Watanabe, Gail Winar,
Conwell Worthington, III
Teaching Artist Emeritus .... Reneé Flemings
Teaching Artist Apprentices .... Carrie Ellman-Larsen,
  Deanna Frieman, Meghan O'Neill
Education Interns .... Kali DiPippo, Devin Shacket

ADMINISTRATIVE STAFF
GENERAL MANAGER .... Sydney Beers
Associate Managing Director .... Greg Backstrom
General Manager,
  American Airlines Theatre .... Rebecca Habel
General Manager, Steinberg Center .... Rachel E. Ayers
Human Resources Manager .... Stephen Deutsch
Operations Manager .... Valerie D. Simmons
Associate General Manager .... Maggie Cantrick
Office Manager .... Scott Kelly
Management Associate .... Jill K. Boyd
Archivist .... Tiffany Nixon
Receptionists ...... Dee Beider, Raquel Castillo, Elisa Papa,
  Allison Patrick, Monica Sidorchuk
Messenger .... Darnell Franklin

FINANCE STAFF
DIRECTOR OF FINANCE .... Susan Neiman
Payroll Director .... John LaBarbera
Accounts Payable Manager .... Frank Surdi
Payroll Benefits Administrator .... Yonit Kafka
Manager Financial Reporting .... Joshua Cohen
Business Interns .... Matthew Kagen,
  Rebekah Lashof, Laura Marshall
Business Office Assistant .... Jackie Verbitski

DEVELOPMENT STAFF
Director, Special Events .... Steve Schaeffer
Director, Major Gifts .... Joy Pak
Director, Patron Programs .... Amber Jo Manuel
Manager, Donor Information Systems .... Lise Speidel
Manager, Patron Programs .... Tyler Ennis
Manager, Telefundraising .... Gavin Brown
Manager, Corporate Relations .... Roxana Petzold
Associate Manager, Patron Programs .... Marisa Perry
Development Assistants .. Ryan Hallett, Nick Luckenbaugh
Assistant to the Executive Director .... Jason Butler
Special Events Assistant .... Amy Rosenfield
Institutional Giving Assistant .... Brett Barbour
Major Gifts Intern .... Joseph Jankowski
Special Events Intern .... Gavi Young

INFORMATION TECHNOLOGY STAFF
IT DIRECTOR .... Antonio Palumbo
IT Associate .... Dylan Norden
IT Associate .... Jim Roma
DIRECTOR DATABASE OPERATIONS . Wendy Hutton
Database Administrator/Programmer .... Revanth Anne

MARKETING STAFF
DIRECTOR OF MARKETING
  AND SALES PROMOTION .... David B. Steffen
Associate Director of Marketing .... Tom O'Connor
Marketing/Publications Manager ..... Margaret Casagrande
Assistant Director of Marketing .... Stefanie Schussel
Marketing Manager .... Shannon Marcotte
Website Consultant .... Keith Powell Beyland
Director of Telesales Special Promotions ...... Marco Frezza
Telesales Manager .... Anthony Merced
Telesales Office Coordinator .... Patrick Pastor
Marketing Interns .... Akeem Baisden-Folkes,
  Shoshana Greenberg

TICKET SERVICES STAFF
Director of Sales Operations .... Charlie Garbowski, Jr.
Ticket Services Manager .... Ellen Holt
Subscription Manager .... Ethan Ubell
Box Office Managers .... Edward P. Osborne,
  Jaime Perlman, Krystin MacRitchie,
  Nicole Nicholson
Group Sales Manager .... Jeff Monteith
Assistant Box Office Managers .... Robert Morgan,
  Andrew Clements, Scott Falkowski,
  Catherine Fitzpatrick
Assistant Ticket Services Managers .... Robert Kane,
  Bill Klemm, Lindsay Ericson
Customer Services Coordinator .... Thomas Walsh
Ticket Services .... Solangel Bido, Arianna Boykins,
  Lauren Cartelli, Joseph Clark, Barbara Dente,
  Nisha Dhruna, Adam Elsberry, James Graham,
  Kara Harrington, Tova Heller, Nicki Ishmael,
  Kate Longosky, Michelle Maccarone, Elisa Mala,
  Mead Margulies, Chuck Migliaccio, Carlos Morris,
  Kayrose Pagan, Hillary Parker, Thomas Protulipac,
  Jessica Pruett-Barnett, Kaia Rafoss, Josh Rozett,

Everyday Rapture

Ben Schneider, Kenneth Senn, Heather Siebert, Nalane Singh, Lillian Soto, Ron Tobia, Jacklyn Verbitski, Hannah Weitzman
Intern .... Emily Cole

SERVICES
Counsel .... Paul, Weiss, Rifkind, Wharton and Garrison LLP, Charles H. Googe Jr., Carol M. Kaplan
Counsel .... Rosenberg & Estis
Counsel .... Andrew Lance, Gibson, Dunn, & Crutcher, LLP
Counsel .... Harry H. Weintraub, Glick and Weintraub, P.C.
Counsel .... Stroock & Stroock & Lavan LLP
Counsel .... Daniel S. Dokos, Weil, Gotshal & Manges LLP
Immigration Counsel .... Mark D. Koestler and Theodore Ruthizer
Government Relations .... Law Offices of Claudia Wagner LLC
House Physicians .... Dr. Theodore Tyberg, Dr. Lawrence Katz
House Dentist .... Neil Kanner, D.M.D.
Insurance .... DeWitt Stern Group, Inc.
Accountant .... Lutz & Carr CPAs, LLP
Advertising .... Spotco/ Drew Hodges, Jim Edwards, Tom Greenwald, Kyle Hall, Cory Spinney
Interactive Marketing .... Situation Interactive/ Damian Bazadona, John Lanasa, Eric Bornemann, Randi Fields
Events Photography .... Anita and Steve Shevett
Production Photographer .... Joan Marcus
Theatre Displays .... King Displays, Wayne Sapper
Lobby Refreshments .... Sweet Concessions
Merchandising .... Spotco Merch/ James Decker

MANAGING DIRECTOR EMERITUS .... Ellen Richard

Roundabout Theatre Company
231 West 39th Street, New York, NY 10018
(212) 719-9393.

GENERAL PRESS REPRESENTATIVES
BONEAU/BRYAN-BROWN
Adrian Bryan-Brown
Matt Polk   Jessica Johnson   Amy Kass

STAFF FOR *EVERYDAY RAPTURE*
Company Manager .... Carly DiFulvio
Production Stage Manager .... Richard C. Rauscher
Stage Manager .... Bryce McDonald
Production Management by .... Aurora Productions/ Gene O'Donovan, W. Benjamin Heller II, Rachel Sherbill, Jarid Sumner, Melissa Mazdra, Amanda Raymond, Graham Forden, Liza Luxenberg
Assistant Director .... Austin Regan
Associate Choreographer .... Eric Sean Fogel
Associate Set Designer .... Jonathan W. Collins
Associate Costume Designer .... David Withrow
Associate Lighting Designers .... Aaron Sporer, Paul Toben
Assistant Lighting Designer .... Craig Stelzenmuller
Associate Sound Designer .... Drew Levy
Associate Projection Designer .... Dan Scully
Hair Design .... John Barrett, for John Barrett Salon
Make-Up .... Tiffany Hicks
Dance Captain .... Lindsay Mendez
Magic Consultant .... Steve Cuiffo
Production Properties Supervisor .... Peter Sarafin
Production Carpenter .... Glenn Merwede
Production Electrician .... Brian Maiuri
Running Properties .... Robert W. Dowling II
Deck Sound .... Dann Wojnar
Front Light Operator .... Barb Bartel
Sound Mixer .... Jason McKenna
Wardrobe Supervisor .... Susan J. Fallon
Dressers .... Cathy Cline, Mel Hansen
Wardrobe Dayworker .... Lauren Gallitelli
Hair and Wig Supervisor .... Manuela Laporte
Production Assistant .... McKenzie Murphy
Guardian .... Jenn McNeil
IA Apprentice .... Sarah K. Conyers
Scenery constructed, painted
    and electrified by .... Showmotion, Inc., Norwalk CT, and Daedalus, Brooklyn, NY
Lighting Equipment provided by .... PRG Lighting, a division of Production Resource Group LLC
Sound and Projection Equipment
    provided by .... Sound Associates
Music Clearances by .... Janet Billig Rich
Piano by .... Steinway and Sons

M•A•C Cosmetics
Official Makeup of Roundabout Theatre Company

To learn more about Roundabout Theatre Company,
please visit roundabouttheatre.org
Find us on Facebook.
Follow us on Twitter @RTC_NYC

AMERICAN AIRLINES THEATRE STAFF
Company Manager .... Carly DiFulvio
House Carpenter .... Glenn Merwede
House Electrician .... Brian Maiuri
House Properties .... Robert W. Dowling II
House Sound .... Dann Wojnar
IA Apprentice .... Sarah K. Conyers
Wardrobe Supervisor .... Susan J. Fallon
Box Office Manager .... Ted Osborne
Assistant Box Office .... Robert Morgan
House Manager .... Stephen Ryan
Associate House Manager .... Zipporah Aguasvivas
Head Usher .... Ilia Diaz
House Staff .... Anne Ezell, Denise Furbert, Edlyn Gonzalez, Lee Henry, Paul Krasner, Rebecca Knell, Taylor Martin, Joaquin Melendez, Ariana Murphy, Argenis Peguero, Celia Perez, Fatimah Robinson, Crystal Suarez, Adam Wier
Security .... Julious Russell
Additional Security provided by .... Gotham Security
Maintenance .... Jerry Hobbs, Daniel Pellew, Willie Philips, Magali Western
Lobby Refreshments .... Sweet Concessions

SPECIAL THANKS
Susan Barras, Bobby Mrozek, Bill Herz, Eric Armstrong, David Drake, Michael Friedman, Dan Lipton, Tom Viola, Broadway Cares/Equity Fights AIDS, Jayson Raitt, The Center, Scott Pask, Bobby Pearce, Dan Knechtges, Noah Cornman, Kurt Deutsch and the staff at Sh-K-Boom/Ghostlight Records, Christine Struble, Tyler Maynard, Bill Isler, Family Communications Inc., Joanne Rogers, Ellen Kander, Maxine Lapiduss, Jorge Vargas, Bryan Landrine, Jill Boyd, Heather Cousens, Bethany Russell, Carmel Dean, Jim Hershman, George Farmer, Shannon Ford, Hiroko Taguchi and especially Carole Rothman, Chris Burney and everyone at Second Stage.

CASTING
MelCap Casting
David Caparelliotis, Mele Nagler
Stephanie Yankwitt, Lauren Port, Matt Dittes,
Christina Wright

MUSIC CREDITS
"Elevation" written by Adam Clayton, David Evans, Paul David Hewson and Laurence Mullen. ©Published by Universal Polygram International (ASCAP). "Everybody's Fancy" written by Fred Rogers. ©Published by Family Communications, Inc. "Get Happy" written by Harold Arlen and Ted Koehler. ©Published by SA Music Co. (ASCAP) and Warner Bros. Inc. (ASCAP). "Got a Thing on My Mind" written by Gabriel Alexander Roth. ©Published by Boscosound Music (BMI) and Songs of Kobalt Music Publishing (BMI). "Good Feeling to Know You're Alive" written by Fred Rogers. ©Published by Family Communications, Inc. "I Guess the Lord Must Be in New York City" written by Harry Nilsson. ©Published by Unichappell Music Inc (BMI). "I Like to be Told" written by Fred Rogers. ©Published by Family Communications, Inc. "It's You I Like" written by Fred Rogers. ©Published by Family Communications, Inc. "Killing Me Softly" written by Charles Fox and Norman Gimbel. ©Published by Fox-Gimbel Productions Inc. (BMI) and Rodali Music (BMI). "Life Line" written by Harry Nilsson. ©Published by EMI Blackwood Music Inc. (BMI) and Unichappell Music Inc. (BMI). "Over the Rainbow" written by Harold Arlen and E.Y. Harburg. ©Published by EMI Feist Catalog Inc. (ASCAP). "Overture" (from "The Other Side of This Life") written by David Byrne. ©Published by Malu Music Inc., dba Moldy Fig Music. "On the Atchison, Topeka and the Santa Fe" written by John Mercer and Harry Warren. ©Published by EMI Feist Catalog Inc. (ASCAP). "Rainbow Sleeves" written by Tom Waits. ©Published by Fifth Floor Music. "Strongest Suit" written by Tim Rice and Elton John. ©Published by Wonderland Music Company Inc. (BMI). "Up the Ladder to the Roof" written by Vincent Dimirco and Frank Edward Wilson. Published by Stone Agate Music (a division of Jobete Music Co. Inc.). "The Weight" written by Robbie Robertson. ©Published by Dwarf Music. "Won't You Be My Neighbor" written by Fred Rogers. ©Published by Family Communications, Inc. "Why" written by David Byrne. ©Published by Moldy Fig Music (BMI).

Rehearsed at the
New 42nd Street Studios

Everyday Rapture
Scrapbook

Correspondent: Bryce McDonald, Stage Manager

Memorable Opening Night Letter, Fax or Note: Instead of faxing their notes over, the casts of *American Idiot* and *In the Heights* had someone walk theirs over, so everything was in color and written in different color inks. It was sweet that someone from the show would take the time to do that. It was very cool.

Opening Night Gifts: Sherie Rene Scott and Dick Scanlan gave us each a journal with a silver plate front and silver pen, with a four-leaf clover (as mentioned in the show) on front. It was very poignant to our process and our journey. They also had blue baseball shirts made imprinted with her opening lines. They only made enough for the cast and crew and stage managers. They're one-of-a-kind that you can't buy anyplace else!

Most Exciting Celebrity Visitors: Green Day, Rosie O'Donnell, Lili Taylor, Helen Reddy, Daniel Radcliffe (shirt on, unfortunately). That was super exciting. Also Jim Dale, Stephen Sondheim, Alan Rickman and Kathie Lee and Hoda.

Who Got the Gypsy Robe: Betsy Wolfe. It was her first time. We don't know yet what she's going to put on it.

Special Backstage Rituals: The stage management team runs up and down the tower every day to check in with Sherie when she gets here. "How are you? Do you need anything?" She's the mama of the show. One day we missed it and she came down and said, "Guys, where were you today? I can't start the show if you don't come and talk!" Also when all the girls come down for "places" they gather in the hallway and there's always a hug or a group get-together. Then they talk to the band. We don't get started until Sherie and the girls have talked to the band. Then she says, "I'm ready. Let's get this mother started."

Favorite Moment During Each Performance: Our PA, McKenzie Murphy, and I do our own backstage choreography to two numbers in the show: "The Weight" and "Up the Ladder to the Roof." We pretend we're one of her backup singers, the Mennonettes.

Favorite In-Theatre Gathering Place: Sherie's dressing room or the stage manager's office, that's the clubhouse of the theatre.

Favorite Off-Site Hangout: Every Thursday night it's the upstairs bar at Rosie O'Grady's on 46th Street.

Favorite Snack Foods: Fruit and almonds. The folks on this show are a healthy bunch.

Favorite Therapies: Ours are Raspberry Emergen-C and Grether's Blackcurrant Pastilles.

Most Memorable Ad-Lib: Sherie does magic tricks in the show. One night a balloon popped when it wasn't supposed to, and she just calmly said, "I'll do it again."

Cell Phone Rings, Cell Phone Photos, Tweeting or Texting Incidents During a Performance: No Patti LuPone episodes yet.

Web Buzz: It's been exciting. Daniel Radcliffe heard about us through the web and told his agent, "I keep hearing about this show. I want to know what it is. I want to see it." Buzz has been very good.

Memorable Stage Door Fan Encounter: We haven't had anybody dress up yet; just the normal people requesting photos and signed Playbills. Our stage door is pretty hard to find, so we haven't had a huge amount.

Catchphrase Only the Company Would Recognize: "Yes, honey."

Nicknames: Sherie is called "SHE."

Coolest Thing About Being in This Show: It's a lovefest. And She is just an amazing leader. Her energy is unstoppable. You can't help but be joyous.

1. Sherie Rene Scott gives (and gets) a hand during curtain calls on opening night.
2. Lindsay Mendez (L) and Eamon Foley (R) join Scott for bows.
3. (L-R): Cast members Lindsay Mendez, Sherie Rene Scott, director Michael Mayer, cast members Betsy Wolfe, Eamon Foley and co-author Dick Scanlan at the cast party at the American Airlines Theatre.

Fela!

First Preview: October 19, 2009. Opened: November 23, 2009.
Still running as of May 31, 2010.

CAST

Fela Anikulapo-Kuti	KEVIN MAMBO, SAHR NGAUJAH
Funmilayo Anikulapo-Kuti, his mother	LILLIAS WHITE
Sandra Isadore	SAYCON SENGBLOH
Ismael, Geraldo Piño, Orisha, Ensemble	ISMAEL KOUYATÉ
J.K. Braiman (Tap Dancer), Egungun, Ensemble	GELAN LAMBERT
Ensemble	COREY BAKER, HETTIE VYRINE BARNHILL, LAUREN DE VEAUX, NICOLE CHANTAL DE WEEVER*, ELASEA DOUGLAS, RUJEKO DUMBUTSHENA, RASAAN-ELIJAH "TALU" GREEN, SHANEEKA HARRELL, ABENA KOOMSON, GELAN LAMBERT, SHAKIRA MARSHALL, AFI MCCLENDON, ADESOLA OSAKALUMI, JEFFREY PAGE, JILL M. VALLERY, DANIEL SOTO, IRIS WILSON, AIMEE GRAHAM WODOBODE

*Nicole Chantal de Weever is appearing with the permission of Actors' Equity Association.

SWINGS

CATHERINE FOSTER, CHANON JUDSON, FARAI M. MALIANGA, J.L. WILLIAMS

Continued on next page

EUGENE O'NEILL THEATRE
A JUJAMCYN THEATRE

JORDAN ROTH
President

PAUL LIBIN
Producing Director

JACK VIERTEL
Creative Director

SHAWN "JAY-Z" CARTER AND WILL & JADA PINKETT SMITH
RUTH & STEPHEN HENDEL, ROY GABAY, SONY PICTURES ENTERTAINMENT, EDWARD TYLER NAHEM, SLAVA SMOLOKOWSKI
CHIP MEYRELLES/KEN GREINER, DOUGLAS G. SMITH, STEVE SEMLITZ/CATHY GLASER
DARYL ROTH/TRUE LOVE PRODUCTIONS, SUSAN DIETZ, MORT SWINSKY, KNITTING FACTORY ENTERTAINMENT

PRESENT

FELA!

BOOK
JIM LEWIS & BILL T. JONES

MUSIC AND LYRICS
FELA ANIKULAPO-KUTI

ADDITIONAL LYRICS BY
JIM LEWIS

ADDITIONAL MUSIC BY
AARON JOHNSON & JORDAN McLEAN

BASED ON THE LIFE OF
FELA ANIKULAPO-KUTI

CONCEIVED BY
BILL T. JONES, JIM LEWIS & STEPHEN HENDEL

SAHR NGAUJAH   KEVIN MAMBO
SAYCON SENGBLOH

COREY BAKER, HETTIE VYRINE BARNHILL, LAUREN DE VEAUX, NICOLE CHANTAL DEWEEVER, ELASEA DOUGLAS, RUJEKO DUMBUTSHENA, CATHERINE FOSTER, RASAAN-ELIJAH "TALU" GREEN, SHANEEKA HARRELL, CHANON JUDSON, ABENA KOOMSON, ISMAEL KOUYATÉ, GELAN LAMBERT, FARAI MALIANGA, SHAKIRA MARSHALL, AFI MCCLENDON, ADESOLA OSAKALUMI, JEFFREY PAGE, DANIEL SOTO, JILL M. VALLERY, IRIS WILSON, J.L. WILLIAMS, AIMEE GRAHAM WODOBODE

AND
LILLIAS WHITE

SCENIC & COSTUME DESIGNER	LIGHTING DESIGNER	SOUND DESIGNER	PROJECTION DESIGNER
MARINA DRAGHICI	ROBERT WIERZEL	ROBERT KAPLOWITZ	PETER NIGRINI

WIG, HAIR & MAKEUP DESIGNER	PRODUCTION STAGE MANAGER	CASTING
COOKIE JORDAN	JON GOLDMAN	MUNGIOLI THEATRICALS ARNOLD J. MUNGIOLI, CSA

PRESS REPRESENTATIVE	ADVERTISING & NEW MEDIA SERVICES	MARKETING
RICHARD KORNBERG & ASSOCIATES	ART MEETS COMMERCE	HHC MARKETING WALK TALL GIRL PRODUCTIONS

TECHNICAL SUPERVISION	ASSOCIATE TECHNICAL SUPERVISION	GENERAL MANAGER
HUDSON THEATRICAL ASSOCIATES	JAY JANICKI JOHN TIGGELOVEN	ROY GABAY

MUSIC DIRECTION & SUPERVISION/ORCHESTRATIONS/ARRANGEMENTS	MUSIC COORDINATOR	ASSOCIATE PRODUCER
AARON JOHNSON	MICHAEL KELLER	AHMIR "QUESTLOVE" THOMPSON

ASSOCIATE MUSICAL DIRECTOR & ARRANGER	MUSIC CONSULTANT	ASSOCIATE DIRECTOR	ASSOCIATE CHOREOGRAPHER
JORDAN McLEAN	ANTIBALAS	NIEGEL SMITH	MAIJA GARCIA

DIRECTED AND CHOREOGRAPHED BY
BILL T. JONES

11/23/09

Sahr Ngaujah (center) with the Ensemble

Photo by Monique Carboni

The Playbill Broadway Yearbook 2009-2010

Fela!

MUSICAL NUMBERS

ACT 1

Welcome Na De Shrine
"Everything Scatter" ....Fela and Company
B.I.D. (Breaking It Down)
"Iba Orisa": Traditional Yoruba chant ....Ismael, Fela and Company
Hymn by Reverend J.J. Ransome-Kuti ....Fela, Company and Band
"Medzi Medzi" by E.T. Mensah ....Company and Band
"Mr. Syms" by John Coltrane ....Company and Band
"Manteca" by Chano Pozo ....Company and Band
"I Got the Feeling" by James Brown ....Ismael and Company
Underground Spiritual Game (The Clock)
"Originality/Yellow Fever" ....Fela and Company
Trouble
"Trouble Sleep" ....Fela, Funmilayo and Company
"Teacher Don't Teach Me Nonsense" ....Fela, Funmilayo and Company
Black President
"Lover"* ....Fela and Sandra
"Upside Down" ....Fela, Sandra and Company
"Expensive Shit" ....Fela and Company
"Pipeline"*/"I.T.T. (International Thief Thief)" ....Fela and Company
"Kere Kay" ....Fela and Company

ACT 2

Water
"Water No Get Enemy" ....Fela, Sandra and Company
"Egbe Mio" ....Fela, Queens and Funmilayo
The Game
"Zombie" ....Fela and Company
"Trouble Sleep" (reprise) ....Fela, Funmilayo and Queens
Wedding
"Na Poi" ....Fela and Queens
The Storming of Kalakuta
"Sorrow Tears and Blood" ....Fela and Company
Dance of the Orisas
"Iba Orisa/Shakara" ....Company and Band
"Rain"** ....Funmilayo and Company
B.Y.O.C. (Bring Your Own Coffin)
"Coffin for Head of State" ....Fela and Company
"Kere Kay" (reprise) ....Fela and Company

*"Lover" and "Pipeline," English lyrics by Jim Lewis
**"Rain" music by Aaron Johnson and Jordan McLean, lyrics by Bill T. Jones and Jim Lewis

Cast Continued

DANCE CAPTAINS
JILL M. VALLERY, DANIEL SOTO

UNDERSTUDIES
For Fela Anikulapo-Kuti:
ADESOLA OSAKALUMI
For Funmilayo:
ABENA KOOMSON
For Sandra:
ELASEA DOUGLAS

SETTING
Fela's final concert at the Shrine in Lagos, Nigeria
The Summer of 1978, six months after the death of Funmilayo, Fela's mother

BAND
Conductor/Trombone/Keyboard:
AARON JOHNSON
Assistant Conductor/Drums/Percussion:
GREG GONZALEZ
Trumpet:
JORDAN MCLEAN
Bass/Keyboards/Percussion:
JEREMY WILMS
Guitar/Percussion:
OREN BLOEDOW
Guitar/Percussion:
RICARDO QUINONES
Percussion:
YOSHIHIRO TAKEMASA
Baritone Saxophone/Percussion:
ALEX HARDING
Tenor Saxophone/Percussion/
Featured Saxophone Soloist:
STUART BOGIE
Percussion:
DYLAN FUSILLO
Music Coordinator
MICHAEL KELLER

Sahr Ngaujah
Fela Anikulapo-Kuti

Kevin Mambo
Fela Anikulapo-Kuti

Lillias White
Funmilayo Anikulapo-Kuti

Saycon Sengbloh
Sandra Isadore

Corey Baker
Ensemble

Hettie Vyrine Barnhill
Ensemble

Lauren De Veaux
Ensemble

Fela!

Nicole Chantal de Weever
Ensemble

Elasea Douglas
Ensemble

Rujeko Dumbutshena
Ensemble

Catherine Foster
Swing

Rasaan-Elijah "Talu" Green
Ensemble

Shaneeka Harrell
Ensemble

Chanon Judson
Swing

Abena Koomson
Vocal Captain, Ensemble

Ismael Kouyaté
Ensemble

Gelan Lambert
Ensemble

Farai Malianga
Swing

Shakira Marshall
Ensemble

Afi McClendon
Ensemble

Adesola Osakalumi
Ensemble

Jeffrey Page
Ensemble

Daniel Soto
Ensemble/Assistant Dance Captain

Jill M. Vallery
Ensemble/ Dance Captain

Iris Wilson
Ensemble

J.L. Williams
Swing

Aimee Graham Wodobode
Ensemble

Bill T. Jones
Conceiver/Director/ Choreographer/ Book Writer

Jim Lewis
Conceiver/ Book Writer/ Additional Lyrics

Marina Draghici
Set & Costume Design

Robert Wierzel
Lighting Designer

Robert Kaplowitz
Sound Design

Neil A. Mazzella/ Hudson Theatrical Associates
Technical Supervision

Aaron Johnson
Musical Director

Michael Keller
Music Contractor

Arnold J. Mungioli, Mungioli Theatricals, Inc.
Casting

Richard Kornberg & Associates
Press Representative

Shawn "Jay-Z" Carter
Producer

Will Smith
Producer

Ruth Hendel
Producer

Roy Gabay
Producer/ General Manager

Chip Meyrelles
Producer

Fela!

Ken Greiner
Producer

Daryl Roth
Producer

Jeanne Donovan Fisher/
True Love Productions
Producer

Susan Dietz
Producer

Mort Swinsky
Producer

Oneika Phillips
Swing

Justin Prescott
Swing

Ryan H. Rankine
Swing

MANAGEMENT
(L-R): Jon Goldman (PSM), Linda Marvel (SM), Hilary Austin (ASM)

CREW
Front Row (L-R): Damian Caza-Cleypool, Kevin Maher, Susie Ghebresillassie, Sue Stepnik, Heather Wright, Anna Hoffmann, Linda Marvel, Sue Cerceo, Reid Hall, Hilary Austin
Back Row (L-R): Jordan Gable, James Gardener, Mary Chesterman, Guy Patria, Shannon Slayton, Mary McGregor, Emile LaFargue, Christopher Beck, Ken Keneally, Jon Goldman

Fela!

2009-2010 AWARDS

Tony Awards
Best Choreography
(Bill T. Jones)
Best Costume Design of a Musical
(Marina Draghici)
Best Sound Design of a Musical
(Robert Kaplowitz)

Outer Critics Circle Award
Outstanding Choreography
(Bill T. Jones [tie])

Theatre World Award
First Major New York Appearance
(Sahr Ngaujah)

Fred and Adele Astaire Award
Outstanding Choreographer
(Bill T. Jones)
Outstanding Female Dancers
(The Women's Ensemble)

FRONT OF HOUSE STAFF
Front Row (L-R): Lorraine Wheeler, Verna Hobson, Saime Hodzic, Bruce Lucoff
Second Row (L-R): Pamela Martin, Sandra Palmer, Mili Vela, Heather Gilles
Third Row (L-R): Giovanni Monserrate, Scott Rippe, Dorothy Lennon, Byron Varags
Back Row (L-R): Hal Goldberg, Russ Ramsey, Elise Gainer, Ray Segal

BOX OFFICE
(L-R): Harry Keith Stephenson, Stan Shaffer

DOORMAN
Emir Hodzic

HAIR
(L-R): Heather Wright, Anna Hoffmann

Fela!

STAFF FOR FELA!

GENERAL MANAGEMENT
ROY GABAY THEATRICAL PRODUCTION & MANAGEMENT

Roy Gabay	Chris Aniello	Bobby Driggers
Daniel Kuney	Jennifer Pluff	Mandy Tate

COMPANY MANAGEMENT
Daniel Kuney
Chris Aniello

GENERAL PRESS REPRESENTATIVE
RICHARD KORNBERG & ASSOCIATES
Richard Kornberg   Billy Zavelson
Don Summa   Tommy Wesely

CASTING
MUNGIOLI THEATRICALS
Arnold J. Mungioli, CSA
Alex Hanna   Melanie Lockyer

TECHNICAL SUPERVISION
HUDSON THEATRICAL ASSOCIATES
Neil A. Mazzella   John Tiggeloven

PRODUCTION STAGE MANAGER .... JON GOLDMAN
Stage Manager .... Linda Marvel
Assistant Stage Manager .... Hilary Austin
Associate Technical Supervision .... Jay Janicki, Aduro Productions, Caitlin McInerney
Associate Director .... Niegel Smith
Associate Choreographer .... Maija Garcia
Music Contractor .... Michael Keller
Associate Set Designers ..... Timothy R. Mackabee, Wilson Chin, Katheryn Monthei
Associate Costume Designer .... Amy Clark
Assistant Costume Designer .... Mike Floyd
Costume Intern .... Abby Kong
Associate Lighting Designer .... Paul Hackenmueller
Assistant Lighting Designer .... G. Benjamin Swope
Assistant to the Lighting Designer .... Xavier Pierce
Original Mural and Scenic Art .... IRLO, Omar and Nuclear Fairy
Associate Sound Designer .... Jessica Paz
Assistant Sound Designer .... John Emmett O'Brien
Production Sound Engineers .... Reid Hall, Shannon Slayton
Sound Intern .... Ted Pallas
Associate Projection Designer, Content ... C. Andrew Bauer
Associate Projection Designer, System .... Dan Scully
Projection Programmer .... Benjamin Keightley
Production Projectionist .... Greg Peeler
Additional Content and Editing .... Mirit Tal
Projection Intern .... Barbara Samuels
Head Follow Spot Operator .... Damian Caza-Cleypool
Spot Operator .... James Gardener
Props Master .... Kathy Fabian/Propstar
Associate Props .... Jennifer Breen, Sid King/Propstar
Prop Artisans .... Sarah Bird, Corey Shipler, Hanna Davis, Martin Izquierdo Studio, Arianna Zindler, Emily Walsh
Flame Treatment .... Turning Star, Inc.
Wardrobe Supervisor .... Sue Stepnik
Dressers .... Sue Cerceo, Bobby Clifton, Cathy Cline, Mindy Eng, Alessandro Ferdico, Susie Ghebresillassie, Nesreen Mahmoud
Hair Supervisor .... Heather Wright
Hair Assistant .... Tonya Bodsin
Production Electrician .... Todd D'Aiuto
Automated Lighting Programmer .... Timothy F. Rogers
Assistant Electrician/Board Operator .... Robert Hale
Production Carpenter .... Jordan Gable
Flyman .... Kevin Mar
Automation Operators .... Mark Diaz, Todd Frank, Jordan Gable
House Props .... Christopher Beck
Props Head .... Ken Keneally
Casting Associates .... Alex Hanna, Melanie Lockyer
Legal .... Susan Mindell/Levine, Plotkin & Menin LLP
Accounting .... Fried & Kowgios Partners, LLP/ Robert Fried
Controller .... Galbraith & Co./ Sarah Galbraith
Payroll .... Castellana Services, Inc.
Insurance .... Ventura Insurance Brokerage, Inc./ Jessica Brown
Advertising/New Media Services .... Art Meets Commerce/ Jim Glaub, Laurie Connor, Kevin Keating, Ryan Greer, Brad Coffman, Crystal Chase, Marissa Coronado
Marketing .... HHC Marketing/ Hugh Hysell, Matt Sicoli, Nicole Pando Walk Tall Girl Productions/ Marcia Pendelton, Jesse Wooden, Jr., Marielin Lopez, Sharif Colon
Production Assistants .... Melanie Ganim, Leslie Grisdale, Colleen M. Sherry
Artistic Assistant .... Radha Blank
Physical Therapy .... Performing Arts Physical Therapy
Orthopedic Consultant .... Dr. Phillip Bauman
Car Services .... Elegant Limousine/Joe Cox
Production Photographer .... Monique Carboni

CREDITS
Scenery constructed by Hudson Scenic Studios, Inc. Lighting equipment from PRG Lighting. Sound and projection equipment from Sound Associates. Costumes constructed by Tricorne, John Scheeman Studios, Izquierdo Studios, Jennifer Love Costumes, Monica Vianni Custom Millinery, Bola International Boutique and Brian Hemesath, Costume Armour.

Make-up provided by M·A·C

Additional footwear provided by Dance Paws.

MUSIC RIGHTS
"I Got the Feeling" by James Brown. By arrangement with Fort Knox Music Inc. c/o Carlin America Inc. (BMI). "Manteca" by Dizzy Gillespie, Walter Gil Fuller and Chano Pozo. By arrangement with Boosey & Hawkes, Inc. o/b/o Twenty-Eighth Street Music (ASCAP) and with Music Sales Corporation (ASCAP). "Medzi Medzi" by E.T. Mensah. By arrangement with RetroAfric Music (PRS). "Mr. Syms" by John Coltrane. By arrangement with Jowcol Music (BMI). "Nice 'N Easy" by Alan and Marilyn Bergman and Lew Spence. By arrangement with Spirit Two Music, Inc. o/b/o Lew Spence Music (ASCAP) and with Threesome Music Company (ASCAP). Frank Sinatra video clip from "The Edsel Show" (1957). Produced by CBS Television Network.

SPECIAL THANKS
Rikki Stein, Romanian Cultural Institute in New York, Actors' Equity Association, Link TV, LAByrinth Theater, Culture Project, Atlantic Theater Company, Bill T. Jones/Arnie Zane Dance Company, the Joyce Theater, Public Theater, the New Group, Sean Barlow/AFROPOP, Joe's Pub, S.O.B.'s, Artistic Relations, Noro, Bra*Tenders for hosiery and undergarments, Frank/voodoofunk.com, Aretha Amma/Global Fusion Productions, Rosie Goldman, Dance Paws LLC.

Rehearsed at the New 42nd Street Studios

To learn more about the production, please visit www.felaonbroadway.com

STAFF FOR EUGENE O'NEILL THEATRE
Manager .... Justin L. Karr
Associate Manager .... Hal Goldberg
Treasurer .... Stan Shaffer
Carpenter .... Donald Robinson
Propertyman .... Christopher Beck
Electrician .... Todd D'Aiuto
Engineer .... Frank Italiano

JUJAMCYN THEATERS
JORDAN ROTH
President

PAUL LIBIN	JACK VIERTEL
Producing Director	Creative Director
DANIEL ADAMIAN	**JENNIFER HERSHEY**
General Manager	Director of Operations
MEREDITH VILLATORE	**JERRY ZAKS**
Chief Financial Officer	Resident Director

Lillias White and Sahr Ngaujah

Photo by Monique Carboni

Fela!
Scrapbook

Correspondent: Maija Garcia, Associate Choreographer

Opening Night Gifts: Will and Jada Pinkett Smith generously offered "*Fela!*"-engraved Tiffany's keychains for each member of the cast and crew.

Most Exciting Celebrity Visitors: Sting, Alicia Keys, Spike Lee, Wesley Snipes, Barbara Walters, Denzel Washington...too many more to mention.

Who Got the Gypsy Robe: Adesola Osakalumi received the Gypsy Robe and our costume department put a *Fela!* patch over the Yansh (ass).

Actor Who Performed the Most Roles in This Show: Ismael Kouyaté plays many roles in addition to chorus dancer and singer. He gives a call to prayer, honoring Fela as a rising star. Geraldo Piño. He plays Fela chanting while hanging upside down on a ladder in the General torture. He also plays Eshu, the messenger god—Orisha of the crossroads.

Who Has Done the Most Shows in Their Career: LILLIAS WHITE!!! (again, too many to mention).

Special Backstage Rituals: Pre-show Winding, Water Goddess.

Favorite Moment During Each Performance (On Stage or Off): Lillias White dancing the clock off-stage left.

Favorite In-Theatre Gathering Place: We gather on-stage!

Favorite Off-Site Hangout: Serafina!

Favorite Snack Foods: Coconut water, Emergen-C.

Mascot: Broadway Bear Egungun! (Understudy mascot: Ismael's Scooby Doo slippers).

Favorite Therapies: Tiger Balm and naps.

Memorable Ad-Lib: Puff-Puff-Pass (the magic word in Kalakuta republic).

Memorable Press Encounter: A newspaper interviewer asked Maija G (associate choreographer) what language we were speaking—referring to abstract vocalizations while rehearsing movement.

Memorable Stage Door Fan Encounter: A woman who starting hugging and humping everyone.

Latest Audience Arrival: "ITT!" (right before intermission).

Fastest Costume Change: Fela has about 20 seconds to get into General costume.

Busiest Day at the Box Office: December 30, 2009—the box office was a madhouse!

Who Wore the Heaviest/Hottest Costume: Gelan Lambert's Egungun costume for Orishas.

Who Wore the Least: The Queens.

Catchphrases Only the Company Would Recognize: AGO! AME!

Nicknames: We have many. "Dudo," "Sax Man Al," "Bon Fils."

Sweethearts Within the Company: "What happens in Kalakuta stays in Kalakuta."

Orchestra Member Who Played the Most Instruments: Dylan Fusillo (percussion... too many instruments to mention).

Orchestra Member Who Played the Most Consecutive Performances Without a Sub: Ricardo Quinones (guitar).

Memorable Directorial Note: "Stage Whores of the World, Unite!" —Bill T. Jones, in tech rehearsal.

1. Director/choreographer Bill T. Jones leads the cast in curtain calls on opening night.
2. Sahr Ngaujah comes down the aisle at the premiere.
3. Cast member Saycon Sengbloh at Gotham Hall for the cast party.
4. Cast member Lillias White on opening night.
5. Cast members Daniel Soto and Shaneeka Harrell at Gotham Hall.

Embarrassing Moment: During "Yellow Fever" (improvised solos) Nicole de Weever's ponytail weave flew off as she did her signature head rotation... she picked it up and worked it like a lasso.

Coolest Thing About Being in This Show: The opportunity to improvise onstage, always exploring and developing new ideas. And the Cast is AMAZING! We are Kalakuta warriors.

Photos by Aubrey Reuben

Fences

First Preview: April 14, 2010. Opened: April 26, 2010.
Still playing as of May 31, 2010.

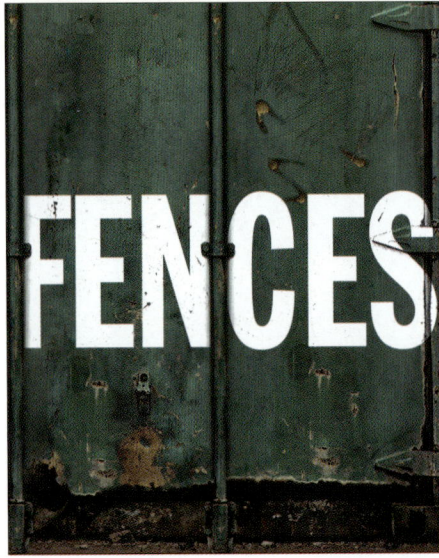

CAST
(in order of appearance)

Troy Maxson .... DENZEL WASHINGTON
Jim Bono, Troy's
 friend ... STEPHEN McKINLEY HENDERSON
Rose, Troy's wife .... VIOLA DAVIS
Lyons, Troy's oldest son
 by a previous marriage ..... RUSSELL HORNSBY
Gabriel, Troy's brother ... MYKELTI WILLIAMSON
Cory, Troy and Rose's son .... CHRIS CHALK
Raynell, Troy's
 daughter .... EDEN DUNCAN-SMITH and
  SaCHA STEWART-COLEMAN
  at alternating performances

The play takes place in Pittsburgh, 1957.

"Confront the dark parts of yourself, and work to banish them with illumination and forgiveness. Your willingness to wrestle with your demons will cause your angels to sing. Use the pain as fuel, as a reminder of your strength." – August Wilson

STANDBYS
For Troy Maxson: KEITH RANDOLPH SMITH
For Rose: ROSLYN RUFF
For Jim Bono, Gabriel: MICHAEL GENET
For Lyons, Cory: JASON DIRDEN

CORT THEATRE
138 West 48th Street
A Shubert Organization Theatre
Philip J. Smith, *Chairman*   Robert E. Wankel, *President*

Carole Shorenstein Hays and Scott Rudin
present

Denzel Washington

August Wilson's
FENCES

Viola Davis

Chris Chalk   Eden Duncan-Smith   Stephen McKinley Henderson
Russell Hornsby   SaCha Stewart-Coleman   Mykelti Williamson

Original Music by
Branford Marsalis

Set Design   Costume Design   Lighting Design   Sound Design
Santo Loquasto   Constanza Romero   Brian MacDevitt   Acme Sound Partners

Production Stage Manager   Press Representative   Casting
Narda E. Alcorn   Boneau/Bryan-Brown   MelCap Casting

Production Management   General Management   Associate Producer
Aurora Productions   Stuart Thompson Productions   Constanza Romero
                                          David Turner

Directed by
Kenny Leon

4/26/10

(L-R): Denzel Washington and Viola Davis

Photo by Joan Marcus

Fences

Denzel Washington
Troy Maxson

Viola Davis
Rose

Chris Chalk
Cory

Stephen McKinley Henderson
Jim Bono

Russell Hornsby
Lyons

Mykelti Williamson
Gabriel

Eden Duncan-Smith
Raynell

SaCha Stewart-Coleman
Raynell

Jason Dirden
Standby Lyons, Cory

Michael Genet
Standby Jim Bono, Gabriel

Roslyn Ruff
Standby Rose

Keith Randolph Smith
Standby Troy Maxson

August Wilson
Playwright

Kenny Leon
Director

Branford Marsalis
Original Music

Santo Loquasto
Set Design

Constanza Romero
Costume Design

Brian MacDevitt
Lighting Design

Tom Clark, Mark Menard and Nevin Steinberg, Acme Sound Partners
Sound Design

Rick Sordelet
Fight Director

Stuart Thompson Productions
General Management

Carole Shorenstein Hays
Producer

Scott Rudin
Producer

CREW
Front Row (L-R): Scott DeVerna (House Electrician), Darin Stillman (Production Sound Engineer), Alissa Zulvergold (Child Wrangler), Lonny Gaddy (House Properties), Dave Cohen (Props)

Back Row (L-R): Michael Zaleski (Stage Manager), Narda Alcorn (Production Stage Manager)

Fences

WARDROBE DEPARTMENT

(L-R): Anita Ali Davis, Ginny Hounsell, Moira MacGregor (Supervisor), Laura Ellington

---

STAFF FOR *FENCES*

CAROLE SHORENSTEIN HAYS-SHN
Duffy Anderson-Rothe
Pip Ngo

GENERAL MANAGEMENT
STUART THOMPSON PRODUCTIONS
Stuart Thompson   David Turner   James Triner

COMPANY MANAGER
Chris Morey

PRODUCTION MANAGEMENT
AURORA PRODUCTIONS INC.
Gene O'Donovan   Ben Heller
Jarid Sumner   Rachel Sherbill   Melissa Mazdra
Amanda Raymond   Graham Forden
Liza Luxenberg

PRESS REPRESENTATIVE
BONEAU/BRYAN-BROWN
Chris Boneau   Heath Schwartz
Kelly Guiod

CASTING
MELCAP CASTING
Mele Nagler, CSA   David Caparelliotis, CSA
Christina Wright   Stephanie Yankwitt
Lauren Port   Matthew Dittes

FIGHT DIRECTOR
Rick Sordelet

WIG DESIGNER
Charles LaPointe

Production Stage Manager	Narda E. Alcorn
Stage Manager	Michael P. Zaleski
Associate Director	Todd Kreidler
Associate Scenic Designer	Jenny Sawyers
Associate Costume Designer	Katie Irish
Associate Lighting Designer	Jennifer Schriever
Associate Sound Designer	Nick Borisjuk
Assistant Scenic Designers	Antje Ellerman, Yoki Lai
Assistant Lighting Designer	Aaron Parsekian
Production Carpenter	Edward Diaz
Production Electrician	Dan Coey
Production Properties Coordinator	Propstar/Kathy Fabian
Production Sound Engineer	Darin Stillman
House Electrician	Scott DeVerna
House Properties	Lonny Gaddy
Wardrobe Supervisor	Moira MacGregor
Dressers	Anita-Ali Davis, Ginny Hounsell, Laura Ellington
Hair Supervisor	Amy Neswald
Child Wrangler	Alissa Zulvergold
Children's Tutoring	On Location Education
Production Assistant	Chelsea Antrim
Propstar Associates	Carrie Mossman, Timothy Ferro
Fight Captain	Chris Chalk
Assistant to Ms. Hays	Paula Miller
Assistants to Mr. Rudin	Tim Kava, David Kennedy, Allie Moore, Matt Nemeth, Nick Zayas
Assistant to Mr. Thompson	Christopher Taggart
General Management Assistants	Megan E. Curren, Geo Karapetyan, Brittany Levasseur
General Management Interns	Erin Byrne, Andrew Lowy
Stage Management Interns	Erica Gambino, Benjamin Bales Karlin
Advertising	Spotco/Drew Hodges, Jim Edwards, Tom Greenwald, Y. Darius Suyama, Kristen Rathbun
Marketing	Walk Tall Girl Productions/ Marcia Pendelton; Jesse Wooden, Jr.; Kojo Ade; Sharif Colon; Marielin Lopez
Website	Spotco/Sara Fitzpatrick, Matt Wilstein, Marc Mettler
Accountant	Fried & Kowgios CPA's LLP/ Robert Fried, CPA
Controller	Joe Kubala
Banking	City National Bank/Michele Gibbons
Insurance	DeWitt Stern Inc.
Legal Counsel	Davis Wright Tremaine LLP/ M. Graham Coleman, Robert Driscoll
Payroll	Castellana Services, Inc.
Production Photographer	Joan Marcus
Theatre Displays	King Displays, Inc.
Transportation	IBA Limousine Inc.
Travel Agent	Tzell Travel/Andi Henig

CREDITS

Scenery by Hudson Scenic Studios, Inc. Costumes by Parsons-Meares, Artur & Tailors, John Kristiansen New York Inc. Lighting by PRG. Sound by Masque Sound. Specialty props by American Foliage and Anything But Costumes. Flame treatment by Turning Star Inc. Uniforms by Jim Korn and Kaufman's Army Navy. Millinery by Lynne Mackey. Special thanks to Bra*Tenders for hosiery and undergarments.

Rehearsed at New 42nd Street Studios.

 THE SHUBERT ORGANIZATION, INC.
Board of Directors

Philip J. Smith Chairman	**Robert E. Wankel** President
Wyche Fowler, Jr.	**John W. Kluge**
Lee J. Seidler	**Michael I. Sovern**

Stuart Subotnick

Elliot Greene Chief Financial Officer	**David Andrews** Senior Vice President – Shubert Ticketing
Juan Calvo Vice President and Controller	**John Darby** Vice President – Facilities
Peter Entin Vice President – Theatre Operations	**Charles Flateman** Vice President – Marketing
Anthony LaMattina Vice President – Audit & Production Finance	**Brian Mahoney** Vice President – Ticket Sales

D.S. Moynihan
Vice President – Creative Projects

CORT THEATRE

House Manager .... Joseph Traina

Fences
SCRAPBOOK

Correspondent: Chris Chalk, "Cory"

Opening Night Gifts: The producers gave us a fantastic gift: A leather-bound copy of the play, including our names and the opening night Playbill information. Wow! What a really classy gift, one that we'll actually keep. At the final performance we hope to sign each others' copies. Denzel gave us a subscription to "The Daily Word," a publication like "Word of the Day," but one that offers an inspirational word, often from Scripture. On recent days we had "teamwork" and "togetherness." There's always something that brings us back to our company and August Wilson's text.

Most Exciting Celebrity Visitors and What They Did/Said: In a single night we had Will Smith, Jada Pinkett Smith, Aretha Franklin, Lenny Kravitz and Matthew Morrison. On various other nights we've had Jerry Bruckheimer, Oprah Winfrey, Alfre Woodard, S. Epatha Merkerson, Eddie Murphy, Halle Berry, Viggo Mortensen and Robert Downey Jr. A lot of them come backstage to visit. A lot of them do not. It's hard to keep track. Courtney Vance, who originated my role on Broadway, contacted me beforehand as an opening night gift from my lady and came opening night. He gave me personal advice to stay loyal to Cory's youth and innocence and the rest will take care of itself. Keep Cory young and present as a 17-year-old. Which is essentially what my director instills, so it's great to have that influence from several directions.

Actors Who Have Done the Most Shows in Their Careers: On Broadway? Stephen, at five. Viola and Denzel have three Broadway shows each and I think the rest of us—Mykelti, Russell and myself—are making our debuts on Broadway.

Special Backstage Ritual: Before every show the cast gathers (and sometimes if Kenny, our director, is in town he joins us) at five minutes and pray together. One person says something special for that day. That keeps us grounded for doing the work and remembering why we do the work. That's where Denzel's gift of "Daily Word" has come in; sometimes we take the word from there and it is always always right on time.

Favorite Moment During Each Performance: We all look forward to the moment when Troy tells his wife that she's supposed to come when he calls, and then he asks his friend Bono, "Don't your wife come when you call?" And Bono just looks away. It's the most well-timed comic moment between the three of them and Stephen's last beat just knocks it out of the ball park. I'm usually doing a quick-change backstage and others are meditating, but we all stop and watch on the monitor. It's one of the best moments in the play, period.

Favorite Off-Site Hangout: We all go to a little bar called 48 right across the street. The food is amazing and they're very good to us.

Favorite Snack Food: Synergy Kombucha—it's an all-natural drink made of fermented mushroom caps and it helps you purify your system. Essentially, it's a five-dollar healthy soda.

Favorite Therapies: I swear by a combination of acupuncture and massage. and for us all I'd say prayer.

Most Memorable Ad-Lib: One night we all had the gremlins. Mykelti Williamson (Gabe) was onstage, and when Lyons said, "Hey Uncle Gabe, where are you goin'?" Mykelti said, "I got my trumpet and...something...I'm just confused." Mykelti kind of left the building for a second. But Lyons saved it by saying, "That's OK, Uncle Gabe, you all right." Very very funny stuff.

Embarrassing Moment: I was answering the phone while putting the football under the chair and I tripped. The ball rolled off the edge of the stage, but an audience member was kind enough to put it back. Backstage they were all like, "What is going on?" "What was so funny?" And I told them, "The audience is helping me out."

Electronic Device Incidents During a Performance: That happens all the time. It's not as bad as I would have thought. There's not so much during the show itself, but at the end it's a sea of red and blue lights and occasionally people take pictures at curtain calls. One time, though, there was a man in the front row with a video camera. He was recording the whole show. He was even leaning to one side to get a better shot! Denzel came backstage and said, "I think someone in the front row is recording the show." They got him at the end.

Memorable Stage Door Fan Encounters: It gets crazy sometimes, especially on weekends.

1. Viola Davis and Denzel Washington at curtain calls on opening night..
2. Child wrangler Alissa Zulvergold with Denzel Washington.
3. Back Row (L-R): guests Idina Menzel, Taye Diggs and Chad Coleman with (L-R): cast members SaCha Stewart-Coleman and Eden Duncan-Smith.

Fences
SCRAPBOOK

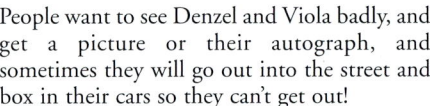

1. Cast members Chris Chalk (*Yearbook* Correspondent) and Mykelti Williamson at The Cellar Bar for the opening night party.
2. Washington and Davis at the premiere.
3. Playwright's family members Azula Wilson and costume designer Constanza Romero.
4. Composer Branford Marsalis and wife Nicole at the cast party.

2009-2010 AWARDS

TONY AWARDS
Best Revival of a Play
Best Leading Actor in a Play
(Denzel Washington)
Best Leading Actress in a Play
(Viola Davis)

OUTER CRITICS CIRCLE AWARDS
Outstanding Revival of a Play
Outstanding Actor in a Play
(Denzel Washington)
Outstanding Actress in a Play
(Viola Davis)

DRAMA DESK AWARDS
Outstanding Featured Actress in a Play
(Viola Davis)
Outstanding Music in a Play
(Branford Marsalis)

THEATRE WORLD AWARD
First Major New York Stage Appearance
(Chris Chalk)

RICHARD SEFF AWARD
Veteran Male Character Actor
(Stephen McKinley Henderson)

People want to see Denzel and Viola badly, and get a picture or their autograph, and sometimes they will go out into the street and box in their cars so they can't get out!

Web Buzz on the Show: We don't do much reading of the reviews and such. We believe in the show and what we are doing. So, I think we are blessed in that we truly just do the work, believe in the work and trust that it will land how it's supposed to land.

Latest Audience Arrivals: Our audiences may be noisy, but they're generally on time. Well, we do start the show like 15 minutes late seating people though.

Fastest Costume Changes: I have a 30-second change from I-3 to I-4, but it's just changing from one shirt and pants to a different shirt and pants. Viola has a change that's much more complicated, and if it's 40 seconds, I'm probably overestimating.

Catchphrases Only the Company Would Recognize: "August Wilson FENCES peace and love....and soooooooul." Also "I'll take it." Also, for a few of us in fight call, Narda, Zaleski, myself and Denzel, there is the great Shakespearean gesture of acting. I'll be teaching a class about it later.

Memorable Directorial Notes: Kenny's main notes were: "Make sure the second act is shorter than the first act," "Tell the truth" and "Let it happen."

Nicknames: Denzel is "D." Viola is "Vi." Mykelti is "T." I'm "Chalk." Russell Hornsby is "Hornsby." And Stephen is..."Stephen."

Coolest Thing About Being in This Show: I think it's the family we have created. Everyone genuinely wants to be at work and talk and laugh and share serious things. It's cool when you go to work and there's genuine love there and no ego. It's inspirational, really. Everyone knows it's a blessing to be a part of this show and we all treat it that way every day, even when we are tired and broken. We give it all that we have. That is special. I have a fractured rib, a numb leg and weird pain in my knee, and others have pains and colds and aches, and we all are still excited to come to work every day. Through the pain and the ailments, we shine as bright as we can to honor the story. Everyone. Every night. Working hard as a family. That is Cool.

Special Thank-You: From the cast, I'd like to say thank you to the people that come out and the Broadway community for welcoming our show so graciously and being receptive to such a gorgeous American story. August Wilson is an amazing artist and we are blessed to share his work with each other, the audience and the universe every night. We are also thankful to bring in people who rarely to never see theatre and allow them the experience of seeing and experiencing their story onstage. Everyone comes for their own reasons and everyone leaves having had a special, personal important experience. That is special and inspirational to be a part of.

Finian's Rainbow

First Preview: October 8, 2009. Opened: October 29, 2009.
Closed January 17, 2010 after 22 Previews and 92 Performances.

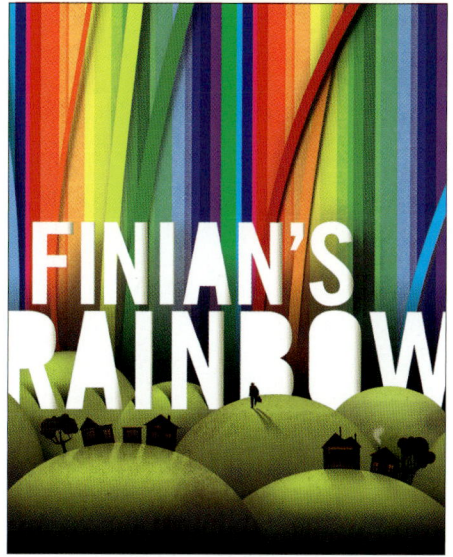

CAST OF CHARACTERS
(in order of appearance)

Sunny	GUY DAVIS
Dottie	TERRI WHITE
Buzz Collins	WILLIAM YOUMANS
Sheriff	BRIAN REDDY
Susan Mahoney	ALINA FAYE
Finian McLonergan	JIM NORTON
Sharon McLonergan	KATE BALDWIN
Woody Mahoney	CHEYENNE JACKSON
Henry	CHRISTOPHER BORGER
Diana	PAIGE SIMUNOVICH
Og	CHRISTOPHER FITZGERALD
Howard	TYRICK WILTEZ JONES
Senator Rawkins	DAVID SCHRAMM
Black Geologist	JOE AARON REID
White Geologist	TAYLOR FREY
Deputy	STEVE SCHEPIS
Bill Rawkins	CHUCK COOPER
Preacher	JAMES STOVALL
Mr. Shears	TIM HARTMAN
Mr. Robust	KEVIN LIGON
First Gospeleer	BERNARD DOTSON
Second Gospeleer	JAMES STOVALL
Third Gospeleer	DEVIN RICHARDS

SHARECROPPERS
(in alphabetical order)

Betty	TANYA BIRL
Meg	MEGGIE CANSLER
George	BERNARD DOTSON
Melinda	LESLIE DONNA FLESNER

Continued on next page

ST. JAMES THEATRE
A JUJAMCYN THEATRE

JORDAN ROTH
President

PAUL LIBIN
Producing Director

JACK VIERTEL
Creative Director

DAVID RICHENTHAL JACK VIERTEL ALAN D. MARKS
MICHAEL SPEYER BERNARD ABRAMS DAVID M. MILCH
STEPHEN MOORE DEBBIE BISNO/MYLA LERNER JUJAMCYN THEATERS

IN ASSOCIATION WITH
MELLY GARCIA JAMIE DEROY JON BIERMAN RICHARD DRIEHAUS
KEVIN SPIRTAS JAY BINDER STAGEVENTURES 2009 LIMITED PARTNERSHIP

PRESENT

FINIAN'S RAINBOW

MUSIC BY
BURTON LANE

LYRICS BY
YIP HARBURG

BOOK BY
YIP HARBURG AND FRED SAIDY

STARRING
JIM NORTON

KATE BALDWIN **CHEYENNE JACKSON**

GUY DAVIS ALINA FAYE BRIAN REDDY

DAVID SCHRAMM TERRI WHITE WILLIAM YOUMANS

WITH
CHUCK COOPER

AND
CHRISTOPHER FITZGERALD

AARON BANTUM	TANYA BIRL	CHRISTOPHER BORGER	MEGGIE CANSLER
BERNARD DOTSON	LESLIE DONNA FLESNER	SARA JEAN FORD	TAYLOR FREY
LISA GAJDA	KEARRAN GIOVANNI	TIM HARTMAN	LAUREN LIM JACKSON
TYRICK WILTEZ JONES	GRASAN KINGSBERRY	KEVIN LIGON	MONICA L. PATTON
JOE AARON REID	DEVIN RICHARDS	STEVE SCHEPIS	RASHIDRA SCOTT
BRIAN SEARS	PAIGE SIMUNOVICH	JAMES STOVALL	ELISA VAN DUYNE

SCENIC DESIGN BY
JOHN LEE BEATTY

COSTUME DESIGN BY
TONI-LESLIE JAMES

LIGHTING DESIGN BY
KEN BILLINGTON

SOUND DESIGN BY
SCOTT LEHRER

HAIR, WIG & MAKEUP DESIGN BY
WENDY PARSON

BOOK ADAPTATION
ARTHUR PERLMAN

ORIGINAL ADAPTATION FOR ENCORES!
DAVID IVES

BASED ON THE PRESENTATION BY
NEW YORK CITY CENTER ENCORES!®

CASTING BY
JAY BINDER/NIKOLE VALLINS

ASSOCIATE CHOREOGRAPHER
PARKER ESSE

PRODUCTION STAGE MANAGER
TRIPP PHILLIPS

ORIGINAL ORCHESTRATIONS BY
ROBERT RUSSELL BENNETT AND DON WALKER

MUSIC COORDINATION BY
SEYMOUR RED PRESS

GENERAL MANAGEMENT
FRANKEL GREEN THEATRICAL MANAGEMENT

TECHNICAL SUPERVISION BY
HUDSON THEATRICAL ASSOCIATES

PRESS REPRESENTATIVE
RICHARD KORNBERG DON SUMMA

ASSOCIATE PRODUCERS
ANDREW HARTMAN AND GAIL LAWRENCE

EXECUTIVE PRODUCER
NICOLE KASTRINOS

MUSIC SUPERVISION AND VOCAL ARRANGEMENTS BY
ROB BERMAN

DIRECTION AND CHOREOGRAPHY BY
WARREN CARLYLE

THE PRODUCERS WISH TO EXPRESS THEIR APPRECIATION TO THE THEATRE DEVELOPMENT FUND FOR ITS SUPPORT OF THIS PRODUCTION.

10/29/09

(Center, L-R): Cheyenne Jackson, Kate Baldwin, Jim Norton with the Cast

Photo by Joan Marcus

Finian's Rainbow

SCENES AND MUSICAL NUMBERS

Time and Place: The Mythical State of Missitucky, 1940s.

ACT ONE

OVERTURE .... Orchestra
Scene 1: The Meetin' Place in Rainbow Valley, Missitucky
  "This Time of the Year" .... Sharecroppers
  "How Are Things in Glocca Morra?" .... Sharon
  "Look to the Rainbow" .... Sharon, Finian, Woody and Sharecroppers
Scene 2: The Meetin' Place, four hours later
  "Old Devil Moon" .... Woody and Sharon
Scene 3: The Colonial Estate of Senator Rawkins, the next morning
Scene 4: The Meetin' Place, late the following afternoon
  "How Are Things in Glocca Morra?" (Reprise) .... Sharon
  "Something Sort of Grandish" .... Og and Sharon
  "If This Isn't Love" .... Woody, Sharon, Finian and Sharecroppers
  "Something Sort of Grandish" (Reprise) .... Og, Henry and Diana
Scene 5: The Meetin' Place, the next morning
  "Necessity" .... Dottie, Women and Sunny
  "That Great 'Come-and-Get-It' Day" .... Woody, Sharon, Preacher, Henry and Sharecroppers

ACT TWO

ENTR'ACTE .... Orchestra
Scene 1: The Meetin' Place, Sunday, a few weeks later
  "When the Idle Poor Become the Idle Rich" .... Finian, Sharon and Sharecroppers
  "Old Devil Moon" (Reprise) .... Woody and Sharon
  "Dance of the Golden Crock" .... Susan and Sunny
Scene 2: A wooded section of the Hills, two weeks later
  "The Begat" .... The Three Gospeleers and Bill
Scene 3: The Meetin' Place
  "Look to the Rainbow" (Reprise) .... Woody, Sharon and Sharecroppers
Scene 4: The Meetin' Place, just before dawn the next morning
  "When I'm Not Near the Girl I Love" .... Og
  Finale: "How Are Things in Glocca Morra?" (Reprise) .... Woody, Sharon and Company

ORCHESTRA

Conductor: ROB BERMAN
Associate Conductor: DAVID GURSKY
Assistant Conductor: JOSHUA CLAYTON

Violins: SUZANNE ORNSTEIN (Concertmistress), MAURA GIANNINI, KRISTINA MUSSER, MINEKO YAJIMA
Violas: RICHARD BRICE, SHELLEY HOLLAND-MORITZ
Cellos: ROGER SHELL, DEBORAH ASSAEL
Harp: ANNA REINERSMAN
Woodwinds: STEVEN KENYON, DENNIS ANDERSON, JAMES ERCOLE, KENNETH ADAMS, JOHN WINDER
Trumpets: DAVE STAHL, KEN RAMPTON
Trombones: WAYNE GOODMAN, ROBERT SUTTMANN
French Horns: NANCY BILLMANN, LEISE ANSCHUETZ BALLOU
Keyboards: DAVID GURSKY, JOSHUA CLAYTON
Bass: JOHN BEAL
Drums and Percussion: BILLY MILLER

Original Dance Music Arrangements: TRUDE RITTMANN
Original Vocal Arrangements: LYN MURRAY

Music Coordinator: SEYMOUR RED PRESS
Additional Orchestrations: LARRY MOORE
Keyboard Programmer: RANDY COHEN
Music Preparation: BRIAN ALLAN HOBBS

Cast Continued

Arlene .... SARA JEAN FORD
Jack .... TAYLOR FREY
Rose .... LISA GAJDA
Suzanne .... KEARRAN GIOVANNI
John .... TIM HARTMAN
Howard .... TYRICK WILTEZ JONES
Frank .... KEVIN LIGON
Charlotte .... MONICA L. PATTON
Jesse .... JOE AARON REID
Eugene .... DEVIN RICHARDS
Sam .... STEVE SCHEPIS
Dolores .... RASHIDRA SCOTT
Willie .... JAMES STOVALL

SWINGS
LAUREN LIM JACKSON, GRASAN KINGSBERRY, ELISA VAN DUYNE

PARTIAL COVERS
BERNARD DOTSON, TAYLOR FREY, KEVIN LIGON, JOE AARON REID, STEVE SCHEPIS

DANCE CAPTAIN
ELISA VAN DUYNE

ASSISTANT DANCE CAPTAIN
GRASAN KINGSBERRY

UNDERSTUDIES
For Finian McLonergan:
WILLIAM YOUMANS, TIM HARTMAN
Sharon McLonergan:
SARA JEAN FORD, ELISA VAN DUYNE
Woody Mahoney:
TAYLOR FREY, BRIAN SEARS
Og:
BRIAN SEARS, STEVE SCHEPIS
Susan Mahoney:
LESLIE DONNA FLESNER, LISA GAJDA
Senator Rawkins:
KEVIN LIGON
Bill:
JAMES STOVALL, BERNARD DOTSON
Buzz Collins, Sheriff:
KEVIN LIGON, BRIAN SEARS
Sunny:
GRASAN KINGSBERRY, DEVIN RICHARDS
Dottie:
RASHIDRA SCOTT, LAUREN LIM JACKSON
Henry and Diana:
AARON BANTUM

Finian's Rainbow

Jim Norton
Finian McLonergan

Kate Baldwin
Sharon McLonergan

Cheyenne Jackson
Woody Mahoney

Christopher Fitzgerald
Og

Chuck Cooper
Bill Rawkins

Guy Davis
Sunny

Alina Faye
Susan Mahoney

Brian Reddy
Sheriff

David Schramm
Senator Rawkins

Terri White
Dottie

William Youmans
Buzz Collins

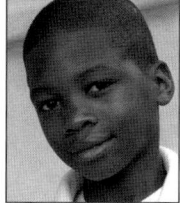
Aaron Bantum
u/s Henry, Diana

Tanya Birl
Betty

Christopher Borger
Henry

Meggie Cansler
Meg

Bernard Dotson
*George,
First Gospeleer*

Leslie Donna Flesner
Melinda

Sara Jean Ford
Arlene

Taylor Frey
*Jack,
White Geologist*

Lisa Gajda
Rose

Kearran Giovanni
Suzanne

Tim Hartman
John, Mr. Shears

Lauren Lim Jackson
Swing

Tyrick Wiltez Jones
Howard

Grasan Kingsberry
*Swing,
Asst. Dance Captain*

Kevin Ligon
Frank, Mr. Robust

Monica L. Patton
Charlotte

Joe Aaron Reid
*Jesse,
Black Geologist*

Devin Richards
*Eugene,
Third Gospeleer*

Steve Schepis
Sam, Deputy

Rashidra Scott
Dolores

Brian Sears
*u/s Woody Mahoney,
Og, Buzz Collins,
Sheriff*

Paige Simunovich
Diana

James Stovall
*Willie, Preacher,
Second Gospeleer*

Elisa Van Duyne
Swing

Finian's Rainbow

Burton Lane
Music

Yip Harburg
Book and Lyrics

Fred Saidy
Book

Warren Carlyle
Director/Choreographer

Rob Berman
Music Supervisor and Vocal Arrangements

John Lee Beatty
Scenic Design

Ken Billington
Lighting Design

Scott Lehrer
Sound Design

Jay Binder
Associate Producer, Casting

Nikole Vallins
Casting

Seth Sklar-Heyn
Associate Director

Robert Russell Bennett
Original Orchestrations

Seymour Red Press
Music Coordinator

Richard Frankel, Frankel Green Theatrical Management
General Management

Laura Green, Frankel Green Theatrical Management
General Management

Neil A. Mazzella/Hudson Theatrical Associates
Technical Supervisor

Richard Kornberg & Associates
Press Representative

Jack Viertel
Producer

Michael Speyer
Producer

Bernard Abrams
Producer

Rocco Landesman, Jujamcyn Theaters
Producer

Jordan Roth, Jujamcyn Theaters
Producer

Jamie deRoy
Associate Producer

2009-2010 AWARD

DRAMA DESK AWARD
Outstanding Featured Actor in a Musical (Christopher Fitzgerald)

BOX OFFICE
(L-R): Vincent Sclafani, Vincent Siniscalchi, George Licata

STAGE MANAGEMENT
(L-R): Thomas Gates (Assistant Stage Manager), Tripp Phillips (Production Stage Manager, Jason Hindelang (Stage Manager), Alissa R. Zulvergold (Child Wrangler)

Finian's Rainbow

CREW

Front Row (L-R): Shanah-Ann Kendall, Anna Hoffman, Alison Wadsworth, Therese Ducey, Samantha Lawrence, Cailin Anderson, Charlie Catanese, Del Miskie

Second Row (L-R): Richard Dunning, Emile LaFargue, Sandy Paradise

Third Row (L-R): Eric Castaldo, Al Sayers, Fraser Weir, Joe Lenihan, Sue Pelkofer, Bob Miller, Barry Doss, "Hello" Dolly Williams, Joshua Burns, Shana Albery, Stacey Haynes

Back Row (L-R): Dave Brown, Ryan McDonough, Tim McDonough Sr., Tim McDonough Jr.

FRONT OF HOUSE STAFF

Front Row (L-R): Donna VanDerlinden, Catherine Junior, Margaret McElroy, Maura Thompson, Amy Wolk, Lane Beauchamp

Second Row (L-R): Kendra MacDuffie, Heather Jewels, James Zannelli, Katie Siegmund, Julia Furay

Third Row (L-R): Cynthia Lopiano, Leonard Baron, Andrew Mackay, Joel Briel

Back Row (L-R): Eddie Dunagan, Jeff Hubbard, Ray Siegel

ORCHESTRA

Back Row (L-R): Ken Adams, Dennis Anderson, David Gursky, Steve Kenyon, Kristina Musser, Billy Miller, John Winder

Second Row (L-R): Rob Berman (Conductor), Nancy Billmann, Leise Anschuetz Ballou

Front Row (L-R): Ken Rampton, Wayne Goodman, David Stahl, Maura Giannini, Richard Brice, Josh Clayton, Anna Reinersman, Roger Shell, John Beal

Not Pictured: Deborah Assael, James Ercole, Shelly Holland-Moritz, Suzanne Ornstein, Bob Suttmann, Mineko Yajima

Photos by Brian Mapp

The Playbill Broadway Yearbook 2009-2010

Finian's Rainbow

STAFF FOR FINIAN'S RAINBOW

GENERAL MANAGEMENT
FRANKEL GREEN THEATRICAL MANAGEMENT
Richard Frankel   Laura Green
Joe Watson   Leslie Ledbetter

COMPANY MANAGER
Kathy Lowe
Associate Company Manager ....Maia Sutton

TECHNICAL SUPERVISION
HUDSON THEATRICAL ASSOCIATES
Neil A. Mazzella
Sam Ellis   Patrick Sullivan   Irene Wang

GENERAL PRESS REPRESENTATIVE
RICHARD KORNBERG & ASSOCIATES
Richard Kornberg   Don Summa
Billy Zavelson   Tommy Wesely

CASTING
JAY BINDER CASTING
Jay Binder CSA
Jack Bowdan CSA, Mark Brandon, Sara Schatz CSA,
Nikole Vallins, Karen Young, Patrick Bell

Production Stage Manager	**Tripp Phillips**
Stage Manager	Jason Hindelang
Assistant Stage Manager	Thomas J. Gates
Associate Director	Seth Sklar-Heyn
Associate Choreographer	Parker Esse
Assistant Choreographer	Angie Canuel
Dance Captain	Elisa Van Duyne
Assistant Dance Captain	Grasan Kingsberry
Magic & Illusions Consultant	Matthew Holtzclaw
Dialect Coach	Deborah Hecht
Assistant Scenic Designer	Kacie Hultgren
Associate Costume Designer	Neno Russell
Assistant Costume Designers	Nicky Tobolski, Christopher Mueller, Bonnie McCoy
Assistants to Ms. James	Cailin Anderson, Josh Quinn
Associate Lighting Designer	Anthony Pearson
Assistant Lighting Designer	Jonathan Spencer
Assistant Sound Designer	Ashley Hanson
Assistant Wig & Hair Designer	Jorie Mars Malan
Company Management Assistant	Katie Pope
Company Management Intern	Jason Styres
Production Carpenter	Donald J. Oberpriller
Deck Automation Carpenter	Ryan McDonough
Flyman	Dave Brown
Production Electrician	Scott De Verna
Head Electrician	Fraser Weir
Moving Light Programmer	Hillary Knox
Front Light Head	Sandy Paradise
Follow Spot Operators	Susan Pelkofer, Bob Miller
Production Sound Engineer	Carin Ford
Deck Sound Man	Joe Lenihan
Production Property Supervisor	Joseph P. Harris, Jr.
Head Properties	Eric Castaldo
Production Wardrobe Supervisor	Shana Albery
Assistant Wardrobe Supervisor	Dolly Williams
Dressers	Cailin Anderson, Joshua Burns, Charlie Catanese, Barry Doss, Samantha Lawrence, Del Miskie
Wig & Hair Supervisor	Shanah-Ann Kendall
Assistant Wig & Hair Supervisor	Anna Hoffman
Hair Stylist	Therese Ducey
Child Wrangler	Alissa Zulvergold
Tutoring	On Location Education/Sonya Finkel
Production Assistants	John Bantay, Andrew Zachary Cohen, John Murdock
Physical Therapy Services	PhysioArts/Jennifer Green
Company Massage Therapist	Russ Beasley
Associate Music Director	David Gursky
Assistant Conductor	Joshua Clayton
Additional Orchestrations	Larry Moore
Music Coordinator	Seymour Red Press
Keyboard Programmer	Randy Cohen
Assistant Keyboard Programmer	Bryan Crook
Music Preparation	Brian Allan Hobbs
Rehearsal Pianist	Mark Mitchell
Rehearsal Drummer	Rich Rosenzweig
Assistant to Mr. Richenthal	Emma Kingaby
Intern to Mr. Richenthal	Julia Sternberg
Assistant to Mr. Viertel	Marisol Rosa-Shapiro
Advertising	Spotco/Drew Hodges, Jim Edwards, Tom Greenwald, Jim Aquino, Stacey Maya
Marketing	Type A Marketing/Anne Rippey, Nick Pramik, Nina Bergelson
Internet Marketing & Web Design	Art Meets Commerce/Jim Glaub, Ryan Greer, Laurie Connor, Kevin Keating, Brad Coffman, Mark Seeley
Merchandising	SpotCo Merchandising/James Decker
Insurance	De Witt Stern Group, Inc.
Legal Counsel	Franklin, Weinrib, Rudell & Vasallo/Dan Wasser
Banking	JP Morgan Chase Bank
Payroll Service	Castellana Services, Inc.
Accounting	Fried & Kowgios Partners, CPAs, LLP
Merchandising	Dewynters, Ltd.
Theatre Displays	King Displays, Inc.
Rehearsal Space	Snapple Theatre Center, Alvin Ailey Dance Center, Ripley/Grier Studios
Group Sales	Theater Direct Group Sales 1.800.BROADWAY

FRANKEL GREEN THEATRICAL MANAGEMENT

Finance Director	Michael Naumann
Assistant to Mr. Frankel	Heidi Libby
Assistant to Ms. Green	Joshua A. Saletnik
Assistant Finance Director	Sue Bartlett
Finance Associate	Heather Allen
Information Technology Manager	Roddy Pimentel
Director of Business Affairs	Michael Sinder
Business Affairs Assistant	Dario Dalla Lasta
Booking	On the Road Booking, LLC/Simma Levine, President
Office Manager	Emily Wright
Receptionists	Rebekah Hughston, Allison Raines
Interns	Danielle Barchetto, Alex Parra, Alex Peyser, Claudia Stuart, James Teal, Laura Valenti, Shannon Winter

The producers would like to acknowledge and thank the parents of each of the juvenile actors in *Finian's Rainbow*: Precious Ballard, Melissa and Joseph Borger, Debbie and Chet Simunovich.

Makeup provided by M•A•C Cosmetics

CREDITS AND ACKNOWLEDGEMENTS
Scenery and automation by Hudson Scenic Studio. Lighting equipment from PRG Lighting. Sound equipment from PRG Audio. Props provided by Spoon Group. Costumes constructed by Barbara Matera Ltd. Menswear by House of Savoia. Additional costumes by Adrienne Wells, Marci Linton, D.L. Cerney and David Samuel Menkes Custom Leatherwear. Custom fabric painting by Jeff Fender. Fabric dyeing by Dye-Namix. Vintage reproduction denim by Sugar Cane Selvage Denim. Millinery by Arnold Levine and Christopher Mueller. Custom shoes by T. O. Dey. Additional footwear by Capezio Dance Theatre Shop and Worldtone Dance Shoes. Special thanks to David Leong, Maura L. Cravey and Kenann Quander.

JUJAMCYN THEATERS

JORDAN ROTH
President

PAUL LIBIN	**JACK VIERTEL**
Producing Director	Creative Director
DANIEL ADAMIAN	**JENNIFER HERSHEY**
General Manager	Director of Operations
MEREDITH VILLATORE	**JERRY ZAKS**
Chief Financial Officer	Resident Director

STAFF FOR THE ST. JAMES THEATRE

Manager	Daniel Adamian
Associate Manager	Jeff Hubbard
Treasurer	Vincent Sclafani
Carpenter	Timothy McDonough Jr.
Propertyman	Timothy McDonough
Electrician	Albert Sayers

Christopher Fitzgerald as Og

Photo by Joan Marcus

Finian's Rainbow
Scrapbook

Correspondent: Steve Schepis, "Deputy"
Opening Night Gifts: Cheyenne commissioned an artist to create a rendering of Kate and him based on a photo taken of the "Old Devil Moon" scene. Cheyenne then took the finished artwork (beautiful and amazingly accurate) and turned it into opening night cards for all of us. Ladies and Gentlemen, there you have it: Cheyenne Jackson, not just a pretty face, he's creative, too! And talented, of course!

Our talented music director Rob Berman definitely has a certain grace and finesse with the conducting baton. Although, he did have one particular recurring problem of thinking, "Glocca Morra" but speaking, "Guacamole." Thus, as an opening night gift, we each received a jar of "Glocca Morra Guacamole."

Most Exciting Celebrity Visitor: The most exciting visitor who came to the St. James was Arlene Anderson (married name: Arlene Skutch). Arlene was in the ensemble of the original Broadway production of *Finian's Rainbow*, more than sixty years ago!

Who Got the Gypsy Robe: The beautiful and talented Lisa Gajda received the Gypsy Robe. This production marks her fourteenth show on Broadway! She is, without a doubt, the most humble and hilarious veteran of the Broadway stage. If you don't think that self-deprecation is an effective form of comedy, seek out Lisa. She will teach you a thing or two.

Actors Who Perform the Most Roles in This Show: Tim Hartman and Kevin Ligon not only played sharecroppers, but also had the duties of portraying the comical characters, Shears and Robust. After the curtain comes down on Act I, Tim and Kevin would have to scramble down to the wig room to get the 'old man character face' applied: white paint in their eyebrows and sideburns, makeup to age their faces, and, of course, the ever popular fake moustache. They would then rush up six flights of stairs to the ensemble men's dressing room to complete the look with top hats, tails, white gloves, and canes (furnished by our brilliant costume designer Toni-Leslie James) and appear on stage at the top of Act II. After their fast (and funny) five minute scene, they had to hurry offstage to take off the makeup and the costumes and appear onstage twenty minutes later, once again, as sharecroppers.

Favorite Moment During Each Performance: Collectively, our favorite moment during the show was the end of Act I when hundreds of credit slips would rain down from the sky. It was exhilarating and also somewhat dangerous. A piece of paper spiraling toward earth and accelerating at the rate of gravity can leave a nasty paper cut.

Favorite In-Theatre Gathering Place: An hour before curtain, the most popular gathering place would actually be onstage. Here you would find dancers performing plies and tendus at the barre and releasing their aching muscles on foam rollers. Oftentime, you would spot a swarm of dancers huddled in the corner gawking at Alina Faye (Susan the Silent) and her beautiful, long, fluid lines. You could also

1. The cast takes bows on the St. James Theatre stage on opening night.
2. Chuck Cooper ("Bill Rawkins") at the cast party at Bryant Park Grill.
3. Jim Norton ("Finian") at the premiere.

find Jim Norton (Finian) warming up his voice with a series of tongue twisters, and Cheyenne Jackson (Woody) practicing Yoga and Pilates.

Favorite Off-Site Hangout: The cast oftentimes went to Angus McIndoe after the performance. Its proximity to the theatre (right next door!) made it a popular hangout spot. We gathered at Angus to celebrate the success of our first preview. It is also where Terri White's (Dottie) reception was held following her wedding ceremony, which took place on the stage of the St. James!

Favorite Snack Foods: In order to bring a snack into the St. James it must fit at least one of the following criteria: 1) it contains an absurd amount of sugar 2) chocolate is a main ingredient 3) the cooking method: DEEP FRYING! That being said, the crew room was always filled with goodies: donuts, potato chips, cookies, candy… et cetera. On occasion, Chris Fitzgerald (Og), would bring in donuts that were jelly-filled, deep fried, and then dipped in sugar. If it clogs the arteries and warms the soul, it was in that crew room and we were eating it. And like true Americans, we were NOT exercising proper portion control. Consequently, we are all looking forward to the inevitable: adult-onset diabetes.

Mascots: Kearran Giovanni announced to the cast a couple weeks into the run of the show that she was pregnant! As the weeks flew by, she got bustier and bustier (as one does when one is pregnant). By the time we closed, her bosom should have had its own zip code. We didn't have one, but two big beautiful mascots.

Favorite Therapy: An amazing amount of Ricola have been consumed during the run of the show. A plethora of bulk-size containers of these 'vocal life savers' are stored in the stage management office.

Most Memorable Ad-Lib: "You tell 'em, Mama." Uttered from the lips of Christopher

Finian's Rainbow
SCRAPBOOK

1. Cast members arrive at Bryant Park Grill for the cast party.
2. Kate Baldwin ("Sharon") and Cheyenne Jackson ("Woody") at the Ailey Studios to meet the New York press corps.
3. Terri White ("Dottie") on opening night.

Photos by Aubrey Reuben

Borger (Henry). This ad-lib (which is spoken during the song "Necessity") snuck into the show during rehearsals. During previews, as Chris became more and more comfortable with his role, the ad-lib got louder and louder. Eventually, our book adapter Arthur Perlman penned the ad-lib into the official script. Perhaps Christopher is a young, budding playwright.

Record Number of Cell Phone Rings, Cell Phone Photos or Texting Incidents During a Performance: Fortunately for us, the large majority of our audience was comprised of senior citizens. Texting on Blackberries and iPhones doesn't seem to be an issue with senior citizens. Unfortunately, falling asleep during the performance is an issue.

Memorable Audience Departure: At one performance, there was an elderly lady sitting third row center. Was she wearing a gigantic, white, furry hat? Yes. Did the hat make her look like a powdered donut? Clearly. Was it distracting? Very. Did she decide to get up and leave during the curtain call? Do I even have to answer that question?

Busiest Day at the Box Office: The busiest day at the box office was Tuesday, December 29, 2009. At that night's performance we enjoyed a standing-room-only audience. Two days later, the producers announced that we were closing. Oh, the irony.

Actor Who Wore the Heaviest/Hottest Costume: The female dancers wore very heavy (and beautiful) dresses in the show. Because of the weight of the dresses, performing clean pirouettes was extremely difficult. You could often find Tanya Birl and Lauren Lim Jackson on stage before the show punching out a set of Pilates 100's. Therefore, all the girls had trim and fit waistlines.

Actor Who Wore the Least: The award for 'most scantily-clad' definitely goes to our beloved dance captain, Elisa Van Duyne. During the opening of Act II ("When the Idle Poor Become The Idle Rich"), she portrayed a beauty pageant contestant. And let's just put it this way: it was not the eveningwear portion of the competition.

Orchestra Member Who Played the Most Consecutive Performances Without a Sub: Josh Clayton (Keyboard II) not only has the distinguished honor of playing the most consecutive shows, but is also the only orchestra member who (drumroll, please) wasn't in the pit. That's right, folks: Because the orchestra was so large, they couldn't fit both Josh and his keyboard in the pit. So instead, he was placed in the basement where the cast members made their quick changes. The downside: He didn't get to mingle with the orchestra members until intermission. The upside: Half-naked dancers running around. Need I say more?

Best In-House Parody Lyrics: Some things are nurture, and others are just nature. In the showstopper, "Necessity," Terri White (Dottie), Monica Patton and Rashidra Scott's intrinsic, soulful ability was put to good use. The skinny white girls in the number, Meggie Cansler and Sara Jean Ford (while being brilliant vocalists in their own right) felt a tad bit like…well, like they were in "someone else's high school," if you know what I mean. In jest, they replaced Harburg's lyric, "Sister, you're so right" with, "Sister, we're so white." Gotta love a funny, white chick!

Memorable Directorial Note: Warren's response to a cast member suggesting an alternate staging to the scene: "Thank you, but I like what I am doing."

Understudy Anecdote: The day of the invited dress rehearsal (the very first time we performed in front of a full house) Alina Faye (Susan the Silent) became violently ill with pneumonia. At this point, no understudy rehearsal had been conducted and yet, Leslie Donna Flesner stepped into the role with grace and poise and a star was born!

Nicknames: Cast members Leslie Donna Flesner, Brian Sears, and Joe Aaron Reid, who spent many nights together at The GAF shooting darts and downing beer, affectionately referred to themselves as "The Three Muskaqueers." Clever? Yes. Accurate? Hardly. As far as we know, none of them are expert swordsmen and only one of them is actually gay.

Sweethearts Within the Company: While we truly all love each other, it's the kind of love one has for a sibling. And last time I checked, incest is illegal in New York.

Ghostly Encounters Backstage: Ghostly encounters? Maybe not. But, both the Patti LuPone and Tyne Daly productions of *Gypsy* were housed in the St. James. We all felt their presence in the theatre encouraging us to sing with resonance in the "mask" and with the widest, most diva-like vibrato possible.

God of Carnage

First Preview: February 28, 2009. Opened: March 22, 2009.
Still running as of May 31, 2010.

CAST
(in alphabetical order)

Veronica	CHRISTINE LAHTI
Annette	ANNIE POTTS
Alan	JIMMY SMITS
Michael	KEN STOTT

STANDBYS

For Alan, Michael:
BRUCE McCARTY
For Annette, Veronica:
CHARLOTTE MAIER

Ken Stott is appearing with the support of Actors' Equity Association pursuant to an exchange program between American Equity and UK Equity.

BERNARD B. JACOBS THEATRE
242 West 45th Street
A Shubert Organization Theatre
Philip J. Smith, *Chairman* Robert E. Wankel, *President*

Robert Fox David Pugh & Dafydd Rogers Stuart Thompson
Scott Rudin Jon B. Platt The Weinstein Company
The Shubert Organization

Present

Christine Lahti
Annie Potts
Jimmy Smits
Ken Stott

God of Carnage

by
Yasmina Reza

translated by
Christopher Hampton

Scenic and Costume Design	Lighting Design	Music
Mark Thompson	Hugh Vanstone	Gary Yershon
Sound Design	Casting	Production Stage Manager
Simon Baker/Christopher Cronin	Daniel Swee	Jill Cordle
Press Representative	Production Management	General Management
Boneau/Bryan-Brown	Aurora Productions	STP / David Turner

Directed By
Matthew Warchus

The Producers wish to express their appreciation to
Theatre Development Fund for its support of this production.

11/16/09

(L-R): Jimmy Smits, Annie Potts, Christine Lahti, Ken Stott

Photo by Joan Marcus

God of Carnage

Christine Lahti
Veronica

Annie Potts
Annette

Jimmy Smits
Alan

Ken Stott
Michael

Charlotte Maier
Standby Annette, Veronica

Bruce McCarty
Standby Alan, Michael

Yasmina Reza
Playwright

Christopher Hampton
Translator

Matthew Warchus
Director

Mark Thompson
Set and Costume Design

Hugh Vanstone
Lighting Design

Simon Baker
Sound Design

Christopher Cronin
Sound Design

Beatrice Terry
Associate Director

Robert Fox
Producer

Stuart Thompson
Producer

Scott Rudin
Producer

Jon B. Platt
Producer

Bob Weinstein, The Weinstein Company
Producer

Harvey Weinstein, The Weinstein Company
Producer

Philip J. Smith, Chairman, The Shubert Organization
Producer

Robert E. Wankel, President, The Shubert Organization
Producer

Jeff Daniels
Alan

Hope Davis
Annette

James Gandolfini
Michael

Marcia Gay Harden
Veronica

Dylan Baker
Alan

Orlagh Cassidy
Standby for Annette, Veronica

Jeff Daniels
Michael

Lucy Liu
Annette

Janet McTeer
Veronica

The Playbill Broadway Yearbook 2009-2010

God of Carnage

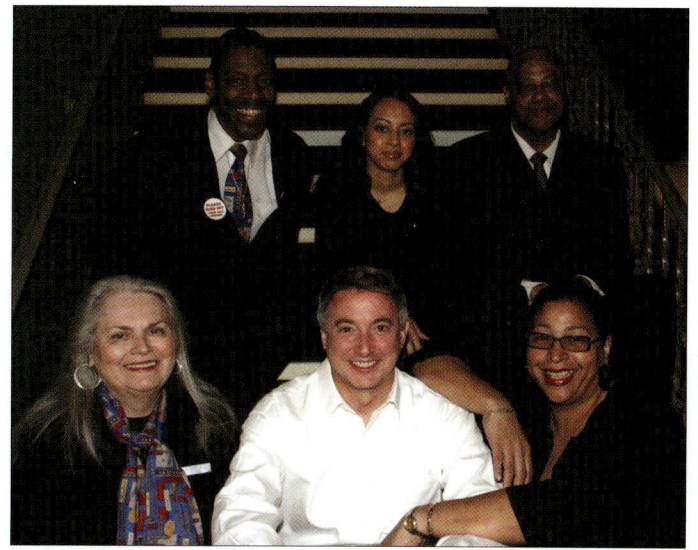

FRONT OF HOUSE STAFF
Front Row (L-R): Patanne McEvoy, John Minore, Martha Rodriguez

Back Row (L-R): Al Peay, Natalie Escalera, Billy Mitchell

Photos by Brian Mapp

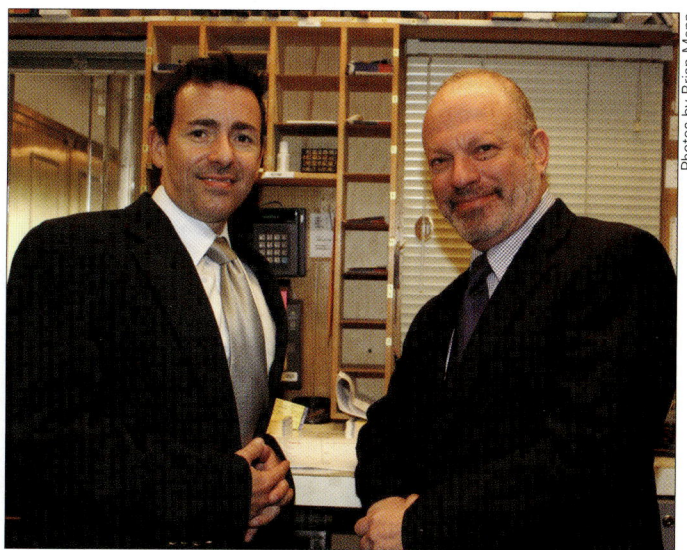

BOX OFFICE
(L-R): Jules Ochoa, Michael Kohlbrenner

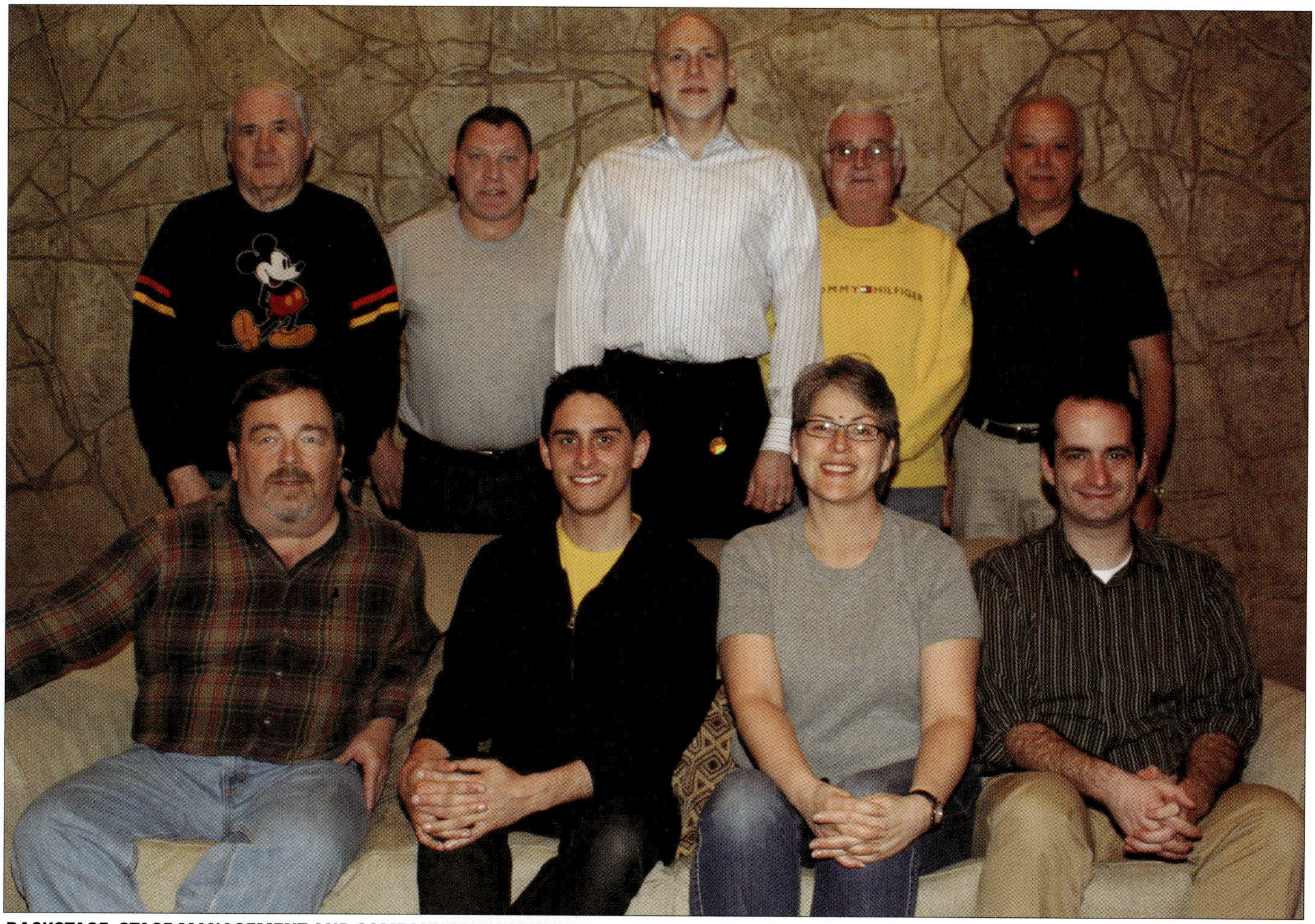

BACKSTAGE, STAGE MANAGEMENT AND COMPANY MANAGEMENT
Front Row (L-R): Tom Ferguson, Justin Scribner, Jill Cordle, Doug Gaeta

Back Row (L-R): Herbert Messing, Michael Van Praagh, Chip White, Terry O'Conner, Alfred Ricci

God of Carnage
Scrapbook

Correspondent: Jill Cordle, Production Stage Manager
Anniversary Parties and/or Gifts: We had a lovely holiday party between shows just before Christmas. We gathered in the basement for a good meal and conversation.
Most Exciting Celebrity Visitor: Gloria Steinem
Actors Who Have Done the Most Shows: Ken Stott (most West End productions) Christine Lahti (most Broadway productions).
Special Backstage Ritual: Actors being called "to the woodshed" to run lines from top of the show (every performance).
Favorite Moment During Each Performance: Vomit.
Favorite In-Theatre Gathering Place: Basement for brunch every Sunday.
Favorite Off-Site Hangout: Bar Centrale.
Favorite Snack Food: Chicken-in-a-Biskit.
Favorite Therapy: Singers Saving Grace throat spray.

New cast members (L-R): Ken Stott, Christine Lahti, Annie Potts and Jimmy Smits at Etcetera Etcetera restaurant December 1, 2009 to meet the press.

STAFF FOR GOD OF CARNAGE

GENERAL MANAGEMENT
STUART THOMPSON PRODUCTIONS
Stuart Thompson
David Turner   James Triner

COMPANY MANAGER
Chris Morey

PRODUCTION MANAGEMENT
AURORA PRODUCTIONS
Gene O'Donovan, W. Benjamin Heller II,
Rachel Sherbill, Melissa Mazdra, Amy Merlino Coey,
Amanda Raymond, Graham Forden, Liza Luxenberg

PRESS REPRESENTATIVE
BONEAU/BRYAN-BROWN
Chris Boneau   Susanne Tighe
Christine Olver

Production Stage Manager	Jill Cordle
Stage Manager	Kenneth J. McGee
Associate Director	Beatrice Terry
Associate Scenic Designer	Nancy Thun
Associate Costume Designer	Daryl A. Stone
Associate Lighting Designer	Ted Mather
Vocal Coach	Deborah Hecht
Makeup Consultant	Judy Chin
Production Electricians	Randall Zaibek, James Fedigan
Production Properties Coordinator	Denise J. Grillo
Production Sound	Brien Brannigan
Wardrobe Supervisor	Kay Grunder
Dresser	Chip White
Assistants to the Lighting Designer	Zack Brown, Michael Megliola
Production Assistants	Nathan K. Claus, Annette Verga-Lagier
RADA Trainee Assistant Director	Caroline (CJay) Ranger
General Management Assistants	Megan E. Curren, Geo Karapetyan, Brittany Levasseur
General Management Interns	Bridget Reddington, Erin Byrne
Casting Associate	Camille Hickman
Assistant to Mr. Fox	Sarah Richardson
Assistant to Mr. Thompson	Christopher Taggart
Assistant to Mr. Rudin	Kevin Graham-Caso
Assistant to Mr. Platt	Terrie Lootens
Banking	City National Bank/Michele Gibbons
Payroll	Castellana Services, Inc.
Accountant	Fried & Kowgios CPA's LLP/ Robert Fried, CPA
Controller	Joe Kubala
Insurance Broker	Stockbridge Risk Management/ Neil Goldstein
Insurance	DeWitt Stern Inc.
Legal Counsel	Davis Wright Tremaine LLP/ M. Graham Coleman, Robert Driscoll
Advertising	Serino Coyne Inc./ Greg Corradetti, Robert Jones, Sean Pomposello, Danielle Boyle
Interactive Marketing Agency	Situation Interactive/ Jenn Elston, John Lanasa
Production Photographer	Joan Marcus
Annie Potts Headshot	Robert Ascroft
Theatre Displays	King Displays, Inc.
Transportation	IBA Limousine Inc.

STAFF FOR DAVID PUGH LIMITED

Chairman	Michael Medwin
Directors	David Pugh, Dafydd Rogers, George Biggs
PA to the Directors	Jane Allen
Accounts	Nick Payne
Casting	Sarah Bird
Dramaturg	Ruth Little
Associate Producer	Mark Jenkyns
Executive Store Manager	Stewart Pugh

CREDITS
Scenery by Miraculous Engineering. Props by Luca Cristani. Floor by Hudson Scenic Studios, Inc. Lighting by Production Resource Group. Sound by Sound Associates. Special Effect Machine by Rorschach PropFX. Custom suit for James Gandolfini by Giliberto Tailors. Makeup provided by M•A•C. BlackBerry devices courtesy of BlackBerry. English Harbour Rum courtesy of Antigua Distillery Ltd. Eyeglasses by Julio Santiago at Artsee Eyewear. Flowers supplied by George Vallo/Portafiori Flowers. Rehearsed at New 42nd Street Studios.

Souvenir merchandise designed and created by The Araca Group.

 **THE SHUBERT ORGANIZATION, INC.**
Board of Directors

Philip J. Smith Chairman	**Robert E. Wankel** President
Wyche Fowler, Jr.	**John W. Kluge**
Lee J. Seidler	**Michael I. Sovern**

Stuart Subotnick

Elliot Greene Chief Financial Officer	**David Andrews –** Senior Vice President Shubert Ticketing
Juan Calvo Vice President and Controller	**John Darby** Vice President – Facilities
Peter Entin Vice President – Theatre Operations	**Charles Flateman** Vice President – Marketing
Anthony LaMattina Vice President – Audit & Production Finance	**Brian Mahoney** Vice President – Ticket Sales

D.S. Moynihan
Vice President – Creative Projects

House Manager ....William Mitchell

Guys and Dolls

First Preview: February 5, 2009. Opened: March 1, 2009.
Closed June 14, 2009 after 28 Previews and 121 Performances.

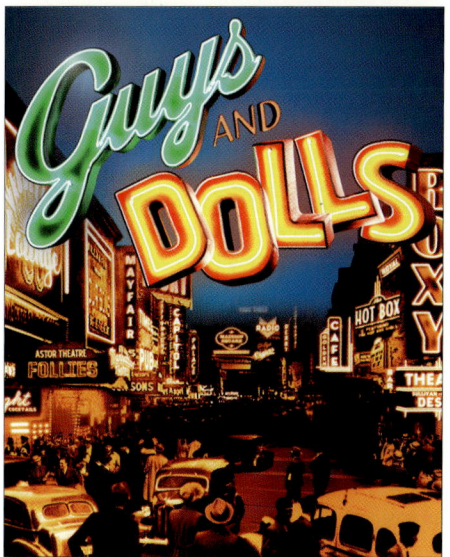

CAST
(in order of appearance)

Nicely-Nicely Johnson	TITUSS BURGESS
Benny Southstreet	STEVE ROSEN
Rusty Charlie	SPENCER MOSES
Sarah Brown	KATE JENNINGS GRANT
Agatha	ANDREA CHAMBERLAIN
Martha	JESSICA RUSH
Calvin	WILLIAM RYALL
Arvide Abernathy	JIM ORTLIEB
Harry the Horse	JIM WALTON
Lt. Brannigan	ADAM LeFEVRE
Nathan Detroit	OLIVER PLATT
Angie the Ox	GRAHAM ROWAT
Society Max	JAMES HARKNESS
Liver Lips Louie	NICK ADAMS
Damon	RAYMOND DEL BARRIO
The Greek	JOSEPH MEDEIROS
Brandy Bottle Bates	RON TODOROWSKI
Scranton Slim	JOHN SELYA
Sky Masterson	CRAIG BIERKO
Mimi	LORIN LATARRO
Joey Biltmore	BRIAN SHEPARD
Adelaide	LAUREN GRAHAM
General Cartwright	MARY TESTA
Big Jule	GLENN FLESHLER
Carmen	KEARRAN GIOVANNI
Hot Box Emcee	GRAHAM ROWAT
Hot Box Girls	KEARRAN GIOVANNI, LORIN LATARRO, RHEA PATTERSON, JESSICA RUSH, JENNIFER SAVELLI, BROOKE WENDLE

Continued on next page

NEDERLANDER THEATRE
UNDER THE DIRECTION OF
JAMES M. NEDERLANDER AND JAMES L. NEDERLANDER

HOWARD PANTER FOR AMBASSADOR THEATRE GROUP
NORTHWATER ENTERTAINMENT
TULCHIN/BARTNER
DARREN BAGERT
BILL KENWRIGHT
TOM GREGORY

NEDERLANDER PRESENTATIONS, INC.
INDEPENDENT PRESENTERS NETWORK
with
DAVID MIRVISH
OLYMPUS THEATRICALS
MICHAEL JENKINS/DALLAS SUMMER MUSICALS
SONIA FRIEDMAN PRODUCTIONS

present

**OLIVER PLATT   LAUREN GRAHAM
CRAIG BIERKO   KATE JENNINGS GRANT**

in

Guys and Dolls

A MUSICAL FABLE OF BROADWAY
BASED ON A STORY AND CHARACTERS OF DAMON RUNYON

Music and Lyrics by
FRANK LOESSER

Book by
JO SWERLING AND **ABE BURROWS**

with

TITUSS BURGESS   GLENN FLESHLER   ADAM LEFEVRE
JIM ORTLIEB   STEVE ROSEN   MARY TESTA

NICK ADAMS   ANDREA CHAMBERLAIN   RAYMOND DEL BARRIO   MELISSA FAGAN   LISA GAJDA   KEARRAN GIOVANNI   JAMES HARKNESS   LORIN LATARRO
BENJAMIN MAGNUSON   JOSEPH MEDEIROS   SPENCER MOSES   RHEA PATTERSON   GRAHAM ROWAT   JESSICA RUSH   WILLIAM RYALL
MARCOS SANTANA   JENNIFER SAVELLI   JOHN SELYA   BRIAN SHEPARD   RON TODOROWSKI   CRAIG WALETZKO   JIM WALTON   BROOKE WENDLE

Scenery Design	Costume Design	Lighting Design	Sound Design
ROBERT BRILL	PAUL TAZEWELL	HOWELL BINKLEY	STEVE CANYON KENNEDY
Video Design	Hair & Wig Design	Fight Director	Casting
DUSTIN O'NEILL	CHARLES LAPOINTE	STEVE RANKIN	TARA RUBIN CASTING
Orchestrations	Dance Arrangements	Conductor	Music Coordinator
BRUCE COUGHLIN	JAMES LYNN ABBOTT	JEFFREY KLITZ	MICHAEL KELLER
Marketing Direction	Technical Supervision	Press Representative	Production Stage Manager
TYPE A MARKETING/ ANNE RIPPEY	DON S. GILMORE	BARLOW•HARTMAN	KELLY A. MARTINDALE
General Management	Associate Producers		Executive Producer
ALCHEMY PRODUCTION GROUP CARL PASBJERG & FRANK SCARDINO	JILL LENHART PETER GODFREY		DAVID LAZAR

Music Direction, Vocal Arrangements and Incidental Music
TED SPERLING

Choreography by
SERGIO TRUJILLO

Directed by
DES McANUFF

6/14/09

The chorus performs "Runyonland."

Photo by Carol Rosegg

Guys and Dolls

MUSICAL NUMBERS

ACT I

Overture	The Orchestra
"Runyonland"	The Company
"Fugue for Tinhorns"	Nicely-Nicely, Benny and Rusty
"Follow the Fold"	Sarah, Arvide, Calvin, Martha and Agatha
"The Oldest Established"	Nicely-Nicely, Benny, Nathan and Crap Shooters
"Follow the Fold" (Reprise)	Sarah, Arvide, Calvin, Martha and Agatha
"I'll Know"	Sarah and Sky
"A Bushel and a Peck"	Adelaide and the Hot Box Girls
"Adelaide's Lament"	Adelaide
"Guys and Dolls"	Nicely-Nicely and Benny
"Havana"	The Company
"If I Were a Bell"	Sarah
"My Time of Day"	Sky
"I've Never Been in Love Before"	Sky and Sarah

ACT II

Entr'acte	The Orchestra
"Take Back Your Mink"	Adelaide and the Hot Box Girls
"Adelaide's Lament" (Reprise)	Adelaide
"More I Cannot Wish You"	Arvide
"The Crapshooter's Dance"	The Crapshooters
"Luck Be a Lady"	Sky and the Crapshooters
"Sue Me"	Adelaide and Nathan
"Sit Down, You're Rockin' the Boat"	Nicely-Nicely and the Company
"Follow the Fold" (Reprise)	The Company
"Marry the Man Today"	Adelaide and Sarah
"Guys and Dolls" (Reprise)	The Company

ORCHESTRA
Conductor: JEFFREY KLITZ
Associate Conductor: JEFF MARDER
Concertmaster: CENOVIA CUMMINS
Violins: LORI MILLER, MING YEH
Cello 1: MAIRI DORMAN-PHANEUF
Cello 2: SARAH HEWITT-ROTH
Lead Trumpet: DON DOWNS
Trumpet: CJ CAMERIERI
Trombone: MIKE DAVIS
Bass Trombone/Tuba: MATT INGMAN
Reed 1: TOM MURRAY
Reed 2: KEN DUBISZ
Reed 3: MARK THRASHER
Keyboard: JEFF MARDER
Guitar/Banjo: GREG UTZIG
Bass: MARK VANDERPOEL
Drums: STEVE BARTOSIK
Percussion: JAVIER DIAZ
Music Coordinator: MICHAEL KELLER
Keyboard Programmer: RANDY COHEN

Cast Continued

Hot Box Waiter .... JOSEPH MEDEIROS
"The Crapshooter's Dance"
   Specialty .... JOHN SELYA

SETTING
New York City in the time of Damon Runyon

ENSEMBLE
NICK ADAMS, ANDREA CHAMBERLAIN, RAYMOND DEL BARRIO, KEARRAN GIOVANNI, JAMES HARKNESS, LORIN LATARRO, JOSEPH MEDEIROS, SPENCER MOSES, RHEA PATTERSON, GRAHAM ROWAT, JESSICA RUSH, WILLIAM RYALL, JENNIFER SAVELLI, JOHN SELYA, BRIAN SHEPARD, RON TODOROWSKI, JIM WALTON, BROOKE WENDLE

SWINGS
MELISSA FAGAN, LISA GAJDA, BENJAMIN MAGNUSON, MARCOS SANTANA, CRAIG WALETZKO

DANCE CAPTAIN
MARCOS SANTANA

UNDERSTUDIES
For Sky Masterson:
GRAHAM ROWAT
For Nathan Detroit:
ADAM LeFEVRE
For Nicely-Nicely Johnson, Lt. Brannigan:
JIM WALTON
For Arvide Abernathy, Big Jule:
WILLIAM RYALL
For Benny Southstreet:
BENJAMIN MAGNUSON
For Sarah Brown:
JESSICA RUSH
For Adelaide:
ANDREA CHAMBERLAIN, LORIN LATARRO
For General Cartwright:
ANDREA CHAMBERLAIN

(L-R): Kate Jennings Grant and Lauren Graham

Guys and Dolls

 Oliver Platt — *Nathan Detroit*
 Lauren Graham — *Miss Adelaide*
 Craig Bierko — *Sky Masterson*
 Kate Jennings Grant — *Sarah Brown*
 Tituss Burgess — *Nicely-Nicely Johnson*
 Glenn Fleshler — *Big Jule*
 Adam LeFevre — *Lt. Brannigan*

 Jim Ortlieb — *Arvide Abernathy*
 Steve Rosen — *Benny Southstreet*
 Mary Testa — *General Cartwright*
 Nick Adams — *Liver Lips Louie, Ensemble*
 Andrea Chamberlain — *Agatha, Ensemble*
 Raymond Del Barrio — *Damon, Ensemble*
 Melissa Fagan — *Swing*

 Kearran Giovanni — *Carmen, Hot Box Girl, Ensemble*
 James Harkness — *Society Max, Ensemble*
 Lorin Latarro — *Mimi, Hot Box Girl, Ensemble*
 Benjamin Magnuson — *Swing*
 Joseph Medeiros — *The Greek, Ensemble*
 Spencer Moses — *Rusty Charlie, Ensemble*
 Rhea Patterson — *Hot Box Girl, Ensemble*

 Graham Rowat — *Angie the Ox, Hot Box Emcee, Ensemble*
 Jessica Rush — *Martha, Ensemble*
 William Ryall — *Calvin, Ensemble*
 Marcos Santana — *Swing/Dance Captain*
 Jennifer Savelli — *Hot Box Girl, Ensemble*
 John Selya — *Scranton Slim, "The Crapshooter's Dance" Specialty, Ensemble*
 Brian Shepard — *Joey Biltmore, Ensemble*

 Ron Todorowski — *Brandy Bottle Bates, Ensemble*
 Jim Walton — *Harry the Horse, Ensemble*
 Brooke Wendle — *Hot Box Girl, Ensemble*
 Frank Loesser — *Music and Lyrics*
 Abe Burrows — *Book*
 Des McAnuff — *Director*
 Sergio Trujillo — *Choreographer*

Guys and Dolls

Ted Sperling
Music Director, Vocal and Incidental Music Arrangements

Robert Brill
Set Design

Paul Tazewell
Costume Design

Howell Binkley
Lighting Designer

Steve Canyon Kennedy
Sound Design

Steve Rankin
Fight Director

Tara Rubin Casting
Casting

Bruce Coughlin
Orchestrations

James Lynn Abbott
Dance Arrangements

Jeffrey Klitz
Conductor

Michael Keller
Music Coordinator

Howard Panter, Ambassador Theatre Group
Producer

Rosemary Squire, Ambassador Theatre Group
Producer

Bill Kenwright
Producer

Darren Bagert
Producer

James L. Nederlander, Nederlander Presentations, Inc.
Producer

Michael A. Jenkins/Dallas Summer Musicals
Producer

Sonia Friedman Productions
Producer

CAST AND CREW

Guys and Dolls

ORCHESTRA
Kneeling (L-R): Lori Miller, Jeff Marder, Mark Thrasher

Standing (L-R): Steve Bartosik, Ming Yeh, Sarah Hewitt-Roth, Matt Ingman, Mairi Dorman-Phaneuf, Greg Thymius, Kory Grossman

Not pictured: Cenovia Cummins, C.J. Camerieri, Don Downs, Mike Davis, Ken Dubisz, Tom Murray, Greg Utzig, Mark Vanderpoel, Javier Diaz, Jeff Klitz

CREW
Front Row (L-R): Kelly Martindale (Production Stage Manager), Jason Bowles (Props), Tasha Cowd (Wardrobe), Kyle Wesson (Wardrobe), Michele Rutter (Hair Supervisor), Alex Lyu Volckhausen (Stage Manager), Andrew C. Gottlieb (ASM)

Back Row (L-R): Michael D. Hannah (Wardrobe), Dave Cohen (Carpenter), Frank (Wardrobe), John (Props), Maureen George (Wardrobe), Gus Poitras (Carpenter), Pamela Pierzina (Wardrobe), Dora Suarez (Wardrobe), Mary Kay Yezerski-Bondoc (Hair), Rick Caroto (Hair), Christel Murdoch (Wardrobe), Paul Wimmer (Carpenter), Chris Pantuso (Props), Jenny Slattery (ASM), Brett Bingman (Sound), Charlie Gravina (Carpenter)

BOX OFFICE
(L-R): Gary Kenny (Treasurer), Erich Stollberger, Christina Kenny

FRONT OF HOUSE STAFF
Front Row (L-R): Sonny Curry, Marlon Pichardo, Louise Angelino (House Manager), Shannon Luker, Iris Cortes, Ralph Hendrix

Middle Row (L-R): Eddie Cuevas, Angel Diaz, Junesse Cartagena

Back Row (L-R): Brian Baeza, Terrence Cummiskey, Katie Spillane, Joaquin Quintana, Joe Santiago

Guys and Dolls

STAFF FOR GUYS AND DOLLS

GENERAL MANAGEMENT
ALCHEMY PRODUCTION GROUP
Carl Pasbjerg   Frank P. Scardino

COMPANY MANAGER
JIM BRANDEBERRY

GENERAL PRESS REPRESENTATIVE
BARLOW•HARTMAN
John Barlow   Michael Hartman
Juliana Hannett   Matt Ross

CASTING
TARA RUBIN CASTING
Tara Rubin CSA, Merri Sugarman CSA, Dale Brown,
Eric Woodall CSA, Laura Schutzel CSA,
Paige Blansfield, Rebecca Carfagna, Kaitlin Shaw

MAKE-UP DESIGNER
ANGELINA AVALLONE

VIDEO CONTENT PRODUCTION
THE ORACLE GROUP/Ari Novak

MARKETING
TYPE A MARKETING
Anne Rippey   Janette Roush   Nick Pramik

Associate General Manager	Chris Morey
Production Stage Manager	Kelly A. Martindale
Stage Manager	Alex Lyu Volckhausen
Assistant Stage Managers	Andrew C. Gottlieb, Jenny Slattery
Assistant Company Manager	Sherra Johnston
Associate to the General Managers	Tegan Meyer
Dance Captain	Marcos Santana
Fight Captain	Graham Rowat
Dialect Coach	Stephen Gabis
Dramaturg	James Magruder
Assistant Director	Shelley Butler
Associate Choreographer	Jane Lanier
Associate Scenic Designer	Dustin O'Neill
Associate Costume Designer	Nancy A. Palmatier
Associate Lighting Designer	Mark Simpson
Associate Sound Designer	Andrew Keister
Associate Hair Designer	Leah Loukas
Assistant Set Designers	Erica Hemminger, Steven Kemp, Caleb Levengood, Angrette McCloskey, Michael Locher, Daniel Meeker
Assistant Costume Designers	Michael Zecker, Court Watson, Maria Zamansky
Assistant to the Costume Designer	Caitlin Hunt
Assistant Lighting Designer	Christian DeAngelis
Moving Light Programmer	David Arch
Video Programmer	Thomas Hague
Sound Programmer	Wallace Flores
Production Carpenter	Fred Gallo
Head Carpenter	Todd Frank
Assistant Carpenters	Scott "Gus" Poitras, David Cohen
Production Electrician	James Fedigan
Head Electrician	Eric Norris
Assistant Electricians	Gary Fernandez, Lorne MacDougall
Production Property Master	Chris Pantuso
Assistant Property Master	Jason Bowles
Head Sound Engineer	Julie Randolph
Assistant Sound Engineer	Brett Bingman
Sound Associate	Stephanie Celustka
Wardrobe Supervisor	Debbie Cheretun
Associate Wardrobe Supervisor	Jim Hall
Dressers	Dora Bonilla, Fred Castner, Tasha Cowd, Suzanne Delahunt, Tara Delahunt, Maureen George, Betty Gillispie, Michael D. Hannah, Jim Hodun, Bob Kwaitkowski, Christel Murdoch, Pamela Pierzina, Kyle Wesson
Hair Supervisor	Michele Rutter
Assistant Hair Supervisor	Mary Kay Yezerski-Bondoc
Hair Stylist	Rick Caroto
Music Copying	Emily Grishman Music Preparation/ Emily Grishman, Katharine Edmonds
Asst. Keyboard Programmers	Jim Mironchik, Bryan Crook
Music Intern	Oran Eldor
Production Assistant	Alissa Zulvergold
Executive Assistant to Des McAnuff	Jay Turton
Physical Therapy	Performing Arts Physical Therapy
Advertising	Spotco/ Drew Hodges, Jim Edwards, Tom Greenwald, Jim Aquino, Stacey Maya
Production Photographer	Carol Rosegg
Accountant	Fried & Kowgios LLC/Robert Fried
Controller	Galbraith & Co/ Sarah Galbraith
Legal Counsel	Franklin Weinrib Rudell & Vassallo PC/ Elliot Brown, Dan Wasser
SDCF Director Observer	David Alpert
SDCF Choreographic Observer	Kevin Hill
Scenic Design Intern	Hannah Hogan
Associate Producer/Infinity Stages	Adam Sansiveri
Payroll Services	Castellana Services, Inc.
Banking	TD Bank/Olivia Cassin
Insurance	Dewitt Stern Inc./ Pete Shoemaker, Rebecca Alspector
Opening Night Coordination	McNabb Roick/ Jim McNabb, Ty Kuppig
Theatre Displays	King Displays, Inc.

CREDITS
Scenic Technologies. Sign-A-Rama. Props provided by The Spoon Group. Lighting equipment from Production Resource Group. Sound by Sound Associates. Men's suits: Brian Hemesath, Jennifer Love, Joe Scafati, Barbara Matera LTD. "Bushel/Mink" costumes: Tricorne Inc. Principal ladies' costumes: Donna Langman Costumes. Ladies' millinery: Lynne Mackey Studio. Men's millinery: Rodney Gordon, Worth & Worth, Arnold Levine. Ensemble ladies' costumes: Jennifer Love, Parsons-Meares, Donna Langman. Men's overcoats: Gilberto Designs. Men's shirts: Beckenstein's, The Shirt Store. Jewelry: Christine McParland. Gloves: LaCrasia. Embroidery: Gigi at Vogue 2. Knitwear: Karen Eifert, Maria Ficalore Knitwear Ltd. Undergarments: Bra*Tenders. Furs: Christie Brothers. Dying/painting: Hochi Asiatico, Gene Mignola Inc. Keyboard by Yamaha. Dental prosthetics: Dr. Marc Beshar.

THE AMBASSADOR THEATRE GROUP LTD.

Chairman	Sir Eddie Kulukundis OBE
Deputy Chairman	Peter Beckwith OBE
Joint Chief Executive & Creative Director	Howard Panter
Joint Chief Executive	Rosemary Squire OBE
Operations & Building Development Director	David Blyth
Finance & Commercial Director	Helen Enright
Executive Director	Michael Lynas
Business Affairs Director	Peter Kavanagh

AMBASSADOR THEATRE GROUP – New York

Chief Executive Officer	David Lazar
Production Associate	Dan Gallagher

TULCHIN/BARTNER PRODUCTIONS, LLC

Robert G. Bartner	Producer
Norman Tulchin	Producer
Steven Tulchin	Producer
Lauren Doll	Associate Producer
Mario Aiello	General Manager
Sarah Nashman	Production Assistant
Anna Parrotta	Assistant to the General Manager

BILL KENWRIGHT LTD.

Managing Director	Bill Kenwright
Finance Director	Alan Sharp
Commercial Director	Steve Potts
Producer	Julius Green
Producer	Richard Temple
Production Manager	David Stothard
Associate Producer	Joshua Andrews

GUYS AND DOLLS
Rehearsed at the New 42nd Street Studios.

Souvenir merchandise designed and created by
The Araca Group.

Chairman	**James M. Nederlander**
President	**James L. Nederlander**

Executive Vice President
Nick Scandalios

Vice President	Senior Vice President
Corporate Development	Labor Relations
Charlene S. Nederlander	**Herschel Waxman**

Vice President	Chief Financial Officer
Jim Boese	**Freida Sawyer Belviso**

STAFF FOR THE NEDERLANDER THEATRE

House Manager	Louise Angelino
Treasurer	Gary Kenny
Assistant Treasurer	Keshave Sattaur
House Carpenter	Joseph Fererri Sr.
Flyman	Joseph Ferreri Jr.
House Electrician	Richard Beck
House Properties	William Wright

Hair

First Preview: March 6, 2009. Opened: March 31, 2009.
Still running as of May 31, 2010.

THE COMPANY
(in order of appearance)

Dionne	JEANNETTE BAYARDELLE
Berger	ACE YOUNG
Woof	JASON WOOTEN
Hud	WALLACE SMITH
Claude	KYLE RIABKO
Sheila	DIANA DeGARMO
Jeanie	ANNALEIGH ASHFORD
Crissy	VANESSA RAY
Mother	RACHEL BAY JONES
Dad	JOSH LAMON
Principal	LEE ZARRETT
Margaret Mead	JOSH LAMON
Hubert	LEE ZARRETT
Abraham Lincoln	ANASTACIA McCLESKEY
John Wilkes Booth	LEE ZARRETT
Buddhadalirama	RACHEL BAY JONES
Tribe Members	JUSTIN BADGER, LARKIN BOGAN, NATALIE BRADSHAW, CATHERINE BROOKMAN, ANTWAYN HOPPER, ERIKA JERRY, RACHEL BAY JONES, MYKAL KILGORE, JOSH LAMON, ANASTACIA McCLESKEY, PARIS REMILLARD, KATE ROCKWELL, CAILAN ROSE, RASHIDRA SCOTT, JEN SESE, LAWRENCE STALLINGS, TERRANCE THOMAS, LEE ZARRETT

Continued on next page

The Playbill Broadway Yearbook 2009-2010

AL HIRSCHFELD THEATRE
A JUJAMCYN THEATRE

JORDAN ROTH
President

PAUL LIBIN
Producing Director

JACK VIERTEL
Creative Director

THE PUBLIC THEATER
Oskar Eustis, Artistic Director   Andrew D. Hamingson, Executive Director

JEFFREY RICHARDS   JERRY FRANKEL
GARY GODDARD ENTERTAINMENT   KATHLEEN K. JOHNSON   NEDERLANDER PRODUCTIONS, INC.
FRAN KIRMSER PRODUCTIONS/JED BERNSTEIN   MARC FRANKEL   BROADWAY ACROSS AMERICA
BARBARA MANOCHERIAN/WENCARLAR PRODUCTIONS   JK PRODUCTIONS/TERRY SCHNUCK
ANDY SANDBERG   JAM THEATRICALS   THE WEINSTEIN COMPANY   NORTON HERRICK
JUJAMCYN THEATERS

JOEY PARNES Executive Producer
by special arrangement with
ELIZABETH IRELAND McCANN

present

HAIR
The American Tribal Love-Rock Musical

Book & Lyrics by
GEROME RAGNI & JAMES RADO

Music by
GALT MacDERMOT

with

ANNALEIGH ASHFORD   JEANNETTE BAYARDELLE   DIANA DeGARMO
VANESSA RAY   KYLE RIABKO   WALLACE SMITH   JASON WOOTEN   ACE YOUNG

and

JUSTIN BADGER   NICHOLAS BELTON   LARKIN BOGAN   NATALIE BRADSHAW
CATHERINE BROOKMAN   BRIANA CARLSON-GOODMAN   ANTWAYN HOPPER
ERIKA JERRY   JAY ARMSTRONG JOHNSON   RACHEL BAY JONES   MYKAL KILGORE
JOSH LAMON   NICOLE LEWIS   ANASTACIA McCLESKEY   PARIS REMILLARD
ARBENDER ROBINSON   KATE ROCKWELL   CAILAN ROSE   RASHIDRA SCOTT   JEN SESE
LAWRENCE STALLINGS   TERRANCE THOMAS   EMMA ZAKS   LEE ZARRETT

Scenic Design	Costume Design	Lighting Design	Sound Design
SCOTT PASK	MICHAEL McDONALD	KEVIN ADAMS	ACME SOUND PARTNERS

Orchestrations	Music Director	Music Coordinator
GALT MacDERMOT	NADIA DIGIALLONARDO	SEYMOUR RED PRESS

Casting	Production Stage Manager	Wig Design
JORDAN THALER & HEIDI GRIFFITHS	NANCY HARRINGTON	GERARD KELLY

Press Representative	Associate Producer	Marketing	Sponsorship
O&M CO.	JENNY GERSTEN	ALLIED LIVE, INC.	ROSE POLIDORO

Associate Producers
ARIELLE TEPPER MADOVER   DEBBIE BISNO/REBECCA GOLD   CHRISTOPHER HART
APPLES AND ORANGES: TIM & PAMELA WINSLOW KASHANI   TONY & RUTHE PONTURO   JOSEPH TRAINA

Choreography by
KAROLE ARMITAGE

Directed by
DIANE PAULUS

ORIGINALLY PRODUCED IN 1967 AND SUBSEQUENTLY REVIVED IN 2008 BY THE PUBLIC THEATER
THE PRODUCERS WISH TO EXPRESS THEIR APPRECIATION TO THEATRE DEVELOPMENT FUND FOR ITS SUPPORT OF THIS PRODUCTION.

3/8/10

The Tribe

Hair

MUSICAL NUMBERS

ACT 1

"Aquarius"	Dionne and Tribe
"Donna"	Berger and Tribe
"Hashish"	Tribe
"Sodomy"	Woof and Tribe
"Colored Spade"	Hud and Tribe
"Manchester, England"	Claude and Tribe
"I'm Black"	Hud, Woof, Berger, Claude and Tribe
"Ain't Got No"	Woof, Hud, Dionne and Tribe
"Sheila Franklin"	Tribe
"I Believe in Love"	Sheila and Trio
"Ain't Got No"	Tribe
"Air"	Jeanie with Crissy and Dionne
"The Stone Age"	Berger
"I Got Life"	Claude and Tribe
"Initials"	Tribe
"Going Down"	Berger and Tribe
"Hair"	Claude, Berger and Tribe
"My Conviction"	Margaret Mead
"Easy to Be Hard"	Sheila
"Don't Put It Down"	Berger, Woof, Lawrence
"Frank Mills"	Crissy
"Hare Krishna"	Tribe
"Where Do I Go"	Claude and Tribe

ACT 2

"Electric Blues"	Badger, Rachel, Josh, Rashidra
"Oh Great God of Power"	Tribe
"Black Boys"	Catherine, Jen, Kate, Wallace, Antwayn, Lawrence
"White Boys"	Dionne, Erika, Rashidra
"Walking in Space"	Tribe
"Minuet"	Orchestra
"Yes, I's Finished on Y'alls Farmlands"	Wallace, Terrance, Antwayn, Lawrence
"Four Score and Seven Years Ago"/"Abie Baby"	Anastacia, Terrance, Wallace, Antwayn, Lawrence
"Give Up All Desires"	Buddhadalirama, Woof, Sheila, Crissy
"Three-Five-Zero-Zero"	Tribe
"What a Piece of Work Is Man"	Paris, Mykal, Claude
"How Dare They Try"	Tribe
"Good Morning Starshine"	Sheila and Tribe
"Ain't Got No" (Reprise)	Claude and Tribe
"The Flesh Failures"	Claude, Sheila, Dionne, Woof
"Eyes Look Your Last"	Tribe
"Let the Sun Shine In"	Tribe

Cast Continued

UNDERSTUDIES
For Claude, Woof:
    JAY ARMSTRONG JOHNSON,
    PARIS REMILLARD
For Berger: JUSTIN BADGER,
    NICHOLAS BELTON
For Hud: ANTWAYN HOPPER
For Sheila: BRIANA CARLSON-GOODMAN,
    NICOLE LEWIS
For Dionne: NICOLE LEWIS,
    ANASTACIA McCLESKEY
For Jeanie: NATALIE BRADSHAW
For Crissy: BRIANA CARLSON-GOODMAN,
    CAILAN ROSE
For Mother, Buddhadalirama:
    NATALIE BRADSHAW, EMMA ZAKS
For Dad: NICHOLAS BELTON, LEE ZARRETT
For Principal, Hubert: NICHOLAS BELTON,
    ARBENDER ROBINSON
For Margaret Mead: NICHOLAS BELTON,
    LEE ZARRETT
For John Wilkes Booth: NICHOLAS BELTON,
    JOSH LAMON
For Abraham Lincoln: NICOLE LEWIS

Dance Captain: ARBENDER ROBINSON
Assistant Dance Captain: NICOLE LEWIS

TRIBE SWINGS
NICHOLAS BELTON,
BRIANA CARLSON-GOODMAN,
JAY ARMSTRONG JOHNSON,
NICOLE LEWIS, ARBENDER ROBINSON,
EMMA ZAKS

MUSICIANS
Conductor/Keyboard: NADIA DIGIALLONARDO
Assistant Conductor/Keyboard: LON HOYT
Guitar: STEVE BARGONETTI,
    ANDREW SCHWARTZ
Bass: WILBUR BASCOMB
Woodwinds: ALLEN WON
Trumpet: ELAINE BURT,
    RONALD BUTTACAVOLI,
    CHRISTIAN JAUDES
Trombone: VINCENT MACDERMOT
Percussion: JOE CARDELLO
Drums: BERNARD PURDIE

Hair

Annaleigh Ashford
Jeanie

Jeannette Bayardelle
Dionne

Diana DeGarmo
Sheila

Vanessa Ray
Crissy

Kyle Riabko
Claude

Wallace Smith
Hud

Jason Wooten
Woof

Ace Young
Berger

Justin Badger
Electric Blues Quartet, Tribe

Nicholas Belton
Swing

Larkin Bogan
Tribe

Natalie Bradshaw
Tribe

Catherine Brookman
Black Boys Trio, Tribe

Briana Carlson-Goodman
Swing

Antwayn Hopper
Tribe

Erika Jerry
White Boys Trio, Tribe

Jay Armstrong Johnson
Swing

Rachel Bay Jones
Mother, Buddhadalirama, Tribe

Mykal Kilgore
What a Piece Duo, Tribe

Josh Lamon
Dad, Margaret Mead, Tribe

Nicole Lewis
Swing, Assistant Dance Captain

Anastacia (Stacy) McCleskey
Abraham Lincoln, Tribe

Paris Remillard
What a Piece Duo, Tribe

Arbender J. Robinson
Swing, Dance Captain

Kate Rockwell
Black Boys Trio, Tribe

Cailan Rose
Tribe

Rashidra Scott
Electric Blues Quartet, White Boys Trio, Tribe

Jen Sese
Black Boys Trio, Tribe

Lawrence Stallings
Tribe

Terrance Thomas
Tribe

Emma Zaks
Swing

Lee Zarrett
Principal, Hubert, John Wilkes Booth, Tribe

Gerome Ragni
Co-Creator

James Rado
Co-Creator

Galt MacDermot
Composer

The Playbill Broadway Yearbook 2009-2010

Hair

Diane Paulus
Director

Karole Armitage
Choreographer

Scott Pask
Scenic Design

Michael McDonald
Costume Design

Kevin Adams
Lighting Design

Tom Clark, Mark Menard and Nevin Steinberg,
Acme Sound Partners
Sound Design

Seymour Red Press
Music Coordinator

Heidi Griffiths and Jordan Thaler
Casting

Tanya Grubich,
Allied Live
Marketing

Laura Matalon,
Allied Live
Marketing

Oskar Eustis
*Artistic Director,
The Public Theater*

Andrew D. Hamingson
*Executive Director,
The Public Theater*

Jeffrey Richards
Producer

Jerry Frankel
Producer

Gary Goddard,
Gary Goddard Entertainment
Producer

Forbes Candlish,
Gary Goddard Entertainment
Producer

James L. Nederlander,
Nederlander Presentations, Inc.
Producer

Jed Bernstein
Producer

John Gore,
CEO,
Broadway Across America
Producer

Thomas B. McGrath,
Chairman,
Broadway Across America
Producer

Barbara Manocherian
Producer

Wendy Federman
WenCarLar
Producer

Carl Moellenberg
WenCarLar
Producer

Larry Hirschhorn
WenCarLar
Producer

Terry Schnuck
Producer

Bob Weinstein,
The Weinstein Company
Producer

Harvey Weinstein,
The Weinstein Company
Producer

Jordan Roth,
President,
Jujamcyn Theaters
Producer

Joey Parnes
Executive Producer

Elizabeth Ireland McCann
Producer

Arielle Tepper Madover
Associate Producer

Tim Kashani,
Apples and Oranges Productions
Producer

Pamela Winslow Kashani,
Apples and Oranges Productions
Producer

Tony Ponturo
Producer

Hair

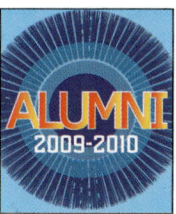

Sasha Allen
Dionne

Ato Blankson-Wood
Tribe Member

Krystal Joy Brown
Abraham Lincoln, Tribe Member

Steel Burkhardt
Tribe Member

Jackie Burns
Tribe Member, Assistant Dance Captain

Heath Calvert
Tribe Member

Allison Case
Crissy

Gavin Creel
Claude

Matt DeAngelis
Tribe Swing

Lauren Elder
Tribe Member

Allison Guinn
Tribe Member

Chasten Harmon
Tribe Swing

Anthony Hollock
Tribe Member

Kaitlin Kiyan
Tribe Member

Andrew Kober
Dad, Margaret Mead, Tribe Member

Megan Lawrence
Buddhadalirama, Mother

Caissie Levy
Sheila

Ryan Link
Tribe Swing

John Moauro
Tribe Member

Darius Nichols
Hud

Brandon Pearson
Tribe Member

Megan Reinking
Tribe Member

Bryce Ryness
Woof

Michael James Scott
Dance Captain, Tribe Member, Tribe Swing

Saycon Sengbloh
Abraham Lincoln, Tribe Member

Hannah Shankman
Tribe Swing

Maya Sharpe
Tribe Member

Kacie Sheik
Jeanie

Theo Stockman
Hubert, John Wilkes Booth, Principal, Tribe Member

Ryan Watkinson
Tribe Swing

Tommar Wilson
Dance Captain, Tribe Member

2009-2010 AWARDS

HENRY HEWES DESIGN AWARD
Lighting Design
(Kevin Adams)

Hair

STAGE CREW
Front Row (L-R): Bonnie Runk, Eric Abbott, Sal Scalfani, Rocco Williams

Middle Row (L-R): John Blixt, Worth Strecker, Doug Earl, Amelia Haywood, Clarion Overmoyer, Joe Maher Jr, Christina Ainge, Scott Sanders

Back Row (L-R): Jim Wilkinson, Gabe Harris, Mike Smanko, Gloria Burke, Cat Dee, Michele Gutierrez, Danny Koye, Tom Burke

FRONT OF HOUSE STAFF
Front Row (L-R): Jennifer DiDonato, Henry Menendez, Elizabeth Harvey, Antonia Marrero, Terry Monahan, Albert Kim

Second Row (L-R): Alexander Gutierrez, Lorraine Feeks, Tereso Avila, Ronan Babbitt

Third Row (L-R): Gloria Diabo, Theresa Lopez, Christopher Rustin, Clinton Kennedy

Fourth Row (L-R): Carrie Brinker, Karen Marshall, Brian Gold, Andi Hopkins

Back Row (L-R): Mary Marzan, Bart Ryan, Jennifer Alam, Peter Davino, William Meyers, Donald Royal, Janice Rodriguez

COMPANY MANAGEMENT
(L-R): Kit Ingui, Kim Sellon and Leslie Glassburn

MUSICIANS
Front Row (L-R): Vincent MacDermot, Steve Bargonetti, Lon Hoyt, Wilbur Bascomb, Andrew Schwartz

Back Row (L-R): Joe Cardello, Bernard Purdie, Ronald Buttacavoli, Alden Banta III

Hair

(L-R): Kyle Riabko, Diana DeGarmo, Ace Young.
Photo by Joan Marcus

STAFF FOR *HAIR*

GENERAL MANAGEMENT
Joey Parnes
John Johnson   S.D. Wagner

COMPANY MANAGER
Kim Sellon

FOR THE PUBLIC THEATER
Artistic Director	Oskar Eustis
Executive Director	Andrew D. Hamingson
Associate Producer	Jenny Gersten
Director of Communications	Candi Adams
Director of Marketing	Nella Vera

PRESS REPRESENTATIVE
O&M Co.
Rick Miramontez
Molly Barnett   Philip Carrubba
Andy Snyder   Elizabeth Wagner

PRODUCTION STAGE MANAGER
Nancy Harrington

ASSOCIATE DIRECTOR
Jeff Whiting

ASSOCIATE CHOREOGRAPHER
Christine O'Grady

Stage Manager	Julie Baldauff
Assistant Stage Manager	Stephen R. Gruse
Associate Company Manager	Leslie A. Glassburn
Assistant Company Manager	Kit Ingui
Assistant Directors	Allegra Libonati, Shira Milikowsky
Associate Set Designer	Orit Jacoby Carroll
Assistant Set Designers	Jeffrey Hinchee, Lauren Alvarez
Assistant to the Set Designer	Warren Stiles
Mural Illustration Associate	Amy Guip
Associate Lighting Designer	Aaron Sporer
Assistant Lighting Designer	Joel Silver
Associate Costume Designer	Lisa Zinni
Assistant Costume Designer	Chloe Chapin
Assistant to the Costume Designer	David Mendizabal
Costume Assistant	Sydney Ledger
Assistant Sound Designer	Alex Hawthorn
Production Carpenter	Larry Morley
Production Electrician	Steve Cochrane/ Richard Mortell
Production Prop Supervisor	Michael Smanko
Production Sound Engineer	Scott Sanders
Head Electrician	Brian Dawson
Moving Light Programmer	Paul J. Sonnleitner
Monitor Mixer	Jim Wilkinson
Wardrobe Supervisor	John A. Robelen, III
Assistant Wardrobe Supervisor	Amelia Haywood
Dressers	Christina Ainge, Cat Dee, Doug Earl, Shannon McDowell, Clarion Overmoyer
Hair/Wig Supervisor	Gloria Burke
Hair Dresser	Danny Koye
Production Assistant	Johnny Milani
Music Consultant	Tom Kitt
Music Copyist	Rob Baumgartner
Associate to Jeffrey Richards	Jeremy Scott Blaustein
Assistant to Jeffrey Richards	Diana Rissetto
Assistant to Jenny Gersten	Eric Louie
Management Associate	Andrew White
Management Associate	Kristen Luciani
Casting Assistant	Amber Wakefield
Casting Intern	Ann Thayer
Advertising	SpotCo/ Drew Hodges, Jim Edwards, Stephen Sosnowski, Tom Greenwald
Interactive Marketing	Situation Interactive/ Damian Bazadona, Jessica Dachille, Jeremy Kraus, John Lanasa, Steve Rovery
Marketing	Allied Live LLC/ Laura Matalon, Tanya Grubich, Victoria Cairl, Sara Rosenzweig
Exclusive Tour Direction	Steven Schnepp, Broadway Booking Office NYC
Sponsorship	Rose Polidoro
Press Associates	Jaron Caldwell, Jon Dimond, Yufen Kung, Richard Hillman
Press Interns	Sam Corbett, Felicia Pollack, Alexandra Rubin
Merchandise	Creative Goods/ Pete Milano, Mary Lee Fowler, Jennifer Alam, Karen Marshall
Legal Counsel	Lazarus & Harris LLP/ Scott Lazarus, Esq., Robert Harris, Esq.
Public Theater Counsel	Paul, Weiss, Rifkind, Wharton & Garrison LLP/ Charles H. Googe Jr., Carolyn J. Casselman, Michael Bogner
Consulting Counsel	Robinson Brog, Leinwand Greene, Genovese & Gluck PC/ Richard M. Ticktin, Esq., Roy A. Jacobs, Esq.
Accountants	RNK/ Mark D'Ambrosi, Pat Pedersen, Ruthie Wagh
Banking	JPMorgan Chase/ Stephanie Dalton, Stefanie Boger, Salvatore Romano
Insurance	AON/Albert G Ruben/ George Walden, Claudia B. Kaufman
Payroll	Castellana Services Inc/ Lance Castellana, James Castellana, Norman Sewell
Opening Night Coordinator	The Lawrence Company
Production Photographer	Joan Marcus
Production Photographer	Robert J. Saferstein
Additional Production Photography	Bruce Glikas
Physical Therapy	Performing Arts Physical Therapy
Mascots	Skye and Franco

Music Advisor
Rob Fisher

CREDITS

Scenery and scenic effects built, painted and electrified by Showmotion, Inc., Norwalk, Connecticut. Set elements fabricated by Cigar Box Studios. Lighting equipment by PRG Lighting. Sound equipment by Sound Associates. Costumes executed by the Public Theater Costume Shop; John Kristiansen, New York Inc.; Tricorne LLC; Marc Happel; Giliberto Custom Tailors. Specialty costumes by Fritz Masten and Barbara Brust. Millinery by Lynne Mackey Studio & T. Michael Hall. Custom embroidery by Jason Hadley. Knitware by Clarion Overmoyer. Custom leatherwear by David Samuel Menkes. Select vintage clothing courtesy of Scaramouche. Military uniforms and accessories supplied by Kaufman's Army & Navy, NYC. Car service by IBA Limousine. Flowers supplied by George Vallo of Portafiori Flowers. Makeup provided by M•A•C.

SPECIAL THANKS

Luke McDonough, Public Theater Costume Master; Jason Hadley, Costume Assistant: 40th Anniversary Concert; Theoni V. Aldredge; Tonne Goodman; Maj. Gabriel J. Zinni, USA; Mary Beth Regan; Grier Coleman; Anne Wingate & Kim Jones; Daybreak Vintage; Amy Carothers; Julian Christenberry; Jane Pfeffer; Don Frantz; Laurie Brown; Stuart Levy; Louise Foisy; Cynthia Ponce; Daniel Rigazzi

Hair is supported, with love, by Levi's©.

Salon services, hair care and styling products provided by Bumble and bumble.

Synthesizers provided by Yamaha Corporation of America.

JUJAMCYN THEATERS

JORDAN ROTH
President

PAUL LIBIN	**JACK VIERTEL**
Producing Director	Creative Director
DANIEL ADAMIAN	**JENNIFER HERSHEY**
General Manager	Director of Operations
MEREDITH VILLATORE	**JERRY ZAKS**
Chief Financial Officer	Resident Director

Staff for the Al Hirschfeld Theatre
Manager	Albert T. Kim
Associate Manager	Willa Burke
Treasurer	Carmine La Mendola
Carpenter	Joseph J. Maher, Jr.
Propertyman	Sal Sclafani
Electrician	Michele Gutierrez
Engineer	Brian DiNapoli

Hair
SCRAPBOOK

Correspondent: Vanessa Ray, "Crissy"

Memorable Holiday Gifts: This year for Christmas the producers went above and beyond for us. I walked into the theater and saw that some people were carrying reusable bags with the *Hair* logo on it, I thought that was what we got and was sooooo excited!! Maybe I'm easily excited. Darius told me to look in the bag in my dressing room, and inside was a white robe with the *Hair* logo and my name. If that wasn't enough there was also a membership to a yoga studio. So thankful.

Most Exciting Celebrity Visitors: We have had some huge stars come to the show. The first night I decided to ...er... bare all... David E. Kelly and Michelle Pfeiffer were in the front row on my side. Yikes. Though I have to say my favorite celeb was Kate Beckinsale. She came with her mom and daughter Lily. Her mother was the first replacement swing in the London cast in 1968, she learned the music off of the original company's LP. Her stories were awesome. Kate and Lily kept calling me Baby Spice.

Who Wrote This Year's "Gypsy of the Year" Sketch: Gavin Creel and Michael James Scott. It was a take on the "trip." In this version, Claude (played by Jay Armstrong Johnson) goes on a journey through Broadway musicals, everything from *Fiddler on the Roof* to *Music Man* with a little bit of original *Mary Poppins* choreography thrown in the mix (thanks Gavin!).

Actor Who Performed the Most Roles in This Show: Mom, played by Rachel Bay Jones: 3. And Dad, played by Andrew Kober: 3.

Special Backstage Rituals: Lots of Ricola and hand sanitizer is used like a drug with the cast.

Favorite Moments During Each Performance: There are really just so many. I love the moment right before the title song starts. The whole cast's backs are to the audience and we are all just silly. Also the first time we sing "this is the dawning of the age of Aquarius" and welcome the audience. Chills and tears.

Favorite In-Theatre Gathering Place: Kacie Sheik's room. Although Paris Remillard and I seem to think that my room is like the genie's lamp—whatever we wish for comes true. Sometimes it is just a treat like a specific type of cookie we wanted, other times it's money or most recently conjuring the drummer of the Spin Doctors...not kidding.

Favorite Off-Site Hangouts: Juice Generation and Kodama.

Memorable Press Encounter: "Let the Sun Shine In" in front of the Capitol Building at the National Equality March in D.C. So inspiring!

Fastest Costume Change: End of the show when Claude changes into his military uniform.

Who Wore the Heaviest/Hottest Costume: None of us wears super heavy costumes for a long period of time, but Woof does wear a huge heavy fur throughout the show.

Who Wore the Least: This is a toss-up between Paris Remillard and Jackie Burns. They basically wear the same thing, but Paris doesn't wear a shirt.

1. The cast plus co-creator James Rado (second from right, holding mockup of the CD) pose on the stage of the Al Hirschfeld Theatre June 23, 2009 at an autograph party for the newly-released cast album.
2. Gavin Creel (L) and Will Swenson receive their portrait for the Broadway Wall of Fame at Tony's di Napoli restaurant on August 6, 2009.

Memorable Ad-Libs: Hud: His actual line: "But some people have called me and my beautiful black brothers and sisters many other things."
Ad-lib: "But some people have caaaallled me, to my FACE, many other things."
Berger & Claude: Actual line: Claude "And I'm gonna spread it around the world, mother."
Ad-lib: "And I'm gonna spread it around the world, mother." Berger: variations of "Aw, I love it when he spreads it! Yeah, Claude, spread that shit!"

Favorite Snack Foods: Whatever candy is in Kacie Sheik's room =).

Mascot: Haha, Frisco...Steel Burkhardt's tribe character.

Record Number of Cell Phone Rings, Cell Phone Photos or Texting Incidents During a Performance: Not totally sure, but word to the wise, during "Oh Great God" though all the lights are out and we are using flashlights it's maybe not the best time to pull out your cell phone and text or return emails or what have you. It is the cast of *Hair*... we WILL shine our flashlights on you and embarrass you and your family. All out of LOVE.

Memorable Stage Door Fan Encounter: Recently a sweet fan made "I love Crissy" pins. LOVE THEM!!

Catchphrases Only the Company Would Recognize: "Get at me!" "There, there."

Sweethearts Within the Company: The saga of John Moauro and Josh Lamon over the intercom. Are they? Aren't they? WHAT'S GONNA HAPPEN??? (It's just a little fake soap opera for us.)

Fan Club Head and Website/Newsletter: Andrew Kober—follow us on Twitter @HairTribe!

Nickname: Baby Spice (Thanks, Kate Beckinsale!)

Best In-House Parody Lyrics: For the first month doing the show I thought the lyrics in "Electric Blues" were "Miles and Miles of the Unicorn, the electronic sonic Flood." The actual lyrics: "Miles and miles of Medusen corn the electronic sonic BOOM." Either way, they don't make much sense.

Memorable Directorial Note: "Sit on the steps faster leading up to 'Frank Mills' and smell the flowers at the end of the song...." Of course every time Diane Paulus comes to the show I manage to trip on the steps. Cool.

Coolest Thing About Being in This Show: Playing with the coolest most inventive cast, crew and band in the world. We are so free up there.

Also: I would just like to say that *Hair* has the most incredible fans imaginable. We are showered with love and support. Whether it be "baby Claude" singing "Frank Mills" on YouTube or the fans at the stage door—you are all extensions of the *Hair* tribe. Thank you for sharing this message of peace, freedom, happiness, and most of all LOVE with us.

Hamlet

First Preview: September 12, 2009. Opened: October 6, 2009.
Closed December 6, 2009 after 25 Previews and 72 Performances.

CAST
(in order of speaking)

Barnardo, Priest, Captain	MICHAEL HADLEY
Francisco, Fortinbras, 4th Player	ALAN TURKINGTON
Marcellus, 3rd Player, 2nd Gravedigger, English Ambassador	HENRY PETTIGREW
Horatio	MATT RYAN
Claudius	KEVIN R. McNALLY
Osric	IAN DRYSDALE
Laertes	GWILYM LEE
Polonius, 1st Gravedigger	RON COOK
Gertrude	GERALDINE JAMES
Hamlet	JUDE LAW
Ophelia	GUGU MBATHA-RAW
Ghost of Hamlet's Father, Player King	PETER EYRE
Reynaldo	SEAN JACKSON
Rosencrantz	JOHN MacMILLAN
Guildenstern	HARRY ATTWELL
Player Queen	JENNY FUNNELL
Cornelius	ROSS ARMSTRONG
Member of the Court	FAYE WINTER
Member of the Court	COLIN HAIGH
Member of the Court	JAMES LE FEUVRE

Continued on next page

The Playbill Broadway Yearbook 2009-2010

BROADHURST THEATRE
235 West 44th Street
A Shubert Organization Theatre

Philip J. Smith, *Chairman*   Robert E. Wankel, *President*

ARIELLE TEPPER MADOVER   THE DONMAR WAREHOUSE   MATTHEW BYAM SHAW
SCOTT M. DELMAN   STEPHANIE P. McCLELLAND   NEAL STREET PRODUCTIONS/CARL MOELLENBERG
RUTH HENDEL/BARBARA WHITMAN   PHILIP MORGAMAN/FRANKIE J. GRANDE

PRESENT

THE DONMAR WAREHOUSE PRODUCTION

HAMLET
BY WILLIAM SHAKESPEARE

ROSS ARMSTRONG   HARRY ATTWELL   RON COOK   IAN DRYSDALE
PETER EYRE   JENNY FUNNELL   MICHAEL HADLEY   COLIN HAIGH
SEAN JACKSON   GERALDINE JAMES   JUDE LAW   GWILYM LEE
JAMES LE FEUVRE   JOHN MacMILLAN   GUGU MBATHA-RAW
KEVIN R. McNALLY   HENRY PETTIGREW   MATT RYAN
ALAN TURKINGTON   FAYE WINTER

SET AND COSTUME DESIGNER	LIGHTING DESIGNER	COMPOSER AND SOUND DESIGNER
CHRISTOPHER ORAM	NEIL AUSTIN	ADAM CORK

DONMAR EXECUTIVE PRODUCER	CASTING	PRESS REPRESENTATIVE	MARKETING DIRECTOR
JAMES BIERMAN	ANNE McNULTY	BONEAU/BRYAN BROWN	ERIC SCHNALL

GENERAL MANAGEMENT	PRODUCTION STAGE MANAGER	U.S. TECHNICAL SUPERVISOR	U.K. TECHNICAL SUPERVISOR
101 PRODUCTIONS, LTD.	FRANK LOMBARDI	AURORA PRODUCTIONS	PATRICK MOLONY

DIRECTED BY
MICHAEL GRANDAGE

10/6/09

Jude Law as Hamlet delivers his soliloquy in the snow.

Photo by Johan Persson

Hamlet

Cast Continued

UNDERSTUDIES

For Laertes, Rosencrantz, Osric:
ROSS ARMSTRONG
For Claudius, Polonius:
IAN DRYSDALE
For Gertrude:
JENNY FUNNELL
For Ghost of Hamlet's Father, 1st Gravedigger, Barnardo:
COLIN HAIGH
For Marcellus, Captain, Priest:
SEAN JACKSON
For Guildenstern, Francisco/4th Player, 3rd Player/2nd Gravedigger/English Ambassador, Reynaldo, Cornelius:
JAMES LE FEUVRE
For Horatio:
JOHN MacMILLAN
For Fortinbras:
HENRY PETTIGREW
For Hamlet:
MATT RYAN
For Player King:
ALAN TURKINGTON
For Ophelia, Player Queen:
FAYE WINTER

The company of *Hamlet* is appearing with the permission of Actors' Equity Association.

This production of *Hamlet* was first performed at the Wyndam's Theatre as part of the Donmar West End season on May 29, 2009.

(L-R): Jude Law and Kevin R. McNally
Photo by Johan Persson

Ross Armstrong
Cornelius

Harry Attwell
Guildenstern

Ron Cook
Polonius, 1st Gravedigger

Ian Drysdale
Osric

Peter Eyre
Ghost of Hamlet's Father, Player King

Jenny Funnell
Player Queen

Colin Haigh
Member of the Court

Michael Hadley
Barnardo, Priest, Captain

Sean Jackson
Reynaldo

Geraldine James
Gertrude

Jude Law
Hamlet

Gwilym Lee
Laertes

James Le Feuvre
Member of the Court

John MacMillan
Rosencrantz

Kevin R. McNally
Claudius

Gugu Mbatha-Raw
Ophelia

Henry Pettigrew
Marcellus, 3rd Player, 2nd Gravedigger, English Ambassador

Matt Ryan
Horatio

Alan Turkington
Francisco, Fortinbras, 4th Player

Faye Winter
Member of the Court

Hamlet

 William Shakespeare
Author

 Michael Grandage
Director

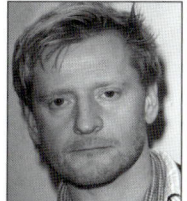 Christopher Oram
Set and Costume Design

 Neil Austin
Lighting Design

 Adam Cork
Composer & Sound Design

 Wendy Orshan, 101 Productions, Ltd.
General Manager

 Arielle Tepper Madover
Producer

 Stephanie P. McClelland; Green Curtain Productions (GCP)
Producer

 Caro Newling
Producer

 Carl Moellenberg
Producer

 Ruth Hendel
Producer

 Barbara Whitman
Producer

 Frankie J. Grande
Producer

STAGE CREW

USHERS

Hamlet

Joe Trepasso
(Doorman)

BOX OFFICE
Cliff Cobb (Treasurer), Noreen Morgan (Assistant Treasurer), Mike Lynch (Assistant Treasurer)

MANAGEMENT
Beverly Edwards (Company Manager), Frank Lombardi (Production Stage Manager), Diane DiVita (Stage Manager)

Carmel Vargyas
(Hair Supervisor)

Photos by Brian Mapp

STAFF FOR HAMLET

GENERAL MANAGEMENT
101 PRODUCTIONS, LTD.
Wendy Orshan   Jeffrey M. Wilson
David Auster
Elie Landau

COMPANY MANAGER
Beverly Edwards

GENERAL PRESS REPRESENTATIVE
BONEAU/BRYAN-BROWN
Adrian Bryan-Brown   Jim Byk
Christine Olver

U.S TECHNICAL SUPERVISION
AURORA PRODUCTIONS
Gene O'Donovan   W. Benjamin Heller II
Rachel Sherbill, Steve Rosenberg, Jarid Sumner
Melissa Mazdra, Amy Merlino Coey, Amanda Raymond
Graham Forden, Liza Luxenberg

WIG AND HAIR DESIGN
Richard Mawbey

Production Stage Manager	Frank Lombardi
Stage Manager	Diane DiVita
Associate Director	Sam Yates
Associate Scenic Designer	Andrew D. Edwards
UK Scenic Associate	Richard Kent
Associate Costume Designer	Barry Doss
UK Associate Lighting Designer/Lighting Programmer	Rob Halliday
Associate Lighting Designer	Pamela Kupper
Associate Sound Designer	Chris Cronin
Production Carpenter	Jim Kane
Production Electrician	Jon Lawson
Head Electrician	Tom Lawrey
Production Props Supervisor	Andrew Meeker
Production Sound	Ed Chapman
House Carpenter	Brian McGarty
House Flyman	Brian Bullard
House Electrician	Charley DeVerna
House Properties	Ron Vitelli
Wardrobe Supervisor	Kelly Saxon
Star Dresser	Lyle Jones
Dressers	Meredith Benson, Sandy Binion, Cesar Porto
Hair Supervisor	Carmel Vargyas
Assistant to Ms. Tepper Madover	Holly Ferguson
Assistant to Mr. Law	Ben Jackson
Production Assistant	Iris D. O'Brien
Legal Counsel	Lazarus & Harris, LLP/ Scott R. Lazarus, Esq., Robert C. Harris, Esq.
Accountant	Fried & Kowgios
Controller	Galbraith & Co Inc./Kenny Noth
Advertising	SPOTCO/ Drew Hodges, Jim Edwards, Pete Duffy, Y Darius Suyama
Marketing	Eric Schnall
101 Productions, Ltd. Staff	Denys Baker, Mark Barna, Beth Blitzer, Clinton Kennedy, Ingrid Kloss, Michael Rudd, Mary Six Rupert, Hannah Wachtel
Banking	City National Bank/Anne McSweeney
Insurance	Ventura Brokerage, Inc./ Christine Sadofsky Walton & Parkinson/ Richard Walton
Immigration	Visa Consultants/Lisa Carr Traffic Control Group/David King
Company Housing	Maison International/ Marie-Claire Martineau Alternative Business Accommodations
Travel Services	Road Rebel
Transportation	IBA Limousine
Theatre Displays	King Displays, Inc.
Payroll Services	Castellana Services, Inc.
Production Photographer	Joan Marcus
UK Production Photographer	Johan Persson
Website Design	Dotmeta/Yujin Asai
Opening Night Coordinator	The Lawrence Company/ Michael P. Lawrence

DONMAR WAREHOUSE

Artistic Director	Michael Grandage
Executive Producer	James Bierman
General Manager	Jo Danvers
PA to the Executive	Miriam Green
Creative & Casting Associate	Anne McNulty
Resident Casting Assistant	Vicky Richardson
Development Director	Kate Mitchell
Development Manager	Deborah Lewis
Development Officer	Rosie Dalling
Development Administrator	Fraser Anderson
Marketing Manager	Jonathan Aplin
Press Representative	Kate Morley for Blueprint PR
Marketing & Press Assistant	Kim Savage
Office Administrator	Frankie Bridges
General Assistant	Nina Segal
Deputy Production Manager	Kate West
Head of Wardrobe	Tansy Blaik-Kelly
Deputy Head of Wardrobe	Morag Pirrie
Associate Director	Jamie Lloyd
Resident Assistant Director	Paul Hart
Education Associates	Dominic Francis, Sophie Watkiss

CREDITS
Scenery by Souvenir Scenery. Lighting by Lights Up & Cue Sound. Sound by Sound Associates. Hosiery and undergarments by Bra*Tenders.

www.Hamletbroadway.com

 THE SHUBERT ORGANIZATION, INC.
Board of Directors

Philip J. Smith Chairman	**Robert E. Wankel** President
Wyche Fowler, Jr.	**John W. Kluge**
Lee J. Seidler	**Michael I. Sovern**

Stuart Subotnick

Elliot Greene Chief Financial Officer	**David Andrews** Senior Vice President – Shubert Ticketing
Juan Calvo Vice President and Controller	**John Darby** Vice President – Facilities
Peter Entin Vice President – Theatre Operations	**Charles Flateman** Vice President – Marketing
Anthony LaMattina Vice President – Audit & Production Finance	**Brian Mahoney** Vice President – Ticket Sales

D.S. Moynihan
Vice President – Creative Projects

House Manager .... Hugh Barnett

Hamlet
Scrapbook

1. Opening night curtain call on the stage of the Broadhurst Theatre.
2. Jude Law (Hamlet) attends the premiere.
3. Cast member Geraldine James (Gertrude) at the opening night party at Gotham Hall.
4. Cast member Ron Cook at Gotham Hall.
5. Gugu Mbatha-Raw (Ophelia) at the premiere.

Photos by Aubrey Reuben

Correspondent: Diane DiVita, Stage Manager
Memorable Opening Night Letter, Fax or Note: All the good wishes from other Broadway shows.
Opening Night Gifts: *Hamlet* hoodies and playing cards.
Most Exciting Celebrity Visitor: Martin Scorsese.
Who Has Done the Most Shows in Their Career: Peter Eyre has appeared in *Hamlet* three times, and twice on Broadway!
Special Backstage Rituals: Poker game in the Men's Ensemble dressing room.
Favorite Moment During Each Performance: Snow falling on Hamlet
Favorite In-Theatre Gathering Place: Wardrobe room.
Favorite Off-Site Hangouts: Angus, Jimmy's Corner.
Favorite Snack Food: Pretzel rods and biscuits (cookies), regular and gluten-free.
Mascot: "Zoe"—an orange furry head owned by Arielle Tepper Madover (our producer).
Favorite Therapy: Alcohol.
Most Memorable Ad-Lib: "Another sword for Hamlet!," "My Lord!"
Memorable Press Encounter: Every day.
Memorable Stage Door Fan Encounter: Japanese fan.
Fastest Costume Change: None really…except James Le Feuvre into a soldier.
Busiest Day at the Box Office: Day after Opening.
Who Wore the Heaviest/Hottest Costume: Peter Eyre.
Who Wore the Least: Gugu Mbatha-Raw: Ophelia in a nightgown.
Catchphrase Only the Company Would Recognize: "Kaboom"—fragrance by John MacMillain.
Memorable Directorial Note: "Don't give an audience what they want. Give them what they need."
Company Legends: Henry Pettigrew / That you get free popcorn at movies if you show your Playbill photo.
Tales from the Put-In: Never take down the brick wall.
Understudy Anecdote: Ross Armstrong got "The Understudy Touch" from Ed Bennet and went on 12 minutes later.
Nicknames: "Laugh Whore."
Sweethearts Within the Company: Everyone including crew, doormen, GMs and Company Manager.
Embarrassing Moments: A company member slept through curtain call.
Ghostly Encounters Backstage: Just Peter Eyre.
Coolest Thing About Being in This Show: JUDE LAW!!!
Any Other Stories or Memories You'd Like To Add! Overheard at a promotional event: "Do you think the writer will come?"

In the Heights

First Preview: February 14, 2008. Opened: March 9, 2008.
Still running as of May 31. 2010.

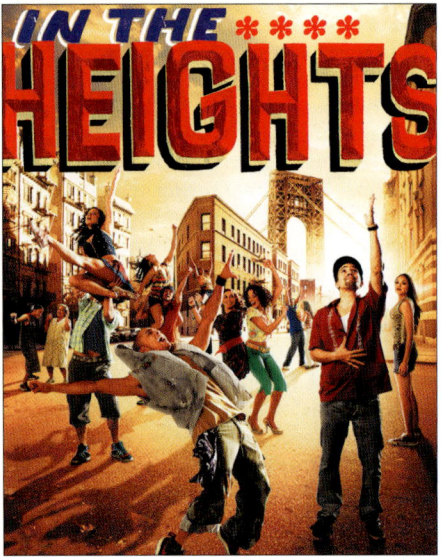

CAST

(in order of appearance)

Graffiti Pete	WILLIAM B. WINGFIELD
Usnavi	JAVIER MUÑOZ
Piragua Guy	ELISEO ROMÁN
Abuela Claudia	OLGA MEREDIZ
Carla	COURTNEY REED
Daniela	ANDRÉA BURNS
Kevin	RICK NEGRÓN
Camila	PRISCILLA LOPEZ
Sonny	ROBIN DE JESÚS
Benny	CHRISTOPHER JACKSON
Vanessa	MARCY HARRIELL
Nina	MANDY GONZALEZ
Bolero Singer	DOREEN MONTALVO
Ensemble	TONY CHIROLDES, DWAYNE CLARK, ROSIE LANI FIEDELMAN, MARCUS PAUL JAMES, NINA LAFARGA, JENNIFER LOCKE, DOREEN MONTALVO, ELISEO ROMÁN GABRIELLE RUIZ, LUIS SALGADO, KEVIN SANTOS, RICKEY TRIPP

SWINGS
MICHAEL BALDERRAMA,
BLANCA CAMACHO,
STEPHANIE KLEMONS,
ALEJANDRA REYES, JON RUA,
MARCOS SANTANA

Continued on next page

RICHARD RODGERS THEATRE
UNDER THE DIRECTION OF JAMES M. NEDERLANDER AND JAMES L. NEDERLANDER

KEVIN McCOLLUM   JEFFREY SELLER   JILL FURMAN
SANDER JACOBS GOODMAN/GROSSMAN PETER FINE EVERETT/SKIPPER

PRESENT

IN THE HEIGHTS

MUSIC AND LYRICS BY
LIN-MANUEL MIRANDA

BOOK BY
QUIARA ALEGRÍA HUDES

CONCEIVED BY
LIN-MANUEL MIRANDA

WITH
ANDRÉA BURNS   ROBIN DE JESÚS   MANDY GONZALEZ
MARCY HARRIELL CHRISTOPHER JACKSON PRISCILLA LOPEZ OLGA MEREDIZ
JAVIER MUÑOZ RICK NEGRÓN COURTNEY REED WILLIAM B. WINGFIELD

AND
TONY CHIROLDES   DWAYNE CLARK   ROSIE LANI FIEDELMAN
MARCUS PAUL JAMES NINA LAFARGA JENNIFER LOCKE DOREEN MONTALVO
ELISEO ROMÁN GABRIELLE RUIZ LUIS SALGADO KEVIN SANTOS RICKEY TRIPP
MICHAEL BALDERRAMA BLANCA CAMACHO STEPHANIE KLEMONS
ALEJANDRA REYES JON RUA MARCOS SANTANA

SET DESIGN	COSTUME DESIGN	LIGHTING DESIGN	SOUND DESIGN
ANNA LOUIZOS	PAUL TAZEWELL	HOWELL BINKLEY	ACME SOUND PARTNERS

ARRANGEMENTS & ORCHESTRATIONS	MUSIC COORDINATOR	MUSIC DIRECTOR
ALEX LACAMOIRE & BILL SHERMAN	MICHAEL KELLER	ZACHARY DIETZ

CASTING	PRESS REPRESENTATIVE	MARKETING	COMPANY MANAGER
TELSEY + COMPANY	THE HARTMAN GROUP	SCOTT A. MOORE	BRIG BERNEY

GENERAL MANAGEMENT	TECHNICAL SUPERVISOR	PRODUCTION STAGE MANAGER	ASSOCIATE PRODUCERS
JOHN S. CORKER LIZBETH CONE	BRIAN LYNCH	J. PHILIP BASSETT	RUTH HENDEL HAROLD NEWMAN

MUSIC SUPERVISION
ALEX LACAMOIRE

CHOREOGRAPHED BY
ANDY BLANKENBUEHLER

DIRECTED BY
THOMAS KAIL

DEVELOPMENT OF *IN THE HEIGHTS* WAS SUPPORTED BY THE EUGENE O'NEILL THEATER CENTER
DURING A RESIDENCY AT THE MUSIC THEATER CONFERENCE OF 2005.

INITIALLY DEVELOPED BY BACK HOUSE PRODUCTIONS.

INTHEHEIGHTSTHEMUSICAL.COM
BROADWAY CAST ALBUM AVAILABLE ON GHOSTLIGHT RECORDS.

10/1/09

Javier Muñoz (center) with members of the cast

Photo by Joan Marcus

In the Heights

MUSICAL NUMBERS

ACT I

"In the Heights"	Usnavi, Company
"Breathe"	Nina, Company
"Benny's Dispatch"	Benny, Nina
"It Won't Be Long Now"	Vanessa, Usnavi, Sonny
"Inutil"	Kevin
"No Me Diga"	Daniela, Carla, Vanessa, Nina
"96,000"	Usnavi, Benny, Sonny, Vanessa, Daniela, Carla, Company
"Paciencia y Fe" ("Patience and Faith")	Abuela Claudia, Company
"When You're Home"	Nina, Benny, Company
"Piragua"	Piragua Guy
"Siempre" ("Always")	Camila
"The Club/Fireworks"	Company

ACT II

"Sunrise"	Nina, Benny, Company
"Hundreds of Stories"	Abuela Claudia, Usnavi
"Enough"	Camila
"Carnaval del Barrio"	Daniela, Company
"Atencion"	Kevin
"Alabanza"	Usnavi, Nina, Company
"Everything I Know"	Nina
"No Me Diga (Reprise)"	Daniela, Carla, Vanessa
"Piragua (Reprise)"	Piragua Guy
"Champagne"	Vanessa, Usnavi
"When the Sun Goes Down"	Nina, Benny
"Finale"	Usnavi, Company

Cast Continued

UNDERSTUDIES

For Usnavi:
MICHAEL BALDERRAMA, JON RUA, KEVIN SANTOS
For Abuela Claudia, Camila, Daniela:
BLANCA CAMACHO, DOREEN MONTALVO
For Nina:
NINA LAFARGA, COURTNEY REED, GABRIELLE RUIZ
For Benny:
DWAYNE CLARK, MARCUS PAUL JAMES
For Kevin:
TONY CHIROLDES, ELISEO ROMÁN
For Vanessa:
COURTNEY REED, GABRIELLE RUIZ
For Carla:
STEPHANIE KLEMONS, GABRIELLE RUIZ
For Sonny:
JON RUA, KEVIN SANTOS
For Graffiti Pete:
MICHAEL BALDERRAMA, JON RUA, RICKEY TRIPP
For Piragua Guy:
TONY CHIROLDES, KEVIN SANTOS

Dance Captains:
MICHAEL BALDERRAMA, STEPHANIE KLEMONS

BAND

Conductor:
ZACHARY DIETZ
Associate Conductor:
JOSEPH CHURCH
Lead Trumpet:
RAUL AGRAZ
Trumpet:
SCOTT WENDHOLT
Trombones:
JOE FIEDLER, RYAN KEBERLE
Reeds:
DAVE RICHARDS, KRISTY NORTER
Drums:
ANDRES FORERO
Percussion:
DOUG HINRICHS, WILSON TORRES
Bass:
IRIO O'FARRILL
Guitar:
MANNY MOREIRA
Keyboard 1:
ZACHARY DIETZ
Keyboard 2:
JOSEPH CHURCH

(L-R: Olga Merediz and Mandy Gonzalez)
Photo by Joan Marcus

The Playbill Broadway YEARBOOK 2009-2010

In the Heights

 Andréa Burns *Daniela*
 Robin De Jesús *Sonny*
 Mandy Gonzalez *Nina*
 Marcy Harriell *Vanessa*
 Christopher Jackson *Benny*
 Priscilla Lopez *Camila*
 Olga Merediz *Abuela Claudia*

 Javier Muñoz *Usnavi*
 Rick Negrón *Kevin*
 Courtney Reed *Carla*
 William B. Wingfield *Graffiti Peter*
 Tony Chiroldes *Ensemble*
 Dwayne Clark *Ensemble*
 Rosie Lani Fiedelman *Ensemble*

 Marcus Paul James *Ensemble*
 Nina Lafarga *Ensemble*
 Jennifer Locke *Ensemble*
 Doreen Montalvo *Bolero Singer/ Ensemble*
 Eliseo Román *Piragua Guy/ Ensemble*
 Gabrielle Ruiz *Ensemble*
 Luis Salgado *Ensemble; Latin Assistant Choreographer*

 Kevin Santos *Ensemble*
 Rickey Tripp *Ensemble*
 Michael Balderrama *Swing; Dance Captain/ Fight Captain*
 Blanca Camacho *Swing*
 Stephanie Klemons *Swing*
 Alejandra Reyes *Swing*
 Jon Rua *Swing*

 Marcos Santana *Swing*
 Lin-Manuel Miranda *Music and Lyrics; Original Concept*
 Quiara Alegría Hudes *Book*
 Thomas Kail *Director*
 Andy Blankenbuehler *Choreographer*
 Alex Lacamoire *Music Supervisor, Arranger, Orchestrator*
 Anna Louizos *Set Designer*

In the Heights

Paul Tazewell
Costume Designer

Howell Binkley
Lighting Designer

Tom Clark, Mark Menard and Nevin Steinberg,
Acme Sound Partners
Sound Designer

Bill Sherman
Arranger/Orchestrator

Bernard Telsey,
Telsey+Company
Casting

John S. Corker
General Manager

Brian Lynch/
Theatretech, Inc.
Technical Supervisor

Ron Piretti
Fight Director

Casey Hushion
Assistant Director

Joey Dowling
Associate Choreographer

Kevin McCollum
Producer

Jeffrey Seller
Producer

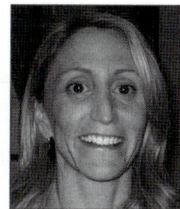
Jill Furman
Producer

Sander Jacobs
Producer

Robyn Goodman,
Goodman/Grossman
Producer

Walt Grossman,
Goodman/Grossman
Producer

Sonny Everett,
Everett/Skipper
Producer

Ruth Hendel
Associate Producer

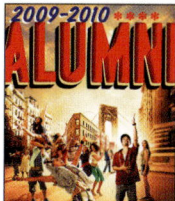
Afra Hines
Ensemble

Antuan Raimone
Swing

Elise Santora
Daniela

Janet Dacal
Carla

José-Luis Lopez
Swing

Justina Machado
Daniela

Noemi Del Rio
Swing

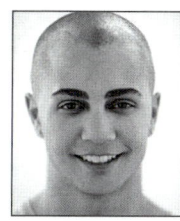
Seth Stewart
Graffiti Pete

Shaun Taylor-Corbett
Ensemble, Swing

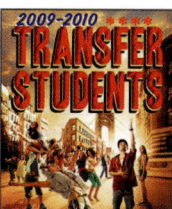

Afra Hines
Ensemble, Swing

Allison Thomas Lee
Swing

Antuan Raimone
Swing

Corbin Bleu
Usnavi

David Del Rio
Sonny

The Playbill Broadway Yearbook 2009-2010

In the Heights

Janet Dacal
Nina

Nancy Ticotin
Swing

Noah Rivera
Ensemble

Noemi Del Rio
Swing

Rubén Flores
Ensemble, Swing

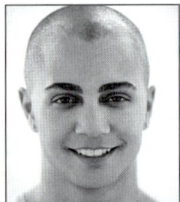
Seth Stewart
Dance Captain, Swing

WARDROBE
Seated: Alon Ben-David

Standing (L-R): Leslie Moulton, Kirsten Solberg, Susan Checklick

CREW
Seated (L-R): Dan Tramontozzi, Justin Rathbun, Chris Kurtz, David Speer, Brian Frankel

Standing (L-R): Steve DeVerna, Kevin Camus, Jae Day

ORCHESTRA
Front Row (L-R): Joe Fiedler, Doug Hinrichs, Andres Forero, Zachary Dietz

Back Row (L-R): Richard Bouka, Dave Miller, Irio O'Farrill, Kristy Norter, Wilson Torres, Matt Gallagher, Carl Fischer

STAGE AND COMPANY MANAGEMENT
Front: Heather Hogan

Back Row (L-R): Kenneth J. McGee, Brig Berney, Beverly Jenkins

In the Heights

Left: Jamie Stewart (Hair)
Right: Angelo Gonzalez (Stage Door)

Photos by Brian Mapp

STAFF FOR *IN THE HEIGHTS*

GENERAL MANAGEMENT
John S. Corker
Lizbeth Cone

GENERAL PRESS REPRESENTATIVES
THE HARTMAN GROUP
Michael Hartman
Wayne Wolfe   Matt Ross

DIRECTOR OF MARKETING
Scott A. Moore

CASTING
TELSEY + COMPANY
Bernie Telsey CSA, Will Cantler CSA, David Vaccari CSA,
Bethany Knox CSA, Craig Burns CSA,
Tiffany Little Canfield CSA, Rachel Hoffman CSA,
Carrie Rosson CSA, Justin Huff CSA, Bess Fifer CSA,
Patrick Goodwin, Abbie Brady-Dalton

COMPANY MANAGER	Brig Berney
TECHNICAL SUPERVISION	Brian Lynch/Theatretech, Inc.
PRODUCTION STAGE MANAGER	J. Philip Bassett
WIG DESIGNER	Charles LaPointe
Assistant Director	Casey Hushion
Associate Choreographer	Joey Dowling
Fight Director	Ron Piretti
Dance Captains	Michael Balderrama, Stephanie Klemons
Stage Manager	Amber Wedin
Assistant Stage Manager	Michael T. Clarkston
Latin Assistant Choreographer	Luis Salgado
Fight Captain	Michael Balderrama
Associate Scenic Designers	Donyale Werle, Todd Potter
Assistant Scenic Designers	Hilary Noxon, Heather Dunbar
Associate Costume Designer	Michael Zecker
Assistant Costume Designer	Caitlin Hunt
Associate Lighting Designer	Mark Simpson
Assistant Lighting Designer	Greg Bloxham, Ryan O'Gara
Associate Sound Designer	Sten Severson
Moving Light Programmer	David Arch
Advance Carpenter	McBrien Dunbar
Advance Flyman	Cheyenne Benson
Production Electrician	Keith Buchanan
Head Electrician	Christopher Kurtz
Production Sound	Dan Robillard
Production Propmaster	George Wagner
Head Propmaster	David Speer
Follow Spot Operator	Jason Wilkosz
Sound Engineer	Justin Rathbun
Wardrobe Supervisor	Susan Checklick
Hair Supervisor	Jamie Stewart
Dressers	Alon Ben-David, Gary Biangone, Jennifer Hohn, Leslie Moulton
Rehearsal Pianists	Joseph Church, Cian McCarthy, Daniel Moctezuma, Kat Sherrell, Charity Wicks
Musical Coordinator	Michael Keller
Copyist	Emily Grishman Music Preparation/Emily Grishman, Katharine Edmonds
Keyboard Programming	Randy Cohen
Rehearsal Drummer	Doug Hinrichs
Music Assistant	Colleen Darnell
Management Assistant	Andy Jones
Production Assistants	Jess Slocum, Mark Barna
Assistant to Messrs. McCollum & Seller	Caitlyn Thomson
Assistant to Mr. Corker	Kim Marie Vasquez
Legal Counsel	Levine Plotkin Menin, LLP/Loren Plotkin, Susan Mindell, Conrad Rippy, Cris Criswell
Marketing Associate	Joshua Lee Poole
Advertising	SpotCo/Drew Hodges, Jim Edwards, Darius Suyama, Pete Duffy, Tom Greenwald
Press Interns	Matt Sinsheimer, Jacob Matsumiya
Accountant	FK Partners/Robert Fried
Controller	Sarah Galbraith and Co.
Insurance	D.R. Reiff & Associates
Banking	Signature Bank/Margaret Monigan, Mary Ann Fanelli
Payroll	Castellana Services
Merchandise	Marquee Merchandise LLC/Matt Murphy
Travel Arrangements	Tzell Travel
Flyer Distribution	Laura Cosentino/Roselily
Website/Internet Marketing	SpotCo/Sara Fitzpatrick, Matt Wilstein
Production Photographer	Joan Marcus
Physical Therapy	Mark Hunter Hall
Merchandising	George Fenmore/More Merchandising International

---

THE PRODUCING OFFICE
Kevin McCollum   Jeffrey Seller
John S. Corker   Debra Nir
Caitlyn Thomson

SPECIAL THANKS
Luis Miranda; John Buzzetti; Mark Sendroff;
Nick Lugo; LaVie Productions/R. Erin Craig,
Off-Broadway General Manager

CREDITS
Scenery constructed by Centerline Studio, Inc. Lighting equipment from PRG Lighting. Sound equipment from PRG Audio. New York Daily News, L.P., used with permission. Chain motors from Show Motion. Trucking by Clark Transfer, Inc. Percussion equipment and drum programming by Dan McMillan. Latin percussion supplied by Pearl Drum Company. Andres Patrick Forero plays Yamaha Drum heads, Sabian cymbals, Vic Firth sticks and Reunion Blues, exclusively. Wireless handsets by Verizon. Costumes built by Donna Langman Costumes; Tricorne, Inc.; Paul Chang Custom Taylor. Millinery by Lynne Mackey Studio. Hosiery and undergarments from Bra*Tenders. Goya products furnished by Goya Foods, Inc. Lottery items courtesy of NY State Lottery. Cell phones courtesy of Motorola. Cups, straws and stirrers courtesy of Solo, Inc. Mars Inc. products used. Adams gum and Cadbury chocolates used. Werthers Original courtesy of Storck USA. MASTERFOODS USA products used. Unilever N.A. products used. Kraft Foods products used. Massimo-Zanetti beverages used. Country Club cola products and Iberia Food products courtesy of Luis Botero, North Shore Bottling Company, Brooklyn, NY. Beauty salon supplies provided by Ray Beauty Supply. Piragua Cart, artificial food props, other props provided by John Creech Design and Production. Local trucking provided by Prop Transport. Flicker candles provided by Clara Sherman, Kinnelon, NJ. Car service counter, bodega counter provided by Blackthorne Studio. Various bodega prop dressing courtesy of Rock Ice Café and Catering, Dunellen, NJ. Food display hanging racks courtesy of Green Acres Health Food Store, Piscataway, NJ. Additional set and hand props courtesy of George Fenmore, Inc. Steel security gates by Steelcraft Folding Gate Corp. Raul Agraz and Trevor Neumann exclusively use Cannonball trumpets.

Makeup provided by M•A•C

Bolero singer is Doreen Montalvo. Radio voices by Joshua Henry, Elisáo Roman and Daphne Rubin-Vega.

Smoke, haze and strobe lights are used
in this production.

In the Heights rehearsed at
The New 42nd Street Studios.

NEDERLANDER

Chairman	James M. Nederlander
President	James L. Nederlander

Executive Vice President
Nick Scandalios

Vice President Corporate Development	Senior Vice President Labor Relations
Charlene S. Nederlander	**Herschel Waxman**

Vice President	Chief Financial Officer
Jim Boese	**Freida Sawyer Belviso**

HOUSE STAFF FOR
THE RICHARD RODGERS THEATRE

House Manager	Timothy Pettolina
Box Office Treasurer	Fred Santore Jr.
Assistant Treasurer	Corinne Dorso
Electrician	Steve Carver
Carpenter	Kevin Camus
Propertymaster	Stephen F. DeVerna
Engineer	Sean Quinn

In the Heights
SCRAPBOOK

Correspondents: Blanca Camacho, "Swing"; Corbin Bleu, "Usnavi"

Memorable Fan Letter: We got a letter from a teacher who had brought her high school students to the show. She talked about how much her class had enjoyed the show. Then she mentioned one student in particular. He'd had no intention of applying to colleges. He never even considered it an option for himself until he saw our show which deals with a neighborhood girl going away to Stanford. The teacher added that the young man had just gotten his first college acceptance letter and was awaiting what would probably be a few more! That's why we do what we do....

Anniversary Parties and/or Gifts: This year we celebrated our second anniversary with amazing cream puffs and sparkling cider before the show. We LOVE to snack!

Most Exciting Celebrity Visitors: How about a double whammy? Ex-President AND Senator Clinton! The whole building turned out to meet them! Then there were our theatrical forebears: Chita Rivera and Rita Moreno—Latin ROYALTY! These icons, through their talent, generosity, and perseverance, made a show like ours possible.

Who Has Done the Most Shows: Our Grande Dame and icon in her own right Ms. Priscilla (PLo) Lopez, numbering 12 Broadway shows.

Favorite In-Theatre Gathering Place: Goodness Gracious, it's the basement! That's where the food is! Lots of food, always food. Anytime anyone comes back from vacation they bring a little taste of the place to share. Yep, just like your Mom would.

Favorite Off-Site Hangout: Oh sure, we do Bourbon Street and Brazil, Brazil, but if you wanna talk off-site, it's PR, baby! I estimate close to half the cast has been to Puerto Rico on vacation; during one recent seven-week stretch there was someone from *Heights* there at any given moment! Lately, the little Puerto Rican island of Culebra has seen a lot of action from us, but keep it a secret!

Favorite Snack Providers: Reed player Kristy Norter's friend Grace who gifts us the most delicious assortments of cookies! Lately, a newbie has come in a close second: Corbin's girlfriend Reba and her Red Velvet Chocolate Balls.

Favorite Therapy: Ricola by the tub-full! It's the duct tape of throat maladies—fixes anything!

Memorable Ad-Lib: The inimitable Priscilla Lopez! The line as written: "One day I'm going to open my 'Restaurante Boricua' but until then you are all my guinea pigs. Serve yourselves, the plates are in the kitchen." Which was replaced with "BUT UNTIL THEN YOU ARE ALL SUBJECT TO MY MICE. Serve yourselves the plates are in the kitchen!" Yum....

Latest Audience Arrival: 9:45 for an 8 PM curtain! Show finishes at 10:30. They were out-of-towners and weren't able to accept our House Manager's (Tim Pettolina) generous offer for them to return. Also, we always get a few stragglers who think our 2 PM show starts at 3 or our 7 PM show at 8.

Orchestra Member Who Played the Most

(L-R): Janet Dacal, Marcy Harriell, *Yearbook* co-correspondent Corbin Bleu and David Del Rio attending the after-party to celebrate the opening night for Bleu and the new cast members February 23, 2010.

Consecutive Performances Without a Sub: Starting with previews, percussionist Wilson Torres logged in 93 shows without respite.

Actor Who Performed the Most Roles in This Show: No one performs more than one role in a show at *ITH*, HOWEVER, the swings are something else. Jon Rua covers nine roles and has performed 8 1/2 of them. Yes, a split track. Dance Captain Michael "Superman" Balderrama has been on for 9 male roles (counting a turn as Piragua Guy during the Off-Broadway run) AND a turn at part of the Woman 5 track in a pinch!

Record Number of Texting Incidents During a Performance: During a matinee with Corbin Bleu as Usnavi, our audience had about a thousand students in attendance, half of whom were texting!

Busiest Day at the Box Office: In general, Saturdays, but the busiest ever was the day after our Tony Award win for Best Musical.

Who Wore the Heaviest/Hottest Costume: Piragua Guy, Eliseo Román, who overdresses his PG costume with heavy winter 1943 outerwear á la Fiorello LaGuardia.

Who Wore the Least: Nina Lafarga: midriff halter, teeny, tiny skirt. It's the summer's hottest day, after all....

Sweethearts Within the Company: Jon Rua and Gabrielle Ruiz. Recently engaged Shaun Taylor-Corbett and Noemi Del Rio literally met on our stage. He proposed there, and both are now part of our touring company after being with the Broadway company. How romantic!

Orchestra Member Who Played the Most Instruments: Percussionist Doug Hinrichs manipulates 26 instruments: the sample pad, samba whistle, congas, bongos, djembe, cymbals, tambourine, guiro, cowbells, agogo bells, woodblocks, caxixis, shakers, claves, timbal, floor tom, concert bass drum, timpani, vibraphone, vibra-slap, mark tree, chimes, shekere, finger cymbal, triangles, and the tam-tam, all with just 2 hands!

Memorable Directorial Notes: Director Thomas Kail: "So we get to do the show again tomorrow," "That's a change."

Musical Director Alex Lacamoire: "sforte-piano," "soft serve ending."

Backstage Rituals: Perhaps more like habits or vices? On Saturdays, Alex Lacamoire would play and sing a little ditty at our five-minute call: "Saturday night on Broadway—they ain't ready!" Over time, different cast members expanded the idea and eventually Javier Muñoz took the helm. It became a little parody, or a heartfelt sentiment, or a full production, depending on what was going on with our show or in the world. It would still always end with Alex's same two lines. When Javi left, selections from the "archives" were re-played until Corbin took over the task.

Also, our new stage manager, Beverly Jenkins, instituted "Dollar Fridays." We all put a dollar in the pot, the winner gets all the $, but not before spending some of it on a bagel buffet for everyone on Saturday morning. More goodies—yeeees! (Musicians seem uncannily lucky at this.)

We celebrate everyone's birthday with goodies ranging from cake, to flan, to banana pudding but there's always the singing of "Happy Birthday" followed by "Que te crezca el pipí"—a wish for bigger things to come for the honoree! We love holidays! We have Secret Santas, Secret Valentines, and we hold door-decorating contests. The SM office always sports a holiday theme (hearts, eggs, shamrocks, etc) and hair supervisor Jamie Stewart turns the basement into a winter wonderland every year!

And yes, we still hold hands at our prayer circle before every show.

Memorable Stage Door Fan Encounter: A young Latina greeted me after a performance when I went on for "Abuela." With tears welling up in her eyes she told me of her dreams of someday being a performer and how inspiring I was to her. I could barely keep my own tears in check as I recalled my own inspiration when I had stood outside a stage door, myself then a

In the Heights
Scrapbook

young Latina, and presented an *A Chorus Line* PLAYBILL to Priscilla Lopez to sign. I am now her understudy and I could not believe how lucky I was to be helping pass on Priscilla's gift to someone else. And, yes, I still have that PLAYBILL Priscilla signed.

Fastest Costume Change: Man 3 and Woman 5 (currently Noah Rivera and Rosie Lani Fiedelman) change from contemporay clothes to Havana 1943 to NY 1943 and back all in the course of one number, "Paciencia y Fe."

Embarrassing Moments: Corbin, as Usnavi, likes to lovingly stroke the arms of all us ladies who play Abuela. Well, I had been back from my Puerto Rican vacation about a week when I went on. During the dinner scene Corbin rubbed and rubbed my bare arm. Little did he know that the effects of the Caribbean sun had taken effect and that my tan was peeling. He was actually doing a buff and polish! I kept wondering if under the lights the audience was seeing a billowing cloud of dead skin cells! Of course one could argue that Robin De Jesús farting on stage while playing "Sonny" takes the embarrassment prize!

Superstition That Turned Out To Be True: One night, early in our run, a butterfly flew on stage from the audience, flitted about, and calmly landed on the shoulder of "Sonny" (Robin De Jesús) during the touching, culminating moment of our show: the lowering of the bodega grate. I'm sure members of the audience thought it was part of the show! I thought this MUST be a good omen—and it has been, as we've been here for two years now and have won numerous awards and critical acclaim. Plus a bit more to come.

Nicknames: In addition to previously published ones we have Javier "Usjavi" Muñoz, Blanca "Blanchameleon" Camacho, Michael "Superman" Balderrama, and I'd like to coin Stephanie "Wonder Woman" Klemons!

Who Wrote This Year's "Easter Bonnet" Sketch: It takes a village: Brig Berney, Rickey Tripp, Marcus Paul James, Blanca Camacho, Allison Thomas Lee, Corbin Bleu, and Bill Sherman. "Heights Cool Musical" was the title and it was Corbin Bleu's nightmare about what happens to a "celebrity" when he joins a Broadway show.

Catchphrases Only the Company Would Recognize: We have names for sections of choreography that confuse every new person that ever joins the company. They were coined by choreographer Andy Blankenbuehler as a communications shortcut: "Soft Porn Circle," "Shawshank," "Superfriends Circle," "Matrix," "Cowbell," "Soft Flags," "Maypole," "Snakes on a Plane," to name a few!

Memorable Press Encounter: Well, being food-centric around here, Olga Merediz DID get to be a celebrity judge on Bobby Flay's Throwdown—a Cuban sandwich competition. Lucky girl!

Singer Jordin Sparks (center, long earrings) visits backstage with the cast February 11, 2010.

Best In-House Parody Lyric: "You're done for the day" "No way" "Cause we've got a date" "OK!" becomes: "You're done for the day" "No way" "Cause we've got a date" "I'm Gay...."

Understudy Anecdote: They all go on before they're scheduled to. By happenstance, usually the day they have their put-in a call comes in from an ailing cast member and next thing, they're on!

Ghostly Encounters Backstage: I was almost embarrassed to poll *Heights* folk with this question as I was certain I would get blank stares or quizzical looks—I'd never heard any such rumors at our theatre UNTIL I ASKED! The house staff had PLENTY to say: Dottie, Beverly, Rosie, Ralph, Jimmy, and Nadia all had stories to share. There are reappearing red lipstick smudges in the ladies room. They get painted and wiped but inevitably return. Stall doors open by themselves. Dressing rooms have strange sounds, and things spontaneously fall off shelves in one of them. After hours brings bizarre howling sounds, chandeliers moving, the sound of people walking. Jimmy, our doorman, armed himself with a baseball bat one such evening. Guess he was gonna take a few of them with him! Then three different people told me about the "Redheads." Ralph sees "her" in Box B about 2 AM. Beverly saw "him" in Mezzanine Row H. Cast member Tony Chiroldes has twice felt the presence of his Mom, an actress and also, at times, a redhead. None of these people knew of the others' stories! Our beautiful red theatre must be a beacon for them. I myself, during a company meeting in the house, saw a door open fully and close slowly all by itself but nervously dismissed it til I heard these stories. However, I was assured that these are benevolent beings that like musicals as nothing bad ever happens during those times when music fills the Richard Rodgers Theatre.

Company Legends: Michael "Superman" Balderrama—period. He is the dance captain, and covers several roles including the lead. He has kept us on our toes and enabled our company to surmount any challenge thrown at us. No matter what, we can always do the show. He's split-tracked roles, suddenly realizing onstage that the piragua he was about to sell was to himself! He's torn down the house as Usnavi while simultaneously keeping an eye on a newbie or calling for a quick rehearsal for a change during the intermission. All in the spirit of cooperation and the benevolent, gentle firmness of a shepherd with his flock. What a mind! What a talent! What a man! Thank you, Michael Balderrama—*Heights* Legend!

The Name of the Club in Act I: La Cueva de Cuca.

Company Member with the Show the Longest: Doreen Montalvo since reading in September 2002.

Loudest Belcher: Marcus Paul James.

Biggest Appetite: Wilson Torres, always munching.

Cookie Monster: Manny Moreira.

Favorite Pizza: Grandma Slice from Patzeria's.

Longest Medical Leave: Rickey Tripp, injured doing show, out 10 months.

Unofficial Understudy: PSM Beverly Jenkins, knows almost all the parts.

Unofficial "Captain" of our *ITH* family: Chris Jackson.

Shortest Short-Shorts: Alum Krysta Rodriguez sported shorts that left little to the imagination!

Other Stories and Memories: Corbin recounts: I received a letter from a woman saying that she had heard the announcement that "Corbin Bleu from *High School Musical* was to be taking over the role of Usnavi in *In The Heights*." In her opinion it wasn't a very good promotional idea. She was highly skeptical, however she wanted to see the show itself so she came prepared to see a mediocre performance. But she said that what she saw shocked her and couldn't have been farther from what she expected. It was one of her favorite performances she had ever seen and she admitted to it, changing a jaded perspective she had obtained from possibly being in NYC for too long. She finished the letter by wishing me luck in the rest of what she believes will be a very prosperous career and that she will be following it from now on. I hung the letter up in my dressing room and look to it for inspiration every now and then. It's very uplifting to have supportive fans, and it's a whole other fulfillment to know your work has turned a skeptic. I'm just grateful to be a part of a project that gives me the opportunity to strive to work for that type of respect.

In the Next Room or the vibrator play

First Preview: October 22, 2009. Opened: November 19, 2009.
Closed January 10, 2010 after 31 Previews and 60 Performances.

CAST
(in order of speaking)

Mrs. Givings	LAURA BENANTI
Dr. Givings	MICHAEL CERVERIS
Annie	WENDY RICH STETSON
Mr. Daldry	THOMAS JAY RYAN
Mrs. Daldry	MARIA DIZZIA
Elizabeth	QUINCY TYLER BERNSTINE
Leo Irving	CHANDLER WILLIAMS

PLACE
A prosperous spa town outside of New York City, perhaps Saratoga Springs

TIME
The dawn of the age of electricity, and after the Civil War; circa 1880s

Assistant Stage Manager .... DENISE YANEY

UNDERSTUDIES
For Mrs. Givings:
ERICA SULLIVAN
For Dr. Givings: NATHAN DARROW,
PAUL NIEBANCK
For Annie: EMILY DORSCH, ERICA SULLIVAN
For Mr. Daldry: PAUL NIEBANCK
For Mrs. Daldry: EMILY DORSCH
For Elizabeth: DONNETTA LAVINIA GRAYS
For Leo Irving: NATHAN DARROW

LYCEUM THEATRE
149 West 45th Street
A Shubert Organization Theatre
Philip J. Smith, *Chairman*   **Robert E. Wankel**, *President*

LINCOLN CENTER THEATER
under the direction of
André Bishop and Bernard Gersten
presents

IN THE NEXT ROOM
or
the vibrator play

by
Sarah Ruhl

with (in alphabetical order)
Laura Benanti   Quincy Tyler Bernstine
Michael Cerveris   Maria Dizzia   Thomas Jay Ryan
Wendy Rich Stetson   Chandler Williams

sets	costumes	lighting
Annie Smart	David Zinn	Russell H. Champa

sound	music
Bray Poor	Jonathan Bell

production stage manager	casting	general press agent
Roy Harris	Daniel Swee	Philip Rinaldi

director of development	director of marketing
Hattie K. Jutagir	Linda Mason Ross

general manager	production manager
Adam Siegel	Jeff Hamlin

directed by
Les Waters

Special thanks to The Harold and Mimi Steinberg Charitable Trust for supporting new American work at LCT.
American Airlines is the official airline of Lincoln Center Theater.
LCT wishes to express its appreciation to Theatre Development Fund for its support of this production.
IN THE NEXT ROOM or the vibrator play was originally commissioned and produced by Berkeley Repertory Theatre, Berkeley, CA, Tony Taccone, Artistic Director/ Susan Medak, Managing Director.

11/19/09

Michael Cerveris (C) induces a "paroxysm" in Maria Dizzia (L) while Laura Benanti listens at a door, as in the show's logo.

Photo by Joan Marcus

In the Next Room or the vibrator play

 Laura Benanti
Mrs. Givings

 Quincy Tyler Bernstine
Elizabeth

 Michael Cerveris
Dr. Givings

 Maria Dizzia
Mrs. Daldry

 Thomas Jay Ryan
Mr. Daldry

 Wendy Rich Stetson
Annie

 Chandler Williams
Leo Irving

 Nathan Darrow
Understudy

 Emily Dorsch
Understudy

 Donnetta Lavinia Grays
Understudy

 Paul Niebanck
Understudy

 Erica Sullivan
Understudy

 Sarah Ruhl
Playwright

 Les Waters
Director

 David Zinn
Costumes

 Paul Huntley
Wigs & Hair

 André Bishop and Bernard Gersten, Lincoln Center Theater
Producer

(L-R): Quincy Tyler Bernstine and Laura Benanti

Photo by Joan Marcus

The Playbill Broadway Yearbook 2009-2010

USHERS AND FRONT OF HOUSE CREW

Front Row (L-R):
Elsie Grosvenor,
Joann Swanson (House Manager),
Jessica Cooke

Middle Row (L-R):
Merida Colon,
Rose Ann Cipriano,
Victoria Heslin

Back Row (L-R):
Gerry Belitsis,
Victor Beaulieu,
Joe Pittman,
Carmen Sanchez,
Security (unidentified)

STAGE MANAGERS AND RUNNING CREW

Front Row (L-R):
Laura McGarty (Props),
Vanessa Poggioli (Production Assistant),
Leah Nelson (Props)

Back Row (L-R): Roy Harris (Production Stage Manager), Adam Braunstein (Carpenter), Wallace Flores (Production Sound), David Karlson (Production Electrician), Jonathan Cohen (Electrician), Denise Yaney (Stage Manager)

BOX OFFICE

(L-R): Kathy Cadunz,
Viji Cadunz (Head Treasurer)

In the Next Room or the vibrator play

COSTUME CREW
(L-R): Tree Sarvay, Moira MacGregor-Conrad (Wardrobe Supervisor) and Erick Medinilla

LINCOLN CENTER THEATER
ANDRÉ BISHOP — BERNARD GERSTEN
ARTISTIC DIRECTOR — EXECUTIVE PRODUCER

ADMINISTRATIVE STAFF
GENERAL MANAGER ....ADAM SIEGEL
   Associate General Manager ....Jessica Niebanck
   General Management Assistant ....Meghan Lantzy
   Facilities Manager ....Alex Musteliar
   Associate Facilities Manager ....Michael Assalone
GENERAL PRESS AGENT ....PHILIP RINALDI
   Press Associate ....Barbara Carroll
PRODUCTION MANAGER ....JEFF HAMLIN
   Associate Production Manager ....Paul Smithyman
DIRECTOR OF
   DEVELOPMENT ....HATTIE K. JUTAGIR
   Associate Director of Development ......Rachel Norton
   Manager of Special Events and
     Young Patron Program ....Karin Schall
   Grants Writer ....Neal Brilliant
   Manager, Patron Program ....Sheilaja Rao
   Assistant to the
     Director of Development ....Raelyn Lagerstrom
   Development Associate/
     Special Events and
     Young Patron Program ....Jennifer H. Rosenbluth
   Development Assistant/
     Patron Program ....Terra Gillespie
DIRECTOR OF FINANCE ....DAVID S. BROWN
   Controller ....Susan Knox
   Systems Manager ....Stacy Valentine
   Finance Associate ....Joan Glazer
DIRECTOR OF MARKETING .LINDA MASON ROSS
   Marketing Associate ....Kristin Miller
   Marketing Assistant ....Ashley M. Dunn
DIRECTOR OF EDUCATION ....KATI KOERNER
   Associate Director of Education ....Alexandra Lopez
Assistant to the Executive Producer ......Barbara Hourigan

Office Manager ....Brian Hashimoto
Office Assistant ....Rhonda Lipscomb
Messenger ....Esau Burgess
Reception ....Brenden Rogers, Michelle Metcalf

ARTISTIC STAFF
ASSOCIATE DIRECTORS ......GRACIELA DANIELE,
   NICHOLAS HYTNER,
   JACK O'BRIEN,
   SUSAN STROMAN,
   DANIEL SULLIVAN
RESIDENT DIRECTOR ....BARTLETT SHER
DRAMATURG and DIRECTOR,
   LCT DIRECTORS LAB ....ANNE CATTANEO
CASTING DIRECTOR ....DANIEL SWEE, CSA
MUSICAL THEATER
   ASSOCIATE PRODUCER ....IRA WEITZMAN
DIRECTOR OF LCT3 ....PAIGE EVANS
Artistic Administrator ....Julia Judge
Casting Associate ....Camille Hickman
Lab Assistant ....Kate Marvin

SPECIAL SERVICES
Advertising ....Serino-Coyne/
   Jim Russek, Roger Micone,
   Becca Goland-Van Ryn
Principal Poster Artist ....James McMullan

Poster Artwork for *In the Next Room
   or the vibrator play* ....James McMullan
Counsel ....Peter L. Felcher, Esq.;
   Charles H. Googe, Esq.;
   and Carol Kaplan, Esq. of
   Paul, Weiss, Rifkind, Wharton & Garrison
Immigration Counsel ....Theodore Ruthizer, Esq.;
   Mark D. Koestler, Esq.
   of Kramer, Levin, Naftalis & Frankel LLP
Labor Counsel ....Michael F. McGahan, Esq.
   of Epstein, Becker & Green, P.C.
Auditor ....Frederick Martens, CPA
   Lutz & Carr, L.L.P.
Insurance ....Jennifer Brown of
   DeWitt Stern Group
Photographer ....Joan Marcus
Video Services ....Fresh Produce Productions/
   Frank Basile
Travel ....Tygon Tours
Consulting Architect ....Hugh Hardy,
   H3 Hardy Collaboration Architecture
Construction Manager ....Yorke Construction
Payroll Service ....Castellana Services, Inc.
Merchandising ....Marquee Merchandise, LLC/
   Matt Murphy

STAFF FOR *IN THE NEXT ROOM or the vibrator play*
COMPANY MANAGER.........MATTHEW MARKOFF
Assistant Company Manager ....Daniel Hoyos
Assistant Director ....Sarah Rasmussen
Assistant Set Designer ....Andrew Kaufman
Assistant Costume Designer ....Jacob Climer
Assistant Lighting Designer ....Justin Partier
Assistant Sound Designer ....Charles Coes
Production Carpenter ....John Weingart
Production Electrician ....David Karlson
Production Propertyman ....Mark Dignam
Production Soundman ....Wallace Flores
Make-up Design ....Jon Carter
Props ....Susan Barras
Wardrobe Supervisor ....Moira MacGregor-Conrad
Dressers ....Erick Medinilla, Tree Sarvay
Hair Supervisor ....Cindy Demand
Costume Intern ....Joshua Marsh
Production Assistant ....Vanessa Poggioli

Technical Supervision by
William Nagle and Patrick Merryman

Wig & Hair Design
Paul Huntley

CREDITS
Scenery fabrication by PRG-Scenic Technologies, a division of Production Resource Group, LLC. Show control and scenic motion control featuring Stage Command Systems® by PRG-Scenic Technologies, a division of Production Resource Group, LLC., New Windsor, NY. Costumes by Tricorne Costumes, Carelli Costumes, Marc Happel, Jared Leese, Paul Chang Custom Tailors, Berkeley Costume Shop and the TDF Costume Collection. Sound equipment by Sound Associates. Lighting equipment from PRG Lighting. Natural herb cough drops courtesy of Ricola USA, Inc.

Visit www.lct.org

For groups of 20 or more:
Caryl Goldsmith Group Sales
(212) 889-4300

THE SHUBERT ORGANIZATION, INC.
Board of Directors

Philip J. Smith — **Robert E. Wankel**
Chairman — President

Wyche Fowler, Jr. — **John W. Kluge**

Lee J. Seidler — **Michael I. Sovern**

Stuart Subotnick

Elliot Greene — **David Andrews**
Chief Financial — Senior Vice President
Officer — Shubert Ticketing

Juan Calvo — **John Darby**
Vice President — Vice President –
and Controller — Facilities

Peter Entin — **Charles Flateman**
Vice President – — Vice President –
Theatre Operations — Marketing

Anthony LaMattina — **Brian Mahoney**
Vice President – — Vice President –
Audit & Production Finance — Ticket Sales

D.S. Moynihan
Vice President – Creative Projects

House Manager ....Joann Swanson

Irving Berlin's White Christmas

First Preview: November 13, 2009. Opened: November 22, 2009.
Closed January 3, 2010 after 13 Previews and 51 Performances.

CAST
(in order of appearance)

Bob Wallace	JAMES CLOW
Phil Davis	TONY YAZBECK
Ralph Sheldrake	PETER REARDON
General Henry Waverly	DAVID OGDEN STIERS
Ed Sullivan Announcer	REMY AUBERJONOIS
Rita	KIIRA SCHMIDT
Rhoda	BETH JOHNSON NICELY
Tessie	LEAH HOROWITZ
Betty Haynes	MELISSA ERRICO
Judy Haynes	MARA DAVI
Jimmy	MATTHEW LaBANCA
Quintet	LEAH HOROWITZ, DENNIS O'BANNION, DREW HUMPHREY, ANNA AIMEE WHITE, CLIFF BEMIS
Mr. Snoring Man	CLIFF BEMIS
Mrs. Snoring Man	DENISE NOLIN
Train Conductor	DREW HUMPHREY
Martha Watson	RUTH WILLIAMSON
Susan Waverly	MADELEINE ROSE YEN
Ezekiel	CLIFF BEMIS
Mike Nulty	REMY AUBERJONOIS
Sheldrake's Secretary	DENISE NOLIN
Regency Room Announcer	REMY AUBERJONOIS

Continued on next page

MARQUIS THEATRE
UNDER THE DIRECTION OF JAMES M. NEDERLANDER AND JAMES L. NEDERLANDER

Kevin McCollum John Gore Thomas B. McGrath Paul Blake
The Producing Office Dan Markley Sonny Everett
Broadway Across America

in association with
Paramount Pictures
present

Irving Berlin's WHITE CHRISTMAS

Based upon the Paramount Pictures film written for the screen by
Norman Krasna, Norman Panama, and Melvin Frank

Music and Lyrics by
Irving Berlin

Book by
David Ives and Paul Blake

starring
**James Clow Melissa Errico
Tony Yazbeck Mara Davi**

also starring
Ruth Williamson Peter Reardon
Remy Auberjonois Cliff Bemis Madeleine Rose Yen

and
David Ogden Stiers

with
Kelli Barclay Abby Church Sara Edwards Mary Giattino Chad Harlow
Tori Heinlein Leah Horowitz Drew Humphrey Matthew J. Kilgore
Matthew LaBanca Jason Luks Joseph Medeiros Taryn Molnar Beth Johnson Nicely
Denise Nolin Dennis O'Bannion Con O'Shea-Creal Kristyn Pope Kiira Schmidt
Kelly Sheehan Anna Aimee White Ryan Worsing Richard Riaz Yoder

Set Design	Costume Design	Lighting Design	Sound Design
Anna Louizos	Carrie Robbins	Ken Billington	Acme Sound Partners
Orchestrations	Vocal and Dance Arrangements	Music Coordinator	Music Director
Larry Blank	Bruce Pomahac	Seymour Red Press	Steven Freeman
Technical Supervisor	Production Stage Manager	Marketing	Press Representative
Brian Lynch	Peter Wolf	Scott A. Moore	Boneau/Bryan-Brown
Casting	General Management	Associate Director	Associate Choreographer	Associate Producers
Jay Binder	John S. Corker	Marc Bruni	Kelli Barclay	Richard A. Smith
Nikole Vallins	Barbara Crompton			Douglas L. Meyer
				James D. Stern

Music Supervisor
Rob Berman

Choreographer
Randy Skinner

Directed by
Walter Bobbie

A developmental production of Irving Berlin's White Christmas was presented at the MUNY in St. Louis, MO.

11/22/09

(L-R): James Clow, Melissa Errico, Tony Yazbeck and Mara Davi

Photo by Joan Marcus

Irving Berlin's White Christmas

SCENES

ACT ONE
Prologue	An Army Camp in Europe, Christmas Eve, 1944
Scene One	The Ed Sullivan Show, 1954
Scene Two	Bob & Phil's Dressing Room; Betty & Judy's Dressing Room
Scene Three	Jimmy's Back Room
Scene Four	A Train
Scene Five	The Front Desk at the Columbia Inn
Scene Six	The Barn Theatre
Scene Seven	The Front Porch of the Inn
Scene Eight	Sheldrake's Office; Martha's Switchboard
Scene Nine	The Barn Theatre

ACT TWO
Scene One	The Barn Theatre
Scene Two	Betty's Bedroom
Scene Three	The Barn Theatre
Scene Four	The Regency Room
Scene Five	The Ed Sullivan Show
Scene Six	The Front Desk at the Columbia Inn
Scene Seven	The Barn Theatre, Christmas Eve

MUSICAL NUMBERS

ACT ONE
Overture
- "Happy Holiday" .... Bob & Phil
- "White Christmas" .... Bob, Phil, Sheldrake & Ensemble
- "Let Yourself Go" .... Bob, Phil & Ensemble
- "Love and the Weather" .... Bob & Betty
- "Sisters" .... Betty & Judy
- "The Best Things Happen While You're Dancing" .... Phil, Judy & Quintet
- "Snow" .... Bob, Phil, Betty, Judy, Mr. Snoring Man, Mrs. Snoring Man & Ensemble
- "What Do You Do With a General?" .... Martha, Bob & Phil
- "Let Me Sing and I'm Happy" .... Martha & Ensemble
- "Count Your Blessings" .... Bob & Betty
- "Blue Skies" .... Bob & Ensemble

ACT TWO
Entr'acte
- "I Love a Piano" .... Phil, Judy & Ensemble
- "Falling Out of Love Can Be Fun" .... Martha, Betty & Judy
- "Sisters" (Reprise) .... Bob & Phil
- "Love, You Didn't Do Right By Me/How Deep Is the Ocean" .... Betty & Bob
- "We'll Follow the Old Man" .... Bob & Male Ensemble
- "Let Me Sing and I'm Happy" (Reprise) .... Susan
- "How Deep Is the Ocean" (Reprise) .... Bob & Betty
- "We'll Follow the Old Man" (Reprise) .... Bob, Phil, Sheldrake & Male Ensemble
- "White Christmas" (Reprise) .... Bob & Company
- Finale: "I've Got My Love to Keep Me Warm" .... Full Company

---

Cast Continued

ENSEMBLE
ABBY CHURCH, SARA EDWARDS, CHAD HARLOW, LEAH HOROWITZ, DREW HUMPHREY, MATTHEW LaBANCA, JOSEPH MEDEIROS, TARYN MOLNAR, BETH JOHNSON NICELY, DENISE NOLIN, DENNIS O'BANNION, CON O'SHEA-CREAL, KRISTYN POPE, KIIRA SCHMIDT, KELLY SHEEHAN, ANNA AIMEE WHITE, RYAN WORSING, RICHARD RIAZ YODER

UNDERSTUDIES
For Bob Wallace: PETER REARDON
For Betty Haynes: LEAH HOROWITZ
For Phil Davis: DREW HUMPHREY
For Judy Haynes: ANNA AIMEE WHITE
For General Waverly: CLIFF BEMIS
For Susan Waverly: TORI HEINLEIN
For Ralph Sheldrake: REMY AUBERJONOIS
For Martha Watson: DENISE NOLIN
For Mike, Ed Sullivan Announcer: CHAD HARLOW
For Ezekiel, Mr. Snoring Man: DREW HUMPHREY

SWINGS
KELLI BARCLAY, MARY GIATTINO, MATTHEW J. KILGORE, JASON LUKS

DANCE CAPTAINS
Dance Captain: KELLI BARCLAY
Assistant Dance Captain: MARY GIATTINO

MUSIC DIRECTOR
STEVEN FREEMAN

ASSOCIATE MUSIC DIRECTOR
MATTHEW PERRI

ORCHESTRA
Violin: MARILYN REYNOLDS
Trumpets: DAVE TRIGG, ANTHONY GORRUSO, MIKE PONELLA
Keyboards: MATTHEW PERRI, MICHA YOUNG
Cello: DANNY MILLER
Woodwinds: DAVE PIETRO, HARRY HASSELL, AARON HEICK, SCOTT SCHACHTER, EUGENE SCHOLTENS
Trombones: LARRY FARRELL, CLINT SHARMAN, JEFF NELSON
French Horn: DAVID BYRD-MARROW
Percussion: BILL HAYES
Bass: LOU BRUNO
Drums: ERIC HALVORSON

Irving Berlin's White Christmas

 James Clow — *Bob Wallace*
 Melissa Errico — *Betty Haynes*
 Tony Yazbeck — *Phil Davis*
 Mara Davi — *Judy Haynes*
 David Ogden Stiers — *General Henry Waverly*
 Ruth Williamson — *Martha Watson*
 Peter Reardon — *Ralph Sheldrake*

 Remy Auberjonois — *Mike Nulty, Ed Sullivan Announcer*
 Cliff Bemis — *Ezekiel, Mr. Snoring Man*
 Madeleine Rose Yen — *Susan Waverly*
 Kelli Barclay — *Swing, Associate Choreographer, Dance Captain*
 Abby Church — *Ensemble*
 Sara Edwards — *Ensemble*
 Mary Giattino — *Swing, Asst. Choreographer, Asst. Dance Captain*

 Chad Harlow — *Ensemble*
 Tori Heinlein — *u/s Susan*
 Leah Horowitz — *Tessie, Ensemble*
 Drew Humphrey — *Ensemble*
 Matthew J. Kilgore — *Swing*
 Matthew LaBanca — *Jimmy, Ensemble*
 Jason Luks — *Swing*

 Joseph Medeiros — *Ensemble*
 Taryn Molnar — *Ensemble*
 Beth Johnson Nicely — *Rhoda*
 Denise Nolin — *Mrs. Snoring Man, Ensemble*
 Dennis O'Bannion — *Ensemble*
 Con O'Shea-Creal — *Ensemble*
 Kristyn Pope — *Ensemble*

 Kiira Schmidt — *Rita*
 Kelly Sheehan — *Ensemble*
 Anna Aimee White — *Ensemble*
 Ryan Worsing — *Ensemble*
 Richard Riaz Yoder — *Ensemble*
 Irving Berlin — *Music & Lyrics*
 David Ives — *Book*

Irving Berlin's White Christmas

 Paul Blake
Book & Producer

 Walter Bobbie
Director

 Randy Skinner
Choreographer

 Anna Louizos
Set Design

 Carrie Robbins
Costume Design

 Ken Billington
Lighting Design

 Larry Blank
Orchestrations

 Tom Clark, Mark Menard and Nevin Steinberg, Acme Sound Partners
Sound Design

 Rob Berman
Musical Supervisor

 Seymour Red Press
Music Coordinator

 Marc Bruni
Associate Director

 Jay Binder
Casting

 Nikole Vallins
Casting

 Brian Lynch/Theatretech, Inc.
Technical Supervisor

 John Corker
General Manager

 Kevin McCollum
Producer

 John Gore
Producer

 Thomas B. McGrath
Producer

 Jeffrey Seller, The Producing Office
Producer

 Sonny Everett
Associate Producer

 Douglas L. Meyer
Associate Producer

DOORMAN
Juan "Cisco" Garcia

MANAGEMENT
(L-R): Jim Athens (Assistant Stage Manager), Jay McLeod (Stage Manager), Andy Jones (Assistant Company Manager), Barbara Crompton (Company Manager), Unknown.

The Playbill Broadway Yearbook 2009-2010

Irving Berlin's White Christmas

STAFF FOR *IRVING BERLIN'S WHITE CHRISTMAS*

GENERAL MANAGEMENT
John S. Corker
Barbara Crompton

MARKETING
Scott A. Moore

CASTING
JAY BINDER CASTING
Jay Binder CSA
Jack Bowdan CSA, Mark Brandon,
Sara Schatz CSA, Nikole Vallins,
Karen Young, Patrick Bell

PRESS REPRESENTATIVE
BONEAU/BRYAN-BROWN
Chris Boneau   Joe Perrotta
Kelly Guiod

ASSOCIATE DIRECTOR
Marc Bruni

ASSOCIATE CHOREOGRAPHER
Kelli Barclay

COMPANY MANAGER
Barbara Crompton

PRODUCTION STAGE MANAGER	Peter Wolf
Technical Supervisor	Brian Lynch/Theatretech, Inc.
Stage Manager	Jay McLeod
Assistant Stage Manager	Jim Athens
Associate Company Manager	Andrew Jones
Associate Musical Director	Matthew Perri
Additional Orchestrations	Peter Myers
Assistant Director	David Ruttura
Assistant Choreographer	Mary Giattino
Executive Assistant to Mr. McCollum and Mr. Seller	Caitlyn Thomson
Assistant to Mr. Blake	Michael Bosner
Assistant to the General Manager	Kim Marie Vasquez
Marketing Assistant	Joshua Poole
Production Assistants	Danny Sharron, Danielle Teague-Daniels
Associate Set Designer	Mike Carnahan
Associate Lighting Designer	Ed McCarthy
Assistant Lighting Designer	Jonathan Spencer
Moving Light Programmer	Hillary Knox
Associate Sound Designer	Nicholas Borisjuk
Assistant Sound Designer	Bridget O'Connor
Associate Costume Designer	Lee Austin
Production Carpenter	Lehan Sullivan
Head Carpenter	Joe Valentino
Flyman	Jeremy Palmer
Automation	Robert Valli
Production Electrician	Manny Becker
Head Electrician	Craig Caccamise
Assistant Electrician	Jason Wilkosz
Spot Light Operator	Christopher Robinson
Production Sound	Dan Robillard
Sound Engineer	Brad Gyorgak
Assistant Sound Engineer	Elizabeth Coleman
Production Properties Master	George Wagner
Prop Master	Jacob White
Production Wardrobe Supervisor	Lee Austin
Wardrobe Supervisor	Jessica Worsnop
Assistant Wardrobe	Cherie Cunningham
Dressers	Jenny Barnes, Jason Bishop, Diana Calderazzo, Tracey Diebold, Barry Hoff, William Hubner, Jeffrey Johnson, Cindy Steffens-Kubala, Jean Steinlein, John Webber
Stitchers	Deborah Black, Amy Kitzhaber
Principal Wigs Designed by	Paul Huntley Enterprises, Inc.
Ensemble Wigs Designed by	Howard Leonard/Wigboys, Inc.
Production Hair Supervisor	Elisa Acevedo
Assistant Hair	Nathaniel Hathaway
Music Preparation	Chelsea Music Service/Paul Holderbaum
Synthesizer Programmer	Bruce Samuels
Rehearsal Pianists	Andrew Graham, Paul Masse
Education Service	On Location Education
New York Child Guardian	Alison Roberts
NYC Studio Teacher	Amy Wolk
Advertising	Spotco/Drew Hodges, Jim Edwards, Tom Greenwald, Y. Darius Suyama, Stacey Maya
Website/Internet Marketing	Spotco/Sara Fitzpatrick, Matt Wilstein, Marc Mettler
Merchandise	Creative Goods LLC/Pete Milano
Legal Counsel	Levine Plotkin & Menin LLP/Loren H. Plotkin, Esq.; Susan Mindell, Esq.
Accounting	FK Partners/Robert Fried
Comptroller	Galbraith and Company/Sarah Galbraith, Tabitha Falcone
Insurance	D.R. Reiff & Associates/Dennis Reiff, Regina Newsome
Banking	JP Morgan Chase
Payroll	CSI Payroll Services, Inc./Lance Castellana

THE PRODUCING OFFICE
Kevin McCollum	Jeffrey Seller
John S. Corker	Debra Nir
Scott A. Moore	Caitlyn Thomson

Irving Berlin's White Christmas on Broadway
is dedicated to
Sonny Everett,
our friend and fellow producer.

THE ST. LOUIS MUNY
Dennis Regan, President and CEO
Paul Blake, Executive Producer

CREDITS
Scenery built by Hudson Scenic. Certain scenery built by Centerline. Drops painted by Scenic Art Studios, Inc. Certain scenery and scenic effects built, painted, electrified and automated by ShowMotion Inc. Lighting equipment by PRG Lighting. Sound equipment by PRG Audio. Women's clothing by Parsons-Meares Ltd. Jimmy's sequence by CMC & Design. Men's custom tailoring by Scafati. Additional tailoring by Saint Laurie Merchant Tailors. Custom knitwear by Maria Ficalora. Oxydol ensembles by Martin Izquierdo Studio. Dance shoes by Capezio, NYC; Worldtone Dance Shoes. Millinery by Arnold S. Levine, Inc.; Studio Rouge; Timberlake Studios. Sisters' shoes by Phil LaDuca NYC. Principal wigs by Paul Huntley Enterprises, Inc. Ensemble wigs built by Wigboys, Inc. Snow effects by Snowmasters Inc. Chain motors from ShowMotion, Inc. Radios from Production Radio Rentals. Quick-Ice packs provided by Medi-Ice. Spike tape provided by Garden Hardware.

SPECIAL THANKS
Mary Ellin Barrett, Linda Emmet, Elizabeth Peters, Ted Chapin, Victoria Traube, Bert Fink, Neil Mazzella, William M. Mensching, Joseph Forbes, Roger Gray, Darren DeVerna, David Strang, Eric Pearce, Kevin Branch, Kevin Collins of Capezio NYC, Ricola natural herb cough drops courtesy of Ricola USA, Inc., Linda at Medi, Emergen-C products courtesy of Alacer Corporation. Special thanks to Actors' Equity Association and SSD&C for their special consideration on this production.

Performance rights to *Irving Berlin's White Christmas* are licensed by R&H Theatricals:
www.rnhtheatricals.com.

Rehearsed at New 42nd Street Studios.

NEDERLANDER

Chairman	James M. Nederlander
President	James L. Nederlander

Executive Vice President
Nick Scandalios

Vice President Corporate Development **Charlene S. Nederlander**	Senior Vice President Labor Relations **Herschel Waxman**
Vice President **Jim Boese**	Chief Financial Officer **Freida Sawyer Belviso**

STAFF FOR THE MARQUIS THEATRE
Manager	David Calhoun
Associate Manager	Austin Nathaniel
Treasurer	Rick Waxman
Assistant Treasurer	John Rooney
Carpenter	Joseph P. Valentino
Electrician	James Mayo
Property Man	Scott Mecionis

Irving Berlin's White Christmas
Scrapbook

Correspondent: Kelly Sheehan, Ensemble
Opening Night Gift: Massage chair from David Ogden Stiers.
Most Exciting Celebrity Visitor and What They Did/Said: Jimmy Fallon...he said he was very happy to be there because his wife used to tap dance.
Who Has Done the Most Shows: Drew Humphrey has performed in the show (on tour) for six [?] consecutive years. (I don't think he has missed one yet.)
Special Backstage Rituals: During overture we had a special dance.
Before Act II started, someone was "assigned" the job of wrangling the dancers so no one would get hit by the drop flying in!
Visits from our dance team Kelli and Mary!
Favorite Moment During Each Performance: Santa Freeman's "surprise" visit from the orchestra every night!!!!
Favorite In-Theatre Gathering Place: The greenroom, right by the massage chair.
Favorite Off-Site Hangout: Glass House Tavern
Favorite Snack Foods: Holiday baked goods and the candy drawer.
Mascot: Mickey the magical mouse. He would visit all the dressing rooms and liked chocolate kisses.
Favorite Therapy: Reflexology sessions generously donated by David Ogden Stiers.
Memorable Ad-Lib: The fantastic Remy Auberjonois ad-libs during the number "Blue Skies."
Memorable Stage Door Fan Encounter: The man that called our ethnic female the "token." (No one was offended in the making of this comment!)
Fastest Costume Change: From "Sisters" reprise into "Regency," six ensemble members change out of rehearsal wear into evening attire, with lots of accessories included!
Busiest Day at the Box Office: Jason Luks' Broadway Debut.
Who Wore the Biggest Costume? Melissa Errico's "Big Red."
Who Wore the Least?: We are not that kind of show!
Catchphrases Only the Company Would Recognize: Broadway POW!
Sweethearts Within the Company: A love story in progress!
Memorable Directorial Note: "Don't let me catch you acting" by Walter Bobbie.
Nickname: "No Bow Clow." One day after a long matinee Jim Clow forgot to lead us in our final company bow! Oops!
Embarrassing Moments: It's a *White Christmas* tradition that if someone drops a cane during "Blue Skies" they buy the dancing ensemble a round of drinks. And yes, it happened this year!
Coolest Things About Being in This Show: Celebrating the Holidays in the middle of Times Square. Getting to work with the nicest bunch of people in New York.

1. The folks making their Broadway debut! Back Row (L-R): Richard Riaz Yoder, Chad Harlow, Jason Luks, Matt Kilgore. Middle Row (L-R): Abby Church, Taryn Molnar, Dennis O'Bannion, Denise Nolin, Sara Edwards. Front Row (L-R): Madeleine Rose Yen and Tori Heinlein.
2. Clockwise from top: Yearbook correspondent Kelly Sheehan, Sara Edwards, Anna Aimee White, Abby Church, Kristyn Pope, and Taryn Molnar.
3. Dennis O'Bannion in his dressing room.
4. Members of the cast backstage.
5. (L-R): Abby Church, Matt LaBanca, Kristyn Pope, Chad Harlow and Taryn Molnar.
6. (L-R): Beth Johnson Nicely, Kristyn Pope

Photos courtesy Kelly Sheehan

The Playbill Broadway Yearbook 2009-2010

Jersey Boys

First Preview: October 4, 2005. Opened: November 6, 2005.
Still running as of May 31, 2010.

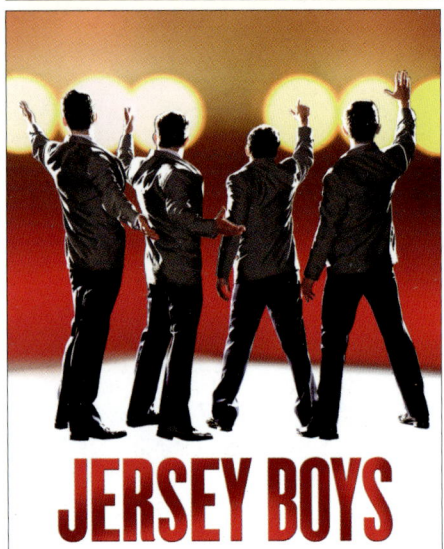

CAST

Bob Gaudio	SEBASTIAN ARCELUS
Nick Massi	MATT BOGART
Tommy DeVito	DOMINIC NOLFI
Frankie Valli	JARROD SPECTOR
Frankie Valli (Wed. & Sat. matinees)	CORY GRANT
Bob Crewe (and others)	PETER GREGUS
Gyp DeCarlo (and others)	MARK LOTITO
Nick DeVito, Stosh, Billy Dixon, Norman Waxman, Charlie Calello (and others)	MILES AUBREY
Officer Petrillo, Hank Majewski, Crewe's PA, Joe Long (and others)	ERIK BATES
Mary Delgado, Angel (and others)	BRIDGET BERGER
French Rap Star, Detective One, Hal Miller, Barry Belson, Police Officer, Davis (and others)	KRIS COLEMAN
Church Lady, Miss Frankie Nolan, Bob's Party Girl, Angel, Lorraine (and others)	HEATHER FERGUSON
Joey, Recording Studio Engineer (and others)	RUSSELL FISCHER
Frankie's Mother, Nick's Date, Angel, Francine (and others)	SARA SCHMIDT
Thugs	KEN DOW, JOE PAYNE

SWINGS
MICHELLE ARAVENA, JOHN HICKMAN,
KATIE O'TOOLE, JAKE SPECK,
TAYLOR STERNBERG

Continued on next page

AUGUST WILSON THEATRE
A JUJAMCYN THEATRE

JORDAN ROTH
President

PAUL LIBIN
Producing Director

JACK VIERTEL
Creative Director

Dodger Theatricals Joseph J. Grano Tamara and Kevin Kinsella Pelican Group
in association with Latitude Link Rick Steiner/Osher/Staton/Bell/Mayerson Group

present

JERSEY BOYS
The Story of Frankie Valli & The Four Seasons

Book by
Marshall Brickman & Rick Elice

Music by
Bob Gaudio

Lyrics by
Bob Crewe

with
Sebastian Arcelus Matt Bogart Dominic Nolfi Jarrod Spector

Michelle Aravena Miles Aubrey Erik Bates Bridget Berger Kris Coleman Ken Dow
Heather Ferguson Russell Fischer Cory Grant John Hickman Katie O'Toole Joe Payne
Sara Schmidt Jake Speck Taylor Sternberg with Peter Gregus and Mark Lotito

Scenic Design	Costume Design	Lighting Design	Sound Design
Klara Zieglerova	Jess Goldstein	Howell Binkley	Steve Canyon Kennedy

Projection Design	Wig and Hair Design	Fight Director	Production Supervisor
Michael Clark	Charles LaPointe	Steve Rankin	Richard Hester

Orchestrations	Music Coordinator	Conductor	Production Stage Manager
Steve Orich	John Miller	Adam Ben-David	Michelle Bosch

Technical Supervisor	East Coast Casting	West Coast Casting	Company Manager
Peter Fulbright	Tara Rubin Casting	Sharon Bialy C.S.A. Sherry Thomas C.S.A.	Sandra Carlson

Associate Producers	Executive Producer	Promotions	Press Representative
Lauren Mitchell Rhoda Mayerson Stage Entertainment	Sally Campbell Morse	HHC Marketing	Boneau/Bryan-Brown

Music Direction, Vocal Arrangements & Incidental Music
Ron Melrose

Choreography
Sergio Trujillo

Directed by
Des McAnuff

World Premiere Produced by La Jolla Playhouse, La Jolla, CA
Christopher Ashley, Artistic Director & Steven B. Libman, Managing Director
The producers wish to thank Theatre Development Fund for its support of this production.

10/1/09

(L-R): Sebastian Arcelus, Jarrod Spector, Dominic Nolfi and Matt Bogart

Photo by Joan Marcus

Jersey Boys

MUSICAL NUMBERS

ACT ONE

"Ces Soirées-La (Oh What a Night)" – Paris, 2000 .... French Rap Star, Backup Group
"Silhouettes" .... Tommy DeVito, Nick Massi, Nick DeVito, Frankie Castelluccio
"You're the Apple of My Eye" .... Tommy DeVito, Nick Massi, Nick DeVito
"I Can't Give You Anything But Love" .... Frankie Castelluccio
"Earth Angel" .... Tommy DeVito, Full Company
"Sunday Kind of Love" .... Frankie Valli, Tommy DeVito, Nick Massi, Nick's Date
"My Mother's Eyes" .... Frankie Valli
"I Go Ape" .... The Four Lovers
"(Who Wears) Short Shorts" .... The Royal Teens
"I'm in the Mood for Love/Moody's Mood for Love" .... Frankie Valli
"Cry for Me" .... Bob Gaudio, Frankie Valli, Tommy DeVito, Nick Massi
"An Angel Cried" .... Hal Miller and The Rays
"I Still Care" .... Miss Frankie Nolan and The Romans
"Trance" .... Billy Dixon and The Topix
"Sherry" .... The Four Seasons
"Big Girls Don't Cry" .... The Four Seasons
"Walk Like a Man" .... The Four Seasons
"December, 1963 (Oh What a Night)" .... Bob Gaudio, Full Company
"My Boyfriend's Back" .... The Angels
"My Eyes Adored You" .... Frankie Valli, Mary Delgado, The Four Seasons
"Dawn (Go Away)" .... The Four Seasons
"Walk Like a Man" (reprise) .... Full Company

ACT TWO

"Big Man in Town" .... The Four Seasons
"Beggin'" .... The Four Seasons
"Stay" .... Bob Gaudio, Frankie Valli, Nick Massi
"Let's Hang On (To What We've Got)" .... Bob Gaudio, Frankie Valli
"Opus 17 (Don't You Worry 'Bout Me)" .... Bob Gaudio, Frankie Valli and The New Seasons
"Bye Bye Baby" .... Frankie Valli and The Four Seasons
"C'mon Marianne" .... Frankie Valli and The Four Seasons
"Can't Take My Eyes Off You" .... Frankie Valli
"Working My Way Back to You" .... Frankie Valli and The Four Seasons
"Fallen Angel" .... Frankie Valli
"Rag Doll" .... The Four Seasons
"Who Loves You" .... The Four Seasons, Full Company

Cast Continued

Dance Captain:
PETER GREGUS
Assistant Dance Captain:
KATIE O'TOOLE

UNDERSTUDIES

For Tommy DeVito:
ERIK BATES, JAKE SPECK
For Nick Massi:
MILES AUBREY, JOHN HICKMAN, JAKE SPECK
For Frankie Valli:
RUSSELL FISCHER, CORY GRANT, TAYLOR STERNBERG
For Bob Gaudio:
JOHN HICKMAN, JAKE SPECK
For Gyp DeCarlo:
MILES AUBREY, JOHN HICKMAN
For Bob Crewe:
ERIK BATES, JOHN HICKMAN

ORCHESTRA

Conductor:
ADAM BEN-DAVID
Associate Conductor:
DEBORAH N. HURWITZ
Keyboards:
DEBORAH N. HURWITZ, STEPHEN "HOOPS" SNYDER
Guitars:
JOE PAYNE
Bass:
KEN DOW
Drums:
KEVIN DOW
Reeds:
MATT HONG, BEN KONO
Trumpet:
DAVID SPIER
Music Coordinator:
JOHN MILLER

Sebastian Arcelus
Bob Gaudio

Matt Bogart
Nick Massi

Dominic Nolfi
Tommy DeVito

Jarrod Spector
Frankie Valli

Peter Gregus
Bob Crewe and others

Mark Lotito
Gyp DeCarlo and others

Michelle Aravena
Swing

Jersey Boys

Miles Aubrey
Norman Waxman and others

Erik Bates
Hank Majewski and others

Bridget Berger
Mary Delgado and others

Kris Coleman
Hal Miller and others

Ken Dow
Thug, Bass

Heather Ferguson
Lorraine and others

Russell Fischer
Joey, Recording Studio Engineer and others

Cory Grant
Frankie Valli on Wed. & Sat. Mats.

John Hickman
Swing

Katie O'Toole
Swing

Joe Payne
Thug, Guitars

Sara Schmidt
Francine and others

Jake Speck
Swing

Taylor Sternberg
Swing

Marshall Brickman
Book

Rick Elice
Book

Bob Gaudio
Composer

Bob Crewe
Lyricist

Des McAnuff
Director

Sergio Trujillo
Choreographer

Ron Melrose
Music Direction, Vocal Arrangements and Incidental Music

Klara Zieglerova
Scenic Design

Jess Goldstein
Costume Design

Howell Binkley
Lighting Design

Steve Canyon Kennedy
Sound Design

Steve Rankin
Fight Director

Steve Orich
Orchestrations

John Miller
Music Coordinator

Adam Ben-David
Conductor

Tara Rubin Casting
Casting

Stephen Gabis
Dialect Coach

Sharon Bialy and Sherry Thomas
West Coast Casting

Michael David,
Dodger Theatricals
Producer

Edward Strong,
Dodger Theatricals
Producer

Jersey Boys

Rocco Landesman,
Dodger Theatricals
Producer

Kevin and Tamara Kinsella
Producers

Ivor Royston,
The Pelican Group
Producer

Rick Steiner
Producer

John and Bonnie Osher
Producer

Dan Staton
Producer

Marc Bell
Producer

Frederic H. Mayerson
Producer

Lauren Mitchell
Associate Producer

Rhoda Mayerson
Associate Producer

Joop van den Ende,
Stage Entertainment
Producer

Christopher Ashley
*Artistic Director
La Jolla Playhouse*

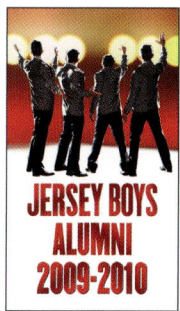
JERSEY BOYS ALUMNI 2009-2010

Michelle Knight
Swing

Andrew Rannells
Bob Gaudio

Matthew Scott
*Stanley,
Hank Majewski,
Crewe's PA,
Joe Long
(and others)*

JERSEY BOYS TRANSFER STUDENTS 2009-2010

Douglas Crawford
Swing

Drew Gehling
Bob Gaudio

(L-R): Matt Bogart as Nick Massi, Jarrod Spector as Frankie Valli, Sebastian Arcelus as Bob Gaudio and Dominic Nolfi as Tommy DeVito.

Photo by Joan Marcus

The Playbill Broadway Yearbook 2009-2010

Jersey Boys
SCRAPBOOK

Correspondent: Russell Fischer, "Joey"
Memorable Fan Letter: A letter and photo from a fan whose kids did a Four Seasons medley for their eighth grade assembly/talent show.
Anniversary Parties: Four-Year Anniversary Party at Lucky Strike Lanes and the Jujamcyn Holiday Party.
Most Exciting Celebrity Visitors: The Beckhams, John Stamos, and the Vice President of Guatemala.
Actor Who Performed the Most Roles in This Show: Heather Ferguson is the female who plays the most roles...18, perhaps?
Actor Who Has Done the Most Shows in Their Career: Peter Gregus...since La Jolla Playhouse.
Special Backstage Ritual: Tapping fingers through the fence.
Favorite Moments During Each Performance: On Stage: "Dawn," "The Finale." Off Stage: Half-hour and/or intermission.
Favorite In-Theatre Gathering Place: Stage management office, car seats off stage, the fourth and fifth floor dressing rooms/swing room.
Favorite Off-Site Cast Hangouts: House of Flavored Vodkas, House of Brews, Sosa Borella, Disiac, Bossa Nova.
Favorite Snack Foods: Bowl Appetit, anything our talented stage managers and/or crew make, nuts/trail mix, anything covered in chocolate.
Favorite Therapies: Throat-Coat Tea, massages (Avanti), chiropractic care.
Memorable Ad-Lib: "Dip-s**t" "We're goin' to Atlantic City...it's gonna be awesome."
Record Number of Cell Phone Rings, Cell Phone Photos or Texting Incidents During a Performance: Too many to count...programs and ticket stubs left on the edge of the stage, too!
Who Wore the Heaviest/Hottest Costume: Whoever has to wear a three-piece suit...you know who you are.
Who Wore the Least: The ladies of the company...it's usually chilly for them on stage.
Embarrassing Moments: Tripping up/down stairs in serious moments. Thanks! Russell

Photo by James Zielinski

Russell Fischer and Taylor Sternberg offered spoken word renditions of Broadway showtunes à la William Shatner for the December 2009 "Gypsy of the Year" competition.

Company Legends: Original company members.
Understudy Anecdote: One of our swings told us he had the "swing's nightmare" where he covered *Phantom of the Opera* a couple blocks down and knew it even though he never rehearsed it.
Nicknames: Dominooch, Grey Goose, Russinator, Bud, TayTay, Coco, NuVonda, La Zveisha, et cetera.
Fan Club Head: Audrey Rau Rockman, JerseyBoysBlog.com.

STAFF FOR JERSEY BOYS

GENERAL PRESS REPRESENTATION
BONEAU/BRYAN-BROWN
Adrian Bryan-Brown   Susanne Tighe
Heath Schwartz

COMPANY MANAGER
Sandra Carlson

PRODUCTION STAGE
 MANAGER ....MICHELLE BOSCH
Stage Manager ....Michelle Reupert
Assistant Stage Manager ....Brendan M. Fay
Senior Associate General Manager ......Jennifer F. Vaughan
Associate General Manager ....Flora Johnstone
Assistant General Manager ....Dean A. Carpenter
Assistant Production Supervisor ....Jeff Parvin
Associate Company Manager ....Tim Sulka
Technical Supervision ....Tech Production Services/
 Peter Fulbright, Mary Duffe,
 Colleen Houlehen, Lauren A. Duffy
Music Technical Design ....Deborah N. Hurwitz
Musician Swing ....Steve Gibb
Assistant Directors ....Holly-Anne Ruggiero,
 West Hyler, Daisy Walker
Second Assistant Director ....Alex Timbers

Associate Choreographer ....Kelly Devine
Assistant Choreographers ....Danny Austin,
 Caitlin Carter
Associate Music Supervisor ....Michael Rafter
Dialect Coach ....Stephen Gabis
Fight Captain ....Peter Gregus
Associate Scenic Designers ....Nancy Thun, Todd Ivins
Assistant Scenic Designers ....Sonoka Gozelski,
 Matthew Myhrum
Associate Costume Designer ....Alejo Vietti
Assistant Costume Designers ....China Lee,
 Elizabeth Flauto
Associate Lighting Designer ....Patricia Nichols
Assistant Lighting Designer ....Sarah E. C. Maines
Associate Sound Designer ....Andrew Keister
Associate Projection Designer ....Jason Thompson
Assistant Projection Designer ....Chris Kateff
Story Board Artist ....Don Hudson
Casting Directors ....Tara Rubin, CSA;
 Merri Sugarman, CSA
Casting Associates ....Eric Woodall, CSA;
 Laura Schutzel, CSA
Casting Assistants ....Paige Blansfield, Dale Brown,
 Kaitlin Shaw
Automated Lighting Programmer ....Hillary Knox
Projection Programming ....Paul Vershbow
Set Model Builder ....Anne Goelz

Costume Intern ....Jessica Reed
Production Carpenter ....Michael W. Kelly
Deck Automation ....Greg Burton
Fly Automation ....Ron Fucarino
Flyman ....Peter Wright
Production Electrician ....James Fedigan
Head Electrician ....Brian Aman
Assistant Electrician ....Gary L. Marlin
Follow Spot Operator ....Sean Fedigan
Production Sound Engineer ....Andrew Keister
Head Sound Engineer ....Julie M. Randolph
Production Props ....Emiliano Pares
Assistant Props ....Kenneth Harris Jr.
Production Wardrobe Supervisor ....Lee J. Austin
Assistant Wardrobe Supervisor ....Nancy Ronan
Wardrobe Department ......Davis Duffield, Kelly Kinsella,
 Shaun Ozminski, Michelle Sesco,
 Nicholas Staub, Ricky Yates
Hair Supervisor ....Frederick G. Waggoner
Hair Department ....Hazel Higgins, Richard Fabris
Assistant to John Miller ....Charles Butler
Synthesizer Programming ....Deborah N. Hurwitz,
 Steve Orich
Music Copying ....Anixter Rice Music Service
Music Production Assistant ....Alexandra Melrose
Dramaturg ....Allison Horsley

Jersey Boys

Associate to Messrs. Michael David and Ed Strong	Pamela Lloyd
Advertising	Serino Coyne, Inc./ Scott Johnson, Sandy Block, Lauren D'Elia
Marketing	Dodger Marketing/ Jessica Ludwig, Jessica Morris
Promotions	HHC Marketing/ Hugh Hysell, Michael Redman
Banking	Commerce Bank/Barbara von Borstel
Payroll	Castellana Services Inc./ Lance Castellana, Norman Seawell, James Castellana
Accountants	Schall and Ashenfarb, C.P.A.
Finance Director	Paula Maldonado
Insurance	AON/Albert G. Rubin Insurance Services/ George Walden, Claudia Kaufman
Counsel	Nan Bases, Esq.
Special Events	John L. Haber
Travel Arrangements	The "A" Team at Tzell Travel/ Andi Henig
MIS Services	Rivera Technics: Sam Rivera
Web Design	Curious Minds Media, Inc.
Production Photographer	Joan Marcus
Theatre Displays	King Displays

DODGERS
DODGER THEATRICALS

Richard Biederman, Sandra Carlson, Dean A. Carpenter, Benjamin Cohen, Michael David, Anne Ezell, Lauren Freed, John L. Haber, Richard Hester, Flora Johnstone, Jennifer Hindman Kemp, Abigail Kornet, Pamela Lloyd, James Elliot Love, Jessica Ludwig, Paula Maldonado, Lauren Mitchell, Jessica Morris, Sally Campbell Morse, Dustin T. Norris, Jeff Parvin, Samuel Rivera, R. Doug Rodgers, Maureen Rooney, Bill Schaeffer, Andrew Serna, David Ryan Spry, Bridget A. Stegall, Edward Strong, Tim Sulka, Ashley Tracey, Ann E. Van Nostrand, Jennifer F. Vaughan, Laurinda Wilson, Josh Zeigler.

LA JOLLA PLAYHOUSE

Artistic Director	Christopher Ashley
Managing Director	Steven B. Libman
Associate Artistic Director	Shirley Fishman
Director Emeritus	Des McAnuff
General Manager	Debby Buchholz
Associate General Manager	Jenny Case
Director of Marketing	Joan Cumming
Director of Development	Ellen Kulik
Director of Finance	John T. O'Dea
Director of Education & Outreach	Steve McCormick
Production Manager	Peter J. Davis
Associate Production Manager	Linda S. Cooper
Technical Director	Brian Busch
Associate Technical Directors	Chris Borreson, Chris Kennedy
Costume Shop Manager	Susan Makkoo
Sound Supervisor	Peter Hashagen
Lighting Supervisor	Mike Doyle
Prop Master	Debra Hatch
Charge Scenic Artist	Mark Jensen
Theatre Operations Manager	Ned Collins

Dodger Group Sales	1-877-5DODGER
Exclusive Tour Direction	Steven Schnepp/ Broadway Booking Office NYC

CREDITS

Scenery, show control and automation by ShowMotion, Inc., Norwalk, CT. Lighting equipment from PRG Lighting. Sound equipment by Masque Sound. Projection equipment by Sound Associates. Selected men's clothing custom made by Saint Laurie Merchant Tailors, New York City. Costumes executed by Carelli Costumes, Studio Rouge, Carmen Gee, John Kristiansen New York, Inc. Selected menswear by Carlos Campos. Props provided by The Spoon Group, Downtime Productions, Tessa Dunning. Select guitars provided by Gibson Guitars. Laundry services provided by Ernest Winzer Theatrical Cleaners. Additional set and hand props courtesy of George Fenmore, Inc. Rosebud matches by Diamond Brands, Inc., Zippo lighters used. Rehearsed at the New 42nd Street Studios. Natural herb cough drops courtesy of Ricola USA, Inc. Emergen-C by Alacer Corporation. PLAYBILL® cover photo by Chris Callis.

www.jerseyboysinfo.com

Scenic drops adapted from *George Tice: Urban Landscapes*/W.W. Norton. Other photographs featured are from *George Tice: Selected Photographs 1953–1999*/David R. Godine. (Photographs courtesy of the Peter Fetterman Gallery/Santa Monica.)

SONG CREDITS

"Ces Soirees-La ("Oh What a Night")" (Bob Gaudio, Judy Parker, Yannick Zolo, Edmond David Bacri). Jobete Music Company Inc., Seasons Music Company (ASCAP). "Silhouettes" (Bob Crewe, Frank Slay, Jr.), Regent Music Corporation (BMI). "You're the Apple of My Eye" (Otis Blackwell), EMI Unart Catalog Inc. (BMI). "I Can't Give You Anything But Love" (Dorothy Fields, Jimmy McHugh), EMI April Music Inc., Aldi Music Company, Cotton Club Publishing (ASCAP). "Earth Angel" (Jesse Belvin, Curtis Williams, Gaynel Hodge), Embassy Music Corporation (BMI). "Sunday Kind of Love" (Barbara Belle, Anita Leanord Nye, Stan Rhodes, Louis Prima), LGL Music Inc./Larry Spier, Inc. (ASCAP). "My Mother's Eyes" (Abel Baer, L. Wolfe Gilbert), Abel Baer Music Company, EMI Feist Catalog Inc. (ASCAP). "I Go Ape" (Bob Crewe, Frank Slay, Jr.), MPL Music Publishing Inc. (ASCAP). "(Who Wears) Short Shorts" (Bob Gaudio, Bill Crandall, Tom Austin, Bill Dalton), EMI Longitude Music, Admiration Music Inc., Third Story Music Inc., and New Seasons Music (BMI). "I'm in the Mood for Love" (Dorothy Fields, Jimmy McHugh), Famous Music Corporation (ASCAP). "Moody's Mood for Love" (James Moody, Dorothy Fields, Jimmy McHugh), Famous Music Corporation (ASCAP). "Cry for Me" (Bob Gaudio), EMI Longitude Music, Seasons Four Music (BMI). "An Angel Cried" (Bob Gaudio), EMI Longitude Music (BMI). "I Still Care" (Bob Gaudio), Hearts Delight Music, Seasons Four Music (BMI). "Trance" (Bob Gaudio), Hearts Delight Music, Seasons Four Music (BMI). "Sherry" (Bob Gaudio), MPL Music Publishing Inc. (ASCAP). "Big Girls Don't Cry" (Bob Gaudio, Bob Crewe), MPL Music Publishing Inc. (ASCAP). "Walk Like a Man" (Bob Crewe, Bob Gaudio), Gavadima Music, MPL Communications Inc. (ASCAP). "December, 1963 (Oh What a Night)" (Bob Gaudio, Judy Parker), Jobete Music Company Inc, Seasons Music Company (ASCAP). "My Boyfriend's Back" (Robert Feldman, Gerald Goldstein, Richard Gottehrer), EMI Blackwood Music Inc. (BMI). "My Eyes Adored You" (Bob Crewe, Kenny Nolan), Jobete Music Company Inc, Kenny Nolan Publishing (ASCAP), Stone Diamond Music Corporation, Tannyboy Music (BMI). "Dawn, Go Away" (Bob Gaudio, Sandy Linzer), EMI Full Keel Music, Gavadima Music, Stebojen Music Company (ASCAP). "Big Man in Town" (Bob Gaudio), EMI Longitude Music (BMI), Gavadima Music (ASCAP). "Beggin'" (Bob Gaudio, Peggy Farina), EMI Longitude Music, Seasons Four Music (BMI). "Stay" (Maurice Williams), Cherio Corporation (BMI). "Let's Hang On (To What We've Got)" (Bob Crewe, Denny Randell, Sandy Linzer), EMI Longitude Music, Screen Gems-EMI Music Inc., Seasons Four Music (BMI). "Opus 17 (Don't You Worry 'Bout Me)" (Denny Randell, Sandy Linzer) Screen Gems-EMI Music Inc, Seasons Four Music (BMI). "Everybody Knows My Name" (Bob Gaudio, Bob Crewe), EMI Longitude Music, Seasons Four Music (BMI). "Bye Bye Baby" (Bob Crewe, Bob Gaudio), EMI Longitude Music, Seasons Four Music (BMI). "C'mon Marianne" (L. Russell Brown, Ray Bloodworth), EMI Longitude Music and Seasons Four Music (BMI). "Can't Take My Eyes Off You" (Bob Gaudio, Bob Crewe), EMI Longitude Music, Seasons Four Music (BMI). "Working My Way Back to You" (Denny Randell, Sandy Linzer), Screen Gems–EMI Music Inc, Seasons Four Music (BMI). "Fallen Angel" (Guy Fletcher, Doug Flett), Chrysalis Music (ASCAP). "Rag Doll" (Bob Crewe, Bob Gaudio), EMI Longitude Music (BMI), Gavadima Music (ASCAP). "Who Loves You?" (Bob Gaudio, Judy Parker), Jobete Music Company Inc, Seasons Music Company (ASCAP).

SPECIAL THANKS

Peter Bennett, Elliot Groffman, Karen Pals, Janine Smalls, Chad Woerner of La Jolla Playhouse, Alma Malabanan-McGrath and Edward Stallsworth of the New 42nd Street Studios, David Solomon of the Roundabout Theatre Company, Dan Whitten. The authors, director, cast and company of *Jersey Boys* would like to express their love and thanks to Jordan Ressler.

IN MEMORY

It is difficult to imagine producing anything without the presence of beloved Dodger producing associate James Elliot Love. Friend to everyone he met, James stood at the heart of all that is good about the theatrical community. He will be missed, but his spirit abides.

Grammy Award-winning cast album now available on Rhino Records.

 JUJAMCYN THEATERS

JORDAN ROTH
President

PAUL LIBIN	JACK VIERTEL
Producing Director	Creative Director
DANIEL ADAMIAN	**JENNIFER HERSHEY**
General Manager	Director of Operations
MEREDITH VILLATORE	**JERRY ZAKS**
Chief Financial Officer	Resident Director

STAFF FOR THE AUGUST WILSON THEATRE

Manager	Matt Fox
Treasurer	Nick Russo
Associate Manager	Justin L. Karr
Carpenter	Dan Dour
Propertyman	Scott Mulrain
Electrician	Robert Fehribach
Engineer	Ralph Santos

The Playbill Broadway Yearbook 2009-2010

La Cage aux Folles

First Preview: April 6, 2010. Opened: April 18, 2010.
Still running as of May 31, 2010.

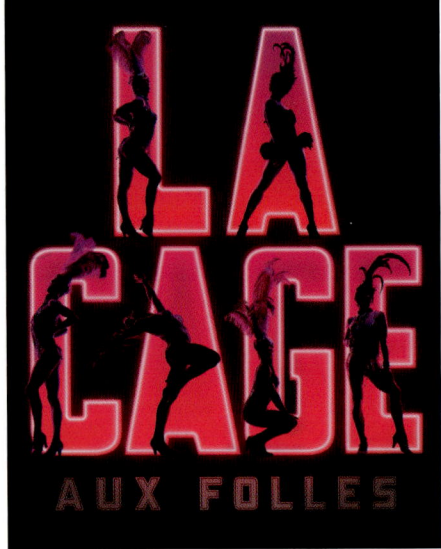

LONGACRE THEATRE
220 West 48th Street
A Shubert Organization Theatre
Philip J. Smith, *Chairman*   Robert E. Wankel, *President*

SONIA FRIEDMAN PRODUCTIONS, DAVID BABANI, BARRY and FRAN WEISSLER and
EDWIN W. SCHLOSS, BOB BARTNER/NORMAN TULCHIN, BROADWAY ACROSS AMERICA, MATTHEW MITCHELL,
RAISE THE ROOF 4 RICHARD WINKLER/BENSINGER TAYLOR/LAUDENSLAGER BERGÈRE,
ARLENE SCANLAN/JOHN O'BOYLE, INDEPENDENT PRESENTERS NETWORK, OLYMPUS THEATRICALS,
ALLEN SPIVAK, JERRY FRANKEL/BAT-BARRY PRODUCTIONS, NEDERLANDER PRESENTATIONS, INC/HARVEY WEINSTEIN
Present the MENIER CHOCOLATE FACTORY Production

KELSEY GRAMMER with DOUGLAS HODGE
in
LA CAGE AUX FOLLES

MUSIC & LYRICS BY **JERRY HERMAN**   BOOK BY **HARVEY FIERSTEIN**
BASED ON THE PLAY "LA CAGE AUX FOLLES" BY JEAN POIRET

Starring
FRED APPLEGATE   VEANNE COX
CHRIS HOCH   ELENA SHADDOW   A.J. SHIVELY

with
CHRISTINE ANDREAS
and
ROBIN De JESÚS

DALE HENSLEY   HEATHER LINDELL   CAITLIN MUNDTH   BILL NOLTE   DAVID NATHAN PERLOW   CHERYL STERN

And featuring the notorious and dangerous Cagelles
NICK ADAMS   CHRISTOPHE CABALLERO   SEAN A. CARMON   NICHOLAS CUNNINGHAM   SEAN PATRICK DOYLE   LOGAN KESLAR   TODD LATTIMORE   TERRY LAVELL

Scenic Design   Costume Design   Lighting Design   Sound Design   Wig & Makeup Design
TIM SHORTALL   MATTHEW WRIGHT   NICK RICHINGS   JONATHAN DEANS   RICHARD MAWBEY

Associate Choreographer   Technical Supervisors   Production Stage Manager   Associate Producers
NICHOLAS CUNNINGHAM   ARTHUR SICCARDI   KRISTEN HARRIS   CARLOS ARANA
                           & PATRICK SULLIVAN   ROBERT DRIEMEYER

Music Director   Musical Coordinator
TODD ELLISON   JOHN MILLER

Casting   Press Representative   Advertising   UK General Management
DUNCAN STEWART   BONEAU/BRYAN-BROWN   SPOTCO   DIANE BENJAMIN,
                                                           PAM SKINNER & TOM SIRACUSA

General Manager   Executive Producer
B.J. HOLT   ALECIA PARKER

Music Supervision, Orchestrations & Dance Arrangements
JASON CARR

Choreography by
LYNNE PAGE

Directed by
TERRY JOHNSON

This production premiered at the Menier Chocolate Factory November 23, 2007
and transferred to the Playhouse Theatre October 30, 2008.
Original Chocolate Factory Set Design by David Farley.

4/18/10

CAST
(in order of appearance)

Georges	KELSEY GRAMMER
"Les Cagelles"	
Angelique	NICK ADAMS
Bitelle	LOGAN KESLAR
Chantal	SEAN PATRICK DOYLE
Hanna	NICHOLAS CUNNINGHAM
Mercedes	TERRY LAVELL
Phaedra	SEAN A. CARMON
Francis	CHRIS HOCH
Babette	CHERYL STERN
Jacob	ROBIN De JESÚS
Albin	DOUGLAS HODGE
Jean-Michel	A.J. SHIVELY
Anne	ELENA SHADDOW
Colette	HEATHER LINDELL
Etienne	DAVID NATHAN PERLOW
Tabarro	BILL NOLTE
Jacqueline	CHRISTINE ANDREAS
M. Renaud	FRED APPLEGATE
Mme. Renaud	VEANNE COX
M. Dindon	FRED APPLEGATE
Mme. Dindon	VEANNE COX
Waiter	DALE HENSLEY

SWINGS
CHRISTOPHE CABALLERO,
TODD LATTIMORE, CAITLIN MUNDTH

DANCE CAPTAIN
NICHOLAS CUNNINGHAM

Continued on next page

Kelsey Grammer (L) sings "Song on the Sand" to Douglas Hodge.

Photo by Matt Crockett

164   The Playbill Broadway Yearbook 2009-2010

La Cage aux Folles

MUSICAL NUMBERS

ACT ONE

Scene 1 La Cage Aux Folles Nightclub
"We Are What We Are" .... Cagelles, Georges
Scene 2 Georges and Albin's Apartment
"A Little More Mascara" .... Albin, Georges
Scene 2a La Cage Aux Folles Nightclub
Scene 3 Georges and Albin's Apartment
"With Anne on My Arm" .... Georges, Jean-Michel
"With You on My Arm" .... Albin, Georges
Scene 4 The Promenade
"Song on the Sand" .... Georges
Scene 5 Backstage at La Cage Aux Folles
Scene 5a La Cage Aux Folles Nightclub
"La Cage aux Folles" .... Company
Scene 6 Backstage at La Cage Aux Folles
Scene 6a La Cage Aux Folles Nightclub
"I Am What I Am" .... Albin

ACT TWO

Scene 1 Promenade
"Song on the Sand" (Reprise) .... Albin, Georges
"Masculinity" .... Albin, Georges, M. Renaud, Mme. Renaud, Tabarro
Scene 2 Georges and Albin's Apartment
"Look Over There" .... Georges
"Cocktail Counterpoint" .... Anne, M. Dindon, Mme. Dindon, Georges, Jacob, Jean-Michel
Scene 3 Chez Jacqueline Restaurant
"The Best of Times" .... Company
Scene 4 Georges and Albin's Apartment
"Look Over There" (Reprise) .... Georges, Jean-Michel
Scene 5 La Cage Aux Folles Nightclub
Finale .... Company

2009-2010 AWARDS

TONY AWARDS
Best Revival of a Musical
Best Actor in a Musical
(Douglas Hodge)
Best Direction of a Musical
(Terry Johnson)

DRAMA DESK AWARDS
Outstanding Revival of a Musical
Outstanding Actor in a Musical
(Douglas Hodge)
Outstanding Costume Design
(Matthew Wright)

OUTER CRITICS CIRCLE AWARDS
Outstanding Revival of a Musical
Outstanding Actor in a Musical
(Douglas Hodge)
Outstanding Director of a Musical
(Terry Johnson)
Outstanding Costume Design
(Matthew Wright)

DRAMA LEAGUE AWARD
Distinguished Revival of a Musical

Les Cagelles
Photo by Joan Marcus

Cast Continued

UNDERSTUDIES

For Georges:
CHRIS HOCH, BILL NOLTE
For Albin:
DALE HENSLEY, CHRIS HOCH
For M. Dindon/M. Renaud:
DALE HENSLEY, BILL NOLTE
For Mme. Dindon/Mme. Renaud:
HEATHER LINDELL, CHERYL STERN
For Francis:
CHRISTOPHE CABALLERO, DALE HENSLEY
For Anne:
HEATHER LINDELL, CAITLIN MUNDTH
For Jean-Michel:
NICK ADAMS, DAVID NATHAN PERLOW
For Jacqueline:
HEATHER LINDELL, CHERYL STERN
For Jacob:
CHRISTOPHE CABALLERO,
SEAN PATRICK DOYLE

Douglas Hodge and Nicholas Cunningham are appearing with the permission of Actors' Equity Association.

ORCHESTRA

Conductor:
TODD ELLISON

Associate Conductor:
ANTONY GERALIS

Keyboards:
TODD ELLISON, ANTONY GERALIS
Woodwinds:
STEVE KENYON, ROGER ROSENBERG
Trumpet:
DON DOWNS
Tenor Trombone:
KEITH O'QUINN
Acoustic Bass:
MARC SCHMIED
Drums/Percussion:
SEAN MCDANIEL

Synthesizer Programmer:
RANDY COHEN

Music Coordinator:
JOHN MILLER

La Cage aux Folles

Kelsey Grammer
Georges

Douglas Hodge
Albin

Fred Applegate
*M. Dindon/
M. Renaud*

Veanne Cox
*Mme. Dindon/
Mme. Renaud*

Chris Hoch
Francis

Elena Shaddow
Anne

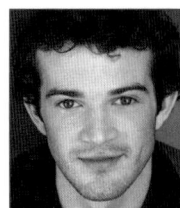
A.J. Shively
Jean-Michel

Christine Andreas
Jacqueline

Robin De Jesús
Jacob

Heather Lindell
Colette

Bill Nolte
Tabarro

David Nathan Perlow
Etienne

Nick Adams
Angelique

Sean A. Carmon
Phaedra

Nicholas Cunningham
*Hanna, Associate Choreographer/
Dance Captain*

Sean Patrick Doyle
Chantal

Logan Keslar
Bitelle

Terry Lavell
Mercedes

Christophe Caballero
Swing

Dale Hensley
Waiter, Swing

Todd Lattimore
Swing

Caitlin Mundth
Swing

Cheryl Stern
Babette

Jerry Herman
Music and Lyrics

Harvey Fierstein
Book

Terry Johnson
Director

Lynne Page
Choreographer

Todd Ellison
Music Director

Tim Shortall
Scenic Design

Matthew Wright
Costume Design

Nick Richings
Lighting Design

Jonathan Deans
Sound Design

Jason Carr
*Musical Supervision,
Orchestrations &
Dance Arrangements*

John Miller
Musical Coordinator

Duncan Stewart
Casting Director

La Cage aux Folles

Arthur Siccardi
Theatrical Services,
Inc.
Technical Supervisor

Sonia Friedman
Productions Ltd.
Producer

Barry and Fran Weissler
Producer

Edwin W. Schloss
Producer

John Gore,
Broadway Across
America
Producer

Thomas B. McGrath,
Broadway Across
America
Producer

Harriet Newman
Leve,
Raise The Roof 4
Producer

Jennifer
Manocherian,
Raise The Roof 4
Producer

Chris Bensinger
Producer

Jane Bergère
Producer

Arlene Scanlan
Producer

John O'Boyle
Producer

Allen Spivak
Producer

Jerry Frankel
Producer

Barry Weisbord
Producer

REFRESHMENTS

James L.
Nederlander,
Nederlander
Presentations Inc.
Producer

Bob Weinstein,
The Weinstein
Company
Producer

CREW
Front Row (L-R): Joe Goldman, Kristen Harris, Neveen Mahmoud, Karl Schuberth, Andre Gray, Scott Mendelsohn

Back Row (L-R): Wilbur Graham, Wayne Smith, Glynn David Turner, Jessica Worsnop, Jason Bishop, John Lofgren, Carin Ford, Kimberly Mark, Cherie Cunningham, Jack Curtin, Jorie Malan, Drayton Allison, Rob Presley, Ric Rogers

Harvey Weinstein,
The Weinstein
Company
Producer

La Cage aux Folles

FRONT OF HOUSE STAFF

STAFF FOR *LA CAGE AUX FOLLES*

COMPANY MANAGER
Kimberly Kelley

GENERAL PRESS REPRESENTATIVE
BONEAU/BRYAN-BROWN
Adrian Bryan-Brown Jim Byk Michael Strassheim

Production Stage Manager	Kristen Harris
Stage Manager	Glynn David Turner
Assistant Stage Manager	Neveen Mahmoud
Associate General Manager	Hilary Hamilton
General Management Associates	Dana Sherman, Stephen Spadaro
Assistant Company Manager	Dominic Shiach
Associate Scenic Designer	Bryan Johnson
Associate Lighting Designer	Vivien Leone
Assistant Lighting Designer	Ben Hagen
Moving Lights Programmer	Michael Hill
UK Production Consultant	Kirsten Turner
Head Carpenter	Karl Schuberth
Production Electricians	James J. Fedigan, Randall Zaibek
Head Electrician	Eric Norris
Head Properties	Robert Presley
Sound Engineer	Carin M. Ford
Advance Sound	Simon Matthews
Production Costume Coordinator	Brigid Guy
Wardrobe Supervisor	Jessica Worsnop
Dressers	Jason Bishop, Cherie Cunningham, Tracey Diebold, Kimberly Santos Mark, William Hubner, Deborah Black, Anastasya Jula
Hair & Make-Up Supervisor	John Curtin
Hair & Make-Up Assistants	Wanda Gregory, Jorie Malan
Production Assistants	Aaron Elgart, Beth Stegman
Casting Associate	Benton Whitely
Vice President of Marketing	Todd Stuart
Director of Marketing	Ken Sperr
Advertising	SpotCo/ Drew Hodges, Jim Edwards, Tom Greenwald, Vinny Sainato, Jim Aquino, Stacey Maya
Website Design/ Online Marketing Strategy	SpotCo/ Sara Fitzpatrick, Matt Wilstein, Marc Mettler, Christine Sees
Production Photography	Joan Marcus
Legal Counsel	Loeb & Loeb, Seth Gelblum
Merchandising	SpotCo Merch/Dewynters
Insurance	Stockbridge Risk Management DeWitt Stern
Accounting	Rosenberg, Neuwirth & Kuchner/ Mark D'Ambrosi, Marina Flom
Business Affairs Consultant	Daniel Posener
Banking	City National Bank/ Michele Gibbons
Stunt Coordinator	Tom Schall
Skating Instruction	Lezly Skate School
Skate Trainer	James H. Singley
Physical Therapy	Performing Arts Physical Therapy
Travel Services	Tzell Travel/Andi Henig
Payroll Service	Castellana Services, Inc.
Promotional Support	Maybelline New York

SONIA FRIEDMAN PRODUCTIONS

Creative Producer	Lisa Makin
Associate Producer	Sharon Duckworth
Literary Associate	Jack Bradley
Production Associate	Lucie Lovatt
Assistant General Manager	Martin Ball
Production Accountant	Melissa Hay
Chief Executive Officer-NY	David Lazar
Executive Assistant-NY	Dan Gallagher

MENIER CHOCOLATE FACTORY

Marketing & Production Coordinator	Lucy McNally
Marketing & Production Assistant	Sarah Mannion
Restaurant General Manager	Nik Whybrew
Head Chef	Anthony Falla
Restaurant Manager	Douglas Hyde
Box Office Supervisor	Jane Elizabeth

NATIONAL ARTISTS MANAGEMENT COMPANY

Chief Financial Officer	Bob Williams
International Manager	Nina Skriloff
Executive Assistant to the Weisslers	Brett England
Accounting Associate	Marian Albarracin
Receptionist	Michelle Coleman
Assistant to B.J. Holt	Tuey Connell
Creative Associate	Eli Gonda
Assistant to Barry Weissler	Roger Kuch
Executive Assistant to Barry Weissler	Eddie Pisapia
Messenger	Victor Ruiz
Assistant to Alecia Parker	Laura Sisk
Accounting Associate	Marion Taylor

CREDITS

Scenery executed by Hudson Scenic Studio, RK Resource. Plumage by Mark Wheeler. Lighting equipment from PRG Lighting. Sound equipment from PRG Audio. Costumes executed by Jane Gonin, Dennis & Shirley Fitzgerald, Theatrical Shoemakers, Theatre Royal Plymouth, Amanda Barrow, Keith Watson, Richard Handscombe, Glenn Hills, Judy Ward, Caroline Hughes, Elsa Threadgold, Sten Vollmuller, Shultz & Wiremu, Saint Laurie Merchant Tailors New York City. Millinery by Jenny Adey. Shoes by T.O. Dey, Capezio. Rollerskates by Lezly. Acrylic drinkware by U.S. Acrylic, LLC. Additional hand props by George Fenmore, Inc. Special thanks to Bra*Tenders for hosiery and undergarments. Make-up provided by M•A•C Cosmetics.

SPECIAL THANKS

Gary Murphy, Stas Iavorski at Ripley-Grier Studios, Tony Spinoza, Elizabeth Helke, Will Dailey, John Darby.

 THE SHUBERT ORGANIZATION, INC.
Board of Directors

Philip J. Smith	**Robert E. Wankel**
Chairman	President
Wyche Fowler, Jr.	**John W. Kluge**
Lee J. Seidler	**Michael I. Sovern**

Stuart Subotnick

Elliot Greene	**David Andrews**
Chief Financial Officer	Senior Vice President- Shubert Ticketing
Juan Calvo	**John Darby**
Vice President and Controller	Vice President – Facilities
Peter Entin	**Charles Flateman**
Vice President – Theatre Operations	Vice President – Marketing
Anthony LaMattina	**Brian Mahoney**
Vice President – Audit & Production Finance	Vice President – Ticket Sales

D.S. Moynihan
Vice President – Creative Projects

House Manager ....Bob Reilly

La Cage aux Folles
Scrapbook

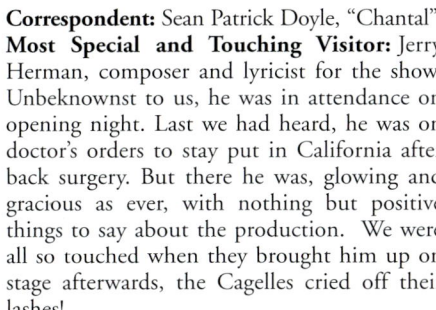

1. The Cagelles prepare for the OUT Magazine shoot.
2. Out of drag, the Cagelles pose with Regis Philbin outside the theatre.
3. Dale Hensley blesses the dressing rooms with the Gypsy Robe.
4. (L-R): Todd Lattimore and Logan Keslar in their dressing room.
5. Cast members relax with Kelsey Grammer (R) after the sitzprobe.

Correspondent: Sean Patrick Doyle, "Chantal"

Most Special and Touching Visitor: Jerry Herman, composer and lyricist for the show. Unbeknownst to us, he was in attendance on opening night. Last we had heard, he was on doctor's orders to stay put in California after back surgery. But there he was, glowing and gracious as ever, with nothing but positive things to say about the production. We were all so touched when they brought him up on stage afterwards, the Cagelles cried off their lashes!

Most Bizarre Celebrity Visitor and What He Did/Said: The most bizarre celebrity visitor was the notorious conservative pundit Glenn Beck. He was visiting Kelsey and reached for my hand to congratulate me and say how much he enjoyed the performance. As I walked away, it hit me how strange it was that I met someone from the Fox network while dressed in full drag.

Special Backstage Rituals: At the "places" call of every show, most of the cast gathers behind the rose-colored show curtain to say a prayer for our bodies, voices, minds and give thanks for the gifts that we've been given. Then we form a pagan circle and recite a long (and ever growing) string of superstitious phrases, some of which are a carry-over from the London company. By the time we reached opening night, the chant had grown to include, "Un Deux Trois—OOOH—Booyayakasha—[Swahili tongue clicks]—Allergies Schmal-lergies—Gooorrrgeous—WE GOT THIS!" Now it has morphed and grown even further! Kelsey then squeezes all of the "girls" breasts for luck and fellow Cagelle Nick Adams christens the show with a new subtitle (example: "Tonight is Wing-It Wednesday" or "Savor It Sunday," which was used on opening night).

Favorite Therapy: I sling back some coffee before the show, but most of the Cagelles have an IV of Red Bull hooked up before the "Can-Can"!

Memorable Press Encounter: Our first press outing, being shot for Out Magazine's HOT LIST, which we Cagelles topped this year at #1. It was an early day, but so much fun!

Who Wore the Least: Undoubtedly—the Cagelles. You can see our SOULS in some of those outfits!

Catchphrases Only the Company Would Recognize: Too many to name, but if I could choose one, "Get used to it!"

Memorable Directorial Note: "Never let the showbiz of the play infect the scenes outside of the club. Everything for truth, nothing for laughs." I also appreciated when Terry said, (and I paraphrase) "There's no such thing as 110 percent. There's only 100 percent. You were all hired because you are wonderful and capable of doing this, so aim for the safe completion of this show and take the pressure off yourselves."

The Biggest Blooper: During the evening performance on April 25, this resounding thud echoed throughout the auditorium. Our sound board had gone out—keyboards, microphones, the works. We Merman-ed through the "Can-Can" with wonky accompaniment, but stage management decided to stop the show during the scene preceding "I Am What I Am." Kelsey saved the day by delivering a five minute standup routine while the sound board was rebooting. Of course it was recorded for posterity by an audience member and reared its head on YouTube days later. The highlight was a lengthy joke featuring an Italian and a Greek boasting about their respective cultures' contributions to society. In a pissing contest of sorts, they argued over who had the greatest food, pasta and parmesan versus filo and feta,

La Cage aux Folles
SCRAPBOOK

1. Cheryl Stern displays a old resume photo of herself with "70's hair."
2. The Cagelles in special costumes for the 2010 "Easter Bonnet" competition at the Minskoff Theatre.
3. *Yearbook* correspondent Sean Patrick Doyle (L) reunites backstage with composer Jerry Herman.
4. Specially designed cookies sent by the producers after the show earned 11 Tony Award nominations.

et cetera. It culminated in the Greek saying, "Well, the Greeks invented sex." To which the smirking Italian replied, "Ah yes, but WE introduced it to WOMEN!" The audience roared, and moments later his mic clicked on. We had them in the palm of our hand for the rest of the show. Audiences love when something goes haywire!

Off-Site Hangout: The cast can often be found next door at Hurley's, which transforms into Club *La Cage* on the weekends. On the night of the Drama Desk Awards, much of the cast had drinks while we religiously checked the Twitter feed. We were all cheering when Doug won, and after I texted to congratulate him, he had his car make a stop at Hurley's. He slung back a beer, bought a round for everyone, said we were the top, and bolted off to the after-party. Doug and Kelsey often have a drink at the end of the bar when the curtain comes down. Their relationship is quite funny because one moment they'll be making out together onstage and the next, Doug will pop backstage, still wearing his frock, and say "Hey Kelsey, did you see that blonde at the cabaret table?"

Wardrobe Mishaps: The athletic "Can-Can" has become notorious among the Cagelles for the wardrobe malfunctions that plague it. Once during a Sunday evening performance, my snap broke and I lost my skirt. Later in the number, I lost my wig with my microphone attached. I have no idea what sort of performance I served up that evening—I was too busy trying to keep my body from repelling my costume pieces. More recently, the shoe strap of a fellow Cagelle broke and he performed half of the number with only one heel, like Cinderella hobbling around the steps of the palace. Finally, he threw the other shoe offstage and danced the rest of the number barefoot. It was quite hilarious, and no small feat—pun intended.

Composer/Librettist Anecdote: It's worth mentioning what a full circle experience this has been for me...in so many ways. I first worked with Jerry Herman very briefly when I was 12. I played Young Patrick in a production of *Mame* that opened the Jerry Herman Ring Theatre in Miami and Jerry flew in to finesse the show during tech. He was really the first composer whose name and work I knew. When we met, he was shocked that such a young boy knew so much about his life and had read his biography. We wrote each other letters on and off for about two years after that, but had since lost touch completely. When he came to visit us for opening, I reminded him about that and his eyes lit up! Also, prior to *La Cage*, I was on the road as Fruma-Sarah in *Fiddler on the Roof*; *La Cage* Librettist Harvey Fierstein was announced as our new Tevye (stepping in for an ailing Topol) on the very day that I received my offer to do this production, so we got to work together for five weeks before I departed the tour! It's a small, small world.

Favorite Moments: Choreographically, my favorite moment is the caged-bird sequence in the title number. In most productions of *La Cage*, the Cagelles' dances are showy and athletic, but rarely are they choreographed with as much nuance as they are here. In this moment, through economy of movement, Lynne Page has created a wonderful iconic moment of us standing there in avian fashion. There's a sense of restraint, a contained energy, that's quite sexy and alluring. Another favorite moment comes after the curtain call when we get to sing "Best of Times" right to the audience, who often sing along. We can see the show lights reflecting in their eyes. It's two minutes of getting to soak up how you have affected this thousand-person crowd, and it's very gratifying to end the evening on that note.

Lend Me a Tenor

First Preview: March 12, 2010. Opened: April 4, 2010.
Still running as of May 31, 2010.

CAST
(in order of appearance)

Maggie	MARY CATHERINE GARRISON
Max	JUSTIN BARTHA
Saunders	TONY SHALHOUB
Tito Merelli	ANTHONY LaPAGLIA
Maria	JAN MAXWELL
Bellhop	JAY KLAITZ
Diana	JENNIFER LAURA THOMPSON
Julia	BROOKE ADAMS

The action takes place in a hotel suite in Cleveland, Ohio, in 1934.

ACT I
Scene One: Early afternoon on a Saturday in September
Scene Two: Four hours later, about 6:30pm

ACT II
Scene One: That night, about 11 o'clock
Scene Two: Fifteen minutes later

UNDERSTUDIES
For Maggie/Diana: JESSIE AUSTRIAN
For Saunders/Tito: TONY CARLIN
For Maria/Julia: DONNA ENGLISH
For Max/Bellhop: BRIAN SEARS

THE MUSIC BOX
239 W. 45th Street
A Shubert Organization Theatre

Philip J. Smith, *Chairman*   Robert E. Wankel, *President*

The Araca Group
Stuart Thompson   Carl Moellenberg   Rodney Rigby
Olympus Theatricals   Broadway Across America
The Shubert Organization
In Association With
Wendy Federman/Jamie deRoy/Richard Winkler   Lisa Cartwright
Spring Sirkin   Scott and Brian Zeilinger
present

Anthony LaPaglia   Tony Shalhoub   Justin Bartha

in

Ken Ludwig's

with

Brooke Adams   Mary Catherine Garrison   Jennifer Laura Thompson
Jay Klaitz
and
Jan Maxwell

Scenic Design	Costume Design	Lighting Design	Sound Design
John Lee Beatty	Martin Pakledinaz	Kenneth Posner	Peter Hylenski

Wig & Hair Design	Casting	Dialect Coach	Production Stage Manager
Paul Huntley	MelCap/ David Caparelliotis	Stephen Gabis	David O'Brien

Press Representative	Production Management	General Management	Executive Producer
Boneau/Bryan-Brown	Juniper Street Productions/ Kevin Broomell	STP/ David Turner	Amanda Watkins

Directed by
Stanley Tucci

The producers wish to express their appreciation to the Theatre Development Fund for its support of this production

4/4/10

(L-R): Brooke Adams, Mary Catherine Garrison, Tony Shalhoub and Jay Klaitz

Photo by Joan Marcus

Lend Me a Tenor

 Anthony LaPaglia
Tito Merelli

 Tony Shalhoub
Saunders

 Justin Bartha
Max

 Jan Maxwell
Maria

 Brooke Adams
Julia

 Mary Catherine Garrison
Maggie

 Jennifer Laura Thompson
Diana

 Jay Klaitz
Bellhop

 Jessie Austrian
u/s Maggie/Diana

 Tony Carlin
u/s Saunders/Tito

 Donna English
u/s Maria/Julia

 Brian Sears
u/s Max/Bellhop

 Ken Ludwig
Author

 Stanley Tucci
Director

 John Lee Beatty
Set Design

 Martin Pakledinaz
Costume Design

 Kenneth Posner
Lighting Design

 Peter Hylenski
Sound Design

 Paul Huntley
Wig & Hair Design

 Joseph Dulude II
Makeup Design

 Patrick Vaccariello
Musical Supervisor

 Stephen Gabis
Dialect Coach

 Guy Kwan, John Paull III, Hillary Blanken, Kevin Broomell, Ana Rose Greene, Juniper Street Productions
Production Management

 Stuart Thompson
Producer

 Carl Moellenberg
Producer

 John Gore,
CEO,
Broadway Across America
Producer

 Thomas B. McGrath,
Chairman,
Broadway Across America
Producer

 Philip J. Smith,
Chairman,
The Shubert Organization
Producer

 Robert E. Wankel,
President,
The Shubert Organization
Producer

 Wendy Federman
Producer

 Jamie deRoy
Producer

 Spring Sirkin
Producer

 Scott Zeilinger
Producer

 Brian Zeilinger
Producer

Lend Me a Tenor

2009-2010 AWARD

OUTER CRITICS CIRCLE AWARD
Outstanding Featured Actress in a Play
(Jan Maxwell)

FRONT OF HOUSE STAFF
Front Row (L-R): Lottie Dennis, Laura Scanlon, Dennis Scanlon, Kenneth T. Kelly, Joseph M. Amato

Back Row (L-R): Michael L. Composto, Michael A. Concepcion, John J. Seid, Steven A. Staszewski, Joseph A. Lopez

CREW
Front Row (L-R): Rosemary Keough, David O'Brien, Rachel A. Wolff, Chris Sanders

Back Row (L-R): Billy Rowland, Kim Garnett, Dennis Maher, Karen L. Eifert, Rob Brenner, Dan Foss, Paul Delcioppo

Lend Me a Tenor

MANAGEMENT
(L-R): Adam Miller (Company Manager), Jonathan Shulman (House Manager)

BOX OFFICE
(L-R): John J. Dunn Jr., Robert D. Kelly

STAFF FOR LEND ME A TENOR

GENERAL MANAGEMENT
STUART THOMPSON PRODUCTIONS
Stuart Thompson   David Turner   James Triner

COMPANY MANAGER
Adam J. Miller

MUSICAL SUPERVISOR
Patrick Vaccariello

MAKEUP DESIGNER
Joe Dulude II

PRESS REPRESENTATIVE
BONEAU/BRYAN-BROWN
Adrian Bryan-Brown   Jackie Green   Emily Meagher

MARKETING DIRECTION
TYPE A MARKETING
Anne Rippey   Nick Pramik   Elyce Henkin

PRODUCTION MANAGEMENT
JUNIPER STREET PRODUCTIONS
Hillary Blanken   Kevin Broomell
Guy Kwan   Ana Rose Greene   Sue Semaan

INTERNET MARKETING/MERCHANDISING
THE ARACA GROUP

Production Stage Manager	David O'Brien
Stage Manager	Rachel A. Wolff
Assistant Director	Kristin McLaughlin
Associate Scenic Designer	Kacie Hultgren
Associate Costume Designer	Sarah Sophia Lidz
Associate Lighting Designer	Aaron Spivey
Associate Sound Designer	Keith Caggiano
Production Carpenter	Erik Hansen
Production Electrician	Dan Coey
Production Properties Supervisor	Chris Pantuso
Production Sound Engineer	Simon Matthews
Sound Engineer	Paul Delcioppo
Wardrobe Supervisor	Karen L. Eifert
Hair Supervisor	Edward Wilson
Dressers	Dan Foss, Rosemary Keough, Chris Sanders
Production Assistant	Colleen Danaher
Costume Assistant	Tescia Seufferlein
Assistant to Mr. Pakledinaz	Inci Kangal
Costume Interns	Carly Bradt, Jaime Torres
Production Management Assistants	Alexandra Paull, Steve Chazaro
Assistant to Mr. Zeilinger	Robert Wachsberger

THE ARACA GROUP

Chief Business Affairs Officer	Marisa Sechrest
Director of Development	Amanda Watkins
Internet Marketing Acct Exec	Kristen Butler
Business Affairs Associate	Lindsay Meck
Executive Assistants	Sarah Grace Welbourn, Danielle Von Gal

STUART THOMPSON PRODUCTIONS

Assistant to Mr. Thompson	Christopher Taggart
Director of Creative Development	Kevin Emrick
General Management Assistants	Geo Karapetyan, Brittany Levasseur
General Management Interns	Erin Byrne, Andrew Lowy

Banking	City National Bank/Michele Gibbons
Payroll	Castellana Services, Inc.
Accountant	Fried & Kowgios CPA's LLP/Robert Fried, CPA
Controller	Joe Kubala
Insurance	DeWitt Stern Group
Legal Counsel	Loeb & Loeb, LLP
Advertising	Serino Coyne/Greg Corradetti, Sandy Block, Joaquin Esteva, Lauren D'Elia Pressman
Production Photographer	Joan Marcus
Theatre Displays	King Displays, Inc.
Ground Transportation	IBA Limousines
Air Transportation	Tzell Travel Group/Andi Henig

CREDITS

All scenery constructed by Global Scenic Services, Inc., Bridgeport, CT. Lighting equipment provided by PRG Lighting, North Bergen, NJ. Sound equipment provided by PRG Audio, Mt. Vernon, NY. Props executed by The Spoon Group, Rahway, NJ. Women's clothing executed by Tricorne Inc. Otello and Bellhop costumes executed by Eric Winterling, Inc. Men's tailoring by Paul Chang Tailors, Chicago. Shirts by Anto. Millinery by Lynne Mackey Studio. Men's hats by Gary J. White - The Custom Hatter and JJ Hat Center. Furs by Sharnelle. Shoes by LaDuca, WORLDTONE Dance Shoes. Boots by Handmade Shoes. Gloves by Sermoneta Gloves and LaCrasia Gloves. Special thanks to Bra*Tenders for hosiery and undergarments. Jewelry by Larry Vrba and Kenneth J. Lane. Special thanks to Early Halloween, NY Vintage, Family Jewels, JJ Hat Center, Sol Moscot, Fabulous Fanny's, Timberlake Studios and Mitchell Travers. Makeup provided by M•A•C Cosmetics. Rehearsed at the New 42nd Street Studios. Special thanks to Robert Miller.

THE SHUBERT ORGANIZATION, INC.
Board of Directors

Philip J. Smith Chairman	**Robert E. Wankel** President
Wyche Fowler, Jr.	**John W. Kluge**
Lee J. Seidler	**Michael I. Sovern**

Stuart Subotnick

Elliot Greene Chief Financial Officer	**David Andrews** Senior Vice President – Shubert Ticketing
Juan Calvo Vice President and Controller	**John Darby** Vice President – Facilities
Peter Entin Vice President – Theatre Operations	**Charles Flateman** Vice President – Marketing
Anthony LaMattina Vice President – Audit & Production Finance	**Brian Mahoney** Vice President – Ticket Sales

D.S. Moynihan
Vice President – Creative Projects

House Manager	Jonathan Shulman

Lend Me a Tenor
SCRAPBOOK

1. (L-R): Jan Maxwell, Mary Catherine Garrison, Tony Shalhoub, Brooke Adams, Jennifer Laura Thompson and Anthony LaPaglia attend the opening night party at Espace.
2. Author Ken Ludwig on opening night.
3. Co-star Justin Bartha at Espace.
4. Maxwell, *Yearbook* correspondent Jay Klaitz and Thompson recreate a scene from the show for the cameras after the premiere.

Correspondent: Jay Klaitz, "Bellhop"
Memorable Opening Night Letter, Fax or Note: Maxwell's note said something to the effect of "I've written a lot of notes, so I got nothing left. Sorry I'm phoning in your opening night card. But have a great time and all." I love that woman.
Opening Night Gifts: For our Easter Sunday opening, I received a 5-foot tall, pink bunny. The bunny arrived sporting a custom made t-shirt. Pictured on this t-shirt are my three best friends from back home, and their girlfriends, all of whom were giving me the middle finger. Truly, it's a blessing to have good friends.
Most Exciting Celebrity Visitor and What They Did/Said: Steve Buscemi. He was very complimentary about the show. He's one of my favorite actors. Meryl Streep complimented my voice, which was awfully nice.
Who Wrote the Easter Bonnet Sketch: Jesus?
Who Has Done the Most Shows in Their Career: Jan Maxwell, who has been a working actor since 1834.
Special Backstage Rituals: Mary Catherine Garrison always pretends to kick me in the junk and throat-punch me when I get exit applause for my first scene...just to keep me in check.
Favorite Moment During Each Performance (On Stage or Off): Tony Shalhoub's (purposeful) mispronunciation of the Italian greeting: "Bean vinuto a Cleveland."
Favorite In-Theatre Gathering Place: The floor I share with Jen Laura Thompson and Mary Catherine...it's where the party's at, y'all!
Favorite Off-Site Hangout: Café Un Deux Trois. The manager, Jose, is the greatest man alive, and he keeps us in martinis.
Favorite Snack Food: Babies.
Mascot: Me, wearing my pink onesie with kittens. I sometimes throw it on and run around to everyone's dressing room, just to keep the gang on their toes.
Favorite Therapy: Martinis.
Most Memorable Ad-Lib: Shalhoub: "My chilluns!"
Memorable Stage Door Fan Encounter: Some dude had been to the stage door to get autographs more than once. I saw him one night, and he said "I know you...," and for a moment, I thought he was an old friend, so I grabbed his hand and very enthusiastically said "Hey, man!! How ya been?! Great to see you!" Turns out he was a complete stranger. I think I frightened him.
Who Wore the Least: Tie between MCG and JLT in their sexy underwear.
Understudy Anecdote: Brian Sears is the greatest man alive.
Nicknames: Stanley Tucci: "The Tooch."
Coolest Thing About Being in This Show: The people. Our cast, crew, and director are all such great people. I'm so happy to be working with each one!!

The Lion King

First Preview: October 15, 1997. Opened: November 13, 1997.
Still running as of May 31, 2010.

MINSKOFF THEATRE

UNDER THE DIRECTION OF
JAMES M. NEDERLANDER, JAMES L. NEDERLANDER,
SARA MINSKOFF ALLAN AND THE MINSKOFF FAMILY

Disney PRESENTS

THE LION KING

Music & Lyrics by
ELTON JOHN & TIM RICE

Additional Music & Lyrics by
LEBO M, MARK MANCINA, JAY RIFKIN, JULIE TAYMOR, HANS ZIMMER

Book by
ROGER ALLERS & IRENE MECCHI

Starring
DEREK SMITH NATHANIEL STAMPLEY TSHIDI MANYE
CAMERON POW BEN LIPITZ DANNY RUTIGLIANO
DASHAUN YOUNG TA'REA CAMPBELL
JAMES BROWN-ORLEANS BONITA J. HAMILTON ENRIQUE SEGURA
ALPHONSO ROMERO JONES II SHEREEN PIMENTEL MARQUIS KOFI RODRIGUEZ SHANNON SKYE TAVAREZ

SANT'GRIA BELLO CAMILLE M. BROWN MICHELLE BRUGAL ALVIN CRAWFORD GABRIEL CROOM
GARLAND DAYS CHARITY de LOERA LINDIWE DLAMINI BONGI DUMA ANGELICA EDWARDS JIM FERRIS
CHRISTOPHER FREEMAN JEAN MICHELLE GRIER KENNY INGRAM TONY JAMES NICOLE ADELL JOHNSON
DENNIS JOHNSTON JOEL KARIE CHARLAINE KATSUYOSHI RON KUNENE BRIAN M. LOVE SHERYL McCALLUM
RAY MERCER BRENDA MHLONGO WILLIA-NOEL MONTAGUE S'BU NGEMA SELLOANE A. NKHELA
BRANDON CHRISTOPHER O'NEAL SOPHIA STEPHENS L. STEVEN TAYLOR NATALIE TURNER PHILLIP TURNER
THOM CHRISTOPHER WARREN REMA WEBB KENNY REDELL WILLIAMS CAMILLE WORKMAN

Adapted from the screenplay by
IRENE MECCHI & JONATHAN ROBERTS & LINDA WOOLVERTON

Produced by
PETER SCHNEIDER & THOMAS SCHUMACHER

Scenic Design	Costume Design	Lighting Design	Mask & Puppet Design
RICHARD HUDSON	JULIE TAYMOR	DONALD HOLDER	JULIE TAYMOR & MICHAEL CURRY
Sound Design	Hair & Makeup Design	Associate Director	Associate Choreographer
STEVE CANYON KENNEDY	MICHAEL WARD	JOHN STEFANIUK	MAREY GRIFFITH
Associate Producer	Technical Director	Production Stage Manager	Production Supervisor
ANNE QUART	DAVID BENKEN	RON VODICKA	DOC ZORTHIAN
Music Supervisor	Music Director	Associate Music Producer	Music Coordinator	Orchestrators
CLEMENT ISHMAEL	KARL JURMAN	ROBERT ELHAI	MICHAEL KELLER	ROBERT ELHAI DAVID METZGER BRUCE FOWLER
Music Produced for the Stage & Additional Score by	Additional Vocal Score, Vocal Arrangements & Choral Director	Casting	Fight Director
MARK MANCINA	LEBO M	BINDER CASTING/ MARK BRANDON	RICK SORDELET

Choreography by
GARTH FAGAN

Directed by
JULIE TAYMOR

CAST
(in order of appearance)

RAFIKI	Tshidi Manye
MUFASA	Nathaniel Stampley
SARABI	Jean Michelle Grier
ZAZU	Cameron Pow
SCAR	Derek Smith
YOUNG SIMBA	Alphonso Romero Jones II
	(Thurs., Fri., Sat. Eve., Sun. Mat.)
YOUNG SIMBA	Marquis Kofi Rodriguez
	(Tues., Wed., Sat. Mat., Sun. Eve.)
YOUNG NALA	Shereen Pimentel
	(Tues., Fri., Sat. Eve., Sun. Eve.)
YOUNG NALA	Shannon Skye Tavarez
	(Wed., Thurs., Sat. Mat., Sun. Mat.)
SHENZI	Bonita J. Hamilton
BANZAI	James Brown-Orleans
ED	Enrique Segura
TIMON	Danny Rutigliano
PUMBAA	Ben Lipitz
SIMBA	Dashaun Young
NALA	Ta'Rea Campbell
ENSEMBLE SINGERS	Alvin Crawford, Lindiwe Dlamini, Bongi Duma, Jean Michelle Grier, Joel Karie, Ron Kunene, Sheryl McCallum, Brenda Mhlongo, S'bu Ngema, Selloane A. Nkhela, L. Steven Taylor, Rema Webb, Kenny Redell Williams
ENSEMBLE DANCERS	Sant'gria Bello, Camille M. Brown, Michelle Brugal, Gabriel Croom, Charity de Loera, Christopher Freeman, Nicole Adell Johnson,

Continued on next page

(L-R): S'Bu Ngema, Bongi Duma and Ron Kunene with the Ensemble

The Lion King

SCENES AND MUSICAL NUMBERS

ACT ONE

Scene 1	Pride Rock	
	"Circle of Life" with "Nants' Ingonyama"	Rafiki, Ensemble
Scene 2	Scar's Cave	
Scene 3	Rafiki's Tree	
Scene 4	The Pridelands	
	"The Morning Report"	Zazu, Young Simba, Mufasa
Scene 5	Scar's Cave	
Scene 6	The Pridelands	
	"I Just Can't Wait to Be King"	Young Simba, Young Nala, Zazu, Ensemble
Scene 7	Elephant Graveyard	
	"Chow Down"	Shenzi, Banzai, Ed
Scene 8	Under the Stars	
	"They Live in You"	Mufasa, Ensemble
Scene 9	Elephant Graveyard	
	"Be Prepared"	Scar, Shenzi, Banzai, Ed, Ensemble
Scene 10	The Gorge	
Scene 11	Pride Rock	
	"Be Prepared" (Reprise)	Scar, Ensemble
Scene 12	Rafiki's Tree	
Scene 13	The Desert/The Jungle	
	"Hakuna Matata"	Timon, Pumbaa, Young Simba, Simba, Ensemble

ACT TWO

Entr'acte	"One by One"	Ensemble
Scene 1	Scar's Cave	
	"The Madness of King Scar"	Scar, Zazu, Banzai, Shenzi, Ed, Nala
Scene 2	The Pridelands	
	"Shadowland"	Nala, Rafiki, Ensemble
Scene 3	The Jungle	
Scene 4	Under the Stars	
	"Endless Night"	Simba, Ensemble
Scene 5	Rafiki's Tree	
Scene 6	The Jungle	
	"Can You Feel the Love Tonight"	Timon, Pumbaa, Simba, Nala, Ensemble
	"He Lives in You" (Reprise)	Rafiki, Simba, Ensemble
Scene 7	Pride Rock	
	"King of Pride Rock"/"Circle of Life" (Reprise)	Ensemble

SONG CREDITS

All songs by Elton John (music) and Tim Rice (lyrics) except as follows:

"Circle of Life" by Elton John (music) and Tim Rice (lyrics) with "Nants' Ingonyama" by Hans Zimmer and Lebo M

"He Lives in You" ("They Live in You"): Music and lyrics by Mark Mancina, Jay Rifkin, and Lebo M

"One by One": Music and lyrics by Lebo M

"Shadowland": Music by Lebo M and Hans Zimmer, lyrics by Mark Mancina and Lebo M

"Endless Night": Music by Lebo M, Hans Zimmer, and Jay Rifkin, lyrics by Julie Taymor

"King of Pride Rock": Music by Hans Zimmer, lyrics by Lebo M

ADDITIONAL SCORE

Grasslands chant and Lioness chant by Lebo M
Rafiki's chants by Tsidii Le Loka

Cast Continued

Charlaine Katsuyoshi, Ray Mercer, Brandon Christopher O'Neal, Phillip Turner, Camille Workman

SWINGS AND UNDERSTUDIES
RAFIKI: Angelica Edwards, Sheryl McCallum, Brenda Mhlongo, Selloane A. Nkhela, Rema Webb
MUFASA: Alvin Crawford, L. Steven Taylor
SARABI: Camille M. Brown, Sheryl McCallum, Rema Webb
ZAZU: Jim Ferris, Enrique Segura, Thom Christopher Warren
SCAR: Thom Christopher Warren
SHENZI: Angelica Edwards, Sophia Stephens, Rema Webb
BANZAI: Garland Days, Kenny Ingram, Kenny Redell Williams
ED: Gabriel Croom, Kenny Ingram, Dennis Johnston
TIMON: Jim Ferris, Enrique Segura
PUMBAA: Jim Ferris, Thom Christopher Warren
SIMBA: Dennis Johnston, Joel Karie, Brian M. Love
NALA: Nicole Adell Johnson, Selloane A. Nkhela, Sophia Stephens, Rema Webb

SWINGS: Garland Days, Angelica Edwards, Kenny Ingram, Tony James, Dennis Johnston, Brian M. Love, Willia-Noel Montague, Sophia Stephens, Natalie Turner

DANCE CAPTAINS
Garland Days, Willia-Noel Montague

SPECIALTIES
CIRCLE OF LIFE VOCALS: Bongi Duma, S'bu Ngema
MOUSE SHADOW PUPPET: Joel Karie
ANT HILL LADY: Michelle Brugal
GUINEA FOWL: Sant'gria Bello
BUZZARD POLE: Christopher Freeman
GAZELLE WHEEL: Charity de Loera
BUTTERFLIES: Charity de Loera
GAZELLE: Brandon Christopher O'Neal
LIONESS CHANT VOCAL: S'bu Ngema
ACROBATIC TRICKSTER: Ray Mercer
STILT GIRAFFE CROSS: Gabriel Croom
GIRAFFE SHADOW PUPPETS: Brandon Christopher O'Neal, Kenny Redell Williams
CHEETAH: Charlaine Katsuyoshi
SCAR SHADOW PUPPETS: Sant'gria Bello, Brandon Christopher O'Neal, Kenny Redell Williams
SIMBA SHADOW PUPPETS: Christopher Freeman, Ray Mercer, Phillip Turner

The Lion King

Cast Continued

ONE BY ONE VOCAL: Bongi Duma,
　Selloane A. Nkhela
ONE BY ONE DANCE: Bongi Duma,
　Ron Kunene, S'bu Ngema
FIREFLIES: Camille M. Brown
PUMBAA POLE PUPPET: Kenny Redell Williams
NALA POLE PUPPET: Charlaine Katsuyoshi
FLOOR DANCERS: Sant'gria Bello,
　Michelle Brugal
FLYING DANCERS: Gabriel Croom,
　Charlaine Katsuyoshi, Charity de Loera,
　Brandon Christopher O'Neal
LIONESS/HYENA SHADOW PUPPETS:
　Lindiwe Dlamini, Ron Kunene,
　Sheryl McCallum, Brenda Mhlongo,
　Selloane A. Nkhela, Rema Webb

Bongi Duma, Tshidi Manye, Brenda Mhlongo, S'bu Ngema and Selloane A. Nkhela are appearing with the permission of Actors' Equity Association.

ORCHESTRA
CONDUCTOR: Karl Jurman
KEYBOARD SYNTHESIZER/ASSOCIATE
　CONDUCTOR: Cherie Rosen
SYNTHESIZERS: Ted Baker, Paul Ascenzo
WOOD FLUTE SOLOIST/FLUTE/PICCOLO:
　David Weiss
CONCERTMASTER: Francisca Mendoza
VIOLINS: Krystof Witek, Avril Brown
VIOLIN/VIOLA: Ralph Farris
CELLOS: Eliana Mendoza, Bruce Wang
FLUTE/CLARINET/BASS CLARINET:
　Robert DeBellis
FRENCH HORNS: Patrick Milando,
　Alexandra Cook, Greg Smith
TROMBONE: Rock Ciccarone
BASS TROMBONE/TUBA: Morris Kainuma
UPRIGHT AND ELECTRIC BASSES:
　Tom Barney
DRUMS/ASSISTANT CONDUCTOR:
　Tommy Igoe
GUITAR: Kevin Kuhn
PERCUSSION/ASSISTANT CONDUCTOR:
　Rolando Morales-Matos
MALLETS/PERCUSSION: Valerie Dee Naranjo,
　Tom Brett
PERCUSSION: Junior "Gabu" Wedderburn
MUSIC COORDINATOR: Michael Keller

Based on the Disney film *The Lion King*
Directed by Roger Allers and Rob Minkoff
Produced by Don Hahn
Special thanks to all the artists and staff of Walt Disney Feature Animation

Derek Smith
Scar

Nathaniel Stampley
Mufasa

Tshidi Manye
Rafiki

Cameron Pow
Zazu

Ben Lipitz
Pumbaa

Danny Rutigliano
Timon

Dashaun Young
Simba

Ta'rea Campbell
Nala

James Brown-Orleans
Banzai

Bonita J. Hamilton
Shenzi

Enrique Segura
Ed

Alphonso Romero Jones II
Young Simba

Shereen Pimentel
Young Nala

Marquis Kofi Rodriguez
Young Simba

Shannon Skye Tavarez
Young Nala

Sant'gria Bello
Ensemble

Camille M. Brown
Ensemble

Michelle Brugal
Ensemble

Alvin Crawford
Ensemble

Gabriel Croom
Ensemble

The Lion King

Garland Days
Swing, Dance Captain

Charity de Loera
Ensemble

Lindiwe Dlamini
Ensemble

Bongi Duma
Ensemble

Angelica Edwards
Swing

Jim Ferris
Standby Zazu, Timon, Pumbaa

Christopher Freeman
Ensemble

Jean Michelle Grier
Sarabi/Ensemble

Kenny Ingram
Swing

Tony James
Swing

Nicole Adell Johnson
Ensemble

Dennis Johnston
Swing

Joel Karie
Ensemble

Charlaine Katsuyoshi
Ensemble

Ron Kunene
Ensemble

Brian M. Love
Swing

Sheryl McCallum
Ensemble

Ray Mercer
Ensemble

Brenda Mhlongo
Ensemble

Willia-Noel Montague
Swing, Dance Captain

S'Bu Ngema
Ensemble

Selloane A. Nkhela
Ensemble

Brandon Christopher O'Neal
Ensemble

Sophia Stephens
Swing

L. Steven Taylor
Ensemble

Natalie Turner
Swing

Phillip W. Turner
Ensemble

Thom Christopher Warren
Standby Zazu, Scar, Pumbaa

Rema Webb
Ensemble

Kenny Redell Williams
Ensemble

Camille Workman
Ensemble

Sir Elton John
Music

Tim Rice
Lyrics

Roger Allers
Book

Irene Mecchi
Book

The Lion King

Julie Taymor
Director, Costume Design, Mask/Puppet Co-Design, Additional Lyrics

Garth Fagan
Choreographer

Lebo M
Additional Music & Lyrics, Additional Vocal Score, Vocal Arrangements, Choral Director

Mark Mancina
Additional Music & Lyrics, Music Produced for the Stage, Additional Score

Hans Zimmer
Additional Music & Lyrics

Jay Rifkin
Additional Music & Lyrics

Richard Hudson
Scenic Design

Donald Holder
Lighting Design

Michael Curry
Mask & Puppet Design

Steve Canyon Kennedy
Sound Design

Mark Brandon/Binder Casting
Casting

David Benken
Technical Director

John Stefaniuk
Associate Director

Karl Jurman
Music Director/Conductor

Jen Bender
Resident Director

Ruthlyn Salomons
Resident Dance Supervisor

Robert Elhai
Associate Music Producer, Orchestrator

Michael Keller
Music Coordinator

Thomas Schumacher, Disney Theatrical Productions

Jeff Binder
Zazu

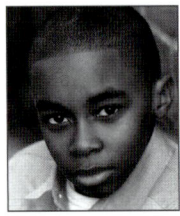
Sean Bradford
Swing

Clifford Lee Dickson
Young Simba

Jeremy Gumbs
Young Simba

Christine Horn
Lioness/Hyena Shadow Puppets, Ensemble Singer

Chantylla Johnson
Young Nala

Lisa Lewis
Cheetah, Flying Dancer, Nala Pole Puppet, Ensemble Dancer

Jennifer Harrison Newman
Ensemble Dancer

Tom Alan Robbins
Pumbaa

LaQuet Sharnell
Ensemble Dancer

Mpume Sikakane
Lioness/Hyena Shadow Puppets, One by One Vocal, Ensemble Singer

Cypress Eden Smith
Young Nala

Lisa Nicole Wilkerson
Lioness/Hyena Shadow Puppets, Ensemble Singer

Damian Baldet
Timon

The Lion King

Jeff Binder
Zazu

Izell O. Blunt
Buzzard Pole Speciality, Simba Shadow Puppets, Ensemble Dancer

John E. Brady
u/s Pumbaa, Timon, Zazu

Khail Toi Bryant
Young Nala

Robert Creighton
Timon

Joshua J. Jackson
Young Simba

Cornelius Jones Jr.
Swing

Lisa Lewis
Cheetah, Flying Dancer, Nala Pole Puppet, Ensemble Dancer

Jade Milan
Young Nala

James A. Pierce III
Swing

Jacqueline René
Swing

Tom Alan Robbins
Pumbaa

Kellen Stancil
Swing

Torya
Ensemble Dancer

Lisa Nicole Wilkerson
Swing

FRONT OF HOUSE STAFF
Front Row (L-R): David Eschinger, Mathew Maine, Marion Mooney
Second Row (L-R): Magdelana Clavano, Ada Ocasio, Judy Pirouz
Third Row (L-R): Maria Compton, Cheryl Budd
Back Row (L-R): Victor Irving, Megan Mulligan

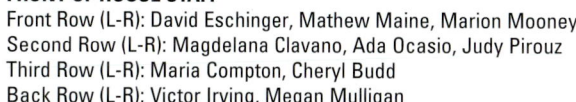

ORCHESTRA
Front Row (L-R): Avril Brown, Patrick Milando, Lara Hicks
Back Row (L-R): Greg Smith, Robert Debellis, Cherie Rosen, Morris Kainuma

CREW
Kneeling (L-R): David Lynch, Alphonso Romero Jones II (Young Simba), Don McKennan, Niki White, Ron Vodicka, Maria Shrime, Richard McQuail, Michael Lavaia, Carmen I. Abrazado, Dave Tisue, Pixie Esmonde, Walter Weiner, April Taylor-Stackle, William Brennan, Joseph P. Lynch

Standing (L-R): Frank Illo, Sheila Little Terrell, Scott Scheidt, Theresa DiStasi, Mark Houston, Doug Graf, Edward Greenberg, Aldo "Butch" Servilio, David Holliman, Douglas Hamilton, Stephen Speer, Michael Lynch, Ruthlyn Salomons, George Zegarsky, Donna Doiron, Alain Van Achte, Sean Strohmeyer

The Playbill Broadway Yearbook 2009-2010

The Lion King
SCRAPBOOK

Correspondent: Jean Michelle Grier, "Sarabi"
Most Vivid Memories of Recent Performances: Whoopi Goldberg joining the cast for an evening of cameos. The "concert" version of the show after Pride Rock broke down center stage.
Memorable Fan Letter: A fan letter apologizing to Scar (Derek Smith) for booing him at the curtain call—they wanted to clarify that he was indeed, a delightfully convincing villain.
Milestone Party: The annual Gemini Birthday Party; those amazing 5,000th Show lapel pins—woo hoo!; free martinis and pizza at the 5,000th Show party.
Most Exciting Celebrity Visitor: Michelle Brugal: Common—I imagined him saying, "I love you, Michelle"!
Special Backstage Rituals: All the backstage social cues.
Derek Smith: "Every show my tail pays a special visit to a certain part of Sheryl McCallum. It's been a long, happy, volatile relationship."
Special Intermission Activity: Eating snacks; There is a birthday almost every day—there is ALWAYS birthday cake at intermission.
Favorite Moment in the Show: Michelle Brugal: "The ballet duet with my partner."
Anonymous: Scar's line, "I'm surrounded by idiots."
Favorite Off-Site Hangouts: Room Service; Bond 45; St. Andrews; my couch; anywhere with an Equity discount, especially on drinks!
Favorite Snack Foods: Stage Managers' chocolate; popcorn; anything free; sangria.
Memorable Stage Door Fan Encounters: Derek Smith: "Who were you?"—I played Scar. "No you didn't!" —Yes, I did. "You did?" —Yep. ... "I thought you were black!"
Tom Reynolds, Stage Manager: "I'm white and ignored."
Catchphrases Only the Company Would Recognize: "Yes, we are indeed at places!" "We gwine!" "Are you mechanical or non-mechanical?" "Five minutes! Five minutes, ladies and gentlemen, five minutes. Five five five five minutes. Thank you. FIVE!!!"

Whoopi Goldberg (front) takes a curtain call as Rafiki with the cast after a special cameo performance January 14, 2010.

Memorable Stage Management Note: "Remember to be quiet backstage." Yeah, right.
Embarrassing Moment: Simba to Scar: "Give me one good reason why I shouldn't rip your clothes off!"
Derek Smith (Scar): I screamed, "Sarabi!", and fell flat on my face.

Staff for THE LION KING Worldwide

Associate Producer	Anne Quart
Production Supervisor	Doc Zorthian
Production Manager	Myriah Perkins
Associate Director	John Stefaniuk
Associate Choreographer	Marey Griffith
Music Supervisor	Clement Ishmael
Dance Supervisor	Celise Hicks
Associate Music Supervisor	Jay Alger
Associate Scenic Designer	Peter Eastman
Associate Costume Designer	Mary Nemecek Peterson
Associate Mask & Puppet Designer	Louis Troisi
Associate Sound Designer	John Shivers
Associate Hair & Makeup Designer	Carole Hancock
Associate Lighting Designer	Jeanne Koenig
Assistant Lighting Designer	Marty Vreeland
Assistant Sound Designer	Shane Cook
Automated Lighting Programmer	Aland Henderson
Production Coordinator	Tara Engler
Management Assistant	Elizabeth Fine

DISNEY ON BROADWAY PUBLICITY

Senior Publicist	Dennis Crowley
Publicist	Adriana Douzos

Staff for THE LION KING New York

Company Manager	THOMAS SCHLENK
Assistant Company Manager	Fred Hemminger
Production Stage Manager	Ron Vodicka
Resident Director	Jen Bender
Resident Dance Supervisor	Ruthlyn Salomons
Musical Director/Conductor	Karl Jurman
Stage Managers	Carmen I. Abrazado, Narda E. Alcorn, Antonia Gianino, Tom Reynolds
Dance Captains	Garland Days, Willia-Noel Montague
Fight Captain	Ray Mercer
Assistant Choreographers	Norwood J. Pennewell, Natalie Rogers
South African Dialect Coach	Ron Kunene
Casting Associates	Jack Bowdan, C.S.A.; Mark Brandon; Sara Schatz, C.S.A.; Nikole Vallins
Casting Assistants	Karen Young, Patrick Bell
Corporate Counsel	Michael Rosenfeld
Physical Therapy	Neuro Tour Physical Therapy/ Maria Shrime
Consulting Orthopedist	Philip Roth, M.D.
Child Wrangler	Niki White
Executive Travel	Robert Arnao, Patt McRory
Production Travel	Jill Citron
Web Design Consultant	Joshua Noah
Advertising	Serino/Coyne Inc.
Interactive Marketing	Situation Marketing/ Damian Bazadona, Lisa Cecchini, Miriam Gardin
Production Carpenter	Drew Siccardi
Head Carpenter	Michael Trotto
House Carpenter	Patrick Sullivan
Assistant Carpenters	Kirk Bender, Michael Phillips
Automation Carpenters	Aldo "Butch" Servilio, George Zegarsky
Carpenters	Giuseppe Iannello, Daniel Macormack, Terry McGarty, Duane Mirro
Flying Supervision	Dave Hearn
Production Flymen	Kraig Bender, Dylan Trotto
House Flyman	Richard McQuail
Production Electrician	James Maloney
House Electrician	Michael Lynch
Board Operator	Edward Greenberg
House Assistant Electrician	Stephen Speer
Automated Lighting Technician	Sean Strohmeyer
Key Spot Operator	Doug Graf
Assistant Electricians	William Brennan, David Holliman, David Lynch, Joseph P. Lynch
Production Propman	Victor Amerling
House Propman	Frank Illo
Props	Matthew Lavaia, Michael Lavaia, Robert McCauley
Head Sound	Alain Van Achte
Sound Assistants	Donald McKennan, Scott Scheidt
Production Wardrobe Supervisor	Kjeld Andersen
Assistant Wardrobe Supervisor	Cynthia Boardman
Puppet Supervisor	Anne Salt
Puppet Dayworkers	Islah Abdul-Rahiim, Ilya Vett
Mask/Puppet Studio	Jeff Curry
Dressers	Meredith Chase-Boyd, Andy Cook, Tom Daniel, Donna Doiron,

The Lion King

	Pixie Esmonde, April Fernandez-Taylor, Michelle Gore-Butterfield, Douglas Hamilton, Mark Houston, Sara Jablon, Mark Lauer, Dawn Reynolds, Kathryn Rohe, Sheila Terrell, Dave Tisue, Steven Washington, Walter Weiner
Stitcher	Janeth Iverson
Production Hair Supervisor	Jon Jordan
Assistant Hair Supervisor	Adenike Wright
Production Makeup Supervisor	Elizabeth Cohen
Assistant Makeup Supervisor	Marian Torre
Makeup Artist	Rebecca Kuzma
Music Development	Nick Glennie-Smith
Music Preparation	Donald Oliver and Evan Morris/Chelsea Music Service, Inc.
Synthesizer Programmer	Ted Baker
Orchestral Synthesizer Programmer	Christopher Ward
Electronic Drum Programmer	Tommy Igoe
Addt'l Percussion Arrangements	Valerie Dee Naranjo
Music Assistant	Elizabeth J. Falcone
Personal Assistant to Elton John	Bob Halley
Assistant to Tim Rice	Eileen Heinink
Assistant to Mark Mancina	Chuck Choi
Associate Scenic Designer	Jonathan Fensom
Assistant Scenic Designer	Michael Fagin
Lighting Design Assistant	Karen Spahn
Automated Lighting Tracker	Lara Bohon
Projection Designer	Geoff Puckett
Projection Art	Caterina Bertolotto
Assistant Sound Designer	Kai Harada
Assistant Costume Designer	Tracy Dorman
Stunt Consultant	Peter Moore
Children's Tutoring	On Location Education
Production Photography	Joan Marcus, Marc Bryan-Brown
Associate Producer 1996–1998	Donald Frantz
Project Manager 1996–1998	Nina Essman
Associate Producer 1998–2002	Ken Denison
Associate Producer 2000-2003	Pam Young
Associate Producer 2002-2007	Todd Lacy
Associate Producer 2003-2008	Aubrey Lynch
Original Music Director	Joseph Church

Disney's *The Lion King* is a registered trademark owned by The Walt Disney Company and used under special license by Disney Theatrical Productions.

HOUSE STAFF FOR THE MINSKOFF THEATRE

House Manager	Victor Irving
Treasurer	Nicholas Loiacono
Assistant Treasurer	Cheryl Loiacono

CREDITS

Scenery built and mechanized by Hudson Scenic Studio, Inc. Additional scenery by Chicago Scenic Studios, Inc.; Edge & Co., Inc.; Michael Hagen, Inc.; Piper Productions, Inc.; Scenic Technologies, Inc.; I. Weiss & Sons, Inc. Lighting by Westsun, vari*lite® automated lighting provided by Vari-Lite, Inc. Props by John Creech Design & Production. Sound equipment by Pro-Mix, Inc. Additional sound equipment by Walt Disney Imagineering. Rehearsal Scenery by Brooklyn Scenic & Theatrical. Costumes executed by Barbara Matera Ltd., Parsons-Meares Ltd., Donna Langman, Eric Winterling, Danielle Gisiger, Suzie Elder. Millinery by Rodney Gordon, Janet Linville, Arnold Levine. Ricola provided by Ricola, Inc. Shibori dyeing by Joan Morris. Custom dyeing and painting by Joni Johns, Mary Macy, Parsons-Meares Ltd., Gene Mignola. Additional Painting by J. Michelle Hill. Knitwear by Maria Ficalora. Footwear by Sharlot Battin, Robert W. Jones, Capezio, Vasilli Shoes. Costume Development by Constance Hoffman. Special Projects by Angela M. Kahler. Custom fabrics developed by Gary Graham and Helen Quinn. Puppet Construction by Michael Curry Design, Inc. and Vee Corporation. Shadow puppetry by Steven Kaplan. Pumbaa Puppet Construction by Andrew Benepe. Flying by Foy. Trucking by Clark Transfer. Wigs created by Wig Workshop of London. Marimbas by De Morrow Instruments, Ltd. Latin Percussion by LP Music Group. Drumset by DrumWorkshop. Cymbals by Zildjian. Bass equipment by Eden Electronics. Paper products supplied by Green Forest.

SONG EXCERPTS (used by permission): "Supercalifragilisticexpialidocious" written by Richard M. Sherman and Robert B. Sherman; "Five Foot Two, Eyes of Blue" written by Sam Lewis, Joe Young, and Ray Henderson; "The Lion Sleeps Tonight" written by Hugo Peretti, George David Weiss, Luigi Creatore and Solomon Linda.

NEDERLANDER

Chairman	James M. Nederlander
President	James L. Nederlander

Executive Vice President
Nick Scandalios

Vice President Corporate Development **Charlene S. Nederlander**	Senior Vice President Labor Relations **Herschel Waxman**
Vice President **Jim Boese**	Chief Financial Officer **Freida Sawyer Belviso**

DISNEY THEATRICAL PRODUCTIONS

President	Thomas Schumacher
EVP & Managing Director	David Schrader
Senior Vice President, Creative Affairs	Michele Steckler
Senior Vice President, International	Ron Kollen
Vice President, Operations	Dana Amendola
Vice President, Labor Relations	Allan Frost
Vice President, Worldwide Publicity & Communications	Joe Quenqua
Vice President, Domestic Touring	Jack Eldon
Vice President, Theatrical Licensing	Steve Fickinger
Vice President, Human Resources	June Heindel
Director, Domestic Touring	Michael Buchanan
Director, Publicity & Communications	Jay Carducci
Manager, Labor Relations	Stephanie Cheek
Manager, Human Resources	Jewel Neal
Manager, Film Development	Dusty Bennett
Manager, Information Systems	Scott Benedict
Senior Computer Support Analyst	Kevin A. McGuire
IT/Business Analyst	William Boudiette

Production

Executive Music Producer	Chris Montan
Director, International	Michael Cassel
Manager, Physical Production	Karl Chmielewski
Dramaturg & Literary Manager	Ken Cerniglia

Marketing

Vice President, Broadway	Andrew Flatt
Vice President, International	Fiona Thomas
Director, Internet Strategy & Online Marketing	Kyle Young
Director, Broadway	Michele Groner
Director, Domestic Tour Marketing	Deborah Warren
Website Manager	Eric W. Kratzer
Assistant Manager, Advertising	Lauren Daghini

Sales

Director, National Sales	Bryan Dockett
Manager, New Business Development	Jacob Lloyd Kimbro
Manager, Sales & Ticketing	Nick Falzon
Manager, Group Sales	Juil Kim

Business and Legal Affairs

Senior Vice President	Jonathan Olson
Director	Daniel M. Posener
Senior Counsel	Seth Stuhl
Paralegal	Jessica White

Finance

VP Finance & Business Development	Mario Iannetta
Director	Joe McClafferty
Senior Manager, Finance	Dana James
Manager, Finance	John Fajardo
Production Accountants	Joy Sims Brown, Nick Judge, Barbara Toben
Assistant Production Accountant	Isander Rojas
Senior Sales Analyst	Liz Jurist Schwarzwalder
Senior Business Planner	Shaan Akbar
Director, Accounting	Leena Mathew
Sr. Financial Analyst	Adrineh Ghoukassian

Administrative Staff

Sarah Bills, Dayle Bland, Lindsay Braverman, Amy Caldamone, Michael Dei Cas,, Alanna Degner, Jessica Doina, Cristi Finn, Gregory Hanoian, Abbie Harrison, Cyntia Leo, Colleen McCormack, Janine McGuire, Lisa Mitchell, Dimitri Pankas, Ryan Pears, David Scott, Benjy Shaw, Christina Tuchman, Kyle Wilson, Jason Zammit

DISNEY THEATRICAL MERCHANDISE

Vice President	Steven Downing
Operations Manager	Shawn Baker
Merchandise Manager	Neil Markman
Associate Buyer	Violet Burlaza
Assistant Manager, Inventory	Suzanne Jakel
District Manager	Alyssa Somers
On-Site Retail Manager	Jeff Knizner
On-Site Assistant Retail Manager	Jana Cristiano

Disney Theatrical Productions
c/o New Amsterdam Theatre
214 W. 42nd St.
New York, NY 10036

guestmail@disneytheatrical.com

The Little Mermaid

First Preview: November 3, 2007. Opened: January 10, 2008.
Closed August 30, 2009 after 50 Previews and 685 Performances.

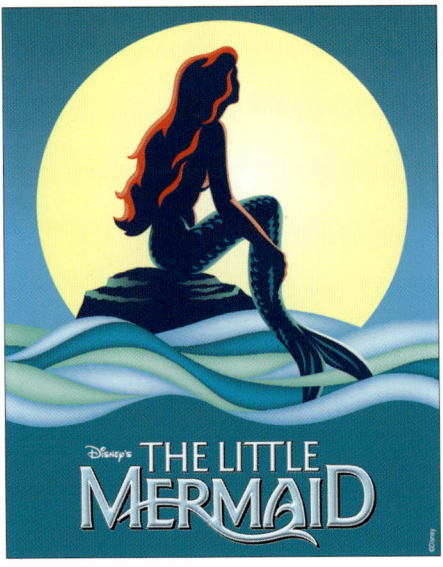

CAST OF CHARACTERS
(in order of appearance)

Pilot	MERWIN FOARD
Prince Eric	DREW SEELEY
Grimsby	JONATHAN FREEMAN
King Triton	NORM LEWIS
Mersisters	CATHRYN BASILE, MEGAN CAMPANILE, CICILY DANIELS, MICHELLE LOOKADOO, ZAKIYA YOUNG MIZEN, KAY TRINIDAD
Sebastian	ROGELIO DOUGLAS JR.
Ariel	CHELSEA MORGAN STOCK
Flounder	BRIAN D'ADDARIO (Tues. eve., Wed. eve., Fri. eve., Sat. mat., Sun. mat.) MAJOR CURDA (Wed. mat., Thurs. eve., Sat. eve.)
Scuttle	EDDIE KORBICH
Gulls	JOE ABRAHAM, ENRIQUE BROWN, RHETT GEORGE
Ursula	FAITH PRINCE
Flotsam	TYLER MAYNARD
Jetsam	ERIC LaJUAN SUMMERS
Carlotta	JULIE BARNES
Chef Louis	ROBERT CREIGHTON

LUNT-FONTANNE THEATRE
UNDER THE DIRECTION OF
JAMES M. NEDERLANDER AND JAMES L. NEDERLANDER

Disney Theatrical Productions
under the direction of
Thomas Schumacher
presents

CHELSEA MORGAN STOCK   DREW SEELEY
and
FAITH PRINCE
as Ursula

Disney's THE LITTLE MERMAID

Music: ALAN MENKEN
Lyrics: HOWARD ASHMAN & GLENN SLATER
Book: DOUG WRIGHT

Based on the Hans Christian Andersen story and the Disney film produced by Howard Ashman & John Musker and written & directed by John Musker & Ron Clements.

Starring
NORM LEWIS   ROGELIO DOUGLAS JR.   EDDIE KORBICH   JONATHAN FREEMAN
TYLER MAYNARD   ERIC LAJUAN SUMMERS   ROBERT CREIGHTON
MAJOR CURDA   BRIAN D'ADDARIO

JOE ABRAHAM   JULIE BARNES   CATHRYN BASILE   ENRIQUE BROWN   JAMES BROWN III   MEGAN CAMPANILE
CICILY DANIELS   J. AUSTIN EYER   MERWIN FOARD   LYNDY FRANKLIN   RHETT GEORGE   AMY HALL
BEN HARTLEY   TYRONE A. JACKSON   MICHELLE LOOKADOO   ALAN MINGO, JR   ZAKIYA YOUNG MIZEN
JC MONTGOMERY   MICHELLE PRUIETT   BRET SHUFORD   JASON SNOW   KAY TRINIDAD

Scenic Design: GEORGE TSYPIN
Costume Design: TATIANA NOGINOVA
Lighting Design: NATASHA KATZ
Sound Design: JOHN SHIVERS
Hair Design: DAVID BRIAN BROWN
Makeup Design: ANGELINA AVALLONE
Projection & Video Design: SVEN ORTEL
Dance Arrangements: DAVID CHASE
Music Coordinator: MICHAEL KELLER
Fight Director: RICK SORDELET
Casting: TARA RUBIN CASTING

Associate Producer: TODD LACY
Associate Director: BRIAN HILL
Associate Choreographer: TARA YOUNG

Technical Director: DAVID BENKEN
Production Supervisor: CLIFFORD SCHWARTZ

Orchestrations by DANNY TROOB

Music Director
Incidental Music & Vocal Arrangements by
MICHAEL KOSARIN

Choreography by
STEPHEN MEAR

Directed by
FRANCESCA ZAMBELLO

8/30/09

(L-R): Chelsea Morgan Stock and Drew Seeley

Continued on next page

The Little Mermaid

MUSICAL NUMBERS

ACT I

Overture	
"Fathoms Below"†	Pilot, Sailors, Prince Eric, Grimsby
"Daughters of Triton"*	Mersisters
"The World Above"	Ariel
"Human Stuff"	Scuttle, Gulls
"I Want the Good Times Back"	Ursula, Flotsam, Jetsam, Eels
"Part of Your World"*	Ariel
"Storm at Sea"	
"Part of Your World" (Reprise)*	Ariel
"She's in Love"	Mersisters, Flounder
"Her Voice"	Prince Eric
"The World Above" (Reprise)	King Triton
"Under the Sea"*	Sebastian, Sea Creatures
"Sweet Child"	Flotsam, Jetsam
"Poor Unfortunate Souls"*	Ursula

ACT II

Entr'acte	
"Positoovity"	Scuttle, Gulls
"Beyond My Wildest Dreams"	Ariel, Carlotta, Maids
"Les Poissons"*	Chef Louis
"Les Poissons" (Reprise)	Chef Louis, Chefs
"One Step Closer"	Prince Eric
"I Want the Good Times Back" (Reprise)	Ursula, Flotsam, Jetsam
"Kiss the Girl"*	Sebastian, Animals
"Sweet Child" (Reprise)	Flotsam, Jetsam
"If Only"	Ariel, Prince Eric, Sebastian, King Triton
"The Contest"	Grimsby, Princesses
"Poor Unfortunate Souls" (Reprise)	Ursula
"If Only" (Reprise)	King Triton, Ariel
"Finale"†	Prince Eric, Ariel, Ensemble

Music by Alan Menken
* Lyrics by Howard Ashman
† Lyrics by Howard Ashman and Glenn Slater
All other lyrics by Glenn Slater

ENSEMBLE

JOE ABRAHAM; CATHRYN BASILE; ENRIQUE BROWN; MEGAN CAMPANILE; CICILY DANIELS; MERWIN FOARD; RHETT GEORGE; AMY HALL; BEN HARTLEY; TYRONE A. JACKSON; MICHELLE LOOKADOO; ALAN MINGO, JR.; ZAKIYA YOUNG MIZEN; JC MONTGOMERY; BRET SHUFORD; KAY TRINIDAD

SWINGS

JULIE BARNES, JAMES BROWN III, J. AUSTIN EYER, LYNDY FRANKLIN, MICHELLE PRUIETT, JASON SNOW

DANCE CAPTAINS

JAMES BROWN III, JASON SNOW

UNDERSTUDIES

Ariel:
MEGAN CAMPANILE, MICHELLE LOOKADOO, MICHELLE PRUIETT
Ursula:
CICILY DANIELS
Prince Eric:
J. AUSTIN EYER, BRET SHUFORD
King Triton, Grimsby:
MERWIN FOARD, JC MONTGOMERY
Sebastian:
RHETT GEORGE, ALAN MINGO, JR.
Scuttle:
JOE ABRAHAM, JASON SNOW
Flotsam:
BRET SHUFORD, JASON SNOW
Jetsam:
JAMES BROWN III, J. AUSTIN EYER
Chef Louis:
JOE ABRAHAM, MERWIN FOARD

ORCHESTRA

Conductor: MICHAEL KOSARIN
Associate Conductor: GREG ANTHONY

Concertmaster: SUZANNE ORNSTEIN
Violin: MINEKO YAJIMA
Cello 1: ROGER SHELL
Cello 2: DEBORAH ASSAEL-MIGLIORE
Lead Trumpet: NICHOLAS MARCHIONE
Trumpet: FRANK GREENE
Trombone: GARY GRIMALDI
Bass Trombone/Tuba: JEFF CASWELL
Reed 1: STEVE KENYON
Reed 2: DAVID YOUNG
Reed 3: MARC PHANEUF
French Horn: ZOHAR SCHONDORF
Keyboard 1: ARON ACCURSO
Keyboard 2: GREG ANTHONY
Keyboard 3: ANDREW GROBENGIESER
Bass: RICHARD SARPOLA
Drums: JOHN REDSECKER
Percussion: JOE PASSARO

Electronic Music Design: ANDREW BARRETT
Music Coordinator: MICHAEL KELLER

Faith Prince as Ursula

Photo by Joan Marcus

The Little Mermaid

Chelsea Morgan Stock
Ariel

Faith Prince
Ursula

Drew Seeley
Prince Eric

Norm Lewis
King Triton

Rogelio Douglas Jr.
Sebastian

Eddie Korbich
Scuttle

Jonathan Freeman
Grimsby

Tyler Maynard
Flotsam

Eric LaJuan Summers
Jetsam

Robert Creighton
Chef Louis

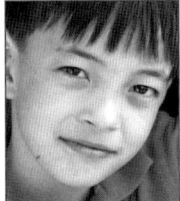
Major Curda
Flounder at certain performances

Brian D'Addario
Flounder at certain performances

Joe Abraham
Ensemble

Julie Barnes
Swing

Cathryn Basile
Ensemble

Enrique Brown
Ensemble

James Brown III
Swing/Dance Captain

Megan Campanile
Ensemble

Cicily Daniels
Ensemble

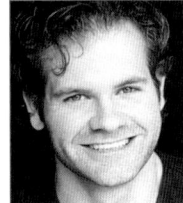
J. Austin Eyer
Swing

Merwin Foard
Pilot/Ensemble

Lyndy Franklin
Swing

Rhett George
Ensemble

Amy Hall
Ensemble

Ben Hartley
Ensemble

Tyrone A. Jackson
Ensemble

Michelle Lookadoo
Ensemble

Alan Mingo, Jr.
Ensemble

Zakiya Young Mizen
Ensemble

JC Montgomery
Ensemble

Michelle Pruiett
Swing

Bret Shuford
Ensemble

Jason Snow
Swing

Kay Trinidad
Ensemble

Alan Menken
Composer

The Little Mermaid

Howard Ashman
Lyrics

Glenn Slater
Lyrics

Doug Wright
Book

Francesca Zambello
Director

Stephen Mear
Choreographer

George Tsypin
Scenic Design

Tatiana Noginova
Costume Design

Natasha Katz
Lighting Design

John H. Shivers
Sound Design

Danny Troob
Orchestrator

Michael Kosarin
Music Direction/ Vocal and Incidental Music Arrangements

David Brian Brown
Wig/Hair Design

Angelina Avallone
Make-up Design

Sven Ortel
Projection & Video Design

Michael Keller
Music Coordinator

Rick Sordelet
Fight Director

Pichón Baldinu
Aerial Design

Tara Rubin
Tara Rubin Casting
Casting

Brian Hill
Associate Director

Tara Young
Associate Choreographer

David Benken
Technical Director

Clifford Schwartz
Production Supervisor

Andrew Barrett
Electronic Music Design

Thomas Schumacher
Disney Theatrical Productions

ALUMNI 2009-2010

Trevor Braun
Flounder at certain performances

Meredith Inglesby
Carlotta, Ensemble

Sean Palmer
Prince Eric

John Mara (kneeling) backstage with (L-R) Michelle Lookadoo, Zakiya Young Mizen, Cathryn Basile, Brian D'Addario, Chelsea Morgan Stock, Kay Trinidad, and Cicily Daniels on Stock's final performance as a "Mersister" before she took over the lead role of Ariel.

The Playbill Broadway Yearbook 2009-2010

The Little Mermaid

Staff for THE LITTLE MERMAID
COMPANY MANAGER ....EDUARDO CASTRO
Production Manager ....Jane Abramson
Assistant Company Manager ....Margie McGlone
Production Supervisor ....Clifford Schwartz
Stage Manager ....Theresa Bailey
Assistant Stage Managers ....Robert M. Armitage,
Alexis Shorter, Matthew Aaron Stern
Dance Captains ....James Brown III, Jason Snow
Fight Captain ....James Brown III
Assistant to the Associate Producer ....Kerry McGrath

DISNEY ON BROADWAY PUBLICITY
Senior Publicist ....Dennis Crowley
Publicist ....Adriana Douzos

Associate Scenic Designer ....Peter Eastman
Assistant Scenic Designer ....Denny Moyes
Scenic Design Assistants ....Gaetane Bertol,
Larry Brown, Kelly Hanson,
Niki Hernandez-Adams,
Nathan Heverin, Rachel Short Janocko,
Jee an Jung, Mimi Lien,
Frank McCullough, Arnulfo Maldonado,
Robert Pyzocha, Chisato Uno
Sculptor ....Arturs Virtmanis
Associate Costume Designer ....Tracy Christensen
Assistant Costume Designers ....Brian J. Bustos,
Amy Clark
Costume Shoppers ....Leon Dobkowski, Vanessa Leuck
Associate Lighting Designer ....Yael Lubetzky
Lighting Design Assistant ....Craig Stelzenmuller
Automated Lighting Programmer ....Aland Henderson
Automated Lighting Tracker ....Joel Shier
Assistant to the Lighting Designer ....Richard Swan
Associate Sound Designer ....David Patridge
Associate Hair Designer ....Jonathan Carter
Assistant Hair Designer ....Thomas Augustine
Projection Design Assistants ....Peter Acken,
Katy Tucker
Associate Aerial Designer ....Angela Phillips
Magic/Illusion Designer ....Joe Eddie Fairchild
Associate to Technical Director ....Rose Palombo
Production Carpenter ....Stephen Detmer
Head Carpenter ....Patrick Eviston
Fly Automation ....Jeff Zink
Deck Automation ....Michael L. Shepp, Jr.
Rigger ....Rick Howard
Production Electrician ....Rick Baxter
Head Electrician ....Joseph Pearson
Assistant Electrician ....Damian Caza-Cleypool
Moving Light Technician ....Jesse Hancox
Production Props ....Jerry L. Marshall
Assistant Props ....Steven E. Wood
Production Sound Engineer ....David Patridge
Head Sound ....George Huckins
Deck Sound ....Scott Anderson
Wardrobe Supervisor ....Nancy Schaefer
Assistant Wardrobe Supervisor ....Edmund Harrison
Wardrobe Staff ....Rachael Garrett, Sue Hamilton,
Melanie Hansen, Barbara Hladsky,
Franklin Hollenbeck, Greg Holtz,
Teresia Larsen, Terry LaVada,
Robert J. Malkmus III, Paul Riner,
Erin Brooke Roth, Eric Rudy,
Rita Santi, Rodd Sovar, Claire Verlaet

Hair Supervisor ....Wanda Gregory
Assistant Hair Supervisor ....Lisa Fraley
Hairdressers ....Joshua First, Jennifer Pendergraft
Make-Up Supervisor ....Tiffany Hicks
Assistant Make-Up Supervisor ....Jorge Vargas
Associate Music Director ....Greg Anthony
Additional Orchestrations ....Larry Hochman,
Michael Starobin
Music Preparation ....Anixter Rice Music Service
Electronic Music Design ....Andrew Barrett,
for Lionella Productions, Ltd.
Electronic Music Design Assistant ....Jeff Marder
Associate to Mr. Menken ....Rick Kunis
Rehearsal Drummer ....John Redsecker
Rehearsal Pianists .....Aron Accurso, Brent-Alan Huffman,
Andrew Grobengieser, Brian Hertz
Children's Vocal Coach ....Marianne Challis
Chaperone ....John Mara
Children's Tutoring ....On Location Education/
Serena Stanley

CASTING
TARA RUBIN CASTING
Tara Rubin, CSA, Eric Woodall, CSA
Laura Schutzel, CSA, Merri Sugarman, CSA
Rebecca Carfagna, Paige Blansfield, Dale Brown

AERIAL DESIGNER ....**PICHÓN BALDINU**

DIALOGUE &
VOCAL COACH ....**DEBORAH HECHT**

Advertising ....Serino Coyne, Inc.
Interactive Marketing ....Situation Marketing/
Damian Bazadona, Lisa Cecchini, Miriam Gardin
Web Design Consultant ....Joshua Noah
Logo Art ....Scott Thornley + Company
Production Photography ....Joan Marcus
Acoustic Consultant ....Paul Scarbrough, A'Kustiks
Structural Engineering Consultant ....Bill Gorlin,
McLaren, P.C.
Executive Travel ....Robert Arnao, Patricia McRory
Production Travel ....Jill L. Citron
Payroll Managers ....Anthony DeLuca, Cathy Guerra
Counsel – Immigration ....Michael Rosenfeld
Physical Therapy ....The Green Room P.T./Heidi Green
Consulting Orthopedic Surgeon ....Dr. Phillip Bauman

CREDITS
Scenery by Showman Fabricators, Inc.; Show Canada Industries; Adirondack Studios, Inc.; The Paragon Innovation Group, Inc.; Proof Productions. Automation of scenery and rigging by Showman Fabricators, Inc., Long Island City, NY featuring Raynok Motion Control. Lighting equipment by PRG Lighting. Projection equipment by PRG Lighting. Sound equipment by Sound Associates Inc. Costume construction by Parsons-Meares Ltd.; Barbara Matera, Ltd.; Eric Winterling, Inc.; Tricorne, Inc.; Martin Izquierdo Studio. Custom millinery provided by Lynne Mackey Studio; Rodney Gordon; Arnold S. Levine, Inc.; Marian Jean Hose. Custom fabric dyeing and printing by Gene Mignola, Hochi Asiatico, Martin Izquierdo Studio, Olympus Flag and Banner. Costume painting by Hochi Asiatico, Virginia Clow, Claudia Dzundza, Martin Izquierdo Studio, Mary Macy, Parmelee Welles Tolkan, Margaret Peot. Custom footwear by Capri Shoes by Oscar Navarro; Handmade Shoes by Fred Longtin; LaDuca Shoes; Pluma Shoes by Walter Raimundo; Capezio. Custom jewelry and crafts by Arnold S. Levine, Inc.; Marian Jean Hose; Martin Izquierdo Studios; Gaetane Bertol; Larry Vrba. Undergarments by Bra*Tenders; On Stage Dancewear. Ursula mechanics by Jon Gellman Effects. Mermaid tails by Michael Curry Design, Inc. Eel electrics by Birtek Specialty Lighting. Knitwear provided by Karen Eifert and Maria Ficalora Knitwear, Ltd. Wigs by Bob Kelly Wigs; Ray Marston Wigs; Victoria Wood. Props by Arnold S. Levine, Inc.; Jerard Studio; Michael Curry Design, Inc.; The Paragon Innovation Group, Inc.; Provost Displays; I.C.B.A; Puppet Heap; Rabbit's Choice; Vogue Too; Zoë Morsette. Ricola natural herb cough drops courtesy of Ricola USA, Inc. Emergen-C health and energy drink mix provided by Alacer Corp.

Make Up Provided By M•A•C.

Gliding By Heelys®.

THE LITTLE MERMAID originally premiered at the Ellie Caulkins Opera House, Denver Center for the Performing Arts, Colorado.

THE LITTLE MERMAID
rehearsed at the New 42nd Street Studios.

SPECIAL THANKS
Kate Boucher, Ian Galloway and Dan Murtha of Bolt Action Five, Michael Curry, Jackie Galloway, Helen Goddard, Green Hippo, Nichol Hignite, Courtney Hoffman, Diana Kuriyama, Anna Ledwich, Calvin Klein Inc., Jim Haag/Vendura, Larry Sonn, Georgia Stitt, Crystal Thompson, Walt Disney Imagineering R&D.

DISNEY THEATRICAL PRODUCTIONS
President ....Thomas Schumacher
EVP & Managing Director ....David Schrader
SVP, Creative Affairs ....Michele Steckler
Senior Vice President, International ....Ron Kollen
Vice President, Operations ....Dana Amendola
Vice President, Labor Relations ....Allan Frost
Vice President, Worldwide Publicity
& Communications ....Joe Quenqua
Vice President, Domestic Touring ....Jack Eldon
Vice President, Theatrical Licensing ....Steve Fickinger
Vice President, Human Resources ....June Heindel
Director, Domestic Touring ....Michael Buchanan
Director, Casting & Development ....Jennifer Rudin, CSA
Director, Publicity & Communications ....Jay Carducci
Manager, Labor Relations ....Stephanie Cheek
Manager, Human Resources ....Jewel Neal
Manager, Film Development ....Dusty Bennett
Manager, Information Systems ....Scott Benedict
Senior Computer Support Analyst ....Kevin A. McGuire
IT/Business Analyst ....William Boudiette

Production
Executive Music Producer ....Chris Montan
Vice President, Physical Production ....John Tiggeloven
Director, International ....Michael Cassel
Senior Manager, Safety ....Canara Price
Manager, Physical Production ....Karl Chmielewski
Dramaturg & Literary Manager ....Ken Cerniglia

The Little Mermaid
Scrapbook

Correspondent: Chelsea Morgan Stock, "Ariel"
The Final Performance: My most vivid memory of the final performance was when I made my final entrance onstage for the wedding/finale. Usually, as I walked down the center, I would always look at the Mersisters to my left. At the final performance, that is the moment I got very emotional. Looking into the eyes of all my fellow actors, most of whom I worked with from day one, was quite overwhelming. All the original Mersisters were there, singing their hearts out, enjoying these final moments of a beautiful show. From that point on, I was very choked up and had a hard time singing.

During the last weeks of the show I got around to some of my fan mail. Two boys had sent me blown up pictures of me as Ariel to sign. On one of the last shows, they were both outside with the same picture for me to sign. They hadn't received my response yet, and they were so dedicated they were back at the show, at the front of the autograph line waiting for me to sign. I was so flattered that it meant that much to them, and now they have two pictures signed!

I had a blast at the closing night party, which was held on the roof of the Empire Hotel. All of the close friends I made in the show were there with me to celebrate. On top of that, so many of the original company members, designers and our crew were there. It was truly amazing to talk to composer Alan Menken at the party and hear his response to my performance. He has known me from my first audition when I was

Chelsea Morgan Stock (center) with the Mersisters backstage during the show's final performance.

cast as Andrina. Now, to be able to sing the music he wrote for Ariel and get his feedback was unbelievable. He was very positive and complimentary. He definitely made a huge impression on me.

During the final performance the energy backstage before the show was thrilling! People were sad, and excited. A few original cast members rehashed an old ritual we had back in the Denver pre-Broadway engagement. When the set was placed behind the opening curtain, a bunch of us would dance in the middle of the stage. Original cast member Derrick Baskin had a dance that would make us laugh so hard. A few people offstage were dancing that crazy dance again as we all geared up for an emotional last show.

During the run of the show, I always liked to sit outside in front of the theater on the stoop and take in the crowd. During the final weeks of the show, I was out there daily. A few people started to call a certain area the "Chelsea stoop." These were favorite moments of mine. I love to people watch in New York. You can learn so much just from taking things in. While I was out there during the final week, it was so

Marketing
Vice President, Broadway .... Andrew Flatt
Vice President, International .... Fiona Thomas
Director, Broadway .... Kyle Young
Director, Broadway .... Michele Groner
Director, Domestic Tour Marketing .... Deborah Warren
Website Manager .... Eric W. Kratzer
Assistant Manager, Marketing .... Lauren Daghini

Sales
Director, National Sales .... Bryan Dockett
Manager,
 New Business Development .... Jacob Lloyd Kimbro
Manager, Sales & Ticketing .... Nick Falzon
Manager, Group Sales .... Juil Kim

Business and Legal Affairs
Senior Vice President .... Jonathan Olson
Director .... Daniel M. Posener
Senior Counsel .... Seth Stuhl

Finance
VP Finance & Business Development .... Mario Iannetta
Director .... Joe McClafferty
Senior Manager, Finance .... Dana James
Manager, Finance .... John Fajardo
Production Accountants .... Joy Sims Brown,
 Nick Judge, Barbara Toben
Assistant Production Accountant .... Isander Rojas

Senior Sales Analyst .... Liz Jurist Schwarzwalder
Senior Business Planner .... Shaan Akbar
Director, Accounting .... Leena Mathew
Sr. Financial Analyst .... Adrineh Ghoukassian

Administrative Staff
Sarah Bills, Dayle Bland, Lindsay Braverman, Amy Caldamone, Alanna Degner, Michael Dei Cas, Jessica Doina, Cristi Finn, Gregory Hanoian, Abbie Harrison, Tom Kingsley, Cyntia Leo, Colleen McCormack, Janine McGuire, Lisa Mitchell, Dimitri Pankas, Ryan Pears, David Scott, Benjy Shaw, Christina Tuchman, Colleen Verbus, Kyle Wilson, Jason Zammit

DISNEY THEATRICAL MERCHANDISE
Vice President .... Steven Downing
Operations Manager .... Shawn Baker
Merchandise Manager .... Neil Markman
Associate Buyer .... Violet Burlaza
Assistant Manager, Inventory .... Suzanne Jakel
Retail Supervisor .... Alyssa Somers
On-Site Retail Manager .... Jeff Knizner
On-Site Assistant Retail Manager .... Mark Murynec

Disney Theatrical Productions
c/o New Amsterdam Theatre
214 W. 42nd St.
New York, NY 10036

guestmail@disneytheatrical.com

NEDERLANDER
Chairman .... James M. Nederlander
President .... James L. Nederlander

Executive Vice President
Nick Scandalios

Vice President
Corporate Development
Charlene S. Nederlander

Senior Vice President
Labor Relations
Herschel Waxman

Vice President
Jim Boese

Chief Financial Officer
Freida Sawyer Belviso

STAFF FOR THE LUNT-FONTANNE
House Manager .... Tracey Malinowski
Treasurer .... Joe Olcese
Assistant Treasurer .... Gregg Collichio
House Carpenter .... Terry Taylor
House Electrician .... Dennis Boyle
House Propertyman .... Andrew Bentz
House Flyman .... Matt Walters
House Engineers .... Robert MacMahon,
 Joseph Riccio III

The Little Mermaid
Scrapbook

amazing to see everyone lined up and filled with anticipation, waiting to go inside. It was saddening considering we were closing, but the excitement of the audience members who were about to see such a beloved Disney classic was so fulfilling. It would get me very prepared to put on the best performance I could!

My favorite place to hang out after the show would have to be Bar Centrale. You usually have to make a reservation to go there, so whenever my parents come to NYC, or for a special occasion, I love to go there. It is so classy and the food and drinks are really great!

I didn't keep very many snack foods at the theatre, but one thing I loved about this company was its passion for baking. I am definitely a part of that group. I love to try new things, and just the other week I made a few pies and brownies for the crew loading out our show at the Lunt. There were often cupcakes, lemon squares, and cakes to be tasted by many of the amazing bakers in the theater.

I will never forget one encounter I had at the stage door after a show. I was working my way down the line signing autographs and taking pictures. I could hear this little boy being held by his mother yelling "Ariel, Ariel, Ariel." I couldn't really respond yet so when I finally got to him, I said "yes" with a big smile on my face and he shouted "Boo!" It made me laugh so hard! He was very exited to see me, and he was just playing around. I loved that he surprised me.

One term that only members of *The Little Mermaid* would understand is "Merblades." This is the term we voted on to describe the shoes we glided around on. They were shoes that were custom made for us, taken from the idea of Heelys.

I can't think of one specific directorial note that is memorable. However, I will always remember the way Francesca would hype up the company. She is an amazing speaker and inspirational director. In Denver, we had many moments where the cast was brought together and by the end of her talk, she would have the cast pumped and excited to work even harder.

I am not sure if I can specify one cool thing about this show. There were so many amazing things about this show. I met so many amazing people in all aspects of the process. I made friends that will be with me forever, and memories to last a lifetime. It was a dream come true portraying Ariel in *The Little Mermaid*. In the fall of 2006, I was hoping that one day in my life I would get to make it to Broadway. And now fall of 2009, I have made my Broadway debut, and starred in a show, playing a character that means so much to so many people. I honestly can't believe it is over, or that I was lucky enough to have such an amazing life experience. I can't wait for what is to come next, and I only hope that with what I have learned from this experience, I can once again bring a bit of joy to more people's lives.

Taking their final bow (L-R): Jonathan Freeman, Rogelio Douglas Jr., Drew Seeley, Chelsea Morgan Stock, Faith Prince and Norm Lewis.

(L-R): Drew Seeley, Eric LaJuan Summers and Norm Lewis hanging out after the show.

Correspondent: Drew Seeley, "Prince Eric"
Most Vivid Memory of the Final Performance: All the flashbulbs at the end! It was a proper finale, went out with a bang and felt great!
Most Exciting Celebrity Visitor and What They Did/Said: I was kind of star-struck when I stepped out of my dressing room and Billy Crudup was sitting there. Seemed like he enjoyed the show as much as his son and the kids with him. That's what I loved so much about *Mermaid*, anyone could enjoy it.
Favorite Off-Site Hangout: All about Blockheads for some good Mexican and cheap margaritas.
Favorite Snack Foods: I think I said once in an interview that I liked Gummi worms. So I got those at the stage door at least five or six times over the summer. Ended up being my snack by default. Ha!
Memorable Stage Door Fan Encounters: All these little girls dressed up as mermaids and princesses—that was precious to see every night.
Embarrassing Moment: Twisted my ankle right in the beginning of 'Her Voice'... Went down pretty hard and had to be replaced for Act II. Oops.
Coolest Thing About Being in This Show: Reconnecting with people I hadn't seen in a long time, and making new friends. Loved every second, onstage and off. Counting the days until the next one!

A Little Night Music

First Preview: November 24, 2009. Opened: December 13, 2009.
Still running as of May 31, 2010.

CAST
(in order of appearance)

Henrik Egerman	HUNTER RYAN HERDLICKA
Mr. Lindquist	STEPHEN R. BUNTROCK
Mrs. Nordstrom	JAYNE PATERSON
Mrs. Anderssen	MARISSA McGOWAN
Mr. Erlanson	KEVIN DAVID THOMAS
Mrs. Segstrom	BETSY MORGAN
Fredrika Armfeldt	KATHERINE LEIGH DOHERTY (Wed., Fri., Sun.)
	KEATON WHITTAKER (Tues., Thurs., Sat.)
Madame Armfeldt	ANGELA LANSBURY
Frid	BRADLEY DEAN
Anne Egerman	RAMONA MALLORY
Fredrik Egerman	ALEXANDER HANSON
Petra	LEIGH ANN LARKIN
Desirée Armfeldt	CATHERINE ZETA-JONES
Count Carl-Magnus Malcolm	AARON LAZAR
Countess Charlotte Malcolm	ERIN DAVIE

SWINGS
KAREN MURPHY, ERIN STEWART, KEVIN VORTMANN

DANCE CAPTAIN
MARY MacLEOD

Continued on next page

WALTER KERR THEATRE
A JUJAMCYN THEATRE

JORDAN ROTH
President

PAUL LIBIN
Producing Director

JACK VIERTEL
Creative Director

Tom Viertel Steven Baruch Marc Routh Richard Frankel The Menier Chocolate Factory
Roger Berlind David Babani Sonia Friedman Productions Andrew Fell
Daryl Roth/Jane Bergère Harvey Weinstein/Raise the Roof 3
Beverly Bartner/Dancap Productions, Inc. Nica Burns/Max Weitzenhoffer
Eric Falkenstein/Anna Czekaj Jerry Frankel/Ronald Frankel James D. Stern/Douglas L. Meyer

present

CATHERINE ZETA-JONES   ANGELA LANSBURY

ALEXANDER HANSON

in

A Little Night Music

Music and Lyrics by
Stephen Sondheim

Book by
Hugh Wheeler

Suggested by a film by Ingmar Bergman
Originally Produced and Directed on Broadway by Harold Prince

starring
Erin Davie   Leigh Ann Larkin
Hunter Ryan Herdlicka   Ramona Mallory

and
Aaron Lazar

Stephen R. Buntrock   Bradley Dean   Katherine Leigh Doherty   Marissa McGowan
Betsy Morgan   Jayne Paterson   Kevin David Thomas   Keaton Whittaker
Karen Murphy   Erin Stewart   Kevin Vortmann

Set and Costume Design by	Lighting Design by	Sound Design by
David Farley	Hartley T A Kemp	Dan Moses Schreier / Gareth Owen
Wigs and Hair Design by	Make-up Design by	Casting by
Paul Huntley	Angelina Avallone	Tara Rubin Casting
Production Stage Manager	Associate Director	Associate Choreographer
Ira Mont	Seth Sklar-Heyn	Scott Taylor
Music Direction by	Orchestrations by	Music Coordination by
Tom Murray	Jason Carr	John Miller
General Management by	Technical Supervision by	Press Representative	Associate Producers
Frankel Green Theatrical Management	Aurora Productions	Boneau/Bryan-Brown	Broadway Across America / Dan Frishwasser / Jam Theatricals / Richard Winkler

Music Supervision by
Caroline Humphris

Choreography by
Lynne Page

Directed by
Trevor Nunn

This production premiered at the Menier Chocolate Factory November 22, 2008; transferred to the Garrick Theatre on March 28, 2009.

12/13/09

The Company
Photo by Joan Marcus

A Little Night Music

MUSICAL NUMBERS

Overture .... Mr. Lindquist, Mrs. Nordstrom, Mrs. Anderssen, Mr. Erlanson, Mrs. Segstrom

ACT ONE

"Night Waltz" .... Company
"Now" .... Fredrik
"Later" .... Henrik
"Soon" .... Anne, Henrik, Fredrik
"The Glamorous Life" .... Fredrika, Desirée, Madame Armfeldt, Mrs. Nordstrom, Mrs. Segstrom, Mrs. Anderssen, Mr. Lindquist, Mr. Erlanson
"Remember?" .... Mr. Lindquist, Mrs. Nordstrom, Mrs. Segstrom, Mr. Erlanson, Mrs. Anderssen
"You Must Meet My Wife" .... Fredrik, Desirée
"Liaisons" .... Madame Armfeldt
"In Praise of Women" .... Carl-Magnus
"Every Day a Little Death" .... Charlotte, Anne
"A Weekend in the Country" .... Company

ACT TWO

"The Sun Won't Set" .... Mrs. Anderssen, Mrs. Segstrom, Mrs. Nordstrom, Mr. Lindquist, Mr. Erlanson
"It Would Have Been Wonderful" .... Fredrik, Carl-Magnus
"Night Waltz II" .... Mrs. Nordstrom, Mr. Erlanson, Mr. Lindquist, Mrs. Segstrom, Mrs. Anderssen
"Perpetual Anticipation" .... Mrs. Nordstrom, Mrs. Segstrom, Mrs. Anderssen
"Send in the Clowns" .... Desirée
"The Miller's Son" .... Petra
Finale .... Company

Cast Continued

UNDERSTUDIES

For Henrik Egerman:
KEVIN DAVID THOMAS
For Madame Armfeldt:
KAREN MURPHY
For Frid:
STEPHEN R. BUNTROCK,
KEVIN VORTMANN
For Anne Egerman and Petra:
MARISSA McGOWAN, ERIN STEWART
For Fredrik Egerman:
STEPHEN R. BUNTROCK
For Desirée Armfeldt:
JAYNE PATERSON
For Count Carl-Magnus Malcolm:
BRADLEY DEAN
For Countess Charlotte Malcolm:
BETSY MORGAN, ERIN STEWART

Alexander Hanson is appearing with the support of Actors' Equity Association pursuant to an exchange program between American Equity and UK Equity.

TIME
Turn of the last century

PLACE
Sweden

ORCHESTRA

Conductor/Keyboard:
TOM MURRAY
Associate Conductor:
PAUL STAROBA
Concert Master:
MATTHEW LEHMANN
Viola:
DAVID BLINN
Cello:
MAIRI DORMAN-PHANEUF
Woodwind:
DAVID YOUNG
Bassoon:
THOMAS SEFCOVIC
Harp:
SUSAN JOLLES
Bass:
DICK SARPOLA
Music Coordinator:
JOHN MILLER

(L-R): Angela Lansbury and Catherine Zeta-Jones

Photo by Joan Marcus

A Little Night Music

Catherine Zeta-Jones
Desirée Armfeldt

Angela Lansbury
Madame Armfeldt

Alexander Hanson
Fredrik Egerman

Aaron Lazar
Count Carl-Magnus Malcolm

Erin Davie
Countess Charlotte Malcolm

Leigh Ann Larkin
Petra

Hunter Ryan Herdlicka
Henrik Egerman

Ramona Mallory
Anne Egerman

Stephen R. Buntrock
Mr. Lindquist

Bradley Dean
Frid

Katherine Leigh Doherty
Fredrika Armfeldt

Marissa McGowan
Mrs. Anderssen

Betsy Morgan
Mrs. Segstrom

Jayne Paterson
Mrs. Nordstrom

Kevin David Thomas
Mr. Erlanson

Keaton Whittaker
Fredrika Armfeldt

Karen Murphy
Swing

Erin Stewart
Swing

Kevin Vortmann
Swing

Stephen Sondheim
Music & Lyrics

Harold Prince
Original Director & Producer

Trevor Nunn
Director

Lynne Page
Choreographer

Caroline Humphris
Music Supervisor

David Farley
Set & Costume Design

Hartley T A Kemp
Lighting Design

Dan Moses Schreier
Sound Design

Gareth Owen
Sound Design

Paul Huntley
Wig & Hair Design

Angelina Avallone
Make-up Design

Jason Carr
Orchestrations

Tara Rubin Casting
Casting

John Miller
Music Coordinator

Seth Sklar-Heyn
Associate Director

Laura Green, Frankel Green Theatrical Management
General Management

A Little Night Music

 Tom Viertel *Producer*

 Steven Baruch *Producer*

 Marc Routh *Producer*

 Richard Frankel *Producer*

 Roger Berlind *Producer*

 Sonia Friedman Productions Ltd. *Producer*

 Daryl Roth *Producer*

 Jane Bergère *Producer*

 Bob Weinstein, The Weinstein Company *Producer*

 Harvey Weinstein, The Weinstein Company *Producer*

 Harriet Newman Leve, Raise the Roof 3 *Producer*

 Jennifer Manocherian, Raise the Roof 3 *Producer*

 Aubrey Dan, Dancap Productions, Inc. *Producer*

 Nica Burns *Producer*

 Max Weitzenhoffer *Producer*

 Eric Falkenstein *Producer*

 Jerry Frankel *Producer*

 Douglas L. Meyer *Producer*

 Heather Ayers *Swing*

 Alma Cuervo *u/s Madame Armfeldt*

 Matthew Dengler *Swing*

 Katherine McNamara *Fredrika Armfeldt*

Catherine Zeta-Jones prepares to sing "Send in the Clowns."
Photo by Joan Marcus

194 The Playbill Broadway Yearbook 2009-2010

A Little Night Music

CREW
Sitting (L-R): Brian McGarity, Enrique Vega, Samantha Lawrence, Mary MacLeod, Douglas Petitjean, Lolly Totero, Julia Jones

Standing (L-R): Tony Menditto, Ira Mont, Allen Sanders, George Fullum, Vinnie Valvo, Rachel Maier, John Dory, Josh Burns, Matt Maloney, Tanya Guercy-Blue, Karl Lawrence, Jim Kane, Maeve Butler, Tim Bennet, Mike Bennet

BOX OFFICE
(L-R): Gail Yerkovich, Michael Loiacono

FRONT OF HOUSE STAFF
Front Row (L-R): Juliette Cipriatti, T.J. D'Angelo

Back Row (L-R): Adam Ferguson, Dayris Fana, Brandon Houghton, Joy Sandell

2009-2010 AWARD

TONY AWARD
Best Leading Actress in a Musical
(Catherine Zeta-Jones)

A Little Night Music

STAFF FOR *A LITTLE NIGHT MUSIC*

GENERAL MANAGEMENT
FRANKEL GREEN THEATRICAL MANAGEMENT
Richard Frankel   Laura Green
Joe Watson   Leslie Ledbetter

COMPANY MANAGER
Sammy Ledbetter
Associate Company Manager ....Grant A. Rice

GENERAL PRESS REPRESENTATIVE
BONEAU/BRYAN-BROWN
Chris Boneau   Heath Schwartz   Michael Strassheim

CASTING
TARA RUBIN CASTING
Tara Rubin CSA   Eric Woodall CSA   Dale Brown
Merri Sugarman CSA   Laura Schutzel CSA
Paige Blansfield   Kaitlin Shaw

TECHNICAL SUPERVISION
AURORA PRODUCTIONS
Gene O'Donovan   Ben Heller   Rachel Sherbill
Jarid Sumner   Melissa Mazdra   Amy Merlino Coey
Amanda Raymond   Graham Forden   Liza Luxenberg

Production Stage Manager ....Ira Mont
Stage Manager ....Julia P. Jones
Assistant Stage Manager ....Mary MacLeod
UK Stage Management Consultant ....Ciara Fanning
Associate Director ....Seth Sklar-Heyn
Associate Choreographer ....Scott Taylor
Dance Captain ....Mary MacLeod
US Associate Set Designer ....Josh Zangen
UK Assistant Set Designers ....Machiko Hombu, Cara Newman
UK Set Design Intern ....Vicki Stevenson
US Associate Costume Designer ......Tracy Christensen
US Assistant Costume Designer ....Brian J. Bustos
UK Associate Costume Designer ....Poppy Hall
UK Assistant Costume Designer ....Ellan Perry
UK Costume Supervisor ....Binnie Bowerman
Associate Lighting Designer ....Vivien Leone
Assistant Lighting Designer ....Ben Hagen
Associate Sound Designer ....David Bullard
Assistant to the Wig Designer ....Giovanna Calabretta
Company Management Assistant .....Andrew Michaelson
Company Management Intern ....Travis Ferguson

Head Carpenter ....Tony Menditto
Advance Electrician ....Scott Anderson
Production Electrician ....Brian GF McGarity
Head Electrician ....Justin McClintock
Moving Light Programmer ....Michael Hill
Assistant Electrician ....Stephen Allain
Head Sound Engineer ....Francis Elers
Head Props ....Vera Pizzarelli
Props Shopper ....Peter Sarafin
Wardrobe Supervisor ....Douglas Petitjean
Assistant Wardrobe Supervisor ....Deirdre LaBarre
Miss Zeta-Jones's Dresser ....Lolly Totero
Miss Lansbury's Dresser ....Maeve Fiona Butler
Dressers ....Adam Girardet, Tanya Guercy-Blue, John Rinaldi, Mark Trezza
Hair & Wig Supervisor ....Ruth Carsch
Assistant Hair & Wig Supervisor ....Enrique Vega
Production Assistant ....Stuart Shefter
Children's Tutoring ....On Location Education
Children's Guardian ....Rachel Maier
Dialect Coach ....Deborah Hecht

Music Director/Conductor ....Tom Murray
Music Coordinator ....John Miller
Music Consultant ....Kristen Blodgette
US Music Preparation ....Emily Grishman
UK Music Preparation ....Colin Rae
Synthesizer Programmer ....Bruce Samuels
Music Copying ....Katharine Edmonds/ Emily Grishman Music Preparation
Rehearsal Pianist ....Paul Staroba, Mathew Eisenstein

Assistant to Stephen Sondheim ....Steven Clar
Assistant to Mr. Viertel ....Tania Senewiratne
Assistant to Mr. Baruch ....Sonja Soper
Assistant to Mr. Routh ....Katie Adams
Assistant to Mr. Berlind ....Jeffrey Hillock
Advertising ....Serino Coyne, Inc./ Sandy Block, Scott Johnson, Robert Jones
Campaign Management-
  Marketing & Promotions ......aka/Liz Furze, Adam Jay
Online Advertising,
  Marketing & Design ....Art Meets Commerce/ Jim Glaub, Ryan Greer, Laurie Connor, Kevin Keating, Brad Coffman, Mark Seeley, Marissa Coronado
Production Photography ....Joan Marcus
Insurance ....DeWitt Stern Group, Inc./Mary DeSpirt
Legal Counsel ....Patricia Crown, Esq./ Coblence & Associates
Banking ....JP Morgan Chase Bank
Payroll Service ....Castellana Services, Inc.
Accounting ....Fried & Kowgios Partners, CPAs, LLP
Merchandising ....Marquee Merchandise, LLC
Theatre Displays ....King Displays
Rehearsal
  Studio ....Manhattan Theatre Club Creative Center
Group Sales ....Theatre Direct International

FRANKEL GREEN THEATRICAL MANAGEMENT
Finance Director ....Michael Naumann
Assistant to Mr. Frankel ....Heidi Libby
Assistant to Ms. Green ....Joshua A. Saletnik
Assistant Finance Director ....Sue Bartelt
Finance Associate ....Heather Allen
Information Technology Manager ....Roddy Pimentel
Director of Business Affairs ....Michael Sinder
Business Affairs Assistant ....Dario Dalla Lasta
Booking ....On the Road Booking, LLC/ Simma Levine, President
Office Manager ....Emily Wright
Receptionists ....Rebekah Hughston, Allison Raines
Interns ....Danielle Barchetto, Alex Parra, Alex Peyser, Claudia Stuart, Jason Styres, James Teal, Laura Valenti, Shannon Winter

Makeup provided by M•A•C Cosmetics

CREDITS AND ACKNOWLEDGEMENTS
Scenery and scenic effects built, painted, electrified and automated by Show Motion, Inc., Norwalk, Connecticut. Scenic photography by Chris Bean and Jody Kingzett. Automation and show control by Show Motion, Inc., Norwalk, CT, using the AC² computerized motion control system. Lighting equipment provided by PRG Lighting, North Bergen, NJ. Scenic painting by Scenic Art Studios. Sound equipment provided by Sound Associates. Women's costumes constructed by Tricorne. Men's tailoring by Scafati. Select costumes constructed by Seams Unlimited and Crystal Thompson. Custom knitting by Mary Pat Klein. Fabric painting by Jeff Fender. Millinery by Lynne Mackey and Arnold Levine. Custom footwear by LaDuca and Celebrity Dance Shoes. Props by Almeida Theatre, National Theatre, Giraffe Live, Donmar Warehouse, Newman Hire, Cigar Box Studios, Downtime Productions. Special thanks to Bra*Tenders for undergarments and hosiery.

JUJAMCYN THEATERS

JORDAN ROTH
President

PAUL LIBIN	JACK VIERTEL
Producing Director	Creative Director
DANIEL ADAMIAN	**JENNIFER HERSHEY**
General Manager	Director of Operations
MEREDITH VILLATORE	**JERRY ZAKS**
Chief Financial Officer	Resident Director

STAFF FOR THE WALTER KERR THEATRE
Manager ....Susan Elrod
Treasurer ....Harry Jaffie
Carpenter ....George E. Fullum
Propertyman ....Timothy Bennet
Electrician ....Vincent Valvo, Jr.
Engineer ....Vladimir Belenky

Alexander Hanson and Catherine Zeta-Jones

Photo by Joan Marcus

A Little Night Music
Scrapbook

Correspondent: Hunter Ryan Herdlicka, "Henrik Egerman"
Opening Night Gifts: Customized puzzles from Stephen Sondheim.
Most Exciting Celebrity Visitors: Catherine Zeta-Jones (nightly), Tony Bennett, Kirk Douglas and Donald Trump.
Who Got the Gypsy Robe: Stephen R. Buntrock
Which Actor Performed the Most Roles in This Show: Betsy Morgan - 3
Who Has Done the Most Shows in Their Career: Angela Lansbury—too many to count!
Special Backstage Rituals: Yelling at each other to stop warming up. "Steaming, vocal rest, steaming, vocal rest, drinking tea, vocalizing, then vocal rest."—Leigh Ann Larkin
Favorite Moment During Each Performance: "Ah, there you are Mr. Egerman!!!!" (Catherine sighs)
Favorite In-Theatre Gathering Place: Stage left staircase, anywhere with food!
Favorite Off-Site Hangout: Hurley's (right across from the theatre).
Favorite Snack Food: "Anything edible, we've been known to sweat cookie dough onstage"—Betsy Morgan
Mascot: Figaro, Zeta's puppy who is also at the show nightly.
Favorite Therapies: Throat-Coat Tea, Pastilles, Steaming—Leigh Ann Larkin
Memorable Ad-Libs: Angela: "There was a Caucasian count…." "Frid, we cannot be caught squatting on the ground like Bulgarians." "He deeded me ANOTHER Duchy." CZJ: "I see 'em, they're a-comin'!"
Web Buzz on Our Show: "Reading anything on the web is bad news bears"—Leigh Ann Larkin
Memorable Press Encounter: The first "Meet the Press" day at Etcetera Etcetera.
Memorable Stage Door Fan Encounter: From a fan to Hunter: "If this show doesn't win the Tony for Best Revival, I'm going to hang myself from the Walter Kerr." Yikes.
Latest Audience Arrival: A hungover audience member arrived late, vomited everywhere, and we had to hold the curtain for 15 minutes.
Fastest Costume Change: Betsy Morgan and Marissa McGowan "from blacks to brights in 15 seconds."
Busiest Day at the Box Office: The day after our "mixed" reviews. Someone was overheard at the box office saying, "Hi, is there where we get tickets for *The Catherine Zeta-Jones Show*?"
Heaviest/Hottest Costume: Nothing is hotter than Catherine in pasties, come see for yourself.
Who Wore the Least: Catherine. See above.
Catchphrases Only the Company Would Recognize: "Malla's magical jacket." "Bone chilling." "Botched." "Farce."
Company In-Jokes: Crickets.

1. Cast members and creative team at a photo opportunity at Etcetera Etetera.
2. Curtain call on opening night.
3. Catherine Zeta-Jones and composer Stephen Sondheim at the opening night party at Tavern on the Green.

Orchestra Member Who Played the Most Instruments: David Young—bass clarinet, clarinet, alto sax, flute.
Orchestra Member Who Played the Most Consecutive Performances Without A Sub: David Young.
Best In-House Parody Lyrics: (*Tempo di "Send in the Clowns"*) "Was that a fart? My fault I fear."
Memorable Directorial Notes: "It will all make sense once you see the lighting." "I wanted you to come on with a purpose, not as if you were sprinting the Olympic 100 Meter Dash." "Therefore…."
Company Legend: Angela Lansbury.
Nicknames: "Bunty"—Stephen Buntrock
Embarrassing Moments: "Hitting my head on the tree and forgetting the words to "The Miller's Son" after spilling grapes all over the stage. Oh, and my boob popped out of my corset."—Leigh Ann Larkin

Superstition That Turned Out To Be False: Whistling onstage isn't bad luck. Alex, Catherine and Aaron whistle every night, and we are doing just fine.
Coolest Thing About Being in This Show: Having such a wonderful job. Truly a blessing.
Fan Club Info: NightMusicOnBroadway.com, Facebook and Twitter fan pages.

Looped

First Preview: February 19, 2010. Opened: March 14, 2010.
Closed April 11, 2010 after 27 Previews and 33 Performances.

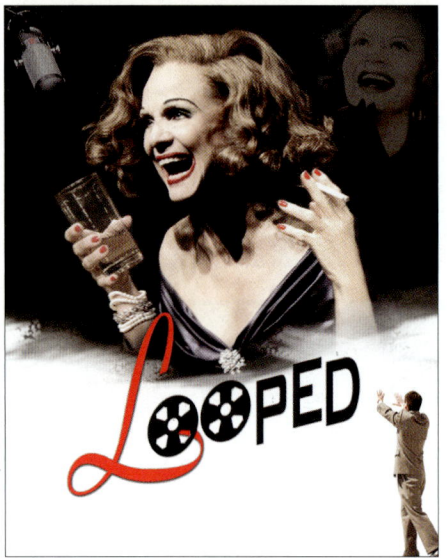

CAST
(in order of appearance)

Steve	MICHAEL MULHEREN
Danny	BRIAN HUTCHISON
Tallulah Bankhead	VALERIE HARPER

UNDERSTUDIES

For Valerie Harper:
GLYNIS BELL
For Brian Hutchison/Michael Mulheren:
TIM ALTMEYER

TIME:
Summer 1965

PLACE:
A Recording Studio. Los Angeles, California

LYCEUM THEATRE
149 West 45th Street
A Shubert Organization Theatre
Philip J. Smith, *Chairman*   Robert E. Wankel, *President*

TONY CACCIOTTI   CHASE MISHKIN   BARD THEATRICALS   LAUREN CLASS SCHNEIDER   LAWRENCE S. TOPPALL   LEONARD SOLOWAY

present

VALERIE HARPER
in

Looped
A New Comedy

by

MATTHEW LOMBARDO

with

BRIAN HUTCHISON
and
MICHAEL MULHEREN

Sets by	*Costumes by*	*Lighting by*	*Sound by*	
ADRIAN W. JONES	WILLIAM IVEY LONG	KEN BILLINGTON	MICHAEL HOOKER & PETER FITZGERALD	

Wig Designer	*Production Supervisor*	*Production Stage Manager*	*Casting*
CHARLES LAPOINTE	ARTHUR SICCARDI & PATRICK SULLIVAN	BESS MARIE GLORIOSO	JAY BINDER CASTING

Press Representative	*Associate Producers*	*Marketing*	*General Management*
BONEAU/ BRYAN BROWN	BARBARA FREITAG DAVID MIRVISH	HHC MARKETING	LEONARD SOLOWAY

Directed by

ROB RUGGIERO

WORLD PREMIERE PRODUCED AT PASADENA PLAYHOUSE
SHELDON EPPS, *Artistic Director*   BRIAN COLBURN, *Managing Director*
TOM WARE, *Producing Director*

THE PRODUCERS WISH TO THANK THEATRE DEVELOPMENT FUND
FOR ITS SUPPORT OF THE PRODUCTION.

3/14/10

(L-R): Brian Hutchison and Valerie Harper.

Looped

Valerie Harper
Tallulah Bankhead

Brian Hutchison
Danny

Michael Mulheren
Steve

Glynis Bell
u/s Tallulah Bankhead

Tim Altmeyer
u/s Danny/Steve

Matthew Lombardo
Playwright

Rob Ruggiero
Director

William Ivey Long
Costume Designer

Ken Billington
Lighting Design

Michael Hooker
Sound Design

Jay Binder CSA
Casting

Arthur Siccardi Theatrical Services, Inc.
Production Supervisor

Tony Cacciotti
Producer

Chase Mishkin
Producer

Leonard Soloway
Producer/General Manager

Barbara Freitag
Associate Producer

CAST AND CREW

Photo by Samantha Souza

The Playbill Broadway Yearbook 2009-2010

Looped
SCRAPBOOK

Correspondent: Valerie Harper, "Tallulah Bankhead"

Most Vivid Memory of the Final Performance: When I made my entrance I was almost completely thrown by the power, volume and length of the entrance applause. All this for just Valerie in a Tallulah get-up?! It went on so long and was so full of loving acknowledgement; I wanted to burst into tears. Poor Brian was staring up at me with his back to the audience, waiting to go ahead. I just had to wait it out, collect myself and be the best Tallulah I could muster this last time.

Memorable Fan Letter: In the play, a line that Tallulah is supposed to be re-recording for the film *Die, Die My Darling* is as follows: "And so Patricia, as I was telling you, that deluded rector has, in literal effect, closed the church to me." I know, a humdinger! A real-life priest who was a major theatre fan sent me flowers. The accompanying note stated, "Congratulations. This is one rector who will never close the church to you. (Signed) Father Jim Paisley."

Opening Night Gifts: We were in rehearsals shortly after the terrible earthquake in Haiti and decided to forego opening night gifts and send donations to the relief effort instead. Michael Mulheren, who played Steve the sound man, collected the checks and I sent the money to the American Red Cross. Generously, the producers gave us all beautifully framed window cards and the show poster image of Tallulah. So we have our memento of the show's opening night after all.

Most Exciting Celebrity Visitors: Rosie O'Donnell drove in from Nyack and we went to Joe Allen's. She sent a mountain of roses, lilies and tulips. Lily Tomlin brought her brother who had worked with Tallulah. He's got Lily's face—so adorable! Stefanie Powers, who had been in the film *Die, Die, My Darling* with Tallulah also came. She's was the "Patricia" I'm addressing in the line I keep looping throughout the play. Rep. Barney Frank, one of my favorite Congressmen, came backstage and was so damn funny and so damn smart.

Special Backstage Ritual: Although I didn't come on until well into Scene 1, I would come down to the stage at "places" and sit quietly in my full Tallulah regalia (fur, scarf, sunglasses) just offstage listening to the scene. To make sure my voice was placed at a proper Tallulah depth I would practice saying "Hello, dahling,"

STAFF FOR LOOPED

GENERAL MANAGEMENT
Leonard Soloway

COMPANY MANAGER
Judith Drasner

GENERAL PRESS REPRESENTATIVE
BONEAU/BRYAN-BROWN
Chris Boneau   Jackie Green   Michael Strassheim

CASTING
JAY BINDER CASTING
Jay Binder CSA
Jack Bowdan CSA, Mark Brandon, Sara Schatz CSA, Nikole Vallins
Assistants: Karen Young, Patrick Bell

PRODUCTION SUPERVISOR
Arthur Siccardi/Patrick Sullivan

Production Stage Manager ....Bess Marie Glorioso
Stage Manager ....Ana M. Garcia
Production Assistant ....Melanie T. Morgan
Assistant Director ....Nick Eilerman
Associate Costume Designer ....Catherine A. Parrott
Director, William Ivey Long Studios ....Donald Sanders
Assistant to the Scenic Designer ....Ann Bartek
Associate Lighting Designer ....Anthony Pearson
Assistant to the Sound Designer ....Megan Henninger

Production Properties ....Michael Pilipski
Head Carpenter ....Adam Braunstein
Head Properties ....Leah Nelson
Production Electrician ....Neil McShane
Head Electrician ....Jonathan Cohen
Production Sound ....Wally Flores
Wardrobe Supervisor ....Jesse Galvan
Dresser ....Erin Brooke Roth
Makeup Consultant ....Cookie Jordan

Legal Counsel ....Cowan, DeBaets, Abrahams & Sheppard LLP, Attorneys at Law/ Fred Bimbler
Accountants ....Rosenberg, Neuwirth & Kuchner CPAs/ Mark A. D'Ambrosi, Patricia Pedersen
Advertising ....Eliran Murphy Group/ Barbara Eliran, Frank Verlizzo, Elizabeth Findlay, Caraline Sogliuzzo
Artwork ....Fraver
Cover Photography ....Scott Suchman
Production Photographer ....Carol Rosegg
Marketing ....HHC Marketing/ Hugh Hysell, Michael Redman, Todd Briscoe
Website and Interactive Media ....Bay Bridge Productions/ Laura Wagner, Jean Strong
Assistant to Mr. Cacciotti ....Emily McGill
Press Office ....Adrian Bryan-Brown, Jim Byk, Joe Perrotta, Matt Polk, Susanne Tighe, Aaron Meier, Jessica Johnson, Heath Schwartz, Kelly Guiod, Amy Kass, Emily Meagher, Christine Olver, Brandi Cornwell, Linnae Hodzic, Kevin Jones
Banking ....JPMorgan Chase/Salvatore Romano
Insurance ....C&S International Insurance Brokers/ Debra Kozee
Theatre Displays ....King Displays
Payroll ....CSI/Lance Castellana
Rehearsal Studio ....Roy Arias Studios
Group Sales ....Group Sales Box Office

CREDITS
Scenery by Hudson Scenic Studio, Inc. Lighting equipment from PRG Lighting. Sound equipment from Sound Associates. Miss Harper's costume by Tricorne. Vintage wear by Gary Franke at Steppin' Out. Vintage jewelry by Ilene Chazanof. Props by the Spoon Group. Makeup provided by M•A•C Cosmetics.

MUSIC CREDITS
"It's Only a Paper Moon" by Billy Rose, E.Y. "Yip" Harburg and Harold Arlen ©1933 (copyright renewed), published by Glocca Morra Music Inc., SA Music and Chappell & Co. (ASCAP), administered by Next Decade Entertainment Inc. All rights reserved. Used by permission.

SPECIAL THANKS
Chad Allen, Elizabeth Ashley, Bob Cuillo, Amber Dickerson, Edgar Dobie, Christopher Durham, Sheldon Epps, Tony Ferchak, Chuck Fox, Michael Gilliam, Jay Goede, Eric Goldman, Jim Goshen, Neal Huff, Carey Lawless, Christopher "Daddy" Nutile, Michael Orensten, Mark Sendroff, Derek Smith, Molly Smith, Snooty, John Tillinger, Tom Ware, Alex Yaeger.

To learn more about the production, please visit
www.LoopedonBroadway.com

THE SHUBERT ORGANIZATION, INC.
Board of Directors

Philip J. Smith
Chairman

Robert E. Wankel
President

Wyche Fowler, Jr.

John W. Kluge

Lee J. Seidler

Michael I. Sovern

Stuart Subotnick

Elliot Greene
Chief Financial Officer

David Andrews
Senior Vice President - Shubert Ticketing

Juan Calvo
Vice President and Controller

John Darby
Vice President – Facilities

Peter Entin
Vice President – Theatre Operations

Charles Flateman
Vice President – Marketing

Anthony LaMattina
Vice President – Audit & Production Finance

Brian Mahoney
Vice President – Ticket Sales

D.S. Moynihan
Vice President – Creative Projects

House Manager ....Joann Swanson

Looped
Scrapbook

but only when Michael or Brian would get a laugh, so there'd be no chance of the audience hearing my warm-up over the sound system.

Favorite Moment: I loved watching Brian Hutchison, as Danny the film editor, squirm with discomfort and valiantly try to maintain his composure in moments when Tallulah is causing him to lose it. The laughs would build and build as the audience could see Danny struggle to keep his equilibrium and try to figure out, "Did this woman really just say that?" He made funny moments shockingly hilarious by his very genuine human reactions. I so enjoyed playing those scenes with Brian.

Favorite In-Theatre Gathering Place: Our theatre had a greenroom way upstairs, but we generally gathered at the offstage-right desk of our glorious, aptly-named stage manager, Bess Glorioso. She always kept an overflowing box of candies for the whole company on that desk and she was the best Den Mother ever.

Favorite Off-Site Hangouts: We were painfully traditional and predictable. We hung out at Orso's and Joe Allen, had a company dinner at Angus McIndoe, and our opening night party at the legendary Sardi's.

Favorite Snack Foods: My dresser Erin Roth is an extraordinary baker. She brought fantastic creations every Wednesday matinee: Midwestern "Gooey Cake," brownies, sometimes miniature loaves. She said, "People have to have something special to get through Wednesday matinee day.

Mascot: Bess Glorioso's adorable little black pup named Louie.

Favorite Therapy: Dr. Scott Kessler's vapors—Drops put in hot water: just terrific for keeping your vocal cords clear and functioning.

Naps—We must remember, along with food and exercise, the third pillar of health is sleep. I always rested between shows on matinee days. On a chaise that formerly belonged to Christopher Plummer, I might add. He'd kindly left it at the Lyceum for the next occupant.

Memorable Ad Lib: I was hit with a coughing fit, severe and seemingly endless, and it was my line!! Thank God, and our director Rob Ruggiero, there was a pitcher of water and glasses on the set. When I finally got my voice back I said, "Goddam L.A. smog!!" Since Tallulah was a chain smoker and hated California the audience thought it was all part of the show.

Memorable Press Encounter: *The Wall Street Journal* was doing a feature on anger management in the workplace and they sent a photographer to take pictures of me making various facial expressions conveying anger. It was one of the oddest requests for a photo shoot, particularly from such a dry, austere publication. So for a half an hour I sat there in a red sweater set (which I had selected as the color of rage) grimacing in anger, resentment, fury, doing a "slow burn," then screaming,

(L-R): Cast members Michael Mulheren, *Yearbook* correspondent Valerie Harper and Brian Hutchison visit Sardi's restaurant on opening night.

gritting my teeth, yelling, and pulling my hair in a rage. What fun! They put it on the front page!

Memorable Stage Door Fan Encounters: The most fun was meeting people I had not seen in decades. One was a boy I had not seen since 9th grade, who would ride the bus with me. Another was an acting classmate I hadn't seen since the 1960s. But most were people I didn't know at all, but love was in their eyes because they remembered my TV show, "Rhoda." They greeted me like a long-lost member of their family.

Company In-Jokes: The use of "Dahling." In honor of Tallulah everyone called each other "Dahling" backstage.

Another catchphrase was "Who was 'HE'?! A GUY?!!?!" During the second act of *Looped*, Tallulah confronts Danny about being gay, asking him "Who was he?" And Danny replies, "Just a guy." In our very first production at Pasadena Playhouse an elderly gentleman in the audience completely startled by this possibility yelled out "Who was 'HE'?!" We got by this interruption and Danny replied to Tallulah, "Just a guy." The same man incredulously shouted, "A 'GUY'?!!?" It was a company joke ever since.

Sweethearts Within the Company: My husband Tony, lead producer of *Looped*, and me, the old marrieds.

Memorable Directorial Note: Director Rob Ruggiero was constantly vigilant, as I begged him to be, about the "Tallulah voice." "Lower, Val, lower, lower in pitch." At a moment of fatigue and frustration I said, "I'm not a man. How low can I go?" Rob shrugged, "As low as Tallulah." A wise man. "Don't play it—live it."

Nicknames: A close family friend dubbed me "Vallulah."
I called Rob Ruggiero "Peachy" after the peachfuzz that his shaved head occasionally sprouted.

Embarrassing Moment: Unaware that my dressing room door was wide open, I was sitting, putting on my makeup naked to waist. Wally the sound man, bringing me my microphone, walked in and made an immediate about-face and walked right out. Poor guy—it was completely my fault.

Coolest Things About Being in This Show: Getting to play this outrageous, hilarious, phenomenal plum of a character—and she was a real, actual person!!! A dream of a dame and a nightmare, too. As she called herself, "Deliciously impossible." Although she's thought of as a movie star, she spent most of her life in the theatre. How fitting in 2010 she was here, back where she belonged, and in this great theatre, the Lyceum, which opened in 1902, the same year Tallulah was born.

The laughs in this show are monumental—as big as any I've encountered in my career. And I've done a lot of comedy. In *Looped*, in order that we be heard, we repeatedly had to hold and hold to allow the audience time to finish laughing. It's wonderful indeed to have those lovely people out front enjoying themselves so much!

The 2010 Tony Nomination: Although *Looped* lasted for only two months, this prestigious nomination [Best Actress in a Play] acknowledges that indeed we were here—not just a ship that passed in the night, but from now on, forever, we're a part of Broadway history. That thrills me. I love that.

Mamma Mia!

First Preview: October 5, 2001. Opened: October 18, 2001.
Still running as of May 31, 2010.

CAST
(in order of speaking)

Sophie Sheridan	ALYSE ALAN LOUIS
Ali	AMINA ROBINSON
Lisa	HALLE MORSE
Tanya	JUDY McLANE
Rosie	ALLISON BRINER
Donna Sheridan	BETH LEAVEL
Sky	ERIC WILLIAM MORRIS
Pepper	MICHAEL MINDLIN
Eddie	RAYMOND J. LEE
Harry Bright	DAVID ANDREW MacDONALD
Bill Austin	PATRICK BOLL
Sam Carmichael	JOHN DOSSETT
Father Alexandrios	BRYAN SCOTT JOHNSON

THE ENSEMBLE

BRENT BLACK, TIMOTHY BOOTH,
ALLYSON CARR, FELICITY CLAIRE,
MARK DANCEWICZ, ANNIE EDGERTON,
NATALIE GALLO, HEIDI GODT,
COREY GREENAN,
BRYAN SCOTT JOHNSON, ROBIN LEVINE,
IAN PAGET, GERARD SALVADOR,
SHARONE SAYEGH, TRACI VICTORIA

Continued on next page

WINTER GARDEN
1634 Broadway
A Shubert Organization Theatre

Philip J. Smith, *Chairman* Robert E. Wankel, *President*

JUDY CRAYMER, RICHARD EAST AND BJÖRN ULVAEUS
FOR LITTLESTAR IN ASSOCIATION WITH UNIVERSAL

PRESENT

MAMMA MIA!

MUSIC AND LYRICS BY
BENNY ANDERSSON
BJÖRN ULVAEUS
AND SOME SONGS WITH STIG ANDERSON

BOOK BY CATHERINE JOHNSON

PRODUCTION DESIGNED BY
MARK THOMPSON

LIGHTING DESIGNED BY
HOWARD HARRISON

SOUND DESIGNED BY
ANDREW BRUCE &
BOBBY AITKEN

MUSICAL SUPERVISOR, ADDITIONAL MATERIAL
& ARRANGEMENTS
MARTIN KOCH

CHOREOGRAPHY
ANTHONY VAN LAAST

DIRECTED BY
PHYLLIDA LLOYD

10/1/09

(L-R): Judy McLane, Beth Leavel and Allison Briner

Mamma Mia!

MUSICAL NUMBERS

(in alphabetical order)

CHIQUITITA
DANCING QUEEN
DOES YOUR MOTHER KNOW
GIMME! GIMME! GIMME!
HONEY, HONEY
I DO, I DO, I DO, I DO, I DO
I HAVE A DREAM
KNOWING ME, KNOWING YOU
LAY ALL YOUR LOVE ON ME
MAMMA MIA
MONEY, MONEY, MONEY
ONE OF US
OUR LAST SUMMER
SLIPPING THROUGH MY FINGERS
S.O.S.
SUPER TROUPER
TAKE A CHANCE ON ME
THANK YOU FOR THE MUSIC
THE NAME OF THE GAME
THE WINNER TAKES IT ALL
UNDER ATTACK
VOULEZ-VOUS

Cast Continued

UNDERSTUDIES
For Sophie Sheridan:
FELICITY CLAIRE, NATALIE GALLO
For Ali:
NATALIE GALLO, TRACI VICTORIA
For Lisa:
FELICITY CLAIRE, SHARONE SAYEGH
For Tanya:
ANNIE EDGERTON, HEIDI GODT,
CORINNE MELANÇON
For Rosie:
ANNIE EDGERTON, HEIDI GODT
For Donna Sheridan:
ANNIE EDGERTON, HEIDI GODT,
CORINNE MELANÇON
For Sky:
MATTHEW FARVER, COREY GREENAN,
RYAN SANDER
For Pepper:
IAN PAGET, GERARD SALVADOR
For Eddie:
MARK DANCEWICZ, MATTHEW FARVER,
RYAN SANDER
For Harry Bright:
TIMOTHY BOOTH,
BRYAN SCOTT JOHNSON
For Bill Austin:
BRENT BLACK, TIMOTHY BOOTH,
BRYAN SCOTT JOHNSON
For Sam Carmichael:
BRENT BLACK, TIMOTHY BOOTH
For Father Alexandrios:
BRENT BLACK, TIMOTHY BOOTH,
MATTHEW FARVER

SWINGS
MATTHEW FARVER,
RACHEL FRANKENTHAL, RYAN SANDER,
COLLETTE SIMMONS

DANCE CAPTAIN
JANET ROTHERMEL

On a Greek Island, a wedding is about to take place...

PROLOGUE
Three months before the wedding

ACT ONE
The day before the wedding

ACT TWO
The day of the wedding

THE BAND
Music Director/Conductor/Keyboard 1:
WENDY BOBBITT CAVETT
Associate Music Director/Keyboard 3:
ROB PREUSS
Keyboard 2:
STEVE MARZULLO
Keyboard 4:
MYLES CHASE
Guitar 1:
DOUG QUINN
Guitar 2:
JEFF CAMPBELL
Bass:
PAUL ADAMY
Drums:
RAY MARCHICA
Percussion:
DAVID NYBERG
Music Coordinator:
MICHAEL KELLER
Synthesizer Programmer:
NICHOLAS GILPIN

(L-R): Halle Morse, Alyse Alan Louis and Amina Robinson

(L-R): John Dossett, David Andrew MacDonald and Patrick Boll

Photos by Joan Marcus

Mamma Mia!

 Beth Leavel *Donna Sheridan*
 Alyse Alan Louis *Sophie Sheridan*
 Allison Briner *Rosie*
 Judy McLane *Tanya*
 John Dossett *Sam Carmichael*
 Patrick Boll *Bill Austin*
 David Andrew MacDonald *Harry Bright*

 Eric William Morris *Sky*
 Amina Robinson *Ali*
 Halle Morse *Lisa*
 Michael Mindlin *Pepper*
 Raymond J. Lee *Eddie*
 Brent Black *Ensemble*
 Timothy Booth *Ensemble*

 Allyson Carr *Ensemble*
 Felicity Claire *Ensemble*
 Mark Dancewicz *Ensemble*
 Annie Edgerton *Ensemble*
 Matthew Farver *Swing*
 Rachel Frankenthal *Swing*
 Natalie Gallo *Ensemble*

 Heidi Godt *Ensemble*
 Corey Greenan *Ensemble*
 Bryan Scott Johnson *Father Alexandrios, Ensemble*
 Robin Levine *Ensemble*
 Ian Paget *Ensemble*
 Janet Rothermel *Dance Captain*
 Gerard Salvador *Ensemble*

 Ryan Sander *Assistant Dance Captain, Swing*
 Sharone Sayegh *Ensemble*
 Collette Simmons *Swing*
 Traci Victoria *Ensemble*
 Björn Ulvaeus *Music & Lyrics*
 Benny Andersson *Music & Lyrics*
 Catherine Johnson *Book*

Mamma Mia!

Phyllida Lloyd
Director

Anthony Van Laast, MBE
Choreographer

Mark Thompson
Production Designer

Howard Harrison
Lighting Designer

Andrew Bruce
Sound Designer

Bobby Aitken
Sound Designer

Martin Koch
Musical Supervisor; Additional Material; Arrangements

David Holcenberg
Associate Music Supervisor

Nichola Treherne
Associate Choreographer

Martha Banta
Resident Director

Tara Rubin
Tara Rubin Casting
Casting

David Grindrod
Casting Consultant

Arthur Siccardi
Theatrical Services, Inc.
Production Manager

Judy Craymer
Producer

Richard East
Producer

Nina Lannan
Nina Lannan Associates
General Management

Pearce Bunting
Bill Austin

Brandi Burkhardt
Sophie

Carolee Carmello
Donna Sheridan

Lanene Charters
Swing

Meghann Dreyfuss
Ensemble

Samantha Eggers
Lisa

Gina Ferrall
Rosie

Lori Haley Fox
Rosie, Ensemble

Ben Gettinger
Pepper

Jon-Erik Goldberg
Swing

Tony Gonzalez
Dance Captain, Swing

Sean Allan Krill
Sam Carmichael

Ben Livingston
Harry Bright

Corinne Melançon
Donna Sheridan, Ensemble

Chris Peluso
Sky

Courtney Reed
Ensemble

Elizabeth Share
Ensemble

Leah Zepel
Lisa, Ensemble

Mamma Mia!

Jen Burleigh-Bentz
Ensemble

Stacia Fernandez
Ensemble

Gina Ferrall
Rosie

Lori Haley Fox
Ensemble

Eric Giancola
Ensemble

Jon-Erik Goldberg
Swing

Adam Michael Hart
Ensemble

Monica Kapoor
Ensemble

Ian Knauer
Ensemble

Erica Mansfield
Swing

Monette McKay
Ensemble

Corinne Melançon
Ensemble

CAST and MANAGEMENT
Front Row (L-R): Heidi Godt, Collette Simmons, Adam M. Hart

Middle Row (L-R): J. Anthony Magner (company manager), Andrew Fenton (production stage manager), Corinne Melançon, Rachel Frankenthal, Ian Paget, Halle Morse, Alyse Alan Louis, Mark Dancewicz, Felicity Claire, John Dossett

Back Row (L-R): Shaun Colledge, Ryan Sander, Natalie Gallo, Gerard Salvador, Traci Victoria, Sharone Sayegh, Monette McKay, Matthew Farver, Allyson Carr, Monica Kapoor, Bryan Scott Johnson, Stacia Fernandez, Sherry Cohen (stage manager), Timothy Booth

Mamma Mia!

CREW
Front Row (L-R): Craig Cassidy, Christine Richmond
Back Row (L-R): Frank Lofgren, Aarne Lofgren, Mai-Linh Lofgren, Art Soyk, Vickey Walker, Chasity Neutze, Irene L. Bunis, Don Lawrence, Carey Bertini, Meredith Kievit, Stephen Burns

FRONT OF HOUSE STAFF
Back Row (L-R): Dennis Marion, Michael Cleary, Craig Dawson, John Mitchell, Ken Costigan, Michael Bosch
Front Row: Unidentified

In loving memory of Daniel McDonald, a cast member of the *Mamma Mia!* Broadway Company 2004-2005.

LITTLESTAR SERVICES LIMITED

Directors .... Judy Craymer
Richard East
Benny Andersson
Björn Ulvaeus
International Executive Producer .... Andrew Treagus
Business & Finance Director .... Ashley Grisdale
Administrator .... Peter Austin
PA to Judy Craymer .... Katie Wolfryd
Marketing & Communications Manager .... Claire Teare
Marketing & Communications
Coordinator .... Liz McGinity
Head of Accounts .... Jo Reedman
Accountant .... Sheila Egbujie
Accounts Assistant .... Sarah Whittaker
Administrative Assistant .... Matthew Willis
Receptionist .... Kimberley Wallwork
Legal Services .... Barry Shaw
Howard Jones at Sheridans
Production Insurance
Services .... Walton & Parkinson Ltd.
Business Manager for Benny Andersson and
Björn Ulvaeus & Scandinavian Press ...... Görel Hanser

NINA LANNAN ASSOCIATES

GENERAL MANAGERS .... DEVIN M. KEUDELL,
AMY JACOBS
COMPANY MANAGER .... J. ANTHONY MAGNER
Assistant Company Manager .... Liza Garcia

Mamma Mia!

ANDREW TREAGUS ASSOCIATES LIMITED

GENERAL MANAGER	JULIAN STONEMAN
Production Coordinator	Stella Warshaw
Production & Contracts Administrator	Philip Effemey
PA to Andrew Treagus	Jacki Harding
Production Assistant & PA to Julian Stoneman	Ffion Jones
Administrative Assistant	James Mullan
International Travel Manager	Lindsay Jones

PRODUCTION TEAM

ASSOCIATE CHOREOGRAPHER	NICHOLA TREHERNE
DANCE SUPERVISOR	JANET ROTHERMEL
RESIDENT DIRECTOR	MARTHA BANTA
ASSOCIATE MUSIC SUPERVISOR	DAVID HOLCENBERG
ASSOCIATE SCENIC DESIGNER (US)	NANCY THUN
ASSOCIATE SCENIC DESIGNER (UK)	JONATHAN ALLEN
ASSOCIATE COSTUME DESIGNERS	LUCY GAIGER / SCOTT TRAUGOTT
ASSOCIATE HAIR DESIGNER	JOSH MARQUETTE
ASSOCIATE LIGHTING DESIGNERS	DAVID HOLMES / ED MCCARTHY / ANDREW VOLLER
ASSOCIATE SOUND DESIGNERS	BRIAN BEASLEY / DAVID PATRIDGE
MUSICAL TRANSCRIPTION	ANDERS NEGLIN
CASTING CONSULTANT	DAVID GRINDROD

CASTING
TARA RUBIN CASTING
Tara Rubin CSA, Eric Woodall CSA,
Laura Schutzel CSA, Merri Sugarman CSA,
Dale Brown, Paige Blansfield, Kaitlin Shaw

PRESS REPRESENTATIVE
BONEAU/BRYAN-BROWN
Adrian Bryan-Brown   Joe Perrotta
Kelly Guiod

MARKETING U.S.
TMG – THE MARKETING GROUP
TANYA GRUBICH   LAURA MATALON
Victoria Cairl

MUSIC PUBLISHED BY EMI GROVE PARK MUSIC, INC. AND EMI WATERFORD MUSIC, INC.

STAFF FOR MAMMA MIA!

PRODUCTION STAGE MANAGER	ANDREW FENTON
Stage Managers	Sherry Cohen, Dean R. Greer
Assistant Dance Captain	Ryan Sander
PRODUCTION MANAGER	ARTHUR SICCARDI
Head Carpenter	Chris Nass
Assistant Carpenters	Stephen Burns, Clark Middleton
Production Electrician	Rick Baxter
Head Electrician	Don Lawrence
Assistant Electrician	Andy Sather
Vari*Lite Programmer	Andrew Voller
Production Sound	David Patridge
Head Sound	Craig Cassidy
Assistant Sound	Pitsch Karrer
Production Properties	Simon E.R. Evans
Head Properties	Gregory Martin
Wardrobe Supervisor	Irene L. Bunis
Assistant Wardrobe	Ron Glow
Dressers	Carey Bertini, Jim Collum, Lauren Kievit, Robert Krauss, Trevor McGinness, Chasity Neutze, Christine Richmond, I Wang
Hair Supervisor	Sandy Schlender
Assistant Hair Supervisor	Vickey Walker
Assistant Lighting Designer	Jeffrey Lowney
Assistant Costume Designer	Angela Kahler
House Crew	Richard Carney, Reginald Carter, Holly Hanson, Mai-Linh Lofgren, Meredith Kievit, Aarne Lofgren, Francis Lofgren, John Maloney, Michael Maloney, Glenn Russo, Dennis Wiener
Rehearsal Pianist	Sue Anschutz
Box Office	Mary Cleary, Lee Cobb, Steve Cobb, James Drury, Sue Giebler, Bob McCaffrey, Ron Schroeder
Casting Directors	Tara Rubin CSA, Eric Woodall
Casting Associates	Laura Schutzel, Merri Sugarman
Casting Assistants	Rebecca Carfagna, Jeff Siebert, Paige Blansfield
Canadian Casting	Stephanie Gorin Casting, C.D.C.
Associate to Casting Consultant	Stephen Crockett
London Casting Assistant	James Orange
Legal Counsel (U.S.)	Lazarus & Harris LLP Scott Lazarus, Esq. Robert Harris, Esq.
Immigration Counsel	Mark D. Koestler/ Kramer Levin Naftalis & Frankel LLP
Accounting	Rosenberg, Neuwirth & Kuchner, Chris Cacace, In Woo
Advertising	Serino Coyne, Inc./ Nancy Coyne, Greg Corradetti, Andrea Prince, Ruth Rosenberg
Press Office Staff	Chris Boneau, Jim Byk, Brandi Cornwell, Jackie Green, Linnae Hodzic, Jessica Johnson, Amy Kass, Kevin Jones, Emily Meagher, Aaron Meier, Christine Olver, Matthew Polk, Heath Schwartz, Rachel Stange, Michael Strassheim, Susanne Tighe
Production Photographer	Joan Marcus
Merchandising	Max Merchandise, LLC/ Randi Grossman, Victor Romero
Theater Displays	King Display
Insurance	Dewitt, Stern/ Walton & Parkinson Ltd.
Orthopedic Consultant	Dr. Phillip Bauman
Banking	J.P. Morgan Trust
Travel Agent	Tzell Travel
Original Logo Design	© Littlestar Services Limited

CREDITS AND ACKNOWLEDGMENTS

Scenery constructed and painted by Hudson Scenic Studio, Inc. and Hamilton Scenic Specialty. Computer motion control and automation by Feller Precision, Inc. SHOWTRAK computer motion control for scenery and rigging. Sound equipment supplied by Masque Sound. Lighting equipment supplied by Fourth Phase and Vari*Lite, Inc. Soft goods by I. Weiss and Sons. Costumes by Barbara Matera, Ltd., Tricorne New York City and Carelli Costumes, Inc. Additional costume work by Allan Alberts Productions. Millinery by Lynne Mackey. Wet suits by Aquatic Fabricators of South Florida. Custom men's shirts by Cego. Custom knitting by C.C. Wei. Custom fabric printing and dyeing by Dye-namix and Gene Mignola. Shoes by Native Leather, Rilleau Leather and T. O. Dey. Gloves by Cornelia James - London. Hair color by Redken. Properties by Paragon Theme and Prop Fabrication. Cough drops provided by Ricola U.S.A. Physical therapy provided by Sean Gallagher. Drums provided by Pearl. Cymbals provided by Zildjian. Drumsticks provided by Vic Firth. Drum heads provided by Remo.

Mamma Mia! was originally produced in London by LITTLESTAR SERVICES LIMITED on April 6, 1999.

Experience *Mamma Mia!* in these cities:
London/Prince of Wales Theatre/mamma-mia.com
Broadway/Winter Garden Theatre/telecharge.com
North American Tour/ticketmaster.com
International Tour/mamma-mia.com
For more information visit:
www.mamma-mia.com

 **THE SHUBERT ORGANIZATION, INC.**
Board of Directors

Philip J. Smith Chairman	**Robert E. Wankel** President
Wyche Fowler, Jr.	**John W. Kluge**
Lee J. Seidler	**Michael I. Sovern**

Stuart Subotnick

Elliot Greene Chief Financial Officer	**David Andrews** Senior Vice President – Shubert Ticketing
Juan Calvo Vice President and Controller	**John Darby** Vice President – Facilities
Peter Entin Vice President – Theatre Operations	**Charles Flateman** Vice President – Marketing
Anthony LaMattina Vice President – Audit & Production Finance	**Brian Mahoney** Vice President – Ticket Sales

D.S. Moynihan
Vice President – Creative Projects

House Manager	Manuel Levine

Mamma Mia!
Scrapbook

Correspondent: Beth Leavel, "Donna Sheridan"
Favorite Moment in the Show: When I scream "Oo you want to hear one more?" (during the "mega-mix") and the audience response is a wonderfully deafening "YES!!" I feel like a big rock star!
Favorite Therapy: Ricola and rolling out with tennis balls!
Orchestra Member Who Played the Most Consecutive Performances Without a Sub: Doug Quinn – guitar.
Orchestra Member Who Played the Most Instruments: Percussionist with 21!
Tale From the Put-In: During my put-in after I finished "Money, Money," the PSM (Andy Fenton) told us to "Hold Please." I thought, "Oh dear. I have done something terribly wrong!" Then, down the aisle walk Benny and Björn of ABBA, who came by to say hello and welcome the new members of the company! Sweet! And thrilling!

Correspondent: Alyse Alan Louis, "Sophie Sheridan"
Fastest Costume Change: Mine happens onstage during Act I. I do not leave the stage from "Lay All Your Love" through "Voulez Vous," the end of Act I. My costume during "Lay All Your Love," a pair of blue pants and a white wraparound shirt, covers a whole other costume underneath. After "Lay All Your Love" I run off and exit through a door behind one of the revolving set pieces. When I am behind the set, I have just enough time to pull off my "Lay All Your Love" costume and reveal the beaded jeans and green tank top that I will wear for the rest of Act I. As the set pieces revolve, I grab the costume that I just pulled off and place it on a stoop that the audience cannot see. During the next number, "Super Trouper," my shoes and accessories are pre-set so that I can put them on during this number and continue on through the act. Sometimes, my quick-change goes slower than planned. In the past, I have knotted the ties on the shirt that I wear in "Lay All Your Love" and was not able to get that off in time. But the unexpected is what makes a show like *Mamma Mia!* so fun and I learn so much from moments that don't go as planned.
Memorable Fan Encounter: A few months into my time with *Mamma Mia*, I got to meet an 8-year-old girl who I will never forget. After a Saturday matinee she and her mom were waiting at the stage door. They were the only ones outside and had waited so patiently to meet some of the cast. "I told my mom that I knew you would come!" the little girl said. The three of us talked about the show and the little girl asked me for my autograph and asked so many questions about me and about playing Sophie. Then she asked for a souvenir from my dressing room. After coming back with a souvenir, the little girl asked, "Can I please see your dressing room? Can we come inside?" And of course I said yes because she was just so excited and I remember being her age and how excited I was when I got to see a Broadway show! I showed her my dressing room and she wanted her mom to take pictures of everything: my costumes, my shoes, my dressing table. She asked so many wonderful questions! We also took a little video for her class back home. And we played dress-up with my jewelry from the show. I wanted her to experience what it was like to get ready for the show as Sophie! A couple of weeks after our visit together, the little girl and her mom sent me a photo booklet that they had made from our time together. It includes pictures of us together and pictures of the little girl in her show at school and her classmates' signatures. It means so much to me and when I look at it I am reminded of how much I love what I do and how grateful I am for the support and love from our audience each night.

1. The new star trio, Judy McLane, Beth Leavel and Allison Briner, take a curtain call after the September 22, 2009 performance.
2. Alyse Alan Louis and Eric William Morris at a champagne reception following the first regular performance with the new leads.
3. (L-R) John Dossett, Beth Leavel, Patrick Boll and David Andrew MacDonald pose at the reception.

Correspondent: David MacDonald, "Harry Bright"
Special Backstage Ritual: I make a cup of tea, Lapsang Souchong, and fill my water bottle. I massage my neck, upper- and lower-back, and my legs with a hard foam roller. I vocalize and then open the door to extend apologies for having done so. I put on my mic pack and fit the microphone into my hair. I caution Patrick Boll, with whom I share my dressing room, against applying as much make-up as he so often does. I listen to Patrick discuss, at some length, how handsome he is. I vocalize again, to reassure Patrick of my inadequacies, and then listen to him discuss, at some length (for indeed what could be discussed at a greater one) how comforting he finds this. I put on my costume for my first scene. I play the guitar. And finally I open the door, tell Patrick that he is indeed a very handsome man, and head downstairs

Mamma Mia!
Scrapbook

1. Cast member Brandi Burkhardt prepares to toss the bouquet to ten brides-to-be after the June 27, 2009 performance.
2. Ten brides-to-be show their engagement rings.
3. (L-R) Cast member Judy McLane. producer Judy Craymer and cast members Beth Leavel and Allison Briner celebrate the show's eighth anniversary.

Photos by Aubrey Reuben

and featured the cast of *Mamma Mia* singing an acoustic version of "Live High" by Jason Mraz.

Catchphrase Only the Company Would Recognize: "Work!" Written phonetically: "WERQ!!!"

Favorite In-Theater Gathering Place: The greenroom. We celebrate birthdays, do our top tens, eat meals, and take tons of naps in our greenroom.

Favorite Off-Site Hangout: Emmet O'Lunney's on 50th Street and Landmarc at the Time Warner Center.

Correspondent: Bryan Scott Johnson, "Father Alexandrios"

Actor Who Performed the Most Roles in This Show: Apart from swings, who can cover not only all ensemble but also some principal roles, it would probably have to be an ensemble man who, apart from his own track, covers all three dads as well as Father Alexandrios. There have been several over the years. In the current company, that ensemble man is Timothy Booth.

Memorable Anniversary Party/Gift: Last fall's eighth anniversary party at Toloache, where they closed down the place for us and served unlimited margaritas and fabulous tapas all night long. Gift? This past holiday season, we had a "green" Christmas, as everyone was given a set of reusable bags and a gift card to Whole Foods.

Actor Who Has Done the Most Shows: Since he has been with the show since its Broadway opening, that would have to be Brent Black.

Best In-House Parody Lyric: "I was in jail just before we met—" the opening line from "Lay All Your Love On Me." (Actual line is "I wasn't jealous before we met.")

Understudy Anecdote: There was one time when an actress who covered Tanya was set to go on; however, in between the matinee and evening shows, she had turned off her dressing room monitor so she could nap. When the show began, she didn't hear it, thinking it was still sometime during "half-hour." Then, when people came running up and down the hall calling her name, and she realized that she had missed her entrance in the Dynamos' arrival scene, she bolted down three and a half flights of stairs, and—shoes in hand (not having had a chance to put them on)—ran onstage mid-scene, from the opposite side of the stage (after numerous ad libs by the other actors trying to keep the scene going without her). At the same time, another Tanya understudy was actually onstage during that same scene that night—dressed as the old Greek lady knitting in her chair—and as she saw that Tanya hadn't shown up—she momentarily considered throwing off her old lady shawl and joining the scene, shouting, "Sophie! It's me! Your crazy Auntie Tanya!"

calling back to him over my shoulder in a thick Scottish accent, "See you doon the stairs, laddie."

Correspondent: Patrick Boll, "Bill Austin"
Coolest Thing About Being in This Show: Spending every night on a Greek Island with this great group of people!
Memorable Directorial Note: "Just be aware, every night 15 housewives from New Jersey will fall in love with you and be waiting outside the stage door. Deal with it."

Correspondent: Ray Lee, "Eddie"
What Did You Think of the Web Buzz On Your Show: We are excited for the new Facebook group that has been launched recently!
"Gypsy of the Year" Sketch: "Gypsy '09" was written by Gerard Salvador and Raymond J. Lee

Mary Poppins

First Preview: October 14, 2006. Opened: November 16, 2006.
Still running as of May 31, 2010.

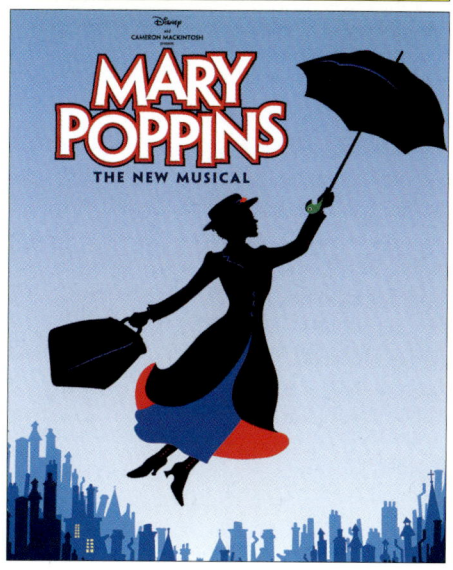

NEW AMSTERDAM THEATRE

Disney and CAMERON MACKINTOSH present

MARY POPPINS

A MUSICAL BASED ON THE STORIES OF P.L. TRAVERS AND THE WALT DISNEY FILM

With

SCARLETT STRALLEN ADAM FIORENTINO
DANIEL JENKINS REBECCA LUKER
ANN ARVIA MARK PRICE RUTH GOTTSCHALL JEFF STEITZER
and
JENNY GALLOWAY

JULIETTE ALLEN ANGELO ALEXANDRA BERRO JEREMIAH KISSANE CASSADY LEONARD MATTHEW SCHECHTER ANDREW SHIPMAN
JAMES HINDMAN NICK KEPLEY SEAN McCOURT JANELLE ANNE ROBINSON JESSICA SHERIDAN COREY SKAGGS SAM STRASFELD

AARON J. ALBANO DAVID BAUM PAM BRADLEY CATHERINE BRUNELL KATHY CALAHAN KATE CHAPMAN BRIAN COLLIER BARRETT DAVIS
ELIZABETH DeROSA SUZANNE HYLENSKI MARK LEDBETTER MATT LOEHR MELISSA LONE JEFF METZLER DENNIS MOENCH
KATHLEEN NANNI AMBER OWENS ROMMY SANDHU JONATHAN RICHARD SANDLER LAURA SCHUTTER CHAD SEIB

Original Music and Lyrics by
RICHARD M. SHERMAN and ROBERT B. SHERMAN
Book by
JULIAN FELLOWES
New Songs and Additional Music and Lyrics by
GEORGE STILES and ANTHONY DREWE
Co-created by
CAMERON MACKINTOSH

Produced for Disney Theatrical Productions by
THOMAS SCHUMACHER

Music Supervisor Music Director
DAVID CADDICK BRAD HAAK

Orchestrations by
WILLIAM DAVID BROHN

Broadway Sound Design Dance and Vocal Arrangements
STEVE CANYON KENNEDY GEORGE STILES

Associate Choreographer Associate Director Associate Producer Makeup Design
GEOFFREY GARRATT ANTHONY LYN TODD LACY NAOMI DONNE

Technical Director Production Stage Manager Casting
DAVID BENKEN MARK DOBROW TARA RUBIN CASTING

Co-choreographer Lighting Design
STEPHEN MEAR HOWARD HARRISON

Scenic and Costume Design
BOB CROWLEY

Co-direction and Choreography
MATTHEW BOURNE

Directed by
RICHARD EYRE

CAST OF CHARACTERS

(in order of appearance)

Bert	ADAM FIORENTINO
George Banks	DANIEL JENKINS
Winifred Banks	REBECCA LUKER
Jane Banks	JULIETTE ALLEN ANGELO, ALEXANDRA BERRO or CASSADY LEONARD
Michael Banks	JEREMIAH KISSANE, MATTHEW SCHECHTER or ANDREW SHIPMAN
Katie Nanna	KATE CHAPMAN
Policeman	COREY SKAGGS
Miss Lark	JESSICA SHERIDAN
Admiral Boom	JEFF STEITZER
Mrs. Brill	JENNY GALLOWAY
Robertson Ay	MARK PRICE
Mary Poppins	SCARLETT STRALLEN
Park Keeper	JAMES HINDMAN
Neleus	NICK KEPLEY
Queen Victoria	RUTH GOTTSCHALL
Bank Chairman	JEFF STEITZER
Miss Smythe	RUTH GOTTSCHALL
Von Hussler	SEAN McCOURT
Northbrook	SAM STRASFELD
Bird Woman	ANN ARVIA
Mrs. Corry	JANELLE ANNE ROBINSON
Fannie	AMBER OWENS
Annie	CATHERINE BRUNELL
Valentine	DENNIS MOENCH
William	MARK LEDBETTER
Mr. Punch	JAMES HINDMAN

Continued on next page

(L-R): Scarlett Strallen and Adam Fiorentino

Photo by Joan Marcus

Mary Poppins

MUSICAL NUMBERS

Mary Poppins takes place in and around the Banks' household somewhere in London at the turn of the last century.

ACT I

"Chim Chim Cher-ee" † ....Bert
"Cherry Tree Lane" (Part 1)* ....George and Winifred Banks, Jane and Michael, Mrs. Brill, and Robertson Ay
"The Perfect Nanny" ....Jane and Michael
"Cherry Tree Lane" (Part 2) ....George and Winifred Banks, Jane, and Michael, Mrs. Brill, and Robertson Ay
"Practically Perfect"* ....Mary Poppins, Jane, and Michael
"Jolly Holiday" † ....Bert, Mary Poppins, Jane, Michael, Neleus, and the Statues
"Cherry Tree Lane" (Reprise),
   "Being Mrs. Banks,"*
   "Jolly Holiday" (Reprise) ....George, Winifred, Jane, and Michael
"A Spoonful of Sugar" ....Mary Poppins, Jane, Michael, Robertson Ay, and Winifred
"Precision and Order"* ....Bank Chairman and the Bank Clerks
"A Man Has Dreams" † ....George Banks
"Feed the Birds" ....Bird Woman and Mary Poppins
"Supercalifragilisticexpialidocious" † ....Mary Poppins, Mrs. Corry, Bert, Jane, Michael, Fannie, Annie, and Customers
"Temper, Temper"* ....Valentine, William, Mr. Punch, the Glamorous Doll, and other Toys
"Chim Chim Cher-ee" (Reprise) ....Bert and Mary Poppins

ACT II

"Cherry Tree Lane" (Reprise) ....Mrs. Brill, Michael, Jane, Winifred, Robertson Ay, and George
"Brimstone and Treacle" (Part 1)* ....Miss Andrew
"Let's Go Fly a Kite" ....Bert, Park Keeper, Jane, and Michael
"Cherry Tree Lane" (Reprise),
   "Being Mrs. Banks" (Reprise) ....George and Winifred
"Brimstone and Treacle" (Part 2) ....Mary Poppins and Miss Andrew
"Practically Perfect" (Reprise) ....Jane, Michael, and Mary Poppins
"Chim Chim Cher-ee" (Reprise) ....Bert
"Step in Time" † ....Bert, Mary Poppins, Jane, Michael, and the Sweeps
"A Man Has Dreams,"
   "A Spoonful of Sugar" (Reprise) ....George and Bert
"Anything Can Happen"* ....Jane, Michael, Mary Poppins, and the Company
"A Spoonful of Sugar" (Reprise) ....Mary Poppins
"A Shooting Star" † ....Orchestra

* New Songs   † Adapted Songs

SONG CREDITS

"The Perfect Nanny," "A Spoonful of Sugar," "Feed the Birds," "Let's Go Fly a Kite" written by Richard M. Sherman and Robert B. Sherman.

"Chim Chim Cher-ee," "Jolly Holiday," "A Man Has Dreams," "Supercalifragilisticexpialidocious," "Step in Time" written by Richard M. Sherman and Robert B. Sherman, with new material by George Stiles and Anthony Drewe.

"Cherry Tree Lane," "Practically Perfect," "Being Mrs. Banks," "Precision and Order," "Temper, Temper," "Brimstone and Treacle," "Anything Can Happen" written by George Stiles and Anthony Drewe.

Cast Continued

Glamorous Doll ....ELIZABETH DeROSA
Jack-In-A-Box ....SEAN McCOURT
Miss Andrew ....RUTH GOTTSCHALL

ENSEMBLE

AARON J. ALBANO, DAVID BAUM, CATHERINE BRUNELL, KATE CHAPMAN, BARRETT DAVIS, ELIZABETH DeROSA, JAMES HINDMAN, NICK KEPLEY, MARK LEDBETTER, MATT LOEHR, MELISSA LONE, SEAN McCOURT, JEFF METZLER, DENNIS MOENCH, KATHLEEN NANNI, AMBER OWENS, JANELLE ANNE ROBINSON, LAURA SCHUTTER, JESSICA SHERIDAN, COREY SKAGGS, SAM STRASFELD

SWINGS

PAM BRADLEY, KATHY CALAHAN, BRIAN COLLIER, SUZANNE HYLENSKI, ROMMY SANDHU, JONATHAN RICHARD SANDLER, CHAD SEIB

Statues, bank clerks, customers, toys, chimney sweeps, lamp lighters and inhabitants of Cherry Tree Lane played by members of the company.

Scarlett Strallen is appearing with the permission of Actors' Equity Association pursuant to an exchange program between American Equity and UK Equity.

UNDERSTUDIES

Mary Poppins: CATHERINE BRUNELL, ELIZABETH DeROSA
Bert: BRIAN COLLIER, MATT LOEHR, SAM STRASFELD
George Banks: JAMES HINDMAN, SEAN McCOURT, COREY SKAGGS
Winifred Banks: MELISSA LONE, LAURA SCHUTTER
Mrs. Brill: ANN ARVIA, PAM BRADLEY
Robertson Ay: AARON J. ALBANO, BRIAN COLLIER, DENNIS MOENCH
Bird Woman: KATE CHAPMAN, JANELLE ANNE ROBINSON, JESSICA SHERIDAN
Miss Andrew/Queen Victoria/Miss Smythe: ANN ARVIA, KATE CHAPMAN, JANELLE ANNE ROBINSON, JESSICA SHERIDAN
Admiral Boom/Bank Chairman: JAMES HINDMAN, SEAN McCOURT, COREY SKAGGS

Continued on next page

Mary Poppins

Cast Continued

Mrs. Corry: PAM BRADLEY,
  CATHERINE BRUNELL, KATHY CALAHAN
Katie Nanna: PAM BRADLEY,
  KATHY CALAHAN, SUZANNE HYLENSKI
Miss Lark: PAM BRADLEY,
  KATHY CALAHAN, LAURA SCHUTTER
Neleus: BRIAN COLLIER, BARRETT DAVIS,
  JONATHAN RICHARD SANDLER
Von Hussler: ROMMY SANDHU,
  COREY SKAGGS
Jack-in-a-Box: BRIAN COLLIER,
  ROMMY SANDHU,
  JONATHAN RICHARD SANDLER,
  CHAD SEIB
Northbrook: JAMES HINDMAN,
  JONATHAN RICHARD SANDLER,
  CHAD SEIB
Policeman/Mr. Punch: SEAN McCOURT,
  ROMMY SANDHU
Park Keeper: ROMMY SANDHU, CHAD SEIB,
  COREY SKAGGS
William: BRIAN COLLIER, ROMMY SANDHU,
  JONATHAN RICHARD SANDLER
Valentine: BRIAN COLLIER,
  JONATHAN RICHARD SANDLER
Glamorous Doll: KATHY CALAHAN,
  SUZANNE HYLENSKI

DANCE CAPTAIN
BRIAN COLLIER

ASSISTANT DANCE CAPTAIN
JONATHAN RICHARD SANDLER

ORCHESTRA
Conductor: BRAD HAAK
Associate Conductor/2nd Keyboard:
  DALE RIELING
Assistant Conductor/Piano: MILTON GRANGER
Bass: PETER DONOVAN
Drums: DAVE RATAJCZAK
Percussion: DANIEL HASKINS
Guitar/Banjo/E-Bow: NATE BROWN
Horns: RUSSELL RIZNER,
  LAWRENCE DiBELLO
Trumpets: JASON COVEY, JOHN SHEPPARD
Trombone/Euphonium: MARC DONATELLE
Bass Trombone/Tuba: RANDY ANDOS
Clarinet: PAUL GARMENT
Oboe/English Horn: ALEXANDRA KNOLL
Flutes: BRIAN MILLER
Cello: STEPHANIE CUMMINS
Music Contractor: DAVID LAI

Scarlett Strallen
Mary Poppins

Adam Fiorentino
Bert

Daniel Jenkins
George Banks

Rebecca Luker
Winifred Banks

Jenny Galloway
Mrs. Brill

Ann Arvia
Bird Woman

Mark Price
Robertson Ay

Ruth Gottschall
*Miss Andrew,
Queen Victoria,
Miss Smythe*

Jeff Steitzer
*Admiral Boom,
Bank Chairman*

Juliette Allen Angelo
*Jane Banks at
certain
performances*

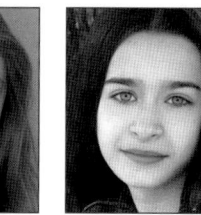
Alexandra Berro
*Jane Banks
at certain
performances*

Jeremiah Kissane
*Michael Banks
at certain
performances*

Cassady Leonard
*Jane Banks
at certain
performances*

Matthew Schechter
*Michael Banks
at certain
performances*

Andrew Shipman
*Michael Banks
at certain
performances*

James Hindman
*Park Keeper,
Mr. Punch, Ensemble*

Nick Kepley
Neleus, Ensemble

Sean McCourt
*Von Hussler,
Ensemble*

Janelle Anne
Robinson
Mrs. Corry, Ensemble

Jessica Sheridan
Miss Lark, Ensemble

Mary Poppins

Corey Skaggs
Policeman, Northbrook, Ensemble

Sam Strasfeld
Northbrook, Ensemble

Aaron J. Albano
Ensemble

David Baum
Ensemble

Pam Bradley
Swing

Catherine Brunell
Annie, Ensemble

Kathy Calahan
Swing

Kate Chapman
Katie Nanna, Ensemble

Brian Collier
Swing, Dance Captain

Barrett Davis
Ensemble

Elizabeth DeRosa
Glamorous Doll, Ensemble

Suzanne Hylenski
Swing

Mark Ledbetter
William, Ensemble

Matt Loehr
Ensemble

Melissa Lone
Ensemble

Jeff Metzler
Ensemble

Dennis Moench
Valentine, Ensemble

Kathleen Nanni
Ensemble

Amber Owens
Fannie, Ensemble

Rommy Sandhu
Swing

Jonathan Richard Sandler
Swing

Laura Schutter
Ensemble

Chad Seib
William, Ensemble

P.L. Travers
Author of the Mary Poppins stories

Cameron Mackintosh
Producer and Co-Creator

Thomas Schumacher
Producer snd President Disney Theatrical Group

Richard M. Sherman and Robert B. Sherman
Original Music & Lyrics

Julian Fellowes
Book

George Stiles
New Songs, Additional Music, Dance & Vocal Arrangements

Anthony Drewe
New Songs & Additional Lyrics

Richard Eyre
Director

Matthew Bourne
Co-Director & Choreographer

Bob Crowley
Scenic and Costume Design

Stephen Mear
Co-Choreographer

Mary Poppins

 Howard Harrison
Lighting Designer

 Steve Canyon Kennedy
Broadway Sound Designer

 William David Brohn
Orchestrations

 David Caddick
Music Supervisor

 Brad Haak
Music Director

 Naomi Donne
Makeup Designer

 Angela Cobbin
Wig Creator

 Geoffrey Garratt
Associate Choreographer

 Anthony Lyn
Associate Director

 David Benken
Technical Director

 Tara Rubin Casting
Casting

 Kristin Carbone
Katie Nanna, Ensemble

Jane Carr
Mrs. Brill

 Kelsey Fowler
Jane Banks

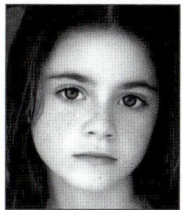 Alison Jaye Horowitz
Jane Banks

 Tony Mansker
Ensemble

 Neil McCaffrey
Michael Banks

 Zach Rand
Michael Banks

 T. Oliver Reid
William, Ensemble

 Marlon Sherman
Michael Banks

 Chaterine Walker
Glamorous Doll, Ensemble

 Rozi Baker
Jane Banks

 Brandon Bieber
Ensemble

Jeff Binder
George Banks

 Christian Borle
Bert

 Valerie Boyle
Mrs. Brill

 Kristin Carbone
Katie Nanna, Ensemble

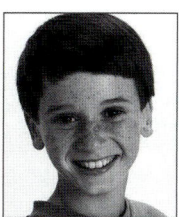 Christopher Flaim
Michael Banks

 Kelsey Fowler
Jane Banks

 Jonathan Freeman
Admiral Boom, Bank Chairman

 Ethan Haberfield
Michael Banks

 Laura Michelle Kelly
Mary Poppins

 Karl Kenzler
George Banks

The Playbill Broadway Yearbook 2009-2010

Mary Poppins

Michelle Lookadoo
Ensemble

Tony Mansker
Ensemble

Neil McCaffrey
Michael Banks

Michael McCarty
Admiral Boom, Bank Chairman

Catherine Missal
Jane Banks

Megan Osterhaus
Winifred Banks

T. Oliver Reid
Ensemble

Rachel Resheff
Jane Banks

James Tabeek
Swing

MERCHANDISE STAFF
Front Row (L-R): Scott Koonce, Greg Rose, Shane Bland

Back Row (L-R): Tatiana Diaz, Stacey Rockwell

FRONT OF HOUSE STAFF
Front Row (L-R): Bryan Plummer, Jeryl Costello (Head Usher)

Middle Row (L-R): James Teal, David Costello, Debbie Vogel, Carla Dawson, Tony Serra

Back Row (L-R): Michael Gilbert, Kenneth Miller, Audrey Terrell

---

THE ORIGINAL FILM SCREENPLAY
FOR WALT DISNEY'S *MARY POPPINS*
BY BILL WALSH * DON DA GRADI

DESIGN CONSULTANT
TONY WALTON

STAFF FOR MARY POPPINS

COMPANY MANAGER	DAVE EHLE
Assistant Company Manager	Laura Eichholz
Production Manager	Jane Abramson
Production Stage Manager	Mark Dobrow
Stage Manager	Jason Trubitt
Assistant Stage Managers	Terence Orleans Alexander, Valerie Lau-Kee Lai, Michael Wilhoite
Dance Supervisor	Brian Collier
Assistant Dance Captain	Jonathan Richard Sandler
Assistant to the Associate Producer	Kerry McGrath

DISNEY ON BROADWAY PUBLICITY

Senior Publicist	Dennis Crowley
Publicist	Adriana Douzos
Associate Scenic Designer	Bryan Johnson
Scenic Design Associate	Rosalind Coombes
US Scenic Assistants	Dan Kuchar, Rachel Short Janocko, Frank McCullough
UK Scenic Assistants	Al Turner, Charles Quiggin, Adam Wiltshire
Associate Costume Designer	Christine Rowland
Associate Costume Designer	Mitchell Bloom
Assistant Costume Designer	Patrick Wiley
Assistant Costume Designer	Rick Kelly
Associate Lighting Designer	Daniel Walker
Assistant Lighting Designer	Kristina Kloss
Lighting Programmer	Rob Halliday
Associate Sound Designer	John Shivers
Wig Creator	Angela Cobbin
Illusions Designer	Jim Steinmeyer
Technical Director	David Benken
Scenic Production Supervisor	Patrick Eviston
Assistant Technical Supervisor	Rosemarie Palombo
Production Carpenter	Drew Siccardi
Production Flyman	Michael Corbett
Foy Flying Operator	Raymond King
Automation	Steve Stackle, David Helck
Carpenters	Eddie Ackerman, Frank Alter, Brett Daley, Tony Goncalves, Gary Matarazzo
Production Electrician	James Maloney
Key Spot Operator	Joseph P. Garvey
Lighting Console Operator	Carlos Martinez
Pyro Operator	Kevin Strohmeyer
Automated Lighting Technician	Andy Catron

Mary Poppins

Assistant Electricians	Gregory Dunkin, Al Manganaro, Chris Passalacqua
Production Propman	Victor Amerling
Assistant Propman	Tim Abel
Props	Joe Bivone, John Saye, John Taccone, Gary Wilner
Production Sound Engineer	Andrew Keister
Sound Engineer	Kurt Fischer
Sound Engineer	Marie Renee Foucher
Sound Assistant	Bill Romanello, Karen Zabinski
Production Wardrobe Supervisor	Helen Toth
Assistant Wardrobe Supervisor	Abbey Rayburn
Dressers	Richard Byron, Vivienne Crawford, Marjorie Denton, Russell Easley, Steven Epstein, Kathy Gallagher, Maya Hardin, Peggie Kurz, Jennifer Molloy, Janet Netzke, Tom Reiter, Frank Scaccia, Gary Seibert, Jean Steinlein
Production Hair Supervisor	Tod L. McKim
Hair Dept. Assistants	Chris Calabrese, Ashley Leitzel-Reichenbach, Matthew B. Wilson
Production Makeup Supervisor	Amy Porter
Child Guardian	Christina Huschle
UK Prop Coordinators	Kathy Anders, Lisa Buckley
UK Wig Shop Assistant	Beatrix Archer
Music Copyist	Emily Grishman Music Preparation – Emily Grishman/Katharine Edmonds
Keyboard Programming	Stuart Andrews

MUSIC COORDINATOR	**DAVID LAI**
DIALECT & VOCAL COACH	**DEBORAH HECHT**

Associate General Manager	Alan Wasser
Production Co-Counsel	F. Richard Pappas
Casting Directors	Tara Rubin, Eric Woodall
Children's Tutoring	On Location Education, Muriel Kester
Physical Therapy	Physioarts
Advertising	Serino Coyne, Inc
Interactive Marketing	Situation Marketing/Damian Bazadona, Lisa Cecchini, Miriam Gardin
Web Design Consultant	Joshua Noah
Production Photography	Joan Marcus
Production Travel	Jill L. Citron
Payroll Managers	Anthony DeLuca, Cathy Guerra
Corporate Counsel	Michael Rosenfeld

CREDITS
Scenery by Hudson Scenic, Inc.; Adirondack Studios, Inc.; Proof Productions, Inc.; Scenic Technologies, a division of Production Resource Group, LLC, New Windsor NY. Drops by Scenic Arts. Automation by Hudson Scenic, Inc. Lighting equipment by Hudson Sound & Light, LLC. Lighting truss by Showman Fabricators, Inc. Sound Equipment by Masque Sound. Projection equipment by Sound Associates Inc. Magic props by William Kennedy of Magic Effects. Props by The Spoon Group, LLC; Moonboots Productions Inc.; Russell Beck Studio Ltd. Costumes by Barbara Matera Ltd.; Parsons-Meares, Ltd.; Eric Winterling; Werner Russold; Studio Rouge; Seamless Costumes. Millinery by Rodney Gordon, Arnold Levine, Lynne Mackey Studio. Shoes by T.O. Dey. Shirts by Cego. Puppets by Puppet Heap. Flying by Foy. Ricola cough drops courtesy of Ricola USA, Inc. Emergen-C super energy booster provided by Alcer Corp. Makeup provided by M•A•C.

MARY POPPINS rehearsed at the New 42nd Street Studios.

THANKS
Thanks to Marcus Hall Props, Claire Sanderson, James Ince and Sons, Great British Lighting, Bed Bazaar, The Wakefield Brush Company, Heron and Driver, Ivo and Kay Covney, Mike and Rosi Compton, Bebe Barrett, Charles Quiggin, Nicola Kileen Textiles, Carl Roberts Shaw, David Scotcher Interiors, Original Club Fenders Ltd., Lauren Pattison, Robert Tatad.

FOR CAMERON MACKINTOSH LIMITED

Directors	Nicholas Allott, Richard Johnston
Deputy Managing Director	Robert Noble
Executive Producer & Casting Director	Trevor Jackson
Technical Director	Nicolas Harris
Financial Controller	Richard Knibb
Associate Producer	Darinka Nenadovic
Sales & Marketing Manager	David Dolman
Head of Musical Development	Stephen Metcalfe
Production Associate	Shidan Majidi

DISNEY THEATRICAL PRODUCTIONS

President	Thomas Schumacher
EVP & Managing Director	David Schrader
Senior Vice President, Creative Affairs	Michele Steckler
Senior Vice President, International	Ron Kollen
Vice President, Operations	Dana Amendola
Vice President, Labor Relations	Allan Frost
Vice President, Worldwide Publicity & Communications	Joe Quenqua
Vice President, Domestic Touring	Jack Eldon
Vice President, Theatrical Licensing	Steve Fickinger
Vice President, Human Resources	June Heindel
Director, Domestic Touring	Michael Buchanan
Director, Casting & Development	Jennifer Rudin, CSA
Director, Publicity & Communications	Jay Carducci
Manager, Labor Relations	Stephanie Cheek
Manager, Human Resources	Jewel Neal
Manager, Film Development	Dusty Bennett
Manager, Information Systems	Scott Benedict
Senior Computer Support Analyst	Kevin A. McGuire
IT/Business Analyst	William Boudiette

Production

Executive Music Producer	Chris Montan
Vice President, Physical Production	John Tiggeloven
Director, International	Michael Cassel
Senior Manager, Safety	Canara Price
Manager, Physical Production	Karl Chmielewski
Dramaturg & Literary Manager	Ken Cerniglia

Marketing

Vice President, Broadway	Andrew Flatt
Vice President, International	Fiona Thomas
Director, Internet Strategy & Online Marketing	Kyle Young
Director, Broadway	Michele Groner
Director, Domestic Tour Marketing	Deborah Warren
Website Manager	Eric W. Kratzer
Assistant Manager, Marketing	Lauren Daghini

Sales

Director, National Sales	Bryan Dockett
New Business Development Manager	Jacob Lloyd Kimbro
Manager, Sales & Ticketing	Nick Falzon
Manager, Group Sales	Juil Kim

Business and Legal Affairs

Senior Vice President	Jonathan Olson
Director	Daniel M. Posener
Senior Counsel	Seth Stuhl
Paralegal	Jessica White

Finance

VP Finance & Business Development	Mario Iannetta
Director	Joe McClafferty
Senior Manager, Finance	Dana James
Manager, Finance	John Fajardo
Production Accountants	Joy Sims Brown, Nick Judge, Barbara Toben
Assistant Production Accountant	Isander Rojas
Senior Business Planner	Shaan Akbar
Director, Accounting	Leena Mathew
Sr. Financial Analyst	Adrineh Ghoukassian
Senior Sales Analyst	Liz Jurist Schwarzwalder

Administrative Staff
Sarah Bills, Dayle Bland, Lindsay Braverman, Amy Caldamone, Michael Dei Cas, Alanna Degner, Jessica Doina, Cristi Finn, Gregory Hanoian, Abbie Harrison, Cyntia Leo, Colleen McCormack, Janine McGuire, Lisa Mitchell, Dimitri Pankas, Ryan Pears, David Scott, Benjy Shaw, Christina Tuchman, Kyle Wilson, Jason Zammit

DISNEY THEATRICAL MERCHANDISE

Vice President	Steven Downing
Operations Manager	Shawn Baker
Merchandise Manager	Neil Markman
Associate Buyer	Violet Burlaza
Assistant Manager, Inventory	Suzanne Jakel
District Manager	Alyssa Somers
On-Site Assistant Retail Manager	Scott Koonce

Disney Theatrical Productions
c/o New Amsterdam Theatre
214 W. 42nd St.
New York, NY 10036
guestmail@disneytheatrical.com

STAFF FOR THE NEW AMSTERDAM THEATRE

Theatre Manager	John M. Loiacono
Guest Services Manager	Kenneth Miller
Box Office Treasurer	Andrew Grennan
Assistant Treasurer	Anthony Oliva
Chief Engineer	Frank Gibbons
Engineer	Dan Milan
Security Manager	Carl Lembo
Head Usher	Jeryl Costello
Lobby Refreshments	Sweet Concessions
Special thanks	Sgt. Arthur J. Smarsch, Det. Adam D'Amico

Mary Poppins
SCRAPBOOK

Correspondent: Catherine Brunell, "Mary Poppins" understudy, "Annie," one of Mrs. Corry's daughters, ensemble.

Most Vivid Memory: Watching the show a couple of weeks after I had been cast. I went with my husband, Chris and my twin sons, Gus and Charlie. They were 3 years old at the time and were mesmerized by the performance. They both started crying because it was over...they didn't want the show to end.

Milestone Parties, Celebrations and/or Company Gifts: Dan Jenkins' Pork Bun Parties, any party at Scarlett Strallen's lovely apartment, Adam Fiorentino buying an enormous cake for our 1000th performance.

Most Exciting Celebrity Visitors: Jude Law, Cate Blanchett, the Jonas Brothers, Sen. Chris Dodd, and the best of all, Brad and Angelina. The best was seeing Angelina sitting in the aisle of the orchestra during the second act with two of her children.

Special Backstage Rituals: At half-hour, stretching on stage and doing 20 push-ups before every show with Matt Loehr, Nick Kepley and Sam Strasfeld.

Special Intermission Activity: Washing off a pound of "monkey" greasepaint, reapplying my "Fly a Kite" makeup, sitting and eating an apple for about 45 seconds, changing tights, shoes, putting on a dress, wig, and hat, and then starting the second act. There's no break.

Favorite Moment in the Show: When Mary flies out over the audience. It makes me tear up every time.

Catchphrase Only the Company Would Recognize: "SIP-A-Dee-Do-Dah."

Favorite Snack Foods: Anything from Trader Joe's! I'm obsessed with their food.

(L-R): Juliette Allen Angelo and *Yearbook* correspondent Catherine Brunell backstage at the New Amsterdam Theatre.

Memorable Stage Door Fan Encounter: When I go on for Mary, no one at the stage door asks for my autograph because I'm blonde in real life and look so different from the character. It's a buzzkill. You can have a great show, feel terrific, and the 25 people at the stage door don't know who you are. It's humbling, to say the least.

Favorite Off-Site Hangout: My couch. I don't go out anymore...I have kids who wake up at 7 AM every day.

Memorable Stage Management Note: "Act better, sing better, dance better" ...No, I can't remember any.

Embarrassing Moment: Blanking out during "Supercal" and forgetting the letters. It happened a few months after I was in the show. Mortified!

Coolest Thing About Being in This Show: Getting to be in a Broadway show that is appropriate for my children to watch. Also, the simple fact of having a job (in a show that is running). During the state of our economy, this is a GIFT!!

CREW
Seated (L-R): Tony Goncalves, Michael Wilhoite, Alexis Prussack, Alan Cabrera, Valerie Lau-Kee Lai, Carly Hirschberg, Mark Dobrow, Midge Denton, Jason Trubitt, Karen Zabinski, Bill Romanello, Greg Matteis

Standing (L-R): Gary Seibert, Marie Renee Foucher, Jimmy Maloney, John Saye, Frank Alter, Terry Alexander, Ashley Reichenbach, Andy Catron, Gary Wilner, Kevin Strohmeyer, Carlos Martinez, Steve Stackle, Joe Bivone, Joe Garvey, Chris Passalacqua

Memphis

First Preview: September 23, 2009. Opened: October 19, 2009.
Still running as of May 31, 2010.

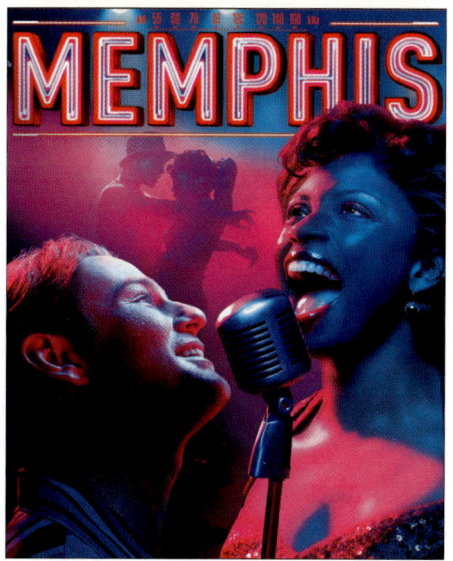

CAST
(in order of appearance)

White DJ/Mr. Collins/ Gordon Grant/Ensemble	JOHN JELLISON
Black DJ/Ensemble	RHETT GEORGE
Delray	J. BERNARD CALLOWAY
Gator	DERRICK BASKIN
Bobby	JAMES MONROE IGLEHART
Ensemble/Wailin' Joe/ Reverend Hobson	JOHN ERIC PARKER
Ensemble	TRACEE BEAZER
Ensemble	DIONNE FIGGINS
Ensemble	VIVIAN NIXON
Ensemble/Ethel	LaQUET SHARNELL
Ensemble	EPHRAIM M. SYKES
Ensemble	DANNY TIDWELL
Ensemble	DANIEL J. WATTS
Ensemble	DAN'YELLE WILLIAMSON
Felicia	MONTEGO GLOVER
Huey	CHAD KIMBALL
Mr. Simmons	MICHAEL McGRATH
Clara/Ensemble	JENNIFER ALLEN
Buck Wiley/Ensemble/ Martin Holton	KEVIN COVERT
Ensemble	HILLARY ELK
Ensemble	BRYAN FENKART
Ensemble	CARY TEDDER
Ensemble	KATIE WEBBER
Ensemble	CHARLIE WILLIAMS
Perry Como/Ensemble/Frank Dryer	BRAD BASS
Mama	CASS MORGAN

Continued on next page

SAM S. SHUBERT THEATRE
225 West 44th Street
A Shubert Organization Theatre

Philip J. Smith, *Chairman*   Robert E. Wankel, *President*

JUNKYARD DOG PRODUCTIONS BARBARA AND BUDDY FREITAG MARLEEN AND KENNY ALHADEFF
LATITUDE LINK JIM AND SUSAN BLAIR DEMOS BIZAR ENTERTAINMENT LAND LINE PRODUCTIONS
APPLES AND ORANGES PRODUCTIONS DAVE COPLEY DANCAP PRODUCTIONS, INC ALEX AND KATYA LUKIANOV TONY PONTURO 2 GUYS PRODUCTIONS RICHARD WINKLER

IN ASSOCIATION WITH
LAUREN DOLL ERIC AND MARSI GARDINER LINDA AND BILL POTTER BROADWAY ACROSS AMERICA JOCKO PRODUCTIONS PATTY BAKER DAN FRISHWASSER
BOB BARTNER/SCOTT AND KAYLIN UNION LORAINE BOYLE/CHASE MISHKIN REMMEL T. DICKINSON/MEMPHIS ORPHEUM GROUP SHADOWCATCHER ENTERTAINMENT/VIJAY AND SITA VASHEE

PRESENT

MEMPHIS

BOOK AND LYRICS BY
JOE DiPIETRO

MUSIC AND LYRICS BY
DAVID BRYAN

BASED ON A CONCEPT BY
GEORGE W. GEORGE

STARRING
CHAD KIMBALL   **MONTEGO GLOVER**

DERRICK BASKIN J. BERNARD CALLOWAY WITH JAMES MONROE IGLEHART MICHAEL McGRATH CASS MORGAN

JENNIFER ALLEN BRAD BASS TRACEE BEAZER KEVIN COVERT HILLARY ELK BRYAN FENKART DIONNE FIGGINS RHETT GEORGE
JOHN JELLISON CANDICE MONET McCALL SYDNEY MORTON VIVIAN NIXON JOHN ERIC PARKER JERMAINE R. REMBERT LAQUET SHARNELL
EPHRAIM M. SYKES CARY TEDDER DANNY TIDWELL DANIEL J. WATTS KATIE WEBBER DAN'YELLE WILLIAMSON CHARLIE WILLIAMS

SCENIC DESIGN	COSTUME DESIGN	LIGHTING DESIGN	SOUND DESIGN
DAVID GALLO	PAUL TAZEWELL	HOWELL BINKLEY	KEN TRAVIS

PROJECTION DESIGN	HAIR & WIG DESIGN	FIGHT DIRECTOR	CASTING	ASSOCIATE CHOREOGRAPHER
DAVID GALLO & SHAWN SAGADY	CHARLES G. LaPOINTE	STEVE RANKIN	TELSEY + COMPANY	KELLY DEVINE

ORCHESTRATIONS	MUSICAL DIRECTOR	DANCE ARRANGEMENTS	MUSIC CONTRACTOR	PRODUCTION STAGE MANAGER
DARYL WATERS & DAVID BRYAN	KENNY J. SEYMOUR	AUGUST ERIKSMOEN	MICHAEL KELLER	ARTURO E. PORAZZI

GENERAL MANAGER	PRODUCTION MANAGEMENT	PRESS AGENT	MARKETING DIRECTION
ALCHEMY PRODUCTION GROUP CARL PASBJERG & FRANK SCARDINO	JUNIPER STREET PRODUCTIONS, INC.	THE HARTMAN GROUP	TYPE A MARKETING ANNE RIPPEY

ASSOCIATE PRODUCERS
EMILY AND AARON ALHADEFF ALISON AND ANDI ALHADEFF KEN CLAY JOSEPH CRAIG RON AND MARJORIE DANZ CYRENA ESPOSITO BRUCE AND JOANNE GLANT MATT MURPHY

MUSIC PRODUCER/MUSIC SUPERVISOR
CHRISTOPHER JAHNKE

CHOREOGRAPHER
SERGIO TRUJILLO

DIRECTOR
CHRISTOPHER ASHLEY

This Production of MEMPHIS Originally Co-produced by La Jolla Playhouse, Christopher Ashley, Artistic Director, Michael S. Rosenberg, Managing Director and 5th Avenue Theatre, Seattle, WA, David Armstrong, Producing Artistic Director, Marilynn Sheldon, Managing Director
Originally Produced as a Joint World Premiere at North Shore Music Theatre, Jon Kimbell, Executive Producer and TheatreWorks, Robert Kelley, Artistic Director and Phil Santora, Managing Director

10/19/09

Montego Glover (center) and Chad Kimball (right) with the cast

Photo by Joan Marcus

Memphis

MUSICAL NUMBERS

ACT I

"Underground"	Delray, Felicia and Company
"The Music of My Soul"	Huey, Felicia and Company
"Scratch My Itch"	Wailin' Joe and Company
"Ain't Nothin' But a Kiss"	Felicia and Huey
"Hello, My Name Is Huey"	Huey
"Everybody Wants to Be Black on a Saturday Night"	Company
"Make Me Stronger"	Huey, Mama, Felicia and Company
"Colored Woman"	Felicia
"Someday"	Felicia and Company
"She's My Sister"	Delray and Huey
"Radio"	Huey and Company
"Say a Prayer"	Gator and Company

ACT II

"Crazy Little Huey"	Huey and Company
"Big Love"	Bobby
"Love Will Stand When All Else Falls"	Felicia and Company
"Stand Up"	Delray, Felicia, Huey, Gator, Bobby and Company
"Change Don't Come Easy"	Mama, Delray, Gator and Bobby
"Tear Down the House"	Huey and Company
"Love Will Stand/Ain't Nothin' But a Kiss" (Reprise)	Felicia and Huey
"Memphis Lives in Me"	Huey and Company
"Steal Your Rock 'n' Roll"	Huey, Felicia and Company

(L-R): J. Bernard Calloway and Montego Glover

Photo by Joan Marcus

2009-2010 AWARDS

TONY AWARDS
Best Musical
Best Original Score
(David Bryan and Joe DiPietro)
Best Book
(Joe DiPietro)
Best Orchestrations
Daryl Waters and David Bryan

DRAMA DESK AWARDS
Outstanding Musical
Outstanding Actress in a Musical
(Montego Glover [tie])
Outstanding Music
(David Bryan)
Outstanding Orchestrations
(Daryl Waters and David Bryan)

OUTER CRITICS CIRCLE AWARDS
Outstanding New Broadway Musical
Outstanding Actress in a Musical
(Montego Glover [tie])
Outstanding New Score (Broadway or Off-Broadway)
Outstanding Choreographer
(Sergio Trujillo [tie])

Cast Continued

SWINGS
CANDICE MONET McCALL,
SYDNEY MORTON, JERMAINE R. REMBERT

UNDERSTUDIES
For Mama:
JENNIFER ALLEN, KATIE WEBBER
For Huey:
BRAD BASS, BRYAN FENKART
For Felicia:
TRACEE BEAZER, DAN'YELLE WILLIAMSON
For Gator:
JERMAINE R. REMBERT, EPHRAIM M. SYKES
For Bobby, Delray:
RHETT GEORGE, JOHN ERIC PARKER
For Mr. Simmons:
JOHN JELLISON, KEVIN COVERT

DANCE CAPTAIN
JERMAINE R. REMBERT

TIME
The 1950s

BAND
Conductor:
KENNY J. SEYMOUR
Associate Conductor:
SHELTON BECTON
Keyboard 1:
KENNY J. SEYMOUR
Keyboard 2:
SHELTON BECTON
Guitars:
MICHAEL AARONS
Bass:
GEORGE FARMER
Drums:
CLAYTON CRADDOCK
Trumpet:
NICHOLAS MARCHIONE
Trombone:
MIKE DAVIS
Reeds:
TOM MURRAY, KEN HITCHCOCK
Music Coordinator:
MICHAEL KELLER

Memphis

Chad Kimball
Huey

Montego Glover
Felicia

Derrick Baskin
Gator

J. Bernard Calloway
Delray

James Monroe Iglehart
Bobby

Michael McGrath
Mr. Simmons

Cass Morgan
Mama

Jennifer Allen
Ensemble

Brad Bass
Ensemble

Tracee Beazer
Ensemble

Kevin Covert
Ensemble

Hillary Elk
Ensemble

Bryan Fenkart
Ensemble

Dionne Figgins
Ensemble, Assistant Dance Captain

Rhett George
Ensemble

John Jellison
Ensemble

Candice Monet McCall
Swing

Sydney Morton
Swing

Vivian Nixon
Ensemble

John Eric Parker
Ensemble

Jermaine R. Rembert
Swing, Dance Captain, Fight Captain

LaQuet Sharnell
Ensemble

Ephraim M. Sykes
Ensemble

Cary Tedder
Ensemble

Danny Tidwell
Ensemble

Daniel J. Watts
Ensemble

Katie Webber
Ensemble

Charlie Williams
Ensemble

Dan'yelle Williamson
Ensemble

Joe DiPietro
Book, Lyrics

David Bryan
Music, Lyrics

Christopher Ashley
Director

Sergio Trujillo
Choreographer

Christopher Jahnke
Music Producer/ Music Supervisor

David Gallo
Set and Co-Projections Design

The Playbill Broadway Yearbook 2009-2010

Memphis

Howell Binkley
Lighting Design

Paul Tazewell
Costume Design

Ken Travis
Sound Design

Steve Rankin
Fight Director

Bernard Telsey,
Telsey + Company
Casting

Kelly Devine
Associate Choreographer

Daryl Waters
Co-Orchestrator

Kenny J. Seymour
Music Director/Conductor

Michael Keller
Music Coordinator

Edgar Godineaux
Associate Choreographer

Guy Kwan, John Paull III, Hillary Blanken,
Kevin Broomell, Ana Rose Greene,
Juniper Street Productions
Production Manager

Beatrice Terry
Associate Director

Randy Adams,
Junkyard Dog Productions
Producer

Kenny Alhadeff,
Junkyard Dog Productions
Producer

Sue Frost,
Junkyard Dog Productions
Producer

Barbara Freitag
Producer

Buddy Freitag
Producer

Marleen Alhadeff
Producer

Nick Demos,
Demos Bizar Entertainment
Producer

Tim Kashani,
Apples and Oranges Productions
Producer

Pamela Winslow Kashani,
Apples and Oranges Productions
Producer

Aubrey Dan,
Dancap Productions Inc.
Producer

Tony Ponturo
Producer

Lauren Doll
Producer

Linda and Bill Potter
Producers

John Gore,
CEO,
Broadway Across America
Producer

Thomas B. McGrath,
Chairman,
Broadway Across America
Producer

Patty Baker,
Good Productions
Producer

Loraine Alterman Boyle
Producer

Chase Mishkin
Producer

Remmel T. Dickinson
Producer

Vijay Vashee
Producer

Sita Vashee
Producer

Memphis

Ken Clay
Associate Producer

Marilynn Sheldon
Managing Director, The 5th Avenue Theatre

David Armstrong
Producing Artistic Director, The 5th Avenue Theatre

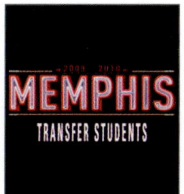

James Brown III
Ensemble

Tyrone A. Jackson
Swing

Betsy Struxness
Ensemble/ Double Dutch Girl

STAGE DOORMAN
Leon Mossen

HAIR
(L-R): Charlene Belmond, Mary Kay Yezerski-Bondoc, Cory McCutcheon, Michele Rutter

STAGE MANAGEMENT
(L-R): Monica Cuoco, Gary Mickelson, Arturo Porazzi

AUDIO
(L-R): Randy Morrison, Jens McVoy, Ty Lackey

Memphis

ELECTRICS, CARPENTERS, PROPS
Front Row (L-R): Peter Drummond, Scott "Gus" Poitras, Eric Norris, Gary Fernandez, Hank Hale, Bobby Miller, Joe Manoy, Geoff Vaughn

Back Row (L-R): Patrick Ainge, Jim Spradling, Randy Morrison, John Paull, Tommy Maher, Donnie Wright, Tommy Manoy

FRONT OF HOUSE STAFF
Front Row (L-R): Karen Diaz, Henry Bethea, Maura Gaynor, Susan Maxwell, Stephen Ivelja

Middle Row (L-R): Joanne Blessington, Alexis Stewart, Elizabeth Reed, Elvis Caban, Paul Rodriguez

Back Row (L-R): Delia Pozo, Melvin Caban, Tomas Ortiz, Katherine Benoit, Erin O'Donnell

WARDROBE
(L-R): Kim Kaldenberg, Maureen George, Jim Hodun, Charles van de Craats (in back), Dora Bonilla, Maureen Leshley, Rick Ortiz, Betty Gillespie and Debbie Cheretun

Memphis

(L-R): Derrick Baskin, Cass Morgan, James Monroe Iglehart
Photo by Joan Marcus

STAFF for *MEMPHIS*

GENERAL MANAGEMENT
ALCHEMY PRODUCTION GROUP
Carl Pasbjerg   Frank P. Scardino

COMPANY MANAGER
Jim Brandeberry

PRODUCTION MANAGEMENT
JUNIPER STREET PRODUCTIONS
Hillary Blanken   Guy Kwan
Kevin Broomell   Ana Rose Greene

GENERAL PRESS REPRESENTATIVE
THE HARTMAN GROUP
Michael Hartman
Juliana Hannett   Frances White

CASTING
TELSEY + COMPANY
Bernie Telsey CSA, Will Cantler CSA, David Vaccari CSA,
Bethany Knox CSA, Craig Burns CSA,
Tiffany Little Canfield CSA, Rachel Hoffman CSA,
Carrie Rosson CSA, Justin Huff CSA, Bess Fifer CSA,
Patrick Goodwin CSA, Abbie Brady-Dalton

MARKETING
TYPE A MARKETING
Anne Rippey   Nick Pramik   Janette Roush
Nina Bergelson

ASSOCIATE DIRECTOR
Beatrice Terry

ASSOCIATE CHOREOGRAPHER
Edgar Godineaux

Production Stage Manager ....Arturo E. Porazzi
Stage Manager ....Gary Mickelson
Assistant Stage Manager ....Monica A. Cuoco
Assistant Company Manager ....Tegan Meyer
Junkyard Dog Associate ....Carolyn D. Miller
Associate to the General Managers ....Sherra Johnston
Dance Captain ....Jermaine R. Rembert
Assistant Dance Captain ....Dionne Figgins
Assistant Fight Director ....Shad Ramsey
Fight Captain ....Jermaine Rembert
Dramaturg ....Gabriel Greene
Dialect Coach ....Stephen Gabis
Make-Up Designer ....Angelina Avallone
Associate Scenic Designer ....Steven C. Kemp
Associate Costume Designer ....Rory Powers
Associate Lighting Designer ....Mark Simpson
Associate Hair Designer ....Leah Loukas
Assistant Costume Designer ....Maria Zamansky
Assistant to the Costume Designer ....Kara Harmon
Assistant to the Lighting Designer ....Amanda Zieve
Assistant Sound Designer ....Alex Hawthorn
Assistant Projection Designer ....Steve Channon
Moving Light Programmer ....David Arch
Projections Programmer ....Florian Mosleh
Production/Head Carpenter ....Hank Hale
Flyman ....Erik Hansen
Assistant Carpenter (Automation) ......Scott "Gus" Poitras
Production Electrician ....James Fedigan
Head Electrician ....Patrick Ainge
Production Property Master ....Mike Pilipski
Head Property Master ....John Paull
Assistant Property Master ....Peter Drummond
Production Sound Engineer ....Phillip Lojo
FOH Sound Engineer ....Ty Lackey
Assistant Sound Engineer ....Jens McVoy
Wardrobe Supervisor ....Deborah Cheretun
Associate Wardrobe Supervisor ....Fred Castner
Dressers ....Dora Bonilla, Maureen George,
Betty Gillespie, James Hodun,
Franklin Hollenbeck, Kim Kaldenberg,
Franc Weinperl, Kyle Wesson
Hair Supervisor ....Michele Rutter
Assistant Hair Supervisor ....Cory McCutcheon
Hair Stylists ....Mary Kay Yezerski-Bondoc,
Charlene Belmond
Music Copying ....Christopher Deschene
Keyboard Programmer ....Kenny J. Seymour
Music Assistant ....Clare Cooper
Rehearsal Drummer ....Clayton Craddock
Production Assistants .....Megan J. Alvord, Meg Friedman
Scenic/Projection Studio Manager ....Sarah Zeitler
Production Intern ....Kendra Stockton
Lighting Interns ....Avery Lewis, Jeff Kastenbaum
Scenic Design Interns ....Tiffany Dalian, Caite Hevner
Projection Design Intern ....Wolfram Ott
Sound Interns ....Stephanie Celustka, Cynthia Hannon
Physical Therapy ....Performing Arts Physical Therapy
Advertising ....Spotco/
Drew Hodges, Jim Edwards,
Tom Greenwald, Jim Aquino, Stacey Maya
Website/Internet Marketing ....Spotco/
Sara Fitzpatrick, Matt Wilstein,
Marc Mettler, Christina Sees
Production Photographer ....Joan Marcus
Accountant ....Fried & Kowgios LLC
Controller ....Joe Kabula
Legal Counsel ....Beigelman Feldman & Associates PC
Payroll Services ....Castellana Services, Inc.
Banking...TD Bank
Insurance .........D.R. Rieff & Associates/Sonny Everett
Hotel Broker ....Road Concierge/
Lisa Morris
Air Travel Broker ....Tzell Travel/
Andi Henig
Opening Night
  Coordination ....The Lawrence Company Events
Merchandising ....Marquee Merchandise, LLC/
Matt Murphy
Theatre Displays ....King Displays Inc.

CREDITS

Scenery constructed by Showman Fabricators, Inc., Long Island City, NY. Show control and scenic motion control featuring Stage Command® Systems by PRG Scenic Technologies, New Windsor, NY. Additional scenery painted by Scenic Arts Studios, Cornwall, NY. Soft goods built by I. Weiss and Sons, Inc., Long Island City, NY. Lighting equipment provided by PRG Lighting, North Bergen, NJ. Sound equipment provided by Masque Sound, East Rutherford, NJ. Projection equipment provided by Scharff Weisberg Inc., Long Island City, NY. Props built by the Spoon Group, Rahway, NJ. Ms. Glover and Ms. Morgan's costumes by Donna Langman. Additional ladies costumes by Euro Co Costumes, Inc.; D. Barak Stribling; Tricorne, Inc.; and Eric Winterling, Inc. Mr. Kimball, Mr. Calloway, and Mr. Iglehart's tailoring by Brian Hemesath. Additional men's tailoring by Jennifer Love Costumes, Inc.; Scafati, Inc.; and D. L. Cerney. Men's finale suits by Top Hat Imagewear. Custom shirts by Cego. Dance shoes by Worldtone Dance. 'Gator' head by Rodney Gordon, Inc. ©Ernest C. Withers Estate, courtesy Panopticon Gallery, Boston, MA: Dewey Phillips of WHQB, Red Hot and Blue Program, The Hippodrome, Beale Street, Memphis, early 1950s #LV61C. Clarence Gatemouth Brown at Club Handy, Memphis, TN. Count Basie, Ruth Brown, Billy Eckstine, The Hippodrome, 1950s. Percy Mayfield (with drumsticks) and band, The Hippodrome, 1951. Special thanks to Edgar Godineaux, Gabriel Barre, Sarah Nashman, Kent Nicholson, Marilynn Sheldon, TeamTastic, Adam Arian, Mo Brady, Michael Finkle, Debra Hatch, Sue Makkoo and the many folks that made it happen at NSMT, TheatreWorks, La Jolla Playhouse and the 5th Avenue Theatre.

THE SHUBERT ORGANIZATION, INC.
Board of Directors

Philip J. Smith	**Robert E. Wankel**
Chairman	President
Wyche Fowler, Jr.	**John W. Kluge**
Lee J. Seidler	**Michael I. Sovern**

Stuart Subotnick

Elliot Greene	**David Andrews**
Chief Financial	Senior Vice President –
Officer	Shubert Ticketing
Juan Calvo	**John Darby**
Vice President	Vice President –
and Controller	Facilities
Peter Entin	**Charles Flateman**
Vice President –	Vice President –
Theatre Operations	Marketing
Anthony LaMattina	**Brian Mahoney**
Vice President –	Vice President –
Audit & Production Finance	Ticket Sales

D.S. Moynihan
Vice President – Creative Projects

House Manager ....Brian Gaynair

Memphis
SCRAPBOOK

1. (L-R): Composer David Bryan, leads Montego Glover and Chad Kimball, and librettist Joe DiPietro at a concert performance in Shubert Alley.
2. Members of the cast at Avatar Studios November 16, 2009 to record the original cast album.
3. *Yearbook* correspondent Derrick Baskin at the Hard Rock Cafe for the cast party.
4. Curtain calls on opening night.

Correspondent: Derrick Baskin, "Gator"
Memorable Opening Night Letter: Cass Morgan wrote one that said, "I love watching you on stage."
Memorable Opening Night Gift: Composer David Bryan and book writer Joe DiPietro gave the cast necklaces holding a record with the engraving "*Memphis*! 10-19-09 Opening Night! The Shubert Theatre." Really nice gift.
Celebrity Visitor: Whoopi Goldberg! After the show, I asked her if she had a good time and she said, "What?! You didn't see me out there in the audience smiling?! I LOVED IT!!"
Who Got the Gypsy Robe: John Jellison.
"Easter Bonnet" Skit: Choreographed by Ephraim Sykes.
Who Performs the Most Roles in This Show: John Jellison, 7 roles!! Crazy!
Most Shows in Their Career: Shocker. John Jellison, 18 Broadway shows!!
Backstage Ritual: After the opening number Ephraim Sykes, Daniel Watts, James Brown III, and myself travel from stage left to stage right and each of us pass John Eric Parker. We walk past him in a certain order and each have a particular saying we do with him. Ephraim says mmm-hmm in a high-pitched voice, followed by JB III's mmm-hmm in a low-pitched voice, followed by me giving John Eric a high-five, and anchored by Daniel Watt's low-five. We do that every show! Every show.
Favorite Moment During Each Performance: Michael McGrath, J. Bernard Calloway and I always share a joke before our entrance in Act II. Michael is a funny man.
Favorite Snack Foods: Plantain chips, animal cookies and a juice box.

Favorite Gathering Place: My dressing room.
Off-Site Hangout: We gravitated to Emmett's and Angus McIndoe on 44th, across the street from the theatre.
Mascot: GATOR, of course
Favorite Therapy: Nothing beats a good yoga class and massage!
Memorable Ad-lib: "One if by land, two if by sea, my Lord! Hold my mule while I shout!" During the church scene! LOL
Record Number of Cell Phone Rings: Around 8-10 cell phone rings, texts and photos in one show! Oy vey!
Web Buzz on Our Show: I didn't realize there was so much internet buzz until I Googled the show! WOW!!! Overwhelming.
Memorable Press Encounter: Walking the red carpet and doing the press junket for the first time. So cool!
Memorable Stage Door Fan Encounter: Someone said to me, "OMG I loved you in *Spelling Bee* and *Mermaid*...what's your name again?"
Latest Audience Arrival: About 15 minutes.
Fastest Costume Change: Chad Kimball has a 26-27-second costume change.
Busiest Day at the Box Office: During the holiday season we had a day when more than 200 people walked up to the box office for that day's show! We had to hold the curtain for everyone to get in.
Who Wears the Hottest Costumes: The ensemble men dance in wool suits at the top of Act II! They're usually drenched after 2-3 minutes.
Who Wears the Least: Montego Glover wears the least: '50s lingerie!

Insider Catchphrase: "Make that water break."
Most Instruments Played by One Musician: Three instruments by our reed player: tenor and bari-sax and bass clarinet.
Most Consecutive Performances by a Musician Without a Sub: Our music director.
Favorite Backstage Parody Lyrics: "Do you want some tacos? Yes I want some tacos! Do you want some tacos? YEAH!!" Sung to the Gator Dance.
Memorable Stage Direction: "You know that thing I told you to do here? Yeah, don't do that."
Company In-Joke: There is a box that I roll on stage. We refer to this box as "The Juilliard Box" because it has more moves and blocking on stage than some trained Broadway actors!
Understudy Anecdote: When Bryan Fenkart was on for Chad Kimball. He was in the radio booth during a scene and as James Iglehart was squeegeeing the window, Bryan stuck his head right through said window. There's an imaginary window there, Bryan. Try not to stick your head through it. Kinda ruins the picture. LOL.
Nicknames: Dan'yelle Williamson: "Foots." LaQuet Sharnell: "Liquidacious." Tracee Beazer: "Hoops."
Embarrassing Moment: During my and J. Bernard's scene, he made me laugh so hard I forgot my lines. The audience got a kick out of that.
Superstition: Daniel Watts is superstitious about kissing Dionne Figgins on her shoulder every show because the one time he didn't everything went awry.
Coolest Thing About Being in This Show: No brainer! I get to sing music written by a real bona fide rockstar!!!!

Million Dollar Quartet

First Preview: March 13, 2010. Opened: April 11, 2010.
Still playing as of May 31, 2010.

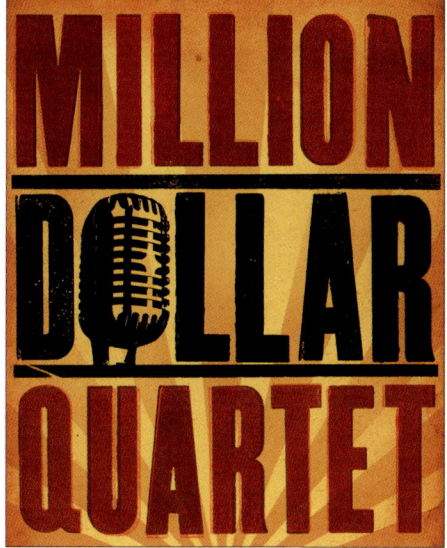

CAST
(in order of appearance)

Carl Perkins	ROBERT BRITTON LYONS
Johnny Cash	LANCE GUEST
Jerry Lee Lewis	LEVI KREIS
Elvis Presley	EDDIE CLENDENING
Sam Phillips	HUNTER FOSTER
Dyanne	ELIZABETH STANLEY

UNDERSTUDIES
For Johnny Cash:
CHRISTOPHER RYAN GRANT
For Elvis Presley, Carl Perkins:
ERIK HAYDEN
For Jerry Lee Lewis, Carl Perkins:
JARED MASON
For Dyanne:
VICTORIA MATLOCK
For Sam Phillips:
JAMES MOYE

Production Stage Manager:
ROBERT WITHEROW
Assistant Stage Managers:
CAROLYN KELSON, ERIK HAYDEN

TIME:
December 4, 1956
PLACE:
Sun Records, Memphis

NEDERLANDER THEATRE
UNDER THE DIRECTION OF
JAMES M. NEDERLANDER AND JAMES L. NEDERLANDER

RELEVANT THEATRICALS, JOHN COSSETTE PRODUCTIONS, AMERICAN POP ANTHOLOGY,
BROADWAY ACROSS AMERICA AND JAMES L. NEDERLANDER
PRESENT

MILLION DOLLAR QUARTET

BOOK BY **COLIN ESCOTT & FLOYD MUTRUX**

ORIGINAL CONCEPT AND DIRECTION BY **FLOYD MUTRUX**

INSPIRED BY
ELVIS PRESLEY, JOHNNY CASH, JERRY LEE LEWIS AND CARL PERKINS

FEATURING
EDDIE CLENDENING   LANCE GUEST   LEVI KREIS   ROBERT BRITTON LYONS

WITH
ELIZABETH STANLEY
AND
HUNTER FOSTER

SCENIC DESIGN	COSTUME DESIGN	LIGHTING DESIGN	SOUND DESIGN
DEREK McLANE	JANE GREENWOOD	HOWELL BINKLEY	KAI HARADA
HAIR AND WIG DESIGN	**ASSOCIATE MUSIC SUPERVISOR**		**CASTING**
TOM WATSON	AUGUST ERIKSMOEN		TELSEY + COMPANY
MARKETING DIRECTOR	**PRESS REPRESENTATION**		**MARKETING**
CAROL CHIAVETTA	BONEAU/BRYAN-BROWN		ALLIED LIVE, LLC
PRODUCTION STAGE MANAGER	**PRODUCTION MANAGER**		**GENERAL MANAGEMENT**
ROBERT WITHEROW	JUNIPER STREET PRODUCTIONS		ALAN WASSER · ALLAN WILLIAMS

MUSICAL ARRANGEMENTS AND SUPERVISION
CHUCK MEAD

DIRECTED BY
ERIC SCHAEFFER

DEVELOPED AND PRODUCED AT VILLAGE THEATRE, ISSAQUAH, WASHINGTON
ROBB HUNT, PRODUCER · STEVE TOMKINS, ARTISTIC DIRECTOR

ORIGINALLY PRESENTED BY SEASIDE MUSIC THEATER
TIPPIN DAVIDSON, PRODUCER
LESTER MALIZIA, ARTISTIC DIRECTOR

(L-R): Levi Kreis, Elizabeth Stanley, Eddie Clendening, Hunter Foster, Lance Guest and Robert Britton Lyons

Photo by Joan Marcus

Million Dollar Quartet

MUSICAL NUMBERS

"Blue Suede Shoes"	COMPANY
"Real Wild Child"	JERRY LEE LEWIS
"Matchbox"	CARL PERKINS
"Who Do You Love?"	CARL PERKINS
"Folsom Prison Blues"	JOHNNY CASH
"Fever"	DYANNE
"Memories Are Made of This"	ELVIS PRESLEY
"That's All Right"	ELVIS PRESLEY
"Brown Eyed Handsome Man"	COMPANY
"Down by the Riverside"	COMPANY
"Sixteen Tons"	JOHNNY CASH
"My Babe"	CARL PERKINS
"Long Tall Sally"	ELVIS PRESLEY
"Peace in the Valley"	COMPANY
"I Walk the Line"	JOHNNY CASH
"I Hear You Knocking"	DYANNE
"Party"	CARL PERKINS & COMPANY
"Great Balls of Fire"	JERRY LEE LEWIS
"Down by the Riverside" (Reprise)	COMPANY
"Hound Dog"	ELVIS PRESLEY
"Riders in the Sky"	JOHNNY CASH
"See You Later Alligator"	CARL PERKINS
"Whole Lotta Shakin' Goin' On"	JERRY LEE LEWIS

(L-R): Levi Kreis, Robert Britton Lyons, Corey Kaiser, Eddie Clendening and Lance Guest

ORCHESTRA
Bass:
COREY KAISER
Drummer:
LARRY LELLI

Additional arrangements by
LEVI KREIS

Eddie Clendening
Elvis Presley

Lance Guest
Johnny Cash

Levi Kreis
Jerry Lee Lewis

Robert Britton Lyons
Carl Perkins

Elizabeth Stanley
Dyanne

Hunter Foster
Sam Phillips

Christopher Ryan Grant
u/s Johnny Cash

Erik Hayden
u/s Elvis Presley, u/s Carl Perkins, Assistant Stage Manager

Jared Mason
u/s Jerry Lee Lewis, u/s Carl Perkins

Victoria Matlock
u/s Dyanne

James Moye
u/s Sam Phillips

Corey Kaiser
Bass

Larry Lelli
Drummer

Eric Schaeffer
Director

Million Dollar Quarter

Colin Escott
Co-Author

Floyd Mutrux
Co-Author, Original Concept and Direction

Derek McLane
Scenic Design

Howell Binkley
Lighting Design

Jane Greenwood
Costume Design

Kai Harada
Sound Design

Chuck Mead
Musical Arrangements and Supervision

Michael Keller
Music Contractor

Tom Watson
Hair and Wig Design

David Ruttura
Assistant Director

Bernard Telsey,
Telsey + Company
Casting

Alan Wasser
General Management

Guy Kwan, John Paull III, Hillary Blanken, Kevin Broomell, Ana Rose Greene, Juniper Street Productions
Production Manager

Gigi Pritzker,
Relevant Theatricals
Producer

Ted Rawlins,
Relevant Theatricals
Producer

John Cossette
Productions
Producer

John Gore,
CEO,
Broadway Across America
Producer

Thomas B. McGrath,
Chairman,
Broadway Across America
Producer

James L.
Nederlander
Producer

BOX OFFICE
(L-R): Keshave Sattaur, Anne Huston, Augie Pugliese

WARDROBE & HAIR
Ryan Rossetto, Shanah Ann Kendall, Francine Schwartz-Buryiak, Aughra Moon

Photos by Brian Mapp

The Playbill Broadway Yearbook 2009-2010

Million Dollar Quartet

2009-2010 AWARDS

TONY AWARD
Best Featured Actor in a Musical
(Levi Kreis)

OUTER CRITICS CIRCLE AWARD
Outstanding Featured Actor in a Musical
(Levi Kreis)

CREW
(L-R): Robert Witherow, Johnny Van, Joe Ferreri Jr,. Billy Wright Jr., Patrick Pummill, Aaron Straus

FRONT OF HOUSE STAFF
Front Row (L-R): Louise Angelino, Veronica Figaroa, Ralph Hendrix, Iris Cortes, Elena Mavoides, Renee Fleetwood

Middle Row (L-R): John Rowe, Austin Presanda, Brian Baeza, Erin

Back Row (L-R): Katie Spillane, Marlon Pichardo, Kyle Luker, Mike Rios

---

STAFF FOR MILLION DOLLAR QUARTET

GENERAL MANAGEMENT
ALAN WASSER ASSOCIATES
Alan Wasser   Allan Williams
Mark Shacket   Dawn Kusinski

COMPANY MANAGER
Jolie Gabler

GENERAL PRESS REPRESENTATIVE
BONEAU/BRYAN-BROWN
Adrian Bryan-Brown   Aaron Meier   Amy Kass

CASTING
TELSEY + COMPANY
Bernie Telsey CSA, Will Cantler CSA, David Vaccari CSA, Bethany Knox CSA, Craig Burns CSA, Tiffany Little Canfield CSA, Rachel Hoffman CSA, Carrie Rosson CSA, Justin Huff CSA, Bess Fifer CSA, Patrick Goodwin CSA, Abbie Brady-Dalton

PRODUCTION MANAGEMENT
Juniper Street Productions
Hillary Blanken   Kevin Broomell
Guy Kwan   Ana Rose Greene   Sue Semaan

ASSISTANT DIRECTOR
David Ruttura

ASSOCIATE PRODUCERS FOR BROADWAY ACROSS AMERICA
Jennifer Costello   Sara Skolnick

UK CONSULTING PRODUCERS
Joseph Smith/Michael McCabe

JAPAN CONSULTING PRODUCER
TBS Services, Inc.

Production Stage Manager	Robert Witherow
Stage Manager	Carolyn Kelson
Associate Set Designer	Shoko Kambara
Associate Costume Designer	Moria Clinton
Associate Lighting Designer	Ryan O'Gara
Assistant Lighting Designers	Amanda Zieve, Sean Beach
Music Contractor	Michael Keller
Production Carpenter	Todd Frank
Advance Carpenter	John Riggins
Automation Carpenter	Scott "Gus" Poitras

Million Dollar Quarter

Production Electricians	James J. Fedigan, Randall Zaibek
Head Electrician	Ron Martin
Production Sound Engineer	Patrick Pummill
Production Properties Supervisor	Will Sweeney
Moving Light Programmer	David Arch
Wardrobe Supervisor	Ryan Rossetto
Dresser	Francine Buryiak
Hair & Wig Supervisor	Shanah-Ann Kendall
Guitars provided by	Gibson Guitar Corporation
Bass provided by	Engelhardt-Link
Drums provided by	Yamaha Corporation of America
Drum Heads provided by	Remo Drumheads
Cymbals provided by	Sabian Cymbals
Makeup by	M•A•C Cosmetics
Makeup Consultant	Ashley Ryan
Technical Production Assistants	Alexandra Paull, Steve Chazaro, Jennie Bownan
Legal Counsel	Levine Plotkin & Menin, LLP/ Loren H. Plotkin, Cris Criswell Loeb & Loeb LLP/Douglas Mirell
Accountant	Rosenberg, Neuwirth & Kuchner, CPAs/Christopher Cacace, Marina Flom, Kirill Baytalskiy
Advertising	Spotco/Drew Hodges, Jim Edwards, Tom Greenwald, Stephen Sosnowski, Meghan Ownbey
Marketing	Carol Chiavetta, Elizabeth Kandel Allied Live/ Tanya Grubich, Victoria Cairl, Sara Rosenzweig
Website Design	Spotco/ Sara Fitzpatrick, Matt Wilstein, Stephen Santore
Payroll Services	Castellana Services, Inc.
Production Photographer	Joan Marcus
Management Associate	Mark Barna
General Management Office	Christopher Betz, Jake Hirzel, Jennifer Mudge, Aurora Segura
Opening Night Coordination	The Lawrence Company/ Michael Lawrence
Banking	Signature Bank, Barbara von Borstel, Margaret Monigan, Mary Ann Fanelli
Insurance	DeWitt Stern Group, Inc./ Peter Shoemaker, Cathy Dumancela
Rehearsed at	New 42nd Street Studios
Theatre Displays	King Displays
Merchandising	Creative Goods Merchandise/ Pete Milano, Jennifer Alam
Tour Bookings	The Booking Group/ Meredith Blair

SPECIAL THANKS

John R. Cash Revocable Trust. Johnny Cash is a registered trademark of John R. Cash Revocable Trust. Image and likeness of Johnny Cash used with permission.

Jerry Lee Lewis™, The Killer ™ and the image and likeness of Jerry Lee Lewis are used with permission. Courtesy Pont Neuf, Inc.

Carl Perkins Enterprises. Image and likeness of Carl Perkins used with permission.

Elvis Presley Enterprises, Inc. Elvis Presley is a registered trademark of EPE, Inc. Image and likeness of Elvis Presley used with permission.

CREDITS

Scenery and scenic effects built and electrified by PRG Scenic Technologies, New Windsor, NY. Scenery painted by Scenic Art Studios, Cornwall, NY. Costumes built by Eric Winterling, Inc. Show control and scenic motion control featuring Stage Command Systems® by PRG Scenic Technologies, New Windsor, NY. Lighting equipment provided by PRG Lighting, North Bergen, NJ. Sound equipment provided by PRG Audio, Mt. Vernon, NY. Music license consulting by Jill Meyers.

MUSIC COPYRIGHTS

"Blue Suede Shoes" (Carl Perkins), ©MPL Music Publishing Inc. All rights reserved. Used by permission of Wren Music Co. o/b/o Carl Perkins Music Inc. "Real Wild Child" (John Greenan, John O'Keefe, David Owens), ©MPL Music Publishing Inc. All rights reserved. Used by permission of Wren Music Co. "Matchbox" (Carl Perkins), ©MPL Music Publishing Inc. All rights reserved. Used by permission of Wren Music Co. o/b/o Carl Perkins Music Inc. "Who Do You Love?" (Ellas McDaniel), ©ARC Music Corp. All rights reserved. Used by permission. "Folsom Prison Blues" written by John R. Cash. Published by House of Cash, Inc. Administered by Bug Music Inc. All rights reserved. Used by permission. "Fever" (John Davenport, Eddie Cooley), ©Carlin America Music/Windswept Pacific Music Publishing. Published by Fort Knox Music, Inc. All rights reserved. Used by permission. "Memories Are Made of This" (Richard Dehr, Terry Gilkyson, Frank Miller), ©EMI Blackwood Music, Inc. (BMI). All rights reserved. Used by permission. "That's All Right" (Arthur Crudup), ©1947 (renewed). Unichappell Music Inc. (BMI) and Crudup Music (BMI). All rights administered by Unichappell Music Inc. All rights reserved. Used by permission. "Brown Eyed Handsome Man" (Chuck Berry), ©Arc Music Corp. All rights reserved. Used by permission. "Down by the Riverside" (Traditional; arranged by Chuck Mead), ©Zoilink Music. All rights administered by Coburn Music. All rights reserved. Used by permission. "Sixteen Tons" (Merle Travis), ©Merle's Girls Music. All rights reserved. Used by permission. "My Babe" (Willie Dixon), ©Bug Music, Inc. o/b/o Hoochie Coochie Music (BMI). All rights reserved. Used by permission. "Long Tall Sally" (Robert Blackwell, Enotris Johnson, Richard Penniman), ©Sony/ATV Music Publishing LLC. All rights reserved. Used by permission. "(There Will Be) Peace in the Valley for Me" (Thomas A. Dorsey), ©(renewed) 1939 Warner-Tamerlane Publishing Corp. (BMI). All rights reserved. Used by permission. "I Walk the Line" written by John R. Cash. Published by House of Cash, Inc. Administered by Bug Music Inc. All rights reserved. Used by permission. "I Hear You Knocking" (Dave Bartholomew, Pearl King), ©EMI Unart Catalog Inc. All rights reserved. Used by permission. "Party" (Jessie Mae Robinson), ©MPL Music Publishing Inc. All rights reserved. Used by permission. "Great Balls of Fire" (Otis Blackwell, Jack Hammer), ©1957 (renewed), Unichappell Music Inc. (BMI), Mijac Music (BMI), Chappell & Co., Inc. (ASCAP) and Mystical Light Music (ASCAP). All rights reserved on behalf of itself and Mijac Music, administered by Unichappell Music Inc. All rights reserved on behalf of itself and Mystical Light Music, administered by Chappell & Co., Inc. All rights reserved. Used by permission. "Hound Dog" (Jerry Leiber and Mike Stoller). Published by Sony/ATV Songs LLC. Copyright 1953 Sony/ATV Music Publishing LLC. All rights administered by Sony/ATV Music Publishing LLC, 8 Music Square West, Nashville TN 37203. All rights reserved. Used by permission. "Riders in the Sky" (Stan Jones), ©MPL Music Publishing Inc. All rights reserved. Used by permission of Edwin H. Morris & Company. "See You Later Alligator" (Robert Guidry), ©]Arc Music Corp. All rights reserved. Used by permission. "Whole Lotta Shakin' Goin' On" (Curly Williams), ©1997 N'Mani Entertainment Co. (ASCAP). All rights reserved. Used by permission.

To learn more about the production, please visit www.MillionDollarQuartetLive.com
Find us on Facebook.
Follow us on Twitter @MillionDQuartet

NEDERLANDER

Chairman	James M. Nederlander
President	James L. Nederlander

Executive Vice President
Nick Scandalios

Vice President Corporate Development **Charlene S. Nederlander**	Senior Vice President Labor Relations **Herschel Waxman**
Vice President **Jim Boese**	Chief Financial Officer **Freida Sawyer Belviso**

STAFF FOR THE NEDERLANDER THEATRE

House Manager	Louise Angelino
Treasurer	Gary Kenny
Assistant Treasurer	Keshave Sattaur
House Carpenter	Joseph Ferreri Sr.
Flyman	Joseph Ferreri Jr.
House Electrician	Richard Beck
House Properties	William Wright

(L-R): Hunter Foster and Levi Kreis

Photo by Joan Marcus

The Miracle Worker

First Preview: February 12, 2010. Opened: March 3, 2010.
Closed April 4, 2010 after 21 Previews and 28 Performances.

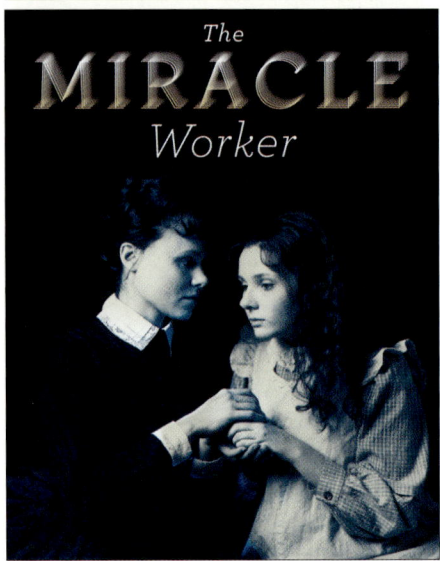

CAST
(in alphabetical order)

Helen Keller	ABIGAIL BRESLIN
Jimmie	LANCE CHANTILES-WERTZ
Percy	MICHAEL CUMMINGS
Aunt Ev	ELIZABETH FRANZ
Viney	YVETTE GANIER
Martha	SIMONE JOY JONES
Captain Keller	MATTHEW MODINE
Kate Keller	JENNIFER MORRISON
Doctor/Anagnos	DANIEL ORESKES
Annie Sullivan	ALISON PILL
James	TOBIAS SEGAL

UNDERSTUDIES
For Percy, Martha: ARU BANKS
For Captain Keller, Doctor/Anagnos: BILL CHRIST
For Viney: SANDRA DALEY
For Annie Sullivan, Kate Keller: KATRINA LENK
For Jimmie: ANTHONY SCARPONE-LAMBERT
For Helen Keller: KYRA YNEZ SIEGEL

TIME:
1880s

PLACE:
In and around the Keller homestead
in Tuscumbia, Alabama;
also, briefly, the Perkins Institute for the Blind
in Boston

CIRCLE IN THE SQUARE
UNDER THE DIRECTION OF
THEODORE MANN and PAUL LIBIN
SUSAN FRANKEL, General Manager

DAVID RICHENTHAL ERIC FALKENSTEIN RANDALL L. WREGHITT
BARBARA & BUDDY FREITAG/DAN FRISHWASSER JOE & KATHY GRANO
MALLORY FACTOR CHERYL LACHOWICZ MARTHA FALKENBERG
BRUCE J. CARUSI & SUSAN ALTAMORE CARUSI DAVID & SHEILA LEHRER LYNN SHAW
in association with
CONNIE BARTLOW KRISTAN JAMIE deROY/REMMEL T. DICKINSON
Present

ABIGAIL BRESLIN   ALISON PILL

in

The MIRACLE Worker

By
WILLIAM GIBSON

Also Starring
JENNIFER MORRISON   ELIZABETH FRANZ

and
MATTHEW MODINE

Featuring
TOBIAS SEGAL DANIEL ORESKES MICHAEL CUMMINGS
SIMONE JOY JONES YVETTE GANIER LANCE CHANTILES-WERTZ

Scenic Design	Costume Design	Lighting Design	Original Music & Sound Design
DEREK McLANE	PAUL TAZEWELL	KENNETH POSNER	ROB MILBURN & MICHAEL BODEEN

Hair Design	Physical Coaching & Movement by	Production Stage Manager
CHARLES LaPOINTE	LEE SHER	J. PHILIP BASSETT

Casting by	Marketing	Company Manager	Production Management
JAY BINDER/ JACK BOWDAN	TYPE A MARKETING	PENELOPE DAULTON	JUNIPER STREET PRODUCTIONS KEVIN BROOMELL

Executive Producer	Associate Producers	Press Representation	General Management
RED AWNING	ROSALIND PRODUCTIONS, INC. PATTY BAKER/ANNA CZEKAJ GOODE PRODUCTIONS	BONEAU/BRYAN-BROWN	ALAN WASSER • ALLAN WILLIAMS AARON LUSTBADER

Directed by
KATE WHORISKEY

The producers wish to express their appreciation to Theatre Development Fund for its support of this production.

3/3/10

(L-R): Elizabeth Franz, Tobias Segal, Yvette Ganier, Matthew Modine, Jennifer Morrison, Abigail Breslin and Alison Pill

Photo by Joan Marcus

The Miracle Worker

Abigail Breslin
Helen Keller

Alison Pill
Annie Sullivan

Matthew Modine
Captain Keller

Jennifer Morrison
Kate Keller

Elizabeth Franz
Aunt Ev

Tobias Segal
James

Daniel Oreskes
Doctor/Anagnos

Michael Cummings
Percy

Simone Joy Jones
Martha

Yvette Ganier
Viney

Lance Chantiles-Wertz
Jimmie

Aru Banks
u/s Percy/Martha

Bill Christ
u/s Captain Keller, Doctor/Anagnos

Sandra Daley
u/s Viney

Katrina Lenk
u/s Annie Sullivan, Kate Keller

Anthony Scarpone-Lambert
u/s Jimmie

Kyra Ynez Siegel
u/s Helen Keller

William Gibson
Playwright

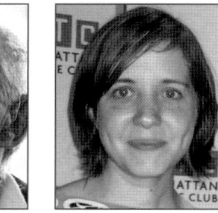
Kate Whoriskey
Director

Derek McLane
Scenic Design

Paul Tazewell
Costume Design

Kenneth Posner
Lighting Design

Rob Milburn and Michael Bodeen
Original Music & Sound Design

Lee Sher
Physical Coaching & Movement

Jay Binder CSA
Casting

Jack Bowdan CSA
Casting

Alan Wasser
General Manager

Guy Kwan, John Paull III, Hillary Blanken, Kevin Broomell, Ana Rose Greene, Juniper Street Productions
Production Management

Eric Falkenstein
Producer

Randall L. Wreghitt
Producer

Barbara Freitag
Producer

Buddy Freitag
Producer

Mallory Factor
Producer

The Miracle Worker

David Lehrer
Producer

Lynn Shaw
Producer

Jamie deRoy
Producer

Remmel T. Dickinson
Producer

Theodore Mann

Paul Libin

STAFF FOR THE MIRACLE WORKER

GENERAL MANAGEMENT
ALAN WASSER ASSOCIATES
Alan Wasser   Allan Williams   Aaron Lustbader

GENERAL PRESS REPRESENTATIVE
BONEAU/BRYAN-BROWN
Chris Boneau   Adrian Bryan-Brown
Joe Perrotta   Kelly Guiod

MARKETING DIRECTION
TYPE A MARKETING
Anne Rippey   Nick Pramik
Janette Roush   Nina Bergelson

PRODUCTION MANAGEMENT
JUNIPER STREET PRODUCTIONS
Hillary Blanken   Kevin Broomell
Guy Kwan   Ana Rose Greene

CASTING
JAY BINDER CASTING
Jay Binder CSA
Jack Bowdan CSA, Mark Brandon, Sara Schatz CSA,
Nikole Vallins
Assistants: Karen Young, Patrick Bell

COMPANY MANAGER
Penelope Daulton

PRODUCTION STAGE MANAGER
J. Philip Bassett

Stage Manager .... Amber Wedin
Gaga coaching to Ms. Breslin & Ms. Pill .... Lee Sher
Assistant Director .... Andrew Russell
Dialect Coach .... Deborah Hecht
Fight Consultant .... Ron Piretti
Associate Scenic Designer .... Shoko Kambara
Assistant Scenic Designer .... Erica Hemminger
Associate Costume Designer .... Daryl Stone
Associate Lighting Designer .... Philip Rosenberg
Associate Sound Designer .... Christopher Cronin
Assistant Sound Designer .... Valerie Spradling
Production Carpenter .... Anthony Menditto
Automation Carpenter .... David Cohen
Production Electrician .... Dan Coey
Production Properties .... Christopher Pantuso
Makeup Designer .... Cookie Jordan
Wardrobe Supervisor .... Eileen Miller
Dressers .... Laura Beattie, Barry Hoff
Hair & Makeup Supervisor .... Cory McCutcheon
Assistant Hair & Makeup .... Christina Grant

Chaperone .... Bridget Mills
Fight Captain .... Michael Izquierdo
Sign Language Consultant .... Anne Tomasetti
Advertising .... SpotCo/
Drew Hodges, Jim Edwards,
Tom Greenwald, Stephen Sosnowski
Website Design &
Internet Marketing .... Art Meets Commerce/
Jim Glaub, Laurie Connor,
Kevin Keating, Chip Meyrelles,
Whitney J. Manalio, Crystal Chase,
Brad Coffman, Marissa Coronado
Legal Counsel .... Franklin, Weinrib, Rudell & Vassallo/
Dan Wasser, Esq.
Accounting .... Rosenberg, Neuwirth & Kuchner/
Chris Cacace, Pat Pedersen
Assistant to Mr. Richenthal .... Emma Kingaby
Assistant to Mr. Falkenstein .... Jeffrey Golde
Assistant to Mr. Wreghitt .... Tom Keegan
Assistant General Manager .... Mark Barna
General Management Associates . Jake Hirzel, Lane Marsh,
Thom Mitchell, Mark Shacket
General Management Office .... Christopher Betz,
Dawn Kusinski, Patty Montesi,
Jennifer Mudge
Spark Productions Interns .... Jaki Silver, Heather Lanza
Wreghitt Productions Staff .... DR Mann Hanson,
Alexis Qualls
Production Photographer .... Joan Marcus
Artwork Photography .... John Dugdale
Production Assistant .... Raynelle Wright
Technical Production Assistant .... Alexandra Paull
Insurance .... Ventura Insurance Brokerage/
Christine Sadofsky
Banking .... Signature Bank/Barbara von Borstel
Payroll .... Castellana Services, Inc.
Children's Tutoring .... On Location Education
Merchandising .... Dewynters
Usability Consultant .... Christopher Roberts
Sponsorship Consultant .... Kim Styler
Niche Marketing/
Corporate Sponsorships .... Joe McGowan
Theatre Displays .... Bam Signs
Opening Night Coordination .... The Lawrence Company/
Michael Lawrence
Group Sales .... Telecharge.com Group Sales/
800-432-7780
TTY: 888-889-TKTS (8587)

CREDITS AND ACKNOWLEDGEMENTS

Scenery fabrication by Scenic Technologies, a division of Production Resource Group, LLC, New Windsor, NY. Show control and scenic motion control featuring Stage Command Systems® by Scenic Technologies, a division of Production Resource Group LLC, New Windsor, NY. Lighting equipment provided by PRG Lighting. Sound equipment provided by Sound Associates. Furniture and props executed by the Spoon Group. Costumes by Donna Langman Costumes; Tricorne, Inc.; Scafati Theatrical Tailors; Artur & Tailors, Inc. Millinery by Lynne Mackey Studio and Rodney Gordon Millinery. Rehearsed at 440 Studios.

Makeup provided by M·A·C

SPECIAL THANKS
American Foundation for the Blind, Helen Keller National Center, Sharon Jensen

www.MiracleWorkerOnBroadway.com

◯ CIRCLE IN THE SQUARE THEATRE
Thespian Theatre, Inc.
Under the direction of
Theodore Mann and Paul Libin
Susan Frankel, *General Manager*

House Manager .... Cheryl Dennis
Head Carpenter .... Anthony Menditto
Head Electrician .... Stewart Wagner
Prop Master .... Owen E. Parmele
FOH Sound Engineer .... Jim Bay
Box Office Treasurer .... Linda Canavan
Administrative Assistant .... Courtney Kochuba
Assistant to Paul Libin .... Clark Mims Tedesco
Assistant to Theodore Mann .... Eric P. Vitale

◯ CIRCLE IN THE SQUARE THEATRE SCHOOL

President .... Paul Libin
Artistic Director .... Theodore Mann
Theatre School Director .... E. Colin O'Leary
Arts Education/Development .... Jonathan Mann
Administrative Assistant .... David Pleva
Administrative Assistant .... Virginia Tuller

(L-R): Abigail Breslin and Alison Pill
Photo by Joan Marcus

234   The Playbill Broadway Yearbook 2009-2010

The Miracle Worker

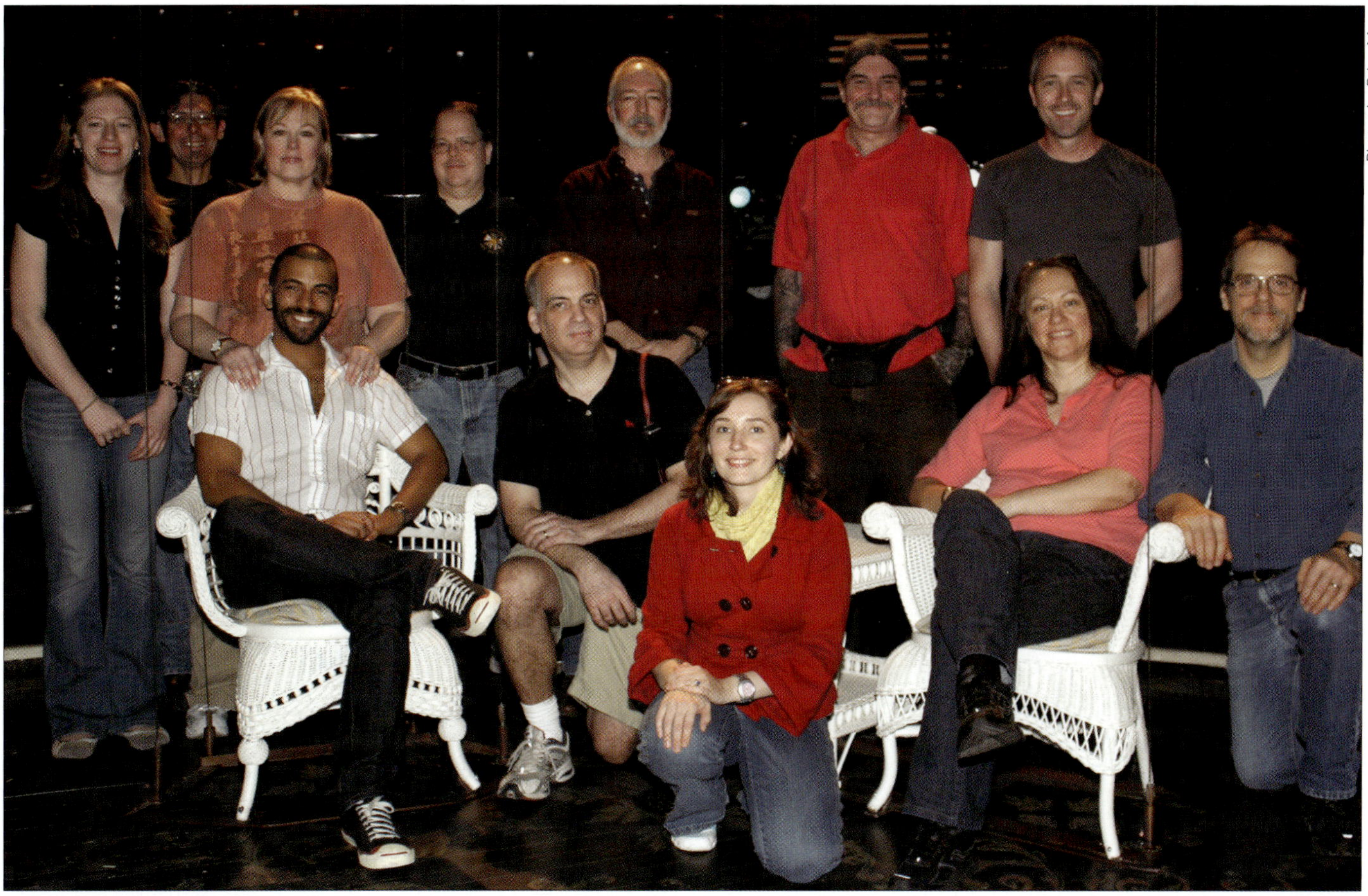

Photos by Brian Mapp

CREW and STAGE MANAGERS
Front Row (L-R): Cory McCutcheon, David Cohen, Christina Grant, Eileen Miller, Owen Parmele

Back Row (L-R): Amber Wedin, Tony Menditto, Laura Beattie, Jim Bay, Rob Dagna, Stewart Wagner, J. Philip Bassett

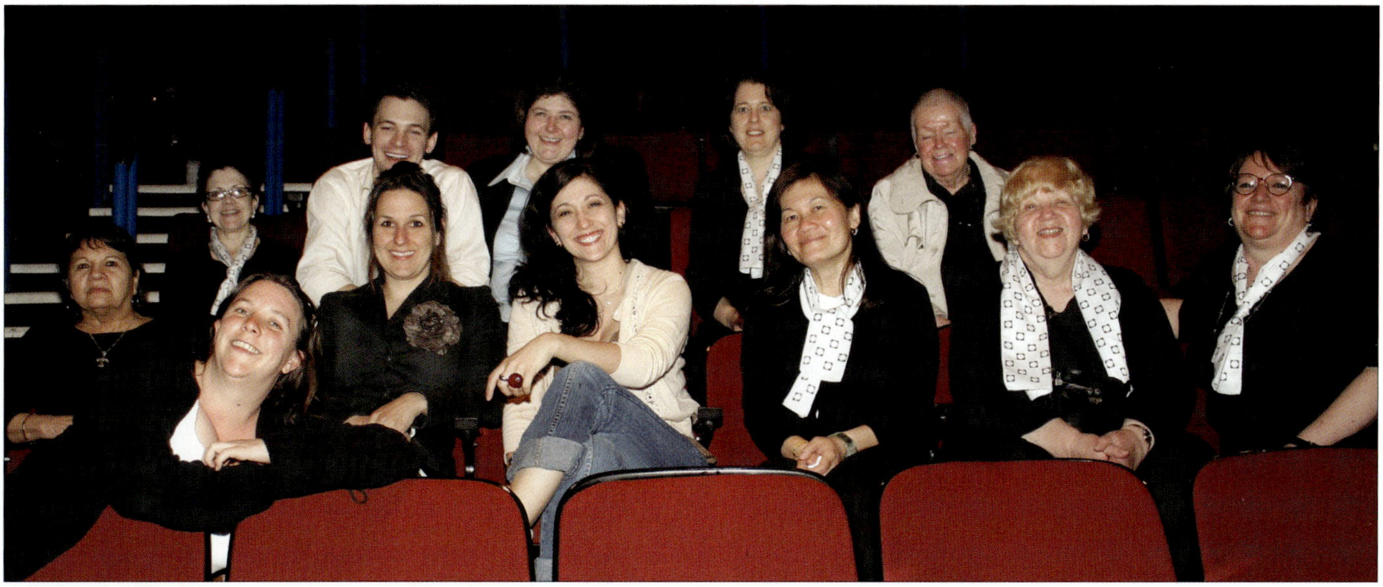

FRONT OF HOUSE STAFF
Front Row (L-R): Margarita Caban, Cheryl C. Dennis, Jennifer S, Ganske, Cristina Marie, Mei Y. Kohn, Laurel T. Brevoort, Patricia Cuocci

Back Row (L-R): Rosetta M. Jlelaty, Michael Liam Stabeno, Kelly Varley, Laura D. Middleton, Patricia A. Kennedy

Next Fall

First Preview: February 16, 2010. Opened: March 11, 2010.
Still running as of May 31, 2010.

CAST
(in order of appearance)

Holly	MADDIE CORMAN
Brandon	SEAN DUGAN
Arlene	CONNIE RAY
Butch	COTTER SMITH
Adam	PATRICK BREEN
Luke	PATRICK HEUSINGER

STANDBYS
For Adam/Butch:
DAVID ADKINS
For Luke/Brandon:
CLAYTON APGAR
For Holly/Arlene:
KRISTIE DALE SANDERS

2009-2010 AWARDS

OUTER CRITICS CIRCLE AWARD
John Gassner Award
for an American Play
preferably by a new playwright
(Geoffrey Nauffts)

THE HELEN HAYES THEATRE
MARTIN MARKINSON   DONALD TICK

Elton John and David Furnish
Barbara Manocherian   Richard Willis
Tom Smedes   Carole L. Haber/Chase Mishkin   Ostar   Anthony Barrile
Michael Palitz   Bob Boyett   James Spry/Catherine Schreiber
Probo Productions   Roy Furman

in association with
Naked Angels

PRESENT

next fall

BY

Geoffrey Nauffts

with

Patrick Breen   Maddie Corman   Sean Dugan
Patrick Heusinger   Connie Ray   Cotter Smith

SCENIC DESIGN	COSTUME DESIGN	LIGHTING DESIGN	ORIGINAL MUSIC AND SOUND DESIGN
Wilson Chin	Jess Goldstein	Jeff Croiter	John Gromada
CASTING	PRODUCTION STAGE MANAGER	PRESS REPRESENTATIVE	MARKETING, PROMOTIONAL & DIGITAL SERVICES
Howie Cherpakov, C.S.A.	Charles Means	Boneau/Bryan-Brown	Allied Live, LLC
PRODUCTION MANAGEMENT	EXECUTIVE PRODUCER	GENERAL MANAGEMENT	
Aurora Productions	Susan Mindell	Stuart Thompson Productions/ David Turner	

DIRECTED BY

Sheryl Kaller

The producers wish to express their appreciation to the Theatre Development Fund for its support of this production.

3/11/10

(L-R): Patrick Heusinger and Patrick Breen

Photo by Carol Rosegg

Next Fall

 Patrick Breen
Adam

 Maddie Corman
Holly

 Sean Dugan
Brandon

 Patrick Heusinger
Luke

 Connie Ray
Arlene

 Cotter Smith
Butch

 David Adkins
Standby for Adam/Butch

 Clayton Apgar
Standby for Luke/Brandon

 Kristie Dale Sanders
Standby for Holly/Arlene

 Geoffrey Nauffts
Playwright

 Sheryl Kaller
Director

 Wilson Chin
Scenic Design

 Jess Goldstein
Costume Design

 Jeff Croiter
Lighting Design

 John Gromada
Original Music and Sound Design

 Joe Langworth
Associate Director

 Tanya Grubich, Allied Live
Marketing, Promotional & Digital Services

 Laura Matalon, Allied Live
Marketing, Promotional & Digital Services

 Stuart Thompson Productions
General Management

 Elton John
Producer

 David Furnish
Producer

 Barbara Manocherian
Producer

 Richard Willis
Producer

 Chase Mishkin
Producer

 Bob Boyett
Producer

 Catherine Schreiber
Producer

 Roy Furman
Producer

STAGE MANAGEMENT
(L-R): Katrina Herrmann (Sub ASM/Production Assistant), Elizabeth Moloney (Stage Manager), Charles Means (Production Stage Manager)

Next Fall

(L-R): Patrick Heusinger, Cotter Smith and Patrick Breen

STAFF FOR *NEXT FALL*

GENERAL MANAGEMENT
STUART THOMPSON PRODUCTIONS
Stuart Thompson   David Turner   James Triner

COMPANY MANAGER
Bobby Driggers

PRODUCTION MANAGEMENT
AURORA PRODUCTIONS
Gene O'Donovan, Ben Heller
Rachel Sherbill, Jarid Sumner,
Melissa Mazdra, Amanda Raymond,
Graham Forden, Liza Luxenberg

PRESS REPRESENTATIVE
BONEAU/BRYAN-BROWN
Chris Boneau   Heath Schwartz   Michael Strassheim

MARKETING, PROMOTIONAL & DIGITAL SERVICES
ALLIED LIVE

FIGHT DIRECTOR
Drew Leary

Production Stage Manager	**Charles Means**
Stage Manager	Elizabeth Moloney
Associate Director	Joe Langworth
Associate Scenic Designer	Mikiko Suzuki MacAdams
Associate Costume Designer	China Lee
Associate Lighting Designer	Grant W.S. Yeager
Associate Sound Designer	Christopher Cronin
Assistant Sound Designer	Alex Neumann
Production Carpenter	Doug Purcell
Production Electrician	Joe Beck
Advance Props	Pete Sarafin
Production Props	Roger Keller
Production Sound	Bob Etter
Wardrobe Supervisor	James Strunk
Dresser	Katie Chihaby
Production Assistant	Katrina Herrmann
Production Intern	Sam Kramer
Costume Intern	Ramsey Scott
General Management Assistants	Geo Karapetyan, Brittany Levasseur
General Management Interns	Erin Byrne, Andrew Lowy
Assistant to Mr. Thompson	Christopher Taggart
Banking	City National Bank/Michele Gibbons
Payroll	Castellana Services, Inc.
Accountant	Fried & Kowgios CPA's LLP/Robert Fried, CPA
Controller	Joe Kubala
Insurance	Tanenbaum-Harber of Florida, LLC
Legal Counsel	Levine, Plotkin & Menin LLP
Advertising	SPOTCO/Drew Hodges, Jim Edwards, Tom Greenwald, Beth Watson, Tim Falotico
Production Photographer	Carol Rosegg
Theatre Displays	King Displays, Inc.
Transportation	IBA Limousines
Housing	Road Concierge/Lisa Morris

NAKED ANGELS STAFF

Artistic Director	Geoffrey Nauffts
Managing Director	John Alexander
Associate Artistic Director	Andy Donald
Producer	Brittany O'Neill

SPECIAL THANKS

Art Meets Commerce, Beth Israel Medical Center, The Blanche and Irving Laurie Foundation, Boris Berlin and Jacob Shnayder, Maria Boshetti and VANS, Matthew Broderick & Sarah Jessica Parker, Francesco Carrozzini, Jeff Davis, Suzi Dietz, Elizabeth Dowling, Bart Fasbender, Edie Falco, Tom Fontana, Joseph Gagliano, Jr, GLAAD, Mariska Hargitay, Michael Hewitson, Robert & Ashley Jansen, Al Larson, Richard Lobel - CBS Radio and CBS Outdoors, Jim Mandler, Rick Miramontez, The Naked Angels Board of Directors, Dave Nelson, Cynthia Nixon, Ken Olin & Patricia Wettig, John Pankow, Laura Peterson, Johanna Pfaelzer - New York Stage and Film, David Schwimmer, Frank Selvaggi & Bill Shea, Rebecca Spinac, Neil Patrick Stewart, Ben Stiller & Christine Taylor Stiller, True Love Productions, Jessica Wegener, Brian Willimans, Scott Zaretsky

CREDITS

Scenery and scenic effects built, painted and electrified by Show Motion, Inc., Norwalk, CT. Equipment supplied by Lights Up & Cue Sound, LLC, West Hempstead, NY. Sound equipment by Sound Associates. Prop furniture by Craig Grigg. Costumes by Studio Rouge. Makeup provided by M•A•C. Rehearsed at Manhattan Theatre Club's Creative Center.

THE HELEN HAYES THEATRE STAFF

Owned and Operated by Little Theatre Group LLC
Martin Markinson and Donald Tick

General Manager and Counsel	Susan S. Myerberg
House Manager	Alan R. Markinson
Engineer	Hector Angulo
Treasurer	David Heveran
Assoc. Gen. Manager	Sharon Fallon
Assistant Treasurer	Chuck Stuis
Head Ushers	John Biancamano, Linda Maley, Berd Vaval
Stage Door	Robert Seymour, Jonathan Angulo, Robert Seymour III
Accountant	Chen-Win Hsu, CPA, PC

Next Fall
Scrapbook

Correspondent: Sean Dugan, "Brandon"
Opening Night Gifts: Mariska's flowers, Whoopi's cookies and Elton & David's champagne.
Most Exciting Celebrity Visitor: Bishop Gene Robinson sharing his story and immense heart at a talkback.
Special Backstage Rituals: The Equity cots, the gay/straight high five with Chuck before the show, Patrick Heusinger's *Lion King* animals Off-Broadway.
Favorite Moment During Each Performance (On Stage or Off): Maddie: Right before the curtain goes up each night looking at Sean.
Connie: Giving Sean the Bible in the Temple scene.
Cotter: My look with Sean in the hospital scene.
Patrick Breen: The scene in the park with Sean.
Favorite In-Theatre Gathering Place: Maddie and Connie's dressing room
Favorite Off-Site Hangout: Kodama EVERY Saturday. For a year. Sardi's between shows on Wednesdays. Angus and Joe Allen after shows.
Favorite Snack Food: Anthony's cheesecake; Barbara's cookies; the stage-left crew food; chicken salad on pumpernickel bagel from Bread Factory
Mascot: Baby Huey.
Favorite Therapies: Eating together between shows; Zicam; back rubs; Dr. K's baking soda, honey, salt and warm water gargle
Most Memorable Ad-Lib: "That bitch sure is a pustule."
Cell Phone Rings, Cell Phone Photos or Texting Incidents During a Performance: During one performance, a cell phone rang for the entire first scene of Act II. Literally from start to finish...then there was the Eagles song ringtone that went on and on in the opening scene.
Fastest Costume Change: Maddie and Paddy Breen. Thank God for James and Katie.
Busiest Day at the Box Office: The day after opening.
Who Wore the Least: Patrick Heusinger shirtless for a minute.
Catchphrases Only the Company Would Recognize: "Boston Market" and "Barbara Bush."
Memorable Directorial Note: "This is a change and change is good."
Company In-Jokes: "Cotter is SO good; Drink!"
Nicknames: Lord Underplay, Lady Overdone, Sir Nibbles McChompsalot, Baron Von Footinmouth, DMD, MQ.
Fan Club Info: facebook.com/nextfall
Sweethearts Within the Company: Cotter and Sean are adorable together.
Coolest Thing About Being in This Show: Feeling the support and goodwill towards our show from the Broadway community. Thank you!!!

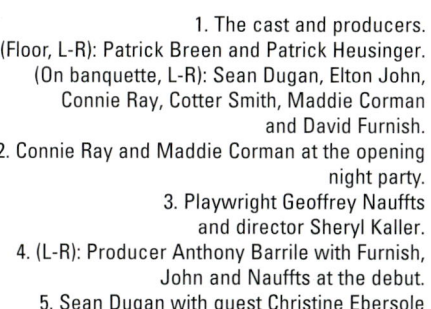

1. The cast and producers. (Floor, L-R): Patrick Breen and Patrick Heusinger. (On banquette, L-R): Sean Dugan, Elton John, Connie Ray, Cotter Smith, Maddie Corman and David Furnish.
2. Connie Ray and Maddie Corman at the opening night party.
3. Playwright Geoffrey Nauffts and director Sheryl Kaller.
4. (L-R): Producer Anthony Barrile with Furnish, John and Nauffts at the debut.
5. Sean Dugan with guest Christine Ebersole at the premiere.

Correspondents: Chuck Means and Beth Moloney, Stage Management
Catchphrases Only the Company Would Recognize: "Lockdown." "Wonder Twin Powers—Activate!" "Set Condition One Throughout the Ship!"
Off-Site Hangout: The Westway Diner.
Mascot: The Screaming Chicken.

Next to Normal

First Preview: March 27, 2009. Opened: April 15, 2009.
Still running as of May 31, 2010.

CAST
(in alphabetical order)

Henry	ADAM CHANLER-BERAT
Natalie	JENNIFER DAMIANO
Dr. Madden/Dr. Fine	LOUIS HOBSON
Diana	ALICE RIPLEY
Dan	J. ROBERT SPENCER
Gabe	KYLE DEAN MASSEY

UNDERSTUDIES

For Dan, Dr. Madden/Dr. Fine: MICHAEL BERRY
For Natalie: MEGHANN FAHY
For Diana: JESSICA PHILLIPS
For Gabe, Henry: TIM YOUNG

DANCE CAPTAIN
JESSICA PHILLIPS

BAND
Conductor/Piano: CHARLIE ALTERMAN
Violin/Keyboard: YUIKO KAMAKARI
Cello: BENJAMIN KALB
Guitars: ERIC B. DAVIS
Bass: MICHAEL BLANCO
Drums/Percussion: SHANNON FORD

Drum and Additional Percussion Arrangements by
DAMIEN BASSMAN
Additional Guitar Arrangements by
MICHAEL AARONS
Music Coordinator: MICHAEL KELLER
Copyist: EMILY GRISHMAN
MUSIC PREPARATION

BOOTH THEATRE
222 West 45th Street
A Shubert Organization Theatre
Philip J. Smith, *Chairman*   Robert E. Wankel, *President*

DAVID STONE
JAMES L. NEDERLANDER BARBARA WHITMAN PATRICK CATULLO
SECOND STAGE THEATRE
Carole Rothman   Ellen Richard
present

ALICE RIPLEY   J. ROBERT SPENCER

next to normal

music by
TOM KITT

book and lyrics by
BRIAN YORKEY

also starring
KYLE DEAN MASSEY
JENNIFER DAMIANO
ADAM CHANLER-BERAT   LOUIS HOBSON

MICHAEL BERRY   MEGHANN FAHY   JESSICA PHILLIPS   TIM YOUNG

set design by	costume design by	lighting design by	sound design by
MARK WENDLAND	JEFF MAHSHIE	KEVIN ADAMS	BRIAN RONAN

orchestrations by
MICHAEL STAROBIN and TOM KITT

vocal arrangements	music director	music coordinator
ANNMARIE MILAZZO	CHARLIE ALTERMAN	MICHAEL KELLER

casting   press representative
TELSEY + COMPANY   THE HARTMAN GROUP

production stage manager	company manager	technical supervisor	general management
JUDITH SCHOENFELD	MARC BORSAK	LARRY MORLEY	321 THEATRICAL MANAGEMENT

musical staging by
SERGIO TRUJILLO

directed by
MICHAEL GREIF

The World Premiere of **next to normal** was presented by Second Stage Theatre on February 13, 2008.
next to normal was subsequently presented at Arena Stage, Washington D.C. in November 2008.
The producers wish to express their appreciation to Theatre Development Fund for its support of this production.
Original Broadway Cast Recording on GHOSTLIGHT RECORDS

1/4/10

(L-R): Kyle Dean Massey, Alice Ripley and J. Robert Spencer

Photo by Joan Marcus

Next to Normal

Alice Ripley
Diana

J. Robert Spencer
Dan

Kyle Dean Massey
Gabe

Jennifer Damiano
Natalie

Adam Chanler-Berat
Henry

Louis Hobson
Dr. Madden/Dr. Fine

Michael Berry
*u/s Dan,
Dr. Madden/Dr. Fine*

Meghann Fahy
u/s Natalie

Jessica Phillips
*u/s Diana,
Dance Captain*

Timothy Young
u/s Gabe/Henry

Tom Kitt
*Composer/
Co-Orchestrator*

Brian Yorkey
Librettist/Lyricist

Michael Greif
Director

Sergio Trujillo
Musical Staging

Mark Wendland
Set Design

Jeff Mahshie
Costume Design

Kevin Adams
Lighting Design

Brian Ronan
Sound Design

Michael Starobin
Co-Orchestrator

AnnMarie Milazzo
Vocal Arrangements

Michael Keller
Music Coordinator

Bernard Telsey,
Telsey + Company
Casting

Marcia Goldberg, Nancy Nagel Gibbs and
Nina Essman,
321 Theatrical Management
General Management

Laura Pietropinto
Assistant Director

Dontee Kiehn
*Associate
Choreographer*

David Stone
Producer

James L.
Nederlander
Producer

Barbara Whitman
Producer

Patrick Catullo
Producer

Carole Rothman,
Artistic Director,
Second Stage
Theatre
Producer

Brian Crum
u/s Gabe, Henry

Brian d'Arcy James
Dan

Adam Kantor
u/s Henry

The Playbill Broadway Yearbook 2009-2010

Next to Normal

MacKenzie Mauzy
u/s Natalie

Asa Somers
u/s Dan, Dr. Madden/Dr. Fine

Asa Somers
u/s Dan, Dr. Madden/Dr. Fine

Aaron Tveit
Gabe

2009-2010 AWARD

PULITZER PRIZE FOR DRAMA

CREW
Front Row (L-R): Robert Witherow, Sally E. Sibson, Sara Jayne Darneille, Christopher Sloan, Susan Goulet, Judith Schoenfeld

Back Row (L-R): Vangeli Kaseluris, Jenny Scheer-Montgomery, Kyle LaColla, Elizabeth Berkeley, Angelo Grasso, Kenneth McDonough, Timmy McWilliams

BAND
Hiroko Taguchi (Violin/Synth sub), Yuiko Kamakari (Violin/Synth), Eric Davis (Guitar), Charlie Alterman (Piano/Conductor), Michael Blanco (Bass), Alisa Horn (Cello), Shannon Ford (Drums/Percussion)

STAFF FOR NEXT TO NORMAL

GENERAL MANAGEMENT
321 THEATRICAL MANAGEMENT
Nina Essman   Nancy Nagel Gibbs
Marcia Goldberg

CASTING
TELSEY + COMPANY
Bernie Telsey CSA, Will Cantler CSA, David Vaccari CSA, Bethany Knox CSA, Craig Burns CSA, Tiffany Little Canfield CSA, Rachel Hoffman CSA, Carrie Rosson CSA, Justin Huff CSA, Bess Fifer CSA, Patrick Goodwin, Abbie Brady-Dalton

GENERAL PRESS REPRESENTATIVE
THE HARTMAN GROUP
Michael Hartman
Tom D'Ambrosio   Michelle Bergmann

TECHNICAL SUPERVISOR .... Larry Morley

COMPANY MANAGER .... Marc Borsak

PRODUCTION STAGE MANAGER .. Judith Schoenfeld
Stage Manager .... Martha Donaldson
Assistant Stage Manager .... Sally E. Sibson
Assistant Director .... Laura Pietropinto
Associate Choreographer .... Dontee Kiehn
Assistant Music Director .... Mat Eisenstein
Associate Lighting Designer .... Joel E. Silver

Associate Sound Designer .... David Stollings
Assistant Scenic Designer .... Rachel Nemec
Assistant Lighting Designers .... Paul Toben, Aaron Sporer
Lighting Programmer .... Michael Pitzer
Scenic Design Assistants .... Jonathan Collins, Shoko Kambara
Associate Technical Supervisor .... Bradley Thompson
Dance Captain .... Jessica Phillips
Assistant to Mr. Kitt and Mr. Yorkey .... Brandon Ivie
Production Carpenter .... Bill Craven
Production Electrician .... Richard Mortell
Production Audio .... Mike Farfalla
Carpenter .... Kenneth McDonough
Flyman .... Ed White
Electrician .... Susan Goulet

Next to Normal

Props	James Keane
Sound Engineer	Christopher C. Sloan
Asst. Sound Engineer	Elizabeth Berkeley
Wardrobe Supervisor	Kyle LaColla
Dressers	Sara Jayne Darneille, Vangeli Kaseluris
Music Preparation	Emily Grishman/ Emily Grishman Music Preparation Inc.
Assistant to Mr. Stone	Aaron Glick
Assts. to the General Managers	Tara Geesaman, John Vermeer
Assistant to the Company Manager	Meredith Morgan
Production Assistant	Stuart Shefter
Advertising	Serino Coyne Inc./ Greg Corradetti, Joaquin Esteva
Interactive Marketing	Situation Interactive
Merchandising	The Araca Group
Legal Counsel	Schreck, Rose and Dapello/ Nancy Rose, David Berlin
Director of Finance	John DiMeglio
Accountant	FK Partners CPA's LLP/ Robert Fried
Banking	JPMorgan Chase/ Stefanie Boger, Salvatore Romano
Insurance	AON/Albert G. Ruben Insurance/ Claudia Kaufman, Susan Weiss
Payroll Service	Castellana Services Inc.
Production Photography	Joan Marcus

Group Sales: Shubert Group Sales
800-432-7780

321 THEATRICAL MANAGEMENT
Bob Brinkerhoff, Mattea Cogliano-Benedict, John DiMeglio, Nicholas Porche, Susan Sampliner, Greg Schaffert, Ken Silverman, Elizabeth Talmadge

Earlier development of *Next to Normal*
was made possible by:

THE JONATHAN LARSON FOUNDATION

THE NEW YORK MUSIC THEATRE FESTIVAL
Isaac Robert Hurwitz, Executive Producer

VILLAGE THEATRE
Issaquah, Washington
Robb Hunt, Executive Producer/
Steve Tomkins, Artistic Director

SECOND STAGE THEATRE

Artistic Director	Carole Rothman
Associate Artistic Director	Christopher Burney
Production Manager	Jeff Wild
Technical Director	Robert Mahon
Director of Finance	Janice B. Cwill
General Manager	Don-Scott Cooper
Director of Development	Sarah Bordy
Literary Manager	Sarah Steele
Ticket Services Manager	Greg Turner

SECOND STAGE THEATRE BOARD OF TRUSTEES
Anthony C.M. Kiser, Chairman Emeritus
Stephen C. Sherrill, Chairman
David A. Ackert, Elizabeth C. Berens, Elizabeth H. Berger, Tavener Holmes Berry, Susan Braddock, Jeffrey H. Bunzel, Sally D. Clement, Lawrence G. Creel, Suzanne Schwartz Davidson, Judy Davis, Carla Emil, Frances D. Fergusson, Richard C. Gay, Hamilton E. James, Wendy Evans Joseph, Steven B. Klinsky, George S. Loening, Patti LuPone, Timothy J. McClimon, Anne McMillen, Mary P. Moran, John Partilla, Bambi Putnam, Kirk A. Radke, Lynne Randall, Donna Rosen, Michael Rothfeld, Carole Rothman, Joshua Ruch, Nathan E. Saint-Amand, Didi Schafer, John Schmidt, Denise V. Seegal, Michael E. Singer, John M. Sullivan, Jr., Ann Tenenbaum, James E. Thomas, Nancy Walker

The development of *Next to Normal* at Second Stage Theatre was supported by the Edgerton Foundation, the Jonathan Larson Foundation, the National Endowment for the Arts and the New York City Department of Cultural Affairs.

ARENA STAGE

Artistic Director	Molly Smith
Managing Director	Edgar Dobie
Director of Communications	Chad M. Bauman
Director of Finance and Administration	Joe Berardelli
Associate Artistic Director	David Dower
Technical Director	Jim Glendinning
Production Manager	Carey Lawless
Director of Community Engagement	Anita Maynard-Losh
Chief Development Office	Carmel Owen

ARENA STAGE BOARD
Chair: Mark Shugoll. Vice Chairs: Guy Bergquist, Michele G. Berman, Susan Haas Bralove, John M. Derrick Jr., Terry R. Peel, Les Silverman. Secretary: Ronald A. Paul, M.D. Treasurer: Hubert M. Schlosberg. Andrew R. Ammerman, Ashok Bajaj, Steven R. Bralove, David S. Broder, Donald de Laski, Nancy de Laski, Gina H. Despres, Wendy L. Farrow, Nancy M. Folger, Ellen K. Harrison, Fruzsina Harsanyi, Joseph H. Jarboe, Margot Kelly, W. Buford Lewis, B. Thomas Mansbach, Beverly Perry, William S. Sessions, David E. Shiffrin, Molly Smith, Richard W. Snowdon, Roderic L. Woodson. Honorary Board: Susan Clampitt, Allan D. Cors, Fred Grandy, Priscilla Dewey Houghton, Judy Lansing Kovler, David O. Maxwell, Joan P. Maxwell, Stacey J. Mobley, Judy Lynn Prince, Beth Newburger Schwartz, Margaret Tomlinson. Life Trustees: Norman Bernstein, Zelda Fichandler, J. Burke Knapp, Dr. Jaylee M. Mead, Lee G. Rubenstein. Emeritus: Joan & Peter Andrews, Arlene Kogod, Jonathan M. Weisgall

Official Opening Night Party at
THE EDISON BALLROOM

CREDITS
Scenery constructed by Daedalus Design and Production Inc. Show control and scenic motion control featuring stage command system ®by PRG Scenic Technologies. Lighting equipment by PRG Lighting. Sound equipment by PRG Audio. Additional wardrobe provided by Julianna Margulies and Jessica Weinstein. Ms. Ripley's hair by John Barrett. Prop body by Den Design Studio. Wig for prop body by J. Jared Janas.

SPECIAL THANKS
The authors would like to thank the following for their invaluable medical expertise: Dr. Anthony Pietropinto, MD., Dr. Nancy Elman, PhD., Dr. Quentin Van Meter, MD.

Piano provided by Steinway & Sons

www.NextToNormal.com

THE SHUBERT ORGANIZATION, INC.
Board of Directors

Philip J. Smith Chairman	**Robert E. Wankel** President
Wyche Fowler, Jr.	**John W. Kluge**
Lee J. Seidler	**Michael I. Sovern**

Stuart Subotnick

Elliot Greene Chief Financial Officer	**David Andrews** Senior Vice President – Shubert Ticketing
Juan Calvo Vice President and Controller	**John Darby** Vice President – Facilities
Peter Entin Vice President – Theatre Operations	**Charles Flateman** Vice President – Marketing
Anthony LaMattina Vice President – Audit & Production Finance	**Brian Mahoney** Vice President – Ticket Sales

D.S. Moynihan
Vice President – Creative Projects

House Manager	Laurel Ann Wilson

(L-R): Adam Chanler-Berat and Jennifer Damiano

Photo by Joan Marcus

Next to Normal
SCRAPBOOK

Cast and creators join Alice Ripley as she receives her caricature at Sardi's restaurant September 24, 2009. Pictured (L-R): director Michael Greif, costume designer Jeff Mahshie, Ripley, composer Tom Kitt, actor Louis Hobson, actor Adam Chanler-Berat and producer David Stone.

Correspondent: J. Robert Spencer, "Dan Good-man"

Memorable Note, Fax or Fan Letter: I was amazed at the amount of people that reached out to me after seeing the show. So many people could relate to the show and had said over and over again that they were or could relate to the role I play. Thanking me for my honest portrayal and that they had lived EXACTLY what they saw me deliver on stage. What an unexpected impact this show and role has had therapeutically to hundreds and hundreds of people. How many shows can do that!?!?!? Not many.

Memorable Gift: Whoopi Goldberg gave us all cupcakes after seeing the show.

Most Exciting Celebrity Visitors: The greatest thing about being an actor is when you have the opportunity to strut your stuff to the "Ones" who inspired you to become an actor in the first place. Whether it's DeNiro, Glenn Close, Ben Stiller, Martin Short, Steve Martin, Bruce Willis, Julianna Margulies, Nicole Kidman, Whoopi Goldberg....at some point all these talents have driven me to do what I do. So, it's incredibly rewarding to thank them for coming to the show, and also being able to thank them for having inspired me with such great work they've accomplished for so long.

Favorite In-Theatre Gathering Place: We usually hang in Louis and Adam's dressing room. Nice room with intimate lighting and great tunes.

Special Backstage Ritual: For me, I like to paint before each show. I sometimes do a new painting every night.

Favorite Moment During Each Performance: From the moment I smash the music box to the end is my favorite!

Favorite Off-Site Hangout: Kodama Sushi for their Hot Sake.

Favorite Snack Foods: Ginger candy.

Mascot: For me, it's John Cassavetes.

Favorite Therapy: Like I said before, hot sake!

Record Number of Cell Phone Rings, Cell Phone Photos or Texting Incidents During a Performance: 82...kidding.

Memorable Stage Door Fan Encounters: People who have traveled all over because they saw our performance on the Tony Awards. Australia, Brazil, Switzerland, Mexico, Ireland...those are the fans I love meeting. Traveling all that distance just to see me and the show...that's amazing.

What We Thought of the Web Buzz on the Show: I think it's wonderful and it's a continual visual aid to keep the cult buzz alive and kicking forevermore.

Latest Audience Arrival: When Neil Patrick Harris showed up for a 7 PM Tuesday night show with his family at 7:45 PM...thinking it was an 8 PM show. Ooooopppsssssss!

Who Wore the Heaviest/Hottest Costume: Me. It's all wool and layers upon layers of shirts, sweaters and jackets.

Fastest Costume Change: From "Song of Forgetting" into "Better than Before."

Who Wore the Least: I think Aaron.

Sweethearts Within the Company: All of our musicians, crew members, and stage managers. Truly loving people.

Orchestra Member Who Played the Most Instruments: Our percussionist, Shannon Ford, is like Neil Peart of the rock group Rush up there. He's jamming on drums, then standing up and playing bells, and gongs, and everything under the sun. He's got a lot on his plate.

Memorable Directorial Note: Michael Grief during tech: "Again please, Louis."

Company In-Jokes: A song I wrote during our run in D.C. "Whoa expanding our horizons. Are you riiiiiiiiiisiiiiiiinnnnnnggggg!"

Tales From the Put-in: Laughs, laughs, and more LAUGHS!

Nicknames: Alice - Al
Jennifer - DAMIANO (in your best/worst Italian accent EVER)
Adam - ACB
Louis - Louis

Embarrassing Moment: My fly was down once during "Better than Before."

Ghostly Encounter Backstage: Halloween when my dresser Vangeli had on a mask and black hood. Scared the crap out of me!

Coolest Thing About Being in This Show: Being able to do it over and over again!

Other Stories or Memories: I've said enough. The rest is for me.

9 to 5: The Musical

First Preview: April 7, 2009. Opened: April 30, 2009.
Closed September 6, 2009 after 24 Previews and 148 Performances.

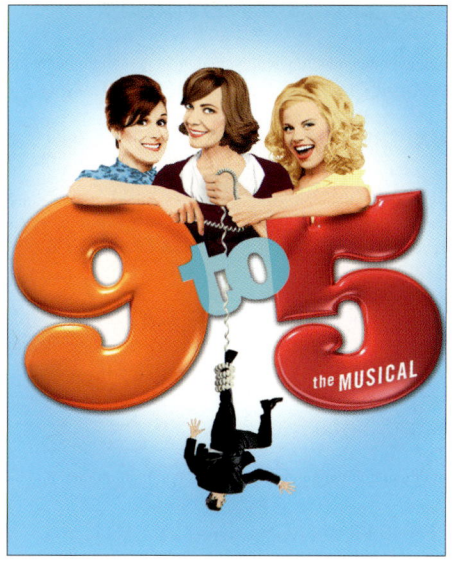

CAST
(in order of appearance)

Violet Newstead	ALLISON JANNEY
Doralee Rhodes	MEGAN HILTY
Dwayne	CHARLIE POLLOCK
Judy Bernly	STEPHANIE J. BLOCK
Roz Keith	KATHY FITZGERALD
Kathy	JILL ABRAMOVITZ
Anita	MAIA NKENGE WILSON
Daphne	TORY ROSS
Franklin Hart, Jr.	MARC KUDISCH
Missy	LISA HOWARD
Maria	IOANA ALFONSO
Joe	ANDY KARL
Margaret	KAREN MURPHY
Josh	VAN HUGHES
Dick	DAN COONEY
Bob Enright	JEREMY DAVIS
Detective	WAYNE SCHRODER
Candy Striper	TORY ROSS
Tinsworthy	MICHAEL X. MARTIN
Ensemble	JILL ABRAMOVITZ, IOANA ALFONSO, JUSTIN BOHON, PAUL CASTREE, DAN COONEY, JEREMY DAVIS, AUTUMN GUZZARDI, LISA HOWARD, VAN HUGHES, SPENCER LIFF, MICHAEL X. MARTIN, MICHAEL MINDLIN, KAREN MURPHY, JESSICA LEA PATTY, HERMAN PAYNE, CHARLIE POLLOCK, TORY ROSS, WAYNE SCHRODER, MAIA NKENGE WILSON, BRANDI WOOTEN

Continued on next page

⇥N⇤ MARQUIS THEATRE
UNDER THE DIRECTION OF JAMES M. NEDERLANDER AND JAMES L. NEDERLANDER

GREEN STATE PRODS.   RICHARD LEVI   JOHN McCOLGAN/MOYA DOHERTY/EDGAR DOBIE
JAMES L. NEDERLANDER/TERRY ALLEN KRAMER   INDEPENDENT PRESENTERS NETWORK   JAM THEATRICALS
BUD MARTIN   MICHAEL WATT   THE WEINSTEIN CO./SONIA FRIEDMAN/DEDE HARRIS
NORTON HERRICK/MATTHEW C. BLANK/JOAN STEIN   CENTER THEATRE GROUP   TONI DOWGIALLO   AND   GFOUR PRODUCTIONS

present

Music and Lyrics by
DOLLY PARTON

Book by
PATRICIA RESNICK

BASED ON THE 20TH CENTURY FOX PICTURE

STARRING
ALLISON JANNEY
STEPHANIE J. BLOCK
MEGAN HILTY

KATHY FITZGERALD   ANDY KARL
AND
MARC KUDISCH

with
JILL ABRAMOVITZ   IOANA ALFONSO   JENNIFER BALAGNA   NATHAN BALSER
JUSTIN BOHON   PAUL CASTREE   DAN COONEY   JEREMY DAVIS   GAELEN GILLILAND
AUTUMN GUZZARDI   LISA HOWARD   VAN HUGHES   SPENCER LIFF   MICHAEL X. MARTIN
MICHAEL MINDLIN   KAREN MURPHY   MARK MYARS   JUSTIN PATTERSON   JESSICA LEA PATTY
HERMAN PAYNE   CHARLIE POLLOCK   TORY ROSS   WAYNE SCHRODER   MAIA NKENGE WILSON   BRANDI WOOTEN

Scenic Design	Costume Design	Lighting Design	Sound Design
SCOTT PASK	WILLIAM IVEY LONG	JULES FISHER & KENNETH POSNER	JOHN H. SHIVERS

Casting	Imaging	Hair Design	Make-Up Design
TELSEY + COMPANY	PETER NIGRINI & PEGGY EISENHAUER	PAUL HUNTLEY & EDWARD J. WILSON	ANGELINA AVALLONE

Technical Supervisor	Scenic Design Associate	Production Supervisor	Associate Director	Associate Choreographer
NEIL A. MAZZELLA	EDWARD PIERCE	WILLIAM JOSEPH BARNES	DAVE SOLOMON	RACHEL BRESS

General Management	Press Agent	Marketing	Music Coordinator
NINA LANNAN ASSOCIATES	THE HARTMAN GROUP	TYPE A MARKETING SITUATION INTERACTIVE	MICHAEL KELLER

Orchestrator	Additional Orchestrations & Incidental Music Arrangements	Dance Music Arrangements	Additional Music Arrangements
BRUCE COUGHLIN	STEPHEN OREMUS & ALEX LACAMOIRE	ALEX LACAMOIRE	KEVIN STITES & CHARLES duCHATEAU

Music Direction and Vocal Arrangements by
STEPHEN OREMUS

Produced by
ROBERT GREENBLATT

Choreographed by
ANDY BLANKENBUEHLER

Directed by
JOE MANTELLO

9/6/09

(L-R): Stephanie J. Block, Allison Janney and Megan Hilty

Photo by Joan Marcus

9 to 5: The Musical

MUSICAL NUMBERS

ACT ONE

"9 to 5"	Violet, Doralee, Dwayne, Judy and Ensemble
"Around Here"	Violet and Ensemble
"Here for You"	Hart
"I Just Might"	Judy, Doralee, Violet
"Backwoods Barbie"	Doralee
"The Dance of Death"	Judy, Hart and Ensemble
"Cowgirl's Revenge"	Doralee, Hart and Ensemble
"Potion Notion"	Violet, Hart and Ensemble
"Joy to the Girls"	Judy, Doralee, Violet, Hart and Ensemble
"Heart to Hart"	Roz and Ensemble
"Shine Like the Sun"	Doralee, Judy, Violet

ACT TWO

Entr'acte	Orchestra
"One of the Boys"	Violet and Boys
"5 to 9"	Roz
"Always a Woman"	Hart and Men's Ensemble
"Change It"	Doralee, Violet, Judy and Ensemble
"Let Love Grow"	Joe, Violet
"Get Out and Stay Out"	Judy
Finale: "9 to 5"	The Company

ORCHESTRA

Conductor:
STEPHEN OREMUS
Associate Conductor:
MATT GALLAGHER
Keyboard 1:
STEPHEN OREMUS
Keyboard 2 and Organ:
MATT GALLAGHER
Keyboard 3:
JODIE MOORE (Assistant Conductor)
Guitars:
MICHAEL AARONS, JAKE EZRA SCHWARTZ
Guitars/Pedal Steel:
JOHN PUTNAM
Bass:
DAVE PHILLIPS
Drums:
SEAN McDANIEL
Percussion:
DAVE MANCUSO
Reeds:
VINCENT DELLA ROCCA, AARON HEICK, DAVE RIEKENBERG
Trumpets:
BOB MILLIKAN, BRIAN PARESCHI
Trombones:
KEITH O'QUINN, JENNIFER WHARTON
Violins:
SUZY PERELMAN, CHRIS CARDONA
Cello:
AMY RALSKE
Music Coordinator:
MICHAEL KELLER
Keyboard Programming:
RANDY COHEN
Music Copying:
EMILY GRISHMAN MUSIC PREPARATION–
EMILY GRISHMAN/KATHARINE EDMONDS

Cast Continued

SWINGS
JENNIFER BALAGNA, NATHAN BALSER, MARK MYARS, JUSTIN PATTERSON

Dance Captain: MARK MYARS
Assistant Dance Captain: JENNIFER BALAGNA

UNDERSTUDIES
Violet:
JILL ABRAMOVITZ, LISA HOWARD
Judy:
GAELEN GILLILAND, JESSICA LEA PATTY, TORY ROSS
Doralee:
GAELEN GILLILAND, AUTUMN GUZZARDI
Hart:
MICHAEL X. MARTIN, WAYNE SCHRODER
Roz:
KAREN MURPHY, TORY ROSS
Joe:
PAUL CASTREE, JUSTIN PATTERSON
Anita, Candy Striper, Daphne, Kathy:
JENNIFER BALAGNA, GAELEN GILLILAND
Detective:
NATHAN BALSER, DAN COONEY, JUSTIN PATTERSON
Bob Enright:
MARK MYARS, JUSTIN PATTERSON
Dwayne:
JUSTIN BOHON, JUSTIN PATTERSON
Dick:
NATHAN BALSER, JEREMY DAVIS, JUSTIN PATTERSON, WAYNE SCHRODER
Josh:
JUSTIN BOHON, MICHAEL MINDLIN
Margaret:
GAELEN GILLILAND, TORY ROSS
Maria:
JENNIFER BALAGNA, JESSICA LEA PATTY
Missy:
GAELEN GILLILAND, BRANDI WOOTEN
Tinsworthy:
NATHAN BALSER, DAN COONEY, JUSTIN PATTERSON, WAYNE SCHRODER

TIME
1979

Allison Janney
Violet Newstead

Stephanie J. Block
Judy Bernly

Megan Hilty
Doralee Rhodes

Marc Kudisch
Franklin Hart, Jr.

Kathy Fitzgerald
Roz Keith

Andy Karl
Joe

Jill Abramovitz
Kathy/Ensemble

9 to 5: The Musical

 Ioana Alfonso
Maria/Ensemble

 Jennifer Balagna
Swing, Assistant Dance Captain

 Nathan Balser
Swing

 Justin Bohon
Ensemble

 Paul Castree
Ensemble

 Dan Cooney
Dick

 Jeremy Davis
Bob Enright/Ensemble

 Gaelen Gilliland
u/s Judy, Doralee

 Autumn Guzzardi
Ensemble

 Lisa Howard
Missy/Ensemble

 Van Hughes
Josh/Ensemble

 Spencer Liff
Ensemble

 Michael X. Martin
Tinsworthy/Ensemble

 Michael Mindlin
Ensemble

 Karen Murphy
Margaret/Ensemble

 Mark Myars
Swing; Dance Captain

 Justin Patterson
Swing

 Jessica Lea Patty
Maria/Ensemble

 Herman Payne
Ensemble

 Charlie Pollock
Dwayne/Ensemble

 Tory Ross
Daphne/Candy Striper/Ensemble

 Wayne Schroder
Detective/Ensemble

 Maia Nkenge Wilson
Anita/Ensemble

 Brandi Wooten
Ensemble

 Dolly Parton
Composer and Lyricist

 Patricia Resnick
Book

 Joe Mantello
Director

 Andy Blankenbuehler
Choreographer

 Scott Pask
Scenic Designer

 William Ivey Long
Costume Designer

 Kenneth Posner
Lighting Designer

 Jules Fisher and Peggy Eisenhauer
Lighting Designer/Imaging

 John H. Shivers
Sound Designer

 Stephen Oremus
Music Director, Additional Orchestrations, Vocal and Incidental Music Arrangements

9 to 5: The Musical

 Bruce Coughlin
Orchestrations

 Alex Lacamoire
Dance Arrangements/ Additional Orchestrations

 Michael Keller
Music Coordinator

 Bernard Telsey, Telsey + Company
Casting

 Paul Huntley
Wig and Hair Designer

 Angelina Avallone
Make-up Designer

 Neil A. Mazzella/ Hudson Theatrical Associates
Technical Supervision

 Dave Solomon
Associate Director

 Rachel Bress
Associate Choreographer

 William Joseph Barnes
Production Supervisor

 Nina Lannan Associates
General Management

 Robert Greenblatt
Producer

 John McColgan
Producer

 Moya Doherty
Producer

 Edgar Dobie
Producer

 James L. Nederlander
Producer

 Terry Allen Kramer
Producer

 Arny Granat, Jam Theatricals
Producer

 Steve Traxler, Jam Theatricals
Producer

 Bob Weinstein, The Weinstein Company
Producer

 Harvey Weinstein, The Weinstein Company
Producer

 Sonia Friedman Productions Ltd.
Producer

 Dede Harris
Producer

 Michael Ritchie
Artistic Director, Center Theatre Group

 Charles Dillingham
Managing Director, Center Theatre Group

 Gordon Davidson
Founding Artistic Director, Center Theatre Group

 Kenneth Greenblatt, GFour Productions
Producer

BOX OFFICE
(L-R): Rick Waxman, Mike Kane, John Rooney

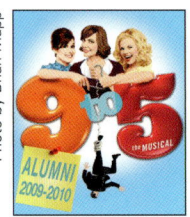 Timothy George Anderson
Ensemble

 Rachel Bress
Ensemble

 Ann Harada
Kathy, Ensemble

9 to 5: The Musical

FRONT OF HOUSE STAFF
Front Row (L-R): Frank Feliciano, Dorothy Marguette

Second Row (L-R): Charlie Spencer, Jamie Lee Fitze, Odalis Concepcion

Third Row (L-R): Frank Tupper, Phyllis Weinsaft, Hugh Dill

Fourth Row (L-R): Stanley Seidman, unidentified, Nancy Diaz, John Clark

Back Row (L-R): Daisy Irizarry, David Cox, Omar Aguilar, Rosaire Caso

HAIR AND WARDROBE
Front Row (L-R): Samantha Lawrence, Tree Sarvay, Steven Kirkham, Charlene Belmond

Middle Row (L-R): Laura Beattie, Ed Wilson, Deirdre LaBarre

Back Row (L-R): Tanya Guercy-Blue, Maggie Horkey, Stephanie Luette, Therese Ducey, Douglas Petitjean

MANAGEMENT
Front Row (L-R): Chris Zaccardi, William Joseph Barnes, Kathryn L. McKee, Adam Jackson

Back Row (L-R): Timothy R. Semon, Kimberly Kelley

CREW
Front Row (L-R): Pat Amari, Scott Mecionis, Michael Bernstein, Stephen Reid, Mark Diaz, Eileen MacDonald, unidentified

Back Row (L-R): Joseph Valentino, Russ Mecionis, Dan Robillard, Dan Tramontozzi

9 to 5: The Musical

STAFF FOR 9 to 5 THE MUSICAL

GENERAL MANAGER
NINA LANNAN ASSOCIATES
Nina Lannan Maggie Brohn

COMPANY MANAGER
Kimberly Kelley

Associate Company Manager ....Adam Jackson

GENERAL PRESS REPRESENTATIVE
THE HARTMAN GROUP
Michael Hartman
Wayne Wolfe   Matt Ross

CASTING
TELSEY + COMPANY
Bernie Telsey CSA, Will Cantler CSA, David Vaccari CSA,
Bethany Knox CSA, Craig Burns CSA,
Tiffany Little Canfield CSA, Rachel Hoffman CSA,
Carrie Rosson CSA, Justin Huff CSA, Bess Fifer CSA,
Patrick Goodwin, Abbie Brady-Dalton

Associate Director	Dave Solomon
Associate Choreographer	Rachel Bress
Production Supervisor	William Joseph Barnes
Production Stage Manager (Pre-Production)	C. Randall White
Stage Manager	Timothy R. Semon
Assistant Stage Managers	Chris Zaccardi, Kathryn L. McKee
Production Assistants	Christopher Paul, Raynelle Wright, Stuart Shefter, McKenzie Murphy
Assistant Producer	Brian Salb
Dance Captain	Mark Myars
Assistant Dance Captain	Jennifer Balagna
Associate Technical Supervisors	Irene Wang, Frank Illo
Associate Scenic Designer	Nick Francone
Assistant Scenic Designers	Orit Jacoby Carroll, Frank McCullough, Lauren Alvarez, Jeffrey Hinchee
Associate Costume Designer	Scott Traugott
Assistant Costume Designer	Robert J. Martin
Costume Design Assistant	Brenda Abbandandolo
Associate Wig and Hair Designer	Giovanna Calabretta
Associate Lighting Designer	Philip Rosenberg
Assistant Lighting Designer	Aaron Spivey, Carl Faber
Automated Lighting Programmer	David Arch
Associate Sound Designer/ Production Sound Engineer	David Patridge
Imaging Associate	C. Andrew Bauer
Imaging Assistant	Dan Scully
LED Image Wall Programmer	Laura Frank for Luminous FX LLC
Additional Character & Castle Animation	Illum Productions
	Creative Director: Jerry Chambless
	Animation Director: Joseph Merideth
Production Carpenter	Donald J. Oberpriller
Carpenters	Eric "Speed" Smith, Chad Hershey, Mark Diaz
Production Electrician	Gregory Husinko
Head Electrician	Eric Abbott
Assistant Electrician/Vari*Lite Tech	Derek Healy
Head of Sound	Dan Tramontozzi
Assistant Sound	Dan Robillard
Production Properties	Timothy M. Abel
Head Properties	Michael Bernstein
Assistant Properties	Ken Keneally
Wardrobe Supervisor	Douglas Petitjean
Assistant Wardrobe Supervisor	Deirdre LaBarre
Dressers	Laura Beattie, Tracey Diebold, Adam Girardet, Kay Gowenlock, Timothy Greer, Barry Hoff, Maggie Horkey, Samantha Lawrence, John Rinaldi, Tree Sarvay, Kelly Smith, Ron Tagert
Hair Supervisor	Edward J. Wilson
Assistant Hair Supervisor	Steven Kirkham
Hairdressers	Charlene Belmond, Therese Ducey
Rehearsal Musicians	Jodie Moore, Sean McDaniel
Music Assistant	Colleen Darnall
Advertising	Spotco/Drew Hodges, Jim Edwards, Tom Greenwald, Tom McCann, Josh Fraenkel
Marketing	Type A Marketing/ Anne Rippey, Janette Roush, Nick Pramik
Interactive Marketing	Situation Interactive/ Damian Bazadona, John Lanasa, Rebecca Spears, Maris Smith
Comptroller	Sarah Galbraith/ Sarah Galbraith Company
Accountant	Robert Fried CPA/ Fried & Kowgios CPAs LLP
General Management Associates	Steve Dow, David Roth, Libby Fox
General Management Interns	Mattea Cogliano, Erica Ruff
Press Associates	Leslie Baden, Michelle Bergmann, Tom D'Ambrosio, Juliana Hannett, Alyssa Hart
Press Interns	Matt Sinsheimer, Jacob Matsumiya
Production Photographer	Joan Marcus
Insurance	Dewitt Stern
Banking	City National Bank, Michele Gibbons
Payroll	Castellana Services, Inc.
Associate to William Ivey Long	Donald Sanders
Orthopaedic Medical Coverage	David S. Weiss, M.D.
Company Physical Therapist	PhysioArts
Merchandising	The Araca Group
Travel Agent	Tzell Travel/ The "A" Team, Andi Henig
Concierge/Chauffeur	get services llc
Legal Counsel	Carolyn J. Casselman/ Paul, Weiss, Rifkind, Wharton & Garrison

www.9to5themusical.com

Special Thanks to
Linda Wallem

ACKNOWLEDGEMENTS
Scenery and automation constructed by Hudson Scenic Studios and PRG Scenic Technologies. Flying by Foy. Costumes by Scafati Inc., Carelli Costumes, Tricorne, John David Ridge, EuroCo Costumes, Valentina, Jennifer Love Costumes, Maria Ficalora Custom Knitwear, Muto-Little, Giliberto Designs Inc. Shoes by T.O. Dey and Capezio. Undergarments provided by Bra*Tenders. Lighting equipment by PRG Lighting. Sound equipment supplied by Sound Associates. Props provided by Spoon Group and Proof Productions, Inc. Special effects equipment by Jauchem & Meeh Inc. Trucking by Clark Transfers. Graphic arts and special assistance by Megan Abel. Video Wall by XL Video. Keyboards provided by Yamaha. "Days of Our Lives" text courtesy of Corday Productions, Inc., Sony Pictures Television.

SPECIAL THANKS
Peter Chernin, John Breglio,
Caroline Andersen, Ellen Campion

American premiere produced at
The Ahmanson Theatre by Centre Theatre Group,
L.A. Theatre Company

9 to 5 (The Movie)
Story by Patricia Resnick

Screenplay by
Colin Higgins and Patricia Resnick

Produced by
Jane Fonda and Bruce Gilbert

Directed by Colin Higgins

Rehearsed at the New 42nd Street Studios

NEDERLANDER

Chairman	James M. Nederlander
President	James L. Nederlander

Executive Vice President
Nick Scandalios

Vice President Corporate Development	Senior Vice President Labor Relations
Charlene S. Nederlander	**Herschel Waxman**
Vice President	Chief Financial Officer
Jim Boese	**Freida Sawyer Belviso**

STAFF FOR THE MARQUIS THEATRE

Manager	David Calhoun
Associate Manager	Austin Nathaniel
Treasurer	Rick Waxman
Assistant Treasurer	John Rooney
Carpenter	Joseph P. Valentino
Electrician	James Mayo
Property Man	Scott Mecionis

(L-R): Megan Hilty and Marc Kudisch

Photo by Joan Marcus

9 to 5
Scrapbook

Correspondent: Tory Ross, "Daphne"

The Final Performance: September 6 was a terrible, horrible, no good, very bad day; the type of day you either float through or experience every agonizing, aching moment. I arrived at the theater with my BFF Justin Bohon (Milton & Daphne forever!) and there were swarms of fans at the stage door collecting autographs, taking pictures, telling stories of how the show brought them closer to each other and their mothers, and crying. Yes, the fans were crying. That's when the lump in my throat really started to grow. After a girl from Belgium, who flew in especially for the closing, handed me chocolates and a cake for the cast, we headed up to Allison's dressing room (the cast's favorite hangout) and found her in a state of complete shock.

Intellectually, we all knew this day was coming, but emotionally, we had all been in complete denial. Kathy Fitzgerald arrived with her daughter Hope, who had written homemade thank-you cards for basically everyone in the building. She read some aloud, which pushed Allison and I over the edge to our first real tears. We didn't really know what to do, so we all sat there and did Allison's warm-up with her, which was actually kind of hilarious. Those warm-up tapes are insane (make a lion face?).

Actually getting ready for the show is a complete blur. Everyone was running late and there were all sorts of people backstage from the creative team in search of some kind of closure: hugs and stories all around (T-Tat).

At the "places" call, we all gathered onstage in our pajamas. I don't know if it was having done tech in L.A., or starting the show in pajamas, or Joe and Bob assembling the nicest, funniest, generous, most incredibly talented group of people I have ever worked with—we all shared an incredible intimacy with each other. We stood in a circle, holding hands (as we did before every show), though on this special occasion we were joined by the dressers, crew and stage management, and we passed actor energy for the last time.

Marc Kudisch was the recipient of the final squeeze (the person whose hands were squeezed at the same time) and he chose the final word of the day: love. (More tears.) Coincidentally enough, Marc was also the recipient of our first circle in L.A. (His choice of word was: "fantasmigoricaldouchecock.")

The show started and every character got ridiculous entrance applause and hoots and hollers that bordered on heckling. The audience was even better than opening night. There was a moment in the opening number when the entire ensemble happened to be upstage in stillness during Stephanie's verse. As the opening number was randomly incredibly aerobic, this was the moment in the show when we would all collectively breathe as a group. During that last show, the breathing was unsteady, mixed with hiccupped tears. I think that's when we all realized we were doing it for the last time.

The show was crazy… with added moments:

1. (L-R): Allison Janney, Stephanie J. Block, Megan Hilty and Marc Kudisch pose for photographers at the *9 to 5* CD-signing event at Barnes & Noble Lincoln Triangle July 14, 2009.
2. Correspondent Tory Ross (L) with Allison Janney.
3. Ross with Dolly Parton.

Kathy shoving her tongue down Lisa's throat in the finale; some Tattletales choreography in the bow; Ann Harada (fresh from her *Avenue Q* matinee) singing in the final "Shine Like the Sun" backup circle); and tears (Megan singing "Backwoods Barbie," Allison's monologue, Stephanie's photocopy scene).

When the final curtain came down at the end, no one knew what to do. We all just stood there and organically returned to the circle. We squeezed each other's hands over and over again until Marc picked a final-final word: "family forever." Then Megan, Stephanie and I collapsed on the stage floor and started chanting, "Hell no, we won't go."

After being picked up (literally) by Allison and Kathy, I convinced one of the stagehands (who wishes to remain anonymous for purposes of future employment) to take my Employee of the Month plaque off the set and give it to me. I would have done it myself, but my power drill skills suck and he didn't want me to ruin the set.

The debaucherous last evening (for this was a group who enjoyed the cocktails!) started with a shot of illegal moonshine that Io's mom smuggled into the country and ended at my house, where I showed the final Daphne video to some peeps. Set to "Over the Rainbow," Andy Karl amassed clips of footage taken from Daphne's desk and all around the theater. The short is one of the saddest, most amazing things I've ever seen. Daphne finds a crystal (from Dollywood!) hidden in her desk and it teleports her to moments at Consolidated. Flashbacks?

Fantasy? Silliness? We don't know.

But I do know that *9 to 5* was the best theatrical experience of my career thus far and it closed too soon. I sit here, devastated, thinking about the words of the inimitable and lovely Dolly Parton: "What to do and where to start? Things are falling all apart. Trying hard to move ahead, but keep losing ground instead. But I have to get a grip and hold onto it like a vice. Have to face the fallen chips; I just might make it, I just might."

The Norman Conquests

First Preview: April 7, 2009. Opened: April 23, 2009.
Closed July 26, 2009 after 18 Previews and 109 Performances.

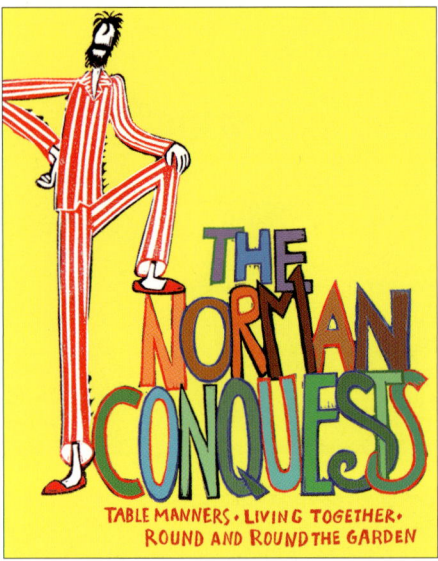

CAST
(in alphabetical order)

Ruth	AMELIA BULLMORE
Annie	JESSICA HYNES
Norman	STEPHEN MANGAN
Tom	BEN MILES
Reg	PAUL RITTER
Sarah	AMANDA ROOT

The actors in *The Norman Conquests* are appearing with the permission of Actors' Equity Association.

UNDERSTUDIES
For Annie: CASSIE BECK
For Norman: PETER BRADBURY
For Ruth/Sarah: ANGELA PIERCE
For Tom/Reg: TONY WARD

TABLE MANNERS
The action takes place in the dining room of a Victorian house in England during a weekend in July.

Act I	Act II
Scene I: Saturday, 6pm	Scene I: Sunday, 8pm
Scene II: Sunday, 9am	Scene II: Monday, 8am

Continued on next page

 **CIRCLE IN THE SQUARE**
UNDER THE DIRECTION OF
THEODORE MANN and PAUL LIBIN
SUSAN FRANKEL, General Manager

Sonia Friedman Productions
Steven Baruch   Marc Routh   Richard Frankel   Tom Viertel
Dede Harris   Tulchin/Bartner/Lauren Doll
Jamie deRoy   Eric Falkenstein   Harriet Newman Leve   Probo Productions
Douglas G. Smith   Michael Filerman/Jennifer Manocherian   Richard Winkler

In association with
Dan Frishwasser   Pam Laudenslager/Remmel T. Dickinson
Jane Dubin/True Love Productions   Barbara Manocherian/Jennifer Isaacson

Present

The Old Vic Theatre Company
Production of

THE NORMAN CONQUESTS

by
Alan Ayckbourn

Starring
**Amelia Bullmore   Jessica Hynes   Stephen Mangan
Ben Miles   Paul Ritter   Amanda Root**

Scenery and Costumes Designed by	Lighting Designed by	Music by
Rob Howell	**David Howe**	**Gary Yershon**

Sound Designed by	Original Casting by	Production Stage Manager
Simon Baker	**Gabrielle Dawes, CDG**	**Ira Mont**

US General Management	UK General Management	Production Manager	Press Representative
Frankel Green Theatrical Management	**Diane Benjamin for SFP**	**Aurora Productions**	**Boneau/ Bryan-Brown**

Directed by
Matthew Warchus

 This production was first performed as a trilogy on October 6, 2008 produced by The Old Vic Theatre Company (Artistic Director Kevin Spacey, Chair Sally Greene, Producers John Richardson and Kate Pakenham)

7/26/09

Stephen Mangan in *Table Manners*

Photo by Joan Marcus

The Norman Conquests

(L-R): Ben Miles, Stephen Mangan and Paul Ritter in *Living Together*.

Scenes Continued

LIVING TOGETHER

The action takes place in the sitting room of a
Victorian house in England
during a weekend in July.

Act I	Act II
Scene I: Saturday, 6:30pm	Scene I: Sunday, 9pm
Scene II: Saturday, 8pm	Scene II: Monday, 8am

ROUND AND ROUND THE GARDEN

The action takes place in the garden of a
Victorian house in England
during a weekend in July.

Act I	Act II
Scene I: Saturday, 5:30pm	Scene I: Sunday, 11am
Scene II: Saturday, 9pm	Scene II: Monday, 9am

Amelia Bullmore
Ruth

Jessica Hynes
Annie

Stephen Mangan
Norman

Ben Miles
Tom

Paul Ritter
Reg

Amanda Root
Sarah

Cassie Beck
u/s Annie

Peter Bradbury
u/s Norman

Angela Pierce
u/s Ruth, Sarah

Tony Ward
u/s Tom, Reg

Alan Ayckbourn
Playwright

Matthew Warchus
Director

Rob Howell
Scenery and Costume Designer

David Howe
Lighting Designer

Simon Baker for Autograph
Sound Designer

Kevin Spacey,
Artistic Director,
The Old Vic
Original Producer

Laura Green,
Frankel Green
Theatrical
Management
General Management

Sonia Friedman
Productions Ltd.
Producer

Steven Baruch
Producer

Marc Routh
Producer

Richard Frankel
Producer

The Playbill Broadway Yearbook 2009-2010   253

The Norman Conquests

Tom Viertel
Producer

Dede Harris
Producer

Lauren Doll
Producer

BOX OFFICE
(L-R): Michael McCarthy, Cheryl Dennis, Michael Kumor

Jamie deRoy
Producer

Remmel T. Dickinson
Producer

Eric Falkenstein
Producer

Harriet Newman Leve
Producer

CREW
Seated (L-R): Andrew Michaelson, Jessica Worsnop, Sue Stepnik, Julia P. Jones, Townsend Teague

Standing (L-R): Jim Bay, Stewart Wagner, Ira Mont, Bobby Clifton, Tony Menditto, Joe Caputo, Owen Parmele

Michael Filerman
Producer

Jennifer Manocherian
Producer

Jeanne Donovan Fisher,
True Love Productions
Producer

Barbara Manocherian
Producer

FRONT OF HOUSE STAFF
Front Row (L-R): Cristina Marie, Amy Wolk, Sophie Koufakis, Denise Demirjian

Middle Row (L-R): Roxanne Gayol, Katherine Maldonado, Xavier Young, Rosetta M. Jlelaty, Michael Trupia

Back Row (L-R): Patricia Kennedy, Patricia Cuocci, Laurel Brevoort, Georgia Keghlian, Travis Libin

The Norman Conquests

STAFF FOR THE NORMAN CONQUESTS

GENERAL MANAGEMENT
FRANKEL GREEN THEATRICAL MANAGEMENT
Richard Frankel   Laura Green   Joe Watson
Leslie Ledbetter

COMPANY MANAGER
Kathy Lowe
Associate Company Manager .... Townsend Teague

GENERAL PRESS REPRESENTATIVE
BONEAU BRYAN-BROWN
Adrian Bryan-Brown   Jim Byk
Aaron Meier   Rachel Stange

New York Casting by Jim Carnahan, C.S.A.

Production Stage Manager	Ira Mont
Stage Manager	Julia P. Jones
Associate Director	Annabel Bolton
Associate Director	Mark Schneider
Production Manager	Aurora Productions/ Gene O'Donovan, Ben Heller, Bethany Weinstein
Video Designer	Duncan McLean
Dialect Consultant	Elizabeth A. Smith
Vocal Coach	Deborah Hecht
Associate Set Designer	Paul Weimer
Associate Costume Designer	Daryl Stone
Associate Lighting Designer	Vivien Leone
Associate Sound Designer	Christopher Cronin
Assistant Props	Joe Caputo
Management Assistant	Andrew Michaelson
Production Assistant	Nathan K. Claus
Wardrobe Supervisor	Sue Stepnik
Dressers	Bobby Clifton, Jessica Worsnop

Asst. to Ms. Friedman	Lucie Lovatt
Asst. to Mr. Routh	Katie Adams
Asst. to Mr. Baruch	Sonja Soper
Asst. to Mr. Viertel	Tania Senewiratne
Asst. to Ms. Harris	Matthew Parent
Asst. to Mr. Bartner	Sarah Nashman
Advertising	Spotco, Inc./ Drew Hodges, Tom Greenwald, Jim Edwards, Jim Aquino, Stacey Maya
Promotions/Marketing	Broadway Print and Mail
Insurance	DeWitt Stern Group
Legal	Patricia Crown, Coblence and Associates
Payroll Service	Castellana Service, Inc.
Accounting	Fried and Kowgios Partners, LLP

FRANKEL GREEN THEATRICAL MANAGEMENT STAFF

Finance Director	Michael Naumann
Assistant to Mr. Frankel	Heidi Libby
Assistant to Ms. Green	Joshua A. Saletnik
Assistant Finance Director	Sue Bartelt
Finance Associate	Heather Allen
IT Manager	Roddy Pimentel
Sales & Marketing Director	Adam Jay
Director of Business Affairs	Michael Sinder
Business Affairs Assistant	Dario Dalla Lasta
Booking	On the Road Booking, LLC/ Simma Levine, President
Office Manager	Emily Wright
Receptionists	Christina Cataldo, Allison Raines
Interns	Carrie Brinker, Burke Campbell, Caitlin Fahey, Stephanie Halbedel, Beky Hughston, Collin Kim, Sue Lippa, Katie Pope, Baile Slevin

SONIA FRIEDMAN PRODUCTIONS

Producer	Sonia Friedman
General Manager	Diane Benjamin
Creative Producer	Lisa Makin
Head of Production	Pam Skinner
Associate Producer	Sharon Duckworth
Literary Associate	Jack Bradley
Production Assistant	Lucie Lovatt
Production Assistant	Martin Ball
Production Assistant	Bailey Lock
Production Accountant	Melissa Hay
Chief Executive Officer-NY	David Lazar
Executive Assistant-NY	Dan Gallagher
SFP Board	Helen Enright, Howard Panter, Rosemary Squire

CREDITS AND ACKNOWLEDGEMENTS
Set construction by Souvenir Scenic Studios. U.S. scenic by Showmotion, Inc. Costumes made by Kevin Matthias and Kathy Pedersen. Lighting equipment provided by PRG Lighting. Sound and video equipment provided by Sound Associates, Inc. Thanks to Jane Semark, Lorna Earl, Anna Maria Casson and the staff at The Old Vic Theatre. Makeup provided by M•A•C.

MUSIC CREDITS
"Here Comes the Sun" (George Harrison), Harrisongs, Ltd. All rights administered by Wixen Music Publishing, Inc. "Here Comes the Sun" performed by Nina Simone courtesy of the RCA Records label by arrangement with Sony Music Entertainment. "Here Comes the Sun" performed by Steve Harley & Cockney Rebel; courtesy of EMI Records, Ltd., under license from EMI Film & Television Music. "Here Comes the Sun" performed by Charles Wright & the Watts 103rd Street Rhythm Band; courtesy of Warner Bros. Records, Inc. by arrangement with Warner Music Group Film & TV Licensing. "One" (Harry Nilsson), ©1968 (renewed), Golden Syrup Music (BMI). All rights administered by Warner-Tamerlane Publishing Corp. All rights reserved. Used by permission.

THE OLD VIC

Chief Executive	Sally Greene
Artistic Director	Kevin Spacey
Producers	Kate Pakenham, John Richardson
Development Director	Vivien Wallace
General Manager, OVTC	Ros Brooke-Taylor
Production Manager	Dominic Fraser
Finance Director	Vanessa Harrison
Marketing Director	Catrin John
Manager, American Associates & New Voices Network	Rachael Stevens
Head of Development, American Associates of The Old Vic	Amanda Woods
U.S. Legal Counsel	David Friedlander
Associates	Edward Hall, David Liddiment, Matthew Warchus, Anthony Page

☐ CIRCLE IN THE SQUARE THEATRE
Under the direction of
Theodore Mann and Paul Libin
Susan Frankel, *General Manager*

House Manager	Cheryl Dennis
Head Carpenter	Anthony Menditto
Head Electrician	Stewart Wagner
Prop Master	Owen E. Parmele
Sound Engineer	Jim Bay
Box Office Treasurer	Michael G. McCarthy
Administrative Assistant	Courtney Kochuba
Assistant to Paul Libin	Clark Mims Tedesco
Assistant to Theodore Mann	Eric P. Vitale

☐ CIRCLE IN THE SQUARE THEATRE SCHOOL

President	Paul Libin
Artistic Director	Theodore Mann
Theatre School Director	E. Colin O'Leary
Arts Education/Development	Jonathan Mann
Administrative Assistant	David Pleva
Administrative Assistant	Virginia Tuller

GOVERNMENT, FOUNDATION & PATRON SUPPORT
Stephen & Mary Birch Foundation; Jewels of Charity; Patrick J. Patek Scholarship Fund; Thomas L. Kelly Foundation; Blanche & Irving Laurie Foundation; Frederick Loewe Foundation; Edith Meiser Foundation, Newman's Own; Jerome Robbins Foundation; Ross Family Fund; Geraldine Stutz Foundation; John Veitch Bequest; Arthur N. Wiener Trust; Martin E. Segal; Vera Stern; New York City Department of Cultural Affairs

Amelia Bullmore in *Round and Round the Garden*

Photo by Richard Termine

Oleanna

First Preview: September 29, 2009. Opened: October 11, 2009.
Closed December 6, 2009 after 15 Previews and 65 Performances.

CAST
(in alphabetical order)
John .... BILL PULLMAN
Carol .... JULIA STILES

SETTING
The play takes place in John's office.

STANDBYS
For Carol:
BLAIR BAKER

For John:
MARTY LODGE

(L-R): Bill Pullman and Julia Stiles

GOLDEN THEATRE
A Shubert Organization Theatre
Philip J. Smith, *Chairman*   Robert E. Wankel, *President*

JEFFREY FINN
ARLENE SCANLAN   JED BERNSTEIN
KEN DAVENPORT   CARLA EMIL   ERGO ENTERTAINMENT
HARBOR ENTERTAINMENT   ELIE HIRSCHFELD   RACHEL HIRSCHFELD
HOP THEATRICALS   BRIAN FENTY/MARTHA H. JONES   CENTER THEATRE GROUP

present

BILL PULLMAN   JULIA STILES

in

OLEANNA

by

DAVID MAMET

| Scenic Design | Costume Design | Lighting Design |
| NEIL PATEL | CATHERINE ZUBER | DONALD HOLDER |

| Fight Direction | Production Stage Manager | Marketing Services |
| RICK SORDELET | CHARLES MEANS | B&B MARKETING |

| Production Management | Press Representative | General Management |
| JUNIPER STREET PRODUCTIONS | THE PUBLICITY OFFICE | ALAN WASSER - ALLAN WILLIAMS MARK SHACKET |

Directed by
DOUG HUGHES

The Producers wish to express their appreciation to Theatre Development Fund for its support of this production.

Bill Pullman
John

Julia Stiles
Carol

Blair Baker
Standby for Carol

Marty Lodge
Standby for John

Oleanna

David Mamet
Playwright

Doug Hughes
Director

Neil Patel
Scenic Designer

Catherine Zuber
Costume Designer

Donald Holder
Lighting Designer

Rick Sordelet
Fight Director

Guy Kwan, John Paull III, Hillary Blanken, Kevin Broomell, Ana Rose Greene, Juniper Street Productions
Production Manager

Alan Wasser
General Manager

Jeffrey Finn
Producer

Arlene Scanlan
Producer

Jed Bernstein
Producer

Ken Davenport
Producer

Donny Epstein,
Ergo Entertainment
Producer

Yeeshai Gross,
Ergo Entertainment
Producer

Elie Landau,
Ergo Entertainment
Producer

David Broser and Aaron Harnick,
Harbor Entertainment
Producers

Elie Hirschfeld
Producer

Larry Kaye,
HOP Theatricals
Producer

Michael Ritchie,
Artistic Director,
Center Theatre Group
Producer

Charles Dillingham,
Managing Director,
Center Theatre Group
Producer

Gordon Davidson,
Founding Artistic Director,
Center Theatre Group
Producer

FRONT OF HOUSE STAFF
Front Row (L-R): Patricia Kenary, Patricia Byrne, Shelia Miller, Cookie Harlin, Nilsa Nairn

Middle Row (L-R): House Manager Carolyne Jones-Barnes, Rita Russell, Veronica Morrissey, Mae Smith, Helen Bentley

Back Row (L-R): Lena White, Lars Jorgensen, Yuri Fernandez, Timothy Moran

Oleanna

BACKSTAGE STAFF
(L-R): Michael Borowski (press agent), Paul Delcioppo (sound), Penny Daulton (company manager), Carrie Kamerer (wardrobe), Marti McIntosh (stage manager), Steve McDonald (props), Sylvia Yoshioka (house electrician), Charles Means (production stage manager)

STAFF FOR OLEANNA

GENERAL MANAGEMENT
ALAN WASSER ASSOCIATES
Alan Wasser   Allan Williams
Mark Shacket

COMPANY MANAGER
Penelope Daulton

GENERAL PRESS REPRESENTATIVE
THE PUBLICITY OFFICE
Marc Thibodeau   Michael S. Borowski
Jeremy Shaffer   Matt Fasano

PRODUCTION STAGE MANAGER
Charles Means

TECHNICAL SUPERVISION
JUNIPER STREET PRODUCTIONS
Hillary Blanken   Ana Rose Greene
Kevin Broomell   Guy Kwan

Stage Manager .... Marti McIntosh
Assistant to the Director .... Jenny Slattery
Associate Scenic Designer .... Caleb Levengood
Associate Lighting Designer .... Carolyn Wong
Assistant to the Lighting Designer .... Carla Linton
Production Carpenter .... Dave Fulton
Automation Carpenter .... Geoff Vaughn
Production Electrician .... Jimmy Maloney
Production Properties .... Chris Pantuso
Wardrobe Supervisor/
  Mr. Pullman's Dresser .... Patrick Bevilacqua
Ms. Stiles' Dresser .... Carrie Kamerer
Fight Captain .... Charles Means
Advertising .... SpotCo/
   Drew Hodges, Jim Edwards,
   Tom Greenwald, Stephen Sosnowski,
   Meghan Ownbey
Marketing .... B&B Marketing/
   Betsy Bernstein, Jed Bernstein
Website Design &
  Internet Marketing .... Jamie Lynn Ballard/
   Davenport Theatrical Enterprises, Inc.
Legal Counsel .... Sendroff & Baruch LLP/
   Jason Baruch, Esq.
Accounting .... Rosenberg, Neuwirth & Kuchner/
   Chris Cacace, Pat Pedersen
Assistant to Mr. Finn .... Richard Rainville
General Management Associates .... Aaron Lustbader,
   Lane Marsh, Thom Mitchell
General Management Office .... Christopher Betz,
   Jake Hirzel, Dawn Kusinski,
   Patty Montesi, Jennifer Mudge
Production Photographer .... Craig Schwartz
Production Assistant .... Raynelle Wright
Technical Production Assistant .... Alexandra Paull
Insurance .... Ventura Insurance Brokerage/
   Christine Sadofsky
Banking .... Signature Bank/Barbara von Borstel
Payroll .... Castellana Services, Inc.
Merchandising .... Marquee Merchandise, LLC/
   Matt Murphy
Theatre Displays .... King Displays
Opening Night Consultant .... Suzanne Tobak
Group Sales .... Group Sales Box Office
   BestOfBroadway.com 212-398-8383/
   800-223-7565

Makeup provided by M•A•C

CREDITS AND ACKNOWLEDGEMENTS
Scenery built and painted by PRG Scenic Technologies. Lighting equipment provided by PRG Lighting. Sound equipment provided by PRG Audio. Furniture and props executed by the Spoon Group.

Rehearsed at the New 42nd Street Studios

SPECIAL THANKS
Jessica Alvarez, Ron Gwiazda, Toni Howard, George Lane, Tom Katzenmeyer, Elise Konialian, L. Glenn Poppleton, Graciella Sanchez, Adam Schweitzer and a special thanks to Jamie deRoy.

JOIN THE OLEANNA CONVERSATION
www.OleannaOnBroadway.com
and
http://oleannaonbroadway.com/sides.html
www.Twitter.com/OleannaBroadway
www.facebook.com/pages/New-York-NY/Oleanna/94023919490

Oleanna was originally produced on the New York stage by Frederick Zollo, Mitchell Maxwell, Alan J. Schuster, Peggy Hill Rosenkranz, Ron Kastner, Thomas Viertel, Steven Baruch and Frank and Wojo Gero, in association with Patricia Wolff.

THE SHUBERT ORGANIZATION, INC.
Board of Directors

Philip J. Smith
Chairman

Robert E. Wankel
President

Wyche Fowler, Jr.

John W. Kluge

Lee J. Seidler

Michael I. Sovern

Stuart Subotnick

Elliot Greene
Chief Financial Officer

David Andrews
Senior Vice President – Shubert Ticketing

Juan Calvo
Vice President and Controller

John Darby
Vice President – Facilities

Peter Entin
Vice President – Theatre Operations

Charles Flateman
Vice President – Marketing

Anthony LaMattina
Vice President – Audit & Production Finance

Brian Mahoney
Vice President – Ticket Sales

D.S. Moynihan
Vice President – Creative Projects

Oleanna
SCRAPBOOK

Oleanna
Scrapbook

Photos and Page Design by Marti McIntosh

The Phantom of the Opera

First Preview: January 9, 1988. Opened: January 26, 1988
Still running as of May 31, 2010.

CAST

The Phantom of the Opera	JOHN CUDIA
Christine Daaé	JENNIFER HOPE WILLS
Christine Daaé	SUSAN OWEN
	(Mon. eve. performance)
Christine Daaé	KIMILEE BRYANT
	(Thurs. eve. performance)
Raoul, Vicomte de Chagny	RYAN SILVERMAN
Carlotta Giudicelli	PATRICIA PHILLIPS
Monsieur André	GEORGE LEE ANDREWS
Monsieur Firmin	DAVID CRYER
Madame Giry	CRISTIN J. HUBBARD
Ubaldo Piangi	EVAN HARRINGTON
Meg Giry	HEATHER McFADDEN
Monsieur Reyer/ Hairdresser ("Il Muto")	GEOFF PACKARD
Auctioneer	JOHN KUETHER
Jeweler ("Il Muto")	FRANK MASTRONE
Monsieur Lefèvre/Firechief	KENNETH KANTOR
Joseph Buquet	RICHARD POOLE
Don Attilio ("Il Muto")	JOHN KUETHER
Passarino ("Don Juan Triumphant")	JEREMY STOLLE
Slave Master ("Hannibal")	ANTON HARRISON LaMON
Flunky/Stage Hand/Solo Dancer ("Il Muto")	JACK HAYES
Page ("Don Juan Triumphant")	TONNA MILLER
Porter/Fireman	CHRIS BOHANNON
Spanish Lady ("Don Juan Triumphant")	KIMILEE BRYANT
Wardrobe Mistress/Confidante ("Il Muto")	RAYANNE GONZALES
Princess ("Hannibal")	SUSAN OWEN
Madame Firmin	MELODY RUBIE
Innkeeper's Wife ("Don Juan Triumphant")	MARY ILLES
Marksman	PAUL A. SCHAEFER
The Ballet Chorus of the Opéra Populaire	POLLY BAIRD, AMANDA EDGE, GIANNA LOUNGWAY, MABEL MODRONO, JESSICA RADETSKY, CARLY BLAKE SEBOUHIAN, DIANNA WARREN

Continued on next page

MAJESTIC THEATRE
247 West 44th Street
A Shubert Organization Theatre
Philip J. Smith, *Chairman*   Robert E. Wankel, *President*

CAMERON MACKINTOSH and
THE REALLY USEFUL THEATRE COMPANY, INC.
present

The PHANTOM of the OPERA

starring
JOHN CUDIA
JENNIFER HOPE WILLS
RYAN SILVERMAN

GEORGE LEE ANDREWS   DAVID CRYER   PATRICIA PHILLIPS
CRISTIN J. HUBBARD   EVAN HARRINGTON   HEATHER McFADDEN

At certain performances
MARNI RAAB
plays the role of "Christine"

Music by
ANDREW LLOYD WEBBER
Lyrics by **CHARLES HART**
Additional lyrics by RICHARD STILGOE
Book by RICHARD STILGOE & ANDREW LLOYD WEBBER
Based on the novel 'Le Fantôme de L'Opéra' by GASTON LEROUX
Production Design by MARIA BJÖRNSON   Lighting by ANDREW BRIDGE
Sound Design by MICK POTTER   Original Sound Design by MARTIN LEVAN
Musical Supervision & Direction DAVID CADDICK   Musical Director KRISTEN BLODGETTE
Production Supervisor PETER von MAYRHAUSER
Orchestrations by DAVID CULLEN & ANDREW LLOYD WEBBER
Casting by TARA RUBIN CASTING   Original Casting by JOHNSON-LIFF ASSOCIATES
General Management ALAN WASSER ASSOCIATES

Musical Staging & Choreography by GILLIAN LYNNE
Directed by **HAROLD PRINCE**

10/1/09

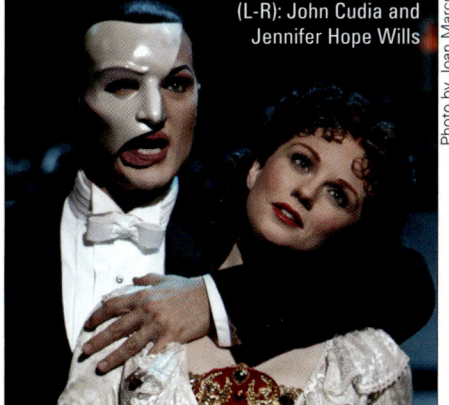

(L-R): John Cudia and Jennifer Hope Wills

Photo by Joan Marcus

The Phantom of the Opera

MUSICAL NUMBERS

PROLOGUE
The stage of the Paris Opéra House, 1911

OVERTURE

ACT ONE—PARIS 1881

Scene 1—The dress rehearsal of "Hannibal"
"Think of Me"..Carlotta, Christine, Raoul
Scene 2—After the Gala
"Angel of Music"..Christine and Meg
Scene 3—Christine's dressing room
"Little Lotte/The Mirror" (Angel of Music)................Raoul, Christine, Phantom
Scene 4—The Labyrinth underground
"The Phantom of the Opera"....................................Phantom and Christine
Scene 5—Beyond the lake
"The Music of the Night"..Phantom
Scene 6—Beyond the lake, the next morning
"I Remember/Stranger Than You Dreamt It"............Christine and Phantom
Scene 7—Backstage
"Magical Lasso"..................Buquet, Meg, Madame Giry and Ballet Girls
Scene 8—The Managers' office
"Notes/Prima Donna"......................Firmin, André, Raoul, Carlotta, Giry, Meg,
Piangi and Phantom
Scene 9—A performance of "Il Muto"
"Poor Fool, He Makes Me Laugh"..........................Carlotta and Company
Scene 10—The roof of the Opéra House
"Why Have You Brought Me Here/Raoul, I've Been There"...........Raoul and Christine
"All I Ask of You"..Raoul and Christine
"All I Ask of You" (Reprise)..Phantom

ENTR'ACTE

ACT TWO—SIX MONTHS LATER

Scene 1—The staircase of the Opéra House, New Year's Eve
"Masquerade/Why So Silent"..Full Company
Scene 2—Backstage
Scene 3—The Managers' office
"Notes/Twisted Every Way"...............André, Firmin, Carlotta, Piangi, Raoul,
Christine, Giry and Phantom
Scene 4—A rehearsal for "Don Juan Triumphant"
Scene 5—A graveyard in Peros
"Wishing You Were Somehow Here Again"..........................Christine
"Wandering Child/Bravo, Bravo"..............Phantom, Christine and Raoul
Scene 6—The Opéra House stage before the Premiere
Scene 7—"Don Juan Triumphant"
"The Point of No Return"..................................Phantom and Christine
Scene 8—The Labyrinth underground
"Down Once More/Track Down This Murderer"..................Full Company
Scene 9—Beyond the lake

Cast Continued

Ballet Swing ....LAURIE V. LANGDON
Swings ....SCOTT MIKITA, JAMES ROMICK,
JANET SAIA, KRISTIE DALE SANDERS

UNDERSTUDIES
For the Phantom: JAMES ROMICK,
JEREMY STOLLE
For Christine: KIMILEE BRYANT,
SUSAN OWEN
For Raoul: GEOFF PACKARD, JAMES ROMICK,
PAUL A. SCHAEFER, JEREMY STOLLE
For Firmin: KENNETH KANTOR,
JOHN KUETHER, JAMES ROMICK
For André: FRANK MASTRONE,
SCOTT MIKITA, RICHARD POOLE,
JAMES ROMICK
For Carlotta: KIMILEE BRYANT, JANET SAIA,
JULIE SCHMIDT
For Mme. Giry: KIMILEE BRYANT, JANET SAIA,
KRISTIE DALE SANDERS, JULIE SCHMIDT
For Piangi: CHRIS BOHANNON,
FRANK MASTRONE, JEREMY STOLLE
For Meg Giry: POLLY BAIRD, AMANDA EDGE,
CARLY BLAKE SEBOUHIAN
For Slave Master: JACK HAYES
For Solo Dancer ("Il Muto"):
ANTON HARRISON LaMON
Dance Captain: LAURIE V. LANGDON
Assistant Dance Captain: HEATHER McFADDEN

ORCHESTRA
Conductors: DAVID CADDICK,
KRISTEN BLODGETTE, DAVID LAI,
TIM STELLA, NORMAN WEISS
Violins: JOYCE HAMMANN (Concert Master),
ALVIN E. ROGERS, CLAIRE CHAN,
KURT COBLE, JAN MULLEN,
KAREN MILNE
Violas: STEPHANIE FRICKER,
VERONICA SALAS
Cellos: TED ACKERMAN, KARL BENNION
Bass: MELISSA SLOCUM
Harp: HENRY FANELLI
Flute: SHERYL HENZE
Flute/Clarinet: ED MATTHEW
Oboe: MELANIE FELD
Clarinet: MATTHEW GOODMAN
Bassoon: ATSUKO SATO
Trumpets: LOWELL HERSHEY,
FRANCIS BONNY
Bass Trombone: WILLIAM WHITAKER
French Horns: DANIEL CULPEPPER,
PETER REIT, DAVID SMITH
Percussion: ERIC COHEN, JAN HAGIWARA
Keyboards: TIM STELLA, NORMAN WEISS

The Phantom of the Opera

 John Cudia
The Phantom of the Opera

 Jennifer Hope Wills
Christine Daaé

 Ryan Silverman
Raoul, Vicomte de Chagny

 George Lee Andrews
Monsieur André

 David Cryer
Monsieur Firmin

 Patricia Phillips
Carlotta Giudicelli

 Cristin J. Hubbard
Madame Giry

 Evan Harrington
Ubaldo Piangi

 Heather McFadden
Meg Giry/Assistant Dance Captain

 Marni Raab
Christine Daaé at certain performances

 Polly Baird
Ballet Chorus

 Chris Bohannon
Porter/Fireman

 Kimilee Bryant
Spanish Lady and Christine Daaé at certain performances

 Amanda Edge
Ballet Chorus

 Rayanne Gonzales
Wardrobe Mistress/Confidante

 Jack Hayes
Flunky/Stage hand/Solo Dancer

 Mary Illes
Innkeeper's Wife

 Kenneth Kantor
Monsieur Lefèvre/Firechief

 John Kuether
Auctioneer/Don Attilio

 Anton Harrison LaMon
Slave Master

 Laurie V. Langdon
Dance Captain/Ballet Swing

 Gianna Loungway
Ballet Chorus

 Frank Mastrone
Jeweler

 Scott Mikita
Swing

 Tonna Miller
Page

 Mabel Modrono
Ballet Chorus

 Susan Owen
Princess and Christine Daaé at certain performances

 Geoff Packard
Monsieur Reyer/Hairdresser

 Richard Poole
Joseph Buquet

 Jessica Radetsky
Ballet Chorus

 James Romick
Swing

 Melody Rubie
Madame Firmin

 Janet Saia
Swing

 Kristie Dale Sanders
Swing

 Paul A. Schaefer
Marksman

The Phantom of the Opera

Carly Blake Sebouhian
Ballet Chorus

Jeremy Stolle
Passarino

Dianna Warren
Ballet Chorus

Andrew Lloyd Webber
Composer/Book/Co-Orchestrator

Harold Prince
Director

Charles Hart
Lyrics

Richard Stilgoe
Book and Additional Lyrics

Gillian Lynne
Musical Staging and Choreography

Maria Björnson (1949-2002)
Production Design

Andrew Bridge
Lighting Designer

Mick Potter
Sound Designer

Martin Levan
Original Sound Designer

David Cullen
Co-Orchestrator

David Caddick
Musical Supervision and Direction

Kristen Blodgette
Associate Musical Supervisor/Musical Director

Peter von Mayrhauser
Production Supervisor

Denny Berry
Production Dance Supervisor

Craig Jacobs
Production Stage Manager

Bethe Ward
Stage Manager from the beginning

David Lai
Conductor

Tara Rubin Casting
Casting

Vincent Liff and Geoffrey Johnson, Johnson-Liff Associates
Original Casting

Alan Wasser Associates
General Manager

Cameron Mackintosh
Producer

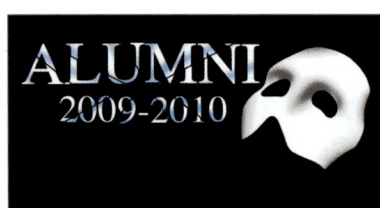

Dara Adler
Ballet Chorus

Kyle Barisch
Swing

Wren Marie Harrington
Innkeeper's Wife ("Don Juan Triumphant")

Satomi Hofmann
Madame Giry, Page ("Don Juan Triumphant")

Rebecca Judd
Madame Giry

Anna Laghezza
Ballet Chorus

Elizabeth Loyacano
Christine Daaé at certain performances

Howard McGillin
The Phantom of the Opera

The Phantom of the Opera

Janice Niggeling
Ballet Chorus

Stephen Tewksbury
Joseph Buquet, Porter/Fireman

Jim Weitzer
Swing

Bruce Winant
Monsieur Firmin

James Zander
Flunky/Stage Hand/ Solo Dancer ("Il Muto")

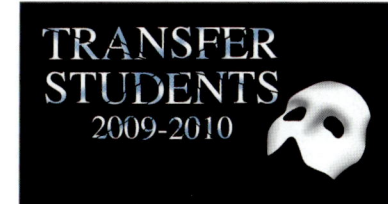

Emily Adonna
Ballet Chorus

Kyle Barisch
Jeweler ("Il Muto"), Marksman, Monsieur Reyer/Hairdresser ("Il Muto"), Passarino ("Don Juan Triumphant")

Melanie Field
Page ("Don Juan Triumphant")

Julie Hanson
Princess ("Hannibal")

Jessy Hendrickson
Ballet Chorus

Rebecca Judd
Madame Giry

Ted Keegan
Monsieur André, Monsieur Reyer/Hairdresser ("Il Muto")

Kfir
Slave Master ("Hannibal"), Solo Dancer ("Il Muto") at certain performances

Kara Klein
Meg Giry at certain performances, Ballet Chorus

Kris Koop
Madame Firmin, Page ("Don Juan Triumphant")

Anna Laghezza
Ballet Chorus

Mykal D. Laury, II
Flunky/Stage Hand/Solo Dancer ("Il Muto"), Slave Master ("Hannibal")

Sarah Anne Lewis
Madame Firmin, Swing

Michele McConnell
Wardrobe Mistress/Confidante ("Il Muto")

Justin Peck
Flunky/Stage Hand/Solo Dancer ("Il Muto"), Slave Master ("Hannibal")

Carly Blake Sebouhian
Meg Giry at certain performances

Jimmy Smagula
Porter/Fireman, Ubaldo Piangi

Stephen Tewksbury
Joseph Buquet, Porter/Fireman

Jim Weitzer
Monsieur Reyer/Hairdresser ("Il Muto"); Raoul, Vicomte de Chagny at certain performances

James Zander
Slave Master ("Hannibal"), Solo Dancer ("Il Muto") at certain performances

CREW
Front Row (L-R): Frank Billings, John Hulbert, Craig Evans, Fred Smith, Matt Mezick, Eric Carney
Back Row (L-R): Jack Farmer, George Dummitt, Brian Colonna, Rob Wallace

The Phantom of the Opera

ORCHESTRA
Front Row (L-R): Kristen Blodgette (Musical Director), Suzanne Gilman, Lowell Hershey, Eddie Malave, Henry Fanelli, Jill de Vos, Karen Milne, Melanie Feld, Karl Bennion
Back Row (L-R): Christine MacDonnell, Claire Chan, Sheryl Henze, Matthew Goodman, Francis Bonny, Joyce Hammann, Peter Reit, Chris Thompson, Dan Culpepper, Will De Vos
Not Pictured: David Lai, Ted Ackerman, Kurt Coble, Eric Cohen, Jan Hagiwara, Jan Mullen, Veronica Salas, Atsuko Sato, Debra Shufelt-Dine, Melissa Slocum, David Smith, Tim Stella, Norman Weiss, William Whitaker

FRONT OF HOUSE STAFF
Front Row (L-R): Deanna Sorenson, Lucia Cappelletti, Karen Starken, Gwen Coley, Sylvia Bailey, Dorothy Curich, Virginia Kinard

Back Row (L-R): Lawrence Darden, Devin Elting, James Muro, Perry Dell'Aquila, Emilio Benoit, Abigail Smith, Taka Ono, Cynthia Carlin, Peter Kulok (House Manager)

HAIR, WARDROBE & MAKEUP
Front Row (L-R): Annette Lovece, Sarah Stamp, Jameson Eaton, Erika Smith, Shazia Saleem

Middle Row (L-R): Jessica Reiner, Michael Piscitelli, Ron Flemming, Marylou Rios, Ron Blakely

Back Row (L-R): Michael Jacobs, Thelma Pollard (Makeup Supervisor)

Not Pictured: Julie Ratcliffe (Wardrobe Supervisor) and Leone Gagliardi (Hair Supervisor)

MANAGEMENT
Front Row (L-R): Josh Blye (Assistant Stage Manager), Brendan Smith (Stage Manager), Karen Parlato (Assistant Stage Manager), Brian Westmoreland (Assistant Stage Manager)

Middle Row (L-R): Craig Jacobs (Production Stage Manager), Michael Borowski (Press Agent), Bethe Ward (Stage Manager), Katherine McNamee (Assistant Company Manager), Steve Greer (Company Manager)

Top: Laurie Volny Langdon (Dance Captain)

Not Pictured: Peter von Mayrhauser (Production Supervisor)

The Phantom of the Opera

STAFF FOR *THE PHANTOM OF THE OPERA*

General Manager
ALAN WASSER ASSOCIATES
Alan Wasser   Allan Williams

General Press Representative
THE PUBLICITY OFFICE
Marc Thibodeau   Michael S. Borowski
Jeremy Shaffer   Matt Fasano

Assistant to Mr. Prince
RUTH MITCHELL

Production Supervisor
PETER von MAYRHAUSER

Production Dance Supervisor
DENNY BERRY

Associate Musical Supervisor
KRISTEN BLODGETTE

Casting
TARA RUBIN CASTING

Technical Production Manager .... JAKE BELL
Company Manager .... STEVE GREER
Production Stage Manager .... CRAIG JACOBS
Stage Managers .... Bethe Ward, Brendan Smith
Assistant Company Manager .... Cathy Kwon

U.S. Design Staff
Associate Scenic Designer .... DANA KENN
Associate Costume Designer .... SAM FLEMING
Associate Lighting Designer .... DEBRA DUMAS
Associate Sound Designer .... PAUL GATEHOUSE
Sculptures Consultant .... Stephen Pyle
Pro Tools Programmer .... Lee McCutcheon

Casting Associates .... Dale Brown, Eric Woodall, CSA;
Laura Schutzel, CSA;
Merri Sugarman, CSA
Casting Assistants .... Paige Blansfield, Kaitlin Shaw
Dance Captain .... Laurie V. Langdon
Production Carpenter .... Joseph Patria
Production Electrician .... Robert Fehribach
Production Propertyman .... Timothy Abel
Production Sound Engineer .... Shannon Slaton
Production Wig Supervisor .... Leone Gagliardi
Production Make-up Supervisor .... Thelma Pollard
Make-up Assistants .... Pearleta N. Price,
Shazia J. Saleem
Head Carpenter .... Russell Tiberio III
Automation Carpenters .... Santos Sanchez,
Michael Girman
Assistant Carpenter .... Giancarlo Cottignoli
Flyman .... Daryl Miller
Head Electrician .... Alan Lampel
Assistant Electrician .... JR Beket
Head Props .... Matthew Mezick
Asst. Props./Boat Captain .... Joe Caruso
Sound Operator .... Eric Carney
Wardrobe Supervisor .... Julie Ratcliffe
Assistant Wardrobe Supervisor .... Robert Strong Miller
Hair Supervisor .... Leone Gagliardi

Hairdressers .... Charise Champion,
Kathleen A. Kurz, Erika Smith,
Sarah Stamp

Conductor .... David Lai
Associate Conductor .... Tim Stella
Assistant Conductor .... Norman Weiss
Musical Preparation
  Supervisor (U.S.) .... Chelsea Music Service, Inc
Synthesizer Consultant .... Stuart Andrews

Assistants to the Gen. Mgr. .... Christopher Betz,
Jake Hirzel, Patty Montesi, Jennifer Mudge

Legal Counsel .... F. Richard Pappas
Accounting .... Rosenberg, Neuwirth and Kutchner
Christopher A. Cacace
Logo Design and Graphics .... Dewynters Plc
London
Merchandising .... Dewynters Advertising Inc.
Advertising .... Serino Coyne Inc.,
Greg Corradetti, Andrea Prince
Marketing Direction .... Type A Marketing
Anne Rippey
Director of Ticket Services .... Janette Roush
Displays .... King Displays, Wayne Sapper
Insurance (U.S.) .... DeWitt Stern Group
Peter K. Shoemaker
Insurance (U.K.) .... Walton & Parkinson Limited
Richard Walton
Banking .... TD Bank
Payroll Service .... Castellana Services, Inc.

Original Production Photographer .... Clive Barda
Additional Photography .... Joan Marcus,
Bob Marshak, Peter Cunningham
House Manager .... Peter Kulok

CREDITS AND ACKNOWLEDGMENTS
Scenic construction and boat automation by Hudson Scenic Studios.
Scenery automation by Jeremiah J. Harris Associates, Inc./East Coast Theatre Supply, Inc. Scenery painted by Nolan Scenery Studios. Set and hand properties by McHugh Rollins Associates, Inc. Sculptural elements by Costume Armour. "Opera Ball" newell post statues and elephant by Nino Novellino of Costume Armour. Proscenium sculptures by Stephen Pyle. Draperies by I. Weiss and Sons, Inc. Soft goods provided by Quartet Theatrical Draperies. Safety systems by Foy Lighting equipment and special lighting effects by Four Star Lighting, Inc. Sound equipment and technical service provided by Masque Sound and Recording Corp. Special effects designed and executed by Theatre Magic, Inc., Richard Huggins, President. Costumes executed by Barbara Matera, Ltd. Costumes for "Hannibal" and "Masquerade" executed by Parsons/Meares, Ltd. Men's costumes by Vincent Costumes, Inc. Costume crafts for "Hannibal" and "Masquerade" by Janet Harper and Frederick Nihda. Fabric painting by Mary Macy. Additional costumes by Carelli Costumes, Inc. Costume accessories by Barak Stribling. Hats by Woody Shelp. Millinery and masks by Rodney Gordon. Footwear by Sharlot Battin of Montana Leatherworks, Ltd. Shoes by JC Theatrical and Costume Footwear and Taffy's N.Y. Jewelry by Miriam Haskell Jewels. Eyeglasses by H.L. Purdy. Wigs by The Wig Party. Garcia y Vega cigars used. Makeup consultant Kris Evans. Emer'gen-C super energy booster provided by Alacer Corp.

Champagne courtesy of Champagne G.H. Mumm

Furs by Christie Bros.

Shoes supplied by Peter Fox Limited

"The Phantom" character make-up created and designed by Christopher Tucker

Magic Consultant—Paul Daniels

CAMERON MACKINTOSH, INC.
Managing Director .... Nicholas Allott
Production Associate .... Shidan Majidi

THE REALLY USEFUL COMPANY INC
Public Relations .... BROWN LLOYD JAMES/
PETER BROWN

THE REALLY USEFUL GROUP
Directors .... LORD LLOYD WEBBER
LADY LLOYD WEBBER
ANDRÉ PTASZYNSKI
JONATHAN HULL
HOWARD WITTS
MARK WORDSWORTH

 THE SHUBERT ORGANIZATION, INC.
Board of Directors

Philip J. Smith	Robert E. Wankel
Chairman	President
Wyche Fowler, Jr.	John W. Kluge
Lee J. Seidler	Michael I. Sovern

Stuart Subotnick

Elliot Greene	David Andrews
Chief Financial Officer	Senior Vice President – Shubert Ticketing
Juan Calvo	John Darby
Vice President and Controller	Vice President – Facilities
Peter Entin	Charles Flateman
Vice President – Theatre Operations	Vice President – Marketing
Anthony LaMattina	Brian Mahoney
Vice President – Audit & Production Finance	Vice President – Ticket Sales

D.S. Moynihan
Vice President – Creative Projects

Phantom of the Opera
SCRAPBOOK

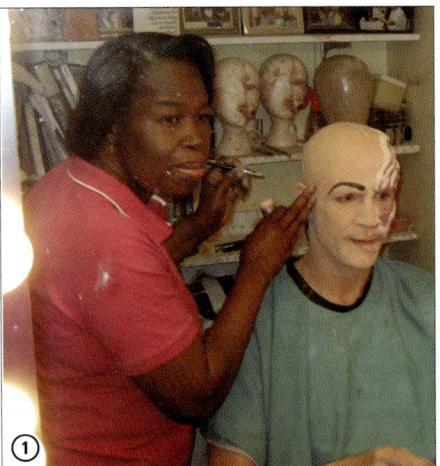

Correspondent: Kris Koop Ouellette, "Page"

Memorable Anniversary Gift: We get yummy brownies every year, although we think our producers are trying to help us watch our weight —each year, the size of the treats is a bit smaller. Perhaps they are superstitious and wish to prevent the show from ever ending (you know: It ain't over 'til the FAT LADY SINGS…?)

Most Exciting Celebrity Visitor: We all had the pleasure of entertaining—and being entertained by—Jude Mason, son of Broadway dancers/choreographers/et cetera Dana Solimando and Buck Mason. (Jude is also the grandson of Broadway star and Tony nominee Cathy Rigby and Theatre Producer Tom McCoy). Seriously, the first thing this charming 5-year old asked his Aunt Koopie was to see the PROPS! He asked everyone in the hair department very thoughtful questions about the silly wigs and had the rest of the company wrapped around his finger before the curtain went up and the chandelier came down. John Cudia, our wonderful Phantom, allowed Jude to stand next to him while make-up artist Thelma Pollard applied the latex pieces that make this handsome man into a bit of a beast. Jude was never shy with his questions, but always polite, saying "Excuse me…" before he spoke. When the curtain came down at 10:30 that night, Jude sat bolt upright in his seat and said, "I have to see John!" and then asked a million more questions about the Phantom's magic. SOOOOO SWEET!!!

Favorite Moment During Performance: Post Auction, pre-Hannibal: The ensemble and Mme. Giry, Piangi, etc. all assemble to "enter stage left" after Carlotta's initial solo entrance. We get to watch the Diva "prep" while lightning flashes upstage and heavy curtains rise to her right. Patricia Phillips raises a hand or her gaze up to the heavens right before her entrance, reminding herself—and the rest of us—how precious this performance opportunity is for the entire cast, crew and audience.

Favorite In-Theatre Gathering Place: Dick

1. Makeup artist Pearleta Price viewed in dressing room mirror as she prepares Howard McGillin for his final performance as The Phantom.
2. McGillin (left) backstage behind the curtain, about to make his entrance for "Masquerade."
3. McGillin's pup, Teddy, with his own dressing room door.
4. McGillin holds a commemorative urn created in his honor by longtime Phantom cover James Romick using a "segmented turning" technique utilizing 2,544 separate pieces of wood—the number of McGillin's performances as the Phantom.
5. Jennifer Hope Wills visits McGillin in his dressing room before his final peformance.

Miller's office is his own, and because he is who he is, that means that all are welcome—if they PLAY like good sports. We watch our college basketball, our NFL (Go STEELERS!), and Russell Tiberio and the Miller Clan often make a big crock-pot of MEAT to share with anyone who asks nicely. Some serious pork loin or hot dogs and sauerkraut, etc. make the entire company drool until dinner is served!

Favorite Off-Site Hangout: Ryan Silverman created a new off-site hangout for us *Phantom* Folk, plus a thriving group of lucky out-of-towners and a few locals, too! The EDISON BALLROOM, after-hours on a Saturday Night, features BIG BAND music via the real-deal – JOE BATTAGLIA AND THE NEW YORK BIG BAND—a full, luscious orchestra with a gorgeous singer (with a gorgeous voice) and food and drinks galore! And a shout-out to trombonist Jason Ingram, a pal to many of us *Phantom* Folk! Stop in and check it out!

Favorite Snack Food for Each Group:
Ballet Corps: Anything Kara Klein bakes
Principals: Ditto
Ensemble: Ditto
Crew: Ditto
Orchestra: Anything Norman Weiss bakes—so if Kara and Norman get together, they will RULE THE WORLD!!!!

Phantom of the Opera
SCRAPBOOK

Mascot: Still (and maybe always) Lucky Lai, now 11, who draws more $$$ for Broadway Cares/Equity Fights AIDS during collections than the rest of the cast put together. The kid is cute, and he's a maniac-salesman for our beloved charity! And bless us all—*The Phantom of the Opera*, Broadway, will have raised over four MILLION DOLLARS for BC/EFA on its own, thanks to the generosity of our audiences.

Favorite Therapy: We have to give props to the talented staff at Performing Arts Physical Therapy for keeping our show on its feet—literally! From healing our "tweaks" and "twinges" to rehabilitating our more serious injuries, we couldn't do this eight-shows-a-week, 52-weeks-a-year without PAPT!!!

Memorable Ad-Libs: So, we have to let Kenneth Kantor off the hook in a category in which he usually finds himself reluctantly starring…this year, we salute Ryan Silverman, who, as Raoul, found himself a bit distracted on stage after learning that his Mother had a serious accident (she's healing nicely by the way). Instead of the written lyric: "Christine, Christine, don't think that I don't care, but every hope and every prayer rests on you now!" he sang: "Christine, Christine don't think that I don't care…" and then he finished the phrase sounding like an electric pencil sharpener instead of saying another word.

'Caps'-off to Richard Poole who spat his front teeth at the feet of Carlotta while singing as Joseph Buquet in the *Hannibal* scene. Get it? CAPS OFF??? No, seriously. His front teeth were on the floor. And so, pro that he is, Richard reached down, shoved his teeth back in his mouth and finished the scene. Yes. He shoved them back in his mouth. And he alone finished the scene while everyone else peed in their pants.

Who Wore the Least: Mykal D. Laury II dropped his skirt (that's right, his SKIRT) in the *Hannibal* scene during a performance. Mykal plays the already-scantily-clad Slave Master role…but we all agree that this unexpected onstage costume change should become a permanent part of the show!

Catchphrases: "MEH…Meh Meh Meh…" That's all of the Raoul understudies speaking everything that Raoul might think or say. They are one part Monocled Monopoly Millionaire and one part Beeker from the Muppets (but very wealthy and a baritone.) We now just all greet each other backstage with "MEH."

Infamous Directorial Note: We are so fortunate to have the lovely and talented Kristen Blodgette conducting us again! There is a tricky spot in the show where the entire ensemble runs onstage in a blackout and begins singing the atonal Sitzprobe scene with many of us having no view of the conductor. Kristen got on the PA system to address an intended tempo change for the piece, acknowledging that we are all in the dark, with only a few singers able to make eye contact with the conductor. She stated with a big grin on her face: "I may be a bit more deliberate than you are used to…so just know that and be BETTER."

Principals (L-R) Jennifer Hope Wills, John Cudia and Ryan Silverman onstage at the Majestic Theatre sampling a cake marking the 9,000th performance, September 16, 2009.

Company Legends: Christine Dresser, Erna Dias, proud member of Local 764, has been with this company from the very beginning. Recently honored on stage in Times Square by presenter New York City Council Speaker Christine Quinn, Erna finally got to take a well-deserved bow for her many years of hard work. Erna treats every one of her 'Christine's like a star, and protects her girls from any troubles. During previews of *Phantom* on Broadway, the show's composer asked to visit with the 'Christine,' and Miss Erna made him wait until she could verify that the star wished to have such a visit. Lord Lloyd Webber cooled his heels in the hall while Erna asked Sarah Brightman (a.k.a. Mrs. Lloyd Webber at the time) if her husband would be welcome in her dressing room. After a few moments, ALW was escorted in with a smile. That's our girl!!!

We have another legend in our midst—the ever-smiling Sylvia Bailey—an usher at the Majestic for this show's entire run. Sylvia was a dancer at the Roxy Theatre in New York in the early 1940's, helping to support her family after her father fell ill. She graced the stage alongside the likes of Lana Turner, never missing a day of school despite her heavy performance schedule. In the midst of a blizzard in 1986, Sylvia offered a ride to chilly fellow-bus-mate Rose Heslin, and the rest is history. Rose recognized the goodness in this lovely lady and offered her a job when times were getting tough—ushering at the Majestic Theatre. Now Sylvia works alongside Dorothy Heslin, Rose's daughter.

Audition/Casting/Hiring Process: We have a new cast member who has a bit of a history with auditioning for this show. We recently and proudly welcomed Michele McConnell in the role of the Wardrobe Mistress/Confidante after her first audition in 1989. In a show that is still a hit after all of these years, Michele is not alone in being made to wait for this sweet success! In fact, she has this and a lot else in common with at least two other cast mates! At one point, Michele and fellow cast-mate Cristin J. Hubbard subleased a shabby apartment on 14th Street and Second Avenue from Kris Koop. None of these ladies had yet to grace the stage of the Majestic in this beautiful show, but now all three get to perform eight shows a week together. Small, lovely world, yes?

Traditions: Karen Milne of the orchestra has begun a new favorite tradition this year! She has begun to add a little sparkle into the basic black uniform the orchestra members wear. (Our show, unlike many on Broadway, has the entire orchestra seated in the orchestra pit, a thing that might seem obvious, but no—some more recent productions have their instrumentalists placed throughout the theatre, playing via the sound system, watching the conductor on a tv screen). To add a little beloved spice to lesser-loved holidays, Karen will don a groundhog puppet or Irish hat and beard during the first long blackout, just to shake things up. No one in the audience will ever see it, but we all get a big boost from her spontaneity!

A much-longer-running tradition is conducted by original cast-member George Lee Andrews. George Lee recites a piece or two of Irish poetry every Saint Patrick's Day, after the half-hour call. His lilting, honeyed voice makes our tired PA system SING—and every voice in the theatre is hushed for a few blessed moments. In the days leading up to these precious events, George can be seen in his usual haunts, whispering to himself, making certain that he will be word-perfect without any hint of a script on hand.

Present Laughter

First Preview: January 2, 2010. Opened: January 21, 2010.
Closed March 21, 2010 after 23 Previews and 69 Performances.

CAST
(in order of appearance)

Daphne Stillington	HOLLEY FAIN
Miss Erikson	NANCY E. CARROLL
Fred	JAMES JOSEPH O'NEIL
Monica Reed	HARRIET HARRIS
Garry Essendine	VICTOR GARBER
Liz Essendine	LISA BANES
Roland Maule	BROOKS ASHMANSKAS
Morris Dixon	MARC VIETOR
Henry Lyppiatt	RICHARD POE
Joanna Lyppiatt	PAMELA JANE GRAY
Lady Saltburn	ALICE DUFFY

TIME AND PLACE
Late 1930's London. Garry Essendine's flat.

ACT I
The morning

ACT II
Scene 1: Midnight, three days later
Scene 2: The following morning

ACT III
Evening, a week later

Continued on next page

AMERICAN AIRLINES THEATRE
ROUNDABOUT THEATRE COMPANY
Todd Haimes, Artistic Director
Harold Wolpert, Managing Director
Julia C. Levy, Executive Director

Presents

Victor Garber
in

PRESENT LAUGHTER

By
Noël Coward

with
Brooks Ashmanskas

Lisa Banes Nancy E. Carroll Alice Duffy Holley Fain
Pamela Jane Gray James Joseph O'Neil Richard Poe Marc Vietor

and
Harriet Harris

Set Design	Costume Design	Lighting Design	Sound Design	Hair & Wig Design
Alexander Dodge	Jane Greenwood	Rui Rita	Drew Levy	Tom Watson

Dialect Coach	Production Stage Manager	Production Management	Original Casting by
Deborah Hecht	Stephen M. Kaus	Aurora Productions	Alaine Alldaffer C.S.A.

Additional Casting by	General Manager	Press Representative
Jim Carnahan C.S.A. Carrie Gardner C.S.A.	Rebecca Habel	Boneau/Bryan-Brown

Director of Marketing & Sales Promotion	Founding Director	Associate Artistic Director
David B. Steffen	Gene Feist	Scott Ellis

Directed by
Nicholas Martin

Lead support provided by Roundabout's Play Production Fund partners: Beth and Ravenel Curry, Steven and Liz Goldstone, The Blanche and Irving Laurie Foundation, Mary and David Solomon.

This production of *Present Laughter* was originally produced in May 2007 by the Huntington Theatre Company.

Roundabout Theatre Company is a member of the League of Resident Theatres.
www.roundabouttheatre.org

1/21/10

(L-R): Victor Garber reclines as Harriet Harris screens his calls

Photo by Joan Marcus

Present Laughter

(L-R): Brooks Ashmanskas and Victor Garber

Photo by Joan Marcus

Cast Continued

UNDERSTUDIES

For Morris Dixon, Fred, Henry Lyppiatt:
PETER BRADBURY
For Daphne Stillington:
KATHLEEN McELFRESH
For Miss Erikson, Monica Reed, Lady Saltburn:
ROBIN MOSELEY
For Roland Maule:
JAMES JOSEPH O'NEIL
For Liz Essendine, Joanna Lyppiatt:
NICOLE ORTH-PALLAVICINI

Production Stage Manager:
STEPHEN M. KAUS
Stage Manager:
JAMIE GREATHOUSE

Victor Garber
Garry Essendine

Harriet Harris
Monica Reed

Brooks Ashmanskas
Roland Maule

Lisa Banes
Liz Essendine

Nancy E. Carroll
Miss Erikson

Alice Duffy
Lady Saltburn

Holley Fain
Daphne Stillington

Pamela Jane Gray
Joanna Lyppiatt

James Joseph O'Neil
Fred

Richard Poe
Henry Lyppiatt

Marc Vietor
Morris Dixon

Peter Bradbury
u/s Morris Dixon, Fred, Henry Lyppiatt

Kathleen McElfresh
u/s Daphne Stillington

Robin Moseley
u/s Miss Erikson, Monica Reed, Lady Saltburn

Nicole Orth-Pallavicini
u/s Liz Essendine, Joanna Lyppiatt

Noël Coward
Playwright

Nicholas Martin
Director

Alexander Dodge
Set Design

Jane Greenwood
Costume Design

Tom Watson
Hair and Wig Design

Peter DuBois
Artistic Director, Huntington Theatre Company

Present Laughter

Michael Maso
Managing Director, Huntington Theatre Company

Gene Feist
Founding Director, Roundabout Theatre Company

Todd Haimes
Artistic Director, Roundabout Theatre Company

STAGE AND COMPANY MANAGEMENT
(L-R): Stephen M. Kaus, Kelly Beaulieu, Carly DiFulvio

BOX OFFICE
(L-R): Solangel La Bido, Heather Siebert, Robert Morgan, Ted Osborne

WARDROBE
(L-R): Susan Fallon, Dale Carman, Kat Martin, Lauren Gallitelli, Cathy Cline

272   The Playbill Broadway Yearbook 2009-2010

Present Laughter

HAIR AND WIG SUPERVISOR
Nellie LaPorte

CREW
(Clockwise, from bottom left): Sarah Conyers, Mike Allen, Glenn Merwede, Brian Maiuri, Dann Wojnar, Robert Dowling

ROUNDABOUT THEATRE COMPANY STAFF
ARTISTIC DIRECTOR ....TODD HAIMES
MANAGING DIRECTOR ....HAROLD WOLPERT
EXECUTIVE DIRECTOR ....JULIA C. LEVY
ASSOCIATE ARTISTIC DIRECTOR ...SCOTT ELLIS

ARTISTIC STAFF
DIRECTOR OF ARTISTIC DEVELOPMENT/
　DIRECTOR OF CASTING ....Jim Carnahan
Artistic Consultant ....Robyn Goodman
Resident Director ....Doug Hughes
Associate Artists ....Scott Elliott, Bill Irwin,
　　　　　　　　　　　Joe Mantello, Mark Brokaw,
　　　　　　　　　　　　　　　　Kathleen Marshall
Literary Manager ....Jill Rafson
Casting Director ....Carrie Gardner
Casting Associate ....Kate Boka
Casting Associate ....Stephen Kopel
Artistic Assistant ....Amy Ashton
Literary Associate ....Josh Fiedler
The Blanche and Irving Laurie Foundation
　Theatre Visions Fund Commissions ....Julia Cho,
　　　　　　　　　　Stephen Karam, Lewis Black,
　　　　　　　　　　　　　　　Nathan Louis Jackson
Educational Foundation of
　America Commissions ....Bekah Brunstetter,
　　　　　　　　　　　Lydia Diamond, Diana Fithian,
　　　　　　　　　　　　　　　　　Julie Marie Myatt
New York State Council
　on the Arts Commission ....Nathan Louis Jackson
Roundabout Commissions ....Steven Levenson,
　　　　　　　Robert Lopez & Kristen Anderson-Lopez
Artistic Intern ....Benjamin Izzo

Casting Interns ....Kyle Bosley, Jillian Cimini,
　　　　　　　　　　　　Erin Drake, Andrew Femenella,
　　　　　　　　　　　　Lauren Lewis, Quinn Meyers
Script Readers ....Jay Cohen, Hillary Dixler,
　　　　　　　　　　　　　　　　　Nicholas Stimler

EDUCATION STAFF
EDUCATION DIRECTOR ....Greg McCaslin
Associate Education Director ....Jennifer DiBella
Education Associate
　for Theatre-Based Programs ....Jay Gerlach
Education Program Associate ....Aliza Greenberg
Education Dramaturg ....Ted Sod
Teaching Artists ....Cynthia Babak, Victor Barbella,
　　　　　　　　　　　Grace Bell, LaTonya Borsay,
　　　　　　　　Mark Bruckner, Joe Clancy, Vanessa Davis,
　　　　　　　　　Joe Doran, Elizabeth Dunn-Ruiz,
　　　　　　　　　Carrie Ellman-Larsen, Kevin Free,
　　　　　　　　　Tony Freeman, Deanna Frieman,
　　　　　　　　　Natalie Gold, Sheri Graubert,
　　　　　　　Matthew A.J. Gregory, Melissa Gregus,
　　　　　　　　　Adam Gwon, Devin Haqq,
　　　　　　　　Carrie Heitman, Karla Hendrick,
　　　　　　Jim Jack, Jason Jacobs, Lisa Renee Jordan,
　　　　　　　　　Jamie Kalama, Alvin Keith,
　　　　Tami Mansfield, Erin McCready, Kyle McGinley,
　　　　　　Andrew Ondrejcak, Meghan O'Neill,
　　　　　　Laura Poe, Nicole Press, Jennifer Rathbone,
　　　　　　　Leah Reddy, Amanda Rehbein,
　　　　　Bernita Robinson, Christopher Rummel,
　　　　　Cassy Rush, Nick Simone, Heidi Stallings,
　　　　　Daniel Sullivan, Carl Tallent, Vickie Tanner,
　　　　Jolie Tong, Cristina Vaccaro, Jennifer Varbalow,
　　　　　Leese Walker, Eric Wallach, Michael Warner,
　　　　　　　Christina Watanabe, Gail Winar,
　　　　　　　　　Conwell Worthington, III
Teaching Artist Emeritus ....Reneé Flemings
Teaching Artist Apprentices ....Carrie Ellman-Larsen,
　　　　　　　　　　Deanna Frieman, Meghan O'Neill
Education Interns ....Nicole Bournas-Ney,
　　　　　　　　　　　　　　　　　　Mandy Menaker

ADMINISTRATIVE STAFF
GENERAL MANAGER......................Sydney Beers
Associate Managing Director ....Greg Backstrom
General Manager,
　American Airlines Theatre ....Rebecca Habel
General Manager,
　Steinberg Center ....Rachel E. Ayers
Human Resources Manager ....Stephen Deutsch
Operations Manager ....Valerie D. Simmons
Associate General Manager ....Maggie Cantrick
Office Manager ....Scott Kelly
Management Associate ....Jill K. Boyd
Archivist ....Tiffany Nixon
Receptionists ....Dee Beider, Raquel Castillo,
　　　　　　　　　　　　Elisa Papa, Allison Patrick,
　　　　　　　　　　　　　　　　Monica Sidorchuk
Messenger ....Darnell Franklin
Management Interns ....Samara Harand,
　　　　　　　　　　　　　　　　　Jennifer Levine

FINANCE STAFF
DIRECTOR OF FINANCE................Susan Neiman
Assistant Controller.........................John LaBarbera
Accounts Payable Administrator ....Frank Surdi

The Playbill Broadway Yearbook 2009-2010　　273

Present Laughter

Financial Associate	Yonit Kafka
Business Office Assistant	Joshua Cohen
Business Interns	Davin DeSantis, Stephanie Jaccarino, Laura Marshall

DEVELOPMENT STAFF

Director, Institutional Giving	Julie K. D'Andrea
Director, Special Events	Steve Schaeffer
Director, Major Gifts	Joy Pak
Director, Patron Programs	Amber Jo Manuel
Manager, Donor Information Systems	Lise Speidel
Manager, Patron Programs	Tyler Ennis
Manager, Telefundraising	Gavin Brown
Manager, Corporate Relations	Roxana Petzold
Associate Manager, Patron Programs	Marisa Perry
Special Events Manager	Ashley Firestone
Patron Services Associate	David Pittman
Institutional Giving Associate	Nick Nolte
Development Assistants	Ryan Hallett, Nick Luckenbaugh
Assistant to the Executive Director	Jason Butler
Major Gifts Intern	Kayla Carpenter
Special Events Intern	Amy Rosenfield

INFORMATION TECHNOLOGY STAFF

IT DIRECTOR	Antonio Palumbo
IT Associate	Dylan Norden
IT Associate	Jim Roma
DIRECTOR DATABASE OPERATIONS	Wendy Hutton
Database Administrator/Programmer	Revanth Anne

MARKETING STAFF

DIRECTOR OF MARKETING AND SALES PROMOTION	David B. Steffen
Associate Director of Marketing	Tom O'Connor
Marketing/Publications Manager	Margaret Casagrande
Assistant Director of Marketing	Stefanie Schussel
Marketing Manager	Shannon Marcotte
Website Consultant	Keith Powell Beyland
Director of Telesales Special Promotions	Marco Frezza
Telesales Manager	Anthony Merced
Telesales Office Coordinator	Patrick Pastor
Marketing Interns	Akeem Baisden-Folkes, Shoshana Greenberg

TICKET SERVICES STAFF

Director of Sales Operations	Charlie Garbowski, Jr.
Ticket Services Manager	Ellen Holt
Subscription Manager	Ethan Ubell
Box Office Managers	Edward P. Osborne, Jaime Perlman, Krystin MacRitchie, Nicole Nicholson
Group Sales Manager	Jeff Monteith
Assistant Box Office Managers	Robert Morgan, Andrew Clements, Scott Falkowski, Catherine Fitzpatrick
Assistant Ticket Services Managers	Robert Kane, Bill Klemm, Lindsay Ericson
Customer Services Coordinator	Thomas Walsh
Ticket Services	Solangel Bido, Arianna Boykins, Lauren Cartelli, Joseph Clark, Barbara Dente, Nisha Dhruna, Adam Elsberry, James Graham, Kara Harrington, Tova Heller, Nicki Ishmael, Kate Longosky, Michelle Maccarone, Elisa Mala, Mead Margulies, Chuck Migliaccio, Carlos Morris, Kayrose Pagan, Thomas Protulipac, Jessica Pruett-Barnett, Kaia Rafoss, Josh Rozett, Ben Schneider, Kenneth Senn, Heather Siebert, Nalane Singh, Lillian Soto, Ron Tobia, Jacklyn Verbitski, Hannah Weitzman
Intern	Melissa Cohen

SERVICES

Counsel	Paul, Weiss, Rifkind, Wharton and Garrison LLP, Charles H. Googe Jr., Carol M. Kaplan
Counsel	Rosenberg & Estis
Counsel	Andrew Lance, Gibson, Dunn, & Crutcher, LLP
Counsel	Harry H. Weintraub, Glick and Weintraub, P.C.
Counsel	Stroock & Stroock & Lavan LLP
Counsel	Daniel S. Dokos, Weil, Gotshal & Manges LLP
Immigration Counsel	Mark D. Koestler and Theodore Ruthizer
Government Relations	Law Offices of Claudia Wagner LLC
House Physicians	Dr. Theodore Tyberg, Dr. Lawrence Katz
House Dentist	Neil Kanner, D.M.D.
Insurance	DeWitt Stern Group, Inc.
Accountant	Lutz & Carr CPAs, LLP
Advertising	Spotco/Drew Hodges, Jim Edwards, Tom Greenwald, Kyle Hall, Cory Spinney
Interactive Marketing	Situation Interactive/Damian Bazadona, John Lanasa, Eric Bornemann, Randi Fields
Events Photography	Anita and Steve Shevett
Production Photographer	Joan Marcus
Theatre Displays	King Displays, Wayne Sapper
Lobby Refreshments	Sweet Concessions
Merchandising	Spotco Merch/James Decker

MANAGING DIRECTOR EMERITUS .... Ellen Richard

Roundabout Theatre Company
231 West 39th Street, New York, NY 10018
(212) 719-9393.

GENERAL PRESS REPRESENTATIVES
BONEAU/BRYAN-BROWN
Adrian Bryan-Brown
Matt Polk   Jessica Johnson   Amy Kass

STAFF FOR *PRESENT LAUGHTER*

Company Manager	Carly DiFulvio
Production Stage Manager	Stephen M. Kaus
Stage Manager	Jamie Greathouse
Production Management by	Aurora Productions/Gene O'Donovan, W. Benjamin Heller II, Rachel Sherbill, Jarid Sumner, Melissa Mazdra, Amy Merlino Coey, Amanda Raymond, Graham Forden, Liza Luxenberg
Assistant Director	Erick Herrscher
Associate Scenic Designer	Kevin Judge
Assistant Scenic Designer	Melissa Shakun
Associate Costume Designer	Moria Clinton
Associate Lighting Designer	Carl Faber
Assistant Lighting Designer	Matthew Taylor
Associate Sound Designer	Will Pickens
Production Properties	Peter Sarafin
Production Carpenter	Glenn Merwede
Production Electrician	Brian Maiuri
Running Properties	Robert W. Dowling II
Sound Operator	Dann Wojnar
Wardrobe Supervisor	Susan J. Fallon
Dressers	Kat Martin, Lauren Gallitelli, Cathy Cline
Wardrobe Dayworker	Dale Carman
Hair and Wig Supervisor	Manuela Laporte
Production Assistant	Morgan R. Holbrook
IA Apprentice	Sarah K. Conyers
Scenery built, painted and electrified by	Show Motion, Inc., Norwalk, CT
Sound equipment provided by	Sound Associates
Lighting equipment provided by	PRG Lighting, a division of Production Resource Group LLC
Costumes constructed by	Eric Winterling
Additional Costumes by	Angels the Costumiers, Bobby From Boston
Millinery by	Alexis Weglowski
Piano by	C. Bechstein
Mr. Garber's portrait by	Rainer Andreesen
Special thanks to	Nathan Lane & Kristine Holmes, Sarah Hudnut, Richard Snee, Justin Waldman

M•A•C Cosmetics
Official Makeup of Roundabout Theatre Company

MUSIC CREDITS

"The Younger Generation," "This Is a Changing World," "Twentieth Century Blues," "You Were There," "Words and Music," "Try to Learn Love," "World Weary," "I'll See You Again." All music and lyrics by Noël Coward.

AMERICAN AIRLINES THEATRE STAFF

Company Manager	Carly DiFulvio
House Carpenter	Glenn Merwede
House Electrician	Brian Maiuri
House Properties	Robert W. Dowling II
House Sound	Dann Wojnar
IA Apprentice	Sarah K. Conyers
Wardrobe Supervisor	Susan J. Fallon
Box Office Manager	Ted Osborne
Assistant Box Office Manager	Robert Morgan
House Manager	Steve Ryan
Associate House Manager	Zipporah Aguasvivas
Head Usher	Ilia Diaz
House Staff	Anne Ezell, Adam Wier, Rebecca Knell, James Watanachaiyot, Ernesto Sanchez, Celia Perez, Kareem McRae, Jacklyn Rivera, Crystal Suarez, Fatimah Robinson, Paul Krasner
Security	Julious Russell
Additional Security provided by	Gotham Security
Maintenance	Jerry Hobbs, Daniel Pellew, Willie Philips, Magali Western
Lobby Refreshments	Sweet Concessions

Present Laughter
SCRAPBOOK

1. The cast takes its opening night curtain call on Alexander Dodge's set.
2. Comedy royalty congratulates the cast on opening night (L-R): Matthew Broderick, Victor Garber, Marc Shaiman (mostly obscured), Nathan Lane, Sarah Jessica Parker and Mario Cantone.
3. Cast member Brooks Ashmanskas at B. B. King Blues Club for the opening night party.
4. Cast member Harriet Harris arrives at the premiere.

Correspondent: Lisa Banes, "Liz Essendine"

Memorable Opening Night Letters, Faxes and Notes: I got quite a few. All managed to wish me warmth and broken bones.

Opening Night Gifts: We all got a lovely framed photo of the whole cast and crew. Strangely enough, many people also gave me bottles of champagne. Anytime you come by it will be in the Frigidaire!

Actor Who Performed the Most Roles in This Show: It seems like Brooks Ashmanskas does, but no. We each play one role.

Most Broadway Shows in Their Career: Probably Victor Garber, but Alice Duffy is making her Broadway debut at the age of 81, a far more telling and wonderful fact.

Special Backstage Rituals: We are a cast who just adore each other unabashedly. The American Airlines Theatre does not have a greenroom, so Stage Management has fashioned us a greenroom on stage right. We sit there and yak and drink coffee and eat egg-on-a-roll before we do the show. Everyone comes by and we just laugh. Several of us do a little dance backstage as the music starts. If that doesn't happen the show doesn't go on, that's clear!

Favorite Moment/Embarrassing Moment: During the last couple of moments at the end of Act II when we're all on stage (except two members) and we have been known, shockingly, to break up during these moments. You just never know if were going to hang on to the end. Last night we didn't make it. I hope the audience doesn't know and thinks we're just having a grand time up there. Meanwhile, we're trying not to collapse.

Favorite Off-Site Hangout: Café Un Deux Trois, for sure. That's the gathering place. And José makes it all happen.

Favorite Snack Foods: Chocolate, and Sue Fallon's birthday cakes. Fallon has a reputation for being a great baker and, honey, she lives up to every bit of it!

Mascot: I think we have each other.

Favorite Therapy: Gin.

Most Memorable Ad-Lib: There is a line that is supposed to go, "It's delicious." But instead the person once said, "You're delicious." Now backstage we all say, "You're delicious."

Memorable Stage Door Fan Encounters: Victor Garber is Canadian by birth, and he has received several gifts pertaining to Canada and the upcoming Olympics.

Record Number of Cell Phone Rings, Cell Phone Photos or Texting Incidents During a Performance: I think the audience of the Roundabout is so well versed in what can happen, they make sure we really don't have a lot. They're educated. They don't want to be bothered.

Fastest Costume Change: Pamela changes from beautiful evening gown into men's pajamas in the blink of an eye, and does it with great aplomb. There's always great applause and laughter when she comes out of the door.

Heaviest/Hottest Costumes: All the men are in wool suits, so they can all share that one.

Who Wore the Least: Pamela Gray is in an evening dress that is very simple and off-the shoulder, shall we say.

Memorable Press Coverage: It's all been extremely respectful and extremely fabulous.

Catchphrase Only the Company Would Recognize: "I'm out."

Company Legends: We all fell in love with each other.

Coolest Things About Being in This Show: The cast. And now that we're in the theatre, the crew. They're just wonderful.

Promises, Promises

First Preview: March 28, 2010. Opened: April 25, 2010.
Still running as of May 31, 2010.

BROADWAY THEATRE
1681 Broadway
A Shubert Organization Theatre
Philip J. Smith, *Chairman*   Robert E. Wankel, *President*

BROADWAY ACROSS AMERICA   CRAIG ZADAN   NEIL MERON
THE WEINSTEIN COMPANY / TERRY ALLEN KRAMER   CANDY SPELLING   PAT ADDISS
BERNIE ABRAMS / MICHAEL SPEYER   TAKONKIET VIRAVAN / SCENARIO THAILAND
NORTON HERRICK / BARRY & FRAN WEISSLER / TBS SERVICE / LAUREL OZTEMEL

SEAN HAYES   KRISTIN CHENOWETH

Promises, Promises
The Musical Comedy

Book by **NEIL SIMON**   Music by **BURT BACHARACH**   Lyrics by **HAL DAVID**

Based on the screenplay "The Apartment" by BILLY WILDER and I. A. L. DIAMOND
By arrangement with MGM ON STAGE

TONY GOLDWYN

KATIE FINNERAN   **DICK LATESSA**

BROOKS ASHMANSKAS   PETER BENSON   SEÁN MARTIN HINGSTON   KEN LAND

CAMERON ADAMS   ASHLEY AMBER   HELEN ANKER   NATHAN BALSER   WENDI BERGAMINI   NIKKI RENEE DANIELS
SARAH JANE EVERMAN   CHELSEA KROMBACH   KEITH KÜHL   MATT LOEHR   MAYUMI MIGUEL   BRIAN O'BRIEN
SARAH O'GLEBY   ADAM PERRY   MEGAN SIKORA   MATT WALL   RYAN WATKINSON   KRISTEN BETH WILLIAMS

Scenic Design by **SCOTT PASK**   Costume Design by **BRUCE PASK**   Lighting Design by **DONALD HOLDER**   Sound Design by **BRIAN RONAN**

Hair and Wig Design by **TOM WATSON**   Music Coordinator **HOWARD JOINES**   Dance Music Arranger **DAVID CHASE**

Casting by **TARA RUBIN CASTING**   Production Stage Manager **MICHAEL J. PASSARO**   Associate Director / Choreographer **CHRISTOPHER BAILEY**

Production Manager **JUNIPER STREET PRODUCTIONS**   Press Representative **THE HARTMAN GROUP**   Marketing **TYPE A MARKETING / ANNE RIPPEY**

General Management **ALAN WASSER - ALLAN WILLIAMS MARK SHACKET**   Associate Producers **MICHAEL MCCABE / JOSEPH SMITH STAGE VENTURES 2009 NO. 2 LIMITED PARTNERSHIP**   Executive Producer **BETH WILLIAMS**

Music Director **PHIL RENO**

Orchestrations by **JONATHAN TUNICK**

Directed and Choreographed by **ROB ASHFORD**

4/25/10

CAST
(in order of appearance)

Chuck Baxter	SEAN HAYES
J.D. Sheldrake	TONY GOLDWYN
Fran Kubelik	KRISTIN CHENOWETH
Eddie Roth	KEITH KÜHL
Mr. Dobitch	BROOKS ASHMANSKAS
Sylvia Gilhooley, Miss Polansky	MEGAN SIKORA
Mike Kirkeby	PETER BENSON
Ginger, Miss Della Hoya, Lum Ding Hostess	CAMERON ADAMS
Mr. Eichelberger	SEÁN MARTIN HINGSTON
Vivien, Miss Wong	MAYUMI MIGUEL
Dr. Dreyfuss	DICK LATESSA
Jesse Vanderhof	KEN LAND
Miss Kreplinski, Helen Sheldrake	ASHLEY AMBER
Company Doctor, Karl Kubelik	BRIAN O'BRIEN
Miss Olson	HELEN ANKER
Kathy, Orchestra Voice	SARAH JANE EVERMAN
Patsy, Orchestra Voice	KRISTEN BETH WILLIAMS
Barbara, Orchestra Voice	NIKKI RENEE DANIELS
Sharon, Orchestra Voice	CHELSEA KROMBACH
Night Watchman, New Young Executive	RYAN WATKINSON
Lum Ding Waiter	MATT LOEHR
Eugene	ADAM PERRY
Marge MacDougall	KATIE FINNERAN

SWINGS
NATHAN BALSER, WENDI BERGAMINI, SARAH O'GLEBY, MATT WALL

Continued on next page

Kristin Chenoweth and the women's chorus

Promises, Promises

MUSICAL NUMBERS

Manhattan, 1962

ACT I

"Half As Big As Life"	Chuck
"Grapes of Roth"	Chuck, Bar Patrons
"Upstairs"	Chuck
"You'll Think of Someone"	Fran, Chuck
"Our Little Secret"	Chuck, Sheldrake
"I Say a Little Prayer"	Fran, Girls
"She Likes Basketball"	Chuck
"Knowing When to Leave"	Fran
"Where Can You Take a Girl?"	Dobitch, Kirkeby, Eichelberger, Vanderhof
"Wanting Things"	Sheldrake
"Turkey Lurkey Time"	Miss Polansky, Miss Wong, Miss Della Hoya and the Employees of Consolidated Life
"A House Is Not a Home"	Fran

ACT II

"A Fact Can Be a Beautiful Thing"	Chuck, Marge, Bar Patrons
"Whoever You Are"	Fran
"Christmas Day"	Sheldrake, Mrs. Sheldrake, Party Guests
"A House Is Not a Home" (Reprise)	Chuck
"A Young Pretty Girl Like You"	Chuck, Dr. Dreyfuss
"I'll Never Fall in Love Again"	Fran, Chuck
"Promises, Promises"	Chuck
"I'll Never Fall in Love Again" (Reprise)	Fran, Chuck

(L-R): Sean Hayes and Katie Finneran
Photo by Joan Marcus

2009-2010 AWARDS

Tony Award
Best Featured Actress in a Musical
(Katie Finneran)

Drama Desk Award
Outstanding Featured Actress in a Musical
(Katie Finneran)

Outer Critics Circle Award
Outstanding Featured Actress in a Musical
(Katie Finneran)

Cast Continued

UNDERSTUDIES

For Chuck Baxter: MATT LOEHR
For Fran Kubelik: SARAH JANE EVERMAN, MEGAN SIKORA
For J.D. Sheldrake: KEN LAND, BRIAN O'BRIEN
For Dr. Dreyfuss: KEN LAND
For Marge MacDougall: MEGAN SIKORA, KRISTEN BETH WILLIAMS
For Mr. Dobitch, Vanderhof: NATHAN BALSER, BRIAN O'BRIEN, MATT WALL
For Eichelberger, Mike Kirkeby: NATHAN BALSER, MATT LOEHR, MATT WALL
For Karl Kubelik: NATHAN BALSER, MATT WALL, RYAN WATKINSON
For Night Watchman, Eugene, Lum Ding Waiter: NATHAN BALSER, MATT WALL
For Miss Olson, Miss Polansky: ASHLEY AMBER, WENDI BERGAMINI, SARAH O'GLEBY
For Miss Della Hoya, Ginger, Miss Wong, Vivian, Miss Kreplinski, Helen Sheldrake, Sylvia, Orchestra Voices: WENDI BERGAMINI, SARAH O'GLEBY

Dance Captain: SARAH O'GLEBY
Assistant Dance Captain: MATT WALL

ORCHESTRA

Conductor: PHIL RENO
Associate Conductor: MAT EISENSTEIN
Music Coordinator: HOWARD JOINES
Reeds: LES SCOTT, JAMES ERCOLE, KENNETH DYBISZ, JACQUELINE HENDERSON
Trumpets: DAVID TRIGG, DAN URNESS, BARRY DANIELIAN
Trombone: JASON JACKSON
Drums: PERRY CAVARI
Bass: MICHAEL KUENNEN
Guitar: ED HAMILTON
Percussion: BILL HAYES
Concertmaster: RICK DOLAN
Violin: ELIZABETH LIM-DUTTON
Viola: LIUH-WEN TING
Cello: LAURA BONTRAGER
Keyboard 1: MATTHEW PERRI
Keyboard 2/Associate Conductor: MAT EISENSTEIN
Synthesizer Programmer: BRUCE SAMUELS
Music Copying: EMILY GRISHMAN MUSIC PREPARATION – KATHARINE EDMONDS/ EMILY GRISHMAN

The Playbill Broadway Yearbook 2009-2010

Promises, Promises

 Sean Hayes
Chuck Baxter

 Kristin Chenoweth
Fran Kubelik

 Tony Goldwyn
J.D. Sheldrake

 Katie Finneran
Marge MacDougall

 Dick Latessa
Dr. Dreyfuss

 Brooks Ashmanskas
Mr. Dobitch

 Peter Benson
Mike Kirkeby

 Seán Martin Hingston
Mr. Eichelberger

 Ken Land
Jesse Vanderhof

 Cameron Adams
Miss Della Hoya

 Ashley Amber
Miss Kreplinski, Helen Sheldrake

 Helen Anker
Miss Olson

 Nathan Balser
Swing

 Wendi Bergamini
Swing

 Nikki Renee Daniels
Barbara, Orchestra Voice

 Sarah Jane Everman
Kathy, Orchestra Voice

 Chelsea Krombach
Sharon, Orchestra Voice

 Keith Kühl
Eddie Roth

 Matt Loehr
Lum Ding Waiter

 Mayumi Miguel
Miss Wong, Vivien

 Brian O'Brien
Company Doctor, Karl Kubelik

 Sarah O'Gleby
Swing, Dance Captain

 Adam Perry
Eugene

 Megan Sikora
Miss Polansky, Sylvia Gilhooley, Nurse

 Matt Wall
Swing, Assistant Dance Captain

 Ryan Watkinson
Night Watchman, New Young Executive

 Kristen Beth Williams
Patsy, Orchestra Voice

 Neil Simon
Book

 Burt Bacharach
Music

 Hal David
Lyricist

 Rob Ashford
Director/Choreographer

 Phil Reno
Music Director

 Scott Pask
Scenic Design

 Donald Holder
Lighting Design

 Brian Ronan
Sound Design

Promises, Promises

Tom Watson
Hair and Wig Design

Jonathan Tunick
Orchestrations

David Chase
Dance Music Arranger

Howard Joines
Music Coordinator

Guy Kwan, John Paull III, Hillary Blanken, Kevin Broomell, Ana Rose Greene, Juniper Street Productions
Production Management

Tara Rubin Casting
Casting

Alan Wasser
General Management

John Gore, CEO, Broadway Across America
Producer

Thomas B. McGrath, Chairman, Broadway Across America
Producer

Craig Zadan and Neil Meron
Producers

Candy Spelling
Producer

Pat Flicker Addiss
Producer

Bob Weinstein, The Weinstein Company
Producer

Harvey Weinstein, The Weinstein Company
Producer

Terry Allen Kramer
Producer

ORCHESTRA
Front Row (L-R): Phil Reno, Rick Dolan, Jackie Henderson, Mat Eisenstein

Back Row (L-R): Barry Danielian, Joe Choroszewski, Richard Brice, Mike Kuennen, Les Scott, Jimmy Ercole, Ken Dybisz, Matt Perri, Ed Hamilton

Bernard Abrams
Producer

Michael Speyer
Producer

Norton Herrick
Producer

Barry and Fran Weissler
Producers

Beth Williams
Executive Producer

COMPANY MANAGEMENT AND STAGE MANAGEMENT
Front Row: Cathy Kwon

Back Row (L-R): Penny Daulton, Alex Lyu Volckhausen, Michael J. Passaro, Pat Sosnow, Shannon Hammons

Photos by Brian Mapp

Promises, Promises

FRONT OF HOUSE STAFF
Back Row (L-R): Mattie Robinson, John Hall, Andrew Sanford, Mae Park, Sean Lanigan, Ron (Security), Jerry Gallagher, Tony (Security), Kathleen Powell, Selene Nelson
Middle Row (L-R): William Phelan, Barbara Arias, Andie (Infra-Red), Ulises Santiago, Tiffany Murphy, Lisa Maisonet, Mario Carillo, Jorge Colon, Svetlana Pinkhas
Front Row (L-R) Dom Giovanni, Ismeal Tirado, Isaac Trujillo, Michael S. R. Harris, Casey Ademick, Brook Bokun, Lori Bokun

STAGE CREW
Front Row (L-R): Mike Bernstein, Devin Biggart, Rick DalCortivo, Rick DalCortivo Jr, Peter Becker
Back Row (L-R): Charles Rasmussen, George Milne, Scott "Gus" Poitras, Alan Grudzinski, Tommy Cole, Mike Farfalla, Chris Sloan, Tyler Ricci, Mike Cornell

WARDROBE
Front Row (L-R): Jay Woods, Barry Hoff, Dolly Williams, Eugene Nicks, Veneda Truesdale
Back Row (L-R): Brendan Cooper, Christel Murdock, Melanie McClintock, Shana Albery, Fred Castner, Michael Harrell

STAFF FOR *PROMISES, PROMISES*

GENERAL MANAGEMENT
ALAN WASSER ASSOCIATES
Alan Wasser   Allan Williams
Mark Shacket

GENERAL PRESS REPRESENTATIVE
THE HARTMAN GROUP
Michael Hartman
Wayne Wolfe   Matt Ross

COMPANY MANAGER
Laura Kirspel

CASTING
TARA RUBIN CASTING
Tara Rubin CSA, Merri Sugarman CSA,
Eric Woodall CSA, Laura Schutzel CSA, Dale Brown CSA,
Paige Blansfield, Kaitlin Shaw

PRODUCTION MANAGEMENT
JUNIPER STREET PRODUCTIONS
Hillary Blanken   Guy Kwan
Kevin Broomell   Ana Rose Greene

FIGHT DIRECTOR
Thomas Schall

Production Stage Manager	Michael J. Passaro
Stage Manager	Pat Sosnow
Assistant Stage Manager	Alex Lyu Volckhausen
Assistant Company Manager	Cathy Kwon
Assistant Director	Stephen Sposito
SDC Ockrent Directing Fellow	Gregg Wiggans
Dance Captain	Sarah O'Gleby
Assistant Dance Captain	Matt Wall
Associate Scenic Designer	Orit Jacoby Carroll
Assistant Scenic Designer	Lauren Alvarez
Assistant to the Scenic Designer	G. Warren Stiles
Associate Costume Designer	Matthew Pachtman
Assistant Costume Designers	Katie Irish, Jessica Pabst
Costume Shopper	Amanda Bujak
Associate Lighting Designer	Karen Spahn
Associate Lighting Designer	Carolyn Wong
Assistant to the Lighting Designer	R. Christopher Stokes
Associate Sound Designer	Joanna Staub
Moving Lighting Programmer	Richard Tyndall
Make-up Design	Ashley Ryan
Technical Director	Fred Gallo
Head Carpenter	Jack Anderson
Flyman	Geoffrey Vaughn
Automation Carpenter	Hugh Hardyman
Assistant Carpenters	Andrew Elman, Alan Grudzinski, Matty Lynch
Production Electricians	Randall Zaibek, James Fedigan
Head Electrician	Michael Cornell
Production Properties Supervisor	Tim Abel
Head Properties Supervisor	David Fulton
Production Sound Engineer	Christopher Sloan
Deck Audio	Mike Farfalla
Advance Audio	Jason McKenna
Wardrobe Supervisor	Dolly Williams
Assistant Wardrobe Supervisor	Fred Castner
Dresser to Mr. Hayes	Barry Hoff

Photos by Brian Mapp

Promises, Promises

Dresser to Ms. Chenoweth	Jay Woods
Dressers	Shana Albery, Brendan Cooper, Melanie McClintock, Christel Murdock, Virginia Neinenger, David Oliver, Veneda Truesdale
Hair Supervisor	Thomas Augustine
Assistant Hair Supervisor	Carmel Vargyas
Hair Dresser	Joshua First
House Carpenter	Charles Rasmussen
House Electrician	George D. Milne
House Properties	Rick DalCortivo
House Flyman	Thomas Cole Jr.
Music Coordinator	Howard Joines
Music Copying	Emily Grishman Music Preparation – Katharine Edmonds/Emily Grishman
Advertising	Serino Coyne/Nancy Coyne, Sandy Block, Greg Corradetti, Robert Jones, Danielle Boyle
Marketing	Type A Marketing/ Anne Rippey, Nick Pramik, Janette Roush, Elyce Henkin
Website Design & Internet Marketing	Art Meets Commerce/ Jim Glaub, Laurie Connor, Kevin Keating, Chip Meyrelles, Whitney Manalio Creighton, Mark Seeley
Theatre Displays	King Displays
Legal Counsel	Levine Plotkin & Menin LLP/ Loren Plotkin, Esq.
Accounting	Rosenberg, Neuwirth & Kuchner/ Chris Cacace, Marina Flom, Kirill Baytalskiy
Assistant to Ms. Chenoweth	Julie Trussell
General Management Associates	Aaron Lustbader, Lane Marsh, Thom Mitchell
General Management Office	Mark Barna, Christopher Betz, Jake Hirzel, Dawn Kusinski, Patty Montesi, Jennifer O'Connor
Production Photographer	Joan Marcus
Technical Production Assistant	Alexandra Paull
Production Assistants	John Ferry, Shannon Hammons, Libby Unsworth
Physical Therapist	Encore Physical Therapy PC
Orthopaedist	David S. Weiss, M.D.
Insurance	Ventura Insurance Brokerage/ Christine Sadofsky
Banking	Signature Bank/Barbara von Borstel, Margaret Monigan, Mary Ann Fanelli, Janett Urena
Payroll	Castellana Services, Inc.
Opening Night Coordination	The Lawrence Company/ Michael P. Lawrence
Specialty Promotional Partners	The Sponsor Company/ Keith Hurd, Christopher Raphael
Group Sales	Telecharge.com Group Sales/ 800-432-7780 TTY: 888-889-TKTS (8587)
Transportation	I.B.A. Limousine, Carmine Lucariello Inc., Get Services

CREDITS AND ACKNOWLEDGEMENTS

Show control and scenic motion control featuring stage command systems by Scenic Technologies, a division of Production Resource Group, LLC, New Windsor, NY. Scenic elements constructed by Global Scenic Services, Inc., Bridgeport, CT. Engineering review by McLaren Engineering Group, West Nyack, NY. Audio equipment from PRG Audio, Mount Vernon, NY. Lighting equipment from PRG Lighting, North Bergen, NJ. Props built by The Spoon Group, Rahway, NJ, and Cigarbox Studios, Newburgh, NY. Soft goods built by I. Weiss and Sons, Inc., Long Island City, NY. Costumes by Euroco Costumes, Inc.; Gayle Palmieri; House of Savoia; Jennifer Love Costumes; Katrina Patterns; Maria Ficalora Knitwear, Ltd.; Tricorne, Inc. Custom shirting by Brooks Brothers. Fur by Fur & Furgery. Millinery by Lynne Mackey Studios, Inc. Gloves by Daniel Storto. Custom fabric dyeing & painting by Gene Mignola, Inc. Custom footwear by J.C. Theatrical, LaDuca Shoes, Worldtone Dance. Leather jacket provided by Schott, Inc.; Harris tweed fabrics supplied by HTT (manufacturing), Carloway Mills, Scotland. Mr. Hayes' wristwatch provided by Hamilton Watch. Special thanks to Bra*Tenders for hosiery & undergarments.

SPECIAL THANKS

Autumn Olive, Ava Lounge, Brooks Brothers, Jennifer Costello, Jim David, Dream Hotel, Ben Famiglietti, Florsheim, Holland & Sherry Fabrics, Ilene Chazanof, Imogene & Willie, Kaufman's Army Navy, Scott Mauro, Erin McMurrough, NY Vintage, Serafina Broadway, Michelle Singer, Kevin Spirtas, David Stern, Dean Stolber and Darcie Denkert, Adam Waring, Chad Woerner

---

Makeup provided by M•A•C Cosmetics

Certain scenery and scenic effects built, painted and electrified by Show Motion, Inc., Norwalk, Connecticut.

Rehearsed at the New 42nd Street Studios

Souvenir Merchandise designed and created by The Araca Group

www.PromisesPromisesBroadway.com

THE SHUBERT ORGANIZATION, INC.
Board of Directors

Philip J. Smith Chairman	**Robert E. Wankel** President
Wyche Fowler, Jr.	**John W. Kluge**
Lee J. Seidler	**Michael I. Sovern**

Stuart Subotnick

Elliot Greene Chief Financial Officer	**David Andrews** Senior Vice President – Shubert Ticketing
Juan Calvo Vice President and Controller	**John Darby** Vice President – Facilities
Peter Entin Vice President – Theatre Operations	**Charles Flateman** Vice President – Marketing
Anthony LaMattina Vice President – Audit & Production Finance	**Brian Mahoney** Vice President – Ticket Sales

D.S. Moynihan
Vice President – Creative Projects

Theatre Manager .... Michael S. R. Harris

BOX OFFICE
(L-R): James Toguville, Debbie Giarratano

STAGE DOOR
Ellsworth Butts

WIG/HAIR DEPARTMENT
Joshua First, Carmel Vargyas, Tom Augustine

Race

First Preview: November 17, 2009. Opened: December 6, 2009.
Still running as of May 31, 2010.

CAST
(in order of appearance)

Jack Lawson	JAMES SPADER
Henry Brown	DAVID ALAN GRIER
Susan	KERRY WASHINGTON
Charles Strickland	RICHARD THOMAS

UNDERSTUDIES/STANDBYS

For Jack Lawson, Charles Strickland:
JORDAN LAGE

For Henry Brown:
RAY ANTHONY THOMAS

For Susan:
AFTON C. WILLIAMSON

ETHEL BARRYMORE THEATRE
243 West 47th Street
A Shubert Organization Theatre
Philip J. Smith, *Chairman*   Robert E. Wankel, *President*

Jeffrey Richards   Jerry Frankel   Jam Theatricals
JK Productions   Peggy Hill & Nicholas Quinn Rosenkranz   Scott M. Delman
Terry Allen Kramer/James L. Nederlander   Swinsky Deitch
Bat-Barry Productions   Ronald Frankel   James Fuld Jr.
Kathleen K. Johnson   Terry Schnuck   The Weinstein Company
Marc Frankel   Jay & Cindy Gutterman/Stewart Mercer

present

James Spader   David Alan Grier   Kerry Washington
and
Richard Thomas
in

RACE

Written and Directed by
David Mamet

Scenic Design	Costume Design	Lighting Design
Santo Loquasto	**Tom Broecker**	**Brian MacDevitt**

Production Stage Manager	Casting	Technical Supervision	Company Manager
Matthew Silver	**Telsey + Company**	**Hudson Theatrical Associates**	**Bruce Klinger**

Press Representative	Associate Producer	General Management
Jeffrey Richards Associates	**Jeremy Scott Blaustein**	**Richards/Climan, Inc.**
Irene Gandy/Alana Karpoff		

The Producers wish to express their appreciation to the Theatre Development Fund for its support of this production.

12/6/09

(L-R): James Spader, David Alan Grier and Richard Thomas

Photo by Robert J. Saferstein

Race

James Spader
Jack Lawson

David Alan Grier
Henry Brown

Kerry Washington
Susan

Richard Thomas
Charles Strickland

Jordan Lage
u/s Jack, Charles

Ray Anthony Thomas
u/s Henry

Afton C. Williamson
u/s Susan

David Mamet
Playwright/Director

Santo Loquasto
Scenic Design

Brian MacDevitt
Lighting Design

Bernard Telsey,
Telsey + Company
Casting

Sharon Bialy and Sherry Thomas
West Coast Casting

Neil A. Mazzella,
Hudson Theatrical
Associates
Technical Supervision

David R. Richards
and Tamar Haimes,
Richards/Climan Inc.
General Manager

Jeffrey Richards
Producer

Jerry Frankel
Producer

Arny Granat,
Jam Theatricals
Producer

Steve Traxler,
Jam Theatricals
Producer

Peggy Hill
Producer

Terry Allen Kramer
Producer

James L.
Nederlander
Producer

Mort Swinsky
Producer

Barry Weisbord,
Bat-Barry
Productions
Producer

Terry Schnuck
Producer

Bob Weinstein,
The Weinstein
Company
Producer

Kerry Washington as Susan.

Photo by Robert J. Saferstein

Harvey Weinstein,
The Weinstein
Company
Producer

Jay and Cindy Gutterman
Producer

Jeremy Scott
Blaustein
Associate Producer

The Playbill Broadway Yearbook 2009-2010

Race

FRONT OF HOUSE STAFF
Front Row (L-R): Pamela Gittlitz (Usher), Dan Landon (House Manager), Aileen Kilburn (Usher)

Back Row (L-R): Dexter Luke (Head Usher), John Cashman (Usher), John Barbaretti (Ticket Taker)

BOX OFFICE
(L-R): Chuck Loesche, Diane Heatherington, Steve Deluca

CREW
Sitting (L-R): Jillian Oliver (Stage Manager), Sandy Binion (Wardrobe Supervisor)

Standing (L-R): Victor Verdejo (House Carpenter), Matthew Silver (Production Stage Manager), Phillip Feller (House Props), Bruce Klinger (Company Manager), Al Galvez (Flyman), David Marques (Dresser)

Not pictured: John Randolph Ferry (Production Assistant)

Race
Scrapbook

Correspondent: David Alan Grier, "Henry Brown"
Opening Night Gift: The offer of sexual favors from a true fan.
Most Exciting Celebrity Visitors: Bootsy Collins, Sidney Poitier.
Who Has Done the Most Shows in Their Career: Richard Thomas.
Special Backstage Rituals: Going over, and over my lines…compulsively.
Favorite Moment During Each Performance: Curtain call. It's where I feel I give my best performance each evening.
Favorite In-Theatre Gathering Place: My dressing room which has been kidnapped by unscrupulous stage managers.
Mascot: The Ku Klux Klan hood we keep backstage. All the famous people who come back and visit get to put it on, and we take pics with them.
Catchphrase Only the Company Would Recognize: "Because, white man, he was guilty."

David Alan Grier meets the press at an open rehearsal at Atlantic Theater Company Studios October 22, 2009.

Memorable Press Encounter: No press encounter is ever memorable.
Record Number of Cell Phone Rings, Cell Phone Photos or Texting Incidents During a Performance: I can't hear them. I let the audience sort that out.
Internet Buzz: I didn't pay attention to any of that.
Who Wore the Heaviest/Hottest Costume: Kerry?
Memorable Directorial Note: Act better
Company Legend: Me.
Understudy Anecdote: I don't talk to THOSE people.
Nickname: DAG.
Sweethearts Within the Company: Me.
Embarrassing Moments: Every day of my life!
Coolest Thing About Being in This Show: Well, it's David Mamet, I'm in it, and it's on Broadway. And I get to do it…over, and over, and over again!
Other Stories or Memories: Chita Rivera told me long ago in regards to my first Broadway show, "Don't be afraid, it's only your career that's at stake!"

STAFF FOR RACE

GENERAL MANAGEMENT
RICHARDS/CLIMAN, INC.
David R. Richards   Tamar Haimes

COMPANY MANAGER
BRUCE KLINGER

GENERAL PRESS REPRESENTATIVE
JEFFREY RICHARDS ASSOCIATES
IRENE GANDY/ALANA KARPOFF
Elon Rutberg   Diana Rissetto

CASTING
TELSEY + COMPANY, C.S.A.
Bernie Telsey, Will Cantler, David Vaccari,
Bethany Knox, Craig Burns,
Tiffany Little Canfield, Rachel Hoffman,
Carrie Rosson, Justin Huff, Joe Langworth,
Bess Fifer, Patrick Goodwin

WEST COAST CASTING
Sharon Bialy & Sherry Thomas, C.S.A.

PRODUCTION MANAGEMENT
HUDSON THEATRICAL ASSOCIATES
Neil Mazzella   Sam Ellis   Irene Wang

PRODUCTION STAGE MANAGER ....MATTHEW SILVER
Stage Manager ....Jillian M. Oliver
Assistant to the Director ....Justin Fair
Associate Scenic Designer ....Jenny Sawyers
Associate Costume Designer ....David Withrow
Associate Lighting Designer ....Driscoll Otto
Associate General Manager ....Michael Sag
General Management Associate ....Jeromy Smith
General Management Assistant ....Cesar Hawas
Production Assistant ....John Ferry
Production Carpenter ....Don Oberpriller
Production Electrician ....Jimmy Maloney
Production Props ....Kathy Fabian/Propstar
Wardrobe Supervisor ....Rob Bevenger
Dresser ....Sandy Binion
Associate Props Coordinator ....Carrie Mossman
Props Assistants ....Tim Ferro, Sarah Bird
Assistant to Mr. Mamet ....Pam Susemiehl
Assistant to Mr. Traxler ....Brandi Preston
Press Interns ....Charlie McAteer, Andy Drachenberg
Advertising ....Serino Coyne, Inc./ Greg Corradetti, Tom Callahan, Robert Jones, Vanessa Javier
Interactive Marketing Agency ....Situation Marketing/ Damian Bazadona, John Lanasa, Ryan Klink
Website ....Robert J. Saferstein
Banking ....City National Bank/Michele Gibbons
Accountants ....Fried & Kowgios, CPA's LLP/ Robert Fried, CPA
Comptroller ....Elliott Aronstam, CPA
Legal Counsel ....Lazarus & Harris LLP/ Scott R. Lazarus, Esq., Robert C. Harris, Esq.
Insurance ....DeWitt Stern Group Inc./ Jolyon F. Stern, Joseph Bower
Payroll ....CSI/Lance Castellana
Production Photographers ....Brigitte Lacombe, Robert J. Saferstein
Company Mascots ....Skye and Lottie (in memoriam)
Opening Night Sponsor ....Movado

CREDITS
Scenery constructed by Hudson Scenic Studios. Lighting equipment from PRG Lighting. Flame treatment by Turning Star Inc. James Spader and David Alan Grier's suits from Saint Laurie. James Spader's shoes from John Lobb. Kerry Washington and David Alan Grier's shoes from Cole Haan. Richard Thomas' suit and overcoat from Hugo Boss.

SPECIAL THANKS
Shelby Steele, Stan Coleman, Rabbi Mordecai Finley, Cynthia Silver, The Atlantic Theater Company, Jennifer Brennan, Peter Johnson, The Law Book Exchange, Anything But Costumes

www.RaceOnBroadway.com
www.BroadwaysBestShows.com

 THE SHUBERT ORGANIZATION, INC.
Board of Directors

Philip J. Smith   **Robert E. Wankel**
Chairman   President

Wyche Fowler, Jr.   **John W. Kluge**

Lee J. Seidler   **Michael I. Sovern**

Stuart Subotnick

Elliot Greene   **David Andrews**
Chief Financial   Senior Vice President –
Officer   Shubert Ticketing

Juan Calvo   **John Darby**
Vice President   Vice President –
and Controller   Facilities

Peter Entin   **Charles Flateman**
Vice President –   Vice President –
Theatre Operations   Marketing

Anthony LaMattina   **Brian Mahoney**
Vice President –   Vice President –
Audit & Production Finance   Ticket Sales

D.S. Moynihan
Vice President – Creative Projects

Staff for The Ethel Barrymore
House Manager ....Dan Landon

Ragtime

First Preview: October 23, 2009. Opened: November 15, 2009.
Closed January 10, 2010 after 28 Previews and 65 Performances.

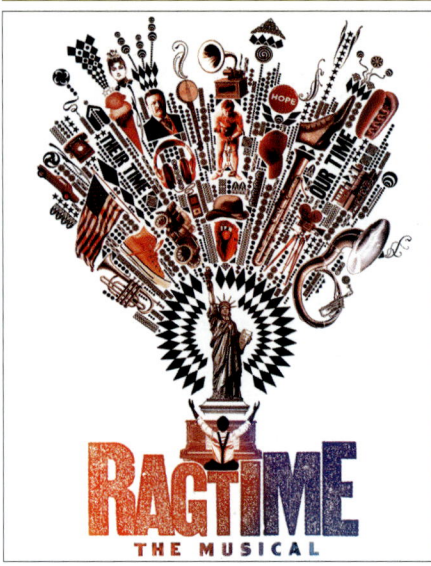

CAST
(in order of appearance)

The Little Boy	CHRISTOPHER COX
Father	RON BOHMER
Mother	CHRISTIANE NOLL
Mother's Younger Brother	BOBBY STEGGERT
Grandfather	DAN MANNING
Coalhouse Walker Jr.	QUENTIN EARL DARRINGTON
Sarah	STEPHANIE UMOH
Booker T. Washington	ERIC JORDAN YOUNG
Tateh	ROBERT PETKOFF
The Little Girl	SARAH ROSENTHAL
Harry Houdini	JONATHAN HAMMOND
J.P. Morgan	MICHAEL X. MARTIN
Henry Ford	AARON GALLIGAN-STIERLE
Emma Goldman	DONNA MIGLIACCIO
Evelyn Nesbit	SAVANNAH WISE
Admiral Peary	MICHAEL X. MARTIN
Matthew Henson	TERENCE ARCHIE
Stanford White	MIKE McGOWAN
Harry K. Thaw	JOSH WALDEN
Kathleen	JENNIFER EVANS
Sarah's Friend	BRYONHA PARHAM
Willie Conklin	MARK ALDRICH
Brigit	TRACY LYNN OLIVERA
Charles S. Whitman	MIKE McGOWAN
Coalhouse Walker III	JAYDEN BROCKINGTON, KYLIL CHRISTOPHER WILLIAMS

Continued on next page

NEIL SIMON THEATRE
UNDER THE DIRECTION OF JAMES M. NEDERLANDER AND JAMES L. NEDERLANDER

Kevin McCollum Roy Furman Scott Delman Roger Berlind
Max Cooper Tom Kirdahy/Devlin Elliott Jeffrey A. Sine Stephanie McClelland
Roy Miller Lams Productions Jana Robbins Sharon Karmazin Eric Falkenstein/Morris Berchard
RialtoGals Productions Independent Presenters Network Held-Haffner Productions HRH Foundation
and Emanuel Azenberg

IN ASSOCIATION WITH
The John F. Kennedy Center for the Performing Arts

PRESIDENT
Michael Kaiser

VICE PRESIDENT
Max Woodward

PRESENT

RAGTIME THE MUSICAL

BOOK BY **Terrence McNally**   MUSIC BY **Stephen Flaherty**   LYRICS BY **Lynn Ahrens**

BASED ON THE NOVEL *RAGTIME* BY
E.L. Doctorow

STARRING
Ron Bohmer Quentin Earl Darrington Christiane Noll
Robert Petkoff Bobby Steggert Stephanie Umoh
Christopher Cox Sarah Rosenthal

WITH
Jonathan Hammond Donna Migliaccio Savannah Wise Eric Jordan Young
Mark Aldrich Sumayya Ali Terence Archie Corey Bradley Jayden Brockington Jennifer Evans
Aaron Galligan-Stierle Carly Hughes Valisia Lekae Dan Manning Michael X. Martin Mike McGowan
Tracy Lynn Olivera Bryonha Parham Mamie Parris Nicole Powell Arbender J. Robinson
Benjamin Schrader Wallace Smith Josh Walden Catherine Walker Kylil Christopher Williams
Carey Rebecca Brown Benjamin Cook Lisa Karlin James Moye Kaylie Rubinaccio Jim Weaver

SCENIC DESIGN	COSTUME DESIGN	LIGHTING DESIGN	SOUND DESIGN
Derek McLane	Santo Loquasto	Donald Holder	Acme Sound Partners
HAIR AND WIG DESIGN	ORCHESTRATIONS	VOCAL ARRANGEMENTS	MUSIC COORDINATOR
Edward J. Wilson	William David Brohn	Stephen Flaherty	John Miller
CASTING	PRESS REPRESENTITIVE	MARKETING	ASSOCIATE DIRECTOR/CHOREOGRAPHER
Laura Stanczyk Casting	Boneau/Bryan-Brown	Scott A. Moore	Josh Walden
GENERAL MANAGER	TECHNICAL SUPERVISOR		PRODUCTION SUPERVISOR
John S. Corker	Brian Lynch		Peter Lawrence

MUSIC DIRECTION BY
James Moore

DIRECTED AND CHOREOGRAPHED BY
Marcia Milgrom Dodge

11/15/09

Quentin Earl Darrington (center) with members of the Ensemble

Photo by Joan Marcus

Ragtime

SCENES & MUSICAL NUMBERS

ACT ONE

Prologue:	RAGTIME	The Company
Scene 1:	Dock in New York Harbor/At Sea	
	GOODBYE, MY LOVE	Mother
	JOURNEY ON	Father, Tateh, Mother
Scene 2:	A vaudeville theatre, New York City	
	THE CRIME OF THE CENTURY	Evelyn Nesbit, Younger Brother, Ensemble
Scene 3:	Mother's garden, New Rochelle	
	WHAT KIND OF WOMAN	Mother
Scene 4:	Ellis Island/Lower East Side	
	A SHTETL IZ AMEREKE	Tateh, The Little Girl, Ensemble
	SUCCESS	Tateh, J.P. Morgan, Harry Houdini, Ensemble
Scene 5:	The Tempo Club, Harlem/Ford's assembly line	
	GETTIN' READY RAG	Coalhouse, Ensemble
	HENRY FORD	Henry Ford, Coalhouse, Ensemble
Scene 6:	Railroad station, New Rochelle	
	NOTHING LIKE THE CITY	Tateh, Mother, The Little Boy, The Little Girl
Scene 7:	Emerald Isle Firehouse	
Scene 8:	Mother's house, New Rochelle	
	YOUR DADDY'S SON	Sarah
	NEW MUSIC	Father, Mother, Younger Brother, Coalhouse, Sarah, Ensemble
Scene 9:	A hillside above New Rochelle	
	THE WHEELS OF A DREAM	Coalhouse, Sarah
Scene 10:	A union hall in New York City/Lawrence, Massachusetts/A train	
	THE NIGHT THAT GOLDMAN SPOKE AT UNION SQUARE	Younger Brother, Emma Goldman, Ensemble
	GLIDING	Tateh
Scene 11:	New Rochelle and New York City	
	JUSTICE	Coalhouse, Ensemble
	PRESIDENT	Sarah
	TILL WE REACH THAT DAY	Sarah's Friend, Coalhouse, Emma Goldman, Younger Brother, Mother, Tateh, Ensemble

ACT TWO

Entr'acte		Orchestra
Scene 1:	The streets of New Rochelle/Mother's house	
	COALHOUSE'S SOLILOQUY	Coalhouse
	COALHOUSE DEMANDS	The Company
Scene 2:	The Polo Grounds	
	WHAT A GAME!	Father, The Little Boy, Ensemble
Scene 3:	Mother's house	
	ATLANTIC CITY	Evelyn Nesbit, Harry Houdini, Father
	NEW MUSIC (Reprise)	Father
Scene 4:	Atlantic City/Million Dollar Pier/Boardwalk	
	ATLANTIC CITY, PART II	Evelyn Nesbit, Harry Houdini, Ensemble
	BUFFALO NICKEL PHOTOPLAY, INC.	Baron Ashkenazy
	OUR CHILDREN	Mother, Baron Ashkenazy
Scene 5:	Harlem/Coalhouse's hideout	
	SARAH BROWN EYES	Coalhouse, Sarah
	HE WANTED TO SAY	Emma Goldman, Younger Brother, Coalhouse, Coalhouse's Gang
Scene 6:	The beach, Atlantic City	
	BACK TO BEFORE	Mother
Scene 7:	The Morgan Library, New York City	
	LOOK WHAT YOU'VE DONE	Booker T. Washington, Coalhouse, Coalhouse's Gang
	MAKE THEM HEAR YOU	Coalhouse
Epilogue:	RAGTIME/THE WHEELS OF A DREAM (Reprise)	The Company

Cast Continued

ENSEMBLE

New Rochelle Citizens, Harlem Men and Women, Immigrants, Vaudevillians and Stagehands, Judge, Reporters, Child Buyer, Policemen, Ford Workers, Firemen, Trolley Conductor, Millworkers, Strikers, Militia, Train Conductor, Bureaucrats and Lawyers, Baron's Assistant, Coalhouse Gang, Spectators, Welfare Official, Hotel Staff, Vacationers, Bathing Beauties and Camera Crew ..... MARK ALDRICH, SUMAYYA ALI, TERENCE ARCHIE, COREY BRADLEY, JENNIFER EVANS, AARON GALLIGAN-STIERLE, JONATHAN HAMMOND, CARLY HUGHES, VALISIA LEKAE, DAN MANNING, MICHAEL X. MARTIN, MIKE McGOWAN, DONNA MIGLIACCIO, TRACY LYNN OLIVERA, BRYONHA PARHAM, MAMIE PARRIS, NICOLE POWELL, ARBENDER J. ROBINSON, BENJAMIN SCHRADER, WALLACE SMITH, JOSH WALDEN, CATHERINE WALKER, SAVANNAH WISE, ERIC JORDAN YOUNG

SWINGS

CAREY REBECCA BROWN, LISA KARLIN, JAMES MOYE, JIM WEAVER

DANCE CAPTAIN

JOSH WALDEN

ASSISTANT DANCE CAPTAIN

JIM WEAVER

UNDERSTUDIES

For Father:
MIKE McGOWAN, JAMES MOYE
For Coalhouse Walker Jr.:
TERENCE ARCHIE, WALLACE SMITH, ERIC JORDAN YOUNG
For Mother:
MAMIE PARRIS, CATHERINE WALKER
For Tateh:
JONATHAN HAMMOND, MIKE McGOWAN
For Mother's Younger Brother:
BENJAMIN SCHRADER, JOSH WALDEN
For Sarah:
CARLY HUGHES, VALISIA LEKAE
For The Little Boy:
BENJAMIN COOK
For The Little Girl:
KAYLIE RUBINACCIO

Ragtime

Cast Continued

ORCHESTRA
Conductor:
JAMES MOORE
Associate Conductor:
JAMIE SCHMIDT
Assistant Conductor:
SUE ANSCHUTZ
Concert Master:
RICK DOLAN
Violins:
ELIZABETH LIM-DUTTON,
CENOVIA CUMMINS, ASHLEY HORN,
UNA TONE, KIKU ENOMOTO
Violas:
MAXINE ROACH, DEBRA SHUFELT-DINE
Celli:
LAURA BONTRAGER,
SARAH HEWITT-ROTH
Bass:
JEFF COOPER
Harp:
BARBARA BIGGERS
Woodwinds:
KATHERINE FINK, LYNNE COHEN,
JONATHAN LEVINE, TODD GROVES
Trumpets:
TIMOTHY SCHADT, DANIEL URNESS
French Horns:
PATRICK PRIDEMORE, WILL De VOS
Trombones:
ALAN FERBER, DAN LEVINE
Tuba:
MARCUS ROJAS
Percussion:
CHARLES DESCARFINO
Drums:
RICH ROSENZWEIG
Guitar:
GREG UTZIG
Keyboards:
JAMIE SCHMIDT, SUE ANSCHUTZ
Music Coordinator:
JOHN MILLER

2009-2010 AWARDS

DRAMA DESK AWARD
Outstanding Sound Design in a Musical
(Acme Sound Partners)

THEATRE WORLD AWARD
First Major New York Appearance
(Stephanie Umoh)

Ron Bohmer
Father

Quentin Earl Darrington
Coalhouse Walker Jr.

Christiane Noll
Mother

Robert Petkoff
Tateh

Bobby Steggert
Mother's Younger Brother

Stephanie Umoh
Sarah

Christopher Cox
The Little Boy

Sarah Rosenthal
The Little Girl

Jonathan Hammond
Harry Houdini, Ensemble

Donna Migliaccio
Emma Goldman, Ensemble

Savannah Wise
Evelyn Nesbit, Ensemble

Eric Jordan Young
Booker T. Washington, Ensemble

Mark Aldrich
Willie Conklin, Ensemble

Sumayya Ali
Soprano Soloist, Ensemble

Terence Archie
Matthew Henson, Ensemble

Corey Bradley
Ensemble

Jayden Brockington
Coalhouse Walker III

Jennifer Evans
Kathleen, Ensemble

Aaron Galligan-Stierle
Henry Ford, Ensemble

Carly Hughes
Ensemble

Ragtime

Valisia Lekae
Ensemble

Dan Manning
Grandfather, Ensemble

Michael X. Martin
J.P. Morgan, Ensemble

Mike McGowan
Charles S. Whitman

Tracy Lynn Olivera
Brigit

Bryonha Parham
Sarah's Friend, Ensemble

Mamie Parris
Ensemble

Nicole Powell
Ensemble

Arbender J. Robinson
Ensemble

Benjamin Schrader
Ensemble

Wallace Smith
Ensemble

Josh Walden
Harry K. Thaw, Ensemble, Associate Director/Choreographer

Catherine Walker
Ensemble

Kylil Christopher Williams
Coalhouse Walker III

Carey Rebecca Brown
Swing

Benjamin Cook
u/s Little Boy

Lisa Karlin
Swing

James Moye
Swing

Kaylie Rubinaccio
u/s Little Girl

Jim Weaver
Swing, Asst. Dance Captain

Terrence McNally
Book

Stephen Flaherty and Lynn Ahrens
Music and Vocal Arrangements; Lyrics

E.L. Doctorow
Original Novel

Marcia Milgrom Dodge
Director & Choreographer

Derek McLane
Scenic Design

Santo Loquasto
Costume Design

Donald Holder
Lighting Design

Tom Clark, Mark Menard and Nevin Steinberg, Acme Sound Partners
Sound Designer

William David Brohn
Orchestrations

John Miller
Music Coordinator

Brian Lynch
Technical Supervisor

Peter Lawrence
Production Supervisor

John S. Corker
General Manager

Ragtime

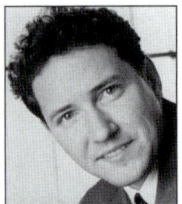

Kevin McCollum
Producer

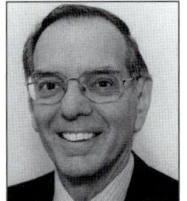

Roy Furman
Producer

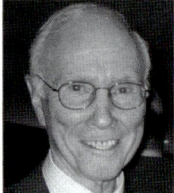

Roger Berlind
Producer

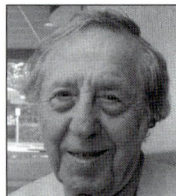

Max Cooper
Producer

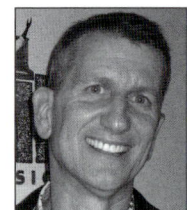

Tom Kirdahy
Producer

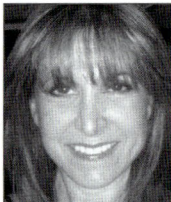

Stephanie P. McClelland
Producer

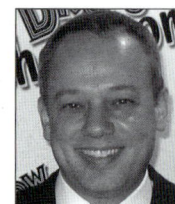

Roy Miller
Producer

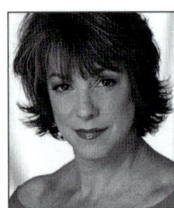

Jana Robbins
Producer

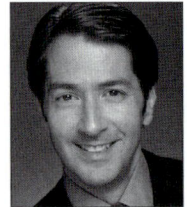

Bradley Reynolds, Lams Productions

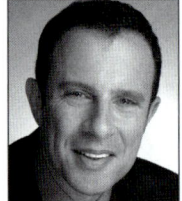

David Siesko, Lams Productions

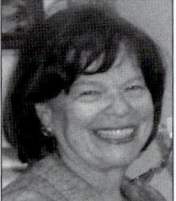

Sharon Karmazin
Producer

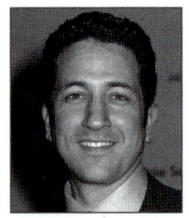

Eric Falkenstein
Producer

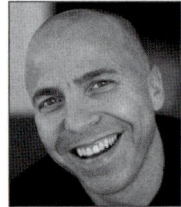

Morris Berchard
Producer

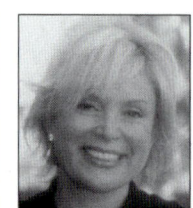

Wendy Federman, Rialtogals Productions
Producer

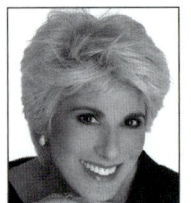

Jamie deRoy, Rialtogals Productions
Producer

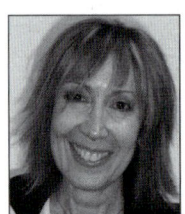

Lauren Stevens, Rialtogals Productions
Producer

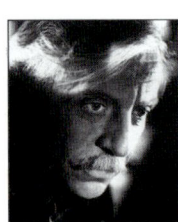

Emanuel Azenberg
Producer

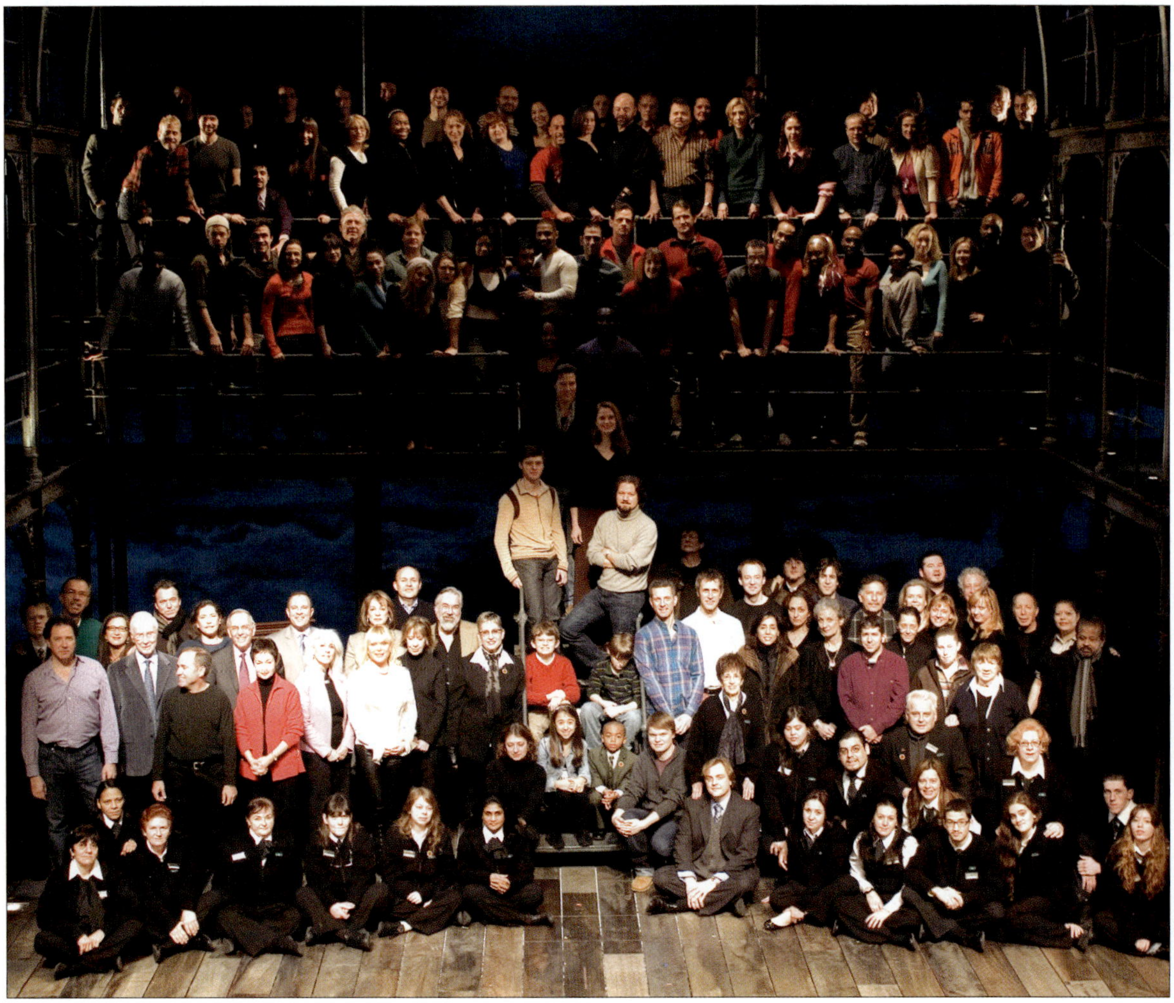
Photo by Brian Mapp

CAST, CREW AND PRODUCERS ON THE STAGE OF THE NEIL SIMON THEATRE

Ragtime

STAFF FOR RAGTIME

GENERAL MANAGEMENT
John S. Corker
Lizbeth Cone

GENERAL PRESS REPRESENTATIVE
BONEAU/BRYAN-BROWN, INC.
Chris Boneau   Joe Perrotta   Michael Strassheim

DIRECTOR OF MARKETING
Scott A. Moore

CASTING
LAURA STANCZYK CASTING
Laura Stanczyk
Clare Drobot, Benton Whitley, Anna Strasser, CJ Tropp

COMPANY MANAGER
Roeya Banuazizi

Production Supervisor	Peter Lawrence
Technical Supervisor	Brian Lynch/Theatretech, Inc.
Stage Manager	Karen Moore
Assistant Stage Manager	Jim Woolley
Associate Conductor	Jamie Schmidt
Assistant Company Manager	Michael Bolgar
Dance Captain	Josh Walden
Fight Captain	Aaron Galligan-Stierle
Assistant Dance Captain	Jim Weaver
Assistant to the Director	Josie Bray
Casting Dance Assistant	Ann Cooley-Presley
Associate Scenic Designer	Shoko Kambara
Assistant Scenic Designers	Erica Hemminger, Brett Banakis
Associate Costume Designer	Matthew Pachtman
Assistant Costume Designer	Sophia Lidz
Costume Assistant	Noah Marin
Original Broadway Associate Costume Designer	Mitchell Bloom
Associate Lighting Designers	Caroline Chao, Jeanne Koenig
Assistant Lighting Designers	Michael Jones, Karen Spahn
Associate Sound Designer	Alexander Ritter
Associate Hair & Wig Designer	Giovanna Calabretta
Assistant Hair & Wig Designer	Susan Corrado
Moving Light Programmer	Elfin Lighting/Richard Tyndall
Technical Consultant	Douglas Grekin
Production Carpenter	Chris Kluth
Flyman	Justin Garvey
Automation	Michael Shepp
Production Electrician	Keith Buchanan
Follow Spot Operator/Moving Lights	Patrick Harrington
Sound Engineer	John Dory
Advance Sound Engineer	Greg Freedman
Production Propmaster	Ron Groomes
Wardrobe Supervisor	Michael D. Hannah
Assistant Wardrobe Supervisor	Christel Murdock
Dressers	Alicia Aballi, Christina Ainge, Samanthe Burrow, Alexa K. Burt, Anita Ali Davis, Jackie S. Freeman, Rachael Garrett, Bobby Gerard, Rosemary Keough, Yleana Nuñez, Jerome Parker, Danny Paul, Kyle Stewart, Ron Tagert, Arlene Watson, Cheryl Lyn Widner
Hair Supervisor	Edward J. Wilson
Assistant Hair Supervisor	Steven Kirkham
Hair Dressers	Brannon Gray, Jeanette Harrington
Education Service	On Location Education/Susan Feltman
Tutor	Priscilla Richardson
Child Guardian	John Mara
Dialect Coach	Anita Maynard-Losh
Assistant Conductor/Rehearsal Pianist	Sue Anschutz
Music Coordinator	John Miller
Assistant to John Miller	Nichole Jennino
Music Prep	Holly Carroll
Keyboard Programming	Synthlink LLC/Jim Harp
Music Assistants	Shawn James Bolduc, Hannah Kohl
Production Assistants	Lisa Chernoff, Bryan Rountree
Assistant to Mr. McCollum	Caitlyn Thomson
Assistant to Mr. Corker	Kim Marie Vasquez
Legal Counsel	Levine Plotkin Menin, LLP/Loren Plotkin, Susan Mindell, Conrad Rippy, Cris Criswell
Advertising	Spotco/Drew Hodges, Jim Edwards, Tom Greenwald, Y. Darius Suyama, Pete Duffy
Website/Internet Marketing	Spotco/Sara Fitzpatrick, Matt Wilstein, Marc Mettler, Christina Sees
Marketing Associate	Joshua Lee Poole
Accountant	FK Partners/Robert Fried, Anthony Moore
Controller	Sarah Galbraith
Insurance	D.R. Reiff & Associates
Banking	Signature Bank/Margaret Monigan, Mary Anne Fanelli
Payroll	Castellana Services Inc.
Merchandise	Creative Goods/Jennifer Alam, Peter Milano
Production Photographer	Joan Marcus
Travel/Accommodations	Andi Henig/A Team Travel

SPECIAL THANKS
Michael Kaiser, Max Woodward

CREDITS
Scenery constructed by Global Scenic Studios. Lighting equipment from PRG Lighting. Sound equipment from Sound Associates. Scenery automation and show control by Show Motion, Inc. Norwalk CT, using the AC2 computerized Motion Control System. Chain motors from United Staging & Rigging. Trucking by Argularia. Percussion equipment and drum programming by Dan McMillan. Wireless handsets by Verizon. Original Broadway costumes and millinery construction by Livent Costumes, Inc. Costumes by EuroCo Costumes, Inc.; Seamless Costumes; Werner Russold; Giliberto Designs, Inc.; Katrina Patterns. Millinery by Kaz Maxine, Hellen Flower, Carelli Costumes, Inc. Wig construction by Paul Huntley Enterprises, Inc. Custom fabric dyeing and painting by Jeff Fender. Custom footwear by J.C. Theatrical, Worldtone Dance. Hosiery and undergarments from Bra*Tenders. Natural herb cough drops courtesy of Ricola USA, Inc.

Stock and amateur performance rights are available through Music Theatre International, New York, NY.

Ragtime rehearsed at the Hilton Theatre Rehearsal Studios.

www.RagtimeBroadway.com

NEDERLANDER

Chairman	James M. Nederlander
President	James L. Nederlander

Executive Vice President
Nick Scandalios

Vice President Corporate Development	Senior Vice President Labor Relations
Charlene S. Nederlander	**Herschel Waxman**
Vice President	Chief Financial Officer
Jim Boese	**Freida Sawyer Belviso**

STAFF FOR THE NEIL SIMON THEATRE

Theatre Manager	Steve Ouellette
Treasurer	Eddie Waxman
Associate Treasurer	Marc Needleman
House Carpenter	John Gordon
Flyman	Douglas McNeill
House Electrician	James Travers, Sr.
House Propman	Danny Viscardo
House Engineer	John Astras

Christiane Noll as Mother
Photo by Joan Marcus

Ragtime
Scrapbook

Correspondent: Christiane Noll, "Mother"

Memorable Fan Letter: "The only other fan letter I've ever written was to the Divine Miss RuPaul!"—Kirk Douglas's note praising the show with an original drawing of his profile.

Most Exciting Celebrity Visitors and What They Did/Said: Lea Michele, the original "Little Girl" and star of TV's "Glee." Sarah Rosenthal, our "Little Girl" flipped out!! Whoopi Goldberg!!—She loved it! and said so on "The View."

Actor Who Performed the Most Roles in This Show: Aaron Galligan-Stierle: 13 roles / 19 costume changes.

Special Backstage Rituals: Saturday Night Surprise!! A few of the ladies in the ensemble who sing the offstage aahhs during "Back to Before" dress up in funny themes, including Living Menorah, Living Nativity, Thanksgiving Day Parade, slumber party, stuffed animals, flashers with Happy Opening fig leaves (see photo, right), '80s cartoon characters, et cetera.

Young Coalhouse (both of them) walk Christiane Noll from her dressing room to the stage every show before the finale.

Various hand-jives, fist-pumps and hand-slaps abound on a regular basis backstage.

Eric Jordan Young does an interpretive dance during "Journey On."

Christopher Cox says "Hi" to everyone EVERY TIME he sees them—and needs to hug everyone—all the time. Ritual?

Favorite Moments During Each Performance: Watching "Baseball," the end of the opening number, and the end of "New Music."

Favorite In-Theatre Gathering Places: The wardrobe room. Also, the downstairs stage left water cooler.

Favorite Snack Foods: There are ALWAYS baked goods backstage—thanks mostly to the orchestra!!!!

Mascot: Gene!! Thank you Ben Schrader!!!

Record Number of Cell Phone Rings; Other Audience Technology Issues: There have been quite a few recording devices in the front row! Shameless!!

Memorable Press Encounters: "Broadway on Broadway"—when we were all together for the first time!! Singing on "The View"!!

Memorable Stage Door Fan Encounters: Lots of crying and shaking college students. John Ratzenberger—Cliff Claven from "Cheers"—one of our investors! A teenager who said that Willie Conklin was his dream role! Ah youth!

Latest Audience Arrival: Whoopi Goldberg! Held the curtain over 15 minutes—But heck—we got to be on "The View"!

Who Wore the Heaviest/Hottest Costume: Debatable—but either the underdressed Reporters or Michael X. Martin's J.P. Morgan costume!!

1. Cast members horse around in costume at a special CBS-TV Thanksgiving Day filming two songs from the show in Battery Park, across from the Statue of Liberty.
2. Donna Migliaccio and Savannah Wise get into costume backstage at the Neil Simon Theatre.
3. Sarah Rosenthal, child wrangler John Mara and Christopher Cox at the Battery Park event, with Liberty Island and Ellis Island in the background.
4. Composer Stephen Flaherty with Music Director/Conductor Jim Moore.
5. Jennifer Evans, Mamie Parris, Tracy Lynn Olivera, and Catherine Walker enact one of their "Saturday Night Surprise" stunts for opening night.
6. Dan Manning and Robert Petkoff in costume, plus sunglasses, head out to shoot the Thanksgiving Day Parade segment in Battery Park.

Ragtime
SCRAPBOOK

1. Director Marcia Milgrom Dodge surveys the set for the first time.
2. Ron Bohmer waves from his dressing room window at the Neil Simon Theatre.
3. Lyricist Lynn Ahrens greets Robert Petkoff on opening night.
4. Jayden Brockington and Stephanie Umoh hug backstage.
5. *Yearbook* correspondent Christiane Noll (center) and members of the ensemble prepare for their appearance on TV's "The View."

Fastest Costume Change: Mark Aldrich—less than 5 seconds from Baseball back into Willie Conklin and a close second Savannah Wise—10 seconds.
Actresses With Most Wig Changes: Savannah Wise and Mamie Parris: 12.
Who Wore the Least: Savannah Wise as Evelyn Nesbit, and Jonathan Hammond as Harry Houdini.
What Did You Think of the Web Buzz on Your Show: On the one hand harmful—on the other overwhelmingly supportive!
Busiest Day at the Box Office: The day we posted our closing notice—go figure!
Catchphrases Only the Company Would Recognize: "Who's Peter?" "Short pants are for little boys." "I know how to blow things up." "The Geshrei of the day is...."
Memorable Directorial Notes: "Be Ferocious." "Both Little Coalhouses scratch their noses on stage excessively, please tell them not to." "Don't be precious."
Embarrassing Moments: The Baby's leg fell off in the beach scene—bounced on the floor—Ron Bohmer picked it up, handed it to Christopher Cox and continued on with the scene. Wow! Christiane Noll had to sing "Back to Before" with the audience still all a-titter and a-twitter!
Corey Bradley bent over to pick up 'dead' Sarah in the funeral and split his pants. He was wearing attractive underwear and made people in the front row giddy!
Coolest Thing About Being in This Show: The amazing, positive, committed, supportive, gifted, loving Company that is *Ragtime*!!
Other Stories and Memories: Stage Manager Karen Moore sprinting to Stephanie Umoh's apartment to get her to the show by 15 minutes to curtain because Stephanie had forgotten it was a 7 PM curtain instead of 8 PM.
One of the Young Coalhouses created and drew up a ticket for "Jaydentime."
Swing Jim Moye dressed up as Santa for Christmas Eve.
The Kids had a scavenger hunt on Halloween and Christiane Noll gave them a food challenge—they had to eat carrots. Christopher Cox and Ben Cook almost didn't make it through that one.
On opening night, *Jersey Boys* (across the street) welcomed us to Broadway 15 minutes before curtain by yelling out of their windows "Break Legs," "Happy Opening," et cetera.
Orchestra members were given to passing out tissues to patrons in the front row because there was so much crying going on in the audience.

Ragtime Facts:

Cast: 40, including swings and understudies
Stage Managers: 3
Wardrobe: 18, including crew heads
Carpenters: 5
Electricians: 5
Props: 4
Sound: 3
Orchestra: 28 plus 1 conductor
Costumes: 350-plus
Number of Wigs: 86
Facial Hair Pieces: 112
Wireless Mics: 37
Orchestra Mics: 58
Stage Manager Cues: 550-plus

Red

First Preview: March 11, 2010. Opened: April 1, 2010.
Still running as of May 31, 2010.

CAST
(in order of speaking)

Mark Rothko .... ALFRED MOLINA
Ken .... EDDIE REDMAYNE

UNDERSTUDIES

For Mark Rothko: STEPHEN ROWE
For Ken: GABRIEL EBERT

Eddie Redmayne is appearing with the permission of Actors' Equity Association. The producers gratefully acknowledge Actors' Equity Association for its assistance to this production.

GOLDEN THEATRE
A Shubert Organization Theatre
Philip J. Smith, *Chairman*   Robert E. Wankel, *President*

ARIELLE TEPPER MADOVER   STEPHANIE P. McCLELLAND   MATTHEW BYAM SHAW   NEAL STREET
FOX THEATRICALS   RUTH HENDEL / BARBARA WHITMAN
PHILIP HAGEMANN / MURRAY ROSENTHAL   THE DONMAR WAREHOUSE

PRESENT
THE DONMAR WAREHOUSE PRODUCTION

ALFRED MOLINA   EDDIE REDMAYNE
IN

RED

A NEW PLAY BY
JOHN LOGAN

SET AND COSTUME DESIGNER: **CHRISTOPHER ORAM**
LIGHTING DESIGNER: **NEIL AUSTIN**
COMPOSER AND SOUND DESIGNER: **ADAM CORK**

DONMAR EXECUTIVE PRODUCER: **JAMES BIERMAN**
CASTING: **ANNE McNULTY**
PRESS REPRESENTATIVE: **BONEAU / BRYAN-BROWN**
MARKETING DIRECTOR: **ERIC SCHNALL**

GENERAL MANAGEMENT: **101 PRODUCTIONS, LTD.**
PRODUCTION STAGE MANAGER: **ARTHUR GAFFIN**
PRODUCTION MANAGEMENT: **AURORA PRODUCTIONS**

DIRECTED BY
MICHAEL GRANDAGE

THE PRODUCERS WISH TO EXPRESS THEIR APPRECIATION TO THEATRE DEVELOPMENT FUND FOR ITS SUPPORT OF THIS PRODUCTION.

4/1/10

(L-R): Alfred Molina and Eddie Redmayne

Red

Alfred Molina
Mark Rothko

Eddie Redmayne
Ken

Stephen Rowe
Understudy

Gabriel Ebert
Understudy

John Logan
Playwright

Michael Grandage
Director

Christopher Oram
Set and Costume Design

Neil Austin
Lighting Design

Adam Cork
Composer & Sound Design

Wendy Orshan, 101 Productions, Ltd.
General Manager

Arielle Tepper Madover
Producer

Stephanie P. McClelland
Producer

Caro Newling for Neal Street
Producer

Ruth Hendel
Producer

Barbara Whitman
Producer

BOX OFFICE
(L-R): Melissa Jorgensen, Chip Jorgensen

CREW
(L-R): Barry Doss (Associate Costume Designer/Dresser), Kelly Saxon (Wardrobe Supervisor), Mark Trezza (Star Dresser), Steve McDonald (House Props), Vera Pizzarelli (Head Props), Tom Lawrey (Head Electrician), Sylvia Yoshioka (House Electrician), Barbara Crompton (Company Manager), Artie Gaffin (Production Stage Manager), Jamie Greathouse (Stage Manager)

(Not pictured: Brad Gyorgak, Jon Lawson)

Red

USHERS
Back Row (L-R):
Carolyne Jones (House Manager), Mae Smith, Helen Bentley, Shelia Miller

Front Row (L-R):
Unidentified, Patricia Byrne, Cookie Harlin, Felicia Masias

Photo by Brian Mapp

STAFF FOR RED

GENERAL MANAGEMENT
101 PRODUCTIONS, LTD.
Wendy Orshan   Jeffrey M. Wilson
David Auster
Elie Landau

COMPANY MANAGER
Barbara Crompton

GENERAL PRESS REPRESENTATIVE
BONEAU/BRYAN-BROWN
Adrian Bryan-Brown   Jim Byk
Christine Olver

PRODUCTION MANAGEMENT
AURORA PRODUCTIONS
Gene O'Donovan, W. Benjamin Heller II,
Rachel Sherbill, Steve Rosenberg, Jarid Sumner,
Melissa Mazdra, Amy Merlino Coey,
Amanda Raymond,
Graham Forden, Liza Luxenberg

Production Stage Manager	Arthur Gaffin
Stage Manager	Jamie Greathouse
Associate Director	Paul Hart
UK Scenic Associate	Richard Kent
Associate Costume Designer	Barry Doss
UK Associate Lighting Designer/ Lighting Programmer	Rob Halliday
US Associate Lighting Designer	Pamela Kupper
Lighting Design Intern	Kelly Smith
Associate Sound Designer	Chris Cronin
Dialect Coach	Kate Wilson

Production Electrician	Jon Lawson
Production Props Supervisor	Vera Pizzarelli
Production Sound	Brad Gyorgak
Head Electrician	Tom Lawrey
Wardrobe Supervisor	Kelly Saxon
Star Dresser	Mark Trezza
Dresser	Mickey Abbate
Assistant to Ms. Tepper Madover	Holly Ferguson

Legal Counsel	Lazarus & Harris, LLP/ Scott R. Lazarus, Esq., Robert C. Harris, Esq.
Accountant	Fried & Kowgios
Controller	Galbraith & Co Inc./Kenny Noth
Advertising	SPOTCO/ Drew Hodges, Jim Edwards, Tom Greenwald, Beth Watson, Tim Falotico
Marketing	Eric Schnall
Marketing Associate	Holly Ferguson
Production Assistant	Jenny Kennedy
101 Productions, Ltd. Staff	Michael Rudd, Ingrid Kloss, Meredith Morgan, Mary Six Rupert
Banking	City National Bank/Anne McSweeney
Insurance	Ventura Brokerage, Inc./Christine Sadofsky
Immigration	Visa Consultants/Lisa Carr Traffic Control Group/David King
Company Housing	BridgeStreet Worldwide, Alternative Business Accommodations
Theatre Displays	King Displays, Inc.
Payroll Services	Castellana Services, Inc.
Production Photographer	Joan Marcus
UK Production Photographer	Johan Persson
Website Design	Dotmeta/Yujin Asai
Opening Night Coordinator	The Lawrence Company/ Michael P. Lawrence

DONMAR WAREHOUSE

Artistic Director	Michael Grandage
Executive Producer	James Bierman
General Manager	Jo Danvers
PA to the Executive	Miriam Green
Creative & Casting Associate	Anne McNulty
Casting Assistant	Vicky Richardson
Development Director	Kate Mitchell
Development Manager	Deborah Lewis
Development Officer	Rosie Dalling
Development Administrator	Fraser Anderson
Marketing Manager	Jonathan Aplin
Press Representative	Kate Morley for Blueprint PR
Office Administrator	Frankie Bridges
General Assistant	Nina Segal
Deputy Production Manager	Kate West
Head of Wardrobe	Tansy Blaik-Kelly
Deputy Head of Wardrobe	Morag Pirrie
Associate Director	Rob Ashford, Jamie Lloyd
Resident Assistant Director	Titas Halder
Education Associates	Dominic Francis, Sophie Watkiss

CREDITS

Scenery built by Bowerwood Production Services and ShowMotion, Inc. Set and canvases painted by Richard Nutbourne. Additional scenery painted by Scenic Art Studios. Lighting by PRG. Sound by Sound Associates. Period lighting equipment provided by PRG Europe, Ancient Lights and Props, Steve Huttly and Nick Peal. Costumes supplied by Carlo Manzi.

Likeness of Rothko Seagram mural panels: Copyright ©1998 Kate Rothko Prizel and Christopher Rothko/Artists Rights Society (ARS), New York

SPECIAL THANKS
Greg Shimmin, Nicole (Tinky) Walker, Laura Sully

www.RedOnBroadway.com

 THE SHUBERT ORGANIZATION, INC.
Board of Directors

Philip J. Smith
Chairman

Robert E. Wankel
President

Wyche Fowler, Jr.

John W. Kluge

Lee J. Seidler

Michael I. Sovern

Stuart Subotnick

Elliot Greene
Chief Financial Officer

David Andrews
Senior Vice President - Shubert Ticketing

Juan Calvo
Vice President and Controller

John Darby
Vice President – Facilities

Peter Entin
Vice President – Theatre Operations

Charles Flateman
Vice President – Marketing

Anthony LaMattina
Vice President – Audit & Production Finance

Brian Mahoney
Vice President – Ticket Sales

D.S. Moynihan
Vice President – Creative Projects

House Manager	Carolyne Jones

Red
Scrapbook

Correspondent: Artie Gaffin, Production Stage Manager

Forty-Five Minutes Before the House Opens: The smell of turpentine is released into the theatre. This is part of Michael Grandage and Christopher Oram's desire to make the audience feel they are entering Mark Rothko's studio. Tremendous attention and respect for detail. And it wasn't easy to get a company to create that smell!

"Half hour everyone. This is your half hour call." Vera brings up the "priming bucket" with that distinct smell of rabbit skin glue. Jamie quietly and thoroughly checks all the props—she opens the phonograph for the fourth time just to make sure the right record is on and spinning. Eddie is finishing up his warm up—"BECAUSE NATURAL LIGHT ISN'T GOOD ENOUGH FOR YOU." Many actors are just arriving at theatres all over Broadway and signing in—but Alfred Molina is taking his place in the Adirondack chair where he will spend the next 35 minutes until the show starts. What is he thinking during all that time? He has shared with us what he is mostly hearing: People not quite sure if they are in the right seat! Is this BB 102 or 104? One time he heard an audience member say to her friend: "That's Alfred Molina, the actor." "What's he doing?" "Getting into the mood."

Eddie and Fred hug. In London they would say "See you in New York." Now that they are IN New York, they say "See you in '58." Fred and Vera hug. "Have a good one."

The house is given to Carolyne; "The house is yours." Carolyne turns to the ushers and says, "The house is open." In unison, Fred and the ushers respond, "Long live the house."

At five minutes after the curtain time, the show begins. Ninety-three minutes, no intermission. Audiences are rapt throughout. Sometimes, the audience is listening so intently, you cannot hear a cough or a candy wrapper. Even cell phones are afraid to go off. Lots of laughs throughout and then whistling, cheering, bravos at the standing curtain call.

Who could ask for a better way to spend the spring and summer? Even the red paint that somehow ends up on your clothes and under your fingernails after every performance could not take away the joy of being a part of this project—a beautifully directed, written and designed production, lovely and talented actors, a hard-working, thoughtful and caring crew, generous general managers and wonderful producers.

And if that's not "good enough for you," there are the Sunday brunches (bagels, muffins, coffee cake, fruit—not just red-colored food) provided every week courtesy of Arielle.

Seventeen weeks full of the smell of turpentine and love!

1. (L-R): Director Michael Grandage, actors Alfred Molina and Eddie Redmayne with author John Logan at Gotham Hall for the opening night party.
2. (L-R): Guests David Hyde Pierce and Victor Garber at Gotham Hall.
3. Redmayne and Molina on the Golden Theatre stage for curtain calls at the premiere.

Photos by Joe Marzullo

2009-2010 AWARDS

Tony Awards
Best Play
(Author: John Logan)
Best Featured Actor in a Play
(Eddie Redmayne)
Best Direction of a Play
(Michael Grandage)
Best Scenic Design of a Play
(Christopher Oram)
Best Lighting Design of a Play
(Neil Austin)
Best Sound Design of a Play
(Adam Cork)

Outer Critics Circle Award
Outstanding New Broadway Play

Drama Desk Awards
Outstanding Play
Outstanding Director of a Play
(Michael Grandage)
Outstanding Lighting Design
(Neil Austin)

Drama League Awards
Distinguished Production of a Play
Distinguished Performance (Alfred Molina)

Theatre World Award
First Major New York Appearance
(Eddie Redmayne)

Rock of Ages

First Preview: March 17, 2009. Opened: April 7, 2009.
Still running as of May 31, 2010

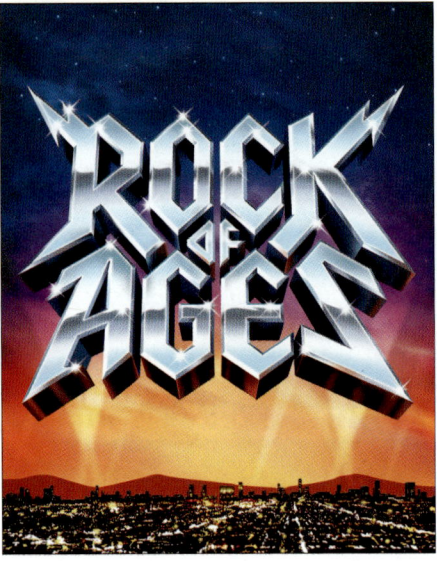

CAST
(in order of appearance)

Lonny	MITCHELL JARVIS
Justice	MICHELE MAIS
Dennis	ADAM DANNHEISSER
Drew	CONSTANTINE MAROULIS
Sherrie	KERRY BUTLER
Father	JAMES CARPINELLO
Mother	MICHELE MAIS
Regina	LAUREN MOLINA
Mayor	ANDRE WARD
Hertz	DON STEPHENSON
Franz	TOM LENK
Stacee Jaxx	JAMES CARPINELLO
Waitress #1	ERICKA HUNTER
Reporter	KATHERINE TOKARZ
Ja'Keith Gill	ANDRE WARD
Record Company Men	ADAM DANNHEISSER/ MITCHELL JARVIS
Sleazy Producer	JEREMY WOODARD
Joey Primo	JEREMY WOODARD
Candi	LAUREN MOLINA
Strip Club DJ	TAD WILSON
Young Groupie	ANGEL REED

THE ENSEMBLE
ERICKA HUNTER, ANGEL REED,
KATHERINE TOKARZ,
ANDRE WARD, JEREMY WOODARD

Continued on next page

BROOKS ATKINSON THEATRE
UNDER THE DIRECTION OF JAMES M. NEDERLANDER AND JAMES L. NEDERLANDER

MATTHEW WEAVER   CARL LEVIN   JEFF DAVIS   BARRY HABIB   SCOTT PRISAND   RELATIVITY MEDIA
in association with
CORNER STORE FUND   JANET BILLIG RICH   HILLARY WEAVER   RYAN KAVANAUGH   TONI HABIB
PAULA DAVIS   SIMON AND STEFANY BERGSON/JENNIFER MALONEY   CHARLES ROLECEK
SUSANNE BROOK   CRAIG COZZA   ISRAEL WOLFSON   SARA KATZ/JAYSON RAITT   MAX GOTTLIEB/JOHN BUTLER
DAVID KAUFMAN/JAY FRANKS   MICHAEL WITTLIN   PROSPECT PICTURES   LAURA SMITH/BILL BODNAR
WIN SHERIDAN   HAPPY WALTERS   ADAM SMITH/MICHELLE CARD   and   THE ARACA GROUP
present

ROCK OF AGES

book by
CHRIS D'ARIENZO

starring
CONSTANTINE MAROULIS
and
KERRY BUTLER as SHERRIE

ADAM DANNHEISSER   MITCHELL JARVIS   TOM LENK   MICHELE MAIS
LAUREN MOLINA   DON STEPHENSON   *with* JAMES CARPINELLO

BAHIYAH SAYYED GAINES   ERICKA HUNTER   JEREMY JORDAN
MICHAEL MINARIK   ANGEL REED   BECCA TOBIN   KATHERINE TOKARZ
ANDRE WARD   TAD WILSON   JEREMY WOODARD

set design	costume design	lighting design	sound design	projection design
BEOWULF BORITT	GREGORY GALE	JASON LYONS	PETER HYLENSKI	ZAK BOROVAY

hair/wig design	make-up design	casting	production stage manager
TOM WATSON	ANGELINA AVALLONE	TELSEY+COMPANY	CLAUDIA LYNCH

associate choreographer	associate director	associate producer
ROBERT TATAD	ADAM JOHN HUNTER	DAVID GIBBS

general management	press representative	technical supervisor
FRANKEL GREEN THEATRICAL MANAGEMENT LESLIE LEDBETTER	THE HARTMAN GROUP	PETER FULBRIGHT

music director	music coordinator	original arrangements
HENRY ARONSON	JOHN MILLER	DAVID GIBBS

music supervision, arrangements & orchestrations by
ETHAN POPP
choreographed by
KELLY DEVINE
directed by
KRISTIN HANGGI

10/1/09

Constantine Maroulis (center) and the Company

Photo by Joan Marcus

Rock of Ages

Cast Continued

OFFSTAGE VOICES
BAHIYAH SAYYED GAINES,
ERICKA HUNTER, BECCA TOBIN,
TAD WILSON

UNDERSTUDIES
For Sherrie:
ERICKA HUNTER, BECCA TOBIN
For Drew/Franz:
JEREMY JORDAN, JEREMY WOODARD
For Stacee Jaxx:
MICHAEL MINARIK, JEREMY JORDAN,
JEREMY WOODARD
For Lonny/Dennis/Hertz:
MICHAEL MINARIK, TAD WILSON
For Regina/Justice:
BAHIYAH SAYYED GAINES,
KATHERINE TOKARZ

SWINGS
JEREMY JORDAN,
BAHIYAH SAYYED GAINES,
MICHAEL MINARIK, BECCA TOBIN

DANCE CAPTAIN
BAHIYAH SAYYED GAINES

BAND
Conductor/Keyboard:
HENRY ARONSON
Guitar 1:
JOEL HOEKSTRA
Guitar 2:
TOMMY KESSLER
Drums:
JON WEBER
Bass:
WINSTON ROYE

Synthesizer Programming:
RANDY COHEN
Music Coordinator:
JOHN MILLER
Copyist:
FIREFLY MUSIC SERVICE/
BRIAN ALLAN HOBBS

Constantine Maroulis
Drew

Kerry Butler
Sherrie

James Carpinello
Stacee Jaxx/Father

Adam Dannheisser
Dennis

Mitchell Jarvis
Lonny

Tom Lenk
Franz

Michele Mais
Justice/Mother

Lauren Molina
Regina/Candi

Don Stephenson
Hertz

Bahiyah Sayyed Gaines
Ensemble

Ericka Hunter
Ensemble

Jeremy Jordan
Ensemble

Michael Minarik
Swing

Angel Reed
Ensemble

Becca Tobin
Swing

Katherine Tokarz
Ensemble

Andre Ward
Ensemble

Tad Wilson
Ensemble

Jeremy Woodard
Ensemble

Henry Aronson
Music Direction, Keyboard

Rock of Ages

 Chris D'Arienzo — *Book*
 Kristin Hanggi — *Director*
 Kelly Devine — *Choreographer*
 Beowulf Boritt — *Set Designer*
 Gregory Gale — *Costume Design*
 Jason Lyons — *Lighting Design*
 Peter Hylenski — *Sound Designer*

 Zak Borovay — *Projection Design*
 Tom Watson — *Hair and Wig Design*
 Angelina Avallone — *Make-up Designer*
 Ethan Popp — *Music Supervisor, Arranger, Orchestrator*
 John Miller — *Music Coordinator*
 Bernard Telsey, Telsey + Company — *Casting*
 Robert Tatad — *Associate Choreographer*

 Liz Caplan Vocal Studios, LLC — *Production Vocal Coach*
 Richard Frankel, Frankel Green Theatrical Management — *General Management*
 Laura Green, Frankel Green Theatrical Management — *General Management*
 Barry Habib — *Producer*
 Toni Habib — *Producer*
 Stefany Bergson — *Producer*
 Jennifer Maloney — *Producer*

 Jayson Raitt — *Producer*
 Bill Bodnar — *Producer*
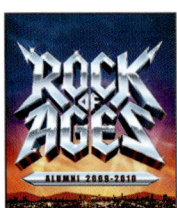
 Paul Schoeffler — *Hertz*
 Eric Sciotto — *Swing*
 Amy Spanger — *Sherrie*
 Wesley Taylor — *Franz*

 Savannah Wise — *Sherrie, Waitress, Ensemble*

 Callie Carter — *Offstage Voice, Swing*
 Jenifer Foote — *Dance Captain, Offstage Voice, Swing*
 Geoff Packard — *Swing*
 Emily Padgett — *Sherrie, Waitress #1, Ensemble*
Paul Schoeffler — *Hertz*

300   The Playbill Broadway Yearbook 2009-2010

Rock of Ages

Eric Sciotto
Swing

Derek St. Pierre
Franz

Matthew Stocke
Strip Club DJ, Offstage Voice

Katie Webber
Waitress #1, Ensemble

MANAGEMENT
(L-R): Adam John Hunter, Claudia Lynch, Marisha Ploski, Matt DiCarlo, Robert Tatad

HAIR AND WARDROBE
Front Row (L-R): Dawn Marcoccia, Ali Psiuk, Renee Borys

Back Row (L-R): Josh Schwartz, Barry Lee Moe, Danny Mura, Robert Guy, Michael Louis, Wendall Goings

BAND
(L-R): Tommy Grasso, Jerry Kops, Joel Hoekstra, Jon Weber, Winston Roye, Matt Gallagher, Jason DeBord (not pictured: Tommy Kessler and Henry Aronson)

BOX OFFICE
(L-R): Michelle Smith, Peter Attanasio, Jillian Gloven

Rock of Ages

FRONT OF HOUSE STAFF
Front Row (L-R): James Holley, Marie Gonzalez, Kimberlee Imperato, Ilona Figueroa, Angel Diaz, Barbara Hart

Middle Row (L-R): Manuel Prensa, Michelle Gonzalez, Marilyn Christie, Arlene Reill, Tara McCormack, Jamie, Marion Danton

Back Row (L-R): Roberto Rivera, Brenda Brauer, Sam Figert, Austin Branda, Robin Mates, Susan Martin

CREW
(L-R): Michael Attianese, Jeff Koger, Brent Oakley, Joe Pfifferling, Tommy Lavaia, Tommy Grasso, Joe DePaulo, Craig Van Tassel, Victor Seastone, Jesse Stevens, Brian Munroe

Rock of Ages
Scrapbook

Correspondent: Adam Dannheisser, "Dennis"
Memorable Opening Night Message: Friends of mine broke out huge "#1 Fannheisser" signs at curtain call on opening night.
Most Exciting Celebrity Visitor: We've had a lot of schmancy folks come through but I was most excited by David Lee of the New York Knicks. Is that weird? I said something funny to him and he completely ignored me. Yey! I'd like to think that he just didn't hear me... he's a lot taller.
Favorite Moment During Each Performance: Well, you never know what you're going to get with the lead-in to "I Can't Fight This Feeling." It's a semi-unscripted moment for me to interact with the audience. Keeps things a little dangerous and fun.
Favorite In-Theatre Gathering Place: Round the card table.
Favorite Off-Site Hangout: Glass House Tavern.
Mascot: Boobs.
Favorite Therapies: Ricola, Ben-Gay, Throat-Coat Tea, massage, Pilates, all of the above. With just a liiiiittle splash of bourbon.
Memorable Ad-Lib: Here's your f-ing "free bird."
Record Number of Cell Phone Rings, Cell Phone Photos or Texting Incidents During a Performance: Ask Constantine. He's the hall monitor. Patti LuPone ain't got jack on him.
Memorable Press Encounter: When the Australian press stopped me outside the stage door and asked me if I had liked the show.
Memorable Stage Door Fan Encounter: Well, let's just say I never signed boobs at Lincoln Center.

In attendance when Constantine Maroulis (C) gets his portrait hung at Sardi's Restaurant March 18, 2010 are cast members (L-R): Mitch Jarvis, Katherine Tokarz, Maroulis, Derek St. Pierre and Michele Mais.

Who Wore the Heaviest Costume: I believe that would be my GIANT set of angel's wings.
Who Wore the Least: All the women.
Catchphrase Only the Company Would Recognize: "Hooray for Boobies."
Best In-House Parody Lyrics: "I shoulda had flan" instead of "I shoulda been gone."
Who Heads Your Fan Club and What Is Their Website/Newsletter: Oh, my Fannheissers? I'm still reviewing applications. It's between my friend Debbie and David Lee.
Coolest Thing About Being in This Show: There is never a sense of "punching in" at work. This show feeds on spontaneity and the energy from the crowd. It is truly a different show every night.

STAFF FOR ROCK OF AGES

GENERAL MANAGEMENT
FRANKEL GREEN THEATRICAL MANAGEMENT
Richard Frankel Laura Green Joe Watson
Leslie Ledbetter

COMPANY MANAGER
Tracy Geltman
Assistant Company Manager .... Susan Keappock

TECHNICAL SUPERVISOR
TECH PRODUCTION SERVICES, INC.
Peter Fulbright, Colleen Houlehen
Mary Duffe, Miranda Wigginton

GENERAL PRESS REPRESENTATIVE
THE HARTMAN GROUP
Michael Hartman
Leslie Baden Alyssa Hart

CASTING
TELSEY + COMPANY, C.S.A.
Bernie Telsey CSA, Will Cantler CSA, David Vaccari CSA, Bethany Knox CSA, Craig Burns CSA, Tiffany Little Canfield CSA, Rachel Hoffman CSA, Carrie Rosson CSA, Justin Huff CSA, Bess Fifer CSA, Patrick Goodwin, Abbie Brady-Dalton

Associate General Manager .... Aliza Wassner
Production Stage Manager .... Claudia Lynch
Stage Manager .... Adam John Hunter
Assistant Stage Manager .... Marisha Ploski
Assistant Stage Manager .... Matthew DiCarlo
Production Manager .... Peter Fulbright
Production Management Associate ...... Colleen Houlehen
Associate Scenic Designer .... Jo Winiarski
Assistant Scenic Designers .... Maiko Chii, Alexis Distler, Buist Bickley
Associate Costume Designer .... Karl Ruckdeschel
Assistant Costume Designers .... Julia Broer, Colleen Kesterson
Assistant Lighting Designer .... Driscoll Otto
Assistant to the Lighting Designer .... Barbara Samuels
Lighting Programmer .... Victor Seastone
Associate Sound Designer .... Keith Caggiano
Associate Projection Designer/
 Projection Programmer .... Austin Switser
Assistant Projection Designer .... Daniel Brodie
Associate Choreographer .... Robert Tatad
Creative Advisor .... Wendy Goldberg
Production Carpenter .... Brian P. Munroe
Assistant Production Carpenter .... Ray Harold
Production Electrician .... Michael S. LoBue
Head Electrician .... Brent Oakley
Production Sound Engineer .... Phillip Lojo
Head Sound Engineer .... Jesse Stevens
Production Property Master .... Michael Pilipski
Head Propman .... Jacob White
Wardrobe Supervisor .... Robert Guy
Dressers .... Renee Borys, Michael Louis, Dawn Marcoccia, Danny Mura, Susan Cook, Marisa LeRette
Hair & Wig Supervisor .... Thomas Augustine
Hair & Wig Assistant .... Joshua Speed Schwartz
Production Assistant .... Samantha Saltzman
Script Supervisor .... Justin Mabardi
Assistants to Mr. Weaver .... Tom Pelligrini, Leigh Huser
Assistants to Mr. Levin .... B. Dannheisser, Anna Wood
Company Management Assistant .... Caitlin Fahey
Company Management Intern .... Danielle Barchetto
Music Director/Conductor .... Henry Aronson
Music Coordinator .... John Miller
Assistant to John Miller .... Nichole Jennino

Rock of Ages

Synthesizer Programmer	Randy Cohen
Music Copying/ Music Preparation	FireFly Music Service/ Brian Allan Hobbs
Rehearsal Pianist	Keith Cotton
Advertising	Serino Coyne, Inc./ Scott Johnson, Sandy Block, Ryan Cunningham, Andrea Prince, Jill Falcone
Marketing & Promotions	The Pekoe Group/ Amanda Pekoe, Kerry Minchinton
Marketing	Leanne Schanzer Promotions, Inc./ Leanne Schanzer, Justin Schanzer, Kara Laviola
Internet Marketing/ Web Design	Art Meets Commerce/ Jim Glaub, Ryan Greer, Laurie Connor, Kevin Keating, Brad Coffman, Mark Seeley
Press Associates	Edward Allen, Nicole Capatasto, Frances Connelly, Tom D'Ambrosio, Juliana Hannett, Holly Kinney, Matt Ross, Wayne Wolfe
Production Photography	Joan Marcus
Insurance	DeWitt Stern Group, Inc./ Peter Shoemaker, Mary E. De Spirt
Legal Counsel	Sendroff and Baruch, LLP/ Jason Baruch
Banking	Chase Manhattan Bank
Payroll Service	Castellana Services, Inc.
Accounting	Fried & Kowgios Partners, CPAs, LLP
Additional New York Rehearsals	Ripley-Grier Studios
Group Sales	Theatre Direct Group Sales 1.800.BROADWAY

FRANKEL GREEN THEATRICAL MANAGEMENT

Finance Director	**Michael Naumann**
Assistant to Mr. Frankel	Heidi Libby
Assistant to Ms. Green	Joshua A Saletnik
Assistant Finance Director	Sue Bartelt
Finance Associate	Heather Allen
Information Technology Manager	**Roddy Pimentel**
National Sales and Marketing Director	**Ronni Mandell**
Director of Business Affairs	**Michael Sinder**
Business Affairs Assistant	Dario Dalla Lasta
Booking	On the Road Booking, LLC/ Simma Levine, President
Office Manager	**Emily Wright**
Receptionists	Rebekah Hughston, Allison Raines
Interns	Alex Parra, Alex Peyser, Claudia Stuart, Jason Styres, James Teal, Laura Valenti, Shannon Winter

CREDITS AND ACKNOWLEDGEMENTS

Avalon Salon & Day Spa, Gibson, Ernie Ball, Baldwin Piano, Vic Firth, Vans, PRG Audio, Showmotion and Spoon Group. Lighting equipment from Hudson Sound and Light LLC, Mimi Bilinski. Costumes constructed by Jennifer Love Costumes and Jennifer Jacob. Custom leatherwear by www.rawhides.com, Shoes and boots constructed by T.O. Dey and Worldtone. Fabric painting and costume crafts by Jeffrey Fender. Hosiery and undergarments by Bra*Tenders. Keyboards by Yamaha. Daddy-O scenery. Dany Margolies.

A special thanks to
Trash and Vaudeville
for the rock 'n' roll gear.

Rehearsed at the New 42nd Street Studios

MUSIC CREDITS

"Anyway You Want It" written by Steve Perry and Neal Schon. © Published by Lacey Boulevard Music and Weed High Nightmare Music.
"Can't Fight This Feeling" written by Kevin Cronin. © Published by Fate Music (ASCAP).
"Cum on Feel the Noize" written by Neville Holder and James Lea. © Barn Publishing (Slade) Ltd.
"Don't Stop Believin'" written by Jonathan Cain, Stephen Ray Perry, Neal J. Schon © Published by Weed High Nightmare Music and Lacey Boulevard Music.
"Every Rose Has Its Thorn" written by Bobby Dall, Bruce Anthony Johannesson, Bret Michaels, Rikki Rocket. © All rights owned or administered by Universal Music-Z Songs on behalf of Cyanide Publ./BMI. Used by permission.
"The Final Countdown" written by Joey Tempest. © Screen Gems-EMI Music Inc.
"Harden My Heart" written by Marvin Webster Ross. © 1980 WB Music Corp. (ASCAP), Narrow Dude Music (ASCAP) and Bonnie Bee Good Music. All rights administered by WB Music Corp. All rights reserved. Used by permission.
"Heat of the Moment" written by Geoffrey Downes and John K. Wetton. © 1982 WB Music Corp. (ASCAP), Almond Legg Music Corp (ASCAP) and Pallan Music. All rights on behalf of itself and Almond Legg Music Corp. administered by WB Music Corp. All rights reserved. Used by permission.
"Heaven" written by Jani Lane, Erik Turner, Jerry Dixon, Steven Sweet and Joey Allen ©.
"Here I Go Again" written by David Coverdale and Bernard Marsden. © 1982 C.C. Songs Ltd. (PRS) and Seabreeze Music Ltd. Administered by WB Music Corp. (ASCAP). All rights reserved. Used by permission.
 "High Enough" written by Jack Blades, Ted Nugent and Tommy R. Shaw. © Published by Bicycle Music Company, Broadhead Publishing and Wixen Music.
"Hit Me With Your Best Shot" written by E. Schwartz. © Sony/ATV Tunes LLC/ASCAP.
"I Hate Myself for Loving You" written by Desmond Child and Joan Jett. © All rights owned or administered by Universal-PolyGram Int. Publ., Inc./ASCAP. Used by permission.
"I Wanna Rock" written by Daniel Dee Snider. © All rights owned or administered by Universal Music-Z Melodies on behalf of Snidest Music/SESAC. Used by permission.
"I Want to Know What Love Is" written by Michael Leslie Jones. © Published by Somerset Songs Publishing, Inc.
"Just Like Paradise" written by David Lee Roth and Brett Tuggle. © Diamond Dave Music c/o RS Plane Music.
"Keep on Lovin' You" written by Kevin Cronin. © Published by Fate Music (ASCAP).
"Kiss Me Deadly" written by Mick Smiley. © Published by The Twin Towers Co. and Mike Chapman Publishing Enterprises.
"More Than Words" written by Nuno Bettencourt and Gary F. Cherone. © All rights owned or administered by Almo Music Corp. on behalf of Color Me Blind Music/ASCAP. Used by permission.
"Nothin' But a Good Time" written by Bobby Dall, Bruce Anthony Johannesson, Bret Michaels, Rikki Rocket. © All rights owned or administered by Universal Music-Z Songs on behalf of Cyanide Publ./BMI. Used by permission.
"Oh Sherrie" written by Steve Perry, Randy Goodrum, Bill Cuomo, Craig Krampf. © Published by Street Talk Tunes, April Music Inc & Random Notes, Pants Down Music and Phosphene Music.
"Renegade" written by Tommy Shaw. © All rights owned or administered by Almo Music Corp. on behalf of itself and Stygian Songs /ASCAP. Used by permission.
"The Search Is Over" written by Frank Sullivan and Jim Peterik. © Published by Ensign Music LLC (BMI). Used by permission. All rights reserved.
"Shadows of the Night" written by D.L. Byron. ©Zen Archer/ASCAP.
"Sister Christian" written by Kelly Keagy. © Published by Bicycle Music Company.
"To Be With You" written by David Grahame and Eric Martin. ©EMI April Music, Inc. obo itself, Dog Turner Music and Eric Martin Songs (ASCAP).
"Too Much Time on My Hands" written by Tommy Shaw. © Stygian Songs/ASCAP.
"Waiting for a Girl Like You" written by Michael Leslie Jones and Louis Gramattico. © Published by Somerset Songs Publishing, Inc.
"Wanted Dead or Alive" written by Jon Bon Jovi and Richard S. Sambora. © All rights owned or administered by Universal-Polygram Int. Publ., Inc. on behalf of itself and Bon Jovi Publishing/ASCAP. Used by permission.
"We Built This City" written by Dennis Lambert, Martin George Page, Bernie Taupin and Peter Wolf. © All rights owned or administered by Universal-Polygram Int. Publ., Inc. on behalf of Little Mole Music Inc./ASCAP. Used by permission.
"We're Not Gonna Take It" written by Daniel Dee Snider. © All rights owned or administered by Universal Music-Z Melodies on behalf of Snidest Music/SESAC. Used by permission.

NEDERLANDER

Chairman	James M. Nederlander
President	James L. Nederlander

Executive Vice President
Nick Scandalios

Vice President Corporate Development	Senior Vice President Labor Relations
Charlene S. Nederlander	**Herschel Waxman**
Vice President	Chief Financial Officer
Jim Boese	**Freida Sawyer Belviso**

STAFF FOR THE BROOKS ATKINSON THEATRE

House Manager	Susan Martin
Treasurer	Peter Attanasio
Assistant Treasurer	Anthony Giannone
House Carpenter	Thomas A. Lavaia
House Flyman	Joseph J. Maher
House Electrician	Manuel Becker
House Properties	Joseph P. DePaulo
Engineer	Reynold Barriteau

The Royal Family

First Preview: September 15, 2009. Opened: October 8, 2009.
Closed December 13, 2009 after 26 Previews and 77 Performances.

CAST
(in alphabetical order)

Perry Stewart	FREDDY ARSENAULT
Gwen Cavendish	KELLI BARRETT
Della	CAROLINE STEFANIE CLAY
McDermott, Gunga	RUFUS COLLINS
Kitty Dean	ANA GASTEYER
Herbert Dean	JOHN GLOVER
Jo	DAVID GREENSPAN
Fanny Cavendish	ROSEMARY HARRIS
Julie Cavendish	JAN MAXWELL
Chauffeur	ANTHONY NEWFIELD
Gilbert Marshall	LARRY PINE
Oscar Wolfe	TONY ROBERTS
Tony Cavendish	REG ROGERS
Miss Peake	HENNY RUSSELL
Hallboy	CAT WALLECK
Hallboy	JOHN WERNKE

The action passes in the duplex apartment of the Cavendishes, in the East Fifties, New York City

Act I: A Friday in November. Early Afternoon
Act II: Saturday. Between Matinee and Night
Act III: A Year Later

Stage Manager .... ELIZABETH MOLONEY

Continued on next page

MANHATTAN THEATRE CLUB
Samuel J. Friedman Theatre

ARTISTIC DIRECTOR
Lynne Meadow

EXECUTIVE PRODUCER
Barry Grove

PRESENTS

THE ROYAL FAMILY

BY

George S. Kaufman & Edna Ferber

WITH

Ana Gasteyer   John Glover   Rosemary Harris
Jan Maxwell   Larry Pine   Tony Roberts   Reg Rogers

Freddy Arsenault   Kelli Barrett   Caroline Stefanie Clay
Rufus Collins   David Greenspan   Anthony Newfield
Henny Russell   Cat Walleck   John Wernke

SCENIC DESIGN — John Lee Beatty
COSTUME DESIGN — Catherine Zuber
LIGHTING DESIGN — Kenneth Posner
SOUND DESIGN — Darron L West

ORIGINAL MUSIC — Maury Yeston
HAIR & WIG DESIGN — Tom Watson
FIGHT DIRECTOR — Rick Sordelet

ANIMALS — William Berloni
PRODUCTION STAGE MANAGER — Rick Steiger
CASTING — David Caparelliotis

DIRECTED BY
Doug Hughes

GENERAL MANAGER — Florie Seery
ASSOCIATE ARTISTIC DIRECTOR — Mandy Greenfield
DIRECTOR OF ARTISTIC DEVELOPMENT — Jerry Patch
DIRECTOR OF MARKETING — Debra Waxman-Pilla
PRESS REPRESENTATIVE — Boneau/Bryan-Brown
PRODUCTION MANAGER — Kurt Gardner
DIRECTOR OF CASTING — Nancy Piccione
DIRECTOR OF DEVELOPMENT — Jill Turner Lloyd

Special funding for *The Royal Family* was provided by The Blanche and Irving Laurie Foundation.
Additional support was provided by American Express.
Manhattan Theatre Club wishes to express its appreciation to Theatre Development Fund for its support of this production.

10/8/09

(L-R): Jan Maxwell, Kelli Barrett and Rosemary Harris

Photo by Joan Marcus

The Royal Family

(L-R): Rufus Collins, Rosemary Harris and Reg Rogers
Photo by Joan Marcus

Cast Continued

UNDERSTUDIES
For Gilbert Marshall, Tony Cavendish:
RUFUS COLLINS
For Fanny Cavendish:
BETH DIXON
For Herbert Dean, Jo, Oscar Wolfe:
ANTHONY NEWFIELD
For Della, Kitty Dean, Julie Cavendish:
HENNY RUSSELL
For Gwen Cavendish, Hallboy, Miss Peake:
CAT WALLECK
For Perry Stewart, McDermott, Gunga:
JOHN WERNKE

Ana Gasteyer
Kitty Dean

John Glover
Herbert Dean

Rosemary Harris
Fanny Cavendish

Jan Maxwell
Julie Cavendish

Larry Pine
Gilbert Marshall

Tony Roberts
Oscar Wolfe

Reg Rogers
Tony Cavendish

Freddy Arsenault
Perry Stewart

Kelli Barrett
Gwen Cavendish

Caroline Stefanie Clay
Della

Rufus Collins
McDermott, Gunga

David Greenspan
Jo

Anthony Newfield
Chauffeur

Henny Russell
Miss Peake

Cat Walleck
Hallboy

John Wernke
Hallboy

Beth Dixon
u/s Fanny Cavendish

George S. Kaufman
(1889-1961)
Playwright

Edna Ferber
(1885-1963)
Playwright

Doug Hughes
Director

John Lee Beatty
Scenic Design

The Royal Family

Catherine Zuber
Costume Design

Kenneth Posner
Lighting Design

Darron L West
Sound Design

Maury Yeston
Original Music

Tom Watson
Hair & Wig Design

Rick Sordelet
Fight Director

William Berloni
Animals

Lynne Meadow
Artistic Director, Manhattan Theatre Club, Inc.

Barry Grove
Executive Producer, Manhattan Theatre Club, Inc.

Joel Rooks
u/s Oscar Wolfe, Jo, Chauffeur

2009-2010 AWARDS

Tony Award
Outstanding Costume Design of a Play
(Catherine Zuber)

Drama Desk Award
Outstanding Actress in a Play
(Jan Maxwell)

CREW
Front Row (L-R): Seth Shepsle, Cathy Prager, Angie Simpson, Natasha "Nabba" Steinhagen, Elizabeth Moloney, Brian Hoffman

Back Row (L-R): Jack Curtin, Eunice Dugan, Vaughn Preston, Jason Dodds, Jeff Dodson, Ian Harbor, Tim Walters, Lou Shapiro, Chris Munnell, Rick Steiger

BOX OFFICE
(L-R): David Dillon, Jeffrey Davis

FRONT OF HOUSE STAFF
Front Row (L-R): Wendy Wright, Ron Albanese, Vivian Goldring, Teff Nichols
Back Row (L-R): John Wyffels, Ed Brashear, Dinah Glorioso, Jim Joseph, Luis Sapien

Photos by Brian Mapp

The Royal Family

Ana Gasteyer as Kitty Dean

Photo by Joan Marcus

MANHATTAN THEATRE CLUB STAFF

Artistic Director	Lynne Meadow
Executive Producer	Barry Grove
General Manager	Florie Seery
Associate Artistic Director	Mandy Greenfield
Director of Artistic Development	Jerry Patch
Artistic Consultant	Daniel Sullivan
Director of Artistic Administration/ Assistant to the Artistic Director	Amy Gilkes Loe
Artistic Associate	Lisa McNulty
Artistic Assistant	Kevin Emrick
Administrative Assistant	Kristi Taylor
Assistant to the Executive Producer	Emily Hammond
Director of Casting	Nancy Piccione
Casting Associate	Kelly Gillespie
Literary Manager/Sloan Project Manager	Annie MacRae
Play Development Assistant	Alex Barron
Director of Development	Jill Turner Lloyd
Director, Individual Giving	Jeremy Blocker
Director, Institutional Giving	Roger Kingsepp
Director, Special Events	Antonello Di Benedetto
Manager, Individual Giving	Emily Fleisher
Manager, Institutional Giving	Andrea Gorzell
Development Associate/Individual Giving	Allison Taylor
Development Associate/Institutional Giving	Laurel Bear
Development Associate/Special Events	Samantha Mascali
Development Associate/Database Coordinator	Kelly Haydon
Patrons' Liaison	Chad Jones
Director of Marketing	Debra Waxman-Pilla
Assistant Director of Marketing	Sunil Ayyagari
Marketing Associate	Caitlin Baird
Director of Finance	Jeffrey Bledsoe
Human Resources Manager	Darren Robertson
Finance Associate	Adam Cook
Business Assistant	Gillian Campbell
IT Manager	Mendy Sudranski
Systems Administrator	Carsten Losse
Receptionist/Studio Coordinator	Thatcher Stevens
Associate General Manager	Lindsey Brooks Sag
Company Manager/ NY City Center	Erin Moeller
General Management Assistant	Ann Mundorff
General Management Consultant	Deborah Hartnett
Director of Subscriber Services	Robert Allenberg
Associate Subscriber Services Manager	Andrew Taylor
Subscriber Services Representatives	Mark Bowers, Matthew Praet, Rosanna Consalva Sarto, Amber Wilkerson
Director of Telesales and Telefunding	George Tetlow
Assistant Manager	Terrence Burnett
Telemarketing Staff	Stephen Brown, Kel Haney, Kate Sessions
Director of Education	David Shookhoff
Asst. Director of Education/ Coordinator, Paul A. Kaplan Theatre Management Program	Amy Harris
Education Assistant, TheatreLink Coordinator	Julia Davis
Education Assistant	Kelli Bragdon
MTC Teaching Artists	Stephanie Alston, Carl Capatoro, Chris Ceraso, Charlotte Colavin, Dominic Colon, Allison Daugherty, Gilbert Girion, Andy Goldberg, Elise Hernandez, Jeffrey Joseph, Julie Leedes, Kate Long, Louis D. Moreno, Andres Munar, Melissa Murray, Angela Pietropinto, Alexa Polmer, Alfonso Ramirez, Carmen Rivera, Judy Tate, Candido Tirado, Joe White
Theatre Management Interns	Alex Bisker, Katie Chambers, Annah Feinberg, Barbara Harrison, Jennifer Hoguet, Robert Intile, Rebecca Kahane, Michelle Karst, Vinh Le, Andrew Lowy, Teff Nichols, Madeleine Parsigian, Luis Sapien, Bee Shaffer

Production Manager	Kurt Gardner
Associate Production Manager	Joshua Helman
Assistant Production Manager	Kelsey Martinez
Properties Supervisor	Scott Laule
Assistant Properties Supervisor	Julia Sandy
Props Carpenter	Peter Grimes
Costume Supervisor	Erin Hennessy Dean

GENERAL PRESS REPRESENTATION
BONEAU/BRYAN-BROWN

Chris Boneau Aaron Meier
Christine Olver

Script Readers	Jeff Augustin, Aaron Grunfeld, Liz Jones, Portia Krieger

SERVICES

Accountants	ERE, LLP
Advertising	SpotCo/Drew Hodges, Tom Greenwald, Jim Edwards, Beth Watson, Tim Falotico
Web Design	Calico Systems
Legal Counsel	Charles H. Googe, Jr.; Carol M. Kaplan/ Paul, Weiss, Rifkind, Wharton and Garrison LLP
Real Estate Counsel	Marcus Attorneys
Labor Counsel	Harry H. Weintraub/ Glick and Weintraub, P.C.
Immigration Counsel	Theodore Ruthizer/ Kramer, Levin, Naftalis & Frankel, LLP
Sponsorship Consultant	Above the Title Entertainment/ Jed Bernstein
Insurance	Dewitt Stern Group, Inc./ Anthony Pittari
Maintenance	Reliable Cleaning
Production Photographer	Joan Marcus
Event Photography	Bruce Glikas
Cover Art	Lara Tomlin
Cover Design	SpotCo
Theatre Displays	King Display

PRODUCTION STAFF FOR THE ROYAL FAMILY

Company Manager	Seth Shepsle
Production Stage Manager	Rick Steiger
Stage Manager	Elizabeth Moloney
Assistant Director	David Hilder
Make-up Designer	Angelina Avallone
Rosemary Harris' Wig	Paul Huntley
Assistant Scenic Designer	Yoshinori Tanokura
Assistant Costume Designers	Brian Hemesath, Nikki Moody, David Newell
Associate Lighting Designer	Aaron Spivey
Assistant Lighting Designer	Alex Fogel
Assistant Sound Designer	Matt Hubbs
Hair/Make-up Supervisor	Natasha Steinhagen
Assistant Hair Supervisor	Ruth Carsch
Assistant Props	Cathy Prager
Dressers	Eunice Dugan, Virginia Neininger
Lightboard Programmer	Jane Masterson
Animal Handler	Brian Hoffman
Production Assistant	Christopher Munnell

CREDITS

All scenery constructed by Global Scenic Services, Inc., Bridgeport, CT. Lighting equipment provided by PRG Lighting. Sound equipment provided by Masque Sound. Men's and women's costumes provided by Angel's, the Costumiers. Men's tailoring by Brian Hemesath. Women's costumes provided by EuroCo Costumes and John Cowles. Millinery by Arnold Levine. Makeup provided by M•A•C.

For more information visit
www.ManhattanTheatreClub.org

SPECIAL THANKS
Ostar Productions, Philip Morgaman

MANHATTAN THEATRE CLUB
SAMUEL J. FRIEDMAN THEATRE STAFF

Theatre Manager	Jim Joseph
Assistant House Manager	Richard Ponce
Box Office Treasurer	David Dillon
Assistant Box Office Treasurers	Jeffrey Davis, John Skelly
Head Carpenter	Chris Wiggins
Head Propertyman	Timothy Walters
Sound Engineer	Louis Shapiro
Master Electrician	Jeff Dodson
Wardrobe Supervisor	Angela Simpson
Apprentices	Jason Dodds, Ian Harbor
Chief Engineer	Deosarran
Maintenance Engineer	Ricky Deosarran
Security	Allied Barton
Lobby Refreshments	Sweet Concessions

The Royal Family
Scrapbook

Correspondent: John Wernke, "Hallboy," with answers submitted by the cast.

Who Has Done the Most Shows: Rosemary Harris…countless. She was part of a touring company in England that would do a different show each week with only four weeks off over the Christmas holiday. So 48 different shows in one year, and she had to provide her own costumes. There would be ads in the paper looking for a juvenile or ingénue with "extensive wardrobe" as a requirement for getting the part!

Special Backstage Ritual: John Glover does a glorious dance to the opening anthem every day. He parades with hat in hand and cane a-twirl and makes us all giggle.

Favorite Moments During Each Performance (On Stage or Off): There are three really: David Greenspan (Jo) plays a butler of sorts and has this brief exchange with Reg Rogers (Tony) and does this hand clap to take him off stage while they are plotting Tony's escape from the paparazzi–it is small but always gets a nice laugh and well I love it. Second is Jan Maxwell's (Julie's) speech at the end of Act II which is just unbelievable. A genuine show-stopper.

The third would have to be Reg's speech about how he has to escape or Zeta Zaydack will clap some papers on him. He does a full bodied bit explaining how he must "GET! OUT! of HERE!" It is brilliant and hilarious.

Favorite In-Theatre Gathering Place: Ian and Jay's (our two stalwart prop apprentices) "Lounge" upstage right. Dressing Room #5 after the show. Usual suspects Rufus Collins, Tony Newfield, Larry Pine, Freddy Arsenault, Cat Walleck, Kelli Barrett, Caroline Clay and Henny Russell.

Favorite Off-Site Hangout: The Glass House Tavern…it's conveniently right across the street.

Favorite Snack Foods: Our PSM Rick Steiger always has an endless supply of various morsels of candy in an aesthetically pleasing tall Tupperware container under his seat in the call booth.

Who Wore the Heaviest/Hottest Costume: A tie between Reg's Raccoon Coat and Tony Roberts' Overcoat.

Memorable Ad-Lib: Tony Roberts has a line "Don't go back on me like these other loafers!" in the third act addressing Rosemary. During rehearsal one day, he said, "Don't go DOWN on me like these other loafers!" Rosemary hid her head behind the piano convulsing with laughter. HA!

Memorable Stage Door Fan Encounter: The most memorable moment had to be the patrons that thought the two Scottish Deerhounds we have in the show (Phoebe and Izzy) were Disney Animatronics! Folks have also thought they were all sorts of different animals. One woman even said she believed they were small baby camels!

1. Cast members at rehearsal (L-R): Tony Roberts, John Glover, Kelli Barrett, Ana Gasteyer, Jan Maxwell, Rosemary Harris, Reg Rogers and Larry Pine.
2. Harris and Maxwell take a curtain call on opening night.

Mascot: The Monkey. (Sorry – gotta vote for the monkey on this one!)

Favorite Therapy: Ricola, Ricola, Ricola (especially for John, Ana, Rosemary and Jan).

Catchphrases Only the Company Would Recognize: "Say P***y!" Ask Rosemary Harris about that one… the asterisks stand for two ss and you find the vowel.
"Mister Ishi!"

Sweethearts Within the Company: Phoebe and Izzy–our doggie divas.

Memorable Directorial Notes: "We assign blame but give credit." "You're the director."

Company In-Jokes: Sergei!!! The mad bicycle terrorist Jan Maxwell!
"I changed it to splendid.... IF I say it."

Company Legends: It feels like this whole cast is made up of legends. Rosemary Harris, Tony Roberts, John Glover, Ana Gasteyer, Jan Maxwell, Larry Pine, David Greenspan… and soon to be, if he isn't already, Reg Rogers!

Tales From the Put-in: As many know, we had a scary experience with Tony Roberts falling ill on the Sunday afternoon just before we opened. (He made the opening, which is a testament to his constitution and fortitude.) We had a put-in rehearsal just before our final Sunday evening preview. The entire company–actors, dressers, stage hands, stage managers, house managers–were assembled on stage in utter silence. Doug Hughes, after finding the nod of approval from PSM Rick Steiger that all were present, delivered an eloquent address to us all. It was short but surely left us all with our hearts suspended and yearning to triumph over the frightening incident. When he finished, Rosemary Harris just quoted the show aptly: "When one drops out there will always be another." That long Sunday at the beginning of October put me in mind that the family created in this wonderful profession is an exquisite ephemeral trust not to be found in any other calling.

Understudy Anecdote: Well, almost all of us went on. There are a million stories. Three of us went on before we even opened. Each and every time there was a grand round of applause from the cast when the final curtain descended. My personal story is just to have been happy and relieved that I got through the sword fight. The first performance Reg and I fought we received a nice round of applause at its finale and, well, I was smiling inside.

Nicknames: "Sergei!!" (a.k.a. The mad bicycle terrorist Jan Maxwell.)
"Jacked-Up Hair."
"Baby Fat."

Coolest Thing About Being in This Show: It simply is a wonderful company to be around. I am filled with glee entering the Friedman each and every night. There is nothing like it.

Fan Club President: I have a Craigslist ad looking for someone but no takers as of yet.

Shrek The Musical

First Preview: November 8, 2008. Opened: December 14, 2008.
Closed January 3, 2010 after 37 Previews and 441 Performances.

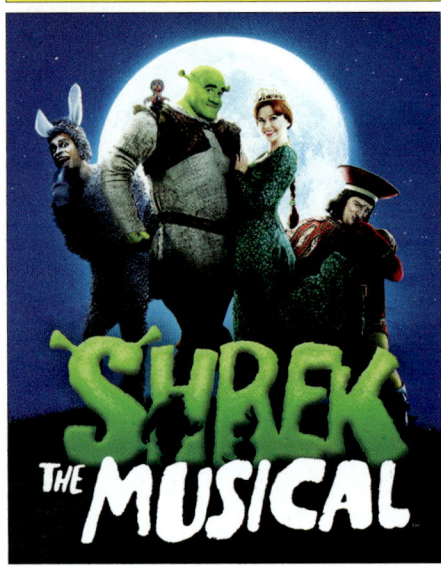

CAST
(in alphabetical order)

Ensemble	CAMERON ADAMS
Teen Fiona	TESSA ALBERTSON
Young Fiona (Wed., Thurs., Sat.); Young Shrek, Dwarf (Tues., Fri., Sun.)	RŌZI BAKER
Donkey	DANIEL BREAKER
Sugar Plum Fairy, Gingy, Dragonette	HAVEN BURTON
Sticks, Bishop	BOBBY DAYE
Bricks, Skeleton	RYAN DUNCAN
Ugly Duckling, Blind Mouse	SARAH JANE EVERMAN
Princess Fiona	SUTTON FOSTER
Young Fiona (Tues., Fri., Sun.); Young Shrek, Dwarf (Wed., Thurs., Sat.)	MAYA GOLDMAN
Fairy Godmother, Bluebird	COLLEEN HAWKS
Baby Bear, Blind Mouse	LISA HO
Big Bad Wolf, Captain of the Guard	CHRIS HOCH
Shrek	BRIAN D'ARCY JAMES
Guard	MARTY LAWSON
Papa Ogre, Straw	JACOB MING-TRENT
Peter Pan, Skeleton	DENNY PASCHALL
Gnome, Skeleton, Pied Piper	KEVEN QUILLON
White Rabbit, Skeleton	NOAH RIVERA
Pinocchio, The Magic Mirror, Dragon Puppeteer	ROBB SAPP
Lord Farquaad	CHRISTOPHER SIEBER
Wicked Witch	JENNIFER SIMARD
Mama Ogre, Humpty Dumpty, Dragonette	RACHEL STERN
Papa Bear, Thelonius, Skeleton	DENNIS STOWE

Continued on next page

BROADWAY THEATRE
1681 Broadway
A Shubert Organization Theatre
Philip J. Smith, *Chairman*   Robert E. Wankel, *President*

DREAMWORKS THEATRICALS
NEAL STREET PRODUCTIONS
present

SHREK THE MUSICAL

Based on the DreamWorks Animation Motion Picture and the Book by William Steig

Book and Lyrics by
DAVID LINDSAY-ABAIRE

Music by
JEANINE TESORI

Starring
BRIAN D'ARCY JAMES   SUTTON FOSTER   CHRISTOPHER SIEBER   DANIEL BREAKER

CAMERON ADAMS   TESSA ALBERTSON   RŌZI BAKER   HAVEN BURTON   BOBBY DAYE   RYAN DUNCAN   SARAH JANE EVERMAN
MAYA GOLDMAN   JUSTIN GREER   COLLEEN HAWKS   LISA HO   CHRIS HOCH   MARTY LAWSON   JACOB MING-TRENT
CAROLYN OCKERT-HAYTHE   DENNY PASCHALL   KEVEN QUILLON   NOAH RIVERA   HEATHER JANE ROLFF   JENNIFER SIMARD
RACHEL STERN   DENNIS STOWE   DAVID F.M. VAUGHN   MAIA NKENGE WILSON   RYAN WORSING   KIRSTEN WYATT

and
ROBB SAPP

Scenic & Costume Design
TIM HATLEY

Lighting Design
HUGH VANSTONE

Sound Design
PETER HYLENSKI

Hair/Wig Design
DAVID BRIAN-BROWN

Make-up Design
NAOMI DONNE

Puppet Design
TIM HATLEY

Casting
TARA RUBIN CASTING, CSA

Illusions Consultant
MARSHALL MAGOON

Associate Director
EVAN ENSIGN

Associate Choreographer
SLOAN JUST

Dance Arrangements
MATTHEW SKLAR

Associate Orchestrator
JOHN CLANCY

Music Supervisor & Incidental Music Arrangements
TIM WEIL

Music Coordinator
MICHAEL KELLER

Vocal Arrangements
JEANINE TESORI & TIM WEIL

Music Director
ERIC STERN

Production Stage Manager
BEVERLY JENKINS

Production Management
AURORA PRODUCTIONS

Press Representative
BONEAU/BRYAN-BROWN

Marketing Director
CLINT BOND JR.

General Management
STUART THOMPSON PRODUCTIONS/
JAMES TRINER

Orchestrations
DANNY TROOB

Choreographed by
JOSH PRINCE

Directed by
JASON MOORE

10/1/09

(L-R): Brian d'Arcy James and Daniel Breaker

Photo by Joan Marcus

Shrek The Musical

MUSICAL NUMBERS

ACT I
"Big Bright Beautiful World"
"Story of My Life"
"The Goodbye Song"
"Don't Let Me Go"
"I Know It's Today"
"What's Up, Duloc?"
"Travel Song"
"Donkey Pot Pie"
"This Is How a Dream Comes True"
"Who I'd Be"

ACT II
"Morning Person"
"I Think I Got You Beat"
"The Ballad of Farquaad"
"Make a Move"
"When Words Fail"
"Morning Person" (Reprise)
"Build a Wall"
"Freak Flag"
"Big Bright Beautiful World" (Reprise)
"This Is Our Story"

Cast Continued

Mama Bear,
　Dragonette ....MAIA NKENGE WILSON
Shoemaker's Elf, Blind Mouse ...KIRSTEN WYATT

UNDERSTUDIES
Standby for Shrek: BEN CRAWFORD
For Shrek: JACOB MING-TRENT
For Princess Fiona: HAVEN BURTON,
　SARAH JANE EVERMAN
For Donkey: BOBBY DAYE, RYAN DUNCAN
For Lord Farquaad: CHRIS HOCH,
　DAVID F.M. VAUGHN
For Pinocchio: DENNY PASCHALL,
　NOAH RIVERA
For Teen Fiona: HAVEN BURTON,
　KIRSTEN WYATT

SWINGS
JUSTIN GREER,
CAROLYN OCKERT-HAYTHE,
HEATHER JANE ROLFF,
DAVID F.M. VAUGHN,
RYAN WORSING

DANCE CAPTAIN
JUSTIN GREER

ASSISTANT DANCE CAPTAIN
CAROLYN OCKERT-HAYTHE

ORCHESTRA
Conductor: ERIC STERN
Associate Conductor: JASON DeBORD

Concertmaster: ANTOINE SILVERMAN
Violins: JONATHAN DINKLAGE,
　ENTCHO TODOROV, SEAN CARNEY
Cellos: JEANNE LeBLANC, ANJA WOOD
Acoustic Bass: BILL ELLISON
Flutes: ANDERS BOSTROM
Reeds: CHARLES PILLOW, JACK BASHKOW,
　RON JANNELLI
Trumpets: ANTHONY KADLECK,
　BUD BURRIDGE
Trombones: BRUCE EIDEM,
　MICHAEL CHRISTIANSON
French Horn: ADAM KRAUTHAMER
Keyboards: JOHN DELEY, JASON DEBORD
Guitars: KEN BRESCIA, BOB BAXMEYER
Electric Bass: LUICO HOPPER
Drums: WARREN ODZE
Percussion: SHANE SHANAHAN

Electronic Music Design: ANDREW BARRETT FOR LIONELLA MUSIC LLC
Music Copying: KAYE-HOUSTON MUSIC/ ANNE KAYE & DOUG HOUSTON

Brian d'Arcy James
Shrek

Sutton Foster
Princess Fiona

Christopher Sieber
Lord Farquaad

Daniel Breaker
Donkey

Robb Sapp
*Pinocchio,
The Magic Mirror,
Dragon Puppeteer*

Cameron Adams
Ensemble

Tessa Albertson
Teen Fiona

Rōzi Baker
*Young Fiona,
Young Shrek, Dwarf*

Haven Burton
*Sugar Plum Fairy,
Gingy, Dragonette*

Bobby Daye
Sticks, Bishop

Ryan Duncan
Bricks, Skeleton

Sarah Jane Everman
*Ugly Duckling,
Blind Mouse*

Maya Goldman
*Young Shrek,
Young Fiona, Dwarf*

Justin Greer
*Dance Captain/
Swing*

Shrek The Musical

 Colleen Hawks
Fairy Godmother, Bluebird

 Lisa Ho
Baby Bear, Blind Mouse

 Chris Hoch
Big Bad Wolf, Captain of the Guard

 Marty Lawson
Guard

 Jacob Ming-Trent
Papa Ogre, Straw

 Carolyn Ockert-Haythe
Swing, Assistant Dance Captain

 Denny Paschall
Peter Pan, Skeleton

 Keven Quillon
Gnome, Pied Piper, Skeleton

 Noah Rivera
White Rabbit, Skeleton

 Heather Jane Rolff
Swing

 Jennifer Simard
Wicked Witch

 Rachel Stern
Mama Ogre, Humpty Dumpty, Dragonette

 Dennis Stowe
Papa Bear, Thelonius, Skeleton

 David F.M. Vaughn
Swing

 Ryan Worsing
Swing

 Maia Nkenge Wilson
Mamma Bear, Dragonette

 Kirsten Wyatt
Shoemaker's Elf, Blind Mouse

 David Lindsay-Abaire
Book & Lyrics

 Jeanine Tesori
Music

 Jason Moore
Director

 Josh Prince
Choreographer

 Tim Hatley
Set, Costume & Puppet Design

 Hugh Vanstone
Lighting

 Peter Hylenski
Sound Designer

 Danny Troob
Orchestrator

 David Brian-Brown
Wig/Hair Design

 Naomi Donne
Makeup Design

 Tara Rubin Casting
Casting

 Matthew Sklar
Dance Music Arranger

 Michael Keller
Music Coordinator

 Andrew Barrett
Electronic Music Design

 Stuart Thompson Productions
General Management

 James Triner
General Manager

 Sam Mendes, Neal Street Productions
Producer

 Caro Newling, Neal Street Productions
Producer

Shrek The Musical

Bill Damaschke
Producer

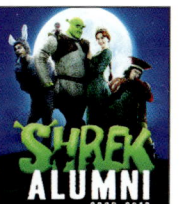

Jennifer Cody
Shoemaker's Elf, Blind Mouse

Aymee Garcia
Mama Bear, Dragonette

Leah Greenhaus
Young Fiona (select performances)

Danette Holden
Fairy Godmother, Bluebird

Marissa O'Donnell
Teen Fiona

Frankie Paparone
White Rabbit, Skeleton

Eric Petersen
Papa Ogre, Straw

Rachel Resheff
Young Fiona (select performances)

Greg Reuter
Gnome, Skeleton, Pied Piper

Adam Riegler
Young Shrek, Dwarf

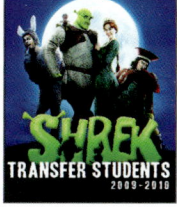
John Tartaglia
Pinocchio, The Magic Mirror, Dragon Puppeteer

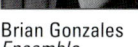

Brian Gonzales
Ensemble

Eric Petersen
Papa Ogre, Straw

Greg Reuter
Gnome, Skeleton, Pier Piper

John Tartaglia
Pinocchio, The Magic Mirror, Dragon Puppeteer

CREW
Front Row (L-R): Roy Franks, James Cariot, Jason McKenna, Tommy Cole, Alan Grudzinski, Mike Martinez

Back Row (L-R): Bob Beimers, Bryan Davis, Charlie Grieco, Andy Miller, Peter Becker, Paul Davila, Mike Cornell, Declan McNeil, Drew Lanzarotta

STAGE MANAGEMENT
(L-R): Chad Lewis (holding picture of Peter Lawrence), Stacey Zaloga, Rachel A. Wolff, Beverly Jenkins

Photos by Brian Mapp

Shrek The Musical

COMPANY MANAGEMENT
(L-R): Roeya Banuazizi, Scott Armstrong

DOORMAN
Fernando Sepulveda

FRONT OF HOUSE STAFF
Back Row (L-R): Freddie Matos, Sean McMonoco, Karen Banyai, Mae Park, William Denson, Michael Harris, Lori Bokun, Ismeal Tirado, Robert Evans

Front Row (L-R): Lana Pinkhas, Ulises Santiago, Mattie Robinson, Andi Hopkins, John Hall, Nathan Wright, Jorge Colon

WARDROBE/HAIR/MAKE-UP
Front Row (L-R): Michael Sancineto, Julien Havard, Megan Bowers, Meghan Carsella, Angela Johnson, Christina Grant, David Presto, Jack Scott, Hiro Hosomizu

Back Row (L-R): Liz Mathews, Pam Hughes, James Roy, Joan Weiss, Dan Foss, Emily Ockenfels, Adam Bailey, Victoria Tjoelker, Cleo Matheos, Alessandro Ferdico, Pam Kurz, Richard Orton, Anthony Hoffman, Joel Hawkins, Julienne Schubert-Blechman

STAFF FOR SHREK THE MUSICAL

GENERAL MANAGEMENT
Stuart Thompson James Triner
David Turner

PRESS REPRESENTATIVE
BONEAU/BRYAN-BROWN
Adrian Bryan-Brown Heath Schwartz
Matt Polk Kelly Guiod

CASTING
TARA RUBIN CASTING
Tara Rubin, CSA Laura Schutzel, CSA
Eric Woodall, CSA Merri Sugarman, CSA
Paige Blansfield Dale Brown Kaitlin Shaw

PRODUCTION MANAGEMENT
AURORA PRODUCTIONS INC.
Gene O'Donovan W. Benjamin Heller II
Rachel Sherbill Melissa Mazdra Amy Merlino Coey
Amanda Raymond Graham Forden Liza Luxenberg

PRODUCTION STAGE MANAGER	BEVERLY JENKINS
Stage Manager	Rachel A. Wolff
Assistant Stage Managers	Chad Lewis, Stacey Zaloga
Company Manager	Scott Armstrong
Associate Company Manager	Doug Gaeta
Assistant Company Manager	Megan Curren
Assistant Director	Stephen Sposito
Associate Director	Evan Ensign
Associate Choreographer	Sloan Just
Dance Captain	Justin Greer
Assistant Dance Captain	Carolyn Ockert-Haythe
Puppet Captain	Ryan Worsing
Assistant to Stage Managers	Bryan Rountree
Associate Scenic Designer	Paul Weimer
UK Scenic Associate	Andrew Edwards
UK Scenic Assistant	Tim Blazdell
UK Model Makers	Ben Davies, Paul Tulley
Assistant Scenic Designers	Derek Stenborg, Zhanna Gervich
US Associate Costume Designers	Tracy Christensen, Brian J. Bustos
Associate Costume Designer	Jack Galloway
Assistant Costume Designers	Jessica Wegener, Sarah Laux
Costume Department Assistants	Leon Dobkowski, Katie Irish, Roxana Ramseur
Associate Lighting Designer	Philip Rosenberg
Assistant Lighting Designer	Anthony Pearson
Moving Light Programmer	Sharon Huizinga
Associate Sound Designer	Keith Caggiano
Associate Hair/Wig Designer	Susan Corrado
Associate Makeup Designer	Angela L. Johnson
Associate Prosthetics Designer	Dave Presto
Assistant to the Makeup Designer	Nicky Pattison
Media Associate and Programmer	Laura Frank
Media Assistant	Joshua Fleitell
Production Carpenter	Mike Martinez
Deck Carpenter	Rick Styles
Fly Automation Carpenter	Alan Grudzinski
Deck Automation Carpenter	Bryan S. Davis
Production Electricians	James J. Fedigan, Randall Zaibek

Shrek The Musical

Head Electrician	Mike Cornell
Deck Electrician	Paul D.J. Davila
Follow Spot Operator	Andrew Dean
Pyro/Special Effects Electrician	Roy Franks
Production Sound	Phil Lojo
Head Sound Engineer	Jason Strangfeld
Assistant Sound Engineer	Jason McKenna
Production Props	Jerry Marshall
Assistant Props	Andrew Miller
Wardrobe Supervisor	Michael Sancineto
Assistant Wardrobe Supervisors	Meghan Carsella, Sara Foster
Dressers	Megan Bowers, Alessandro Ferdico, Dan Foss, Tony Hoffman, Hiro Hosomizu, Pamela Hughes, Kurt Kielmann, Pamela Kurz, Emily Ockenfels, Julienne Schubert-Blechman, Joan Weiss
Brian d'Arcy James' Dresser	Jack Scott
Sutton Foster's Dresser	Julien Havard
Production Hair Supervisor	Carole Morales
Assistant Hair Supervisor	Richard Orton
Hairdressers	Joel Hawkins, Liz Mathews
Hair Day Worker	Chelsea Roth
Production Makeup Supervisor	Angela L. Johnson
Assistant Makeup Supervisor	Christina Grant
Shrek Makeup Artist	Dave Presto
Dialect Coach	Stephen Gabis
Electronic Music Design Associate	Jeff Marder
Rehearsal Pianists	Jodie Moore, Matt Perri, John Deley
Rehearsal Percussion	Warren Odze
Production Assistant	Jacqueline Prats
Music Department Assistant	Michael Gacetta
General Management Assistants	Geo Karapetyan, Brittany Levasseur, Christopher Taggart
Management Intern	Bridget Reddington
Child Wrangler	Bridget Walders
Scenic Design Intern	Melissa Shakun
Costume Interns	Thomas Legalley, Robert Croghan
Banking	JPMorgan/Chase
Payroll	Castellana Services, Inc.
Production Accountant	Caitlin McCambridge
Insurance	Marsh Risk and Insurance Services
Legal Counsel	Paul, Weiss, Rifkind, Wharton & Garrison
Merchandising	Max Merchandising
Advertising	SPOTCO/ Drew Hodges, Jim Edwards, Tom Greenwald, Tom McCann, Josh Fraenkel
Production Photographer	Joan Marcus
NY Company Physical Therapists	PhysioArts
NY Company Orthopaedist	David S. Weiss, M.D.
Children's Tutoring	On Location Education
Broadway Group Sales	Shubert Group Sales

Prosthetic Makeup Design
Michael Marino
Prosthetic Renaissance
Hayes Vilandry   Roland Blancafor
Chris Kelly   Paul Komoda

CREDITS
Scenery fabrication by PRG-Scenic Technologies, a division of Production Resource Group, LLC, New Windsor, NY. Additional scenery and fly automation by Hudson Scenic Studios. Additional scenery by Scenic Art Studios, Inc., Souvenir Scenic Studios Ltd., Arquepoise Limited, Seattle Repertory Theatre. Deck effect show control and scenic motion control featuring Stage Command Systems® by PRG Scenic Technologies, a division of Production Resource Group, LLC, New Windsor, NY. Lighting equipment from PRG Lighting. Audio equipment from PRG Audio. Video projection system provided by Scharff Weisberg Inc. Pyrotechnical effects by Kelly Sticksel/Excitement Technologies Group. Props fabricated by Arnold S. Levine, Inc.; Zoe Morsette; Moonboots Productions, Inc.; Randy Carfagno Productions; Jerard Studio, Inc.; ICBA, Inc.; Paragon Innovation Group; Cigar Box Studios, Inc.; Peter Sarafin; Craig Grigg; Proof Productions; Seattle Repertory Theatre; Sean McArdle; Lewis Shaw; Spoon Group. Costumes executed by Tricorne, Inc.; Parsons-Meares, Ltd.; Eric Winterling, Inc.; Barbara Matera, Ltd.; Seams Unlimited; Crystal Thompson. Costume crafts by Marian Jean Hose, Leigh Cranston, Erik Andor. Costume mechanics by Jon Gellman Effects, Perfection Electricks, Michael Curry Design, Inc. Knitwear by Maria Ficalora Knitwear, Ltd. Custom fabric printing by Gene Mignola. Armor by Costume Armor. Custom millinery provided by Lynne Mackey Studio; Arnold S. Levine, Inc.; Rodney Gordon. Custom footwear by Capri Shoes by Oscar Navarro. Handmade shoes by Fred Longtin, LaDuca, Capezio, JC Theatrical. Custom and fabric painting by Jose Asiatico, Jeff Fender, Virginia Clow, Claudia Dzundza, Mary Macy, Parmalee Welles Tolkan, Margaret Peot. Costume flameproofing by Turning Star, Inc. Hosiery and undergarments by Bra*Tenders. Airbrushes supplied by Iwata. Mehron makeup. Wigs by Ray Marston Wig Studio, Victoria Wood Wigs, Bob Kelly Wigs. Drums from Yamaha Corporation of America. Performing Arts Short Term Housing. Road Rebel. Natural herb cough drops courtesy of Ricola USA, Inc.

Dragon and Travel Song puppets by Rick Lazzarini/The Character Shop.

Rehearsed at the New 42nd Street Studios.

Makeup Provided by
MAKE UP FOR EVER

Magic Mirror Technology by
AUTODESK
Brett Ineson   Kamal Mistry
Kevin Smith   Jason Walter

CHASE is the official credit card of Shrek the Musical.

Sheraton Hotels & Resorts is the official hotel of *Shrek the Musical.*

"Escape (The Pina Colada Song)" (Rupert Holmes), ©1979 WB Music Corp. (ASCAP) and Holmes Line of Music Inc. (ASCAP). All rights administered by WB Music Corp. All rights reserved. Used by permission.

SPECIAL THANKS
Andrew Adamson, Guillaume Aretos, Denise Cascino, Ann Daly, Philippe Denis, Anne Globe, Vicky Jenson, Jim Mainard, Chris Miller, Terry Press, Chip Sullivan, Aron Warner, Sunny Ye.

A very special thanks to the amazing and talented artists at DreamWorks and PDI DreamWorks who contributed to the show: Sean Bishop, Doug Cooper, Martin Costello, David Doepp, John Dorst, Corban Gossett, Daniel Hashimoto, Anthony Hodgson, Pam Hu, Lucas Janin, Andrew Kim, Gina Lawes, Betsy Nofsinger, Alex Ongaro, Jason Reisig, Jason Schleifer, Scott Singer, Bill Stahl, Munira Tayabji, Mike Yamada

DREAMWORKS THEATRICALS
President	Bill Damaschke
President's Office	Carole Sue Lipman, Richard Hamilton
Marketing (NY)	Clint Bond, Jr., David Carpenter, Steven Rummer, Ritchie Bermudez
Promotions	Susan Spencer, Linda Kehn, Chris Fahland
Consumer Products	Kerry Phelan, Joel Ward
Operations/Finance	Bruce Daitch
Business Affairs/Operations	Jamie Kershaw
Finance	Gary Raksis, Laura Fratianne, Kathleen Frederickson
Insurance	Ross Pebley
Administrative	Cynthia Park, Belinda Arge, Diane Stromer, Susan Souther, Richard Hamner, Andy Areffi

NEAL STREET PRODUCTIONS LTD.
Directors	Sam Mendes, Caro Newling, Pippa Harris
Associate Producer Theatre	Beth Byrne
Executive Coordinator	Milly Leigh
General Assistant	Caroline Reynolds

 ### THE SHUBERT ORGANIZATION, INC.
Board of Directors

Philip J. Smith Chairman	**Robert E. Wankel** President
Wyche Fowler, Jr.	**John W. Kluge**
Lee J. Seidler	**Michael I. Sovern**

Stuart Subotnick

Elliot Greene Chief Financial Officer	**David Andrews** Senior Vice President – Shubert Ticketing
Juan Calvo Vice President and Controller	**John Darby** Vice President – Facilities
Peter Entin Vice President – Theatre Operations	**Charles Flateman** Vice President – Marketing
Anthony LaMattina Vice President – Audit & Production Finance	**Brian Mahoney** Vice President – Ticket Sales

D.S. Moynihan
Vice President – Creative Projects

Theatre Manager .... Michael S. R. Harris

Shrek The Musical
Scrapbook

Correspondents: Lisa Ho, "Baby Bear," "Blind Mouse" and Ryan Duncan, "Bricks," "Skeleton"

Memorable Fan Encounter: The boy who wore a mask because of his illness and was ashamed of it. After the show, which he loved, we gave him a signed poster and a freak flag which he proudly waved. His parents sent a follow-up letter saying how the show really helped him and how he has a much easier time being in public wearing his mask.

Anniversary Parties and/or Gifts: For Christmas we got a nice navy blue bag that listed the name of EVERY fairytale creature including all the swing fairy tale creatures: the Imp, Mad Hatter, Sprite, Ugly Stepsister, AND the Gizzard (Justin Greer's beloved gay Wizard) plus the tap dancing Rats. All had a place on this lovely bag.

Most Exciting Celebrity Visitors: Catherine Zeta-Jones was great and told her kids how hard it was to do eight shows a week. She remembered doing that in London and wanted to make sure her kids knew the difficulties of the job. She was so nice. Kate Hudson and A-Rod also came to the show with their kids. A lot of celebrities that come to Broadway shows get special treatment: free tickets, backstage privileges, photo ops, etc. The two of them didn't have any of that arranged and just came to the show like everyone else. One of our swings, Carolyn, spotted them in the audience and asked if they were planning to come backstage. They were not, so she offered to give them a tour. They accepted and were very appreciative of the opportunity. They were a class act!

Actors Who Performed the Most Roles in This Show: The swings of course. Our male swings David Vaughn and Justin Greer have gone on for all nine male ensemble members PLUS some female ensemble members as well. Each ensemble member already has multiple roles so you can imagine how many roles it adds up to when you are a swing.

Most Shows: Brian d'Arcy James did an amazing number of shows. He is a workhorse. Others that missed the fewest shows: Lisa Ho, Marty Lawson and Ryan Duncan.

Special Backstage Rituals: Marty Lawson sings "Build a Wall" in the wings after a guard scene. If swings are on for him, they also do this. At the end of the run, the pigs took to attacking Baby Bear. Johnny T. also loved to do offstage shows for people on stage.

Favorite Moment: Saturday Night Comedy at the Outhouse!! Bobby Daye arranged stand-up comedy sketches performed by various members of cast and crew. The best night was the "Yo Mama" battle between Ryan Duncan/Greg Reuter and Noah Rivera/David Vaughn. Yo Mama jokes like you've never heard them before.

In-Theatre Gathering Place: Girls' dressing room for Saturday Night Soirees and Sutton's room for Shot Night.

Off-Site Hangouts: Swizz, El Azteca, Maison, Divine Bar, Bamboo 52 for work parties.

Favorite Snack Foods: Ketchup chips and dill pickle chips from Canada. Also, Bobby Daye's homemade red velvet cake, banana pudding, and other delights.

1. The ladies ensemble at the audio recording of "I'm A Believer," which was added as an encore.
2. Ben Crawford as Shrek right before Macy's Thanksgiving Day Parade performance.
3. Chris Hoch getting out of the cab, post-Macy's performance/stuck on the bus debacle.
4. Stage management and our head of wardrobe on Halloween.

Favorite Therapies: COFFEE before the show. Alcohol after the show. PT also helps.

Memorable Ad-Lib: Chris Sieber in Duloc on closing night: instead of singing "Yes I'm growing," he sang "Yes we're closing." It got a good chuckle from the audience and a few of the ensemble may have flubbed their lyrics that came after.

Web Buzz: One girl did that one-woman webcam abridged version of the show in her room complete with costume pieces, wigs and fake Shrek eyebrows. Another teenage boy did an "I can't believe *Shrek* is closing" video. He hadn't even seen the show and the video was priceless!

Fastest Costume Changes: Sutton into Ogress, Wolf into captain of the guards, Baby Bear/Ugly

Shrek The Musical
Scrapbook

1. Yearbook correspondent Lisa Ho (L) and Sutton Foster at the Macy's Thanksgiving Day Parade.
2. Backstage, dresser Kurt Kielman helps one of the skeletons with his costume.
3. Keven Quillon and Marty Lawson at the Macy's Thanksgiving Day Parade.
4. (L-R): Ben Crawford, Aymee Garcia and Sarah Jane Everman at one of our Saturday Night Soirees.

Photos courtesy Lisa Ho

Memorable Directorial Note: During character work improv: "OK. You guys (fairytale creatures) are all in line at Starbucks. Go!" That happened over a year ago when we were putting up the show, but I thought it was worth mentioning because you can imagine the hilarity that ensued.
Company In-Jokes: Assassin Night. Cosmic Diner orders. "Turn in your underwear," Chris Hoch's tie-dyed underwear—he swears it was accidental because he cleans his kitchen with his underwear and a little bleach. Frankie Paparone fake sexual harassment write-up. Eric Petersen "you're on, start putting on your makeup" practical joke, chunky ass!
Tales From the Put-in: Eric Petersen became the standby for Shrek in November. We did not have a Fiona during his put-in, so our trusty old Dance Captain, Justin Greer, stepped up to the plate. The big moment came for the Shrek and Fiona kiss, and like any good actor should, Eric laid a nice fat kiss on Justin. The rest of us were screaming for joy. Nobody likes going to rehearsal, but THAT made it totally worth it!
Nickname: "Action Petersen" for Eric Petersen and his gutsy poker bets.
Embarrassing Moments: During the Magic Mirror scene a very large cockroach-type bug was crawling up Dennis Stowe's face mask when he was playing Thelonius. None of the guards could keep it together on stage. The bug eventually fell to the floor and Denny Paschall tried to stomp it out with his dance moves. Fun times at *Shrek The Musical*!
Coolest Thing About Being in This Show: We have a wonderful cast and you never know what to expect on stage. There are new choices every day and it keeps it fresh for everyone. We've also had some wonderful opportunities this year like performing at the Tonys and the Macy's Thanksgiving Day Parade. We also get to wear Tony Award winning costumes!
Also: After the Thanksgiving Parade we all boarded the bus to go back to the theatre. None of us have anything with us other than the costumes on our back. Between the roads being blocked and the Spider-Man balloon being deflated we got stuck on Broadway and 40th St. The cops would not let the bus move in any direction. Forward, back, right, left was not an option, so we all sat on the bus in costume and waited. It was very fish bowl-esque. Passersby started to walk up and stare into the window of the bus. Some took pictures. We waited for about 30 minutes while management was frantically trying to get Macy's on the phone to figure out how to get out of the situation. None of us had money or Metrocards so cabs and subways weren't much of an option either. Some lucky folk with easy costumes were able to walk back to the theatre while the rest of us waited. Eventually the company managers gave us cash to take cabs. All of us in costume walked to Port Authority through the crowds to catch cabs back to the theatre. Three Blind Mice and the Big Bad Wolf get into a cab....it was all like a bad joke. Anyways, we made it back to the theatre!! And everyone was able to get back home in time for Thanksgiving dinner. A happy ending.

Duckling/Elf into Blind Mouse for "I'm A Believer" finale."
Heaviest/Hottest Costume: Daniel Breaker as Donkey. Brian d'Arcy James/Ben as Shrek. Pigs, Bears, Duloc, EVERYONE at one point wears a heavy, hot, and/or uncomfortable costume.
Catchphrases Only the Company Would Recognize: "Smizing." "Sex clump." "Get low and party." "Telesis." "Bond off." "Jelly from your eyes." "My rib is out." "Under armor."
Best In-House Parody Lyric: "Yo mama's a beaver."
Sweethearts Within the Company: Peter Pan and Sugar Plum Fairy.

Sondheim on Sondheim

First Preview: March 19, 2010. Opened: April 22, 2010.
Still running as of May 31, 2010.

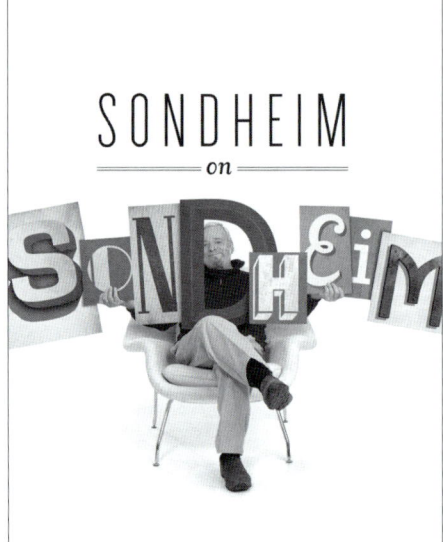

STUDIO 54

ROUNDABOUT THEATRE COMPANY
Todd Haimes, Artistic Director
Harold Wolpert, Managing Director
Julia C. Levy, Executive Director

Presents

Barbara Cook Vanessa Williams Tom Wopat

in

SONDHEIM on SONDHEIM

Music and Lyrics by
Stephen Sondheim

with

Leslie Kritzer Norm Lewis Euan Morton
Erin Mackey Matthew Scott

Set Design	Costume Design	Lighting Design	Sound Design
Beowulf Boritt	Susan Hilferty	Ken Billington	Dan Moses Schreier

Video & Projection Design	Orchestrations	Music Coordinator
Peter Flaherty	Michael Starobin	John Miller

Production Stage Manager	Casting	Technical Supervisor	Executive Producer
Peter Hanson	Jim Carnahan c.s.a. & Stephen Kopel	Steve Beers	Sydney Beers

Press Representative	Director of Marketing & Sales Promotion	Founding Director	Associate Artistic Director
Boneau/Bryan-Brown	David B. Steffen	Gene Feist	Scott Ellis

Music Direction/Arrangements
David Loud

Musical Staging
Dan Knechtges

Conceived and Directed by
James Lapine

Major support provided by The Shen Family Foundation, Perry and Marty Granoff, Tom and Diane Tuft, Areté Foundation, FirstService Williams, and The Horace W. Goldsmith Foundation.

Inspired by a concept by David Kernan
Roundabout Theatre Company is a member of the League of Resident Theatres.
www.roundabouttheatre.org

4/22/10

CAST
(in alphabetical order)
BARBARA COOK
LESLIE KRITZER
NORM LEWIS
ERIN MACKEY
EUAN MORTON
MATTHEW SCOTT
VANESSA WILLIAMS
TOM WOPAT

UNDERSTUDIES
For Euan Morton, Matthew Scott: KYLE HARRIS

For Vanessa Williams, Leslie Kritzer, Erin Mackey:
N'KENGE

Production Stage Manager: PETER HANSON
Stage Manager: SHAWN PENNINGTON

ORCHESTRA
Conductor/Piano: ANDY EINHORN
Assistant Conductor/Keyboard: MARK HARTMAN
Violin/Concert Master: CHRISTIAN HEBEL
Cello: SARAH SEIVER
Woodwinds: RICK HECKMAN, ALDEN BANTA
French Horn: R.J. KELLEY
Bass: BILL ELLISON
Music Coordinator: JOHN MILLER
Synthesizer Programmer: RANDY COHEN
Music Copying: EMILY GRISHMAN
MUSIC PREPARATION –
EMILY GRISHMAN/KATHARINE EDMONDS

(L-R): Vanessa Williams, Tom Wopat, Matthew Scott, Erin Mackey, Barbara Cook, Euan Morton, Norm Lewis, Leslie Kritzer

Photo by Richard Termine

Sondheim on Sondheim

MUSICAL CHRONOLOGY

By George (1946) performed at the George School.
- "I'll Meet You at the Donut"

Saturday Night (1954), unproduced until 1997, book by Julius J. Epstein and Philip G. Epstein.
- "So Many People"

West Side Story (1957), music by Leonard Bernstein, book by Arthur Laurents.
- "Something's Coming"

Gypsy (1959), music by Jule Styne, book by Arthur Laurents.
- "Smile, Girls"

A Funny Thing Happened on the Way to the Forum (1962), book by Burt Shevelove and Larry Gelbart.
- "Invocation/Forget War"
- "Love Is in the Air"
- "Comedy Tonight"

Anyone Can Whistle (1964), book by Arthur Laurents.
- "Anyone Can Whistle"

Do I Hear a Waltz? (1965), music by Richard Rodgers, book by Arthur Laurents.
- "Do I Hear a Waltz?"

Evening Primrose (1966), originally broadcast November 16, 1966; written by John Collier & James Goldman for the television series "ABC Stage 67."
- "Take Me to the World"

Company (1970), book by George Furth.
- "You Could Drive a Person Crazy"
- "The Wedding Is Off"
- "Multitudes of Amys"
- "Happily Ever After"
- "Being Alive"
- "Company"

Follies (1971), book by James Goldman.
- "Ah, But Underneath" (London production, 1987)
- "Waiting for the Girls Upstairs"
- "Losing My Mind"
- "In Buddy's Eyes"

A Little Night Music (1973), book by Hugh Wheeler.
- "Send in the Clowns"
- "A Weekend in the Country"

Pacific Overtures (1976), book by John Weidman, additional material by Hugh Wheeler.
- Entr'acte

Sweeney Todd (1979), book by Hugh Wheeler.
- "Epiphany"

Merrily We Roll Along (1981), book by George Furth.
- "Now You Know"
- "Franklin Shepard, Inc."
- "Good Thing Going"
- "Opening Doors"
- "Not a Day Goes By"
- "Old Friends"

Sunday in the Park with George (1984), book by James Lapine.
- "Finishing the Hat"
- "Sunday"
- "Beautiful"

Into the Woods (1987), book by James Lapine.
- "Children Will Listen"
- "Ever After"

Assassins (1990), book by John Weidman.
- "Something Just Broke"
- "The Gun Song"

Passion (1994), book by James Lapine.
- "Fosca's Entrance (I Read)"
- "Is This What You Call Love?"
- "Loving You"
- "Happiness"

Road Show (2008), book by John Weidman, formerly titled **Bounce** (2003).
- "The Best Thing That Ever Has Happened"

Barbara Cook — Vanessa Williams

Tom Wopat — Leslie Kritzer

Norm Lewis — Euan Morton

Erin Mackey — Matthew Scott

Kyle Harris
u/s Euan Morton,
Matthew Scott

N'Kenge
u/s Vanessa Williams,
Leslie Kritzer,
Erin Mackey

Sondheim on Sondheim

Stephen Sondheim
Music & Lyrics

James Lapine
Conceived & Directed

Dan Knechtges
Musical Staging

Beowulf Boritt
Set Design

Susan Hilferty
Costume Design

Ken Billington
Lighting Design

Dan Moses Schreier
Sound Design

Peter Flaherty
Video & Projection Design

Michael Starobin
Orchestrations

John Miller
Musical Coordinator

Jim Carnahan
Casting

Gene Feist
Founding Director, Roundabout Theatre Company

Todd Haimes
Artistic Director, Roundabout Theatre Company

WARDROBE/HAIR
Seated (L-R): Tara Delahunt, Julie Tobia, Mary Ann Oberpriller
Standing (L-R): Suzanne Lunney-Delahunt, John James (Hair Supervisor), Nadine Hettel

MUSICIANS
(L-R): Bill Ellison, Rick Heckman, Andy Einhorn, Mark Hartman, Alden Banta

CREW
Seated (L-R): Mike Widmer, Jenn Fagant, Ann Cavanaugh, Paul Coltoff, Dorion Fuchs
Standing (L-R): T.J. McEvoy, Steve Jones, Dan Hoffman, John Wooding, Scott Anderson, Larry Jennino

HOUSE STAFF
Front Row (L-R): Linda Gjonbalaj, Zaydee Cruz, LaConya Robinson, Diana Trent
Middle Row (L-R): Stella Varrialle, Jose Cuello, Valerie Simmons
Back Row (L-R): Amy, Nicholas Wheatley

Sondheim on Sondheim

STAGE MANAGEMENT
(L-R): Peter Hanson, Emmy Frank, Shawn Pennington

BOX OFFICE
(L-R): Ben Schneider, Scott Falkowski, Joe Clark

Photos by Brian Mapp

ROUNDABOUT THEATRE COMPANY STAFF
ARTISTIC DIRECTOR .... TODD HAIMES
MANAGING DIRECTOR .... HAROLD WOLPERT
EXECUTIVE DIRECTOR .... JULIA C. LEVY
ASSOCIATE ARTISTIC DIRECTOR .. SCOTT ELLIS

ARTISTIC STAFF
DIRECTOR OF ARTISTIC DEVELOPMENT/
   DIRECTOR OF CASTING .... Jim Carnahan
Artistic Consultant .... Robyn Goodman
Resident Director .... Doug Hughes
Associate Artists ...... Scott Elliott, Bill Irwin, Joe Mantello,
   Mark Brokaw, Kathleen Marshall
Literary Manager .... Jill Rafson
Casting Director .... Carrie Gardner
Casting Associate .... Kate Boka
Casting Associate .... Stephen Kopel
Artistic Assistant .... Amy Ashton
Literary Associate .... Josh Fiedler
The Blanche and Irving Laurie Foundation
   Theatre Visions Fund Commissions .... Julia Cho,
   Stephen Karam, Lewis Black,
   Nathan Louis Jackson
Educational Foundation of
   America Commissions .... Bekah Brunstetter,
   Lydia Diamond, Diana Fithian,
   Julie Marie Myatt
New York State Council
   on the Arts Commission .... Nathan Louis Jackson
Roundabout Commissions .... Steven Levenson,
   Robert Lopez & Kristen Anderson-Lopez
Artistic/Literary Intern .... Liz Malta
Casting Interns .... Kyle Bosley, Jillian Cimini,
   Erin Drake, Andrew Femenella,
   Lauren Lewis, Quinn Meyers
Script Readers .... Jay Cohen, Hillary Dixler,
   Nicholas Stimler

EDUCATION STAFF
EDUCATION DIRECTOR .... Greg McCaslin
Associate Education Director .... Jennifer DiBella
Education Associate
   for Theatre-Based Programs .... Jay Gerlach
Education Program Associate .... Aliza Greenberg
Education Dramaturg .... Ted Sod
Teaching Artists .... Cynthia Babak, Victor Barbella,
   Grace Bell, LaTonya Borsay,
   Mark Bruckner, Joe Clancy, Vanessa Davis,
   Joe Doran, Elizabeth Dunn-Ruiz,
   Carrie Ellman-Larsen, Kevin Free,
   Tony Freeman, Deanna Frieman,
   Natalie Gold, Sheri Graubert,
   Matthew A.J. Gregory, Melissa Gregus,
   Adam Gwon, Devin Haqq,
   Carrie Heitman, Karla Hendrick,
   Jim Jack, Jason Jacobs, Lisa Renee Jordan,
   Jamie Kalama, Alvin Keith,
   Tami Mansfield, Erin McCready, Kyle McGinley,
   Andrew Ondrejcak, Meghan O'Neill,
   Laura Poe, Nicole Press, Jennifer Rathbone,
   Leah Reddy, Amanda Rehbein,
   Bernita Robinson, Christopher Rummel,
   Cassy Rush, Nick Simone, Heidi Stallings,
   Daniel Sullivan, Carl Tallent, Vickie Tanner,
   Jolie Tong, Cristina Vaccaro, Jennifer Varbalow,
   Leese Walker, Eric Wallach, Michael Warner,
   Christina Watanabe, Gail Winar,
   Conwell Worthington, III
Teaching Artist Emeritus .... Reneé Flemings
Teaching Artist Apprentices .... Carrie Ellman-Larsen,
   Deanna Frieman, Meghan O'Neill
Education Interns .... Kali DiPippo, Devin Shacket

ADMINISTRATIVE STAFF
GENERAL MANAGER .... Sydney Beers
Associate Managing Director .... Greg Backstrom
General Manager,
   American Airlines Theatre .... Rebecca Habel
General Manager, Steinberg Center .... Rachel E. Ayers
Human Resources Manager .... Stephen Deutsch
Operations Manager .... Valerie D. Simmons
Associate General Manager .... Maggie Cantrick
Office Manager .... Scott Kelly
Management Associate .... Jill K. Boyd
Archivist .... Tiffany Nixon
Receptionists ...... Dee Beider, Raquel Castillo, Elisa Papa,
   Allison Patrick, Monica Sidorchuk
Messenger .... Darnell Franklin

FINANCE STAFF
DIRECTOR OF FINANCE .... Susan Neiman
Assistant Controller .... John LaBarbera
Accounts Payable Administrator .... Frank Surdi
Financial Associate .... Yonit Kafka
Business Office Assistant .... Joshua Cohen
Business Interns .... Matthew Kagen, Rebekah Lashof,
   Laura Marshall

DEVELOPMENT STAFF
Director, Special Events .... Steve Schaeffer
Director, Major Gifts .... Joy Pak
Director, Patron Programs .... Amber Jo Manuel
Manager, Donor Information Systems .... Lise Speidel
Manager, Patron Programs .... Tyler Ennis
Manager, Telefundraising .... Gavin Brown
Manager, Corporate Relations .... Roxana Petzold
Associate Manager, Patron Programs .... Marisa Perry
Patron Services Associate .... David Pittman
Development Assistants .. Ryan Hallett, Nick Luckenbaugh
Assistant to the Executive Director .... Jason Butler
Special Events Assistant .... Amy Rosenfield
Major Gifts Intern .... Joseph Jankowski
Special Events Intern .... Gavi Young

INFORMATION TECHNOLOGY STAFF
IT DIRECTOR .... Antonio Palumbo
IT Associate .... Dylan Norden
IT Associate .... Jim Roma
DIRECTOR DATABASE
   OPERATIONS .... Wendy Hutton
Database Administrator/Programmer .... Revanth Anne

MARKETING STAFF
DIRECTOR OF MARKETING
   AND SALES PROMOTION .... David B. Steffen
Associate Director of Marketing .... Tom O'Connor
Marketing/Publications Manager ..... Margaret Casagrande
Assistant Director of Marketing .... Stefanie Schussel
Marketing Manager .... Shannon Marcotte
Website Consultant .... Keith Powell Beyland
Director of Telesales Special Promotions ...... Marco Frezza
Telesales Manager .... Anthony Merced
Telesales Office Coordinator .... Patrick Pastor
Marketing Interns .... Akeem Baisden-Folkes,
   Shoshana Greenberg

TICKET SERVICES STAFF
Director of Sales Operations .... Charlie Garbowski, Jr.
Ticket Services Manager .... Ellen Holt
Subscription Manager .... Ethan Ubell
Box Office Managers .... Edward P. Osborne,
   Jaime Perlman, Krystin MacRitchie,
   Nicole Nicholson
Group Sales Manager .... Jeff Monteith
Assistant Box Office Managers .... Robert Morgan,
   Andrew Clements, Scott Falkowski,
   Catherine Fitzpatrick
Assistant Ticket Services Managers .... Robert Kane,
   Bill Klemm, Lindsay Ericson
Customer Services Coordinator .... Thomas Walsh

Sondheim on Sondheim

Ticket Services ....Solangel Bido, Arianna Boykins, Lauren Cartelli, Joseph Clark, Barbara Dente, Nisha Dhruna, Adam Elsberry, James Graham, Kara Harrington, Tova Heller, Nicki Ishmael, Kate Longosky, Michelle Maccarone, Elisa Mala, Mead Margulies, Chuck Migliaccio, Carlos Morris, Kayrose Pagan, Hillary Parker, Thomas Protulipac, Jessica Pruett-Barnett, Kaia Rafoss, Josh Rozett, Ben Schneider, Kenneth Senn, Heather Siebert, Nalane Singh, Lillian Soto, Ron Tobia, Jacklyn Verbitski, Hannah Weitzman
Intern ....Emily Cole

SERVICES

Counsel ..Paul, Weiss, Rifkind, Wharton and Garrison LLP, Charles H. Googe Jr., Carol M. Kaplan
Counsel ....Rosenberg & Estis
Counsel ..Andrew Lance, Gibson, Dunn, & Crutcher, LLP
Counsel ..Harry H. Weintraub, Glick and Weintraub, P.C.
Counsel ....Stroock & Stroock & Lavan LLP
Counsel ...Daniel S. Dokos, Weil, Gotshal & Manges LLP
Immigration Counsel ....Mark D. Koestler and Theodore Ruthizer
Government Relations ....Law Offices of Claudia Wagner LLC
House Physicians ....Dr. Theodore Tyberg, Dr. Lawrence Katz
House Dentist ....Neil Kanner, D.M.D.
Insurance ....DeWitt Stern Group, Inc.
Accountant ....Lutz & Carr CPAs, LLP
Advertising ....Spotco/ Drew Hodges, Jim Edwards, Tom Greenwald, Kyle Hall, Cory Spinney
Interactive Marketing ....Situation Interactive/ Damian Bazadona, John Lanasa, Eric Bornemann, Randi Fields
Events Photography ....Anita and Steve Shevett
Production Photographer ....Joan Marcus
Theatre Displays ....King Displays, Wayne Sapper
Lobby Refreshments ....Sweet Concessions
Merchandising ....Spotco Merch/ James Decker
Theatre and Lobby Rentals available by calling ......David Solomon at Roundabout

MANAGING DIRECTOR EMERITUS ....Ellen Richard

Roundabout Theatre Company
231 West 39th Street, New York, NY 10018
(212) 719-9393.

GENERAL PRESS REPRESENTATIVES
BONEAU/BRYAN-BROWN
Adrian Bryan-Brown
Matt Polk   Jessica Johnson   Amy Kass

CREDITS FOR SONDHEIM ON SONDHEIM

Company Manager ....Denise Cooper
Company Manager Assistant ....David Solomon
Production Stage Manager ....Peter Hanson
Stage Manager ....Shawn Pennington
Assistant Director ....Sarna Lapine
Assistant Musical Stager ....DJ Gray
Assistant to Stephen Sondheim ....Steve Clar
Assistant Technical Supervisor ....Chad Woerner
Associate Set Designer ....Jo Winiarski
Assistant Set Designers ....Jason Lajka, Maiko Chii
Associate Costume Designer ....Tricia Barsamian
Assistant to the Costume Designer ....Becky Lasky
Costume Shopper ....Brooke Cohen
Associate Lighting Designer ....John Demous
Assistant Lighting Designer ....Jeremy Cunningham
Associate Sound Designer ....David Bullard
Production Sound Engineer ....Scott Anderson
Associate Video Designer/Programmer ....Austin Switser
Lead Video Animator ....Michael Bell-Smith
Video Associate ....Joshua Higgason
Assistant Video Designer ....Daniel Brodie
Wig Design by ....Tom Watson
Hair Design by ....John Barrett
Rehearsal Pianist ....Andy Einhorn
Musical Assistant ....David Ben Dabbon
Assistant to John Miller ....Nichole Jennino
Production Carpenter ....Dan Hoffman
Automation Carpenter ....Ann Cavanaugh
Flyman ....Steve Jones
Production Electrician ....John Wooding
Moving Light Programmer ....Timothy F. Rogers
Conventional Light Programmer ....Jessica Morton
Followspot Operators ....Paul Coltoff, Jenn Fagant
Deck Sound ....T.J. McEvoy
Production Properties Coordinator ....Buist Bickley
House Properties ....Lawrence Jennino
Wardrobe Supervisor ....Nadine Hettel
Dressers ....Mary Ann Oberpriller, Suzanne Lunney-Delahunt, Julie Tobia
Hair Supervisor ....John James
Local ONE IATSE Apprentice ....Michael Widmer
Production Assistant ....Emmy Frank
Clearances ....BZ/Rights & Permissions, Inc.

Clips from "The Mike Douglas Show" courtesy of CBS Television Distribution; clip from the *Bernard Levin Interviews* courtesy of BBC and the Levin Estate; clip from "The David Frost Show" courtesy of CBS Television Distribution and David Frost; clips from "The South Bank Show" are courtesy of ITV Studios Limited; clips showing actors and Stephen Sondheim rehearsing for *Company* and clip showing Ethel Merman and various cast members from *Gypsy* courtesy of Pennebaker Hegedus Films, Pamela Myers and the Estate of Ethel Merman; clips From "20/20" courtesy of ABC News; clips from "60 Minutes" courtesy of CBS News Archive and Diane Sawyer; *West Side Story* footage is courtesy of MGM, the Estate of Natalie Wood and Richard Beymer; "Send in the Clowns Montage": Clip of Glynis Johns courtesy of Glynis Johns; clip of Frank Sinatra courtesy of South Bay Music and the Frank Sinatra Estate; clip of Judy Collins courtesy of the "Muppet Show" and Judy Collins; clip of Patti LaBelle courtesy of Pattonium, Inc.; clip of *A Little Night Music* courtesy of Sascha films and Elizabeth Taylor; clip of Judi Dench from *A Little Night Music* courtesy of ITV Studios Limited and Judi Dench; clip of The Treorchy Male Choir courtesy of Frederick O'Brien and Dean Powell; clip from *One Voice* courtesy of Barbra Streisand; clips of Olivia Broderick courtesy of Miriam Ascarelli and James Broderick; clip of Aldo Blaga courtesy of Aldo Blaga; clip of ice skater, Joan Chanel, choreography Bobby Beauchamp, courtesy of Joan Chanel; clip of Bernadette Peters courtesy of Bernadette Peters; clip of Sarah Vaughan courtesy of the Estate of Sarah Vaughan; clip of Warren Freeman courtesy of Warren Freeman. Various photos courtesy of Black Star, Friedman-Abeles Studio, Getty Images, Martha Swope, Peter Cunningham, Rivka Katvan, Mary Rodgers Guettel and RHO/Imagem. Photograph by Richard Avedon, Stephen Sondheim, composer, New York, June 12, 1961© 2010 The Richard Avedon Foundation.

Interview footage with Mr. Sondheim created for *Sondheim on Sondheim*: DP: Adam Feinstein, Tim Smith, Ben Wolf. Line Producers: Danielle Blumstein, Sarna Lapine, Joel Viertel. Makeup Artists: Angelina Avallone, Annie Mistak. Sound: Nara Garber, Trokon Nagbe. AC: Marshall Stief. Transferring Footage: Alex Serpico. Continuity: Shawn Pennington. Production Assistants: David Blazina, Emmy Frank, Lyslynn Lacoste, Kaley McMahon, Andrew McMullen

CREDITS

Scenery fabrication by PRG Scenic Technologies, a division of Production Resource Group L.L.C., New Windsor, NY. Show control and scenic motion control featuring Stage Command Systems® by Scenic Technologies, a division of Production Resource Group L.L.C. Scenery constructed by Global Scenic Services, Inc., Bridgeport, CT. Lighting equipment by PRG Lighting. Audio and video equipment by Sound Associates, Inc. Video monitors by NEC Display Solutions. Costumes by Euroco Costumes, Inc.; Eric Winterling, Inc.; and Giliberto Designs. Crafts by Brent Barkhaus. Shoes by WORLDTONE DANCE. Yamaha piano provided by Bondy Piano.

TARA RUBIN CASTING
Tara Rubin CSA, Eric Woodall CSA,
Merri Sugarman CSA, Laura Schutzel CSA,
Dale Brown, Paige Blansfield, Kaitlin Shaw

SPECIAL THANKS
Dodger Theatricals, Joy Abbott, Kate Best, Beyond Our Reality, Bob Brown, Carol Cornicelli, Mark Horowitz, Peter Jones, Jane Klain, Arthur Laurents, Les Moonves, Playwrights Horizons, Mary Rodgers, Juliana Rosati, Diane Sawyer, Topiary Productions, Inc., Carmen Marc Valvo, David Westin, William Baldwin Young

Make-up Provided by M•A•C Cosmetics
Official Makeup of Roundabout Theatre Company

STUDIO 54 THEATRE STAFF

House Carpenter ....Dan Hoffman
House Electrician ....John Wooding
House Properties ....Lawrence Jennino
Box Office Manager ....Krystin MacRitchie
Assistant Box Office Manager ....Scott Falkowski
House Manager ....LaConya Robinson
Associate House Manager ....Jack Watanachaiyot
Head Usher ....Jonathan Martineaz
Ushers ....Justin Brown, Linda Gjonbalaj, Jennifer Kneeland, Hajjah Karriem, Essence Mason, Nicole Ramirez, Diana Trent, Stella Varrialle, Nicholas Wheatley
Security ....Gotham Security
Maintenance ....Jason Battle, Ralph Mohan, Eddie Perez, Reliable Cleaning
Lobby Refreshments ....Sweet Concessions

Sondheim on Sondheim
Scrapbook

Correspondent: Erin Mackey, Various Roles

Memorable Opening Night Faxes: We had a lot of those come in from *Wicked, Behanding in Spokane, South Pacific, Fela, Race, Promises, Promises, The Phantom of the Opera, Come Fly Away, Jersey Boys* and several others.

Memorable Opening Night Gifts: Steve is known for being a huge puzzle fan, so he gave everybody in the cast puzzles with our *Sondheim on Sondheim* logo, but each one was customized with our initials. It's a really cool memory. Roundabout gave us engraved framed pictures of the whole company. James gave us a digital photo album programmed with photos he took of us during tech.

Web Buzz on the Show: I do sometimes check out interviews we do and I thought what was on the web was celebratory. It came at the time when Sondheim was turning 80. There was stuff everywhere about it and our show was an important part of that. Steve was around our show quite a bit. He worked with us several times, and he wrote a new song for the show. He came one day and worked with Euan and Tom on their songs. We all came and sat in the house and watched. It was like a big master class from Stephen Sondheim himself.

Most Exciting Celebrity Visitors: Carol Burnett came and when she was in Tom's dressing room we all snuck in and took pictures. Elaine Stritch came backstage and visited each of us in our dressing rooms. A lot of Vanessa's cast mates from "Ugly Betty" visited her. Mandy Patinkin came and was so kind: he just raved about the show. Barbra Streisand was spotted in the audience.

Actor Who Has Done the Most Shows in Their Career: Barbara Cook, definitely.

Backstage Rituals: Leslie Kritzer and I share a dressing room. Before each show the boys stop by and we all chat about our lives. Then, just before we go on, we all kind of encourage each other: "Have a great show!" It's very informal, but we do it every time.

Favorite Moment During Each Performance: Singing the *Sunday* sequence at the end of Act I. It comes after a medley of so many great songs. All eight of us are on stage singing together, and it makes for a very full, beautiful sound.

Favorite In-Theatre Gathering Place: Aside from my dressing room, for birthdays we go to the greenroom below the stage.

Favorite Snack Foods: Euan loves popcorn, so he always has popcorn. Vanessa has a wonderful bakery in her neighborhood in upstate New York and she's always bringing us treats from there. Also, tamari almonds from Westerly.

2009-2010 AWARDS

Drama Desk Award
Outstanding Musical Revue

Drama League Award
Distinguished Production of a Musical

1. (L-R): Tom Wopat, Leslie Kritzer, "Yearbook" correspondent Erin Mackey, Barbara Cook, Norm Lewis, Vanessa Williams, and Matthew Scott at the cast party.
2. Barbara Cook takes a curtain call on opening night.
3. Vanessa Williams takes her first-night curtain call on the Studio 54 stage.

Favorite Therapies: We have PT at the theatre once a week, and then Ricolas backstage. Gypsy Cold Care and Throat Coat tea are also common. Grether's Pastilles are usually around too.

Memorable Ad-Libs: There's not a whole lot of ad-libbing you can do in a Sondheim song, but there are moments where people kind of jumble the lyrics. In "Waiting for the Girls," Leslie and I have the lyric "ta, ta goodbye you'll find us at Tony's" and she accidently switched it to "cha, cha goodbye...." Small things like that!

Memorable Press Encounters: Reporters always wanted to know what was my favorite Sondheim song. That was certainly hard to answer! It was always one question that tripped me up. In the end, I changed my answer every interview because I have so many.

Memorable Stage Door Fan Encounters: There are usually fans at the stage door and every so often Barbara, Vanessa or Tom will have fans there that didn't see the show, but want autographs.

Fastest Costume Change: The fastest one for me is probably between *Assassins* and *Do I Hear a Waltz?*, which is about 45 seconds. The boys have a pretty quick change during the "Ah, But Underneath" narration.

Best In-House Parody Lyrics: It's not different lyrics, but Leslie and I have created a *Sweeney Todd* "Epiphany" rap while Tom sings onstage.

Catchphrase Only the Company Would Recognize: "I've been Cook'd."

Memorable Directorial Speech: Just before we opened, James Lapine called us into Barbara Cook's dressing room for a pre-show gathering. He will tell you, he's not much of a complimenter. But he told us all he was proud of the show and proud of our work. That was a very special thing to hear from James.

Coolest Things About Being in This Show: One thing is that the show is a big celebration. Everybody is so excited to celebrate what Stephen's done for musical theatre. That's a great way to start a show. But, more personally, the coolest thing is the people and we have a great group of people, both crew and cast. The eight of us onstage look like buddies and we are. It's a really special group of people and that's the best way to go to work.

South Pacific

First Preview: March 1, 2008. Opened: April 3, 2008.
Still running as of May 31, 2010.

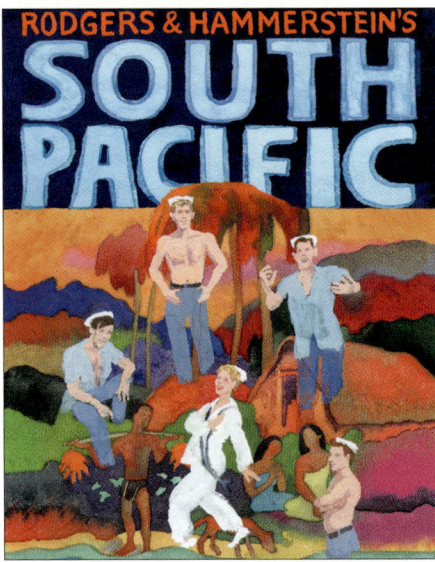

LINCOLN CENTER THEATER AT THE VIVIAN BEAUMONT
under the direction of
ANDRÉ BISHOP and BERNARD GERSTEN
in association with
BOB BOYETT
presents

RODGERS & HAMMERSTEIN'S SOUTH PACIFIC

Music
RICHARD RODGERS

Lyrics
OSCAR HAMMERSTEIN II

Book OSCAR HAMMERSTEIN II and JOSHUA LOGAN
Adapted from the Pulitzer Prize-winning novel *Tales of the South Pacific* by JAMES A. MICHENER
Original stage production directed by JOSHUA LOGAN

with
LAURA OSNES   PAULO SZOT

DANNY BURSTEIN   LORETTA ABLES SAYRE   ANDREW SAMONSKY
ERIC ANDERSON   SEAN CULLEN   CHRISTIAN DELCROIX   MURPHY GUYER
LUKA KAIN   LI JUN LI   LAURISSA ROMAIN
and
MICHAEL ARNOLD   BECCA AYERS   CRAIG BENNETT   WENDI BERGAMINI   CHARLIE BRADY
CHRISTIAN CARTER   TODD CERVERIS   HELMAR AUGUSTUS COOPER   MARGOT DE LA BARRE
LAURA MARIE DUNCAN   ROB GALLAGHER   MARYANN HU   ROBERT LENZI   DEBORAH LEW
PETER LOCKYER   GARRETT LONG   NICK MAYO   LIZ McCARTNEY   GEORGE MERRICK
WILLIAM MICHALS   MARLA MINDELLE   KIMBER MONROE   ALFIE PARKER, JR.   GEORGE PSOMAS
GREG RODERICK   JASON MICHAEL SNOW   JEROLD E. SOLOMON   CORREY WEST

Sets	Costumes	Lighting	Sound
MICHAEL YEARGAN	CATHERINE ZUBER	DONALD HOLDER	SCOTT LEHRER

Orchestrations	Dance & Incidental Music Arrangements	Conductor
ROBERT RUSSELL BENNETT	TRUDE RITTMANN	FRED LASSEN

Casting	Production Stage Manager	General Press Agent	Musical Theater Associate Producer
TELSEY + COMPANY	MICHAEL BRUNNER	PHILIP RINALDI	IRA WEITZMAN

General Manager	Production Manager	Director of Development	Director of Marketing
ADAM SIEGEL	JEFF HAMLIN	HATTIE K. JUTAGIR	LINDA MASON ROSS

Music Direction
TED SPERLING

Musical Staging
CHRISTOPHER GATTELLI

Directed by
BARTLETT SHER

LINCOLN CENTER THEATER GRATEFULLY ACKNOWLEDGES THE CONTRIBUTORS WHOSE EXTRAORDINARY GENEROSITY HAS MADE SOUTH PACIFIC POSSIBLE:
Debra and Leon Black • The Susan and Elihu Rose Foundation • Catherine and Ephraim Gildor
The Joseph and Joan Cullman Arts Foundation • The Blanche and Irving Laurie Foundation • WolfBlock
Sir Thomas Moore/Laurence Levine Charitable Fund • Henry Nias Foundation courtesy of Dr. Stanley Edelman
The New York Community Trust - Mary P. Oenslager Foundation Fund • Leon Levy Foundation
Blanchette Hooker Rockefeller Fund • National Endowment for the Arts

American Airlines is the official airline of Lincoln Center Theater.

10/1/09

CAST OF CHARACTERS

Ensign Nellie Forbush	LAURA OSNES
Emile de Becque	PAULO SZOT
Ngana, his daughter	LAURISSA ROMAIN
Jerome, his son	LUKA KAIN
Henry	HELMAR AUGUSTUS COOPER
Bloody Mary	LORETTA ABLES SAYRE
Liat, her daughter	LI JUN LI
Bloody Mary's Assistants	MARYANN HU, DEBORAH LEW, KIMBER MONROE
Luther Billis	DANNY BURSTEIN
Stewpot (Carpenter's Mate Second Class, George Watts)	ERIC ANDERSON
Professor	CHRISTIAN DELCROIX
Lt. Joseph Cable, United States Marine Corps	ANDREW SAMONSKY
Capt. George Brackett, United States Navy	MURPHY GUYER
Cmdr. William Harbison, United States Navy	SEAN CULLEN
Lt. Buzz Adams	GEORGE MERRICK
Yeoman Herbert Quale, Sailor	JASON MICHAEL SNOW
Radio Operator Bob McCaffrey, Sailor	PETER LOCKYER
Morton Wise, Seabee	TODD CERVERIS
Richard West, Seabee	NICK MAYO
Johnny Noonan, Seabee	MICHAEL ARNOLD
Billy Whitmore, Seabee	ROBERT LENZI
Tom O'Brien, Sailor	ALFIE PARKER, JR.
James Hayes, Sailor	JEROLD E. SOLOMON
Kenneth Johnson, Sailor	CHRISTIAN CARTER

Continued on next page

(L-R): Paulo Szot and Laura Osnes

Photo by Joan Marcus

South Pacific

MUSICAL NUMBERS

The action of the play takes place on two islands in the South Pacific during World War II. There is one week's lapse of time between the two acts.

ACT I

OVERTURE
- Scene 1: The Terrace of Emile de Becque's Plantation Home
  - DITES-MOI .... Ngana and Jerome
  - A COCKEYED OPTIMIST .... Nellie
  - TWIN SOLILOQUIES .... Nellie and Emile
  - SOME ENCHANTED EVENING .... Emile
  - Reprise: DITES-MOI .... Ngana, Jerome and Emile
- Scene 2: Another Part of the Island
  - BLOODY MARY .... Seabees
  - THERE IS NOTHIN' LIKE A DAME .... Billis and Seabees
  - BALI HA'I .... Bloody Mary
- Scene 3: The Company Street
- Scene 4: Inside the Island Commander's Office
- Scene 5: The Company Street
  - MY GIRL BACK HOME .... Cable and Nellie
- Scene 6: The Beach
  - I'M GONNA WASH THAT MAN RIGHT OUTA MY HAIR .... Nellie and Nurses
  - Reprise: SOME ENCHANTED EVENING .... Emile and Nellie
  - A WONDERFUL GUY .... Nellie and Nurses
- Scene 7: Inside the Island Commander's Office
- Scene 8: On Bali Ha'i
  - Reprise: BALI HA'I .... Island Women
- Scene 9: Inside a Hut on Bali Ha'i
  - YOUNGER THAN SPRINGTIME .... Cable
- Scene 10: Near the Beach on Bali Ha'i
- Scene 11: Emile's Terrace
  - FINALE ACT I .... Nellie and Emile

ACT II

ENTR'ACTE
- Scene 1: A Performance of "The Thanksgiving Follies" .... Nellie, Nurses and G.I.'s
- Scene 2: Backstage at "The Thanksgiving Follies"
  - HAPPY TALK .... Bloody Mary and Liat
- Scene 3: The Stage
  - HONEY BUN .... Nellie, Billis and Ensemble
- Scene 4: Backstage
  - YOU'VE GOT TO BE CAREFULLY TAUGHT .... Cable
  - THIS NEARLY WAS MINE .... Emile
- Scene 5: The Radio Shack
- Scene 6: The Beach
  - Reprise: SOME ENCHANTED EVENING .... Nellie
- Scene 7: The Company Street
- Scene 8: Emile's Terrace
  - FINALE ULTIMO .... Emile, Nellie, Ngana and Jerome

Cast Continued

Petty Officer Hamilton Steeves .. CHARLIE BRADY
Marine Staff Sgt.
  Thomas Hassinger .... CRAIG BENNETT
Lt. Eustis Carmichael,
  Shore Patrolman .... ROB GALLAGHER
Lt. Genevieve Marshall,
  Head Nurse .... LIZ McCARTNEY
Ensign Dinah Murphy .. LAURA MARIE DUNCAN
Ensign Janet MacGregor ..... WENDI BERGAMINI
Ensign
  Connie Walewska ..... MARGOT DE LA BARRE
Ensign Sue Yaeger .... GARRETT LONG
Ensign Cora MacRae .... MARLA MINDELLE
Islanders, Sailors, Seabees,
  Party Guests .... ERIC ANDERSON,
    MICHAEL ARNOLD, CRAIG BENNETT,
    WENDI BERGAMINI, CHARLIE BRADY,
    CHRISTIAN CARTER, TODD CERVERIS,
    HELMAR AUGUSTUS COOPER,
    MARGOT DE LA BARRE, ROB GALLAGHER,
    MARYANN HU, ROBERT LENZI,
    DEBORAH LEW, PETER LOCKYER,
    GARRETT LONG, NICK MAYO,
    LIZ McCARTNEY, GEORGE MERRICK,
    MARLA MINDELLE, KIMBER MONROE,
    ALFIE PARKER, JR., JEROLD E. SOLOMON

1st Assistant Stage Manager ...... DANA WILLIAMS
2nd Assistant
  Stage Manager .... SAMANTHA GREENE

Dance Captain .... WENDI BERGAMINI
Asst. Dance Captain .... GEORGE PSOMAS
Swings .... BECCA AYERS, GEORGE PSOMAS,
  GREG RODERICK, CORREY WEST

Paulo Szot is appearing with the permission of Actors' Equity Association.

UNDERSTUDIES

For Nellie Forbush: WENDI BERGAMINI,
  LAURA MARIE DUNCAN,
  GARRETT LONG
For Emile de Becque: ROB GALLAGHER,
  WILLIAM MICHALS
For Ngana and Jerome: KIMBER MONROE
For Henry: CHRISTIAN CARTER,
  ALFIE PARKER, JR.
For Bloody Mary: MARYANN HU,
  LIZ McCARTNEY
For Liat: WENDI BERGAMINI,
  DEBORAH LEW
For Luther Billis: NICK MAYO,
  GEORGE MERRICK

South Pacific

Cast Continued

For Stewpot: MICHAEL ARNOLD,
    TODD CERVERIS
For Lt. Joseph Cable: CHARLIE BRADY,
    ROBERT LENZI, PETER LOCKYER
For Capt. George Brackett: ERIC ANDERSON,
    TODD CERVERIS
For Professor: GEORGE MERRICK,
    JASON MICHAEL SNOW
For Cmdr. William Harbison: ROB GALLAGHER,
    GEORGE MERRICK
For Bob McCaffrey and Yeoman Herbert Quale:
    GEORGE PSOMAS, GREG RODERICK
For Ensign Dinah Murphy: BECCA AYERS,
    WENDI BERGAMINI, GARRETT LONG
For Lt. Eustis Carmichael and Lt. Buzz Adams:
    CHARLIE BRADY, NICK MAYO

ORCHESTRA
Conductor: FRED LASSEN
Associate Conductor: CHARLES DU CHATEAU
Violins: BELINDA WHITNEY (Concertmaster),
    KARL KAWAHARA,
    KATHERINE LIVOLSI-LANDAU,
    JAMES TSAO, LISA MATRICARDI,
    RENA ISBIN, MICHAEL NICHOLAS,
    LOUISE OWEN
Violas: DAVID BLINN, DAVID CRESWELL
Cellos: PETER SACHON, CARYL PAISNER,
    CHARLES DU CHATEAU
Bass: LISA STOKES-CHIN
Flute/Piccolo: LIZ MANN
Clarinet: TODD PALMER, SHARI HOFFMAN
Oboe/English Horn: KELLY PERAL
Bassoon: DAMIAN PRIMIS
French Horns: ROBERT CARLISLE,
    DANIEL GRABOIS, SHELAGH ABATE
Trumpets: DOMINIC DERASSE,
    GARETH FLOWERS, WAYNE DUMAINE
Trombones: MARK PATTERSON,
    NATE MAYLAND
Tuba: MARCUS ROJAS
Harp: GRACE PARADISE
Drums/Percussion: BILL LANHAM

Music Coordinator: DAVID LAI

Richard Rodgers' music is being presented in the 30-player orchestration created for the original production. The scores and orchestral parts were restored by The Rodgers & Hammerstein Organization using all existing material, including manuscripts (Rodgers, Trude Rittmann), the full orchestral scores (Robert Russell Bennett) and the individual instrumental parts played by the original orchestra.

Laura Osnes
Ensign Nellie Forbush

Paulo Szot
Emile de Becque

Danny Burstein
Luther Billis

Loretta Ables Sayre
Bloody Mary

Andrew Samonsky
Lt. Joseph Cable

Eric Anderson
Stewpot

Sean Cullen
Cmdr. William Harbison

Christian Delcroix
Professor

Murphy Guyer
Capt. George Brackett

Luka Kain
Jerome

Li Jun Li
Liat

Laurissa Romain
Ngana

Michael Arnold
Johnny Noonan

Becca Ayers
Swing

Craig Bennett
Thomas Hassinger

Wendi Bergamini
Ensign Janet MacGregor/ Dance Captain

Charlie Brady
Petty Officer Hamilton Steeves

Christian Carter
Kenneth Johnson

Todd Cerveris
Morton Wise

Helmar Augustus Cooper
Henry

South Pacific

Margot De La Barre
Ensign Connie Walewska

Laura Marie Duncan
Ensign Dinah Murphy

Rob Gallagher
Ensemble

Maryann Hu
Bloody Mary's Assistant

Robert Lenzi
Billy Whitmore

Deborah Lew
Bloody Mary's Assistant

Peter Lockyer
Ensemble

Garrett Long
Ensign Sue Yaeger

Nick Mayo
Richard West

Liz McCartney
Lt. Genevieve Marshall

George Merrick
Lt. Buzz Adams

William Michals
Understudy for Emile de Becque

Marla Mindelle
Ensign Cora MacRae

Kimber Monroe
Bloody Mary's Assistant

Alfie Parker, Jr.
Tom O'Brien

George Psomas
Swing/Asst. Dance Captain

Greg Roderick
Swing

Jason Michael Snow
Yeoman Herbert Quale

Jerold E. Solomon
James Hayes

Correy West
Swing

Joshua Logan
(1908-1988)
Co-Author

Richard Rodgers (1902-1979)
Music

Oscar Hammerstein II (1895-1960)
Lyrics and Co-Author

James A. Michener (1907-1997)
Author, Tales of the South Pacific

Bartlett Sher
Director

Christopher Gattelli
Musical Staging

Ted Sperling
Music Direction

Michael Yeargan
Sets

Catherine Zuber
Costumes

Donald Holder
Lighting

Scott Lehrer
Sound

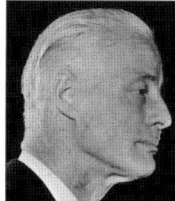
Robert Russell Bennett (1894-1981)
Orchestrations

Trude Rittmann (1908-2005)
Dance and Incidental Music Arrangements

David Lai
Music Coordinator

Bernard Telsey, Telsey+Company
Casting

The Playbill Broadway Yearbook 2009-2010

South Pacific

Bob Boyett

André Bishop and Bernard Gersten, Lincoln Center Theater
Producer

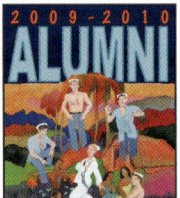

Genson Blimline
Morton Wise, Ensemble

Matt Caplan
Professor

Eric L. Christian
Swing

Mike Evariste
Tom O'Brien Ensemble

Julie Foldesi
Swing

David Pittsinger
Emile de Becque

Matt Wall
Morton Wise, Ensemble

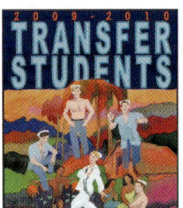

Jacqueline Bayne
Swing

Julie Foldesi
Swing

Taylor Frey
Petty Officer Hamilton Steeves, Ensemble

Kelli O'Hara
Ensign Nellie Forbush

David Pittsinger
Emile de Becque

Samantha Shafer
Ensign Janet MacGregor, Ensembe

Skipp Sudduth
Capt. George Brackett

HAIR CREW
(L-R): John McNulty, Carrie Rohm (Hair Supervisor), and Isaac Grnya

COSTUME CREW
Front Row (L-R): Linda McAllister, Tamara Kopko, Mark Klein

Back Row (L-R): Stacia Williams, Liam O'Brien, Patti Luther, Lynn Bowling (Wardrobe Supervisor)

Not Pictured: James Nadeaux, Leo Namba, Chuck ReCar

South Pacific

STAGE MANAGEMENT
(L-R): Andrea O. Saraffian (ASM), Rolt Smith (PSM) and Dana Williams (ASM)

FRONT OF HOUSE STAFF
Front Row (L-R): Paula Gallo, Amy Yedowitz, Ann Danilovics, Susan Lehman, Officer Steve Spear

Middle Row (L-R): Ruby Jaggernauth, Margie Blair, Jeff Goldstein

Back Row (L-R): Beatrice Gilliard, Nick Andors

RUNNING CREW
Kneeling (L-R): Bruce Rubin (Electrician/Board Operator), Andrew Belits (Carpenter), Mark Dignam (Props), Rudy Wood (Props), John Weingart (Production Flyman), Jeff Ward (Follow Spot Operator), John Ross (Props), Kristina Clark (Electrics), Julia Rubin (Sound Deck), Fred Bredenbeck (Carpenter)

Standing (L-R): Charles Rausenberger (Props), Bill Nagle (Production Carpenter), Paul Gruen (Flyman), Greg Cushna (Flyman), Ray Skillin (Deck Carpenter), Matt Altman (Followspot), Joe Pizzuto (Follow Spot Operator), Pat Merryman (Production Electrician), Juan Bustamante (Deck Automation), John Howie (Carpenter), Bill Burke (Deck Automation), Frank Linn (Electrician/Automation Tech), Nick Irons (Follow Spot), Marc Salzberg (Production Soundman), Gary Simon (Sound Deck)

Not pictured: Karl Rausenberger (Production Propman), Kevin McNeil (Flyman), Takuda Moody (Sound Deck)

The Playbill Broadway Yearbook 2009-2010

South Pacific

LINCOLN CENTER THEATER
ANDRÉ BISHOP — ARTISTIC DIRECTOR
BERNARD GERSTEN — EXECUTIVE PRODUCER

ADMINISTRATIVE STAFF
GENERAL MANAGER .... ADAM SIEGEL
Associate General Manager .... Jessica Niebanck
General Management Assistant .... Meghan Lantzy
Facilities Manager .... Alex Mustelier
Associate Facilities Manager .... Michael Assalone
GENERAL PRESS AGENT .... PHILIP RINALDI
Press Associate .... Barbara Carroll
PRODUCTION MANAGER .... JEFF HAMLIN
Associate Production Manager .... Paul Smithyman
DIRECTOR OF DEVELOPMENT .... HATTIE K. JUTAGIR
Associate Director of Development ...... Rachel Norton
Manager of Special Events and
 Young Patron Program .... Karin Schall
Grants Writer .... Neal Brilliant
Manager, Patron Program .... Sheilaja Rao
Assistant to the
 Director of Development .... Raelyn R. Lagerstrom
Development Associate/
 Special Events .... Jennifer H. Rosenbluth
Development Assistant/Patron Program .. Terra Gillespie
DIRECTOR OF FINANCE .... DAVID S. BROWN
Controller .... Susan Knox
Systems Manager .... Stacy Valentine
Finance Associate .... Joan Glazer
DIRECTOR OF MARKETING .LINDA MASON ROSS
Marketing Associate .... Kristin Miller
Marketing Assistant .... Ashley M. Dunn
DIRECTOR OF EDUCATION .... KATI KOERNER
Associate Director of Education .... Alexandra Lopez
Assistant to the Executive Producer ..... Barbara Hourigan
Office Manager .... Brian Hashimoto
Office Assistant .... Rhonda Lipscomb
Messenger .... Esau Burgess
Reception .... Brenden Rogers, Michelle Metcalf

ARTISTIC STAFF
ASSOCIATE DIRECTORS ...... GRACIELA DANIELE,
 NICHOLAS HYTNER,
 JACK O'BRIEN,
 SUSAN STROMAN,
 DANIEL SULLIVAN
RESIDENT DIRECTOR .... BARTLETT SHER
DRAMATURG and DIRECTOR,
 LCT DIRECTORS LAB .... ANNE CATTANEO
CASTING DIRECTOR .... DANIEL SWEE, CSA
MUSICAL THEATER
 ASSOCIATE PRODUCER .... IRA WEITZMAN
DIRECTOR OF LCT3 .... PAIGE EVANS
Artistic Administrator .... Julia Judge
Casting Associate .... Camille Hickman
Lab Assistant .... Kate Marvin

HOUSE STAFF
HOUSE MANAGER .... RHEBA FLEGELMAN
Production Carpenter .... William Nagle
Production Electrician .... Patrick Merryman
Production Propertyman .... Karl Rausenberger
Production Flyman .... John Weingart
House Technician .... Linda Heard
Chief Usher .... M.L. Pollock
Box Office Treasurer .... Fred Bonis

Assistant Treasurer .... Robert A. Belkin

SPECIAL SERVICES
Advertising .... Serino-Coyne/Jim Russek
 Roger Micone, Becca Goland-Van Ryn
Principal Poster Artist .... James McMullan
Poster Art for *Rodgers & Hammerstein's*
 South Pacific .... James McMullan
Counsel .... Peter L. Felcher, Esq.;
 Charles H. Googe, Esq.;
 and Carol Kaplan, Esq. of
 Paul, Weiss, Rifkind, Wharton & Garrison
Immigration Counsel .... Theodore Ruthizer, Esq.;
 Mark D. Koestler, Esq.
 of Kramer, Levin, Naftalis & Frankel LLP
Labor Counsel .... Michael F. McGahan, Esq.
 of Epstein, Becker & Green, P.C.
Auditor .... Frederick Martens, C.P.A.
 Lutz & Carr, L.L.P.
Insurance .... Jennifer Brown of DeWitt Stern Group
Photographer .... Joan Marcus
Video Services .... Fresh Produce Productions/
 Frank Basile
Travel .... Tygon Tours
Consulting Architect .... Hugh Hardy,
 H3 Hardy Collaboration Architecture
Construction Manager .... Yorke Construction
Payroll Service .... Castellana Services, Inc.
Merchandising .... Marquee Merchandise, LLC/
 Matt Murphy
Lobby Refreshments .... Sweet Concessions

STAFF FOR
RODGERS & HAMMERSTEIN'S SOUTH PACIFIC
COMPANY MANAGER ...... Jessica Perlmeter Cochrane
Assistant Company Manager .... Daniel Hoyos
Assistant Director .... Sarna Lapine
Associate Choreographer .... Joe Langworth
Associate Set Designer .... Lawrence King
Assistant Set Designer .... Mikiko Suzuki
Assistant Costume Designers .... Holly Cain,
 David Newell, Court Watson
Associate Lighting Designer .... Karen Spahn
Assistant Lighting Designer .... Caroline Chao
Automated Light Programmer .... Victor Seastone
Associate Sound Designer .... Leon Rothenberg
Assistant Sound Designer .... Bridget O'Connor
Music Copyist .... Emily Grishman Music Preparation/
 Emily Grishman, Katharine Edmonds
Production Soundman .... Marc Salzberg
Wig and Hair Design .... Tom Watson
Make-up Designer .... Cookie Jordan
Properties Coordinator .... Kathy Fabian
Associate Props Coordinators .... Rose A.C. Howard,
 Carrie Mossman, and Propstar Associates
Prop Scenic Artist .... Curt Tomczyk
Wardrobe Supervisor .... Lynn Bowling
Dressers .... Mark Caine, Mark Klein,
 Tamara Kopko, Patti Luther,
 Linda McAllister, James Nadeaux,
 Leo Namba, Chuck ReCar, Stacia Williams
Hair Supervisor .... Carrie Rohm
Hair Assistants .... Pat Marcus, John McNulty
Production Assistant .... Brandon Kahn
Children's Guardian .... Vanessa Brown
Children's Tutoring .... On Location Education
Costume Shopper .... Nicole Moody

Electronic Percussion Programming .... Randy Cohen
Rehearsal Pianist .... Jonathan Rose
Vocal Coach .... Deborah Hecht

Telsey + Company
Bernie Telsey CSA, Will Cantler CSA, David Vaccari CSA,
Bethany Knox CSA, Craig Burns CSA,
Tiffany Little Canfield CSA, Rachel Hoffman CSA,
Carrie Rosson CSA, Justin Huff CSA, Bess Fifer CSA,
Patrick Goodwin, Abbie Brady-Dalton

FOR THE RODGERS & HAMMERSTEIN ORGANIZATION
President & Executive Director .... Ted Chapin
Senior Vice President & General Manager ...... Bill Gaden
Senior Vice President &
 General Counsel .... Victoria G. Traube
Senior Vice President/Communications .... Bert Fink
Director of Music .... Bruce Pomahac

Performance rights to *South Pacific* are licensed by R&H Theatricals: www.rnhtheatricals.com

For help with Michener matters, thanks to Selma Luttinger, Shirley Soenksen at the University of Northern Colorado, Alice Birney (Manuscript Division) and Mark Eden Horowitz (Music Division) of the Library of Congress, and the Vice President's Office at Swarthmore College.

The producers wish to thank the Naval Historical Center; the Navy Medical Department; the CEC/Seabee Historical Foundation; the Intrepid Sea, Air and Space Museum; the New York City Marines; Major Seth Lapine, USMC; Dr. Regina Anna Sekinger, Ph.D; and Katie McGerr for their invaluable assistance with the military research for this production.

CREDITS
Scenery construction by Hudson Scenic Studio, Inc. Show control and scenic motion control featuring Stage Command Systems® by PRG Scenic Technologies, a division of Production Resource Group, LLC, New Windsor, NY. Scenery fabrication by PRG Scenic Technologies, a division of Production Resource Group, LLC, New Windsor, NY. Costumes by Jennifer Love Costumes; Angels the Costumiers; Parsons-Meares, Ltd.; Euro Co. Costumes; and John Cowles. Men's tailoring by Brian Hemesath and Edward Dawson. Millinery by Rodney Gordon, Inc. and Arnold S. Levine, Inc. Fabric painting and distressing by Jeffrey Fender. Fabric painting by Gene Mignola, Inc. Undergarments and hosiery by Bra*Tenders. Tattoos by Louie Zakarian. Sound equipment by Masque Sound. Lighting equipment from PRG Lighting. Specialty props construction by Costume Armour. Specific military props and accessories provided by Jim Korn & Kaufman's Army Navy. Special thanks to Frank Cwiklik at Metropolis Collectibles, South Sea Rattan Collections and Carris Reels. Cymbals provided courtesy of Paiste America Inc. Drumheads provided by Remo Inc. Drum sticks and mallets provided by Vic Firth Inc. Natural herb cough drops courtesy of Ricola USA, Inc. Emergen-C is the official health and energy drink of *South Pacific*.

For groups of 20 or more:
Caryl Goldsmith Group Sales, (212) 889-4300

Visit www.SouthPacificMusical.com

South Pacific
SCRAPBOOK

1. Vanessa Brown with (L-R): Laurissa Romain, Kimber Monroe and Luka Kain at the anniversary party.
2. (L-R): Luka and Laurissa recording the cast album.
3. (L-R): Alice Hammerstein and Mary Rodgers, daughters of the original songwriters, at the first day of rehearsal for the national tour of *South Pacific*.
4. (L-R): Loretta Ables Sayre and Laura Osnes in their Easter Bonnets.

Correspondents: Luka Kain, "Jerome"; Laurissa Romain, "Ngana"; and their understudy, Kimber Monroe

Most Exciting Celebrity Visitors: We've met Captain Sully Sullenberger, Daniel Radcliffe, Hillary Clinton, James Taylor, Matthew Broderick and Sarah Jessica Parker...so many others, too!

Special Backstage Rituals: Laurissa and Laura Osnes have a special moment where they have to shout: "Toot! Toot-a-loo!" Kimber does "Wang Chung" with the other Island Ladies and for his last entrance, Luka raises the curtain magically by whispering "Wingardium Leviosa." Without these rituals, the show just couldn't go on!

Anniversary Party: We celebrated our two-year Anniversary with a Bowling Party at Lucky Strike. It just may have been the Best Party Ever.

"Easter Bonnet" Sketch: Our wrangler Vanessa Brown wrote the sketch, Rebecca Larkin is building our bonnet, and Kimber, Luka and Laurissa are performing it. It's called: "All I Need To Know I Learned On Broadway."

Catchphrases Only Us Kids Would Recognize: "Meep!" "Yazeedaz!" "Stringbean Custard!" "Fools give you raisins...." "Really, Mira?" "Axe me!" "Brussell Sprouts make me want to...Belgium!" "Mr. Man, you are an unmade bed and a Discounted Flapdoodle" (special thanks to our fabulous dresser, Linda McAllister for that last one).

Favorite Snack Foods: No, Laura didn't make them, but take one anyway!

Favorite Way To Spend Downtime: When we're done with homework, we draw, make movies, memorize State Capitals, torture Tammy, play Apples To Apples or Jenga, or work on our newsletter, "The Island Times."

Charity Involvement: Aside from collecting money for BC/EFA (of course), we joined up with the kids from *Happiness* last year and had a Valentine's Day Bake Sale. We raised more than $400 for The Children's Aid Society.

Favorite In-Theatre Gathering Place: Luka and Vanessa's room. Not only can you find us kids there, playing board games, making stop-motion movies and generally being goofy kids (AFTER we've done our homework, of course), but other members of the company have been known to stop by to play games or watch "Buffy, the Vampire Slayer" or "Survivor" or just to take a nap... Correy!

Favorite Off-Site Hangout: After every Wednesday matinee, we love to hang out with kids from other Broadway shows at Broadway Kids Care.

Memorable Fan Encounter: A girl named Brooke has written a few times and come to see the show with her family, like, five times! We gave her a backstage tour and she gave us sweatshirts.

Reptilian Encounters Backstage: On April Fool's Day Luka found a very large SNAKE in his toilet. You can see the video at: http://www.youtube.com/watch?v=80PxpuoAZx8. It was extra creepy because we had been watching *Jurassic Park* at the time!

Coolest Thing About Being in This Show: Everything!! We've had so many good times and met so many great people. We've been so lucky that the three of us original kids have been able to be here the WHOLE run. Two and a half years is a long time when you're a kid! We will remember our *South Pacific* Family for the rest of our lives.

A Steady Rain

First Preview: September 10, 2009. Opened: September 29, 2009.
Closed December 6, 2009 after 21 Previews and 80 Performances.

CAST

Joey .... DANIEL CRAIG
Denny .... HUGH JACKMAN

UNDERSTUDIES

For Joey:
C.J. WILSON

For Denny:
DANNY MASTROGIORGIO

SETTING

Chicago. The not-too-distant past.

GERALD SCHOENFELD THEATRE
236 West 45th Street
A Shubert Organization Theatre

Philip J. Smith, *Chairman*   Robert E. Wankel, *President*

FREDERICK ZOLLO   MICHAEL G. WILSON   BARBARA BROCCOLI
RAYMOND L. GASPARD   FRANK GERO   CHERYL WIESENFELD
JEFFREY SINE   MICHAEL ROSE LTD   THE SHUBERT ORGANIZATION, INC.   AND   ROBERT COLE

PRESENT

DANIEL CRAIG   HUGH JACKMAN

IN

A STEADY RAIN

BY

KEITH HUFF

SCENIC AND COSTUME DESIGN BY
SCOTT PASK

LIGHTING DESIGN BY
HUGH VANSTONE

ORIGINAL MUSIC AND SOUND DESIGN BY
MARK BENNETT

PRODUCTION MANAGEMENT   PRODUCTION STAGE MANAGER
AURORA PRODUCTIONS   **MICHAEL J. PASSARO**

PRESS REPRESENTATIVE   ADVERTISING   COMPANY MANAGER
THE HARTMAN GROUP   **SPOTCO**   **LISA M. POYER**

DIRECTED BY
JOHN CROWLEY

A STEADY RAIN WAS ORIGINALLY PRESENTED BY NEW YORK STAGE AND FILM COMPANY AND THE POWERHOUSE THEATER AT VASSAR. IT WAS SUBSEQUENTLY PRESENTED AT CHICAGO DRAMATISTS.

9/29/09

(L-R): Hugh Jackman and Daniel Craig

Photo by Joan Marcus

A Steady Rain

Daniel Craig
Joey

Hugh Jackman
Denny

C.J. Wilson
u/s Joey

Danny Mastrogiorgio
u/s Denny

Keith Huff
Playwright

John Crowley
Director

Scott Pask
Scenic and Costume Design

Hugh Vanstone
Lighting Design

Mark Bennett
Original Music & Sound Design

David Brian Brown
Hair Design

Naomi Donne
Makeup Designer

Jim Carnahan
Casting

Philip J. Smith,
Chairman,
The Shubert Organization
Producer

Robert Cole
Producer/ General Manager

FRONT OF HOUSE STAFF

Front Row (L-R): Raya Konyk, Marie Teresa Farnesbath, Ramona Maben, Gillian Sheffler, David Conte

Middle Row: Francine Kramer, Roz Cobbs, Milagros Vargas, Denise Demirjian

Top Row: Anthony Martinez, Marion Mooney

CREW

Front Row (L-R): Tim McWilliams, Dave Cohen, Glenn Ingram, Heidi Brown, Brien Brannigan, Geoffrey Polischuk

Back Row (L-R): Leslie Kilian, Dan Coey, Chris Keene, Pat Sosnow, Kathleen Gallagher, Yvonne Jensen, Scott Pask, Michael J. Passaro

A Steady Rain

BOX OFFICE
(L-R): Brian Goode, Rodney Giebler, Michael DelVecchio

STAFF FOR *A STEADY RAIN*

GENERAL MANAGEMENT
COLE PRODUCTIONS LLC

COMPANY MANAGEMENT
LISA M. POYER
Kyle Bonder

PRESS REPRESENTATIVE
THE HARTMAN GROUP
Michael Hartman   Wayne Wolfe   Matt Ross

PRODUCTION MANAGEMENT
AURORA PRODUCTIONS
Gene O'Donovan   W. Benjamin Heller II
Rachel Sherbill   Steve Rosenberg   Jarid Sumner
Melissa Mazdra   Amy Merlino Coey
Amanda Raymond   Graham Forden   Liza Luxenberg

HAIR DESIGN
David Brian Brown

MAKEUP DESIGN
Naomi Donne

NEW YORK CASTING
Jim Carnahan, C.S.A.

DIALECT COACH
Jess Platt

Production Stage Manager .... Michael J. Passaro
Stage Manager .... Pat Sosnow

Associate Scenic Designer .... Orit J. Carroll
Assistant Scenic Designers .... Frank M. McCullough,
Lauren M. Alvarez
Associate Costume Designer .... Daryl A. Stone
Associate Lighting Designer .... Philip S. Rosenberg
Associate Sound Designer .... Tony Smolenski IV
Guitarist .... Brien Brannigan

Production Carpenter .... Tony Menditto
Flyman .... David Cohen
Production Electrician .... Dan Coey
Electrics Programmer .... Laura Frank

Prop Coordinator .... Propstar/Kathy Fabian
Associate Prop Coordinator .... Jennifer Breen
Prop Master .... Heidi L. Brown
Production Sound Engineer .... Brien Brannigan
Sound Programmer .... Tony Smolenski IV
Wardrobe Supervisor .... Kathleen Gallagher
Mr. Craig's Dresser .... Yvonne Jensen
Mr. Jackman's Dresser .... Geoffrey Polischuk

Assistant to the Producer &
  General Manager .... Gabriel Flateman
Production Assistant .... Alison M. Roberts
Assistant to Mr. Jackman .... Alexandra Ducocq
Assistant to the Director .... Meg Griffiths
Assistant to the Scenic &
  Costume Designer .... Roman Palyk
Assistant to the Lighting Designer .... Isabella F. Byrd
Assistant to the Composer .... Phillip Owen
Press Associates .... Edward Allen, Leslie Baden,
Nicole Capatasto, Frances Connelly,
Tom D'Ambrosio, Juliana Hannett,
Alyssa Hart, Holly Kinney,
Casting Assistant .... Jillian Cimini

Advertising .... SpotCo/Drew Hodges, Jim Edwards,
Tom Greenwald,
Tom McCann, Josh Fraenkel
Legal Counsel .. Franklin, Weinrib, Rudell & Vassallo, P.C./
Jonathan Lonner, Heather C. Reid
Additional
  Legal Counsel .... Law Offices of George Sheanshang
Immigration Counsel .... Fragomen, Del Rey,
Bernsen & Loewy, LLP/
Freddi M. Weintraub, Susanah Wade
UK Visa
  Consultant .... Specialist Visa Consultants Ltd./
Lisa Carr
Accountant .... Fried & Kowgios CPA's LLP/
Robert Fried, CPA
Comptroller .... Anne Stewart FitzRoy, CPA
Banking .... City National Bank/
Anne McSweeney, Sylvia Gibbons
Insurance .... Dewitt Stern Group/
Peter Shoemaker, Rebecca Alspector
Payroll Service .... Castellana Payroll Services, Inc./
Lance Castellana
Production Photographer .... Joan Marcus

Advertising & Portrait Photography .... Greg Williams
Rehearsal Studio .... Steiner Studios
Opening Night
  Coordination .... The Lawrence Company Events, Inc./
Michael P. Lawrence
Theatre Displays .... King Display, Inc.
Group Sales .... Telecharge.com Group Sales/
212-239-6262, 1-800-432-7780,
www.telecharge.com/groups

WEBSITE
www.asteadyrain.com

CREDITS
Scenery, automation and show control by Show Motion, Inc., Norwalk, CT, using the AC2 Computerized Motion Control System. Lighting equipment from PRG Lighting. Sound equipment by Masque Sound. Soft goods provided by Aurora Productions Inc. Upholstery by Mimi New York. Lighting fixtures from City Knickerbocker. Flame treatment by Turning Star. Music recorded and engineered at John Kilgore Studios. Skincare and makeup from SENSAI by Kanebo and Hommage. Tattoo by Jenai Chin for Temptu.

SPECIAL THANKS
Russell Nardozza, Geoffrey Beene; Chéri DaLuz, Philip Van Heusen Sportswear Group; John Kammeier, Randa Accessories; Scott Bray, Philip Van Heusen, The Designer Group; David Napoli, Lanier Clothes; Yamaha Pianos.

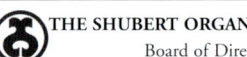 **THE SHUBERT ORGANIZATION, INC.**
Board of Directors

Philip J. Smith
Chairman

Robert E. Wankel
President

Wyche Fowler, Jr.

John W. Kluge

Lee J. Seidler

Michael I. Sovern

Stuart Subotnick

Elliot Greene
Chief Financial
Officer

David Andrews
Senior Vice President –
Shubert Ticketing

Juan Calvo
Vice President
and Controller

John Darby
Vice President –
Facilities

Peter Entin
Vice President –
Theatre Operations

Charles Flateman
Vice President –
Marketing

Anthony LaMattina
Vice President –
Audit & Production Finance

Brian Mahoney
Vice President –
Ticket Sales

D.S. Moynihan
Vice President – Creative Projects

Theatre Manager .... David M. Conte

Superior Donuts

First Preview: September 16, 2009. Opened: October 1, 2009.
Closed January 3, 2010 after 17 Previews and 109 Performances.

CAST
(in order of appearance)

Max Tarasov	YASEN PEYANKOV
Officer Randy Osteen	KATE BUDDEKE
Officer James Hailey	JAMES VINCENT MEREDITH
Lady Boyle	JANE ALDERMAN
Arthur Przybyszewski	MICHAEL McKEAN
Franco Wicks	JON MICHAEL HILL
Luther Flynn	ROBERT MAFFIA
Kevin Magee	CLIFF CHAMBERLAIN
Kiril Ivakina	MICHAEL GARVEY

SETTING

"Superior Donuts," a small donut shop in Chicago's Uptown neighborhood

UNDERSTUDIES/STANDBYS

For Officer Randy Osteen, Lady Boyle:
MARILYN DODDS FRANK
For Arthur Przybyszewski:
STEPHEN PAYNE
For Max Tarasov, Luther Flynn, Kevin Magee:
SEAN PATRICK REILLY
For Kiril Ivakina:
MICHAEL ROSSMY
For Officer James Hailey, Franco Wicks:
SAMUEL STRICKLEN

THE MUSIC BOX
239 W. 45th Street
A Shubert Organization Theatre

Philip J. Smith, *Chairman* **Robert E. Wankel**, *President*

JEFFREY RICHARDS   JEAN DOUMANIAN   JERRY FRANKEL
AWAKEN ENTERTAINMENT   DEBRA BLACK   CHASE MISHKIN   KARMICHELLE PRODUCTIONS / ROBERT G. BARTNER
CAROLE & BARRY KAYE / IRV WELZER   ANDREW ASNES   REBECCA GOLD   DASHA THEATRICALS, INC.
KATHLEEN K. JOHNSON   GEORGE KAUFMAN   CHARLIE McATEER   TERRY SCHNUCK
MICHAEL GARDNER / DAVID JAROSLOWICZ   ROY GOTTLIEB / RAISE THE ROOF TWO
DENA HAMMERSTEIN / PAM PARISEAU   STEWART F. LANE / BONNIE COMLEY

PRESENT

THE STEPPENWOLF THEATRE COMPANY PRODUCTION OF

BY TRACY LETTS

JANE ALDERMAN   KATE BUDDEKE   CLIFF CHAMBERLAIN   MICHAEL GARVEY   JON MICHAEL HILL
ROBERT MAFFIA   MICHAEL McKEAN   JAMES VINCENT MEREDITH   YASEN PEYANKOV

SCENIC DESIGN	COSTUME DESIGN	LIGHTING DESIGN	SOUND DESIGN
JAMES SCHUETTE	ANA KUZMANIC	CHRISTOPHER AKERLIND	ROB MILBURN & MICHAEL BODEEN

HAIR & WIG DESIGN	DRAMATURG	ORIGINAL CASTING	NEW YORK CASTING
CHARLES LaPOINTE	EDWARD SOBEL	ERICA DANIELS	TELSEY + COMPANY

FIGHT DIRECTOR	PRODUCTION STAGE MANAGER	TECHNICAL SUPERVISION
RICK SORDELET	ARTHUR GAFFIN	HUDSON THEATRICAL ASSOCIATES

PRESS REPRESENTATIVE	ASSOCIATE PRODUCERS	GENERAL MANAGEMENT
IRENE GANDY / JEFFREY RICHARDS ASSOCIATES	JEREMY SCOTT BLAUSTEIN PATRICK DALY SUSAN JEAN STEIGER DONNA ROEHN WARD	RICHARDS / CLIMAN, INC.

DIRECTED BY
TINA LANDAU

THE WORLD PREMIERE OF *SUPERIOR DONUTS* WAS PRESENTED AT STEPPENWOLF THEATRE COMPANY, CHICAGO, IL.
MARTHA LAVEY, ARTISTIC DIRECTOR AND DAVID HAWKANSON, EXECUTIVE DIRECTOR.
THE PRODUCERS WISH TO EXPRESS THEIR APPRECIATION TO
THE THEATRE DEVELOPMENT FUND FOR ITS SUPPORT OF THIS PRODUCTION.

10/1/09

(L-R): Kate Buddeke, Michael McKean, Jon Michael Hill

Superior Donuts

Michael McKean
Arthur Przybyszewski

Jane Alderman
Lady Boyle

Kate Buddeke
Officer Randy Osteen

Cliff Chamberlain
Kevin Magee

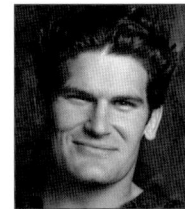
Michael Garvey
Kiril Ivakina

Jon Michael Hill
Franco Wicks

Robert Maffia
Luther Flynn

James Vincent Meredith
Officer James Hailey

Yasen Peyankov
Max Tarasov

Marilyn Dodds Frank
u/s Lady Boyle, Officer Randy Osteen

Stephen Payne
u/s Arthur

Sean Patrick Reilly
u/s Max, Luther, Kevin

Michael Rossmy
u/s Kiril, Fight Captain

Samuel Stricklen
u/s James, Franco

Tracy Letts
Playwright

Tina Landau
Director

Ana Kuzmanic
Costume Design

Christopher Akerlind
Lighting Design

Rob Milburn and Michael Bodeen
Sound Design

Bernard Telsey, Telsey + Company
Casting

Rick Sordelet
Fight Director

Neil A. Mazzella/ Hudson Theatrical Associates
Technical Supervision

David R. Richards and Tamar Haimes, Richards/Climan, Inc.
General Management

Jeffrey Richards
Producer

Jean Doumanian
Producer

Jerry Frankel
Producer

Jennifer Maloney, Awaken Entertainment
Producer

Debra Black
Producer

Chase Mishkin
Producer

Sharon Karmazin
Producer

Irving Welzer
Producer

Andrew Asnes
Producer

Terry Schnuck
Producer

Superior Donuts

Michael Gardner
Producer

Jennifer Manocherian,
Raise the Roof Two
Producer

Harriet Newman Leve,
Raise the Roof Two
Producer

Stewart Lane and Bonnie Comley
Producers

Jeremy Scott Blaustein
Associate Producer

Martha Lavey
*Artistic Director,
Steppenwolf Theatre Company*

David Hawkanson
*Executive Director,
Steppenwolf Theatre Company*

BOX OFFICE
(L-R): Brendan Berberich, Robert D. Kelly

FRONT OF HOUSE STAFF
Front Row (L-R): Lottie Dennis, Kenneth Kelly
Middle Row (L-R): Jonathan Shulman, Thomas Murdoch, Michael Concepcion
Back Row (L-R): Joseph Lopez, Christopher Scopo, Justin Perez, Steven Staszewski, Joseph Amato

CREW
(L-R): Dennis Maher, Brian Laube, William Rowland, Kim Garnett, Billy Rowland

WARDROBE
(L-R): Kim Prentice, Rob Bevenger

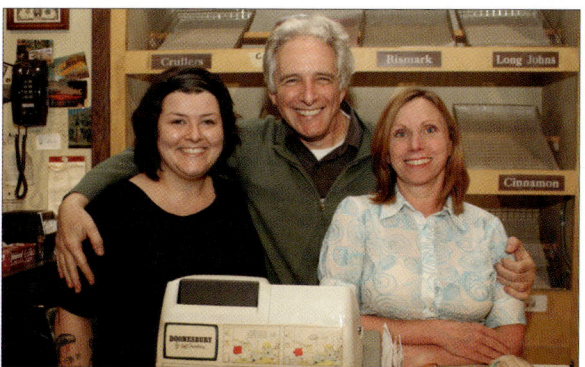
STAGE AND COMPANY MANAGEMENT
(L-R): Lauren Hickman, Artie Gaffin, Mary Miller

CREW
Front Row (L-R): Lauren Hickman, Kim Prentice, Mary Miller, Alana Karpoff
Back Row (L-R): Brian Laube, Dennis Maher, Billy Rowland, William Rowland, Rob Bevenger, Artie Gaffin, Kim Garnett.

The Playbill Broadway Yearbook 2009-2010

Superior Donuts

ENTIRE CAST AND CREW ON THE STAGE OF THE MUSIC BOX

STAFF FOR SUPERIOR DONUTS

GENERAL MANAGEMENT
RICHARDS/CLIMAN, INC.
David R. Richards   Tamar Haimes

GENERAL PRESS REPRESENTATIVE
JEFFREY RICHARDS ASSOCIATES
IRENE GANDY
Alana Karpoff   Elon Rutberg   Diana Rissetto

COMPANY MANAGER
MARY MILLER

Production Stage Manager	Arthur Gaffin
Stage Manager	Lauren Hickman
Assistant Director	Robert Quinlan
Assistant Set Designers	Jonathan Collins, Andrew Boyce
Assistant Costume Designer	Kristina Lucka
Associate Lighting Designer	Ben Krall
Associate Sound Designer	Jeremy J. Lee
Production Properties Coordinator	Jeremy Chernick
Associate Props Coordinator	Jeremy Lydic
Associate General Manager	Michael Sag
General Management Associate	Jeromy Smith
General Management Assistant	Cesar Hawas
Press Intern	Kristin Piacentile
Production Assistant	Jamie Greathouse
Production Electrician	Jimmy Maloney
Associate Production Electrician	Brad Robertson
Production Sound	Valerie Spradling
House Carpenter	Dennis Maher
House Electrician	William Rowland
House Props	Kim Garnett
Wardrobe Supervisor	Rob Bevenger
Dresser	Kim Prentice
Hair & Makeup Supervisor	Amy Neswald
Advertising	SpotCo./Drew Hodges, Jim Edwards Stephen Sosnowski, Meghan Ownbey
Interactive Marketing Services	Situation Interactive/Damian Bazadona, John Lanasa, Ryan Klink, Kristen Butler
Banking	City National Bank/Michele Gibbons
Accountants	FK Partners/Robert Fried, CPA
Comptroller	Elliott Aronstam
Legal Counsel	Lazarus & Harris, LLP/ Scott R. Lazarus, Esq., Robert C. Harris, Esq.
Insurance	DeWitt Stern Group, Inc./Joseph Bower
Payroll	CSI/Lance Castellana
Group Sales	Broadway Inbound
Production Photographer	Robert J. Saferstein
Company Mascots	Lottie, Skye, Mr. Moon, Mr. Arcati

CREDITS
Scenery constructed by Hudson Scenic Studio, Inc. Lighting equipment by Hudson Sound & Light LLC. Sound equipment by Sound Associates. "Higher Ground" (100%) written by Stevie Wonder. Published by Jobete Music Co., Inc., and Black Bull Music.

SPECIAL THANKS
Atlantic Theater Company, Barrow Street Theatre, Manhattan Class Company, The Public Theater, Roundabout Theatre Company, The Doughnut Plant.

STEPPENWOLF THEATRE COMPANY
Founders: Terry Kinney, Jeff Perry and Gary Sinise
Ensemble Members: Joan Allen, Kevin Anderson, Alana Arenas, Randall Arney, Kate Arrington, Ian Barford, Robert Breuler, Gary Cole, Kathryn Erbe, K. Todd Freeman, Frank Galati, Francis Guinan, Moira Harris, Jon Hill, Tim Hopper, Tom Irwin, Ora Jones, Tina Landau, Martha Lavey, Tracy Letts, John Mahoney, John Malkovich, Mariann Mayberry, James Vincent Meredith, Laurie Metcalf, Amy Morton, Sally Murphy, Austin Pendleton, Yasen Peyankov, Martha Plimpton, Rondi Reed, Molly Regan, Anna D. Shapiro, Eric Simonson, Lois Smith, Rick Snyder, Jim True-Frost, Alan Wilder

THE SHUBERT ORGANIZATION, INC.
Board of Directors

Philip J. Smith Chairman	**Robert E. Wankel** President
Wyche Fowler, Jr.	**John W. Kluge**
Lee J. Seidler	**Michael I. Sovern**

Stuart Subotnick

Elliot Greene Chief Financial Officer	**David Andrews** Senior Vice President – Shubert Ticketing
Juan Calvo Vice President and Controller	**John Darby** Vice President – Facilities
Peter Entin Vice President – Theatre Operations	**Charles Flateman** Vice President – Marketing
Anthony LaMattina Vice President – Audit & Production Finance	**Brian Mahoney** Vice President – Ticket Sales

D.S. Moynihan
Vice President – Creative Projects

House Manager .... Jonathan Shulman

Photo by Robert J. Saferstein

Superior Donuts
SCRAPBOOK

Photos by Aubrey Reuben

Correspondent: Jon Michael Hill, "Franco Wicks"
Memorable Note: Dustin Hoffman: "To the cast of *Superior Donuts*, one word: 'Superior.'"
Most Exciting Celebrity Visitor and What They Did: Kate Winslet: Hugged me.
Special Backstage Rituals: Playing grab-ass.
Favorite Moment on Stage or Off: Improvising with Jane Alderman (as her character) on the subway.
Favorite In-Theatre Gathering Place: Jon Michael Hill's dressing room.
Favorite Off-Site Hangout: The Hourglass Tavern.
Favorite Snack Foods: Honey Wheat Twist pretzels.
Favorite Therapy: Argentinian Bug Juice (ginger, honey and lemon tea).
Memorable Ad-Lib: Kate Buddeke: "James, you wanna go get that table?"
Who Wore the Heaviest/Hottest Costume: Jane Alderman, complete with newspaper in her bag lady boots.
Catchphrase Only the Company Would Recognize: "We can be rich and have enemies or be poor and have friends" (James Meredith doing Robert Maffia doing Armand Assante).
Sweethearts Within the Company: Jon Michael Hill and Jane Alderman.
Company Legend: Michael McKean's beard.
Nicknames: Jane Alderman: "Lady Jane"
Kate Buddeke: "Red Snapper"
Cliff Chamberlain: "Chuck"
Jon Michael Hill: "Li'l Wanko Ficks"
James Vincent Meredith: "Big Chocolate"
Yasen "The Bear" Peyankov
Embarrassing Moment: James coming on as the cop without his gunbelt.
Coolest Thing About Being in This Show: Going to work every day with people I love.

1. Cast member (and *Yearbook* correspondent) Jon Michael Hill at the opening night party at the Redeye Grill.
2. Cast member Michael McKean on opening night.
3. Cast members (L-R) Yasen Peyankov, Cliff Chamberlain, Michael Garvey, Robert Maffia, James Vincent Meredith meet the press at Snapple Theatre Rehearsal Studio.
4. Author Tracy Letts at the Redeye Grill.
5. Director Tina Landau at the opening night party.

2009-2010 AWARDS

OUTER CRITICS CIRCLE AWARD
Outstanding Featured Actor in a Play
(Jon Michael Hill)

THEATRE WORLD AWARD
First Major New York Appearance
(Jon Michael Hill)

The 39 Steps

First Preview: January 4, 2008. Opened: January 15, 2008.
Closed January 10, 2010 after 23 Previews and 771 Performances. (Transferred to an Off-Broadway run.)

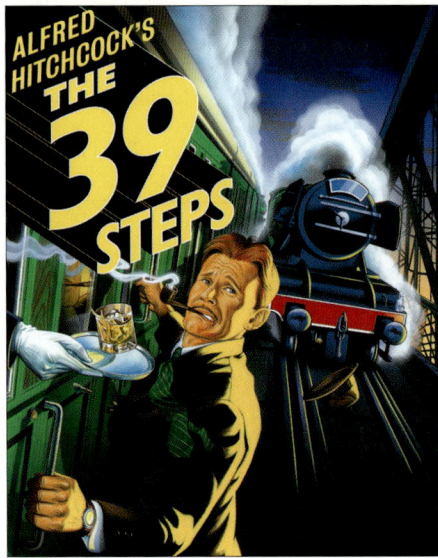

CAST
(in order of appearance)

Man #1	JEFFREY KUHN
Man #2	ARNIE BURTON
Richard Hannay	SEAN MAHON
Annabella Schmidt/Pamela/Margaret	JILL PAICE

UNDERSTUDIES

For Richard Hannay:
ROB BRECKENRIDGE
For Man #1 & #2:
CAMERON FOLMAR
For Annabella Schmidt/Pamela/Margaret:
NISI STURGIS

Production Stage Manager:
NEVIN HEDLEY
Stage Manager:
JANET TAKAMI

THE HELEN HAYES THEATRE
MARTIN MARKINSON   **DONALD TICK**

Bob Boyett, Harriet Newman Leve/Ron Nicynski, Stewart F. Lane/Bonnie Comley, Manocherian Golden Prods., Olympus Theatricals/Douglas Denoff, Pam Laudenslager/Pat Addiss, Tim Levy/Remmel T. Dickinson

IN ASSOCIATION WITH
Roundabout Theatre Company
(Todd Haimes, Artistic Director; Harold Wolpert, Managing Director; Julia C. Levy, Executive Director)
Huntington Theatre Company
(Nicholas Martin, Artistic Director; Michael Maso, Managing Director)
Edward Snape for Fiery Angel Ltd.

PRESENT

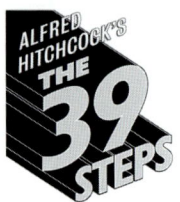

ADAPTED BY **Patrick Barlow**

BASED ON AN ORIGINAL CONCEPT BY **Simon Corble and Nobby Dimon**
BASED ON THE BOOK BY **John Buchan**

with

Arnie Burton   **Jeffrey Kuhn**   **Sean Mahon**   **Jill Paice**

LIGHTING DESIGN	SOUND DESIGN
Kevin Adams	Mic Pool

ORIGINAL MOVEMENT CREATED BY	ADDITIONAL MOVEMENT CREATED BY	PRODUCTION MANAGER	PRODUCTION STAGE MANAGER
Toby Sedgwick	Christopher Bayes	Aurora Productions	Nevin Hedley

CASTING	MARKETING	PRESS REPRESENTATIVE
Jay Binder/Jack Bowdan	HHC Marketing	Boneau/Bryan-Brown

DIALECT COACH	ASSOCIATE PRODUCER	EXECUTIVE PRODUCER	GENERAL MANAGER
Stephen Gabis	Marek J. Cantor	101 Productions, Ltd.	Roy Gabay

SET & COSTUME DESIGN
Peter McKintosh

DIRECTED BY
Maria Aitken

This production of *The 39 Steps* premiered at the Tricycle Theatre, London in August 2006. We wish to express our appreciation to Theatre Development Fund for its support of this production.

10/1/09

(L-R): Jeffrey Kuhn as a Policeman chases Sean Mahon as Richard Hannay.

Photo by Joan Marcus

The 39 Steps

Arnie Burton
Man #2

Jeffrey Kuhn
Man #1

Sean Mahon
Richard Hannay

Jill Paice
Annabella Schmidt/
Pamela/Margaret

Rob Breckenridge
u/s Richard Hannay

Cameron Folmar
u/s Man #1 & #2

Nisi Sturgis
u/s Annabella
Schmidt/Pamela/
Margaret

Maria Aitken
Director

Patrick Barlow
Adaptor

Peter McKintosh
Set and Costume
Design

Kevin Adams
Lighting Design

Mic Pool
Sound Design

Stephen Gabis
Dialect Coach

Jay Binder C.S.A
Casting

Jack Bowdan C.S.A.
Casting

Bob Boyett
Producer

Harriet Newman
Leve
Producer

Ron Nicynski
Producer

Stewart F. Lane and Bonnie Comley
Producer

Jennifer
Manocherian
Producer

Barbara
Manocherian
Producer

Douglas Denoff
Producer

Pat Flicker Addiss
Producer

Edward Snape,
Fiery Angel
Producer

Peter DuBois
Artistic Director,
Huntington Theatre
Company

Michael Maso
Managing Director,
Huntington Theatre
Company

Todd Haimes
Artistic Director,
Roundabout Theatre
Company

Wendy Orshan,
101 Productions, Ltd.
Executive Producers

Roy Gabay
General Manager

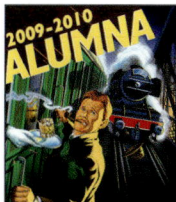

Claire Brownell
u/s Annabella
Schmidt/Pamela/
Margaret

The Playbill Broadway Yearbook 2009-2010

The 39 Steps

(L-R): Sean Mahon, Jill Paice, Arnie Burton and Jeffrey Kuhn.

Photo by Joan Marcus

STAFF FOR THE 39 STEPS

GENERAL MANAGEMENT
ROY GABAY PRODUCTIONS
Roy Gabay   Chris Aniello

COMPANY MANAGER
Bobby Driggers

GENERAL PRESS REPRESENTATIVE
BONEAU/BRYAN-BROWN
Adrian Bryan-Brown   Jim Byk
Jessica Johnson   Rachel Stange

CASTING
JAY BINDER CASTING
Jay Binder CSA
Jack Bowdan CSA, Mark Brandon, Sara Schatz
Nikole Vallins, Allison Estrin

PRODUCTION MANAGEMENT
AURORA PRODUCTIONS
Gene O'Donovan   W. Benjamin Heller II
Rachel Sherbill   Melissa Mazdra   Amy Merlino Coey
Amanda Raymond   Graham Forden   Liza Luxenberg

Production Stage Manager/
  Resident Director .... Nevin Hedley
Stage Manager .... Janet Takami
Assistant to the Director .... Kevin Bigger
Production Assistant .... Rosy Garner
Assistant Sound Designer .... Drew Levy
Associate Scenic Designer .... Josh Zangen
Associate Lighting Designer .... Joel Silver
Assistant Lighting Designer .... Hilary Manners

Movement Director .... Christopher Bayes
Movement Captain .... Cameron Folmar
Wig Design .... Jason Allen

Production Electrician .... Joseph Beck
Production Carpenter .... Doug Purcell
Production Sound .... Bob Etter
Head Properties .... Roger Keller
Assistant Properties .... Joe Redmond, Joe Lavaia
Production Props Shopper .... Pete Sarafin
Wardrobe Supervisor .... Jessie Galvan
Hair and Wig Supervisor .... Alice Ramos
Dressers .... Peggy Donovan, Renee Mariotti

Assistant to Mr. Boyett .... Diane Murphy
Assistants to Ms. Leve .... Jennifer Isaacson, Daniel Krost
Legal Counsel .... Lazarus & Harris LLP/
  Scott Lazarus, Esq.;
  Robert C. Harris, Esq.;
  Andrew Farber, Esq.
Accountants .... Rosenberg Neuwirth & Kuchner CPAs/
  Chris Cacace, Jana Jevnikar
Advertising .... Spotco/
  Drew Hodges, Jim Edwards,
  Denise Ganjou, Kristen Rathbun
Marketing .... HHC Marketing/
  Hugh Hysell, Matt Sicoli,
  Eddie Rabin, Michael Redman,
  Jaime Roberts, James Hewson,
  Brandon Martin, Nicole Pando
Distribution Specialist .... Padraig Haughey/
  The Big Frog Inc.
Banking .... Chase/Richard Callian
Insurance .... DeWitt Stern/Peter Shoemaker
Theatre Displays .... King Displays, Inc.
Merchandising .... Marquee Merchandise, LLC/
  Matt Murphy
Immigration Attorney .... Traffic Control Group/
  David King
Payroll .... CSI/Lance Castellana
Physical Therapist .... Rhonda M. Barkow, PT, MS

Orthopedic Consultant .... Phillip Bauman, MD
Production Photographer .... Joan Marcus
Special Thanks .... Simon Jones

CREDITS
Scenery by Huntington Theatre Company and Hudson Scenic Studio, Inc. Lighting equipment from PRG Lighting. Sound equipment by Masque Sound. Costumes constructed by Huntington Theatre Company and CarmenGee.com. Natural herb cough drops courtesy of Ricola USA, Inc.

THE HELEN HAYES THEATRE STAFF
Owned and Operated by Little Theatre Group LLC
Martin Markinson and Donald Tick
General Manager and Counsel .... Susan S. Myerberg
House Manager .... Alan R. Markinson
Engineer .... Hector Angulo
Treasurer .... David Heveran
Assoc. Gen. Manager .... Sharon Fallon
Assistant Treasurer .... Chuck Stuis
Head Ushers .... John Biancamano, Linda Maley, Berd Vaval
Stage Door .... Robert Seymour, Jonathan Angulo, Robert Seymour III
Accountant .... Chen-Win Hsu, CPA, PC

MUSIC CREDITS
1. "If You Knew Suzie" performed by Jack Shilkret & Orchestra from The Roaring Twenties CD-SDL 344 (www.saydisc.com). 2. "Embassy Stomp" courtesy of Memoir Records. 3. "The 39 Steps" composed by Louis Levy and Jack Beaver; published by Cinephonic Music ©1995 Silva Screen Records Ltd. "Dial M for Murder" composed by Dimitri Tiomkin; published by Warner Chappell Music ©1993 Silva Screen Records Ltd. "The Man Who Knew Too Much" composed by Bernard Herrmann; published by Famous Music ©1995 Silva Screen Records Ltd. Vertigo "Scene d'Amour" composed by

Time Stands Still

First Preview: January 5, 2010. Opened: January 28, 2010.
Closed March 27, 2010 after 28 Previews and 67 Performances.

CAST
(in alphabetical order)

Richard Ehrlich	ERIC BOGOSIAN
James Dodd	BRIAN D'ARCY JAMES
Sarah Goodwin	LAURA LINNEY
Mandy Bloom	ALICIA SILVERSTONE

A loft in Williamsburg, Brooklyn. Recently.

Stage Manager .... SHANNA SPINELLO

UNDERSTUDIES

For Richard/James:
TONY CARLIN

For Sarah/Mandy:
MONICA McCARTHY

MANHATTAN THEATRE CLUB
SAMUEL J. FRIEDMAN THEATRE

ARTISTIC DIRECTOR
LYNNE MEADOW

EXECUTIVE PRODUCER
BARRY GROVE

BY SPECIAL ARRANGEMENT WITH
NELLE NUGENT / WENDY FEDERMAN

PRESENTS

TIME STANDS STILL

BY
DONALD MARGULIES

WITH
ERIC BOGOSIAN   BRIAN D'ARCY JAMES   LAURA LINNEY   ALICIA SILVERSTONE

SCENIC DESIGN	COSTUME DESIGN	LIGHTING DESIGN	SOUND DESIGN
JOHN LEE BEATTY	RITA RYACK	PETER KACZOROWSKI	DARRON L WEST

ORIGINAL MUSIC	FIGHT DIRECTOR	PRODUCTION STAGE MANAGER
PETER GOLUB	THOMAS SCHALL	ROBERT BENNETT

DIRECTED BY
DANIEL SULLIVAN

GENERAL MANAGER	ASSOCIATE ARTISTIC DIRECTOR
FLORIE SEERY	MANDY GREENFIELD

DIRECTOR OF ARTISTIC DEVELOPMENT	DIRECTOR OF MARKETING	PRESS REPRESENTATIVE
JERRY PATCH	DEBRA WAXMAN-PILLA	BONEAU/BRYAN-BROWN

PRODUCTION MANAGER	DIRECTOR OF CASTING	DIRECTOR OF DEVELOPMENT
KURT GARDNER	NANCY PICCIONE	JILL TURNER LLOYD

Originally commissioned and produced by the Geffen Playhouse,
Gil Cates, Producing Director, Randall Arney, Artistic Director.

Special thanks to the Harold and Mimi Steinberg Charitable Trust
for supporting new American plays at Manhattan Theatre Club.

Manhattan Theatre Club wishes to express its appreciation to
Theatre Development Fund for its support of this production.

1/28/10

(L-R): Laura Linney, Brian d'Arcy James and Eric Bogosian

Photo by Joan Marcus

Time Stands Still

Eric Bogosian
Richard Ehrlich

Brian d'Arcy James
James Dodd

Laura Linney
Sarah Goodwin

Alicia Silverstone
Mandy Bloom

Tony Carlin
u/s James/Richard

Monica McCarthy
u/s Sarah/Mandy

Donald Margulies
Playwright

Daniel Sullivan
Director

John Lee Beatty
Scenic Design

Peter Kaczorowski
Lighting Design

Darron L West
Sound Design

Peter Golub
Original Music

Lynne Meadow
*Artistic Director,
Manhattan Theatre
Club, Inc.*

Barry Grove
*Executive Producer,
Manhattan Theatre
Club, Inc.*

Wendy Federman

BOX OFFICE
(L-R): David Dillon, Jeffrey Davis

FRONT OF HOUSE STAFF
Front Row (L-R): Colleen Gallagher, John Wyffels, Nilsa Nairn, Christine Ehren

Back Row (L-R): Richard Ponce, Alicia Mangelsdorf, Jim Joseph, Jackson Ero

CREW
Front Row (L-R): Angela Simpson, Timothy Coffey, Michael Growler

Middle Row (L-R): Ian Harbor (with Monkey), Natasha Steinhagen, Mystery Guest

Back Row (L-R): Jeff Dodson, Chris Wiggins, Tim Walters, Lou Shapiro, Jason Dodds

Time Stands Still

(L-R): Laura Linney and Alicia Silverstone

MANHATTAN THEATRE CLUB STAFF

Artistic Director	Lynne Meadow
Executive Producer	Barry Grove
General Manager	Florie Seery
Associate Artistic Director	Mandy Greenfield
Director of Artistic Development	Jerry Patch
Artistic Consultant	Daniel Sullivan
Director of Artistic Administration/ Assistant to the Artistic Director	Amy Gilkes Loe
Artistic Associate/Artistic Line Producer	Lisa McNulty
Musical Theatre Associate	Kevin Emrick
Administrative Assistant	Nicki Hunter
Assistant to the Executive Producer	Emily Hammond
Director of Casting	Nancy Piccione
Casting Associate	Kelly Gillespie
Literary Manager/Sloan Project Manager	Annie MacRae
Play Development Assistant	Alex Barron
Musical Theatre Consultant	Clifford Lee Johnson III
Director of Development	Jill Turner Lloyd
Director, Individual Giving	Jeremy Blocker
Director, Institutional Giving	Roger Kingsepp
Director, Special Events	Antonello Di Benedetto
Manager, Individual Giving	Emily Fleisher
Manager, Institutional Giving	Andrea Gorzell
Development Associate/Individual Giving	Allison Taylor
Development Associate/Institutional Giving	Laurel Bear
Development Associate/Special Events	Samantha Mascali
Development Associate/Database Coordinator	Kelly Haydon
Patrons' Liaison	Chad Jones
Director of Marketing	Debra Waxman-Pilla
Assistant Director of Marketing	Sunil Ayyagari
Marketing Associate	Caitlin Baird
Director of Finance	Jeffrey Bledsoe
Human Resources Manager	Darren Robertson
Finance Associate	Adam Cook
Business Assistant	Gillian Campbell
IT Manager	Mendy Sudranski
Systems Administrator	Carsten Losse
Receptionist/Studio Coordinator	Thatcher Stevens
Associate General Manager	Lindsey Brooks Sag
Company Manager/NY City Center	Erin Moeller
General Management Assistant	Ann Mundorff
General Management Consultant	Deborah Hartnett
Director of Subscriber Services	Robert Allenberg
Associate Subscriber Services Manager	Andrew Taylor
Subscriber Services Representatives	Mark Bowers, Matthew Praet, Rosanna Consalva Sarto, Amber Wilkerson
Director of Telesales and Telefunding	George Tetlow
Assistant Manager	Terrence Burnett
Telemarketing Staff	Stephen Brown, Kel Haney, Kate Sessions
Director of Education	David Shookhoff
Asst. Director of Education/ Coordinator, Paul A. Kaplan Theatre Management Program	Amy Harris
Education Assistant, TheatreLink Coordinator	Julia Davis
Education Assistant	Kelli Bragdon
MTC Teaching Artists	Stephanie Alston, Carl Capataro, Chris Ceraso, Charlotte Colavin, Dominic Colon, Allison Daugherty, Gilbert Girion, Andy Goldberg, Elise Hernandez, Jeffrey Joseph, Julie Leedes, Kate Long, Louis D. Moreno, Andres Munar, Melissa Murray, Angela Pietropinto, Alexa Polmer, Alfonso Ramirez, Carmen Rivera, Judy Tate, Candido Tirado, Joe White
Theatre Management Interns	Katie Chambers, Tal Drori, Annah Feinberg, Courtney Hammond, Barbara Harrison, Robert Intile, Jane B. Jones, Aisha Jordan, Rebecca Kahane, Michelle Karst, Matthew Troillett
Production Manager	Kurt Gardner
Associate Production Manager	Joshua Helman
Assistant Production Manager	Kelsey Martinez
Properties Supervisor	Scott Laule
Assistant Properties Supervisor	Julia Sandy
Props Carpenter	Peter Grimes
Costume Supervisor	Erin Hennessy Dean

GENERAL PRESS REPRESENTATION
BONEAU/BRYAN-BROWN

Chris Boneau	Aaron Meier
Christine Olver	Emily Meagher

Script Readers .... Jeff Augustin, Aaron Grunfeld, Liz Jones, Portia Krieger, Rachel Slaven, Rebecca Stang

SERVICES

Accountants	ERE, LLP
Advertising	SpotCo/Drew Hodges, Tom Greenwald, Jim Edwards, Beth Watson, Tim Falotico
Web Design	Calico Systems
Legal Counsel	Charles H. Googe, Jr.; Carol M. Kaplan/ Paul, Weiss, Rifkind, Wharton and Garrison LLP
Real Estate Counsel	Marcus Attorneys
Labor Counsel	Harry H. Weintraub/ Glick and Weintraub, P.C.
Immigration Counsel	Theodore Ruthizer/ Kramer, Levin, Naftalis & Frankel, LLP
Sponsorship Consultant	Above the Title Entertainment/ Jed Bernstein
Insurance	Dewitt Stern Group, Inc./ Anthony Pittari
Maintenance	Reliable Cleaning
Production Photographer	Joan Marcus
Event Photography	Bruce Glikas
Cover Art	John Ritter
Cover Design	SpotCo
Theatre Displays	King Display

PRODUCTION STAFF FOR TIME STANDS STILL

Company Manager	Seth Shepsle
Production Stage Manager	Robert Bennett
Stage Manager	Shanna Spinello
Drama League – Assistant Director	Mia Rovegno
Assistant Scenic Designer	Kacie Hultgren
Assistant Costume Designer	Richard Schurkamp
Assistant Lighting Designer	Jake DeGroot
Assistant Sound Designer	Charles Coes
Make-Up Designer to Laura Linney	Mindy Hall
Video Editor	Rocco DiSanti
Hair/Make-Up Supervisor	Natasha Steinhagen
Dresser	Virginia Neininger
Lightboard Programmer	Marc Polimeni
Deck Crew	Timothy Coffey
Production Assistant	Aaron Gonzalez

CREDITS

MTC thanks the following people for sharing their expertise and experience with the company of *Time Stands Still*: Jonathan J. Glasberg, Lori Grinker, Jack Saul, Ph.D., Bruce Shapiro and Bob Woodruff.

Scenery fabrication by Hudson Scenic Studio. Lighting equipment provided by PRG Lighting. Sound equipment provided by Masque Sound. Computers for *Time Stands Still* were generously provided by Tekserve, New York's independent Apple specialist. Special thanks to Matthew Carleton and Lissette Schettini.

MUSIC/VIDEO CREDITS

"Bodysnatchers" (Thomas Edward Yorke, Jonathan Richard, Guy Greenwood, Colin Charles Greenwood, Edward John O'Brien and Philip James Selway) ©2008 Warner/Chappell Music Ltd (PRS). All rights administered by Warner-Tamerlane Publishing Corp. All rights reserved. Used by permission. *Invasion of the Body Snatchers* and *Friday the 13th, Part III* courtesy of Paramount Pictures.

For more information visit
www.ManhattanTheatreClub.com.
Find us on Facebook at "Manhattan Theatre Club,"
or follow us on Twitter @ MTC_NYC.

MANHATTAN THEATRE CLUB
SAMUEL J. FRIEDMAN THEATRE STAFF

Theatre Manager	Jim Joseph
Assistant House Manager	Richard Ponce
Box Office Treasurer	David Dillon
Assistant Box Office Treasurers	Jeffrey Davis, John Skelly
Head Carpenter	Chris Wiggins
Head Propertyman	Timothy Walters
Sound Engineer	Louis Shapiro
Master Electrician	Jeff Dodson
Wardrobe Supervisor	Angela Simpson
Apprentices	Jason Dodds, Ian Harbor
Chief Engineer	Deosarran
Maintenance Engineers	Ricky Deosarran, Maximo Perez
Security	Allied Barton
Lobby Refreshments	Sweet Concessions

Time Stands Still
Scrapbook

Correspondent: Shanna Spinello, Assistant Stage Manager
Opening Night Gifts: Laura Linney's mix CD. The Kind Diet! Good vegan treats.
Most Exciting Celebrity Visitor: Judge Judy!
Which Actor Performed the Most Roles in This Show: Shanna Spinello, ASM, at understudy rehearsal
Who Has Done the Most Shows in Their Career: Bob Bennett!
Mascot: DiDi, the calling desk pony.
Special Backstage Ritual: Pets from DiDi.
Favorite Snack Food: Girl Scout cookies, vegan goodies.
Favorite Therapy: Altoids.
Memorable Ad-Lib: "If you need anything, don't call me."
Fastest Costume Change: 21 seconds.
Catchphrase Only the Company Would Recognize: "Kissy, Kissy."

1. The cast takes bows on the stage of the Samuel J. Friedman Theatre on opening night.

2. Director Daniel Sullivan on hand for the premiere.

3. Brian d'Arcy James arrives at the Times Square Planet Hollywood for the cast party.

4. Laura Linney on opening night.

5. Eric Bogosian at Planet Hollywood.

6. Alicia Silverstone at the opening night party.

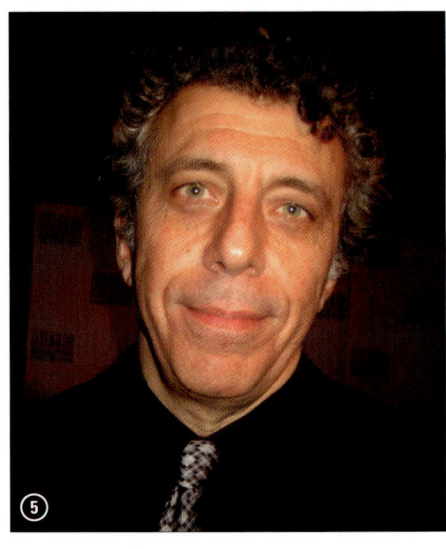

A View From the Bridge

First Preview: December 28, 2009. Opened: January 24, 2010.
Closed April 4, 2010 after 30 Previews and 81 Performances.

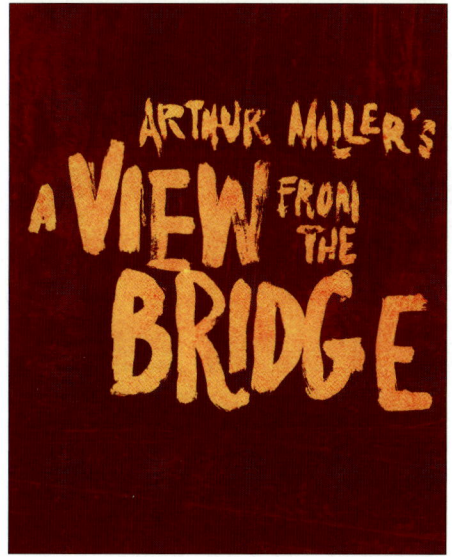

CAST
(in order of appearance)

Louis	ROBERT TURANO
Mike	JOE RICCI
Alfieri	MICHAEL CRISTOFER
Eddie	LIEV SCHREIBER
Catherine	SCARLETT JOHANSSON
Beatrice	JESSICA HECHT
Marco	COREY STOLL
Tony	MATTHEW MONTELONGO
Rodolpho	MORGAN SPECTOR
1st Immigration Officer	ANTHONY DeSANDO
2nd Immigration Officer	MARCO VERNA
Submarines	MATTHEW MONTELONGO, ALEX CENDESE
Mr. Lipari	MARK MORETTINI
Mrs. Lipari	ANTOINETTE LaVECCHIA
Stage Manager	THEA BRADSHAW SCOTT

UNDERSTUDIES
Eddie: ANTHONY DeSANDO
Catherine, Mrs. Lipari: BONNIE DENNISON
Beatrice: ANTOINETTE LaVECCHIA
Alfieri: MARK MORETTINI
Marco: MARCO VERNA, MATTHEW MONTELONGO
Louis, Mike: JIM IORIO, MARCO VERNA
Tony: ALEX CENDESE
1st and 2nd Immigration Officers, Submarines:
ALEX CENDESE, JIM IORIO
Mr. Lipari: JIM IORIO

CORT THEATRE
138 West 48th Street
A Shubert Organization Theatre
Philip J. Smith, *Chairman*   **Robert E. Wankel**, *President*

STUART THOMPSON   THE ARACA GROUP
JEFFREY FINN   BROADWAY ACROSS AMERICA
OLYMPUS THEATRICALS   MARISA SECHREST   THE WEINSTEIN COMPANY
JON B. PLATT   SONIA FRIEDMAN PRODUCTIONS/ROBERT G. BARTNER
MORT SWINSKY/JOSEPH DEITCH   ADAM ZOTOVICH/RUTH HENDEL/ORIN WOLF
SHELTER ISLAND ENTERPRISES   THE SHUBERT ORGANIZATION

PRESENT

LIEV SCHREIBER   **SCARLETT JOHANSSON**
JESSICA HECHT

IN

ARTHUR MILLER'S
A View From the Bridge

WITH

MICHAEL CRISTOFER
MORGAN SPECTOR   COREY STOLL

ALEX CENDESE   ANTHONY DeSANDO   ANTOINETTE LaVECCHIA   MATTHEW MONTELONGO
MARK MORETTINI   JOE RICCI   ROBERT TURANO   MARCO VERNA

SCENIC DESIGN	COSTUME DESIGN	LIGHTING DESIGN	SOUND DESIGN
JOHN LEE BEATTY	JANE GREENWOOD	PETER KACZOROWSKI	SCOTT LEHRER
HAIR & WIG DESIGN	CASTING	DIALECT COACH	PRODUCTION STAGE MANAGER
TOM WATSON	CINDY TOLAN	STEPHEN GABIS	WILLIAM JOSEPH BARNES
PRESS REPRESENTATIVE	PRODUCTION MANAGEMENT		GENERAL MANAGEMENT
BONEAU/BRYAN-BROWN	HUDSON THEATRICAL ASSOCIATES		STP/DAVID TURNER

DIRECTED BY

GREGORY MOSHER

The producers wish to express their appreciation to
Theatre Development Fund for its support of this production.

1/24/10

(L-R): Scarlett Johansson, Jessica Hecht and Liev Schreiber

Photo by Joan Marcus

A View From the Bridge

Liev Schreiber
Eddie

Scarlett Johansson
Catherine

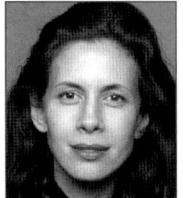
Jessica Hecht
Beatrice

Michael Cristofer
Alfieri

Morgan Spector
Rodolpho

Corey Stoll
Marco

Alex Cendese
Submarine #2, Neighbor

Anthony DeSando
Fed #1/Guard

Antoinette LaVecchia
Mrs. Lipari

Matthew Montelongo
Tony, Submarine #1, Neighbor

Mark Morettini
Mr. Lipari

Joe Ricci
Mike

Robert Turano
Louis

Marco Verna
Fed #2, Guard

Bonnie Dennison
u/s Catherine

Jim Iorio
Understudy

Arthur Miller
Playwright; 1915-2005

Gregory Mosher
Director

John Lee Beatty
Scenic Design

Jane Greenwood
Costume Design

Peter Kaczorowski
Lighting Design

Scott Lehrer
Sound Design

Tom Watson
Hair and Wig Design

Stephen Gabis
Dialect Coach

Neil A. Mazzella/ Hudson Theatrical Associates
Technical Supervision

Stuart Thompson
Producer

Jeffrey Finn
Producer

John Gore,
CEO,
Broadway Across America
Producer

Thomas B. McGrath, Chairman, Broadway Across America
Producer

Marisa Sechrest
Producer

Bob Weinstein, The Weinstein Company
Producer

Harvey Weinstein, The Weinstein Company
Producer

Jon B. Platt
Producer

Sonia Friedman Productions Ltd.
Producer

Mort Swinsky
Producer

A View From the Bridge

 Adam Zotovich, *Producer*

 Ruth Hendel, *Producer*

 Philip J. Smith, Chairman, The Shubert Organization, *Producer*

 Robert E. Wankel, President, The Shubert Organization, *Producer*

 Santino Fontana, *Rodolpho*

 William Connell, u/s 1st and 2nd Immigration Officers, Rodolpho, Submarines, Tony

USHERS
Top Row (L-R): William Denson, Lynette Myers, Robert De Jesus, Robert Evans
Bottom Row (L-R): Tia Hefner, Hilda McQuillen, Taylor Tricarico, Felicia Farr

BOX OFFICE
Mike Lynch, Gerard O'Brien

CREW
Front Row (L-R): Lyle Jones, Jim VanBergen, Billy Barnes, Scott Deverna

Back Row (L-R): Scott Monroe, Jill Heller, Claire Verlaet, Carrie Kamerer, Katie Beatty, Thea Bradshaw Scott, Lonnie Gaddy

The Playbill Broadway Yearbook 2009-2010

A View From the Bridge

2009-2010 AWARDS

TONY AWARD
Best Featured Actress in an Play
(Scarlett Johansson)

DRAMA DESK AWARDS
Outstanding Revival of a Play
Outstanding Actor in a Play
(Liev Schreiber)

DRAMA LEAGUE AWARD
Distinguished Revival of a Play

THEATRE WORLD AWARD
First Major New York Appearance
(Scarlett Johansson)

(L-R): Scarlett Johansson, Liev Schreiber and Morgan Spector

Photo by Joan Marcus

STAFF FOR *A VIEW FROM THE BRIDGE*

GENERAL MANAGEMENT
STUART THOMPSON PRODUCTIONS
Stuart Thompson David Turner James Triner

COMPANY MANAGER
Nathan Gehan

PRODUCTION MANAGEMENT
HUDSON THEATRICALS ASSOCIATES
Neil Mazzella Sam Ellis

PRESS REPRESENTATIVE
BONEAU/BRYAN-BROWN
Chris Boneau Susanne Tighe Christine Olver

MARKETING DIRECTION
TYPE A MARKETING
Anne Rippey Nick Pramik Elyce Henkin

INTERNET MARKETING
THE ARACA GROUP

FIGHT DIRECTOR
Thomas Schall

Production Stage Manager	William Joseph Barnes
Stage Manager	Thea Bradshaw Scott
Associate Scenic Designer	Kacie Hultgren
Associate Costume Designer	Wade Laboissonniere
Associate Lighting Designer	John Viesta
Associate Sound Designer	Alex Hawthorn
Assistant to Mr. Mosher	Christopher Thomasson
Fight Captain	Corey Stoll
Dialect Coach	Stephen Gabis
Production Carpenter	Edward Diaz
Production Electrician	Scott Deverna
Advance Props	Scott Laule
Production Props	Scott Monroe
Production Sound	Jim vanBergen
Makeup Consultant	Cookie Jordan
Wardrobe Supervisor	Lyle Jones
Dresser for Ms. Johansson	Kelly A. Saxon
Hair Supervisor	Katie Beatty
Dressers	Carrie Kamerer, Claire Verlaet
Production Assistants	Kathryn McKee, Ashley Bigge
General Management Assistants	Geo Karapetyan, Brittany Levasseur
General Management Interns	Erin Byrne, Andrew Lowy
Costume Assistants	Luke Brown, Amanda Seymour
Casting Associate	Adam Caldwell
Assistant to Mr. Thompson	Christopher Taggart

The Araca Group

Director of Development	Amanda Guettel
Internet Marketing Acct Exec	Kristen Butler
Executive Assistants	Alyson Zeitz, Sarah Grace Welbourn, Danielle Von Gal
Business Affairs Associate	Lindsay Meck

Banking	City National Bank/Michele Gibbons
Payroll	Castellana Services, Inc.
Accountant	Fried & Kowgios CPA's LLP/Robert Fried, CPA
Controller	Joe Kubala
Insurance	DeWitt Stern Group
Legal Counsel	Davis Wright Tremaine LLP/M. Graham Coleman, Robert Driscoll
Advertising	SpotCo/Drew Hodges, Jim Edwards, Tom Greenwald, Stephen Sosnowski, Meghan Ownbey
Production Photographer	Joan Marcus
Liev Schreiber Headshot	Nigel Parry/CPi
Theatre Displays	King Displays, Inc.
Transportation	Elegant Limousines, IBA Limousines, KSW Transportation

CREDITS

Scenery by Hudson Scenic Studio, Inc. Lighting and sound equipment from PRG. Costumes by Eric Winterling, Inc. Aging and distressing by Izquierdo Studio. Knitwear by Mary Pat Klein. Undergarments by Bra*Tenders. Makeup provided by M•A•C Cosmetics. Rehearsed at Second Stage Theatre. "Paper Doll" performed by the Mills Brothers courtesy of Ranwood Records.

 THE SHUBERT ORGANIZATION, INC.
Board of Directors

Philip J. Smith Chairman	**Robert E. Wankel** President
Wyche Fowler, Jr.	**John W. Kluge**
Lee J. Seidler	**Michael I. Sovern**

Stuart Subotnick

Elliot Greene Chief Financial Officer	**David Andrews** Senior Vice President – Shubert Ticketing
Juan Calvo Vice President and Controller	**John Darby** Vice President – Facilities
Peter Entin Vice President – Theatre Operations	**Charles Flateman** Vice President – Marketing
Anthony LaMattina Vice President – Audit & Production Finance	**Brian Mahoney** Vice President – Ticket Sales

D.S. Moynihan
Vice President – Creative Projects

CORT THEATRE
House Manager .... Joseph Traina

A View From the Bridge
SCRAPBOOK

1. The cast takes a curtain call on opening night.
2. Director Gregory Mosher at Espace for the cast party.
3. Naomi Watts and cast member Liev Schreiber at Espace on opening night.

Photos by Aubrey Reuben

Correspondent: William Joseph Barnes, Production Stage Manager

Memorable Opening Night Messages: It was very cool to see faxes we got from many of the Broadway shows hanging by the call board.

Opening Night Gifts: Hard bound and dated copy of the play complete with cast listing; Brooklyn Bridge photos from Liev.

Most Exciting Celebrity Visitors and What They Did/Said: Meryl Streep told Joe Ricci he was "just hysterical." Bono wanted to know how the set looked like it "continues forever" off stage right. Jim Gandolfini sending a deli spread and shouting "are you naked??" in the stairway.

Actor Who Performed the Most Roles in This Show: Morgan Spector: Tony and Submarine in previews, then Rodolpho.

Special Backstage Rituals: 500 Rummy during intermission. A different quote from the show was posted each night by Kelly Saxon and attributed to our doorman Smitty. Smoking on the fire escape. Shots (AFTER the show).

Actor Who Has Done the Most Shows: Liev Schreiber: five Broadway shows.

Favorite Moments During Each Performance: When Scarlett, Liev and Jessica eat tomato sauce and tofu. When Michael Cristofer clears his throat at the top-of-show stand by call. The death scene... almost everyone is onstage.

In-Theatre Gathering Place: Guys dressing room on the third floor. It's been dubbed Top O' the Cort. There's cocktails, darts and Trivial Pursuit. It like a Boy's and Girl's Clubs of America but without the positive influence.

Favorite Off-Site Hangouts: Hurley's, Glass House Tavern, Bar Centrale.

Favorite Snack Foods: Anything that Corey Stoll's Aunt Cathy bakes. Scarlett's gluten-free banana chocolate chip muffins (with no refined sugar!)

Mascot: Smitty, our 87-year old night doorman.

Favorite Therapies: Ricola, Throat-Coat Tea, cigarettes, the amazing pastries that Corey's Aunt Cathy bakes.

Memorable Ad-libs: "Eh," "Yiz know," "Listen."

Cell Phone Rings, Photos or Texts: There was a ring right after Eddie died. It made us think of the old theatre joke: "Oh dear, I do hope it's not for Eddie Carbone!"

Memorable Press Encounters: Joe Ricci, Robert Turano, Mark Morettini and Alex Cendese walking the press line together at opening night. Scarlett on Letterman.

Memorable Stage Door Fan Encounter: One day after the show, Joe Ricci exited and someone took a picture of him thinking he was someone important and, deciding he wasn't, said "Ughhhh! DELETE!"

Internet Buzz: It was very cool. Having a combination of celebrities and so many great reviews.

Latest Audience Arrival: Top of Act II. Granted, it was a Tuesday and there was a 7 PM curtain, but, come on! Also: The crazy man with the blue guitar charging down the aisle a half hour in.

Fastest Costume Changes: Both 30 seconds: Jessica shoe change and coat Scene 2 into Scene 3. Scarlett into wedding dress.

Busiest Day at the Box Office: The day after opening. We did $500,000 in sales.

Who Wore the Heaviest Costume: Liev wears a scuba vest with blood bag and industrial magnet target for the retractable knife under two shirts and a heavy coat.

Who Wore the Hottest Costume: Joe Ricci wears a T-shirt, Henley shirt, flannel shirt, scarf, boiled wool jacket, fleece jacket and hat.

Who Wore the Least: Scarlett. Just a dress.

Catchphrases Only the Company Would Recognize: "Red Hookers." "PULL THE GATE!!" "He's like a weird."

Memorable Directorial Notes: "I want it to look like you're bumping up against each other in a little apartment, not running around on a Broadway stage." "Don't forget the twirl." "Cleaner, simpler."

Company Legend: The 6'6" drunk guy with the blue guitar who pushed past the ticket taker during the show, walked down the aisle and leaned on the edge of the stage until security removed him.

Nicknames: Smitsters, Bonnie Pants or Boots (Bonnie Dennison).

Sweethearts Within the Company: Liev and Morgan. LOL.

Embarrassing Moment: Liev hocked a loogie on Scarlett.

Ghostly Encounters Backstage: Ours would have to be the Cort Theatre heating system but Scarlett swore she heard a ghost saying, "You have no business on Broadway" on the first day of rehearsal. Turns out it was the five-gallon coffee urn heating up.

Coolest Thing About Being in This Show: Besides the sex and violence, it would have to be the constant stream of celebrities backstage.

Also: Michael Cristofer, who made his Broadway acting debut playing Alfieri, won a Writers Guild Award for "Georgia O'Keefe" during the run.

West Side Story

First Preview: February 23, 2009. Opened: March 19, 2009.
Still running as of May 31, 2010.

CAST

The Jets

Action	WES HART
Anybodys	SARA DOBBS
A-rab	KYLE COFFMAN
Baby John	RYAN STEELE
Big Deal	MIKEY WINSLOW
Diesel	JOSHUA BUSCHER
Graziella	PAMELA OTTERSON
Hotsie	MARINA LAZZARETTO
Kiddo	KYLE BRENN

(Tues., Wed., Fri., Sat. eves.)
MICHAEL KLEEMAN
(Wed., Sat. & Sun. mats. & Thurs. eve.)

Mugsy	AMY RYERSON
Riff	JOHN ARTHUR GREENE
Snowboy	MIKE CANNON
Tony	MATTHEW HYDZIK

(Tues., Thurs., Fri., Sat. eves.; Wed. & Sat. mats.)
JEREMY JORDAN
(Wed. eve. & Sun. mat.)

Velma	LINDSAY DUNN
Zaza	KAITLIN MESH
4H	SAM ROGERS

The Sharks

Alicia	SAMANTHA SHAFER
Anita	KAREN OLIVO
Bebecita	MILEYKA MATEO
Bernardo	GEORGE AKRAM
Bolo	PETER CHURSIN
Chino	MICHAEL ROSEN

Continued on next page

PALACE THEATRE
UNDER THE DIRECTION OF
STEWART F. LANE, JAMES M. NEDERLANDER AND JAMES L. NEDERLANDER

Kevin McCollum   James L. Nederlander   Jeffrey Seller
Terry Allen Kramer   Sander Jacobs
Roy Furman/Jill Furman Willis   Freddy DeMann   Robyn Goodman/Walt Grossman   Hal Luftig
Roy Miller   The Weinstein Company   Broadway Across America

PRESENT

West Side Story
Based on a conception of JEROME ROBBINS

BOOK BY **Arthur Laurents**   MUSIC BY **Leonard Bernstein**   LYRICS BY **Stephen Sondheim**

ENTIRE ORIGINAL PRODUCTION DIRECTED AND CHOREOGRAPHED BY
Jerome Robbins

STARRING
Matthew Hydzik   Josefina Scaglione
Karen Olivo   John Arthur Greene   George Akram

At certain performances
Jeremy Jordan
plays the role of "Tony."

WITH
Steve Bassett   Kyle Brenn   Joshua Buscher   Mike Cannon   Kyle Coffman   Sara Dobbs   Wes Hart   Michael Kleeman
Michael Mastro   Michael Rosen   Lee Sellars   Ryan Steele   Greg Vinkler   Mikey Winslow   Mark Zimmerman
Isaac Calpito   Gabriel Canett   Haley Carlucci   Peter Chursin   Natalie Cortez   Kristine Covillo
Lindsay Dunn   Yurel Echezarreta   Marina Lazzaretto   Mileyka Mateo   Kaitlin Mesh   Shina Ann Morris
Angelina Mullins   Kat Nejat   Pamela Otterson   Colt Prattes   Alex Ringler   Sam Rogers
Amy Ryerson   Jennifer Sanchez   Manuel Santos   Samantha Shafer   Phillip Spaeth
Brendon Stimson   CJ Tyson   Tanairi Sade Vazquez   Michael Williams

SCENIC DESIGN	COSTUME DESIGN	LIGHTING DESIGN	SOUND DESIGN
James Youmans	David C. Woolard	Howell Binkley	Dan Moses Schreier
WIGS & HAIR DESIGN	MAKE-UP DESIGN	CASTING	TRANSLATIONS
Mark Adam Rampmeyer	Angelina Avallone	Howard/Schecter/Hardt	Lin-Manuel Miranda
ASSOCIATE DIRECTOR	ASSOCIATE CHOREOGRAPHER	ASSOCIATE PRODUCER	PRODUCTION STAGE MANAGER
David Saint	Lori Werner	LAMS Productions	Joshua Halperin
ORIGINAL BROADWAY PRODUCTION CO-CHOREOGRAPHED BY	ORCHESTRATIONS	ARRANGEMENTS	GENERAL MANAGEMENT
Peter Gennaro	Leonard Bernstein with Sid Ramin and Irwin Kostal	Stephen Sondheim Patrick Vaccariello and Garth Edwin Sunderland	Charlotte Wilcox Company
MUSIC COORDINATOR	TECHNICAL SUPERVISOR	MARKETING	PRESS REPRESENTATIVE
Michael Keller	Brian Lynch	Scott A. Moore	The Hartman Group

MUSIC SUPERVISOR / MUSIC DIRECTOR
Patrick Vaccariello

CHOREOGRAPHY REPRODUCED BY
Joey McKneely

DIRECTED BY
Arthur Laurents

New Broadway cast recording available on Masterworks Broadway

12/14/09

(L-R): Josefina Scaglione and Matthew Hydzik

Photo by Joan Marcus

West Side Story

SCENES AND MUSICAL NUMBERS

ACT ONE

Scene 1: The Neighborhood
  "Prologue" .... The Sharks and the Jets
  "Jet Song" .... Riff and the Jets
Scene 2: Outside Doc's Drugstore
  "Something's Coming" .... Tony
Scene 3: Bridal Shop
Scene 4: The Gym
  "Dance at the Gym" .... Company
  "Maria" .... Tony
Scene 5: Alleyways
  "Tonight" .... Tony and Maria
  "America" .... Anita, Rosalia and Shark Girls
Scene 6: The Drugstore
  "Cool" .... Riff, Jet Boys and Jet Girls
Scene 7: Bridal Shop
  "One Hand, One Heart" .... Tony and Maria
Scene 8: The Neighborhood
  "Tonight" (Quintet) .... Company
Scene 9: Under the Highway
  "The Rumble"

ACT TWO

Scene 1: Maria's Bedroom
  "Me Siento Hermosa" ("I Feel Pretty") .... Maria, Rosalia, Consuela and Fernanda
  "Somewhere" .... Kiddo, Tony, Maria and Company
Scene 2: The Neighborhood
  "Gee, Officer Krupke" .... Action and the Jets
Scene 3: Maria's Bedroom
  "A Boy Like That"/"I Have a Love" .... Anita and Maria
Scene 4: The Drugstore
Scene 5: The Cellar
Scene 6: The Neighborhood

Cast Continued

Consuela	SHINA ANN MORRIS
Federico	PHILLIP SPAETH
Fernanda	KAT NEJAT
Inca	ISAAC CALPITO
Indio	MANUEL SANTOS
Lupe	TANAIRI SADE VAZQUEZ
Maria	JOSEFINA SCAGLIONE
Pepe	GABRIEL CANETT
Rosalia	JENNIFER SANCHEZ
Tio	YUREL ECHEZARRETA

The Adults

Doc	GREG VINKLER
Glad Hand	MICHAEL MASTRO
Krupke	LEE SELLARS
Lt. Schrank	STEVE BASSETT

SWINGS
HALEY CARLUCCI, NATALIE CORTEZ, KRISTINE COVILLO, ANGELINA MULLINS, COLT PRATTES, ALEX RINGLER, BRENDON STIMSON, CJ TYSON, MICHAEL WILLIAMS

UNDERSTUDIES
For Action: COLT PRATTES
For Anita: NATALIE CORTEZ, KAT NEJAT, JENNIFER SANCHEZ
For Anybodys: PAMELA OTTERSON, KAITLIN MESH
For A-rab and Baby John: SAM ROGERS, BRENDON STIMSON
For Bernardo: GABRIEL CANETT, MANUEL SANTOS
For Big Deal: JOSHUA BUSCHER, SAM ROGERS
For Chino: MANUEL SANTOS, PHILLIP SPAETH
For Consuela: SAMANTHA SHAFER, TANAIRI SADE VAZQUEZ
For Diesel: COLT PRATTES, ALEX RINGLER
For Fernanda: HALEY CARLUCCI, SAMANTHA SHAFER
For Glad Hand: LEE SELLARS
For Graziella: AMY RYERSON, LINDSAY DUNN
For Maria: HALEY CARLUCCI, KAT NEJAT
For Riff: MIKE CANNON, WES HART, COLT PRATTES
For Rosalia: HALEY CARLUCCI, KAT NEJAT, SAMANTHA SHAFER
For Snowboy: ALEX RINGLER, BRENDON STIMSON
For Tony: MIKE CANNON
Standby for Doc, Glad Hand, Krupke, Lt. Schrank: MARK ZIMMERMAN

Dance Captain .... MARINA LAZZARETTO
Fight Captain .... JOSHUA BUSCHER

Josefina Scaglione appears with the permission of Actors' Equity Association.

SETTING
Upper West Side of New York City

ORCHESTRA
Conductor: PATRICK VACCARIELLO
Associate Conductor: MAGGIE TORRE
Concertmaster: MARTIN AGEE
Violins: PAUL WOODIEL, ROB SHAW, VICTORIA PATERSON, FRITZ KRAKOWSKI, DANA IANCULOVICI, PHILIP PAYTON
Cellos: PETER PROSSER, VIVIAN ISRAEL, DIANE BARERE, JENNIFER LANG
Bass: BILL SLOAT
Reed 1: LAWRENCE FELDMAN
Reed 2: LINO GOMEZ
Reed 3: DAN WILLIS
Reed 4: ADAM KOLKER
Reed 5: GILBERT DeJEAN
Lead Trumpet: JOHN CHUDOBA
Trumpets: TREVOR NEUMANN, MATT PETERSON
Trombone: TIM ALBRIGHT
Bass Trombone: JEFF NELSON
French Horns: CHRIS KOMER, THERESA MacDONNELL
Piano: MAGGIE TORRE
Keyboard: JIM LAEV
Drums: ERIC POLAND
Percussion: DAN McMILLAN, PABLO RIEPPI
Music Coordinator: MICHAEL KELLER
Keyboard Programmer: RANDY COHEN

West Side Story

 Matthew Hydzik *Tony at certain performances*

 Josefina Scaglione *Maria*

 Karen Olivo *Anita*

 John Arthur Greene *Riff*

 George Akram *Bernardo*

 Jeremy Jordan *Tony at certain performances*

 Steve Bassett *Lt. Schrank*

 Mike Cannon *Snowboy*

 Kyle Coffman *A-rab*

 Sara Dobbs *Anybodys*

 Wes Hart *Action*

 Michael Mastro *Glad Hand*

 Michael Rosen *Chino*

 Lee Sellars *Krupke*

 Ryan Steele *Baby John*

 Greg Vinkler *Doc*

 Mikey Winslow *Big Deal*

 Mark Zimmerman *Adult Standby*

 Kyle Brenn *Kiddo at certain performances*

 Joshua Buscher *Diesel*

 Isaac Calpito *Inca*

 Gabriel Canett *Pepe*

 Haley Carlucci *Maria Standby*

 Peter Chursin *Bolo*

 Natalie Cortez *Swing*

 Kristine Covillo *Swing*

 Lindsay Dunn *Velma*

 Yurel Echezarreta *Tio*

 Michael Kleeman *Kiddo at certain performances*

 Marina Lazzaretto *Hotsie; Dance Captain*

 Mileyka Mateo *Bebecita*

 Kaitlin Mesh *Zaza*

 Shina Ann Morris *Consuela*

 Angelina Mullins *Swing*

 Kat Nejat *Fernanda*

West Side Story

 Pamela Otterson
Graziella

 Colt Prattes
Swing

 Alex Ringler
Swing

 Sam Rogers
4H

 Amy Ryerson
Mugsy

 Jennifer Sanchez
Rosalia

 Manuel Santos
Indio

 Samantha Shafer
Alicia

 Phillip Spaeth
Federico

 Brendon Stimson
Swing

 CJ Tyson
Swing

 Tanairi Sade Vazquez
Lupe

 Michael Williams
Swing

 Arthur Laurents
Book, Director

 Leonard Bernstein
Music

 Stephen Sondheim
Lyrics

 Jerome Robbins
Choreography

 Joey McKneely and Lori Werner
Reproduction Choreographer; Associate Choreographer

 Patrick Vaccariello
Music Supervisor/ Music Director

 James Youmans
Scenic Design

 David C. Woolard
Costume Design

 Howell Binkley
Lighting Design

 Dan Moses Schreier
Sound Design

 David Saint
Associate Director

 Lin-Manuel Miranda
Translations

 The Charlotte Wilcox Company
General Manager

 Michael Keller
Music Coordinator

 Brian Lynch
Technical Supervision

 Kevin McCollum
Producer

 James L. Nederlander
Producer

 Jeffrey Seller
Producer

 Terry Allen Kramer
Producer

 Sander Jacobs
Producer

 Freddy DeMann
Producer

West Side Story

 Roy Furman
Producer

 Jill Furman Willis
Producer

 Robyn Goodman
Producer

 Walt Grossman
Producer

 Hal Luftig
Producer

 Roy Miller
Producer

 Bob Weinstein, The Weinstein Company
Producer

 Harvey Weinstein, The Weinstein Company
Producer

 John Gore, CEO, Broadway Across America
Producer

 Thomas B. McGrath, Chairman, Broadway Across America
Producer

 Bradley Reynolds, Lams Productions
Associate Producer

 David Siesko, Lams Productions
Associate Producer

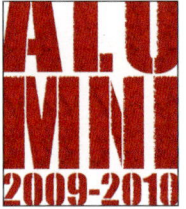 Nicholas Barasch
Kiddo

 J.R. Bruno
Swing

 Matt Cavenaugh
Tony

 Stephen Diaz
Swing

 Cody Green
Riff

 Joey Haro
Chino

 Eric Hatch
Big Deal

 Manuel Herrera
Pepe

 Curtis Holbrook
Action

 Chase Madigan
Swing

 Yanira Marin
Alicia

 Lauralyn McClelland
Swing

 Joseph Medeiros
Swing

 Janice Niggeling
Swing

 Christian Elán Ortiz
Swing

 Danielle Polanco
Consuela

 Tro Shaw
Anybodys

 Michaeljon Slinger
Assistant Dance Captain, Swing

 Jessica Bishop
Velma

 Jace Coronado
Tio

Stephen Diaz
Bolo

358   The Playbill Broadway Yearbook 2009-2010

West Side Story

Sean Ewing
Pepe

Yanira Marin
Alicia

Skye Mattox
Mugsy

Lauralyn McClelland
Swing

Alex Michael Stoll
Swing

2009-2010 AWARDS

GRAMMY AWARD
Best Musical Show Album

ACTORS EQUITY ACC AWARD
Outstanding Broadway Chorus

MANAGEMENT
(L-R): Jason Brouillard, Lisa Dawn Cave (in photo), Joshua Halperin, Tom Capps

FRONT OF HOUSE STAFF
Front Row (L-R): Paula Vanderlinden, Maria Agurto, Verne Shayne, Gina Sanabria, Gloria Syracuse

Back Row (L-R): Catherine Larocco, Diana Hosang, Scott Muso, Mike D'Arcy, Jennifer Kina

HAIR
(L-R): Pat Marcus, Armando Licon, Paula Schaffer

The Playbill Broadway Yearbook 2009-2010

West Side Story

WARDROBE
Front Row (L-R): Herb Ouellette, Allison Rogers, Sarah Hench, David Grevengoed

Back Row (L-R): Christopher Thorton, Roy Seiler, Hilda Suli-Garcia, Scott Westervelt, Stephanie Fox, Keith Shaw, Aryn Lawrence, Hector Lugo

CREW
Front Row (L-R): Tim Kovalenko, Dan Gaudreau, Rob Toscano, Cory Schmidt, Chuck Fields

Back Row (L-R): Jesse Hancox, Paul Baker, McBrien Dunbar, Chris Kluth, Steve Clem, Keith Buchanan, John Cullen

ORCHESTRA
Front Row: Patrick Vaccariello

Middle Row: Martin Agee

Back Row (L-R): Lawrence Feldman, Igor Scedrov, Karen Banos, Jennifer Baxmeyer, Vivian Israel, Gilbert DeJean, Jeremy Miloszewicz

West Side Story

BOX OFFICE
(L-R): Louie Waldron, Anne Wilson, John Yerkovich

STAFF FOR WEST SIDE STORY

GENERAL MANAGEMENT
THE CHARLOTTE WILCOX COMPANY
Charlotte W. Wilcox
Seth Marquette
Matthew W. Krawiec Dina S. Friedler Margaret Wilcox

GENERAL PRESS REPRESENTATIVE
THE HARTMAN GROUP
Michael Hartman
Wayne Wolfe   Alyssa Hart

COMPANY MANAGER
James Lawson

ASSOCIATE COMPANY MANAGER
Erica Ezold

DIRECTOR OF MARKETING
Scott A. Moore

CASTING
STUART HOWARD ASSOCIATES, LTD.
Stuart Howard   Amy Schecter   Paul Hardt

Production Stage Manager	Joshua Halperin
Stage Manager	Lisa Dawn Cave
Assistant Stage Manager	Jason Brouillard
Assistant to the Director	Isaac Klein
Assistant to Mssrs. McCollum & Seller	Caitlyn Thomson
Assistant to Mr. Nederlander	Ken Happel
Fight Director	Ron Piretti
Associate Scenic Designer	Jerome Martin
Assistant Costume Designers	Robert Martin, Daryl A. Stone, Maria Zamansky
Assistants to the Costume Designer	Sara James, Yuri Cataldo, Angela Harner
Associate Lighting Designer	Ryan O'Gara
Assistant Lighting Designer	Carrie Wood
Associate Sound Designer	David Bullard
Moving Light Programmer	David Arch
Head Carpenter/TheatreTech Associate	Cory Schmidt
Production Flyman	Bob Griffin
Automation Carpenters	McBrien Dunbar, Robert M. Hentze
Head Electrician	Jack Culver
Moving Light Technician	Chuck Fields
Spotlight Operator	Steve Clem
Production Properties Supervisor	George Wagner
Head Properties	Chuck Dague
Sound Engineer	Lucas Indelicato
Wardrobe Supervisor	Scott Westervelt
Assistant Wardrobe Supervisor	Jessica Dermody
Dressers	Scotty Cain, Stephanie Fox, Kasey Graham, David Grevengoed, Sarah Hench, Hector Lugo, Dorothy Manning, Herb Ouellette, Roy Seiler, Keith Shaw, Hilda Suli-Garcia
Hair Supervisor	Paula Schaffer
Assistant Hair Supervisors	Armando Licon, Pat Marcus
Assistant Keyboard Programmers	Bryan Cook, Jim Mironchik
Production Assistants	Rachel E. Miller, Zac Chandler
Language Consultant	Desiree Rodriguez
Legal Counsel	Levin, Plotkin & Menin, LLP
Accountants	Fried & Kowgios LLP/ Robert Fried
Controller	Galbraith & Co./ Sarah Galbraith
Advertising	SpotCo/ Drew Hodges, Jim Edwards, Tom Greenwald, Y. Darius Suyama, Pete Duffy
Website	SpotCo/ Sara Fitzpatrick, Matt Wilstein, Marc Mettler
Children's Tutoring	On Location Education
Children's Guardian	Libby Stevens
Press Office Associates	Leslie Baden, Michelle Bergmann, Nicole Capatasto, Tom D'Ambrosio, Juliana Hannett, Bethany Larsen, Matt Ross, Frances White
Marketing Associate	Joshua Lee Poole
Production Photography	Joan Marcus
Banking	JP Morgan Chase/ Stephanie Daulton
Payroll Service	Castellana Services, Inc.
Physical Therapy	PhysioArts/ Jennifer Green
Massage Therapist	Russell Beasley
Orthopedist	Phillip Bauman, MD
Group Sales	Nederlander Group Sales
Merchandise	Creative Goods/ Mike D'Arcy, Pete Milano
Insurance Consultant	Stockbridge Risk Management
Information Management Services	Marion Finkler Taylor
Travel Services	Tzell Travel/ Andi Henig, Road Rebel
Tour Booking Agency	The Booking Group/ Meredith Blair

Rehearsed at New 42nd Street Studios

CREDITS
Scenery built by Hudson Scenic Studio, Inc.; Show Motion, Inc.; Blackthorn Scenic Studio, Inc.; Scenic Art Studios, Inc.; Blackwalnut; Center Line Studios, Inc. Costumes by Tricorne Inc., Barbara Matera Ltd., Eric Winterling Inc., Timberlake Studios Inc., Giliberto Designs Inc., Beckenstein Men's Fabrics Inc. Custom knitwear by Maria Ficalora Knitwear Ltd. Footwear by JC Theatrical & Custom Footwear Inc., Capezio. Millinery by Arnold S. Levine Inc. Undergarments by Bra*Tenders. Costume ageing and distressing by Hochi Asiatico Studio. Accessories by David Samuel Menkes Custom Leatherwear New York. Lighting equipment from PRG Lighting. Sound equipment from PRG Sound. Mannequins and sewing machine provided by Fox Sewing Machines, New York, NY. Cigarette lighters courtesy of Zippo Lighters. Certain props constructed by John Creech Design and Production, Brooklyn, NY. Doc's window and interior shelves set dressing provided by Ann Pinkus, Monmouth Antiques, Red Bank, NJ.

Makeup provided by M•A•C

SPECIAL THANKS
Tom Hatcher, Federico del Piño Gonzales,
Fernando Masorllones

Chairman	**James M. Nederlander**
President	**James L. Nederlander**

Executive Vice President
Nick Scandalios

Vice President Corporate Development **Charlene S. Nederlander**	Senior Vice President Labor Relations **Herschel Waxman**
Vice President **Jim Boese**	Chief Financial Officer **Freida Sawyer Belviso**

STAFF FOR THE PALACE THEATRE

Theatre Manager	Dixon Rosario
Treasurer	Cissy Caspare
Assistant Treasurer	Anne T. Wilson
Carpenter	Thomas K. Phillips
Flyman	Robert W. Kelly
Electrician	Eddie Webber
Propertymaster	Steve Camus
Engineer	Rob O'Connor
Chief Usher	Gloria Hill

Wicked

First Preview: October 8, 2003. Opened: October 30, 2003.
Still running as of May 31, 2010.

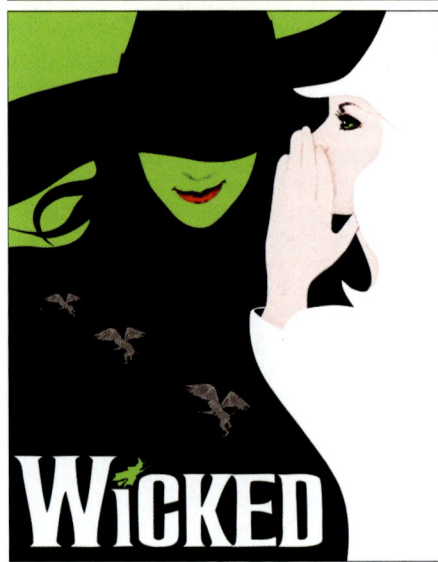

THE CAST
(in order of appearance)

Glinda	ERIN MACKEY
Witch's Father	MICHAEL DeVRIES
Witch's Mother	KRISTEN LEIGH GORSKI
Midwife	KATHY SANTEN
Elphaba	DEE ROSCIOLI
Nessarose	MICHELLE FEDERER
Boq	ALEX BRIGHTMAN
Madame Morrible	RONDI REED
Doctor Dillamond	TIMOTHY BRITTEN PARKER
Fiyero	KEVIN KERN
Ozian Official	MICHAEL DeVRIES
The Wonderful Wizard of Oz	P.J. BENJAMIN
Chistery	MARK SHUNKEY

Monkeys, Students, Denizens of the Emerald City, Palace Guards and Other Citizens of Oz .... NOVA BERGERON, SARAH BOLT, JERAD BORTZ, MICHAEL DeVRIES, MAIA EVWARAYE-GRIFFIN, ADAM FLEMING, KRISTEN LEIGH GORSKI, CHELSEA KROMBACH, KENWAY HON WAI K. KUA, KYLE DEAN MASSEY, JONATHAN McGILL, LINDSAY K. NORTHEN, RHEA PATTERSON, EDDIE PENDERGRAFT, ROBERT PENDILLA, ADAM PERRY, ALEXANDER QUIROGA, KATHY SANTEN, MARK SHUNKEY, HEATHER SPORE, RON TODOROWSKI, BRIAN WANEE, ROBIN WILNER

Continued on next page

GERSHWIN THEATRE
UNDER THE DIRECTION OF
JAMES M. NEDERLANDER AND JAMES L. NEDERLANDER

Marc Platt
Universal Pictures
The Araca Group   and   Jon B. Platt
David Stone
present

WICKED

Music and Lyrics
Stephen Schwartz

Book
Winnie Holzman

Based on the novel by Gregory Maguire

starring
Dee Roscioli   **Erin Mackey**

also starring
Kevin Kern

Alex Brightman   Michelle Federer   Timothy Britten Parker

Nova Bergeron Sarah Bolt Jerad Bortz Michael DeVries Maia Evwaraye-Griffin
Adam Fleming Anthony Galde Kristen Leigh Gorski Brenda Hamilton Lindsay Janisse
Chelsea Krombach Kenway Hon Wai K. Kua Kyle Dean Massey Jonathan McGill
Lindsay K. Northen Rhea Patterson Eddie Pendergraft Robert Pendilla Adam Perry
Alexander Quiroga Kathy Santen Mark Shunkey Heather Spore Ron Todorowski
Brian Wanee Jonathan Warren Robin Wilner Briana Yacavone

and
Rondi Reed   **P.J. Benjamin**

Settings	Costumes	Lighting	Sound
Eugene Lee	Susan Hilferty	Kenneth Posner	Tony Meola
Projections	Wigs & Hair	Production Supervisor	Technical Supervisor
Elaine J. McCarthy	Tom Watson	Thom Widmann	Jake Bell
Music Arrangements	Associate Music Supervisor	Dance Arrangements	Music Coordinator
Alex Lacamoire & Stephen Oremus	Dominick Amendum	James Lynn Abbott	Michael Keller
Associate Set Designer	Special Effects	Associate Choreographer	Associate Director
Edward Pierce	Chic Silber	Corinne McFadden Herrera	Lisa Leguillou
Casting	Production Stage Manager	General Management	Press	Executive Producers
Telsey + Company	Marybeth Abel	321 Theatrical Management	The Hartman Group	Marcia Goldberg & Nina Essman

Orchestrations
William David Brohn

Music Supervisor
Stephen Oremus

Musical Staging by
Wayne Cilento

Directed by
Joe Mantello

Grammy Award-winning Original Cast Recording on DECCA BROADWAY

10/1/09

(L-R): Erin Mackey as Glinda and Dee Roscioli as Elphaba.

Photo by Joan Marcus

Wicked

MUSICAL NUMBERS

ACT I
"No One Mourns the Wicked" .... Glinda and Citizens of Oz
"Dear Old Shiz" .... Students
"The Wizard and I" .... Morrible, Elphaba
"What Is This Feeling?" .... Galinda, Elphaba and Students
"Something Bad" .... Dr. Dillamond and Elphaba
"Dancing Through Life" .... Fiyero, Galinda, Boq, Nessarose, Elphaba and Students
"Popular" .... Galinda
"I'm Not That Girl" .... Elphaba
"One Short Day" .... Elphaba, Glinda and Denizens of the Emerald City
"A Sentimental Man" .... The Wizard
"Defying Gravity" .... Elphaba, Glinda, Guards and Citizens of Oz

ACT II
"No One Mourns the Wicked" (reprise) .... Citizens of Oz
"Thank Goodness" .... Glinda, Morrible and Citizens of Oz
"The Wicked Witch of the East" .... Elphaba, Nessarose and Boq
"Wonderful" .... The Wizard and Elphaba
"I'm Not That Girl" (reprise) .... Glinda
"As Long As You're Mine" .... Elphaba and Fiyero
"No Good Deed" .... Elphaba
"March of the Witch Hunters" .... Boq and Citizens of Oz
"For Good" .... Glinda and Elphaba
"Finale" .... All

ORCHESTRA
Conductor: DOMINICK AMENDUM
Associate Conductor: DAVID EVANS
Assistant Conductor: BEN COHN

Concertmaster: CHRISTIAN HEBEL
Violin: VICTOR SCHULTZ
Viola: KEVIN ROY
Cello: DANNY MILLER
Harp: LAURA SHERMAN
Lead Trumpet: JON OWENS
Trumpet: TOM HOYT
Trombones: DALE KIRKLAND,
  DOUGLAS PURVIANCE
Flute: HELEN CAMPO
Oboe: TUCK LEE
Clarinet/Soprano Sax: JOHN MOSES
Bassoon/Baritone Sax/Clarinets: CHAD SMITH
French Horns: THEO PRIMIS,
  CHAD YARBROUGH
Drums: MATT VANDERENDE
Bass: KONRAD ADDERLEY
Piano/Synthesizer: BEN COHN
Keyboards: PAUL LOESEL, DAVID EVANS
Guitars: RIC MOLINA, GREG SKAFF
Percussion: ANDY JONES

Music Coordinator: MICHAEL KELLER

Cast Continued

UNDERSTUDIES and STANDBYS
Standby for Elphaba:
JENNIFER DiNOIA
Standby for Glinda:
LAURA WOYASZ

Understudy for Elphaba:
CHELSEA KROMBACH
For Glinda:
LINDSAY K. NORTHEN, HEATHER SPORE
For Fiyero:
JERAD BORTZ, ANTHONY GALDE,
KYLE DEAN MASSEY
For the Wizard and Dr. Dillamond:
MICHAEL DeVRIES, ANTHONY GALDE
For Madame Morrible:
SARAH BOLT, KATHY SANTEN
For Boq:
ADAM FLEMING, EDDIE PENDERGRAFT
For Nessarose and Midwife:
ROBIN WILNER, BRIANA YACAVONE
For Chistery:
BRIAN WANEE, JONATHAN WARREN
For Witch's Father and Ozian Official:
ANTHONY GALDE, ALEXANDER QUIROGA
For Witch's Mother:
LINDSAY JANISSE, ROBIN WILNER
For Midwife:
BRENDA HAMILTON.

Swings:
ANTHONY GALDE, BRENDA HAMILTON,
ROBERT PENDILLA, BRIANA YACAVONE

Dance Captains/Swings:
LINDSAY JANISSE, JONATHAN WARREN

Rondi Reed as Madame Morrible

Wicked

 Dee Roscioli *Elphaba*
 Erin Mackey *Glinda*
 Rondi Reed *Madame Morrible*
 P.J. Benjamin *The Wizard*
 Kevin Kern *Fiyero*
 Alex Brightman *Boq*
 Michelle Federer *Nessarose*

 Timothy Britten Parker *Doctor Dillamond*
 Jennifer DiNoia *Standby for Elphaba*
 Laura Woyasz *Standby for Glinda*
 Nova Bergeron *Ensemble*
 Sarah Bolt *Ensemble*
 Jerad Bortz *Ensemble*
 Michael DeVries *Witch's Father/Ozian Official*

 Maia Evwaraye-Griffin *Ensemble*
 Adam Fleming *Ensemble*
 Anthony Galde *Swing*
 Kristen Leigh Gorski *Ensemble; Witch's Mother*
 Brenda Hamilton *Swing*
 Lindsay Janisse *Dance Captain; Swing*
 Chelsea Krombach *Ensemble*

 Kenway Hon Wai K. Kua *Ensemble*
 Kyle Dean Massey *Ensemble*
 Jonathan McGill *Ensemble*
 Lindsay K. Northen *Ensemble*
 Rhea Patterson *Ensemble*
 Eddie Pendergraft *Ensemble*
 Robert Pendilla *Ensemble/Swing*

 Adam Perry *Ensemble*
 Alexander Quiroga *Ensemble*
 Kathy Santen *Midwife*
 Mark Shunkey *Chistery*
 Heather Spore *Ensemble*
 Ron Todorowski *Ensemble*
 Brian Wanee *Ensemble*

Wicked

Jonathan Warren
Dance Captain; Swing

Robin Wilner
Ensemble

Briana Yacavone
Swing

Stephen Schwartz
Music and Lyrics

Winnie Holzman
Book

Joe Mantello
Director

Wayne Cilento
Musical Staging

Eugene Lee
Scenic Designer

Susan Hilferty
Costume Designer

Kenneth Posner
Lighting Designer

Tony Meola
Sound Designer

Tom Watson
Wig and Hair Designer

Joe Dulude II
Makeup Designer

Thom Widmann
Production Supervisor

Stephen Oremus
Music Supervisor; Music Arrangements

William David Brohn
Orchestrations

Alex Lacamoire
Music Arrangements

James Lynn Abbott
Dance Arrangements

Michael Keller
Music Coordinator

Chic Silber
Special Effects

Corinne McFadden Herrera
Associate Choreographer

Bernard Telsey, Telsey + Company
Casting

Gregory Maguire
Author of Original Novel

Marcia Goldberg, Nancy Nagel Gibbs and Nina Essman, 321 Theatrical Management
General Management

Marc Platt
Producer

Jon B. Platt
Producer

David Stone
Producer

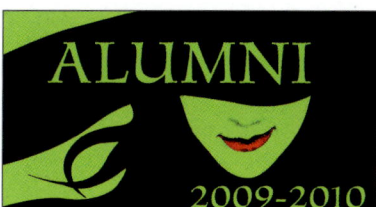

Todd Anderson
Swing

Sam J. Cahn
Chistery, Ensemble

Cristy Candler
Nessarose

Maria Eberline
Ensemble

Kristina Fernandez
Ensemble

The Playbill Broadway Yearbook 2009-2010

Wicked

Lauren Haughton
Swing

Alli Mauzey
Glinda

Brian Munn
Swing

Nicole Parker
Elphaba

Charlie Sutton
Ensemble

Samantha Zack
Swing

Todd Anderson
Swing

Cristy Candler
Witch's Mother, Ensemble

Katie Rose Clarke
Glinda

Michael Drolet
Ensemble

Jenny Fellner
Nessarose

Mandy Gonzalez
Elphaba

Manuel Herrera
Ensemble

David Hull
Ensemble

Andy Karl
Fiyero

Brian Munn
Swing

Nathan Peck
Ensemble

Julie Reiber
Standby for Elphaba

Amanda Rose
Ensemble, Swing

Betsy Struxness
Ensemble

Stephanie Torns
Ensemble

Bryan West
Ensemble

Samantha Zack
Witch's Mother, Ensemble, Dance Captain/Swing

Wicked

STAGE AND COMPANY MANAGEMENT
(L-R): Marybeth Abel (PSM), Christy Ney, Jason Daunter, Jennifer Marik, Eric Cornell, Susan Sampliner (Co. Mgr)

FRONT OF HOUSE STAFF
Front Row (L-R): Eileen Roig, Siobhan Dunne, Maureen Dabreo, Rick Kaye, Martha Boniface, Elisabeth Ford, James Madden, Mariana Casanova, Jason Navarro

Middle Row (L-R): Carmen Rodriguez, Penny Bonacci, Heather Farrell, Jacob Korder, Gregory Woolard, Michele Belmond, Philippa Koopman, Carlos Buelto, Joyce Pena

Back Row (L-R): Brenda Denaris, Albert Cruz, Peggy Boyles, Derek Holland, Leonila Guity, Miguel Buelto, Charles Thompson, Ivan Rodriguez, Maria Szymanski

Wicked

CREW
Front Row (L-R): Nick Garcia, Val Menz, Brendan Quigley, Craig Aves

Back Row (L-R): Jeff Sigler, Bill Nimmo, John Riggins, Steve Caputo, Kevin Anderson, Henry Brisen

HAIR AND MAKEUP
(L-R): Ryan P. McWilliams (Hair Asst), Beverly Belletieri, Nora Martin (Hair Head), Jenny Pendergraft, Craig Jessup (Makeup Head)

WARDROBE
Front Row (L-R): Laurel Parrish, Alyce Gilbert Briggs (Head), Nancy Lawson, Dennis Birchall

Middle Row (L-R): Barbara Rosenthal, Kathe Mull, Shahnaz Khan, Teri Pruitt

Back Row (L-R): Dianne Hylton, Kevin Hucke (Asst), Karen Lloyd, Bobbye Sue Albrecht, James Byrne, Michael Michalski

Wicked

STAFF FOR WICKED

GENERAL MANAGEMENT
321 THEATRICAL MANAGEMENT
Nina Essman   Nancy Nagel Gibbs
Marcia Goldberg

GENERAL PRESS REPRESENTATIVE
THE HARTMAN GROUP
Michael Hartman
Tom D'Ambrosio   Edward Allen

CASTING
TELSEY + COMPANY
Bernie Telsey CSA, Will Cantler CSA, David Vaccari CSA,
Bethany Knox CSA, Craig Burns CSA,
Tiffany Little Canfield CSA, Rachel Hoffman CSA,
Carrie Rosson CSA, Justin Huff CSA, Bess Fifer CSA,
Patrick Goodwin, Abbie Brady-Dalton

TECHNICAL SUPERVISION
JAKE BELL PRODUCTION SERVICES LTD.

COMPANY MANAGER .... SUSAN SAMPLINER

Stage Manager .... Jennifer Marik
Assistant Stage Managers .... J. Jason Daunter, Christy Ney
Assistant Company Manager .... Elizabeth Talmadge
Assistant Director .... Paul Dobie
Dance Supervisor .... Patrick McCollum
Assistant to Mr. Schwartz .... Michael Cole
Assistant Scenic Designer .... Nick Francone
Dressing/Properties .... Kristie Thompson
Scenic Assistant .... Christopher Domanski
Oz Map Design .... Francis Keeping
Draftsman .... Ted LeFevre
Set Model Construction .... Miranda Hardy
Associate Costume Designers .... Michael Sharpe, Ken Mooney
Assistant Costume Designers .... Maiko Matsushima, Amy Clark
Costume Coordinator .... Amanda Whidden
Wig Coordinator .... J. Jared Janas
Associate Lighting Designer .... Karen Spahn
Associate Lighting Designer/
  Automated Lights .... Warren Flynn
Assistant Lighting Designer .... Ben Stanton
Lighting Assistant .... Jonathan Spencer
Associate Sound Designer .... Kai Harada
Sound Assistant .... Shannon Slaton
Projection Programmer .... Mark Gilmore
Assistant Projection Designer .... Anne McMills
Projection Animators .... Gareth Smith, Ari Sachter Zeltzer
Special Effects Associate .... Aaron Waitz
Associate Hair Designer .... Charles LaPointe
Fight Director .... Tom Schall
Flying Effects .... ZFX Flying Illusions
Production Carpenter .... Rick Howard
Head Carpenter .... C. Mark Overton
Deck Automation Carpenter .... William Breidenbach
Production Electrician .... Robert Fehribach
Head Electrician .... Brendan Quigley
Deck Electrician/Moving Light Operator .... Craig Aves
Follow Spot Operator .... Valerie Gilmore
Production Properties .... George Wagner
Property Master .... Joe Schwarz
Assistant Property Master .... Augie Mericola
Production Sound Engineer .... Douglas Graves
Sound Engineer .... Jordan Pankin
Assistant Sound Engineer .... Jack Babin
Production Wardrobe Supervisor ...... Alyce Gilbert
Assistant Wardrobe Supervisor .... Kevin Hucke
Dressers .... Bobbye Sue Albrecht, Dennis Birchall, James Byrne, Dianne Hylton, Nancy Lawson, Michael Michalski, Kathe Mull, Laurel Parrish, Teresa Pruitt, Barbara Rosenthal, Jason Viarengo, Randy Witherspoon
Hair Supervisor .... Nora Martin
Assistant Hair Supervisor .... Ryan P. McWilliams
Hairdressers .... Beverly Belletieri, Cheri Tiberio
Makeup Design .... Joe Dulude II
Makeup Supervisor .... Craig Jessup
Music Preparation Supervisor .... Peter R. Miller, Miller Music Service
Synthesizer Programming .... Andrew Barrett for Lionella Productions, Ltd.
Rehearsal Pianists .... Matthew Doebler, Paul Masse
Rehearsal Drummer .... Gary Seligson
Music Intern .... Joshua Salzman
Production Assistants .... Timothy R. Semon, David Zack
Advertising .... Serino Coyne/Greg Corradetti, Joaquin Esteva
Marketing .... Betsy Bernstein
Online Marketing .... Situation Interactive
Website .... Istros Media Corporation
Merchandise .... The Araca Group
Theatre Display .... King Displays
Group Sales .... Julia Zaborowski (212-768-8255)
Banking .... JP Morgan Chase Bank/ Salvatore A. Romano
Payroll .... Castellana Services, Inc.
Director of Finance .... John DiMeglio
Production Administrator .... Robert Brinkerhoff
Accountant .... Robert Fried, C.P.A.
Insurance .... AON/Albert G. Ruben Insurance
Legal Counsel .... Loeb & Loeb/Seth Gelblum
Legal Counsel for Universal Pictures .... Keith Blau
Physical Therapy .... Encore Physical Therapy, P.C.
Orthopaedist .... David S. Weiss, MD
Onstage Merchandising .... George Fenmore, Inc.

Makeup provided by MAC Cosmetics

MARC PLATT PRODUCTIONS
Adam Siegel, Greg Lessans, Joey Levy,
Jared LeBoff, Nik Mavinkurve, Tia Maggini,
Dana Krupinski, Conor Welch

STONE PRODUCTIONS
David Stone   Patrick Catullo   Aaron Glick

321 THEATRICAL MANAGEMENT
Marc Borsak, Mattea Cogliano-Benedict, Tara Geesaman,
Nicholas Porche, Greg Schaffert, Ken Silverman, John Vermeer

UNIVERSAL PICTURES
President & COO, Universal Studios, Inc. ...... Ron Meyer
Chairman .... Marc Shmuger
Co-Chairman .... David Linde
President of Marketing & Distribution ..... Adam Fogelson
President of Marketing .... Eddie Egan
Co-President, Production
  & EVP, Universal Pictures .... Jimmy Horowitz

To find out more about the world of *Wicked*
and to take our Broadway survey, visit
www.wickedthemusical.com.

CREDITS

Scenery built by F&D Scene Changes, Calgary, Canada. Show control and scenic motion control featuring Stage Command Systems© and scenery fabrication by Scenic Technologies, a division of Production Resource Group, New Windsor, NY. Lighting and certain special effects equipment from Fourth Phase and sound equipment from ProMix, both divisions of Production Resource Group LLC. Other special effects equipment by Sunshine Scenic Studios and Aztec Stage Lighting. Video projection system provided by Scharff Weisberg Inc. Projections by Vermilion Border Productions. Costumes by Barbara Matera Ltd., Parsons-Meares Ltd., Scafati, TRICORNE New York City and Eric Winterling. Millinery by Rodney Gordon and Lynne Mackey. Shoes by T.O. Dey, Frederick Longtin, Pluma, LaDuca Shoes NYC, and J.C. Theatrical. Flatheads and monkey wings built by Michael Curry Design Inc. Natural herb cough drops courtesy of Ricola USA, Inc. Masks and prosthetics by W.M. Creations, Inc., Matthew W. Mungle and Lloyd Matthews; lifecasts by Todd Kleitsch. Fur by Fur & Furgery. Undergarments and hosiery by Bra*Tenders, Inc. Antique jewelry by Ilene Chazanof. Specialty jewelry and tiaras by Larry Vrba. Custom Oz accessories by LouLou Button. Custom screening by Gene Mignola. Certain props by John Creech Designs and Den Design Studio. Environmentally friendly detergent provided by Arm & Hammer. Additional hand props courtesy of George Fenmore. Confetti supplied by Artistry in Motion. Puppets by Bob Flanagan. Musical instruments from Manny's and Carroll Musical Instrument Rentals. Drums and other percussion equipment from Bosphorus, Black Swamp, PTECH, D'Amico and Vater. Emer'gen'C provided by Alacer Corp. Rehearsed at the Lawrence A. Wien Center, 890 Broadway, and the Ford Center for the Performing Arts.

NEDERLANDER

Chairman .... James M. Nederlander
President .... James L. Nederlander

Executive Vice President
Nick Scandalios

Vice President	Senior Vice President
Corporate Development	Labor Relations
Charlene S. Nederlander	**Herschel Waxman**

| Vice President | Chief Financial Officer |
| **Jim Boese** | **Freida Sawyer Belviso** |

STAFF FOR THE GERSHWIN THEATRE
Manager .... Richard D. Kaye
Assoc. Manager .... Steven Ouellette
Treasurer .... John Campise
Assistant Treasurer .... Anthony Rossano
Carpenter .... John Riggins
Electrician .... Henry L. Brisen
Property Master .... Mark Illo
Flyman .... Dennis Fox
Fly Automation Carpenter .... Michael J. Szymanski
Head Usher .... Martha McGuire Boniface

Wicked
SCRAPBOOK

Correspondents: Jason Viarengo, Star Dresser to The Wizard, and Rondi Reed, "Madame Morrible"

Milestones: On May 21, 2010 *Wicked* became the 18th-longest-running Broadway show passing *My Fair Lady*. This year we also surpassed *Annie, Hairspray, The Producers* and *Avenue Q*.

Wicked shattered box office records on three separate occasions during the holiday season:
Thanksgiving Week: $2,086,135
Christmas Week: $2,092,745
New Year's Week: $2,125,740

Wicked currently holds the record for the highest grossing Broadway show for an eight-performance week.

Anniversary Parties and Gifts: The holiday gift from producers this year was a pair of yoga pants with the *Wicked* logo on them. We hope to receive the matching top next year.

Wicked producers threw a "Shiz" mixer/holiday party for the Broadway company and the two national tours at the nightclub M2.

On October 30 the producers threw us a party at the Palm Restaurant to celebrate our sixth anniversary on Broadway.

Celebrity Visitors: The following celebrities came to see *Wicked* this year: talk show host Oprah Winfrey, singer Paula Abdul, musician Melissa Etheridge, comedian Jerry Seinfeld, and actors John Travolta, Katie Holmes, Halle Berry, Jimmy Fallon and Abigail Breslin.

Fundraising: The "Gypsy of the Year" sketch "In Your Own Grace" featured Samantha Zack, Kenway Kua and Carrie Manolakos. *Wicked* raised $147,611 for "Gypsy of the Year" to benefit BC/EFA.

Wicked was the top money-raiser for The 24th Annual Easter Bonnet Competition among Broadway shows, bringing in $208,880. The Easter Bonnet Sketch "Let's Recycle" was conceived by stage managers Christy Ney and Jason Daunter with music and lyrics by Andy Karl and staging by Adam Fleming.

Backstage Fun: Production Stage Manager Marybeth Abel created the stunning Shiz University Alumni Wall in the stage left stairwell, with the help of various stage management interns. Every Equity member who has been here at *Wicked* gets their name added to the wall when they leave.

We have had a few company contests here at *Wicked*. For Thanksgiving we had a Hand Turkey Contest, and Christmas we had a Recycled Materials Ornament Contest. All entries were shared with fans on our Facebook page.

We held two baking contests this year—Bars & Brownies and Loaf Cakes! Winners were selected by an elite group of judges within the company. There were five different categories each time: Best Overall, Best Appearance, Best Texture, Best Taste and Best Olfactory Satisfaction.

"Let's Recycle," the sketch for the annual "Easter Bonnet" competition, featured Andy Karl as "Captain Green" (center), a superhero who leads characters from other Broadway shows, including *Phantom of the Opera, Annie, Pippin, The King and I* and *Mary Poppins*, to "go green" literally and figuratively.

Carols for a Cure Carol: "Carol of the Bells"

Special Backstage Ritual: Going into Rondi Reed's dressing room and spinning her Tony Award for good luck!!!

Double Duty: On June 28 Rondi Reed received a call that Elizabeth Ashley was ill and would miss the closing performance of *August: Osage County*. She was invited to fill in and reprise her Tony Award-winning role. *Wicked* producer David Stone gave his blessing for her to miss her matinee to do *August: Osage County* if she would return that evening for the Actors' Fund performance of *Wicked*. Rondi may be the only performer to appear in a Broadway Musical and Play in the same day.

Favorite Moment During Each Performance: The curtain call.

Favorite In-Theatre Gathering Place: The greenroom seems to be the place where everyone can hang out, eat their dinner, and relax. Most of the company's birthday celebrations are held here.

Favorite Snack Foods: Randy Witherspoon's fried macaroni & cheese balls. The candy jar in the principal hallway is always filled with delicious treats.

Sweethearts Within the Company: Music Director/Conductor Dominick Amendum is engaged to ensemble member Lindsay Janisse.

Wicked Phenomenon: There are currently six ladies in the female ensemble who got engaged this past year. Wonder if there's something in the green elixir after all?????

Memorable Incident During a Performance: A young lady in the front row decided to finish her dinner during the show. She happened to be eating the largest New York slice of pizza on record. It lasted through the entire opening number, until it was confiscated. At intermission it was announced that there was pizza in the greenroom for the company courtesy of Alli Mauzey (Glinda), Kevin Kern (Fiyero) and Rondi Reed (Madame Morrible) in honor of the young lady who distracted everyone on stage.

Catchphrases Only the Company Would Recognize: "Living the Dream."

Ghostly Encounter Backstage: Stage Manager Jason Daunter and ensemble member Eddie Pendergraft were standing on stage left and happened to look up thinking they saw a swing performer watching the show. Then suddenly that person disappeared behind the curtain. The person they thought they saw was actually only a few feet away from them on the stage.

Coolest Thing About Being in This Show: When someone asks you where you work, you just say *Wicked*... and they scream!!

Wishful Drinking

First Preview: September 22, 2009. Opened: October 4, 2009.
Closed January 17, 2010 after 15 Previews and 118 Performances.

PLAYBILL

CAST

Creator & Performer .... CARRIE FISHER

Production Stage Manager: DANIEL J. KELLS

2009-2010 AWARD

OUTER CRITICS CIRCLE AWARD
Outstanding Solo Performance
(Carrie Fisher)

Carrie Fisher
Photo by Joan Marcus

STUDIO 54

ROUNDABOUT THEATRE COMPANY

Todd Haimes, Artistic Director
Harold Wolpert, Managing Director
Julia C. Levy, Executive Director

In association with
Jonathan Reinis
Jamie Cesa   Eva Price
&
Berkeley Repertory Theatre

Present

CARRIE FISHER
in
WISHFUL DRINKING

Created and Performed by
Carrie Fisher

Scenic/Lighting/Projection Design	Production Stage Manager	Associate Producer
Alexander V. Nichols	Daniel J. Kells	Garret Edington
Technical Supervisor	General Manager	Press Representative
Steve Beers	Sydney Beers	Boneau/Bryan-Brown
Director of Marketing & Sales Promotion	Founding Director	Associate Artistic Director
David B. Steffen	Gene Feist	Scott Ellis

Directed by
Tony Taccone

The World Premiere of "Wishful Drinking" was presented
at the Geffen Playhouse Los Angeles 2006
Gil Cates   Randall Arney   Stephen Eich
Producing Director   Artistic Director   Managing Director

Roundabout Theatre Company is a member of the League of Resident Theatres.
www.roundabouttheatre.org
10/4/09

Carrie Fisher
Creator, Performer

Tony Taccone
Director

Jonathan Reinis

Gene Feist
Founding Director, Roundabout Theatre Company

Todd Haimes
Artistic Director, Roundabout Theatre Company

The Playbill Broadway Yearbook 2009-2010

Wishful Drinking

FRONT OF HOUSE STAFF
Front Row (L-R): Nicholas Wheatley, Jose Cuello, LaConya Robinson, Christopher Burgos, Jack Watanachaiyot.
Back Row (L-R): Alvin Vega, Essence Mason, Justin Brown, Stella Varrialle, Linda Gjonbalaj, Hajjah Karriem.

BOX OFFICE
(L-R): Scott Falkowski, Krystin MacRitchie, Ben Schneider, Joseph Clark.

ROUNDABOUT THEATRE COMPANY STAFF

ARTISTIC DIRECTOR	TODD HAIMES
MANAGING DIRECTOR	HAROLD WOLPERT
EXECUTIVE DIRECTOR	JULIA C. LEVY
ASSOCIATE ARTISTIC DIRECTOR	SCOTT ELLIS

ARTISTIC STAFF
DIRECTOR OF ARTISTIC DEVELOPMENT/
  DIRECTOR OF CASTING .... Jim Carnahan
Artistic Consultant .... Robyn Goodman
Resident Director .... Doug Hughes
Associate Artists ..... Scott Elliott, Bill Irwin, Joe Mantello, Mark Brokaw, Kathleen Marshall
Literary Manager .... Jill Rafson
Casting Director .... Carrie Gardner
Casting Associate .... Kate Boka
Casting Associate .... Stephen Kopel
Artistic Assistant .... Amy Ashton
Literary Associate .... Josh Fiedler
The Blanche and Irving Laurie Foundation
  Theatre Visions Fund Commissions ...... Julia Cho, Stephen Karam, Lewis Black, Nathan Louis Jackson
Educational Foundation of
  America Commissions .... Bekah Brunstetter, Lydia Diamond, Diana Fithian, Julie Marie Myatt
New York State Council
  on the Arts Commission .... Nathan Louis Jackson
Roundabout Commissions .... Steven Levenson, Robert Lopez & Kristen Anderson-Lopez
Artistic Intern .... Benjamin Izzo
Casting Interns .... Kyle Bosley, Jillian Cimini, Erin Drake, Andrew Femenella, Lauren Lewis, Quinn Meyers
Script Readers Jay Cohen, Hillary Dixler, Nicholas Stimler

EDUCATION STAFF
EDUCATION DIRECTOR .... Greg McCaslin
Education Program Manager .... Jennifer DiBella
Education Associate
  for Theatre-Based Programs .... Jay Gerlach
Education Coordinator .... Aliza Greenberg
Education Dramaturg .... Ted Sod
Teaching Artists .... Cynthia Babak, Victor Barbella, LaTonya Borsay, Mark Bruckner, Joe Clancy, Vanessa Davis, Joe Doran, Elizabeth Dunn-Ruiz, Janet Edwards, Kevin Free, Tony Freeman, Sheri Graubert, Matthew A.J. Gregory, Melissa Gregus, Adam Gwon, Devin Haqq, Carrie Heitman, Karla Hendrick, Jim Jack, Jason Jacobs, Lisa Renee Jordan, Jamie Kalama, Alvin Keith, Tami Mansfield, Erin McCready, Deidre O'Connor, Andrew Ondrejcak, Maya Parra, Laura Poe, Jennifer Rathbone, Leah Reddy, Amanda Rehbein, Bernita Robinson, Christopher Rummel, Cassy Rush, Nick Simone, Heidi Stallings, Daniel Sullivan, Carl Tallent, Vickie Tanner, Jolie Tong, Cristina Vaccaro, Jennifer Varbalow, Leese Walker, Eric Wallach, Christina Watanabe, Gail Winar, Conwell Worthington, III
Teaching Artist Apprentices .... Carrie Ellman-Larsen, Deanna Frieman, Meghan O'Neill
Education Interns .... Nicole Bournas-Ney, Mandy Menaker

ADMINISTRATIVE STAFF
GENERAL MANAGER .... Sydney Beers
Associate Managing Director .... Greg Backstrom
General Manager,
  American Airlines Theatre .... Rebecca Habel
General Manager, Steinberg Center ...... Rachel E. Ayers
Human Resources Manager .... Stephen Deutsch
Operations Manager .... Valerie D. Simmons
Associate General Manager .... Maggie Cantrick
Office Manager .... Scott Kelly
Management Associate .... Jill K. Boyd
Archivist .... Tiffany Nixon
Receptionists ...... Dee Beider, Raquel Castillo, Elisa Papa, Allison Patrick, Monica Sidorchuk
Messenger .... Darnell Franklin
Management Interns .... Samara Harand, Jennifer Levine

FINANCE STAFF
DIRECTOR OF FINANCE .... Susan Neiman
Assistant Controller .... John LaBarbera
Accounts Payable Administrator .... Frank Surdi
Financial Associate .... Yonit Kafka
Business Office Assistant .... Joshua Cohen
Business Interns .... Davin DeSantis, Stephanie Jaccarino

DEVELOPMENT STAFF
Director, Institutional Giving .... Julie K. D'Andrea
Director, Special Events .... Steve Schaeffer
Director, Major Gifts .... Joy Pak
Director, Patron Programs .... Amber Jo Manuel
Manager, Donor Information Systems .... Lise Speidel
Manager, Patron Programs .... Tyler Ennis
Manager, Telefundraising .... Gavin Brown
Manager, Corporate Relations .... Roxana Petzold
Associate Manager, Patron Programs .... Marisa Perry
Special Events Associate .... Ashley Firestone
Patron Services Associate .... David Pittman
Institutional Giving Associate .... Nick Nolte
Development Assistants .. Ryan Hallett, Nick Luckenbaugh
Assistant to the Executive Director .... Jason Butler
Major Gifts Intern .... Kayla Carpenter
Special Events Intern .... Amy Rosenfield

INFORMATION TECHNOLOGY STAFF
IT DIRECTOR .... Antonio Palumbo
IT Associate .... Dylan Norden
IT Associate .... Jim Roma
DIRECTOR DATABASE OPERATIONS . Wendy Hutton
Database Administrator/Programmer .... Revanth Anne

MARKETING STAFF
DIRECTOR OF MARKETING
  AND SALES PROMOTION .... David B. Steffen
Associate Director of Marketing .... Tom O'Connor
Marketing/Publications Manager ...... Margaret Casagrande
Assistant Director of Marketing .... Stefanie Schussel
Marketing Manager .... Shannon Marcotte
Website Consultant .... Keith Powell Beyland
Director of Telesales Special Promotions ...... Marco Frezza

Wishful Drinking

Telesales Manager	Anthony Merced
Telesales Office Coordinator	Patrick Pastor
Marketing Interns	H.L. Ray, Sean Burpee

TICKET SERVICES STAFF

Director of Sales Operations	Charlie Garbowski, Jr.
Ticket Services Manager	Ellen Holt
Subscription Manager	Ethan Ubell
Box Office Managers	Edward P. Osborne, Jaime Perlman, Krystin MacRitchie, Nicole Nicholson
Group Sales Manager	Jeff Monteith
Assistant Box Office Managers	Robert Morgan, Andrew Clements, Scott Falkowski, Catherine Fitzpatrick
Assistant Ticket Services Managers	Robert Kane, Bill Klemm, Lindsay Ericson
Customer Services Coordinator	Thomas Walsh
Ticket Services	Solangel Bido, Arianna Boykins, Lauren Cartelli, Joseph Clark, Barbara Dente, Nisha Dhruna, Adam Elsberry, James Graham, Kara Harrington, Tova Heller, Nicki Ishmael, Kate Longosky, Elisa Mala, Mead Margulies, Chuck Migliaccio, Carlos Morris, Kayrose Pagan, Thomas Protulipac, Jessica Pruett-Barnett, Kaia Rafoss, Josh Rozett, Ben Schneider, Kenneth Senn, Heather Siebert, Nalane Singh, Lillian Soto, Ron Tobia, Hannah Weitzman
Intern	Melissa Cohen

SERVICES

Counsel	Paul, Weiss, Rifkind, Wharton and Garrison LLP, Charles H. Googe Jr., Carol M. Kaplan
Counsel	Rosenberg & Estis
Counsel	Andrew Lance, Gibson, Dunn, & Crutcher, LLP
Counsel	Harry H. Weintraub, Glick and Weintraub, P.C.
Counsel	Stroock & Stroock & Lavan LLP
Counsel	Daniel S. Dokos, Weil, Gotschal & Manges LLP
Immigration Counsel	Mark D. Koestler and Theodore Ruthizer
Government Relations	Law Offices of Claudia Wagner LLC
House Physicians	Dr. Theodore Tyberg, Dr. Lawrence Katz
House Dentist	Neil Kanner, D.M.D.
Insurance	DeWitt Stern Group, Inc.
Accountant	Lutz & Carr CPAs, LLP
Advertising	Spotco/ Drew Hodges, Jim Edwards, Tom Greenwald, Kyle Hall, Cory Spinney
Interactive Marketing	Situation Interactive/ Damian Bazadona, John Lanasa, Ryan Klink, Kristen Butler
Events Photography	Anita and Steve Shevett
Production Photographer	Joan Marcus
Theatre Displays	King Displays, Wayne Sapper
Lobby Refreshments	Sweet Concessions
Merchandising	Marquee Merchandise, LLC/ Matt Murphy

MANAGING DIRECTOR EMERITUS ....Ellen Richard

Roundabout Theatre Company
231 West 39th Street, New York, NY 10018
(212) 719-9393.

GENERAL PRESS REPRESENTATIVES
BONEAU/BRYAN-BROWN
Adrian Bryan-Brown
Matt Polk   Jessica Johnson   Amy Kass
Emily Meagher

STAFF FOR WISHFUL DRINKING

Assistant Company Manager	Chris Minnick
Production Stage Manager	Daniel J. Kells
Production Carpenter	Dan Hoffman
Production Electrician	John Wooding
Followspot Operators	Jenn Fagent, Mike Widmer
Production Consultant	Josh Weitzman
Running Properties	Lawrence Jennino
Wardrobe Supervisor	Markus Fokken
Sound Mixer	Francis Elers
Sound Equipment provided by	PRG Audio
Lighting Equipment provided by	PRG Lighting

CARRIE FISHER would like to thank:

Billie Lourd: for her intellect, imperturbability and fashion tips.
Debbie Reynolds: for her endless affection and her endless advice (some even solicited) and overall endlessness in general.
Todd Fisher: for his even (and thus odd to me) disposition, shared history and co-dependence.
Eddie Fisher: Thanks for bringing your drug dealer to my opening in Berkeley. His notes were inspirational.
Elizabeth Taylor: for getting Eddie Fisher out of our house.
Josh Ravetch: For the countless hours we worked together. And his inspiration. I will always be grateful.
Paul Slansky: for editing, inspiration and political guidance.
Garret Edington, a.k.a. Lew Ayres: my astrologer, associate producer, and all around go-to guy.
Also: Gloria Crayton, Beatrice Foster, Michael Rodriguez, The Tolkins, Melissa North, Bruce Cohen, Bruce Wagner, Helen Fielding, Dave Mirkin, Abe Gurko, Cyndi Sayre, Clancy Ismislund and Gregory Stevens, Dreyfuss, Warren, Beverly, Buck, Graham, Teresa, Victor, Meryl, Rufus, Sean and all 12 of my shrinks.

STAFF FOR WISHFUL DRINKING JV

GENERAL MANAGER	CESA Entertainment, Inc.
Marketing Coordinator	Eva Price
Production Manager	Daniel J. Kells
Bookkeeping	Alyssa Seiden
Legal Counsel	Beigelman, Feldman & Feiner/ Ron Feiner, Esq.
Piano Recording	Billy Philadelphia
Set & Prop Construction	Berkeley Repertory Theatre Shops

Ms. Fisher's makeup provided by
MAKE UP FOR EVER

BOOKING CONTACT FOR WISHFUL DRINKING:
JONATHAN REINIS PRODUCTIONS 510-647-8033

BOOKING AGENT CONTACT FOR MS. FISHER:
ROLAND SCAHILL, THE GERSH AGENCY,
212-634-8122

TOURING STAFF FOR BERKELEY REPERTORY THEATRE

Artistic Director	Tony Taccone
Managing Director	Susan Medak
General Manager	Karen Racanelli
Director of Communications	Robert Sweibel
Production Manager	Tom Pearl
Assoc. Production Manager	Amanda Williams

STUDIO 54 THEATRE STAFF

Assistant Company Manager	Chris Minnick
House Carpenter	Dan Hoffman
House Electrician	John Wooding
House Properties	Lawrence Jennino
Box Office Manager	Krystin MacRitchie
Assistant Box Office Manager	Scott Falkowski
House Manager	LaConya Robinson
Associate House Manager	Jack Watanachaiyot
Head Usher	Jonathan Martineaz
Ushers	Justin Brown, Linda Gjonbalaj, Jennifer Kneeland, Hajjah Karriem, Essence Mason, Nicole Ramirez, Diana Trent, Stella Varrialle, Nicholas Wheatley
Security	Gotham Security
Maintenance	Jason Battle, Ralph Mohan, Eddie Perez, Reliable Cleaning
Lobby Refreshments	Sweet Concessions

CREW
Front Row (L-R): Lawrence Jennino, Mai-Linh Lofgren, Jennifer Pesce Fagant, Christopher Clay Minnick.
Back Row (L-R): TJ McEvoy, Patrick Shea, Princess Leia Sex Doll, Daniel J. Kells, Markus Fokken, John Wooding, Mike Widmer.

Photo by Brian Mapp

The following shows opened in 2008-2009 and closed shortly after the start of the 2009-2010 season with no changes to their casts or crews. For complete details and photographs from these shows, please consult the 2008-2009 Playbill Broadway Yearbook.

First Preview:
April 7, 2009
Opened: April 29, 2009
Friedman Theatre
Closed June 28, 2009 after
24 Previews and
71 Performances.

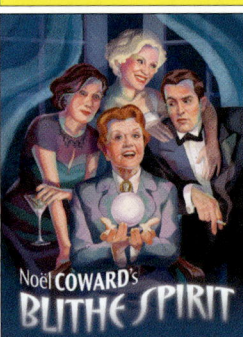

First Preview:
February 26, 2009
Opened: March 15, 2009
Shubert Theatre
Closed July 19, 2009 after
20 Previews and
145 Performances.

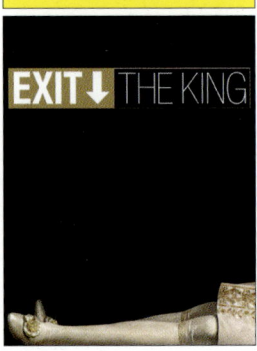

First Preview:
March 7, 2009
Opened: March 26, 2009
Barrymore Theatre
Closed June 14, 2009 after
21 Previews and
93 Performances.

First Preview:
March 10, 2009
Opened: March 29, 2009
Walter Kerr Theatre
Closed June 28, 2009 after
23 Previews and
105 Performances.

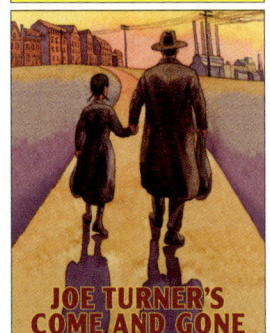

First Preview:
March 19, 2009
Opened: April 16, 2009
Belasco Theatre
Closed June 14, 2009 after
31 Previews and
69 Performances.

First Preview:
March 30, 2009
Opened: April 19, 2009
Broadhurst Theatre
Closed August 16, 2009 after
22 Previews and
137 Performances.

First Preview:
April 10, 2009
Opened: April 26, 2009
American Airlines Theatre
Closed June 28, 2009 after
19 Previews and
73 Performances.

First Preview:
March 13, 2009
Opened: April 2, 2009
Lyceum Theatre
Closed June 14, 2009 after
21 Previews and
85 Performances.

First Preview:
April 3, 2009
Opened: April 30, 2009
Studio 54
Closed July 12, 2009 after
32 Previews and
84 Performances.

Shows • Events • Faculty • In Memoriam • Index

The American Theatre Wing's Spring Gala 377
Fred and Adele Astaire Awards 393
Born for Broadway 377
Broadway Backwards 378
Broadway Bares 19.0: "Click It" 376
Broadway Bears XIII 379
Broadway Flea Market and Grand Auction 381
Broadway on Broadway 2009 380
Broadway Winners: The Award-Winning Music of Broadway! 382
Clarence Derwent Awards 393
Drama Desk Awards 392
Drama Desk Panel: The Play's the Thing 382
Drama League Awards 393
Drama League Gala: A Musical Celebration of Broadway 382
Easter Bonnet Competition 386
Gypsy of the Year 383
Henry Hewes Design Awards 393
Irene Sharaff Awards 393
Jim Caruso's Cast Party/Liza Minnelli's Birthday 385
14th Annual Kids' Night on Broadway 379
Miscast 2010 378
New York Drama Critics' Circle Awards 392
Nothing Like a Dame 377
Outer Critics Circle Awards 392
Pulitzer Prize for Drama 392
Richard Seff Awards 393
Sondheim: The Birthday Concert 385
38th Annual Theater Hall of Fame Induction 384
Theatre World Awards 393
2010 Tony Awards 387-391

The Playbill Broadway Yearbook 2009 • 6 • 2010

Broadway Bares 19.0: "Click It!"

June 21, 2009 at Roseland Ballroom

Broadway Bares 19.0: "Click It!," the latest edition of the annual burlesque-style fundraiser for Broadway Cares/Equity Fights AIDS, earned $808,819 for the charity. The event was billed thus: "Broadway's hottest boiz are grabbing their hard drives and the grlz are ready to play with some brand new software for what is sure to be a Broadway Bares that will fry more than your motherboard."

Peter Gregus (*Jersey Boys*) directed this year's fundraiser, which was executive-produced by Tony winner Jerry Mitchell. The evening featured the work of 18 choreographers and 243 of the "sexiest male and female dancers from Broadway's biggest shows."

This year $172,284 of the total was raised through an online "Strip-A-Thon" that allowed fans to make contributions to see more of their favorite dancers. Frankie James Grande raised the most of any single performer, $14,161. Others who brought in high figures included Steven Bratton ($9,685), Jennifer Cody ($7,210) and Holly Ann Butler ($4,560).

Highlights of this year's event included performances by Daniel Reichard (*Jersey Boys*), Heidi Blickenstaff (*[title of show]*), Kevin Chamberlin (*The Addams Family*), Gavin Creel (*Hair*), Sutton Foster (*Shrek The Musical*), Allison Janney (*9 to 5*), Norm Lewis (*The Little Mermaid*), Darius Nichols (*Hair*) and pop singer Jason Walker.

Tony Award nominee Hunter Bell (*[title of show]*) wrote sketches for the event, with David Nehls (*The Great American Trailer Park Musical*) contributing the opening number, "Click It!"

1. "Thank You, Uncle Sam" a.k.a. "Stimulus Package," featured Miss Liberty played by Sarrah Strimel.
2. Daniel Reichard (front) and Heidi Blickenstaff (top) perform in the opening number.
3. Perennial Bares showstoppers "The Living Art of Armando" offered a dance number called "The World Wide Web."
4. Jennifer Cody backstage.
5. Masked cast members prepare to go on.
6. Members of the chorus sport beehives.

Nothing Like a Dame
June 15, 2009 at New World Stages

The "all-new" "Nothing Like a Dame" concert, billed as an intimate benefit concert event for The Phyllis Newman Women's Health Initiative, featured Tony Award winners Betty Buckley, Audra McDonald and Bebe Neuwirth; three-time Tony nominee Kelli O'Hara; *9 to 5* star Stephanie J. Block; and original *Annie* star Andrea McArdle, among others.

Hosted by Seth Rudetsky, the evening featured a new format of songs and stories from the women of Broadway, as well as rare video clips from earlier days in each of their remarkable careers, accompanied by commentary from Rudetsky and the women themselves.

(L-R): Stephanie J. Block, Andrea McArdle, Seth Rudetsky, Betty Buckley and Brian Stokes Mitchell at the "Nothing Like a Dame" after party.

The American Theatre Wing Gala
June 1, 2009 at Cipriani 42nd Street

The American Theatre Wing's annual spring gala featured performances by Tony Award winners Kristin Chenoweth, Barbara Cook and Audra McDonald.

Tony winner Hugh Jackman served as the gala's honorary chair. Co-chairs were Mrs. Schuyler G. Chapin, Lucia Hwong Gordon and Anthony D. Leeds. The evening included cocktails, dinner and performances. All proceeds benefited the education and outreach programs of the American Theatre Wing.

(L-R): Audra McDonald, Will Swenson and Gavin Creel at the American Theatre Wing's 2009 Annual Spring Gala at Cipriani 42nd St.

Born for Broadway
June 22, 2009 at New World Stages

"Born for Broadway," the first in what's planned as an annual series of Broadway fundraisers for the Christopher and Dana Reeve Foundation, boasted performances by James Naughton, Randy Graff, Douglas Sills, Malcolm Gets, Julia Murney, Aaron Lazar, Kate Baldwin, Annaleigh Ashford, Adrian Bailey, Patrick Boyd, Doug Kreeger, Marissa Perry, Michele Ragusa, Michael Rice, Steve Rosen, Rob Sutton, Noah Weisberg, Kathleen Monteleone, Ali Stroker and others. Richard Kind served as host. The evening was staged by Marcia Milgrom Dodge with musical direction by Larry Yurman.

(L-R): Producer Sarah Galli (L) and director Marcia Milgrom Dodge backstage at "Born for Broadway."

The Playbill Broadway Yearbook 2009-2010

Broadway Backwards 2010
February 22, 2010 at the Vivian Beaumont Theatre

The fifth annual "Broadway Backwards" concert gave actresses the chance to sing showtunes usually associated with men, and vice versa.

The gender-reversed show was created, directed and choreographed by Robert Bartley as a benefit for The Center (The Lesbian, Gay, Bisexual and Transgender Community Center) & Broadway Cares/Equity Fights Aids (BC/EFA).

Florence Henderson hosted the evening and sang "Shipoopi" from *The Music Man* and "Luck Be a Lady" from *Guys and Dolls*. Among other performances, Len Cariou and Lee Roy Reams duetted on "I Remember It Well" (*Gigi*), Gary Beach sang "I'm Not at All in Love" (*The Pajama Game*), Tonya Pinkins sang "Too Many Mornings" (*Follies*), Aaron Lazar did "As Long as He Needs Me" (*Oliver!*) and Douglas Sills performed "I Could Have Danced All Night" (*My Fair Lady*).

1. (L-R): Len Cariou and Lee Roy Reams.
2. (L-R): Tonya Pinkins and Michele Lee.
3. (L-R): Eve Plumb and host Florence Henderson.

Miscast 2010
March 1, 2010 at the Hammerstein Ballroom

Broadway performers young and old got a chance to perform songs against type in the concert event "Miscast 2010" to benefit the MCC Theater.

Mo Rocca hosted the gala, which also honored actor Julianna Margulies "for her commitment to taking risks as an artist and for her long-standing support of MCC's mission."

Performers included Raúl Esparza (*Company*) who sang "Where Is the Warmth" from *The Baker's Wife*; Sutton Foster (*Thoroughly Modern Millie*) who sang "Maria" from *West Side Story*; Montego Glover (*Memphis*) who sang "If I Were a Rich Man" from *Fiddler on the Roof*; Marin Mazzie (*Kiss Me, Kate*) who sang "Where Is the Life That Late I Led?" from *Kate*; Aaron Tveit (*Next to Normal*) who sang "Buenos Aires" from *Evita*; and Kelsey Fowler (*Sunday in the Park with George*) and Alison Horowitz (*Mary Poppins*) who sang "We Do Not Belong Together" from *Sunday in the Park*.

1. (L-R): Alison Horowitz and Kelsey Fowler
2. Aaron Tveit
3. Jackie Burns (*Hair*), Anastacia McCleskey (*Tarzan*) and Jordan Ballard (*Hairspray*).
4. George S. Irving (*Enter Laughing*).

Broadway Bears XIII
February 14, 2010 at B.B. King's Blues Club & Grill

The 13th annual Broadway Bears auction of teddy bears costumed like characters from Broadway shows (many autographed by the original stars) raised more than $101,000 for Broadway Cares/Equity Fights AIDS.

Hosted by John Bolton (*Curtains, Spamalot*), the event offered bears from *Billy Elliot* (signed by Haydn Gwynne, Stephen Daldry and Elton John), *Exit The King* (signed by Geoffrey Rush, Susan Sarandon, Lauren Ambrose and Andrea Martin), *Hair* (signed by Will Swenson and Gavin Creel), *Liza's at the Palace* (signed by Liza Minnelli), *A Little Night Music* (signed by Catherine Zeta-Jones and Stephen Sondheim), *9 to 5* (signed by Dolly Parton and Megan Hilty), *Rent* (signed by Adam Pascal and Anthony Rapp), *Rock of Ages* (signed by Constantine Maroulis), *A Steady Rain* (signed by Daniel Craig and Hugh Jackman), *33 Variations* (signed by Jane Fonda), *Victor/Victoria* (signed by Julie Andrews and Blake Edwards), *Wishful Drinking* (signed by Carrie Fisher), *Xanadu* (signed by Cheyenne Jackson), among many more.

1. Host John Bolton with bears from *Curtains* and *Spamalot*.
2. BC/EFA Executive Director Tom Viola with auctioneer Lorna Kelly at the event.
3. Christopher Sieber with the Lord Farquaad bear from his show *Shrek The Musical*.
4. Jim Caruso with the Liza Minnelli bear.

14th Annual Kids' Night on Broadway
February 2, 2010 at Madame Tussaud's

Young dancers from the Broadway Bodies dance company kick off Kids' Night with a number from *Billy Elliot*, performed with cast members from the show.

Hundreds of young performers helped kick off the 14th annual Kids' Night on Broadway event in a show hosted by TV personality Meredith Viera at Madame Tussaud's on 42nd Street.

The show was designed to attract kids ages 6 to 18 to Kids' Night, at which they could attend a Broadway show for free February 2, 3, and 7 when accompanied by a full-paying adult.

Broadway performers from Broadway Kids Care and Camp Broadway made an appearance at the opening event. Corbin Bleu, who appeared in TV's *High School Musical* and recently debuted on Broadway in *In the Heights*, also made a guest appearance at the event and then led the way to the FanFest where dancers from *In the Heights* gave a dance lesson.

At the various participating theatres, children received a special-edition Kids' PLAYBILL written entirely by kids.

Broadway on Broadway

September 13, 2009 in Times Square

Michael McKean (*Superior Donuts*) hosted the annual "Broadway on Broadway" concert in Times Square, which drew an estimated 50,000 to hear performers from more than 20 Broadway shows. The free outdoor event highlighted the new Broadway theatre season.

The 18th annual lunchtime concert featured current and upcoming shows performing numbers backed by a 30-piece orchestra.

Among those in attendance were cast members of *Billy Elliot*, *Bye Bye Birdie*, *Chicago*, *Fela!*, *In the Heights*, *Irving Berlin's White Christmas*, *Jersey Boys*, *The Lion King*, *The Little Mermaid*, *Mamma Mia!*, *Mary Poppins*, *Memphis*, *The Phantom of the Opera*, *Ragtime* and *Wicked*.

The concert was presented by the Broadway League and the Times Square Alliance.

1. Confetti and streamers fall on the stage and crowd in Times Square.
2. (L-R): Tim Tompkins (president of the Times Square Alliance), John Stamos (*Bye Bye Birdie*), NY Mayor Michael Bloomberg, Charlotte St. Martin (executive director of the Broadway League), and Michael McKean (*Superior Donuts*).
3. The cast of *Fela!*
4. Quentin Earl Darrington and Stephanie Umoh perform a musical number from *Ragtime*.
5. Dancers from *Irving Berlin's White Christmas*.
6. Haydn Gwynne and the cast of *Billy Elliot*.
7. The cast of *In the Heights*.

Broadway Flea Market and Grand Auction

September 27, 2009 at Roseland Ballroom

The 23rd Annual Broadway Flea Market and Grand Auction, which was moved from Shubert Alley to Roseland Ballroom owing to inclement weather, raised a total of $403,929 for Broadway Cares/Equity Fights AIDS.

Sixty-four tables selling a variety of theatre memorabilia raised a total of $192,429. The booth that raised the most money this year was again "Broadway Beat," which raised $12,640. The show booth that raised the most money was again *Wicked*, with $9,663.

The Silent Auction included 103 items and raised $36,590. The top item sold was a *Les Misérables* "I Dreamed a Dream" musical phrase, handwritten and signed by the composers that went for $2,450. Other top earners were an *A Chorus Line* "What I Did for Love" musical phrase, handwritten and signed by Marvin Hamlisch, which went for $1,475, and a *Jersey Boys* "Big Girls Don't Cry" musical phrase, handwritten and signed by "Jersey Boys" Bob Gaudio and Frankie Valli that went for $1,150. The grand auction featured 64 "lots" which raised $175,000. The top-selling lot was a set of VIP tickets to *A Steady Rain*, for $7,500.

Among the Broadway and daytime TV stars who raised $14,770 at the Autograph Table and Celebrity Photo Booths: John Stamos, Alice Ripley, Anthony Rapp, Bernadette Peters, Brian Stokes Mitchell, Bryan Batt, Chita Rivera, Christiane Noll, Christopher Sieber, Constantine Maroulis, Gavin Creel, Gregory Jbara, Jessica Hecht, John Glover, Jonathan Groff, Kathleen Chalfant, Kevin Chamberlin, Marin Mazzie, Priscilla Lopez, Rebecca Luker, Rosemary Harris, Susan Blackwell, Tovah Feldshuh, Victoria Clark and Will Chase.

1. (L-R): Kerry Butler and James Carpinello before signing autographs.
2. The *Wicked* booth.
3. Michael Cerveris of *In the Next Room* at the autograph booth.
4. Rebecca Luker of *Mary Poppins*.
5. Autographed PLAYBILL posters were available for collectors.

Broadway Winners: The Award-Winning Music of Broadway!
July 13, 2009 at Town Hall

The third annual Summer Broadway Festival kicked off with "Broadway Winners: The Award-Winning Music of Broadway." Scott Siegel narrated the evening, which featured "music created on the Great White Way that won Tonys, Grammys and Oscars."

The roster of talent included Megan Hilty, James Barbour, Donna Lynne Champlin, Jenn Colella, Tovah Feldshuh, Alexander Gemignani, Debbie Gravitte, Ute Lemper, Jeff McCarthy, Jack Noseworthy and Martin Vidnovic.

(L-R): Performers with host Scott Siegel (seventh from left).

Drama Desk Panel: The Play's the Thing
June 12, 2009 at Sardi's Restaurant

The Drama Desk hosted a symposium at Sardi's restaurant, exploring "the impressive number of plays presented during the 2008-2009 season."

The panel comprised playwright Annie Baker, and actors Marcia Gay Harden, Condola Rashad, Geoffrey Rush and Bill Irwin. Elysa Gardner, theatre critic for *USA Today*, moderated the discussion.

(L-R): Drama Desk President William Wolf, moderator Elysa Gardner, Bill Irwin, Marcia Gay Harden, Geoffrey Rush, Annie Baker and Condola Rashad at Sardi's.

Drama League Gala: A Musical Celebration of Broadway
February 8, 2010 at the Pierre Hotel

The Drama League's annual Benefit Gala honored actress Angela Lansbury at The Pierre Hotel. The annual black-tie gala features a cocktail reception, a silent auction, a three-course meal and a one-night-only musical revue celebrating the career of the year's Gala Honoree.

Lansbury's Broadway career spans 52 years, beginning in 1957 with *Hotel Paradiso*, and includes work in *Anyone Can Whistle, Mame, Dear World, Gypsy, Sweeney Todd, Deuce, Blithe Spirit* and this season's run in *A Little Night Music*. The actress is also known for her work in both film and television starring in "Murder, She Wrote," *Bedknobs and Broomsticks* and supplying the voice for Mrs. Potts in Disney's *Beauty and the Beast*.

Onetime *Sweeney Todd* co-stars Angela Lansbury and Len Cariou reunited at the Drama League event.

21st Annual "Gypsy of the Year"
December 7-8, 2009 at the Palace Theatre

Hugh Jackman and Daniel Craig earned a unique place for themselves in the history of Broadway Cares/Equity Fights AIDS fundraising by raising $1,549,952 for the 21st annual Gypsy of the Year competition in six weeks of curtain appeals at their hit Broadway drama, *A Steady Rain*. The figure is not only the most ever collected by a single show in the history of BC/EFA fundraisers, but totaled more than was raised in entire Broadway-wide "Gypsy of the Year" events in any of its first nine years.

The *Steady Rain* bonanza boosted the 2009 Gypsy of the Year total to a record $4,630,695, far outdistancing the previous record of $3,927,000 set in pre-recession 2007. This year's event was hosted by Julie White and Seth Rudetsky.

Actors from the long-running Broadway production of *Chicago* won the Gypsy of the Year's Best Stage Presentation award with a gay-themed interpretation of the *West Side Story* song "I Have a Love," titled "9th Avenue Story," and featuring Ryan Lowe performing the Maria part in a countertenor that brought down the house.

First runner-up for Best Stage Presentation went to the actual *West Side Story* cast for "Gypsy Nation," in which the chorus danced in a series of different, tightly choreographed styles.

Top national tour fundraisers: *Rent* with $242,383, *Wicked* (Emerald City Tour) with $237,000, *Jersey Boys* (Sherry Company) with $225,225, and *Jersey Boys* (Chicago) with $190,466.

Top Broadway musical fundraisers: *Phantom of the Opera* with $161,060, *Billy Elliot* with $153,677, *Hair* with $153,648, and *Wicked* with $147,611.

The top fundraiser among Off-Broadway shows was *Avenue Q*, which gathered $27,918.

As has become custom, the event featured a mixture of satirical skits, inspirational songs and virtuoso dance numbers, all performed by the "gypsies," the Broadway dancers who go from show to show and provide singing and dancing support to the leads.

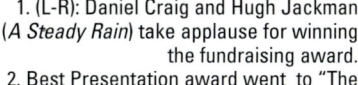

1. (L-R): Daniel Craig and Hugh Jackman (*A Steady Rain*) take applause for winning the fundraising award.
2. Best Presentation award went to "The Merry Men of *Chicago*," featuring vocals from Ryan Lowe (L).
3. Gypsies of *West Side Story* paid homage to Michael and Janet Jackson in a rendition of "Rhythm Nation," retitled "Gypsy Nation."
4. Hosts Julie White and Seth Rudetsky.
5. The cast of *Bye Bye Birdie* honored artists lost to AIDS with a tribute to Freddie Mercury and the Queen classic "Bohemian Rhapsody."
6. Gavin Creel and the cast of *Hair* presented a cannabis-influenced medley of show tunes.

Photos by James Zielinski

The Playbill Broadway Yearbook 2009-2010

39th Annual Theater Hall of Fame Induction

January 25, 2010 at the Gershwin Theatre and the Friars Club

The 39th Annual Theater Hall of Fame induction ceremony welcomed actors Jim Dale (*Barnum*), John McMartin (*Sweet Charity*) and Lynn Redgrave (*Shakespeare for My Father*); producers Roger Berlind (dozens of productions including the current *A Little Night Music*) and Ted Mann (Circle in the Square); composers Stephen Schwartz (*Wicked, Godspell*) and Andrew Lloyd Webber (*Cats, Phantom of the Opera*); and, posthumously, playwright/actor Charles Ludlam (Ridiculous Theatrical Company).

Veteran Broadway publicist Shirley Herz accepted the Founders Award for Outstanding Contribution to the Theatre. Pia Lindström hosted the event. An Honorees Dinner followed at the New York Friars Club.

Presenters included playwright John Guare; directors Frank Dunlop, Joseph Hardy and Michael Montel; actor Everett Quinton; and producers Paul Libin, David Stone, Marc Platt and Nick Scandalios.

Nominees for the Theater Hall of Fame must have had a minimum of five major credits and 25 years in the Broadway theatre. Inductees are elected by the American Theater Critics Association and the living members of the Theater Hall of Fame.

1. Composer Stephen Schwartz at the Friars Club.
2. Publicist Shirley Herz.
3. Actor John McMartin.
4. Producer Roger Berlind with his Hall of Fame medallion.
5. Charlotte St. Martin and Nick Scandalios at the Honorees Dinner.
6. Actor Jim Dale.

Photos by Aubrey Reuben

Sondheim: The Birthday Concert
March 15 and 16, 2010 at Avery Fisher Hall

1. Composer Stephen Sondheim (center) accepts an ovation while backed by members of the New York Philharmonic and flanked by stars associated with his shows, marking his 80th birthday.
2. Elaine Stritch performs "I'm Still Here."
3. The cast of the current *West Side Story* performs a number from the show.

Jim Caruso's Cast Party/Liza Minnelli's Birthday
March 15, 2010 at Birdland Jazz Club

1. (L-R): Jim Caruso and Billy Stritch, who organized and performed a birthday concert for singer Liza Minnelli as a special edition of Caruso's "Cast Party" series at Birdland Jazz Club, with special appearances by friends and co-stars from throughout her career.
2. Minnelli's *Cabaret* co-star, Joel Grey.
3. The guest of honor.
4. Caruso performs for Minnelli.

The 24th Annual Easter Bonnet Competition

April 26-27, 2010 at the Minskoff Theatre

The 24th annual Broadway Cares/Equity Fights AIDS Easter Bonnet Competition raised $3,265,700 in six weeks of nightly curtain-call appeals, capped by two days of skits, songs, dances and imaginatively designed hats.

This year's total was raised by 55 participating Broadway, Off-Broadway and touring shows.

The various companies of the musical *Wicked* took three of the top fundraising awards. The Oz musical was the top moneyraiser among Broadway shows, bringing in $208,880. The "Emerald City" company was also a big moneymaker among national tours, taking in $239,883. But the "Munchkinland" touring company of *Wicked* stood the tallest of all, winning the grand fundraising prize with $251,332.

The award for outstanding bonnet design went to the cast of *Fela!* for a huge turban of brightly colored African cloth.

The company of *Memphis* took the top prize for performances, with "Love Terrorists," in which the company danced in army fatigues to a glowering song about the militant spreading of love. Their bonnet consisted of a stack of dynamite sticks and a timer that tilted up to reveal a heart.

1. Montego Glover of *Memphis* sings "Help Is on the Way" as bonnets are displayed in the finale.
2. Performers from *Memphis* don their controversial heart-full-of-dynamite bonnet in the skit "Love Terrorists."
3. Leslie Jordan (C) of Off-Broadway's *My Trip Down the Pink Carpet*, in his dressing room with, among others, Constantine Maroulis (far left) of *Rock of Ages* and Chad Kimball (far right) of *Memphis*.
4. Original *Follies* girl Doris Eaton Travis makes her final "Easter Bonnet" appearance, riding in a basket, two weeks before her death at age 106.
5. The cast of *Next Fall* in their skit "*Next Fall* Goes Down."
6. The *South Pacific* bonnet is introduced by young cast members (L-R): Laurissa Romain, Luka Kain and Kimber Monroe (also that show's *Yearbook* correspondents).

The Antoinette Perry (Tony) Awards

June 13, 2009 at Radio City Music Hall

Memphis, Red, La Cage aux Folles and *Fences* won the major production categories at the 2010 Tony Awards.

The 64th annual awards, representing excellence in Broadway theatre for the 2009-2010 season, were presented at Radio City Music Hall in a ceremony hosted by Sean Hayes and broadcast on CBS. The nominees and recipients of the 64th annual Antoinette Perry "Tony" Awards follow. Winners are listed in **boldface** with an asterisk (*).

Best Musical
American Idiot
Fela!
* ***Memphis***
Million Dollar Quartet

Best Play
In the Next Room or the Vibrator Play by Sarah Ruhl
Next Fall by Geoffrey Nauffts
* ***Red* by John Logan**
Time Stands Still by Donald Margulies

Best Revival of a Musical
Finian's Rainbow
* ***La Cage aux Folles***
A Little Night Music
Ragtime

Best Revival of a Play
* ***Fences***
Lend Me a Tenor
The Royal Family
A View from the Bridge

Best Performance by a Leading Actor in a Musical
Kelsey Grammer, *La Cage aux Folles*
Sean Hayes, *Promises, Promises*
* **Douglas Hodge, *La Cage aux Folles***
Chad Kimball, *Memphis*
Sahr Ngaujah, *Fela!*

Best Performance by a Leading Actress in a Musical
Kate Baldwin, *Finian's Rainbow*
Montego Glover, *Memphis*
Christiane Noll, *Ragtime*
Sherie Rene Scott, *Everyday Rapture*
* **Catherine Zeta-Jones, *A Little Night Music***

1. Winners (L-R): Denzel Washington and Viola Davis of *Fences*, Catherine Zeta-Jones of *A Little Night Music*, Douglas Hodge of *La Cage aux Folles*.
2. (L-R): *Red* author John Logan with his producer, Arielle Tepper Madover.
3. Katie Finneran with her Tony for *Promises, Promises*
4. (L-R): *Memphis* creators Joe DiPietro, David Bryan and Daryl Waters.

The Tony Awards

Best Performance by a Leading Actor in a Play
Jude Law, *Hamlet*
Alfred Molina, *Red*
Liev Schreiber, *A View from the Bridge*
Christopher Walken, *A Behanding in Spokane*
* **Denzel Washington**, *Fences*

Best Performance by a Leading Actress in a Play
* **Viola Davis**, *Fences*
Valerie Harper, *Looped*
Linda Lavin, *Collected Stories*
Laura Linney, *Time Stands Still*
Jan Maxwell, *The Royal Family*

Best Performance by a Featured Actor in a Musical
Kevin Chamberlin, *The Addams Family*
Robin De Jesús, *La Cage aux Folles*
Christopher Fitzgerald, *Finian's Rainbow*
* **Levi Kreis**, *Million Dollar Quartet*
Bobby Steggert, *Ragtime*

Best Performance by a Featured Actress in a Musical
Barbara Cook, *Sondheim on Sondheim*
* **Katie Finneran**, *Promises, Promises*
Angela Lansbury, *A Little Night Music*
Karine Plantadit, *Come Fly Away*
Lillias White, *Fela!*

Best Performance by a Featured Actor in a Play
David Alan Grier, *Race*
Stephen McKinley Henderson, *Fences*
Jon Michael Hill, *Superior Donuts*
Stephen Kunken, *Enron*
* **Eddie Redmayne**, *Red*

Best Performance by a Featured Actress in a Play
Maria Dizzia, *In the Next Room or the Vibrator Play*
Rosemary Harris, *The Royal Family*
Jessica Hecht, *A View from the Bridge*
* **Scarlett Johansson**, *A View from the Bridge*
Jan Maxwell, *Lend Me a Tenor*

Best Direction of a Musical
Christopher Ashley, *Memphis*
Marcia Milgrom Dodge, *Ragtime*
* **Terry Johnson**, *La Cage aux Folles*
Bill T. Jones, *Fela!*

Best Direction of a Play
* **Michael Grandage**, *Red*
Sheryl Kaller, *Next Fall*
Kenny Leon, *Fences*
Gregory Mosher, *A View from the Bridge*

Best Choreography
Rob Ashford, *Promises, Promises*
* **Bill T. Jones**, *Fela!*
Lynne Page, *La Cage aux Folles*
Twyla Tharp, *Come Fly Away*

1. Nominee and Tony host Sean Hayes of *Promises, Promises*.

2. Choreographer Bill T. Jones with his Tony for *Fela!*

3. Nominee Barbara Cook of *Sondheim on Sondheim* on the red carpet.

4. Scarlett Johansson with her Tony for Best Featured Actress in a Play for *A View from the Bridge*.

5. Eddie Redmayne with his Tony Award for *Red*.

Best Scenic Design of a Musical
Marina Draghici, *Fela!*
* **Christine Jones**, *American Idiot*
Derek McLane, *Ragtime*
Tim Shortall, *La Cage aux Folles*

Best Scenic Design of a Play
John Lee Beatty, *The Royal Family*
Alexander Dodge, *Present Laughter*
Santo Loquasto, *Fences*
* **Christopher Oram**, *Red*

Best Costume Design of a Musical
* **Marina Draghici**, *Fela!*
Paul Tazewell, *Memphis*
Matthew Wright, *La Cage aux Folles*

Best Costume Design of a Play
Martin Pakledinaz, *Lend Me a Tenor*
Constanza Romero, *Fences*
David Zinn, *In the Next Room or the Vibrator Play*
* **Catherine Zuber**, *The Royal Family*

388   The Playbill Broadway Yearbook 2009-2010

The Tony Awards

Best Lighting Design of a Musical
* Kevin Adams, *American Idiot*
Donald Holder, *Ragtime*
Nick Richings, *La Cage aux Folles*
Robert Wierzel, *Fela!*

Best Lighting Design of a Play
Neil Austin, *Hamlet*
* Neil Austin, *Red*
Mark Henderson, *Enron*
Brian MacDevitt, *Fences*

Best Sound Design of a Musical
Jonathan Deans, *La Cage aux Folles*
* Robert Kaplowitz, *Fela!*
Dan Moses Schreier and Gareth Owen, *A Little Night Music*
Dan Moses Schreier, *Sondheim on Sondheim*

Best Sound Design of a Play
Acme Sound Partners, *Fences*
Adam Cork, *Enron*
* Adam Cork, *Red*
Scott Lehrer, *A View from the Bridge*

Best Book of a Musical
Everyday Rapture, Dick Scanlan and Sherie Rene Scott
Fela! Jim Lewis and Bill T. Jones
* *Memphis,* Joe DiPietro
Million Dollar Quartet, Colin Escott and Floyd Mutrux

Best Original Score (Music and/or Lyrics) Written for the Theatre
The Addams Family, Music & Lyrics: Andrew Lippa
Enron, Music: Adam Cork, Lyrics: Lucy Prebble
Fences, Music: Branford Marsalis
* *Memphis,* Music: David Bryan, Lyrics: Joe DiPietro, David Bryan

Best Orchestrations
Jason Carr, *La Cage aux Folles*
Aaron Johnson, *Fela!*
Jonathan Tunick, *Promises, Promises*
* **Daryl Waters & David Bryan, *Memphis***

Special Tony Awards for Lifetime Achievement in the Theatre
Alan Ayckbourn
Marian Seldes

Tony Honors for Excellence in the Theatre
The Alliance of Resident Theatres/New York
Fight Director B.H. Barry
BC/EFA Executive Director Tom Viola
Midtown North and South, New York City Police Precincts

Isabelle Stevenson Award
David Hyde Pierce

Regional Theatre Tony Award
Eugene O'Neill Theater Center, Waterford, Connecticut

Here's a tally of the 2009 Tony Award winners:

Red 6
Memphis 4
Fences 3
Fela! 3
La Cage aux Folles 3
American Idiot 2
A View from the Bridge 1
Promises, Promises 1
Million Dollar Quartet 1
The Royal Family 1
A Little Night Music 1

1. On the Red Carpet: Mike Dirnt, Billie Joe Armstrong and Tré Cool of Green Day and *American Idiot*.
2. Costume designer Catherine Zuber holds her Tony for *The Royal Family*.
3. Karine Plantadit (*Come Fly Away*).
4. Honoree Alan Ayckbourn.

The Playbill Broadway Yearbook 2009-2010

The Tony Awards

1. Nominees Montego Glover and Chad Kimball of *Memphis*

2. Daniel Radcliffe

3. Nominee Christopher Walken of *A Behanding in Spokane*

4. Antonio Banderas

5. Nominee Kelsey Grammer of *La Cage aux Folles*, with his wife Camille

6. Tony Shalhoub of *Lend Me a Tenor*, with his daughter

7. Idina Menzel

The Tony Awards

1. Presenter Bernadette Peters
2. Nominee Sahr Ngaujah of *Fela!*
3. Nominee Christiane Noll of *Ragtime*
4. Nominee Lillias White of *Fela!*
5. Lea Michele
6. Kristin Chenoweth
7. Lifetime Achievement honoree Marian Seldes

Other Theatre Awards

Covering the 2009-2010 Broadway Season

THE PULITZER PRIZE FOR DRAMA
Next to Normal by Tom Kitt and Brian Yorkey

NY DRAMA CRITICS' CIRCLE AWARDS
Best Play: *The Orphans' Home Cycle* (Off-Broadway)
Best Musical: *No award*
Best Foreign Play: *No award*

DRAMA DESK AWARDS
Outstanding Play: *Red* by John Logan
Outstanding Musical: *Memphis* by Joe DiPietro and David Bryan
Outstanding Revival of a Play: [tie] *Fences* by August Wilson and *A View from the Bridge* by Arthur Miller
Outstanding Revival of a Musical: *La Cage aux Folles* by Harvey Fierstein and Jerry Herman
Outstanding Actor in a Play: Liev Schreiber, *A View from the Bridge*
Outstanding Actress in a Play: Jan Maxwell, *The Royal Family*
Outstanding Actor in a Musical: Douglas Hodge, *La Cage aux Folles*
Outstanding Actress in a Musical: [tie] Montego Glover, *Memphis* and Catherine Zeta-Jones, *A Little Night Music*
Outstanding Featured Actor in a Play: Santino Fontana, *Brighton Beach Memoirs*
Outstanding Featured Actress in a Play: Viola Davis, *Fences*
Outstanding Featured Actor in a Musical: Christopher Fitzgerald, *Finian's Rainbow*
Outstanding Featured Actress in a Musical: Katie Finneran, *Promises, Promises*
Outstanding Director of a Play: Michael Grandage, *Red*
Outstanding Director of a Musical: Michael Mayer, *American Idiot*
Outstanding Choreography: Twyla Tharp, *Come Fly Away*
Outstanding Music: David Bryan, *Memphis*

(L-R): Catherine Zeta-Jones and Montego Glover, who tied for Outstanding Actress in a Musical in the Outer Critics Circle Awards, presented at Sardi's May 27, 2010.

Outstanding Lyrics: John Kander & Fred Ebb, *The Scottsboro Boys* (OB)
Outstanding Book of a Musical: Alex Timbers, *Bloody Bloody Andrew Jackson* (OB)
Outstanding Orchestrations: Daryl Waters & David Bryan, *Memphis*
Outstanding Musical Revue: *Sondheim on Sondheim*
Outstanding Music in a Play: Branford Marsalis, *Fences*
Outstanding Set Design in a Musical: Phelim McDermott, Julian Crouch and Basil Twist, *The Addams Family*
Outstanding Set Design in a Play: Fitz Patton, *When the Rain Stops* (OB)
Outstanding Costume Design: Matthew Wright, *La Cage aux Folles*
Outstanding Lighting Design: Neil Austin, *Red*

Outstanding Sound Design: Acme Sound Partners, *Ragtime*
Outstanding Solo Performance: Jim Brochu, *Zero Hour* (OB)
Unique Theatrical Experience: *Love, Loss, and What I Wore* (OB)
Outstanding Ensemble Performance: The cast of *Circle Mirror Transformation* (OB)
Outstanding Ensemble Performance: The cast of *The Temperamentals* (OB)
Special Award to the cast, creative team and producers of Horton Foote's epic *The Orphans' Home Cycle*
Special Award to Jerry Herman
Special Award to Godlight Theatre Company (OB)
Special Award to Ma-Yi Theater Company (OB)

OUTER CRITICS CIRCLE AWARDS
Outstanding New Broadway Play: *Red*
Outstanding New Broadway Musical: *Memphis*
Outstanding New Off-Broadway Play: *The Orphans' Home Cycle* (OB)
Outstanding New Off-Broadway Musical [tie]: *Bloody Bloody Andrew Jackson* (OB) *The Scottsboro Boys* (OB)
Outstanding New Score: *Memphis*
Outstanding Revival of a Play: *Fences*
Outstanding Revival of a Musical: *La Cage aux Folles*
Outstanding Director of a Play (Lucille Lortel Award): Michael Wilson, *The Orphans' Home Cycle* (OB)
Outstanding Director of a Musical: Terry Johnson, *La Cage aux Folles*
Outstanding Choreographer [tie]: Bill T. Jones, *Fela!* Sergio Trujillo, *Memphis*

(L-R): Edward Albee, Hallie Foote and the team from *The Orphans' Home Cycle*, at the 55th Annual Drama Desk Awards held at LaGuardia Concert Hall May 23, 2010.

Other Theatre Awards
Covering the 2009-2010 Broadway Season

Outstanding Set Design: Phelim McDermott and Julian Crouch, *The Addams Family*
Outstanding Costume Design: Matthew Wright, *La Cage aux Folles*
Outstanding Lighting Design: Kevin Adams, *American Idiot*
Outstanding Actor in a Play: Denzel Washington, *Fences*
Outstanding Actress in a Play: Viola Davis, *Fences*
Outstanding Actor in a Musical: Douglas Hodge, *La Cage aux Folles*
Outstanding Actress in a Musical [tie]: Montego Glover, *Memphis*
Catherine Zeta-Jones, *A Little Night Music*
Outstanding Featured Actor in a Play: Jon Michael Hill, *Superior Donuts*
Outstanding Featured Actress in a Play: Jan Maxwell, *Lend Me a Tenor*
Outstanding Featured Actor in a Musical: Levi Kreis, *Million Dollar Quartet*
Outstanding Featured Actress in a Musical: Katie Finneran, *Promises, Promises*
Outstanding Solo Performance: Carrie Fisher, *Wishful Drinking*
John Gassner Award (New American Play): Geoffrey Nauffts, *Next Fall*

THE DRAMA LEAGUE AWARDS
Distinguished Production of a Play: *Red*
Distinguished Production of a Musical: *Sondheim on Sondheim*
Distinguished Revival of a Play: *A View from the Bridge*
Distinguished Revival of a Musical: *La Cage aux Folles*
Distinguished Performance Award: Alfred Molina, *Red*

THEATRE WORLD AWARDS
For outstanding Broadway or Off-Broadway debuts:
Nina Arianda, *Venus in Fur* (OB)
Chris Chalk, *Fences*
Bill Heck, *The Orphans' Home Cycle* (OB)
Jon Michael Hill, *Superior Donuts*
Scarlett Johansson, *A View from the Bridge*
Keira Keeley, *The Glass Menagerie* (OB)
Sahr Ngaujah, *Fela!*
Eddie Redmayne, *Red*
Andrea Riseborough, *The Pride* (OB)
Heidi Schreck, *Circle Mirror Transformation* (OB)
Stephanie Umoh, *Ragtime*
Michael Urie, *The Temperamentals* (OB)

OTHER ACTORS' EQUITY AWARDS
Joe A. Callaway Award for best performances in a classical play in the New York metropolitan area: Kate Forbes and John Douglas Thompson, both *Othello* (OB)
St. Clair Bayfield Award for the best performance by an actor in a Shakespearean play in the New York metropolitan area: David Pittu, *Twelfth Night* (OB)
ACCA Award for Outstanding Broadway Chorus: the cast of *West Side Story*

THE CLARENCE DERWENT AWARDS
From Actors' Equity for "most promising female and male performers on the New York metropolitan scene."
Nina Arianda, *Venus in Fur* (OB)
Bill Heck, *The Orphans' Home Cycle* (OB)

THE RICHARD SEFF AWARDS
From Actors' Equity, to "female and male character actors 50 years of age or older."

Songwriter John Kander at the 55th Annual Drama Desk Awards, holding the award he won with late collaborator Fred Ebb for Outstanding Lyrics in *Scottsboro Boys*.

Helen Stenborg, *Vigil* (OB)
Stephen McKinley Henderson, *Fences*

THE IRENE SHARAFF AWARDS
From the Theatre Development Fund, for outstanding costume design:
Robert L.B. Tobin Award for Sustained Excellence in Theatrical Design: Ming Cho Lee
Artisan Award: John David Ridge
Lifetime Achievement Award for Costume Design: Albert Wolsky
Young Master Award: Alejo Vietti

FRED AND ADELE ASTAIRE AWARDS
Best Choreographer on Broadway: Bill T. Jones, *Fela!*
Best Female Dancers on Broadway: Nicole Chantal de Weever and the *Fela!* Female Ensemble
Best Male Dancer on Broadway: Charlie Neshyba-Hodges, *Come Fly Away*
Douglas Watt Lifetime Achievement Award: Kenny Ortega

HENRY HEWES DESIGN AWARDS
Given in December 2009 for work in the 2008-2009 season
Scenic Design: David Korins for *Why Torture Is Wrong, and the People Who Love Them* (OB)
Derek McLane for *33 Variations*
Louisa Thompson for *Blasted* (OB)
Costume Design: Clint Ramos for *Women Beware Women* (OB)
Lighting Design: Kevin Adams for *Hair*
Tyler Micoleau for *Blasted* (OB)
Notable Effects (Projection Design): Jeff Sugg for *33 Variation*
Notable Effects (Sound Design): Matt Tierney for *Blasted* (OB)

GRAMMY AWARD
Best Musical Show Album: *West Side Story*

(L-R): Valerie Harper (*Looped*) and Linda Lavin (*Collected Stories*) attending the 76th Annual Drama League Awards Ceremony and Luncheon at the Marriott Marquis Hotel May 21, 2010.

Shows • Events • Faculty • In Memoriam • Index

Actors' Equity Association 401
The Actors Fund 410
American Federation of Musicians
 Local 802 403
The American Theatre Wing 407
Association of Theatrical Press Agents
 and Managers (ATPAM) 401
Roger Berlind 397
Binder Casting 407
Boneau/Bryan-Brown 411
Broadway Cares/
 Equity Fights AIDS 408
The Broadway Channel 414
The Broadway League 397
Bob Boyett 397
Coalition of Broadway Unions
 and Guilds 400
Dodger Theatricals 398
Dramatists Guild 401
Eliran Murphy Group 417
Richard Frankel 397
Bill Haber/Ostar Productions 397
The Hartman Group 412
Hudson Scenic 408
International Alliance of Theatrical
 Stage Employees Local 1 400
IATSE Local 306 404
IATSE Local 751 405
IATSE Local 764 405
IATSE Local 798 404
International Union of Operating
 Engineers Local 30 406
Jujamcyn Theaters 395
Richard Kornberg and Associates 413
Stewart F. Lane
 and Bonnie Comley 397
Cameron Mackintosh 397
Arielle Tepper Madover 397
Manhattan Theatre Club 398
The Nederlander Organization 396
Playbill, Inc. (Manhattan) 419
Playbill, Inc. (Woodside) 420-421

The Publicity Office 413
Jeffrey Richards Associates 413
Roundabout Theatre Company 399
SEIU Local 32BJ 406
Serino Coyne 416
The Shubert Organization 395
Situation Interactive 418
Stage Directors & Choreographers
 Society 403
SpotCo 415
Theatre Development Fund
 and TKTS 409
Theatrical Teamsters, Local 817 406
Tony Award Productions 396
Barry and Fran Weissler 397

The Playbill Broadway Yearbook 2009 • 6 • 2010

Faculty

The Shubert Organization

Philip J. Smith
Chairman and co-CEO

Robert E. Wankel
President and co-CEO

Jujamcyn Theaters

Jordan Roth
President

Paul Libin
Vice President/ Producing Director

Jack Viertel
Creative Director

Faculty

The Nederlander Organization

James M. Nederlander
Chairman

James L. Nederlander
President

Nick Scandalios
Executive Vice President

Freida Belviso
Chief Financial Officer

Jim Boese
Vice President

Susan Lee
Chief Marketing Officer

Jack Meyer
Vice President Programming

Charlene S. Nederlander
Vice President Corporate Development

Kathleen Raitt
Vice President Corporate Relations

Herschel Waxman
Senior Vice President Labor Relations

Tony Award Productions

Alan Wasser
General Manager

Allan Williams
General Manager

Faculty

The Broadway League

Paul Libin
Chair

Charlotte St. Martin
Executive Director

Back Row (L-R): Robert Davis, Tom Ferrugia, Jean Kroeper, Keith Halpern, Colin Gibson, Chris Brockmeyer, Chris Brucato, Erin Rech, Britt Marden, Josh Cacchione

Middle Row (L-R): Ed Sandler, Jan Svendsen, Zenovia Varelis, Rachel Reiner, Lindsay Florestal, Christina Boursiquot, Jennifier Stewart, Laura Grady, Joy Axelrad, Roxanne Rodriguez, Robin Fox

Front Row (L-R): Chelsi Conklin, Ben Pesner, Elisa Shevitz, Charlotte St. Martin, Laura Fayans, Amy Steinhaus, Erica Ryan

Producers and Producing Companies

Roger Berlind

Bob Boyett

Richard Frankel,
Richard Frankel
Productions

Bill Haber
Ostar Productions

Cameron Mackintosh

Arielle Tepper Madover

Barry and Fran
Weissler

Stewart F. Lane and
Bonnie Comley

The Playbill Broadway YEARBOOK 2009-2010

Faculty

Manhattan Theatre Club

Front Row (L-R): Jeffrey Bledsoe, Jerry Patch, Barry Grove, Lynne Meadow, Mandy Greenfield, Florie Seery, Nancy Piccione
Second Row (L-R): Kevin Emrick, Lisa McNulty, Lindsey Brooks Sag, Erin Moeller, Samantha Mascali, Emily Fleisher, Antonello Di Benedetto, Allison Taylor, Jeremy Blocker, Mark Bowers
Third Row (L-R): Kelli Bragdon, Amy Harris, Julia Davis, Gillian Campbell, Thatcher Stevens, Caitlin Baird, Annie MacRae, Emily Hammond, Kelly Gillespie, Debra Waxman, Jill Turner Lloyd, David Shookhoff
Back Row (L-R): Kelsey Martinez, Sunil Ayyagari, Laurel Bear, Vijay Mahadeo, Roger Kingsepp, Andrew Kao, Alex Barron, Chad Jones, Nicki Hunter, Amy Loe

Dodger Theatricals

Front Row (L-R): Linda Wright, Lauren Freed, Ake The Dog, Dean Carpenter, Andrew Serna, Ashley Tracey, Michael David

Second Row (L-R): Pamela Lloyd, Lauren White, Anne Ezell, Annie Van Nostrand, Laurinda Wilson

Third Row (L-R): Jeff Parvin, Jennifer Vaughan, Flora Johnstone, Jessica Ludwig, Jessica Morris

Back Row (L-R): John Haber, Abigail Kornet, Edward Strong, Lauren Mitchell

Faculty

The Roundabout Theatre Company

Front Row (L-R): Harold Wolpert, Todd Haimes, Julia Levy

Second Row (L-R): Greg Backstrom, Jill Rafson, Amy Ashton, Rachel Ayers, Greg McCaslin, Antonio Palumbo, Steve Deutsch, Valerie Simmons, Susan Neiman, Rebecca Habel, Lynne Gugenheim Gregory, Sydney Beers

Third Row (L-R): Ted Sod, Ethan Ubell, Nick Caccavo, Carly DiFulvio, Joy Pak, Joy Magyawe, Elisa Papa, Steve Schaeffer, Frank Surdi, Shannon Marcotte, Lauren Brender, Josh Cohen

Fourth Row (L-R): standing/green scarf: Jennifer DiBella, seated: Jackie Verbitski, Dee Beider, Roxana Petzold, Jennifer Stafford, Julianne Ross, Tiffany Nixon, Tyler Ennis, Gavin Brown, Robert Morgan, Solangel Bido, Gavi Young, Liz Malta, Sophia Hinshelwood

Fifth Row standing (L-R): Wendy Hutton, Maggie Cantrick, Lise Speidel, Steve Ryan, Magali Western, John LaBarbera, Ryan Hallett, Amy Rosenfield, Nick Lyndon, Glenn Merwede, Bobby Dowling, Scott Kelly, Joe Foster, Marisa Perry, unidentified, Yonit Kafka

Sixth Row standing (L-R): Tom O'Connor, Brian Maiuri, Mead Margulies, Zachary Baer, Karl Hinze, Nick Luckenbaugh, Ellen Holt, Marc Grimshaw, Revanth Anne, Bradley Sanchez, Brett Barbour

Faculty

IATSE Local One, Stagehands

Replacement Room Chairperson Daniel Thorn, Administrative Secretary Edmond F. Supple, Sr. and Financial Secretary Anthony Manno

Seated (L-R): Chairman, Board of Trustees John M. Diaz, Sr., Recording-Corresponding Secretary Robert C. Score, President James J. Claffey, Jr., Vice-President William J. Walters, Treasurer Robert McDonough

Standing (L-R): Television Business Manager Robert C. Nimmo, Television Business Manager Edward J. McMahon, III, Theatre Business Manager Michael Wekselblatt, Theatre Business Manager Kevin McGarty, Trustee William Ngai and Trustee Daniel D. Dashman

Coalition of Broadway Unions and Guilds

Seated (L-R): Tino Gagliardi (Local 802/AFM), Nick Kaledin (ATPAM), Valerie Gladstone (Local 798), Carl Mulert (Local 829), Gene McElwain (Local 751), Tony DePaulo (IATSE), Evan Shoemake (SDC), Ira Mont (Actors' Equity), David Faux (Dramatists Guild), Mary Donovan (Local 802).

Standing (L-R): Deborah Allton-Maher (AGMA), Dan Dashman (Local 798), Michael McBride (Local 829), Barbara Wolkoff (SDC), Mauro Melleno (SDC), Carol Wasser (Actors' Equity), Lawrence Paone (Local 751), Pat White (Local 764), Bart Daudelin (Local 764), Paige Price (Actors' Equity), Frank Connolly, Jr. (Local 817 Teamsters), Kirk Kelly (Local 30), Patrick Langevin (Local 829).

Faculty

Actors' Equity Association

Paige Price
Acting President

Carol Waaser
Acting Executive Director

NATIONAL COUNCIL
(L-R): Acting President Paige Price, Third Vice President Ira Mont, Secretary-Treasurer Sandra Karas, and Second Vice President Rebecca Kim Jordan

Front Row (L-R): Ellen Carter, Beverly Sloan, Brett Barbour

Second Row (L-R): Kathy Mercado, Michelle Lehrman, Maria Cameron, Mary Kate Gilrein, Annie Mosbacher, Louise Foisy

Third Row (L-R): Sylvina Persaud, Sara Gretschel, Val LaVarco, Alex Williams-Bellotti, Cathy Jayne, Sarah Zybert, Joanna Spencer, Thomas Kaub

Fourth Row (L-R): Diane Raimondi, Deborah Johnson, Adeola Adegbola, Tatiana Kouloumbis, Zalina Hoosein, Lawrence Lorczak, Pearl Brady, Jessica Palermo, Melissa Colgan, Kenneth Naanep, Dragica Dabo

Back Row (L-R): Kevin Doyel, Barry Rosenberg, Walt Kiskaddon and David Westphal

(L-R): Calandra Hackney, Courtney Godan, Kristine Arwe, David Thorn, Jillian Williams, Jonathan Black, John Fasulo and Karlene Laemmie

Front Row (L-R): Jack Goldstein, Karen Nothmann, Doug Beebe, Marie Gottschall, David Lotz, Ann Fortuno
Second Row (L-R): Thomas Miller, Chris Williams, Jenifer Hills, Rachel Laforest, Stephanie Masucci, Ellen Deutsch
Back Row (L-R): Joseph De Michele, Robert Fowler, Karen Master, Megan McManus, Joseph Chiplock and Steven DiPaola

Faculty

Dramatists Guild

STEERING
Standing (L-R): David Lindsay-Abaire, Julia Jordan, David Ives, John Weidman
Seated (L-R): Peter Parnell, Stephen Schwartz, Theresa Rebeck

STAFF
Seated (L-R): David Faux, Gary Garrison, Ralph Sevush and Abby Marcus
Standing (L-R): Tari Stratton, Patrick Shearer, Robert Ross Parker, Larry Pontius and Amy Von Vett

Association of Theatrical Press Agents and Managers

Seated (L-R): Rina Saltzman, Barbara Carroll, David Calhoun (Vice President), Robert Nolan (President), Nick Kaledin (Secretary-Treasurer), Penny Daulton, Anita Dloniak
Standing (L-R): Jeremy Shaffer, A. Scott Falk, Jonathan Shulman, David Gersten, Adam Miller, Merle Debuskey, Maury Collins, Bill Matson, Jeffrey Pluth and Nance Movsesian

Faculty

American Federation of Musicians, Local 802

Mary Landolfi
President

Bill Dennison
Recording Vice President

(L-R): Bud Burridge, Maxine Roach, Jay Blumenthal, Andy Schwartz, Al Hunt, Ethan Fein, Mary Landolfi, Maura Giannini, Jay Schaffner, Ken Rizzo, Bill Dennison and Mark Johansen

Stage Directors and Choreographers Society

Seated (L-R): Larry Carpenter (Executive Vice President), Kathleen Marshall (Vice President), Karen Azenberg (President), Laura Penn (Executive Director), Doug Hughes (Treasurer)
Second Row (L-R): Marcia Milgrom Dodge, Edie Cowan, Susan Schulman, Kim Rogers, Elizabeth Miller, Gerald Freedman, Lisa Peterson, Barbara Wolkoff, Sue Lawless, Tom Moore, Lena Abrams, John Everson
Back Row (L-R): Walter Bobbie, Sam Bellinger, Mauro Melleno, Daniel Sullivan, Rob Ashford, Randy Anderson, Richard Hamburger, Evan Shoemake, Preston Copley
Board members not present: Julie Arenal, Joe Calarco, Tisa Chang, Michael John Garces, Wendy Goldberg, Paul Lazarus, Ethan McSweeny, Amy Morton, Sharon Ott, Lonny Price, Mary B. Robinson, Susan H. Schulman, Oz Scott, Leigh Silverman, David Warren and Chay Yew

Faculty

IATSE Local 306 Motion Picture Projectionists, Video Technicians and Allied Crafts (Ushers)

Back Row (L-R): Roy DuBose, Rafael Cortes, Hugo Capra, Joe Rivierzo, Mike Satrin
Front Row (L-R): Margie Blair, Lorraine Lowery and Rose Ann Cipriano

Make-up Artists and Hair Stylists, IATSE Local 798

Front Row (L-R): Deborah Bell, Joel Mendenhall, Wendy Evans, Norman Bryn, Valerie Gladstone, Charles McKenna
Second Row (L-R): Pat Moore, Cindy Gardner, Stephanie Barnes, Michael Hanue
Third Row (L-R): Rebecca Kuzma, Mary Lampert, Reo Anderson
Top of the stairs: Joe Cuervo
Back Left Corner (L-R): Victor De Nicola, Stephen Bishop, Werner Sherer, Milton Buras, John James, Todd Kleitsch, Daniel Dashman
Back Right Corner (L-R): Gene Block, Magdalena Kolodziej, Carl Fullerton, Shanah Ann Kendall, Lauzanne Nel, Nick London

Faculty

Treasurers & Ticket Sellers Union, IATSE Local 751

THE EXECUTIVE COUNCIL
Seated (L-R): Fred Bonis, Noreen Morgan, A. Greer Bond, Karen Winer and Diane Heatherington
Standing (L-R): John Nesbitt, Mike McCarthy, Harry Jaffie, Matthew Fearon, Michael Loiacono, Gene McElwain, Lawrence Paone, Peter Attanasio Jr., Stanley Shaffer and Fred Santore Jr.

OFFICE STAFF
Seated (L-R): Kathy McBrearty and Patricia Garrison.
Standing (L-R): Lawrence Paone, Gene McElwain and Jim Sita.

Theatrical Wardrobe Union, IATSE Local 764

Standing (L-R): Bart Daudelin, Warren Wernick, Frank Gallagher, Rochelle Friedman
Seated (L-R): Mary Ferry, Mike Gemignani, Joan Boyce, Binh Hoong

Faculty

Theatrical Teamsters, Local 817

EXECUTIVE BOARD
Front Row (L-R): Francis J. Connolly, Jr. (Business Agent & Union Trustee), Jim Leavey (Recording Secretary), Ed Iacobelli (Vice President).
Back Row (L-R): Mike Hyde (Union Trustee), Thomas R. O'Donnell (President), Thomas J. O'Donnell (Secretary-Treasurer), Kevin Keefe (Union Trustee).

STAFF
Front Row (L-R): Christine Harkerss (Human Resources), Tina Gusmano (Union Secretary).
Back Row (L-R): Terry Casaletta (Casting Director Organizer), Marge Marklin (Fund Secretary).

Not Present: Kathy Kreinbihl (Fund Administrator), Margie Vaeth (Union Secretary).

Service Employees International Union Local 32BJ

EXECUTIVE OFFICERS
(L-R): Kevin Doyle (Executive Vice President), Héctor J. Figueroa (Secretary-Treasurer) and Michael P. Fishman (President).

International Union of Operating Engineers Local 30

BUSINESS MANAGER
John T. Ahern

Faculty

American Theatre Wing

BOARD OF DIRECTORS AND STAFF
Seated (L-R): Enid Nemy, Douglas B. Leeds, Sondra Gilman, Theodore S. Chapin (Chairman), Dasha Epstein, Pia Lindström, Anita Jaffe, Ronald S. Konecky

Standing (L-R): Howard Sherman (Executive Director), James Weinman (Staff), Robb Perry (Staff), Gail Yancosek (Staff), Barbara Toy (Staff), Raisa Ushomirskiy (Staff), David Brown (Treasurer), Michael P. Price (Vice President), David Henry Hwang, Peter Schneider, Lucie Arnaz, Alan Siegel (Secretary), Bruce Redditt, William Craver, Jeffrey Eric Jenkins, Joanna Sheehan (Staff), Randy Ellen Lutterman (Staff), Myra Wong (Staff)

Not Pictured: Kate Burton, Mallory Factor, James Higgins, Jo Sullivan Loesser, Jane Fearer Safer, Marva Smalls, Howard Stringer, Sally Susman.

Binder Casting

Back Row: (L-R) Mark Brandon, Sara Schatz, Scout J. Schatz, Jack Bowdan

Front Row (L-R) Nikole Vallins, Jay Binder, Karen Young, Patrick Bell

The Playbill Broadway YEARBOOK 2009-2010

Faculty

Broadway Cares/Equity Fights AIDS

Front Row (L-R): Andy Halliday; Christopher F. Davis; Bobby McGuire
Second Row (L-R): Madeline Reed; Denise Roberts Hurlin; Frank Conway; Yvonne Ghareeb; Keith Bullock; Scott Tucker
Third Row (L-R): Tom Viola, Executive Director; Meagan Grund; Cat Domiano; Wendy Merritt Kaufman; Carol Ingram; Ngoc Bui; Jody O'Neil
Fourth Row (L-R): Andy Smith; Christopher Economakos; Scott Stevens; Roy Palijaro; Michael Simmons-DeFord; Colyn Fiendel; Skip Lawing; Danny Whitman, Director of Communications & Development
Back Row (L-R): Michael Palm; Nathan Hurlin; Peter Borzotta; Larry Cook, Director of Finance & Administration; Chris Kenney and Michael Graziano, Producing Director.

Hudson Scenic Studio

Faculty

Theatre Development Fund and TKTS

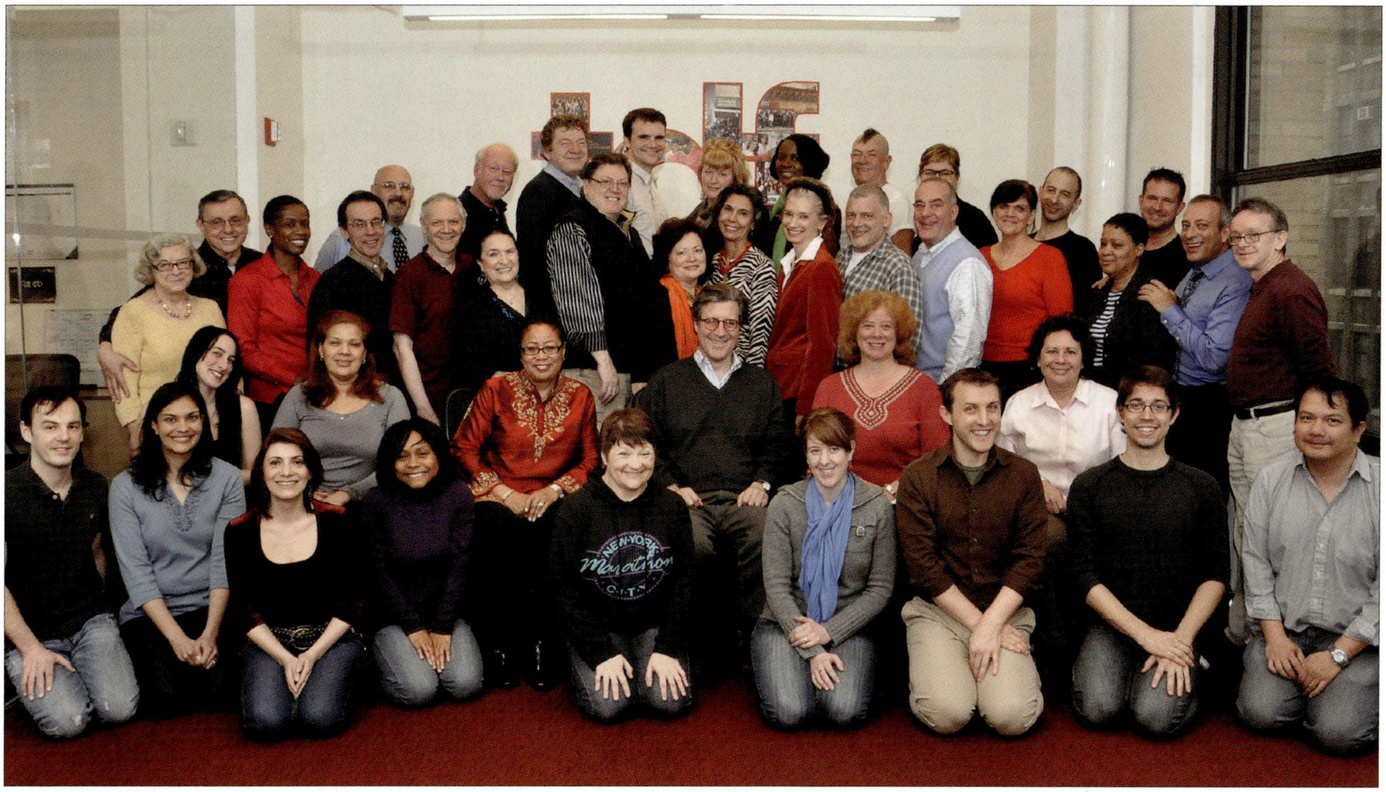

Photo by Anita and Steve Shevett

TDF STAFF

Front Row Kneeling (L-R): Mark Runion, Sarah Aziz, Cherie Samuel, Nikki Duncan-Smith, Nancy Lindeberg, Julie McCabe, Mark Blankenship, Patrick Berger, Jonathan Calindas

Second Row Sitting (L-R): Denyse Owens, Paula Torres, Veronica Claypool, Julian Christenberry, Victoria Bailey, Jane Pfeffer

Third Row Standing (L-R): Ann Mathieson, Joseph Cali, Julie Williams, Howard Marren, George Connolly, Eve Rodriguez, Doug Smith, Joy Cooper, Marianna Houston, Lisa Carling, Sal Polizzi, Eric Sobel, Fran Polino, Joyce Hinds, David LeShay, Richard Price

Back Row Standing: William Castellano, Rob Neely, Costas Michalopoulos, Thomas Adkins, Ginger Meagher, Michele St. Hill, Thomas Westerman, Patty Allen, Michael Yaccarino, Tymand Staggs

Photo by David LeShay

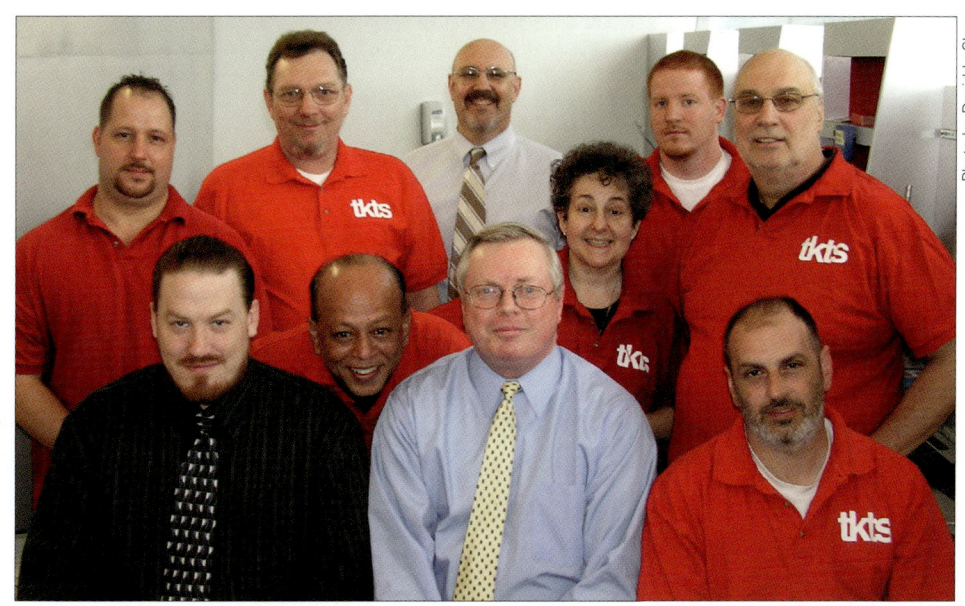

TKTS TREASURERS

Standing (L-R):
Robert Wilamowski,
Joseph McLaughlin,
William Castellano,
Shari Teitelbaum,
Brian Roeder,
James Divone

Seated (L-R):
William Roeder,
Rajesh Sharma (leaning in),
Stephen Banovich,
Michael Campanella

Faculty

The Actors Fund

TRUSTEES
Front Row (L-R): Lynn Redgrave, Jane Powell, Kate Edelman Johnson, Anita Jaffe.
Standing (L-R): Dr. Marc Grodman, Charles Hollerith, George Zuber, Charlotte St. Martin, Jeffrey Bolton, Stewart Lane, Honey Waldman, Alan Levey, Dale Olson, Paul Libin.
Partially Hidden: Merle Debuskey, Scott Weiner, Kristen Madsen, Edward Turen, Brian Stokes Mitchell, B.D. Wong, John Erman.
Back Row: Frank Horak.

NEW YORK STAFF
Front Row (L-R): Suzanne Tobak, Jamie Trachtenberg, Joy Pascua-Kim, Richard Renner, Tamar Shapiro.
Second Row (L-R): Connie Yoo, Gail Perlman, Jay Haddad, Kristen Borg, Alice Vienneau, Erica Chung.
Third Row (L-R): Ell Miocene, Daniel Scholz, Joseph Benincasa, Amy Picar, Zehava Krinsky, Barbara Davis, Karen Ho, Elizabeth Avedon, Elizabeth Tripp.
Fourth Row (L-R): Robert Rosenthal, Paul Riedel, Judy Fish, Marjorie Roop, Thomas Lorio, Amanda Clayman, Jose Delgado, Gloria Jones, Joe Moretti.
Fifth Row (L-R): Tim Pinckney, Kenton Curtis, Amy Wilder, David Engelman, Stephen Joseph, Charlene Nurse, Rick Montero, Carol Wilson, Risa Neuwirth.

NEW JERSEY STAFF
The Actors Fund completed an $11 million expansion and renovation of its nursing home and assisted living care facility in Englewood, New Jersey. Here are some of the staff of the Actors Fund Home team.
Front Row (L-R): Maritza Orellana, Carina Capul, Yalile Chavez, Shanique Wilson, Kourtney Bryant.
Second Row (L-R): Maria Palacios, Aileen Carigo, Zoila Paredes, Maria Box, Alina Arias, Doris Daly, Maritza Bonilla, Susan Kang, John Bautista.
Back Row (L-R): Jordan Strohl, Luis Guirococho, Igor Denisenko, Mandy Williamson, Magnus Tyrell, Grace Park, Susan Langschultz-Maneri, Cathie King, Annmarie De Feis, Rhonda Hunter, Sam Diah.

LOS ANGELES STAFF
Front Row (L-R): Aaron King, Laurhan Beato, Annie Keating, Linda Zimmerman, Joanne Webb, Mike Salerno, Tina Hookom, Roni Blau.
Back Row: Gregory Polcyn, Dan Kitowski, Keith McNutt, Heather Vanian, Jan Kees Van Der Gaag, Joey Shanley.

Faculty

Boneau/Bryan-Brown

Chris Boneau

Adrian Bryan-Brown

Photos by Joan Marcus

Jim Byk

Brandi Cornwell

Jackie Green

Kelly Guiod

Linnae Hodzic

Jessica Johnson

Kevin Jones

Amy Kass

Emily Meagher

Aaron Meier

Christine Olver

Joe Perrotta

Matt Polk

Heath Schwartz

Michael Strassheim

Susanne Tighe

Faculty

The Hartman Group

Michael Hartman

Leslie Baden

Michelle Bergmann

Nicole Capatasto

Tom D'Ambrosio

Juliana Hannett

Alyssa Hart

Bethany Larsen

Matt Ross

Frances White

 Wayne Wolfe

Faculty

Richard Kornberg & Associates

Richard Kornberg

Don Summa

Billy Zavelson

Danielle McGarry

Jeffrey Richards Associates

Standing (L-R): Robert J. Saferstein, Jeremy Scott Blaustein, Jeffrey Richards, Elon Rutberg
Seated (L-R): Kristin Piacentile, Irene Gandy, Alana Karpoff, Diana Rissetto, Charlie McAteer

The Publicity Office

Standing (L-R): Jeremy Shaffer and Michael Borowski

Seated: Marc Thibodeau (with Berger)

The Playbill Broadway Yearbook 2009-2010

Faculty

THE BROADWAY CHANNEL™
One on the aisle and a backstage pass to the best of Broadway

Kate Shindle with Julie Andrews at the 2008 Tony Awards

Ken Hege

Matthew Hege

Melba Silwany

Kate Shindle

Jackie Bales

Paul Dokuchitz

Keith Hurd

Jimmy Merrill

Diovon Pelicot

Brian Piccirillo

Betty Alvarez

John Sawina

Faculty

G. ANDERSON ART CLUB	B. AQUART BASKETBALL	J. AQUINO TRACK & FIELD	M. BARRY BADMINTON
A. BIZJAK JAZZ TEAM	J. BODLEY ROCK BAND	G. COLEMAN THEATRE TECHIE	J. COOPER 4-H
T. COPPOLA CHORUS	D. COX HISTORICAL SOCIETY	G. CRADDOCK EAGLE SCOUTS	T. CREWS VALEDICTORIAN
A. CRUZ GLEE CLUB	A. DAVIS BLACK HISTORY CLUB	M. DELMORE BABYSITTERS CLUB	L. ELLIS SHAMPOO CLUB
T. FALOTICO WATER POLO	C. FENTON THATCHERITE	S. FITZPATRICK CHEERLEADING	J. FOX A.M. ANNOUNCEMENTS
J. FRAENKEL HILLEL	T. FRANCIS STUDY CLUB	R. GASKINS DRILL TEAM	G. GREEN PEP SQUAD
K. HALL WEIGHTLIFTING	J. HESTER BREAKFAST CLUB	I. HILAIRE SYNC. SWIMMING	L. HU SCIENCE OLYMPIAD
L. HUNTER ICE HOCKEY	L. JOHNSON DANCE TEAM		

SpotCo Class of 2010

D. HODGES — PRINCIPAL
J. EDWARDS — VICE PRINCIPAL
B. BERK — DEAN OF STUDENTS
T. GREENWALD — AV SQUAD

L. KAISER YEARBOOK	K. LEVIN HALL MONITOR	N. LINDEMAN PING PONG	S. MAYA FORENSICS
T. McCANN EQUINE CLUB	M. McCRACKEN NERD	J. McNICHOLAS BROADCAST CLUB	M. METTLER CLOGGING
W. MITCHELL DRAMA SOCIETY	M. OWNBEY CHEESE CLUB	D. PRESTON MATHLETES	K. RATHBUN QUIZ BOWL CAPTAIN
S. RAUCHWERGER STEP TEAM	M. RHEAULT WRESTLING	J. ROGERS DRUMLINE	I. ROSEN PROM COMMITTEE
A. ROTHENBERG COLOR GUARD	V. SAINATO DEBATE	S. SANTORE CROSS COUNTRY	C. SEES CLASS CLOWN
C. SHALOIKO SKI CLUB	R. SIMNOWITZ HOME ECONOMICS	C. SKENE COMPUTER CLUB	D. SNYPE BALLET FOLKLORICS
J. SOCHACZEWSKI EXCHANGE STUDENT	S. SOSNOWSKI FENCING	A. SPIELMAN NEWSPAPER	C. SPINNEY BROWNIES
D. SUYAMA SOCCER	L. TAYLOR APIARIST CLUB	E. VICIOSO BAND	B. WATSON YOUNG DEMOCRATS
M. WILSTEIN ASTRONOMY CLUB			

Faculty

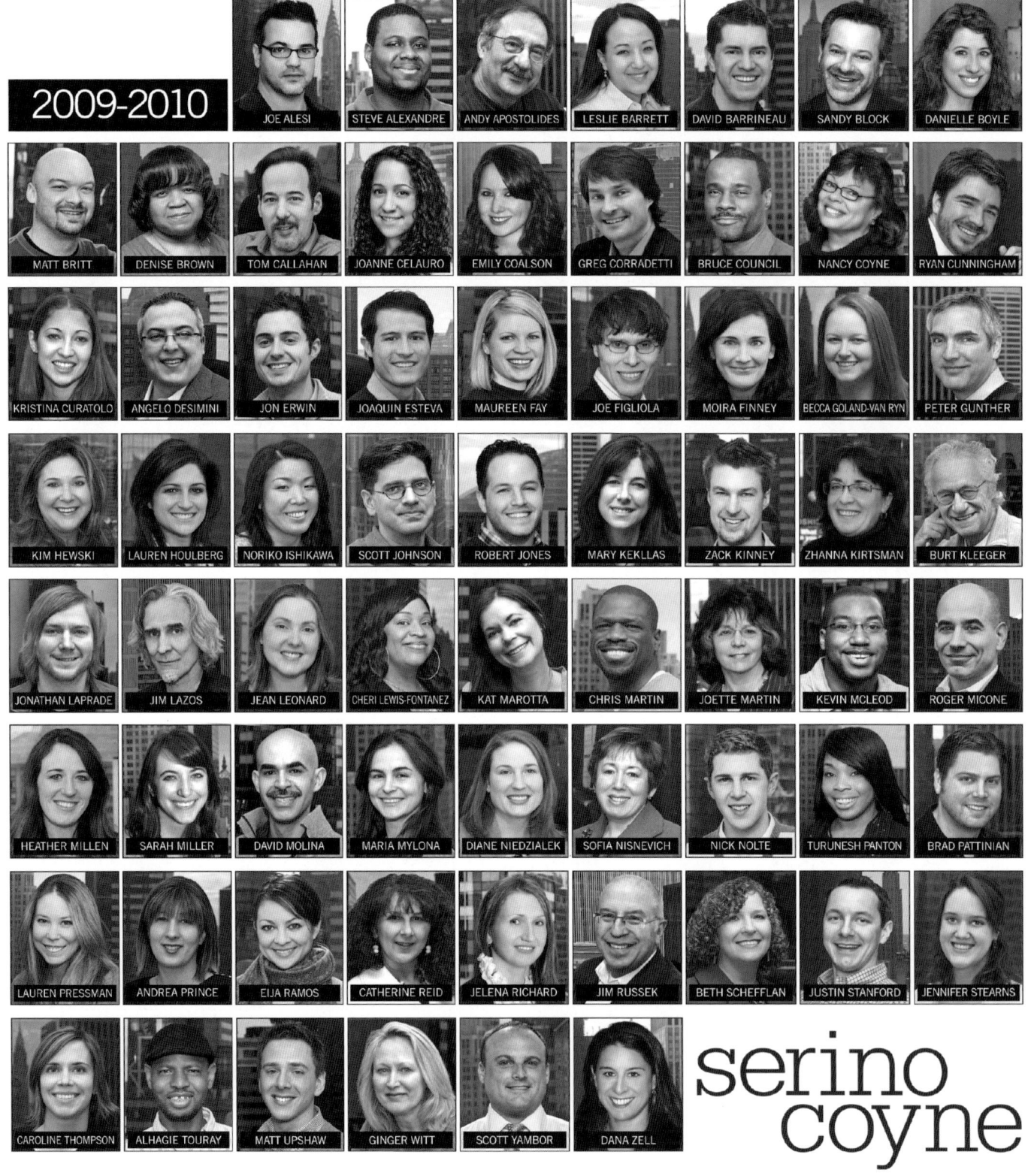

Faculty

Eliran Murphy Group

a) Barbara Eliran b) Ann Murphy c) Richard Robertson d) Elizabeth Findlay
e) Janice Brunell (& Chef John Besh) f) Robert Marlin g) Denise Ganjou h) Cara Sogliuzzo
i) Hannah Speirits j) Greg Cavaluzzo k) Brittinee Phillips l) Alex Walker m) Clint Okayama
n) Suzanne Hereth o) Terry Newberry p) Frank "Fraver" Verlizzo q) Jeff Lilley
r) Pamela Bush s) Matthew Lee t) Amy Lipson u) Patrick Flood v) Shirley

Faculty

Faculty

Playbill

Philip S. Birsh
Publisher

Arthur T. Birsh
Chairman

Clifford S. Tinder
*Senior Vice President/
Publisher, Classic Arts
Division*

Joan Alleman
*Corporate Vice
President*

Blake Ross
*Editor-in-Chief
Playbill*

MANHATTAN OFFICE
Front Row, Seated (L-R): Jil Simon, Blake Ross, Clifford S. Tinder, Diana Leidel, Ari Ackerman
Second Row, Standing (L-R): Oldyna Dynowska, Adam Hetrick, Theresa Holder, Tiffany Feo, Wanda Young, Clara Barragan-Tiburcio, Samantha Souza, Maude Popkin, Andrew Ku, Andrew Gans
Back Row, Standing (L-R): Robert Viagas, Ernio Hernandez, Ben Finane, Alex Near, David Gewirtzman, Daniel Beaver-Seitz, Arturo Gonzalez, Glenn Asciutto, James Cairl, Matt Blank, Irv Winick, Norman Miller, and Jeff Nicholson
Not pictured: Louis Botto, Esvard D'Haiti, Kenneth Jones, Jose Ortiz, Silvija Ozols, Anderson Peguero, Jolie Schaffzin, Glenn Shaevitz, Kesler Thibert and Joel Wyman.

PLAYBILL.COM
(Seated L-R):
Kenneth Jones
and Andrew Gans

(Standing L-R): Adam
Hetrick,
Ernio Hernandez
and David Gewirtzman

Not pictured:
Matt Blank,
Martha Graebner,
Andrew Ku
and Samantha Souza.

Louis Botto
Columnist

Harry Haun
Columnist

Jennifer Lanter
Columnist

Seth Rudetsky
Columnist

Mark Shenton
*London
Correspondent*

Robert Simonson
*Senior
Correspondent*

Steven Suskin
Columnist

Not Pictured: Tom Nondorf.

Faculty

Playbill

CLASSIC ARTS DIVISION and PROGRAM EDITORS

Seated (L-R): Pam Karr, Claire Mangan, Scott Hale, Rori Grable

Standing (L-R): Patrick Cusanelli, Judy Samelson, Amy Asch, Sean Kenny, Ben Hyacinthe, Brian Libfeld, David Porrello

Not pictured: Kristy Bredin, Silvia Cañadas, Maria Chinda, Bill Reese, Andrew Rubin and Eddie Silva

Photos by Brian Mapp

ACCOUNTING
(Clockwise from front left): Lewis Cole, Theresa Bernstein, James Eastman, JoAnn D'Amato, John LoCascio
Not pictured: Beatriz Chitnis

Carolina Diaz
Florida Production Manager

Regional Advertising Salespersons

Kenneth R. Back
*Sales Manager
Cincinnati*

Elaine Bodker
*Sales
St. Louis*

Dory Binyon
*Sales Manager
Chicago*

Carol Brumm
*Sales
St. Louis*

Bob Caulfield
*Sales
San Francisco*

Margo Cooper
*Sales Manager
St. Louis*

Betsy Gugick
*Sales Manager
Dallas*

Ron Friedman
*Sales Manager
Columbus*

Tom Green
*Sales
Florida/Texas, etc.*

Ed Gurien
*Sales
Florida/Dallas*

Michel Manzo
*Sales Manager
Philadelphia*

Marilyn A. Miller
*Sales Manager
Minneapolis*

Judy Pletcher
*Sales Manager
Washington, DC*

John Rosenow
*Sales Manager
Phoenix/Tucson*

Kenneth Singer
*Sales Manager
Houston*

Not Pictured: Jennifer Allington, Dick Coffee, Nancy Hardin, Jeff Ross, Sara Smith and Donald Roberts.

Faculty

Playbill / Woodside Office

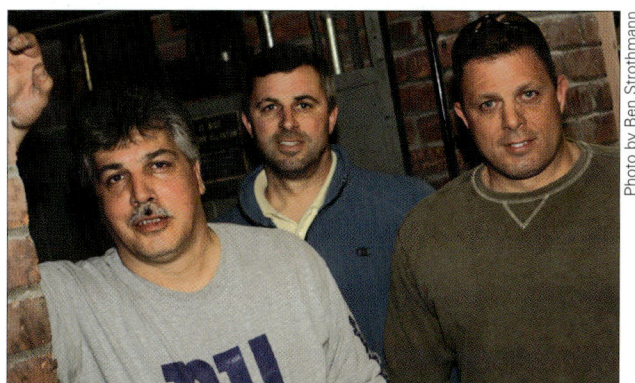

PRODUCTION CHIEFS
(L-R): Louis Cusanelli, Robert Cusanelli and Patrick Cusanelli

PRODUCTION
Standing (L-R): Patrick Cusanelli, Benjamin Hyacinthe, Sean Kenny
Seated: David Porrello

DAY CREW

Back Row (L-R): Robert Cusanelli, Ray Sierra, Larry Przetakiewicz, Steve Ramlall, Mary Roaid, Nancy Galarraga, Scott Cipriano, Janet Moti, John Matthews

Front Row (L-R): Lennox Worrell, David Rodriguez, Chris Toribio, Joseph Lucania

NIGHT CREW

(L-R): Ricardo Garcia, Anna Rincon, Frank Dunn, Jim Ayala, Robert Cusanelli, Louis Cusanelli II, Kenneth Gomez, Lidia Yagual, Elias Garcia

In Memoriam
May 2009 to May 2010

Betty Allen
Ruth Altman
Army Archerd
Claudia Asbury
Val Avery
Guy Babylon
Carl Ballantine
Ernie Banks
Gene Barry
John Battles
Margery Beddow
Leta Bonynge
Ronald Bostick
Martin Brandt
David Brown
Ernest Brown
Michael Buckley
Donald Buka
Douglas Campbell
Carmen Capalbo
Richard Carlyle
Grace Carney
David Carradine
Dixie Carter
Patricia Casterlin
Carol Cole
Dennis Cole
Rik Colitti
Ann Collins
Gene Cooper
Peggy Cooper
Pierre Cossette
Ward Costello
Darryl Croxton
Frank Cruz
T. Scott Cunningham
Joyce Dahl
Carleton Davis
Phil DiMaggio
Robert E. Dixon
Donal Donnelly
John Dorman
Ralph Douglas
Ethelyne Dunfee
Harry Edelstein
Harry Edwards
Max Eisen
Jerome Eskow
Bruce Evans
Sonny Everett

Broadway Dims Its Lights
Broadway theatres dimmed their marquee lights this season upon the passing of the following theatre personalities, listed here along with the date the honor was accorded: Theatre Executive George MacPherson, June 5, 2009. Actor Karl Malden, July 2, 2009. Edison Café co-owner Harry Edelstein, July 15, 2009. Playwright/librettist Larry Gelbart, September 15, 2009. Producer David Brown, February 3, 2010. Actress/playwright Lynn Redgrave, May 4, 2010. Singer/actress Lena Horne, May 11, 2010. Dancer/Actress Doris Eaton Travis, May 12, 2010. Critic Michael Kuchwara, May 25, 2010.

Farrah Fawcett
Ruth Ford
John Forsythe
Conard Fowkes
Clement Fowler
John Franklyn-Robbins
Michael Frazier
Larry French
Larry Gelbart
Douglas Gordon
Morton Gottlieb
Kathryn Grayson
Susan Gregg
Shelly Gross
Birdie M. Hale
Alaina Reed Hall
June Havoc
Marc Hertsens
Jack Holland
Lena Horne
Reby Howells

Lou Jacobi
Patricia Jenkins
Alan Kass
Bernard Kates
Grace Keagy
Betty Lou Keim
John Kenley
Everett King
Lawrence King
Adelaide Klein
Tony Kraber
Michael Kuchwara
Barbara London
Andre Love
Sam Lutfiyya
Mara Lynn
George MacPherson
Karl Malden
William Malone
Jack Manning
Adrienne Marden

Nan Martin
Don Mayo
Bill McIntyre
Caroline M. McWilliams
Dan Merriman
George R. Merritt
Joe Milan
James Mitchell
Zakes Mokae
Bill Mullikin
Brittany Murphy
Karl Nielsen
Craig Noel
Julian Patrick
Carol Perea
Michael Philippi
Joseph Pinckney
David Powers
Harve Presnell
Claude Purdy
Corin Redgrave
Lynn Redgrave
Frances Reid
Shirley Rich
Pernell E. Roberts
Mary Roche
M. Edgar Rosenblum
Budd Schulberg
Dorothy Scott
Jean Simmons
Arnold Stang
Robert V. Straus
Patrick Swayze
Mark A. Taylor
Angela Thornton
Wayne Tippit
Doris Eaton Travis
K.C. Townsend
Mary Mon Toy
Edmond Varrato
Ralph Vucci
Douglas Watt
James R. Whittle
Collin Wilcox
Susan Willis
Joseph Wiseman
Edward Woodward
Conrad Yama
Torrie Zito

Doris Eaton Travis, 106, believed to be the oldest living *Ziegfeld Follies* alumna, blows the audience a kiss while taking her final Broadway bow on the Minskoff Theatre stage April 27, 2010, at the annual "Easter Bonnet" competition, two weeks before her death. She made her Broadway debut in 1917.

Index

A

Aarons, Michael 22, 220, 240, 246
Aballi, Alicia 7, 291
Abate, Shelagh 326
Abbandandolo, Brenda 66, 250
Abbate, Mickey 296
Abbott, Eric 25, 132, 250
Abbott, James 8
Abbott, James Lynn 121, 124, 362, 365
Abbott, Joy 322
Abdul-Rahiim, Islah 182
Abdul, Paula 370
Abel, Marybeth 362, 367, 370
Abel, Megan 250
Abel, Timothy 217, 250, 267, 280
Abraham, Joe 184, 185, 186
Abramovitz, Jill 245, 246
Abrams, Bernard 109, 112, 279
Abrams, Bernie 276
Abrams, Lena 403
Abramson, Jane 188, 216
Abrazado, Carmen I. 181, 182
Accurso, Aron 47, 185, 188
Acevedo, Elisa 156
Acken, Peter 188
Ackerman, Ari 419
Ackerman, Eddie 216
Ackerman, Ted 262, 266
Ackert, David A. 243
Adamian, Daniel 25, 102, 114, 133, 163, 196
Adams, Brooke 171, 172, 175
Adams, Cameron 276, 278, 310, 311
Adams, Candi 133
Adams, Hilary 78
Adams, Katie 58, 196, 255
Adams, Ken 113
Adams, Kevin 21, 23, 24, 91, 92, 127, 130, 131, 240, 241, 340, 341, 389, 393

Adams, Lee vi, 60, 63, 67, 68
Adams, Nick 121-123, 164-166, 169
Adams, Randy 222
Adamson, Andrew 315
Adamy, Paul 203
Addams, Charles viii, 1, 9
Adderley, Konrad 363
Addiss, Pat 276, 340
Addiss, Pat Flicker 279, 341
Adegbola, Adeola 401
Adey, Jenny 168
Adkins, David 236, 237
Adkins, Thomas 409
Adler, Dara 264
Adler, Gary 32-34
Adnitt, Stephen 16, 17
Adonna, Emily 265
Agee, Martin 355, 360
Agosta, Alexandra Gushin 74
Agraz, Raul 141, 145
Aguasvivas, Zipporah 13, 95, 274
Aguilar, Hector 7
Aguilar, Omar 249
Agurto, Maria 359
Ahern, John T. 406
Ahrens, Lynn vii, 286, 289, 293
Aibel, Douglas 34, 36
Aiello, Mario 126
Ainge, Christina 132, 133, 291
Ainge, Patrick 224, 225
Aitken, Bobby 202, 205
Aitken, Maria 340, 341, 343, 344
Akbar, Shaan 183, 189, 217
Akerlind, Christopher 335, 336
Akram, George 354, 356
Alam, Jennifer 132, 133, 231, 291
Albanese, Ron 307
Albano, Aaron J.

211, 212, 214
Albarracin, Marian 74, 168
Albee, Edward 392
Alberts, Allan 208
Albertson, Tessa 310, 311
Albery, Shana 113, 114, 280, 281
Albrecht, Bobbye Sue 368, 369
Albright, Tim 355
Alcorn, Narda 104, 105, 106, 182
Alderman, Jane 335, 336, 339
Aldredge, Theoni V. 133
Aldrich, Mark 286, 287, 288, 293
Aldridge, Rebecca 8
Alexander, John 238
Alexander, Terence Orleans 216
Alexander, Terry 218
Alexander, TV 8
Alfonso, Ioana 245, 247
Alfred, Roy 83
Alger, Jay 182
Alhadeff, Aaron 219
Alhadeff, Alison 219
Alhadeff, Andi 219
Alhadeff, Emily 219
Alhadeff, Kenny 219, 222
Alhadeff, Marleen 219, 222
Ali, Sumayya 286, 287, 288
Allain, Stephen 196
Allan, Sara Minskoff 176
Alldaffer, Alaine 270
Allegro, Joseph 83
Alleman, Joan 419
Allemon, Matt 25
Allen, Betty 422
Allen, Chad 200
Allen, Edward 304, 334, 369
Allen, Heather 58, 114, 196, 255, 304
Allen, Jane 120
Allen, Jason 342
Allen, Jennifer 219, 220, 221
Allen, Joan 31, 338
Allen, Joey 304
Allen, Jonathan 208
Allen, Katherine 8

Allen, Mike 273
Allen, Patty 409
Allen, Sasha 131
Allen, Tasha 73
Allenberg, Robert 78, 308, 347
Allers, Roger 176, 178, 179
Alli Mauzey 366
Allison, Drayton 167
Allott, Nicholas 217, 267
Allton-Maher, Deborah 400
Alpert, David 126
Alspector, Rebecca 334
Alston, Stephanie 78, 308, 347
Altamore, Susan 232
Alter, Frank 216, 218
Alterman, Charlie 240, 242
Alterman, Loraine 222
Altman, Matt 329
Altman, Ruth 422
Altmeyer, Tim 198, 199
Alvarez, David 41-43, 49, 50
Alvarez, Jessica 258
Alvarez, Lauren 8, 39, 133, 250, 280
Alvarez, Lauren M. 334
Alvord, Megan J. 225
Aman, Brian 162
Amarantos, John 418
Amari, Pat 249
Amato, Joseph 31, 173, 337
Amber, Ashley 276, 277, 278
Ambler, Scott 85
Ambrose, Lauren 379
Amendola, Dana 183, 188, 217
Amendum, Dominick 362, 363, 370
Amerling, Victor 182, 217
Amis, Tash 48
Amma, Aretha 102
Ammerman, Andrew R. 243

Anders, Kathy 47, 217
Andersen, Caroline 250
Andersen, Kjeld 182
Anderson-Lopez, Kristen 12, 65, 94, 273, 321, 372
Anderson-Rothe, Duffy 106
Anderson, Arlene 115
Anderson, Cailin 113, 114
Anderson, Carey 34
Anderson, Christian 32, 33
Anderson, Dennis 110, 113
Anderson, Eric 324-326
Anderson, Fraser 138, 296
Anderson, Gail 415
Anderson, Jack 280
Anderson, Jay 80
Anderson, Kevin 31, 338, 368
Anderson, Kristen 36
Anderson, Matt 20
Anderson, Randy 403
Anderson, Reo 404
Anderson, Scott 188, 196, 320, 322
Anderson, Stig 202
Anderson, Todd 365, 366
Anderson, Tom 35, 36
Anderson, Vanessa 64, 66
Andersson, Benny 202, 204, 207
Andor, Erik 315
Andors, Nick 329
Andos, Randy 2, 7, 213
Andreas, Christine 164, 166
Andreesen, Rainer 274
Andres, Emily 47
Andresen, Baxley 8
Andrew Dean 315
Andrews, David 31, 36, 39, 48, 58, 74, 88, 120, 138, 151, 168, 174, 200, 208, 225, 243, 258, 267,

281, 285, 296, 315, 334, 338, 352
Andrews, George Lee 261, 263, 269
Andrews, Joan 243
Andrews, Joshua 126
Andrews, Julie 379
Andrews, Peter 243
Andrews, Stuart 217, 267
Andrien, Lydia 8
Andy Sather 208
Angelino, Louise 53, 125, 126, 230, 231
Angelo, Juliette Allen 44, 211, 213, 218
Angulo, Hector 238, 342
Angulo, Jonathan 238, 342
Angus, Henry James 58
Aniello, Chris 102, 342
Anikulapo-Kuti, Fela vii, 97, 98
Anka, Paul 83
Anker, Helen 276, 278
Anna Louizos 33
Anne, Revanth 66, 94, 274, 321, 372, 399
Anschutz, Sue 208, 288, 291
Anthony, Greg 185, 188
Anthony, Marc 59
Anthony, Mike 6
Antrim, Chelsea 106
Apgar, Clayton 236, 237
Aplin, Jonathan 138, 296
Apostolides, Andy 416
Appleby, Elspeth 35, 36
Applegate, Fred 164, 166
Aquart, Bashan 415
Aquino, Jim 39, 47, 114, 126, 168, 225, 255, 415
Arana, Carlos 164
Arango, Julian
Andres 88
Aravena, Michelle 158, 159
Arcelus, Sebastian 158, 159, 161

The Playbill Broadway Yearbook 2009-2010   423

Index

Arch, David 47, 126, 145, 225, 231, 250, 361
Archer, Beatrix 217
Archerd, Army 422
Archie, Terence 286-288
Arditti, Paul 41, 44
Areffi, Andy 315
Arenal, Julie 403
Arenas, Alana 31, 338
Aretos, Guillaume 315
Arge, Belinda 315
Argota, Ashley 49
Arian, Adam 225
Arianda, Nina 393
Arias, Alina 410
Arias, Barbara 280
Arias, Roy 200
Arlen, Harold 20, 82, 83, 95, 200
Arminio, Danielle 36
Armitage, Karole 127, 130
Armitage, Robert M. 188
Armon, Faye 88
Armon, Marilyn 88
Armstrong, Adrienne 25, 26
Armstrong, Billie Joe 21, 23, 26, 389
Armstrong, Craig McKenzie 58
Armstrong, David 219, 223
Armstrong, Eric 95
Armstrong, Ross 135, 136, 139
Armstrong, Scott 25, 314
Arnao, Robert 182, 188
Arnaz, Lucie 407
Arney, Randall 31, 338, 345, 371
Arnold, Matthew 380
Arnold, Michael 324, 325, 326
Arnold, Philip R. Jr. 48
Arodin, Sidney 20
Aronson, Henry 298, 299, 301, 303
Aronstam, Elliott 31, 53, 88, 285, 338
Arrington, Kate 31, 338
Arsenault, Freddy 305, 306, 309
Arvia, Ann 211-213
Arwe, Kristine 401
Asai, Yujin 296
Asbury, Claudia 422
Asbury, Donna Marie iv, 69-71, 75
Ascarelli, Miriam 322
Ascenzo, Paul 178
Asch, Amy i, iii, iv, 420
Asciutto, Glenn 419
Ascroft, Robert 120
Ashford, Annaleigh 127, 129, 377
Ashford, Rob 276, 278, 296, 403
Ashley, Christopher 158, 161, 163, 219, 221, 388
Ashley, Connie 397
Ashley, Elizabeth 28, 29, 200, 370
Ashman, Howard 184, 185, 187
Ashmanskas, Brooks viii, 270, 271, 275, 276, 278
Ashmore, Catherine 69
Ashton, Amy 12, 65, 94, 273, 321, 372, 399
Ashton, Paul 19, 20, 64, 66
Asiatico, Hochi 39, 188
Asiatico, Jose 315
Askew, Sarah 48
Asnes, Andrew 335, 336
Assael-Migliore, Deborah 113, 185
Assalone, Michael 151, 330
Astaire, Adele 375
Astaire, Fred 375
Astin, John 9
Astras, John 291
Athens, Jim 155, 156
Atkinson, Paul 41, 47
Attanasio, Peter 301, 304
Attanasio, Peter Jr. 405
Attianese, Michael 302
Attridge, Rachel 47
Attwell, Harry 135, 136
Auberjonois, Remy 152-154, 157
Aubrey, Miles 158-160
Augustin, Jeff 308, 347
Augustine, Thomas 188, 281, 303
Auster, David 7, 138, 296
Austin, Danny 162
Austin, Hilary 100, 102
Austin, Lee 156, 162
Austin, Neil 135, 137, 294, 295, 297, 389, 392
Austin, Peter 207
Austin, Tom 163
Austrian, Jessie 171, 172
Avallone, Angelina 1, 5, 13, 39, 60, 63, 78, 126, 184, 187, 191, 193, 225, 245, 248, 298, 300, 308, 322, 354
Avedon, Elizabeth 410
Avedon, Richard 322
Avery, Val 422
Aves, Craig 368, 369
Avila, Tereso 132
Axelrad, Joy 397
Ayala, Jim 421
Ayckbourn, Alan 252, 253, 389
Ayers, Becca 324, 325, 326
Ayers, Heather 194
Ayers, Rachel E. 12, 65, 94, 273, 321, 343, 372, 399
Ayesa, MiG 56
Ayres, Lew 373
Ayyagari, Sunil 78, 308, 347, 398
Azenberg, Emanuel vii, 51, 52, 286, 290
Azenberg, Jessica 53
Azenberg, Karen 403
Aziz, Sarah 409

B

Babak, Cynthia 12, 65, 94, 273, 321, 343, 372
Babani, David 164, 191
Babbitt, Ronan 132
Babin, Jack 369
Babylon, Guy 48, 422
Bacharach, Burt viii, 276, 278
Back, Kenneth R. 420
Backstrom, Greg 12, 20, 65, 94, 273, 321, 343, 372
Backus, Jon 418
Bacri, Edmond David 163
Badame, Judy 19, 20
Baden, Leslie 25, 48, 250, 303, 334, 361, 412
Badger, Justin 127-129
Baer, Abel 163
Baer, Zachary 399
Baeza, Brian 125
Bagert, Darren 86, 121, 124
Bailey, Adam 314
Bailey, Adrian 377
Bailey, Christopher 276
Bailey, Sylvia 266, 269
Bailey, Theresa 188
Bailey, Victoria 409
Bains, Leslie E. 343
Baird, Caitlin 78, 308, 347, 398
Baird, Kimberly 19, 20
Baird, Polly 261-263
Baisden-Folkes, Akeem 94, 274, 321
Bajaj, Ashok 243
Baker, Annie 382
Baker, Blair 256
Baker, Corey 97, 98
Baker, Denys 138
Baker, Dylan 118
Baker, Kate 58
Baker, Patty 219, 222, 232
Baker, Paul 360
Baker, Rozi 215, 310, 311
Baker, Shawn 183, 189, 217
Baker, Simon 117, 118, 252, 253
Baker, Ted 178, 183
Balabanova, Sia 66
Balagna, Jennifer 191
Baldauff, Julie 133
Balderrama, Michael 140-142, 145, 147
Baldet, Damian 180
Baldinu, Pichón 187, 188
Baldwin, Kate vii, 109, 111, 116, 377, 387
Ball, Ernie 25, 304
Ball, Martin 168, 255
Ballantine, Carl 422
Ballard, Jamie Lynn 258
Ballard, Jordan 85, 86, 89, 378
Ballou, Leise Anschuetz 110, 113
Balser, Nathan 245-247, 276-278
Banakis, Brett 291
Banderas, Antonio 390
Banes, Lisa iv, 270, 271, 275
Bankhead, Tallulah iii, viii, ix, 198, 199, 200
Banks, Aru 232, 233
Banks, Clarence 80
Banks, Clive 48
Banks, Ernie 422
Banks, Jean 36
Banos, Karen 360
Banovich, Stephen 409
Banta, Alden 132, 318, 320
Banta, Martha 205
Bantay, John 114
Bantum, Aaron 109-111
Banuazizi, Roeya 291, 314
Banyai, Danielle 73
Banyai, Karen 314
Banyai, Lauren 7
Barasch, Nicholas 358
Barbaretti, John 284
Barbella, Victor 12, 65, 94, 273, 321, 343, 372
Barber, Becky 48
Barbereti, Fran 47
Barbour, Brett 94, 399, 401
Barbour, James 382
Barchetto, Danielle 114, 196, 303
Barclay, Kelli 152-154, 156
Barclay, Shelley 74
Barda, Clive 267
Barere, Diane 355
Barford, Ian 31, 338
Bargeron, Dave 70
Bargonetti, Steve 128, 132
Barisch, Kyle 264, 265
Barkhaus, Brent 322
Barkow, Rhonda M. 342
Barlow, John 48, 126
Barlow, Patrick 340, 341, 343
Barlow, Sean 102
Barna, Mark 138, 145, 231, 234, 281
Barnes, Ben 64, 66
Barnes, Gregg 60, 63
Barnes, Jennifer 7, 8
Barnes, Jenny 156
Barnes, Julie 184-186
Barnes, Stephanie 404
Barnes, William Joseph iv, 245, 248-250, 349, 351-353
Barnett, Hugh 88, 138
Barnett, Molly 133
Barnhart, Jennifer 32, 33
Barnhill, Hettie Vyrine 97, 98
Baron, Leonard 113
Barquet, Arturo 48
Barragan-Tiburcio, Clara 419
Barras, Susan 95, 151
Barre, Gabriel 225
Barrett, Andrew 36, 185, 187, 188, 311, 312, 369
Barrett, Brent 69, 71, 75
Barrett, John 95, 243, 322
Barrett, Kelli 305, 306, 309
Barrett, Mary Ellin 156
Barrile, Anthony 236, 239
Barrineau, David 416

424   The Playbill Broadway Yearbook 2009-2010

Index

Barriteau, Reynold 304
Barron, Alex 78, 308, 347, 398
Barrow, Amanda 168
Barry, B.H. 389
Barry, Gene 422
Barry, Kevin 47
Barry, Melissa 415
Barsamian, Tricia 322
Bart, Lionel 20
Bartek, Ann 200
Bartel, Barbara 13, 14, 58, 93, 94
Bartelt, Sue 58, 196, 255, 304
Bartha, Justin 171, 172, 175
Bartholomew, Dave 231
Bartlett, Sue 114
Bartley, Robert 378
Bartner, Beverly 85, 191
Bartner, Robert 37, 126, 164, 219, 335, 349
Bartosik, Steve 122, 125
Baruch, Jason 258, 304
Baruch, Steven 54, 56, 191, 194, 252, 253, 258
Bascomb, Wilbur 128, 132
Bases, Nan 163
Bashkow, Jack 311
Basie, Count 82
Basile, Cathryn 184-187
Basile, Frank 80, 151, 330
Baskin, Derrick iv, 189, 219, 221, 225, 226
Bass, Brad 219-221
Bassett, J. Philip 140, 145, 232, 234, 235
Bassett, Steve 354-356
Bassman, Damien 2, 7, 8, 10, 240
Bassman, Nili 69, 71
Batchelor, Tommy 41, 43, 49, 50
Bateman, Paul 343
Bates, Erik 158-160
Batt, Bryan 381
Battaglia, Joe 268
Battin, Sharlot 267
Battle, Jason 322, 373
Battles, John 422
Bauder, Rachel 64, 66
Bauer, C. Andrew 102, 250
Bauer, Jessica 8
Baum, David 211, 212, 214
Bauman, Chad M. 243
Bauman, Phillip 31, 47, 83, 102, 188, 208, 342, 361
Baumgartner, Rob 133
Bauner, Brad 54
Bautista, John 410
Baxmeyer, Bob 311
Baxmeyer, Jennifer 360
Baxter, Rick 188, 208
Bay, Jim 234, 235, 254, 255
Bayardelle, Jeannette 127, 129
Bayes, Christopher 340, 342
Bayne, Jacqueline 328
Baytalskiy, Kirill 231, 281
Bazadona, Damian 8, 13, 20, 25, 31, 36, 47, 53, 66, 88, 95, 133, 182, 188, 217, 250, 274, 285, 322, 338, 373, 418
Beach, Gary 378
Beach, Sean 230
Beal, John 110, 113
Bean, Chris 196
Bean, R. 72
Bear, Laurel 78, 308, 347, 398
Beasley, Brian 208
Beasley, Russell 25, 27, 83, 114, 361
Beato, Laurhan 410
Beattie, Laura 234, 235, 249, 250
Beatty, John Lee 51, 52, 69, 71, 109, 112, 171, 172, 305, 345, 346, 349, 350, 388
Beatty, Katie 53, 88, 351, 352
Beauchamp, Bobby 322
Beauchamp, Lane 73, 113
Beaulieu, Kelly 53, 88, 272
Beaulieu, Victor 150
Beaver, Jack 342, 343
Beaver-Seitz, Daniel 419
Beazer, Tracee 219-221, 226
Bebout, Steve 6, 8
Beck, Cassie 252, 253
Beck, Christopher 100, 102
Beck, Glenn 169
Beck, Joseph 238, 342
Beck, Richard 53, 126, 231
Beck, Russell 217
Becker, Bonnie L. 41, 46, 47
Becker, Manuel 156, 304
Becker, Peter 280, 313
Beckinsale, Kate 134
Beckwith, Peter 126
Becton, Shelton 220
Beddow, Margery 422
Beebe, Doug 401
Beene, Geoffrey 334
Beers, Steve 19, 20, 60, 66, 318, 371
Beers, Sydney 12, 20, 60, 65, 94, 273, 318, 321, 343, 371, 372, 399
Beguelin, Chad 18
Beider, Dee 13, 65, 94, 273, 321, 343, 372, 399
Beimers, Bob 313
Beket, JR 267
Bekker, Belen 73
Belenky, Vladimir 196
Belits, Andrew 329
Belitsis, Gerry 47, 150
Belkin, Robert A. 330
Bell-Smith, Michael 322
Bell, Deborah 404
Bell, Glynis 198, 199
Bell, Grace 94, 273, 321
Bell, Hunter 376
Bell, Jake 267, 362, 369
Bell, Jonathan 148
Bell, Marc 30, 161
Bell, Patrick 53, 114, 156, 182, 200, 234, 407
Belle, Barbara 163
Belletieri, Beverly 368, 369
Bellinger, Sam 403
Bello, Jessie 48
Bello, Sant'gria 176-178
Belmond, Charlene 223, 225, 249, 250
Belmond, Michele 367
Belolo, Henri 20
Belsher, Nikki 41
Belton, Nicholas 127-129
Belvin, Jesse 163
Belviso, Freida Sawyer 8, 53, 83, 126, 145, 156, 183, 189, 231, 250, 291, 304, 361, 369, 396
Belzer, Rick 54
Bemis, Cliff 152-154
Ben-David, Adam 158-160
Ben-David, Alon 144, 145
Benanti, Laura vii, ix, 148, 149
Bender, Jen 180, 182
Bender, Kirk 182
Bender, Kraig 182
Bendul, Kristine 79-81, 84
Benedict, Scott 183, 188, 217
Benepe, Andrew 183
Benincasa, Joseph 410
Benito, Manny 58
Benjamin, Diane 164, 252, 255
Benjamin, P.J. 362, 364
Benken, David 79, 81, 176, 180, 184, 187, 211, 215, 216
Benn, Lauren J. 66
Bennet, Mike 195
Bennet, Timothy 195, 196
Bennett-Jones, Peter 48
Bennett, Craig 324-326
Bennett, Declan 21, 23, 27
Bennett, Dusty 183, 188, 217
Bennett, Eddie 72
Bennett, Mark 332, 333
Bennett, Peter 163
Bennett, Robert 345, 347, 348
Bennett, Robert Russell 109, 112, 324, 326, 327
Bennett, Tony 197
Bennion, Karl 262, 266
Benoit, Emilio 266
Benoit, Katherine 224
Bensinger, Chris 24, 167
Benson, Cheyenne 145
Benson, Meredith 25, 138
Benson, Peter 276, 278
Benthal, John 91, 93
Bentley, Dorothea 73
Bentley, Helen 35, 257, 296
Bentz, Andrew 8, 189
Berardelli, Joe 243
Berberich, Brendan 337
Berchard, Morris 286, 290
Berens, Elizabeth C. 243
Bergamini, Wendi 276-278, 324-326
Bergelson, Nina 114, 225, 234
Berger, Bridget 158, 160
Berger, Elizabeth H. 243
Berger, Michael 74
Berger, Patrick 409
Bergère, Jane 167, 191, 194
Bergère, Laudenslager 164
Bergeron, Nova 362, 364
Berglund, Michael 46, 47
Bergman, Alan 83, 102
Bergman, Ingmar 191
Bergman, Marilyn 83, 102
Bergmann, Michelle 25, 83, 242, 250, 361, 412
Bergquist, Guy 243
Bergson, Simon 298
Bergson, Stefany 298, 300
Berk, Albie 18
Berk, Brian 415
Berkeley, Elizabeth 242, 243
Berkowitz, Anne 28, 29
Berkowitz, Elie 6
Berlin, Alec 22
Berlin, Boris 238
Berlin, David 243
Berlin, Irving v, vii, 20, 58, 83, 152, 153, 154, 155, 156, 157, 380
Berlind, Roger 37, 38, 191, 194, 286, 290, 384, 397
Berliner, Jay 70, 75
Berloni, William 305, 307
Berman, Ashley 47
Berman, Michele G. 243
Berman, Rob 109, 110, 112, 113, 115, 152, 155
Bermudez, Ritchie 315
Bernard, Kevin 41, 42, 43
Berne, Kevin 54
Berney, Brig 140, 144, 145, 147
Bernstein, Betsy 258, 369
Bernstein, Cubby 9
Bernstein, Jed 78, 127, 130, 256, 257, 258, 308, 347
Bernstein, Jonathan 74
Bernstein, Leonard 354, 357
Bernstein, Michael 249, 250, 280

Index

Bernstein, Norman 243
Bernstine, Quincy Tyler 148, 149
Berro, Alexandra 211, 213
Berry, Chuck 231
Berry, Denny 264, 267
Berry, Halle 107, 370
Berry, Michael 240, 241
Berry, Patricia 74
Berry, Tavener Holmes 243
Bertini, Carey 207, 208
Bertol, Gaetane 188
Bertolacci, Kevin 83
Bertolotto, Caterina 183
Besh, John 417
Beshar, Marc Dr. 126
Best, Kate 322
Best, Sarah 343
Bethea, Henry 224
Bethell, Jo-Ann 74
Bettencourt, Nuno 304
Betz, Christopher 231, 234, 258, 267, 281
Bevan, Tim 41, 48
Bevenger, Rob 30, 88, 285, 337, 338
Bevilacqua, Patrick 88, 258
Beyland, Keith Powell 66, 94, 274, 321, 343, 372
Beymer, Richard 322
Beyoncé 75
Bialy, Sharon 158, 160, 283, 285
Biancamano, John 238, 342
Biangone, Gary 145
Biasetti, Bob 47
Bickley, Buist 303, 322
Bido, Solangel 13, 14, 66, 92, 94, 272, 274, 343, 373, 399
Bieber, Brandon 215
Biederman, Richard 163
Bierko, Craig 121, 123
Bierman, James 135, 138, 294, 296
Bierman, Jon 16, 17, 109
Biggart, Devin 280
Bigge, Ashley 352
Bigger, Kevin 342
Biggers, Barbara 288
Biggs, George 120
Bilheimer, Chris 25
Bilinski, Mimi 304
Billings, Frank 265
Billington, Ken 60, 63, 69, 71, 75, 109, 112, 152, 155, 198, 199, 318, 320
Billmann, Nancy 110, 113
Bills, Sarah 183, 189, 217
Bimbler, Fred 200
Binder, Jay 51, 52, 53, 69, 109, 112, 114, 152, 155, 156, 176, 198, 199, 200, 232, 233, 234, 340, 341, 342, 407
Binder, Jeff 180, 181, 215
Bingham, Sarah 47
Bingman, Brett 125, 126
Binion, Sandy 138, 284, 285
Binkley, Howell 16, 17, 18, 32, 34, 121, 124, 140, 143, 158, 160, 219, 222, 227, 229, 354, 357
Binyon, Dory 420
Birch, Bob 48
Birchall, Dennis 368, 369
Bird, Sarah 20, 102, 120
Birl, Tanya 109, 111, 116
Birney, Alice 330
Birsh, Arthur T. 419
Birsh, Philip S. 419
Bishop, André 148, 149, 151, 322, 324, 328, 330
Bishop, Jason 156, 167, 168
Bishop, Jessica 358
Bishop, Sean 315
Bishop, Stephen 404
Bisker, Alex 308
Bisno, Debbie 109, 127
Bivone, Joe 217, 218
Björnson, Maria 261, 264
Blaber, Paul 47
Black, Brent 202-204, 210
Black, Deborah 156, 168
Black, Debra 28, 30, 37, 38, 324, 335, 336
Black, Jonathan 401
Black, Leon 324
Black, Lewis 12, 65, 94, 273, 321, 372
Blackburn, Mark 58
Blacksell, Emily 48
Blackwell, Otis 20, 163, 231
Blackwell, Robert 231
Blackwell, Susan 381
Blades, Catherine iv, 60-62, 68
Blades, Jack 304
Blaik-Kelly, Tansy 138, 296
Blair, Jim 219
Blair, Margie 329, 404
Blair, Meredith 231, 361
Blair, Susan 219
Blake, Paul 152, 155, 156
Blakely, Ron 266
Blancafor, Roland 315
Blanchett, Cate 218
Blanco, Michael 240, 242
Bland, Dayle 183, 189, 217
Bland, Shane 216
Blandon, David 48
Blank, Larry 152, 155
Blank, Matt iv, 370, 386, 419
Blank, Matthew 245
Blank, Radha 102
Blanken, Hillary 172, 174, 222, 225, 229, 230, 233, 234, 257, 258, 279, 280
Blankenbuehler, Andy 140, 142, 147, 245, 247
Blankenship, Mark 409
Blankson-Wood, Ato 131
Blansfield, Paige 47, 126, 162, 188, 196, 208, 267, 280, 314, 322
Blau, Keith 48, 369
Blau, Roni 410
Blaustein, Jeremy Scott 16, 17, 19, 31, 85, 87, 133, 282, 283, 335, 337, 413
Blazdell, Tim 314
Blazina, David 322
Bledsoe, Jeffrey 78, 347, 398
Blessington, Joanne 224
Bleu, Corbin iv, viii, 49, 143, 146, 147
Blickenstaff, Heidi 376
Blimline, Genson 328
Blinn, David 192, 326
Blitzer, Beth 138
Blixt, John 132
Block, Gene 404
Block, Sandy 8, 58, 163, 174, 196, 281, 304, 416
Block, Stephanie J. 245, 246, 251, 377
Blocker, Jeremy 78, 308, 347, 398
Blodgette, Kristen 196, 261, 262, 264, 266, 267, 269
Bloedow, Oren 98
Bloodworth, Ray 163
Bloom, Mitchell 216, 291
Bloomberg, Michael vii, viii, 380
Bloxham, Greg 145
Blum, Carlin 47
Blumenthal, Jay 403
Blumstein, Danielle 322
Blunt, Izell O. 181
Blye, Josh 266
Blyth, David 126
Boardman, Cynthia 182
Bobbie, Walter 69, 71, 75, 152, 155, 157, 403
Bodeen, Michael 232, 233, 335, 336
Bodker, Elaine 420
Bodnar, Bill 298, 300
Boese, Jim 8, 53, 83, 126, 145, 156, 183, 189, 231, 250, 291, 304, 361, 369, 396
Bogan, Larkin 127, 129
Bogart, Matt 158, 159, 161
Boger, Stefanie 133, 243
Boggess, Summer 65
Bogie, Stuart 98
Bogin, Brian 20
Bogner, Michael 133
Bogosian, Eric viii, 345, 346, 348
Bohan, Amanda 418
Bohannon, Chris 261, 262, 263
Bohmer, Ron 286, 288, 293
Bohon, Justin 245-247, 251
Bohon, Lara 183
Boka, Kate 12, 39, 60, 65, 94, 273, 321, 343, 372
Bokhour, Raymond 69, 71, 75
Bokun, Brook 280
Bokun, Carol 73
Bokun, Lori 280, 314
Boldon, Sara Schmidt 36
Bolduc, Shawn James 291
Bolgar, Michael 36, 83, 291
Boll, Patrick iv, 202, 203, 204, 209, 210
Bologna, David 44, 50
Bolt, Sarah 362-364
Bolton, Annabel 255
Bolton, Bruce 54, 57
Bolton, Jeffrey 410
Bolton, John 379
Bonacci, Penny 367
Bond, A. Greer 405
Bond, Brittanie 63
Bond, Clint Jr. 310, 315
Bond, Greer 47
Bonder, Kyle 88, 334
Boneau, Chris iv, 39, 53, 58, 78, 106, 120, 156, 196, 200, 208, 234, 238, 291, 308, 347, 352, 411
Boniface, Martha 367, 369
Bonilla, Dora 126, 224, 225
Bonilla, Maritza 410
Bonis, Fred 330, 405
Bon Jovi, Jon 304
Bonny, Francis 262, 266
Bono 353
Bontrager, Laura 277, 288
Bonvissuto, Bruce 70
Bonynge, Leta 422
Booth, Susan V. 79
Booth, Timothy 202-204, 206, 210
Bordy, Sarah 243
Borg, Kristen 410
Borg, Rachel 8
Borger, Christopher 109, 111, 115
Borisjuk, Nick 66, 106, 156
Boritt, Beowulf 298, 300, 318, 320
Borle, Christian 215
Bornemann, Eric 25, 53, 95, 274, 322, 418
Bornstein, David 46, 47
Borovay, Zak 298, 300
Borowski, Michael 74, 258, 266, 267, 413
Borreson, Chris 163
Borsak, Marc 240, 242
Borsay, LaTonya 12, 65, 94, 273, 321, 343, 372
Borstelmann, Jim 1, 2, 4, 9
Bortz, Jerad 362-363, 364
Borys, Renee 301, 303
Borzotta, Peter 408
Bosch, Michael 207
Bosch, Michelle 158, 162
Boshetti, Maria 238
Bosley, Kyle 12, 65, 94, 273, 321, 343, 372
Bosner, Michael 156
Bostick, Ronald 422

Index

Bostrom, Anders 311
Botto, Louis 419
Boubnovskaia, Irina 56
Boucher, Kate 188
Boudiette, William 183, 188, 217
Bouka, Richard 144
Bourgeois, Elizabeth 36
Bournas-Ney, Nicole 12, 65, 273, 372
Bourne, Matthew 211, 214
Boursiquot, Christina 397
Boutsikaris, Dennis 51, 52
Bowdan, Jack 51-53, 114, 156, 182, 200, 232-234, 340-342, 407
Bower, Joseph 88, 285, 338
Bowerman, Binnie 196
Bowers, Mark 78, 308, 347, 398
Bowers, Megan 314, 315
Bowles, Anne 76, 77
Bowles, Jason 125, 126
Bowling, Lynn 328, 330
Bowman, Grady McLeod 44, 45
Bowman, Rob 16, 17, 18
Bownan, Jennie 231
Box, Maria 410
Boyce, Andrew 338
Boyce, Joan 405
Boyd, Guy 28, 29
Boyd, Jill K. 12, 65, 94, 95, 273, 321, 343, 372
Boyd, Patrick 377
Boyett, Bob 85, 86, 236, 237, 324, 328, 340, 341, 397
Boykins, Arianna 13, 66, 94, 274, 322, 373
Boyle, Danielle 20, 88, 120, 281
Boyle, Dennis 8, 189
Boyle, Loraine 219
Boyle, Susan vii
Boyle, Valerie 215
Boyles, Joey 48
Boyles, Peggy 367
Bradbury, Colin 79-81
Bradbury, Peter 252, 253, 271
Braddock, Susan 243
Bradford, Sean 180
Bradley, Brad 45
Bradley, Corey 286-288, 293
Bradley, Jack 168, 255
Bradley, Keith 48
Bradley, Pam 211-214
Bradshaw, Natalie 127-129
Bradt, Carly 174
Bradtke, Hans 83
Brady-Dalton, Abbie 8, 19, 88, 145, 225, 230, 242, 303, 330, 369
Brady, Alexander 79, 80, 81
Brady, Charlie 324, 325, 326
Brady, John E. 181
Brady, Mo 225
Brady, Pearl 401
Bragdon, Kelli 78, 308, 347, 398
Bralove, Steven R. 243
Bralove, Susan Haas 243
Branch, Kevin 156
Brand, Ari 52
Branda, Austin 302
Brandeberry, Jim 126, 225
Brandes, Amanda 36
Brandford, Jay 42
Brandon, Mark 53, 114, 156, 176, 180, 182, 200, 234, 342, 407
Brandt, Martin 422
Brannigan, Brien 39, 120, 333, 334
Brashear, Ed 77, 307
Brattain, Andy 20
Bratton, Steven 376
Brauer, Brenda 302
Brauer, Jenna 73, 74
Braun, Trevor 41, 43, 49, 50, 187
Braunstein, Adam 150, 200
Braverman, Lindsay 183, 189, 217
Braxton, Brenda 72
Bray, Josie 291
Bray, Scott 334
Breaker, Daniel 310, 311, 317
Breckenridge, Rob 340, 341, 344
Bredenbeck, Fred 329
Bredin, Kristy 420
Breen, Jennifer 102, 334
Breen, Patrick viii, ix, 236-239
Breglio, John 250
Breidenbach, William 369
Brender, Lauren 399
Brenman, Greg 48
Brenn, Kyle 354, 356
Brennan, Jennifer 285
Brennan, Nora 41, 47
Brennan, William 181, 182
Brenner, Rob 173
Brent, Joseph 91, 93
Brescia, Ken 311
Breslin, Abigail viii, ix, 232-234, 370
Bress, Rachel 245, 248, 250
Bressi-Cilona, Carol 25
Bressi, Allison 343
Brett, Tom 178
Breuler, Robert 31, 338
Brevoort, Laurel 235, 254
Brian-Brown, David 310, 312
Brians, Sara 48
Brice, Richard 110, 113, 279
Brickman, Ariel 8
Brickman, David 6
Brickman, Marshall viii, 1, 158, 160
Bricusse, Leslie 20
Bridge, Andrew 261, 264
Bridges, Frankie 138, 296
Bridgewater, Nicole 69-71
Briel, Joel 113
Briggs, Cassidy J. 19
Brightman, Alex 362, 364
Brightman, Sarah 269
Brill, Robert 121, 124
Brilliant, Neal 151, 330
Briner, Allison 202, 204, 209, 210
Brinker, Carrie 58, 132, 255
Brinkerhoff, Bob 243, 369
Briscoe, Todd 200
Brisen, Henry 368, 369
Britt, Matt 416
Britten, Benjamin 343
Broccoli, Barbara 332
Brochu, Jim 392
Brockington, Jayden 286, 288, 293
Brockmeyer, Chris 397
Broder, David S. 243
Broderick, James 322
Broderick, Matthew 238, 275, 331
Broderick, Olivia 322
Brodie, Daniel 303, 322
Broecker, Tom 91, 282
Broer, Julia 303
Brog, Robinson 133
Brohn, Maggie 37, 48, 250
Brohn, William David 211, 215, 286, 289, 362, 365
Brokaw, Mark 11, 12, 15, 65, 94, 273, 321, 343, 372
Brook, Susanne 298
Brooke-Taylor, Ros 255
Brookman, Catherine 127, 129
Brooks, Derek 25
Broomell, Kevin 171, 172, 174, 222, 225, 229, 230, 232, 233, 234, 257, 258, 279, 280
Broser, David 257
Brosilow, Michael 31
Brothers, Brooks 281
Brouillard, Jason 359, 361
Brown-Orleans, James 176, 178
Brown, Avril 178, 181
Brown, Bob 322
Brown, Camille M. 176, 177, 178
Brown, Carey Rebecca 286, 287, 289
Brown, Clarence Gatemouth 225
Brown, Dale 47, 126, 162, 188, 196, 267, 280, 314, 322
Brown, Dave 25, 113, 114
Brown, David 407, 422
Brown, David Brian 60, 63, 69, 184, 187, 333, 334
Brown, David S. 151, 330
Brown, Denise 416
Brown, Elliot 48, 126
Brown, Enrique 184, 185, 186
Brown, Ernest 422
Brown, Gavin 13, 65, 94, 274, 321, 343, 372, 399
Brown, Heidi 38, 39, 333, 334
Brown, James 98, 102
Brown, James III 184-186, 188, 223, 226
Brown, Jennifer 151, 330
Brown, Jessica 102
Brown, Joy Sims 183, 189, 217
Brown, Justin 322, 372, 373
Brown, Ken 7, 8, 47
Brown, Krystal Joy 131
Brown, L. Russell 163
Brown, Larry 188
Brown, Laurie 133
Brown, Luke 352
Brown, Michael W. 58
Brown, Nate 213
Brown, Peter 267
Brown, Ruth 225
Brown, Shane Marshall 31
Brown, Sharon 57
Brown, Stephen 78, 308, 347
Brown, Vanessa 330, 331
Brown, Zack 120
Brownell, Claire 341
Brucato, Chris 63, 397
Bruce, Andrew 202, 205
Bruckheimer, Jerry 107
Bruckner, Mark 12, 65, 94, 273, 321, 343, 372
Brugal, Michelle 176-178, 182
Brumm, Carol 420
Brunell, Catherine iv, 211-214, 218
Brunell, Janice 417
Bruni, Marc 152, 155, 156
Brunner, Maria 57
Brunner, Michael 324
Bruno, Ben 58
Bruno, J.R. 358
Bruno, Lou 153
Brunstetter, Bekah 12, 65, 94, 273, 321, 372
Bryan-Brown, Adrian iv, 13, 95, 138, 162, 168, 174, 200, 208, 230, 234, 274, 296, 314, 322, 342, 373, 411
Bryan-Brown, Marc 183
Bryan, David vii, 219-221, 226, 387, 389, 392
Bryan, Ralph 24
Bryant, Khail Toi 181
Bryant, Kimilee 261-263
Bryant, Kourtney 410
Bryn, Norman 404
Buchan, John 340
Buchanan, Keith 145, 291, 360
Buchanan, Michael 183, 188, 217
Buchholz, Debby

The Playbill Broadway YEARBOOK 2009-2010   427

Index

163
Buck, Joe 64
Buck, Randall A. 79, 81
Buckle, Phillip 58
Buckley, Betty 377
Buckley, Erick 1, 2, 4
Buckley, Lisa 47, 217
Buckley, Michael 422
Budd, Cheryl 181
Buddeke, Kate 335, 336, 339
Buelto, Carlos 367
Buelto, Miguel 367
Buffini, Fiona 343
Bui, Ngoc 408
Bujak, Amanda 280
Buka, Donald 422
Bullard, Brian 88, 138
Bullard, David 196, 322, 361
Bullard, Wally 46
Bullmore, Amelia 252, 253, 255
Bullock, Keith 408
Bumbery, Brian 25
Bunis, Irene L. 207, 208
Bunting, Pearce 205
Buntrock, Stephen R. 191-193
Bunzel, Jeffrey H. 243
Buras, Milton 404
Burgess, Esau 151, 330
Burgess, Sharna iv, 54, 55, 59
Burgess, Tituss 121, 123
Burke, Bill 329
Burke, Gloria 132, 133
Burke, James J. Jr. 343
Burke, Johnny 83
Burke, Tom 132
Burke, Willa 133
Burkhardt, Brandi 205, 210
Burkhardt, Steel 131, 134
Burlaza, Violet 183, 189, 217
Burleigh-Bentz, Jen 206
Burnett, Carol 323
Burnett, Terrence 78, 308, 347
Burney, Chris 95
Burney, Christopher 243
Burns, Andréa 140, 142
Burns, Craig 19, 88, 145, 225, 242, 250, 285, 303, 330, 369
Burns, Heather Ann 44
Burns, Jackie 131, 134, 378
Burns, Joshua 113, 114, 195
Burns, Nica 191, 194
Burns, Ralph 69
Burns, Stephen 207, 208
Burnsed, Todd 79, 81
Burpee, Sean 66, 373
Burridge, Bud 2, 7, 311, 403
Burrow, Samantha iv
Burrow, Samanthe 291, 292
Burrows, Abe 121, 123
Burstein, Danny 324, 326
Burt, Alexa K. 291
Burt, Elaine 128
Burton, Arnie 340-342, 344
Burton, Greg 162
Burton, Haven 310, 311
Burton, Kate 407
Burward-Hoy, Kenneth 61
Buryiak, Francine 231
Busackino, Barbara 8
Buscemi, Steve 175
Busch, Brian 163
Buscher, Andrew Hans 25
Buscher, Joshua 354, 355, 356
Bush, Pamela 417
Bustamante, Juan 329
Bustos, Brian J. 188, 196, 314
Butler, Charles 162
Butler, Gregory 16, 17, 18, 69, 70, 71, 75
Butler, Holly Ann 376
Butler, Jason 13, 65, 94, 274, 321, 372
Butler, John 298
Butler, Kerry 298, 299, 381
Butler, Kristen 13, 66, 174, 338, 352, 373
Butler, Maeve Fiona 195, 196
Butler, Shelley 126
Buttacavoli, Ronald 128, 132
Butterly, Susan 48
Butts, Ellsworth 281
Butz, Norbert Leo viii, ix, 85, 86
Buxbaum, Lisa iv, 37-40
Buzzetti, John 36, 145
Byalikov, Henry 54, 55
Byerly, Cleon D. 19, 20
Byk, Jim 53, 138, 168, 200, 208, 255, 296, 342, 411
Byrd-Marrow, David 153
Byrd, Isabella F. 334
Byrne, Beth 315
Byrne, David 95
Byrne, Erin 20, 106, 120, 174, 238, 352
Byrne, James 368, 369
Byrne, Patricia 35, 257, 296
Byron, D.L. 304
Byron, Richard 217

C

Caballero, Christophe 164, 165, 166
Caban, Elvis 224
Caban, Margarita 235
Cabrera, Alan 218
Cacace, Christopher 8, 208, 231, 234, 258, 267, 281, 342
Caccamise, Craig 35, 36, 156
Caccavo, Nick 399
Cacchione, Josh 397
Cacciotti, Tony 198, 199
Caddell, Stacy 48
Caddick, David 211, 215, 261, 262, 264
Cadunz, Kathy 150
Cadunz, Viji 150
Cady, Jeff 25
Cady, Scott 70
Caesar, Irving 20
Caggiano, Keith 174, 303, 314
Cahn, Sam J. 365
Cahn, Sammy 82, 83
Cain, Holly 330
Cain, Jonathan 304
Cain, Scotty 361
Cairl, James 419
Cairl, Victoria 133, 208, 231
Calabrese, Chris 217
Calabretta, Giovanna 196, 250, 291
Calahan, Kathy 211, 212, 213, 214
Calarco, Joe 403
Caldamone, Amy 183, 189, 217
Calderazzo, Diana 156
Calderon, Roberto 7
Caldwell, Adam 36, 352
Caldwell, Jaron 133
Calhoun, David 83, 156, 250, 402
Cali, Joseph 409
Call, Andrew 21, 23, 26, 27
Callahan, Tom 20, 25, 53, 88, 285, 416
Callaway, Joe A. 393
Callian, Richard 31, 342
Calloway, J. Bernard 219-221, 226
Calpito, Isaac 354-356
Calvert, Heath 131
Calvo, Juan 31, 39, 48, 58, 74, 88, 106, 120, 138, 151, 168, 174, 200, 208, 225, 243, 258, 267, 281, 285, 296, 315, 334, 338, 352
Camacho, Blanca iv, 140-142, 146, 147
Cambio, Carmella 7
Camerieri, C.J. 125
Cameron, Maria 401
Campanella, Michael 409
Campanile, Megan 184-186
Campbell, Burke 255
Campbell, Douglas 422
Campbell, Gillian 78, 308, 347, 398
Campbell, Jeff 203
Campbell, Mary-Mitchell 1, 2, 5, 7
Campbell, Ta'rea 176, 178
Campion, Ellen 66, 250
Campise, John 369
Campo, Helen 363
Camus, Kevin 144, 145
Camus, Steve 361
Canavan, Linda 234
Candler, Cristy 365, 366
Candlish, Forbes 130
Canett, Gabriel 354-356
Canfield, Tiffany Little 8, 19, 88, 145, 225, 230, 242, 250, 285, 303, 330, 369
Cannon, Mike 354, 355, 356
Canonico, Gerard 21, 22, 23, 27
Cansler, Meggie 109, 111, 116
Cantler, Will 8, 19, 88, 145, 225, 230, 242, 250, 285, 303, 330, 369
Cantone, Mario 275
Cantor, Marek J. 340
Cantrick, Maggie 12, 65, 94, 273, 321, 343, 372, 399
Canuel, Angie 114
Caoili, Chris 47
Capalbo, Carmen 422
Caparelliotis, David 76, 95, 106, 171, 305
Capatasto, Nicole 25, 304, 334, 361, 412
Capatoro, Carl 78, 308, 347
Capeless, Jodi 16-18
Caplan, Jamie 25
Caplan, Liz 23, 25, 26, 300
Caplan, Matt 328
Cappelletti, Lucia 266
Capps, Tom 359
Capra, Hugo 404
Capul, Carina 410
Caputo, Joe 254, 255
Caputo, Steve 368
Carbo, Caroline 63
Carbone, Kristin 215
Carboni, Monique 97, 102
Cardello, Joe 128, 132
Carducci, Jay 183, 188, 217
Carfagna, Rebecca 126, 188, 208
Carigo, Aileen 410
Carillo, Mario 280
Cariot, James 313
Cariou, Len 378, 382
Carleton, Matthew 347
Carlin, Cynthia 266
Carlin, Tony 171, 172, 345, 346
Carling, Lisa 409
Carlisle, Robert 326
Carlson-Goodman, Briana 127, 128
Carlson, Sandra 158, 162, 163
Carlucci, Haley 354, 355, 356
Carlyle, Richard 422
Carlyle, Warren 109, 112
Carman, Dale 272, 274
Carmello, Carolee viii, 1, 2, 4, 9, 205
Carmichael, Hoagy 20
Carmon, Sean A. 164, 166
Carnahan, Jim 12, 21, 23, 37-39, 65, 91, 92, 94, 270, 273, 318, 320, 321, 333, 334, 343, 372
Carnahan, Jim 23
Carnahan, Mike 20, 156
Carney, Eric 265, 267

Index

Carney, Grace 422
Carney, Richard 208
Carney, Sean 2, 7, 311
Caro, Michelle 298
Caron, Christopher 31
Caroto, Rick 125, 126
Carpenter, David 315
Carpenter, Dean A. 162, 163, 398
Carpenter, Kayla 13, 65, 274, 372
Carpenter, Larry 403
Carpinello, James 298, 299, 381
Carr, Allyson 202, 204, 206
Carr, Jane 215
Carr, Jason 164, 166, 191, 193, 389
Carr, Lisa 138, 296, 334
Carradine, David 422
Carrick, Bill 47
Carroll, Barbara 151, 330, 402
Carroll, Holly 80, 291
Carroll, Nancy E. 270, 271
Carroll, Orit Jacoby 133, 250, 280, 334
Carrozzini, Francesco 238
Carrubba, Philip 133
Carsch, Ruth 196, 308
Carsella, Meghan 314, 315
Cartagena, Junesse 125
Cartelli, Lauren 13, 66, 94, 274, 322, 373, 343
Carter, Caitlin 162
Carter, Callie 48, 300
Carter, Christian 324, 325, 326
Carter, Dixie 422
Carter, Ellen 401
Carter, Jon 151
Carter, Jonathan 188
Carter, Reginald 208
Carter, Shawn "Jay-Z" 97, 99
Cartwright, Lisa 171
Caruba, Glen 58
Carusi, Bruce J. 232
Caruso, Jim 375, 379, 385
Caruso, Joe 267
Carver, Steve 145
Cas, Michael Dei 183, 189
Casagrande, Margaret 66, 94, 274, 321, 343, 372
Casaletta, Terry 406
Casanova, Mariana 367
Cascino, Denise 315
Case, Allison 131
Case, Jenny 163
Cash, Johnny viii, ix, 227, 228, 231
Cashman, John 284
Caso, Rosaire 249
Caspare, Cissy 361
Cassel, Michael 183, 188, 217
Casselman, Carolyn J. 133, 250
Cassidy, Craig 207, 208
Cassidy, Orlagh 118
Cassin, Olivia 126
Casson, Anna Maria 255
Castaldo, Eric 25, 113, 114
Castellana, James 133, 163
Castellana, Lance 25, 31, 36, 88, 133, 156, 163, 200, 285, 334, 338
Castellano, William 409
Casterlin, Patricia 422
Castillenti, Reva 8
Castillo, Raquel 13, 65, 94, 273, 321, 343, 372
Castner, Fred 126, 225, 280
Castree, Paul 245-247
Castro, Eduardo 188
Caswell, Jeff 185
Caswell, John 48
Cataldo, Christina 58, 255
Cataldo, Yuri 361
Catanese, Charles 47, 113, 114
Cates, Gil 345, 371
Catron, Andy 216, 218
Cattaneo, Anne 151
Catullo, Patrick 79, 82, 240, 241, 369
Caulfield, Bob 420
Cavaluzzo, Greg 417
Cavanaugh, Ann 320, 322
Cavari, Perry 277
Cave, Lisa Dawn 83, 359, 361
Cavenaugh, Matt 358
Cavett, Wendy Bobbitt 203
Caza-Cleypool, Damian 100, 102, 188
Cecchini, Lisa 182, 188, 217, 418
Celustka, Stephanie 126, 225
Cendese, Alex 349, 350, 353
Centalonza, Richard 70, 75
Cepler, Joanna 53
Ceraso, Chris 78, 308, 347
Cerceo, Sue 100, 102
Cerney, D. L. 225
Cerniglia, Ken 183, 188, 217
Cervantes, Miguel 21-23, 27
Cerveris, Michael vii, ix, 148, 149, 381
Cerveris, Todd 324-326
Cesa, Jamie 371
Chalfant, Kathleen 381
Chalk, Chris iii, iv, 104-108
Challis, Marianne 188
Chamberlain, Andrea 121-123
Chamberlain, Cliff 335, 336, 339
Chamberlin, Kevin viii, ix, 1, 4, 10, 376, 381, 388
Chambers, Katie 78, 308, 347
Chambless, Jerry 250
Champa, Russell H. 148
Champion, Charise 267
Champlin, Donna Lynne 41-43, 49, 382
Chan, Camille 8
Chan, Claire 262, 266
Chandler, Zac 6, 8, 361
Chanel, Joan 322
Chang, Paul 8
Chang, Tisa 403
Chanler-Berat, Adam 240, 241, 243, 244
Channon, Steve 225
Chantiles-Wertz, Lance 232
Chao, Caroline 83, 291, 330
Chapin, Chloe 25, 133
Chapin, Samuel R. 343
Chapin, Schuyler G. 377
Chapin, Theodore S. 156, 330, 407
Chapman, David F. 8
Chapman, Ed 19, 20, 138
Chapman, Kate 211, 212, 214
Charters, Lanene 205
Chase-Boyd, Meredith 182
Chase, Crystal 102, 234
Chase, David 41, 42, 44, 46, 60, 63, 184, 276, 279
Chase, Myles 203
Chase, Paula Leggett 60-62, 67
Chase, Will 41, 43, 50, 381
Chasin, Liza 48
Chavez, Yalile 410
Chazanof, Ilene 200, 281
Chazaro, Steve 174, 231
Checklick, Susan 144, 145
Cheek, Stephanie 183, 188, 217
Chen, Minglie 32, 33
Chenoweth, Kristin viii, ix, 68, 276, 278, 377, 391
Cheretun, Deborah 126, 225
Chernick, Jeremy 8, 338
Chernin, Peter 250
Chernoff, Lisa 291
Cherone, Gary F. 304
Cherpakov, Howie 236
Cherry, Liz 8
Chesterman, Mary 100
Chiavetta, Carol 227, 231
Chicas, Roy 83
Chigvintsev, Artem 56
Chihaby, Katie 238
Chii, Maiko 303, 322
Child, Desmond 304
Chin, Jenai 39, 334
Chin, Judy 120
Chin, Wilson 102, 236, 237
Chinda, Maria 420
Chiplock, Joseph 401
Chiquito, Hilda 416
Chirillo, James 80
Chiroldes, Tony 140-142, 147
Chitnis, Beatriz 420
Chmerkovskiy, Maksim vi, 54, 55
Chmielewski, Karl 183, 188, 217
Cho, Julia 12, 65, 94, 273, 321, 372
Choi, Chuck 183
Christ, Bill 232, 233
Christenberry, Julian 133, 409
Christensen, Thomas 61, 65
Christensen, Tracy 13, 188, 196, 314
Christian, Charles 82
Christian, Eric L. 328
Christianson, Michael 311
Christie, Ed 36
Christie, Marilyn 302
Christman, Cara 53, 416
Chryst, Gary 69
Chudoba, John 355
Chung, Erica 410
Church, Abby 152-154, 157
Church, Joseph 141, 145, 183
Churchill, Winston 11
Chursin, Peter 354, 356
Ciccarone, Rock 178
Cilento, Wayne 362, 365
Cimini, Jillian 12, 25, 39, 65, 94, 273, 321, 334, 343, 372
Cincotta, Tonianne 58
Cintron, Dennis 73
Cintron, Joey 7
Cipolla, Deanna 60, 62
Cipriano, Rose Ann 150, 404
Cipriano, Scott 421
Cipriatti, Juliette 195
Cirillo-Goldberg, Mary 343
Citron, Jill 182, 188, 217
Claffey, James J. Jr. 400
Claire, Felicity 202-204, 206
Clampitt, Susan 243
Clancy, Joe 12, 65, 94, 273, 321, 343, 372
Clancy, John 310
Clapton, Eric Patrick 31
Clar, Steven 196, 322
Clark, Amy 83, 188, 369
Clark, Bridget Megan 51, 52
Clark, Dick 9, 42, 46
Clark, Dwayne 140-142
Clark, Joseph 13, 66, 94, 274, 321, 322, 343, 372, 373
Clark, Michael 158
Clark, Tom 4, 34, 63, 105, 130, 143, 155, 289

Index

Clark, Victoria 381
Clarke, Katie Rose 366
Clarke, Tracey 13
Clarkson, Katie 8
Clarkston, Michael T. 145
Claus, Nathan K. 120, 255
Clavano, Magdelana 181
Clay, Caroline Stefanie 305, 306
Clay, Ken 219, 223
Clayman, Amanda 410
Claypool, Veronica 409
Clayton, Adam 95
Clayton, Joshua 110, 113, 114, 116
Cleary, Mary 208
Cleary, Michael 207
Clem, Steve 360, 361
Clemens, Ceili 7, 8
Clement, Sally D. 243
Clemente, Jacob 45, 50
Clements, Andrew 20, 66, 94, 274, 321, 343, 373
Clements, Ron 184
Clendening, Eddie 227, 228
Clifton, Bobby 254, 255
Clifton, Clare 57
Clifton, Kevin 54
Climer, Jacob 151
Cline, Cathy 95, 272, 274
Clinton, Hillary 331
Clinton, Moria 230, 274
Close, Glenn 75, 244
Clow, James vii, 152, 154
Clow, Virginia 188, 315
Coats, Janelle 7
Cobb, Bryan 47
Cobb, Clifford 87, 138
Cobb, Lee 208
Cobb, Steve 208
Cobbin, Angela 215, 216
Cobbs, Roz 333
Coble, Kurt 262, 266
Cochrane, Jessica Perlmeter 330
Cochrane, Steve 133
Coco, Edward 25
Cody, Dillon 83
Cody, Jennifer 313, 376
Coes, Charles 151, 347
Coey, Amy Merlino 13, 120, 138, 196, 274, 296, 314, 334, 342
Coey, Dan 106, 174, 234, 333, 334
Coffey, Timothy 346, 347
Coffman, Brad 58, 102, 114, 196, 234, 304
Coffman, Kyle 354, 356
Cogliano-Benedict, Mattea 243, 250, 369
Cohen, Andrew Zachary 114
Cohen, Arthur 48
Cohen, Benjamin 163
Cohen, Brooke 322
Cohen, Bruce 373
Cohen, David 105, 125, 126, 234, 235, 333, 334
Cohen, Elizabeth 183
Cohen, Eric 262, 266
Cohen, Jay 12, 65, 94, 273, 321, 372
Cohen, Jonathan 150, 200
Cohen, Joshua 13, 65, 94, 274, 321, 343, 372, 399
Cohen, Lynne 288
Cohen, Melissa 13, 66, 274, 373
Cohen, Randy 22, 91, 110, 114, 122, 145, 165, 246, 299, 304, 318, 330, 355
Cohen, Sherry 206, 208
Cohn, Ben 363
Coid, Marshall 70
Colavin, Charlotte 78, 308, 347
Colburn, Brian 198
Cole, Carol 422
Cole, Dennis 422
Cole, Emily 95, 322
Cole, Gary 31, 338
Cole, Lewis 420
Cole, Michael 369
Cole, Robert 332, 333
Cole, Thomas Jr. 280, 281, 313
Colella, Jenn 382
Coleman, Aaron 418
Coleman, Chad 107
Coleman, Cy 83
Coleman, Elizabeth 156
Coleman, Grier 133
Coleman, Kris 158, 160
Coleman, M. Graham 39, 106, 120, 352
Coleman, Michelle 74, 168
Coleman, Stan 285
Coley, Gwen 266
Colgan, Melissa 401
Colitti, Rik 422
Colledge, Shaun 206
Collichio, Gregg 5, 8, 189
Collier, Brian 211-214, 216
Collier, John 319
Collins, Ann 422
Collins, Bootsy 285
Collins, Jonathan 95, 242, 338
Collins, Judy 322
Collins, Kevin 156
Collins, Maury 402
Collins, Ned 163
Collins, Rufus 305, 306, 309
Collum, Jim 208
Colon, Dominic 78, 308, 347
Colon, Georgie 7
Colon, Jorge 280, 314
Colon, Merida 150
Colon, Sharif 102, 106
Colonna, Brian 265
Coltoff, Paul 64, 66, 320, 322
Coltrane, John 98, 102
Comley, Bonnie 16, 17, 18, 79, 82, 85, 87, 335, 337, 340, 341, 397
Common 182
Composto, Michael 31, 173
Compton, Maria 181
Compton, Mike 217
Compton, Rosi 217
Conacher, William 47
Concepcion, Michael 173, 337
Concepcion, Odalis 249
Concklin, Eric 74
Cone, Lizbeth 140, 145, 291
Conklin, Chelsi 397
Conlon, Mickey 16, 17
Connell, Tuey 168
Connell, William 351
Connelly, Frances 47, 304, 334
Connelly, Maria 41, 43, 50
Connolly, Francis J. Jr. 406
Connolly, Frank Jr. 400
Connolly, George 409
Connor, Laurie 58, 102, 114, 196, 234, 281, 304
Conte, David 39, 333, 334
Conti, Eva 42, 46
Conway, Frank 408
Conway, Ryan 48
Conyers, Sarah K. 13, 14, 93, 95, 273, 274
Cook, Adam 78, 308, 347
Cook, Alexandra 178
Cook, Andy 182
Cook, Barbara iii, viii, ix, 318, 319, 323, 377, 388
Cook, Benjamin 286, 287, 289, 293
Cook, Bryan 25, 361
Cook, Larry 408
Cook, Ron 135, 136, 139
Cook, Shane 182
Cook, Susan 303
Cooke, Jessica 150
Cooke, Peter 35
Cool, Tré 22, 23, 26, 389
Cooley-Presley, Ann 291
Cooley, Eddie 231
Coombes, Rosalind 216
Cooney, Dan 245-247
Cooper, Brendan 280, 281
Cooper, Chuck vii, ix, 109, 111, 115
Cooper, Clare 225
Cooper, Denise 66, 322
Cooper, Don-Scott 243
Cooper, Doug 315
Cooper, Gary iv
Cooper, Gene 422
Cooper, Helmar Augustus 324, 326
Cooper, Jay 415
Cooper, Jeff 288
Cooper, John 46
Cooper, Joy 409
Cooper, Linda S. 163
Cooper, Margo 420
Cooper, Max 51, 52, 286, 290
Cooper, Peggy 422
Coots, J. Fred 20
Copeland, Carolyn Rossi 66
Copley, Dave 219
Copley, Preston 403
Coppola, Tom 415
Corbett, Michael 216
Corbett, Sam 133
Corbin, Quinn M. 20
Corble, Simon 340, 343
Cordle, Jill iv, 117, 119, 120
Cork, Adam 85, 86, 135, 137, 294, 295, 297, 389
Corker, John 32, 34, 36, 140, 143, 145, 152, 155, 156, 286, 289, 291
Corman, Maddie 236, 237, 239
Cornell, Eric 367
Cornell, Mike 280, 313, 315
Cornicelli, Carol 322
Cornman, Noah 95
Cornwell, Brandi 200, 208, 411
Coronado, Jace 358
Coronado, Marissa 102, 234
Corradetti, Greg 20, 88, 120, 174, 208, 243, 267, 281, 285, 369, 416
Corrado, Susan 46, 47, 291, 314
Cors, Allan D. 243
Cortes, Angalic 7
Cortes, Iris 125, 230
Cortes, Rafael 404
Cortez, Natalie 354-356
Cosentino, Laura 145
Cossette, John 227, 229
Cossette, Pierre 422
Costa, Don 80
Costea, Monica 47
Costello, David 216
Costello, Jennifer 230, 281
Costello, Jeryl 216, 217
Costello, Mark 48
Costello, Martin 315
Costello, Riley iv, 60-62, 68, 91, 92
Costello, Ward 422
Costigan, Ken 207
Costin, Kate 88
Cotillard, Marion vii
Cottignoli, Giancarlo 267
Cotton, Keith 304
Coughlin, Bruce 121, 124, 245, 248
Council, Bruce 416
Cousens, Heather 95
Coverdale, David 304
Covert, Kevin 219, 220, 221
Covey, Jason 213
Covillo, Kristine 354, 355, 356
Covney, Ivo 217
Covney, Kay 217
Cowan, Edie 403
Coward, Noël viii, ix, 270, 271, 274
Cowd, Tasha 125, 126

Index

Cowles, John 330
Cox, Brynn iv
Cox, Christopher 286, 288, 292, 293
Cox, Christopher 293
Cox, Darren 415
Cox, David 249
Cox, Douglas 36
Cox, Jeremy 79-81
Cox, Joe 102
Cox, Veanne 164, 166
Coyl, Chuck 28, 29
Coyne, Nancy 208, 281, 416
Cozier, Jimmy 80
Cozza, Craig 298
Craddock, Clayton 220, 225
Craig, Daniel vi, vii, ix, 332, 333, 379, 383
Craig, Joseph 219
Crandall, Bill 163
Cranston, Leigh 315
Craven, Bill 242
Craven, Kim 79, 81
Craver, William 407
Crawford, Alvin 176-178
Crawford, Douglas 161
Crawford, Kevin 8
Crawford, Vivienne 217
Craymer, Judy 202, 205, 207, 210
Crayton, Gloria 373
Crea, Michael 20, 88
Creatore, Luigi 183
Creel, Gavin 131, 134, 377, 379, 381, 383
Creel, Lawrence G. 243
Creighton, Robert 181, 184, 186
Creighton, Whitney Manalio 281
Creque, Neil 58
Creswell, David 326
Crewe, Bob 158-160, 163
Crews, Taylor 415
Cristiano, Jana 183
Cristofer, Michael 349, 350, 353
Criswell, Cris 8, 53, 83, 145, 231, 291
Crockett, Matt 164
Crockett, Stephen 208
Croghan, Robert 315
Croiter, Jeff 236, 237
Croiter, Michael 33
Croman, Dylis 72
Cromer, David 51, 52
Crompton, Barbara 152, 155, 156, 295, 296
Cronin, Chris 16-18, 88, 117, 118, 138, 234, 238, 255, 296
Cronin, Kevin 304
Crook, Bryan 114, 126
Croom, Gabriel 176-178
Crouch, Julian 1, 4, 10, 392, 393
Crowley, Bob 211, 214
Crowley, Dennis 48, 182, 188, 216
Crowley, John 37, 38, 40, 332, 333
Crown, Patricia 58, 196, 255
Croxton, Darryl 422
Crudup, Arthur 231
Crudup, Billy 190
Cruise, Tom 83, 84
Crum, Brian 241
Cruz, Albert 367
Cruz, Angel 415
Cruz, Frank 422
Cruz, Penélope vii, viii
Cruz, Zaydee 320
Cryer, David 261, 263
Crystal, Billy vi
Cudia, John vi, 261, 263, 268, 269
Cuello, Jose 320, 372
Cuervo, Alma 194
Cuervo, Joe 404
Cuevas, Eddie 125
Cuiffo, Steve 95
Cuillo, Bob 200
Cullen, David 261, 264
Cullen, John 360
Cullen, Sean 324, 326
Cullum, John 28, 29
Culpepper, Daniel 262, 266
Culver, Jack 361
Cumming, Joan 163
Cummings, Michael 232, 233
Cummins, Cenovia 22, 122, 125, 288
Cummins, Stephanie 213
Cummiskey, Terrence 125
Cunliffe, Colin 1, 2, 4
Cunningham, Cherie 156, 167, 168
Cunningham, Jeremy 322
Cunningham, Nicholas 164-166
Cunningham, Peter 267, 322
Cunningham, Ryan 58, 304
Cunningham, T. Scott 422
Cuocci, Patricia 235, 254
Cuoco, Monica A. 225
Cuomo, Bill 304
Curatolo, Kristina 25
Curda, Major 184, 186
Curich, Dorothy 266
Curren, Megan 20, 106, 120, 314
Curry, Beth 270
Curry, Jeff 182
Curry, Michael 176, 180, 183, 188
Curry, Ravenel 270
Curry, Sonny 125
Curtin, Jack 167, 307
Curtin, John 168
Curtis, Kenton 410
Cusanelli, Louis 421
Cusanelli, Patrick 420, 421
Cusanelli, Robert 421
Cushna, Greg 329
Cusumano, Michael 69, 70, 71
Cutler, Jennifer 47
Cwill, Janice B. 243
Czekaj, Anna 191, 232
Czulada, Samantha 41-43, 50

D

D'Addario, Brian 184, 186, 187
D'Aiuto, Todd 102
d'Amboise, Charlotte 72
D'Ambrosi, Mark 74, 83, 133, 168, 200
D'Ambrosio, Tom 25, 48, 83, 242, 250, 304, 334, 361, 369, 412
D'Amico, Adam 217
D'Andrea, Julie K. 13, 65, 274, 343, 372
D'Angelo, Chris 8
D'Angelo, T.J. 195
D'Arcy, Mike 83, 359, 361
D'Arienzo, Chris 298, 300
D'Elia, Lauren 163, 416
D'Haiti, Esvard 419
Da Gradi, Don 216
Dabbon, David Ben 322
Dabo, Dragica 401
Dabreo, Maureen 367
Dacal, Janet 143, 144, 146
Dacchille, Jessica 25, 418
Dacey, Kathy 73, 74
Dachille, Jessica 133
Daghini, Lauren 183, 189, 217
Dagna, Rob 235
Dague, Chuck 361
Dahl, Joyce 422
Dailey, Brandon 25
Dailey, Will 168
Daitch, Bruce 315
DalCortivo, Rick Jr. 280, 281
Daldry, Stephen 41, 44, 48, 49, 379
Dale, Jim 96, 384
Daley, Brett 216
Daley, Sandra 232, 233
Dalian, Tiffany 225
Dall, Bobby 304
Dalla Lasta, Dario 58, 196, 255, 304
Dalling, Rosie 138, 296
Dalton, Bill 163
Dalton, Stephanie 74, 133
DaLuz, Chéri 334
Daly, Ann 315
Daly, Christine 32, 35, 36
Daly, Doris 410
Daly, Patrick 31, 335
Daly, Tyne 116
Damaschke, Bill 313, 315
Dameski, Michael 45
Damiano, Jennifer 240, 241, 243
Dan, Aubrey 194, 222
Danaher, Colleen 174
Dancewicz, Mark 202-204, 206
Daniel, Tom 182
Daniele, Graciela 151, 330
Danielian, Barry 61, 65, 277, 279
Daniels, Cicily 184-87
Daniels, Elizabeth 47
Daniels, Erica 28, 335
Daniels, Jeff 118
Daniels, Nikki Renee 276, 278
Daniels, Paul 267
Danilovics, Ann 329
Dannheisser, Adam iv, 298, 299, 303
Dannheisser, B. 303
Danska, Delores 47
Danton, Marion 302
Danvers, Jo 138, 296
Danz, Marjorie 219
Danz, Ron 219
Darby, John 31, 36, 39, 48, 58, 74, 88, 106, 120, 138, 151, 168, 174, 200, 225, 243, 258, 267, 281, 285, 296, 315, 334, 338, 352
Darden, Lawrence 266
Darling, Peter 41, 44, 48
Darlow, Cynthia 45
Darnall, Colleen 25, 91, 250
Darneille, Sara Jayne 242, 243
Darnell, Colleen 145
Darrington, Quentin Earl vii, 286, 288, 380
Darrow, Nathan 148, 149
Dashman, Daniel 400, 404
Daudelin, Bart 400, 405
Daugherty, Allison 78, 308, 347
Daulton, Penelope 232, 234, 258, 279, 402
Daulton, Stephanie 361
Daunter, Jason 367, 369, 370
Davenport, John 231
Davenport, Ken 31, 256, 257
Davi, Mara vii, 152, 154
David Gewirtzman i, iii, iv
David, Carusi 232
David, Hal viii, 276, 278
David, Jim 281
David, Michael 160, 163, 398
Davidson, Gordon 248, 257
Davidson, Mark 78
Davidson, Suzanne Schwartz 243
Davidson, Tippin 227
Davie, Erin 191, 193
Davies, Ben 314
Davies, Luke Lloyd 48
Davila, Paul 313, 315
Davino, Peter 132
Davis, Aaliytha 415
Davis, Anita Ali 106, 291
Davis, Barbara 410
Davis, Barrett 211, 212, 213, 214
Davis, Bryan 8, 313, 314
Davis, Carleton 422
Davis, Christopher F. 408
Davis, Clive 26
Davis, Eric 242, 240
Davis, Gordon 57

The Playbill Broadway YEARBOOK 2009-2010   431

Index

Davis, Guy 109, 111
Davis, Hanna 102
Davis, Hope 118
Davis, Jeffrey 77, 78, 238, 298, 307, 308, 346, 347
Davis, Jeremy 245-247
Davis, Judy 243
Davis, Julia 78, 308, 347, 398
Davis, Mike 122, 125, 220
Davis, Paula 7, 8, 74, 298
Davis, Penny 58
Davis, Peter J. 163
Davis, Robert 397
Davis, Vanessa 12, 65, 94, 273, 321, 343, 372
Davis, Viola iii, viii, ix, 104, 105, 107, 108, 387, 388, 392, 393
Dawes, Gabrielle 252
Dawson, Brian 133
Dawson, Carla 216
Dawson, Craig 207
Dawson, Diane 48
Dawson, Edward 330
Day-Lewis, Daniel vii
Day, Jae 144
Daye, Bobby 310, 311, 316
Days, Garland 176, 177, 179, 182
de Benedet, Rachel 1, 2, 4
De Feis, Annmarie 410
De Ganon, Clint 91
de Graffenried, Mike 343
De Jesus, Robert 351
De Jesús, Robin 140, 142, 147, 164, 166, 388
De La Barre, Margot 324, 325, 327
de Laski, Donald 243
de Loera, Charity 176-179
De Michele, Joseph 401
De Nicola, Victor 404
De Paul, Gene 83
De Spirt, Mary E. 304
de Vos, Jill 266
De Vos, Will 266, 288
de Weever, Nicole Chantal 97, 99, 103, 393
Deakin, Moira 416
Deal, Frank 28, 29
Dean, Bradley 191-193
Dean, Carmel 21-23, 27, 95
Dean, Erin Hennessy 78, 308, 347
DeAngelis, Christian 126
DeAngelis, Matt 131
Deans, Jonathan 164, 166, 389
Debellis, Robert 178, 181
DeBord, Jason 301, 311
Debuskey, Merle 402, 410
Decker, James 13, 66, 95, 274, 322
Dee, Cat 132, 133
DeGarmo, Diana vii, 127, 129, 133
Degner, Alanna 183, 189, 217
DeGroot, Jake 347
Dehr, Richard 231
Dei Cas, Michael 217
Deitch, Joseph 349
Deitch, Swinsky 282
DeJean, Gilbert 355, 360
Del Barrio, Raymond 121-123
Del Rio, David 143, 146
Del Rio, Noemi 143, 144, 146
Dela Garza, James 42, 46
Delahunt, Suzanne 126
Delahunt, Tara 64, 66, 126, 320
Delcioppo, Paul 173, 174, 258
Delcroix, Christian 324, 326
Deley, John 311, 315
Delgado, Jose 410
Dell'Aquila, Perry 266
Della Rocca, Vincent 246
Delman, Scott M. 1, 21, 51, 85, 135, 282
DeLuca, Anthony 188, 217
Deluca, Steve 284
DelVecchio, Michael 334
Demand, Cindy 151
DeMann, Freddy 354, 357
DeMary, Ava 45
Demirjian, Denise 254, 333
Demos, Nick 222
Demous, John 322
Denaris, Brenda 367
Dench, Judi vii, 322
Dengler, Matthew 194
DeNiro, Robert 244
Denis, Philippe 315
Denisenko, Igor 410
Denison, Ken 183
Denkert, Darcie 281
Dennis, Cheryl 234, 235, 254, 255
Dennis, Lottie 31, 173, 337
Dennison, Bill 403
Dennison, Bonnie 349, 350, 353
Denoff, Douglas 340, 341
Denson, William 314, 351
Dent, John 42, 46
Dente, Barbara 13, 66, 94, 274, 322, 343, 373
Denton, Marjorie 217, 218
Deodato, Emuir 80
Deosarran, Ricky 78, 308, 347
DePaulo, Joseph 302, 304
DePaulo, Tony 400
Depinet, Kevin 31
DePiro, Ann Tuomey 83
Derasse, Dominic 326
Dermody, Jessica 361
Derosa, Elizabeth 211, 212, 214
deRoy, Jamie 5, 16, 17, 18, 37, 38, 85, 86, 109, 112, 171, 172, 232, 234, 252, 254, 258, 290
Derrick, John M. Jr. 243
Deruyter, Joel 46
Derwent, Clarence 375
DeSando, Anthony 349, 350
DeSantis, Davin 13, 65, 274, 372
Descarfino, Charles 288
DesChamps, Kyle 41, 42, 43, 47, 50
Deschene, Christopher 225
Desimini, Angelo 8, 53, 416
Desmond, Paul 83
DeSpirt, Mary 196
Despres, Gina H. 243
Detmer, Stephen 188
Detwiler, Andrea 36
Deutsch, Ellen 401
Deutsch, Kurt 95
Deutsch, Stephen 12, 65, 94, 273, 321, 343, 372, 399
DeVerna, Charles 88, 138
DeVerna, Darren 156
Deverna, Scott 351, 352
DeVerna, Scott 105, 106
DeVerna, Stephen 144, 145
DeVico, Joe 83
Devine, Kelly 162, 219, 222, 298, 300
DeVries, Michael 362, 363, 364
Dey, T.O. 217, 250, 304
Dhruna, Nisha 13, 66, 94, 274, 322, 343, 373
Di Benedetto, Antonello 78, 308, 347, 398
di Laski, Nancy 243
Diabo, Gloria 132
Diah, Sam 410
Diamond, I. A. L. 276
Diamond, Lydia 12, 65, 94, 273, 321, 372
Dias, Erna 269
Diaz, Angel 125, 302
Diaz, Carolina 420
Diaz, Edward 106
Diaz, Ilia 13, 95, 274
Diaz, Javier 122, 125
Diaz, John M. Sr. 400
Diaz, Karen 224
Diaz, Mark 25, 249, 250
Diaz, Nancy 249
Diaz, Stephen 358
Diaz, Tatiana 216
Dibble, Matthew Stockwell 79, 80
DiBella, Jennifer 12, 65, 94, 273, 321, 343, 372, 399
DiBello, Lawrence 213
DiCarlo, Matt 301, 303
Dickerson, Amber 200
Dickinson, Remmel T. 16, 17, 19, 219, 222, 232, 234, 252, 254, 340
Dickson, Clifford Lee 180
DiDonato, Jennifer 132
Diebold, Tracey 156, 168, 250
Dietz, Susan 97, 100, 238
Dietz, Zachary 140, 141, 144
DiFulvio, Carly 13, 14, 93, 95, 272, 274, 399
Diggs, Taye 107
Digiallonardo, Nadia 127, 128
Dignam, Mark 151, 329
Dignazio, David 25
Dill, Hugh 249
Dillingham, Charles 248, 257
Dillon, David 77, 78, 307, 308, 346, 347
DiMaggio, Phil 422
DiMeglio, John 243, 369
Dimirco, Vincent 95
Dimon, Nobby 340, 343
Dimond, Jon 133
DiNapoli, Brian 133
DiNoia, Jennifer 363, 364
DiPaola, Steven 401
DiPietro, Joe vii, 219-221, 226, 387, 389, 392
DiPippo, Kali 94, 321
Dirden, Brandon J. 85, 86
Dirden, Jason 104, 105
Dirnt, Mike 22, 23, 26, 389
DiSanti, Rocco 78, 347
Disney, Walt 211, 216
DiStasi, Theresa 181
Distler, Alexis 303
Ditsky, Stuart 1
Dittes, Matthew 95, 106
DiVita, Diane iv, 138, 139
Divone, James 409
Dixler, Hillary 12, 65, 94, 273, 321, 372
Dixon, Beth 306
Dixon, Jerry 304
Dixon, Robert E. 422
Dixon, Willie 58, 231
Dizzia, Maria 148, 149, 388
Dlamini, Lindiwe 176, 178, 179
Dloniak, Anita 402
Dobbins, Kathleen 31
Dobbs, Sara 354, 356
Dobie, Edgar 200, 243, 245, 248
Dobie, Paul 369
Dobkowski, Leon 188, 314
Dobrow, Mark 211, 216, 218
Dockett, Bryan 183, 189, 217

Index

Doctorow, E.L. vii, 286, 289
Dodd, Chris 218
Dodds, Jason 77, 78, 307, 308, 346, 347
Dodge, Alexander 270, 271, 275, 388
Dodge, Marcia Milgrom 286, 289, 293, 377, 388, 403
Dodgion, Jerry 80
Dodson, Jeff 78, 307, 308, 346, 347
Doebler, Matthew 369
Doepp, David 315
Doerr, Sam 13
Doherty, Carolyn 79, 81, 84
Doherty, Moya 245, 248
Dohery, Katherine Leigh 191, 193
Doina, Jessica 183, 189, 217
Doiron, Donna 181, 182
Dokos, Daniel S. 13, 66, 95, 274, 373
Dolan, Rick 277, 279, 288
Dolce, Frank 45, 50
Doll, Lauren 126, 219, 222, 252, 254
Dolman, David 217
Domanski, Christopher 369
Dombo, Aimee M. 20
Dombrowski, Amelia 31
Domiano, Cat 408
Domo, John 21
Donald, Andy 238
Donaldson, Martha 242
Donaldson, Walter 83
Donatelle, Marc 213
Donnalley, Bob 343
Donne, Naomi 211, 215, 310, 312, 333, 334
Donnelly, Donal 422
Donnelly, Lisa 418
Donovan, Jeanne 254
Donovan, Mary 400
Donovan, Peggy 342
Donovan, Peter 46, 213

Doran, Joe 12, 65, 94, 273, 321, 372
Dorigan, Chloe 48
Dorman-Phaneuf, Mairi 61, 122, 125, 192
Dorman, John 422
Dorman, Tracy 183
Dorsch, Emily 148, 149
Dorsey, Thomas A. 231
Dorso, Corinne 145
Dorst, John 315
Dory, John 195, 291
Doss, Barry 113, 114, 138, 295, 296
Dossett, John 202-204, 206, 209
Dotson, Bernard 109-111
Douglas, Elasea 97-99
Douglas, Kirk 197
Douglas, Ralph 422
Douglas, Rogelio, Jr. 184, 186, 190
Doumanian, Jean 28, 29, 56, 335, 336
Dour, Dan 163
Douzos, Adriana 182, 188, 216
Dow, Ken 158-160
Dow, Kevin 159
Dow, Steve 38, 39, 48, 250
Dower, David 243
Dowgiallo, Toni 245
Dowling, Bobby 399
Dowling, Bryn 72
Dowling, Elizabeth 238
Dowling, Joey 143, 145
Dowling, Robert 13, 14, 93, 95, 273, 274
Downes, Geoffrey 304
Downey, Robert Jr. 107
Downing, Ben 415
Downing, Steven 183, 189, 217
Downs, Donald 61, 65, 125, 165
Dowsett, Marie 57
Doyle, Kathleen 66
Doyle, Kevin 401, 406
Doyle, Matt 60, 61, 62

Doyle, Mike 163
Doyle, Rightor 85, 86, 90
Doyle, Sean Patrick iii, iv, 164, 165, 166, 169, 170
Drabinsky, Garth vi
Drachenberg, Andy 20, 88, 285
Draghici, Marina 97, 99, 101, 388
Drake, David 95
Drake, Erin 12, 65, 94, 273, 321, 343, 372
Drasner, Judith 200
Drewe, Anthony 211, 212, 214
Drewes, Glenn 70
Dreyfuss, Meghann 205
Driehaus, Richard 109
Driemeyer, Robert 164
Driggers, Bobby 102, 238, 342
Driscoll, Jon 85, 86
Driscoll, Robert 39, 106, 120, 352
Driscoll, Russell 8
Drobot, Clare 291
Drolet, Michael 366
Drori, Tal 78, 347
Drummond, Peter 224, 225
Drury, James 208
Drysdale, Ian 135, 136
Dubin, Jane 252
Dubisz, Ken 122, 125
DuBoff, Jill BC 13
Du Chateau, Charles 326
Dubois, Amanda 91
DuBois, Peter 271, 341
DuBose, Roy 404
Ducey, Therese 113, 114, 249, 250
duChateau, Charles 245
Duckworth, Sharon 168, 255
Ducocq, Alexandra 334
Dudgeon, Elizabeth 78
Duffe, Mary 58, 162, 303

Duffield, Davis 162
Duffy, Alice 270, 271, 275
Duffy, Lauren A. 162
Duffy, Peter, 36, 138, 145, 291, 361, 415
Dugan, Chris 25
Dugan, Eunice 307, 308
Dugan, Sean 236, 237, 239
Dugdale, John 234
Dulude, Joseph, II 172, 174, 365, 369
Duma, Bongi 176-179
Duma, Debra 267
Dumaine, Wayne 326
Dumancela, Cathy 231
Dumbutshena, Rujeko 97, 99
Dummitt, George 265
Dunagan, Eddie 113
Dunbar, Bevan 8
Dunbar, Heather 20, 36, 145
Dunbar, McBrien 360, 361
Duncan-Smith, Eden 104, 105, 107
Duncan-Smith, Nikki 409
Duncan, Laura Marie 324, 325, 327
Duncan, Ryan iv, 310, 311, 316
Dunfee, Ethelyne 422
Dunkin, Gregory 217
Dunlop, Frank 384
Dunn-Ruiz, Elizabeth 12, 65, 94, 273, 321, 343, 372
Dunn, Ashley M. 151, 330
Dunn, Frank 421
Dunn, John. J., Jr. 174
Dunn, Kathryn 41
Dunn, Lindsay 354, 355, 356
Dunne, Jennifer 72
Dunne, Siobhan 367
Dunning, Richard 113

Dunning, Tessa 163
Durang, Christopher viii, 16, 17, 18
Durham, Christopher 200
Durst, Douglas 343
Dwyer, Pat 418
Dybisz, Kenneth 277, 279
Dynowska, Oldyna 419
Dzundza, Claudia 188, 315

E
E.R. Evans, Simon 208
Eaker, Timothy 39
Earl, Doug 132, 133
Earl, Lorna 255
Easley, Russell 217
East, Richard 202, 205, 207
Easthill, Tim 48
Eastman, James 420
Eastman, Peter 182, 188
Eaton, Jameson 266
Eaves, Dashiell 37, 38
Eaves, Obadiah 76, 77
Ebb, Fred 20, 69, 71, 83, 392, 393
Ebell, Ernst III 8
Eberline, Maria 365
Ebersole, Christine 239
Ebert, Gabriel 294, 295
Echezarreta, Yurel 354-356
Eck, David 57
Eckstine, Billy 225
Economakos, Christopher 408
Edelman, Stanley 324
Edelstein, Harry 422
Edge, Amanda 79-81, 261-263
Edgerton, Annie 202, 203, 204
Edington, Garret 371, 373
Edmonds, Katharine 80, 126, 145, 196, 217, 246, 277, 281, 318, 330
Edwards, Andrew 138, 314

Edwards, Angelica 176, 177, 179
Edwards, Beverly 38, 39, 138
Edwards, Blake 379
Edwards, C.K. 45, 50
Edwards, Dale 415
Edwards, Eboni 41, 42, 43
Edwards, Harry 422
Edwards, Janet 12, 65, 343, 372
Edwards, Jim 13, 31, 36, 39, 47, 66, 74, 78, 83, 95, 106, 114, 126, 133, 138, 145, 156, 168, 225, 231, 234, 250, 255, 258, 274, 291, 296, 308, 315, 334, 338, 342, 347, 352, 361, 373, 415
Edwards, Sara 152-154, 157
Effemey, Philip 208
Egan, Eddie 48, 369
Egan, John Treacy iv, 60-62
Egbujie, Sheila 207
Eggers, David 41-43
Eggers, Samantha 205
Ehle, Dave 216
Ehren, Christine 346
Eich, Stephen 371
Eichholz, Laura 216
Eidem, Bruce 311
Eifert, Karen 48, 173, 174, 188
Eilerman, Nick 200
Einhorn, Andy 318, 320, 322
Eisen, Max 422
Eisenhauer, Peggy 245, 247
Eisenstein, Mat 61, 66, 242, 277, 279
Elder, Lauren 131
Elder, Suzie 183
Eldon, Jack 183, 188, 217
Eldor, Oran 126
Elers, Francis 196, 373
Elgart, Aaron 168
Elhai, Robert 176, 180
Elice, Rick viii, 1, 158, 160
Eliran, Barbara 200,

Index

417
Elizabeth, Jane 168
Elk, Hillary 219, 221
Ellerman, Antje 39, 106
Ellington, Duke 58
Ellington, Laura 106
Elliot, Bill 20
Elliott, Devlin 286
Elliott, Scott 12, 34, 36, 65, 94, 273, 321, 343, 372
Ellis, Sam 19, 25, 114, 285, 352
Ellis, Scott 11, 12, 60, 65, 91, 94, 270, 273, 318, 321, 343, 371, 372
Ellison, Bill 311, 318, 320
Ellison, Todd 164-166
Ellman-Larsen, Carrie 12, 65, 94, 273, 321, 343, 372
Elman, Andrew 280
Elman, Nancy 243
Elms, Stephen 416
Elrod, Susan 196
Elsberry, Adam 13, 66, 94, 274, 322, 343, 373
Elston, Jenn 8, 47, 120
Elston, Jennifer 418
Elting, Devin 266
Emamjomeh, Shawn 69, 71, 75
Emch, Eric 343
Emil, Carla 243, 256
Emmet, Linda 156
Emond, Linda 31
Emrick, Kevin 174, 308, 347, 398
Engelman, David 410
England, Brett 74, 168
Engler, Tara 182
English, Donna 171, 172
Ennis, Tyler 13, 65, 94, 274, 321, 372, 399
Enomoto, Kiku 288
Enright, Helen 126, 255
Ensign, Evan 310, 314
Entin, Peter 31, 36, 39, 48, 58, 74, 88, 106, 120, 138, 151, 168, 174, 200, 208, 225, 243, 258, 267, 281, 285, 296, 315, 334, 338, 352
Epps, Sheldon 198, 200
Epstein, Dasha 407
Epstein, Donny 257
Epstein, Julius J. 319
Epstein, Philip G. 319
Epstein, Steven 217
Erbe, Kathryn 31, 338
Ercole, James 110, 113, 277, 279
Ericson, Lindsay 66, 94, 274, 321, 343, 373
Eriksmoen, August 1, 8, 219, 227
Erman, John 410
Ernst, Barry 6, 8
Ero, Jackson 77, 346
Errico, Melissa vii, 152, 154, 157
Escalera, Natalie 119
Eschinger, David 181
Escott, Colin 227, 229, 389
Eskow, Jerome 422
Esmonde, Pixie 181, 183
Esparza, Raúl 378
Esper, Michael 21, 22, 24, 26, 27
Esposito, Cyrena 219
Esse, Parker 109, 114
Essman, Nina 183, 241, 242, 362, 365, 369
Esteva, Joaquin 174, 243, 369, 416
Estrin, Allison 342
Etheridge, Melissa 370
Etter, Bob 238, 342
Eustis, Oskar 127, 130, 133
Evans, Bruce 422
Evans, Craig 265
Evans, David 95, 363
Evans, Jennifer iv, 286-288, 292, 293
Evans, Leigh 58
Evans, Paige 151, 330
Evans, Robert 314, 351
Evans, Wendy 404
Evariste, Mike 328
Everage, Dame Edna vii, viii, ix, 16, 18, 20
Everett, Lyssa 47
Everett, Sonny 32, 34, 36, 143, 152, 155, 156, 225, 422
Everman, Sarah Jane 276-278, 310, 311, 317
Everson, John 403
Evins, Dorothy 25
Eviston, Patrick 188, 216
Evwaraye-Griffin, Maia 362, 364
Ewing, Sean 359
Eyer, J. Austin 184-186
Eyre, Peter 135, 136, 139
Eyre, Richard 211, 214
Eyton, Frank 82
Ezell, Anne 13, 95, 163, 274, 398
Ezold, Erica 361

F

Faber, Carl 31, 250, 274
Faber, Mary 21, 22, 26, 27
Fabian, Kathy 20, 39, 66, 102, 106, 285, 330, 334
Fabris, Richard 162
Factor, Mallory 16, 17, 19, 85, 87, 232, 233, 407
Fadjo, Adrienne 418
Fagan, Garth 176, 180
Fagan, Melissa 121, 122, 123
Fagan, Valerie 1, 2, 4
Fagant, Jennifer 320, 322, 373
Fagin, Michael 183
Fahey, Caitlin 255, 303
Fahey, John V. 47
Fahland, Chris 315
Fahy, Meghann 240, 241
Fain, Holley 270, 271
Fair, Justin 285
Fairchild, Joe Eddie 188
Fajardo, John 183, 189, 217
Falco, Edie 238
Falcone, Elizabeth J. 183
Falcone, Jill 304
Falcone, Tabitha 20, 156
Falk, A. Scott 402
Falkenberg, Martha 232
Falkenstein, Eric 191, 194, 232, 233, 252, 254, 286, 290
Falkowski, Scott 66, 94, 274, 321, 322, 343, 372, 373
Falla, Anthony 168
Fallon, Jimmy 370
Fallon, Sharon 238, 342
Fallon, Susan 13, 92, 95, 272, 274
Falotico, Tim 31, 78, 296, 308, 347
Falzon, Nick 183, 189, 217
Famiglietti, Ben 281
Fana, Dayris 195
Fanelli, Henry 262, 266
Fanelli, Mary Ann 145, 231, 281, 291
Fanuele, Vincent 61
Farber, Andrew 342
Farber, Sasha 54, 55
Farbrother, Mindy 74
Farfalla, Mike 242, 280
Farina, Peggy 163
Farley, David 164, 191, 193
Farley, Sian 48
Farmer, George 95, 220
Farmer, Holley viii, 79, 80
Farmer, Jack 265
Farnesbath, Marie Teresa 333
Farnham, John 58
Farr, Felicia 351
Farrell, Freda 25
Farrell, Heather 367
Farrell, Larry 153
Farrell, Matthew 87, 88
Farrell, Tom Riis 72
Farris, Ralph 178
Farrow, Wendy L. 243
Farver, Matthew 203, 204, 206
Fasano, Matthew 7, 74, 267
Fasbender, Bart 238
Fasulo, John 401
Faux, David 400, 402
Fawcett, Farrah 422
Fay, Brendan M. 162
Fayans, Laura 397
Faye, Alina 109, 111, 115, 116
Fayers, Bryony 47
Fearon, Matthew 405
Fedchock, John 18
Federer, Michelle 362, 364
Federle, Tim 45, 48
Federman, Wendy 5, 19, 51, 52, 130, 171, 172, 290, 345, 346
Fedigan, James 74, 120, 126, 162, 168, 225, 231, 280, 314
Fedigan, Sean 162
Feeks, Lorraine 132
Fehribach, Robert 163, 267, 369
Fein, Ethan 403
Feinberg, Annah 78, 308, 347
Feiner, Ron 373
Feinstein, Adam 322
Feinstein, Michael vii, viii, ix, 17, 18, 20
Feist, Gene 11, 12, 60, 63, 91, 92, 270, 272, 318, 320, 371
Felcher, Peter L. 330
Feld, Melanie 262, 266
Feldman, Lawrence 355, 360
Feldman, Robert 163
Feldshuh, Tovah 381, 382
Fell, Andrew 191
Feller, Phillip 284
Fellner, Eric 41, 48
Fellner, Jenny 366
Fellowes, Julian 211, 214
Feltman, Susan 291
Femenella, Andrew 12, 65, 94, 273, 321, 343, 372
Fender, Jeff 8, 48, 66, 196, 291, 304, 315, 330
Fenkart, Bryan 219-221, 226
Fenmore, George 8, 369
Fenn, Steve iv, 182
Fensom, Jonathan 183
Fenton, Andrew 206, 208
Fenty, Brian 256
Fenwick, Chris 2, 7
Feo, Tiffany 419
Ferber, Alan 288
Ferber, Edna vi, 305, 306
Ferchak, Tony 200
Ferdico, Alessandro 314, 315
Fererri, Joseph Sr. 126
Ferguson, Adam 195
Ferguson, Heather 158, 160, 162
Ferguson, Holly 138, 296
Ferguson, Jesse Tyler 26
Ferguson, Tom 119
Ferguson, Travis 88, 196
Fergusson, Frances D. 243
Fernandez-Taylor, April 183
Fernandez, Gary 126, 224
Fernandez, Kristina 365
Fernandez, Lois 47
Fernandez, Stacia 206
Fernandez, Yuri 35, 257
Ferrall, Gina 205, 206
Ferreri, Joe Jr. 53, 126, 230, 231
Ferreri, Joseph Sr. 53, 231
Ferris, Jim 176, 177, 179
Ferro, Tim 20, 39,

Index

66, 106, 285
Ferrugia, Tom 397
Ferry, John 281, 284, 285
Ferry, Mary 405
Fiandaca, Daniel 83
Ficalora, Maria 48, 156, 250, 281
Fichandler, Zelda 243
Fickinger, Steve 183, 188, 217
Fiedelman, Rosie Lani 140, 142, 147
Fiedler, Joe 141, 144
Fiedler, Josh 12, 36, 65, 94, 273, 321, 343, 372
Field, Melanie 265
Fielding, Helen 373
Fields, Chuck 360, 361
Fields, Dorothy 83, 163
Fields, Randi 95, 274, 322, 418
Fiendel, Colyn 408
Fierstein, Harvey viii, 164, 166, 170, 392
Fifer, Bess 8, 19, 88, 145, 225, 230, 242, 250, 285, 303, 330, 369
Figaroa, Veronica 230
Figert, Sam 302
Figgins, Dionne 219, 221, 225, 226
Figliola, Joe 416
Figueroa, Héctor J. 406
Figueroa, Ilona 302
Filerman, Bensinger 21
Filerman, Michael 16, 17, 19, 24, 85, 87, 252, 254
Files, Trey 22
Filteau, Morgan 8
Finane, Ben 419
Finck, David 18
Findlay, Elizabeth 200, 417
Fine, Elizabeth 182
Fine, Peter 140
Finer, Ben 8
Fink, Bert 156, 330
Fink, Katherine 288
Finkel, Sonya 114
Finkle, Michael 225
Finley, Mordecai 285
Finn, Cristi 183, 189, 217
Finn, Jeffrey 21, 24, 256, 257, 349, 350
Finn, Jon 41, 48
Finn, William 26
Finneran, Katie viii, ix, 276-278, 387, 388, 392, 393
Fiorentino, Adam 211, 213, 218
Firestone, Ashley 13, 65, 274, 343, 372
First, Joshua 64, 188, 281
Firth, Vic 208, 304
Fischer, Carl 144
Fischer, Kurt 91, 217
Fischer, Russell iv, 158-160, 162
Fish, Judy 410
Fisher, Carrie vi, ix, 371, 373, 379, 393
Fisher, Eddie vi, ix, 373
Fisher, Jeanne Donovan 100
Fisher, Jules 245, 247
Fisher, Rick 41, 44
Fisher, Rob 69, 71, 133
Fisher, Teresa 78
Fisher, Todd 373
Fishman, Michael P. 406
Fishman, Shirley 163
Fithian, Diana 12, 65, 94, 273, 321, 372
Fitze, Jamie Lee 249
Fitzgerald, Christopher vii, 109, 111, 112, 114, 388, 392
Fitzgerald, Kathy 245, 246, 251
Fitzgerald, Peter 16, 17, 54
Fitzpatrick, Catherine 66, 94, 274, 321, 343, 373
Fitzpatrick, Colleen 60-62
Fitzpatrick, Kevin 418
Fitzpatrick, Sara 39, 74, 83, 06, 145, 156, 168, 225, 231, 291, 361, 415
FitzRoy, Anne Stewart 334
FitzSimmons, James 11, 13, 14
Flaherty, Peter 318, 320
Flaherty, Stephen vii, 286, 289, 292
Flaim, Christopher 215
Flanagan, Bob 369
Flanagan, Kit 76, 77
Flanagan, Margiann 47
Flannery, Terrence 16, 17
Flateman, Charles 31, 39, 48, 58, 74, 88, 106, 120, 138, 151, 168, 174, 200, 208, 225, 243, 258, 267, 281, 285, 296, 315, 334, 338, 352
Flateman, Gabriel 334
Flatt, Andrew 183, 189, 217
Flauto, Elizabeth 162
Fleetwood, Renee 230
Flegelman, Rheba 330
Fleisher, Emily 78, 308, 347, 398
Fleitell, Joshua 314
Fleming, Adam 362-364, 370
Fleming, Sam 267
Flemings, Renée 94, 273, 321, 343
Flemming, Ron 266
Fleshler, Glenn 37, 38, 121, 123
Flesner, Leslie Donna 109, 110, 111, 116
Fletcher, Guy 163
Flett, Doug 163
Flom, Marina 74, 168, 231, 281
Flood, Patrick 417
Flooks, Ian 85
Flores, Madeline 7
Flores, Rubén 144
Flores, Wallace 58, 126, 150, 151, 200
Florestal, Lindsay 397
Flower, Hellen 291
Flowers, Gareth 326
Floyd, Carmen Ruby 34
Floyd, Mike 83, 102
Flynn, Warren 369
Flynt, Mary Kathryn 46, 47
Foard, Merwin 1, 4, 184-186
Focarile, Teresa 36
Fogel, Alex 308
Fogel, Eric Sean 95
Fogelson, Adam 48, 369
Fogerty, John C. 58
Foisy, Louise 133, 401
Fokken, Markus 19, 20, 373
Foldesi, Julie 328
Foley, Eamon 91, 92, 96
Folger, Nancy M. 243
Folmar, Cameron 340-342, 344
Fonda, Jane 250, 379
Fonseca, Jason 7
Fontana, Santino 45, 50-53, 351, 392
Fontana, Tom 238
Foote, Hallie 392
Foote, Horton 392
Foote, Jenifer 300
Forbes, Joseph 156
Forbes, Kate 393
Ford, Carin 114, 167, 168
Ford, Elisabeth 367
Ford, Ruth 422
Ford, Sara Jean 110, 111, 116
Ford, Shannon 95, 240, 242, 244
Forden, Graham 7, 13, 95, 106, 120, 138, 196, 238, 274, 296, 314, 334, 342
Forero, Andres 141, 144, 145
Forlenza, Meredith 37, 38
Forman, Brooke 6
Forste, Andrew 20, 64, 66
Forsythe, John 422
Fortuno, Ann 401
Foss, Dan 173, 174, 314, 315
Fosse, Bob 69-71
Foster, Beatrice 373
Foster, Catherine 97, 99
Foster, Hunter 227, 228, 231
Foster, Joe 399
Foster, Sara 315
Foster, Sutton 310, 311, 315, 317, 376, 378
Foucher, Marie Renee 217, 218
Fowkes, Conard 422
Fowler, Clement 422
Fowler, Kelsey 215, 378
Fowler, Mary Lee 133
Fowler, Robert 401
Fowler, Wyche Jr. 31, 36, 39, 48, 58, 74, 88, 106, 120, 138, 151, 168, 174, 200, 208, 225, 243, 258, 267, 281, 285, 296, 315, 334, 338, 352
Fox, Charles 95, 200
Fox, Dennis 369
Fox, Libby 48, 250
Fox, Lori Haley 205, 206
Fox, Matt 163
Fox, Robert 37, 38, 117, 118
Fox, Robin 397
Fox, Stephanie 360, 361
Fraenkel, Josh 74, 83, 250, 315, 334
Fragomeni, Brianna 41-43
Fraley, Lisa 188
Francis, Dominic 138, 296
Francis, Tanya 415
Francois, Claude 83
Francone, Nick 250, 369
Frank, Barney 200
Frank, Emmy 321, 322
Frank, Laura 250, 314, 334
Frank, Marilyn Dodds 335, 336
Frank, Melvin 152
Frank, Todd 88, 126, 230
Franke, Gary 200
Frankel, Brian 144
Frankel, Jerry 16-18, 28, 29, 79, 82, 85, 86, 127, 130, 164, 167, 191, 194, 282, 283, 335, 336
Frankel, Marc 28, 79, 127
Frankel, Richard 54, 56, 58, 112, 114, 191, 194, 196, 252, 253, 255, 300, 303, 397
Frankel, Ronald 28, 79, 85, 191, 282
Frankel, Susan 232, 234, 252, 255
Frankenthal, Rachel 203, 204, 206
Franklin, Aretha 107
Franklin, Darnell 13, 65, 94, 273, 321, 343, 372
Franklin, Lyndy 184-186
Franklin, Lynnette 8
Franklin, Peter 36
Franklyn-Robbins, John 422
Franks, Jay 298
Franks, Roy 313, 315
Frantz, Don 133, 183
Franz, Elizabeth 232, 233
Fraser, Dominic 255
Fraser, Ross 58
Fratianne, Laura 315
Frazier, Michael 422
Frederickson, Kathleen 315
Free, Kevin 12, 65, 94, 273, 321, 343, 372
Free, Sean 7
Freed, Lauren 163
Freedman, Gerald 403
Freedman, Greg 291
Freeman, Christopher 176, 177, 179
Freeman, Ernie 80
Freeman, Jackie S. 291
Freeman, Jonathan 184, 186, 190, 215
Freeman, K. Todd 31, 338
Freeman, Steven 152, 153
Freeman, Tony 12,

Index

65, 94, 273, 321, 343, 372
Freitag, Barbara 28, 30, 198, 199, 219, 222, 232-234
Freitag, Buddy 219, 222, 232, 233
French, Larry 422
Frey, Taylor 109-111, 328
Frezza, Marco 66, 94, 274, 321
Fricker, Stephanie 262
Fried, Jessica 36
Fried, Robert 20, 25, 31, 36, 39, 47, 53, 88, 102, 106, 120, 126, 156, 174, 243, 250, 285, 291, 334, 338, 352, 361, 369
Friedlander, David 48, 255
Friedler, Dina S. 83, 361
Friedman, Jessica 418
Friedman, Michael 95
Friedman, Rochelle 405
Friedman, Ron 420
Friedman, Sonia 11, 12, 121, 124, 164, 167, 168, 191, 194, 245, 248, 252, 253, 255, 349, 350
Frieman, Deanna 12, 65, 94, 273, 321, 343, 372
Fripp, Jason 58
Frishwasser, Dan 16, 17, 54, 191, 219, 232, 252
Fromowitz, Seth 45, 49, 50
Frost, Allan 183, 188, 217
Frost, David 322
Frost, Sue 222
Fucarino, Ron 162
Fuchs, Dorion 19, 20, 64, 66, 320
Fulbright, Peter 54, 58, 158, 162, 298, 303
Fuld, James Jr. 85, 87, 282
Fuller, Walter Gil 102
Fullerton, Carl 404

Fullum, George 195, 196
Fulton, David 258, 280
Funk, John 47, 49
Funk, Nolan Gerard vii, 60-62, 68
Funnell, Jenny 135, 136
Furay, Julia 113
Furbert, Denise 95
Furey, Ben 47
Furman, Jill 140, 143
Furman, Roy 1, 5, 51, 52, 79, 82, 236, 237, 286, 290, 354, 358
Furnish, David 41, 48, 236, 237, 239
Furth, George 319
Furze, Liz 47, 196
Fusco, Luciana 74
Fusco, Nicholas 73
Fusillo, Dylan 98, 103

G
Gabay, Roy 97, 102, 340, 342, 341
Gabis, Stephen 52, 53, 126, 160, 162, 171, 172, 225, 315, 340, 341, 349, 350, 352
Gable, Jordan 19, 20, 100, 102
Gabler, Jolie 230
Gacetta, Michael 315
Gaddy, Lonnie 351
Gaddy, Lonny 105, 106
Gaden, Bill 330
Gaeta, Doug 119, 314
Gaffin, Arthur iv, 294-297, 335, 337, 338
Gagliano, Joseph Jr. 238
Gagliardi, Leone 266, 267
Gagliardi, Tino 400
Gagnon, Amanda 25
Gaiger, Lucy 208
Gainer, Elise 101
Gaines, Bahiyah Sayyed 298, 299
Gajda, Lisa 109-111, 115, 121, 122

Galarraga, Nancy 421
Galati, Frank 31, 338
Galbraith, Sarah 20, 25, 47, 102, 126, 156, 250, 291, 361
Galde, Anthony 362-364
Gale, Andy 47
Gale, Gregory 298, 300
Galembo, Chelsea 45
Galitelli, Lauren 13
Gallagher, Colleen 346
Gallagher, Dan 126, 168, 255
Gallagher, Frank 405
Gallagher, Jerry 280
Gallagher, John Jr. viii, 21, 22, 24, 26, 27
Gallagher, Kathleen 38, 39, 333, 334
Gallagher, Kathy 217
Gallagher, Matt 144, 246, 301
Gallagher, Rob 324-327
Gallagher, Sean 25, 27, 208
Galli, Sarah 377
Galligan-Stierle, Aaron 286, 287, 291, 292
Gallitelli, Lauren 92, 95, 272, 274
Gallo, David 219, 221
Gallo, Fred 126, 280
Gallo, Natalie 202-204, 206
Gallo, Paula 329
Galloway, Ian 188
Galloway, Jack 314
Galloway, Jackie 188
Galvan, Jesse 200
Galvan, Jessie 342
Galvez, Al 284
Gambino, Erica 106
Gandolfini, James 118, 120, 353
Gandy, Irene 16, 17, 19, 85, 88, 282, 285, 335, 338, 413
Ganier, Yvette 232, 233
Ganim, Melanie 102
Ganjou, Denise 342,

417
Gannon, Angie 418
Gans, Andrew iv, 419
Ganske, Jennifer S. 235
Ganz, Allison 48
Garber, Nara 322
Garber, Victor viii, ix, 270, 271, 275, 297
Garbowski, Charlie Jr. 66, 94, 274, 321, 343, 373
Garces, Michael John 403
Garcia, Ana M. 200
Garcia, Aymee 313, 317
Garcia, Elias 421
Garcia, Gabriela 69-71, 75
Garcia, Juan "Cisco" 155
Garcia, Liza 207
Garcia, Maija iv, 102, 103
Garcia, Melly 109
Garcia, Nick 368
Garcia, Ricardo 421
Gardener, James 100, 102
Gardin, Miriam 182, 188, 217, 418
Gardiner, Eric 219
Gardiner, Marsi 219
Gardner, Carrie 12, 39, 65, 94, 270, 273, 321, 343, 372
Gardner, Cindy 404
Gardner, Earl 80
Gardner, Elysa 382
Gardner, Hilary 79-81
Gardner, Kurt 76, 78, 305, 308, 345, 347
Gardner, Michael 335, 337
Garfield, Alice 66
Gargiulo, Frank 415
Garment, Paul 213
Garner, Bob 6
Garner, Jeremy 54, 55
Garner, Rosy 342
Garnett, Kim 30, 31, 173, 337, 338
Garnis, Anya 56
Garratt, Geoffrey 211, 215

Garrett, Rachael 188, 291
Garrett, Rachel 38, 39
Garrison, Gary 402
Garrison, Mary Catherine viii, 171, 172, 175
Garrison, Patricia 405
Garvey-Blackwell, Jennifer 36
Garvey, Joseph 216, 218
Garvey, Justin 35, 36, 291
Garvey, Michael 335, 336, 339
Gaspard, Raymond L. 332
Gassner, John 236
Gastel, John Van 54
Gasteyer, Ana vi, 305, 306, 308, 309
Gatehouse, Paul 267
Gates, Thomas 112
Gattelli, Christopher 324, 327
Gaudio, Bob 158-161, 163, 381
Gaudreau, Dan 360
Gay, Richard C. 243
Gaynair, Brian 225
Gaynor, Maura 224
Gayol, Roxanne 254
Gdula, Kristin 8
Gearhart, Todd 60-62
Geesaman, Tara 243, 369
Gehan, Nathan 352
Gehling, Drew 161
Gelbart, Larry 319, 422
Gelblum, Seth 47, 74, 168, 369
Geller, Maryanna 48
Gemignani, Alexander 382
Gemignani, Mike 405
Gendron, John E. 51, 53
Geneske, Jay 31
Genet, Michaele 104, 105
Gennaro, Peter 354
George, George W. 219
George, Maureen 125, 126, 224, 225

George, Rhett 184-186, 219-221
George, Timothy 248
Geralis, Antony 165
Gerard, Bobby 291
Gerber, Bill 24
Gerlach, Jay 12, 65, 94, 273, 321, 343, 372
Gero, Frank 258, 332
Gero, Wojo 258
Gershon, Gina vi, vii, ix, 60, 62, 67, 68
Gershwin, George 20, 82
Gershwin, Ira 20, 82
Gersten, Bernard 148, 149, 151, 324, 328, 330
Gersten, David 402
Gersten, Jenny 127, 133
Gervich, Zhanna 314
Gets, Malcolm 377
Gettinger, Ben 205
Gettler, Victoria 20, 88, 418
Getzug, Coby 51, 52
Gewirtzman, David 419
Ghareeb, Yvonne 408
Ghebresillassie, Susie 100, 102
Ghosh, Shefali 48
Ghoukassian, Adrineh 183, 189, 217
Giancola, Eric 206
Gianino, Antonia 182
Giannini, Maura 110, 113, 403
Giannone, Anthony 304
Giarratano, Debbie 281
Giattino, Mary 152-154, 156
Gibb, Steve 162
Gibbons, Frank 217
Gibbons, Michele 20, 39, 83, 88, 106, 120, 168, 174, 250, 285, 338, 352
Gibbons, Sylvia 334
Gibbs, David 298
Gibbs, James W. 16,

Index

17, 19
Gibbs, Nancy Nagel 241, 242, 365, 369
Gibson, Colin 397
Gibson, William viii, 232, 233
Giebler, Rodney 334
Giebler, Sue 208
Giegerich, A.J. 35, 36
Gifford, Kathie Lee 96
Gifford, Vanessa 36
Gilbert, Alyce 368, 369
Gilbert, Bruce 250
Gilbert, L. Wolfe 163
Gilbert, Michael 216
Gilbert, Phil 66
Gildor, Catherine 324
Gildor, Ephraim 324
Gilkison, Jason vi, 54, 56, 57, 59
Gilkyson, Terry 231
Gill, Jay 46, 47
Gilles, Heather 101
Gillespie, Betty 224, 225
Gillespie, Dizzy 102
Gillespie, Haven 20
Gibbs, James 19
Gillespie, Kelly 78, 308, 347, 398
Gillespie, Terra 151, 330
Gilliam, Michael 200
Gilliard, Beatrice 329
Gillibrand, Nicky 41, 44
Gilliland, Gaelen 245-247
Gillis, Duncan 8
Gillispie, Betty 126
Gilman, Sondra 407
Gilman, Suzanne 266
Gilmore, Don S. 121
Gilmore, Mark 369
Gilmore, Valerie 369
Gilpin, Nicholas 203
Gilrein, Mary Kate 401
Gimbel, Norman 95
Ginsberg, Ernest 343
Giovanni, Dom 280
Giovanni, Kearran 109-111, 115, 121-123
Girardet, Adam 196, 250
Girion, Gilbert 78, 308, 347
Girman, Michael 267
Gisiger, Danielle 183
Gittlitz, Pamela 284
Gjonbalaj, Linda 320, 322, 372, 373
Gladstone, Valerie 400, 404
Glant, Joanne 219
Glasberg, Jonathan J. 347
Glaser, Cathy 97
Glasper, Ryanne 47
Glassberg, Deborah 36
Glassburn, Leslie 132, 133
Glaub, Jim 58, 102, 114, 196, 234, 281, 304
Glazer, Diana 74
Glazer, Joan 151, 330
Glendinning, Jim 243
Glennie-Smith, Nick 183
Glick, Aaron 243, 369
Glikas, Bruce 78, 133, 308, 347
Globe, Anne 315
Glorioso, Bess Marie 198, 200
Glorioso, Dinah 77, 307
Gloven, Jillian 301
Glover, John vi, 305, 306, 309, 381
Glover, Montego vii, ix, 219-221, 226, 378, 386, 387, 390, 392, 393
Glow, Ron 208
Goble, Patty 60, 62
Godan, Courtney 401
Goddard, Gary 127, 130
Goddard, Helen 188
Godfrey, Peter 121
Godineaux, Edgar 222, 225
Godt, Heidi 202-204, 206
Godwin, Joe 66
Goede, Jay 200
Goelz, Anne 162
Goings, Wendall 301
Goland-Van Ryn, Becca 151, 330
Gold, Andrew 20
Gold, Brian 132
Gold, Natalie 94, 273, 321
Gold, Rebecca 127, 335
Goldberg, Andy 78, 308, 347
Goldberg, Hal 101, 102
Goldberg, Jay 74
Goldberg, Jon-Erik 205, 206
Goldberg, Marcia 241, 242, 362, 365, 369
Goldberg, Wayne 66
Goldberg, Wendy 303, 403
Goldberg, Whoopi 26, 182, 226, 244, 292
Golde, Jeffrey 234
Goldfeder, Laurie 76-78
Goldman, Eric 200
Goldman, James 319
Goldman, Joe 167
Goldman, Jon 97, 100, 102
Goldman, Maya 310, 311
Goldman, Rosie 102
Goldring, Vivian 307
Goldstein, Gerald 163
Goldstein, Jack 401
Goldstein, Jeff 329
Goldstein, Jess 158, 160, 236, 237
Goldstein, Neil 120
Goldstein, Patricia R. 343
Goldstein, Seth 36
Goldstone, Liz 270
Goldstone, Steven 270, 343
Goldwyn, Tony 276, 278
Golembieski, Lorrin 25
Golia, Nanette 46, 47
Golub, Peter 345, 346
Gomez, Kenneth 421
Gomez, Lino 355
Goncalves, Tony 216, 218
Gonda, Eli 168
Gonin, Jane 168
Gonzales, Brian 313
Gonzales, Federico del Piño 361
Gonzales, Rayanne 261, 263
Gonzalez, Andrea 7, 8
Gonzalez, Angelo 145
Gonzalez, Arturo 419
Gonzalez, Edlyn 95
Gonzalez, Greg 98
Gonzalez, Jessica 7
Gonzalez, Mandy 140-142, 366
Gonzalez, Marie 302
Gonzalez, Michelle 302
Gonzalez, Tony 205
Goode, Brian 47, 334
Goodman, Benny 82
Goodman, Doug 25
Goodman, Jeff 343
Goodman, Matthew 262, 266
Goodman, Robyn 12, 23, 32, 34, 36, 65, 94, 143, 273, 321, 343, 354, 358, 372
Goodman, Tonne 133
Goodman, Wayne 110, 113
Goodrum, Randy 304
Goodson-Thomas, Katie 48
Goodwin, Deidre 69, 71, 75
Goodwin, Patrick 8, 19, 88, 145, 225, 230, 242, 250, 285, 303, 330, 369
Googe, Charles H. 151, 330
Googe, Charles H. Jr. 13, 66, 78, 95, 133, 274, 308, 322, 347, 373
Goold, Rupert 85, 86
Gordon, Adam 57
Gordon, Allan S. 21, 24, 56, 79, 82
Gordon, Douglas 422
Gordon, John 291
Gordon, Kelly L. 83
Gordon, Lucia Hwong 377
Gordon, Mack 20, 83
Gordon, Rodney 183, 217, 234, 267, 315, 369
Gordy, Berry 20
Gore-Butterfield, Michelle 183
Gore, John 130, 152, 155, 167, 172, 222, 229, 279, 350, 358
Gorham, Valerie 416
Gorin, Stephanie 208
Gorlin, Bill 48, 188
Gorman, M. McLaren 58
Gorruso, Anthony 153
Gorski, Kristen Leigh 362, 364
Gorzell, Andrea 78, 308, 347
Goshen, Jim 200
Gossett, Corban 315
Gottehrer, Richard 163
Gottlieb, Andrew 47, 125, 126
Gottlieb, Max 298
Gottlieb, Morton 422
Gottlieb, Myron vi
Gottlieb, Roy 335
Gottschall, Marie 401
Gottschall, Ruth 211-213
Gotwald, David 6, 8
Gough, Shawn 42
Goulet, Susan 242
Gouse, Lauren 8
Gowenlock, Kay 83, 250
Goya, Maria 7
Gozelski, Sonoka 162
Grable, Rori 420
Grabois, Daniel 326
Grady, Laura 397
Graebner, Martha iv, 419
Graf, Doug 181, 182
Graff, Randy 377
Graham-Caso, Kevin 120
Graham, Andrew 156
Graham, Gary 183
Graham, Greg 41-43, 47
Graham, James 13, 66, 94, 274, 322, 343, 373
Graham, Kasey 361
Graham, Lauren 121, 122, 123
Graham, Wilbur 167
Grahame, David 304
Graller, Michael 88
Gramattico, Louis 304
Grammer, Camille 390
Grammer, Kelsey viii, ix, 164, 166, 169, 387, 390
Granat, Arny 5, 82, 87, 248, 283
Grandage, Michael 135, 137, 138, 294, 295, 296, 297, 388, 392
Grande, Frankie 135, 137, 376
Grandison, Anthony 73
Grandosek, Gordana 54, 55
Grandy, Fred 243
Granger, Milton 213
Grano, Joseph 158, 232
Grano, Kathy 232
Granoff, Marty 60, 318
Granoff, Perry 318, 343
Grant, Christina 234, 235, 314, 315
Grant, Christopher Ryan 227, 228
Grant, Cory 158-160
Grant, Kate Jennings 121, 122, 123
Grant, Sharon 7
Grappone, Annie 47
Grasso, Angelo 242
Grasso, Tommy 301, 302

Index

Graubert, Sheri 12, 65, 94, 273, 321, 343, 372
Gravenstine, Laura 39
Graves, Douglas 369
Gravina, Charlie 125
Gravitte, Debbie 382
Gray, Allison Esq. 47
Gray, Andre 167
Gray, Brannon 291
Gray, DJ 322
Gray, Pamela Jane 270, 271
Gray, Roger 156
Grays, Donnetta Lavinia 148, 149
Grayson, Kathryn 422
Graziano, Michael 408
Greathouse, Jamie 271, 274, 295, 296, 338
Grecki, Victoria 64, 66, 88
Green, Amanda 36
Green, Cody 79-81, 358
Green, Gina 415
Green, Heidi 188
Green, Jackie 57, 58, 174, 200, 208, 411
Green, Jennifer 47, 67, 83, 114, 361
Green, Jodi 47
Green, John 82
Green, Julius 126
Green, Laura 56, 58, 112, 114, 193, 196, 253, 255, 300, 303
Green, Miriam 138, 296
Green, Rasaan-Elijah "Talu" 97, 99
Green, Tom 420
Greenan, Corey 202, 203, 204
Greenan, John 231
Greenberg, Aliza 12, 65, 94, 273, 321, 343, 372
Greenberg, Edward 181, 182
Greenberg, Missy 8
Greenberg, Shoshana 94, 274, 321
Greenberg, Steven 36
Greenblatt, Kenneth 248
Greenblatt, Robert 245, 248
Greene, Ana Rose 172, 174, 222, 225, 229, 230, 233, 234, 257, 258, 279, 280
Greene, Elliot 31, 36, 48, 58, 74, 88, 106, 120, 138, 151, 168, 174, 200, 208, 225, 243, 258, 267, 281, 285, 296, 315, 334, 338, 352
Greene, Frank 185
Greene, Gabriel 225
Greene, John Arthur 354, 356
Greene, Leinwand 133
Greene, Sally 41, 48, 252, 255
Greene, Samantha 325
Greenfield, Mandy 76, 78, 305, 308, 345, 347, 398
Greenhaus, Leah 313
Greenspan, David 305, 306, 309
Greenspan, Evan 57
Greenwald, Tom 13, 47, 66, 78, 83, 95, 106, 114, 126, 133, 145, 156, 168, 225, 231, 234, 250, 255, 258, 274, 291, 296, 308, 315, 322, 334, 347, 352, 361, 373, 415
Greenwood, Colin Charles 347
Greenwood, Guy 347
Greenwood, Jane 51, 52, 76, 77, 227, 229, 270, 271, 349, 350
Greer, Dean R. 208
Greer, Justin 310, 311, 314, 316, 317
Greer, Ryan 58, 102, 114, 196, 304, 416
Greer, Steve 266, 267
Greer, Timothy 83, 250
Gregg, Susan 422
Gregory, Lynne Gugenheim 399
Gregory, Matthew A.J. 12, 65, 94, 273, 321, 343, 372
Gregory, Tom 121
Gregory, Wanda 168, 188
Gregus, Melissa 12, 65, 94, 273, 321, 343, 372
Gregus, Peter 158, 159, 162, 376
Greif, Michael 26, 240, 241, 244
Greiner, Ken 97, 100
Grekin, Douglas 291
Grennan, Andrew 217
Grennes, Dan 22
Gretschel, Sara 401
Grevengoed, David 360, 361
Grey, Jane 28, 30, 31
Grey, Jennifer 26
Grey, Joel 26, 385
Grieco, Charlie 313
Grier, David Alan iv, vii, ix, 282, 283, 285, 388
Grier, Jean Michelle iv, 176, 179, 182
Griffin, Beth 416
Griffin, Bob 361
Griffin, Gerard 47
Griffith, Marey 176, 182
Griffiths, Heidi 127, 130
Griffiths, Meg 334
Grigg, Craig 8, 39, 238, 315
Griggs, Jennifer 83
Grillo, Denise J. 8, 120
Grimaldi, Gary 185
Grimes, Peter 78, 308, 347
Grimshaw, Marc 399
Grindrod, David 205, 208
Grinker, Lori 347
Grisdale, Ashley 207
Grisdale, Leslie 102
Grisetti, Josh 51, 52
Grishman, Emily 36, 47, 61, 80, 126, 145, 196, 217, 240, 243, 246, 277, 281, 318, 330
Grnya, Isaac 328
Grobengieser, Andrew 185, 188
Grodman, Marc 410
Grodner, Suzanne 60-62
Groff, Jonathan 381
Groffman, Elliot 163
Gromada, John 236, 237
Groner, Michele 183, 189, 217
Groomes, Ron 291
Grose, Mike 58
Gross, Shelly 422
Gross, Yeeshai 257
Grossman, Kory 125
Grossman, Randi 208
Grossman, Walt 24, 143, 354, 358
Grossman, Walter 32
Grosvenor, Elsie 150
Grove, Barry 76, 77, 78, 305, 307, 308, 345, 346, 347, 398
Groves, Todd 288
Growler, Michael 77, 78, 346
Grubich, Tanya 47, 58, 130, 133, 208, 231, 237
Grudzinski, Alan 280, 313, 314
Gruen, Paul 329
Grunder, Kay 120
Grundy, Amanda 47
Grunfeld, Aaron 78, 308, 347
Grupper, Adam 51, 52
Gruse, Stephen R. 133
Guare, John 384
Guercy-Blue, Tanya 195, 196, 249
Guernsey, Peter 64
Guerra, Cathy 188, 217
Guerrero, Kimberly 28, 29
Guest, Lance 227, 228
Guettel, Amanda 352
Guettel, Mary Rodgers 322
Guggino, Michael 74
Gugick, Betsy 420
Guida, Kathryn 35, 36, 53
Guidry, Robert 231
Guinan, Francis 31, 338
Guinn, Allison 131
Guiod, Kelly 53, 57, 58, 106, 156, 200, 208, 234, 314, 411
Guip, Amy 133
Guirococho, Luis 410
Guity, Leonila 367
Gumbs, Jeremy 180
Gumley, Matthew 1, 2, 4, 6
Gunhus, Eric 41, 42, 43, 50
Gunther, Peter 416
Gurien, Ed 420
Gurko, Abe 373
Gursky, David 110, 113, 114
Gusmano, Tina 406
Gutierrez, Alexander 132
Gutierrez, Michele 132, 133
Gutterman, Cindy 5, 82, 282, 283
Gutterman, Jay 5, 80, 82, 282
Guy, Brigid 168
Guy, Robert 301, 303
Guyer, Murphy 324, 326
Guzman, Marina 88
Guzulescu, Meg 45
Guzzardi, Autumn 245-247
Gwiazda, Ron 258
Gwon, Adam 12, 65, 94, 273, 321, 343, 372
Gwynne, Haydn 41-43, 49, 379, 380
Gyorgak, Brad 156, 295, 296

H

Haag, Jim 188
Haak, Brad 211, 213, 215
Haan, Cole 285
Habel, Rebecca 11, 12, 14, 65, 91, 94, 270, 273, 321, 343, 372, 399
Haber, Bill 12, 30, 397
Haber, Carole L. 236
Haber, John 398
Haber, John L. 163
Haberfield, Ethan 215
Habib, Barry 298, 300
Habib, Toni 298, 300
Hackenmueller, Paul 102
Hackney, Calandra 401
Haddad, Jay 410
Hadley, Jason 133
Hadley, Michael 135, 136
Hagemann, Philip 294
Hagen, Ben 168, 196
Hager, Robert 60-62, 64
Hagiwara, Jan 262, 266
Hague, Thomas 126
Hahn, Don 178
Haigh, Colin 135, 136
Haimes, Tamar 29, 31, 86, 88, 283, 285, 336, 338
Haimes, Todd 11, 12, 60, 63, 65, 91, 92, 94, 270, 272, 273, 318, 320, 321, 340, 341, 343, 371, 372, 399
Halakan, Liz 57, 58
Halbedel, Stephanie 255
Halder, Titas 296
Hale, Birdie M. 422
Hale, Hank 224, 225
Hale, Mariah 48
Hale, Scott 420
Hall, Alaina Reed 422
Hall, Amy 184-186
Hall, Edward 255
Hall, Jake 19, 20
Hall, Jim 126
Hall, John 280, 314
Hall, Kyle 13, 66, 95, 274, 322, 373, 415
Hall, Lee 41, 44, 48
Hall, Marcus 217
Hall, Mindy 347
Hall, Poppy 196
Hall, Reid 100, 102
Hallett, Ryan 13, 65, 94, 274, 321, 343, 372, 399
Halley, Bob 183
Halliday, Andy 408

Index

Halliday, Rob 138, 216, 296
Halperin, Joshua 354, 359, 361
Halperin, Nan 88
Halpern, Keith 397
Halvorson, Eric 153
Hamburger, Richard 403
Hamilton, Bonita J. 176, 178
Hamilton, Brenda 362-364
Hamilton, Douglas 25, 181, 183
Hamilton, Ed 277, 279
Hamilton, Heather 79, 81, 84
Hamilton, Hilary 74, 168
Hamilton, Richard 315
Hamilton, Sue 83, 188
Hamingson, Andrew D. 127, 130, 133
Hamlin, Jeff 148, 151, 324, 330
Hamlisch, Marvin 381
Hamm, Brian 91
Hammann, Joyce 262, 266
Hammer, Jack 20, 231
Hammerstein, Alice 331
Hammerstein, Dena 85, 335
Hammerstein, Oscar II 20, 324, 327
Hammond, Courtney 78, 347
Hammond, Emily 78, 308, 347, 398
Hammond, Jonathan 286, 287, 288, 293
Hammons, Shannon 279, 281
Hamner, Richard 315
Hampton, Christopher 117, 118
Hancock, Carole 182
Hancox, Jesse 188, 360
Handscombe, Richard 168
Haney, Kel 78, 308, 347
Hanggi, Kristin 298, 300
Hanna, Alex 102
Hanna, Stephen 41-43
Hannah, Michael D. 125, 126, 291
Hannett, Juliana 25, 47, 126, 225, 250, 304, 334, 361, 412
Hanoian, Gregory 183, 189, 217
Hansen, Erik 58, 174, 225
Hansen, Mel 95
Hansen, Melanie 188
Hanser, Görel 207
Hanson-Johnston, Izzy 41-43, 49, 50
Hanson, Alexander 191-193, 196
Hanson, Ashley 25, 91, 114
Hanson, Mann 234
Hanson, Holly 208
Hanson, Hugh 8
Hanson, Julie 265
Hanson, Kelly 188
Hanson, Peter 60, 61, 64, 66, 318, 321, 322
Hanue, Michael 404
Happel, Ken 83, 361
Happel, Mark 83
Haqq, Devin 65, 94, 273, 321, 343, 372
Harada, Ann 32, 33, 248, 251
Harada, Kai 183, 227, 229, 369
Harand, Samara 13, 65, 273, 372
Harbor, Ian 77, 78, 307, 308, 346, 347
Harburg, E.Y. "Yip" vii, 95, 109, 200
Harden, Marcia Gay 118, 382
Hardin, Maya 217
Harding, Alex 98
Harding, Jacki 208
Hardt, Paul 28, 79, 83, 361
Hardy, Hugh 151, 330
Hardy, Joseph 384
Hardy, Miranda 369
Hardyman, Hugh 280
Hargitay, Mariska 238
Harker, James 21, 25
Harkerss, Christine 406
Harkness, James 121-123
Harley, Steve 255
Harlin, Cookie 35, 257, 296
Harlow, Chad 152, 153, 154, 157
Harmon, Chasten 131
Harmon, Curtis 58
Harmon, Kara 25, 225
Harner, Angela 361
Harnick, Aaron 257
Haro, Joey 358
Harold, Ray 303
Harp, Jim 291
Harper, Janet 267
Harper, Valerie iii, iv, viii, ix, 198-201, 388, 393
Harrell, Michael 280
Harrell, Shaneeka 97, 99, 103
Harrell, Thaddis 20
Harriell, Marcy 140, 142, 146
Harrington, Evan 261, 263
Harrington, Jeanette 291
Harrington, Kara 13, 66, 94, 274, 322, 343, 373
Harrington, Nancy 127, 133
Harrington, Patrick 291
Harris, Amy 78, 308, 347, 398
Harris, Dede 245, 248, 252, 254
Harris, Gabe 132
Harris, Harriet 270, 271, 275
Harris, Jaki 25
Harris, Jeremiah J. 267
Harris, Joseph Jr. 25, 47, 114
Harris, Kenneth, Jr. 162
Harris, Kristen 164, 167, 168
Harris, Kyle 318, 319
Harris, Michael 314
Harris, Michael S. R. 280, 281, 315
Harris, Moira 31, 338
Harris, Neil Patrick vi, 244
Harris, Nicolas 217
Harris, Pippa 315
Harris, Robert 133, 208
Harris, Robert C. 20, 25, 31, 88, 138, 285, 296, 338, 342
Harris, Rosemary vi, ix, 305, 306, 308, 309, 381, 388
Harris, Roy 148, 150
Harris, Samantha 72
Harrison, Abbie 183, 189, 217
Harrison, Barbara 78, 308, 347
Harrison, Edmund 83, 188
Harrison, Ellen K. 243
Harrison, George 255
Harrison, Howard 202, 205, 211, 215
Harrison, Vanessa 48, 255
Harsanyi, Fruzsina 243
Hart, Adam M. 206
Hart, Alyssa 25, 250, 303, 334, 361, 412
Hart, Barbara 302
Hart, Charles 261, 264
Hart, Christopher 127
Hart, Leslie 343
Hart, Lorenz 20, 83
Hart, Paul 138, 296
Hart, Wes 354-356
Hartley, Ben 85, 86, 88, 90, 184, 185, 186
Hartley, Lenora 48
Hartley, Morgan 83
Hartman, Andrew 109
Hartman, Mark 33, 36, 318, 320
Hartman, Michael iv, 25, 47, 83, 126, 145, 225, 242, 250, 280, 303, 334, 361, 369, 412
Hartman, Tim 109, 110, 111, 115
Hartnett, Deborah 308, 347
Harvey, Elizabeth 132
Harwood, Clinton 25
Hashagen, Peter 163
Hashimoto, Brian 151, 330
Hashimoto, Daniel 315
Haskell, Miriam 267
Haskins, Daniel 213
Hassell, Harry 153
Hatch, Debra 163, 225
Hatch, Eric 358
Hatch, Joel 41, 43
Hatcher, Tom 361
Hathaway, Nathaniel 156
Hatley, Tim 310, 312
Hauer, Karen 56
Haughton, Lauren 366
Haun, Harry 419
Haupt, Paulette 36
Havard, Julien 314, 315
Havoc, June 422
Hawas, Cesar 31, 88, 285, 338
Hawkanson, David 28, 30, 335, 337
Hawkins, Joel 314, 315
Hawkins, Tim 36
Hawks, Colleen 310, 312
Hawthorn, Alex 133, 352
Hay, Melissa 168, 255
Hayden, Erik 227, 228
Haydon, Kelly 308, 347
Hayes, Bill 153, 277
Hayes, Jack 261-263
Hayes, Maureen A. 343
Hayes, Sean viii, ix, 276, 277, 278, 387, 388
Hays, Carole Shorenstein 37, 38, 104-106
369, 412
Hartman, Tim 109, 110, 111, 115
Hayward, Debra 48
Haywood, Amelia 132, 133
Healy, Derek 250
Heard, Linda 330
Hearn, Dave 182
Heatherington, Diane 284, 405
Hebbard, Lindsay 57
Hebel, Christian 318, 363
Hecht, Deborah 11, 114, 120, 188, 196, 217, 234, 255, 270, 330
Hecht, Jessica 51, 52, 349, 350, 381, 388
Heck, Bill 393
Heckman, Rick 42, 318, 320
Hedley, Nevin 340, 342
Hefner, Tia 351
Hefti, Neal 80
Heick, Aaron 18, 153, 246
Heindel, June 183, 188, 217
Heinink, Eileen 183
Heinlein, Tori 152-154, 157
Heitman, Carrie 12, 65, 94, 273, 321, 343, 372
Helck, David 216
Helke, Elizabeth 168
Heller, Ben 7, 106, 196, 255
Heller, Dale R. 36
Heller, Jill 35, 36, 53, 351
Heller, Tova 13, 66, 94, 274, 322, 343, 373
Heller, W. Benjamin II 13, 95, 120, 138, 274, 296, 314, 334, 342
Helm, Patrick 54, 55
Helman, Joshua 78, 308, 347
Helms, Kimberly 25, 27
Hemesath, Brian 102, 225, 308, 330
Hemminger, Erica 126, 234, 291
Hemminger, Fred 182
Hench, Sarah 360,

Index

361
Hendel, Ruth 21, 23, 51, 52, 135, 137, 140, 143, 294, 295, 349, 351
Hendel, Stephen 21, 97
Henderson, Aland 8, 182, 188
Henderson, Florence 378
Henderson, Jacqueline 277
Henderson, Mark 85, 86, 389
Henderson, Ray 183
Henderson, Stephen McKinley 104, 105, 108, 388, 393
Hendrick, Karla 12, 65, 94, 273, 321, 343, 372
Hendricks, Jon 82
Hendrickson, Jessy 265
Hendrix, Ralph 125, 230
Hendrix, Tyrone 73
Henig, Andi 39, 48, 83, 106, 163, 168, 174, 250, 291, 361
Henkin, Elyce 58, 174, 225, 281, 352
Henley, Larry 20
Hennessey, Nina 60, 62
Hennig, Kate 45, 49
Henninger, Megan 200
Henry, Joshua 21, 22, 23, 27, 145
Henry, Lee 95
Henshall, Ruthie 72
Hensley, Dale 164, 165, 166, 169
Henson, Cheryl 36
Henson, Jane 36
Hentze, Robert M. 361
Henze, Sheryl 262, 266
Herdlicka, Hunter Ryan iv, 191, 193, 197
Hereth, Suzanne 417
Herman, Chris 20, 88
Herman, Jerry viii, 164, 166, 169, 170, 392
Hernandez-Adams, Niki 188
Hernandez, Elise 78, 308, 347
Hernandez, Ernio iv, 419, 422
Herrera, Corinne McFadden 362, 365
Herrera, Manuel 358, 366
Herrick, Norton 127, 245, 276, 279
Herrmann, Bernard 342, 343
Herrmann, Katrina 237, 238
Herrscher, Erick 274
Hershey, Jennifer 25, 102, 114, 133, 163, 196
Hershey, Lowell 262, 266
Hershman, Jim 2, 7, 95
Hertsens, Marc 422
Hertz, Brian 188
Herz, Bill 95
Herz, Shirley 384
Heslin, Victoria 150
Hess, Rodger H. 85
Hesselink, Ray 48
Hester, Richard 158, 163
Hetherington, Kylend 45, 50
Hetrick, Adam iv, 419
Hettel, Nadine 64, 66, 320, 322
Heulitt, Charles III 47
Heusinger, Patrick viii, 236-239
Heveran, David 238, 342
Heverin, Nathan 188
Hevner, Caite 225
Hewes, Henry 375
Hewitson, Michael 238
Hewitt-Roth, Sarah 122, 125, 288
Hewitt, Tom 72
Hewson, James 342
Hewson, Paul David 95
Heyman, Edward 82
Heyward, DuBose 20
Hibbard, David 41-43
Hickey, Joe 64, 66, 77
Hickey, Michelle 36
Hickman, Camille 120, 151, 330
Hickman, John 158, 159, 160
Hickman, Lauren 337, 338
Hicks, Celise 182
Hicks, Lara 181
Hicks, Tiffany 95, 188
Higgason, Joshua 322
Higgins, Colin 250
Higgins, Hazel 162
Higgins, James 407
Higgins, Patience 33
Higham, Katie 78
Hignite, Nichol 188
Hilder, David 308
Hilferty, Susan 318, 320, 362, 365
Hill, Brian 184, 187
Hill, Gloria 361
Hill, J. Michelle 183
Hill, Jon Michael iv, 31, 335, 336, 339, 388, 393
Hill, Kevin 126
Hill, Michael 168, 196
Hill, Michele St. 409
Hill, Natalie 60, 61, 62
Hill, Peggy 282, 283
Hill, Rosena M. 79-81
Hillman, Richard 133
Hillock, Jeffrey 196
Hills, Glenn 168
Hills, Jenifer 401
Hilsabeck, Rick 41-43
Hilty, Megan 245, 246, 250, 251, 379, 382
Hinchee, Jeffrey 8, 133, 250
Hindelang, Jason 112, 114
Hindman, James 211-213
Hinds, Joyce 409
Hine, Janet 54
Hines, Afra 143
Hingston, Seán Martin 276, 278
Hinrichs, Doug 141, 144-146
Hinshelwood, Sophia 399
Hinze, Karl 399
Hirschberg, Carly 218
Hirschfeld, Elie 256, 257
Hirschfeld, Rachel 256
Hirschhorn, Larry 5, 130
Hirzel, Jake 231, 234, 258, 267, 281
Hitchcock, Ken 220
Hives, Sarah 54, 55
Hladsky, Barbara 188
Ho, Karen 410
Ho, Lisa iv, 310, 312, 316, 317
Hobbs, Brian Allan 110, 114, 299, 304
Hobbs, Jerry 13, 95, 274
Hobson, Louis 240, 241, 244
Hobson, Verna 101
Hoch, Chris 164-166, 310-312, 316, 317
Hochman, Larry 1, 5, 188
Hochstine, Daniel 83
Hocking, Leah 41, 42, 43
Hodge, Douglas viii, ix, 164-166, 387, 392, 393
Hodge, Gaynel 163
Hodges, Drew 13, 31, 36, 39, 47, 66, 74, 78, 83, 95, 106, 114, 126, 133, 138, 145, 156, 168, 225, 231, 234, 250, 255, 258, 274, 291, 296, 315, 338, 342, 347, 352, 361, 373, 415
Hodgson, Anthony 315
Hodun, James 126, 224, 225
Hodzic, Emir 101
Hodzic, Linnae 200, 208, 411,
Hodzic, Saime 101
Hoekstra, Joel 299, 301
Hoerburger, Peter 53
Hoff, Barry 156, 234, 250, 280
Hoffman, Al 82
Hoffman, Anna 113, 114
Hoffman, Anthony 314
Hoffman, Brian 307, 308
Hoffman, Constance 183
Hoffman, Courtney 188
Hoffman, Dan 64, 66, 320, 322, 373
Hoffman, Dustin 339
Hoffman, Jackie viii, 1, 4
Hoffman, Mark 58
Hoffman, Rachel 8, 19, 88, 145, 225, 242, 250, 285, 303, 330, 369
Hoffman, Shari 326
Hoffman, Tony 315
Hoffmann, Anna 100, 101
Hofmann, Satomi 264
Hogan, Hannah 126
Hogan, Heather 144
Hoggett, Steven 21, 23, 27
Hoguet, Jennifer 308
Hohn, Jennifer 145
Holbrook, Curtis 358
Holbrook, Morgan R. 274
Holcenberg, David 60, 61, 63, 65, 205, 208
Holden, Danette 313
Holder, Donald 79, 81, 176, 180, 256, 257, 276, 278, 286, 289, 324, 327, 389
Holder, Neville 304
Holder, Theresa 419
Holderbaum, Paul 156
Holds, Anthony 85, 86, 89
Holland-Moritz, Shelly 113
Holland, Derek 367
Holland, Jack 422
Hollenbeck, Franklin 188, 225
Hollerith, Charles 410
Holley, James 302
Holliman, David 181, 182
Hollock, Anthony 131
Holmes, Chris 73
Holmes, David 208
Holmes, Katie 84, 370
Holmes, Kristine 274
Holmes, Mikaela 25
Holmes, Rupert 315
Holt, B.J. 69, 74, 164, 168
Holt, Ellen 66, 94, 274, 321, 343, 373, 399
Holton, Alex 42, 46
Holtz, Greg 188
Holtzclaw, Matthew 114
Holzman, Winnie 362, 365
Hombu, Machiko 196
Hong, Matt 159
Hooker, Michael 198, 199
Hookom, Tina 410
Hoong, Binh 405
Hooper, Bret 57
Hooper, Jürgen 51, 52
Hooper, Melanie 54, 55
Hooper, Nellee 58
Hoosein, Zalina 401
Hopkins, Andi 132, 314
Hopper, Antwayn 127-129
Hopper, Luico 311
Hopper, Tim 31, 338
Horak, Frank 410
Horkey, Maggie 83, 249, 250
Horn, Alisa 242
Horn, Ashley 288
Horn, Christine 180
Horn, Emilia 48
Horne, Lena 422
Horner, Joshua 45
Hornsby, Russell 104, 105, 108
Horowitz, Alison 215, 378
Horowitz, Jimmy 48,

Index

369
Horowitz, Leah 152-154
Horowitz, Mark 322, 330
Horrigan, Ben 46
Horrigan, Joby 47
Horsley, Allison 162
Horton, Tiffany 48
Hosang, Diana 359
Hose, Marian Jean 315
Hosomizu, Hiro 314, 315
Hoty, Dee 60, 62, 68
Houdyshell, Jayne 60, 62
Houghton, Brandon 195
Houghton, Jennilee 25
Houghton, Priscilla Dewey 243
Houlehen, Colleen 58, 162, 303
Hounsell, Ginny 58, 106
Hourigan, Barbara 151, 330
Houston, Doug 2, 8, 18, 311
Houston, Marianna 409
Houston, Mark 181, 183
Howard, Bart 82
Howard, Lisa 245-247
Howard, Peter 8, 69
Howard, Rick 188, 369
Howard, Stuart 28, 79, 83, 361
Howe, David 252, 253
Howell, Rob 252, 253
Howells, Reby 422
Howey, Nicholas 79
Howie, John 329
Howle, Richard 47
Hoyos, Daniel 151, 330
Hoyt, Lon 128, 132
Hoyt, Tom 363
Hsu, Chen-Win 238, 342
Hu, Maryann 324, 325, 327
Hu, Pam 315

Hubbard, Cristin J. 261, 263, 269
Hubbard, Jeff 25, 113, 114
Hubbs, Matt 308
Hubner, William 156, 168
Hucke, Kevin 368, 369
Huckins, George 188
Hudes, Quiara Alegría 140, 142
Hudnut, Sarah 274
Hudson, Don 162
Hudson, Kate 316
Hudson, Richard 176, 180
Huff, Justin 8, 19, 88, 145, 225, 230, 242, 250, 285, 303, 330, 369
Huff, Keith vi, 332, 333
Huff, Neal 200
Huffman, Brent-Alan 188
Huggins, Richard 267
Hughes, Carly 286-288
Hughes, Caroline 168
Hughes, Doug vii, 65, 94, 256, 257, 273, 305, 306, 309, 321, 343, 372, 403
Hughes, Pamela 314, 315
Hughes, Van 21, 23, 27, 245, 247
Hughston, Rebekah 114, 196, 255, 304
Huizinga, Sharon 314
Hulbert, John 265
Hulce, Tom 21, 23, 91
Hull, Charlie 54, 57, 58
Hull, David 366
Hull, Jonathan 267
Hultgren, Kacie 53, 114, 174, 347, 352
Humphrey, Drew 152-154, 157
Humphries, Barry viii, 16, 18, 20
Humphris, Caroline 191, 193
Hunt, Al 403

Hunt, Caitlin 83, 126, 145
Hunt, Helen 26
Hunt, Robb 227, 243
Hunter, Adam John 298, 301, 303
Hunter, Ericka 298, 299
Hunter, Lauren 415
Hunter, Nicki 78, 347, 398
Hunter, Rhonda 410
Hunter, Sophie 88
Huntley, Darlene 57
Huntley, Paul 11, 12, 76, 77, 149, 151, 171, 172, 191, 193, 245, 248, 291, 308
Hurd, Keith 281
Hurlin, Denise Roberts 408
Hurlin, Nathan 408
Hurwitz, Deborah N. 159, 162
Hurwitz, Isaac Robert 243
Huschle, Christina 217
Huser, Leigh 303
Hushion, Casey 143, 145
Husinko, Gregory 25, 250
Huston, Anne 229
Hutchison, Brian 46, 47, 198, 199, 201
Huttly, Steve 296
Hutton, Wendy 66, 94, 274, 321, 343, 372, 399
Hwang, David Henry 407
Hyacinthe, Benjamin 420, 421
Hyde, Douglas 168
Hyde, Mike 406
Hyde, Wayne 25
Hydzik, Matthew 354, 356
Hylenski, Peter 171, 172, 298, 300, 310, 312
Hylenski, Suzanne 211-214
Hyler, West 162
Hylton, Dianne 368, 369
Hyman, Marcia 57
Hyman, Mike 6, 8

Hynes, Jessica 252, 253
Hysell, Hugh 102, 163, 200, 342
Hyslop, David 69, 74, 75
Hytner, Nicholas 151, 330

I

Iacobelli, Ed 406
Ianculovici, Dana 355
Iannello, Giuseppe 182
Iannetta, Mario 183, 189, 217
Iavorski, Stas 48, 168
Ibanez, Danny 39
Iglehart, James Monroe 219, 221, 225
Ilies, Mary 261, 263
Illo, Frank 181, 182, 250
Illo, Mark 369
Imhof, Chuck 343
Imperato, Kimberlee 302
Inaba, Carrie Ann 54, 56, 59
Ince, James 217
Indelicato, Lucas 361
Ineson, Brett 315
Ingman, Matt 122, 125
Ingram, Carol 408
Ingram, Glenn 333
Ingram, Kenny 176, 177, 179
Ingui, Kit 132, 133
Inkley, Fred 1, 2, 4, 10
Interland, Todd 48
Intile, Robert 78, 308, 347
Iorio, Jim 349, 350
Irazarry, Diego 46
Ireland, Marin iv, vii, 11, 12, 15
Irish, Katie 106, 280, 314
Irizarry, Daisy 249
Irons, Nick 329
Irving, George S. 378
Irving, Victor 181, 183
Irwin, Bill vii, 12, 60, 62, 65, 67, 68, 94, 273, 321, 343, 372, 382
Irwin, Tom 31, 338
Isaacson, Jennifer 252, 342
Isbin, Rena 326
Ishikawa, Noriko 416
Ishmael, Clement 176, 182
Ishmael, Nicki 13, 66, 94, 274, 322, 343, 373
Isler, Bill 95
Ismislund, Clancy 373
Israel, Vivian 355, 360
Italiano, Frank 102
Itzin, Gregory 85, 86, 89
Ivelja, Stephen 224
Iverson, Janeth 183
Ives, David 109, 152, 154, 402
Ivie, Brandon 242
Ivins, Todd 162
Izquierdo, Martin 102, 188
Izquierdo, Michael 234
Izzo, Benjamin 12, 65, 273, 372

J

Jablon, Sara 183
Jaccarino, Stephanie 13, 65, 274, 372
Jack, Jim 12, 65, 94, 273, 321, 343, 372
Jackman, Hugh vi, vii, ix, 332, 333, 377, 379, 383
Jackness, Andrew 60
Jacknow, Alexis 13
Jackson, Adam 249, 250
Jackson, Andrew 392
Jackson, Ben 138
Jackson, Cheyenne vii, 109, 111, 115, 116, 379
Jackson, Christopher 140, 142, 147
Jackson, Janet 383
Jackson, Jason 277

Jackson, Joshua J. 181
Jackson, Lauren Lim 109-111, 116
Jackson, Michael 383
Jackson, Nathan Louis 12, 65, 94, 273, 321, 372
Jackson, Sean 135, 136
Jackson, Trevor 217
Jackson, Tyrone A. 184-186, 223
Jacob, Jennifer 8, 304
Jacobi, Lou 422
Jacobs, Amy 207
Jacobs, Craig 264, 266, 267
Jacobs, Jason 12, 65, 94, 273, 321, 343, 372
Jacobs, Michael 266
Jacobs, Roy A. 133
Jacobs, Sander 140, 143, 354, 357
Jaffe, Anita 407, 410
Jaffie, Harry 196, 405
Jaggernauth, Ruby 329
Jahnke, Christopher 219, 221
Jakel, Suzanne 183, 189, 217
James-Richardson, Sheron 7
James, Brian d'Arcy viii, ix, 241, 310, 311, 315-317, 345, 346, 348
James, Dana 183, 189, 217
James, Georgi 45, 50
James, Geraldine 135, 136, 139
James, Hamilton E. 243
James, John 320, 322, 404
James, Marcus Paul 140, 142, 147
James, Morgan 1, 2, 4
James, Sara 361
James, Toni-Leslie 109, 115
James, Tony 176, 177, 179
James, Zachary iii,

The Playbill Broadway YEARBOOK 2009-2010   441

Index

iv, 1, 4, 9
Janas, J. Jared 243, 369
Janicki, Jay 97, 102
Janin, Lucas 315
Janisse, Lindsay 362, 363, 364, 370
Jankowski, Joseph 94, 321
Jannelli, Ron 18, 311
Janney, Allison 245, 246, 251, 376
Janocko, Rachel Short 188, 216
Jansen, Ashley 238
Jansen, Robert 238
Jarboe, Joseph H. 243
Jaroslowicz, David 335
Jarus, Tom 77
Jarvis, Brett 36
Jarvis, Mitchell 298, 299, 303
Jaudes, Christian 128
Javier, Vanessa 285
Jay, Adam 47, 196, 255
Jayne, Cathy 401
Jbara, Gregory 41, 43, 381
Jellison, John 219-221, 226
Jenkins, Barry 7
Jenkins, Beverly 35, 144, 146, 147, 310, 313, 314
Jenkins, Daniel 211, 213, 218
Jenkins, Gordon 80
Jenkins, Jeffrey Eric 407
Jenkins, Michael A. 124
Jenkins, Patricia 422
Jenkyns, Mark 120
Jennifer, Valentina, 250
Jennino, Lawrence 320, 322, 373
Jennino, Nichole 291, 303, 322
Jensen, Mark 163
Jensen, Sharon 234
Jensen, Yvonne 333, 334
Jenson, Vicky 315
Jerry, Erika 127, 129
Jessup, Craig 368, 369
Jett, Joan 304
Jevnikar, Jana 8, 83, 342
Jewels, Heather 113
Jhung, Finis 47
Jlelaty, Rosetta M. 235, 254
Jobim, Antonio Carlos 83
Joel, Billy viii
Johannesson, Bruce Anthony 304
Johansen, Mark 403
Johansson, Scarlett viii, ix, 349, 350, 352, 388, 393
John, Catrin 255
John, Elton 41, 44, 48, 58, 95, 176, 177, 179, 183, 236, 237, 239, 379
John, Tricorne, 102
Johns, Glynis 322
Johns, Joni 183
Johnsen, Clark 1, 2, 4
Johnson, Aaron 97-99, 389
Johnson, Angela L. 314, 315
Johnson, Birch 18
Johnson, Brian Charles 21, 23, 27
Johnson, Bryan 168, 216
Johnson, Bryan Scott 202-204, 206, 210
Johnson, Catherine 202, 204
Johnson, Chantylla 180
Johnson, Clifford Lee III 347
Johnson, Craig 7, 18
Johnson, Deborah 401
Johnson, Enotris 231
Johnson, Jay Armstrong 127-129, 134
Johnson, Jeff 88
Johnson, Jeffrey 156
Johnson, Jessica 13, 66, 95, 200, 208, 274, 322, 342, 373, 411
Johnson, John 70, 133
Johnson, Kate Edelman 410
Johnson, Kathleen K. 127, 282, 335
Johnson, Keean 41, 43, 50
Johnson, Kym 56
Johnson, Lavonia 415
Johnson, Lee 36
Johnson, Nicole Adell 176, 177, 179
Johnson, Peter 285
Johnson, Scott 25, 163, 196, 304, 416
Johnson, Terry 164-166, 388, 392
Johnson, Virginia 13
Johnston, Dennis 176, 177, 179
Johnston, Richard 217
Johnston, Sherra 126
Johnstone, Davey 48
Johnstone, Flora 162, 163, 398
Joines, Howard 42, 46, 60, 61, 63, 276, 277, 279, 281
Jolie, Angelina 218
Jolles, Susan 192
Jones-Barnes, Carolyne 35, 257
Jones, Adrian W. 198
Jones, Alphonso Romero, II 176, 178, 181
Jones, Andrew 36, 155, 156
Jones, Andy 145, 363
Jones, Bill T. 97-99, 101-103, 388, 389, 392, 393
Jones, Carolyne 296
Jones, Cass 48
Jones, Chad 78, 308, 347, 398
Jones, Christine 21, 23, 91, 92, 388
Jones, Cornelius, Jr. 181
Jones, David Jr. 343
Jones, Ffion 208
Jones, Gillian 57
Jones, Gloria 410
Jones, Howard 207
Jones, Jane B. 347
Jones, Julia 195, 196, 254, 255
Jones, Kenneth iv, 419
Jones, Kevin 200, 208, 411
Jones, Kim 133
Jones, Lindsay 208
Jones, Liz 78, 308, 347
Jones, Lyle 138, 351, 352
Jones, Mark 7
Jones, Martha H. 256
Jones, Michael 88, 291
Jones, Michael Leslie 304
Jones, Ora 31, 338
Jones, Peter 322
Jones, Quincy 31, 80
Jones, Rachel Bay 127, 129, 134
Jones, Rebecca Naomi viii, 21, 22, 26, 27
Jones, Robert 20, 88, 120, 196, 281, 285
Jones, Simon 342
Jones, Simone Joy 232, 233
Jones, Sophie 48
Jones, Stan 231
Jones, Steve 66, 320, 322
Jones, Ty 85, 86, 90
Jones, Tyrick Wiltez 109-111
Jordan, Aisha 347
Jordan, Cookie 97, 200, 234, 330, 352
Jordan, Jeremy 298, 299, 354, 356
Jordan, Jon 183
Jordan, Julia 402
Jordan, Leslie 386
Jordan, Lisa Renee 12, 65, 94, 273, 321, 343, 372
Jordan, Matthew D. 31
Jordan, Rebecca Kim 401
Jordan, Richard 37
Jordan, Will 61
Jorgensen, Chip 35, 295
Jorgensen, Lars 257
Jorgensen, Melissa 295
Joseph, Jeffrey 78, 308, 347
Joseph, Jim 77, 78, 307, 308, 346, 347
Joseph, Stephen 410
Joseph, Wendy Evans 243
Joubert, Joseph 42, 46, 47
Joyce, Rosalind 7
Judd, Rebecca 264, 265
Judge, Julia 151, 330
Judge, Kevin 274
Judge, Nick 183, 189, 217
Judson, Chanon 97, 99
Jula, Anastasya 168
Jung, Jee an 188
Jungwirth, Erich 37
Junior, Catherine 113
Jurman, Karl 176, 178, 180, 182
Just, Sloan 310, 314
Jutagir, Hattie K. 148, 151, 324, 330

K

Kabula, Joe 225
Kaburick, Aaron 41-43, 49, 50
Kaczorowski, Peter 345, 346, 349, 350
Kadleck, Anthony 2, 311
Kafka, Yonit 13, 65, 94, 274, 321, 343, 372, 399
Kagen, Matthew 78, 94, 321
Kahane, Rebecca 78, 308, 347
Kahler, Angela 183, 208
Kahn, Brandon 53, 330
Kahn, Gus 20, 83
Kahn, Ian 85, 86, 89
Kail, Thomas 140, 142, 146
Kain, Luka iv, 324, 326, 331, 386
Kainuma, Morris 178, 181
Kaiser, Corey 228
Kaiser, Lisbeth 415
Kaiser, Michael 286, 291
Kalafatas, Greg iv
Kalama, Jamie 12, 65, 94, 273, 321, 343, 372
Kalb, Benjamin 240
Kaldenberg, Kim 224, 225
Kaledin, Nick 400, 402
Kaley, David 8
Kaller, Sheryl viii, 236, 237, 239, 388
Kamakari, Yuiko 240, 242
Kambara, Shoko 230, 234, 242, 291
Kamerer, Carrie 258, 351, 352
Kammeier, John 334
Kandel, Elizabeth 231
Kander, Ellen 95
Kander, John 20, 69, 71, 83, 392, 393
Kane, Ellen 47
Kane, Jim 138, 195
Kane, Mike 248
Kane, Robert 66, 94, 274, 321, 343, 373
Kang, Susan 410
Kangal, Inci 174
Kanner, Neil 13, 66, 95, 274, 322, 373
Kantor, Adam 241
Kantor, Kenneth 261-263, 269
Kanyok, Laurie 79-81
Kao, Andrew 78, 398
Kaplan, Carol 13, 66, 78, 95, 151, 274, 308, 322, 330, 347, 373
Kaplan, Gary 1, 21
Kaplan, Steven 183
Kaplan, Van 5, 82
Kaplen, Lawrence 343
Kaplowitz, Robert 97, 99, 101, 389
Kapoor, Monica 206
Kapoor, Raj 54
Karam, Stephen 12, 65, 94, 273, 321, 372
Karapetyan, Geo 106, 120, 174, 238, 315, 352
Karas, Sandra 401
Karasik, Irene 47
Karger, Frederick 58
Karie, Joel 176, 177, 179
Karl, Andy 245, 246, 251, 366, 370

Index

Karlin, Benjamin Bales 106
Karlin, Lisa 286, 287, 289
Karling, Walter 403
Karlson, David 150, 151
Karmazin, Sharon 85, 87, 286, 290, 336
Karp, Warren 13
Karpoff, Alana 16, 17, 19, 31, 85, 88, 282, 285, 337, 338, 413
Karr, Justin L. 102, 163
Karr, Pam iv, 420
Karrer, Pitsch 208
Karriem, Hajjah 322, 372, 373
Karst, Michelle 78, 308, 347
Kaseluris, Vangeli 242, 243
Kashani, Pamela Winslow 127, 130, 222
Kashani, Tim 127, 130, 222
Kass, Alan 422
Kass, Amy 13, 66, 95, 200, 208, 230, 274, 322, 373, 411
Kassoff, Russ 79-81
Kastenbaum, Jeff 225
Kastner, Ron 258
Kastrinos, Nicole 109
Kateff, Chris 162
Kates, Bernard 422
Katsuyoshi, Charlaine 176-179
Katvan, Rivka 322
Katz, Lawrence 13, 66, 95, 274, 322, 373
Katz, Natasha 1, 5, 76, 77, 184, 187
Katz, Sara 298
Katzenmeyer, Tom 258
Kaub, Thomas 401
Kaufman, Andrew 151
Kaufman, Claudia 39, 133, 163, 243
Kaufman, David 298
Kaufman, George 335
Kaufman, George S. vi, 305, 306
Kaufman, Marci 416
Kaufman, Wendy Merritt 408
Kaus, Stephen M. 270-272, 274
Kava, Tim 106
Kavanagh, Peter 126
Kavanaugh, Ryan 298
Kawahara, Karl 326
Kawana, Yasuhiro 79, 82
Kay, Dean 83
Kaye, Anne 2, 8, 18, 311
Kaye, Barry 16, 17, 85, 335
Kaye, Buddy 20
Kaye, Carole 16, 17, 85, 335
Kaye, Kristopher 63
Kaye, Larry 24, 257
Kaye, Richard D. 367, 369
Kazan, Zoe viii, 37, 38, 40
Keagy, Grace 422
Keagy, Kelly 304
Keane, James 243
Keappock, Susan 303
Keating, Annie 410
Keating, Kevin 58, 102, 114, 196, 234, 281, 304
Keclik, Scott 66
Keefe, Kevin 406
Keegan, Ted 265
Keegan, Tom 234
Keeley, Keira 393
Keene, Chris 333
Keeping, Francis 369
Keghlian, Georgia 254
Kehn, Linda 315
Kehr, Donnie 45, 50
Keightley, Benjamin 102
Keim, Betty Lou 422
Keister, Andrew 126, 162, 217
Keith, Alvin 12, 65, 94, 273, 321, 343, 372
Keller, Helen viii, ix, 232-234
Keller, Michael 1, 2, 5, 8, 16-18, 21-23, 32, 34, 41, 42, 44, 91, 92, 97-99, 102, 121, 122, 124, 140, 145, 176, 178, 180, 184, 185, 187, 203, 219, 220, 222, 229, 230, 240, 241, 245, 246, 248, 310, 312, 354, 355, 357, 362, 363, 365
Keller, Roger 238, 342
Kelley, Kimberly 168, 249, 250
Kelley, Robert 219
Kells, Daniel J. 371, 373
Kelly, Chris 39, 315
Kelly, David E. 134
Kelly, Gerard 127
Kelly, Glen 16-18
Kelly, Kenneth 31, 173, 337
Kelly, Kirk 400
Kelly, Laura Michelle 215
Kelly, Lorna 379
Kelly, Margot 243
Kelly, Michael W. 162
Kelly, Rick 216
Kelly, Robert D. 174, 337
Kelly, Robert W. 361
Kelly, Scott 12, 65, 94, 273, 321, 343, 372, 399
Kelly, Thomas L. 255
Kelsch, Nina 8
Kelson, Carolyn 227, 230
Kemp, Hartley T A 191, 193
Kemp, Jennifer Hindman 163
Kemp, Steven 126, 225
Kenary, Patricia 257
Kendall, Shanah-Ann 113, 114, 229, 231, 404
Keneally, Ken 100, 102, 250
Kenley, John 422
Kenn, Dana 267
Kennedy, Chris 163
Kennedy, Clinton 132, 138
Kennedy, David 106
Kennedy, Jenny 296
Kennedy, Patricia 235, 254
Kennedy, Steve Canyon 121, 124, 158, 160, 176, 180, 211, 215
Kennedy, William 217
Kenney, Chris 408
Kenny, Christina 125
Kenny, Gary 53, 125, 126, 231
Kenny, Sean 420, 421
Kent, David 69-71, 75
Kent, Richard 138, 296
Kent, Walter 82
Kenwright, Adam 47, 48
Kenwright, Bill 121, 124, 126
Kenyon, Steve 113, 165, 185
Kenzler, Karl 215
Keough, Rosemary 173, 174, 291
Kepley, Nick 211-213, 218
Kern, Jerome 20, 83
Kern, Kevin 362, 364, 370
Kernan, David 318
Kerns, Michael 8
Kerr, Walter 191, 196, 197
Kershaw, Jamie 315
Kerwin, Brian 28, 29
Keslar, Logan 164, 166, 169
Kessler, Tommy 299, 301
Kester, Muriel 8, 217
Kesterson, Colleen 303
Keudell, Devin 41, 47, 207
Key, Scott 35
Keys, Alicia 103
Kfir 265
Khan, Shahnaz 368
Kickel, Mary 66
Kidman, Nicole vii, 244
Kiehn, Dontee 5, 8, 241, 242
Kielmann, Kurt 315
Kievit, Lauren 208
Kievit, Meredith 207, 208
Kilburn, Aileen 284
Kilday, Ray 61, 65
Kileen, Nicola 217
Kilgore, John 38
Kilgore, Matthew J. 152-154, 157
Kilgore, Mykal 127, 129
Kilian, Leslie 38, 39, 333
Kim, Albert 132, 133
Kim, Andrew 315
Kim, Collin 255
Kim, Juil 183, 189, 217
Kimball, Chad vii, ix, 219, 221, 226, 386, 387, 390
Kimbell, Jon 219
Kimbro, Jacob Lloyd 183, 189, 217
Kimmel, Veronica 66
Kina, Jennifer 359
Kinard, Virginia 266
Kind, Richard 377
King, Aaron 410
King, B.B. 379
King, Cathie 410
King, David 138, 296, 342
King, Everett 422
King, Lawrence 330, 422
King, Pearl 231
King, Raymond 216
King, Sid 102
Kingaby, Emma 114, 234
Kingsberry, Grasan 109-111, 114
Kingsberry, Jones Grasan 109
Kingsepp, Roger 78, 308, 347, 398
Kingsley, Tom 189
Kingzett, Jody 196
Kinney, Holly 304, 334
Kinney, Terry 31, 338
Kinney, Zack 416
Kinsella, Kelly 162
Kinsella, Kevin 158, 161
Kinsella, Tamara 158, 161
Kirchoff, Trey 8
Kirdahy, Tom 286, 290
Kirkham, Steven 249, 250, 291
Kirkland, Dale 363
Kirmser, Fran 127
Kirspel, Laura 280
Kiser, Anthony C.M. 243
Kiskaddon, Walt 401
Kissane, Jeremiah 211, 213
Kitaoka, Mark 57
Kitowski, Dan 410
Kitt, Tom 21, 23, 91, 92, 133, 240, 241, 244, 392
Kittles, Tory 37, 38
Kitzhaber, Amy 156
Kiyan, Kaitlin 131
Kjellman, Cara 41-43, 47, 49
Klaitz, Jay iv, 171, 172, 175
Klausen, Ray 54, 56
Kleeger, Burt 416
Kleeman, Michael 354, 356
Klein, Adelaide 422
Klein, Isaac 361
Klein, Kara 41-43, 265, 268
Klein, Mark 328, 330
Klein, Mary Pat 196, 352
Kleitsch, Todd 369, 404
Klemm, Bill 66, 94, 274, 321, 343, 373
Klemons, Stephanie 140-142, 145
Klenner, John 82
Klinger, Bruce 282, 284, 285
Klink, Ryan 13, 66, 285, 338, 373
Klinsky, Steven B. 243
Klitz, Jeffrey 121, 122, 124, 125
Kloss, Ingrid 8, 138, 296
Kloss, Kristina 31, 47, 216
Kluge, John W. 31, 36, 39, 48, 58, 74, 88, 120, 138, 151, 168, 174, 200, 208, 225, 243, 258, 267, 281, 285, 296, 315, 334, 338, 352
Kluth, Chris 291,

The Playbill Broadway Yearbook 2009-2010   443

Index

360
Knapp, J. Burke 243
Knauer, Ian 206
Knechtges, Dan 95, 318, 320
Kneeland, Jennifer 322
Knell, Rebecca 13, 94, 95, 274
Knibb, Richard 217
Knight, Michelle 161
Knight, Steve 418
Knitel, Julia 60-62, 66
Knizner, Jeff 183, 189
Knoll, Alexandra 213
Knowles, Beyoncé 20, 75
Knox, Bethany 8, 19, 88, 145, 225, 230, 242, 250, 285, 303, 330, 369
Knox, Hillary 114, 156, 162
Knox, Susan 151, 330
Ko, Alex 45, 49, 50
Kobak, Joshua 21-23, 27
Kober, Andrew 131, 134
Koch, David 41-43, 49, 53
Koch, Martin 41, 44, 202, 205
Kochuba, Courtney 234, 255
Kocis, Stephen 36
Koehler, Ted 82, 83, 95
Koenig, Jeanne 83, 182, 291
Koening, Arthur 8
Koerner, Kati 151, 330
Koestler, Mark D. 13, 39, 47, 66, 95, 151, 208, 274, 322, 330, 373
Koger, Jeff 302
Kogod, Arlene 243
Kohl, Hannah 291
Kohlbrenner, Michael 119
Kohn, Amy 36
Kohn, Barry Dr. 47
Kohn, Mei Y. 235
Kohn, Nicholas 32, 33
Kolker, Adam 355
Kollen, Ron 183, 188, 217
Kolnik, Paul iv, 21, 22, 24, 25
Kolodziej, Magdalena 404
Kolomiers, Sergio 58
Komer, Chris 355
Komoda, Paul 315
Konecky, Ronald S. 407
Kong, Abby 83, 102
Konialian, Elise 258
Kono, Ben 159
Konyk, Raya 333
Koomson, Abena 97-99
Koonce, Scott 216, 217
Koonin, Brian 33
Koopman, Philippa 367
Kopel, Stephen 12, 39, 65, 94, 273, 318, 321, 343, 372
Kopko, Tamara 328, 330
Kops, Jerry 301
Korbich, Eddie 184, 186
Korder, Jacob 367
Korf, Gene R. 343
Korins, David 393
Korn, Jim 106, 330
Kornberg, Richard iv, 97, 99, 102, 109, 112, 114, 413
Kornet, Abigail 163, 398
Kosarin, Michael 184, 185, 187
Kosis, Tom 60, 63, 66
Kostal, Irwin 354
Kotb, Hoda 96
Koufakis, Sophie 254
Kouloumbis, Tatiana 401
Kouyaté, Ismael 97, 99, 103
Kovalenko, Tim 360
Kovalev, Pasha 56
Kovler, Judy Lansing 243
Kowalik, Trent 41, 43, 49, 50
Koye, Danny 132, 133
Kozee, Debra 200
Kraber, Tony 422
Krakowski, Fritz 355
Krall, Ben 338
Kramer, Francine 333
Kramer, Sam 238
Kramer, Terry Allen 1, 5, 16, 17, 79, 81, 245, 248, 276, 279, 282, 283, 354, 357
Krampf, Craig 304
Krasna, Norman 152
Krasner, Paul 13, 95, 274
Krass, Michael 11
Kratzer, Eric W. 183, 189, 217
Kraus, Jeremy 8, 133, 418
Krause, Jon 61, 64, 66
Krauss, Ben 8
Krauss, Robert 208
Krauthamer, Adam 311
Kravitz, Lenny 107
Krawiec, Matthew W. 83, 361
Kready, Jeff 41-43, 50
Kreeger, Doug 377
Kreidler, Todd 106
Krcinbihl, Kathy 406
Kreis, Levi 227, 228, 230, 231, 388, 393
Krieger, Portia 78, 308, 347
Krill, Sean Allan 205
Kristan, Connie Bartlow 232
Kristiansen, John 83, 106
Kritzer, Leslie viii, 318, 319, 323
Kroeper, Jean 397
Krombach, Chelsea 276, 278, 362-364
Krost, Daniel 342
Krumland, Carole S. 343
Krupinski, Dana 369
Krupp, Judi 24
Ku, Andrew 419
Kua, Kenway Hon Wai K. 362, 364, 370
Kubala, Joe 106, 120, 174, 352
Kubala, Joseph S. 36
Kuch, Roger 168
Kuchar, Dan 216
Kuchwara, Michael 422
Kudisch, Marc 245, 246, 250, 251
Kuennen, Michael 277, 279
Kuether, John 261-263
Kühl, Keith 276, 278
Kuhn, Dave 2, 7
Kuhn, Jeffrey iv, 340-342, 344
Kuhn, Kevin 178
Kulberg, Eric 25
Kuligowski, Marsha 66
Kulik, Ellen 163
Kulik, Kieron 58
Kulish, Kiril 41, 43, 49, 50
Kulok, Peter 266, 267
Kulukundis, Eddie 126
Kumor, Michael 254
Kunene, Ron 176, 178, 179, 182
Kuney, Daniel 102
Kuney, Scott 61
Kung, Yufen 133
Kunis, Rick 188
Kunken, Stephen 85, 86, 90, 388
Kuo, Jay 21
Kupper, Pamela 138, 296
Kuppig, Ty 126
Kuriyama, Diana 188
Kurtz, Christopher 144, 145
Kurtz, Manny 82
Kurtzuba, Stephanie 45
Kurz, Kathleen A. 267
Kurz, Pamela 314, 315
Kurz, Peggie 217
Kusinski, Dawn 230, 234, 281
Kusner, Jon 74
Kuzma, Rebecca 183, 404
Kuzmanic, Ana 28, 29, 335, 336
Kwaitkowski, Bob 126
Kwan, Guy 172, 174, 222, 225, 229, 230, 233, 234, 257, 258, 279, 280
Kwon, Cathy 267, 279, 280

L
LaBanca, Matthew 152-154, 157
LaBarbera, John 13, 65, 94, 273, 321, 343, 372, 399
LaBarre, Deirdre 196, 249, 250
LaBelle, Patti 322
Laboissonniere, Wade 78, 352
Lacamoire, Alex 36, 140, 142, 146, 245, 248, 362, 365
Lachowicz, Cheryl 16, 17, 85, 232
Lackey, Ty 223, 225
LaColla, Kyle 242, 243
Lacombe, Brigitte 285
Lacoste, Lyslynn 322
Lacy, Todd 183, 184, 211
Lader, Joan 48
Laemmie, Karlene 401
Laev, Jim 83, 355
Lafarga, Nina 140-142, 146
LaFargue, Emile 100, 113
Laforest, Rachel 401
Lage, Jordan 282, 283
Lagerstrom, Raelyn R. 151, 330
Laghezza, Anna 264, 265
Lahti, Christine 117, 118, 120
Lai, David 213, 217, 262, 264, 266, 267, 326, 327
Lai, Valerie Lau-Kee 216, 218
Lai, Yoki 78, 106
Lajka, Jason 322
LaMattina, Anthony 31, 39, 48, 58, 74, 88, 106, 120, 138, 151, 168, 174, 200, 208, 225, 243, 258, 267, 281, 285, 296, 315, 334, 338, 352
Lambert, Dennis 304
Lambert, Gelan 97, 99, 103
La Mendola, Carmine 133
LaMon, Anton Harrison 261-263
Lamon, Josh 127-129, 134
Lampel, Alan 267
Lampert, Mary 404
Lanasa, John 8, 13, 20, 25, 31, 53, 66, 88, 95, 120, 133, 250, 274, 285, 322, 338, 373, 418
Lance, Andrew 13, 95, 274, 373
Land, Ken 276-278
Landau, Elie 7, 138, 257, 296
Landau, Randy 42, 46
Landau, Tina 31, 335, 336, 338, 339
Landesman, Rocco vi, 112, 161
Landis, Scott 51, 52
Landolfi, Mary 403
Landon, Dan 284, 285
Landrine, Bryan 95
Lane, Burton vii, 20, 109, 112
Lane, George 258
Lane, James T. 69, 70, 71
Lane, Jani 304
Lane, Kenneth J. 174
Lane, Nathan viii, ix, 1, 4, 9, 10, 274, 275
Lane, Stewart F. 16, 17, 18, 79, 82, 85, 87, 337, 340, 341, 354, 397, 410
Lang, Jennifer 355
Langdon, Laurie V. 262, 263, 266, 267
Langevin, Patrick 400
Langford, Bonnie 72, 75
Langley, Donna 48
Langman, Donna 183, 225
Langschultz-Maneri, Susan 410
Langworth, Joe 237,

Index

238, 330
Lanham, Bill 326
Lanier, Jane 126
Lanigan, Sean 280
Lannan, Nina 37, 38, 205, 207, 245, 248, 250
Lansbury, Angela vii, ix, 191-193, 197, 382, 388
Lanter, Jennifer 419
Lantzy, Meghan 151, 330
Lanza, Heather 234
Lanzarotta, Drew 313
LaPaglia, Anthony viii, ix, 171, 172, 175
Lapiduss, Maxine 95
Lapine, James viii, 318-320, 323
Lapine, Sarna 322, 330
Lapine, Seth 330
LaPointe, Charles 106, 121, 158, 198, 219, 232, 335, 369
Laporte, Manuela 13, 92, 95, 273, 274
Larkin, Leigh Ann 191, 193, 197
Larocco, Catherine 359
LaRoche, CJ 8
Larsen, Anika 32, 33
Larsen, Bethany 25, 361, 412
Larsen, David 41-43
Larsen, Teresia 188
Larson, Al 238
Larson, Jonathan 243
Larson, Ken 36
Lashof, Rebekah 94, 321
Lasky, Becky 322
Lasry, Cathy 343
Lassen, Fred 48, 324, 326
Latarro, Lorin 21-23, 25-27, 121-123
Latessa, Dick 276, 278
Lathan, Katy 6, 8
Latini, Michael 36
Lattimore, Todd 164, 166, 169
Laube, Brian 337
Laudenslager, Pam 252, 340

Lauer, Andrea 21, 23
Lauer, Mark 183
Laule, Scott 78, 308, 347, 352
Laurents, Arthur 319, 322, 354, 357
Laurie, Blanche 12, 238, 270, 273
Laurie, Irving 12, 238, 270, 273
Laury, Mykal D. II 265, 269
Laux, Sarah 8, 314
LaVada, Terry 188
Lavaia, Joe 342
Lavaia, Matthew 182
Lavaia, Michael 181, 182
Lavaia, Thomas 302, 304
LaVarco, Val 401
LaVecchia, Antoinette 349, 350
Lavell, Terry 164, 166
Laverack, Chelsea 58
Lavey, Martha 28, 30, 31, 335, 337, 338
Lavin, Linda viii, 76-78, 388, 393
Laviola, Kara 58, 304
LaVoy, January iii, iv, 85, 86, 89, 90
Law, Jude vi, ix, 135, 136, 139, 218
Lawes, Gina 315
Lawing, Skip 408
Lawless, Carey 200, 243
Lawless, Margo 46, 47, 50
Lawless, Sue 403
Lawrence, Aryn 360
Lawrence, Don 207, 208
Lawrence, Gail 109
Lawrence, Gracie Bea 51, 52
Lawrence, Karl 195
Lawrence, Megan 131
Lawrence, Michael 48, 138, 231, 234, 281, 296, 334
Lawrence, Peter 286, 289, 291, 313
Lawrence, Samantha 113, 114, 195, 249, 250

Lawrey, Tom 138, 295, 296
Lawson, James 361
Lawson, Jon 138, 295, 296
Lawson, Marty 310, 312, 316, 317
Lawson, Nancy 368, 369
Lazar, Aaron 191, 193, 377, 378
Lazar, David 121, 126, 168, 255
Lazarus, Paul 403
Lazarus, Scott 20, 25, 31, 88, 133, 138, 208, 285, 296, 338, 342
Lazzaretto, Marina 354-356
Lazzarini, Rick 315
Le Feuvre, James 135, 136, 139
Le Loka, Tsidii 177
Le, Vinh 308
Leabo, Matthew 8
Leanza, Vito 8
Leary, Drew 238
Leavel, Beth iv, 202, 204, 209, 210
Leavey, Jim 406
Leavitt, Michael 1, 5
LeBlanc, Jeanne 311
LeBoff, Jared 369
Ledbetter, Leslie 58, 114, 196, 255, 298, 303
Ledbetter, Mark 211, 212, 214
Ledbetter, Sammy 58, 196
Ledesma, Almalina 418
Ledger, Sydney 133
Ledwich, Anna 188
Lee, Allison A. 6, 8
Lee, Allison Thomas 143, 147
Lee, China 162, 238
Lee, David 303, 304
Lee, Eugene 362, 365
Lee, Gwilym 135, 136
Lee, Hanyi 415
Lee, Jeremy J. 338
Lee, Linda 7, 8
Lee, Matthew 417
Lee, Ming Cho 393
Lee, Raymond iv, 202, 204, 210

Lee, Spike 103
Lee, Susan 396
Lee, Tuck 363
Leedes, Julie 78, 308, 347
Leeds, Anthony D. 377
Leeds, Douglas B. 407
LeFevre, Adam 121-123
LeFevre, Ted 369
Leff, Adam 418
Legalley, Thomas 315
Leguillou, Lisa 362
Lehman, Susan 329
Lehmann, Matthew 192
Lehrer, David 234
Lehrer, Scott 69, 71, 109, 112, 324, 327, 349, 350, 389
Lehrer, Sheila 232
Lehrman, Michelle 401
Leiber, Jerry 231
Leibowitz, Neal 416
Leidel, Diana 419
Leigh, Carolyn 83
Leigh, Milly 315
Leitzel-Reichenbach, Ashley 217
Lekae, Valisia 286, 287, 289
Lelli, Larry 228
Lembo, Carl 217
Lemieux, Nicole 418
Lemper, Ute 382
Lenher, Caroline 418
Lenihan, Joe 25, 113, 114
Lenk, Katrina 232, 233
Lenk, Tom 298, 299
Lennon, Dorothy 101
Lenoue, Kiki 46
Lenzi, Robert 324-327
Leo, Cyntia 183, 189, 217
Leon, Kenny viii, 104, 105, 388
Leonard, Cassady 211, 213
Leonard, Howard 156
Leonard, Jean 416
Leone, Vivien 168, 196, 255

Leong, David S. 47
LeProtto, Jess 60-62
LeRette, Marisa 303
Lerner, Alan Jay 20
Lerner, Jennifer 35, 36
Lerner, Myla 109
Leroux, Gaston 261
LeShay, David 409
Leshley, Maureen 224
Lessans, Greg 369
Lesser, Nara 8
Letts, Tracy vi, 28, 29, 31, 335, 336, 338, 339
Leuck, Vanessa 188
Levan, Martin 261, 264
Levasseur, Brittany 20, 106, 120, 174, 238, 315, 352
Leve, Harriet Newman 56, 167, 252, 254, 337, 340, 341
Levengood, Caleb 126, 258
Levenson, Steven 12, 65, 94, 273, 321, 372
Levey, Alan 410
Levi, Richard 54, 245
Levine, Arnold 8, 183, 196, 217, 308
Levine, Dan 288
Levine, Jennifer 65, 273, 372
Levine, Jonathan 288
Levine, Manuel 73, 208
Levine, Robin 202, 204
Levine, Simma 58, 196, 255, 304
Levy, Caissie 131
Levy, Drew 95, 342
Levy, Julia 11, 12, 60, 65, 91, 94, 270, 273, 318, 321, 340, 343, 371, 372, 399
Levy, Louis 342
Levy, Marcy 31
Levy, Stuart 133
Levy, Tim 340
Lew, Deborah 324, 325, 327
Lewis-Evans, Kecia

72, 75
Lewis, Avery 225
Lewis, Chad 313, 314
Lewis, Deborah 138, 296
Lewis, Jerry Lee viii, ix, 227, 228, 231
Lewis, Jim 97-99, 389
Lewis, Lauren 12, 65, 94, 273, 321, 372
Lewis, Lisa 180, 181
Lewis, Nicole 127-129
Lewis, Norm viii, 184, 186, 190, 318, 319, 323, 376
Lewis, Sam 82, 183
Lewis, Sarah Anne 265
Lewis, W. Buford 243
Li, Li Jun 324, 326
Libby, Heidi 58, 114, 196, 255, 304
Libfeld, Brian 420
Libin, Paul 21, 25, 97, 102, 109, 114, 127, 133, 158, 163, 191, 196, 232, 234, 252, 255, 384, 395, 397, 410
Libin, Travis 254
Libman, Steven B. 158, 163
Libonati, Allegra 133
Licata, George 112
Licon, Armando 359, 361
Liddiment, David 255
Lidz, Sarah Sophia 174, 291
Lieb, Dick 20
Lien, Mimi 188
Liff, Spencer 245, 247
Liff, Vincent 264
Ligon, Kevin 109-111, 115
Lille, Barry 8
Lilley, Jeff 417
Lim-Dutton, Elizabeth 277, 288
Limauro, Lindsay 8
Linda, Solomon 183
Lindahl, Jason 66
Linde, David 48, 369

Index

Lindeberg, Nancy 409
Lindell, Heather 164-166
Lindeman, Nikki 415
Lindsay-Abaire, David 310, 312, 402
Lindström, Pia 407
Lingotti, Jessica 58
Link, Ryan 131
Linn, Frank 329
Linney, Laura viii, ix, 345-348, 388
Linton, Carla 258
Linville, Janet 183
Linzer, Sandy 163
Lion, Margo 79, 82
Lipitz, Ben 176, 178
Lipman, Carole Sue 315
Lippa, Andrew viii, 1, 4, 10, 389
Lippa, Sue 255
Lippman, Sid 20
Lipscomb, Rhonda 151, 330
Lipson, Amy 417
Lipton, Dan 95
Littell, Mary 415
Little, Ruth 120
Liu, Elizabeth 8
Liu, Lucy 118
Livingston, Ben 205
Livingstone, David 48
Livolsi-Landau, Katherine 326
Lloyd, James 58
Lloyd, Jamie 138, 296
Lloyd, Jill Turner 76, 78, 305, 308, 345, 347, 398
Lloyd, Karen 368
Lloyd, Pamela 163, 398
Lloyd, Phyllida 202, 205
Lobel, Richard 238
LoBue, Michael S. 303
LoBuono, Dan 72
Locarro, Joe 47
LoCascio, John 420
Locher, Michael 126
Lock, Bailey 255
Locke, Jennifer 140, 142
Lockyer, Melanie 102
Lockyer, Peter 324-327
Lodge, Marty 256
Loe, Amy Gilkes 78, 308, 347, 398
Loeffelholz, J. 69-71
Loehr, Matt 211, 212, 214, 218, 276-278
Loening, George S. 243
Loesche, Chuck 284
Loesel, Paul 363
Loesser, Frank 121, 123
Loesser, Jo Sullivan 407
Loewe, Frederick 255
Lofgren, Aarne 207, 208
Lofgren, Francis 208
Lofgren, Frank 207
Lofgren, John 167
Lofgren, Mai-Linh 207, 208, 373
Logan, John 294, 295, 297, 387, 392
Logan, Joshua 324, 327
Loiacono, Cheryl 183
Loiacono, John M. 217
Loiacono, Michael 195, 405
Loiacono, Nicholas 183
Lojo, Phillip 225, 303, 315
Lombardi, Frank iv, 37-40, 135, 138
Lombardo, Matthew viii, 198, 199
London, Barbara 422
London, Caroline 45
London, Nick 404
Lone, Melissa 211, 212, 214
Long, Garrett 324-327
Long, Kate 78, 308, 347
Long, Stephen 6, 8
Long, William Ivey 69, 71, 198-200, 245, 247, 250
Longbottom, Robert vi, 60, 63, 67
Longosky, Kate 13, 66, 94, 274, 322, 343, 373
Longtin, Fred 315
Lonner, Jonathan 334
Lookadoo, Michelle 184-187, 216
Loomis, David 73
Looney, Zack 418
Lootens, Terrie 16, 17, 120
Lopez-Cepero, Omar 21-23, 27
Lopez, Alexandra 151, 330
Lopez, Janice 25
Lopez, Jennifer 58, 59
Lopez, José-Luis 143
Lopez, Joseph 31, 173, 337
Lopez, Marielin 102, 106
Lopez, Priscilla 140, 142, 146, 147, 381
Lopez, Robert 12, 32-34, 65, 94, 273, 321, 372
Lopez, Theresa 132
Lopiano, Cynthia 113
Loquasto, Santo 76, 77, 104, 105, 282, 283, 286, 289, 388
Lorczak, Lawrence 401
Loren, Sophia vii
Lorenzo, Tom 418
Lorio, Thomas 410
Lortel, Lucille 392
Losse, Carsten 308, 347
Lotito, Mark 158, 159
Lotz, David 401
Loud, David 318
Louie, Eric 133
Louis, Alyse Alan iv, 202-204, 206, 209
Louis, Michael 301, 303
Louise, Merle 41-43
Louizos, Anna 16-18, 32, 140, 142, 152, 155
Loukas, Leah 25, 126, 225
Lounge, Ava 281
Loungway, Gianna 261, 263
Lourd, Billie 373
Lovatt, Lucie 168, 255
Love, Andre 422
Love, Brian M. 176, 177, 179
Love, Courtney 26
Love, James Elliot 163
Love, Jennifer 8, 39, 102, 281, 304
Lovece, Annette 266
Lowe, Ryan 69, 71, 75, 383
Lowery, Lorraine 404
Lowetz, Daniel 418
Lowney, Jeffrey 208
Lowy, Andrew 20, 106, 174, 238, 308, 352
Loyacano, Elizabeth 264
Lubetzky, Yael 8, 188
Lucania, Joseph 421
Lucariello, Carmine 281
Luciani, Kristen 133
Lucido, Tom 418
Lucka, Kristina 338
Luckenbaugh, Nick 13, 65, 94, 274, 321, 343, 372, 399
Lucoff, Bruce 101
Ludick, Paul 46, 47
Ludlam, Charles 384
Ludwig, Jessica 163, 398
Ludwig, Ken viii, 171, 172, 175
Luette, Stephanie 249
Luftig, Hal 79, 82, 354, 358
Lugo, Hector 360, 361
Lugo, Nick 35, 36, 145
Luke, Dexter 284
Luker, Kyle 230
Luker, Rebecca 211, 213
Luker, Shannon 125
Lukianov, Alex 219
Lukianov, Katya 219
Luks, Jason 152-154, 157
Lunney-Delahunt, Suzanne 64, 66, 320, 322
Lunsford, Erin 88
LuPone, Patti 96, 116, 243
Lustbader, Aaron 232, 234, 258, 281
Lustig, Rebecca 47
Lutfiyya, Sam 79, 422
Luther, Patti 328, 330
Lutterman, Randy Ellen 407
Luttinger, Selma 330
Lutwick, Nina 58
Luxenberg, Liza 7, 13, 95, 106, 120, 138, 196, 238, 274, 296, 314, 334, 342
Lydic, Jeremy 338
Lyn, Anthony 211, 215
Lynas, Michael 126
Lynch, Aubrey 183
Lynch, Brendan 6
Lynch, Brian 32, 34, 36, 140, 143, 145, 152, 155, 156, 286, 289, 291, 354, 357
Lynch, Claudia 298, 301, 303
Lynch, David 181, 182
Lynch, Fhara 47
Lynch, Joseph P. 181, 182
Lynch, Marian 48
Lynch, Matty 280
Lynch, Michael 87, 138, 181, 182, 351
Lynch, Michele 91, 92
Lynch, Suzanne 47
Lyndon, Nick 399
Lynn, Mara 422
Lynn, Tracy 286, 287, 289, 292
Lynne, Gillian 261, 264
Lyon, Rick 32, 36
Lyons, Jason 298, 300
Lyons, Jonothan 8
Lyons, Robert Britton 227, 228

M

M, Lebo 176, 177, 180
Mabardi, Justin 303
Maben, Ramona 333
MacAdams, Mikiko Suzuki 238
Maccarone, Michelle 13, 94, 274, 322
MacDermot, Galt 127, 129
MacDermot, Vincent 128, 132
MacDevitt, Brian 37, 38, 51, 52, 104, 105, 282, 283, 389
MacDonald, David Andrew 202-204, 209
MacDonald, Eileen 249
MacDonald, Greg 7
MacDonnell, Christine 266
MacDonnell, Theresa 355
MacDougall, Lorne 126
MacDuffie, Kendra 113
MacGregor, Moira 106, 151
Machado, Justina 143
Mackabee, Timothy R. 102
Mackay, Andrew 113
Mackey, Erin iii, iv, 318, 319, 323, 362, 364
Mackey, Lynne 106, 196, 208, 217, 234, 281, 369
Mackie, Anthony viii, 37, 38, 40
Mackintosh, Cameron 211, 214, 217, 261, 264, 267, 397
MacLachlan, Charles 416
MacLeod, Mary 191, 195, 196
MacLeod, Terra C. 72
MacMahon, Robert 8, 189
MacMillan, John 135, 136
MacNeil, Ian 41, 44
MacPherson, George 422
MacRae, Annie 78, 308, 347, 398
MacRitchie, Krystin 66, 94, 274, 321, 322, 343, 372, 373
Macy, Mary 183,

446   The Playbill Broadway YEARBOOK 2009-2010

Index

267, 315
Madden, James 367
Madigan, Chase 358
Madover, Arielle Tepper 127, 130, 135, 137, 139, 294, 295, 387, 397
Madsen, Kristen 410
Maffia, Robert 335, 336, 339
Maggini, Tia 369
Magnarella, Pat 21
Magner, J. Anthony 206, 207
Magnuson, Benjamin 121-123
Magoon, Marshall 310
Magruder, James 126
Maguire, Bobby iv
Maguire, Gregory 362, 365
Magyawe, Johannah-Joy 20, 63, 66, 399
Mahadeo, Vijay 398
Maher, Dennis 30, 31, 173, 337, 338
Maher, Joseph 132, 133, 304
Maher, Kevin 100
Maher, Tommy 224
Mahmoud, Neveen 167, 168
Mahon, John 48
Mahon, Melissa Rae 69-71, 75
Mahon, Robert 243
Mahon, Sean 340-342, 344
Mahoney, Brian 31, 39, 48, 58, 74, 88, 106, 120, 138, 151, 168, 174, 200, 208, 225, 243, 258, 267, 281, 285, 296, 315, 334, 338, 352
Mahoney, John 31, 338
Mahshie, Jeff 240, 241, 244
Maier, Charlotte 117, 118
Maier, Rachel 195, 196
Maija, Antibalas 97
Mainard, Jim 315
Maine, Mathew 181
Maines, Sarah E. C. 162
Mais, Michele 298, 299, 303

Maisonet, Lisa 280
Maiuri, Brian 13, 95, 273, 274, 399
Majidi, Shidan 217, 267
Makin, Lisa 168, 255
Makkoo, Susan 163, 225
Mala, Elisa 13, 66, 94, 274, 322, 343, 373
Malabanan-McGrath, Alma 163
Malan, Jorie 114, 167, 168
Malave, Eddie 266
Malden, Karl 422
Maldonado, Arnulfo 188
Maldonado, Katherine 254
Maldonado, Paula 163
Maley, Linda 238, 342
Malianga, Farai 97, 99
Malinowski, Tracey 7, 8, 189
Malizia, Lester 227
Malkmus, Robert J., III 188
Malkovich, John 31, 338
Mallory, Ramona 191, 193
Malone, William 422
Maloney, Darrel 21, 91
Maloney, Elizabeth 237
Maloney, Jennifer 24, 298, 300, 336
Maloney, Jimmy Jr. 47, 53, 83, 182, 216, 218, 258, 285, 338
Maloney, John 208
Maloney, Matt 195
Maloney, Michael 208
Maloney, Sue 58
Maloney, Tom 25
Malta, Liz 94, 321, 399
Mambo, Kevin vii, 97, 98
Mamet, David vi, vii, ix, 256, 257,
282, 283, 285
Manalio, Whitney 58, 234
Mancina, Mark 176, 177, 180, 183
Mancuso, Catherine 31
Mandel, Johnny 80
Mandell, Ronni 58, 304
Mandler, Jim 238
Maneein, Earl 55
Mangan, Claire 420
Mangan, Stephen 252, 253
Manganaro, Al 217
Mangelsdorf, Alicia 78, 346
Mann, David 18, 55
Mann, Jonathan 234, 255
Mann, Liz 326
Mann, Terrence viii, ix, 1, 4, 10
Mann, Theodore 232, 234, 252, 255, 384
Manners, Hilary 342
Manning, Dan 286, 287, 289, 292
Manning, Dorothy 361
Manning, Jack 422
Mannion, Sarah 168
Manno, Anthony 400
Manns, Laura 8
Manocherian, Barbara 127, 130, 236, 237, 252, 254, 341
Manocherian, Jennifer 28, 30, 56, 167, 194, 252, 254, 337, 341
Manoff, Mark J. 343
Manolakos, Carrie 370
Manoy, Joe 224
Mansbach, B. Thomas 243
Mansfield, Erica 206
Mansfield, Tami 12, 65, 94, 273, 321, 343, 372
Mansker, Tony 215, 216
Mantello, Joe 12, 65, 94, 245, 247, 273, 321, 343, 362, 365,
372

Manuel, Amber Jo 13, 65, 94, 274, 321, 343, 372
Manye, Tshidi 176, 178
Manzi, Carlo 296
Manzo, Michel 420
Mapp, Brian i, iii, iv, 14, 19, 30, 31, 35, 36, 38, 39, 46, 47, 57, 63-65, 77, 92, 93, 100, 101, 112, 113, 119, 132, 137, 138, 144, 145, 150, 151, 155, 167, 168, 173, 174, 181, 195, 206, 207, 216, 218, 223, 224, 229, 230, 235, 242, 248, 249, 254, 257, 258, 265, 266, 272, 273, 279-281, 284, 295, 296, 301, 302, 307, 313, 314, 320, 321, 328, 329, 333, 334, 337, 346, 351, 359, 360, 361, 367, 368, 372, 373, 396, 398, 400-405, 407, 408, 410, 413, 420, 421
Mara, John iv, 187, 188, 291-293
Marber, Patrick vii, 11, 12, 15
Marchica, Ray 203
Marchione, Nicholas 185, 220
Marclana, Eleanor Wolfe 66
Marcoccia, Dawn 301, 303
Marcotte, Shannon 66, 94, 274, 321, 343, 372, 399
Marcus, Abby 402
Marcus, Joan iv, 1, 2, 8, 11-13, 16, 17, 31, 37, 39, 51, 55, 58, 60, 61, 66, 76, 78, 79, 83, 85, 95, 104, 106, 109, 114, 117, 120, 127, 133, 140, 141, 145, 148, 149, 151, 152, 158, 161, 163, 165, 168, 171, 174, 176, 183-185, 188, 191, 192, 194, 196, 202, 203, 208, 211, 217, 219, 220, 225, 227, 228, 231, 232, 234, 240,

243, 245, 250, 252, 253, 261, 267, 270, 271, 274, 276, 277, 281, 286, 291, 296, 298, 304-306, 308, 310, 315, 322, 324, 330, 332, 334, 340, 342, 345, 347, 349, 352, 354, 361, 362, 363, 371, 373, 411
Marcus, Pat 330, 359, 361
Marden, Adrienne 422
Marden, Britt 397
Marder, Jeff 122, 125, 188, 315
Margolies, Dany 304
Marguette, Dorothy 249
Margulies, Donald viii, 76, 77, 345, 346, 387
Margulies, Julianna 243, 244
Margulies, Mead 13, 14, 66, 94, 274, 322, 343, 373, 399
Marie, Cristina 235, 254
Marie, Wren 264
Marik, Jennifer 367, 369
Marin, Noah 66, 291
Marin, Yanira 358, 359
Maring, Christopher 21, 25
Marino, Michael 39, 315
Marion, Dennis 207
Mariotti, Renee 342
Mark McCullough 11
Mark, Kimberly 64, 66, 167, 168
Markinson, Alan R. 238, 342
Markinson, Martin 236, 238, 340, 342
Markley, Dan 152
Marklin, Marge 406
Markman, Neil 183, 189, 217
Markoff, Matthew 151
Markova, Alla 47
Marks, Alan D. 109
Marley, Susanne 28, 29

Marlin, Gary L. 162
Marlin, Robert 417
Marotta, Kathryn 416
Maroulis, Constantine 298, 299, 303, 379, 381, 386
Marques, David 284
Marquette, Josh 208
Marquette, Seth 83, 361
Marren, Howard 409
Marrero, Antonia 132
Marroquin, Bianca 72, 73
Marsalis, Branford 104, 105, 108, 389, 392
Marsden, Bernard 304
Marsh, Ellyn Marie 85, 86
Marsh, Joshua 151
Marsh, Lane 234, 258, 281
Marshak, Bob 267
Marshall, Alex 25
Marshall, Grantley 58
Marshall, Heidi Miami 5, 8
Marshall, Jerry 83, 188, 315
Marshall, Karen 132, 133
Marshall, Kathleen 12, 65, 94, 273, 321, 343, 372, 403
Marshall, Laura 13, 65, 94, 274, 321, 343
Marshall, Shakira 97, 99
Martens, Frederick 330
Martin, Andrea 379
Martin, Barrett 1, 2, 4
Martin, Brandon 342
Martin, Bud 54, 245
Martin, Eric 304
Martin, Gregory 208
Martin, Jerome 83, 361
Martin, Joette 416
Martin, Kat 13, 14, 272, 274

The Playbill Broadway YEARBOOK 2009-2010 447

Index

Martin, Michael X. 245-247, 286, 287, 289, 292
Martin, Nan 422
Martin, Nicholas 270, 271, 340
Martin, Nora 368, 369
Martin, Pamela 101
Martin, Robert 250, 361
Martin, Ron 231
Martin, Steve 244
Martin, Susan 302, 304
Martin, Taylor 95
Martin, Tracy 57
Martindale, Kelly 121, 125, 126
Martineau, Marie-Claire 13, 48, 138
Martineaz, Jonathan 322
Martinez, Anthony 333
Martinez, Carlos 216, 218
Martinez, Kelsey 78, 308, 347, 398
Martinez, Maria 418
Martinez, Mike 313, 314
Martinez, Stephanie 7
Martinson, Zoey 63
Marvel, Linda 100, 102
Marvin, Kate 151, 330
Marx, Jeff 32, 33, 34
Marzan, Mary 132
Marzullo, Joseph i, iii, iv, vii, viii, 9, 10, 26, 27, 84, 96, 107, 108, 146, 147, 175, 239, 297, 323, 378, 379, 385, 387-393
Marzullo, Steve 203
Mascali, Samantha 78, 308, 347, 398
Masias, Felicia 35, 296
Maso, Michael 272, 340, 341
Mason, Buck 268
Mason, Essence 322
Mason, Janelle 58
Mason, Jared 227, 228
Mason, Jude 268
Mason, Scott 20
Masse, Paul 156, 369
Massengill, David E. 343
Masser, Michael 20
Massey, Kyle Dean 240, 241, 362, 363, 364
Master, Karen 401
Masterson, Jane 308
Mastro, Michael 354-356
Mastrogiorgio, Danny 332, 333
Mastrone, Frank 261-263
Masucci, Stephanie 401
Matalon, Laura 47, 58, 130, 133, 208, 237
Matarazzo, Gary 216
Mateo, Jon-Paul 16-18
Mateo, Mileyka 354, 356
Matera, Barbara 208, 217, 267
Mates, Robin 302
Matheos, Cleo 73, 314
Mather, Ted 120
Mathew, Leena 183, 189, 217
Mathews, Liz 314, 315
Mathieson, Ann 409
Matlock, Victoria 227, 228
Matos, Freddie 314
Matricardi, Lisa 326
Matson, Bill 402
Matsumiya, Jacob 145, 250
Matsushima, Maiko 369
Matteis, Greg 218
Matthew, Ed 262
Matthews, John 421
Matthews, Lloyd 369
Matthews, Simon 168, 174
Matthias, Kevin 255
Mattox, Skye 359
Mauro, Scott 281
Mauzey, Alli 370
Mauzy, MacKenzie 242
Mavoides, Elena 230
Mawbey, Richard 138, 164
Maxine, Kaz 291
Maxwell, David O. 243
Maxwell, Jan vi, viii, ix, 171-173, 175, 305-307, 309, 388, 392, 393
Maxwell, Joan P. 243
Maxwell, Mitchell 258
Maxwell, Susan 224
May, Billy 83
May, Leni 60
Maya, Stacey 47, 114, 126, 156, 168, 225, 255
Maybee, Kevin 25
Mayberry, Mariann 28, 29, 31, 338
Mayer, Henry 83
Mayer, Michael 21, 23, 24, 27, 91, 92, 96, 392
Mayerson, Frederic H. 161
Mayerson, Rhoda 158, 161
Mayfield, Percy 225
Mayland, Nate 326
Maynard-Losh, Anita 243, 291
Maynard, Tyler 95, 184, 186
Mayne, Catherine 57
Mayo, Don 422
Mayo, James 83, 156, 250
Mayo, Nick 324-327
Mazdra, Melissa 7, 13, 95, 106, 120, 138, 196, 238, 274, 296, 314, 334, 342
Mazzei, Michell 58
Mazzella, Neil 16-19, 23, 25, 52, 86, 88, 99, 102, 112, 114, 156, 245, 248, 283, 285, 336, 350, 352
Mazzie, Marin 85, 86, 378, 381
Mbatha-Raw, Gugu 135, 136, 139
McAllister, Élan V. 21, 24, 56, 79, 82
McAllister, Linda 328, 330, 331
McAnuff, Des 121, 123, 126, 158, 160, 163
McArdle, Andrea 377
McArdle, Sean 315
McAteer, Charlie 285, 335, 413
McBoyle, Peter 79, 81
McBrearty, Kathy 405
McBride, Michael 400
McCabe, Julie 409
McCabe, Michael 276
McCaffrey, Bob 208
McCaffrey, Neil 63, 215, 216
McCall, Candice Monet 219-221
McCallum, Sheryl 176-179, 182
McCann, Elizabeth Ireland 127, 130
McCann, Tom 74, 83, 250, 315, 334, 415
McCarthy, Cian 145
McCarthy, Ed 156, 208
McCarthy, Elaine J. 362
McCarthy, Jeff 382
McCarthy, Michael 254, 405
McCarthy, Monica 345, 346
McCarthy, Ryan 11, 12, 15
McCartney, Liz 324, 325, 327
McCarty, Bruce 117, 118
McCarty, Michael 216
McCaslin, Greg 12, 65, 94, 273, 321, 343, 372, 399
McCauley, Robert 182
McClafferty, Joe 183, 189, 217
McClelland, Lauralyn 358, 359
McClelland, Stephanie P. 1, 5, 37, 38, 135, 137, 286, 290, 294, 295
McClendon, Afi 97, 99
McCleskey, Anastacia 127-129, 378
McClimon, Timothy J. 243
McClintock, Justin 83, 196
McClintock, Melanie 46, 47, 280, 281
McCloskey, Angrette 126
McClure, Robert 32, 33
McColgan, John 245, 248
McCollum, Kevin 32, 34, 36, 140, 143, 145, 152, 155, 156, 286, 290, 354, 357
McCollum, Patrick 369
McConnell, Michele 265, 269
McCormack, Colleen 183, 189, 217
McCormack, Tara 302
McCormick, Steve 163
McCourt, Sean 211-213
McCoy, Bonnie 114
McCoy, Tom 268
McCready, Erin 12, 65, 94, 273, 321, 343, 372
McCullough, Frank 8, 188, 216, 250, 334
McCutcheon, Cory 47, 223, 225, 234, 235
McCutcheon, Lee 267
McDaniel, Ellas 231
McDaniel, Sean 165, 246, 250
McDermott, Kathleen 39
McDermott, Phelim 1, 4, 10, 392, 393
McDonagh, Martin viii, 37, 38, 40
McDonald, Audra 377
McDonald, Bryce iv, 11, 13, 14, 91, 93, 95, 96
McDonald, Daniel 207
McDonald, David iv, 60-62
McDonald, Michael 127, 130
McDonald, Stephen 35, 36, 258, 295
McDonel, Leslie 21, 23, 27
McDonough, Kenneth 242
McDonough, Luke 133
McDonough, Robert 400
McDonough, Ryan 113, 114
McDonough, Tim Jr. 25, 26, 113, 114
McDonough, Tim Sr. 113, 114
McDowell, Shannon 133
McElfresh, Kathleen 271
McElroy, Margaret 113
McElwain, Gene 400, 405
McEvoy, Patanne 119
McEvoy, T.J. 320, 322, 373
McFadden, Heather 261-263
McGahan, Michael F. 330
McGarity, Brian 195, 196
McGarry, Danielle 413
McGarry, Gilda 60
McGarry, John P. Jr. 343
McGarty, Brian 88, 138
McGarty, Kevin 400
McGarty, Laura 150
McGarty, Terry 182
McGee, Kenneth J. 120, 144
McGeehan, J.J. 42, 46
McGerr, Katie 330
McGill, Emily 200
McGill, Jonathan 362, 364
McGillin, Howard 264, 268
McGinity, Liz 207
McGinley, Kyle 94, 273, 321

Index

McGinness, Trevor 208
McGlone, Margie 188
McGowan, Carter Ann 58
McGowan, Joe 234
McGowan, Marissa 191-193, 197
McGowan, Mike 286, 287, 289
McGrath, Kerry 188, 216
McGrath, Michael 219, 221, 226
McGrath, Thomas B. 130, 152, 155, 167, 172, 222, 229, 279, 350, 358
McGregor, Mary 100
McGuire, Bobby 408
McGuire, Janine 183, 189, 217
McGuire, Kevin A. 183, 188, 217
McHugh, Jimmy 163
McInerney, Caitlin 102
McIntosh, Marcia 46
McIntosh, Marti iv, 258-260
McIntyre, Bill 422
McKay, Monette 206
McKean, Michael vi, 335, 336, 339, 380
McKee, Kathryn 249, 250, 352
McKenna, Charles 404
McKenna, Gráinne 48
McKenna, Jason 93, 95, 280, 313, 315
McKennan, Donald 181, 182
McKeon, Johanna 21
McKernon, John 74
McKim, Tod L. 217
McKintosh, Peter 340, 341
McKneely, Joey 354, 357
McLane, Derek 227, 229, 232, 233, 286, 289, 388, 393
McLane, Judy 202, 204, 209, 210
McLaughlin, Joseph 409
McLaughlin, Kristin 174
McLean, Duncan 255
McLean, Jordan 97, 98
McLean, Lara 36
McLeod, Jay 155, 156
McMahon, Edward J. III 400
McMahon, Kaley 322
McManus, Megan 401
McMartin, John 384
McMillan, Dan 291, 355
McMillen, Anne 243
McMills, Anne 369
McMonoco, Sean 314
McMullan, James 151, 330
McMullen, Andrew 322
McMurrough, Erin 281
McNabb, Jim 126
Mcnally, Kevin R. 135, 136
McNally, Lucy 168
McNally, Terrence 286, 289
McNamara, Katherine 194
McNamee, Katherine 266
McNeil, Declan 313
McNeil, Jenn 8, 95
McNeil, Kevin 329
McNeill, Douglas 291
McNicholas, Jim 415
McNicholl, BT 41
McNulty, Anne 135, 138, 294, 296
McNulty, John 328, 330
McNulty, Lisa 78, 308, 347, 398
McNutt, Keith 410
McQuail, Richard 181, 182
McQuillen, Hilda 351
McRae, Kareem 13, 94, 274
McRory, Patricia 182, 188
McShane, Neil 31, 200
McSweeney, Anne 8, 138, 296
McSweeney, Maryann 33
McSweeny, Ethan 403
McTeer, Janet 118
McVoy, Jens 223, 225
McWaters, Debra 74
McWilliams, Caroline M. 422
McWilliams, Ryan P. 368, 369
McWilliams, Timmy 38, 39, 242, 333
Mead, Chuck 227, 229, 231
Mead, Jaylee M. 243
Mead, Laura 79, 80
Meadow, Lynne 76-78, 305, 307, 308, 345-347, 398
Meadows, Rick 73, 74
Meagher, Emily 13, 66, 78, 174, 200, 208, 347, 373, 411
Meagher, Ginger 409
Means, Charles 236-239, 256, 258
Mear, Stephen 184, 187, 211, 214
Mecchi, Irene 176, 179
Mecionis, Russ 249
Mecionis, Scott 83, 156, 249, 250
Meck, Lindsay 174, 352
Medak, Susan 21
Medcalf, Harley 54, 57
Medcalf, Jaccinta 57
Medeiros, Joseph 121-123, 152-154, 358
Medico, Dorothy 48
Medinilla, Erick 151
Medwin, Michael 120
Meeh, Gregory 1, 47
Meeker, Andrew 138
Meeker, Daniel 126
Megliola, Michael 120
Meier, Aaron 78, 200, 208, 230, 255, 308, 347, 411
Melançon, Corinne 203, 205, 206
Melendez, Joaquin 95
Melleno, Mauro 400, 403
Mellon, Andrew W. 11
Melrose, Alexandra 162
Melrose, Ron 158, 160
Menaker, Mandy 12, 65, 273, 372
Menard, Mark 4, 34, 63, 105, 130, 143, 155, 289
Mendelhoff, Dan 64, 66
Mendelsohn, Scott 167
Mendenhall, Joel 404
Mendes, Sam 312, 315
Mendez, Lindsay 91, 92, 95, 96
Menditto, Tony 195, 196, 234, 235, 254, 255, 334
Mendizabal, David 133
Mendoza, Eliana 178
Mendoza, Francisca 178
Menendez, Henry 132
Menken, Alan 184-186, 189
Menkes, David Samuel 133
Mensah, E.T. 98, 102
Mensching, William M. 156
Menz, Val 368
Menzel, Idina 107, 390
Menzies, Lee 85
Meola, Tony 362, 365
Mercado, Kathy 401
Mercanti, JV 39
Merced, Anthony 66, 94, 274, 321, 343, 373
Mercer, John 95
Mercer, Johnny 20, 83
Mercer, Ray 176, 177, 179, 182
Mercer, Stewart 282
Merchant, Nicole 418
Mercury, Freddie 383
Meredith, James Vincent 31, 335, 336, 338, 339
Merediz, Olga 140-142, 147
Mericola, Augie 369
Merideth, Joseph 250
Merkerson, S. Epatha 107
Merman, Ethel 322
Meron, Neil 276, 279
Merrick, George 324, 325, 326, 327
Merriman, Dan 422
Merritt, George R. 422
Merryman, Pat 329, 330
Merwede, Glenn 13, 14, 93, 95, 273, 274, 399
Mesh, Kaitlin 354-356
Messing, Herbert 119
Metcalf, Laurie 31, 51, 52, 338
Metcalf, Michelle 151, 330
Metcalfe, Stephen 217
Mettler, Marc 39, 83, 106, 156, 168, 225, 291, 361
Metzler, Jeff 211, 212, 214
Metzloff, Gretchen 35, 36
Meyer, Douglas L. 152, 155, 191, 194
Meyer, Jack 396
Meyer, Ron 48, 369
Meyer, Tegan 126, 225
Meyers, Jill 231
Meyers, Quinn 12, 65, 94, 273, 321, 343, 372
Meyers, William 132
Meyrelles, Chip 97, 99, 234, 281
Mezick, Matthew 265, 267
Mhlongo, Brenda 176-179
Micalizzi, Marina 41-43, 50
Michaels, Bret 304
Michaelson, Andrew 58, 196, 254, 255
Michaliszyn, Mitchell 41, 44, 50
Michalopoulos, Costas 409
Michals, William 324, 325, 327
Michalski, Michael 368, 369
Michele, Lea vi, 292, 391
Michener, James A. 324, 327
Mickelson, Gary 223, 225
Micoleau, Tyler 393
Micone, Roger 58, 151, 330, 416
Middleton, Clark 208
Middleton, Laura D. 235
Migliaccio, Chuck 13, 66, 94, 274, 322, 343, 373
Migliaccio, Donna 286, 287, 288, 292
Migliore, Mike 42
Mignola, Gene 183, 281, 315, 369
Miguel, Mayumi 276, 278
Mikita, Scott 262, 263
Mikumo, Akiko 343
Milan, Dan 217
Milan, Jade 181
Milan, Joe 422
Milando, Patrick 178, 181
Milani, Johnny 133
Milano, Peter 36, 83, 133, 156, 231, 291, 361, 415
Milazzo, AnnMarie 240, 241
Milburn, Rob 232, 233, 335, 336
Milch, David M. 109
Miles, Ben 252, 253
Miles, Meredith 79, 81, 84

Index

Milikowsky, Shira 133
Millen, Heather 416
Miller, Adam 57, 174, 402
Miller, Allan 51, 52
Miller, Andrew 313, 315
Miller, Arthur 349, 350, 392
Miller, Billy 2, 7, 110, 113
Miller, Brian 213
Miller, Carolyn D. 225
Miller, Chris 315
Miller, Danny 153, 363
Miller, Daryl 267
Miller, Dave 144
Miller, Eileen 234, 235
Miller, Elizabeth 403
Miller, Frank 231
Miller, Jim 416
Miller, John 54-56, 158-160, 162, 164-166, 191-193, 196, 286, 288, 289, 291, 298-300, 303, 318, 320, 322
Miller, Jonny Lee vii, ix, 11, 12, 15
Miller, Kenneth 216, 217
Miller, Kristin 151, 330
Miller, Lori 122, 125
Miller, Marilyn A. 420
Miller, Mark 80
Miller, Mary 31, 87, 88, 337, 338
Miller, Meredith 8
Miller, Norman 419
Miller, Peter R. 369
Miller, Rachel E. 361
Miller, Robert 25, 113, 114, 174
Miller, Robert Strong 267
Miller, Ronald 20
Miller, Roy 286, 290, 354, 358
Miller, Sabrina Nan 63
Miller, Shelia 35, 257
Miller, Sienna vii, ix, 11, 12, 15
Miller, Thomas 401
Miller, Tim 46
Miller, Tonna 261, 263
Millhollen, Pilar 72, 73
Milligan, Michael 28, 29
Millikan, Bob 246
Mills, Bridget 234
Mills, Irving 58
Milne, George D. 280, 281
Milne, Karen 262, 266, 269
Miloszewicz, Jeremy 360
Minarik, Michael 298, 299
Minchinton, Kerry 304
Mindell, Susan 8, 36, 53, 83, 102, 145, 156, 236, 291
Mindell,, Susan 291
Mindelle, Marla 324, 325, 327
Mindler, Matthew 41, 44
Mindlin, Michael 202, 204, 245-247
Miner, Gabe 78
Ming-Trent, Jacob 310-312
Mingo, Alan 184-186
Minkoff, Rob 178
Minnelli, Liza 26, 59, 375, 379, 385
Minnick, Christopher Clay 373
Minore, John 119
Miocene, Ell 410
Miramontez, Rick iv, 133, 238
Miranda, Lin-Manuel 140, 142, 354, 357
Miranda, Luis 145
Mirell, Douglas 231
Mirkin, Dave 373
Mironchik, Jim 126, 361
Mirro, Duane 182
Mirvish, David 198
Mishkin, Chase 198, 199, 219, 222, 236, 237, 335, 336
Miskie, Adele 7
Miskie, Del 8, 113, 114
Missal, Catherine 216
Mistak, Annie 322
Mistry, Kamal 315
Mitall, Duduzile 46
Mitchell, Brian Stokes 377, 381, 410
Mitchell, Carol 343
Mitchell, James 422
Mitchell, Jerry 376
Mitchell, John 207
Mitchell, Kate 138, 296
Mitchell, Lauren 158, 161, 163, 398
Mitchell, Lisa 183, 189, 217
Mitchell, Mark 114
Mitchell, Matthew 164
Mitchell, Ruth 267
Mitchell, Thom 234, 258, 281
Mitchell, William 119, 120, 415
Mizen, Zakiya Young 184-187
Mizzy, Vic 8
Moauro, John 131
Mobley, Stacey J. 243
Moctezuma, Daniel 145
Modine, Matthew 232, 233
Modrono, Mabel 261, 263
Moe, Barry Lee 301
Moellenberg, Carl 5, 24, 130, 135, 137, 171, 172
Moeller, Erin 78, 308, 347, 398
Moeller, Jennifer 53
Moench, Dennis 211, 212, 214
Mohan, Ralph 322, 373
Mohrman, Thom 74
Mokae, Zakes 422
Molina, Alfred viii, ix, 294, 295, 297, 388
Molina, David 416
Molina, Lauren 298, 299
Molina, Marielys 79-81
Molina, Ric 363
Molloy, Jennifer 217
Molnar, Taryn 152-154, 157
Moloney, Elizabeth 237-239, 305, 307, 308
Molony, Patrick 135
Monahan, Terry 132
Monigan, Margaret 145, 231, 281, 291
Monroe, Kimber iv, 324, 325, 327, 331, 386
Monroe, Scott 88, 351, 352
Monserrate, Giovanni 101
Mont, Ira 191, 195, 196, 252, 254, 255, 400, 401
Montague, Willia-Noel 176, 177, 179, 182
Montalvo, Doreen 140-142, 145, 147
Montan, Chris 183, 188, 217
Monteith, Jeff 66, 94, 274, 321, 343
Montel, Michael 384
Monteleone, Kathleen 377
Montelongo, Matthew 349, 350
Montero, Rick 410
Montesi, Patty 234, 258, 267, 281
Montgomery, JC 60-62, 184, 185
Montgomery, John 74
Montgomery, Robert H., Jr. 82
Monthei, Katheryn 102
Moody, James 163
Moody, Nicole 88, 308, 330
Moody, Takuda 329
Moon, Aughra 229
Mooney, Ken 369
Mooney, Marion 181, 333
Mooneyham, Joseph 74
Moonves, Les 322
Moore, Allie 106
Moore, Anthony 291
Moore, James 286, 288, 292
Moore, Jason 32-34, 310, 312
Moore, Jodie 246, 250, 315
Moore, Karen 291, 293
Moore, Larry 110, 114
Moore, Pat 404
Moore, Peter 183
Moore, Scott 32, 36, 79, 140, 145, 152, 156, 286, 291, 354, 361
Moore, Sharon 69-71, 75
Moore, Sir Thomas 324
Moore, Stephen 109
Moore, Tom 403
Morales-Matos, Rolando 178
Morales, Carole 315
Morali, Jacques 20
Moran, Mary P. 243
Moran, Timothy 257
Morea, Marguerite 416
Moreira, Manny 141, 147
Moreno, Derek 77, 78
Moreno, Louis D. 78, 308, 347
Moreno, Rita 59, 146
Moretti, Joe 410
Morettini, Mark 349, 350, 353
Morey, Chris 106, 120, 126
Morgaman, Philip 135, 308
Morgan, Betsy 191-193, 197
Morgan, Cass 219, 221, 225, 226
Morgan, Ian 36
Morgan, J.P. 208
Morgan, Jackie 48
Morgan, Melanie T. 200
Morgan, Meredith 8, 243, 296
Morgan, Noreen 87, 138, 405
Morgan, Robert 13, 66, 92, 94, 95, 272, 274, 321, 343, 373, 399
Morley, Kate 138, 296
Morley, Larry 133, 240, 242
Morris, Carlos 13, 63, 66, 94, 322, 343, 373
Morris, Edward 20
Morris, Edwin H. 231
Morris, Eric William 202, 204, 209
Morris, Evan 74, 183
Morris, Jessica 163, 398
Morris, Joan 183
Morris, Lisa 238
Morris, Shina Ann 354-356
Morrison, Angela 41, 48
Morrison, Jennifer 232, 233
Morrison, Matthew vi, 107
Morrison, Randy 223, 224
Morrissey, Veronica 35, 257
Morse, Halle 202-204, 206
Morse, Sally Campbell 158, 163
Morsette, Zoe 8, 315
Mortell, Richard 133, 242
Mortensen, Viggo 107
Morton, Amy 28, 29, 31, 338, 403
Morton, Euan viii, 318, 319
Morton, Sydney 219-221
Mosbacher, Annie 401
Mosca, John 80
Moseley, Robin 271
Moses, John 363
Moses, Larry 80
Moses, Spencer 121-123
Mosher, Gregory viii, 349, 350, 353, 388
Mosleh, Florian 225
Mossen, Leon 223
Mossman, Carrie 20, 39, 106, 285, 330
Mossop, Hannah 8
Moti, Janet 421
Moulton, Leslie 144, 145

Index

Moultrie, Darrell Grand 41, 42, 44
Movsesian, Nance 402
Moye, James 227, 228, 286, 287, 289, 293
Moyer, Allen 11, 12
Moyes, Denny 188
Moynihan, D.S. 31, 36, 39, 48, 58, 74, 88, 106, 120, 138, 151, 168, 174, 200, 208, 225, 243, 258, 267, 281, 285, 296, 315, 334, 338, 352
Mrozek, Bobby 95
Mudge, Jennifer 231, 234, 258, 267
Mueller, Christopher 114
Mueller, Jillian 60, 62
Mueller, Kathleen 6, 8
Mulert, Carl 400
Mulheren, Michael iii, 198-201
Mull, Kathe 368, 369
Mullan, James 208
Mullen, Jan 262, 266
Mullen, Laurence 95
Mulligan, Megan 181
Mullikin, Bill 422
Mullins, Angelina 354-356
Mulrain, Scott 163
Munar, Andres 78, 308, 347
Mundorff, Ann 308, 347
Mundth, Caitlin 164-166
Mundy, Jimmy 82
Mungioli, Arnold J. 97, 99, 102
Mungle, Matthew W. 369
Muniz, Carla 36
Munn, Brian 366
Munnell, Christopher 307, 308
Muñoz, Javier 140, 142, 146
Munro, Martine 58
Munroe, Brian 302, 303

Mura, Danny 301, 303
Murdoch, Christel 125, 126
Murdoch, Thomas 337
Murdock, Christel 280, 281, 291
Murdock, John 114
Murgatroyd, Peta 54, 55
Murney, Julia 377
Muro, James 266
Murphy, Ann 417
Murphy, Ariana 95
Murphy, Brittany 422
Murphy, Claire 41, 47
Murphy, Clarissa 418
Murphy, Diane 342
Murphy, Eddie 107
Murphy, Gary 168
Murphy, Jean Kroeper iv
Murphy, Karen 191-193, 245-247
Murphy, Kenneth F. 343
Murphy, Mary 56
Murphy, Matt 145, 151, 219, 225, 258, 330, 342, 373
Murphy, McKenzie 93, 95, 96, 250
Murphy, Sally 28, 29, 31, 338
Murphy, Tiffany 280
Murray, Cameron J. 58
Murray, Karen 63
Murray, Lyn 110
Murray, Melissa 78, 308, 347
Murray, Tom 122, 125, 191, 192, 196, 220
Murtha, Dan 188
Murynec, Mark 189
Musker, John 184
Muso, Scott 359
Musser, Kristina 110, 113
Mustelier, Alex 151, 330
Mutrux, Floyd 227, 229, 389
Mvondo, Whitney Adkins 6, 8
Myars, Mark 82,

245-247, 250
Myatt, Julie Marie 12, 65, 94, 273, 321, 372
Myerberg, Susan S. 238, 342
Myers, Lynette 351
Myers, Peter 156
Myhrum, Matthew 162
Myrow, Josef 20, 83

N

N'Kenge 318, 319
Naanep, Kenneth 401
Nadeaux, James 328, 330
Naftalis, Kramer Levin 39
Nagbe, Trokon 322
Naggar, Miriam 20, 58, 88, 418
Nagle, William 151, 329, 330
Nagler, Mele 95, 106
Nahem, Edward Tyler 97
Nairn, Nilsa 35, 257, 346
Naja, Robert Del 58
Najera, Cova 58
Namba, Leo 328, 330
Nanni, Kathleen 211, 212, 214
Napoleon, Cedric 58
Napoli, David 334
Naranjo, Valerie Dee 178, 183
Nardozza, Russell 334
Nash, Terius 20
Nashman, Sarah 126, 225, 255
Nass, Chris 208
Nathaniel, Austin 39, 83, 156, 250
Nauffts, Geoffrey viii, 236-239, 387, 393
Naughton, James 377
Naughton, Jeannie 47, 50, 83
Naumann, Michael 58, 114, 196, 255, 304
Navarro, Jason 367
Navarro, Oscar 315
Ndlovu-Mitall,

Duduzile 47
Neal, Jewel 183, 188, 217
Nederlander, Charlene S. 8, 53, 83, 126, 145, 156, 183, 189, 231, 250, 291, 304, 361, 369, 396
Nederlander, James L. 1, 5, 8, 51, 53, 79, 81, 83, 121, 124, 126, 130, 140, 145, 152, 156, 167, 176, 183, 184, 189, 227, 229, 231, 240, 241, 245, 248, 250, 282, 283, 286, 291, 298, 304, 354, 357, 361, 362, 369, 396
Nederlander, James M. 1, 8, 51, 53, 79, 83, 121, 126, 140, 145, 152, 156, 176, 183, 184, 189, 227, 231, 245, 250, 286, 291, 298, 304, 354, 361, 362, 369, 396
Needleman, Marc 291
Neely, Rob 409
Neglin, Anders 208
Negrón, Rick 140, 142
Nehls, David 376
Neiman, Susan 13, 65, 94, 273, 321, 343, 372, 399
Neininger, Virginia 281, 308, 347
Nejat, Kat 354-356
Nel, Lauzanne 404
Nelis, Tom 85, 86
Nelson, Dave 238
Nelson, Jeff 80, 153, 355
Nelson, Justin 27
Nelson, Leah 150, 200
Nelson, Selene 280
Nemec, Rachel 242
Nemeth, Matt 106
Nemy, Enid 407
Nenadovic, Darinka 217
Nesbitt, John 405
Neshyba-Hodges, Charlie 79, 80, 82, 393
Nestico, Sam 80
Neswald, Amy 106,

338
Netchaef, Sophie 48
Netting, Tessa iii, iv, 41, 42, 44, 49, 50
Netzke, Janet 217
Neuburger, Rachel 37
Neumann, Alex 238
Neumann, Trevor 145, 355
Neutze, Chasity 207, 208
Neuwirth, Bebe viii, ix, 1, 2, 4, 9, 10, 377
Neuwirth, Risa 410
Neven, Heidi 83
Newberry, Terry 417
Newell, David 308, 330
Newfield, Anthony 305, 306
Newhouse, Claire 48
Newley, Anthony 20
Newling, Caro 86, 137, 312, 315
Newman, Cara 196
Newman, Harold 140
Newman, Harriet 194
Newman, Jennifer Harrison 180
Newman, Phyllis 377
Newsome, Regina 83, 156
Newsome, Timothy 73
Ney, Christy 367, 369, 370
Ngai, William 400
Ngaujah, Sahr vii, 97, 98, 101-103, 387, 391, 393
Ngema, S'Bu 176-179
Ngo, Pip 106
Nicely, Beth Johnson 152-154, 157
Nicholas, Michael 326
Nicholaw, Casey viii, 16-18
Nichols, Alexander V. 371
Nichols, Darius 131, 376
Nichols, Patricia 162
Nichols, Teff 307, 308

Nicholson, Jeff 419
Nicholson, Kent 225
Nicholson, Nicole 66, 94, 274, 321, 343, 373
Nicklaus, Jill 69-71
Nicks, Eugene 280
Nicynski, Ron 340, 341
Niebanck, Jessica 151, 330
Niebanck, Paul 148, 149
Niedzialek, Diane 416
Nielsen, Karl 422
Niggeling, Janice 265, 358
Nigrini, Peter 97, 245
Nihda, Frederick 267
Nilsson, Harry 95, 255
Nimmo, Bill 368
Nimmo, Robert C. 400
Nir, Debra 145, 156
Nixon, Cynthia 238, 343
Nixon, Tiffany 13, 65, 94, 273, 321, 343, 372, 399
Nixon, Vivian 219, 221
Nkhela, Selloane A. 176-179
Noah, Joshua 182, 188, 217
Noble, Polly 78
Noble, Robert 217
Noel, Craig 422
Nofsinger, Betsy 315
Noginova, Tatiana 184, 187
Nolan, Kenny 163
Nolan, Robert 402
Noland, Dave 80
Nolfi, Dominic 158, 159, 161
Nolin, Denise 152-154, 157
Noll, Christiane iii, iv, vii, 286, 288, 291-293, 381, 387, 391
Nolte, Bill 164-166
Nolte, Nick 13, 65, 274, 343, 372
Norden, Dylan 13, 66, 94, 274, 321,

Index

343, 372
Norris, Dustin T. 163
Norris, Eric 126, 168, 224
Norter, Kristy 141, 144, 146
North, Melissa 373
Northen, Lindsay K. 362-364
Norton, Jim vii, 109, 111, 115
Norton, Rachel 151, 330
Norwood, Dennis 47
Noseworthy, Jack 382
Noth, Kenny 39, 296
Nothmann, Karen 401
Notley, Nic 54, 57
Novak, Ari 126
Novak, Eric 8
Novak, Maddy 41, 42, 44
Novell, Arthur 36
Novelli, Alison 78
Novellino, Nino 267
Noxon, Hilary 20, 145
Nugent, Nelle 345
Nugent, Ted 304
Nuñez, Yleana 25, 291
Nunn, Trevor 191, 193
Nurse, Charlene 410
Nutbourne, Richard 296
Nutile, Christopher "Daddy" 200
Nyberg, David 203
Nye, Anita Leanord 163

O

O'Brien, Gerard 351
O'Brien, Jack 151, 330
O'Brien, Liam 30
O'Conner, Terry 119
O'Donnell, Thomas J. 406
O'Donnell, Thomas R. 406
O'Farrill, Irio 141, 144
O'Bannion, Dennis 152-154, 157
O'Boyle, John 164, 167
O'Brien, Brian 69-71, 75, 276-278
O'Brien, David 171, 173, 174
O'Brien, Edward John 347
O'Brien, Frederick 322
O'Brien, Iris D. 138
O'Brien, John Emmett 102
O'Brien, Liam 328
O'Byrne, Jennifer 83
O'Connor, Bridget 156, 330
O'Connor, Deidre 12, 65, 343, 372
O'Connor, Jennifer 281
O'Connor, Rachel 48
O'Connor, Rob 361
O'Connor, Tom 66, 94, 274, 321, 372, 399
O'Dea, John T. 163
O'Donnell, Erin 224
O'Donnell, Marissa 313
O'Donnell, Rosie 96, 200
O'Donovan, Gene 7, 13, 95, 106, 120, 138, 196, 238, 255, 274, 296, 314, 334, 342
O'Gara, Ryan 20, 36, 145, 230, 361
O'Gleby, Sarah 276, 277, 278, 280
O'Grady, Christine 133
O'Hara, Kelli 328, 377
O'Keefe, John 231
O'Leary, E. Colin 234, 255
O'Malley, Kerry 45, 49
O'Neal, Brandon Christopher 176-179
O'Neil, James Joseph 270, 271
O'Neil, Jody 408
O'Neill, Brittany 238
O'Neill, Dustin 121, 126
O'Neill, Meghan 12, 65, 94, 273, 321, 343, 372
O'Quinn, Keith 165, 246
O'Reilly, Cecilie 28, 31
O'Shea-Creal, Con 152-154
O'Toole, Katie 158-160
Oakley, Brent 302, 303
Oates, Kara 41, 42, 44, 50
Oberpriller, Donald J. 25, 31, 114, 285
Oberpriller, Mary Ann 64, 66, 320, 322
Ocasio, Ada 181
Ocasio, David 7
Ocasio, Melissa 7
Ochoa, Jules 119
Ockenfels, Emily 314, 315
Ockert-Haythe, Carolyn 310-312, 314
Oddo, John 16, 17
Odze, Warren 80, 311, 315
Okamoto, Rika 79, 80
Okayama, Clint 417
Oken, Stuart 1, 5
Olcese, Joe 5, 8, 189
Olin, Ken 238
Oliva, Anthony 217
Olive, Autumn 281
Oliver, David 281
Oliver, Donald 74, 183
Oliver, Jillian M. 284, 285
Olivo, Karen 354, 356
Olsen, Nigel 48
Olsen, Ralph 61, 65
Olson, Dale 410
Olson, Jonathan 183, 189, 217
Olver, Christine 39, 78, 120, 138, 200, 208, 296, 308, 347, 352, 411
Olvera, Tracy Lynn 286, 287, 289, 292
Ondrejcak, Andrew 12, 65, 94, 273, 321, 343, 372
Ongaro, Alex 315
Ono, Taka 266
Oram, Christopher 135, 137, 294, 295, 297, 388
Orange, James 208
Orellana, Maritza 410
Oremus, Stephen 32, 33, 245-247, 362, 365
Orensten, Michael 200
Oreskes, Daniel 41, 42, 44, 232, 233
Orich, Steve 158, 160, 162
Origlio, Tony iv
Orlowicz, Martin Andrew 31
Ornstein, Suzanne 110, 113, 185
Orshan, Wendy 5, 7, 137, 138, 295, 296, 341
Ortega, Kenny 393
Ortel, Sven 184, 187
Orth-Pallavicini, Nicole 271
Ortiz, Christian Elán 358
Ortiz, Jose 419
Ortiz, Rick 224
Ortiz, Tomas 224
Ortlieb, Jim 121, 123
Orton, Richard 314, 315
Osakalumi, Adesola 97-99, 103
Osborne, Edward P. 66, 94, 274, 321, 343, 373
Osborne, Ted 13, 14, 95, 272, 274
Osher, Bonnie 161
Osher, John 161
Oslak, Ryan 25
Osnes, Laura 324, 326, 331
Osterhaus, Megan 216
Otero, Kari iii
Ott, Sharon 403
Otterson, Pamela 354, 355, 357
Otto, Driscoll 13, 285, 303
Otto, Eric Michael 79, 81, 84
Ouellette, Herb 360, 361
Ouellette, Kris Koop iii, iv, 265, 268, 269
Ouellette, Steven 291, 369
Oune, Carol M. 47
Overend, Cambra 30, 31
Overmoyer, Clarion 132, 133
Overton, C. Mark 369
Owen, Carmel 243
Owen, Gareth 191, 193, 389
Owen, Louise 326
Owen, Phillip 334
Owen, Susan 261-263
Owens, Adam 343
Owens, Amber 211, 212, 214
Owens, David 231
Owens, Denyse 409
Owens, John 41, 47
Owens, Jon 363
Ownbey, Meghan 231, 258, 338, 352
Ozminski, Shaun 162
Ozols, Silvija 419
Oztemel, Laurel 276

P

Pabst, Jessica 280
Pace, Michael 343
Pacheco, Jesus 358
Pachtman, Matthew 66, 280, 291
Packard, Geoff 261, 262, 263, 300
Padden, Michael 53
Padgett, Emily 300
Pagan, Kayrose 13, 66, 94, 274, 322, 343, 373
Pagdon, Adam 8, 36
Page, Anthony 255
Page, Jeffrey 97, 99
Page, Lynne 164, 166, 170, 191, 193, 388
Page, Martin George 304
Paget, Ian 202, 203, 204, 206
Paguia, Marco 91, 93
Paice, Jill 340-342, 344
Paisner, Caryl 326
Pak, Joy 13, 65, 94, 274, 321, 343, 372, 399
Pakenham, Kate 252, 255
Pakledinaz, Martin 171, 172, 388
Palacios, Maria 410
Palermo, Jessica 401
Palijaro, Roy 408
Palitz, Michael 236
Pallas, Ted 102
Palm, Michael 408
Palmatier, Nancy A. 126
Palmer, Jeremy 156
Palmer, Sandra 101
Palmer, Todd 326
Palmer, Sean 187
Palmieri, Gayle 53, 281
Palombo, Rosemarie 83, 188, 216
Pals, Karen 163
Palumbo, Antonio 13, 65, 94, 274, 321, 372, 399
Palyk, Roman 334
Panama, Norman 152
Pando, Nicole 102, 342
Pankas, Dimitri 183, 189, 217
Pankin, Jordan 369
Pankow, John 238
Panter, Howard 121, 124, 126, 255
Pantuso, Christopher 53, 125, 126, 174, 234, 258
Paone, Lawrence 400, 405
Papa, Elisa 13, 65, 94, 273, 321, 343, 372, 399
Paparone, Frankie 313, 317
Pappas, F. Richard 217, 267
Paradise, Grace 326
Paradise, Sandy 113, 114
Parè, Laura 36
Paredes, Zoila 410
Parent, Matthew 255
Pares, Emiliano 162
Pareschi, Brian 18, 246
Parham, Bryonha 286, 287, 289
Parham, Olivera

Index

Bryonha 286
Park, Cynthia 315
Park, Grace 410
Park, Mae 280
Park, Mea 314
Parker, Alecia 69, 164, 168
Parker, Alfie Jr. 324, 325, 327
Parker, Bobbi 73
Parker, Hillary 94, 322
Parker, Jerome 291
Parker, John Eric 219-221, 226
Parker, Judy 163
Parker, Nicole 366
Parker, Robert Ross 402
Parker, Sarah Jessica 238, 275, 331
Parker, Timothy Britten 362, 364
Parlato, Karen 266
Parmele, Owen 234, 235, 254, 255
Parnell, Peter 402
Parnes, Joey 127, 130, 133
Parra, Alex 58, 114, 196, 304
Parra, Maya 12, 65, 343, 372
Parris, Mamie 286, 287, 289, 292, 293
Parrish, Laurel 368, 369
Parrott, Catherine A. 200
Parrotta, Anna 126
Parry, Nigel 352
Parsekian, Aaron 106
Parsigian, Madeleine 308
Parson, Wendy 109
Partello, Bill 8
Partier, Justin 151
Partilla, John 243
Parton, Dolly 245, 247, 251, 379
Parvin, Jeff 162, 163, 398
Pasbjerg, Carl 121, 126, 219, 225
Pascal, Adam 379
Paschall, Denny 310-312, 317
Pascua-Kim, Joy 410
Paseka, Chris 48
Pask, Bruce 276
Pask, Scott 37-39,
95, 127, 130, 245, 247, 276, 278, 332, 333
Passalacqua, Chris 217, 218
Passaro, Joe 185
Passaro, Michael J. 276, 279, 280, 332-334
Pastor, Patrick 66, 94, 274, 321, 373
Pastore, Anthony 25
Patch, Jerry 76, 78, 305, 308, 345, 347, 398
Patek, Patrick J. 255
Patel, Neil 256, 257
Paterson, Jayne 45, 191-193
Paterson, Victoria 2, 7, 355
Patinkin, Mandy 26, 323
Patria, Guy 100
Patria, Joseph 267
Patrick, Allison 13, 65, 94, 273, 321, 343, 372
Patrick, Julian 422
Patridge, David 83, 188, 208, 250
Patterson, Justin 245-247
Patterson, Mark 326
Patterson, Rhea 121-123, 362, 364
Patterson, Richard 343
Pattinian, Brad 416
Pattison, Lauren 217
Pattison, Nicky 314
Patton, Fitz 51, 392
Patton, Monica L. 109-111
Patty, Jessica Lea 1, 2, 4, 245-247
Paul, Christopher 250
Paul, Danny 25, 291
Paul, Ronald A. 243
Paull, Alexandra 174, 231, 234, 258, 281
Paull, John III 172, 222, 224, 225, 229, 257, 279
Paulson, Sarah viii, 76, 77
Paulus, Diane 127, 130, 134
Payne, Herman 245,
247
Payne, Joe 158-160
Payne, Nick 120
Payne, Stephen 28, 29, 335, 336
Payton, Philip 355
Paz, Jessica 102
Pazmino, Julie 73
Peacock, Chase 21-23, 27
Peacock, Giselle 54, 55
Peal, Nick 296
Pearce, Bobby 95
Pearce, Eric 156
Pearce, Liz 41, 42, 44, 49, 50
Pearl, Tom 25
Pears, Ryan 183, 189, 217
Pearson, Anthony 66, 114, 200, 314
Pearson, Brandon 131
Pearson, Joseph 188
Peay, Al 119
Pebley, Ross 315
Pechar, Thomas 79
Peck, Justin iv, 79, 81, 84, 265
Peck, Nathan 366
Pedersen, Kathy 255
Pedersen, Pat 133, 200, 234, 258
Pedlingham, Nicola 20
Peel, Terry R. 243
Peeler, Greg 25, 102
Peguero, Anderson 419
Peguero, Argenis 95
Peikoff, Jodi Esq. 36
Pekoe, Amanda 304
Pelkofer, Sue 25, 113
Pelkofer, Susan 114
Pelletier, Damon 25
Pelletier, Dee 28, 29
Pellew, Daniel 13, 95, 274
Pelligrini, Tom 303
Pels, Laura 343
Peluso, Chris 205
Pena, Joyce 367
Pendelton, Marcia 102, 106
Pendergraft, Eddie 362-364, 370
Pendergraft, Jennifer 64, 66, 188, 368
Pendilla, Robert 362, 363, 364
Pendleton, Austin 31, 53, 338
Penfield, Jay 14
Penn, Laura 403
Pennewell, Norwood J. 182
Penniman, Richard 231
Pennington, Shawn 318, 321, 322
Penski, Christine 6
Peot, Margaret 315
Pepe, Neil 38
Peral, Kelly 326
Perea, Carol 422
Perelman, Suzy 246
Peretti, Hugo 183
Perez, Celia 13, 95
Perez, Eddie 322, 373
Perez, Justin 337
Perez, Maritza 7
Perez, Maximo 78, 347
Perez, Paul 7
Perkins, Carl viii, ix, 227, 228, 231
Perkins, Myriah 182
Perlman, Arthur 109, 116
Perlman, Gail 410
Perlman, Jaime 20, 63, 66, 94, 274, 321, 343, 373
Perlow, David Nathan 164-166
Perri, Matthew 153, 156, 277, 279, 315
Perron, Francois 47
Perrotta, Joe 156, 200, 208, 234, 291, 411
Perry, Adam 276, 278, 362, 364
Perry, Antoinette 387
Perry, Beverly 243
Perry, Ellan 196
Perry, Jeff 31, 338
Perry, Marisa 13, 65, 94, 274, 321, 372, 399
Perry, Marissa 343, 377
Perry, P.J. 80
Perry, Robb 407
Perry, Steve 304
Persaud, Sylvina 401
Persson, Johan 135, 136, 138, 294, 296
Pesner, Ben 397
Peter Grimes 308
Peterik, Jim 304
Peters, Bernadette 322, 381, 391
Peters, Christine 8, 88
Peters, Elizabeth 156
Petersen, Eric 313, 317
Peterson, Laura 238
Peterson, Lisa 403
Peterson, Mary Nemecek 182
Peterson, Matt 355
Petitjean, Douglas 195, 196, 249, 250
Petkoff, Robert iv, vii, 286, 288, 292, 293
Petruska, Greg 47
Pettigrew, Henry 135, 136, 139
Pettolina, Timothy 145
Petzold, Roxana 13, 65, 94, 274, 321, 372, 399
Peyankov, Yasen 31, 335, 336, 338, 339
Peyser, Alex 114, 196, 304
Pfaelzer, Johanna 238
Pfeffer, Jane 133, 409
Pfeiffer, Michelle 26, 134
Pfifferling, Joe 35, 36, 302
Pflueger, Tanner 45
Phaneuf, Marc 185
Phelan, Kerry 315
Phelan, William 280

Philadelphia, Billy 373
Philbin, Regis 169
Philippi, Michael 422
Philips, Willie 13, 95, 274
Phillips, Angela 188
Phillips, Brittinee 417
Phillips, Dave 246
Phillips, Dewey 225
Phillips, Jessica 240-242
Phillips, Michael 182
Phillips, Oneika 100
Phillips, Patricia 261,
263, 268
Phillips, Thomas K. 361
Phillips, Tripp iv, 109, 112, 114
Piacentile, Kristin 338, 413
Picar, Amy 410
Piccione, Nancy 76, 78, 305, 308, 345, 347, 398
Pichardo, Marlon 125, 230
Pickens, Will 274
Pickett, Travis 8
Pien, Jane 35, 36
Pierce, Angela 252, 253
Pierce, Dave 79, 81
Pierce, David Hyde 297, 389
Pierce, Edward 245, 362
Pierce, James A., III 181
Pierce, Xavier 102
Pierzina, Pamela 125, 126
Pietro, Dave 153
Pietro, Jackie 46
Pietropinto, Angela 78, 308, 347
Pietropinto, Anthony 243
Pietropinto, Laura 241, 242
Pignone, Charles 79
Pilcz, Paul 60, 62
Pilipski, Michael 200, 303
Pilipski, Mike 225
Pill, Alison viii, 232-234
Pillow, Charles 2, 7, 311
Pimentel, Roddy 58, 114, 196, 255, 304
Pimentel, Shereen 176, 178
Pinckard, John 21
Pinckney, Joseph 422
Pinckney, Tim 410
Pine, Larry 305, 306, 309
Pinkhas, Lana 314
Pinkhas, Svetlana 280
Pinkins, Tonya 378
Pinkus, Ann 361
Piño, Geraldo 97, 103

Index

Piretti, Ron 143, 145, 234, 361
Pirouz, Judy 181
Pirrie, Morag 138, 296
Pisapia, Eddie 168
Piscitelli, Michael 266
Pitocchi, Susan 36
Pitt, Brad 218
Pittari, Anthony 78, 308, 347
Pittelman, Carole 25
Pittelman, Ira 21, 23, 25, 51, 52, 91
Pittman, David 13, 65, 274, 321, 343, 372
Pittman, Joe 150
Pittsinger, David 328
Pittu, David 393
Pitzer, Michael 8, 242
Pizzarelli, Vera 196, 295, 296
Pizzuti, Paul 61, 65, 66
Pizzuto, Joe 329
Plantadit, Karine viii, ix, 79, 80, 84, 388, 389
Plante, Tiffany J. 8
Platt, Jess 334
Platt, Jon B. 79, 82, 85, 87, 117, 118, 349, 350, 362, 365
Platt, Marc 362, 365, 369, 384
Platt, Oliver 121, 123
Pletcher, Judy 420
Pleva, David 234, 255
Plimpton, Martha 31, 338
Ploski, Marisha 301, 303
Plotkin, Loren 8, 36, 53, 83, 145, 156, 231, 281, 291
Pluff, Jennifer 102
Plumb, Eve 378
Plummer, Bryan 216
Pluth, Jeffrey 402
Poe, Laura 65, 94, 273, 321, 372
Poe, Richard 270, 271
Poggioli, Vanessa 150, 151
Poiret, Jean 164

Poitier, Sidney 285
Poitras, Scott "Gus" 125, 126, 224, 225, 230, 280
Polanco, Danielle 358
Poland, Eric 355
Polcyn, Gregory 410
Polhill, Patricia 77
Polidoro, Rose 127, 133
Polimeni, Marc 53, 347
Polino, Fran 409
Polischuk, Geoffrey 38, 39, 333, 334
Polizzi, Sal 409
Polk, Matt 13, 66, 95, 200, 274, 314, 322, 373, 411
Polk, Matthew 208
Pollack, Felicia 133
Pollard, Thelma 266-268
Pollock, Charlie 245, 247
Pollock, M.L. 330
Polmer, Alexa 78, 308, 347
Pomahac, Bruce 152, 330
Pomposello, Sean 120
Ponce, Cynthia 133
Ponce, Richard 77, 78, 308, 346, 347
Ponder, Jon Mark 8
Ponella, Mike 153
Pontius, Larry 402
Ponturo, Ruthe 127
Ponturo, Tony 130, 219, 222
Pool, Mic 340, 341
Poole, Joshua 145, 156, 291, 361
Poole, Richard 261-263, 269
Poole, Russell 31
Poor, Bray 148
Pope, Katie 58, 114, 255
Pope, Kristyn 152-154, 157
Popkin, Maude 419
Popp, Ethan 298, 300
Poppleton, L. Glenn 258
Porazzi, Arturo 219, 223, 225
Porche, Nicholas 243

Porrello, David 420, 421
Port, Lauren 95, 106
Porter, Amy 217
Porter, Cole 82
Porto, Cesar 138
Posener, Daniel 168, 183, 189, 217
Posner, Kenneth 171, 172, 232, 233, 245, 247, 305, 307, 362, 365
Potter, Bill 219, 222
Potter, Linda 219
Potter, Mick 261, 264
Potter, Todd 36, 145
Potts, Annie 117, 118, 120
Potts, Steve 126
Pow, Cameron 176, 178
Powell, Dean 322
Powell, Jane 410
Powell, Kathleen 280
Powell, Nicole 286, 287, 289
Powers, Christopher 25, 53, 418
Powers, David 422
Powers, Rory 225
Powers, Stefanie 200
Poyer, Lisa M. 332, 334
Pozo, Chano 98, 102
Pozo, Delia 224
Praagh, Michael Van 119
Praet, Matthew 308, 347
Prager, Cathy 307, 308
Pramik, Nick 8, 25, 114, 126, 174, 225, 234, 250, 281, 352
Prats, Jacqueline 315
Prattes, Colt 354, 355, 357
Prebble, Lucy viii, ix, 85, 86, 389
Prensa, Manuel 302
Prentice, Kim 31, 337, 338
Prescott, Justin 100
Presland, Frank 48
Presley, Elvis viii, ix, 227, 228, 231
Presley, Robert 167, 168
Presnell, Harve 422
Press, Nicole 94,

273, 321
Press, Seymour Red 69-71, 75, 109, 110, 112, 114, 127, 130, 152, 155
Press, Terry 315
Pressman, Lauren D'Elia 174
Presto, David 314, 315
Preston, Brandi 31, 285
Preston, Denise 415
Preston, Lisa 47
Preston, Vaughn 307
Preuss, Rob 203
Priatno, Trudy 416
Price, Canara 83, 188, 217
Price, Eva 1, 371, 373
Price, Laura 415
Price, Lonny 403
Price, Mark 211, 213
Price, Michael P. 407
Price, Paige 400, 401
Price, Pearleta 267, 268
Price, Richard 409
Pridemore, Patrick 288
Prima, Louis 163
Primis, Damian 326
Primis, Theo 363
Prince, Andrea 208, 267, 304, 416
Prince, Faith 184-186, 190
Prince, Harold 191, 193, 261, 264
Prince, Josh 310, 312
Prince, Judy Lynn 243
Prince, Len 70
Prisand, Scott 298
Pritchard, Dean 58
Pritzker, Gigi 229
Prizel, Kate Rothko 296
Prosser, Peter 355
Protulipac, Thomas 13, 66, 94, 274, 322, 343, 373
Proud, Lee 47
Prouty, Joel 79-81
Provencale, Jessica 20
Pruett-Barnett, Jessica 13, 66, 94,

274, 322, 343, 373
Pruiett, Michelle 184-186
Pruitt, Teresa 368
Prussack, Alexis 36, 218
Przetakiewicz, Larry 421
Psiuk, Ali 301
Psomas, George 324-327
Ptaszynski, André 267
Puckett, Geoff 183
Pugh, David 117, 120
Pugh, Stewart 120
Pugliese, Augie 229
Pullara, Joseph 47, 48
Pullman, Bill vi, 256
Pummill, James Patrick 64
Pummill, Patrick 64, 66, 230, 231
Purcell, Doug 238, 342
Purcell, Terri 46, 47
Purdie, Bernard 128, 132
Purdy, Claude 422
Purdy, H.L. 267
Purviance, Douglas 363
Putnam, Bambi 243
Putnam, John 246
Pyle, Stephen 267
Pyzocha, Robert 188

Q
Quadrino, Daniel iv, 60-062, 68
Qualls, Alexis 234
Quart, Anne 176, 182
Quenqua, Joe 183, 188, 217
Quiggin, Charles 216, 217
Quigley, Brendan 368, 369
Quillon, Keven 310, 312, 317
Quinlan, Robert 338
Quinn, Christine 269
Quinn, David 48
Quinn, Doug 203, 209
Quinn, Helen 183
Quinn, Josh 114

Quinn, Sean 145
Quinones, Ricardo 98, 103
Quintana, Joaquin 125
Quinton, Everett 384
Quiroga, Alexander 362-364

R
Raab, Marni 261, 263
Rabatin, Nancy 53
Rabin, Eddie 342
Racanelli, Karen 373
Rachesky, Jill F. 343
Rada, Mirena 32, 34
Radcliffe, Daniel 96, 331, 390
Radetsky, Jessica 261, 263
Radin, Neila B. 343
Radke, Kirk A. 243
Rado, James 127, 129, 134
Rae, Colin 196
Raffio, Ronald 70
Rafoss, Kaia 13, 66, 94, 274, 322, 343, 373
Rafson, Jill 12, 65, 94, 273, 321, 343, 372, 399
Rafter, Michael 91, 162
Ragni, Gerome 127, 129
Ragusa, Michele 377
Raimondi, Diane 401
Raimone, Antuan 143
Raines, Allison 58, 114, 196, 255, 304
Rainville, Richard 258
Raitt, Jayson 95, 298, 300
Raitt, Kathleen 396
Rakos, Ruby 41, 42, 44, 50
Raksis, Gary 315
Ralske, Amy 22, 246
Ramin, Sid 354
Ramirez, Alfonso 78, 347
Ramirez, Nicole 322
Ramlall, Steve 421
Ramos, Alice 342, 344

Index

Ramos, Clint 393
Ramos, Liz 1, 2, 4, 9
Rampmeyer, Mark Adam 354
Rampton, Ken 18, 110, 113
Ramseur, Roxana 314
Ramsey, Russ 101
Ramsey, Shad 225
Ramshur, Valerie 39
Rand, Zach 215
Randall, Lynne 243
Randell, Denny 163
Randolph-Wright, Charles 343
Randolph, Beverley 1, 5, 6, 8
Randolph, Julie 126, 162
Ranger, Caroline 120
Rankin, Steve 121, 124, 158, 160, 219, 222
Rankine, Ryan H. 100
Rannells, Andrew 161
Rao, Sheilaja 151, 330
Raphael, Christopher 281
Rapp, Anthony 379, 381
Rappaport, Felix 58
Rashad, Condola 382
Rashad, Phylicia 28, 29
Rasmussen, Charles 280, 281
Rasmussen, Sarah 151
Ratajczak, Dave 213
Ratcliffe, Julie 266, 267
Rathbone, Jennifer 12, 65, 94, 321, 343, 372
Rathbun, Justin 144, 145
Rathbun, Kristen 106, 342
Ratray, Ann Willis 48
Ratzenberger, John 292
Rauscher, Richard C. 91, 93, 95
Rausenberger, Karl 329, 330
Rawlins, Ted 229
Ray, Connie 236, 237, 239
Ray, H.L. 66, 373
Ray, Vanessa iv, 127, 129, 134
Rayburn, Abbey 217
Raymond, Amanda 7, 13, 95, 106, 120, 138, 196, 238, 274, 296, 314, 334, 342
Reams, Lee Roy 378
Reardon, Peter 152-154
Rebbeck, Stephen 48
Rebeck, Theresa 402
ReCar, Chuck 328, 330
Rech, Erin 397
Reddington, Bridget 120, 315
Redditt, Bruce 407
Reddy, Brian 109, 111
Reddy, Helen 96
Reddy, Leah 12, 65, 94, 273, 321, 343, 372
Redgrave, Corin 422
Redgrave, Lynn 384, 410, 422
Redhead, Liam 45, 49
Redman, Michael 163, 200, 342
Redmayne, Eddie viii, ix, 294, 295, 297, 388, 393
Redmond, Joe 342
Redmond, Leah 31, 46
Redsecker, John 185, 188
Reed, Angel 298, 299
Reed, Courtney 140-142, 205
Reed, Elizabeth 224
Reed, Jessica 162
Reed, Madeline 408
Reed, Robert 48
Reed, Rondi iv, 31, 338, 362-364, 370
Reedman, Jo 207
Reese, Bill 420
Regan, Austin 25, 95
Regan, David 36
Regan, Dennis 156
Regan, Mary Beth 133
Regan, Molly 31, 338
Rehbein, Amanda 12, 65, 94, 273, 321, 343, 372
Reiber, Julie 366
Reichard, Daniel 376
Reichenbach, Ashley 218
Reid, Catherine 416
Reid, Frances 422
Reid, Heather C. 334
Reid, Joe Aaron 109-111, 116
Reid, Stephen 249
Reid, T. Oliver 215, 216
Reiff, Dennis 36, 83, 156, 291
Reill, Arlene 302
Reilly, Bob 57, 168
Reilly, Sean Patrick 335, 336
Reiner, Jessica 266
Reiner, Rachel 397
Reinersman, Anna 110, 113
Reinis, Jonathan 371, 373
Reinking, Ann 69, 71
Reinking, Megan 131
Reisig, Jason 315
Reit, Peter 262, 266
Reiter, Tom 217
Rembert, Jermaine R. 219-221, 225
Remillard, Paris 127-129, 134
Remler, Pamela 63, 66
Renata, Carla 34
René, Jacqueline 181
Renner, Richard 410
Reno, Phil 276-279
Renschler, Eric 74
Resheff, Rachel 41, 42, 44, 50, 216, 313
Resnick, Judith 16, 17, 85
Resnick, Patricia 245, 247, 250
Ressler, Jordan 163
Rettberg, Seth 32, 33, 36
Retter, Thommie 41, 42, 43, 49
Reuben, Aubrey i, iii, iv, vi, 15, 67, 68, 103, 115, 116, 120, 134, 139, 190, 226, 244, 251, 309, 348, 376, 377, 381, 382, 384, 397
Reuchel, Nicholas 36
Reupert, Michelle 162
Reuter, Greg 73, 313, 316
Revaux, Jacques 83
Reyes, Alejandra 140, 142
Reynolds, Bradley 290, 358
Reynolds, Caroline 315
Reynolds, Dawn 183
Reynolds, Debbie vi, 373
Reynolds, Marilyn 153
Reynolds, Tom 182
Reza, Yasmina 117, 118
Rheault, Mark 415
Rhodes, Josh 72
Rhodes, Stan 163
Riabko, Kyle 127, 129, 133
Ricci, Alfred 119
Ricci, Joe 349, 350, 353
Ricci, Tyler 280
Riccio, Joseph, III 8, 189
Rice, Adena 8
Rice, Grant A. 196
Rice, Michael 377
Rice, Tim 95, 176, 177, 179, 183
Rich, Geoffrey 36
Rich, Janet Billig 95, 298
Rich, Shirley 422
Richard, Ellen 13, 66, 95, 240, 274, 322, 373
Richard, Jonathan 347
Richards, David R. 29, 31, 86, 88, 283, 285, 336, 338
Richards, Devin 109-111
Richards, Jeffrey iv, 16-20, 28, 29, 31, 85, 86, 88, 127, 130, 133, 282, 283, 285, 335, 336, 338, 413
Richardson, John 252, 255
Richardson, Priscilla 291
Richardson, Sarah 39, 120
Richardson, Vicky 138, 296
Richenthal, David 109, 232
Richings, Nick 164, 166, 389
Richmond, Christine 207, 208
Rickles, Don 67
Rickman, Alan 96
Riddle, Nelson 80
Ridge, John David 66, 250, 393
Ridgley, Reed 36
Riebl, Felix 58
Riedel, Paul 410
Rieff, D.R. 225
Riegler, Adam iii, 1, 4, 6, 9, 10, 313
Riekenberg, Dave 246
Rieling, Dale 213
Rieppi, Pablo 355
Rifkin, Jay 176, 177, 180
Rigazzi, Daniel 133
Rigby, Cathy 268
Rigby, Rodney 171
Riggins, John 230, 368, 369
Rinaldi, John 196, 250
Rinaldi, Philip iv, 148, 151, 324, 330
Rincon, Anna 421
Riner, Paul 188
Ringler, Alex 354, 355, 357
Rios, Marylou 266
Rios, Mike 230
Ripley, Alice 240, 241, 244, 381
Rippe, Scott 101
Rippey, Anne 8, 25, 114, 121, 126, 174, 219, 225, 234, 250, 267, 276, 281, 352
Rippy, Conrad 8, 83, 145, 291
Riseborough, Andrea 393
Rissetto, Diana 19, 31, 88, 133, 285, 338, 413
Rita, Rui 270
Ritchie, Michael 248, 257
Ritter, Alexander 291
Ritter, John 78, 347
Ritter, Paul 252, 253
Rittmann, Trude 110, 324, 326, 327
Rivera, Carmen 78, 308, 347
Rivera, Chita 146, 285, 381
Rivera, Jacklyn 13, 274
Rivera, Nicole 36
Rivera, Noah 144, 147, 310-312, 316
Rivera, Roberto 302
Rivera, Samuel 163
Rivers, Joan 78
Rivierzo, Joe 404
Rizner, Russell 213
Rizzo, Ken 403
Roach, Maxine 288, 403
Roaid, Mary 421
Roath, Steve 48
Robbins, Carrie 152, 155
Robbins, Jana 286, 290
Robbins, Jerome 255, 354, 357
Robbins, Lois 343
Robbins, Noah 51, 52
Robbins, Tom Alan 180, 181
Robelen, John A. III 133
Roberson, Ken 32, 33
Roberts, Alison 8, 47, 156, 334
Roberts, Christopher 234
Roberts, Donald 66
Roberts, Jaime 342
Roberts, Jonathan 176
Roberts, Keith viii, 79, 80, 84
Roberts, Pernell E. 422
Roberts, Tony 305, 306, 309
Robertson, Brad 47, 83, 338
Robertson, Darren 78, 308, 347

The Playbill Broadway Yearbook 2009-2010   455

Index

Robertson, Robbie 95
Robillard, Dan 145, 156, 249, 250
Robinson, Amina 202-204
Robinson, Arbender J. 127-129, 286-289
Robinson, Bernita 12, 65, 94, 273, 321, 343, 372
Robinson, Christopher 156
Robinson, Donald 102
Robinson, Fatimah 13, 95, 274
Robinson, Gene 239
Robinson, Janelle Anne 211-213
Robinson, Jessie Mae 231
Robinson, Kristin 343
Robinson, LaConya 320, 322, 372, 373
Robinson, Mary B. 403
Robinson, Mattie 280, 314
Roby, Peta 54, 57
Roby, Robbie 41, 44
Roche, Mary 422
Rocket, Rikki 304
Rockman, Audrey Rau 162
Rockwell, Kate 127, 129
Rockwell, Sam viii, 37, 38, 40
Rockwell, Stacey 216
Roderick, Greg 324-327
Rodgers, Mary 322, 331
Rodgers, R. Doug 163
Rodgers, Richard 20, 83, 319, 324, 326, 327
Rodriguez, Carmen 367
Rodriguez, David 421
Rodriguez, Desiree 361
Rodriguez, Eve 409
Rodriguez, Frank 58
Rodriguez, Ivan 367
Rodriguez, Janice 132
Rodriguez, Krysta 1, 4, 9
Rodriguez, Marquis Kofi 176, 178
Rodriguez, Martha 119
Rodriguez, Matt 6
Rodriguez, Michael 373
Rodriguez, Paul 224
Rodriguez, Roxanne 397
Roeder, William 409
Roeder, Brian 409
Roffe, Mary Lu 1
Rogers, Allison 360
Rogers, Alvin E. 262
Rogers, Brenden 151, 330
Rogers, Dafydd 117, 120
Rogers, Fred 95
Rogers, Joanne 95
Rogers, Kim 403
Rogers, Natalie 182
Rogers, Reg 305, 306, 309
Rogers, Ric 167
Rogers, Sam 354, 355, 357
Rogers, Scott 58
Rogers, Timothy F. 36, 39, 66, 322
Rohe, Kathryn 183
Rohm, Carrie 328, 330
Roig, Eileen 367
Rojas, Giorgio 58
Rojas, Isander 183, 189, 217
Rojas, Louise 57, 58
Rojas, Marcus 288, 326
Rojas, Ricky 54, 55, 59
Rolecek, Charles 298
Rolff, Heather Jane 310-312
Rollison, Scott Taylor 6, 8
Roma, Jim 66, 94, 274, 321, 372
Romain, Laurissa iv, 324, 326, 331, 386
Román, Eliseo 140-142, 145, 146
Romanello, Bill 217, 218
Romano, Salvatore 133, 243, 369
Romero, Constanza 104, 105, 108, 388
Romero, Victor 208
Romick, James iv, 262, 263, 268
Ronan, Brian 21, 23, 91, 92, 240, 241, 276, 278
Ronan, Nancy 162
Rooks, Joel 307
Rooney, Cory 58
Rooney, John 83, 156, 248, 250
Rooney, Maureen 163
Roop, Marjorie 410
Roosa, Kate 48
Root, Amanda 252, 253
Root, Jonathan 34
Rosa-Shapiro, Marisol 114
Rosa, Errolyn 53
Rosario, Dixon 361
Rosati, Juliana 322
Roscioli, Dee 362, 364
Rose, Amanda 366
Rose, Billy 200
Rose, Cailan 127-129
Rose, Greg 216
Rose, Jonathan 330
Rose, Michael 332
Rose, Nancy 243
Rosegg, Carol 32, 33, 36, 47, 91, 121, 122, 126, 198, 200, 236, 238
Rosen, Cherie 178, 181
Rosen, Donna 243
Rosen, Emily 8
Rosen, Michael 354, 356
Rosen, Steve 121, 123, 377
Rosenberg, Barry 401
Rosenberg, Michael S. 219
Rosenberg, Neil 30, 31, 38, 39, 40
Rosenberg, Philip 234, 250, 314, 334
Rosenberg, Roger 165
Rosenberg, Ruth 208
Rosenberg, Steve 13, 138, 296, 334
Rosenblum, M. Edgar 422
Rosenbluth, Jennifer H. 151, 330
Rosenfeld, Michael 182, 188, 217
Rosenfield, Amy 13, 65, 94, 274, 321, 372, 399
Rosenkranz, Nicholas Quinn 282
Rosenkranz, Peggy Hill 258
Rosenow, John 420
Rosenthal, Barbara 368, 369
Rosenthal, Murray 294
Rosenthal, Sarah 286, 288, 292
Rosenthal, Todd 28, 29
Rosenthal, Robert 410
Rosenzweig, Rich 114, 288
Rosenzweig, Sara 47, 133, 231
Ross, Andrew 20
Ross, Blake 419
Ross, Donald 48
Ross, John 329
Ross, Julianne 399
Ross, Linda Mason 148, 151, 324, 330
Ross, Marvin Webster 304
Ross, Matt 25, 48, 126, 145, 250, 280, 304, 334, 361, 412
Ross, Tessa 48
Ross, Tory iv, 59, 245-247, 251
Rossano, Anthony 369
Rosser, Tim 8
Rossetto, Ryan 229, 231
Rossmy, Michael 335, 336
Rosson, Carrie 8, 19, 88, 145, 225, 230, 242, 250, 285, 303, 330, 369
Roth, Chelsea 315
Roth, Daryl 28, 30, 79, 82, 85, 87, 97, 100, 191, 194
Roth, David 39, 48, 250
Roth, David Lee 304
Roth, Philip, Dr. 182
Roth, Erin Brooke 188, 200
Roth, Gabriel Alexander 95
Roth, Jordan vi, 21, 25, 97, 102, 109, 112, 114, 127, 130, 133, 158, 163, 191, 196, 395
Roth, Katherine 79
Rothenberg, Adam 415
Rothenberg, Leon 330
Rothermel, Janet 203, 204, 208
Rothfeld, Michael 243
Rothfield, Rae 16, 17
Rothko, Christopher 296
Rothko, Mark viii, 294, 295, 297
Rothman, Carole 92, 95, 240, 241, 243
Rotstein, Erica 343
Rouch, Janette 25
Rountree, Bryan 291, 314
Roush, Janette 225, 234, 250, 267, 281
Roush, Jeanette 126
Routh, Marc 54, 56, 191, 194, 252, 253
Rovegno, Mia 347
Rovery, Steven 133, 418
Rowat, Graham 121-123, 126
Rowe, Stephen 294, 295
Rowen, Scott 46, 47
Rowland, Christine 216
Rowland, William 30, 31, 173, 337, 338
Rowley, Emma 60, 62
Roy, James 314
Roy, Kevin 363
Royal, Donald 132
Roye, Winston 299, 301
Royston, Ivor 161
Rozett, Josh 13, 66, 94, 274, 322, 343, 373
Rua, Jon 140-142, 146
Ruben, Albert G. 39
Rubens, Herbert 52
Rubenstein, Lee G. 243
Rubie, Melody 261, 263
Rubin-Vega, Daphne 145
Rubin, Alexandra 133
Rubin, Andrew 420
Rubin, Bruce 329
Rubin, Julia 329
Rubin, Tara 41, 44, 47, 121, 124, 126, 158, 160, 162, 184, 187, 188, 191, 193, 196, 205, 208, 211, 215, 217, 261, 264, 267, 276, 279, 280, 310, 312, 314, 322
Rubinaccio, Kaylie 286, 287, 289
Ruch, Joshua 243
Ruckdeschel, Karl 36, 303
Rudd, Michael 8, 138, 296
Rudetsky, Seth 377, 383, 419
Rudin, Jennifer 188, 217
Rudin, Scott 37, 38, 104, 105, 117, 118
Rudy, Eric 188
Rudy, Sam iv, 32, 36
Ruff, Erica 250
Ruff, Roslyn 104, 105
Ruggiero, Holly-Anne 162
Ruggiero, Paul 6
Ruggiero, Rob 198, 199, 201
Ruhl, Sarah vii, 148, 149, 387
Ruiz, Gabrielle 140-142, 146
Ruiz, Victor 168
Rummel, Christopher 12, 65, 94, 321, 343, 372
Rummer, Steven 315
Runion, Mark 409
Runk, Bonnie 132
Runyon, Damon 121, 122
RuPaul 292
Rupert, Mary Six 8, 138, 296
Rush, Cassy 12, 65,

Index

94, 273, 321, 343, 372
Rush, Geoffrey 379, 382
Rush, Jessica 121-123
Russek, Jim 151, 330, 416
Russell, Andrew 234
Russell, Bethany 25, 95
Russell, Francesca 16, 17, 19, 20
Russell, Henny 305, 306, 309
Russell, Julious 13, 95, 274
Russell, Neno 114
Russell, Rita 257
Russman, Brian 47
Russo, Nick 163
Russo, Glenn 208
Russo, Rene 59
Russold, Werner 217, 291
Rustin, Christopher 132
Rutberg, Elon 19, 31, 88, 285, 338, 413
Ruthizer, Theodore 13, 66, 78, 95, 151, 274, 308, 322, 330, 347, 373
Rutigliano, Danny 176, 178
Rutter, Michele 125, 126, 223, 225
Ruttura, David 156, 229, 230
Ryack, Rita 345
Ryall, William 121-123
Ryan, Ashley 88, 231, 280
Ryan, Bart 132
Ryan, Catherine iv
Ryan, Erica 397
Ryan, Kathleen 7
Ryan, Matt 135, 136
Ryan, Roz 69, 71
Ryan, Stephen 13, 95, 274, 399
Ryan, Thomas Jay 148, 149
Ryerson, Amy 354, 355, 357
Rylko, Glen 48
Ryn, Becca Goland-Van 330
Ryness, Bryce 131

S

Sachon, Peter 326
Sack, Domonic 20
Sadofsky, Christine 138, 234, 258, 281
Safer, Jane Fearer 407
Saferstein, Robert J. 28, 31, 133, 282, 283, 285, 335, 338, 413
Sag, Lindsey Brooks 78, 308, 347, 398
Sag, Michael 88, 285, 338
Sagady, Shawn 219
Saget, Bob 67
Saia, Janet 262, 263
Saidy, Fred vii, 109, 112
Sainato, Vinny 168, 415
Saint-Amand, Nathan E. 243
Saint, David 354, 357
Sajous, Christina iv, ix, 21, 22, 26, 27
Saks, Danielle 48
Salas, Veronica 262, 266
Salazar, Hector 47
Salb, Brian 250
Saleem, Shazia 266, 267
Salerno, Mike 410
Saletnik, Joshua A. 58, 114, 196, 255, 304
Salgado, Luis 140, 142, 145
Salkin, Eddie 42
Salomons, Ruthlyn 180-182
Salt, Anne 182
Saltzman, Rina 402
Saltzman, Samantha 303
Salvador, Gerard 202-204, 206, 210
Salyer, Chelsea 53
Salzberg, Marc 329, 330
Salzman, Joshua 369
Sambora, Richard S. 304
Samelson, Judy 420
Samonsky, Andrew 324, 326
Sampliner, Susan 243, 367, 369
Samuel, Cherie 409
Samuels, Barbara 25, 102, 303
Samuels, Bruce 61, 156, 196, 277
Sanabria, Gina 359
Sanchez, Bradley 399
Sanchez, Carmen 150
Sanchez, Ernesto 13, 274
Sanchez, Graciella 258
Sanchez, Jennifer 354, 355, 357
Sanchez, Jose 58
Sanchez, Mark 26, 49, 75
Sanchez, Santos 267
Sancineto, Michael 314, 315
Sandberg, Andy 127
Sandell, Joy 195
Sander, Ryan 203, 204, 206, 208
Sanders, Allen 195
Sanders, Ann 34
Sanders, Chris 173, 174
Sanders, Donald 74, 200, 250
Sanders, Kristie Dale 236, 237, 262, 263
Sanders, Scott 132, 133
Sanders, Steven A. 343
Sanderson, Claire 217
Sanderson, David 39
Sandhu, Rommy 211-214
Sandler, Ed 397
Sandler, Jonathan Richard 211-214, 216
Sands, Jason Patrick 69-71
Sands, Stark 21, 22, 24, 26, 27
Sandy, Julia 78, 308, 347
Sandy, Solange 69-71
Sanford, Andrew 280
Sanok, Justin 46
Sansiveri, Adam 126
Santalucia, Nuria 54, 55
Santamaria, Mongo 58
Santana, Marcos 121-123, 126, 140, 142
Santander, Kike 58
Santen, Kathy 362-364
Santi, Rita 188
Santiago, Joe 125
Santiago, Julio 120
Santiago, Ulises 280, 314
Santora, Elise 143
Santora, Phil 219
Santore, Fred Jr. 145
Santore, Stephen 231
Santos, Kevin 140-142
Santos, Manuel 354, 355, 357
Santos, Ralph 163
Santulli, Michael 88
Sapien, Luis 307, 308
Sapp, Robb 310, 311
Sapper, Wayne 13, 66, 95, 267, 274, 322, 373
Sara, Flesner 109
Saraffian, Andrea O. 329
Sarafin, Peter 13, 95, 196, 238, 342, 274, 315
Sarandon, Susan 379
Sarmiento, Stacey 64
Sarmiento, Stacy 66
Sarpola, Richard 185, 192
Sarto, Rosanna Consalva 78, 308, 347
Sarudiansky, Nico 25
Sarvay, Tree 88, 151, 249, 250
Satalof, Stu 61, 65
Sato, Atsuko 262, 266
Satrin, Mike 404
Sattaur, Keshave 53, 126, 229, 231
Saul, Jack 347
Savage, Kim 138
Savelli, Jennifer 121-123
Sawyer, Diane 322
Sawyers, Jenny 78, 106, 285
Saxon, Kelly 138, 295, 296, 352
Saye, John 217, 218
Sayegh, Sharone 202-204, 206
Sayers, Albert 25, 113, 114
Sayre, Cyndi 373
Sayre, Loretta Ables 324, 326, 331
Scaglione, Josefina 354-356
Scahill, Roland 373
Scales, Tim 343
Scalfani, Sal 132
Scandalios, Nick 8, 53, 83, 126, 145, 156, 183, 189, 231, 291, 304, 361, 369, 384, 396
Scanlan, Arlene 164, 167, 256, 257
Scanlan, Dick 91, 92, 96, 389
Scanlon, Dennis 31, 173
Scanlon, Jenna 31
Scanlon, Laura 173
Scarbrough, Paul 188
Scardino, Frank 121, 126, 219, 225
Scarpone-Lambert, Anthony 232
Scedrov, Igor 360
Schachter, Scott 153
Schadt, Timothy 288
Schaefer, Nancy 188
Schaefer, Paul A. 261-263
Schaeffer, Bill 163
Schaeffer, Eric viii, 227, 228
Schaeffer, Steve 13, 65, 94, 274, 321, 343, 372, 399
Schafer, Didi 243
Schaffer, Paula 359, 361
Schaffert, Greg 56, 243, 369
Schaffner, Jay 403
Schaffzin, Jolie 419
Schall, Karin 151, 330
Schall, Thomas 11, 168, 345, 352, 369
Schanzer, Justin 58, 304
Schanzer, Leanne 58, 304
Schatz, Jack 42, 46
Schatz, Sara 53, 114, 156, 182, 200, 234, 342, 407
Schatz, Scout J. 407
Schechter, Matthew 211, 213
Schecter, Amy 28, 79, 83, 361
Schecter, Samantha 58
Scheer-Montgomery, Jenny 242
Scheer, Rachel 25
Schefflan, Beth 416
Scheidt, Scott 181, 182
Scheinmann, David 41, 42, 47
Schepis, Steve iv, 109-111, 115
Schettini, Lissette 347
Schiro, Chad 66
Schisano, Christine 63
Schleifer, Jason 315
Schlender, Sandy 208
Schlenk, Thomas 182
Schlosberg, Hubert M. 243
Schloss, Edwin W. 164, 167
Schmidt, Cory 360, 361
Schmidt, Jamie 288, 291
Schmidt, John 243
Schmidt, Josh 51, 52
Schmidt, Kiira 152-154
Schmidt, Sara 158, 160
Schmied, Marc 165
Schnall, Eric 135, 138, 294, 296
Schneider, Ben 13, 66, 95, 274, 321, 322, 372, 373
Schneider, Bill 25
Schneider, Lauren Class 198
Schneider, Mark 255
Schneider, Peter 176, 407
Schnepp, Steven 133, 163
Schnuck, Terry 56, 127, 130, 282, 283,

Index

335, 336
Schnurr, Candice 63
Schock, Laura 53
Schoeffler, Paul 300
Schoenfeld, Gerald 36
Schoenfeld, Judith 240, 242
Scholtens, Eugene 153
Scholz, Daniel 410
Schon, Neal J. 304
Schondorf, Zohar 2, 185
Schrader, Benjamin 34, 286, 287, 289, 292
Schrader, David 183, 188, 217
Schramm, David 109, 111
Schreck, Heidi 393
Schreiber, Catherine 236, 237
Schreiber, Liev viii, 349, 350, 352, 353, 388, 392
Schreiber, Matt 32, 33, 35, 36
Schreier, Dan Moses 191, 193, 318, 320, 354, 357, 389
Schriever, Jennifer 39, 106
Schroder, Wayne 245-247
Schroeder, Ron 208
Schroko, Steven 343
Schubert-Blechman, Julienne 25, 314, 315
Schuberth, Karl 167, 168
Schuette, James 335
Schulberg, Budd 422
Schuler, Stephen 1
Schulman, Susan H. 403
Schultz, Victor 363
Schumacher, Thomas 91, 176, 180, 183, 184, 187, 188, 211, 214, 217
Schurkamp, Richard 347
Schussel, Stefanie 66, 94, 274, 321, 343, 372
Schuster, Alan J. 258
Schutter, Laura 211-214
Schutzel, Laura 47, 126, 162, 188, 196, 208, 267, 280, 314, 322
Schwartz-Buryiak, Francine 229
Schwartz, Andrew 128, 132, 403
Schwartz, Beth Newburger 243
Schwartz, Clifford 184, 187, 188
Schwartz, Craig 256, 258
Schwartz, E. 304
Schwartz, Heath 106, 162, 196, 200, 208, 238, 314, 411
Schwartz, Jake Ezra 246
Schwartz, Josh 301
Schwartz, Stephen 362, 365, 384, 402
Schwarz, Joe 369
Schwarzwalder, Liz Jurist 183, 189, 217
Schweitzer, Adam 258
Schwencke, Jake Evan 46, 49, 60, 62
Schwimmer, David 26
Sciolan, Mirko 56
Sciotto, Eric 300, 301
Sclafani, Sal 133
Sclafani, Vincent 25, 112, 114
Scoblick, Jessica 47
Scopo, Christopher 337
Score, Robert C. 400
Scorsese, Martin 139
Scotcher, David 217
Scott, David 183, 189, 217
Scott, Dorothy 422
Scott, Eric 343
Scott, Jack 25, 314, 315
Scott, Jessica 8
Scott, Les 61, 65, 277, 279
Scott, Matthew 161, 318, 319, 323
Scott, Michael James 131, 134
Scott, Oz 403
Scott, Ramsey 238
Scott, Rashidra 34, 109-111, 116, 127, 129
Scott, Sherie Rene 91, 92, 96, 387, 389
Scott, Thea Bradshaw 349, 351, 352
Scribner, Justin 119
Scully, Dan 25, 95, 102, 250
Sean Palmer 187
Sears, Brian 109-111, 116, 171, 172, 175
Seastone, Victor 25, 302, 303, 330
Seawell, Norman 163
Sebesky, Don 79, 81
Sebouhian, Carly Blake 261, 262, 264, 265
Sechrest, Marisa 174, 349, 350
Sedgwick, Toby 340
Seegal, Denise V. 243
Seeley, Drew 184, 186, 190
Seeley, Mark 58, 114, 196, 281, 304
Seelig, Chip 343
Seery, Florie 76, 78, 305, 308, 345, 347, 398
Sees, Christina 39, 168, 225, 291
Sefcovic, Thomas 192
Seff, Richard 375
Segal, Martin E. 255
Segal, Nina 138, 296
Segal, Ray 101
Segal, Tobias 232, 233
Segura, Aurora 231
Segura, Enrique 176-178
Seib, Chad 211-214
Seibert, Gary 217, 218
Seid, John J. 173
Seiden, Alyssa 373
Seidler, Lee J. 31, 36, 39, 48, 58, 74, 88, 106, 120, 138, 151, 168, 174, 200, 208, 225, 243, 258, 267, 281, 285, 296, 315, 334, 338, 352
Seidman, Stanley 249
Seidner, Allison 2, 7, 10
Seifert, Jason 58
Seiler, Roy 360, 361
Seinfeld, Jerry 370
Seiver, Sarah 61, 65, 318
Sekinger, Regina Anna, Dr. 330
Seldes, Marian 389, 391
Seligman, Miles 6
Seligson, Gary 42, 369
Sellars, Lee 354-356
Seller, Jeffrey 32, 34, 36, 140, 143, 145, 155, 156, 354, 357
Sellon, Kim 132, 133
Selway, Philip James 347
Selya, John viii, 79, 81, 84, 121-123
Semaan, Sue 174, 230
Semark, Jane 255
Semlitz, Steve 97
Semon, Timothy R. iv, 76, 77, 78, 249, 250, 369
Sendroff, Mark 145, 200
Senewiratne, Tania 58, 196, 255
Sengbloh, Saycon vii, 97, 98, 103, 131
Senn, Kenneth 13, 66, 95, 274, 322, 343, 373
Sepulveda, Carmen 58
Sepulveda, Fernando 314
Serafini, Matthew 46
Serignese, Alana 47
Serna, Andrew 163, 398
Serota, Natalie 416
Serotsky, Aaron 28, 29
Seroukas, Chris 57
Serpico, Alex 322
Serra, Tony 216
Servilio, Aldo "Butch" 181, 182
Sesco, Michelle 162
Sese, Jen 127, 129
Sessions, Kate 78, 308, 347
Sessions, William S. 243
Settle, Matthew 73
Setzer, Brian 58
Seufferlein, Tescia 66, 174
Severson, Sten 145
Sevush, Ralph 402
Sewell, Norman 133
Seymour, Amanda 352
Seymour, Kenny J. 219, 220, 222, 225
Seymour, Robert 238, 342
Shacket, Devin 94, 321
Shacket, Mark 230, 234, 256, 258, 276, 280
Shaddow, Elena 164, 166
Shaevitz, Glenn 419
Shafer, Samantha 328, 354, 355, 357
Shaffer, Bee 308
Shaffer, Jeremy 6, 7, 69, 73, 74, 267, 402, 413
Shaffer, Stan 101, 102
Shah, Sheeraz 48
Shahzad, Faisal viii
Shaiman, Marc 275
Shakespeare, William 135, 137
Shakun, Melissa 66, 274, 315
Shalhoub, Tony viii, 171, 172, 175, 390
Shalom, Janine 48
Shanahan, Shane 311
Shankman, Hannah 131
Shanley, Joey 410
Shapiro, Anna D. 28, 29, 31, 338
Shapiro, Bruce 347
Shapiro, Louis 77, 78, 307, 308, 347
Shapiro, Tamar 410
Share, Elizabeth 205
Sharma, Rajesh 409
Sharman, Clint 153
Sharnell, LaQuet 180, 219, 221, 226
Sharp, Alan 126
Sharpe, Maya 131
Sharpe, Michael 369
Sharron, Danny 156
Shatner, William 162
Shaw, Barry 207
Shaw, Benjy 183, 189, 217
Shaw, Carl Roberts 217
Shaw, Darryl 70
Shaw, Kaitlin 47, 126, 162, 196, 267, 280, 314, 322
Shaw, Keith 360, 361
Shaw, Lynn 232, 234
Shaw, Matthew Byam 85, 135, 294
Shaw, Rob 355
Shaw, Tommy R. 304
Shaw, Tro 358
Shayne, Verne 359
Shea, Bill 238
Shea, Matt 48
Shea, Patrick 373
Sheanshang, George 334
Shearer, Patrick 402
Sheehan, Joanna 407
Sheehan, Kelly iv, 152-154, 157
Sheffler, Gillian 333
Shefter, Stuart 196, 243, 250
Sheik, Kacie 131, 134
Sheldon, Marilynn 219, 223, 225
Shell, Roger 110, 113, 185
Shelley, Carole 41, 43, 50
Shelp, Woody 267
Shemin, Craig 36
Shenton, Mark 419
Shepard, Brian 121-123
Shepp, Michael L., Jr. 83, 188, 291
Sheppard, John 6, 213
Shepsle, Seth 77, 78, 307, 308
Sher, Bartlett 151, 324, 327, 330
Sher, Lee 232-234
Sherbill, Rachel 7, 13, 95, 106, 120, 138, 196, 238, 274, 296, 314, 334, 342
Sherer, Werner 404
Sheridan, Jessica

Index

211-213
Sheridan, Win 298
Sherman, Bill 140, 143, 147
Sherman, Clara 145
Sherman, Dana 168
Sherman, Laura 363
Sherman, Marlon 215
Sherman, Richard M. 183, 211, 212, 214
Sherman, Robert B. 183, 211, 212, 214
Sherrell, Kat 145
Sherrill, Stephen C. 243
Sherry, Allison 88
Sherry, Colleen M. 102
Shevelove, Burt 319
Shevett, Anita iv, 13, 95, 274, 322, 373, 396, 409
Shevett, Holli 6
Shevett, Steve iv, 13, 66, 95, 274, 322, 373, 396, 409
Shevitz, Elisa 397
Shew, Timothy 60-62, 67
Shiach, Dominic 168
Shier, Joel 8, 188
Shiffrin, David E. 243
Shimmin, Greg 296
Shine, Cara 48
Shipler, Corey 102
Shipman, Andrew 211, 213
Shipman, Madisyn 85, 86, 88
Shively, A.J. 164, 166
Shivers, John 182, 184, 187, 216, 245, 247
Shmuger, Marc 48, 369
Shnayder, Jacob 238
Shoemake, Evan 400, 403
Shoemaker, Peter 53, 231, 267, 304, 334, 342
Shookhoff, David 78, 308, 347, 398
Short, Martin 244
Shortall, Tim 164, 166, 388

Shorter, Alexis 188
Shotwell, Kevin 60-62
Shrime, Maria 181, 182
Shrubsole, David 88
Shufelt-Dine, Debra 266
Shuford, Bret 184-186
Shugoll, Mark 243
Shulman, Jonathan 31, 174, 337, 338, 402
Shultz, Dulce 83
Shunkey, Mark 362, 364
Siataga, Daniela 57
Sibson, Sally E. 242
Siccardi, Arthur 41, 44, 69, 72, 164, 167, 198-200, 205, 208
Siccardi, Drew 182, 216
Sicoli, Matt 102, 342
Sidorchuk, Monica 13, 65, 94, 273, 321, 343, 372
Sieber, Christopher 310, 311, 316, 379, 381
Siebert, Heather 13, 66, 92, 95, 272, 274, 322, 343, 373
Siebert, Jeff 208
Siegel, Adam 148, 151, 324, 330, 369
Siegel, Alan 407
Siegel, Kyra Ynez 232, 233
Siegel, Ray 113
Siegel, Scott 382
Siegmund, Katie 113
Sierra, Ray 421
Siesko, David 290, 358
Sigler, Jeff 368
Sikakane, Mpume 180
Sikora, Megan 276, 277, 278
Silas, Jessica 8
Silbar, Jeff 20
Silber, Chic 362, 365
Sills, Douglas 377, 378
Silva, Eddie 420
Silver, Cynthia 285

Silver, Jaki 234
Silver, Jennifer Esq. 36
Silver, Joel 133, 242, 342
Silver, Matthew 282, 284, 285
Silverman, Antoine 311
Silverman, Ken 243, 369
Silverman, Leigh 403
Silverman, Les 243
Silverman, Melody 88
Silverman, Ryan 261, 263, 268, 269
Silvers, Dolores "Vicki" 83
Silverstone, Alicia viii, 345-348
Silvian, Scott 6, 8
Simard, Jennifer 310, 312
Simmons-DeFord, Michael 408
Simmons, Collette 203, 204, 206
Simmons, Jean 422
Simmons, Valerie D. 12, 20, 65, 66, 94, 273, 320, 321, 343, 372, 399
Simoes, Samantha 8
Simon, Alan 8, 47
Simon, Gary 329
Simon, Jil 419
Simon, Neil vii, viii, 51-53, 276, 278
Simone, Nick 12, 65, 94, 273, 321, 343, 372
Simone, Nina 255
Simonson, Eric 31, 338
Simonson, Robert 419
Simpson-Wentz, Ashlee 69-71, 75
Simpson, Angela 25, 307, 308, 346, 347
Simpson, Jessica 75
Simpson, Mark 126, 145, 225
Simpson, Peter 58
Simunovich, Paige 109, 111
Sinatra, Frank viii, 79, 81, 83, 102, 322
Sinatra, Nancy 84
Sinder, Michael 58,

114, 196, 255, 304
Sine, Jeffrey 51, 286, 332
Singer, David 28, 29, 31
Singer, Kenneth 420
Singer, Michael E. 243
Singer, Michelle 281
Singer, Scott 315
Singh, Nalene 13, 66, 95, 274, 322, 343, 373
Singley, James H. 168
Siniscalchi, Vincent 112
Sinise, Gary 31, 338
Sinsheimer, Matt 145, 250
Siracusa, Tom 164
Sirkin, Spring 171, 172
Sisk, Laura 168
Sita, Jim 405
Siu, Aileen 416
Skaff, Greg 363
Skaggs, Corey 211-214
Skelly, John 78, 308, 347
Skillin, Ray 329
Skillman, Peter 58
Skimelis, Vaidas 56
Skinner, Pam 164
Skinner, Randy 152, 155
Sklar-Heyn, Seth 112, 114, 191, 193, 196
Sklar, Matthew 18, 310, 312
Skoff, Rebecca 343
Skolnick, Sara 230
Skowron, Jeff 85, 86, 89
Skriloff, Nina 74, 168
Slade, Donna J. 343
Slansky, Paul 373
Slaten, Julianna 88
Slater, Emma 56
Slater, Glenn 184, 185, 187
Slaton, Shannon 267, 369
Slattery, Jenny 125, 126, 258
Slaven, Rachel 78, 347
Slay, Frank, Jr. 163

Slayton, Shannon 100, 102
Slevin, Baile 255
Slinger, Michaeljon 358
Sloan, Beverly 401
Sloan, Christopher 242, 243, 280
Sloat, Bill 355
Slocum, Jess 145
Slocum, Melissa 262, 266
Smagula, Jimmy 265
Smalls, Janine 163
Smalls, Marva 407
Smanko, Michael 132, 133
Smarsch, Arthur J. 217
Smart, Annie 148
Smedes, Tom 236
Smerdon, Vic 41, 47
Smiley, Mick 304
Smirnoff, Karina vi, 54, 55, 59
Smith, Abigail 266
Smith, Adam 298
Smith, Alissa 22
Smith, Andy 408
Smith, Brendan 266, 267
Smith, Bryan 25
Smith, Chad 363
Smith, Christopher C. 29, 31, 38
Smith, Cotter 236-239
Smith, Cypress Eden 180
Smith, David 262, 266
Smith, Derek 176, 178, 182, 200
Smith, Doug 409
Smith, Douglas G. 97, 252
Smith, Easton 46, 50
Smith, Elizabeth A. 255
Smith, Erika 266, 267
Smith, Fred 265
Smith, Gareth 369
Smith, Greg 178, 181
Smith, Howie Michael 34
Smith, Jada Pinkett 97, 103, 107
Smith, Jeromy 31, 88, 285, 338

Smith, Jocelyn 20, 64, 66, 93
Smith, Joseph 48, 230, 276
Smith, Keith Randolph 104, 105
Smith, Kelly 250, 296
Smith, Kevin 315
Smith, Laura 298
Smith, Lisa Velten 11, 12, 15
Smith, Lois 31, 338
Smith, Mae 35, 257, 296
Smith, Maris 250, 418
Smith, MaryAnn D. 8
Smith, Michelle 301
Smith, Molly 200, 243
Smith, Niegel 97, 102
Smith, Philip J. 28, 31, 32, 36-39, 41, 48, 54, 58, 69, 74, 85, 87, 88, 104, 106, 117, 118, 120, 135, 138, 148, 151, 164, 168, 171, 172, 174, 198, 200, 202, 208, 219, 225, 240, 243, 256, 258, 261, 267, 276, 281, 282, 285, 294, 296, 310, 315, 332-335, 338, 349, 351, 352, 395
Smith, Richard A. 152
Smith, Rolt 329
Smith, Tim 322
Smith, Wallace 127, 129, 286, 287, 289
Smith, Wayne 167
Smith, Will 97, 103, 107
Smithyman, Paul 88, 151, 330
Smits, Jimmy 117, 118, 120
Smolenski, Tony IV 47, 334
Smolokowski, Slava 97
Snape, Edward 340, 341
Snee, Richard 274
Snider, Daniel Dee 304
Snipes, Wesley 103

Index

Snow, Jason 184-186, 188, 324, 326, 327
Snow, Susan 73
Snow, Tom 58
Snowdon, Richard W. 243
Snyder, Andy 133
Snyder, Rick 31, 338
Snyder, Stephen "Hoops" 159
Sobel, Edward 28, 335
Sobel, Eric 409
Socha, Alexandra 51, 52
Sod, Ted 12, 65, 94, 273, 321, 343, 372, 399
Soenksen, Shirley 330
Sogliuzzo, Cara 200, 417
Solberg, Kirsten 144
Solimando, Dana 268
Solomon, David 66, 163, 245, 248, 250, 270, 322
Solomon, Jerold E. 324, 325, 327
Solomon, Mary 270, 343
Soloway, Leonard 198-200
Somers, Alyssa 183, 189, 217
Somers, Asa 242
Somma, Maria iv
Sondheim, Stephen iii, vi, vii, viii, ix, 20, 96, 191, 193, 196, 197, 318, 320, 322, 323, 354, 357, 375, 379, 385
Sonn, Larry 188
Sonnleitner, Paul J. 133
Soper, Sonja 58, 196
Sordelet, Rick 105, 106, 176, 184, 187, 256, 257, 305, 307, 335, 336
Sorenson, Deanna 266
Sorenson, Stephen T. 31
Soriano, Henry 55
Soriano, Sarah 54, 55
Sosnow, Pat 279, 280, 333, 334
Sosnowski, Stephen 31, 133, 231, 234, 258, 338, 352, 415
Soto, Daniel 97-99, 103
Soto, Lillian 13, 66, 95, 274, 322, 343, 373
Sour, Robert B. 82
Souther, Susan 315
Southern, Ted 8
Souza, Samantha i, iii, iv, 124, 125, 199, 419
Sovar, Rodd 53, 188
Sovern, Michael I. 31, 36, 39, 48, 58, 74, 88, 106, 120, 138, 151, 168, 174, 200, 208, 225, 243, 258, 267, 281, 285, 296, 315, 334, 338, 352
Soyk, Art 207
Spacey, Kevin 252, 253, 255
Spadaro, Stephen 74, 168
Spader, James vii, 282, 283, 285
Spaeth, Phillip 354, 355, 357
Spahn, Karen 183, 280, 291, 330, 369
Spanger, Amy 300
Sparks, Jordin 147
Spear, Steve 329
Spears, Rebecca 250
Speck, Jake 158-160
Spector, Jarrod 158, 159, 161
Spector, Morgan 349, 350, 352, 353
Speer, David 144, 145
Speer, Stephen 181, 182
Speidel, Lise 13, 65, 94, 274, 321, 343, 372, 399
Speirits, Hannah 417
Spelling, Candy 276, 279
Spence, Lew 83, 102
Spencer, Charlie 249
Spencer, Cody 25
Spencer, J. Robert iv, 240, 241, 244
Spencer, Joanna 401
Spencer, Jonathan 114, 156, 369
Spencer, Marieke 48
Spencer, Susan 315
Spender, Lizzie 16, 17, 20
Sperber, Stephanie 48
Sperling, Ted 121, 124, 324, 327
Sperr, Ken 74, 168
Speyer, Michael 109, 112, 276, 279
Spielberg, Steven 26
Spier, David 159
Spillane, Katie 125, 230
Spinac, Rebecca 238
Spinello, Shanna iv, 345, 347, 348
Spinney, Cory 13, 66, 95, 274, 322, 373
Spinoza, Tony 168
Spirtas, Kevin 109, 281
Spitulnik, Brian 69-71, 75
Spivak, Allen 164, 167
Spivey, Aaron 78, 174, 250, 308
Spore, Heather 362-364
Sporer, Aaron 25, 95, 133, 242
Sposito, Stephen 280, 314
Spradling, Jim 224
Spradling, Valerie 30, 31, 88, 234, 338
Sprecher, Ben 51, 52
Springer, Jerry 72
Spry, David Ryan 163
Spry, James 236
Squire, Rosemary 124, 126, 255
Squitero, Roger 55
St. Hill, Michele 409
St. Martin, Charlotte 380, 384, 397, 410
St. Pierre, Derek 301, 303
Stabeno, Michael Liam 235
Stackle, Steve 216, 218
Stafford, Jennifer 399
Staggs, Tymand 409
Stahl, Bill 315
Stahl, David 80, 113
Stallings, Heidi 12, 65, 94, 273, 321, 343, 372
Stallings, Lawrence 127, 129
Stallsworth, Edward 163
Stamos, John vi, vii, ix, 60, 62, 67, 68, 162, 380, 381
Stamp, Sarah 266, 267
Stampley, Nathaniel 176, 178
Stancil, Kellen 181
Stanczyk, Laura 286, 291
Stang, Arnold 422
Stang, Rebecca 78, 347
Stange, Rachel 208, 255, 342
Stanley, Elizabeth 227, 228
Stanley, Serena 188
Stanton, Ben 369
Starken, Karen 266
Staroba, Paul 192, 196
Starobin, Michael 188, 240, 241, 318, 320
Starr, Josh 53
Staszewski, Steven 31, 173, 337
Staton, Dan 30, 161
Staub, Joanna Lynne 31, 280
Staub, Nicholas 162
Stavola, Nicholas 31
Steckler, Michele 183, 188, 217
Steele, Ryan 354, 356
Steele, Sarah 243
Steele, Shelby 285
Steeves, Finnerty 51, 52
Stefaniuk, John 176, 180, 182
Steffen, David B. 11, 13, 60, 66, 91, 94, 270, 274, 318, 321, 343, 371, 372
Steffens-Kubala, Cindy 156
Stegall, Bridget A. 163
Steggert, Bobby 286, 288, 388
Stegman, Beth 168
Steig, William 310
Steiger, Rick 79, 83, 305, 307-309
Steiger, Susan Jean 335
Stein, Corrieanne 45
Stein, Jared 22, 27
Stein, Rikki 102
Steinberg, Harold 11, 12
Steinberg, Mimi 11
Steinberg, Nevin 4, 34, 63, 105, 130, 143, 155, 289
Steinberg, Sheila 51
Steiner, Rick 28, 30, 158, 161
Steingraeber, Ellen 66
Steinhagen, Natasha 77, 78, 307, 308, 346, 347
Steinhaus, Amy 397
Steinlein, Jean 156, 217
Steinmeyer, Jim 216
Steitzer, Jeff 211, 213
Stella, Tim 262, 266, 267
Stelzenmuller, Craig 95, 188
Stenborg, Derek 314
Stenborg, Helen 393
Stephens, Sophia 176, 177, 179
Stephenson, Don 298, 299
Stephenson, Harry Keith 101
Stepnik, Sue 100, 102, 254, 255
Stern, Cheryl 164-166, 170
Stern, David 281
Stern, Dewitt 250
Stern, Eric 310, 311
Stern, James D. 152, 191
Stern, Jolyon F. 88, 285
Stern, Matthew Aaron 188
Stern, Rachel 310, 312
Stern, Sarah 36
Stern, Vera 255
Sternberg, Julia 114
Sternberg, Taylor 158-160, 162
Stetson, Wendy Rich 148, 149
Stevens, Gregory 373
Stevens, Jesse 302, 303
Stevens, Lauren 56, 290
Stevens, Libby 361
Stevens, Rachael 255
Stevens, Scott 408
Stevens, Thatcher 78, 308, 347, 398
Stevenson, Vicki 196
Stewart-Coleman, SaCha 104, 107
Stewart, Alexis 224
Stewart, Christopher 20
Stewart, Duncan 69, 72, 164, 166
Stewart, Erin 191-193
Stewart, Jamie 145, 146
Stewart, Jennifer 397
Stewart, Kyle 291
Stewart, Michael 48, 60, 63
Stewart, Neil Patrick 238
Stewart, Seth 143, 144
Stief, Marshall 322
Stiers, David Ogden 152, 154, 157
Stifelman, Leslie 69, 70, 75
Stiff, Barclay 51, 53, 85, 87, 88
Stiles, G. Warren 280
Stiles, George 211, 212, 214
Stiles, Julia vii, 256
Stiles, Warren 39, 133
Stilgoe, Richard 261, 264
Still, Matt 48
Stiller, Ben 238, 244
Stiller, Christine Taylor 238
Stillman, Darin 8, 105, 106
Stimler, Nicholas 12, 65, 94, 273, 321, 372
Stimson, Brendon 354, 355, 357

Index

Stites, Kevin 245
Stitt, Georgia 188
Stock, Chelsea Morgan iv, 184, 186, 187, 189, 190
Stocke, Matthew 301
Stockman, Theo 21-23, 27, 131
Stockton, Kendra 225
Stokes-Chin, Lisa 326
Stokes, R. Christopher 280
Stolber, Dean 281
Stoll, Alex Michael 359
Stoll, Corey 349, 350, 352, 353
Stollberger, Erich 125
Stolle, Jeremy 261, 262, 264
Stoller, Mike 231
Stollings, David 53, 242
Stone, Amber 46
Stone, Daryl 120, 234, 255, 334, 361
Stone, David 240, 241, 244, 362, 365, 369, 370, 384
Stoneman, Julian 208
Storey, Suzanne 6, 8
Storto, Daniel 281
Stothard, David 126
Stott, Ken 117, 118, 120
Stovall, James 109-111
Stowe, Dennis 310, 312, 317
Strallen, Scarlett 211-213, 218
Strang, David 156
Strangfeld, Jason 315
Strasfeld, Sam 211, 212, 214, 218
Strasser, Anna 291
Strassheim, Michael 168, 196, 200, 208, 238, 239, 291, 386, 411
Strassler, Abbie M. 21, 25
Stratton, Tari 402
Straus, Aaron 20, 64, 66, 230
Straus, Barney 21
Straus, Robert V. 422
Straus, Tracy 21
Strecker, Worth 132
Streep, Meryl 175, 353
Street, Neal 294, 295
Streisand, Barbra 322, 323
Stribling, Barak 225, 267
Stricklen, Samuel 335, 336
Strimel, Sarrah 376
Strindberg, August vii, 11, 12
Stringer, Howard 407
Stritch, Billy 385
Stritch, Elaine 323, 385
Strohl, Jordan 410
Strohmeyer, Kevin 216, 218
Strohmeyer, Sean 181, 182
Stroker, Ali 377
Stroman, Susan 151, 330
Stromer, Diane 315
Strong, Allison 60, 62
Strong, Edward 160, 163, 398
Strong, Jean 200
Strothmann, Ben 395, 400, 406, 413, 421
Strouse, Charles vi, 60, 63, 67, 68
Struble, Christine 95
Strum, Alec 13
Strunk, James 238
Strus, Lusia 85, 86
Struxness, Betsy 223, 366
Stuart, Claudia 58, 114, 196, 304
Stuart, Todd 74, 168
Stuckey, Jack 70, 75
Stuhl, Seth 183, 189, 217
Stuis, Chuck 238, 342
Stump, Christine 8
Stumpfova, Katarina 56
Sturgis, Nisi 340, 341, 344
Sturm, Samantha 1, 2, 4
Stutz, Geraldine 255
Styler, Kim 234
Styles, Rick 314
Styne, Jule 83
Styres, Jason 114, 196, 304
Suarez, Crystal 13, 94, 95, 274
Suarez, Dora 125
Subotnick, Stuart 31, 36, 39, 48, 58, 74, 88, 106, 120, 138, 151, 168, 174, 200, 208, 225, 243, 258, 267, 281, 285, 296, 315, 334, 338, 352
Suchman, Scott 200
Sudduth, Skipp 328
Sudranski, Mendy 78, 308, 347
Sugarman, Merri 47, 126, 162, 188, 196, 208, 267, 280, 314, 322
Sugden, Damon iv, 54, 55, 59
Sugden, Rebecca iv, viii, 54, 55, 59
Sugg, Jeff 393
Suidgeest, Trent 48
Suli-Garcia, Hilda 360, 361
Sulka, Tim 162, 163
Sullivan, Annie viii
Sullivan, Chip 315
Sullivan, Daniel 12, 65, 78, 94, 151, 273, 308, 321, 330, 343, 345, 346, 347, 348, 372, 403
Sullivan, Erica 148, 149
Sullivan, Frank 304
Sullivan, John M. Jr. 243
Sullivan, Julia 36
Sullivan, Kevin 78
Sullivan, Lehan 156
Sullivan, Mary Stewart 85, 86, 89
Sullivan, Patrick 41, 47, 114, 164, 182, 198, 200
Sully, Laura 296
Summa, Don 102, 109, 114, 413
Summers, Eric LaJuan 184, 186, 190
Sumner, Jarid 7, 13, 95, 106, 138, 196, 238, 274, 296, 334
Sunderland, Garth Edwin 354
Supeck, Steve 83
Supple, Edmond F. Sr. 400
Surdi, Frank 13, 65, 94, 273, 321, 343, 372, 399
Susan Medak 373
Susemiehl, Pam 285
Suskin, Steven 419
Susman, Sally 407
Sussman, Rita 73
Suttmann, Robert 110, 113
Sutton, Amy 25
Sutton, Charlie 1, 4, 366
Sutton, Maia 114
Sutton, Rob 377
Suyama, Y. Darius 36, 106, 138, 145, 156, 291, 361, 415
Suzuki, Mikiko 330
Svendsen, Jan 397
Swan, Richard 188
Swanson, Joann 150, 151, 200
Swayze, Patrick 422
Swee, Daniel 117, 148, 151, 330
Sweeney, Will 231
Sweet, Steven 304
Swenson, Will 134, 377, 379
Swerling, Jo 121
Swinsky, Morton 5, 32, 34, 72, 82, 97, 100, 283, 349, 350
Switser, Austin 303, 322
Swope, G. Benjamin 102
Swope, Martha 322
Sykes, Ephraim M. 219-221, 226
Syracuse, Gloria 359
Szot, Paulo 324-326
Szymanski, Maria 367
Szymanski, Michael J. 369

T

Tabeek, James 216
Taccone, John 217
Taccone, Tony 21, 24, 371, 373
Tagert, Ronald 7, 8, 250, 291
Taggart, Christopher 31, 106, 120, 174, 315, 352
Taguchi, Hiroko 2, 7, 95, 242
Takagi, Teruyo 13
Takami, Janet iv, 340, 342, 344
Takemasa, Yoshihiro 98
Tal, Mirit 102
Tallent, Carl 12, 65, 94, 273, 321, 343, 372
Talmadge, Elizabeth 243, 369
Tanner, Vickie 12, 65, 94, 273, 321, 343, 372
Tanokura, Yoshinori 308
Tapia, Rebecca 54, 56, 59
Tartaglia, John 313
Tatad, Robert 217, 298, 300, 301, 303
Tate, Judy 78, 308, 347
Tate, Mandy 102
Tate, Steve 31
Taupin, Bernie 304
Tavares, Dayton 46, 49
Tavarez, Shannon Skye 176, 178
Tayabji, Munira 315
Taylor-Corbett, Shaun 143, 146
Taylor-Stackle, April 181
Taylor, Allison 78, 308, 347, 398
Taylor, Andrew 78, 308, 347
Taylor, Bensinger 164
Taylor, Cathy 31
Taylor, Elizabeth 322, 373
Taylor, Hodge 41, 42, 44
Taylor, James 331
Taylor, Kristi 308
Taylor, L. Steven 176, 177, 179
Taylor, Lili 96
Taylor, Marion Finkler 83, 168, 361
Taylor, Mark A. 422
Taylor, Matthew 274
Taylor, Michael 46
Taylor, Millie 8
Taylor, Moellenberg 21
Taylor, Scott 191, 196
Taylor, Terry 8, 189
Taylor, Wesley 1, 4, 9, 300
Taymor, Julie 176, 177, 180
Tazewell, Paul 121, 124, 140, 143, 219, 222, 232, 233, 388
Teague-Daniels, Danielle 156
Teague, Townsend 254, 255
Teal, James 114, 196, 216, 304
Teare, Claire 207
Tedder, Cary 219, 221
Tedesco, Clark Mims 234, 255
Teitelbaum, Shari 409
Telsey, Bernard 5, 18, 19, 86, 88, 143, 145, 222, 225, 229, 241, 248, 283, 285, 300, 303, 327, 330, 336, 365, 369
Tempest, Joey 304
Temple, Richard 126
Tenenbaum, Ann 243
Tepe, Heather 46
Termine, Richard 255, 318, 385
Terrell, Audrey 216
Terrell, Danny 46
Terrell, Sheila 181, 183
Terry, Beatrice 118, 120, 222, 225
Terry, George E. 31
Tesarck, Bethany Ann 60-62
Tesori, Jeanine 310, 312
Testa, Mary 121, 123
Testa, Stephanie 48
Tetlow, George 78, 308, 347
Tewksbury, Stephen 265
Thaler, Jordan 127, 130
Tharp, Twyla viii, 79, 81, 82, 84, 388,

The Playbill Broadway Yearbook 2009-2010

Index

392
Thayer, Ann 133
Theriault, Vanessa 8
Thibault, Gilles 83
Thibert, Kesler i, iii, iv, 419
Thibodeau, Marc iv, 7, 74, 267, 413
Thione, Lorenzo 21
Thirtle, Rob 8
Thomas, Barbara Schaps 343
Thomas, Danielle K. 32, 33
Thomas, Fiona 183, 189, 217
Thomas, Gemma 48
Thomas, James E. 243
Thomas, Kevin David 191-193
Thomas, Ray Anthony 282, 283
Thomas, Richard vii, 31, 282, 283, 285
Thomas, Rod 57
Thomas, Sherry 158, 160, 283, 285
Thomas, Terrance 127, 129
Thomasson, Christopher 352
Thompson, Ahmir "Questlove" 97
Thompson, Ben 21-23, 25, 27
Thompson, Bradley 242
Thompson, Charles 367
Thompson, Chris 266
Thompson, Crystal 188, 196
Thompson, David 48, 69
Thompson, Jason 162
Thompson, Jennifer Laura viii, 171, 172, 175
Thompson, John Douglas 393
Thompson, Kristie 369
Thompson, Louisa 393
Thompson, Mark 117, 118, 202, 205
Thompson, Maura 113
Thompson, Stuart 16-19, 104-106, 117, 118, 120, 171, 172, 174, 236-238, 310, 312, 314, 349, 350, 352
Thomson, Caitlyn 36, 145, 156, 291, 361
Thorn, Daniel 400
Thorn, David 401
Thorne, Alec 8
Thornton, Angela 422
Thorton, Christopher 360
Thorton, Karen 83
Thrasher, Mark 2, 7, 61, 65, 122, 125
Threadgold, Elsa 168
Thun, Nancy 120, 162, 208
Thymius, Greg 125
Tiberio, Cheri 369
Tiberio, Russell III 267, 268
Tick, Donald 236, 238, 340, 342
Ticotin, Nancy 144
Tidwell, Danny 219, 221
Tierney, Matt 393
Tiggeloven, John 97, 102, 188, 217
Tighe, Susanne 39, 120, 162, 200, 208, 352, 411
Tillinger, John 200
Timbers, Alex 162, 392
Tinder, Clifford S. 419
Ting, Liuh-Wen 61, 65, 277
Tingir, Nicole 78
Tiomkin, Dimitri 342
Tippit, Wayne 422
Tirado, Candido 78, 308, 347
Tirado, Ismeal 280, 314
Tisue, Dave 181, 183
Tiwary, Vivek J. 21
Tjoelker, Victoria 314
Tobak, Suzanne 25, 258, 410
Toben, Barbara 183, 189, 217
Toben, Paul 66, 95, 242
Tobia, Julie 320, 322
Tobia, Ron 13, 66, 95, 274, 322, 373
Tobia, Ronnie 63
Tobin, Becca 298, 299
Tobin, Robert L.B. 393
Tobolski, Nicky 114
Todd, Jaimie 47
Todorov, Entcho 311
Todorowski, Ron 79-81, 121-123, 362, 364
Toguville, James 281
Tokarz, Katherine 298, 299, 303
Tolan, Cindy 32, 36, 349
Tolkan, Parmalee Welles 315
Tomasetti, Anne 234
Tomczyk, Curt 330
Tomkins, Steve 227, 243
Tomlin, Lara 308
Tomlin, Lily 200
Tomlinson, Margaret 243
Tompkins, Kimberly 31
Tompkins, Tim 380
Tone, Una 288
Tong, Jolie 12, 65, 94, 273, 321, 343, 372
Toppall, Lawrence S. 198
Torcellini, Jamie 45
Toribio, Chris 421
Torns, Stephanie 366
Torre, Maggie 355
Torre, Marian 183
Torres, Jaime 174
Torres, Paula 409
Torres, Wilson 141, 144, 146, 147
Torya 181
Toscano, Rob 360
Totero, Laura 58
Totero, Lolly 195, 196
Toth, Helen 217
Towlun, David 66
Townsend, K.C. 422
Townshend, Pete 20
Toy, Mary Mon 422
Tracey, Ashley 163, 398
Trachtenberg, Jamie 410
Traina, Joseph 106, 127, 352
Tramontozzi, Dan 144, 249, 250
Trapasso, Joe 87
Traube, Victoria 156, 330
Traugott, Scott 208, 250
Travers, James Sr. 291
Travers, Mitchell 66
Travis, Benjamin 25
Travis, Doris Eaton 49, 386, 422
Travis, Ken 219, 222
Travis, Merle 231
Travolta, John 370
Traxler, Steve 5, 28, 29, 82, 87, 248, 283
Treagus, Andrew 207, 208
Treherne, Nichola 205, 208
Treisman, Jonathan 48
Tremaine, Davis Wright 39, 106
Trent, Diana 320, 322
Trent, Matt 41, 42, 44
Trepasso, Joe 138
Trevisan, Luke 45, 46, 50
Trezza, Mark 196, 295, 296
Tribble, Sean 66
Tricarico, Taylor 351
Trice, Will 20, 88
Trigg, David 153, 277
Trimm, Allie 60, 62, 67, 68
Triner, James 19, 120, 238, 310, 312, 314, 352
Trinidad, Kay 184-187
Tripp, Elizabeth 410
Tripp, Rickey 140-142, 147
Troillett, Matthew 78, 347
Troisi, Louis 182
Troob, Danny 8, 184, 187, 310, 312
Tropp, CJ 291
Trotto, Dylan 182
Trotto, Michael 182
Trubitt, Jason 216, 218
True-Frost, Jim 31, 338
Truesdale, Veneda 280, 281
Trujillo, Isaac 280
Trujillo, Sergio 1, 4, 121, 123, 158, 160, 219-221, 240, 241, 392
Truman, Rachel 47
Trump, Donald 26, 197
Trupia, Michael 254
Tsao, James 326
Tsypin, George 184, 187
Tucci, Stanley viii, 171, 172, 175
Tuchman, Christina 183, 189, 217
Tucker, Christopher 267
Tucker, Katy 188
Tucker, Scott 408
Tuft, Diane 60, 318
Tuft, Thomas 318, 343
Tuggle, Brett 304
Tulchin, Norman 85, 126, 164
Tulchin, Steven 126
Tuller, Virginia 234, 255
Tulley, Paul 314
Tunick, Jonathan 20, 60, 63, 276, 279, 389
Tupper, Frank 249
Turano, Robert 349, 350, 353
Turen, Edward 410
Turkington, Alan 135, 136
Turner, Al 216
Turner, David 19, 104, 106, 117, 120, 171, 174, 236, 238, 314, 349, 352
Turner, Erik 304
Turner, Glynn David 167, 168
Turner, Grant 45, 46, 50
Turner, Greg 243
Turner, Kirsten 168
Turner, Lana 269
Turner, Natalie 176, 177, 179
Turner, Phillip 176, 177, 179
Turton, Jay 126
Tuss, Jamie 48
Tuttle, Ashley 79-81
Tveit, Aaron 242, 378
Twist, Basil 1, 5, 10, 392
Tyberg, Theodore 13, 66, 95, 274, 322, 373
Tyndall, Richard 280, 291
Tyrell, Magnus 410
Tyson, CJ 354, 355, 357

U

Ubell, Ethan 66, 94, 274, 321, 343, 373, 399
Uffner, Helen 13
Ulmer, Elizabeth 73
Ulvaeus, Björn 202, 204, 207
Umoh, Stephanie 286, 288, 293, 380, 393
Umphress, Alysha 21-23, 27
Underhill, Charles 46, 47
Union, Kaylin 219
Union, Scott 219
Uno, Chisato 188
Unsworth, Libby 281
Upshaw, Matt 8, 53
Urena, Janett 281
Urie, Michael 393
Urness, Daniel 277, 288
Ushomirskiy, Raisa 407
Utzig, Greg 122, 125, 288

V

Vaccari, David 8, 19, 88, 145, 225, 230, 242, 250, 285, 303, 330, 369
Vaccariello, Patrick 79, 80, 81, 172, 174, 354, 355, 357, 360
Vaccaro, Cristina 12, 65, 94, 273, 321, 343, 372
Vaeth, Margie 406

Index

Valada-Viars, Kristina 28, 29
Valenti, Laura 114, 196, 304
Valentine, Jill 66
Valentine, Stacy 151, 330
Valentino, Joseph P. 83, 156, 250
Vallery, Jill M. 97-99
Valli, Frankie 381
Valli, Robert 156
Vallins, Nikole 53, 109, 112, 114, 152, 155, 156, 182, 200, 234, 342, 407
Vallo, George 20, 120, 133
Valvo, Vincent Jr. 195, 196
Van Achte, Alain 181, 182
van de Craats, Charles 224
van den Ende, Joop 161
Van Der Gaag, Jan Kees 410
Van Duyne, Elisa 109-111, 114, 116
Van Dyke, Will 2, 7, 8, 10
Van Heusen, James 82, 83
Van Heusen, Philip 334
Van Laast, Anthony 202, 205
Van Meter, Quentin 243
Van Nostrand, Ann E. 163
Van Nostrand, Annie 398
Van Tassel, Craig 302
Van Tieghem, David 11, 37
Van, Johnny 230
vanBergen, Jim 53, 351, 352
Vance, Courtney 107
VanderEnde, Matt 363
VanDerlinden, Donna 113
Vanderlinden, Paula 359
Vanderpoel, Mark 122, 125
Vanderwoude, Jason 39
Vanian, Heather 410
Vanstone, Hugh 117, 118, 310, 312, 332, 333
Varags, Byron 101
Varbalow, Jennifer 12, 65, 94, 273, 321, 343, 372
Varelis, Zenovia 397
Vargas, Jorge 8, 13, 95, 188
Vargas, Milagros 333
Vargyas, Carmel 138, 281
Varley, Kelly 235
Varrato, Edmond 422
Varrialle, Stella 320, 322, 372, 373
Vashee, Sita 219, 222
Vashee, Vijay 219, 222
Vasili, Sam 8
Vasquez, Eliana 418
Vasquez, Kim 36, 156, 291
Vaughan, Jennifer 162, 163, 398
Vaughan, Sarah 322
Vaughn, David 316
Vaughn, David F.M. 310-312
Vaughn, Geoffrey 224, 258, 280
Vaughn, Nelson 66
Vaval, Berd 238, 342
Vazquez, Tanairi Sade 354, 355, 357
Veaux, Lauren De 97, 98
Vega, Alvin 372
Vega, Enrique 195, 196
Veitch, John 255
Vela, Mili 101
Vellacorta, Georgina 47
Ventura, Frank 13
Vera, Nella 133
Verbitski, Jaclyn 13, 94, 95, 274, 322, 343, 399
Verbus, Colleen 189
Verdejo, Victor 284
Verga-Lagier, Annette 120
Vergara, Sofia 72
Verlaet, Claire 188, 351, 352
Verlizzo, Frank 200, 417
Vermeer, John 243, 369
Verna, Marco 349, 350
Verna, Scott De 114
Vernon, Kathryn 418
Vershbow, Paul 162
Vessey, Reg 46, 47
Vett, Ilya 182
Vetter, Stephanie 46
Viagas, Ben iv
Viagas, Robert i, ii, iii, viii, 35, 419
Vianni, Monica 102
Viarengo, Jason iv, 369, 370
Vicioso, Edgar 415
Victoria, Traci 202-204, 206
Vidnovic, Martin 382
Vienneau, Alice 410
Viertel, Jack 21, 25, 97, 102, 109, 112, 114, 127, 133, 158, 163, 191, 196, 395
Viertel, Joel 322
Viertel, Tom 54, 56, 191, 194, 252, 254, 258
Viesta, John 352
Vietor, Marc 270, 271
Vietti, Alejo 162, 393
Vilandry, Hayes 39, 315
Villano, Mildred 7
Villatore, Meredith 25, 102, 114, 133, 163
Villatore, Meredith 196
Vincent, Aspen 21-23, 27
Vincent, Tony 21, 22, 25-27
Vinci, Mark 18
Vinkler, Greg 354-356
Viola, Elise 35
Viola, Tom 95, 379, 389, 408
Viravan, Takonkiet 276
Virtmanis, Arturs 188
Viscardo, Danny 6, 291
Vitale, Eric P. 234, 255
Vitale, Richie 80
Vitelli, Ron 88, 138
Vo, Erlinda 8
Vodicka, Ron 176, 181, 182
Vogel, D. 73
Vogel, Debbie 216
Vogel, James 36
Vogeley, Mark 48
Volckhausen, Alex Lyu 125, 126, 279, 280
Voller, Andrew 208
Vollmuller, Sten 168
von Borstel, Barbara 163, 231, 234, 258, 281
Von Gal, Danielle 174, 352
Von Kleist, Erica 2, 7
Von Mayrhauser, Peter 261, 264, 266, 267
Von Vett, Amy 402
Vortmann, Kevin 191, 192, 193
Vowles, Andrew Lee 58
Vrba, Larry 174, 369
Vreeland, Marty 182
Vrzala, Tomas iv, 376
Vucci, Ralph 422

W

Waaser, Carol 401
Wachsberger, Robert 174
Wachtel, Hannah 138
Wade, Susanah 334
Wadsworth, Alison 113
Waggoner, Frederick G. 162
Wagh, Ruthie 133
Wagner, Bruce 373
Wagner, Claudia 13, 373
Wagner, Elizabeth 133
Wagner, George 53, 145, 156, 361, 369
Wagner, Laura 200
Wagner, S.D. 133
Wagner, Stewart 234, 235, 254, 255
Wahlers, Jeremy 6, 8
Waits, Tom 95
Waitz, Aaron 369
Wakefield, Amber 133
Walden, George 133, 163
Walden, Josh 286, 287, 289, 291
Walders, Bridget 315
Waldman, Honey 410
Waldman, Justin 274
Waldron, Louie 361
Waletzko, Craig 121, 122
Walken, Christopher viii, ix, 37, 38, 40, 388, 390
Walker, Alex 417
Walker, Catherine 286, 287, 289, 292
Walker, Chaterine 215
Walker, Crystal 47
Walker, Daisy 162
Walker, Daniel 47, 216
Walker, Jasmin 32, 33
Walker, Jason 376
Walker, Leese 12, 65, 94, 273, 321, 343, 372
Walker, Nancy 243
Walker, Nicole 296
Walker, Vickey 207, 208
Wall, Matt 276-278, 280, 328
Wallace, Eric D. 47
Wallace, Katherine 13, 14
Wallace, Rob 265
Wallace, Vivien 255
Wallach, Eric 12, 65, 94, 273, 321, 343, 372
Walleck, Cat 305, 306, 309
Wallem, Linda 250
Wallwork, Kimberley 207
Walsh, Bill 216
Walsh, Emily 102
Walsh, Thomas 66, 94, 274, 321, 343, 373
Walter, Doug 20
Walter, Jason 315
Walters, Barbara 103
Walters, Happy 298
Walters, Jeff 415
Walters, Matt 8, 189
Walters, Timothy 77, 78, 307, 308, 346, 347
Walters, William J. 400
Walton, Emily 28, 29
Walton, Jim 60-62, 67, 121-123
Walton, Richard 138
Walton, Tony 216
Wanee, Brian 362-364
Wang, Bruce 178
Wang, I 208
Wang, Irene 19, 88, 114, 250, 285
Wankel, Robert E. 28, 31, 32, 36, 37, 38, 39, 41, 48, 54, 58, 69, 74, 85, 88, 104, 106, 117, 118, 120, 135, 138, 148, 151, 164, 168, 171, 172, 174, 198, 200, 202, 208, 219, 225, 240, 243, 256, 258, 261, 267, 276, 281, 282, 285, 294, 296, 310, 315, 332, 334, 338, 349, 351, 352, 395
Waranoff, William 20
Warchus, Matthew 117, 118, 252, 253, 255
Ward, Andre 298, 299
Ward, Anthony 85, 86
Ward, Bethe 264, 266, 267
Ward, Cherise R. 8
Ward, Christopher 183
Ward, Donna Roehn 335
Ward, Jeff 329
Ward, Joel 315
Ward, Judy 168
Ward, Michael 39, 176
Ward, Tony 252, 253
Ware, Tom 198, 200
Waring, Adam 281
Warmbrunn, Erica

Index

66
Warner, Aron 315
Warner, Michael 94, 273, 321
Warren, David 403
Warren, Deborah 183, 189, 217
Warren, Dianna 261, 264
Warren, Harry 95
Warren, Jonathan 362, 363, 365
Warren, Thom Christopher 176, 177, 179
Warshaw, Stella 208
Wasbotten, Marilyn 73
Washington, Denzel iii, viii, ix, 103-105, 107, 108, 387, 388, 393
Washington, Kerry vii, 282, 283, 285
Washington, Steven 183
Wasser, Alan 217, 227, 229, 230, 232-234, 256-258, 261, 264, 267, 276, 279, 280, 396
Wasser, Carol 400
Wasser, Dan 114, 126, 234
Wassner, Aliza 303
Watanabe, Christina 12, 65, 94, 273, 321, 343, 372
Watanachaiyot, Jack 322, 372, 373
Watanachaiyot, James 13, 274
Waterman, Peter 48
Waters, Daryl 219, 220, 222, 387, 389, 392
Waters, Julius 58
Waters, Les 148, 149
Watkins, Amanda 171, 174
Watkins, Maurine Dallas 69
Watkinson, Ryan 131, 276-278
Watkiss, Sophie 138, 296
Watson, Arlene 291
Watson, Beth 78, 296, 308, 347
Watson, Court 126, 330
Watson, Joe 54, 58, 114, 196, 255
Watson, Keith 168
Watson, Tom 1, 5, 51, 52, 227, 229, 270, 271, 276, 279, 298, 300, 305, 322, 330, 349, 350, 362, 365
Watt, Douglas 422
Watt, Michael 245
Watters, Aléna 1, 4
Watts, Daniel 219, 221, 226
Watts, Naomi 353
Waugh, Laurie Rae 48
Waxman-Pilla, Debra 76, 78, 305, 308, 345, 347, 398
Waxman, Anita 85, 87
Waxman, Eddie 291
Waxman, Herschel 8, 53, 83, 126, 145, 156, 183, 189, 231, 250, 291, 304, 361, 369, 396
Waxman, Rick 83, 156, 248, 250
Way, Matt 418
Weaver, Hillary 298
Weaver, Jim 286, 287, 289, 291
Weaver, Matthew 298
Webb, Joanne 410
Webb, Rema 176-179
Webber, Andrew Lloyd 261, 264, 267, 269, 384
Webber, Eddie 361
Webber, John 7, 8, 156
Webber, Julian 41
Webber, Katie 219-221, 301
Weber, Jon 299, 301
Wedderburn, Junior "Gabu" 178
Wedin, Amber 145, 234, 235
Wegener, Jessica 238, 314
Weglowski, Alexis 274
Wei, C.C. 208
Weidman, John viii, 319, 402
Weil, Tim 310
Weimer, Paul 255, 314
Weiner, Deanna 8
Weiner, Scott 410
Weiner, Walter 181, 183
Weingart, John 151, 329, 330
Weinman, James 407
Weinsaft, Phyllis 249
Weinstein, Amy 74
Weinstein, Bethany 255
Weinstein, Bob 5, 30, 82, 87, 118, 130, 167, 248, 279, 283, 350, 358
Weinstein, Harvey 5, 30, 82, 87, 118, 130, 164, 167, 191, 194, 248, 279, 283, 350, 358
Weinstein, Jessica 243
Weintraub, Freddi M. 334
Weintraub, Harry H. 13, 66, 78, 95, 274, 308, 347, 373
Weir, Fraser 88, 113, 114
Weisberg, Noah 85, 86, 89, 377
Weisbord, Barry 167, 283
Weisgall, Jonathan M. 243
Weiss, Daniel 343
Weiss, David 178, 183
Weiss, David S. 74, 250, 281, 315, 369
Weiss, George David 183
Weiss, I. 267, 281
Weiss, Joan 314, 315
Weiss, Natalie 91, 92
Weiss, Norman 262, 266-268
Weiss, Susan 48, 243
Weissler, Barry 69, 72, 79, 82, 85, 87, 164, 167, 168, 276, 397
Weissler, Fran 69, 72, 79, 82, 85, 87, 164, 167, 276, 279, 397
Weitzenhoffer, Max 191, 194
Weitzer, Jim 265
Weitzman, Hannah 13, 66, 95, 274, 322, 343, 373
Weitzman, Ira 151, 324, 330
Weitzman, Josh 19, 20, 64, 66
Wekselblatt, Michael 400
Welbourn, Sarah Grace 174, 352
Welch, Conor 369
Welk, Larry 21
Wells, Robert 58
Welzer, Irving 16, 17, 19, 336
Wendland, Mark 240, 241
Wendle, Brooke 121-123
Wendt, Roger 42, 46
Werle, Donyale 36, 145
Werner, Howard 60
Werner, Lori 354, 357
Werner, Martin 47
Wernick, Warren 405
Wernke, John iv, 305, 306, 309
Wesely, Tommy 102, 114
Wesson, Kyle 125, 126, 225
West, Bryan 366
West, Correy 324, 325, 327
West, Darron L. 305, 307, 345, 346
West, Kate 138, 296
West, Ray 6
West, Troy 28, 29
Westerman, Thomas 409
Western, Magali 13, 95, 274, 399
Westervelt, Scott 360, 361
Westin, David 322
Westmoreland, Brian 266
Westphal, David 401
Wettig, Patricia 238
Wetton, John K. 304
Wetzel, Patrick 16-18
Wharton, Jennifer 246
Wharton, Natascha 48
Wheatley, Nicholas 320, 322, 372, 373
Wheatley, Sharon 32, 33
Wheeler, Hugh vii, 191, 319
Wheeler, Mark 168
Wheeler, Lorraine 101
Whidden, Amanda 369
Whiddon, Trent 54, 55
Whitaker, Maggie 25
Whitaker, William 262, 266
Whitchurch, Philip 46, 49
White, Andrew 133
White, Anna Aimee 152, 153, 154, 157
White, C. Randall 250
White, Chip 119, 120
White, Ed 242
White, Frances 25, 225, 361, 412
White, Gary J. 174
White, Jacob 156, 303
White, Jessica 36, 183, 217
White, Joe 78, 308, 347
White, Julie 383
White, Katie Klehr 25
White, Lauren 398
White, Lena 257
White, Lillias vii, 97, 98, 102, 103, 388, 391
White, Niki 181, 182
White, Pat 400
White, Terri vii, 73, 109, 111, 115, 116
Whitely, Benton 168
Whitewood, Damian 54, 55
Whiting, Jeff 133
Whitley, Benton 291
Whitman, Barbara 135, 137, 240, 241, 294, 295
Whitney, Belinda 326
Whittaker, Keaton 191, 193
Whittaker, Sarah 207
Whitten, Dan 163
Whittle, James R. 422
Whitton, Jennifer 343
Whitty, Jeff 32-34
Whoriskey, Kate viii, 232, 233
Whybrew, Nik 168
Whyland, Casey 45, 50
Whyland, Erin 45, 50
Wicks, Charity 145
Widmann, Thom 362, 365
Widmer, Michael 320, 322, 373
Widner, Cheryl Lyn 291
Wiener, Arthur N. 255
Wiener, Dennis 208
Wier, Adam 13, 95, 274
Wierzel, Robert 97, 99, 389
Wiesenfeld, Cheryl 332
Wiggans, Gregg 280
Wiggins, Adam 8
Wiggins, Chris 77, 78, 308, 346, 347
Wigginton, Miranda 303
Wilamowski, Robert 409
Wilcox, Charlotte 79, 81, 83, 354, 357, 361
Wilcox, Collin 422
Wilcox, Margaret 83, 361
Wild, Jeff 243
Wilder, Alan 31, 338
Wilder, Amy 410
Wilder, Billy 276
Wiley, Patrick 216
Wilhoite, Michael 216, 218
Wilkerson, Amber 78, 308, 347
Wilkerson, Lisa Nicole 180, 181
Wilkinson, Jim 132, 133
Wilkosz, Jason 156
Willet, Bethany 8
Williams-Bellotti, Alex 401

Index

Williams, Allan 227, 230, 232, 234, 256, 258, 267, 276, 280, 396
Williams, Amanda 373
Williams, Beth 276-279
Williams, Bob 74, 168
Williams, Brynn 60, 62
Williams, Chandler 148, 149
Williams, Charlie 219, 221
Williams, Chris 401
Williams, Curly 231
Williams, Curtis 163
Williams, Dana 325, 329
Williams, Dolly 113, 114, 280
Williams, Eileen 8
Williams, Greg 334
Williams, J.L. 97, 99
Williams, Jillian 401
Williams, Julie 409
Williams, Kenny Redell 176-179
Williams, Kristen Beth 276-278
Williams, Kylil Christopher 286, 289
Williams, Matt 20
Williams, Maurice 163
Williams, Michael 354, 355, 357
Williams, Michelle T. 73
Williams, Rocco 132
Williams, Samantha 48
Williams, Serena 26
Williams, Stacia 328, 330
Williams, Vanessa iii, viii, ix, 318, 319, 323
Williamson, Afton C. 282, 283
Williamson, Dan'yelle 219-221, 226
Williamson, Mandy 410
Williamson, Mykelti 104, 105, 107, 108
Williamson, Ruth 152, 154
Willimans, Brian 238
Willis, Bruce 244
Willis, Dan 355
Willis, Jill Furman 354, 358
Willis, Matthew 207
Willis, Richard 236, 237
Willis, Susan 422
Willis, Victor 20
Wills, Jennifer Hope 261, 263, 268, 269
Wilms, Jeremy 98
Wilner, Gary 217, 218
Wilner, Robin 362, 363, 365
Wilson, Anne 361
Wilson, August viii, 104, 105, 107, 108, 392
Wilson, Azula 108
Wilson, C.J. 332, 333
Wilson, Carol 410
Wilson, Chandra 72
Wilson, Derek 58
Wilson, Edward 174, 245, 250, 286, 291
Wilson, Frank Edward 95
Wilson, Iris 97, 99
Wilson, Jeffrey M. 7, 138, 296
Wilson, Kate 296
Wilson, Kyle 183, 189, 217
Wilson, Laurel Ann 243
Wilson, Laurinda 163, 398
Wilson, Maia Nkenge 245, 247, 310-312
Wilson, Matthew B. 217
Wilson, Michael 332, 392
Wilson, Robert 47
Wilson, Shanique 410
Wilson, Tad 298, 299
Wilson, Tommar 131
Wilstein, Matt 39, 83, 106, 145, 156, 168, 225, 231, 291, 361, 415
Wiltshire, Adam 216
Wimmer, Paul 6, 8, 125
Winant, Bruce 265
Winar, Gail 12, 65, 94, 273, 321, 343, 372
Winder, John 110, 113
Windsor, Robin iv, 54, 55, 59
Winehouse, Amy 20
Winer, Karen 405
Winfrey, Oprah 107, 370
Wing, Sean 24, 27
Wingate, Anne 133
Wingfield, Garth 415
Wingfield, William B. 140, 142
Winiarski, Jo 303, 322
Winick, Irv 419
Winkler, Mara 418
Winkler, Richard 16, 17, 164, 171, 191, 219, 252
Winslet, Kate 49, 339
Winslow, Mikey 354, 356
Winter, Faye 135, 136
Winter, Shannon 114, 196, 304
Winterling, Eric 8, 13, 83, 183, 188, 217, 225, 231, 274, 352
Winters, Libby 21, 23, 27
Wisdom, Natalie 41, 42, 44, 50
Wise, Fred 20
Wise, Savannah 286-288, 292, 293, 300
Wiseman, Joseph 422
Wishcamper, Henry 31
Witek, Krystof 178
Witherow, Robert 227, 230, 242
Withers, Ernest C. 225
Witherspoon, Randy 369, 370
Withrow, David 95, 285
Witt, Ginger 416
Witter, Terrence J. 74
Wittlin, Michael 298
Witts, Howard 267
Wodobode, Aimee Graham 97, 99
Woerner, Chad 163, 281, 322
Wojchik, Mike 46
Wojnar, Dann 13, 14, 93, 95, 273, 274
Wojtal, James W. Jr. 36
Wolcott, Brandon 78
Wolf, Bobby 20, 63
Wolf, Orin 349
Wolf, Peter 152, 156, 304
Wolf, William 382
Wolfe, Betsy 91, 92, 96
Wolfe, Wayne 25, 48, 145, 250, 280, 304, 334, 361, 412
Wolff, Patricia 258
Wolff, Rachel A. 173, 174, 313, 314
Wolfryd, Katie 207
Wolfson, Andrea 8
Wolfson, Israel 298
Wolk, Amy 113, 156, 254
Wolkoff, Barbara 400, 403
Wolpert, Harold 11, 12, 60, 65, 91, 94, 270, 273, 318, 321, 340, 343, 371, 372, 399
Wolsky, Albert 393
Wolterstorff, Daya 74
Won, Allen 128
Wong, B.D. 410
Wong, Carolyn 258, 280
Wong, Margaret 31
Wong, Myra 407
Wood, Anja 311
Wood, Anna 303
Wood, Carrie 361
Wood, Frank 28, 29
Wood, Natalie 322
Wood, Rudy 329
Wood, Steven E. 188
Woodall, Eric 47, 126, 162, 188, 196, 208, 217, 267, 280, 314, 322
Woodard, Alfre 107
Woodard, Jeremy 298, 299
Woodbury, Richard 28, 29
Wooden, Jesse Jr. 102, 106
Woodiel, Paul 355
Wooding, John 66, 320, 322, 373
Woodman, Branch 60, 61, 63
Woodruff, Bob 347
Woods, Amanda 255
Woods, Harry M. 20
Woods, Jay 280, 281
Woods, Tiger 9
Woodson, Roderic L. 243
Woodward, Edward 422
Woodward, Max 286, 291
Woodworth, Kevin 73, 74
Woolard, David C. 354, 357
Woolard, Gregory 367
Woolley, Jim 291
Woolverton, Linda 176
Wooten, Brandi 245-247
Wooten, Jason 127, 129
Wopat, Tom viii, 318, 319, 323
Wordsworth, Mark 267
Workman, Camille 176, 177, 179
Worrell, Lennox 421
Worsing, Ryan 152-154, 310-312, 314
Worsnop, Jessica 156, 167, 168, 254, 255
Worthington, Conwell III 12, 65, 94, 273, 321, 343, 372
Woyasz, Laura 363, 364
Wreghitt, Randall L. 232, 233
Wright, Adenike 183
Wright, Amra-Faye 69, 72, 73
Wright, Amy Jean 25
Wright, Billy Jr. 230
Wright, Charles 255
Wright, Christina 95, 106
Wright, Donnie 224
Wright, Doug 184, 187
Wright, Emily 114, 196, 255, 304
Wright, Gary 56
Wright, Heather 100-102
Wright, Linda 398
Wright, Matthew 164-166, 388, 392, 393
Wright, Michelle 48
Wright, Nathan 314
Wright, Peter 162
Wright, Raynelle 234, 250, 258
Wright, Robin 26
Wright, Wendy 77, 307
Wright, William 53, 126, 231
Wrightson, Ann G. 28, 29
Wyatt, Kirsten 310-312
Wyffels, John 77, 307, 346
Wyman, Joel 419

Y

Yacavone, Briana 362, 363, 365
Yaccarino, Michael 409
Yaeger, Alex 200
Yagecic, Peter 418
Yagual, Lidia 421
Yajima, Mineko 110, 113, 185
Yama, Conrad 422
Yamada, Mike 315
Yambor, Scott 416
Yancosek, Gail 407
Yaney, Denise 148, 150
Yankwitt, Stephanie 95, 106
Yao, Rita 57
Yarbrough, Chad 363
Yarosh, Danika 41, 42, 44, 50
Yates, Ricky 162
Yates, Sam 138
Yazbeck, Tony vii, 152, 154
Ye, Sunny 315
Yeager, Grant W.S. 238

Index

Yeargan, Michael 324, 327
Yedowitz, Amy 329
Yegen, Chris 16, 17
Yegen, Christian C. 343
Yeh, Ming 122, 125
Yen, Madeleine Rose 152, 154, 157
Yerkovich, Gail 195
Yerkovich, John 361
Yershon, Gary 117, 252
Yeston, Maury viii, ix, 36, 305, 307
Yew, Chay 403
Yezerski-Bondoc, Mary Kay 125, 126, 223, 225
Yoder, Richard Riaz 152-154, 157
Yoo, Connie 410
Yorke, Edward 347
Yorkey, Brian 36, 240, 241, 392
Yoshioka, Sylvia 35, 36, 258, 295
Youmans, James 79, 81, 354, 357
Youmans, William 109-111
Young, Ace 127, 129, 133
Young, Campbell 41, 48
Young, Corey 343
Young, Dashaun 176, 178
Young, David 185, 192, 197
Young, Eric Jordan 286, 287, 288, 292
Young, Gavi 94, 321, 399
Young, Jehan O. 63
Young, Joe 183
Young, Karen 53, 114, 156, 182, 200, 234, 407
Young, Kyle 183, 189, 217
Young, Micha 153
Young, Paloma 25
Young, Pam 183
Young, Tara 184, 187
Young, Timothy 240, 241
Young, Wanda 419
Young, William Baldwin 322
Young, Xavier 254
Yurman, Larry 377

Z

Zabinski, Karen 217, 218
Zaborowski, Julia 369
Zaccardi, Chris 249, 250
Zack, David 369
Zack, Samantha 366, 370
Zadan, Craig 276, 279
Zaibek, Randall 120, 168, 231, 280, 314
Zakarian, Louie 330
Zaks, Emma 127-129
Zaks, Jerry viii, 1, 4, 9, 25, 102, 114, 133, 163, 196
Zaleski, Michael 105, 106
Zaloga, Stacey 313, 314
Zamansky, Maria 126, 225, 361
Zambello, Francesca 184, 187
Zambrano, Adrian 77
Zameryka, John 46, 47
Zammit, Jason 183, 189, 217
Zander, James 265
Zane, Arnie 102
Zaneski, Meghan 47
Zangen, Josh 196, 342
Zannelli, James 113
Zaretsky, Scott 238
Zarobinski, Charles 35, 36
Zarrett, Lee 127-129
Zavelson, Billy 102, 114, 413
Zayas, Nick 106
Zecker, Michael 126, 145
Zeelens, Ron 57
Zegarsky, George 181, 182
Zeigler, Josh 163
Zeilinger, Brian 171, 172
Zeilinger, Scott 172
Zeitler, Sarah 225
Zeitz, Alyson 352
Zeltzer, Ari Sachter 369
Zepel, Leah 205
Zeta-Jones, Catherine vii, ix, 191-197, 316, 379, 387, 392, 393
Zhang, Philip 7
Zieglerova, Klara 158, 160
Zielinski, James 162, 383
Zielinski, Peter James iv
Zielonka, Jana 36
Zieve, Amanda 225, 230
Zimmer, Hans 176, 177, 180
Zimmerman, Linda 410
Zimmerman, Mark 354-356
Zindler, Arianna 102
Zink, Jeff 83, 188
Zinn, David 148, 149, 388
Zinni, Gabriel J. 133
Zinni, Lisa 133
Zito, Ronald 70
Zito, Torrie 80, 422
Zollo, Frederick 258, 332
Zolo, Yannick 163
Zorthian, Doc 176, 182
Zotovich, Adam 1, 5, 69, 70, 71, 349, 351
Zuber, Catherine 256, 257, 305, 307, 324, 327, 388, 389
Zuber, George 410
Zulvergold, Alissa iv, 105-107, 112, 114, 126
Zwicky, Paula 74
Zybert, Sarah 401

Autographs

Autographs

Autographs

Autographs